Computer C
in Action

Log on to the
Online Learning Center
through

glencoe.com!

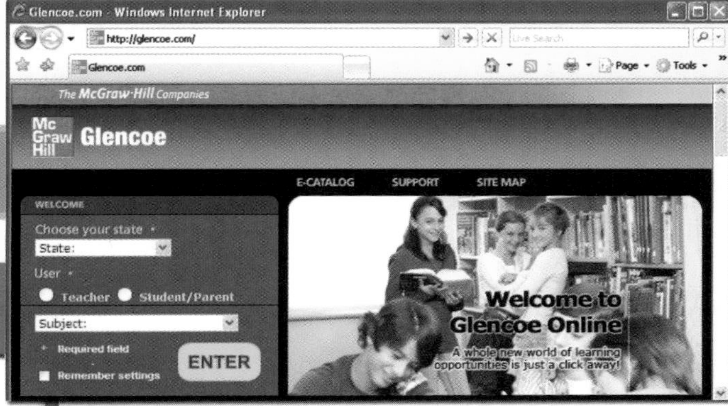

Integrated Academics

- Academic Focus: English Language Arts and Math
- Academic Vocabulary
- Academic Skills Activities
- Projects Across the Curriculum
- Math Skills Handbook

New Student Edition Features

- Real World Projects
- 21st Century Skills Activities
- Real World Features
- TechSavvy Features
- What's New in Office 2007

Reading Skills and Assessments

- Reading Guides
- Reading Strategies
- Reading Checks
- Reading Skills Handbook
- After You Read Activities
- Project Review and Activities
- Unit Portfolio Projects

Online Learning Center

- Self-Check Quizzes and Reviews
- Rubrics
- Data Files
- Worksheets
- Technology Handbook
- *Presentation Plus!*™ PowerPoint Presentations
- Enrichment Activities
- Study-to-Go

IC³ Approved Courseware

Stephen E. Haag, Ph.D.
Daniels College of Business
University of Denver
Denver, CO

glencoe.com

The McGraw-Hill Companies

Between the time that Web site information is gathered and published, it is not unusual for some sites to have changed URLs or closed. URLs will be updated in reprints or on the Online Resource Center when possible.

Printed in the United States of America

Send all inquiries to:

Glencoe/McGraw-Hill
4400 Easton Commons
Columbus, OH 43219

MHID 0-07-880577-5 (Student Edition)
ISBN 978-0-07-880577-6 (Student Edition)

MHID 0-07-880725-5 (Teacher Resource Manual)
ISBN 978-0-07-880725-1 (Teacher Resource Manual)

4 5 6 7 8 9 DOW 12 11

Caution Never shop online without adult supervision. An adult should make sure that the company can be trusted with personal information, such as a home address, telephone number, e-mail address, or credit card number. If a Web site asks you to set up a username and password, check with an adult before doing anything else.

Why It's Important What might an untrustworthy company do with your personal information?

Why Do Businesses and Consumers Use E-Commerce?

Many people still like to visit shopping malls and look at merchandise in person. As you can see in the chart below, e-commerce gives people another way to shop for things. It also gives businesses another way to sell things.

Benefits of E-Commerce

Benefits For Consumers	Easy Shopping	Comparing Prices	Wide Selections
	E-commerce brings your favorite stores into your own house. You do not have to drive or wait in line.	Instead of driving from one store to the next to compare products and prices, you can do your research online.	You can find goods and services anywhere in the world. You can even hunt down rare or hard-to-find items.
Benefits for Businesses	**Doing More with Less**	**Strong Customer Relationships**	**Increased Efficiency**
	Businesses can sell more products without needing to hire more people or open new stores.	By making their Web sites easy to use, businesses invite shoppers to return often.	Businesses can keep track of company expenses and sales and customer information.

▲ Businesses and consumers both have a lot to gain from e-commerce. What do you think is the biggest advantage to doing business online for consumers?

Reading Check

1. **Identify** What are two reasons e-commerce has grown?
2. **Explore** Why do you think some people prefer to shop in stores instead of on a Web site?

E-Commerce

Reading Guide

Before You Read

Memory Aid Successful readers use mental tricks to help them remember what they learn. As you read this unit, make up your own memory aids. For example, when you learn the term *pop-up ad*, imagine a piece of toast popping up from the toaster. This will reinforce the concept.

Key Concepts

- How e-commerce benefits consumers and businesses
- How to compare ways of doing business on the Web
- How to identify elements of a successful e-commerce Web site
- How to evaluate privacy and security on the Internet

Vocabulary

Key Terms

e-commerce
consumer
banner ad
pop-up ad
click-through
database

Academic Vocabulary

percentage
suggest
aware
expert

The Importance of E-Commerce

Today, people can shop on the Internet for almost anything, including many popular items, such as clothes, books, computers, and music. Electronic commerce, or **e-commerce**, refers to buying and selling products and services over the Internet. A person who buys things is called a **consumer**. Consumers use e-commerce to shop for things without leaving their homes. Businesses use e-commerce to reach more consumers, send information quickly, and lower operating expenses.

Why Is E-Commerce So Popular?

In the early days of e-commerce, only a small **percentage**, or proportion, of Internet users bought things online. Gradually, businesses made their Web sites more reliable, secure, and user friendly. When people began to realize that it was safe and easy to shop online, the popularity of e-commerce grew. Eventually, new businesses sprang up that were available only on the Web. Amazon.com®, for example, was one of the first e-commerce businesses to be successful. It became a model for many online businesses that followed.

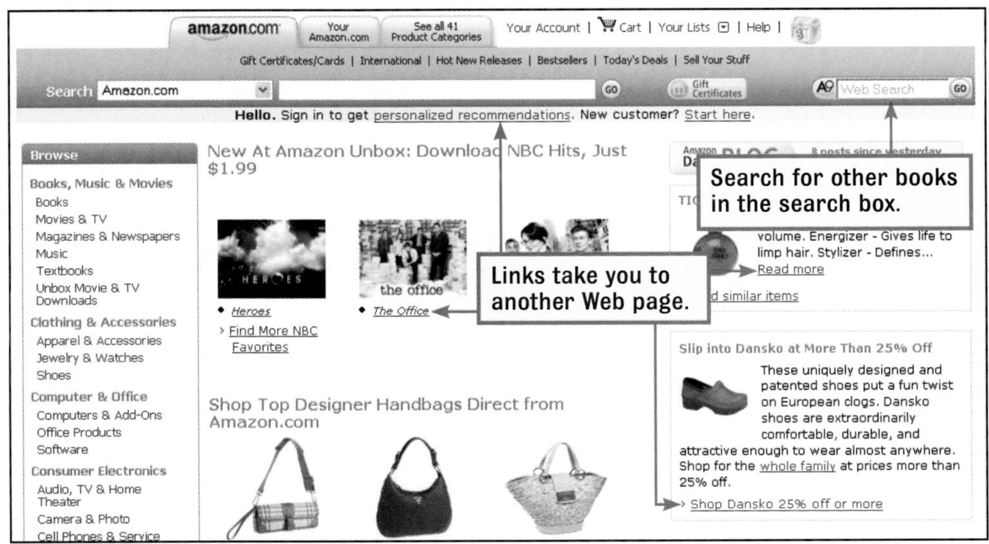

▲ Amazon.com's Web site includes many easy-to-use features, such as links and search boxes. Why do e-commerce businesses make their Web sites easy to use?

Doing Business on the Internet

Businesses know that to keep up with the competition, they need to use the Internet. With the amount of time that people spend on the Internet daily, businesses want to have an Internet address (or a Web "presence") because their competitors probably have Web sites. They also know that the younger generation of shoppers expects to be able to find their company on the Internet.

How they use the Internet depends on the type of business they are. Businesses fit into one of three categories:

- brick-and-mortar
- click-and-mortar
- click-and-order

Brick-and-mortar businesses do not sell goods and services on their Web sites. They might have a Web site for information, but they do all of their business in physical locations.

A brick-and-mortar Web site is used for informational purposes, but it does not sell products. What type of information might you find on a brick-and-mortar Web site?

UNIT 6 Databases

Real World Projects

Go Online **e-QUIZ**

glencoe.com

Starting with You What are the advantages and disadvantages when you shop online? To find out, go to the **Online Learning Center** at glencoe.com. Choose **e-Quizzes**, and take the **Unit 6 Pre-Quiz**.

TECH TALK E-Commerce

Shoppers now have many choices for where to buy things. Why do you think a business would want to sell items in a store and online?

Click-and-mortar businesses exist both on the Internet and in the real world. Many clothing companies, for example, have stores as well as e-commerce Web sites.

You can buy books, clothes, or other items at a store or online. Would you prefer to buy a pair of shoes at a store or through a Web site? Why?

Click-and-order businesses do not have any physical stores. They exist only on the Internet. These businesses often make a lot of sales, but those sales all happen online.

UNIT 5

Build Your Portfolio

Design a Custom Computer

You have just bought a digital camera to make prints, as well as T-shirt transfers, greeting cards, and Web page images. The software has specific computer system requirements, so you decide to buy a new computer. You need to compare two computers to find the best price.

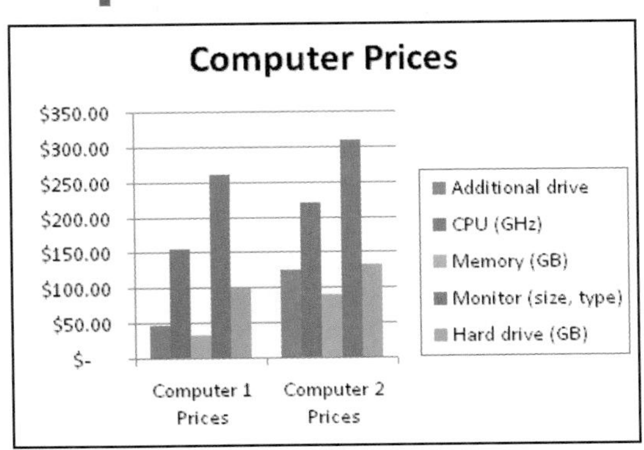

Research

1. Find a software product for your photo needs. Use magazines or catalogs. With your teacher's permission, research on the Internet.
2. Determine the software's computer system requirements.
3. Find out the cost of two different computer systems that could run the software. Identify the cost of each computer component, including printers and monitors.

Prepare

4. Write down the information you need to create a worksheet.
   - **a.** List the costs of the computer components for the two computers.
   - **b.** Determine the column and row headings.
   - **c.** Select formulas or functions to compare prices (the difference in cost for each component, the total price for each computer, and the difference in total price for the two computers).

Build Your Portfolio Use the rubric for this portfolio project to help create and evaluate your work. Go to the **Online Learning Center** at **glencoe.com**. Choose **Rubrics**, then **Unit 5**.

Create

5. Use Excel to create the worksheet.
   - **a.** Enter formulas and functions to evaluate the data.
   - **b.** Sort the worksheet to compare high and low prices.
   - **c.** Create a bar chart comparing the prices of the computers.
   - **d.** Write a report that describes the software and explains which computer you would buy, based on your worksheet data. Include a printout of your worksheet and charts.

Are There Different Kinds of E-Commerce?

E-commerce can be used for different purposes. Some businesses sell to individuals like you, and some sell to other businesses. Individuals also use e-commerce to sell things to each other.

The Three Types of E-Commerce

Type	Business-to-Consumer (B2C)	Business-to-Business (B2B)	Consumer-to-Consumer (C2C)
Definition	In B2C e-commerce, a business uses the Internet to sell things to individual customers like you. There are thousands of B2C e-businesses.	In B2B e-commerce, a business uses the Internet to sell goods and services to other businesses. B2B businesses are a large part of e-commerce, even though they are not well known to the public.	In C2C e-commerce, one person uses the Internet to sell something to another person.
Examples	Wal-Mart Amazon.com iTunes Travelocity FedEx	Ingram Micro sells computer products to major distributors such as CompUSA.	eBay Online classified ads

▲ An e-commerce transaction belongs in one of three categories. Which category would you be most likely to use if you bought a CD online?

Many businesses use a combination of e-commerce methods. For example, a clothing manufacturer might use the Internet to sell to consumers directly, track its products going to other businesses (such as clothing stores), and buy from other businesses (such as zipper manufacturers).

Reading Check

1. **Identify** What do you call businesses that sell on the Web and nowhere else?
2. **Explain** How is B2C e-commerce different from C2C e-commerce?

UNIT 5

Projects Across the Curriculum

Project 2 My Hometown

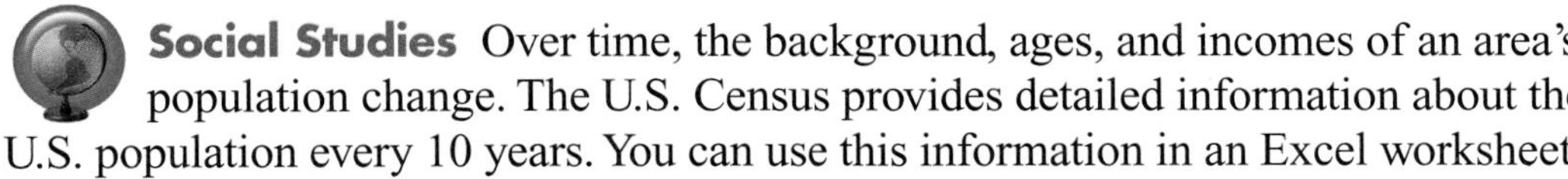

Social Studies Over time, the background, ages, and incomes of an area's population change. The U.S. Census provides detailed information about the U.S. population every 10 years. You can use this information in an Excel worksheet.

Plan

1. Use the information provided in the **Data File** named **5C Census**.
2. Write down the population of five states over at least three time periods.

Create

3. Create an Excel worksheet, using the data you wrote down in Step 2.
   a. Put each time period in a separate column.
   b. Put each state in a separate row.
4. Add line graphs to show the population change of two states over at least two time periods.

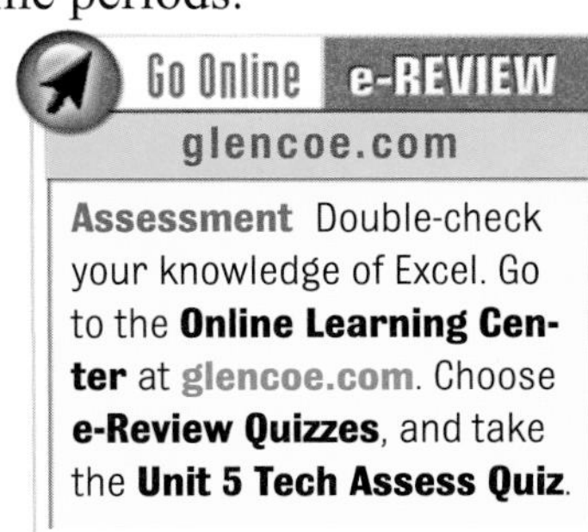

Go Online **e-REVIEW**

glencoe.com

Assessment Double-check your knowledge of Excel. Go to the **Online Learning Center** at glencoe.com. Choose **e-Review Quizzes**, and take the **Unit 5 Tech Assess Quiz**.

Project 3 Animals and Their Habitats

Science Animals can be divided into categories depending on the environment in which they live (habitat) or the type of animal they are (class). Use Excel to compare characteristics of animals.

Research

1. Choose five animals to research. Each animal must live in a different habitat (desert, ocean, tropical, and so on) and belong to a different class (mammal, insect, bird, and so on).
2. Collect information about class, habitat, life expectancy, weight, and diet.

Create

3. Combine your data with data from three other classmates. Use the data to create a worksheet listing 20 animals.
4. Include a row of data for each animal. Include columns with labels for the animal's name, class, habitat, life expectancy, weight, and diet.
5. Use sorts and filters to create bar graphs showing life expectancy and weight for animals in each habitat and class.

Elements of a Successful E-Commerce Site

With so many e-commerce sites on the Internet, businesses are discovering that they have the same kind of competition that they might with physical stores. Just as customers like a clean, well-designed store, they also like a simple, easy-to-use Web site. Good customer service and positive word-of-mouth are important to successful e-commerce.

Caution Pop-up ads are very common ways for businesses to advertise on the Internet. Although most of these are from companies you can trust, some pop-up ads are meant to trick people into giving personal information. They may even look as though they come from a well-known company.

Why It's Important Think about what could happen if you click on a pop-up ad from an untrustworthy source.

How Do Businesses Advertise on the Web?

In addition to using the usual methods of attracting customers, such as newspaper ads, television commercials, and billboards, businesses on the Internet use a variety of new ways to attract customers to their Web sites.

You may see one or more of these popular advertising methods as you use the Internet: banner ads, pop-up ads, or sponsored links.

Similar to a billboard along the side of the road or a movie poster hanging in a shopping mall, a **banner ad** is an easy-to-see, eye-catching graphic advertisement that takes you to another Web site when you click it.

▲ Businesses usually pay a fee to have their banner ads on popular Web sites. What reasons might e-businesses use to decide on which Web sites to post their banner ads?

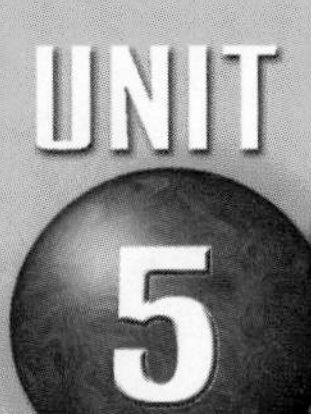

UNIT 5 Projects Across the Curriculum

Use the skills you learned in this unit to help you complete the following projects. Check with your teacher for directions on saving or printing your work.

glencoe.com

Unit Projects Use the rubrics for these projects to help create and evaluate your work. Go to the **Online Learning Center** at **glencoe.com**. Choose **Rubrics**, then **Unit 5**.

Project 1 Keep It Under Budget ★

Math Imagine that you earn an income of $50 each week from a job delivering newspapers. Use Excel to prepare a budget.

Prepare

1. Make a list of your weekly expenses—all the ways you spend your money during the week.

2. Write down how much you think each expense will be.

Research

3. Find out the actual cost for each of your expenses.

Create

4. Use the income and expenses data you listed in Steps 1 through 3 above to create an Excel worksheet with the following columns:

   a. Column A: Each category of expense

   b. Column B: The amount you *expected* to spend for each category

   c. Column C: The amounts that you *actually* spent

   d. Column D: The difference between *expected* and *actual* expenses

5. Total your actual expenses. Find the difference between your total actual expenses and your income of $50. Add this information to the bottom of your worksheet.

6. Filter or sort to find out which expenses are highest.

7. Create a pie chart showing the breakdown of your actual expenses. Save your worksheet.

Continued on page 252

A **pop-up ad** is a small Web page containing an advertisement. It pops up on your screen when you are using a Web site. Be cautious of free offers or ads that say you have won something. Remember pop-up ads are designed to sell you something.

Special software and browser settings can prevent pop-up ads that make your browser less efficient. Why might so many people find pop-up ads annoying and disruptive?

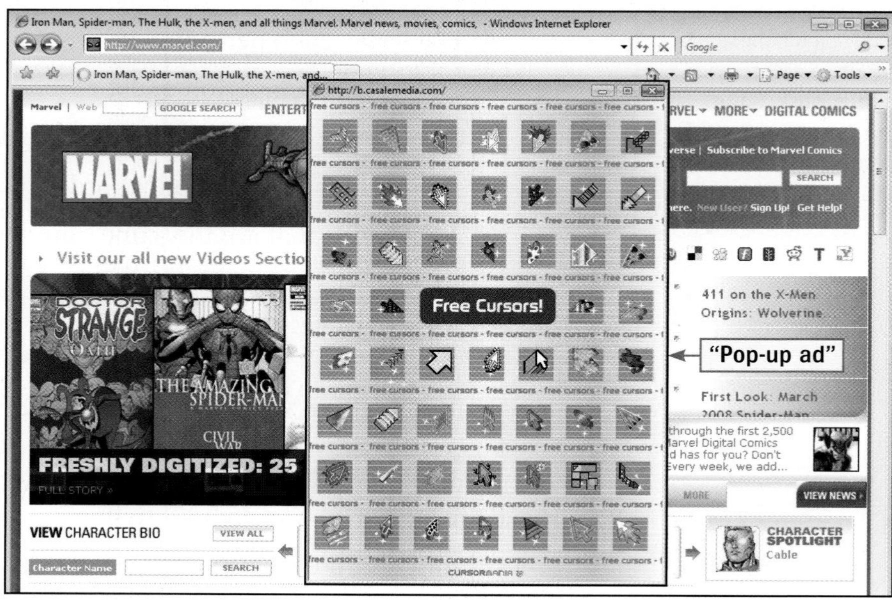

Businesses advertise on search engines, such as Google. These ads are often identified as sponsored links.

Entire fast-paced businesses now exist to auction off sponsored links. Why would having a Web site appear first in a search engine result be worth so much money?

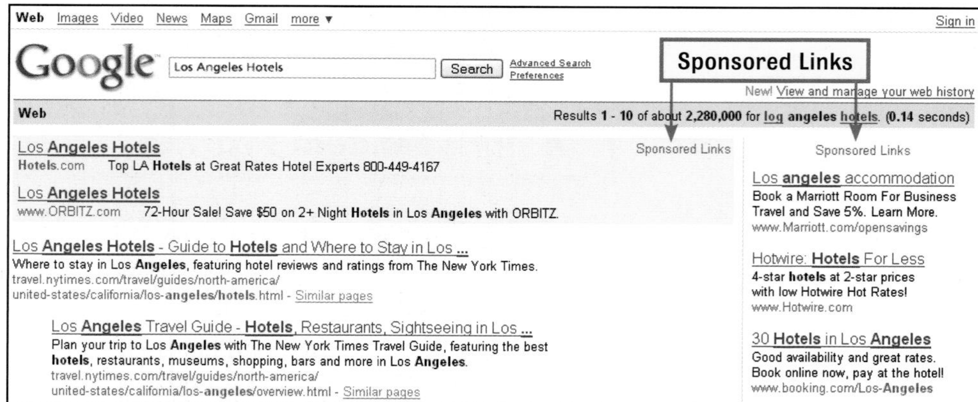

E-commerce sites keep track of click-throughs. A **click-through** refers to the number of customers who click an advertisement to move from one Web site to another. This information is recorded by advertisers to see whether their ads are attracting customers.

Project 3 Assessment

2 Independent Practice 

Go Online RUBRICS
glencoe.com

Independent Practice
Use the rubrics for these projects to help create and evaluate your work. Go to the **Online Learning Center** at **glencoe.com**. Choose **Rubrics**, then **Unit 5**.

Math Show Selected Information Open the **School Day** worksheet you created in Project 2, Independent Practice 2 (page 238). Use a filter, sort, or hide column to show each of the following:

- The times each period starts
- The times each period ends
- Only your classes, not lunch or breaks
- The periods in alphabetical order (A to Z)
- All periods that are the same number of minutes

3 Independent Practice 

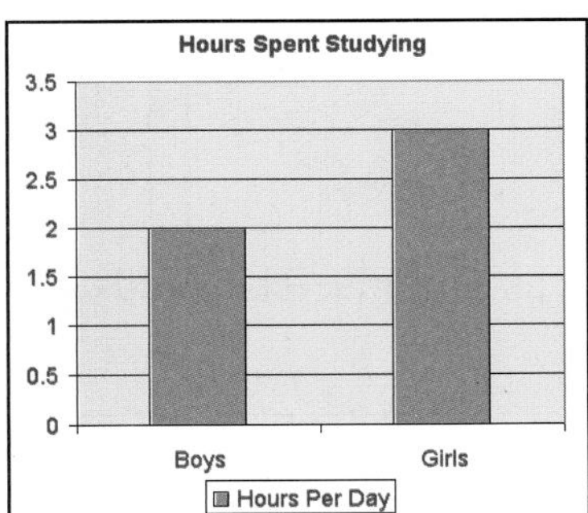

Math Sort, Add Filters, and Add Charts Open the **Survey** worksheet you created in Project 2, Independent Practice 3 (page 238). Add a chart that will compare the boys' survey results to the girls' survey results.

a. Plan First, create filters that compare the number of hours studying, the number of hours watching TV, and the number of hours exercising.

b. Create Use your results to create a column chart that shows the difference in number of hours that boys and girls spend in each of those activities.

4 Independent Practice 

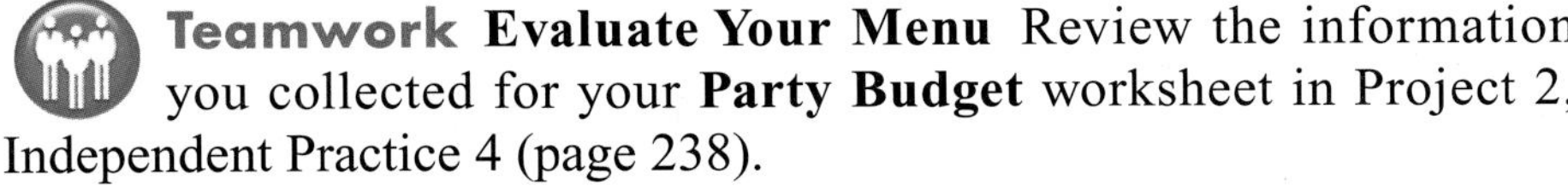

Teamwork Evaluate Your Menu Review the information you collected for your **Party Budget** worksheet in Project 2, Independent Practice 4 (page 238).

- Use filters, sorts, and charts to choose at least two menus that include a drink, a main dish, a side dish, and a dessert for each person in the party.
- The total cost must not be more than $50.
- If your teacher allows, print the two menus that meet your $50 budget.

What Are "Sticky" Web Sites?

E-businesses want to create sites that you will visit again and again. These are called "sticky" Web sites. There are various ways to make a site sticky:

Usability

If Web sites are easy to use, customers will keep coming back.

Personalization

Some sites remember you when you make a return visit. This is made possible by a cookie, which is a file of information about you that a Web site stores on your computer.

Electronic Catalogs

On a site such as Amazon.com, you can browse just as if you were at a retail store. You can even read reviews and book excerpts, and listen to song clips.

Usability On average, most visitors spend fewer than 30 seconds looking at a Web page. Therefore, Web sites should be well organized with clearly marked links. If you cannot find what you are looking for on a site, you probably will not come back to the site.

Personalization When you visit some sites, they greet you by name. The site might **suggest**, or recommend, items for you to buy based on any previous purchases. Reordering becomes quick and easy.

Electronic Catalogs E-commerce sites usually let you see pictures and descriptions of products before you buy.

Customer Service As with any business, an e-commerce business should make it easy for shoppers to get answers to their questions. The ways that customers find answers on Web sites include:

- Reading a FAQ (Frequently Asked Questions) section
- Clicking a Contact Us link that provides phone numbers or e-mail addresses
- Exchanging instant messages with customer service agents

Reading Check

1. **Explain** Why is advertising important to e-commerce businesses?
2. **Draw Conclusions** Imagine that a company has great products but poor customer service. How might that affect the company's online business?

Project 3 Assessment

5 Click **A3**. Then on the **Data** tab, in the **Sort & Filter** group, click the **Filter** button. (Exercise 3-2)

6 In **column A**, filter for the **Memory** of each computer. See Figure 3.14. (Exercise 3-2)

7 On the **Data** tab, in the **Sort & Filter** group, click the **Filter** button to remove the filter. (Exercise 3-2)

8 **Hide columns B** and **D**. (Exercise 3-2)

9 Select cells **A4** through **E8**.

10 On the **Insert** tab, in the **Charts** group, click the **Pie** button. Choose the **Pie** chart. Key Computer 2 Prices as the title of the chart. Add a border to the legend. (Exercise 3-3)

11 Your chart should look like Figure 3.16. Drag the chart below the chart you created in Exercise 3-3.

12 **Save** your worksheet as *Your Name* Computer Price Comparison 2.

13 If your teacher allows, **print** your worksheet. (Exercise 1-4) **Exit Excel**.

Figure 3.14 The worksheet shows only the Memory component.

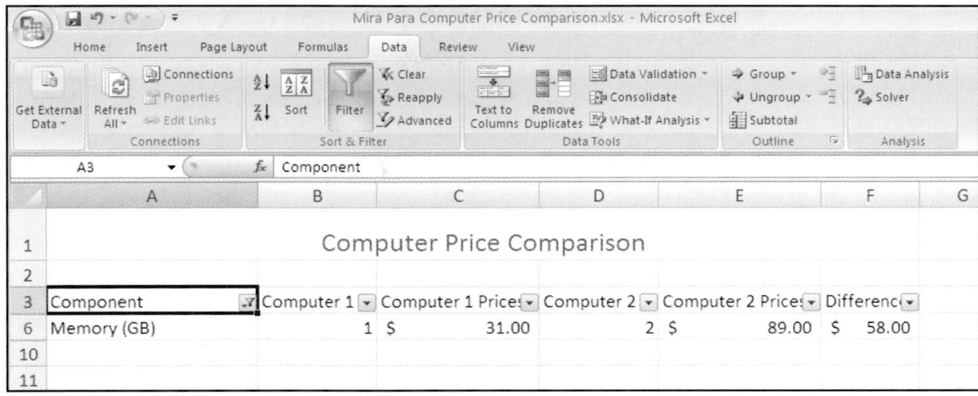

Figure 3.15 Choose Pie for the Chart Type in the Chart Wizard.

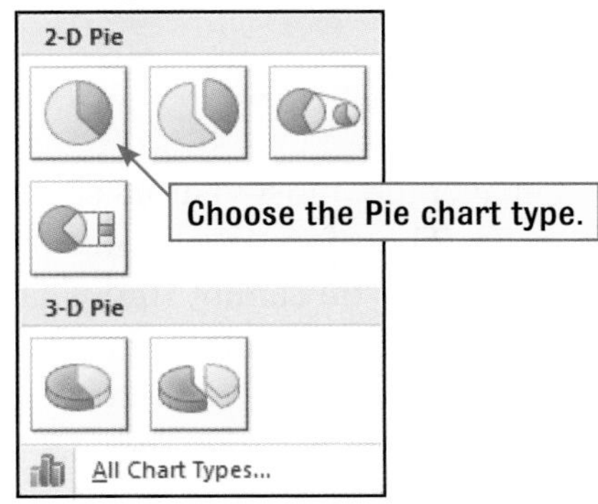

Figure 3.16 The chart displays which components cost the most.

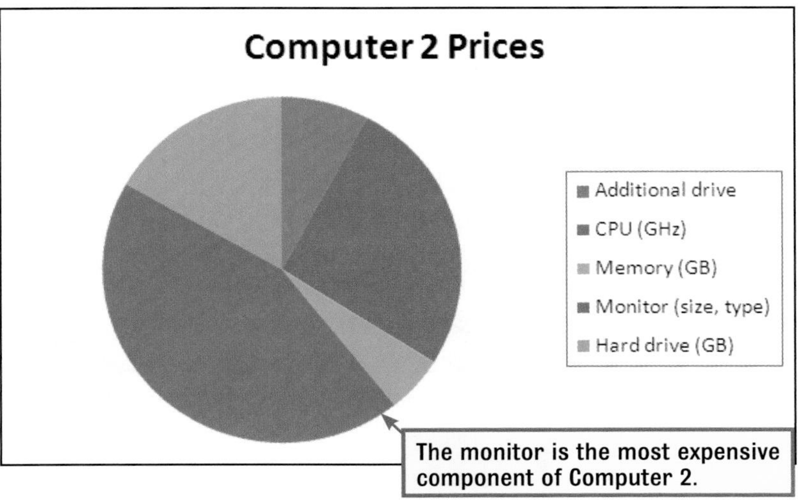

Privacy and Security

Buying products on the Internet is easy, but it does involve risks. Computers might crash, hackers could try to steal data, and dishonest people may try to cheat you. You can greatly reduce the risks by being **aware**, or alert, of simple safety rules.

If you plan to buy something online, keep your security in mind.

- Avoid doing business with unfamiliar companies.
- Make sure the Web site is secure and uses encryption. This is a way of scrambling information to keep it private. Look for the padlock symbol at the bottom of your screen and "https" in the Web address.
- Never provide a credit card number or other personal information unless the site is secure.
- If you create a User ID and password, choose something that would be hard to guess. (Your own birthdate and telephone number are not good passwords.) Never share your password with anyone.

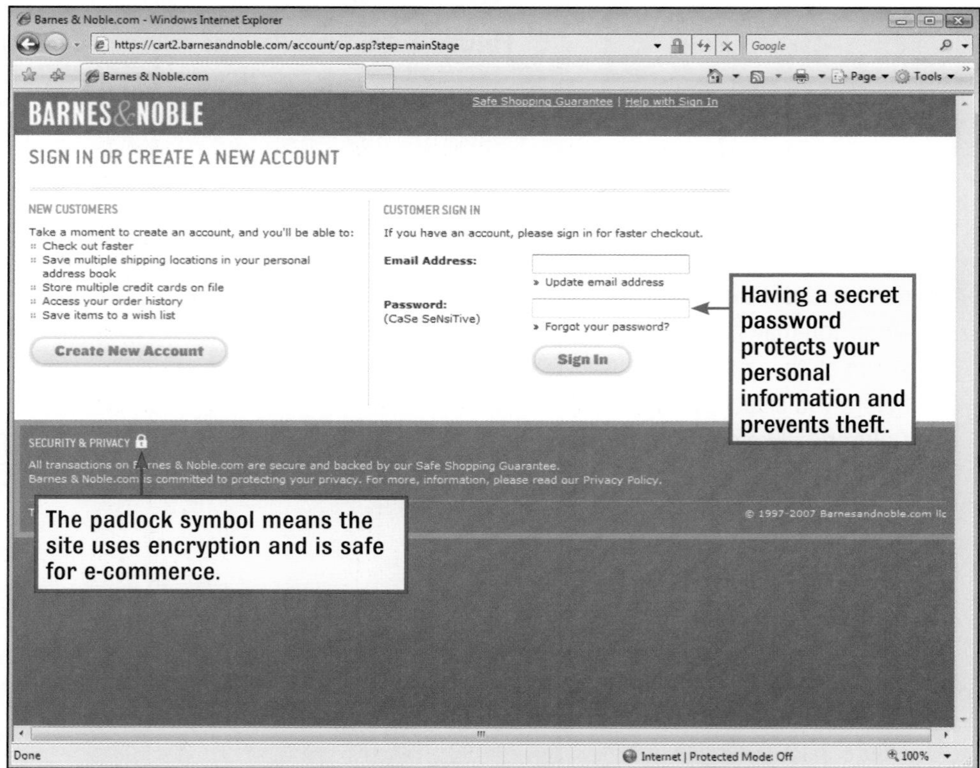

▲ Barnes & Noble has a secure e-commerce Web site. Why is it more secure to buy something from a site with a padlock symbol?

Project 3 Assessment

Key Concepts Check

1. **Identify** What are criteria?
2. **List** What are four types of charts?
3. **Describe** How do you hide a column?
4. **Explain** What are the benefits of using a filter?

Critical Thinking

5. **Compare and Contrast** What is the difference between sorting and filtering?
6. **Draw Conclusions** What type of chart would you use to show the percentage of students in your class who watch MTV?

1 Guided Practice

Sort and Create a Chart Using a sort for the differences in price will help you quickly see which components have the greatest price difference. Creating a pie chart will show each "piece" of the total price of a computer. If you need help, refer back to the exercise in parentheses at the end of the step.

Step-by-Step

1. **Start Excel**, and **open** your **Computer Price Comparison** worksheet.
2. If **column D** is hidden, use the **Unhide** option. **Note:** You may need to select all the data first before you select **Unhide Columns**. (Exercise 3-2)
3. Select **A3** through **F8**. On the **Data** tab, in the **Sort & Filter** group, click the **Sort** button. (Exercise 3-1)
4. Sort the **Difference** column in descending order. See Figure 3.13. (Exercise 3-1)

▼ **Figure 3.13** The Difference column is sorted in descending order.

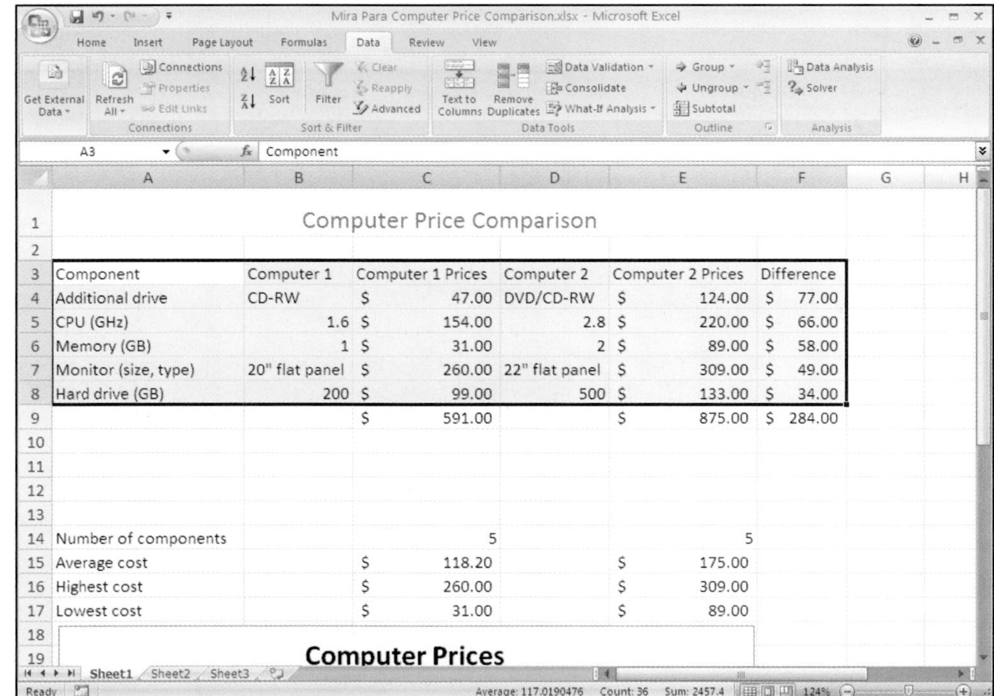

Go Online ACTIVITY
glencoe.com

Network Security
Businesses and individuals deal with hackers, crashes, and other threats. To learn more about how computer networks are protected, go to the **Online Learning Center** at **glencoe.com**. Choose **Tech Talk Activities**, then **Unit 6**.

How Do Businesses Organize Information?

Businesses use databases to keep track of the vast amounts of information involved in e-commerce. A **database** is a collection of files that are organized in a logical way. A database contains hundreds or even thousands of different pieces of data. It allows you to organize the data in a way that helps people easily find information.

Full Name:	Jane Appleseed
Address Line1:	1234 Apple Rd. Street address, P.O. box, company name, c/o
Address Line2:	 Apartment, suite, unit, building, floor, etc.
City:	Apple Tree
State/Province/Region:	NY
ZIP/Postal Code:	01234
Country:	United States
Phone Number:	555-555-1234

▲ Forms like this make it easy to enter information in a database. Why would an e-commerce site use forms?

How Do Businesses Protect Information?

Databases are full of private information such as addresses, account numbers, and health records. To protect your privacy, database information must be:

- **Physically secure** so that a thief cannot carry off or open a computer that contains confidential information.
- **Electronically secure** so that even an **expert**, or skilled, hacker cannot figure out how to break in.

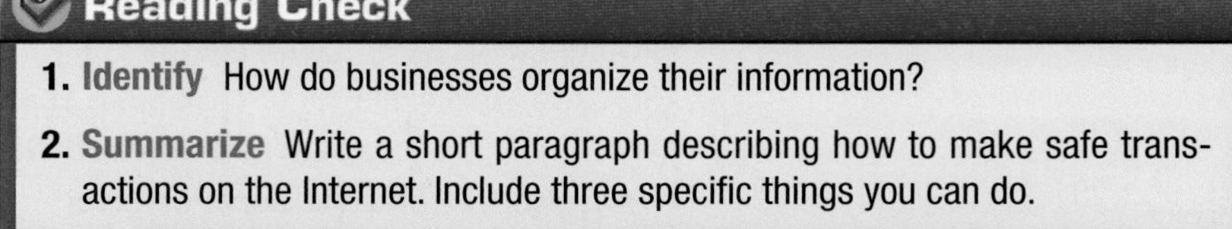

Reading Check

1. **Identify** How do businesses organize their information?
2. **Summarize** Write a short paragraph describing how to make safe transactions on the Internet. Include three specific things you can do.

10. On the **Layout** tab, in the **Labels** group, choose the **Legend** command, then **More Legend Options**. In the **Format Legend** dialog box, under **Legend Options**, choose **Border Color**.

11. Under **Border Color**, click **Solid line**. Click the drop-down arrow next to the **Color** button, and choose **Blue** (Figure 3.11). Click the **Close** button to close the dialog box.

12. Click the chart to select it, if necessary. Your chart should look like the chart shown in Figure 3.12.

13. Drag the chart below the rest of the data. Your worksheet should look similar to Figure 3.12.

14. **Save** your worksheet.

15. **Exit Excel**.

▼ **Figure 3.11** You can format the legend with a line style and color.

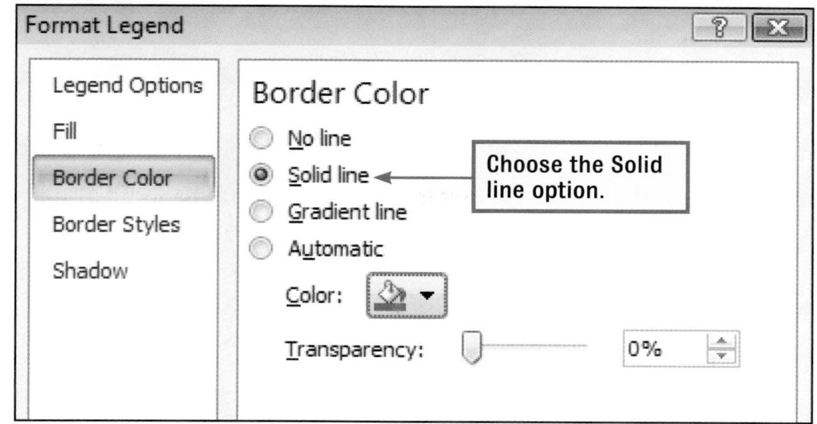

▼ **Figure 3.12** The formatted chart is moved below the worksheet data.

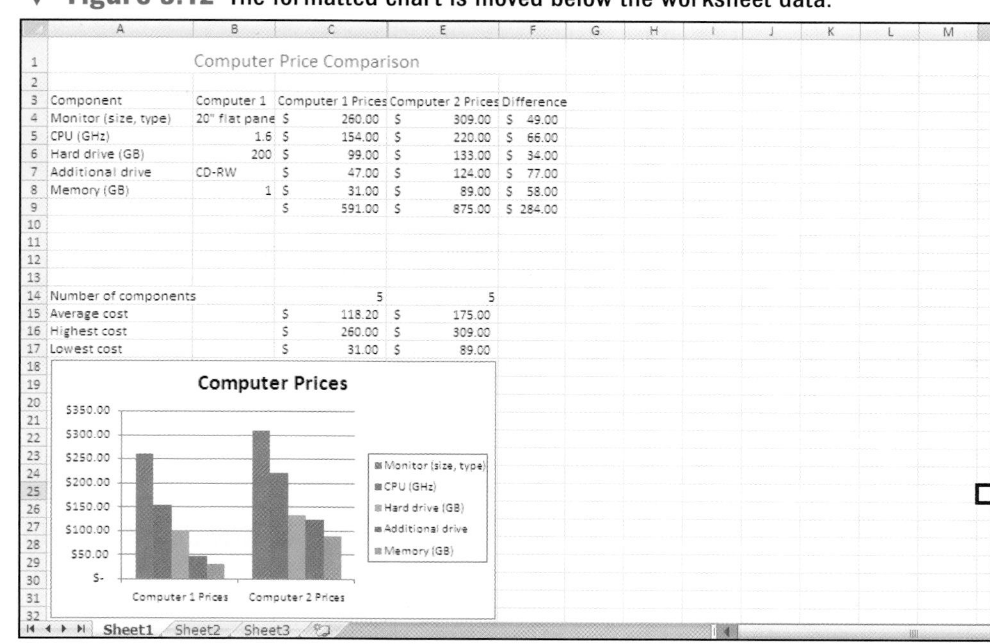

Computer Price Comparison

Component	Computer 1	Computer 1 Prices	Computer 2 Prices	Difference
Monitor (size, type)	20" flat pane	$ 260.00	$ 309.00	$ 49.00
CPU (GHz)	1.6	$ 154.00	$ 220.00	$ 66.00
Hard drive (GB)	200	$ 99.00	$ 133.00	$ 34.00
Additional drive	CD-RW	$ 47.00	$ 124.00	$ 77.00
Memory (GB)	1	$ 31.00	$ 89.00	$ 58.00
		$ 591.00	$ 875.00	$ 284.00
Number of components		5	5	
Average cost		$ 118.20	$ 175.00	
Highest cost		$ 260.00	$ 309.00	
Lowest cost		$ 31.00	$ 89.00	

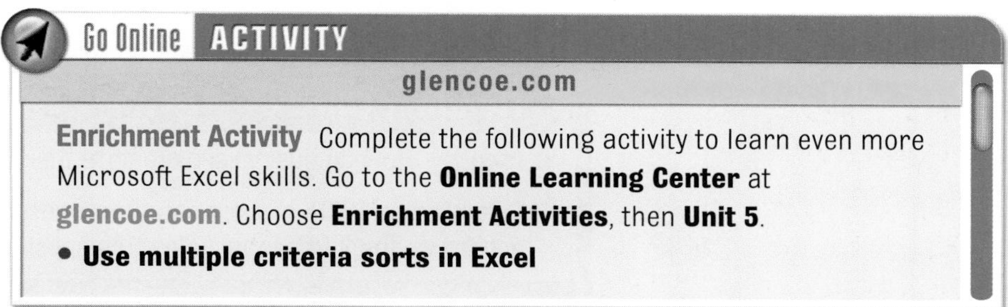

Go Online ACTIVITY

glencoe.com

Enrichment Activity Complete the following activity to learn even more Microsoft Excel skills. Go to the **Online Learning Center** at **glencoe.com**. Choose **Enrichment Activities**, then **Unit 5**.

- **Use multiple criteria sorts in Excel**

After You Read

Key Concepts Check

1. **Compare and Contrast** What are B2B, B2C, and C2C e-commerce?
2. **Identify** Describe three ways that e-commerce benefits consumers.
3. **Describe** What is a database used for?

Critical Thinking

4. **Imagine** You have a friend who is afraid to shop on the Internet because her personal information might get stolen. How would you persuade your friend that e-commerce is usually safe? What precautions would you tell her to take?

21st Century Skills

5. **Evaluate** You own a bookstore that has a Web presence. Write a brief summary about whether you think the Web site is "sticky." Explain why.

Academic Skills

Mathematics

As Web sites become more secure and easier to use, people become more willing to shop online.

a. **Compare** How much more was earned in Year 3 compared to Year 2?

b. **Draw Conclusions** Based on the difference between Year 2 and Year 3, what do you think the Year 4 number will be?

Math Concept

Charts A chart is a graphic that is useful to organize and process data visually so that it is easily understandable. In this case, you are evaluating how quickly business on the internet has grown.

Starting Hint Locate the total amount of e-commerce sales for both Year 3 and Year 2. Then subtract to find how much more was earned in Year 3.

NCTM Number and Operations Compute fluently and make reasonable estimates.

Source: United States Department of Commerce

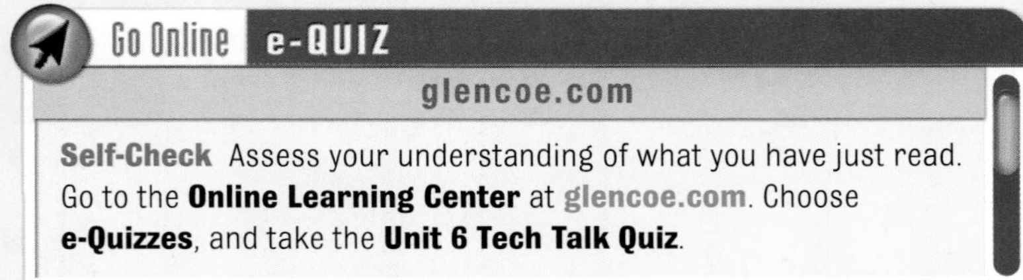

6 The chart displays on the worksheet. The **Chart Tools** display.

7 On the **Design** tab, in the **Data** group, click the **Switch Row/Column** button. Your chart should look like Figure 3.9.

Figure 3.9 The chart is placed on the worksheet as an embedded chart.

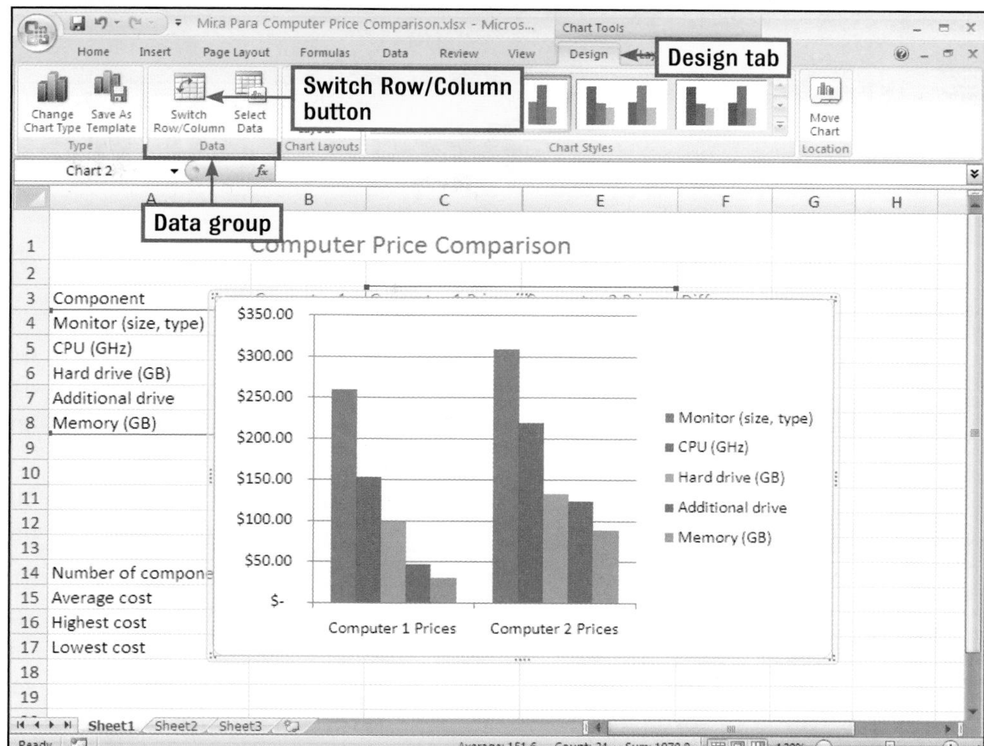

8 On the **Layout** tab, in the **Labels** group, click the **Chart Title** button.

9 Choose the **Above Chart** option. In the **Formula Bar**, key Computer Prices. Press ENTER. See Figure 3.10.

Figure 3.10 Add a chart title.

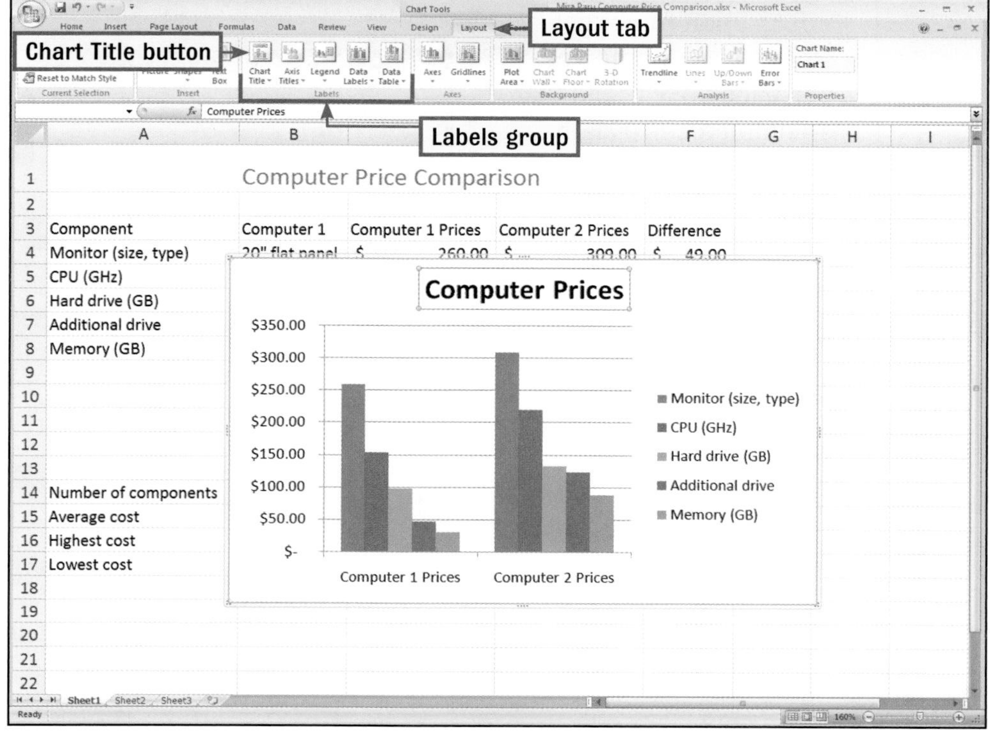

Concepts in Action

Project 1 Create a Database

Key Concepts

Exercise 1-1

- Explain the structure and uses of a database
- Identify the parts of the Access screen

Exercise 1-2

- Identify the objects in a database
- Create a new database file
- Create a table

Exercise 1-3

- Enter information into a field
- Create a new record in a table
- Move through the records in a table

Vocabulary

table
record
field
data type
primary key
relational databases

Before You Begin

Create a Glossary Microsoft Office Access uses many new terms. Keep a glossary of terms just for Access. If necessary, draw a picture to help you understand a term.

For this project, you will use a database program to keep track of products and customers for a school fundraiser.

Enter Your T-Shirt Data

Imagine that your class is planning a trip to Washington, D.C., but you need to raise money for the trip. The class decides to sell T-shirts as a fundraiser. The T-shirts will be available in a variety of sizes and colors. To keep track of your customers, T-shirt orders, and inventory, you will need to set up a database.

Product Number	Color	Size	Cost	Quantity
1	Blue	Small	$5.25	25
2	Blue	Medium	$5.50	35
3	Blue	Large	$5.75	50
4	Red	Small	$5.25	25
5	Red	Medium	$5.50	35
6	Red	Large	$5.75	50

Step-by-Step

1. **Open** your **Computer Price Comparison** worksheet.

2. Click any cell in **column D**. On the **Home** tab, in the **Cells** group, click the **Format** drop-down arrow. Under **Visibility**, choose **Hide & Unhide**, then **Hide Columns.** Column D is hidden.

3. Select cells **A3** through **A8**. Press and hold CTRL, click cell **C3**, and drag the mouse pointer to select **C3** through **E8**. You should now have two ranges selected (Figure 3.7).

4. On the **Insert** tab, in the **Charts** group, click the **Column** button.

5. Under **2-D Column**, click **Clustered Column**. See Figure 3.8.

Figure 3.7 The prices for the two computer systems are now side by side, and column D is hidden.

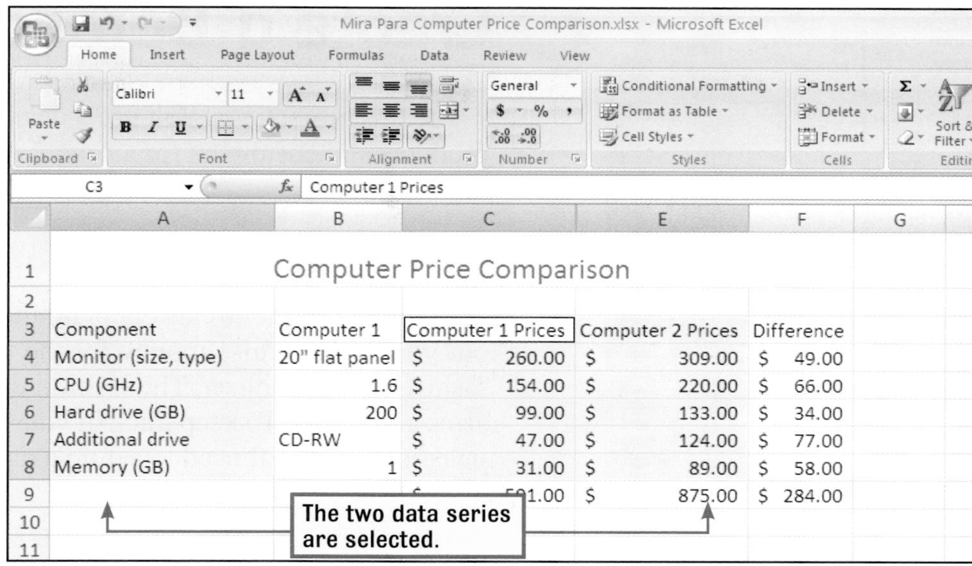

Figure 3.8 Two ranges are selected before you use the Chart Wizard.

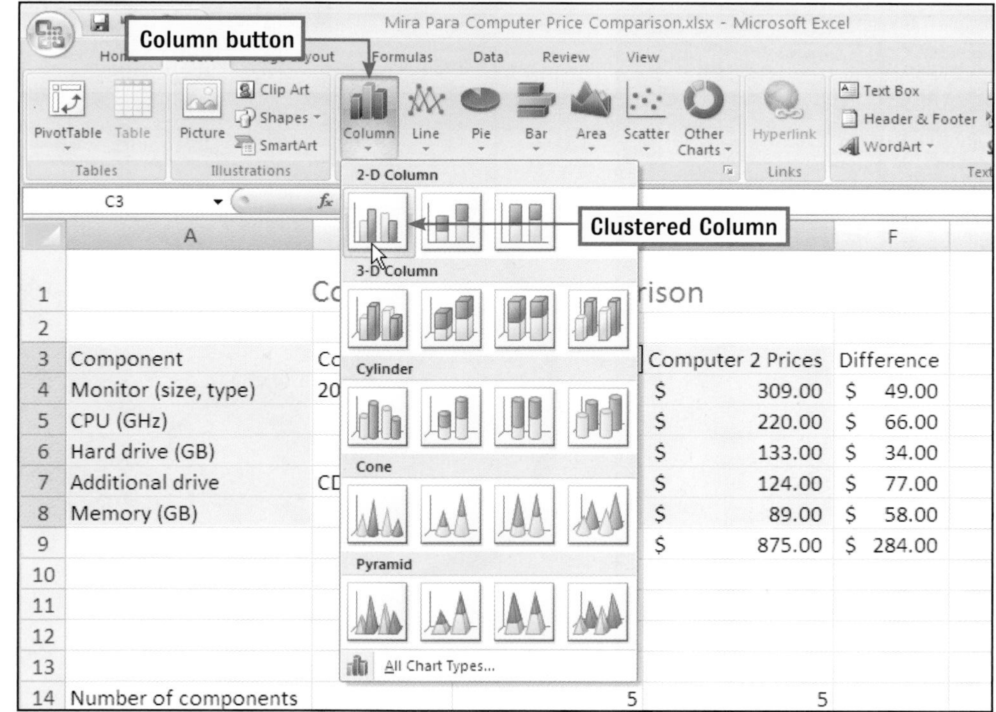

TechSavvy

Data Series To create a chart, you must select the row (or column) headings and each of the ranges to be used as a **data series**.

Exercise 1-1 Get to Know Microsoft Access

You may not know it, but you use databases every day and you are also part of other databases. Your cell-phone and instant-messaging contacts are part of databases, as are your school's student records and your library's catalog.

A database is a software program that organizes data, or information, so that it can be quickly found and displayed. For example, on a cell phone you can:

- Find a person by name or by group
- Search through a list to find a name
- Bring up all of the information you need for one individual

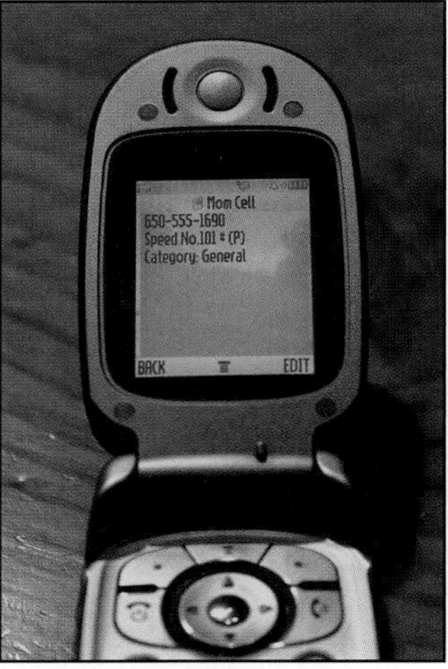

▲ Your phone's contact list is a database.

The building blocks of databases are tables. A **table** is a collection of information, or data, arranged in columns and rows. The data can be classified as a record or a field.

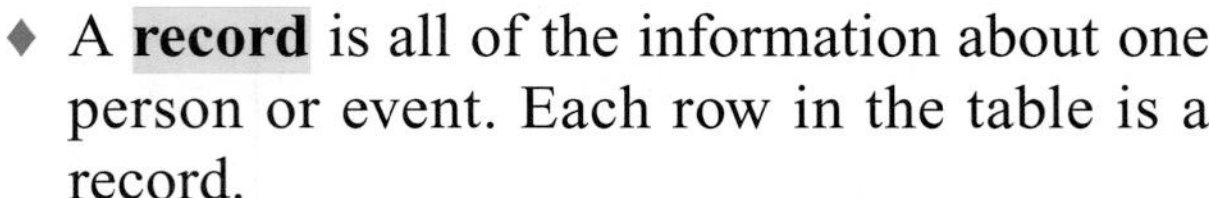

- A **record** is all of the information about one person or event. Each row in the table is a record.
- A **field** is the information contained within each record. Each column lists a specific field.

For example, a cell-phone database could have a table like the one below.

Name	Home Phone	Cell Phone
Dad	662-1578	818-3246
Jenny Tyler	448-7615	442-3218
Mark Adams	652-3821	555-3468
Mom	662-1578	818-3245

Mom's record has three fields.

The cell phone number is one field in Mom's record.

There are a number of commercial database software programs, including Microsoft Office Access, Microsoft SQL Server, and FileMaker® Pro.

In this exercise, you will explore the Access screen and become familiar with the various parts of a database table.

Exercise 3-3 Create Charts

A **chart**, also known as a graph, is a visual way to display and compare data. Excel lets you easily select data in a range of cells to create a chart. Below are examples of different types of charts you can create in Excel.

In this exercise, you will create a column chart that compares the prices of each component of a computer.

▼ A bar chart compares data horizontally (left to right).

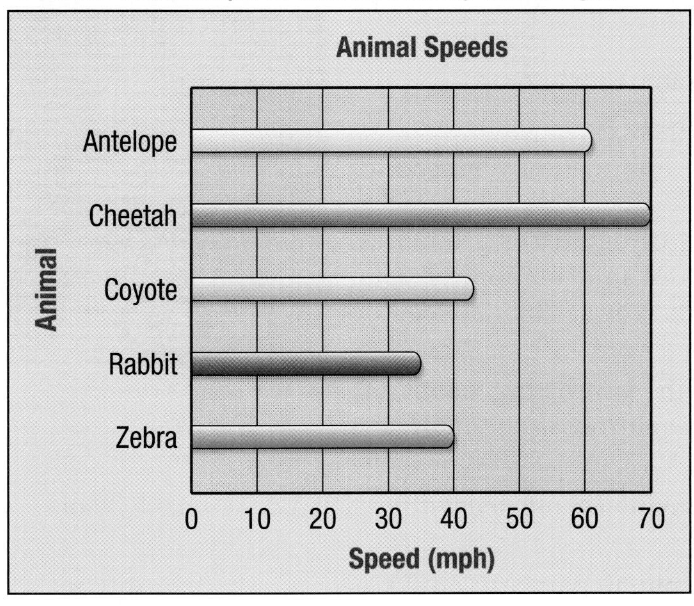

▼ A column chart compares data vertically (top to bottom).

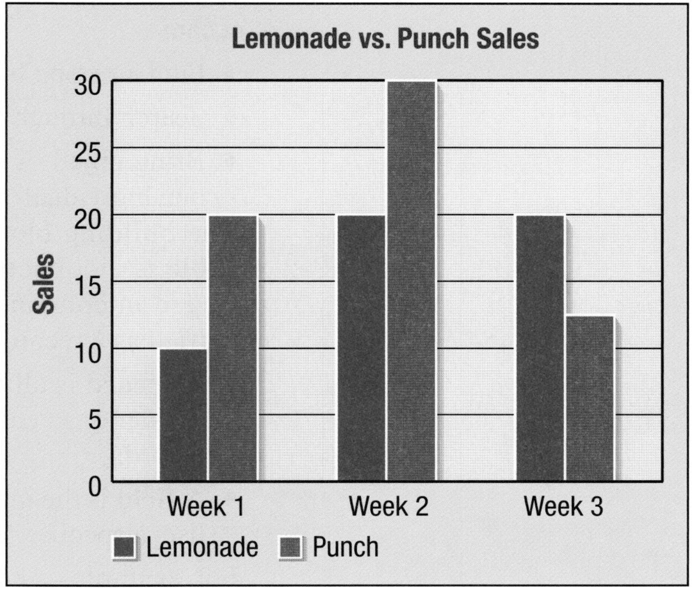

▼ A line chart compares how data change over a period of time.

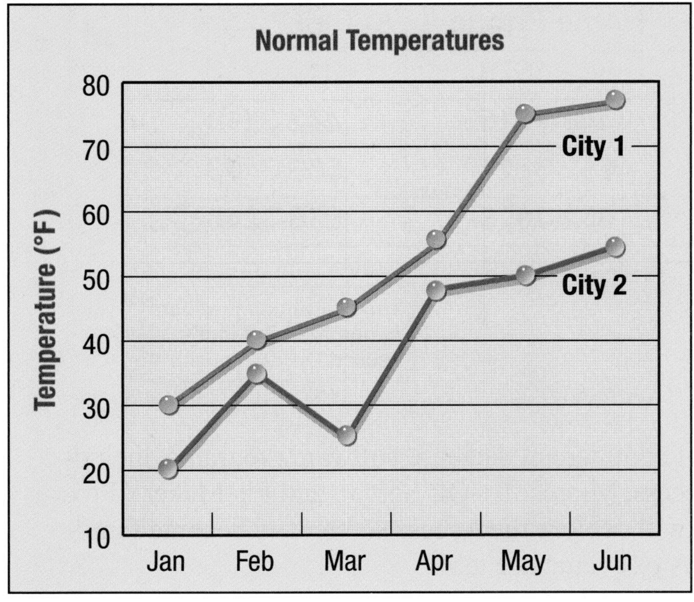

▼ A pie chart compares parts of a whole (in percentages).

Figure 1.1 This is the first window that appears when you start Microsoft Access.

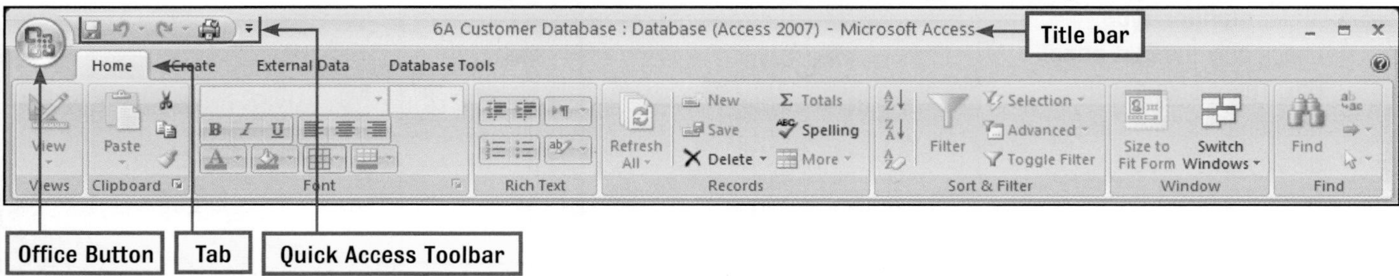

Step-by-Step

1. Start **Microsoft Access**. At the top of the **Getting Started** page, click the **Office Button**. Open the **Data File** named **6A Customer Database.**
2. Use Figure 1.1 to identify key parts of the **Access Ribbon.**
3. On the **Navigation** Pane, click the **Down Arrow** (see Figure 1.2). Read the items in the menu. Click the button again to close the menu.
4. In the **Navigation** Pane, click **Tables**, if necessary. Double-click the **Customer Orders** table. Your screen should look like Figure 1.2.
5. In the **Customer Orders** table, note that there are 20 customers and 7 fields.
6. Click **Close** on the title bar to **exit Access.**

Figure 1.2 The Access screen displays.

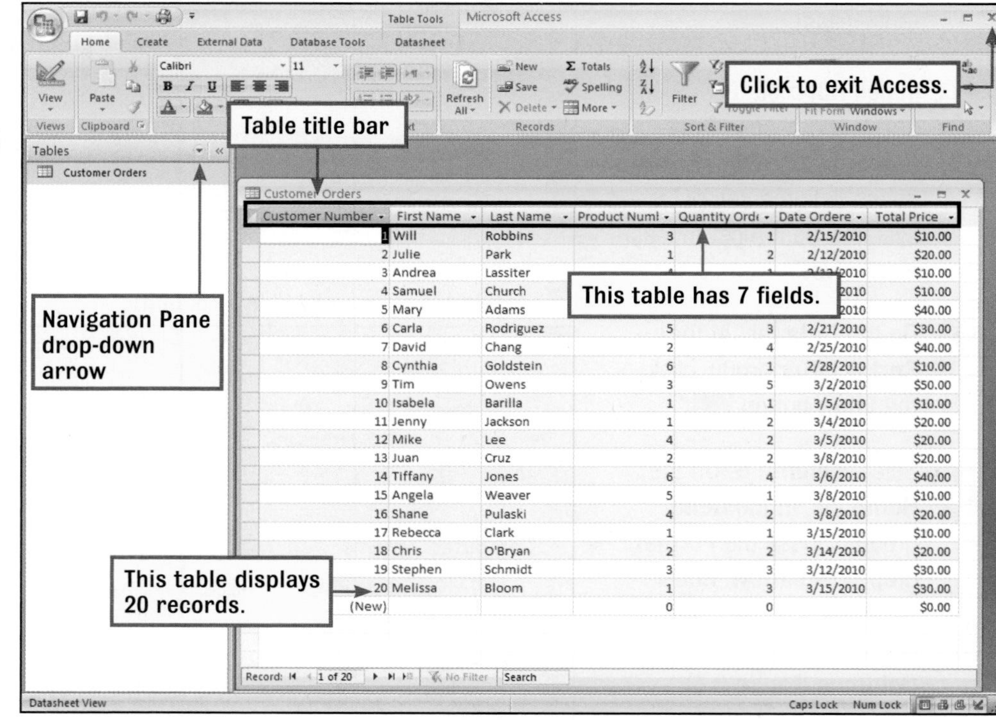

TechSavvy

Ribbon Tabs Notice that the **Ribbon** displays additional features for each tab. The related **Groups** change as you click each tab.

4 Click the drop-down arrow under **Monitor Type**, check only the **Flat panel** box. The systems with flat panel Monitors are displayed. Click **OK** (Figure 3.5).

5 In cell **E3**, click the **Filter** icon. Choose **Clear Filter From "Monitor Type."** All the data is redisplayed.

6 In cell **H3**, click the arrow and choose **Sort Largest to Smallest**. This option lists the computer systems from most to least expensive.

7 On the **Data** tab, in the **Sort & Filter** group, click the **Filter** button.

8 Select **column G**. On the **Home** tab, in the **Cells** group, choose the **Format** drop-down arrow. Under **Visibility**, choose **Hide & Unhide**, then **Hide Columns** (Figure 3.6).

9 Click the **Format** command, choose **Visibility**, **Hide & Unhide**, and click **Unhide Columns**.

10 If you have permission from your teacher, **print** the worksheet.

11 **Save** the worksheet. **Close** the worksheet.

Figure 3.5 The result of the filter displays.

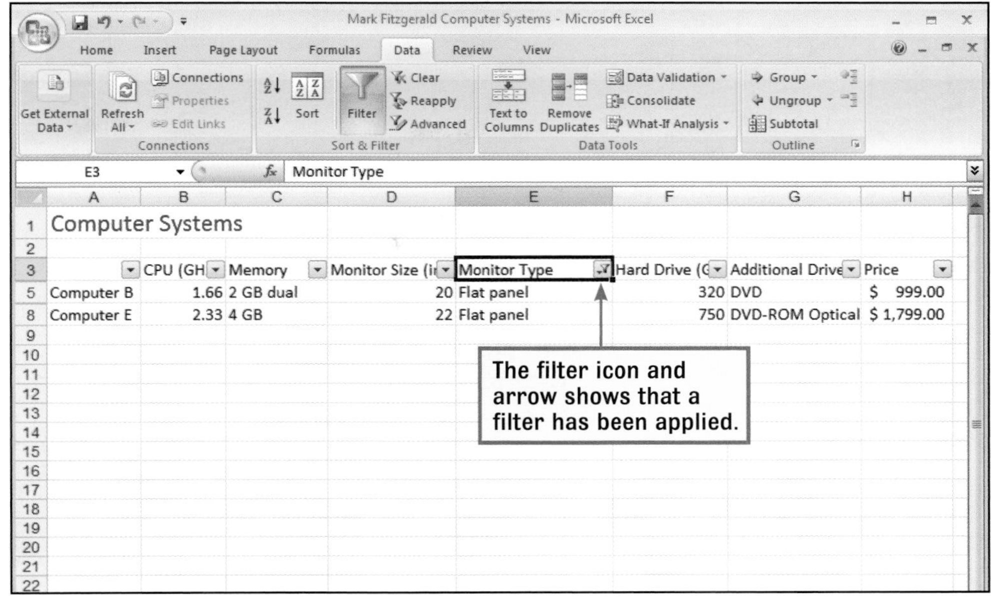

Figure 3.6 You can hide a column.

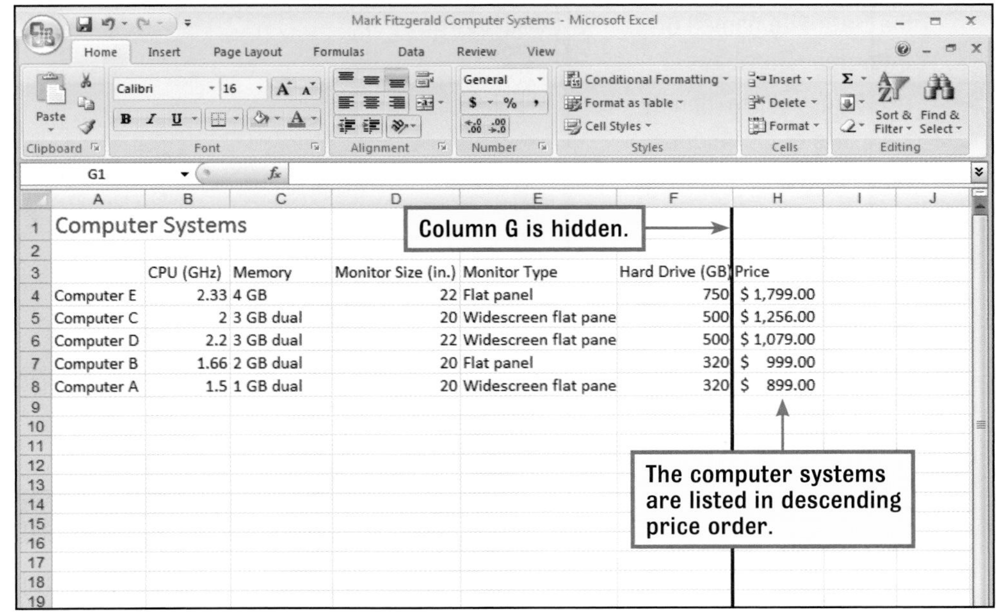

TechSavvy

Advanced Sort The **Sort and Filter** group also has an **Advanced** option. You can use this option to set up more complex criteria, such as checking for a CPU speed of more than 2 GHz or hard drives of less than 100 GB.

Exercise 1-2 Create a Database

To create a database, you will need to build a table to organize your data. When you create a table, you:

- Name the table
- Name each field
- Set the field's data type

The **data type** is the kind of information you display in a field. The four most commonly used data types are shown in the table below.

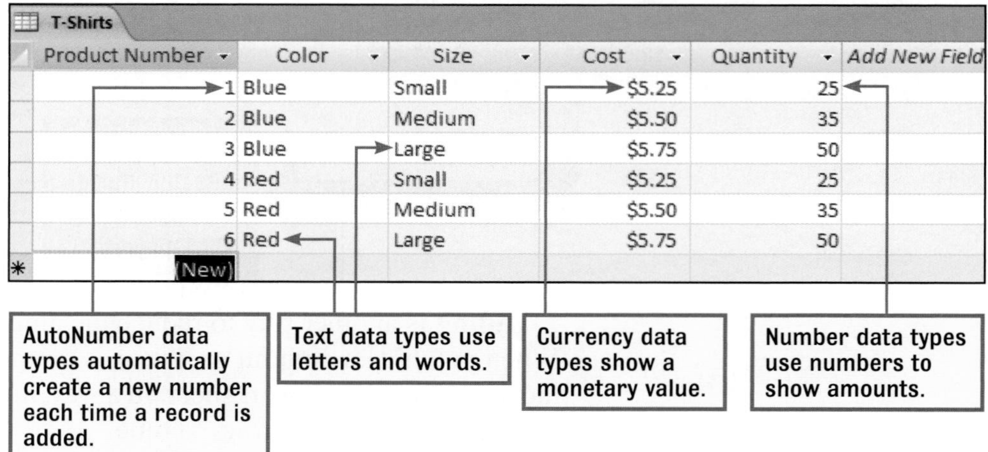

An AutoNumber is often used as a primary key. A **primary key** is a unique number that is created when a new record is added to a database. Just as each of your friends has his or her own phone number, each T-shirt style in the table above has its own product number. If you needed to find out how many medium-sized red T-shirts you have, you would just enter Product Number 5, and the database would find the record for you.

In this exercise, you will create a table for the T-shirts your class will be selling. You will open a new blank database and create a table.

HELP!

Open a Blank Database Your version of Access may not have a Navigation Pane or it may not be visible when you first open Access. You can open a blank database from the opening screen by doing the following: At the top of the page, under the **New Blank Database** heading, click **Blank Database**, name your file, and then click **Create**.

Exercise 3-2 Filter Data

Sometimes the information you need is buried in rows of data. A **filter** finds just the information you need and hides the rest. For example, if you decide you want your computer to have a DVD player, a filter will let you see only those systems that include a DVD player.

	A	F	G	H
1	Computer Systems			
2		Hard Drive	Add'l Drive	Price
3	Computer A	40	CD-R	$ 799.00
4	Computer B	80	DVD	$ 834.00
5	Computer C	160	DVD-RW	$1,256.00
6	Computer D	80	DVD	$1,899.00
7	Computer E	40	CD	$1,099.00

Use a filter to see only those computers with DVD players.

	A	F	G	H
1	Computer Systems			
2		Hard Drive	Add'l Drive	Price
3	Computer B	80	DVD	$ 834.00
5	Computer C	160	DVD-RW	$1,256.00
6	Computer D	80	DVD	$1,899.00

Hiding is another way to reduce the amount of information displayed. When you hide a column or row, it is temporarily hidden from view, but the data is still in the worksheet. In a way, hiding rows is just like filtering, except you choose the rows to hide.

In this exercise, you will use a worksheet that lists five computer systems, each with different components and prices. You will use filters to display the systems that meet your criteria and to hide columns of data that you do not need to see.

Step-by-Step

1. **Open** the **Data File** named **5A Computer Systems**.

2. Click cell **A3**.

3. On the **Data** tab, in the **Sort & Filter** group, click the **Filter** button. The drop-down arrows for the filter appear, as shown in Figure 3.4.

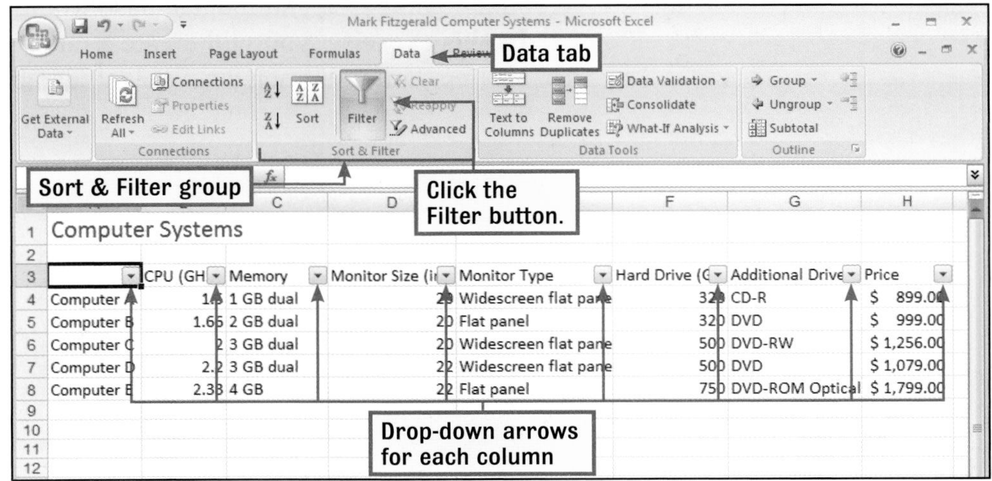

▼ **Figure 3.4** When a filter is applied, drop-down arrows appear over each column of data.

Step-by-Step

1. Start **Access**.

2. On the **Getting Started** page, under **New Blank Database**, click **Blank Database**.

3. Select the text in the **File Name** box on the right side of the screen, and key *Your Name* TShirt Database (Figure 1.3).

4. Click **Create** (Figure 1.3).

5. A new database table opens in a new window (Figure 1.4). Notice that the **Table** tab indicates that the file is in **Datasheet View**. This is the way the screen looks by default.

6. On the **Datasheet** tab, in the **Views** group, click the **View** drop-down arrow (See Figure 1.4), then choose **Design View**.

7. If necessary. Click **Save** on the **QAT**. In the **Save As** dialog box, key T-Shirts, and then click **OK**.

TechSavvy

Blank Table You can also create a new blank table by doing the following: Click the **Create** tab. Then in the **Tables** group, click **Table**.

Figure 1.3 Unlike most Microsoft Office programs, in Access you must key the name of the file when you create a new database.

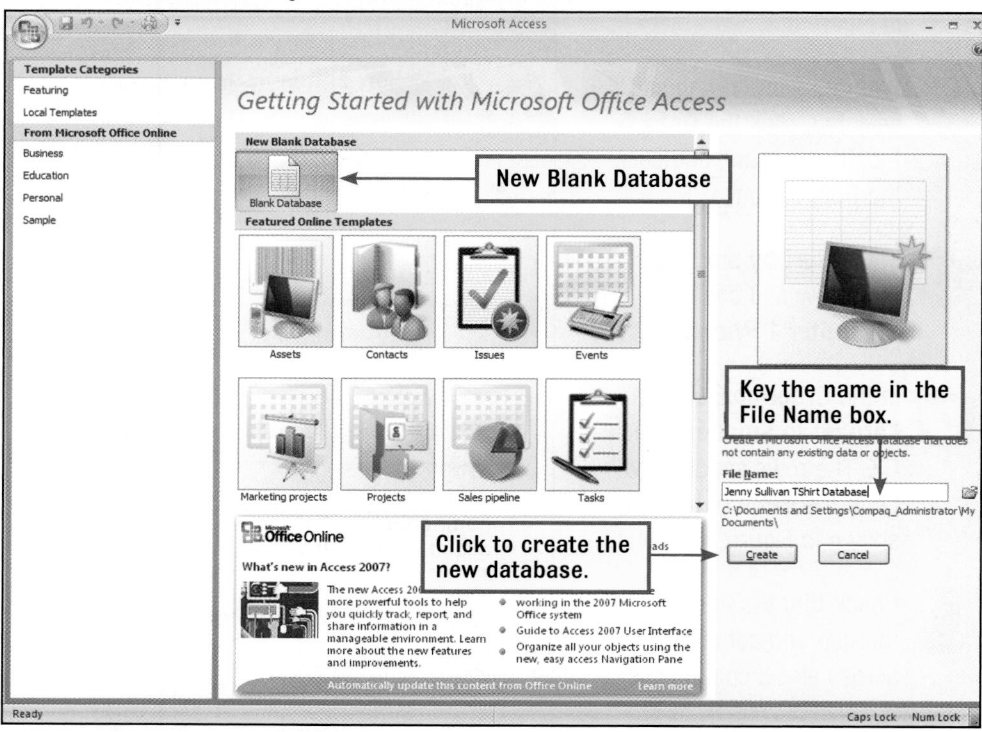

Figure 1.4 The database table automatically opens in Datasheet View.

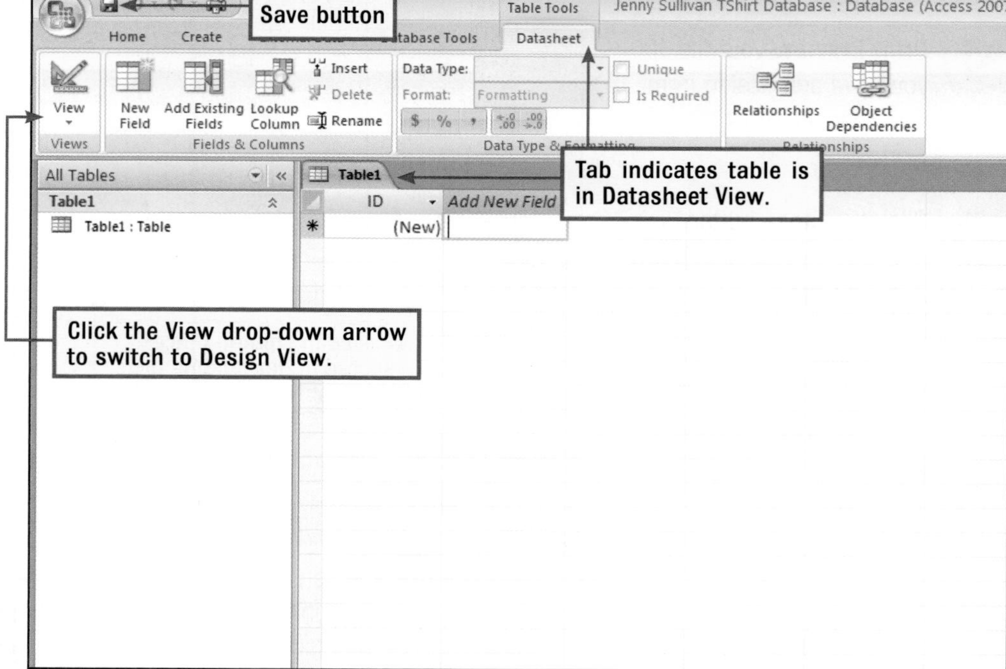

4 The rows should now be in the same order as shown in Figure 3.2.

5 With the same range still selected, click the **Data** tab, if necessary, and click the **Sort** button.

6 In the **Sort by** box, click the arrow and choose **Computer 1 Prices**.

7 In the **Order** box, choose **Largest to Smallest**. Click **OK**. The rows should now be in the same order, as shown in Figure 3.3.

8 Check that the title is merged and centered across all six columns. If not, select cells **A1** to **F1**, then click the **Merge & Center** button. **Save** your worksheet.

9 **Print Preview** your file. If you have permission from your teacher, **print** the worksheet.

10 Click the **Close** button to close the worksheet. (Do *not* exit Excel.)

Figure 3.2 The row headers now appear in alphabetical order.

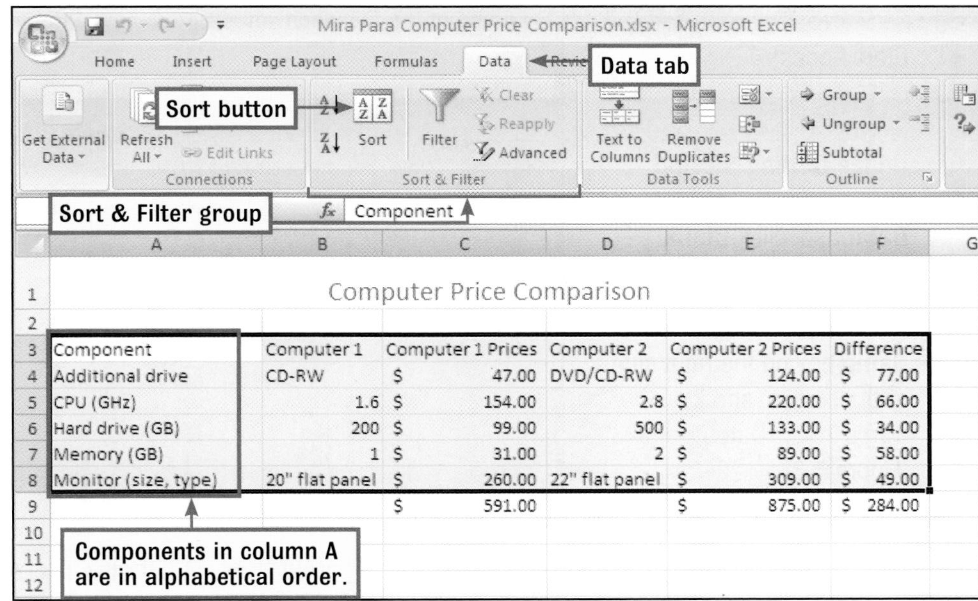

Figure 3.3 Column C shows the highest priced Computer 1 component first.

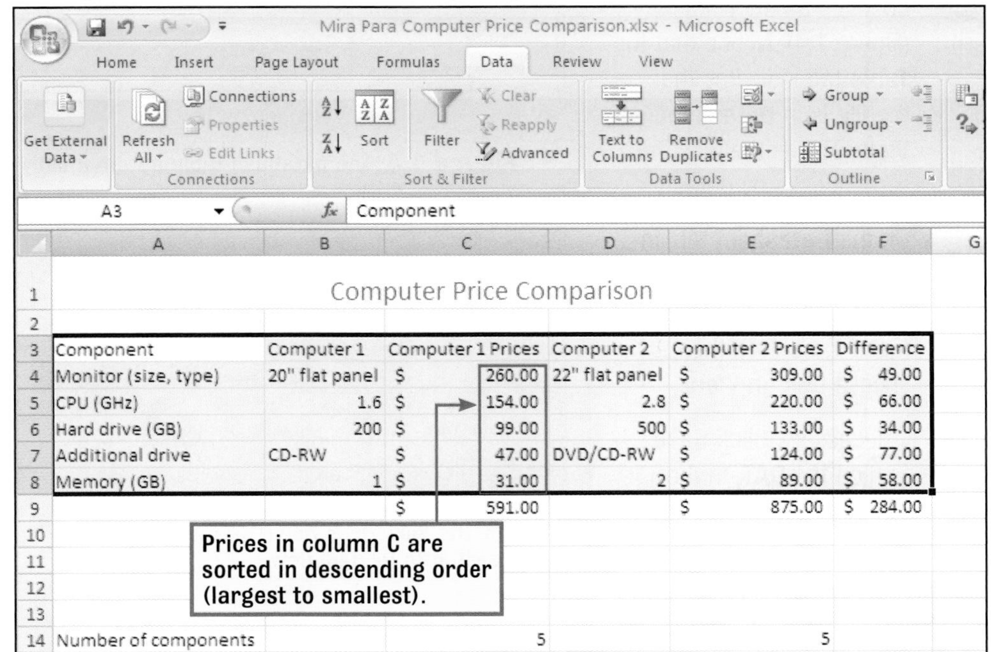

HELP!

Selecting Data If you do not select all of the data in a row before choosing the Sort command, only the selected columns will be rearranged, leaving some data in the original order. In most cases, this is not what you want. Be sure to select the entire row or column before sorting.

8. Under the heading **Field Name**, notice that the text **ID** is selected in the first record (Figure 1.5). Key Product Number.

9. On the keyboard, press TAB to go to the next field.

10. Under the heading **Data Type**, click the drop-down arrow. Notice the data types in the drop-down menu. Then choose **AutoNumber** (Figure 1.6).

11. Click in the first cell of the second row under **Product Number**, then key Color. Press TAB.

12. Under **Data Type**, click the drop-down arrow and choose **Text**.

TechSavvy

Navigation Tip You can minimize the **Navigation** pane by clicking the **Shutter Bar Open/Close** «. Expand the pane by clicking the button again.

Figure 1.5 The field names will display at the top of each column.

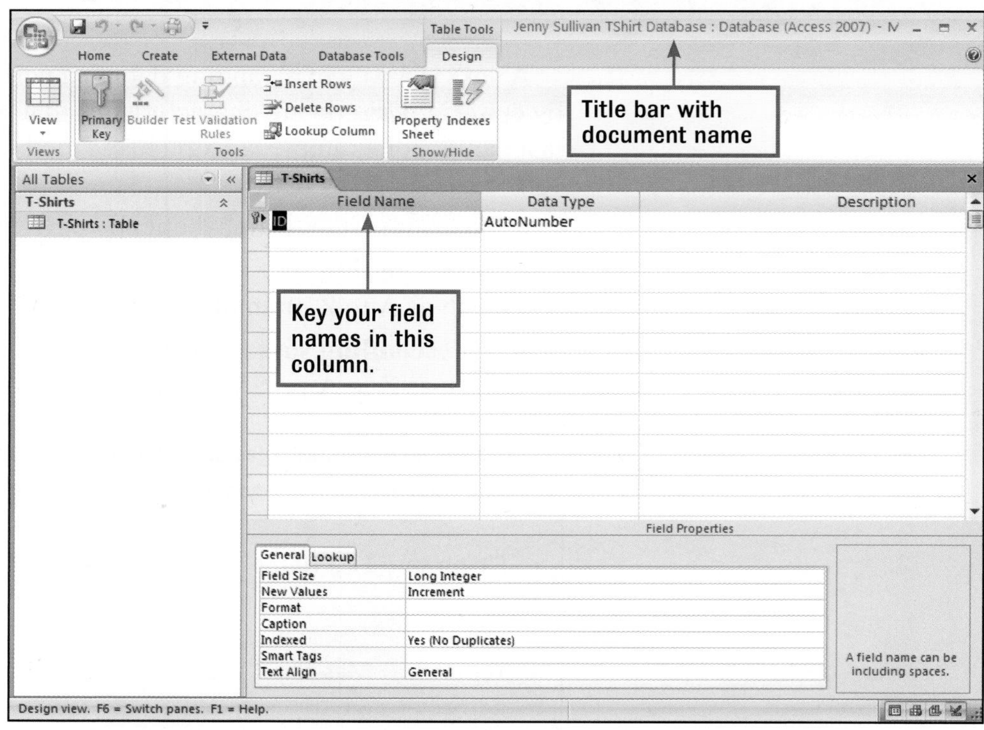

Figure 1.6 "AutoNumber" data type automatically creates new product numbers.

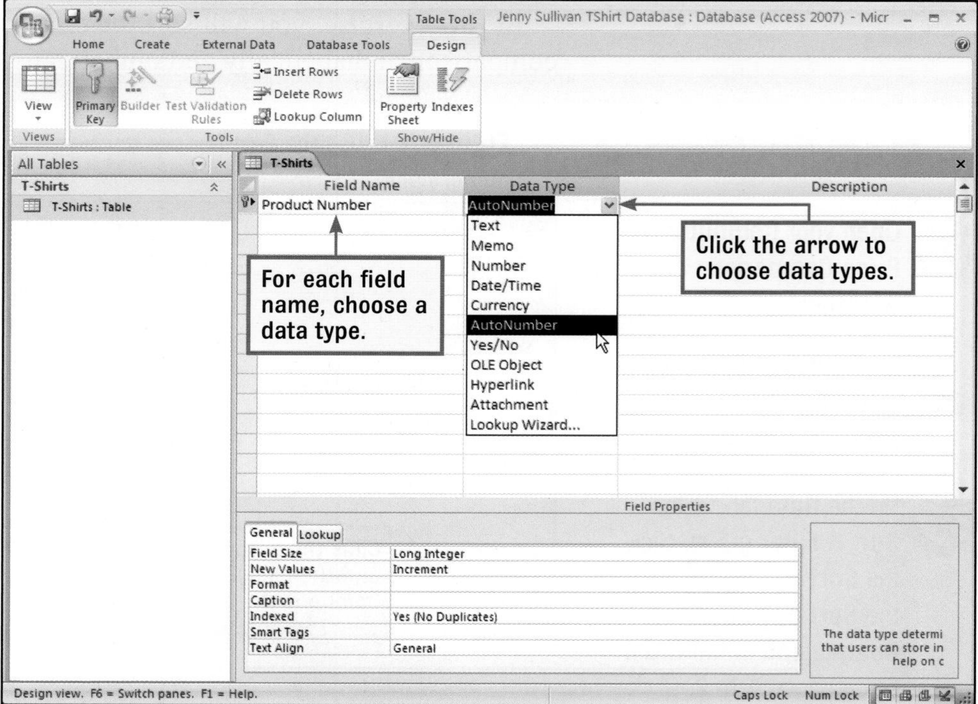

Exercise 3-1 Sort Data

A **sort** is a way of arranging data in a particular order. Rows are sorted by **criteria**. Criteria are characteristics that define an item, such as age or last name. For example, a worksheet filled with names and ages could be sorted by age or by name.

- You can sort data alphabetically or by number.
- An **ascending sort** is a sort to rearrange data from lowest to highest, such as A to Z or smallest number to largest.
- A **descending sort** is a sort to rearrange data from highest to lowest, such as Z to A or largest number to smallest.

▼ **The left image shows ages sorted in ascending order, youngest to oldest. The right image shows last names sorted in descending order, Z to A.**

	A	B	C
1	First Name	Last Name	Age
2			
3	Kieko	Toshima	12
4	Tom	Masiello	14
5	Cornel	Smith	16
6	Mary	Jackson	16
7	Carla	Gomez	18

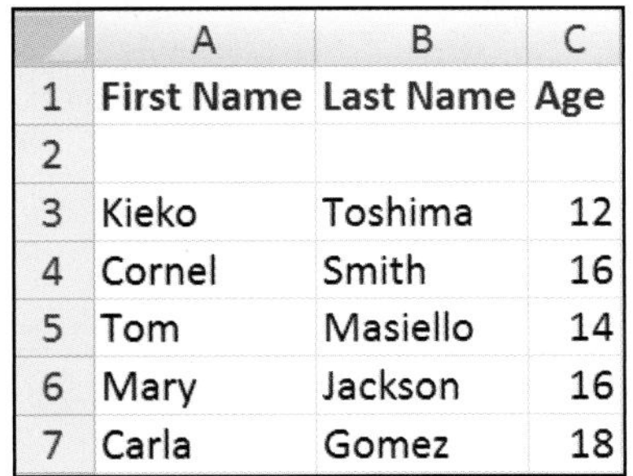

	A	B	C
1	First Name	Last Name	Age
2			
3	Kieko	Toshima	12
4	Cornel	Smith	16
5	Tom	Masiello	14
6	Mary	Jackson	16
7	Carla	Gomez	18

In this exercise, you will sort the components in your computer price comparison alphabetically and numerically.

Step-by-Step

1. **Open** your **Computer Price Comparison** worksheet.
2. Click **A3** and drag to **F8** to select the headers and the data in the worksheet.
3. On the **Data** tab, in the **Sort & Filter** group, click the **Sort** button. In the **Sort by** box, choose **Component**. In the **Order** box, choose **A to Z**. Click **OK** (Figure 3.1).

▼ **Figure 3.1** **Use the Sort feature to rearrange data alphabetically or numerically.**

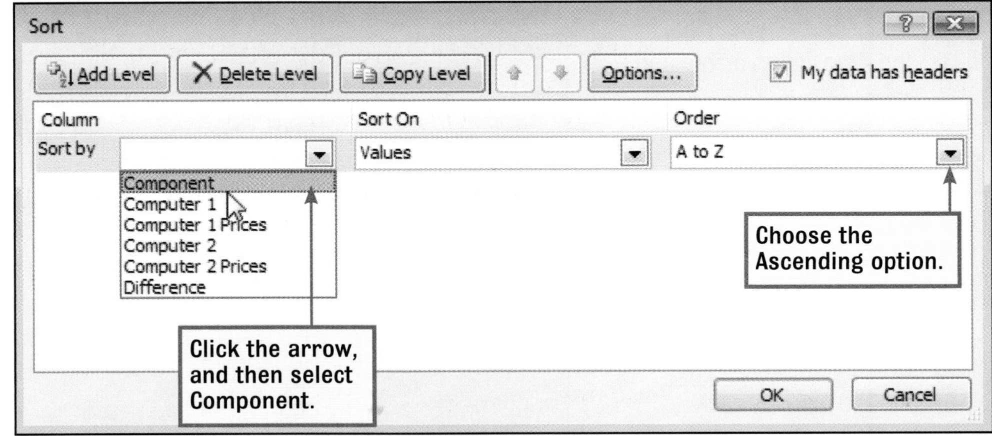

13 Fill out the rest of the **Field Names** and **Data Types** as shown in Figure 1.7.

14 In the Table window, click the **Close** button [X]. Do NOT exit Access!

15 Click **Yes** to save the design of Table 1.

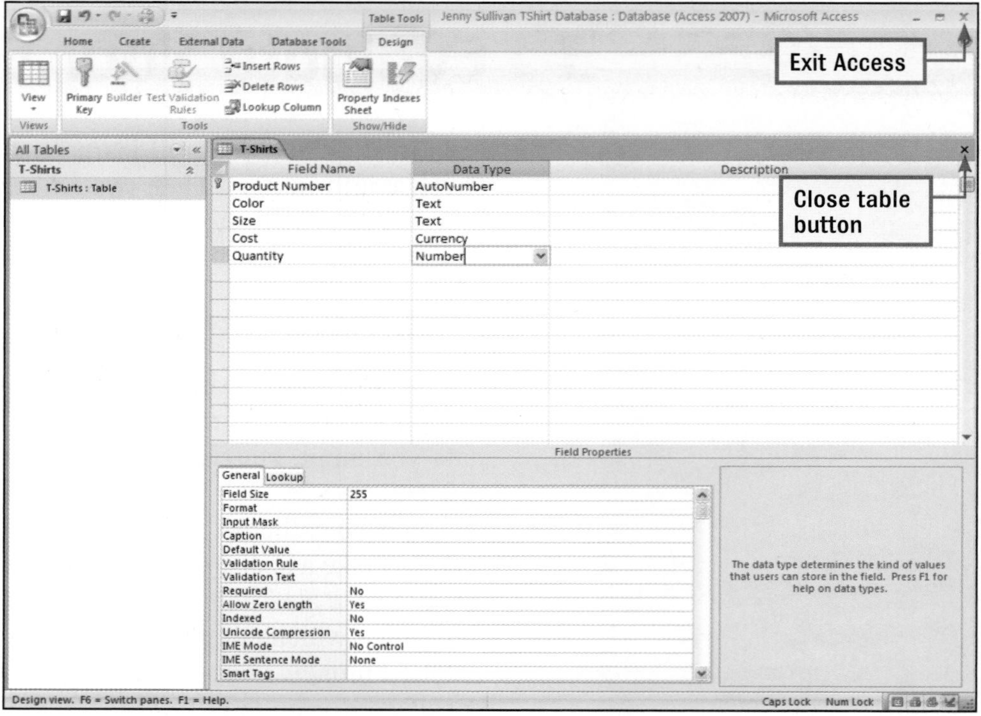

Figure 1.7 The fields for the table are defined with their names and data types.

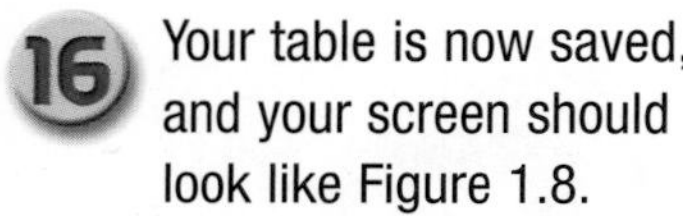

16 Your table is now saved, and your screen should look like Figure 1.8.

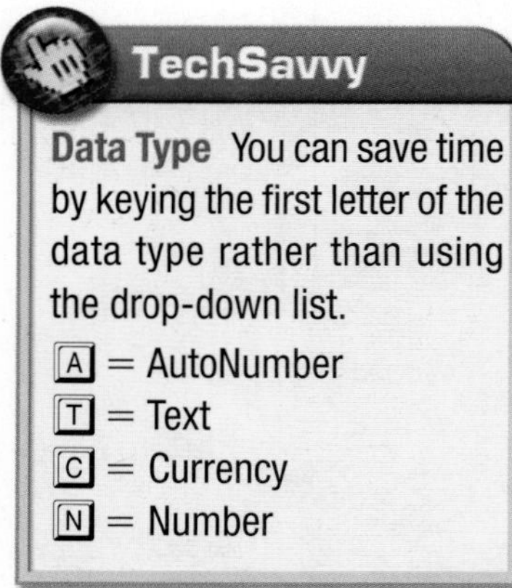

TechSavvy

Data Type You can save time by keying the first letter of the data type rather than using the drop-down list.

[A] = AutoNumber

[T] = Text

[C] = Currency

[N] = Number

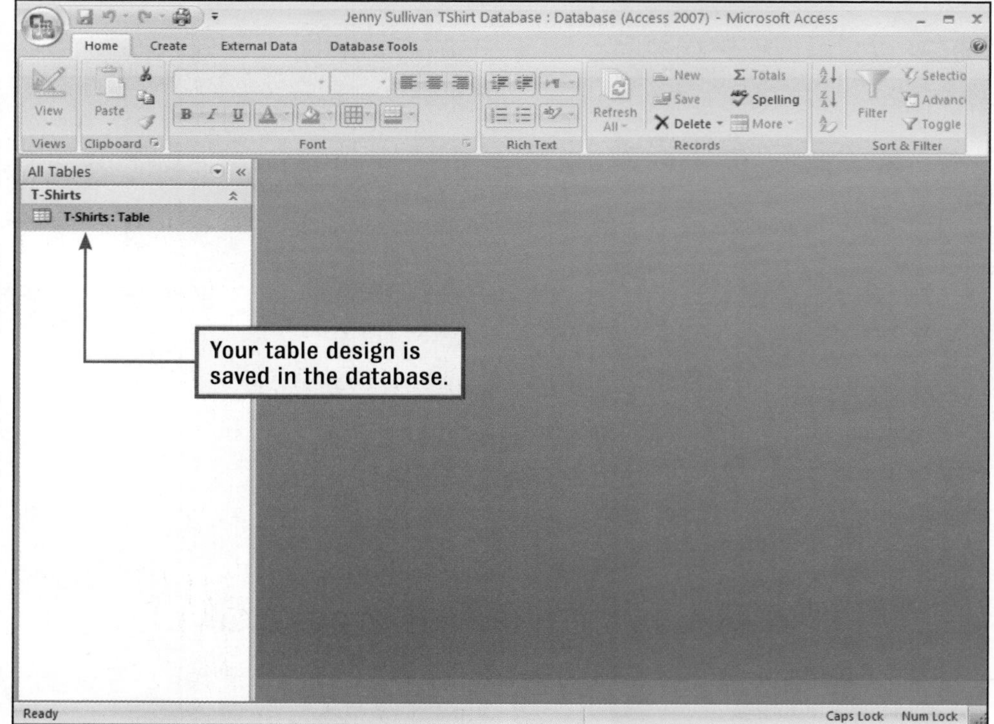

Figure 1.8 The table you just created is listed in the Navigation Pane.

Concepts in Action

Project 3 Evaluate Your Data

Key Concepts

Exercise 3-1
- Select criteria to use in a sort
- Sort in ascending order or descending order

Exercise 3-2
- Display rows that match your needs
- Hide columns

Exercise 3-3
- Create a bar chart
- Select a data series

Vocabulary

Key Terms
sort
criteria
ascending sort
descending sort
filter
hiding
chart

Before You Begin

Using Charts Find examples of charts and graphs in newspapers, magazines, textbooks, or online sources. Evaluate why different charts are used to show different kinds of information.

In this project, you will learn how to sort and filter data to find specific information. Then you will change your data into charts so that you can easily evaluate your results.

Make a Decision with Data

The larger a worksheet gets, the harder it can be to find the information you need. Formulas and functions may add meaning to the data you input, but finding the most important information can be difficult.

You have gathered data for different computer systems. Now you have to make a decision. Which computer is better for you? You need a way to see clearly how the computers compare to each other, and determine which computer gives you the components you need for the least money. Excel has tools that will help you find and evaluate specific information.

Exercise 1-3 Enter Data into a Table

Many companies use databases to keep track of products and customers. For example, airlines need to monitor thousands of passengers and hundreds of flights each day. Their customers have a lot of questions:

- What is my flight number?
- Did the Dallas flight arrive on time?
- Where should I pick up my luggage?

Databases help them answer all of these questions by storing information about passengers, flights, time schedules, airports, and other important data.

Spreadsheets versus Databases Microsoft Access and Excel may seem similar, but there is one big difference: Excel creates spreadsheets, and Access creates databases. Both are good ways to organize information, but if you have hundreds or thousands of records, it would take a long time to find information using a spreadsheet.

A **relational database** links tables through a common field, such as a customer number or product number. It makes it possible to organize and quickly find information that is entered into a number of tables. The information from the different tables can then be displayed as a form. For example, your T-shirt business might use two different database tables to produce a sales receipt. The Product Number creates a relationship between the two tables.

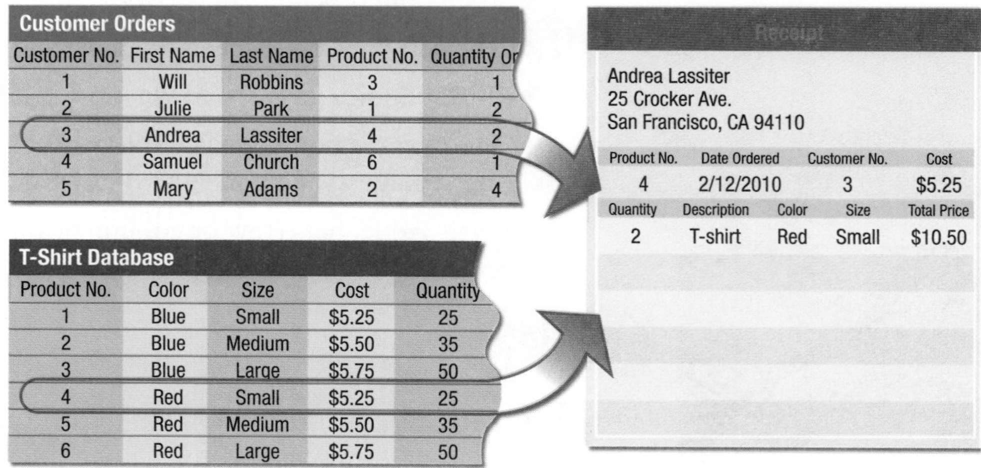

In this exercise, you will add data about the kinds of T-shirts you are selling. This will help you keep track of your inventory. Each T-shirt will have its own record, which you will enter into the table you created in Exercise 1-2.

Project 2 Assessment

2 Independent Practice 

Math Determine Formulas and Functions Add formulas and functions to get more meaning from the data in the **School Day** worksheet you created in Project 1, Independent Practice 2 (page 227).

a. Plan Add labels to the worksheet for the following information. Determine the formulas or functions for each.

- Total minutes spent in all class periods and activities.
- The longest period and the shortest period.
- The difference in time between the longest and shortest periods.

b. Create Apply the formulas and functions to your worksheet.

Independent Practice
Use the rubrics for these projects to help create and evaluate your work. Go to the **Online Learning Center** at **glencoe.com**. Choose **Rubrics**, then **Unit 5**.

3 Independent Practice 

Math Add Formulas and Functions Add formulas and functions to the **Survey** worksheet that you created in Project 1, Independent Practice 3 (page 227).

a. Plan Determine the formulas for the following:

- Total hours spent in all activities for boys and girls.
- The activities boys spend the most and least time doing.
- The activities girls spend the most and least time doing.
- The average number of hours spent in all activities by boys and the average spent in all activities by girls.

b. Create Add labels (row or column headings) for each item above. Apply the formulas and functions to your worksheet.

4 Independent Practice 

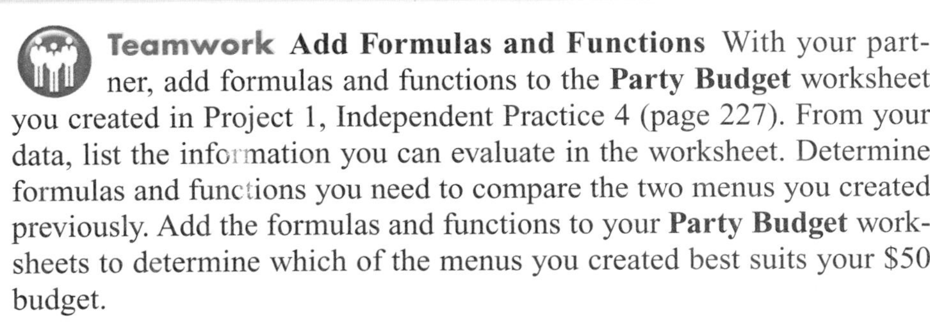
Teamwork Add Formulas and Functions With your partner, add formulas and functions to the **Party Budget** worksheet you created in Project 1, Independent Practice 4 (page 227). From your data, list the information you can evaluate in the worksheet. Determine formulas and functions you need to compare the two menus you created previously. Add the formulas and functions to your **Party Budget** worksheets to determine which of the menus you created best suits your $50 budget.

Step-by-Step

1. **Open** your **TShirt Database** (if it is not open already).

2. In the **Navigation** Pane, double-click the **T-Shirts** table. The table is ready for data entry, as shown in Figure 1.9.

3. To widen the **Product Number** column, place your insertion point on the dividing line next to the field name. The insertion point will change to a double-sided arrow.

4. Click and hold your mouse button and drag the column's title box to the right. Release the mouse when the column is wide enough to see the full title.

5. In the **Color** field, key Blue and press ENTER. Notice that the Product Number is assigned automatically.

6. In the **Size** field, key Small and press ENTER.

7. In the **Cost** field, key 5.25 and press ENTER.

8. In the **Quantity** field, key 25 and press ENTER (Figure 1.10).

Figure 1.9 The table is designed but has no records in.

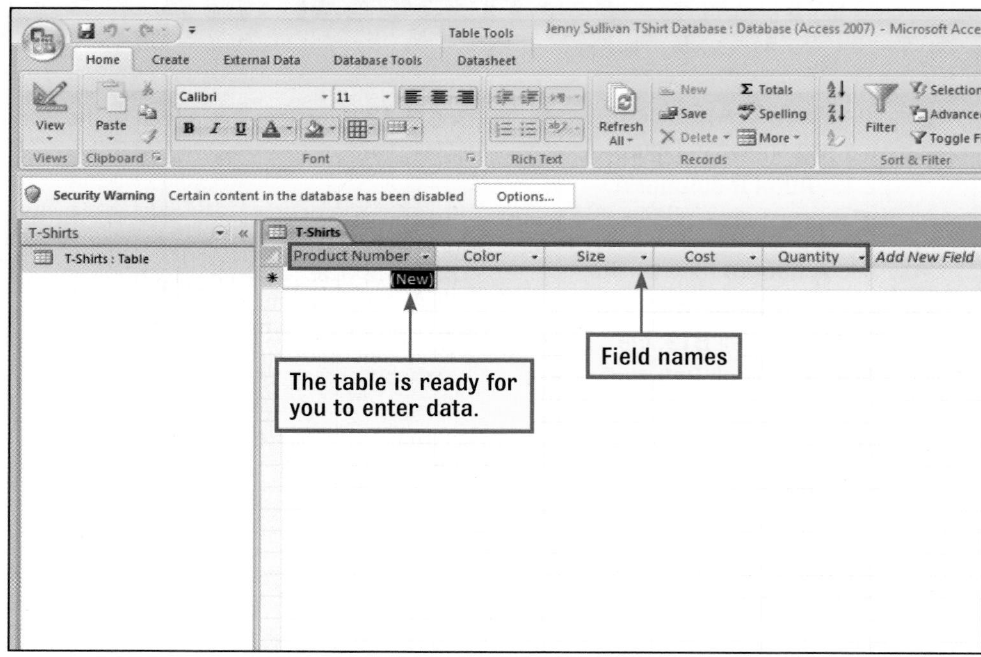

Figure 1.10 The table has one record in it.

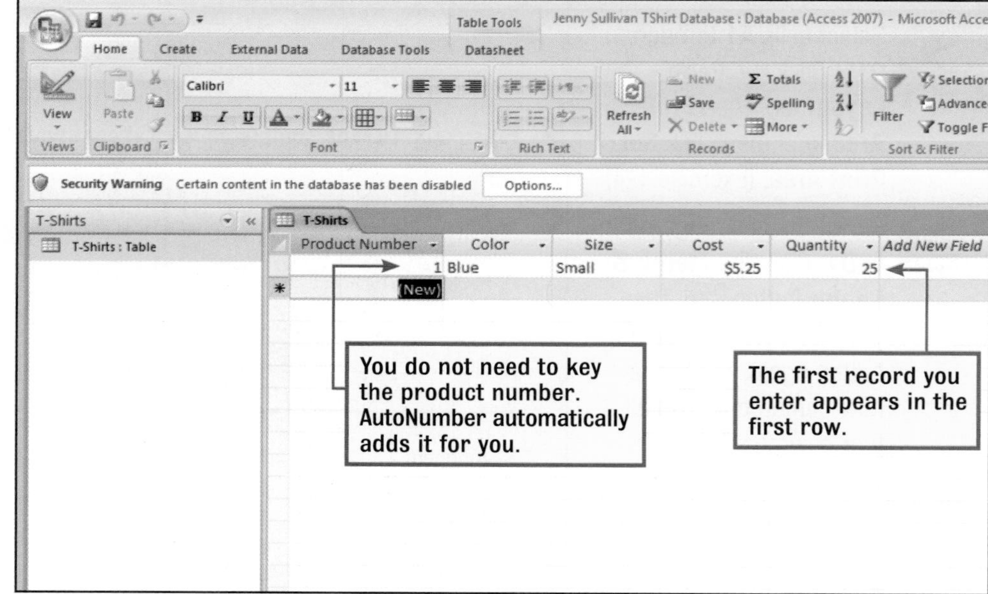

TechSavvy

You Should Know You can arrange open windows by moving them around on the screen. To move a window, drag its title bar.

Project 2 Assessment

5. In cells **A12–A15**, key the text shown in Figure 2.12. **AutoFit column A**. (Exercise 1-3)

6. Use **AutoSum** functions to insert the **Count Numbers** function in cell **B12**, the **Average** in cell **B13**, the **Max** in cell **B14**, and the **Min** in cell **B15**. See Figure 2.12. (Exercise 2-2)

7. Click **D4**. Drag the **fill handle** down through **D8**. (Exercise 2-3)

8. Click **B9**, then drag the **fill handle** through **D9**. See Figure 2.13. (Exercise 2-3)

9. Select cells **A1** through **D15**. Click the **Page Layout** tab, click **Print Area**, and then click **Set Print Area**. (Exercise 1-4)

10. Select the cell range **A1** to **D1**. Click the **Merge & Center** button. Then click the **Merge & Center** button again. The title is now centered across all four columns.

11. **Print Preview** your file. If you have permission to print, click the **Print** button. (Exercise 1-4)

12. **Save** your worksheet. **Exit Excel**.

Figure 2.12 Functions are added to the worksheet.

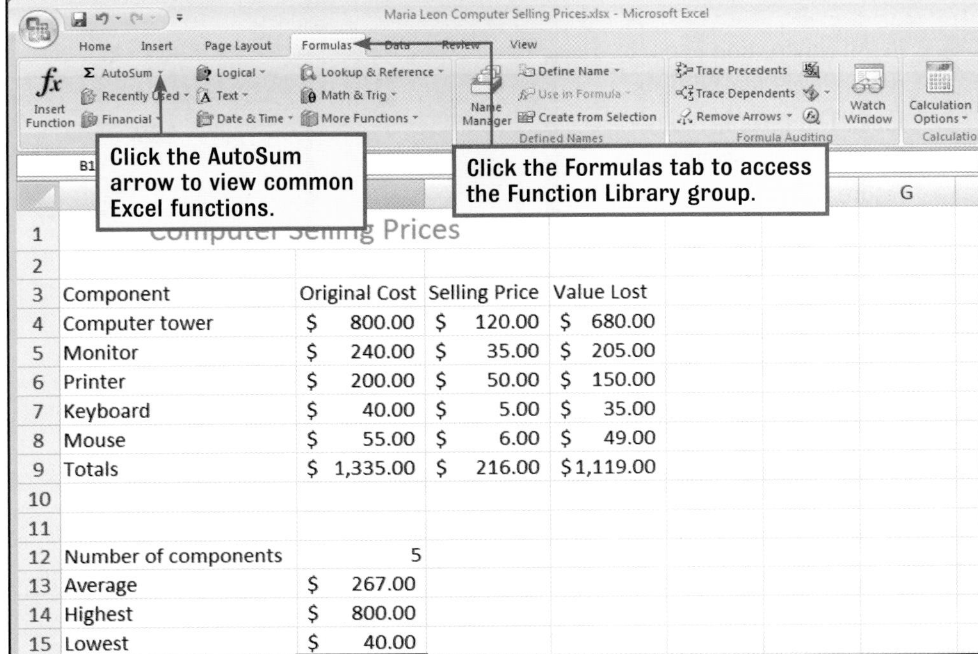

Figure 2.13 The completed worksheet appears below.

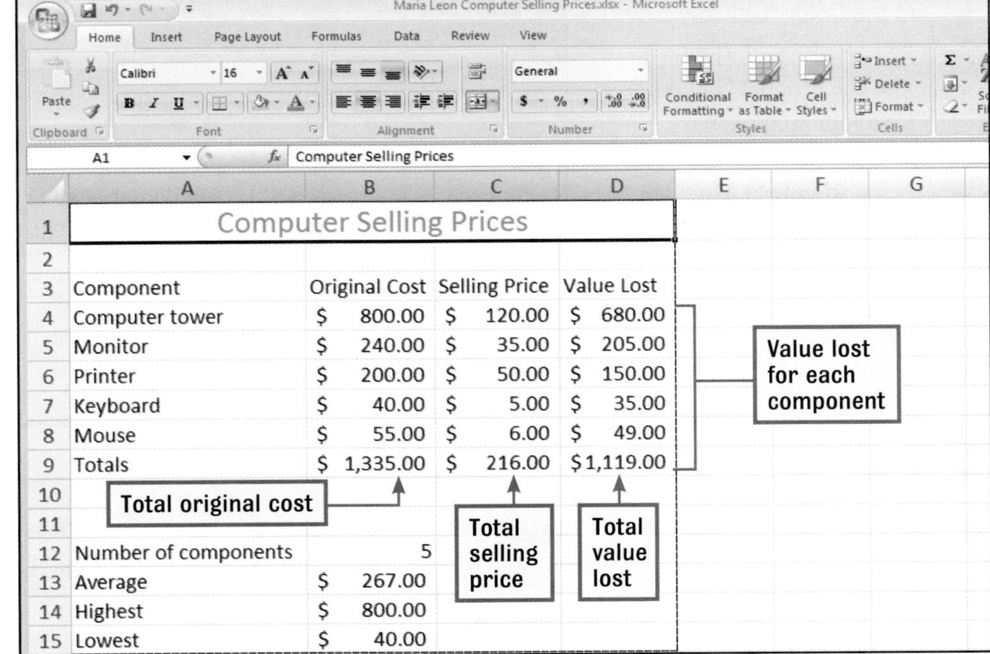

9 In the next row, press ENTER. This will create Product Number 2.

10 Key the rest of the records as shown in Figure 1.11.

Figure 1.11 The complete table has six records in it. Each record has a unique Product Number using the AutoNumber data type.

T-Shirts

Product Number	Color	Size	Cost	Quantity	Add New Field
1	Blue	Small	$5.25	25	
2	Blue	Medium	$5.50	35	
3	Blue	Large	$5.75	50	
4	Red	Small	$5.25	25	
5	Red	Medium	$5.50	35	
6	Red	Large	$5.75	50	
(New)					

11 At the bottom of the T-shirts table, find the Navigation toolbar as shown in Figure 1.12.

12 Click the **First record** button to take you to Product Number 1.

13 Click the **Next record** button three times to go to Record 4.

14 Click inside the **Record number** box, **delete** the **4**, key 2, and press ENTER. You have moved from Record 4 to Record 2, (Figure 1.12).

15 Click the **Close** button to close the table. You do not have to save the table—Access saves tables automatically!

Figure 1.12 The record navigator may not be very useful in a short database, but in a large database it is very important.

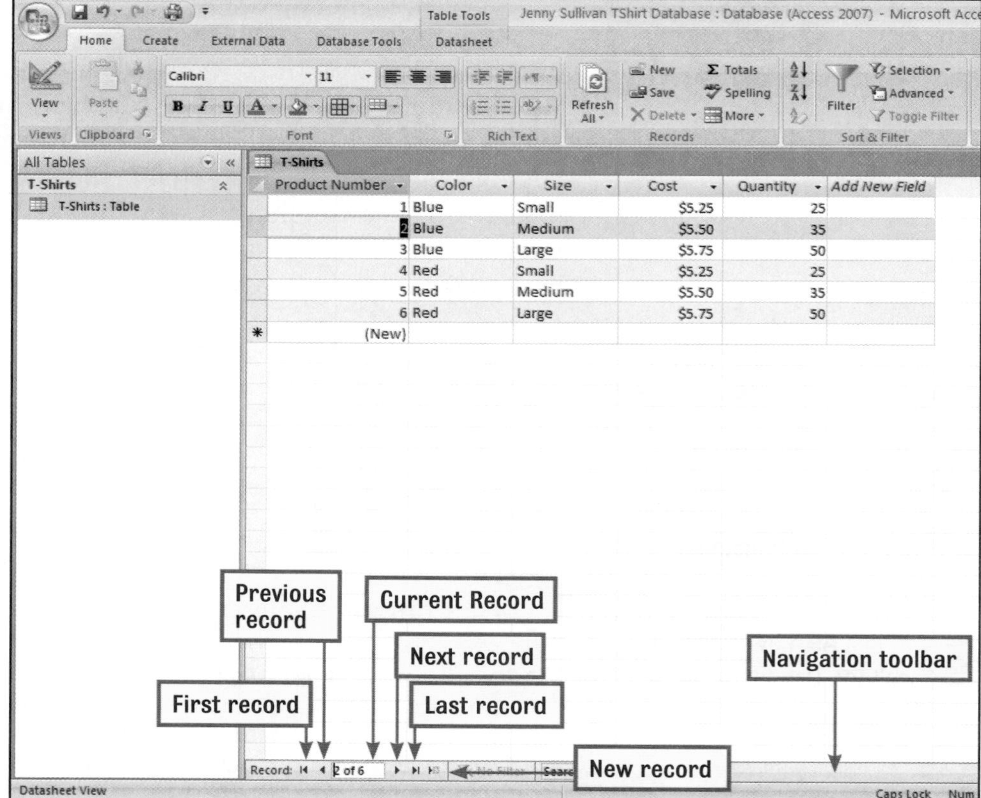

TechSavvy

Caution Entering incorrect data has cost companies millions of dollars in lost business. Companies may lose customers, orders may not be placed, or bills may be overpaid. Be careful to double-check your entries before moving on to the next record. Have someone else proofread your work.

Project 2 Assessment

Key Concepts Check

1. **Identify** List four arithmetic operators and their symbols.
2. **Describe** How does the AutoSum feature work?
3. **Explain** Why would you use AutoSum?

Critical Thinking

4. **Analyze** What is the difference between a formula and a function?
5. **Cause and Effect** What would happen if you copied the function = SUM(B3:C5) two columns to the right and one row down?

1 Guided Practice

Add Formulas to a Worksheet Adding formulas to your Computer Selling Prices worksheet will help you finish determining the selling price for your old computer. In this exercise, you will add formulas to calculate the total cost of the computer system. You will also add the average, maximum, and minimum costs of various components. If you need help, refer back to the exercise in parentheses at the end of the step.

Step-by-Step

1. **Start Excel**. **Open** the **Computer Selling Prices** worksheet you created in the Guided Practice for Project 1.
2. In cell **A9**, key Totals. Click cell **B9**. Use the **AutoSum** button Σ to find the total. (Exercise 2-1)
3. In cell **D3**, key Value Lost. Then **AutoFit column D**. (Exercise 1-3)
4. In cell **D4**, key =. Click **B4**. Key -. Click **C4**. Press ENTER. See Figure 2.11. (Exercise 2-1)

▼ **Figure 2.11** Add formulas to the worksheet.

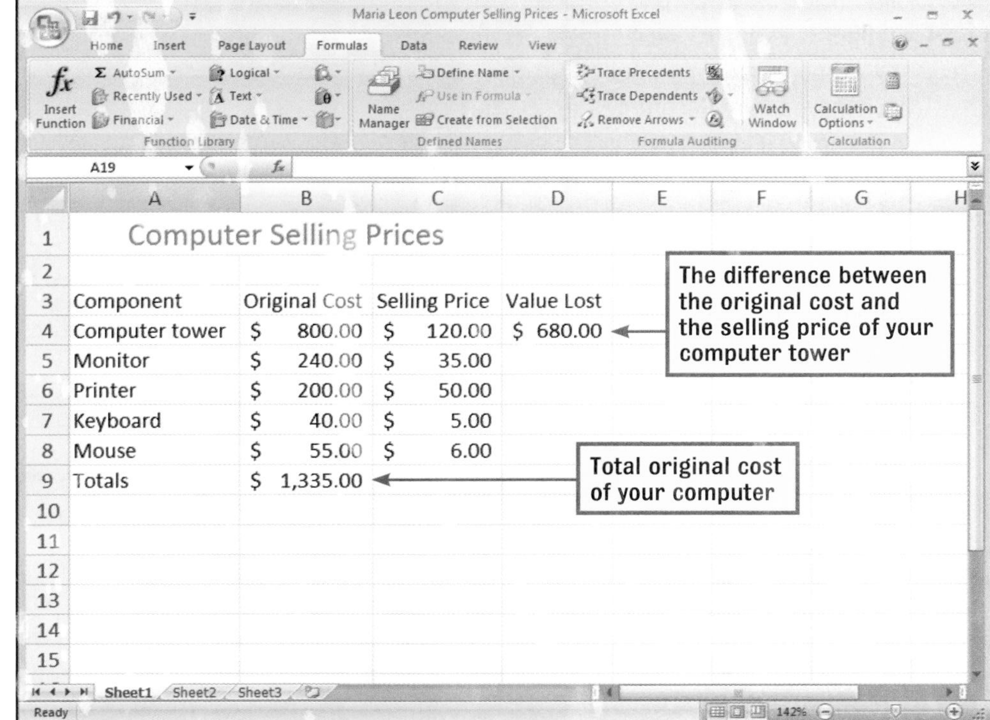

Project 1 Assessment

Key Concepts Check

1. **Define** What is a database?
2. **Explain** When do you name the database file?
3. **List** Name four data types and the kind of information they may store.

Critical Thinking

4. **Compare and Contrast** What is the difference between a table and a database?
5. **Analyze** Besides proofreading, what steps can be taken to reduce the number of data-entry errors?

1 Guided Practice

Create a Customer Database As orders for your T-shirts start pouring in, you decide that a database table of customers and their orders would be very useful.

If you need help completing a step, refer back to the exercise in parentheses at the end of the step.

Step-by-Step

1. **Open** the **TShirt Database** file that you created in Exercises 1-2 and 1-3. On the **Create** tab, in the **Tables** group, click the **Table** button (Figure 1.13).

2. Switch to **Design View**, and save the table with the name **T-Shirt Orders**. **Close** the table. (Exercise 1-2)

▼ **Figure 1.13** Use the Table button to create a new table.

4. Click cell **F4**.

5. Click the fill handle in the bottom-right corner of **F4**, hold the mouse button, drag down to **F9**, and release the mouse button. The formulas are copied to the new cells (Figure 2.9).

6. Select cells **C14** through **C17**, then click the **Copy** button.

▼ **Figure 2.9** Copying formulas can save work and reduce errors.

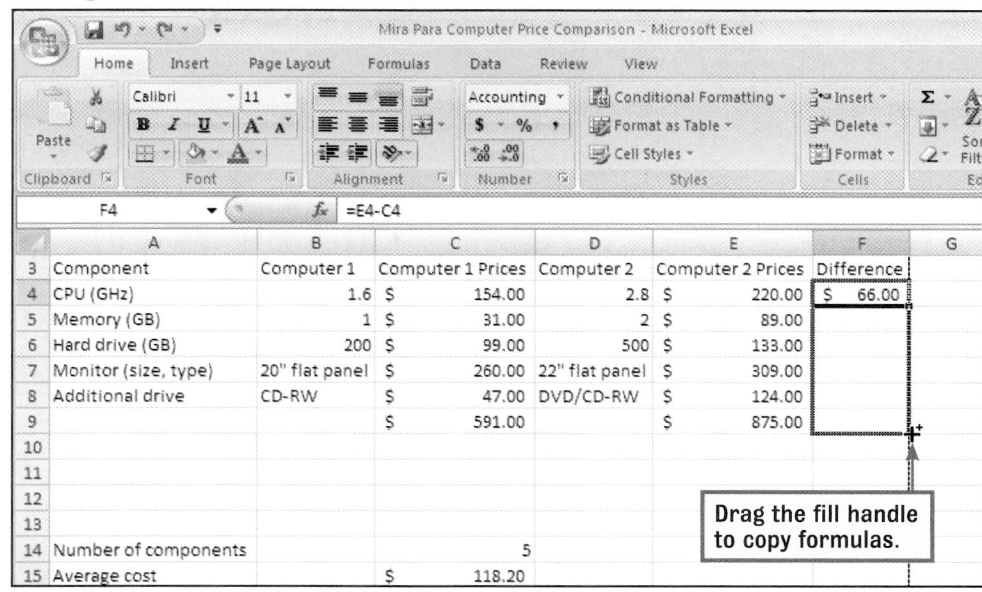

7. Click cell **E14**, and press ENTER. The formulas are copied to the new cells. Your worksheet should look like Figure 2.10.

8. On the **Page Layout** tab, in the **Page Setup** group, click the drop-down arrow on the **Orientation** button. Choose **Landscape**.

9. Select cells **Al** to **Fl**. On the **Home** tab, in the **Alignment** group, click the **Merge & Center** button. If necessary, click the button again.

10. **Print Preview** your worksheet. With your teacher's permission, **print** your worksheet. **Save** your worksheet. **Exit Excel**.

▼ **Figure 2.10** Formulas can be used to summarize data.

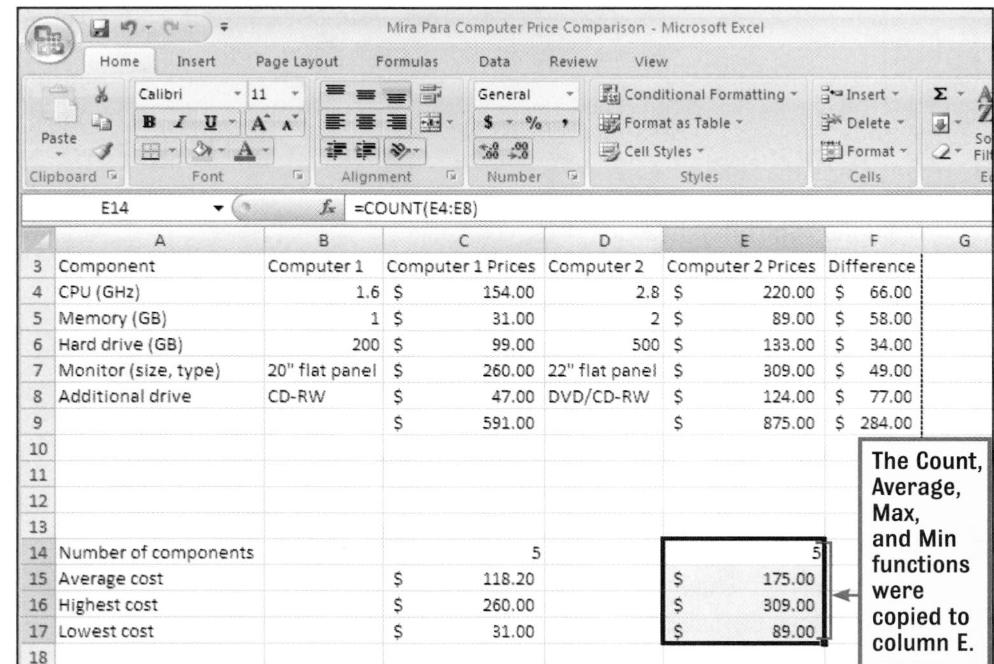

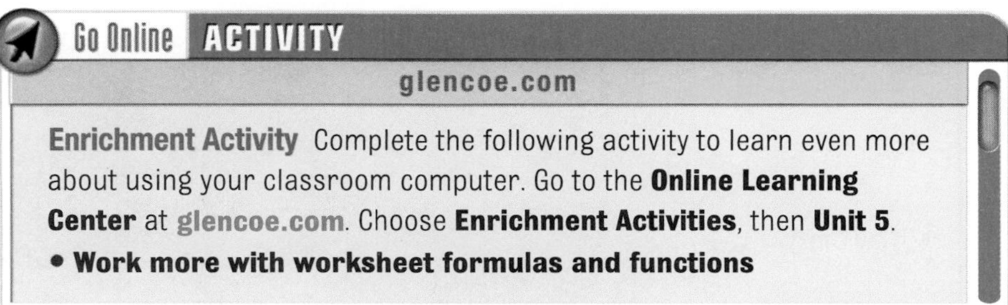
Go Online ACTIVITY

glencoe.com

Enrichment Activity Complete the following activity to learn even more about using your classroom computer. Go to the **Online Learning Center** at glencoe.com. Choose **Enrichment Activities**, then **Unit 5**.

- **Work more with worksheet formulas and functions**

Project 1 Assessment

3. Name the first **Field Name** Customer Number and give it a **Data Type** of **AutoNumber**. (Exercise 1-2)

4. Continue to fill in the **Field Names** and **Data Types** as shown in Figure 1.14. (Exercise 1-2)

5. **Save** the table with the name T-Shirt Orders and **close** the table. Be sure not to create a primary number key. (Exercise 1-2)

6. **Open** the T-Shirt Orders table and enter the data for the first record:
   First Name: Will
   Last Name: Robbins
   Product Number: 3
   Quantity Ordered: 1
   Date Ordered: Feb 15
   (Exercise 1-3)

7. Enter 10 as the Total Price. When you press ENTER, the number is converted to currency. (Exercise 1-3)

8. Key the rest of the records so your table looks like the completed table in Figure 1.15. (Exercise 1-3)

9. **Close** the table, and **exit Access**.

▼ **Figure 1.14** Add new field names to create a T-shirt order form.

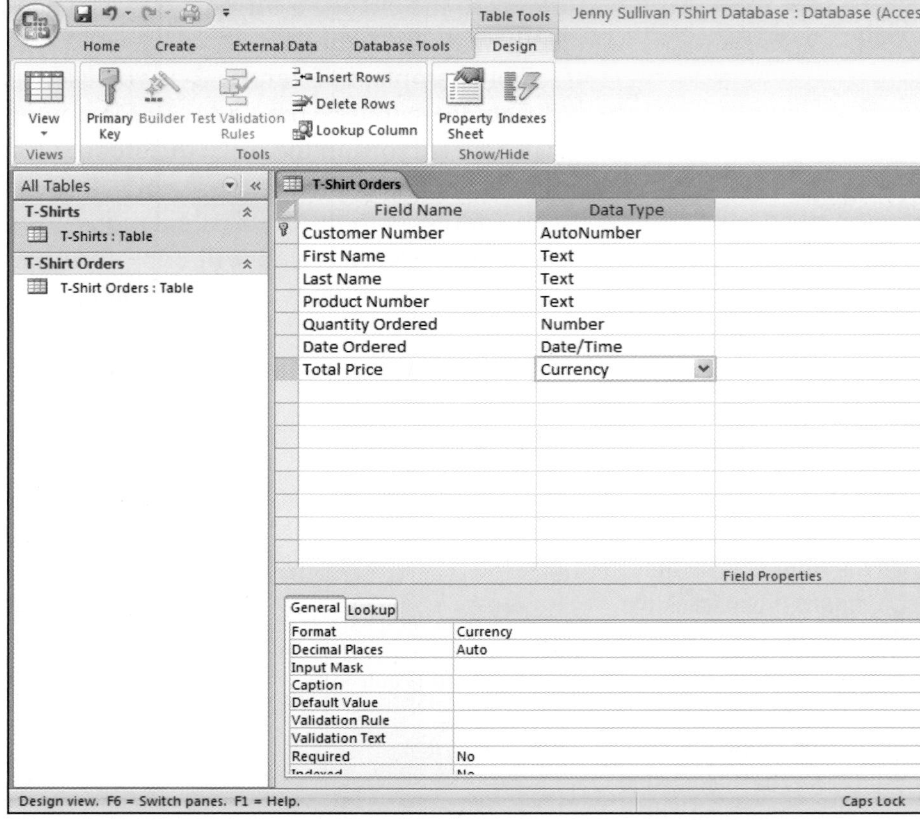

▼ **Figure 1.15** This is the completed T-Shirt Orders table.

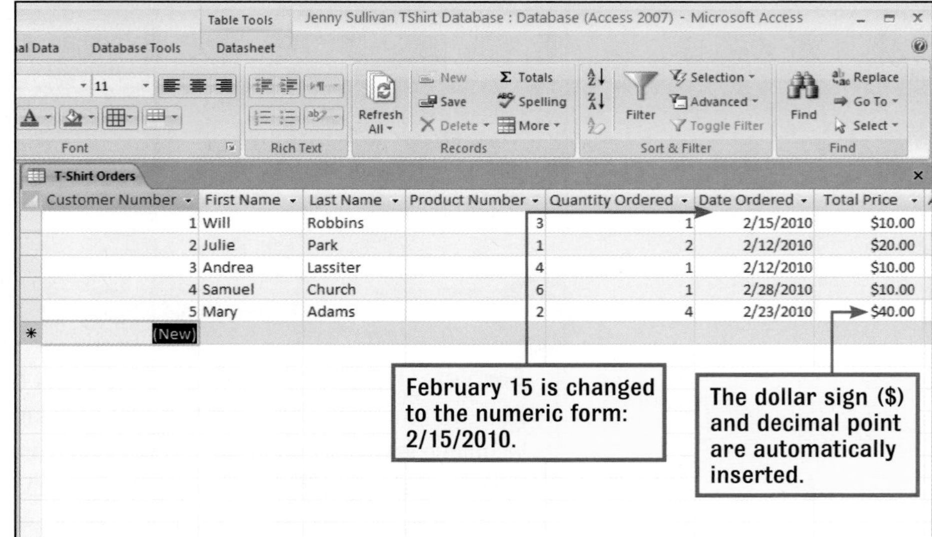

Exercise 2-3 Copy Formulas

In Excel, you can copy formulas from one cell to another. Excel adjusts the formula automatically using **relative addressing**. Relative addressing refers to the change a formula makes when it is moved or copied to other cells with different data.

For example, in Exercise 2-1, you used a formula to calculate the price difference between the CPUs in Computers 1 and 2. The same formula can be used to find the price differences for the other components. When the formula is copied to those cells, it uses the information from the new cell addresses to make its calculations.

In this exercise, you will copy formulas you entered in the previous exercise so that you will not have to enter them again.

Step-by-Step

1. In your worksheet, click cell **C9**.
2. On the **Home** tab, in the **Clipboard** group, click the **Copy** button.
3. Click cell **E9**, and press ENTER. The formula from cell **C9** has been copied to total the component prices of Computer 2 (Figure 2.8).

▼ **Figure 2.8** Notice that the copied formulas automatically change to calculate the correct data.

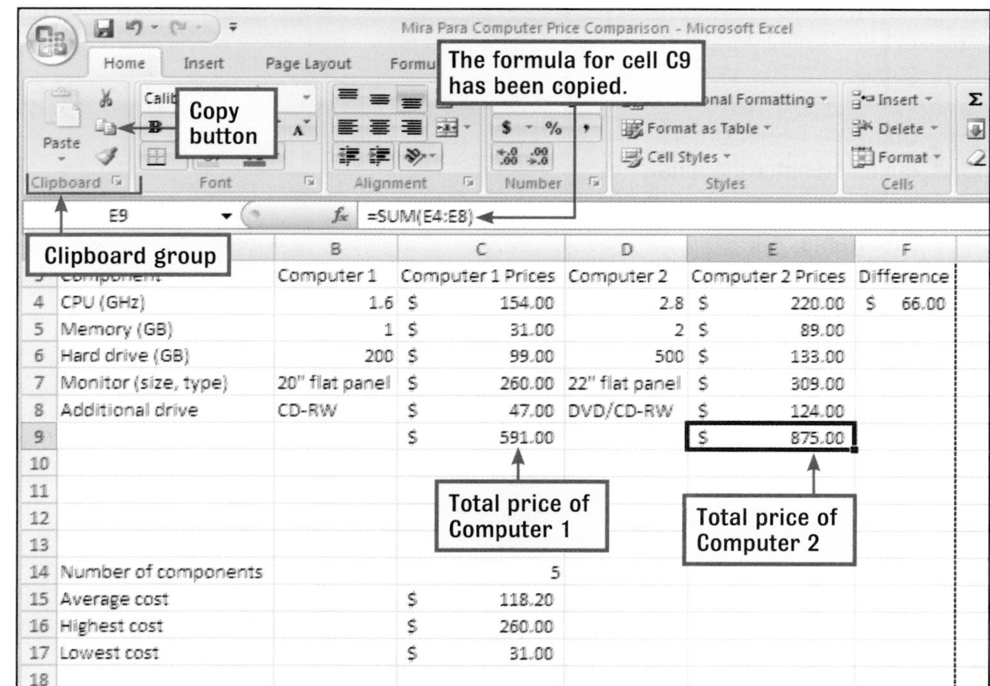

TechSavvy

Absolute Addressing To keep the original row number or column letter when you move or copy a formula, use a dollar sign ($) in the cell address, a technique known as **absolute addressing**. For example, if you use D3 in a formula, the cell address *will not* change when the formula is copied.

Project 1 Assessment

2 Independent Practice 

 **English Language Arts** **Create Records and Fields** To create a database, you need to put information into categories.

a. Plan Write down five to eight field names and data types that you can use to organize a database about your family, friends, or classmates. Fields may include data such as names, birthdays, phone numbers, and so on. (**Note**: If you write an address, the street, city, state, and ZIP Code are all separate fields and data types.)

b. Create Draw a table using paper and pencil. The table should include the records of ten people.

 Go Online RUBRICS

glencoe.com

Independent Practice Use the rubrics for these projects to help create and evaluate your work. Go to the **Online Learning Center** at glencoe.com. Choose **Rubrics**, then **Unit 6**.

3 Independent Practice 

English Language Arts **Create a Personal Database** Complete Independent Practice 2 and put the information you gathered into an Access database. Save this database to use in other Project Assessments later in this unit.

a. Create Create a new database file using the information you gathered in Independent Practice 2.

- Name the database ***Your Name*** **Personal Database**.
- Add the five to eight fields, and key the data into a table.

b. Proofread Check to make sure you entered the data accurately.

4 Independent Practice 

Social Studies **Create a Theme Park Database** You and your team will use a database to compare theme parks. Save this database to use in Project Assessments later in this unit.

a. Research Each team member should use the Internet or other resources to collect the following information about two or more theme parks in the United States: park name, location (city, state, and ZIP Code), ticket price, and number of rides.

b. Create Each team member will create a database with all of the data collected by the entire team.

- Name the file ***Your Name*** **Theme Park Database**.
- Add the fields and enter the data for each record.

9. Click **C15**, then click the **AutoSum** drop-down list and choose **Average**.

10. Select cells **C4** through **C8** (Figure 2.6), then press ENTER.

Figure 2.6 The Average function adds up all the numbers in the range, then divides by the number of cells in the range.

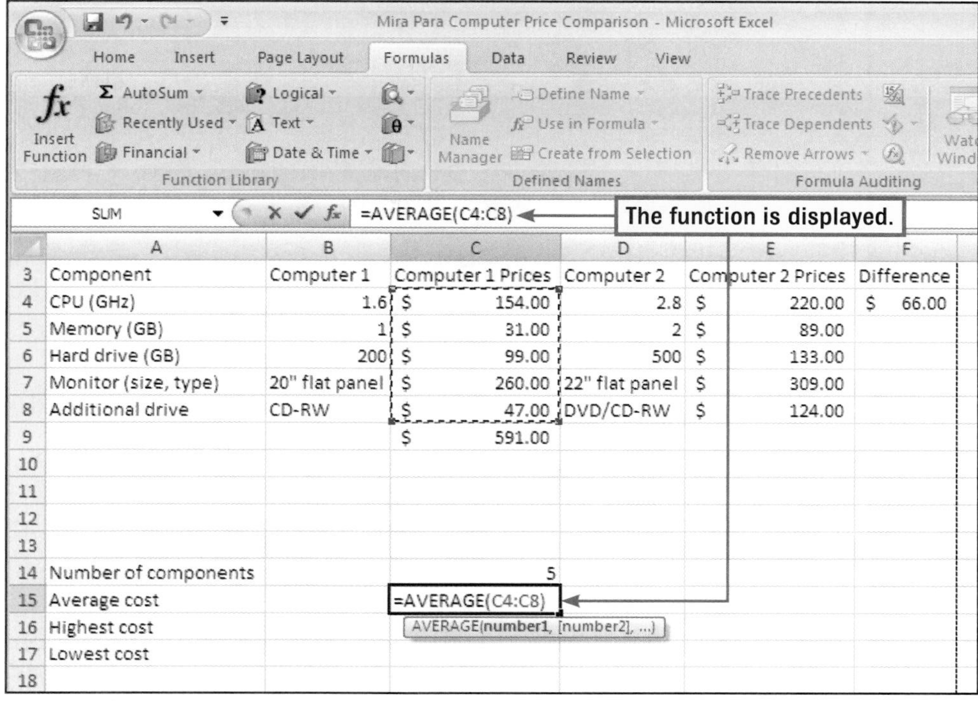

11. Click **C16**, then click the **AutoSum** drop-down list and choose **Max**.

12. Select cells **C4** through **C8**. Press ENTER.

13. Click **C17**, click the **AutoSum** drop-down list, and choose **Min**.

14. Select cells **C4** through **C8**. Press ENTER. Your screen should look like Figure 2.7.

15. **Save** your worksheet.

Figure 2.7 All of the functions have been entered.

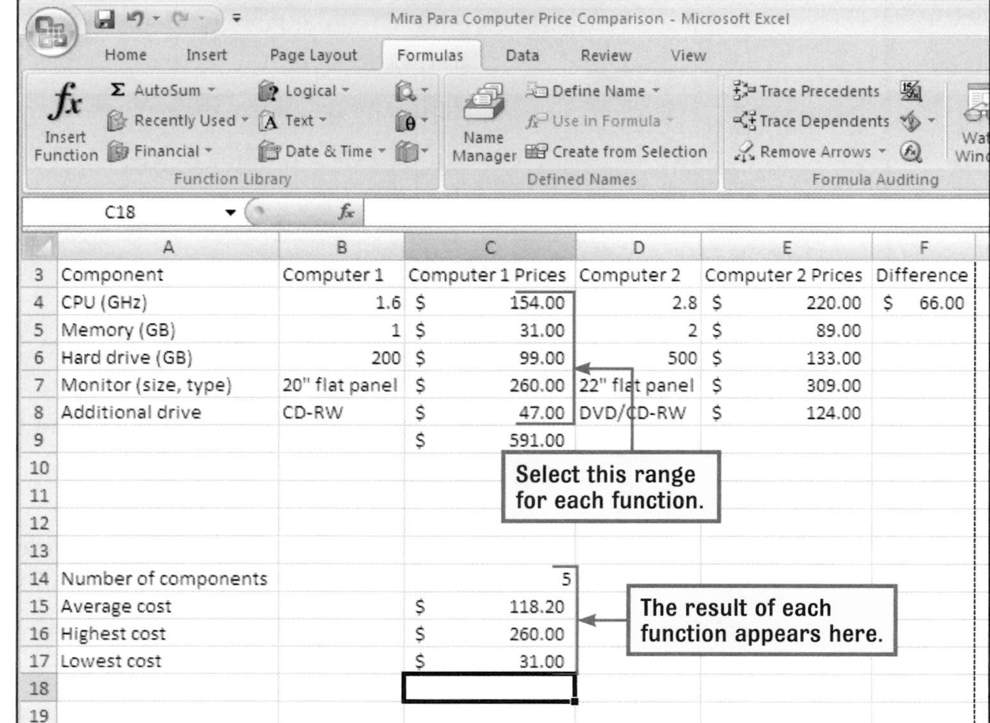

Concepts in Action

Project 2

Key Concepts

Exercise 2-1

- Sort a table in ascending and descending order
- Sort a table by name, quantity, and date

Exercise 2-2

- Use the Filter By Selection method

Exercise 2-3

- Use the Filter By Form method

Vocabulary

Key Terms
sort
filter
query
criteria
Filter By Selection
Filter By Form

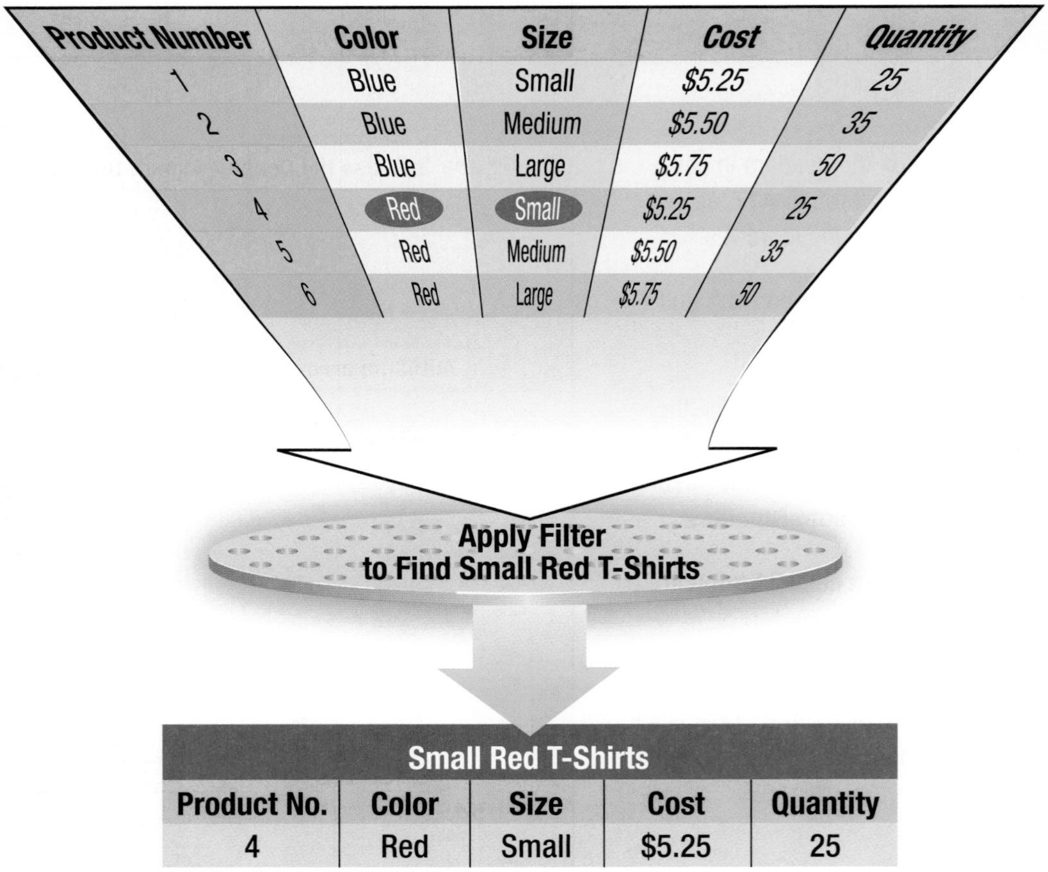

Before You Begin

Sort It Out Think about different ways stores display clothes: by color, by size, by type (shirts, pants, skirts, etc). Remember this example as you learn how to sort data.

Find Information in a Database Table

For this project, you will use your database to organize your records in ways that make it easy to find information.

Organize Your T-Shirts!

You are selling so many T-shirts that you are worried that you might run out. You need to know exactly how many T-shirts you have in each size and color, and whether you need to order more.

You will use Microsoft Access to find the specific information you need in your T-shirts and Customer Orders tables. Remember that with any database, entering data is only half of the job. Using the data to improve your business is the other half.

Product Number	Color	Size	Cost	Quantity
1	Blue	Small	$5.25	25
2	Blue	Medium	$5.50	35
3	Blue	Large	$5.75	50
4	Red	Small	$5.25	25
5	Red	Medium	$5.50	35
6	Red	Large	$5.75	50

Apply Filter
to Find Small Red T-Shirts

Small Red T-Shirts				
Product No.	Color	Size	Cost	Quantity
4	Red	Small	$5.25	25

Step-by-Step

1. In your **Computer Price Comparison** worksheet, **delete** the total in **C9**. Notice that the formula has also been deleted.

2. On the **Formulas** tab, in the **Function Library** group, with your cell pointer in **C9**, click the **AutoSum** button [Σ]. The function is displayed.

3. On the **Formula Bar**, click the **check mark** [✓]. The sum appears in cell C9, and the check mark disappears (Figure 2.4).

▼ **Figure 2.4** **The AutoSum function totals the values in column C.**

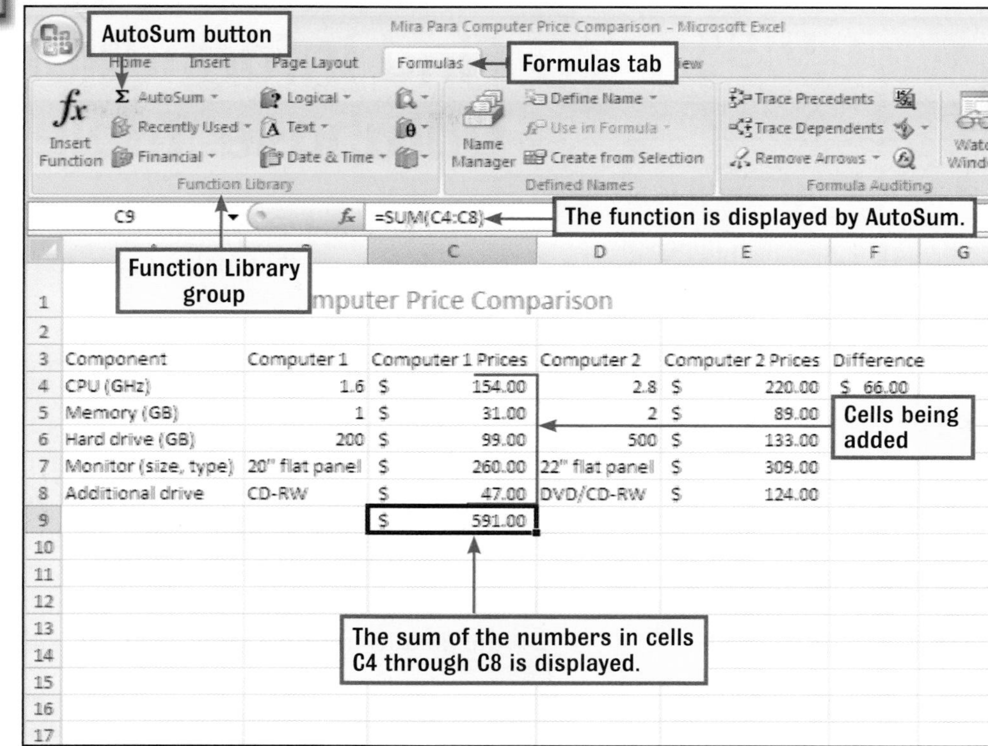

4. Key the headers in cells **A14** through **A17**, as shown in Figure 2.5.

5. **AutoFit columns A** and **F**.

6. Click **C14**, then click the **drop-down arrow** next to the **AutoSum** function and click **Count Numbers**.

7. **Select** cells **C4** through **C8** (Figure 2.5).

8. Press [ENTER]. The number 5 appears in **C14** because there are five components.

▼ **Figure 2.5** **Use the Count Numbers function.**

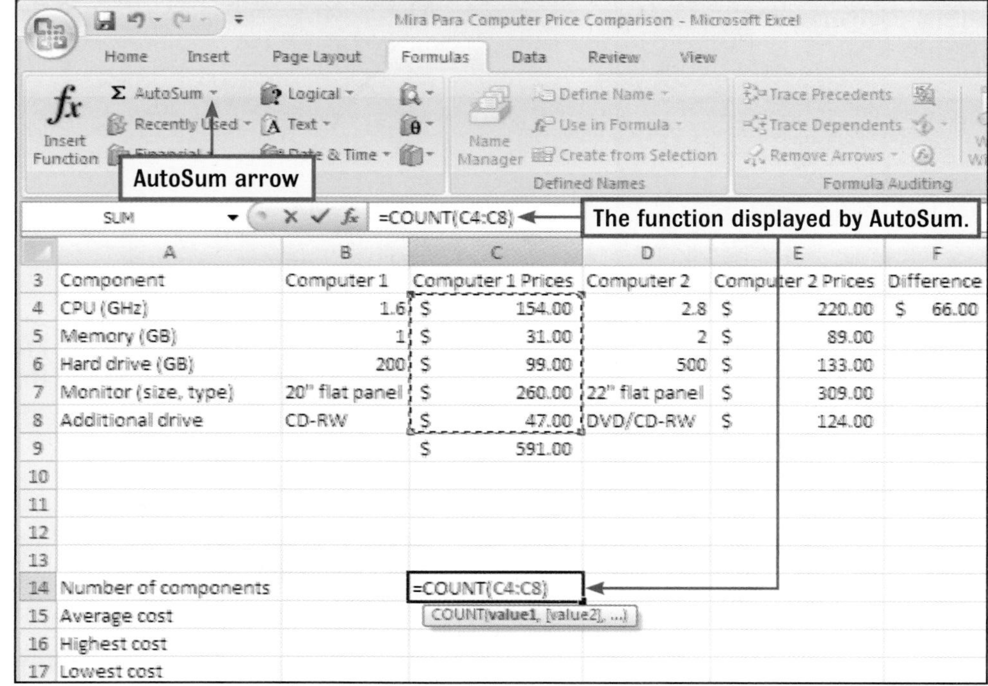

Exercise 2-1 Sort a Database Table

In databases, such as your e-mail message list, you can change how data are organized to suit your needs. You might choose to organize your messages by sender or by the date received, depending on the information you want to find.

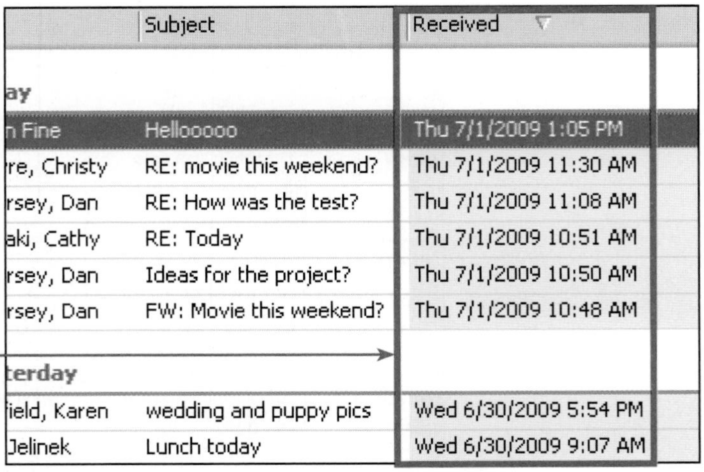

	Subject	Received
ay		
n Fine	Hellooooo	Thu 7/1/2009 1:05 PM
re, Christy	RE: movie this weekend?	Thu 7/1/2009 11:30 AM
rsey, Dan	RE: How was the test?	Thu 7/1/2009 11:08 AM
aki, Cathy	RE: Today	Thu 7/1/2009 10:51 AM
rsey, Dan	Ideas for the project?	Thu 7/1/2009 10:50 AM
rsey, Dan	FW: Movie this weekend?	Thu 7/1/2009 10:48 AM
terday		
ield, Karen	wedding and puppy pics	Wed 6/30/2009 5:54 PM
Jelinek	Lunch today	Wed 6/30/2009 9:07 AM

E-mails are sorted by date in descending order. Here the most recent e-mails appear at the top.

One of the easiest ways to reorganize information in a database is to use the sort command. When you **sort**, you change the order of your information. For example, in your T-shirt database, you can sort your T-shirt orders so that the most recent orders are at the top and the oldest orders are at the bottom, or you can switch so that the most recent orders are on bottom.

The table below shows how information can be organized using two kinds of sorts: descending and ascending.

Sorting by Data Type

Data Type	Ascending Sort	Descending Sort
Number, Currency	Lowest to highest number: 1,2,3,4	Highest to lowest number: 4,3,2,1
Text	Alphabetic order from A to Z: A, B, C, D...	Reverse alphabetic order from Z to A:...D, C, B, A
Date	Oldest date to most recent date: 1/10/10, 1/12/10, 1/15/10	Most recent date to oldest date: 1/15/10, 1/12/10, 1/10/10

In this exercise, you will sort your Customer Orders table in ascending and descending order to help you find information more quickly.

Exercise 2-2 Use Functions to Summarize Data

Some formulas are used so often that Excel has built-in arithmetic operations, such as adding a column of numbers. A built-in formula in Excel is called a **function**. All you have to do to use a function is to tell Excel which cells to use. Some of the most common Excel functions are included in the table below.

Common Excel Functions

Function Name	Description	Example	Result
Sum	Displays the total of the cells above or to the left of it	=SUM(C5:C10)	Adds up all of the cells from C5 through C10 and displays the total
Average	Finds the average number in a range of cells	=AVERAGE(D5:D8)	Adds up the cells from D5 through D8 and divides the total by 4 (the number of cells in the range)
Minimum (Min)	Displays the small-est number in a range of cells	=MIN(A1:C6)	Looks at all of the cells in the range and displays the smallest value
Maximum (Max)	Displays the largest number in a range of cells	=MAX(A1:C6)	Looks at all of the cells in the range and displays the largest value
Count Numbers	Displays how many cells holding numbers are in the range	=COUNT(C3:E8)	Looks at all of the cells in the range and displays how many of the cells contain numbers

The Sum function has a shortcut called AutoSum. When you click the **AutoSum** button on the Formulas tab, Excel automatically knows that you want to add the column of numbers above or add the row of numbers to the left.

▼ The Ribbon in Excel

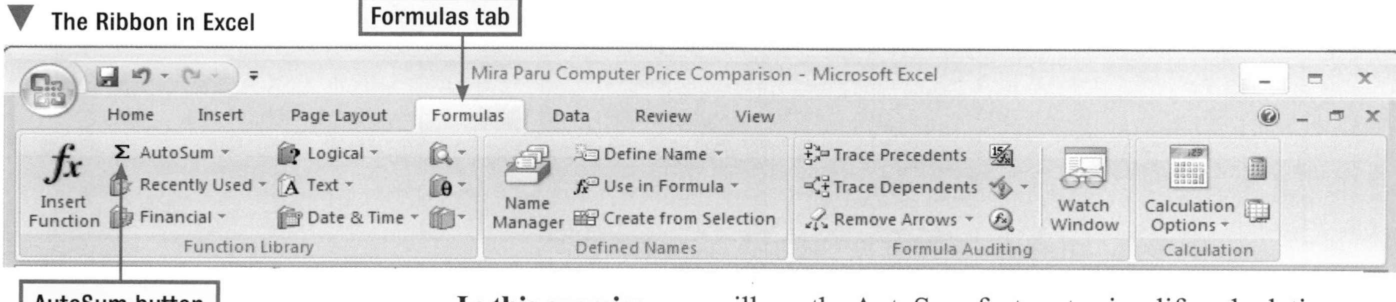

In this exercise, you will use the AutoSum feature to simplify calculations of long columns of numbers. Then you will use the Max, Min, and Count Numbers functions. These formulas will help you organize the data so that you can easily see which computer system is the better choice to buy.

Step-by-Step

1. Following your teacher's instructions, **copy** the **6A Customer Database** file and **paste** it into your folder.

2. Using your mouse, right-click the file.

3. From the pop-up menu, click **Rename**.

4. Change the file name to *Your Name* Customer Database and press ENTER.

5. Double-click *Your Name* Customer Database.

6. Double-click the **Customer Orders** table. Your table should look like Figure 2.1.

7. Click any cell in the **Last Name** column.

8. On the **Home** tab, in the **Sort & Filter** group, click the **Ascending** button. The records are now in alphabetic order by last name, as shown in Figure 2.2.

▼ **Figure 2.1** The records in this table are in the order in which they were originally entered.

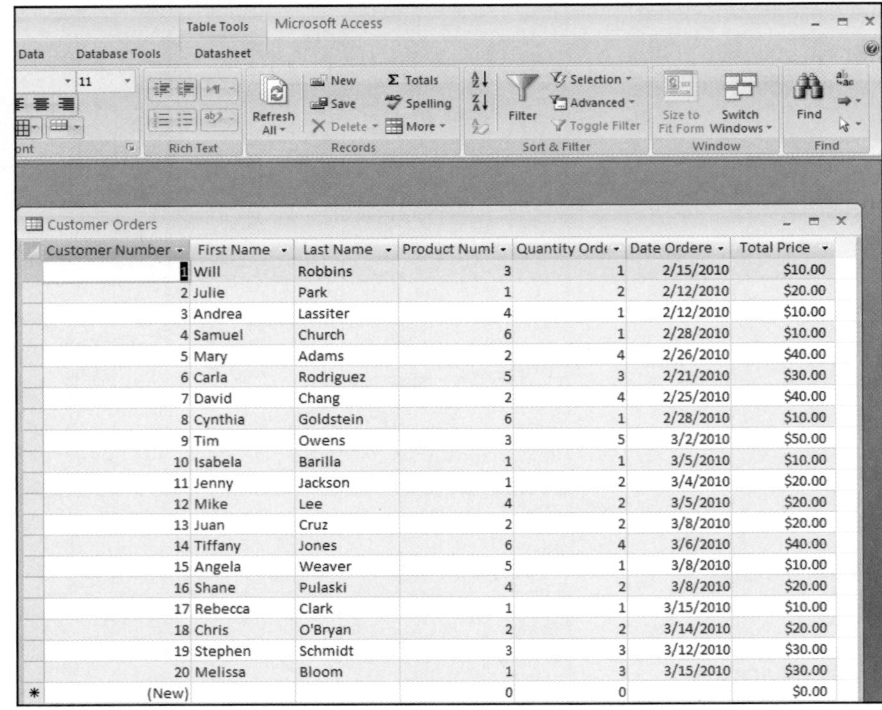

Customer Number	First Name	Last Name	Product Numl	Quantity Ord	Date Ordere	Total Price
1	Will	Robbins	3	1	2/15/2010	$10.00
2	Julie	Park	1	2	2/12/2010	$20.00
3	Andrea	Lassiter	4	1	2/12/2010	$10.00
4	Samuel	Church	6	1	2/28/2010	$10.00
5	Mary	Adams	2	4	2/26/2010	$40.00
6	Carla	Rodriguez	5	3	2/21/2010	$30.00
7	David	Chang	2	4	2/25/2010	$40.00
8	Cynthia	Goldstein	6	1	2/28/2010	$10.00
9	Tim	Owens	3	5	3/2/2010	$50.00
10	Isabela	Barilla	1	1	3/5/2010	$10.00
11	Jenny	Jackson	1	2	3/4/2010	$20.00
12	Mike	Lee	4	2	3/5/2010	$20.00
13	Juan	Cruz	2	2	3/8/2010	$20.00
14	Tiffany	Jones	6	4	3/6/2010	$40.00
15	Angela	Weaver	5	1	3/8/2010	$10.00
16	Shane	Pulaski	4	2	3/8/2010	$20.00
17	Rebecca	Clark	1	1	3/15/2010	$10.00
18	Chris	O'Bryan	2	2	3/14/2010	$20.00
19	Stephen	Schmidt	3	3	3/12/2010	$30.00
20	Melissa	Bloom	1	3	3/15/2010	$30.00
(New)			0	0		$0.00

▼ **Figure 2.2** The records have been sorted into alphabetic order according to the customers' last names.

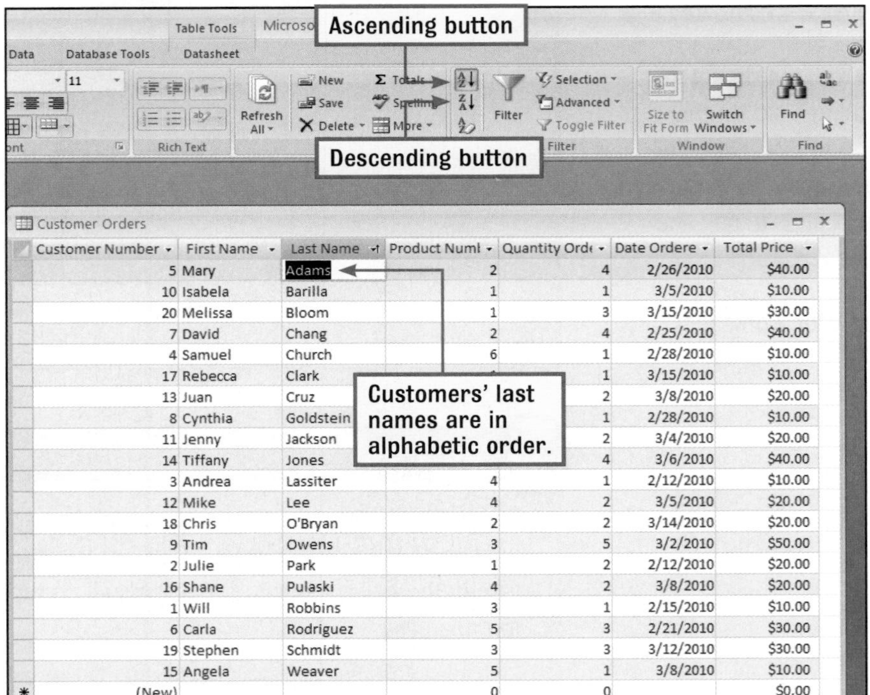

Customer Number	First Name	Last Name	Product Numl	Quantity Ord	Date Ordere	Total Price
5	Mary	Adams	2	4	2/26/2010	$40.00
10	Isabela	Barilla	1	1	3/5/2010	$10.00
20	Melissa	Bloom	1	3	3/15/2010	$30.00
7	David	Chang	2	4	2/25/2010	$40.00
4	Samuel	Church	6	1	2/28/2010	$10.00
17	Rebecca	Clark		1	3/15/2010	$10.00
13	Juan	Cruz		2	3/8/2010	$20.00
8	Cynthia	Goldstein		1	2/28/2010	$10.00
11	Jenny	Jackson		2	3/4/2010	$20.00
14	Tiffany	Jones		4	3/6/2010	$40.00
3	Andrea	Lassiter	4	1	2/12/2010	$10.00
12	Mike	Lee	4	2	3/5/2010	$20.00
18	Chris	O'Bryan	2	2	3/14/2010	$20.00
9	Tim	Owens	3	5	3/2/2010	$50.00
2	Julie	Park	1	2	2/12/2010	$20.00
16	Shane	Pulaski	4	2	3/8/2010	$20.00
1	Will	Robbins	3	1	2/15/2010	$10.00
6	Carla	Rodriguez	5	3	2/21/2010	$30.00
19	Stephen	Schmidt	3	3	3/12/2010	$30.00
15	Angela	Weaver	5	1	3/8/2010	$10.00
(New)			0	0		$0.00

7. On the **Formula Bar**, click the **check mark** ✓. The arrow disappears when it is clicked. Compare your worksheet with Figure 2.2.

▼ **Figure 2.2** The result of the formula displays.

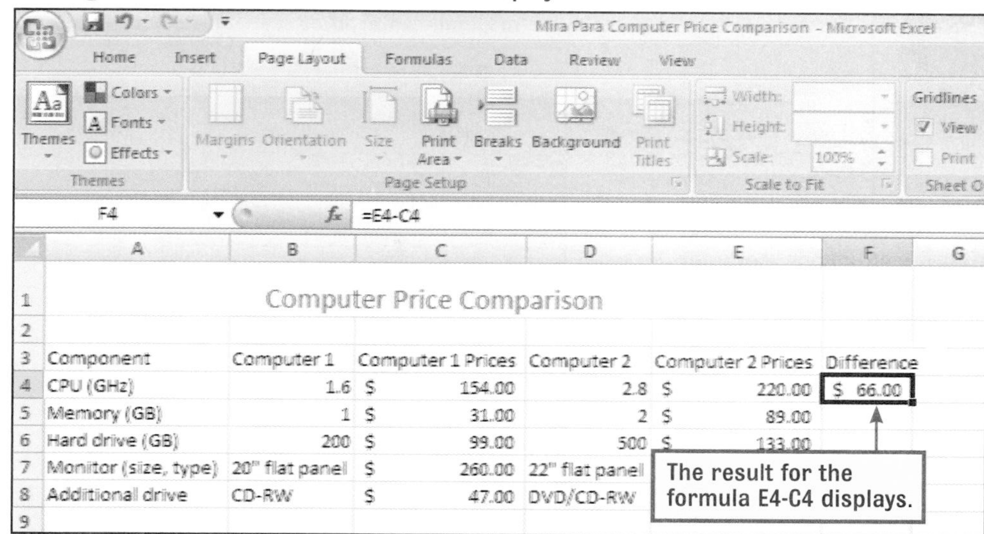

8. In cell **C9**, key = (the equal sign).

9. Click cell **C4** and key + (the plus sign).

10. Click **C5** and key +. Click **C6** and key +, then click **C7** and key +.

11. Click **C8**, but do not key anything else. On the **Formula Bar**, click the **check mark** ✓. Your screen should look like Figure 2.3.

12. **Save** your worksheet.

▼ **Figure 2.3** Find the sum of cells in a column.

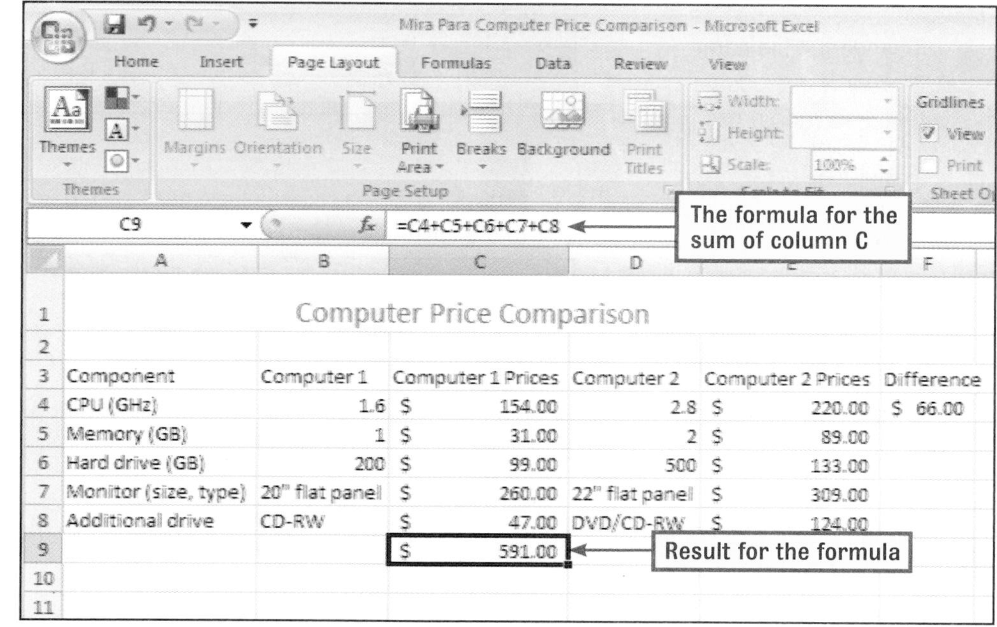

TechSavvy

Formula Tip Pressing **Enter** to complete a formula moves the cell pointer, usually down to the next row. Clicking the **check mark** in the **Formula Bar** leaves the cell pointer in the same cell so that you can format or copy the formula easily.

9 Click any record in the **Quantity Ordered** column.

10 On the **Home** tab, in the **Sort & Filter** group, click the **Descending** button [Z↓A]. Now the records are in order from the largest quantity ordered to the lowest.

11 Click any record in the **Date Ordered** column.

12 Click the **Descending** button [Z↓A]. The results are shown in Figure 2.3.

▼ Figure 2.3 **The newest orders are at the top of the table.**

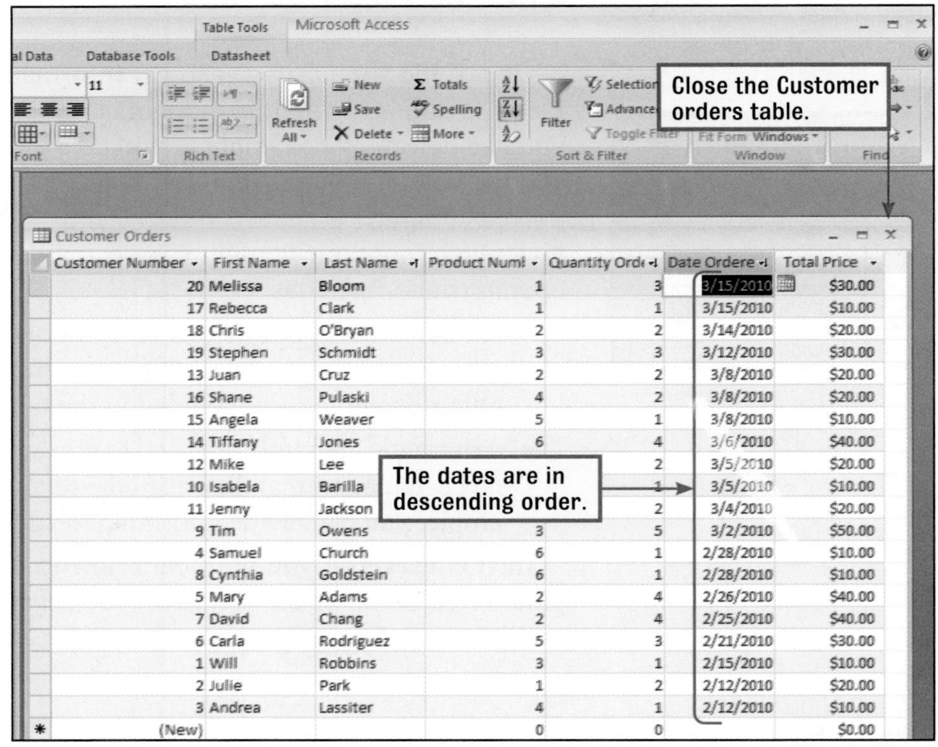

13 Close the **Customer Orders** table by clicking the **Close** button [X].

14 Click **Yes** when prompted to save the changes to the table (Figure 2.4).

▼ Figure 2.4 **Although changes to data are saved automatically by Access, any reorganization of data is NOT saved automatically. You must save the changes yourself.**

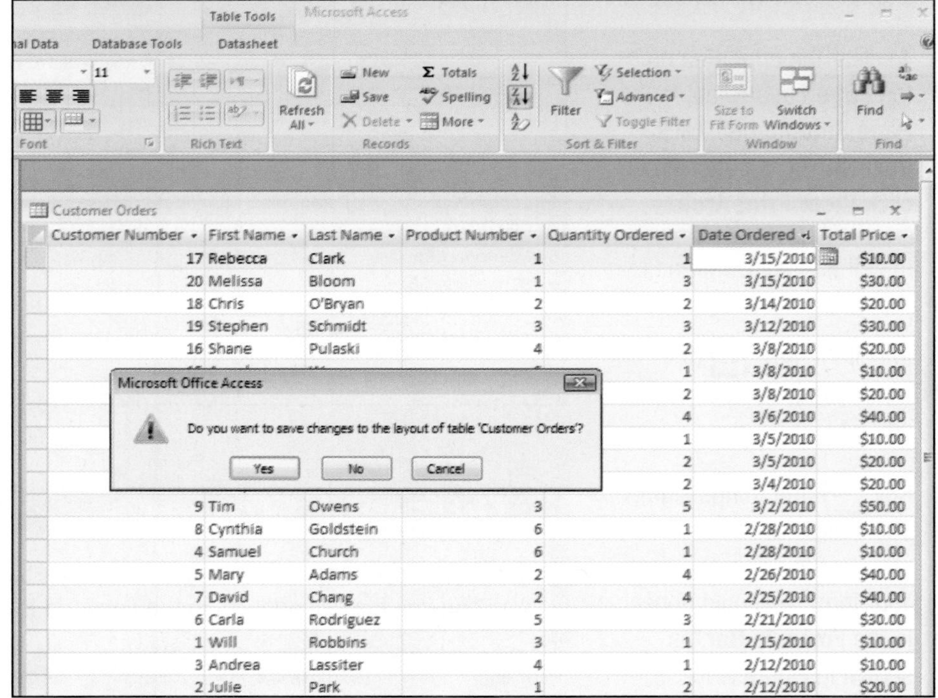

Exercise 2-1 Enter Formulas

Arithmetic Operators	
Sign	**Function**
+	Addition
−	Subtraction
×	Multiplication
÷	Division

One of the simplest ways to get information from data is to use arithmetic. Adding two numbers together gives you more information than you had before. For example, if you take the cost of a basic computer and add the cost of a larger monitor, the result tells you the price of the improved computer system. Similarly, you can use subtraction to figure out how much more one computer costs than another. Excel uses arithmetic operators and formulas.

- An **arithmetic operator** is a symbol that represents a specific action. For instance, the arithmetic symbol for addition is the + sign. Other examples are included in the table to the left.
- Arithmetic operators are used to create formulas. A **formula** in Excel is a calculation that describes the relationship between cells. For example, you can create a formula to add data in cells C4 through C8.

In this exercise, you will learn how to enter formulas into the Computer Price Comparison worksheet you began in Project 1. These formulas will help you determine the total cost of each computer.

Step-by-Step

1. **Start Excel. Open** your **Computer Price Comparison** worksheet.
2. To clear the print area on the **Page Layout** tab, in the **Page Setup** group, click the **Print Area** button. Then click **Clear Print Area**.
3. In cell **F3**, key Difference.
4. In cell **F4**, key = (the equal sign). Then click cell **E4**.
5. Key − (the minus sign). Then click cell **C4**.
6. Your formula should appear in the **Formula Bar**, as shown in Figure 2.1.

Figure 2.1 Enter a formula into a cell.

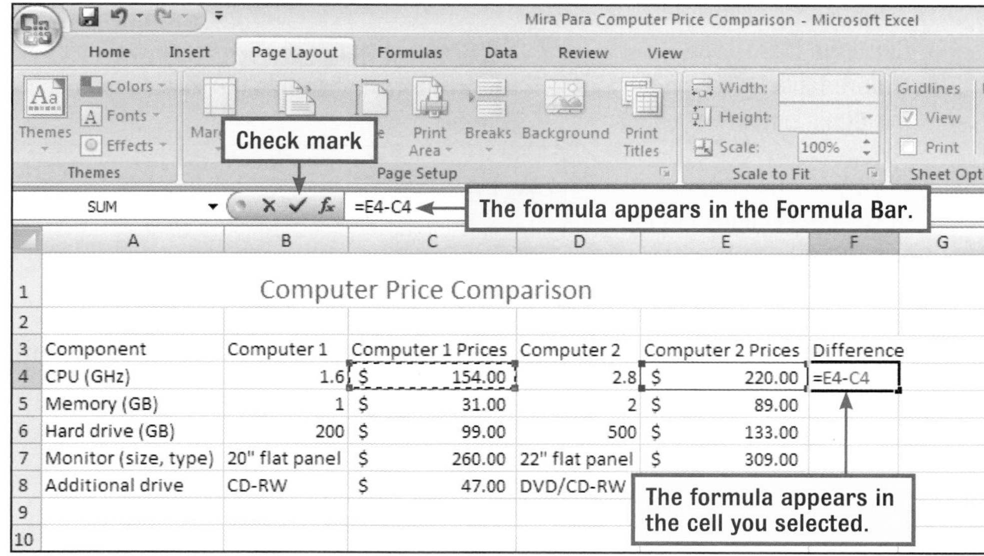

Different Strokes

Entering Formulas You do not have to click the cell to use it in a formula. You can key the cell address in the **Formula Bar** instead.

Exercise 2-2 Filter By Selection

Think of the database of a large company such as Amazon.com. It has hundreds of thousands of customers and thousands of products that it must track. The company's records include customers' names, addresses, orders, and account information. It also needs to track books by their titles, authors, price, and quantity.

When a database is small, it is easy to find information. Searching through a huge database, however, could be like looking for a needle in a haystack. That is why databases have tools such as filters and queries.

You can use a **filter** or a **query** to limit the records you see to only the data you want. If a customer wants to know whether you have any medium, blue T-shirts left, you can apply a filter to quickly find out without having to look through all the other sizes and colors in your table.

The values or conditions that you can choose for your filter are called **criteria**. In the previous example, blue and medium are the criteria.

In this exercise, you will look at one type of filter, called Filter By Selection. **Filter By Selection** displays all of the records that match a specific value you set. For example, if you want to see how many blue T-shirts are available, the filter will show you the records for all blue T-shirts.

Step-by-Step

1. **Open** the **T-Shirts table** in your T-Shirt database.

2. In the first row of the table, click **Blue** in the Color field.

3. On the **Home** tab, in the **Sort & Filter** group, click the **Selection** button. Select **"Blue"** from the list. The results are shown in Figure 2.5.

Figure 2.5 Filtering By Selection displays all "Blue" T-shirts.

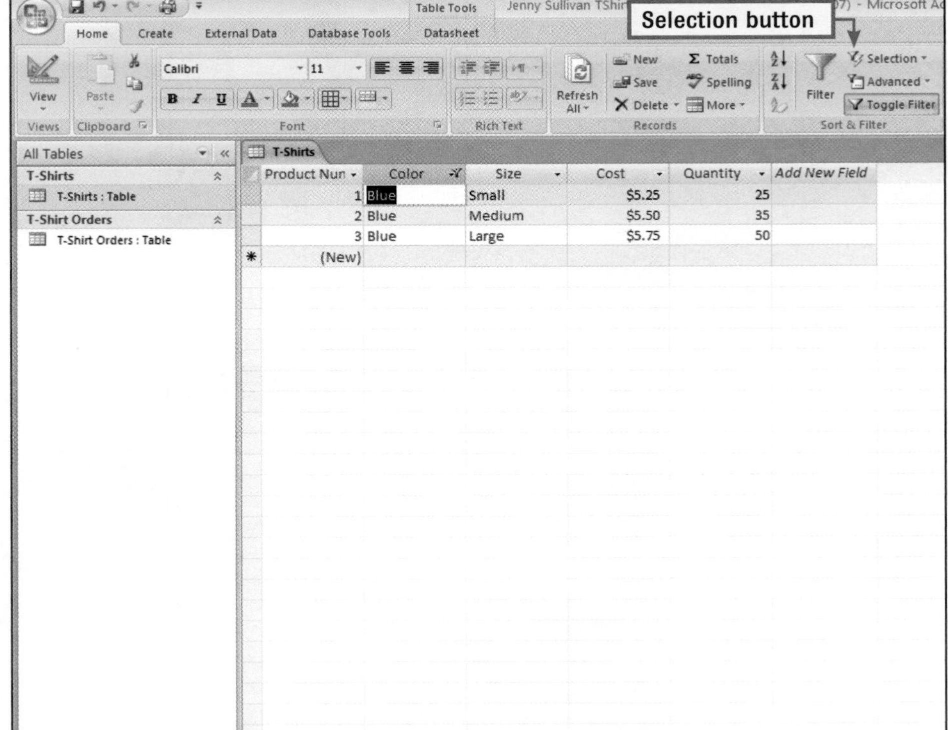

Concepts in Action

Project 2 Apply Formulas

In this project, you will learn how to use formulas and functions to help you evaluate information in different ways.

Does Your Data Add Up?

Before you choose a computer system, you need answers to several questions, such as "How much does each computer cost?" and "Which computer components can I afford?" You have gathered data in the previous Project, but you still do not know all the answers. The data must be calculated to be meaningful. Excel makes calculating data easy!

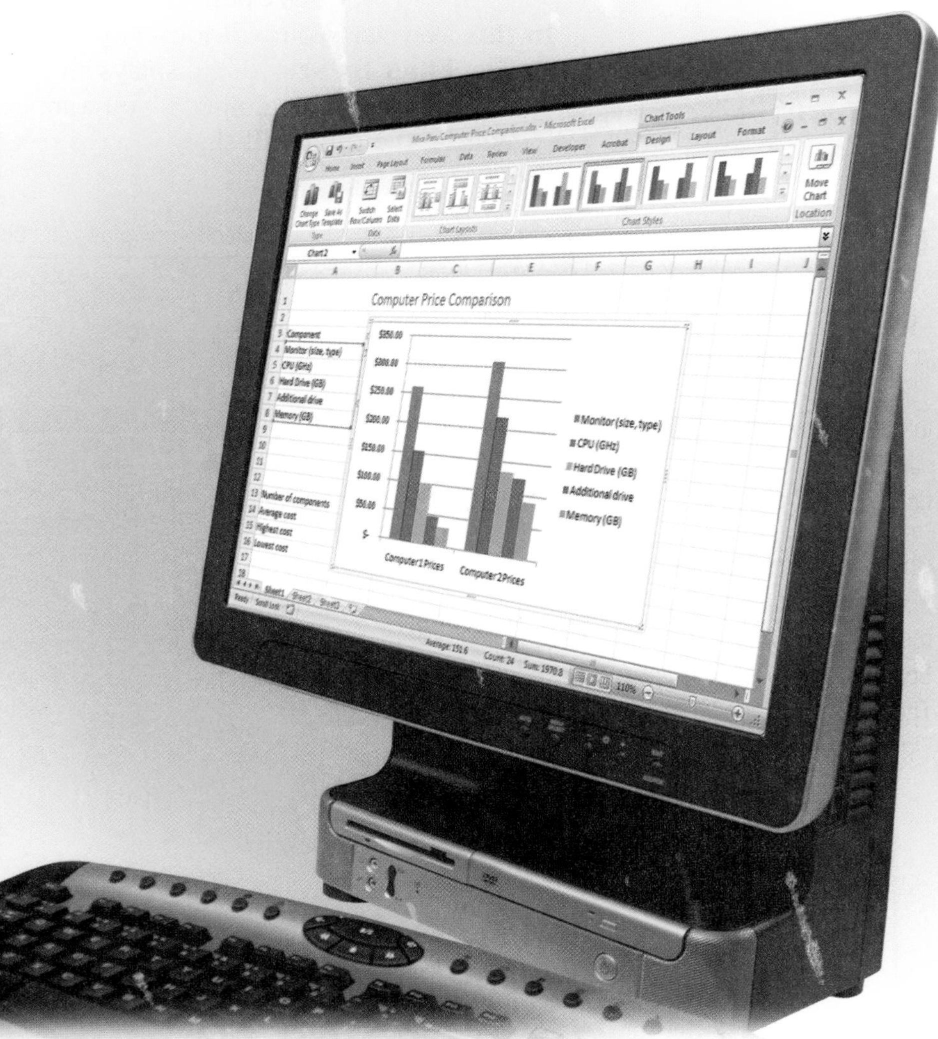

Key Concepts

Exercise 2-1

- Calculate results using arithmetic operators
- Enter formulas in cells

Exercise 2-2

- Add a column of numbers with AutoSum
- Find the minimum and maximum values in a range
- Count and average the numbers in a range

Exercise 2-3

- Explore relative addressing
- Copy formulas

Vocabulary

Key Terms
arithmetic operator
formula
function
AutoSum
relative addressing

Before You Begin

Do the Math Write down two simple arithmetic word problems. Switch papers with a partner, and write down the solution to each problem showing the proper arithmetic symbols (+, −, ÷, ×, =). You will use these symbols in Excel.

4. In the first row of the table, click **Small** in the Size field.

5. Click the **Selection** button. Select **Equals "Small"** from the list. All records with "Small" in the Size field and "Blue" in the Color field are displayed (Figure 2.6). Notice that icons in the column headers and Navigator toolbar indicate that the filter is on.

Figure 2.6 Filter displays all "Small" T-shirts that are "Blue."

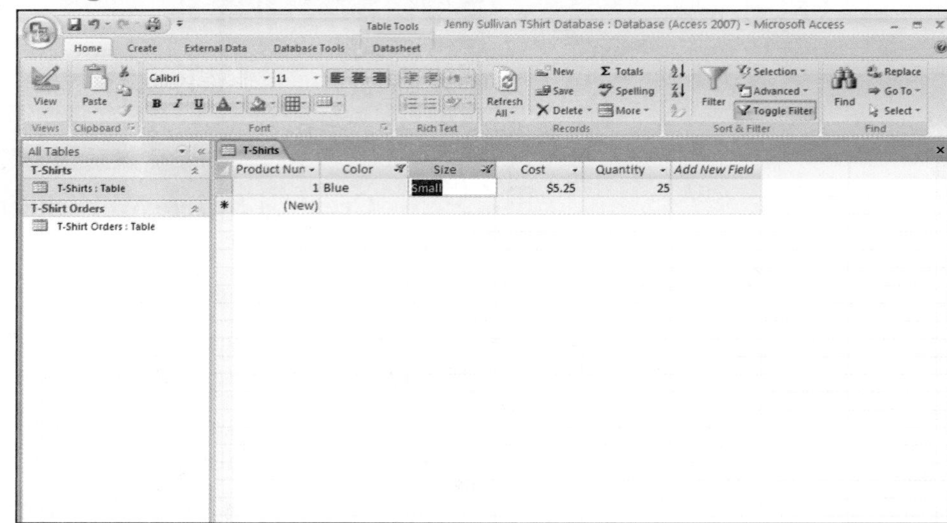

6. Click the **Toggle Filter** button to display all of the records in the table (Figure 2.7).

7. Keep the table open for the next exercise.

Figure 2.7 When you click Toggle Filter, the filter is removed and all the records in the table are displayed.

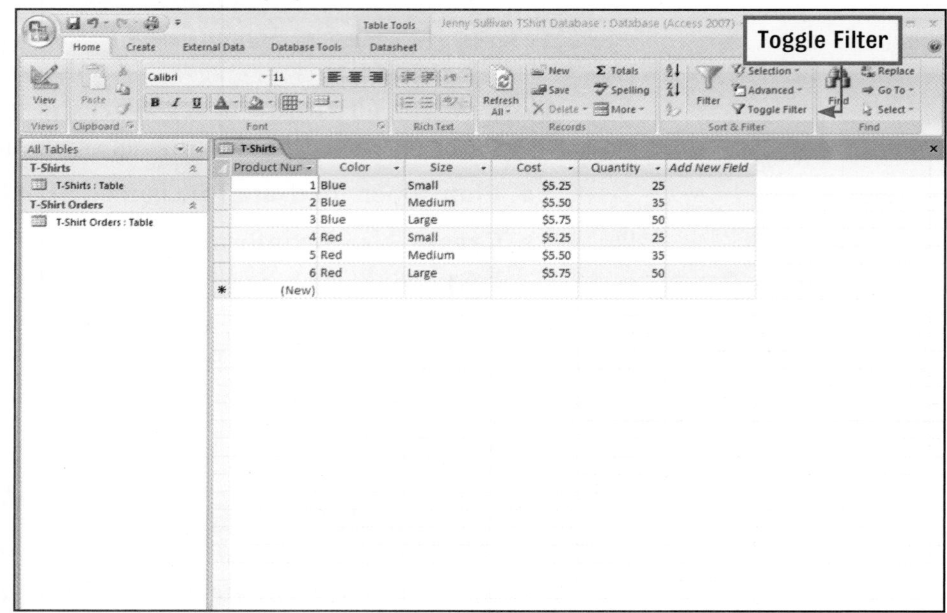

TechSavvy

Toggle Filter The **Toggle Filter** button indicates whether a filter is applied. The button is disabled until there is a filter to apply. If the button is pressed in, a filter is applied.

HELP!

Filtered Button The **Filtered** and **Unfiltered** buttons look similar. When the filter is applied, the button changes to **Filtered**. When the filter is removed, the button changes to **Unfiltered**. Check the **Navigation** toolbar.

Project 1 Assessment

2 Independent Practice 

Math Create a School Worksheet Create a worksheet about your school day.

a. Create Open and save a new worksheet as ***Your Name* School Day**.

- Add four column headings: Period, Time Period Starts, Time Period Ends, Length of Class (minutes).
- In the Period column, add row headings. Enter each class or activity that you participate in during the school day.
- In the correct cells, enter the time each period starts, the time each period ends, and the number of minutes in each class.

b. Proof Make sure your data is entered correctly. Edit, if necessary.

Go Online RUBRICS
glencoe.com

Independent Practice
Use the rubrics for these projects to help create and evaluate your work. Go to the **Online Learning Center** at **glencoe.com**. Choose **Rubrics**, then **Unit 5**.

3 Independent Practice 

Math Create a Survey Worksheet Create a worksheet to enter survey data on how students spend their time.

a. Plan Open the **Data File** named **5B After School Activities**.

b. Create Use the information from the Data File to create a new Excel worksheet. Save it as ***Your Name* Survey**.

- In your new Survey worksheet, add a title. Add three column headings: Activity, Boys, and Girls. In the Activity column, create row headings for each activity listed in the Class Survey.
- In the Boys and Girls columns, enter data from the Data File.

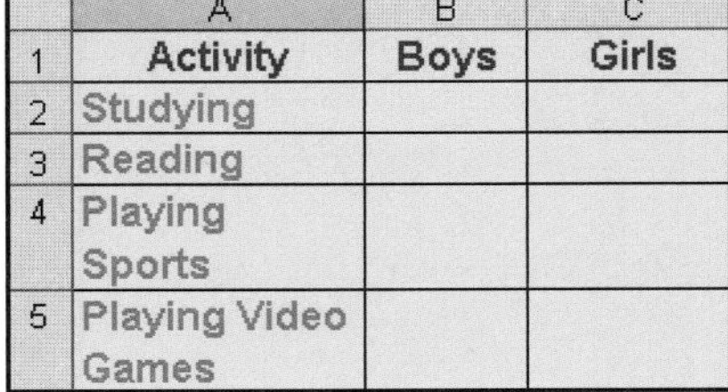

	A	B	C
1	Activity	Boys	Girls
2	Studying		
3	Reading		
4	Playing Sports		
5	Playing Video Games		

4 Independent Practice 

Teamwork Create a Party Budget Worksheet With a partner, plan the menu for a party with ten guests. You have $50 to spend.

a. Research Gather information about the costs of foods you would serve, such as pizza, sandwiches, drinks, and so on.

b. Create Each partner will create a separate menu in a worksheet:

- Open and save a new worksheet as *Your Name* Party Budget. You will use this worksheet later in this unit.
- Enter the information you gathered. Include a title.

Exercise 2-3 Filter By Form

In the previous exercise, you used Filter By Selection. Another way to filter your data is called **Filter By Form**. This method uses a form that allows you to enter two or more criteria at one time. When you used Filter By Selection to find out how many small, blue T-shirts you had, you needed to use two filters: one for blue T-shirts, and then one for small T-shirts. With Filter By Form, you can add both criteria at the same time.

In this exercise, you will use Filter by Form to find out how many large blue T-shirts you have. You will do this by specifying two criteria on the form: *blue* in the Color field and *large* in the Size field.

Step-by-Step

1. On the **Home** tab, in the **Sort & Filter** group, click **Advanced Filter Options**, then choose **Filter By Form**.

2. If your form shows information entered in it, click **Advanced Filter Options**, and choose **Clear Grid**. (Figure 2.8).

▼ **Figure 2.8** Filter By Form opens a form window.

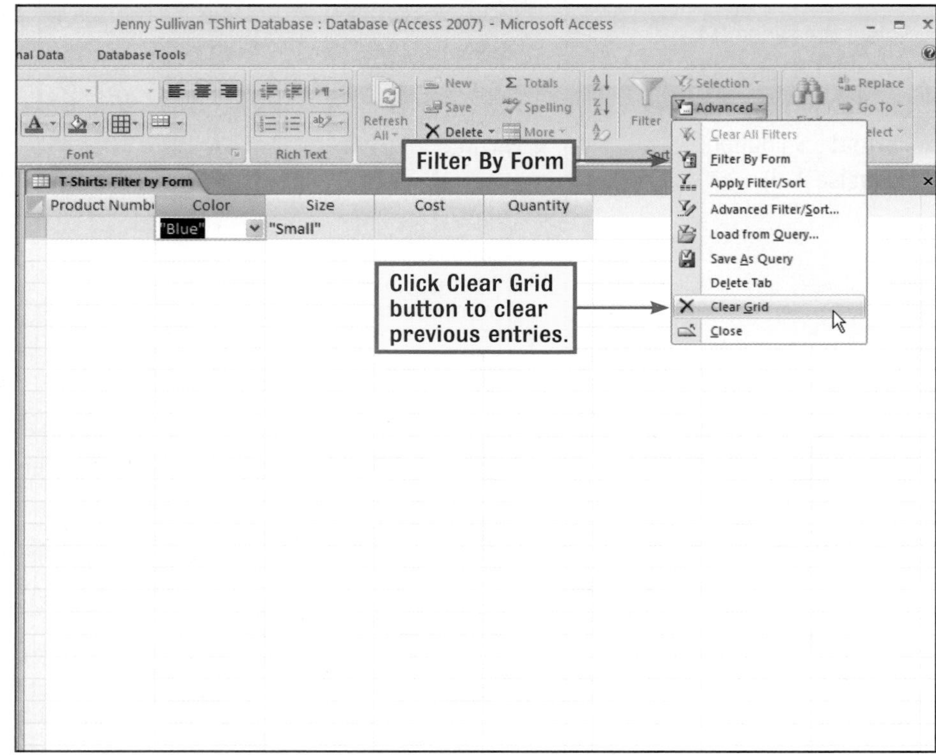

Different Strokes

Faster and Faster If you find using the keyboard more efficient than reaching for the mouse, visit Microsoft Office Access Help for a complete list of keyboard shortcuts that can perform all of the same functions as clicking on-screen command buttons.

Project 1 Assessment

5 Starting in cell **A4**, key the row headers shown in Figure 1.18. (Exercise 1-2)

6 **AutoFit** columns **A**, **B**, and **C**. (Exercise 1-3)

7 Key the data in columns **B** and **C**, as shown in Figure 1.18. (Exercise 1-2)

8 Select the range **B4** through **C8**, and click the **Accounting Number Format** $ button. (Exercise 1-3)

▼ **Figure 1.18** Add data to the worksheet.

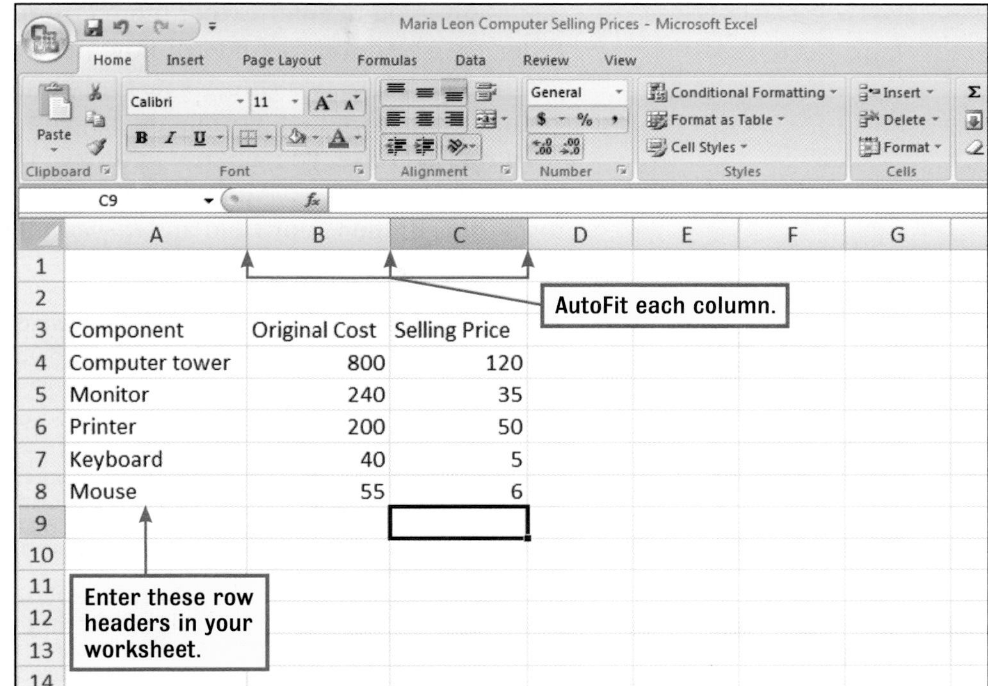

9 Select **A1** to **C1**. Click the **Merge & Center** button. (Exercise 1-4)

10 In cell **A1**, key Computer Selling Prices.

11 Change the **Font Size** to **16** and the **Font Color** to **Green**, as shown in Figure 1.19. (Exercise 1-4)

12 Select cells **A1** to **C8**, and set the **Print Area**. If you have permission to print, **print** your worksheet. (Exercise 1-4)

13 **Save** the worksheet. **Exit Excel**.

▼ **Figure 1.19** This is the completed Computer Selling Prices worksheet.

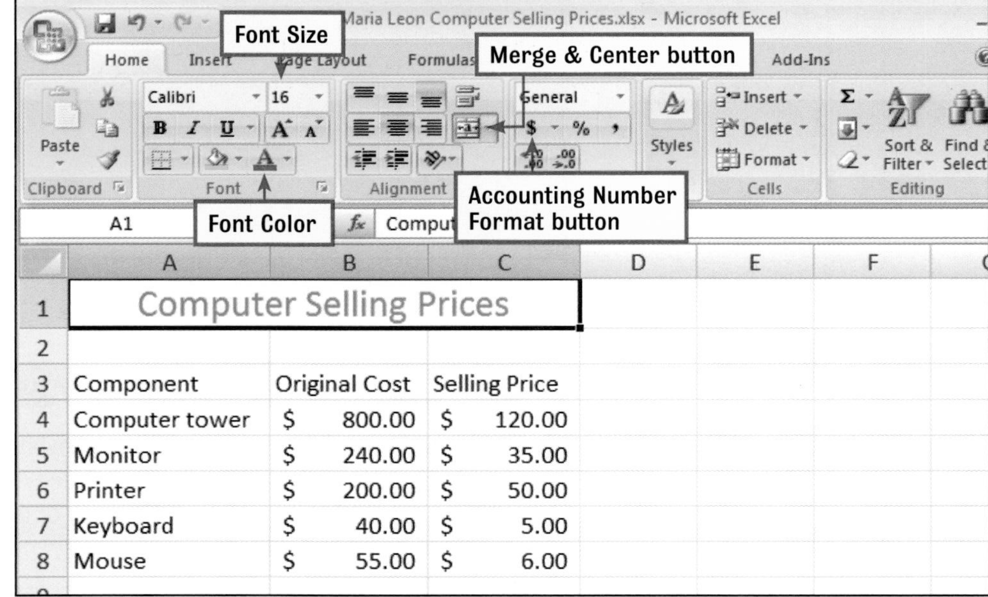

3. Click in the **Size** field, then click the drop-down arrow that appears, and choose **Large** (Figure 2.9).

4. Click in the **Color** field, and choose **"Blue."**

▼ **Figure 2.9** A drop-down menu displays the criteria in a field when you use the Filter By Form option.

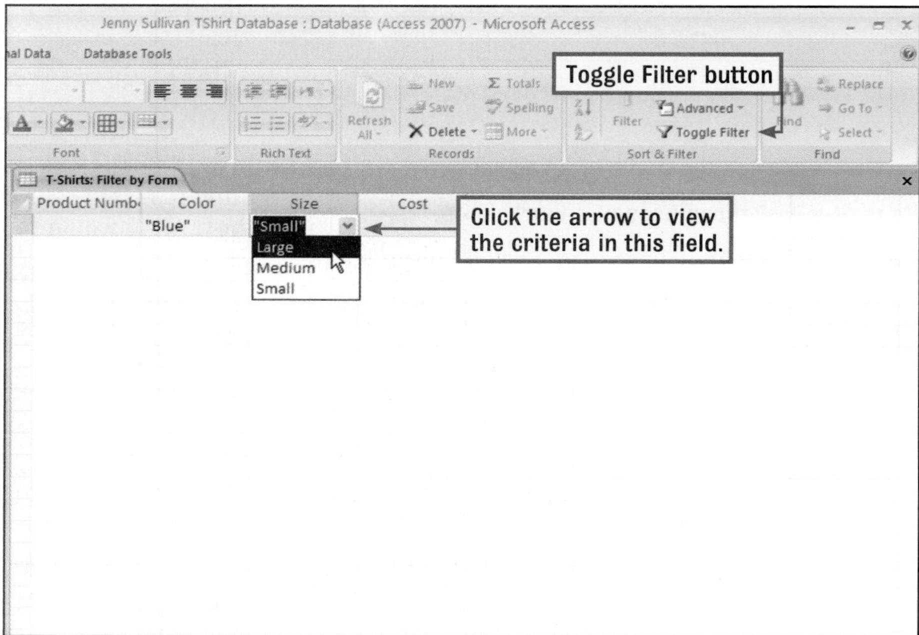

5. Click the **Toggle Filter** [icon]. Your table should look like Figure 2.10.

6. Click the **Toggle Filter** button [icon].

7. To close the table, click the **Close** button [x].

8. Click **Yes** to save the changes.

9. **Exit Access**.

▼ **Figure 2.10** Your table now shows only large blue T-shirts.

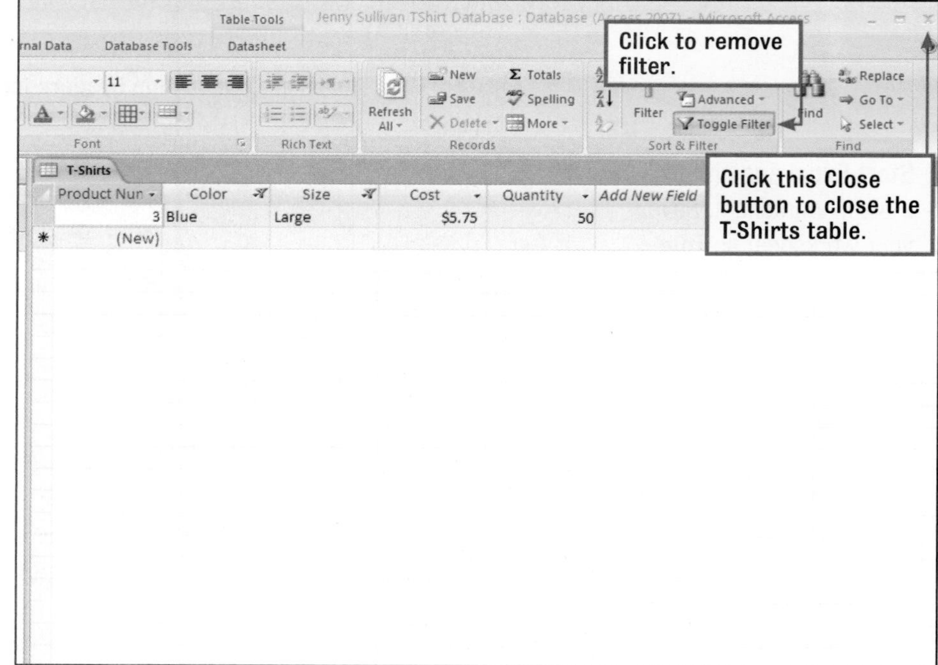

Project 1 Assessment

Key Concepts Check

1. **Define** What are the parts of a worksheet?
2. **Describe** List three uses of a worksheet.
3. **Explain** What is the purpose of a cell address?
4. **Describe** What are two ways to change the width of a column?

Critical Thinking

5. **Draw Conclusions** If you used the fill handle after selecting cells with Saturday and Sunday in them, what would you see in the next cell?
6. **Cause and Effect** What would happen if you AutoFit the width of column A *after* you enter the worksheet title?

1 Guided Practice

Create a Computer Worksheet You want to see whether you can sell your old computer or any of its parts so that you can use the money to help pay for a new computer system. Using a worksheet will help you see how much money you could get by selling your old computer. You will continue creating the worksheet in the next Project Assessment. If you need help, refer back to the exercise in parentheses at the end of the step.

Step-by-Step

1. **Start Excel** and create a blank worksheet. Save your worksheet as *Your Name* Computer Selling Prices. (Exercise 1-1)
2. In cell **A3**, key Component. (Exercise 1-2)
3. In cell **B3**, key Original Cost. (Exercise 1-2)
4. In cell **C3**, key Selling Price. Your worksheet should look like Figure 1.17. (Exercise 1-2)

▼ **Figure 1.17** These are the column headers for the Computer Selling Prices worksheet.

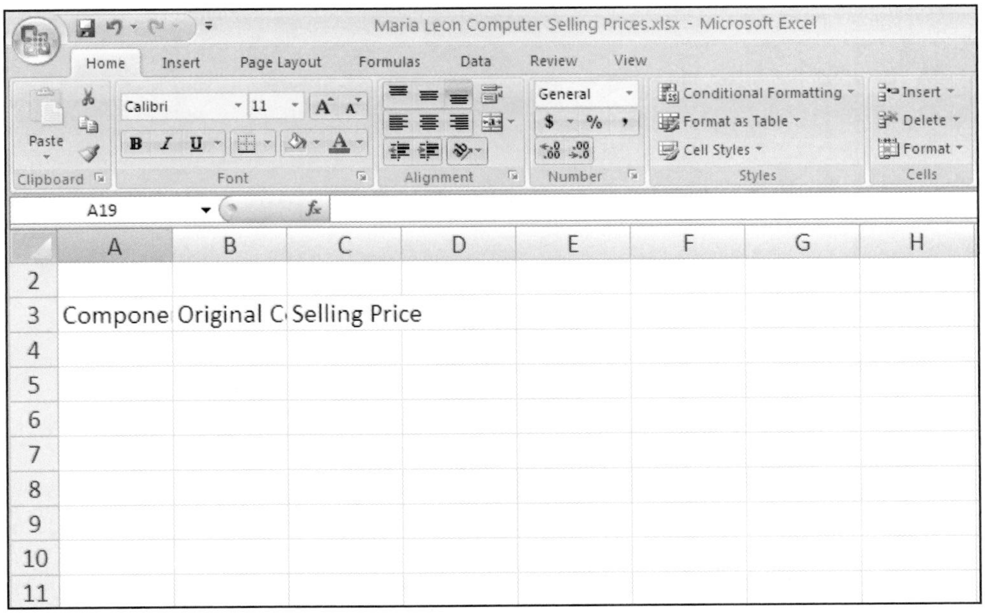

Project 2 Assessment

Key Concepts Check

1. **Compare and Contrast** What is the difference between ascending and descending sorts by number?
2. **Explain** Why are filters and queries important tools in databases?
3. **Describe** What are the two methods of filtering records?

Critical Thinking

4. **Evaluate** What would be the best way to sort your records if you wanted to make sure your very first customers received their orders?
5. **Make Predictions** When might you prefer to use Filter By Selection, and when would Filter By Form be better?

1 Guided Practice

Keeping Up with Orders All of the March 8 orders for small, red T-shirts were not delivered. You will use sorts and filters to find these orders quickly so that your customers get their T-shirts. If you need help, refer back to the exercise in parentheses at the end of the step.

Step-by-Step

1. **Open Access** and open your **Customer Database**.
2. **Open** the **Customer Orders** table.
3. Sort the data in the **Date Ordered** field in ascending order. See Figure 2.11. (Exercise 2-1)

▼ **Figure 2.11** March 8 orders are grouped together.

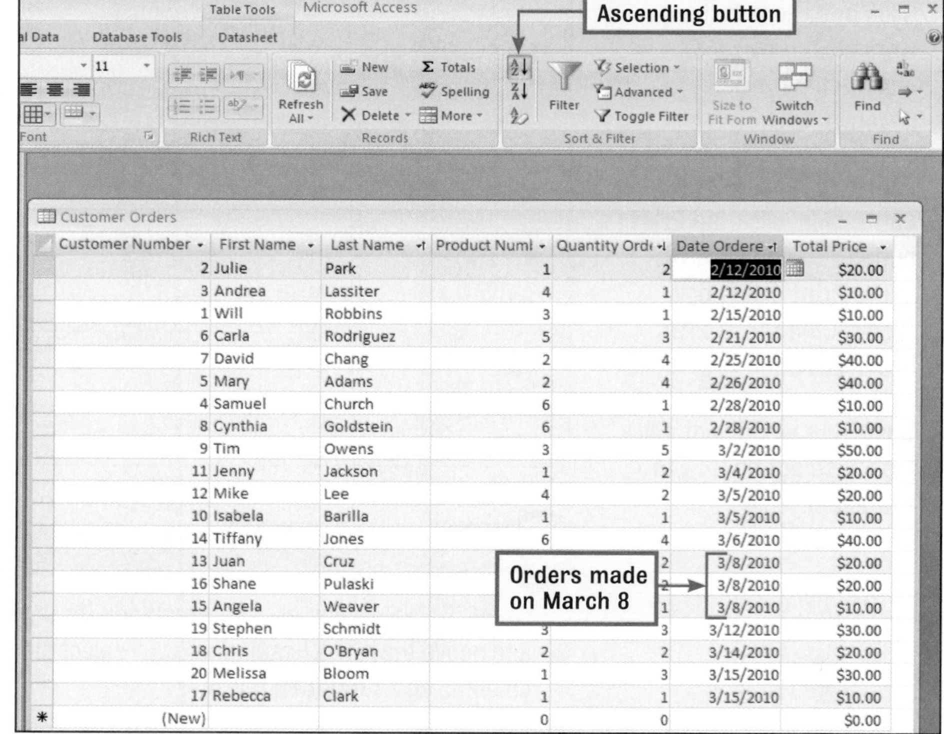

Customer Number	First Name	Last Name	Product Numl	Quantity Ord	Date Ordere	Total Price
2	Julie	Park	1	2	2/12/2010	$20.00
3	Andrea	Lassiter	4	1	2/12/2010	$10.00
1	Will	Robbins	3	1	2/15/2010	$10.00
6	Carla	Rodriguez	5	3	2/21/2010	$30.00
7	David	Chang	2	4	2/25/2010	$40.00
5	Mary	Adams	2	4	2/26/2010	$40.00
4	Samuel	Church	6	1	2/28/2010	$10.00
8	Cynthia	Goldstein	6	1	2/28/2010	$10.00
9	Tim	Owens	3	5	3/2/2010	$50.00
11	Jenny	Jackson	1	2	3/4/2010	$20.00
12	Mike	Lee	4	2	3/5/2010	$20.00
10	Isabela	Barilla	1	1	3/5/2010	$10.00
14	Tiffany	Jones	6	4	3/6/2010	$40.00
13	Juan	Cruz		2	3/8/2010	$20.00
16	Shane	Pulaski		2	3/8/2010	$20.00
15	Angela	Weaver		1	3/8/2010	$10.00
19	Stephen	Schmidt	3	3	3/12/2010	$30.00
18	Chris	O'Bryan	2	2	3/14/2010	$20.00
20	Melissa	Bloom	1	3	3/15/2010	$30.00
17	Rebecca	Clark	1	1	3/15/2010	$10.00
(New)			0	0		$0.00

8 Drag the cell pointer from **A1** to **E8** to select the range of cells.

9 On the **Page Layout** tab, in the **Page Setup** group, click the **Print Area** button. Then click **Set Print Area**. A box encloses your data as seen in Figure 1.15.

10 Click the **Office Button**. Choose **Print**, and then choose **Print Preview**. On the **Print Preview** tab, in the **Print** group, click the **Page Setup** button.

11 In the **Page Setup** dialog box, click the **Sheet** tab. Make sure the **Gridlines** box is checked, and then click **OK**.

12 Click anywhere in the worksheet preview to enlarge the preview (Figure 1.16).

13 With your teacher's permission, click the **Print** button and click **OK** in the **Print** dialog box. Or, click the **Close Print Preview** button.

14 **Save** your worksheet. Click the **Close** button, to exit **Excel**.

Figure 1.15 The Print Area is set.

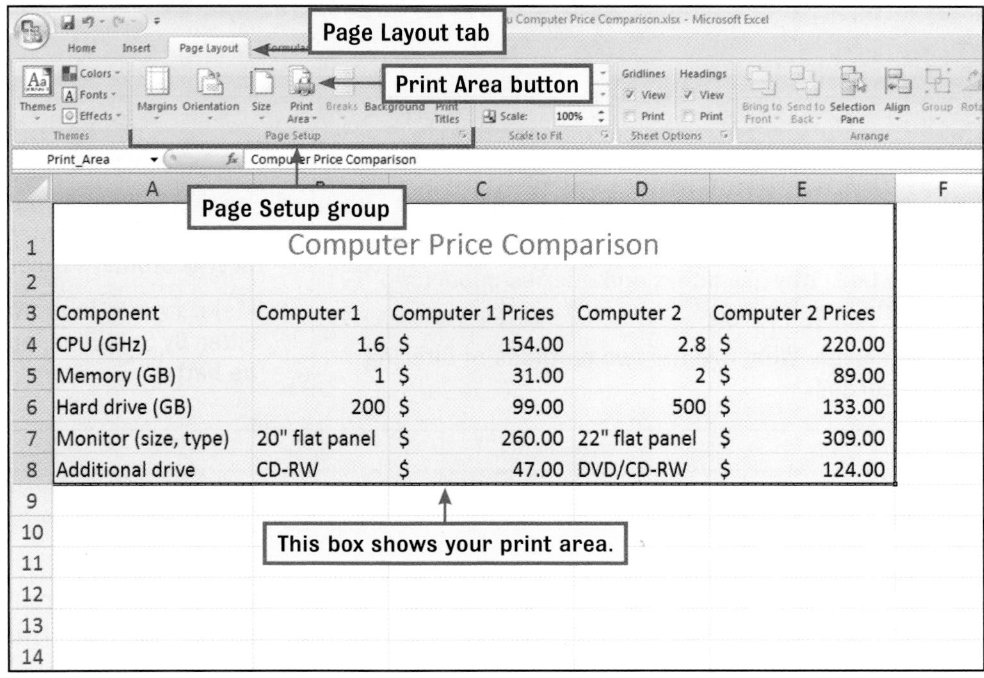

Figure 1.16 The Print Preview shows how your worksheet will look when it is printed.

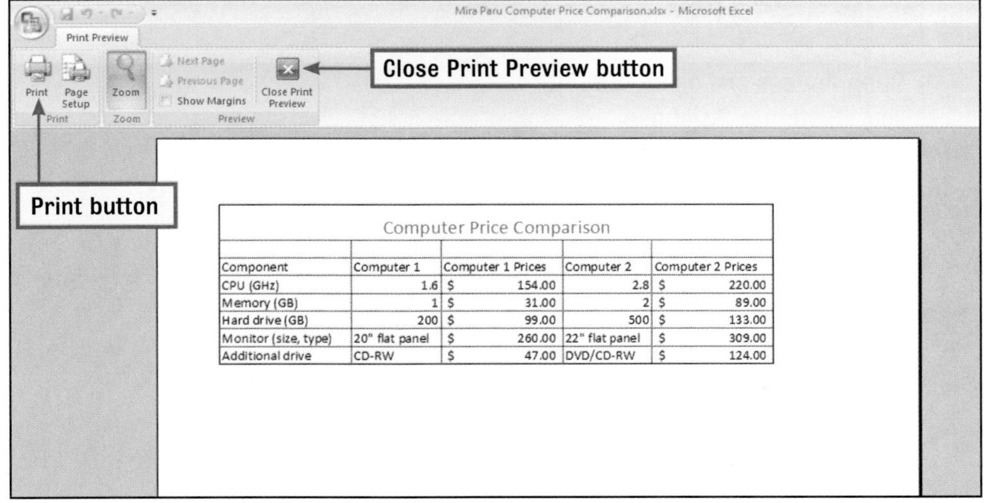

TechSavvy

Quick Select If you click the rectangle to the left of the column A heading and above the row 1 heading, you will select the entire worksheet—all 16,384 columns and 1,048,576 rows!

Project 2 Assessment

4. Click a record with March 8 (3/8) under **Date Ordered**.

5. Use **Filter By Selection** to view all March 8 orders. See Figure 2.12. (Exercise 2-2)

6. **Remove** the filter.

7. Click **Advanced Filter Options** , then choose **Filter By Form**. Click **Advanced Filter Options** , and choose **Clear Grid**.

▼ **Figure 2.12** The table now only displays orders made on March 8.

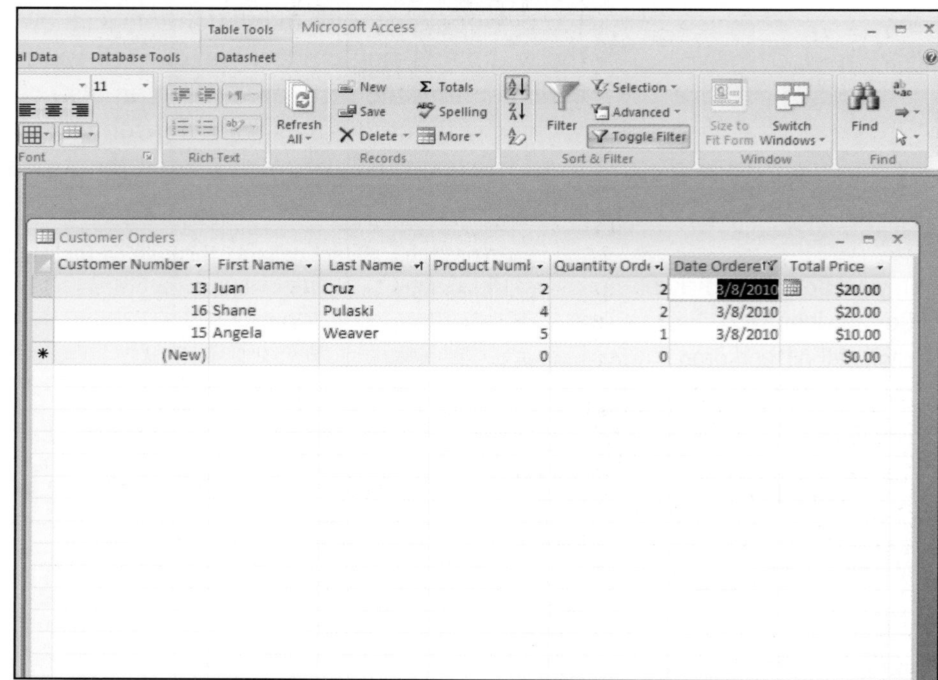

8. Use **Filter By Form** to find March 8 (3/8) orders for small, red T-shirts. Remember that a small, red T-shirt is Product Number 4. See Figure 2.13. (Exercise 2-3)

9. **Remove** the filter, **close** the table, and **save** changes to the design.

10. **Exit Access**.

▼ **Figure 2.13** The table displays only March 8 orders for Product Number 4.

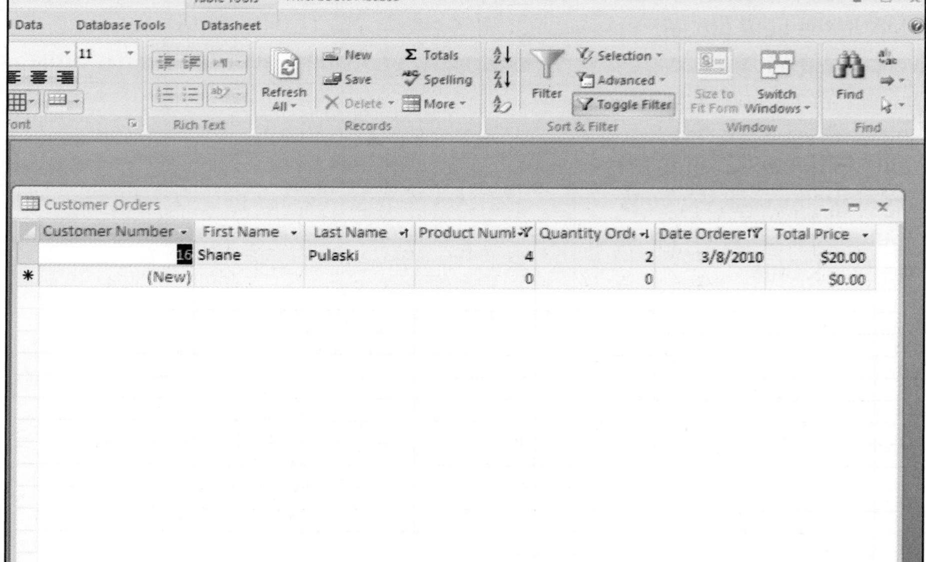

Exercise 1-4 Format and Print a Worksheet

Printing your Excel worksheet is a little different from printing a Word document. Word documents are not usually wider than the paper, but an Excel worksheet with many columns can be several pages wide. To limit the width to a single page, you can tell Excel which cells to print. This is called setting the print area. You can also choose to print the worksheet with or without the lines (called gridlines).

In this exercise, you will format the worksheet with a title and set the print area.

Step-by-Step

1. In your **Computer Price Comparison** worksheet, click cell **A1** and drag the cell pointer to **E1** (Figure 1.13).
2. On the **Home** tab, in the **Alignment** group, click the **Merge & Center** button.
3. Add a title for the worksheet. In cell **A1**, key Computer Price Comparison and press ENTER.
4. Click cell **A1**. On the **Home** tab, in the **Font** group, click the **Font Size** drop-down arrow, and click **16**.
5. On the **Home** tab, in the **Font** group, click the **Font Color** drop-down arrow, and click **Blue**.
6. Move the pointer between **row headings 1** and **2**. The double-arrow pointer appears.
7. Drag the pointer down until the pop-up window says the height is about **30.00** (Figure 1.14).

Figure 1.13 Select cells A1 through E1 for your title. Merging removes the gridlines between cells.

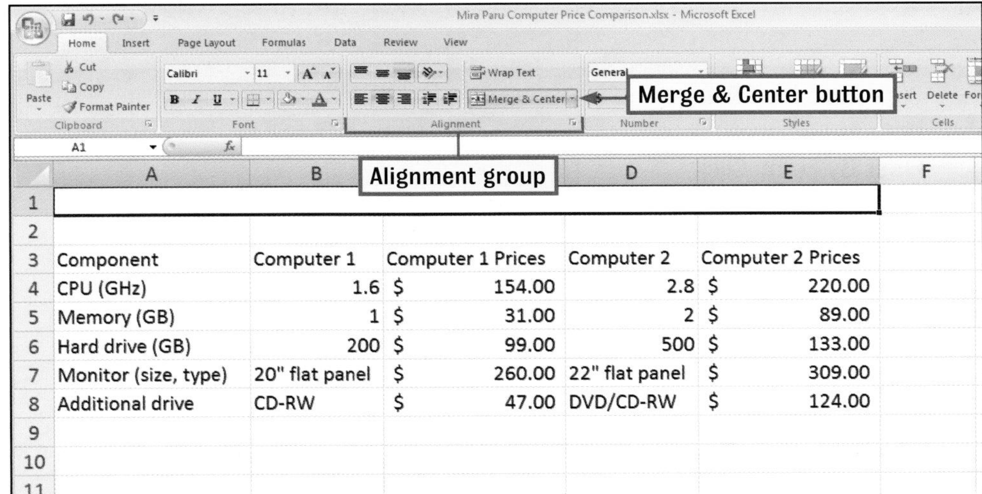

Figure 1.14 A title is added to the top of the worksheet.

Project 2 Assessment

2 Independent Practice ★

Go Online RUBRICS
glencoe.com

Independent Practice
Use the rubrics for these projects to help create and evaluate your work. Go to the **Online Learning Center** at **glencoe.com**. Choose **Rubrics**, then **Unit 6**.

Math **Practice Sorting** Choose the sort or filter to use on your Customer Database (from the Guided Practice on page 287).

a. You want to group customers by ZIP Code to reduce mailing costs.

b. Customers who order five or more T-shirts get a discount. You need to see which customers receive a discount.

c. A lot of your orders are for large, red T-shirts. You have to make sure you are not running out of that style.

3 Independent Practice ★★

Math **Sort Your Personal Database** In Project 1, Independent Practice 3 (page 278), you created a personal database. Now you want to organize that database to make it easier to find information.

a. Plan Decide what criteria would be useful for sorting your personal information.

b. Create Save the new database as ***Your Name* Personal Database 2**, then:

- Sort the table in alphabetic order by last name.
- Use the Filter By Form method to filter the list by two other criteria, such as birthday, street, or city.

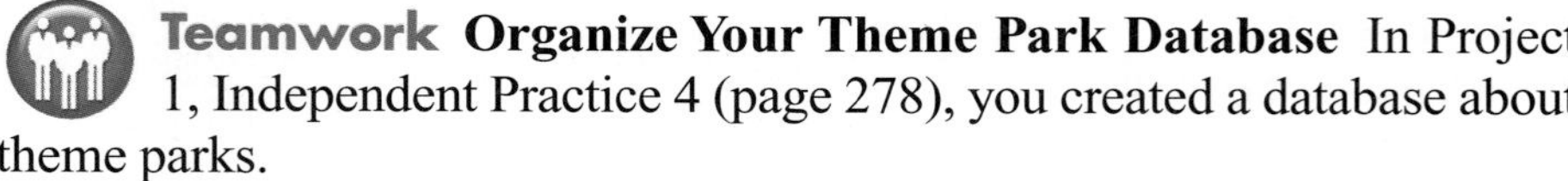

4 Independent Practice ★★★

Teamwork **Organize Your Theme Park Database** In Project 1, Independent Practice 4 (page 278), you created a database about theme parks.

a. Create Each member of your team will use your Theme Park Database to organize the information in the following ways:

- The most expensive park to the least expensive park
- The park with the most number of rides to the park with the least number of rides
- The park that is closest and the park that is farthest

b. Analyze Based on the results of your sorts, rank your theme parks from best to worst.

5 Click **E3**, and key Computer 2 Prices.

6 Starting in **E4** and going down the column, enter the prices as shown in Figure 1.11.

7 Click **E4** and drag to **E8** to select the column range.

▼ **Figure 1.11** More data are entered into the worksheet.

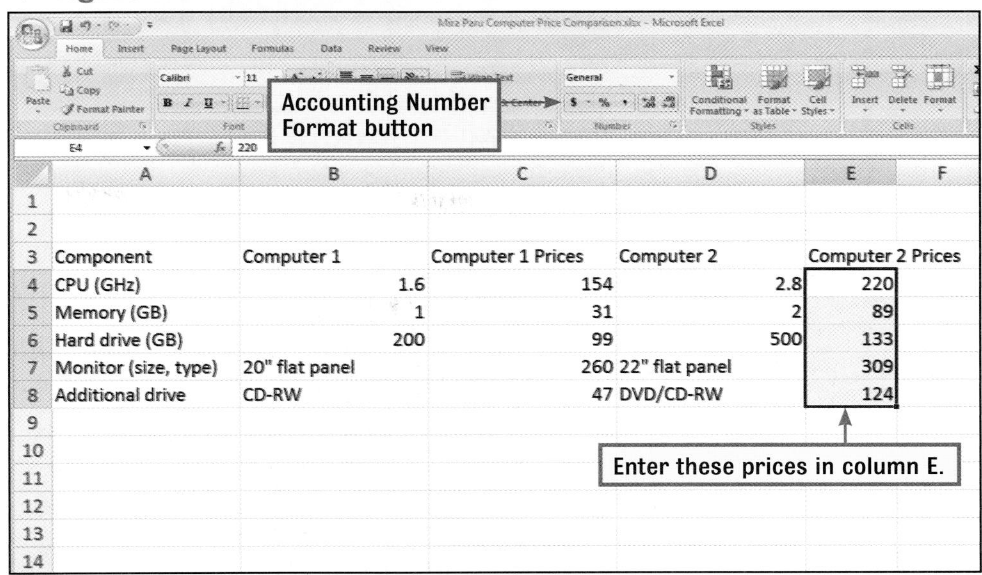

	A	B	C	D	E	F
1						
2						
3	Component	Computer 1	Computer 1 Prices	Computer 2	Computer 2 Prices	
4	CPU (GHz)	1.6	154	2.8	220	
5	Memory (GB)	1	31	2	89	
6	Hard drive (GB)	200	99	500	133	
7	Monitor (size, type)	20" flat panel	260	22" flat panel	309	
8	Additional drive	CD-RW	47	DVD/CD-RW	124	

8 On the **Home** tab, in the **Number** group, click the **Accounting Number Format** [$] button. The data are now formatted as dollars and cents (Figure 1.12).

9 Select **C4** through **C8**, and apply the **Accounting Number Format** style.

10 Double-click the line that separates **column headings A** and **B**. The width will **AutoFit** to the most efficient width.

11 **AutoFit columns B, C, D**, and **E**. Your worksheet should now look like Figure 1.12.

12 **Save** your worksheet.

▼ **Figure 1.12** The data are now formatted with dollars and cents.

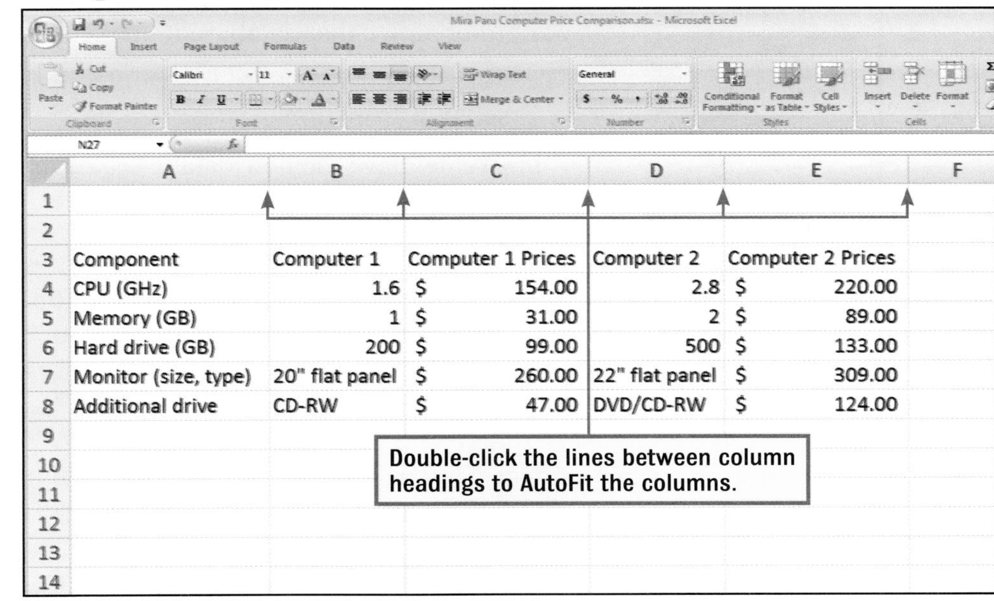

	A	B	C	D	E	F
1						
2						
3	Component	Computer 1	Computer 1 Prices	Computer 2	Computer 2 Prices	
4	CPU (GHz)	1.6	$ 154.00	2.8	$ 220.00	
5	Memory (GB)	1	$ 31.00	2	$ 89.00	
6	Hard drive (GB)	200	$ 99.00	500	$ 133.00	
7	Monitor (size, type)	20" flat panel	$ 260.00	22" flat panel	$ 309.00	
8	Additional drive	CD-RW	$ 47.00	DVD/CD-RW	$ 124.00	

TechSavvy

Cells, Rows, or Columns To insert a new cell, row, or column, click the **Insert** button. Choose **cells**, **rows**, or **columns**. By default, a new row is added *above* the cell pointer. A new column appears to the *left*. If you delete a cell, a Delete box appears, and you can choose how you want the surrounding cells to shift. To delete a cell, highlight the cell and right-click. Choose **Delete**, then click **OK**.

Concepts in Action

Project 3 Display Data in Forms and Reports

Key Concepts

Exercise 3-1

- Use a wizard to create a form
- Change a record
- Add a record

Exercise 3-2

- Create a report
- Organize and total data
- Print a report

Vocabulary

Key Terms
form
wizard
report

Before You Begin

Preview Before creating the forms and reports in this lesson, carefully view the figures in each exercise. After you have "seen" the steps, it will be easier to "do" the steps.

For this project, you will use Access to create forms to enter data easily into your database, and to summarize the information in the database.

Tracking the T-Shirts

T-shirt orders are coming in fast. It is getting difficult to keep your customer order records up-to-date because only a few people in your class know how to add records to the database. You also risk running out of certain colors and sizes, so you need to keep a total of the T-shirts sold by style.

To help manage your record keeping, you will create a data-entry form that will make it easy to update your records. You will also print a report that will show you how well each style of T-shirt is selling. To help manage your record keeping, you will create a data-entry form that will make it easy to update your records. Each form will record a customer's name and order information, and then automatically be added to the database. You will also print a report that can be used to keep your class updated on how well sales are going and which T-shirt styles are selling the fastest.

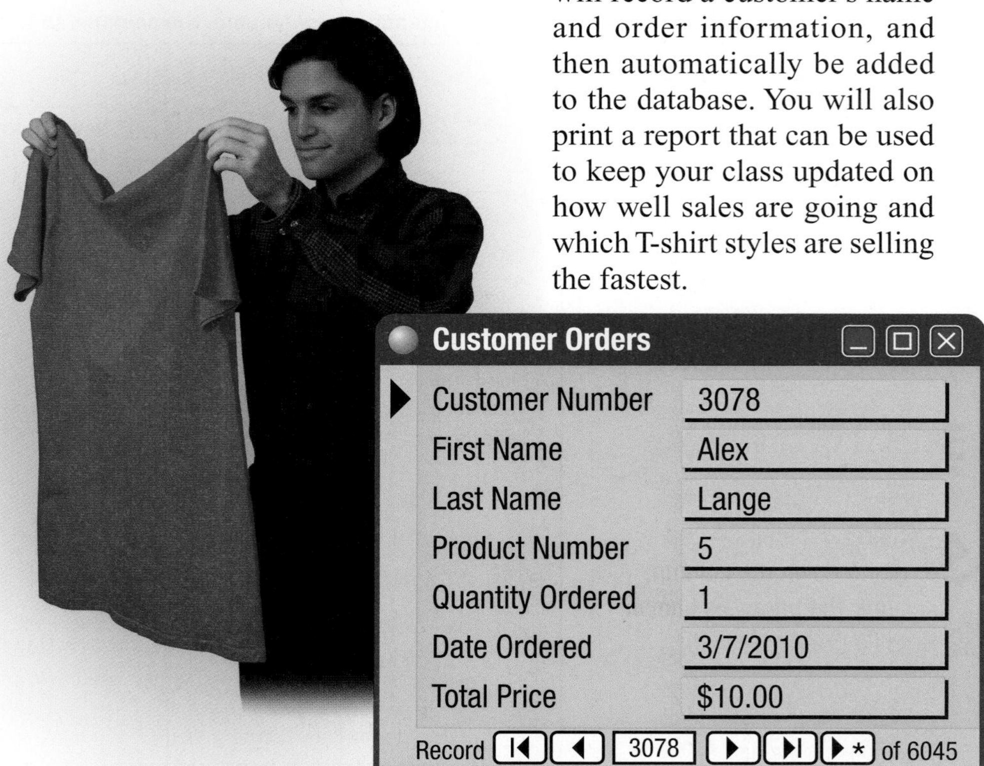

Exercise 1-3 Format a Worksheet

In an Excel worksheet, you can change the formatting, or the appearance, of the data in a cell. For example, the Accounting Number Format and Percent Style buttons on the Excel Home tab, in the Number group, let you easily change a number to dollars, or a percentage. When you select a **range**, which is a group of cells, you can make the same changes to all cells in the range.

Sometimes you will find that you need to add or delete rows, columns, or cells in your worksheet. Excel lets you insert a cell or an entire row, add a new column, and even add a new worksheet. It also lets you easily remove an entire row or column.

All the columns in a new worksheet are the same width. Often, the headers or data do not fit into this standard width. Excel can also automatically change the width of a column to fit the longest entry or change the height of a row to fit the font. This tool is called **AutoFit**.

In this exercise, you will change the appearance of the Computer Price Comparison worksheet by inserting and deleting columns. Then you will format the new data. Finally, you will change the width of a column so that the data fit in each cell.

Step-by-Step

1. Click **column heading C**.
2. On the **Home** tab, in the **Cells** group, click the **Insert** button drop-down arrow. Then click **Insert Sheet Columns**. A new column is added.
3. Click cell **C3**, and key Computer 1 Prices.
4. Starting in cell **C4** and going down the column, enter the prices as shown in Figure 1.10.

▼ **Figure 1.10** **Use the Insert button in the Cells group to add columns or rows. When you add a new column, the columns to the right are automatically renamed.**

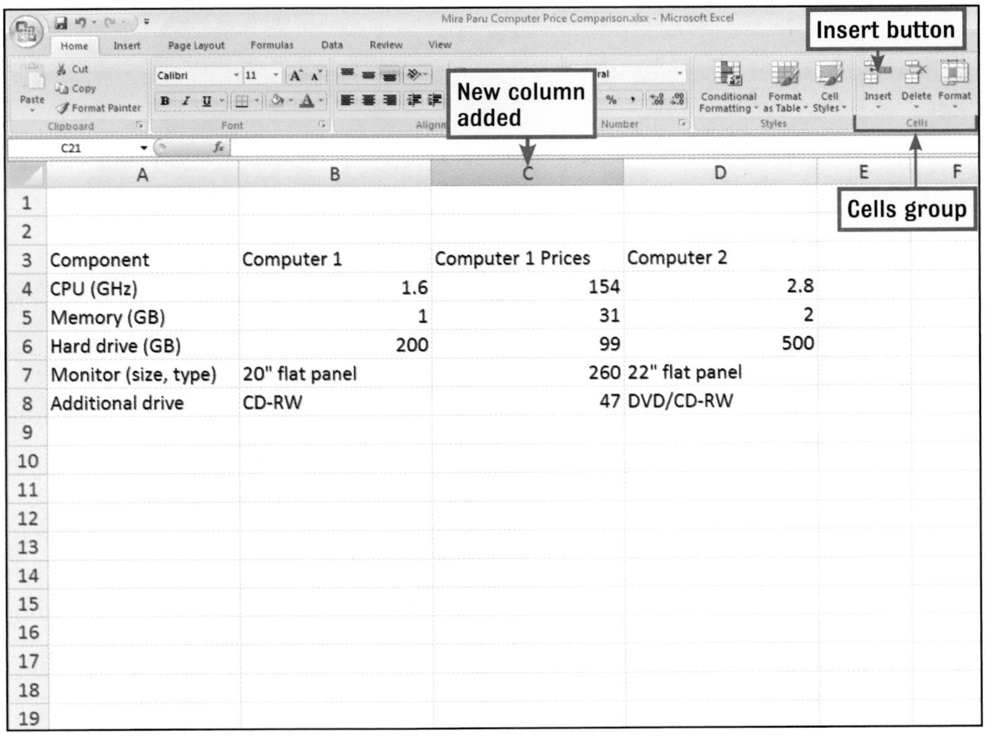

Insert button

New column added

Cells group

	A	B	C	D	E	F
1						
2						
3	Component	Computer 1	Computer 1 Prices	Computer 2		
4	CPU (GHz)	1.6	154	2.8		
5	Memory (GB)	1	31	2		
6	Hard drive (GB)	200	99	500		
7	Monitor (size, type)	20" flat panel	260	22" flat panel		
8	Additional drive	CD-RW	47	DVD/CD-RW		

Exercise 3-1 Create a Form

Adding data to a long table with hundreds of records can take a long time. It is much easier to enter data using forms. A **form** arranges the data from a table in a way that makes it easy for anyone to enter data. For example, when a Web site asks you for information such as your name and address, you are using a form to enter data into that site's database.

Forms let you view records, change a record, add a new record, and delete a record.

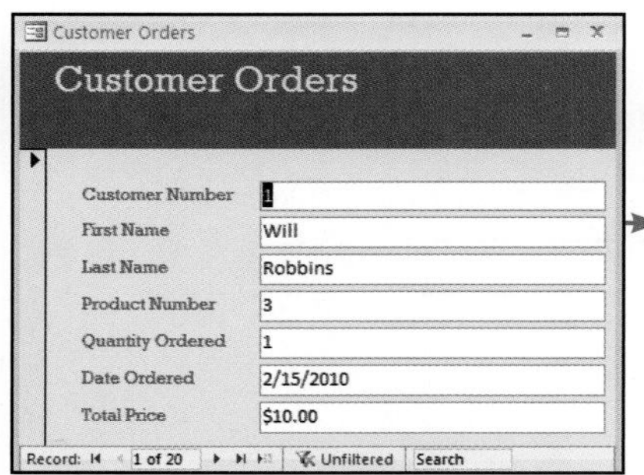

◄ **You can enter new records by using a form.**

In this exercise, you will use a wizard to create a form for your customer database. A **wizard** is a feature that helps you through the series of steps needed to create a helpful tool such as a form. You will then see how easy it is to change and add records.

Step-by-Step

1. In Access, **open** your **Customer Database** file.

2. **Open** the **Customer Orders** table. Click in the first cell of the **Customer Number** column.

3. On the **Home** tab, in the **Sort & Filter** group, click the **Ascending** button [A↓Z]. The customers are now in numerical order (Figure 3.1).

4. **Close** the table. Click **Yes** to save the changes.

▼ **Figure 3.1** **The customers in this database are sorted by customer number.**

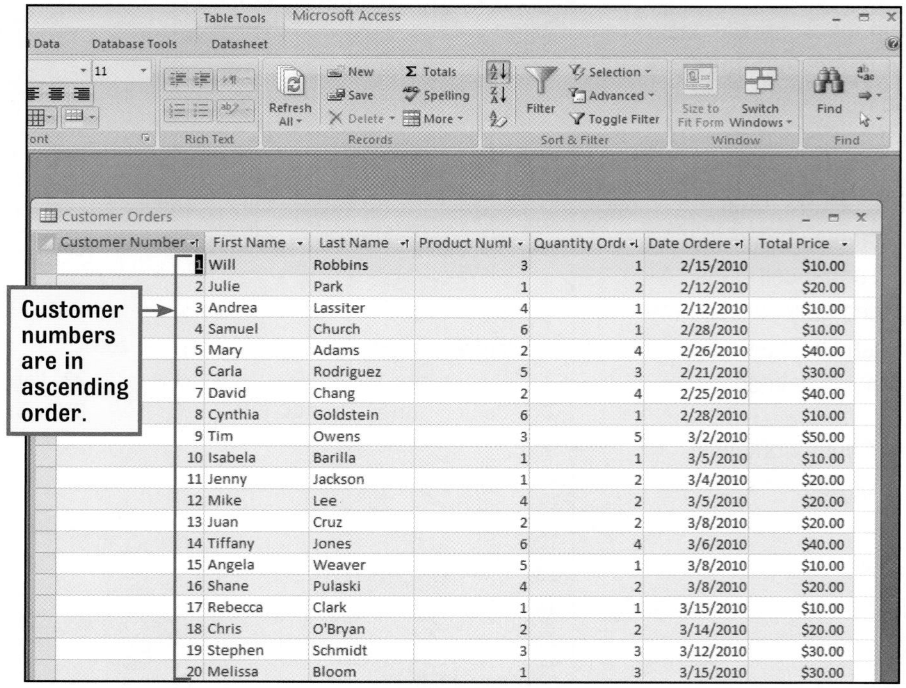

12 Click cell **C6**. The contents of the cell appear in the Formula Bar.

13 In the **Formula Bar**, click between the **3** and the **0** as shown in Figure 1.8. Press BACKSPACE to delete the 3. Key 5.

14 Click the **check mark** ✓ to accept the change. Cell C6 is now 500.

15 Click cell **B7**, and key 20″ flat panel, then press ENTER. By keying directly into the cell, the old contents are deleted.

16 Click cell **C3**. Move the pointer over the dot in the bottom-right corner of the cell (the fill handle). The pointer should change to a thin plus sign.

17 Drag the fill handle one cell to the right (to **D3**), and release the mouse button. See Figure 1.9.

18 Click cell **D3**. Drag the fill handle up and to the left so that cell D3 is shaded gray. Release the fill handle. The Computer 3 label is deleted.

19 **Save** your worksheet.

Figure 1.8 If the Formula Bar is not displayed on your screen, click the View tab. In the Show/Hide group, click the Show/Hide button and click Formula Bar.

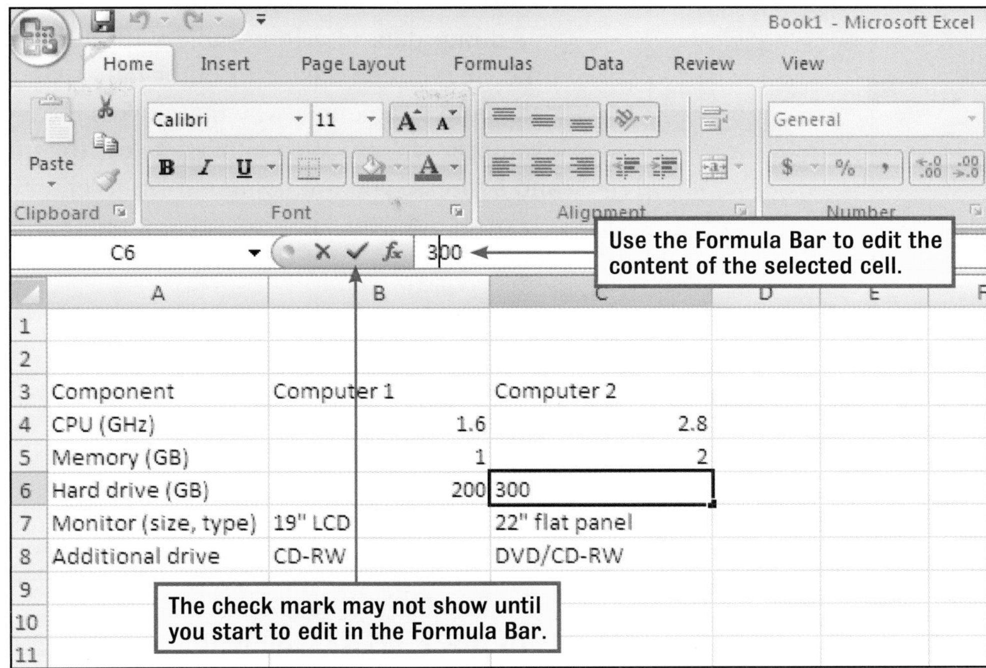

Figure 1.9 Use the fill handle to automatically insert the label "Computer 3" into the cell next to "Computer 2."

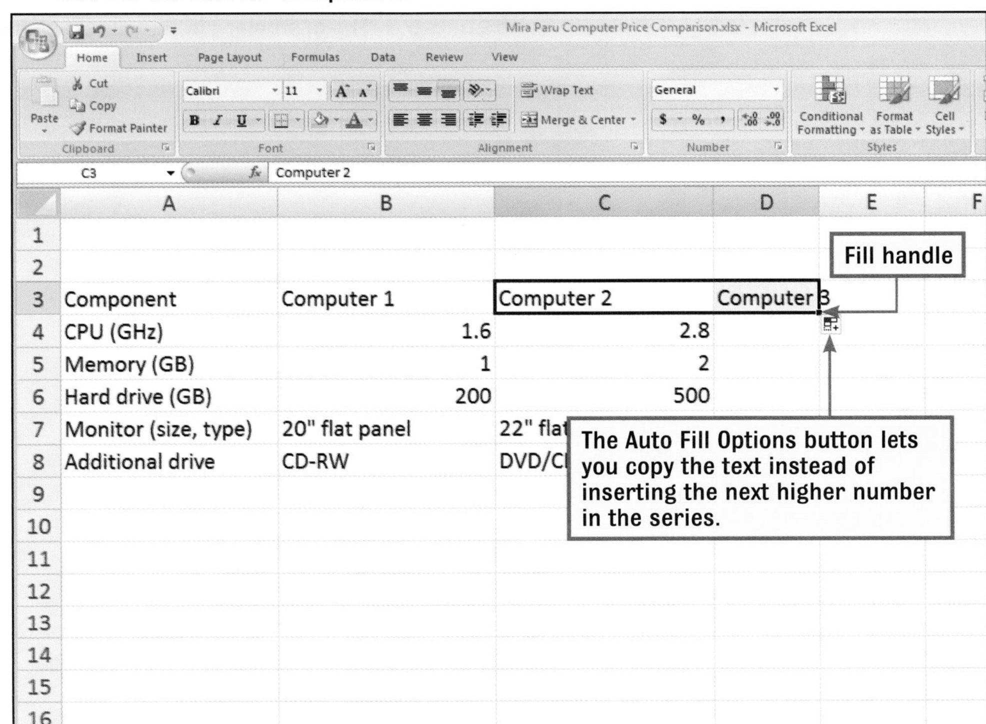

5 In the **Navigation** Pane, click the **Down Arrow** next to **Tables**. Under **Filter By Group**, click **Forms**. Click the **Create** tab.

6 On the **Create** tab, in the **Forms** group, click **More Forms**. Click **Form Wizard**. This takes you to the screen shown in Figure 3.2.

7 In the **Tables/Queries** text box, click the arrow and choose **Table: Customer Orders** (Figure 3.2).

8 Click the **double arrow** button to move all the **Available Fields** to the **Selected Fields** list.

Figure 3.2 To create a Customer Orders form that has all the same fields as the Customer Orders table, click the double arrow.

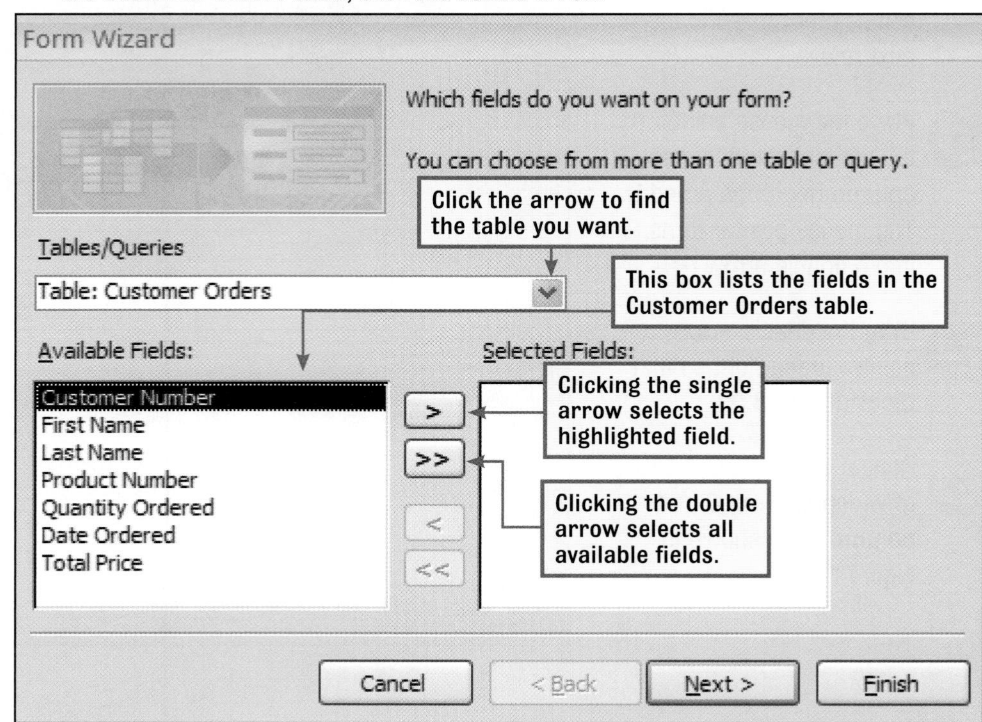

9 When finished, click **Next** to move to the next screen in the **Form Wizard** (Figure 3.3).

10 Choose the **Columnar** layout option, and then click **Next** to move to the next screen.

11 From the list of styles, click **Foundry**. Preview illustrates the effect of your choice.

Figure 3.3 This Form Wizard window lets you choose a layout for your form.

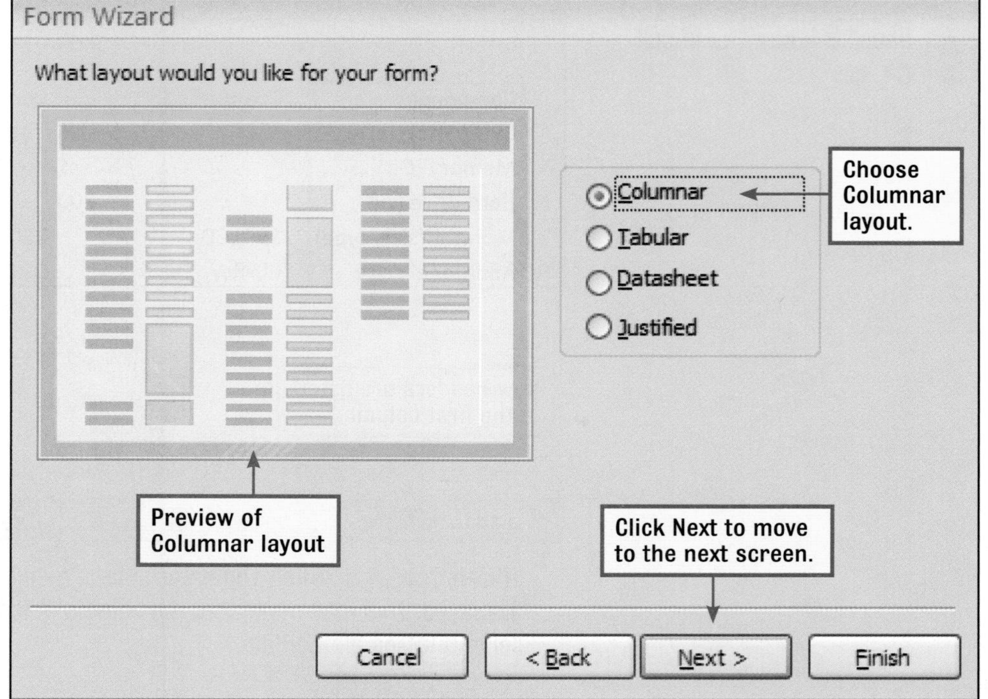

5. In cell **C3**, key Computer 2, and then press ENTER. The cell pointer moves to the next row.

6. Place the mouse pointer on the vertical line between **column headings A** and **B**. The mouse pointer turns into a double arrow.

7. Drag the double-arrow pointer to the right so that the width is **18.00**.

8. Repeat steps 6 and 7 to widen **column B** and **column C**, as shown in Figure 1.6.

Figure 1.6 The columns are wider so that all of the text can be displayed.

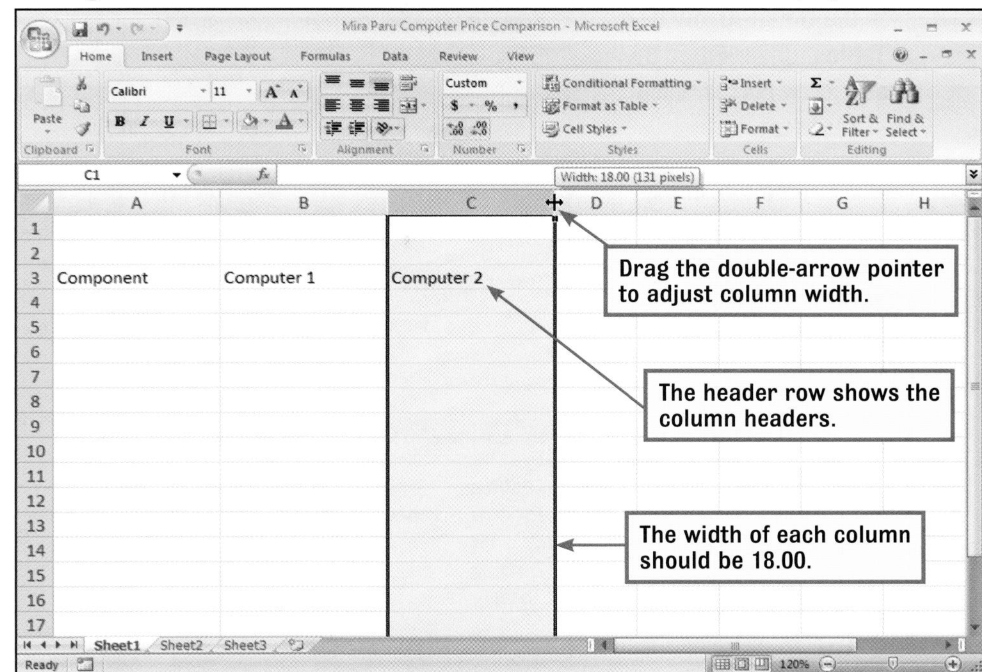

9. In cell **A4**, key CPU (GHz).

10. In cell **B4**, key 1.6. In cell **C4**, key 2.8.

11. Key the next four rows of data, as shown in Figure 1.7.

Figure 1.7 The worksheet shows information comparing two different computer systems.

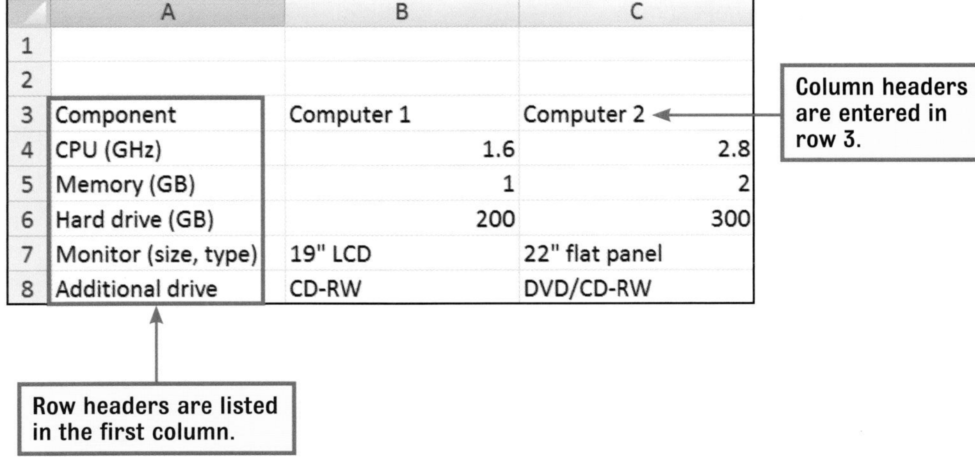

	A	B	C
1			
2			
3	Component	Computer 1	Computer 2
4	CPU (GHz)	1.6	2.8
5	Memory (GB)	1	2
6	Hard drive (GB)	200	300
7	Monitor (size, type)	19" LCD	22" flat panel
8	Additional drive	CD-RW	DVD/CD-RW

HELP!

Widen Columns When you enter data in a cell, you may see #### displayed. This may mean that the column is too narrow. Just widen the column to see all the data.

12 Click **Next** to view the final page of the **Form Wizard** (Figure 3.4).

13 Under **What title do you want for your form?**, leave the title as Customer Orders.

14 Make sure that **Open the form to view or enter information** is selected, then click **Finish**. Your form will be displayed.

Figure 3.4 The Form Wizard has taken you through all the options you need to complete the form.

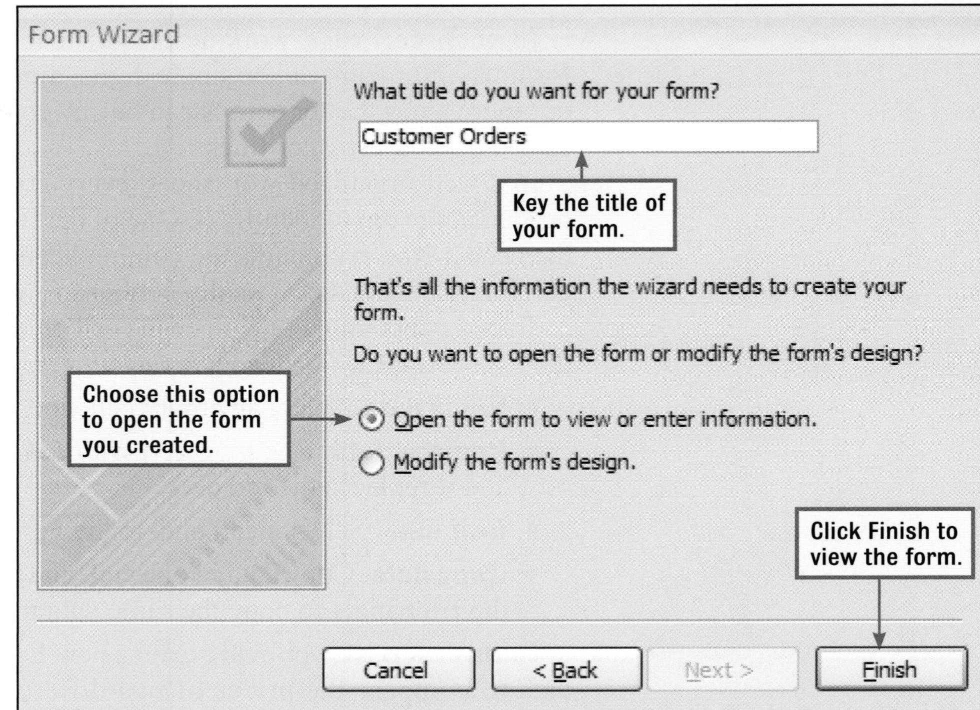

15 In the **Customer Orders** form, change the **Go to Record** box to **5**, and then press ENTER. Record 5 is displayed (Figure 3.5).

16 Change **Quantity Ordered** to **5** and press ENTER.

17 Click the **New Blank Record** button.

Figure 3.5 Your Customer Orders form has the same fields as the Customer Orders table.

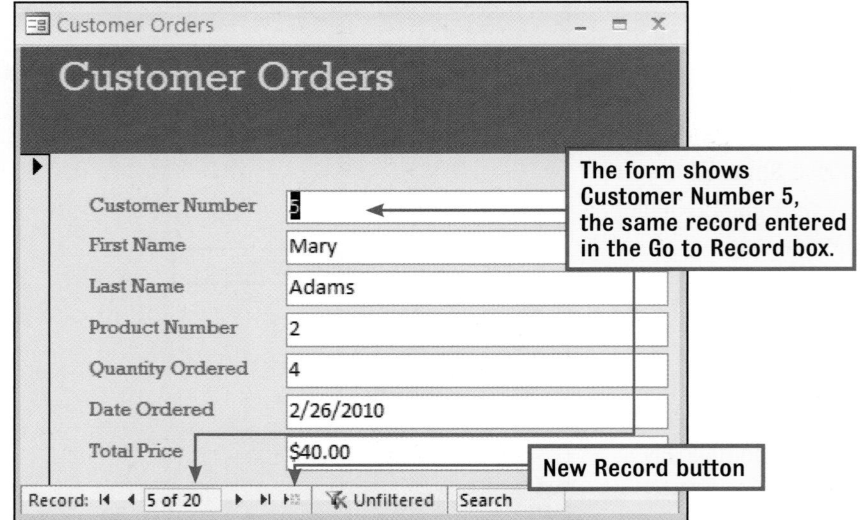

Exercise 1-2 Create a Worksheet

In each cell of a worksheet, you can enter numbers, letters, or formulas. Numbers can be single digits, money amounts, dates, decimals, or other values. Letter entries can be any combination of characters, such as names, addresses, or titles.

In a well-organized worksheet, every column should have a label, or header, at the top to identify it. One of the first few rows in a worksheet is the header row. It contains the column headers (see Figure 1.5). The first column in a worksheet usually contains row headers.

To enter data into a cell, place the cell pointer in the cell where you want the data to appear. Then add, replace, or copy data in the cell.

- **Enter data** Select an empty cell, and key your data.
- **Replace data** Choose a cell with data already in it. Key new data, and it replaces the old data.
- **Edit data** Select a cell and, in the Formula Bar, change the data.
- **Copy data** Copy data in one cell, and then paste it into another. Use the fill handle to copy the same data into multiple cells.

In this exercise, you will create a new Excel workbook. You will enter data to compare the prices of two different computers. You will also change column widths so that you can read all of your data.

Step-by-Step

1. Click the **Office Button**, choose **New**, and select **Blank Workbook**. Then click **Create**.
2. Click the **Office Button** and choose **Save**. Save your file as *Your Name* Computer Price Comparison.
3. Move the cell pointer to cell **A3**, key Component, and press ENTER. The text appears in cell A3, and the cell pointer automatically moves to cell A4.
4. Move the cell pointer to cell **B3**, key Computer 1, then press the **right arrow** key (Figure 1.5).

Figure 1.5 Two new labels are column headers for your data.

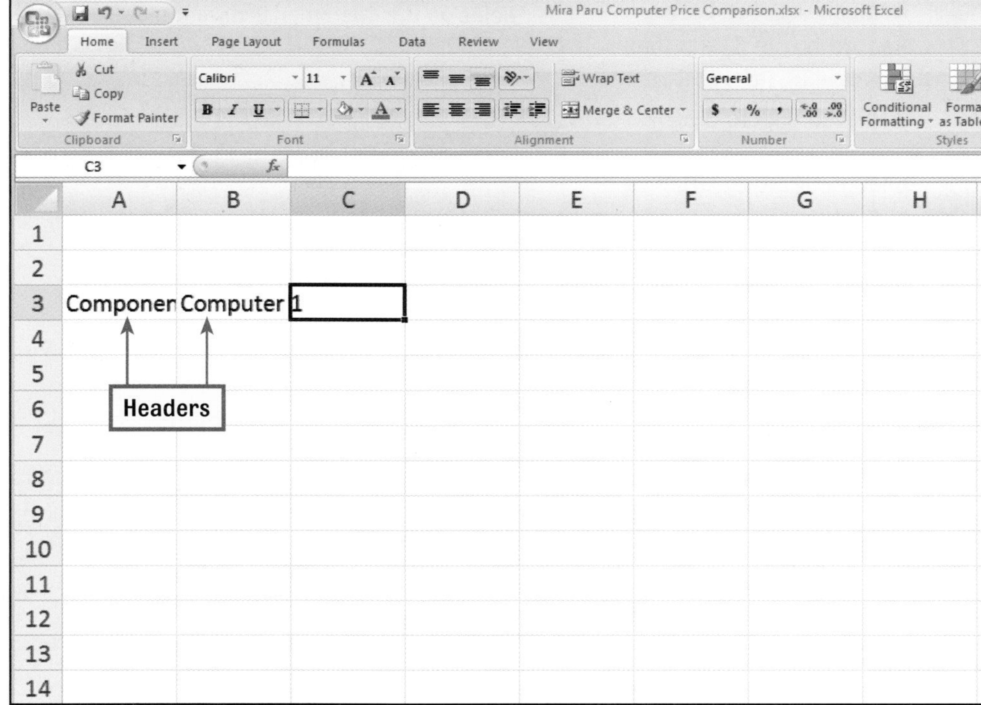

18 In the new record, key the information you see in Figure 3.6. You do not need to enter a Customer Number because **AutoNumber** automatically creates a number when you key information into the form.

19 Click the **Close** button [X] on the form to return to the database window.

20 In the **Navigation** Pane, click the **Down Arrow** next to **Forms**. Under **Filter By Group**, click **Tables**.

21 Double-click the **Customer Orders** table to display your records in **Datasheet View** (Figure 3.7).

22 Notice that the changes you made on the forms are entered in the table. **Close** the table.

▼ **Figure 3.6** A new record is keyed into a table using a form.

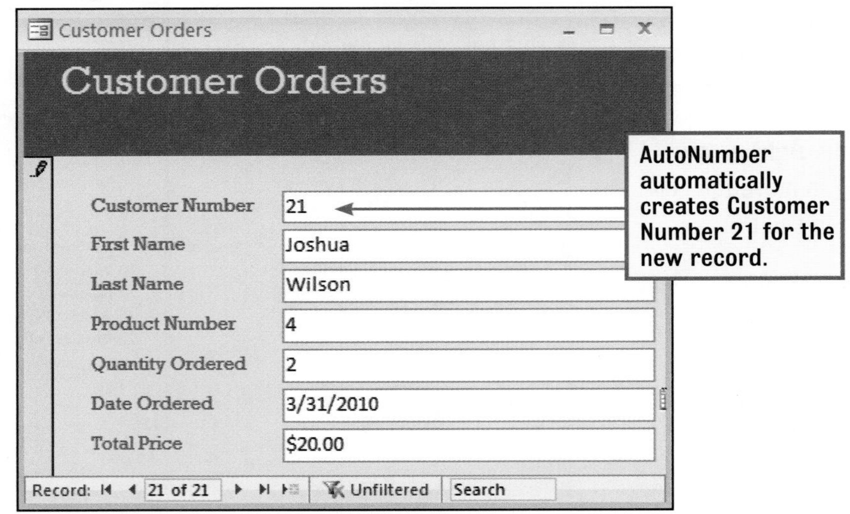

▼ **Figure 3.7** The changes appear in the Datasheet View of the table.

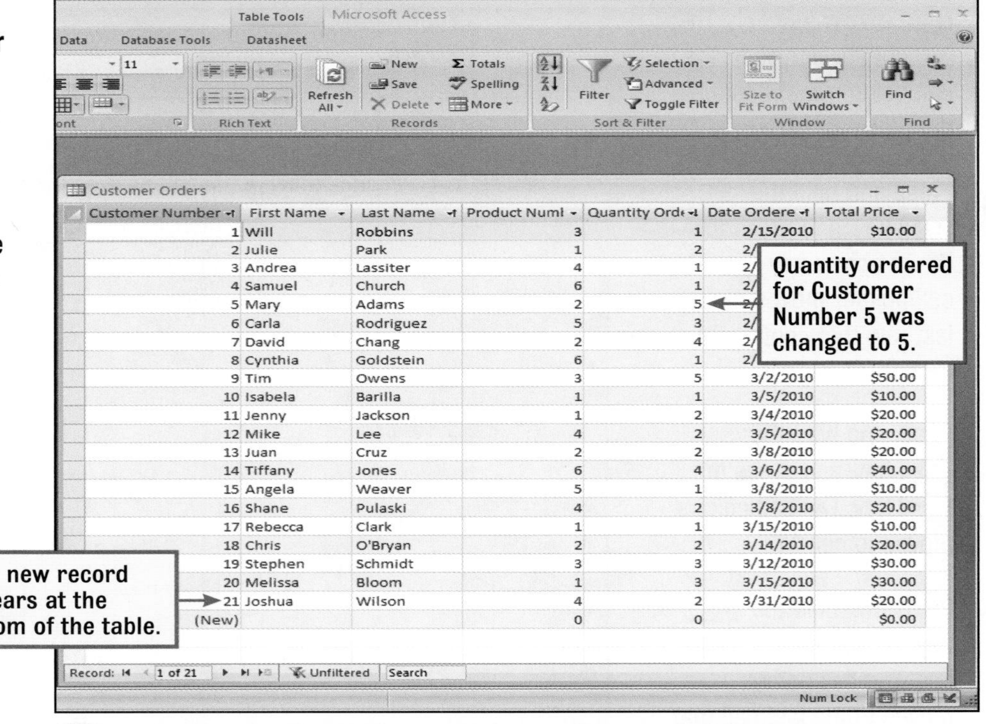

Customer Number	First Name	Last Name	Product Numl	Quantity Orde	Date Ordere	Total Price
1	Will	Robbins	3	1	2/15/2010	$10.00
2	Julie	Park	1	2	2/	
3	Andrea	Lassiter	4	1	2/	
4	Samuel	Church	6	1	2/	
5	Mary	Adams	2	5	2/	
6	Carla	Rodriguez	5	3	2/	
7	David	Chang	2	4	2/	
8	Cynthia	Goldstein	6	1	2/	
9	Tim	Owens	3	5	3/2/2010	$50.00
10	Isabela	Barilla	1	1	3/5/2010	$10.00
11	Jenny	Jackson	1	2	3/4/2010	$20.00
12	Mike	Lee	4	2	3/5/2010	$20.00
13	Juan	Cruz	2	2	3/8/2010	$20.00
14	Tiffany	Jones	6	4	3/6/2010	$40.00
15	Angela	Weaver	5	1	3/8/2010	$10.00
16	Shane	Pulaski	4	2	3/8/2010	$20.00
17	Rebecca	Clark	1	1	3/15/2010	$10.00
18	Chris	O'Bryan	2	2	3/14/2010	$20.00
19	Stephen	Schmidt	3	3	3/12/2010	$30.00
20	Melissa	Bloom	1	3	3/15/2010	$30.00
21	Joshua	Wilson	4	2	3/31/2010	$20.00
(New)			0	0		$0.00

TechSavvy

Viewing Tips You can also open a form in **PivotTable View** or **PivotChart View** to analyze data. In these views, you can change the layout of a form to present data in different ways, by rearranging row headings, column headings, and filter fields until you achieve the best layout for you.

6. In the worksheet, click cell **A5**. Cell A5 is in the first column in the fifth row (Figure 1.3).

7. Press the **right arrow** key [→] to move the cell pointer to cell D5.

8. Press the **down arrow** key [↓] to move to cell D6.

9. Press the [HOME] key, and the cell pointer moves to the beginning of row 6.

10. Press and hold the [END] key, and press the **right arrow** key [→]. The cell pointer moves to the last column that contains data (column H).

11. Press and hold the [END] key, and press the **down arrow** key [↓]. The cell pointer moves to the last row that contains data (row 8).

12. Press and hold the [CTRL] key, and press the [HOME] key. The cell pointer moves to cell A1.

13. Press and hold the [CTRL] key, and press the [END] key. The cell pointer moves to the last cell that contains data (H8). See Figure 1.4.

14. Click the **Close Window** [X] button to **close** the worksheet. Do not close Excel.

▼ **Figure 1.3** **Use the arrow keys to move from cell to cell.**

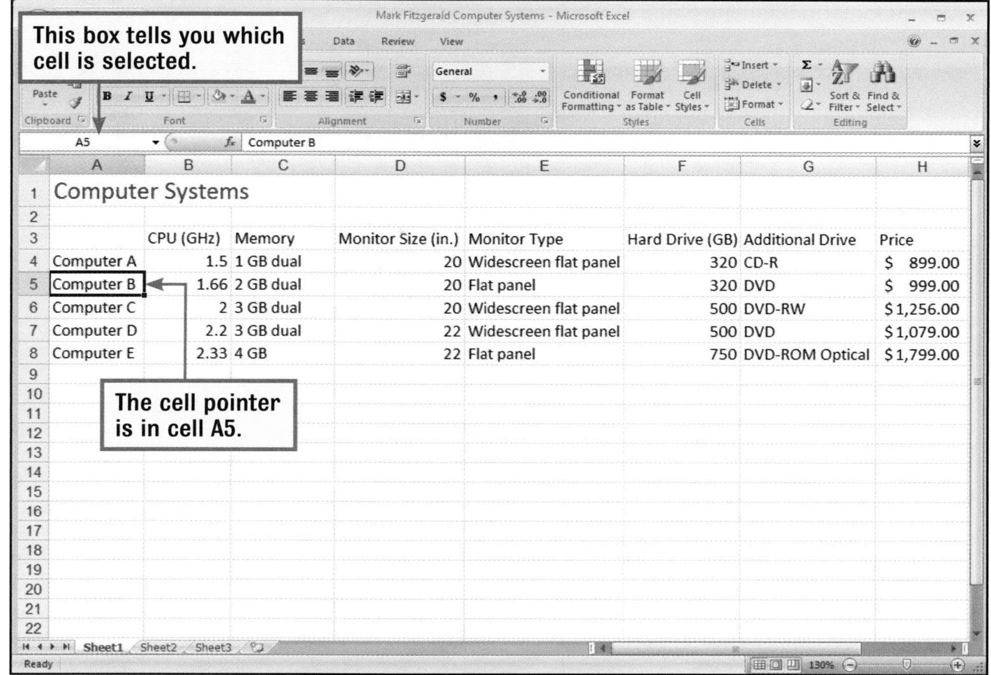

	A	B	C	D	E	F	G	H
1	Computer Systems							
2								
3		CPU (GHz)	Memory	Monitor Size (in.)	Monitor Type	Hard Drive (GB)	Additional Drive	Price
4	Computer A	1.5	1 GB dual	20	Widescreen flat panel	320	CD-R	$ 899.00
5	Computer B	1.66	2 GB dual	20	Flat panel	320	DVD	$ 999.00
6	Computer C	2	3 GB dual	20	Widescreen flat panel	500	DVD-RW	$1,256.00
7	Computer D	2.2	3 GB dual	22	Widescreen flat panel	500	DVD	$1,079.00
8	Computer E	2.33	4 GB	22	Flat panel	750	DVD-ROM Optical	$1,799.00

▼ **Figure 1.4** **Practice moving the cell pointer from the beginning of a row to the end of a row.**

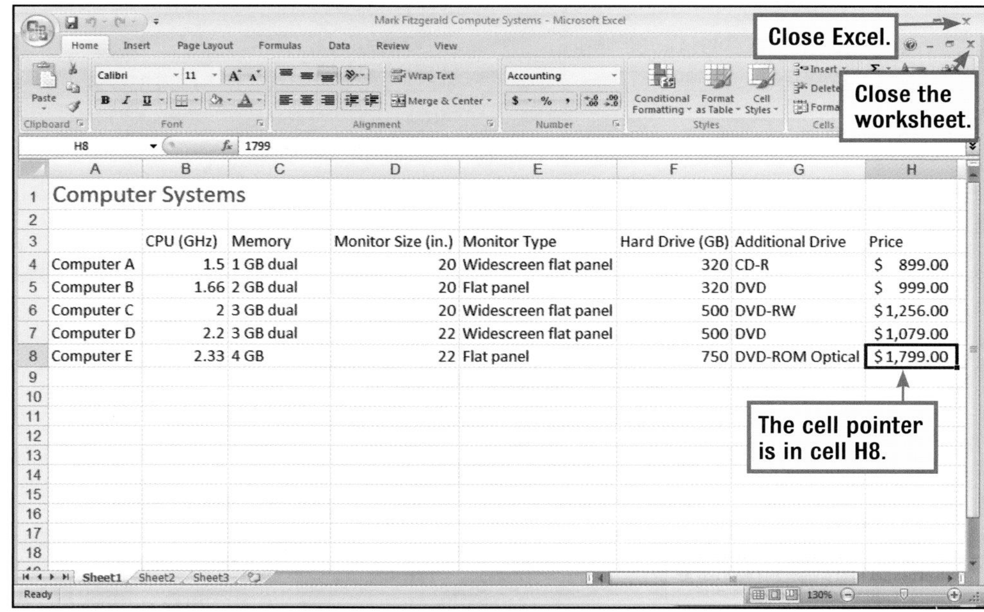

	A	B	C	D	E	F	G	H
1	Computer Systems							
2								
3		CPU (GHz)	Memory	Monitor Size (in.)	Monitor Type	Hard Drive (GB)	Additional Drive	Price
4	Computer A	1.5	1 GB dual	20	Widescreen flat panel	320	CD-R	$ 899.00
5	Computer B	1.66	2 GB dual	20	Flat panel	320	DVD	$ 999.00
6	Computer C	2	3 GB dual	20	Widescreen flat panel	500	DVD-RW	$1,256.00
7	Computer D	2.2	3 GB dual	22	Widescreen flat panel	500	DVD	$1,079.00
8	Computer E	2.33	4 GB	22	Flat panel	750	DVD-ROM Optical	$1,799.00

Exercise 3-2 Create a Report

Every week, the fundraising committee meets to see how many T-shirts have sold and which styles are running low. To show the weekly results, you need to create a report. A **report** is a printable summary of the information in your database. It can highlight the most important information and also add up, or total, any number amounts that you have in a table.

A report can display details of each record and add up total amounts.

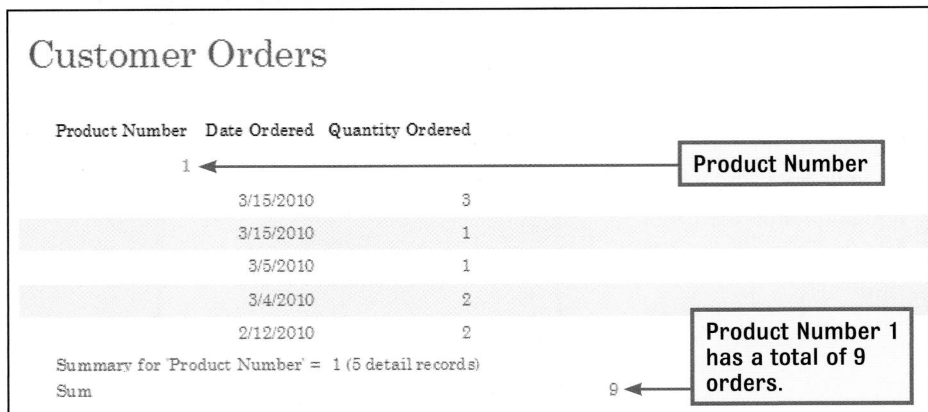

In this exercise, you will use a wizard (similar to the way you created a form) to create a report. In the report, you will total the number of T-shirts you have sold in each style. Because each style has its own product number, you will group the information in the report by product number. Then you will sort each product according to the date of the order, with the most recent orders at the top. That way, you can quickly see how many T-shirts were ordered over the past week.

Step-by-Step

1. In your **Customer Database** file, in the **Navigation** Pane, click the arrow next to **Tables**.

2. Under **Filter By Group**, choose **Reports**. You will see a screen like Figure 3.8.

3. On the **Create** tab, in the **Reports** group, click the **Report Wizard** button.

Figure 3.8 The ways to create a new report are shown on the Ribbon in the Reports group.

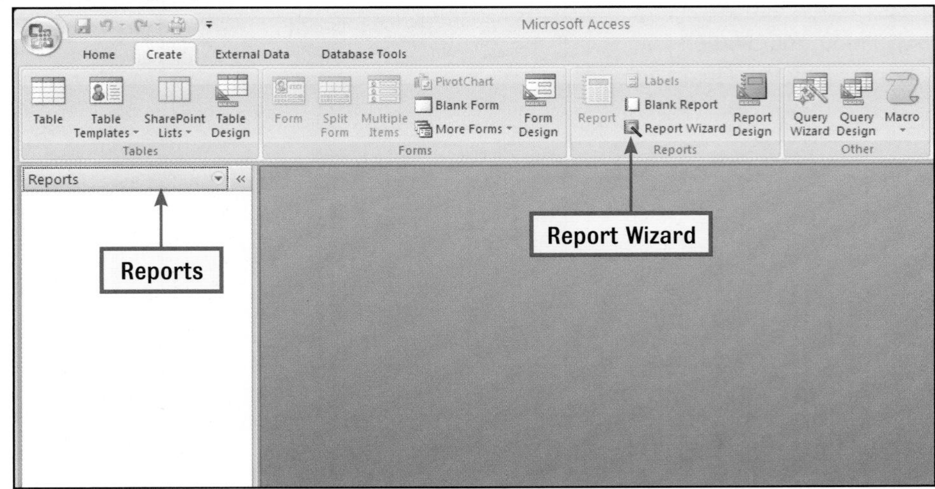

Step-by-Step

1. **Start Microsoft Excel.** If you are using Windows XP, please refer to pages xliv-xlviii in the *Getting Started* section in this book.

2. On your own screen, find and name the Excel features shown in Figure 1.1.

Figure 1.1 A screen like this one appears when you start Microsoft Excel. Excel contains many of the same elements as other Microsoft Office applications.

Title bar
Formula Bar
Quick Access Toolbar
Office Button
Work area
Scroll bars
Status bar

3. Click the **Office Button**, and choose **Open**.

4. **Open** the **Data File** named **5A Computer Systems**.

5. Save the worksheet as *Your Name* Computer Systems. Your screen should look like Figure 1.2.

Figure 1.2 This worksheet compares five computer systems.

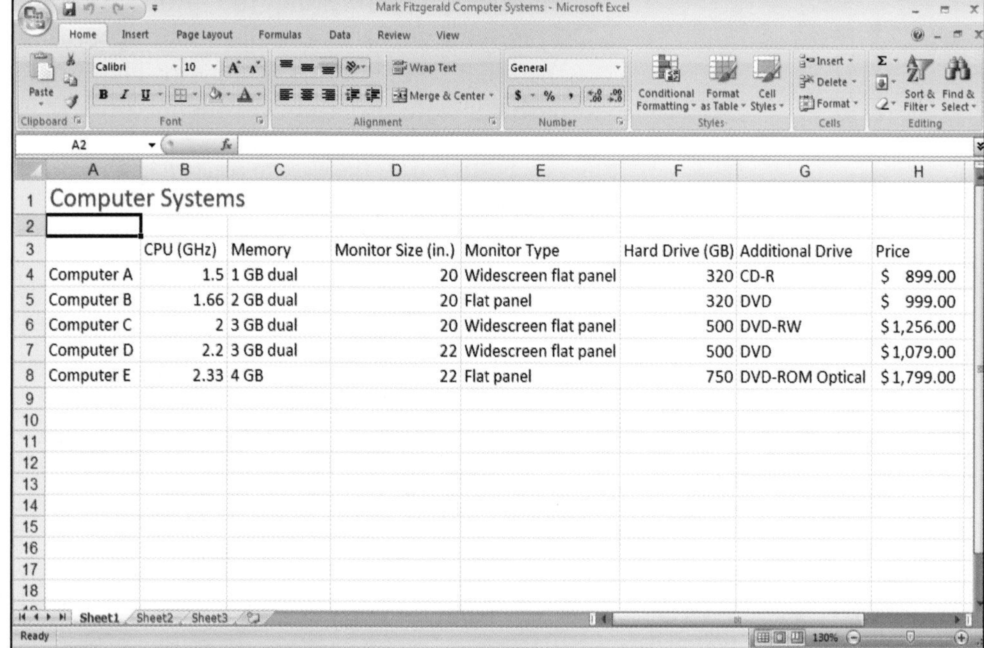
Mark Fitzgerald Computer Systems - Microsoft Excel

Computer Systems

	CPU (GHz)	Memory	Monitor Size (in.)	Monitor Type	Hard Drive (GB)	Additional Drive	Price
Computer A	1.5	1 GB dual	20	Widescreen flat panel	320	CD-R	$ 899.00
Computer B	1.66	2 GB dual	20	Flat panel	320	DVD	$ 999.00
Computer C	2	3 GB dual	20	Widescreen flat panel	500	DVD-RW	$ 1,256.00
Computer D	2.2	3 GB dual	22	Widescreen flat panel	500	DVD	$ 1,079.00
Computer E	2.33	4 GB	22	Flat panel	750	DVD-ROM Optical	$ 1,799.00

4. In the **Tables/Queries** box, click the drop-down arrow and choose **Table: Customer Orders**. The fields in the table appear.

5. Click **Product Number**, then click the **single arrow** [>] to move the **Product Number** field from the **Available Fields** to the **Selected Fields** list.

6. Repeat step 5 to move **Quantity Ordered** and **Date Ordered** from **Available Fields** to **Selected Fields** (Figure 3.9). Click **Next** to move to the next screen.

▼ **Figure 3.9** The Report Wizard lets you choose which fields you want in your report.

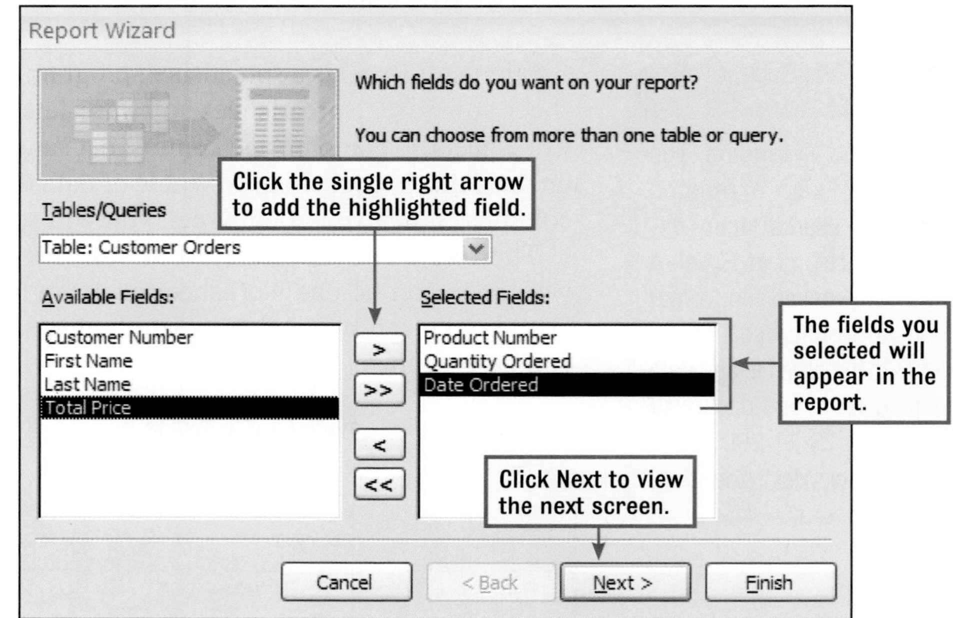

7. Under **Do you want to add any grouping levels?**, double-click **Product Number** to group the records by product number. Click **Next** to move to the next screen (Figure 3.10).

8. In the first text box, click the drop-down arrow, and choose **Date Ordered** (Figure 3.10).

9. Click the **Ascending** button next to the box to change it to **Descending**. (**Note:** If it already says Descending, do NOT click it. If your version of Access does not have the Ascending/Descending button, it should have arrows that you can click to do the same thing.)

▼ **Figure 3.10** You can arrange your dates in ascending or descending order.

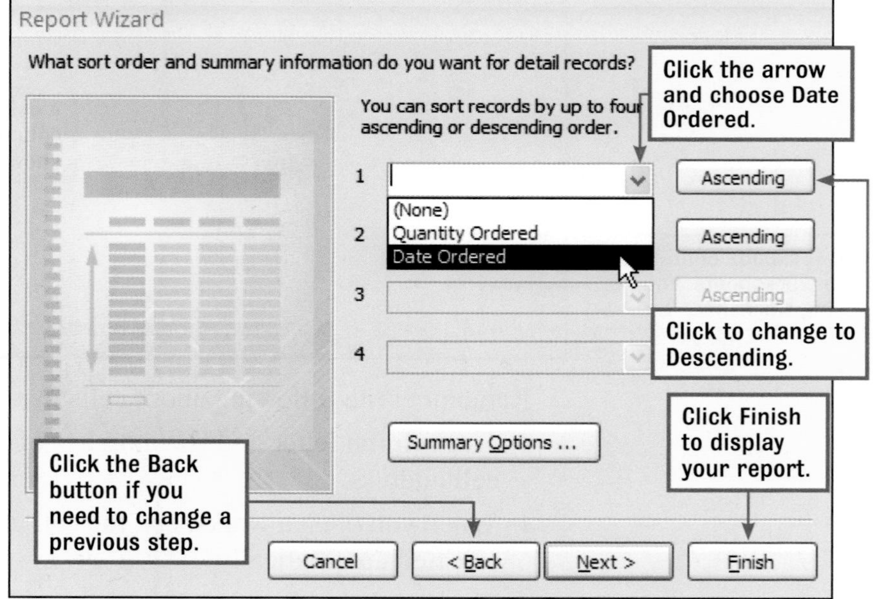

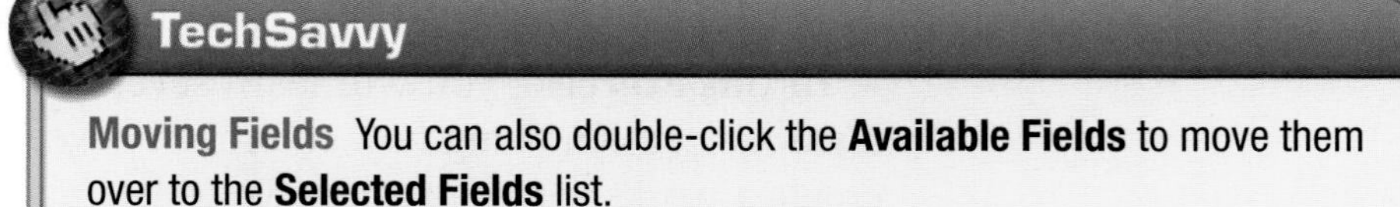

TechSavvy

Moving Fields You can also double-click the **Available Fields** to move them over to the **Selected Fields** list.

Exercise 1-1 Get to Know Microsoft Excel

TechSavvy

File Name Extension The familiar ".xls" extension has been used in many different versions of Excel. A new XML-based file format is used in Microsoft Office 2007 to improve file and data management and document recovery. Excel 2007 files have a new ".xlsx" extension.

Microsoft Excel is a spreadsheet program. It is the most popular spreadsheet software. Spreadsheet software lets you create spreadsheets, or worksheets, to compare and contrast data and perform various calculations on the data. A **worksheet** is a table of data that is organized into rows and columns. When you open Excel, you will see a worksheet on the screen.

The Excel file that holds your worksheets is called a **workbook**. A workbook can be one worksheet or it can hold hundreds of worksheets. Workbooks can be used to create budgets, organize student grades, or compare various products or services.

▼ **A worksheet is made up of columns, rows, and cells.**

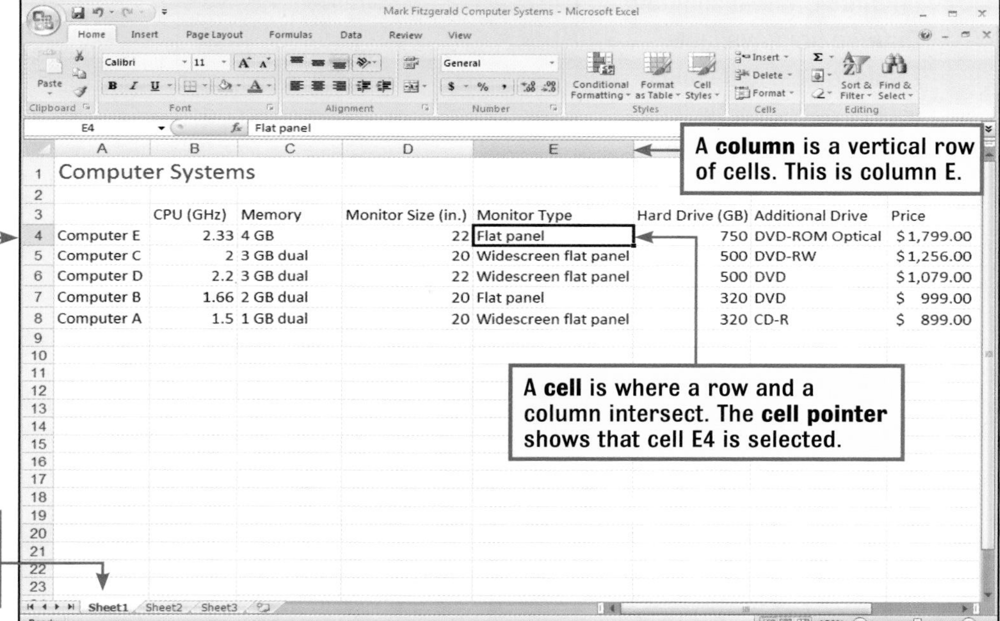

Remember the following about cells in a worksheet:

- The column letter and row number of a cell, such as A1, is called a cell address.
- When you open a worksheet, the cell in the top-left corner is usually selected automatically.
- The box that indicates which cell in a worksheet is selected is called the cell pointer. Use the arrow keys → on your keyboard or click the mouse to move the cell pointer from one cell to another.

In this exercise, you will learn several ways to move between cells in a worksheet. Knowing how to move between cells will help you quickly create a worksheet to organize your data.

10 Click the **Summary Options** button. The **Summary Options** dialog box is displayed (Figure 3.11).

11 Under the **Sum** column, select the check box next to **Quantity Ordered**.

12 Under **Show**, make sure the **Detail and Summary** option is chosen. Click **OK** to return to the **Report Wizard**.

Figure 3.11 This window shows different ways you can calculate information.

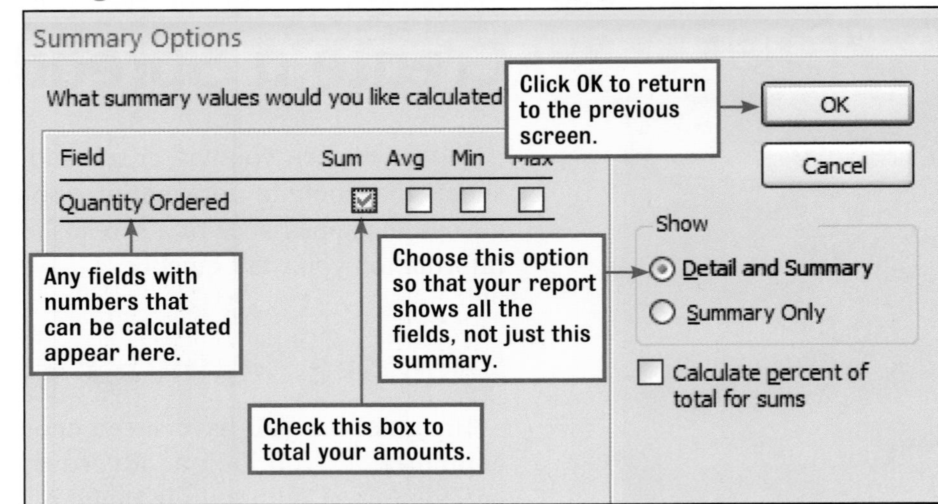

13 Click **Finish** to display your report, which should look similar to Figure 3.12.

14 With your teacher's permission, to print the report, click the **Print** button on the toolbar.

15 Click the **Close** button to save the report and close it.

16 **Exit Access**.

Figure 3.12 Your report shows that Product Number 2 is selling faster.

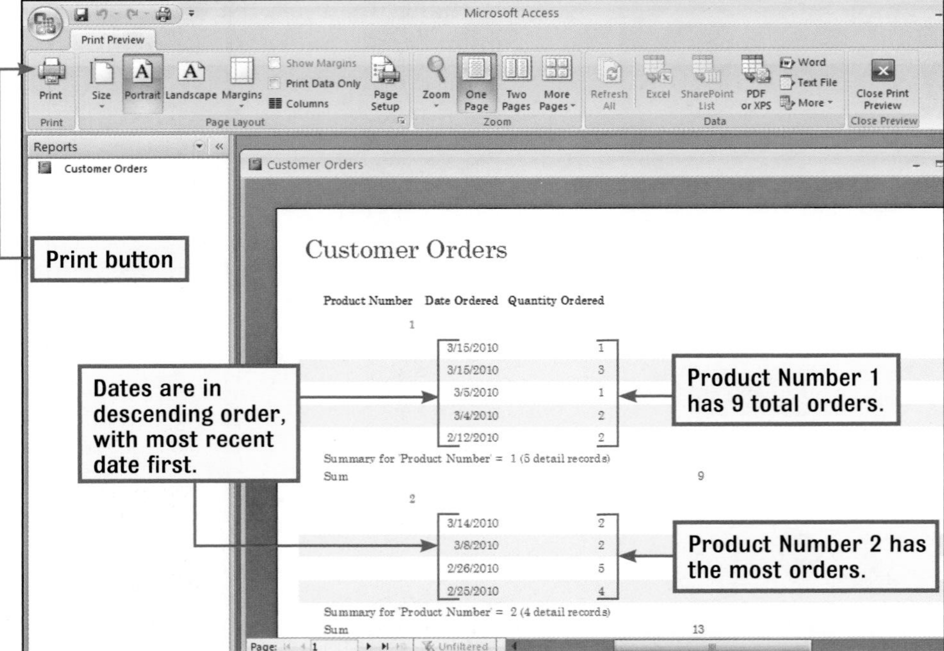

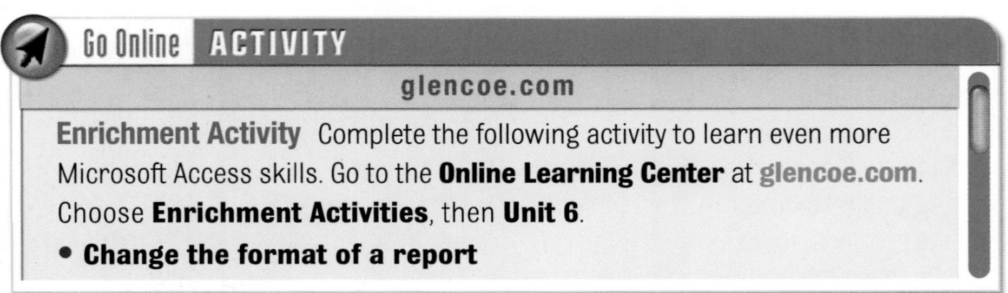

Enrichment Activity Complete the following activity to learn even more Microsoft Access skills. Go to the **Online Learning Center** at glencoe.com. Choose **Enrichment Activities**, then **Unit 6**.

- **Change the format of a report**

Concepts in Action

Project 1 Create a Spreadsheet

Key Concepts

Exercise 1-1
- Identify the parts of the Excel window
- Move between cells in a worksheet

Exercise 1-2
- Create and save a new worksheet
- Enter data into cells
- Edit and delete data

Exercise 1-3
- Format cells
- Define and use ranges
- Insert and delete columns and rows
- Change column width

Exercise 1-4
- Add a title to a worksheet
- Change row height
- Print a worksheet

Vocabulary

Key Terms
worksheet
workbook
range
AutoFit

Before You Begin

Tables Spreadsheets are like tables (grids of information). Find examples of tables in newspapers, magazines, and textbooks. Identify the columns, rows, and cells in these tables.

In this project, you will create and edit Microsoft Excel spreadsheets that include information about computer prices. You will change the appearance of a spreadsheet and use a filter to find the information you want quickly.

Compare Computer Prices

Imagine that you have saved enough money to buy your own computer. As you look at advertisements, you see many different computers with a wide range of prices. Before you buy, you decide to compare computers based on their components, such as memory, hard drives, monitors, and other hardware and software.

Rather than just list the components in a word processing document, you want to create a spreadsheet in which you can easily compare numbers and prices and make calculations.

Project 3 Assessment

Key Concepts Check

1. **Describe** How does a wizard make it easy to create forms and reports?
2. **Explain** Why would you want to enter data using forms rather than a table?
3. **Identify** What type of fields appear in the Summary Options screen?

Critical Thinking

4. **Make Connections** Give two examples of times you have used forms on the Internet to add information to a database.
5. **Make Predictions** What value would you expect to appear if you checked the Average (Avg) button in the Summary Options window?

1 Guided Practice

Create a Report You want to find out how much money you have collected in T-shirt sales and whether sales have gone up since the fundraiser began. Before you create a report, however, you need to add one more customer to your database. If you need help completing a step, refer back to the exercise in parentheses at the end of the step.

Step-by-Step

1. **Open** your **Customer Database** file.
2. Display **Forms** in the **Navigation** Pane. Double-click the **Customer Orders** form. The form is displayed. (Exercise 3-1)
3. **Go to Customer Number 10**. Change the **Quantity Ordered** to 2 and the **Total Price** to $20.00. (Exercise 3-1)
4. Create a **new record** with the information shown in Figure 3.13. (Exercise 3-1)

▼ **Figure 3.13** Use the record navigation buttons at the bottom of the form box to find or add records.

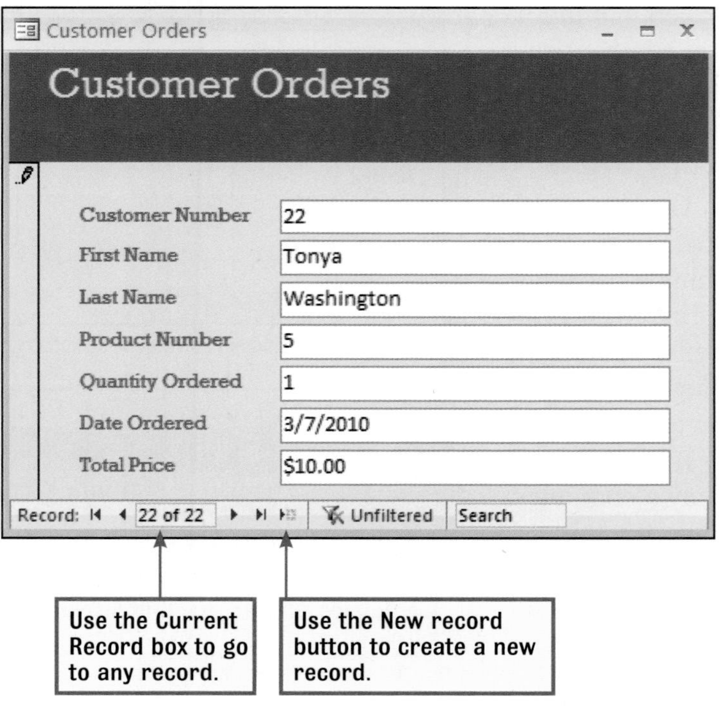

After You Read

Key Concepts Check

1. **Identify** What are three questions to ask yourself before you purchase a computer?
2. **Explain** How can setting up a computer network save money?

Critical Thinking

3. **Evaluate** A friend offers to sell you her three-year-old computer. How will you decide whether to buy it?
4. **Predict** What are two things to keep in mind that computer advertisements may not tell you?

21st Century Skills

5. **Evaluate** Go to glencoe.com to the book's Online Learning Center to find **Web Links** to a computer manufacturer, such as Apple® or Dell®. Navigate through the site as if you were going to buy a computer. Compare the final price of a computer with only basic options to one with all of the best features.

Academic Skills

Mathematics

Every year, more people use the Internet to play online games.

a. **Evaluate** What is the difference in the percentage of gamers between Year 1 and Year 3?

b. **Predict** What do you think the percentage of online gamers in Year 4 might be?

Math Concept

Percentages A percentage is a portion of a whole, which is represented by 100. In the chart below, the value for Year 3 shows that 44 out of every 100 gamers played games online.

Starting Hint To calculate how much online gaming has grown in two years, subtract the value of Year 1 from the value of Year 3.

NCTM Numbers and Operations Compute fluently and make reasonable estimates.

Percentage of Online Gamers in the U.S.

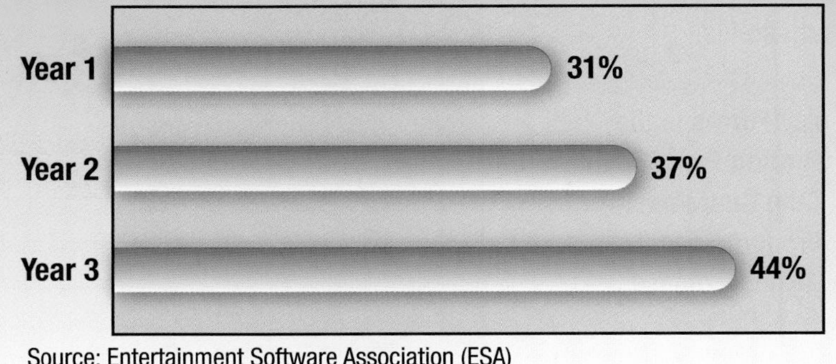

Source: Entertainment Software Association (ESA)

Go Online e-QUIZ

glencoe.com

Self-Check Assess your understanding of what you have just read. Go to the **Online Learning Center** at glencoe.com. Choose **e-Quizzes**, and take the **Unit 5 Tech Talk Quiz**.

5. **Close** the form, check the **Customer Orders** table to see whether the record has been added, then **return** to the Database window. (Exercise 3-1)

6. On the **Create** tab, in the **Reports** group, click **Report Wizard** . (Exercise 3-2)

7. Under **Tables/Queries**, choose the **Table: Customer Orders** table. Add the fields shown in Figure 3.14 to the **Selected Fields** list, then click **Next**. (Exercise 3-2)

8. Click **Date Ordered** as the grouping field, and then click **Next**. (Exercise 3-2)

9. Sort by **Date Ordered, Ascending**. (Exercise 3-2)

10. Click **Summary Options**, then choose the **Total Price** field's **Sum** check box. (Exercise 3-2)

11. Click **OK** to return to the previous screen, and then click **Finish**. Your report should look similar to Figure 3.15. (Exercise 3-2)

12. **Close** your report. **Exit Access.**

Figure 3.14 You can choose the fields you want to display on the record.

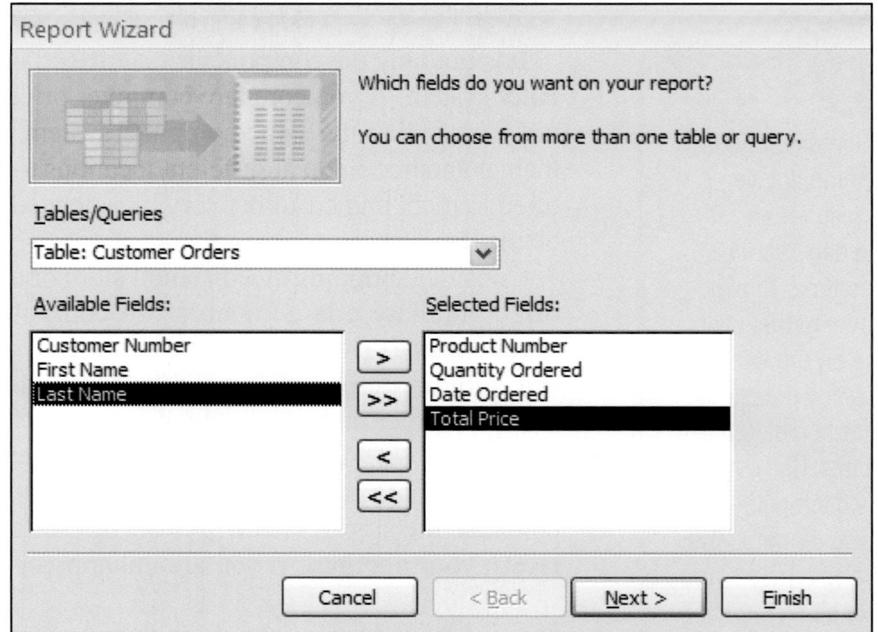

Figure 3.15 The Customer Orders report is displayed.

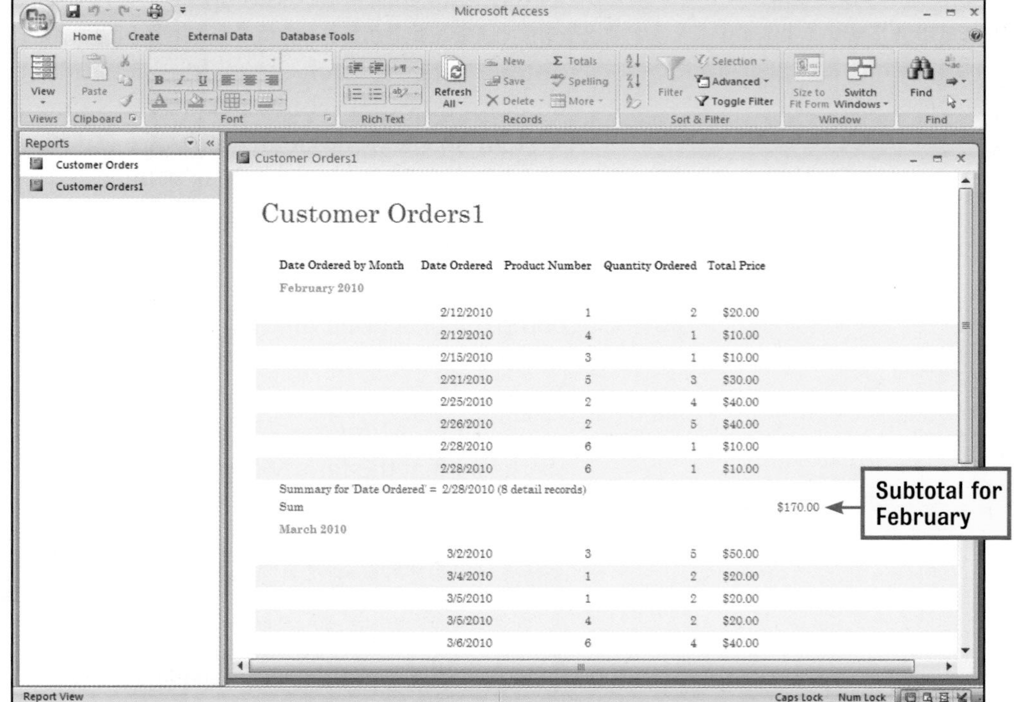

Jargon Some computer games are multiplayer games, which means more than one user can play at one time. To play a multiplayer game, users need to be on the same network. Many people use the Internet to play multi-player games. Use caution if you play such games because you do not know the people you are playing with personally.

Why It's Important Why are safety and ethics important if you are using the Internet for multiplayer games?

Why Are Computer Prices So Different?

It is not only the components that **affect**, or influence, the price of a computer system. If you compare computer prices online or at retail stores, you may notice that the same computer system costs more at one store or site than at another. Shop at different locations to find the best price for the type of equipment and customer service you need. The best deal may not always be the lowest price.

Consider shopping at a discount store or a large retail store. These stores often purchase a large quantity of computers and can then sell them at a lower price. However, some stores may charge more for a system but offer you more personalized service or additional benefits, such as free software, free training, or other services. If you shop online, be aware of shipping costs. A computer may seem inexpensive, but add shipping or handling charges to see what the final cost will be before you buy. Also, consider the store's return **policy**, or guidelines, to see whether you can return your purchase if you are unhappy or if it is damaged.

How Do Networks Affect Price?

A computer by itself is fun to use, but a computer that is hooked up to a network can be even better. A network lets computers "talk" to each other. In a network, computers are all connected to the same system so they can share software, files, and hardware devices such as printers.

Setting up a network can be a way to save money, especially for an organization with many computers, such as a large company or school. Sharing resources cuts down on the amount of equipment needed. You can even set up a small network in your home. Many people use home networks so that the family can share Internet connections or printers.

▲ You can play games such as chess on a network with other players. Why do you think so many people like to play games on a network?

Reading Check

1. **Explain** What is performance?
2. **Identify** Name three components that can affect the price of a computer.

Project 3 Assessment

2 Independent Practice ★

Go Online RUBRICS
glencoe.com

Independent Practice Use the rubrics for these projects to help create and evaluate your work. Go to the **Online Learning Center** at **glencoe.com**. Choose **Rubrics**, then **Unit 6**.

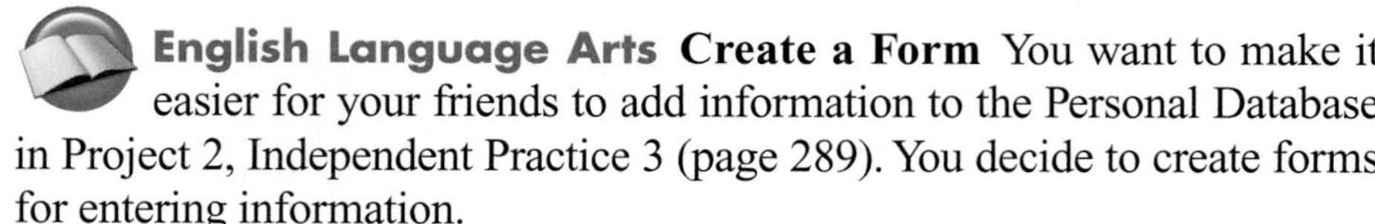

English Language Arts **Create a Form** You want to make it easier for your friends to add information to the Personal Database in Project 2, Independent Practice 3 (page 289). You decide to create forms for entering information.

a. Plan Determine the information that will be on the form.

b. Create Use the fields from your database to create a form.

- Have five classmates use the forms to add information.
- If your classmates have problems entering information, re-do your form to make it easier to use.

3 Independent Practice ★★

Math **Create a Report** Imagine that you want to buy a birthday present for each person in the Personal Database you used in Independent Practice 2 above. You plan to spend $10 per gift.

a. Plan Determine what fields you will need to create a report that shows:

- How many birthdays are celebrated each month
- The total amount you will be spending each month for presents

b. Create Use Access to create and print a report showing:

- The birthdays for each month in ascending order
- The total amount you will be spending per month and per year

4 Independent Practice ★★★

Teamwork **Expand the Theme Park Database** Your team wants to create forms to add new information to the Theme Park Database you created in Project 2, Independent Practice 4 (page 289). You also want to give a printed report to friends so that they can choose the best theme park.

a. Research Each team member should find two more theme parks.

b. Create Each team member should create:

- A form for entering new data. Use this form to enter the data for the new theme parks.
- A printed report totaling the number of rides for each state.

Go Online ACTIVITY
glencoe.com

Company Networks
If you were purchasing computers for a business, the company's networking needs might influence your decision. Learn more about business networks at the **Online Learning Center** at glencoe.com. Choose **Tech Talk Activities**, then **Unit 5.**

Academic Focus
Mathematics

Count Your Costs
Review the table on this page. Think about the benefits of the separate components in relation to the cost of each. When you are ready to purchase a computer, first decide upon what type of components you must have to meet your needs. Decide how much you will spend. Then make a budget to plan for the purchase of your computer system. What else should you consider before making a big purchase such as a computer?

NCTM Problem Solving
Apply and adapt a variety of appropriate strategies to solve problems.

Performance and Price

Performance refers to how fast a computer works. A high-performance computer is one that does things quickly and can run many applications at one time. The key to good performance is good hardware. Generally, the better the hardware components, the more expensive the computer.

Think about what you will do with a computer before you purchase one. Suppose you want to edit digital photos and videos or play games over the Internet. If so, you will probably need a high-performance computer that can handle lots of graphics and animation. If you need only to use basic office applications and send e-mail, you may not need as much RAM or as much hard drive space as a high-performance system offers.

Performance vs. Price

Component	Benefit	Less Expensive	More Expensive
Microprocessor (CPU)	A fast CPU improves overall performance.	2.0 gigahertz (GHz) can process most office applications quickly.	3.5 GHz can process large files, applications, or video games quickly.
Random access memory (RAM)	More RAM lets the computer process information faster and use multiple programs at once.	512 megabytes (MB) is usually enough RAM to run office software, such as Word or Excel, quickly.	2 GB will run complex programs such as video games and graphic programs.
Monitor	A larger monitor lets you display more documents or applications at one time on screen.	A cathode ray tube (CRT) monitor is large and bulky. Lower-priced monitors may have lower resolutions and lower-quality displays.	A flat-panel monitor can be only an inch thick. Games and video may look better on higher-resolution monitors.
Hard disk	A bigger hard disk lets you save more information on your computer.	60 GB will store lots of documents and graphic files, such as art and photos.	200 GB is enough storage space to create movies.
Modem and network connections	These connections can link your computer to the Internet and to other computers.	A 56 K modem (dial-up) will load large data files, such as video, very slowly.	A 56 K modem plus wireless capability allows much faster connection speeds.

▲ A powerful computer with the latest technology available can be a lot more expensive than a basic computer. How will you decide how much to spend on a computer?

UNIT 6 Projects Across the Curriculum

Use your database skills to complete the following projects. Ask your teacher for directions on saving or printing your work.

Go Online RUBRICS

glencoe.com

Unit Projects Use the rubrics for these projects to help create and evaluate your work. Go to the **Online Learning Center** at glencoe.com. Choose **Rubrics**, then **Unit 6**.

Project 1 Create a Weather Database ★

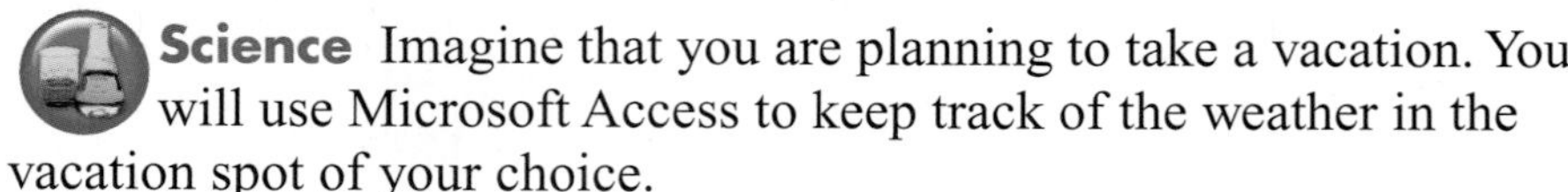

Science Imagine that you are planning to take a vacation. You will use Microsoft Access to keep track of the weather in the vacation spot of your choice.

Research

1. Choose one place, and track the weather in the area every day for a week. With your teacher's permission, use the Internet. The weather report on TV or the newspaper can also be used.

Prepare

2. Write your results in a table that includes the date, a description (cloudy or sunny), the high temperature, the low temperature, and the amount of precipitation (rain or snow).

Create

3. Using the weather data you gathered in your table, create a database table with each of the fields described in Step 2.

Project 2 Build a Personal Library Database

English Language Arts To keep better track of the books, CDs, or movies you own (or the books in your classroom), you will create a database with information about each item, including whether the item has been loaned out.

Plan

1. Write down the field names and data types you will need to create a book (or CD or movie) list table. At a minimum, you will need the following fields:

   a. Title
   b. Author or performer
   c. Genre or style
   d. Person loaned to
   e. Date loaned

Continued on page 302

Go Online ACTIVITY
glencoe.com

Your Computer's Life
The *useful life* of a computer is how long a computer can be used before it becomes outdated. Discover how you can extend your computer's useful life at glencoe.com. Choose **Tech Talk Activities**, then **Unit 5**.

Academic Focus
English Language Arts

Know Your Terms
Ads for computers can provide useful details, but beware of exaggerations. The ad on this page promotes a "free" color printer—but the seller could have raised the price of the computer. Check the prices of similar computers and color printers, and then compare what you find to the advertised price. What other strategies can you use to be sure that you are getting the best deal possible on purchases that you make?

NCTE 3 Apply strategies to interpret texts.

Computer Advertisements

Computer manufacturers provide detailed information in their ads because they realize that buyers want to know exactly what they are getting. A computer ad usually will tell you what you can expect from the machine, such as processor speed, size of the hard drive, and so on.

What Costs Are Not Included?

You can get a great deal on a computer, but it is important to keep in mind that there may be additional costs that do not appear in the ads. When you buy a computer, make sure you can still afford these other costs. They may include:

- **Software** You may wish to purchase additional software programs that are not included with the basic software package.
- **Internet service** This is usually a monthly **fee**, or charge for service, you will have to pay if you want to use the Internet and e-mail.
- **Repairs** Computer makers typically include a basic **warranty** in the price of a computer. The warranty is the computer manufacturer's promise to pay for specific repairs for a certain length of time (such as a year). When the warranty runs out, repair costs must be paid by the owner.

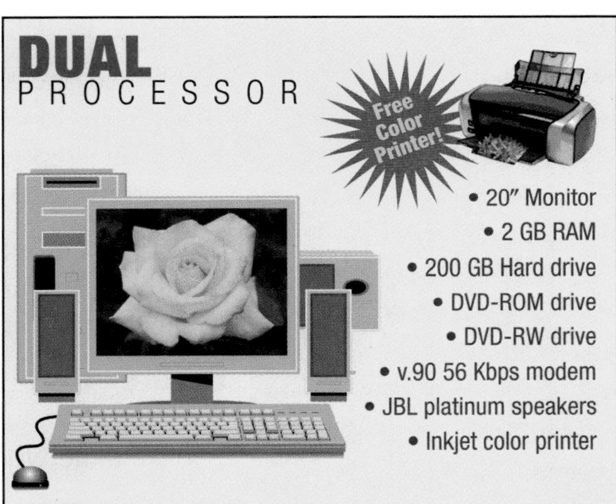

▲ Read computer ads carefully to see what is included with the package. Why do you think some computer makers offer extras, such as printers and speakers?

Reading Check

1. **Explain** Why do computer makers include so much detail in their advertisements?
2. **Describe** What is a warranty, and why is it important to have one?

Projects Across the Curriculum

Create

2. Build a table using the field names and types you chose.
3. Create a form and add at least ten or more books, CDs, or movies to your table.
4. Create reports listing the titles in alphabetic order and by genre.

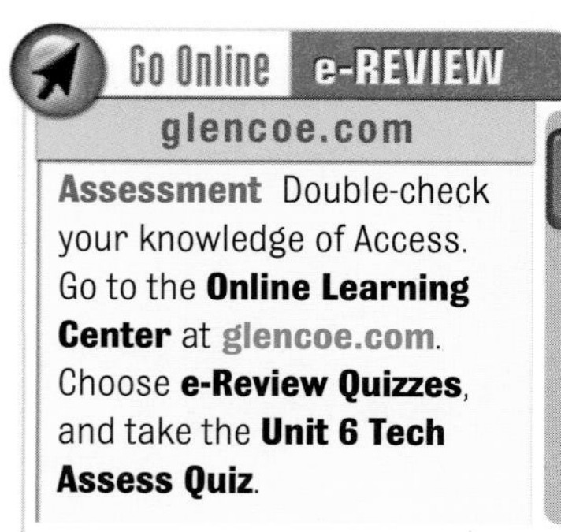

Project 3 Create a United States Database

Social Studies As part of a social studies class project, you and your teammates need to develop a United States database. The project will allow you to print a mini report on each of the states.

Research

1. Following your teacher's instructions, divide the 50 states among the team members. For each team, use an almanac, the Internet, or other resources to find the following:
   - **a.** Capital city
   - **b.** Population
   - **c.** Area (in square miles)
   - **d.** Highest point (in feet)
   - **e.** Order admitted to Union (first, second, third, and so on)

State	Capital City	Population	Area (sq. mi.)	Highest Point	Entered Union
Alabama	Montgomery	4,500,752	50,744	Cheaha Mtn.	22
Alaska	Juneau	648,818	571,951	Mt. McKinley	49
Arizona	Phoenix	5,580,811	113,635	Humphreys Peak	48
Arkansas	Little Rock	2,725,714	52,068	Magazine Mtn.	25
California	Sacramento	35,484,45[illegible]	[illegible]	Mt. Whitney	3[illegible]
Colorado	Denver	4,550,68[illegible]	[illegible]	[illegible]	[illegible]
Connecticut	Hartford	3,483,3[illegible]	[illegible]	[illegible]	5
Delaware	Dover	817,49[illegible]	[illegible]	[illegible]	1
Florida	Tallahassee	17,019,068	[illegible]	[illegible]	27
Georgia	Atlanta	8,68[illegible]	[illegible]	[illegible]	4
Hawaii	Honolulu	1,2[illegible]	6,423	[illegible]	50
Idaho	Boise	1,366,332	82,7[illegible]7	Borah Peak	43

Create

2. Create a database and a table to hold the data collected about each of the states.
3. Make a form for data entry that is easy to use.
4. Use sorts and filters to display the records by state name, area, population, and highest point.
5. Create a report that shows the population of each state, from highest to lowest population.

TECH TALK Buying a Computer

When you shop for a computer, make sure you decide what kind of computer you need and the features you want. Use the questions below to help you. Make a checklist to use as you shop online or when you go to a store.

Questions for a Computer Shopper

What to Ask	What to Know
What can a basic, inexpensive computer do?	A basic computer will let you use: • The Internet. • E-mail. • Simple applications such as word processing and spreadsheets.
What extra features might I need?	Think about what you plan to do with your computer. • Create graphics, music, or videos, you might need a CD or DVD burner. • Play complex computer games, you will need a fast processor and a high-quality video card.
What software comes with the computer?	Many computers come with a preinstalled software package, which can include: • An operating system (such as Windows). • Common applications for word processing and business tasks. • Discounts on other software and on Internet service.
Should I purchase a desktop or laptop computer?	These are some things you should consider before buying a laptop: • A laptop is usually more expensive than a desktop computer. • Do you really need a computer that you can take with you when you leave the house? • Desktops are usually better for playing games, creating complex graphics, and burning DVDs.
What kind of printer and monitor should I buy?	These are some things you should consider before buying a monitor or printer: • A regular CRT monitor is cheaper, but a flat-panel monitor takes up less space. • A color printer makes great-looking documents and photo prints, but the replacement ink cartridges can be expensive.

Smart shoppers ask plenty of questions before they buy. What features and components would you want in your own computer system?

Reading Check

1. **Identify** What are computer components?
2. **Explain** Why is it important to figure out your needs *before* you buy a computer?

UNIT 6

Build Your Portfolio

Create Business Reports

Imagine that you can start an online business that lets people legally view popular movies over the Internet. You might want to review this unit's Tech Talk about e-commerce (pages 255–265). Please also review the Tech Talk article about copyright law (pages 126–132).

Plan

1. Decide what information you would need for your database.

a. Write down what tables you would need.

b. What sorts and filters would you create?

c. What should the data-entry forms and reports look like?

Research

2. Find out about other businesses that rent movies. Find answers to the following questions:

a. What categories do they use to organize their movies?

b. What are the rental prices for new releases? Older movies?

c. What information do they need for each of their customers and their orders?

Prepare

3. Use the information you gathered to design the tables for your database.

a. Write the name of each table on a separate piece of paper.

b. Below the name of the table, list the fields that will be needed.

c. Beside each field name, write the field type.

d. List the criteria you would use to sort and filter the information.

Create

4. Use Access to create a database based on the information you found from your research.

a. Create at least two tables for your database.

b. Make a data-entry form for each table.

c. Enter at least ten movie records and ten customer records.

d. Create filters and sorts to locate movies based on different categories, such as title, director, stars, and so on.

e. Create reports from your database.

Buying a Computer

Reading Guide

Before You Read

Adjust Reading Speed Successful readers adjust the speed of their reading to match the difficulty of the text. If the text is easy, you can read quickly and still understand it all. If the concepts are difficult, slow down to be sure you absorb each word. Sometimes it helps to read out loud or to read a difficult section more than once.

Key Concepts

- How to analyze your computer needs before shopping for equipment
- How to evaluate advertisements for computers
- How to determine how a computer's performance relates to price

Vocabulary

Key Terms

component
warranty
performance

Academic Vocabulary

determine
fee
affect
policy

Computer Components and Your Needs

You know you need a computer, but you are not sure which one to buy. The decision can be overwhelming when there are so many products on the market. Should you choose a desktop or laptop computer? Do you need a regular monitor or a flat-panel monitor? Will you really use a DVD burner? The answers depend on your needs as a computer user.

Your needs **determine**, or establish, the kind of computer components you will want. A **component** is each piece of hardware that is part of a computer system. A basic computer system includes a computer, monitor, keyboard, and mouse. Even these basic components have many variations, and many other hardware components can be added.

What Should I Look for in a Computer?

It is important to determine your needs *before* you buy a computer.

- If you buy the most powerful computer available, you might end up never using all of those expensive features you spent your money on.
- If you buy a computer with limited power, you might be disappointed to find that you cannot do certain things with it, such as play games with 3-D graphics or burn CDs.
- If you buy a computer without the features you need, like software or a DVD burner, you may need to spend even more money to add those features later.

▲ The more you know about your options, the better prepared you will be when you are ready to buy. If you want to buy a computer, how will you make wise buying decisions?

UNIT 7

Presentations

Real World Projects

Go Online **e-QUIZ**

glencoe.com

Starting with You To find out why it is important to identify your audience *before* you create a presentation, go to the **Online Learning Center** at glencoe.com. Choose **e-Quizzes** and take the **Unit 7 Pre-Quiz**.

UNIT 5 Spreadsheets

Real World Projects

Go Online **e-QUIZ**

glencoe.com

Starting with You Why is it important to know how you will use a new computer before you buy one? To find out, go to the **Online Learning Center** at glencoe.com. Choose **e-Quizzes**, and take the **Unit 5 Pre-Quiz**.

Technology in Careers

Reading Guide

Before You Read

Take Notes Keep a note pad handy when you read. If you come across a difficult term or concept, jot it down along with the page number. Later, review your notes and go back to find the information you need. You also can use a note pad to write down thoughts and ideas that occur to you as you read.

Key Concepts

- Why technology is an important job skill
- How to find a job using technology
- How to describe careers in information technology
- How to present your job skills using technology

Vocabulary

Key Terms

information technology (IT)
electronic job market

Academic Vocabulary

require
summary
pursue
demonstrate

Using Technology at Work

Technology plays an essential role in most workplaces today. For this reason, you will need technology skills no matter what career you choose.

Information technology (IT) refers to the creation and installation of computer systems and software. The term IT also refers to the ability to use computers and different types of applications, from basic word processing skills to more complex networking skills. Most jobs today **require**, or demand, employees to have basic IT skills.

Some IT job skills are useful no matter what kind of job you may have. Some of these include:

- Knowing the basics of computer hardware and software, and how to troubleshoot common problems
- Using the Internet and e-mail programs
- Using word-processing software
- Creating and working with spreadsheets
- Working with databases
- Creating and giving presentations

Some professions need more specialized technology skills such as:

- Using computerized machinery
- Creating models using software
- Using diagnostic tools
- Using project management tools

▲ In medicine, it helps to have good people skills and technology skills. How might technology help doctors do their jobs?

UNIT 4

Build Your Portfolio

Create a Research Paper

Read the Tech Talk article on page 129 titled Using and Abusing Technology. The issue of file sharing has led to a lot of debate, and you will continue the debate in a research paper. Go to glencoe.com to find Web Links.

Plan

1. Decide what the consequences should be for people who download music illegally.
2. Support your position with at least five reasons. Write each reason on an index card. As you research, you might want to add more reasons.

Research

3. Research to find facts and examples that support each of your reasons. You should try to find:
   - Interviews with people on both sides of the issue.
   - Data to support or challenge the companies' positions.
   - Legal ways that music and video can be distributed on and off the Internet.
   - Terms of use Web pages that explain how audio and video files can be used legally.

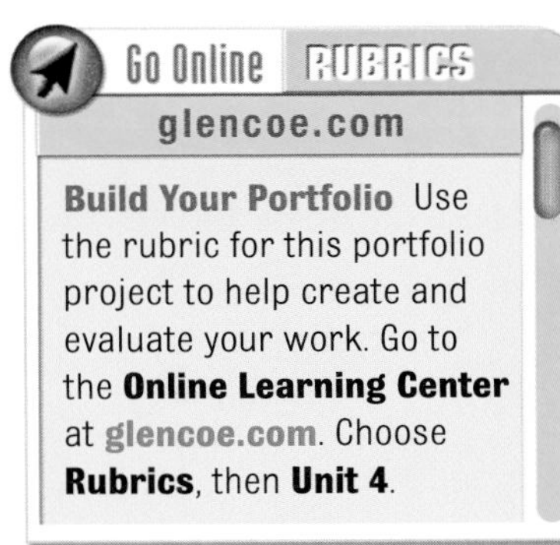

Prepare

4. Add supporting information to your original reasons on the index cards.
5. Make sure to write down the information you will need to cite your sources, including URLs, authors, and titles of publications, Web sites, and articles.

Create

6. Use your index cards to write a two-page research paper defending your point of view on this issue. Include at least two quotations with citations and a works cited page to cite your sources.

Review and Print

7. Proofread and edit your paper before you print it.

TECH TALK Technology in Careers

Academic Focus

English Language Arts

Research Your Future

Each profession has unique technology requirements. For example, medical professionals use special software to help them view x-rays and properly file patient information. What are some ways you can explore the skills and educational requirements for a career that interests you?

NCTE 1 Read texts to acquire new information.

What Careers Use Technology?

From schools to factories to hospitals, people use technology skills for many different tasks, as shown in the table below. Many employers offer training, but most would rather hire someone who already has learned basic computer skills. That is why it is so important for you to learn these skills in school.

How Technology Helps Workers

Job Title	Job Skills	How Technology Is Used
Accountant	Organize information	Spreadsheets and databases help businesses track sales and expenses.
Journalist	Work from anywhere	E-mail and networks can be used to file stories from around the world.
Doctor, Dentist, Lawyer	Keep current with new medical trends	Doctors use the Internet to read the latest research papers in their fields.
Buyer for a Department Store	Evaluate information	Spreadsheets help buyers compare products.
Office Assistant	Work quickly and efficiently	Word-processing software helps workers quickly create letters and documents.
Artist or Photographer	Be creative	Graphic design software helps artists create and present new ideas to clients.
Teacher	Work with others	Presentation software helps teachers create and present lessons. Networks allow teachers to monitor student work.
Construction Project Manager	Solve problems	Databases allow managers to track materials and ensure projects stay on budget.

▲ Computers and the Internet can help people do their jobs more efficiently. How might a construction project manager use technology?

No matter what kind of job you have, you will continue to learn new job skills, including technology skills, throughout your life. Today, advances in technology are constantly—and rapidly—changing how people work.

Reading Check

1. **Identify** Name three IT skills that are useful to have in any kind of career.
2. **Explain** Why is it important to learn technology skills while you are still in school?

UNIT 4

Projects Across the Curriculum

Create

3. Use Word to create a letterhead using these guidelines:
   - Use at least two font styles.
   - Each element in the letterhead should be on a separate line.
   - Include a graphic to add interest. Or, use Word Art.

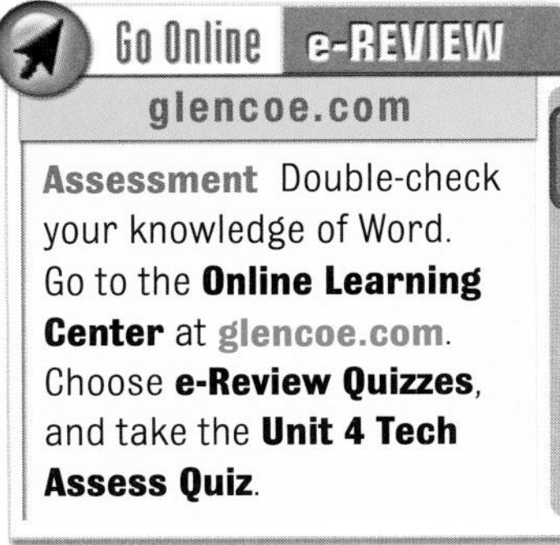

Project 3 Create a Travel Newsletter

Social Studies Create a two-column newsletter about a popular travel destination. The newsletter should provide helpful information about visiting the area.

Plan

1. Determine a place that you would like to feature in the newsletter. It can be a national park or recreation area, a famous city or town, a hotel or resort.

Research

2. With your teacher's permission, use the Internet to find images and information to use in your newsletter.
3. Write the text you will need to describe the location.

Create

4. Your newsletter should include:
   - **a.** A title created with WordArt.
   - **b.** At least two articles. For example, a Grand Canyon newsletter might have articles called *Natural History* and *Things to Do*.
   - **c.** At least one photograph or image. (Remember to give credit!)
   - **d.** One table or chart.
5. Proofread, edit, and print your newsletter.

Use Technology to Find a Job

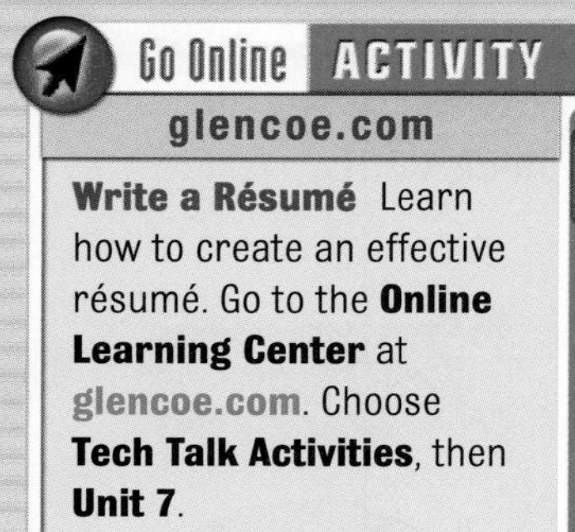

Go Online ACTIVITY
glencoe.com

Write a Résumé Learn how to create an effective résumé. Go to the **Online Learning Center** at glencoe.com. Choose **Tech Talk Activities**, then **Unit 7**.

Today, many people use the **electronic job market** to find work. The electronic job market is made up of Web sites where companies can look for employees, and people can look for jobs.

Job search Web sites such as CareerBuilder.com and Monster.com make it easy to find a job in almost any field that interests you. They often offer special features that make searching for a job easier and faster than using a newspaper's Help Wanted ads. For example, you can let hundreds of employers see your résumé—a **summary**, or review, of your skills and work experience.

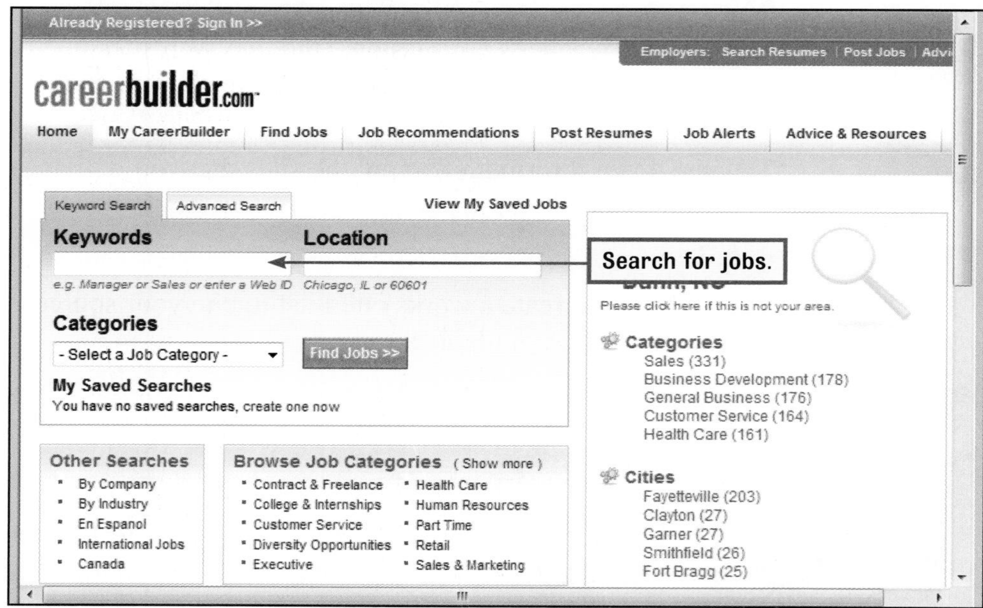

In addition to providing hundreds of thousands of job listings, many job search Web sites offer online tools and advice for job seekers. **If you want to search for a job in a different state, would you look at a newspaper or use an online search? Why?**

If you do not have a computer to search for a job online, libraries and community centers often have computers that the public may use for free. Also, many people use public Internet centers and cafés to access the Internet for free or for a small fee.

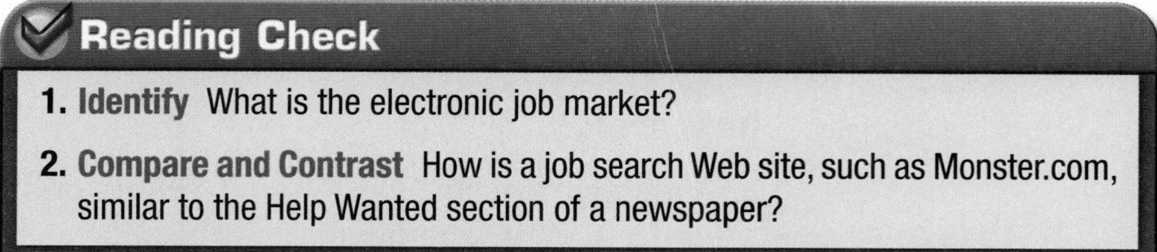

Reading Check

1. **Identify** What is the electronic job market?
2. **Compare and Contrast** How is a job search Web site, such as Monster.com, similar to the Help Wanted section of a newspaper?

Projects Across the Curriculum

Use your word processing skills to complete the following projects. Check with your teacher for directions on saving or printing your work.

Project 1 Cite Resources for a Biography ★

Social Studies Imagine that you are going to create a short biography of an American president that includes career highlights, images, and quotes. The report must include a works cited list.

▲ President Teddy Roosevelt

Research

1. With your teacher's permission, find two Web sites that provide information about the president you have chosen, and choose examples of text or graphics.
2. Write down information about the sites that you will need for the works cited list.

Create

3. Use Word to create a works cited list to cite your sources following MLA guidelines.

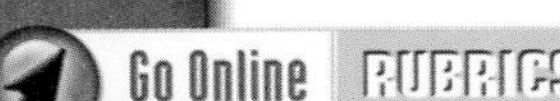

Go Online RUBRICS
glencoe.com

Unit Projects Use the rubrics for these projects to help create and evaluate your work. Go to the **Online Learning Center** at glencoe.com. Choose **Rubrics**, then **Unit 4**.

Project 2 Create a Letterhead ★★

English Language Arts Create a personal letterhead. The letterhead will be used for all your personal and business letters. Please refer to Appendix D, page 494, for one example of a letterhead.

Plan

1. Before you begin, you must determine the information to include in the letterhead.
   - The letterhead must include your name and address.
   - You may also include your phone number (home or cell).

Research

2. With your teacher's permission, search online for a graphic to include on your letterhead.

Continued on page 205

Go Online ACTIVITY
glencoe.com

Find Job Listings
Practice searching for jobs online and find out more about career opportunities in technology. Go to the **Online Learning Center** at **glencoe.com**. Choose **Tech Talk Activities**, then **Unit 7**.

Choose a Career in Technology

For some people, a basic knowledge of technology is all they want or need. Other people, however, take a real interest in technology and choose to **pursue**, or work towards, a career in the information technology field.

There are many types of technology careers. Think of all the ways technology is used and who creates this technology. For example, if you were interested in a career involving video games, you could choose from a variety of jobs. You could be the person who:

- Invents game concepts and storylines
- Creates graphics and special effects
- Invents new kinds of game hardware and software

Video games are only one type of technology. In fact, you can find a technology career in just about every type of business and industry.

▲ There is a need for people who can keep computer networks and other technology systems running smoothly. What kind of technology professionals work in your school?

Technology Careers

Job Title	Job Skills	Why Skills Are Important
Software Programmer	Create software to meet the needs of computer users.	New software is always in demand for office applications, computer performance, games, and so on.
Technical Writer	Learn how technology works, and then write about it so other people can use it.	People need well-written instructions when learning how to use new equipment or software.
Network Administrator	Install computer hardware, set up and maintain networks in businesses.	Businesses need someone to install new equipment and to make sure that all the equipment works well.
Web Designer	Design, create, and update an organization's Web sites.	Businesses want helpful, attractive Web sites so that customers will visit the site or buy products or services.

▲ These are just a few of the career opportunities available in technology. Can you name some other jobs in the technology field?

Reading Check

1. **Identify** Name two tasks performed by video-game creators.
2. **Evaluate** Why is a Web designer important for online businesses?

Project 4 Assessment

Go Online RUBRICS

glencoe.com

Independent Practice
Use the rubrics for these projects to help create and evaluate your work. Go to the **Online Learning Center** at **glencoe.com**. Choose **Rubrics**, then **Unit 4**.

2 Independent Practice

Math Create a Table Create a two-column, six-row table to record your favorite games, music, videos, or books.

a. Create In the first column, list five video games, CDs, movies, or books. Key a title in the top cell of that column. In the second column, identify a specific detail about the listed items. It can be a description, the creator's name, the publisher, or how you rate it. Key a title in the top cell of that column.

b. Format Add an interesting border and shade the table a color of your choice.

3 Independent Practice

English Language Arts Create a Newsletter Create a newsletter about you. Pick any topic: your latest family or school news, your favorite hobby, a sport you play, your family, or a pet. Include:

a. A masthead.

b. A two-column format.

c. One or two articles about the subject.

d. One or two pictures or graphics. Add trademark symbols if you use trademarked names or citations if you use copyrighted sources.

4 Independent Practice

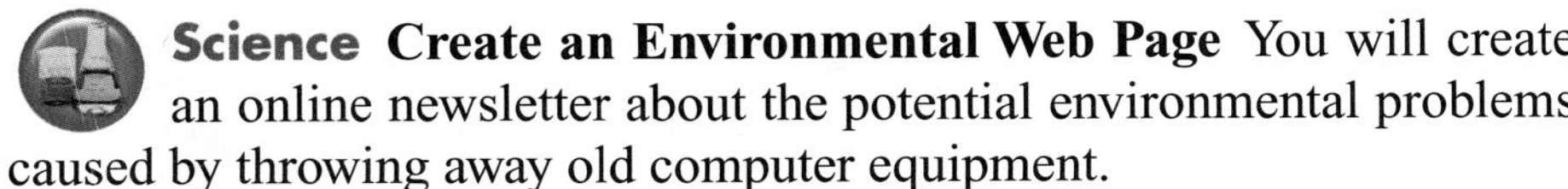

Science Create an Environmental Web Page You will create an online newsletter about the potential environmental problems caused by throwing away old computer equipment.

a. Research Find information and graphics to use on your Web page.

b. Create Use Microsoft Word to create the newsletter. Your finished project should:

- Be one page in length.
- Have at least one graphic and one table.
- Cite your sources for the pictures and information used in your project. Add trademark symbols, if appropriate.

Prepare for a Career

Jargon You may hear the question "What skill set will you bring to this job?" during a job interview. A *skill set* is just what it sounds like—the set of skills that includes all of your areas of knowledge, including information technology.

Why It's Important What skill set will you need to fill the requirements for your dream job?

The earlier you start learning about technology, the more prepared you will be for any career. Technology is always changing, so you will need to keep learning new technology skills even after you leave school.

Prepare for Your Career

While you are in school...	When you begin looking for a job...
• Get the best grades that you can and take some technology-related classes. • Begin to learn about the skills and certifications you will need for jobs that interest you. • Develop your soft skills as well as your technology skills. Soft skills include your communication, problem-solving, and teamwork skills.	• Search the Web. Thousands of Web sites offer databases of job opportunities. • Create your own online portfolio. Use a job search Web site to create one or develop a personal Web site to showcase a résumé and examples of work. • Keep learning! It is important to stay up-to-date with current developments in technology.

▲ The key to getting a great job is to start gaining technology skills today. How can learning technology help you when you want to start a career?

As you look ahead to your future, remember that employers usually prefer to hire people who already have basic technology skills. The more skills you have, the more job opportunities you may have to choose from.

Bill Simmon

Software Engineer

Experience | Skill Set | Contact Me

Welcome to my online portfolio. Please click the links above to learn about my work experience and areas of expertise. To send me an e-mail, click "Contact Me."

I look forward to hearing from you!

An online portfolio can be very effective when looking for work. How is an online portfolio different from a paper résumé? ▶

You can put your portfolio or résumé online so that employers can visit a job search Web site or your own site to learn more about you. An online portfolio can **demonstrate**, or exhibit, your job experience as well as provide samples of your work. An online résumé allows employers to easily contact you through e-mail.

Reading Check

1. **Identify** What is an online portfolio?
2. **Summarize** List three steps you can take while you are still in school to prepare for a career.

Project 4 Assessment

3 **Open** the **Data File** named **4J Trademark Newsletter**.

4 **Copy** the article from the Data File, and **paste** it into the columns in your newsletter. (Exercise 4-2)

5 Create **two columns** under the masthead. (Exercise 4-2)

6 **Bold** the title, and make the **Font Color Blue**.

7 At the end of the article, create a **table** with **two columns** and **seven rows**. (Exercise 4-3)

8 Key the information in Figure 4.25 into your table.

9 Add a **border** and **shading** to your table of your choice. (Exercise 4-3)

10 Insert the **Data File** named **4K Trademark Graphic** below the second paragraph in your newsletter. (Exercise 4-4)

11 Add a trademark notice at the bottom of your newsletter. (Exercise 4-6)

12 **Save** your newsletter.

Figure 4.25 Your final newsletter should look like this.

Ethics Today

Fun with Trademarks

by Ted Jones

Figure out what the following sentences have in common: *Could you pass me a Kleenex? Let's play Frisbee! I love strawberry Jell-O.*

Give up? Here's a hint: find the words that begin with a capital letter within the sentences: Kleenex, Frisbee, Jell-O. Why do these words begin with capital letters? Answer: they are all trademarks.

What is a trademark? A trademark is a name, symbol, or other feature that identifies a product with a specific owner. Businesses usually register the names of the products as trademarks with the government. This means that the trademark name cannot appear on other business's products without the owner's permission.

For example, Pepsi cannot put the words "Coca Cola" on their cans without the Coca Cola Company's permission. (And they probably would not want "Coca Cola" on their cans anyway!)

What is interesting about *Kleenex, Frisbee,* and *Jell-O* is that these trademarks are now used as general words. When someone asks, "Could you pass me a Kleenex?" they usually are not referring to the brand name but to a "facial tissue." The same goes for Frisbee, which is really a disk, and Jell-O, which is really gelatin.

If you want to use a trademark on a product that you are going to sell, you need to ask permission, and you also need to include the trademark ™ or the copyright ® symbol by the word. Not doing so would be unethical and illegal. If you are using a trademark word in a report, you should capitalize the word.

Trademark	Common Word
Kleenex	tissue
Xerox	copy
Jell-O	gelatin
Frisbee	disc
Vaseline	petroleum jelly
Q-Tip	cotton swab

All product names are trademarks of their respective companies.

HELP!

Spacing If your columns do not bottom align (line up at the bottom), then increase or decrease the space around the image or the table.

After You Read

Key Concepts Check

1. **Describe** What is information technology (IT)?
2. **Identify** List three ways that people use technology skills in their careers.
3. **Describe** What are two ways you can use the electronic job market to find a job?

Critical Thinking

4. **Analyze** If you exaggerate on a job application about your technology skills, consider this behavior from an ethical standpoint. What problems could this create after a company hires you?

21st Century Skills

5. **Explore Careers** The U. S. Department of Education groups careers into 16 career clusters based on similar job characteristics. Go to this book's Online Learning Center at **glencoe.com** to find a **Web Link** to the U.S. Department of Education career clusters. Find out what kind of education is required for a career that interests you.

Academic Skills

Mathematics

Technology has played a part in the changes in job demand in the last few years.

a. **Compare** How many more medical assistants are there than medical technologists?

b. **Analyze** Why do you think there are many opportunities in health care and medicine? Do you think the trend will continue?

Math Concept

Tables A table organizes data into columns and rows. The first column lists each occupation, while the second column shows the number of employees.

Starting Hint To determine how many more medical assistants there are than medical technologists, find the values in those two rows, and then subtract.

NCTM Data Analysis and Probability Formulate questions that can be addressed with data and collect, organize, and display relevant data to answer them.

Occupation	Numbers of U.S. Employees
Nurses	2,417,150
Stock Clerks	1,705,450
Software Applications Engineers	472,520
Medical Assistants	409,570
Machinists	385,690
Computer Network Administrators	289,520
Medical Technologists	160,760

Source: Bureau of Labor Statistics

Go Online e-QUIZ

glencoe.com

Self-Check Assess your understanding of what you have just read. Go to the **Online Learning Center** at **glencoe.com**. Choose **e-Quizzes**, and take the **Unit 7 Tech Talk Quiz**.

Project 4 Assessment

Key Concepts Check

1. **Illustrate** Create a table and label the rows, columns, and cells.
2. **Explain** Why would you use WordArt in a newsletter?
3. **Describe** When might you want to use the Find and Replace command?

Critical Thinking

4. **Cause and Effect** Why does organizing information in a table make it easier to understand?
5. **Drawing Conclusions** Describe a situation where it would be better to publish a document as a Web page rather than print it.

1 Guided Practice

Create a Newsletter To keep classmates up to date on important issues in ethics, your teacher wants you to create a newsletter called *Ethics Today*. The newsletter will explain what trademarks are and how to use them ethically. You want to make the newsletter visually interesting by adding WordArt, a graphic, and a table. If you need help completing a step, refer back to the exercise in parentheses at the end of the step.

Step-by-Step

1. **Open** a new Word document, and **save** the file **as** *Your Name* Ethics Newsletter.

2. Create a **WordArt** masthead of your choice titled Ethics Today. Center the masthead. See Figure 4.24. (Exercise 4-1)

▼ **Figure 4.24** Create an eye-catching masthead.

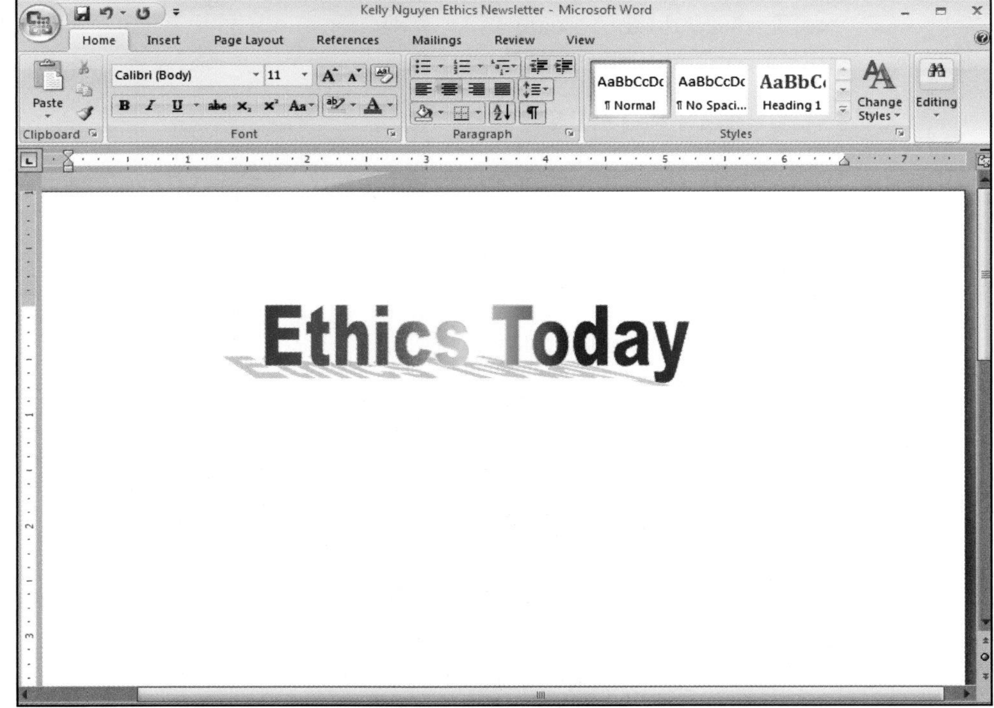

Concepts in Action

Project 1 Create a Presentation

Key Concepts

Exercise 1-1

- Identify PowerPoint features

Exercise 1-2

- Identify PowerPoint views
- Save a presentation

Exercise 1-3

- Apply a theme

Exercise 1-4

- Modify the Slide Master
- Add the date and time to a slide

Exercise 1-5

- Navigate through a slide show
- View a slide show

Vocabulary

Key Terms
presentation software
Slide Master
theme

Before You Begin

Compare Features Note that the Ribbon tabs and command buttons in Microsoft PowerPoint are different from those in Word and Excel. Place your mouse over each command to display a ScreenTip telling you what each one does.

In this project, you will use Microsoft PowerPoint to create a slide show presentation. You will learn the basic features of PowerPoint and practice creating a presentation that your audience will be able to understand.

Present a Road Rally Game

Your dream is to become a video game designer, and you already have great ideas for new games. A video game company is holding a competition for high-school students. They want to find new games that will appeal to teenagers. You have been selected as a finalist and will present your idea for a game called Road Rally to the judges of the competition.

You decide that the best way to present your game is to use Microsoft Office PowerPoint. PowerPoint is software that creates electronic slide shows with text, graphics, animation, special effects, and sound. You want the presentation to be both professional and engaging so that the judges can see why your game is the best. You know that creating a well-written, clearly organized, and neatly designed presentation will reflect well on you and may help you win the contest!

7 If your classroom or school has a Web site, your Web page is ready to be posted with your teacher's permission.

8 **Close** your Word document and **Exit Word**.

9 **Open** your Web page document by double-clicking it. It will open in a browser window and should look similar to Figure 4.23. Do not be concerned that your document is not in column layout. Please review the **Help** box on page 199.

10 **Exit** your Web browser.

▼ **Figure 4.23** **Your newsletter will look different as a Web page than it does as a printed Word document.**

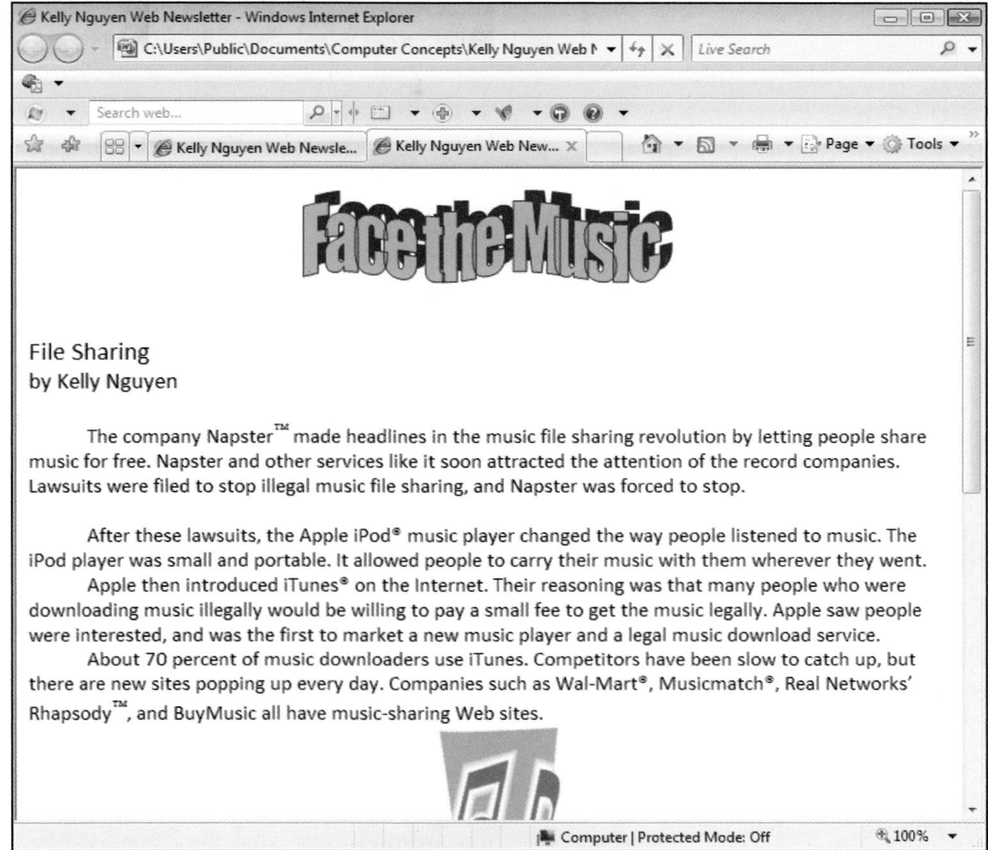

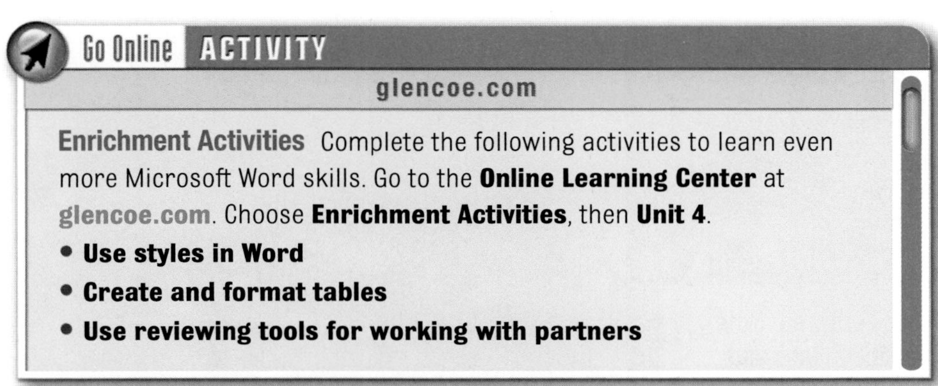

Exercise 1-1 Get to Know Microsoft PowerPoint

TechSavvy

Placeholders Microsoft PowerPoint presentations include five built-in standard layouts to help you create effective presentations. Layouts contain placeholders, which hold text, such as titles, bulleted lists, graphics, tables, charts, and clip art.

Presentation software is used to create a story in words, pictures, sound, and even video to support a speech or public presentation. Although Microsoft PowerPoint is the best-known presentation software, other brands include Apple Keynote®, Corel Presentations™, IBM Lotus® Freelance, and Adobe® Persuasion®.

Microsoft PowerPoint presentations are a series of slides that can be viewed on a computer monitor or displayed on a large screen to an audience. Electronic slides can help a speaker in a number of ways. Slides provide a visual outline of what the speaker is saying. This can help focus the attention of the viewer on key ideas. Slides can also make the content of the presentation more interesting and entertaining. As you complete the projects in this unit, you will learn how to create slides that look professional and present information clearly.

In this exercise, you will create two Microsoft PowerPoint presentation slides. The first will be a title slide. The second will be a slide listing your favorite hobbies. You will then save the presentation.

Step-by-Step

1. **Start Microsoft PowerPoint.**
2. When PowerPoint opens, your screen should look like Figure 1.1. On your own screen, find and name the features identified in Figure 1.1.
3. Click in the space marked **Click to add title**, and key your name.
4. Click in the space marked **Click to add subtitle**, and key the name of your class.

▼ **Figure 1.1** **PowerPoint uses many of the same features as other Microsoft Office applications.**

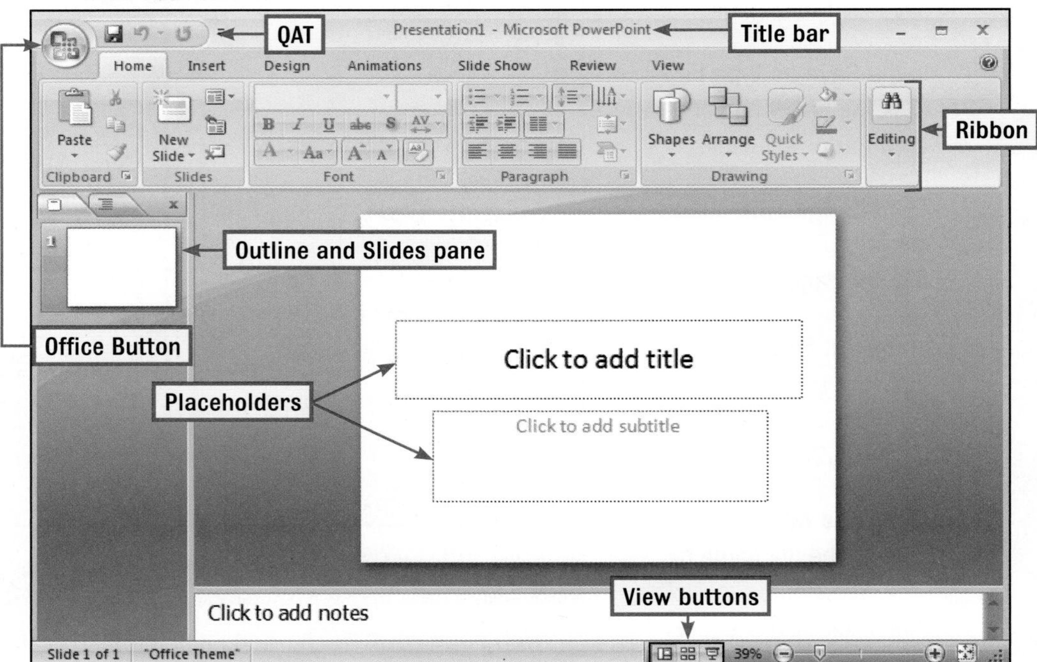

Exercise 4-7 Publish Your Newsletter on the Web

There are two ways to publish your newsletter. You can print many copies and hand them out to people in your class or school. This can take a lot of time and effort and may be costly to print, especially if you use colorful paper and ink.

Another way to get people to see your newsletter is to publish it on the Internet or your school's intranet. Programs in Microsoft Office and many other programs now allow you to save files so that they can be published on the Web. Do not publish anything without your teacher's permission.

In this exercise, you will save your newsletter as a Web page and then view it in your Web browser. This will show you what it would look like on the Internet.

Step-by-Step

1. Click the **Office Button,** then choose **Save As**.
2. In the **Address** bar, choose the folder where you will save your Web page.
3. In the **Save as type** box, click the arrow and choose **Web Page**.
4. The **Change Title** button displays. Click it to display the **Set Page Title** box.
5. In the **Set Page Title** box, key *Your Name* Web Newsletter, then click **OK** (Figure 4.22).
6. In the **File name** box, change the file name to *Your Name* Web Newsletter, then click **Save**.

Figure 4.22 You will need to add a Web page title when you save a Word document as a Web page.

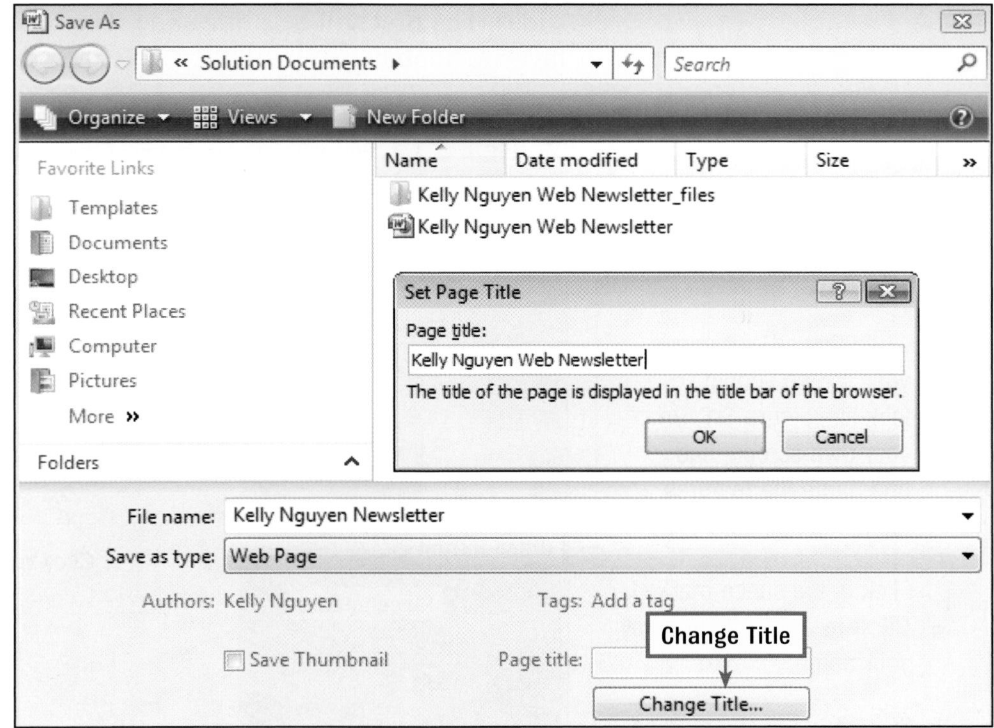

HELP!

Web Page Format The Web page format does not support columns, so your two-column document will look different when it is viewed in a browser. It will, however, be in a format that can be published to the Internet or viewed by anyone with Web browser software and access to your Web page file.

5 Click the **New Slide** button . A new slide appears.

6 On your screen, find and name the features identified in Figure 1.2.

Figure 1.2 The Title and Content slide is usually the second slide in a presentation.

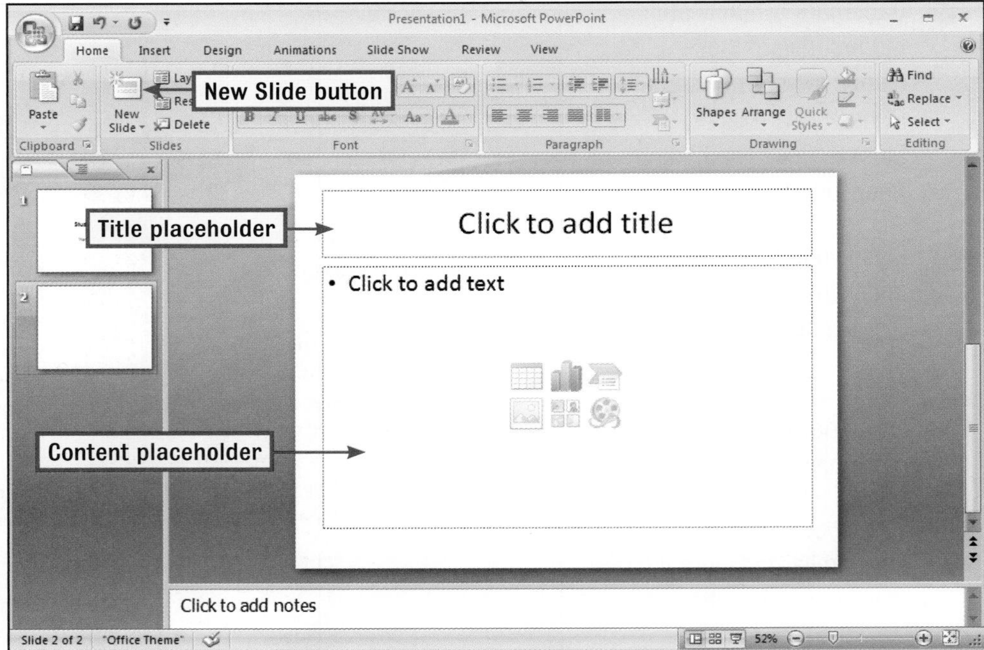

7 Click in the space marked **Click to add title**, and key My Hobbies.

8 Click in the space marked **Click to add text**, and key three of your favorite hobbies. Press ENTER between items on the list (Figure 1.3).

9 **Click the Microsoft Office Button** , and choose **Save As**.

10 Follow your teacher's instructions to **save** your presentation as *Your Name* Hobbies.

11 Click the **Office Button,** and then click **Close** to **close** the presentation. Do not **exit** PowerPoint.

Figure 1.3 The Title and Content slide layout allows you to list the main topic and subtopics for your presentation.

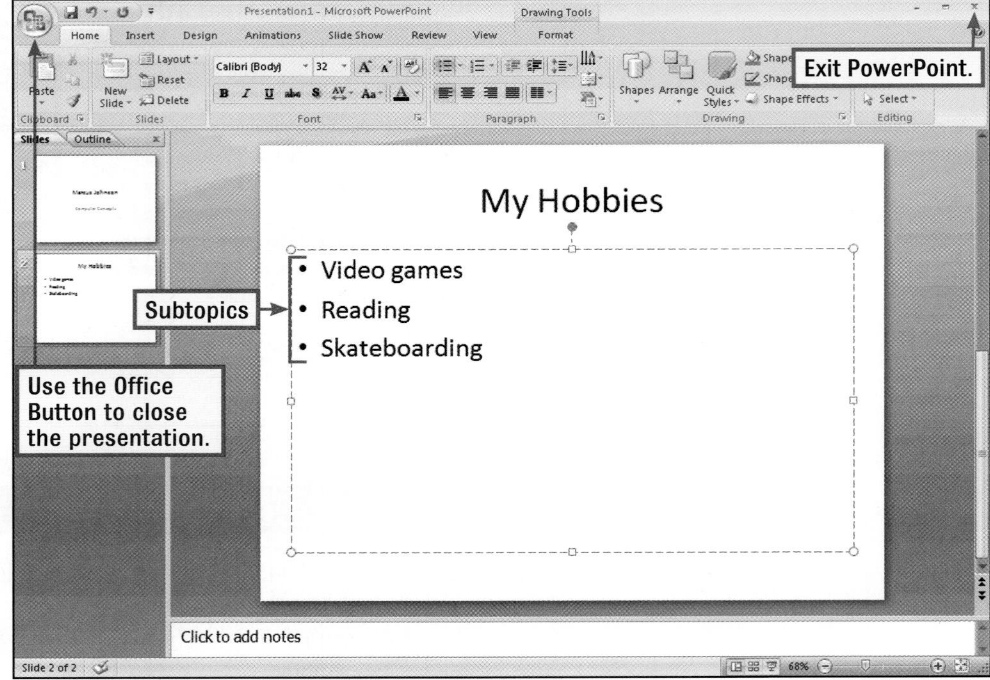

12 Add the following trademark symbols after the first use of these names in your newsletter: iTunes®, Wal-Mart®, Musicmatch®, and Rhapsody™.

13 Place your insertion point under the table, and press ENTER once.

14 Key All product names are trademarks of their respective companies.

15 Your document should look similar to Figure 4.21. Save your newsletter.

16 **Print** your newsletter, with your teacher's permission.

▼ **Figure 4.21** **Your finished newsletter should look like this.**

File Sharing

by Kelly Nguyen

The company Napster™ made headlines in the music file sharing revolution by letting people share music for free. Napster and other services like it soon attracted the attention of the record companies. Lawsuits were filed to stop illegal music file sharing, and Napster was forced to stop.

After these lawsuits, the Apple iPod® music player changed the way people listened to music. The iPod player was small and portable. It allowed people to carry their music with them wherever they went.

Apple then introduced iTunes® on the Internet. Their reasoning was that many people who were downloading music illegally would be willing to pay a small fee to get the music legally. Apple saw people were interested and was the first to market a new music player and a legal music download service.

About 70 percent of music downloaders use iTunes. Competitors have been slow to catch up, but there are new sites popping up every day. Companies such as Wal-Mart®, Musicmatch®, Real Networks' Rhapsody™, and BuyMusic all have music-sharing Web sites.

Napster reemerged as a pay-for-music site. This well-known music site hopes that their brand name will lead to instant market sales and success.

If you download music from the Internet, make sure to use a legal download site, such as those from the companies above. Always follow copyright guidelines to make sure that you are downloading music properly.

Copyright Guidelines	
Can you legally download music for free?	Yes, but only you can play or burn the music to a CD.
Can you legally download music and then sell it?	No, because you are unauthorized to distribute that music.
Can you copy a store-bought CD from a friend?	No, due to the copyright on the CD, you need to pay for it to burn a copy, or else you are stealing.

All product names are trademarks of their respective companies.

Different Strokes

Symbol Shortcuts You can use keyboard shortcuts to insert symbols and change their font to superscript.

- Insert ® symbol ALT + CTRL + R
- Insert ™ symbol ALT + CTRL + T
- Change to superscript CTRL + SHIFT + +

Exercise 1-2 Explore PowerPoint Views

PowerPoint includes many ways to view your presentation. Each type of view is designed to help you complete a specific task.

- **Slide Show view** Use this view to see what each slide looks like.
- **Outline view** Use this view to see an outline of your presentation.
- **Slide Sorter view** Use this view to manage your slides. You can delete, copy, or change the order of your slides.
- **Slide Master view** Use this view to display the **Slide Master**, from which you can make changes to the text, graphics, or background on all slides of the presentaton at one time.

In this exercise, you will practice using the different views in PowerPoint. You can compare each of them to see which view you like best.

Step-by-Step

1. **Open** the **Data File** named **7A Road Rally**. The presentation is in **Normal** view.
2. In the upper-left corner of the workspace, click the **Outline** tab. The left side of the screen shows the presentation in outline form (Figure 1.4).
3. Click the **Slides** tab. **Slides** view allows you to see the layout of each slide.
4. On the status bar, click the **Slide Sorter** button.

Figure 1.4 Outline view allows you to quickly look at the text of all slides at once.

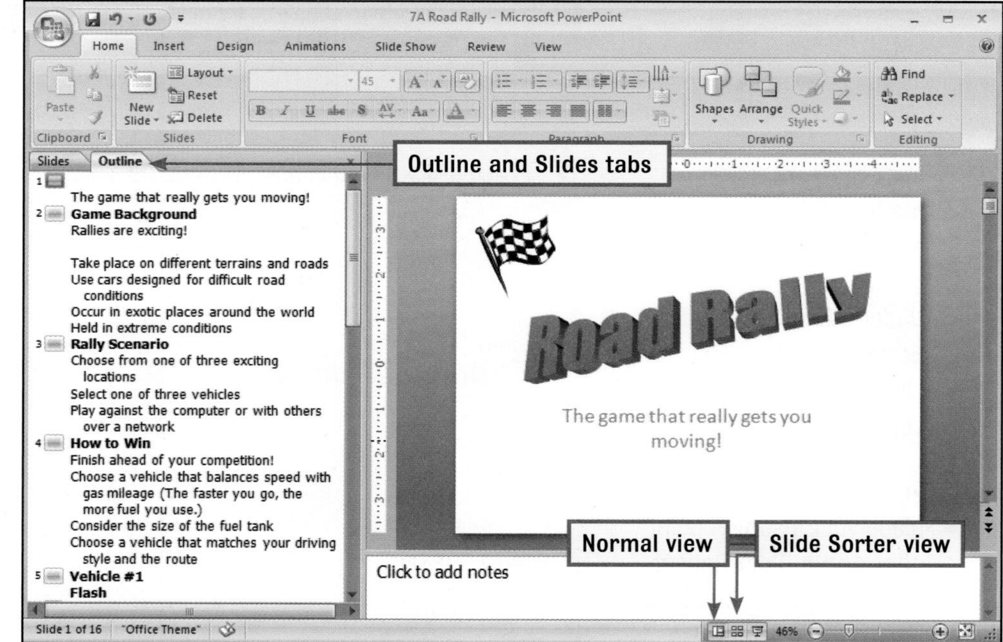

Different Strokes

Ribbon Commands The **Ribbon** provides quick access to commonly used commands. Explore the Ribbon for a complete set of useful commands that you can apply to PowerPoint presentations.

6. Select the ™ symbol. (Figure 4.19).

7. On the **Home** tab, in the **Font** group, click the **Font Dialog Box Launcher**. The **Font** dialog box displays (Figure 4.20).

Figure 4.19 Select the text that you want to format as superscript.

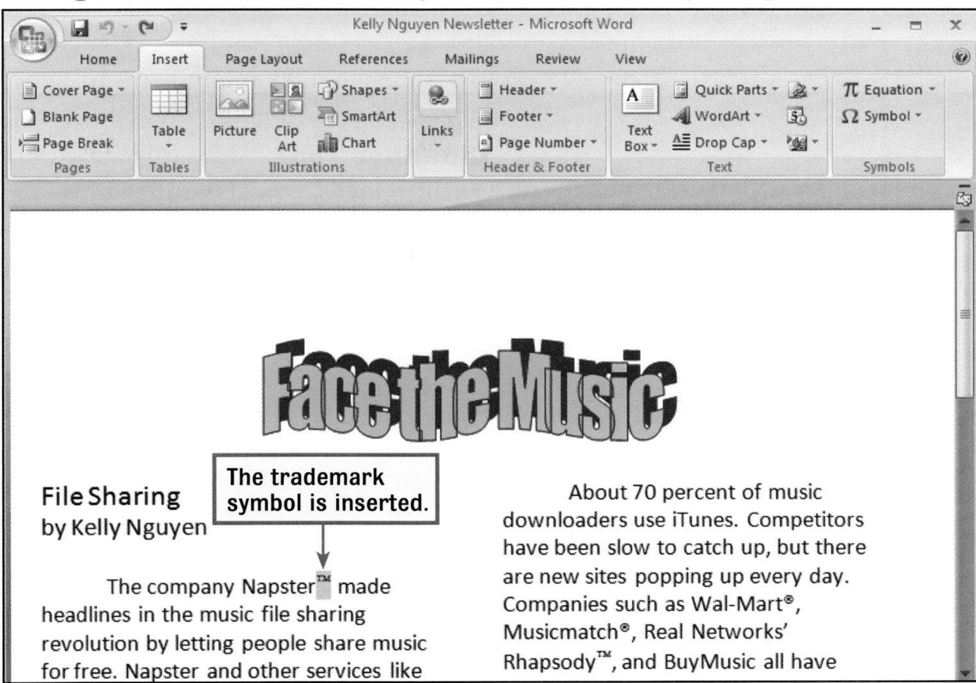

8. Click the **Font** tab at the top of the box, if necessary.

9. Under Effects, select the **Superscript** box. Then click **OK**. The ™ will be superscript in format.

10. In the second paragraph, place your insertion point after **Apple iPod**. Repeat steps 2 to 5, but this time insert the ® symbol.

11. Select the ® symbol. Repeat steps 6 to 9 to change the symbol to superscript.

Figure 4.20 You can apply different effects to your text.

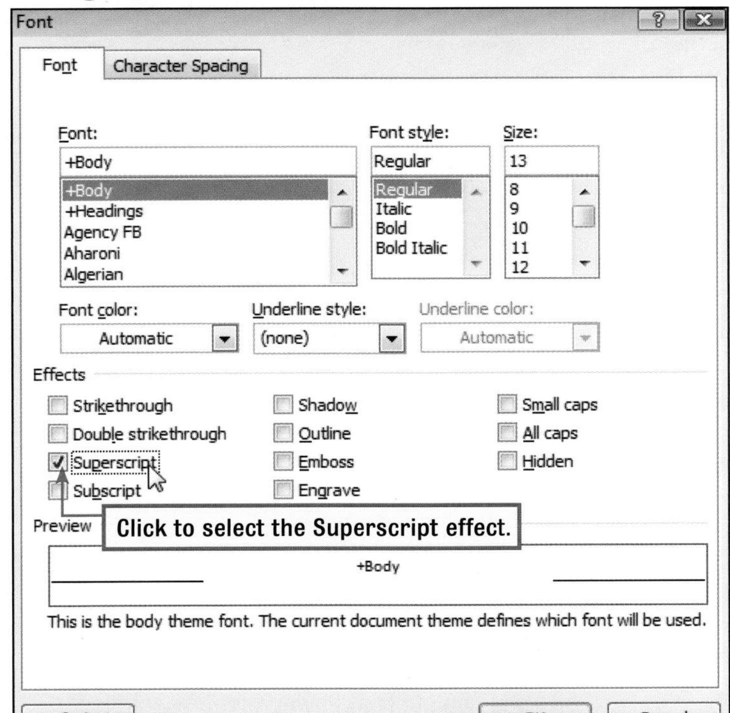

5 Click **Slide 3** and drag it in front of **Slide 5**. Note that a vertical line shows the location of the slide you are moving (Figure 1.5).

6 Release the mouse button. The slides are renumbered and Slide 3 becomes Slide 4.

▼ **Figure 1.5** In Slide Sorter view, it is easy to reorder slides or to delete unneeded slides.

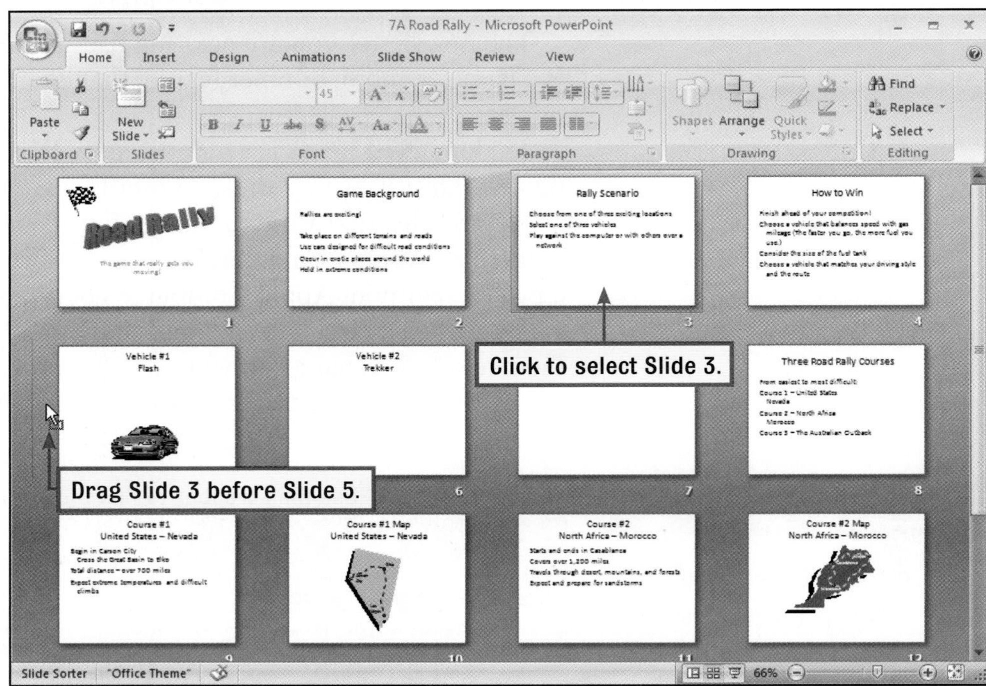

7 Click **Slide 1**.

8 On the status bar, click the **Slide Show** button (Figure 1.6). The slide will fill the screen.

9 To move to the next screen, press the ENTER key on your keyboard.

10 To end the show and return to **Slide Sorter** view, press ESC.

▼ **Figure 1.6** Click Slide Show view to easily preview your presentation.

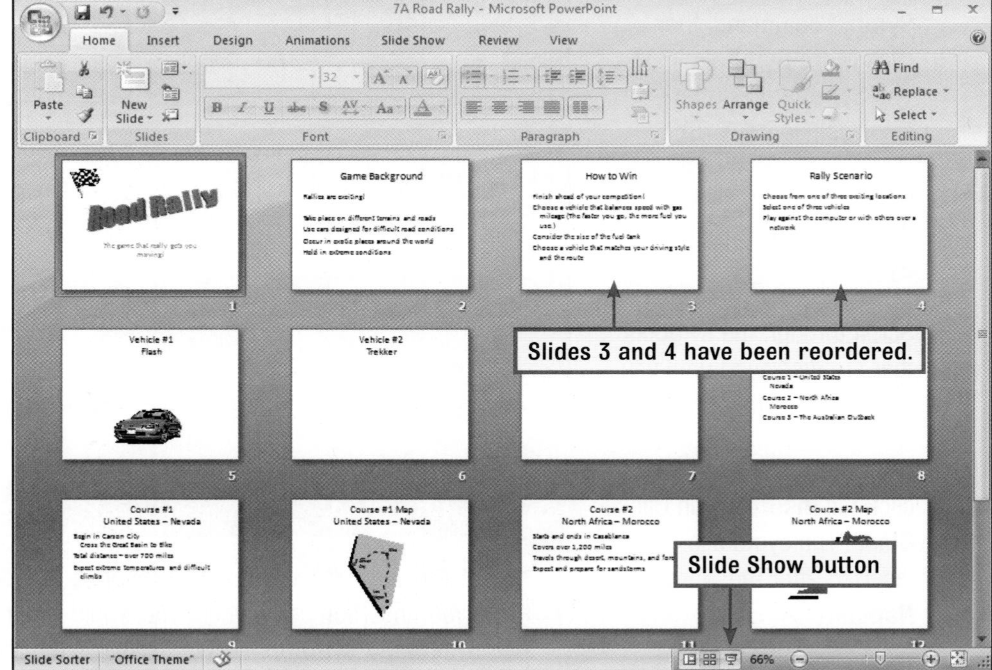

Exercise 4-6 Add a Symbol

The newsletter you are creating uses trademarked names. A trademark is a name, symbol, or other feature that identifies a product with a specific owner.

Trademarked items are identified by the ® or ™ symbols. Many companies like to display these symbols next to their trademarked names, especially the first time the name is used. For example, iPod® is trademarked by Apple Computer, Inc. No one else can use that name to identify a product without Apple Computer's permission.

In this exercise, you will add the ® and ™ symbols to the first use of the trademarked names in your newsletter. These symbols will be formatted as superscript text, which is higher and smaller than the other text.

Step-by-Step

1. In the first line of your article, place your insertion point after the word **Napster**.
2. On the **Insert** tab, in the **Symbols** group, click the **Symbol** command, then click **More Symbols**. The **Symbol** dialog box displays (Figure 4.18).
3. In the **Font** box, click the arrow and scroll to **Symbol**.
4. Scroll through the symbols that are displayed until you find the ™ symbol.
5. Click the ™ symbol, then click the **Insert** button.Click **Close**. The symbol is inserted after the word **Napster**.

▼ **Figure 4.18** Use the scrollbar to find the symbol you need.

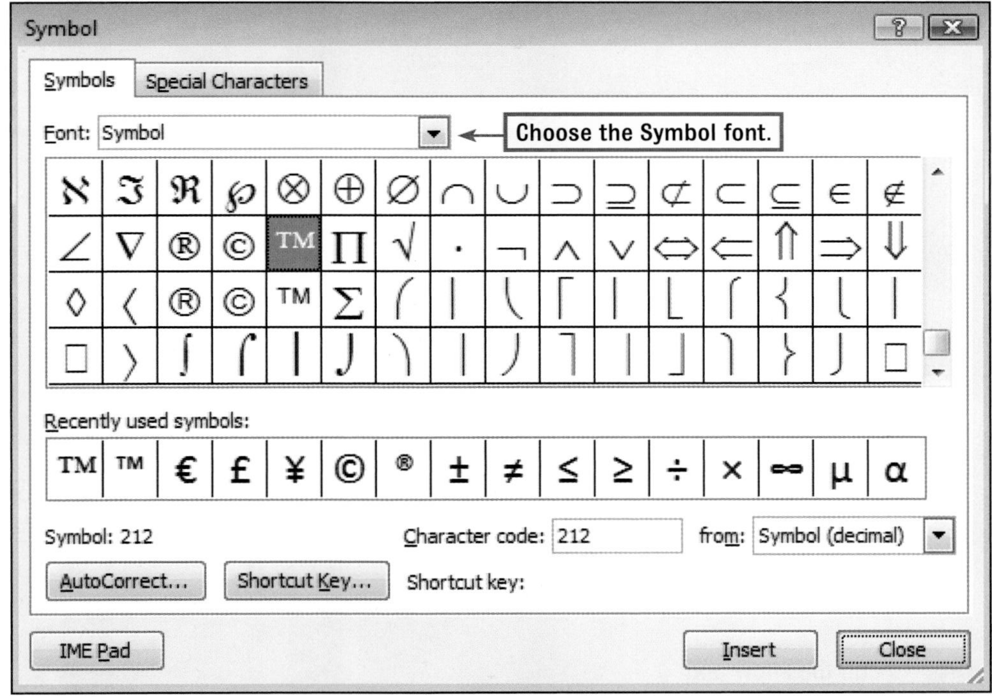

TechSavvy

Insert Symbol You can quickly insert a symbol you have recently used. Place your insertion point where you would like to insert a symbol. Look in the **Recently used symbols** section of the Symbol dialog box. Double-click the symbol to insert it, and then click **Close**.

11 On the **Ribbon**, on the **View** tab, in the **Presentation Views** group, click the **Slide Master View** button. Review the items on the **Slide Master** tab, and notice the slide placeholders.

12 On the **Ribbon**, click the **Close Master View** button (Figure 1.7).

13 Click the **Microsoft Office Button**, and then click **Save As**.

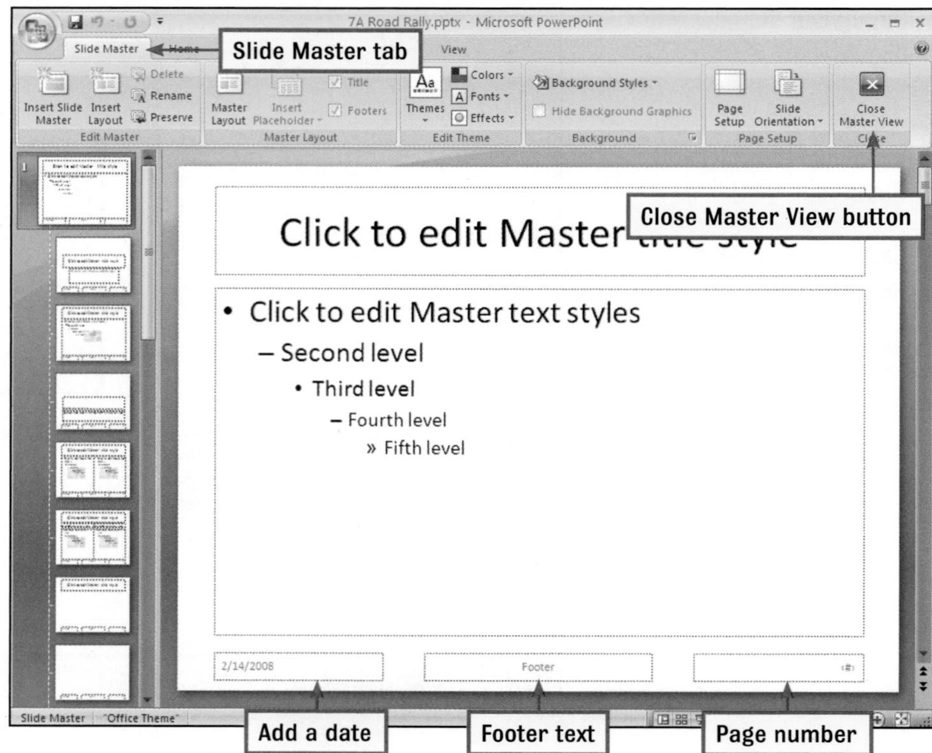

Figure 1.7 Slide Master view allows you to make changes to the entire presentation at one time.

14 Follow your teacher's instructions to **Save** the presentation as *Your Name Road Rally* (Figure 1.8). Make sure you save it to the correct location. If you are using **Windows XP**, refer to the *Getting Started* pages on pages xliv–xlviii of this book.

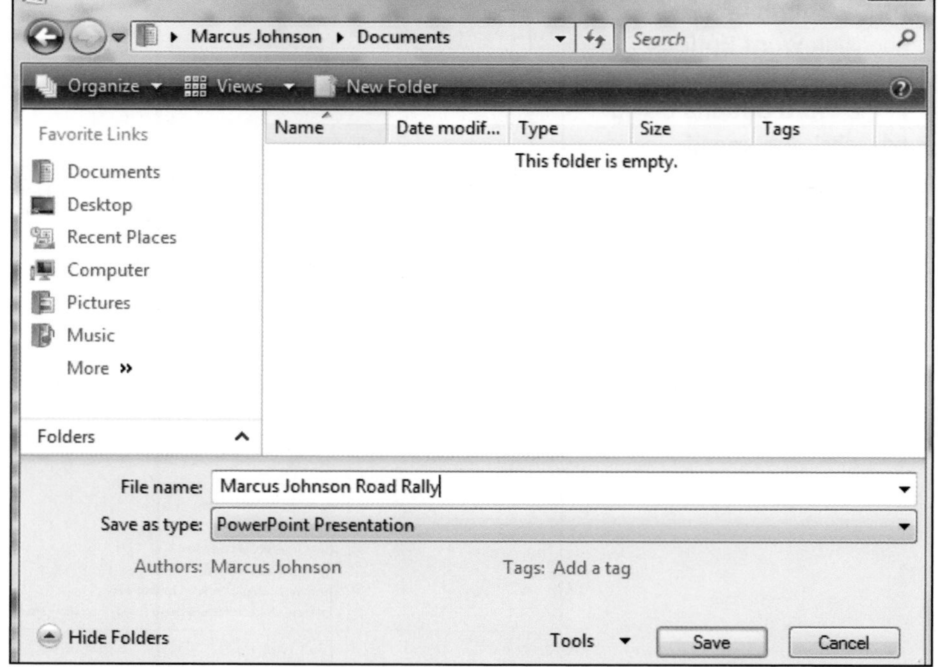

Figure 1.8 You use the same commands to save in PowerPoint as you do in Word.

5. Click **Replace All**. iTunes should appear correctly throughout the newsletter (Figure 4.16).

6. Repeat steps 2 to 5, but this time **Find** *IPod* and **Replace** it with *iPod*.

7. Close the **Find and Replace** box.

▼ **Figure 4.16** Your newsletter should look similar to this.

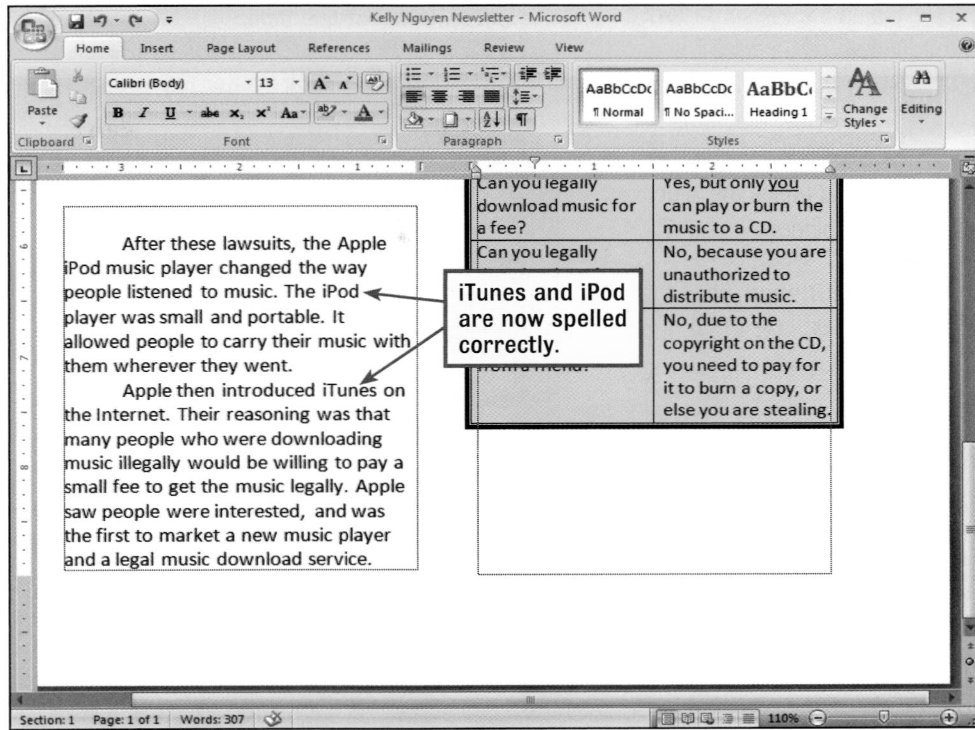

8. If your text boundaries still show, hide them by clicking the **Microsoft Office Button** and choosing **Word Options**.

9. In the **Word Options** dialog box, click **Advanced**. Then scroll to the **Show document content** section. Click to deselect **Show text boundaries**. Click **OK** (Figure 4.17).

10. **Save** your newsletter.

▼ **Figure 4.17** Use Word Options to select the features you view on your screen.

Word Options

Popular
Display
Proofing
Save
Advanced
Customize
Add-Ins
Trust Center
Resources

Show document content

- Show background colors and images in Print Layout view
- Show text wrapped within the document window
- Show picture placeholders
- Show drawings and text boxes on screen
- Show text animation
- Show bookmarks
- Show Smart Tags
- Show text boundaries
- Show crop marks
- Show field codes instead of their values

Field shading: When selected

- Use draft font in Draft and Outline views

Name: Courier New
Size: 10
Font Substitution...

Display

Show this number of Recent Documents: 17
Show measurements in units of: Inches
Style area pane width in Draft and Outline views: 0"

- Show pixels for HTML features
- Show all windows in the Taskbar
- Show shortcut keys in ScreenTips
- Show horizontal scroll bar
- Show vertical scroll bar
- Show vertical ruler in Print Layout view
- Optimize character positioning for layout rather than readability

OK Cancel

Remove the check mark from the Show text boundaries box.

Exercise 1-3 Apply a Theme

A **theme** is a custom design for a presentation. Themes are used to give a unified "look" to all slides in the presentation. They include features such as graphics, colorful backgrounds, and contrasting text colors.

Microsoft themes follow design guidelines to make your slide show attractive and readable. For example, a theme will use a text color that contrasts with the background and a large font size to make text readable. You can use themes to do the following to all of your slides:

- Standardize colors for the text and background
- Standardize text style, size, and alignment
- Repeat images from slide to slide

In this exercise, you will apply a theme to your presentation.

Step-by-Step

1. In your Road Rally presentation, click the **Normal** view button on the status bar.
2. Click **Slide 1**.
3. Click the **Design** tab, and then click the **More** button in the **Themes** group. The **Theme** gallery displays.
4. Point to a thumbnail in the gallery to preview a theme. Click to select the **Metro** theme (Figure 1.9).

Figure 1.9 Themes apply a consistent look throughout a presentation.

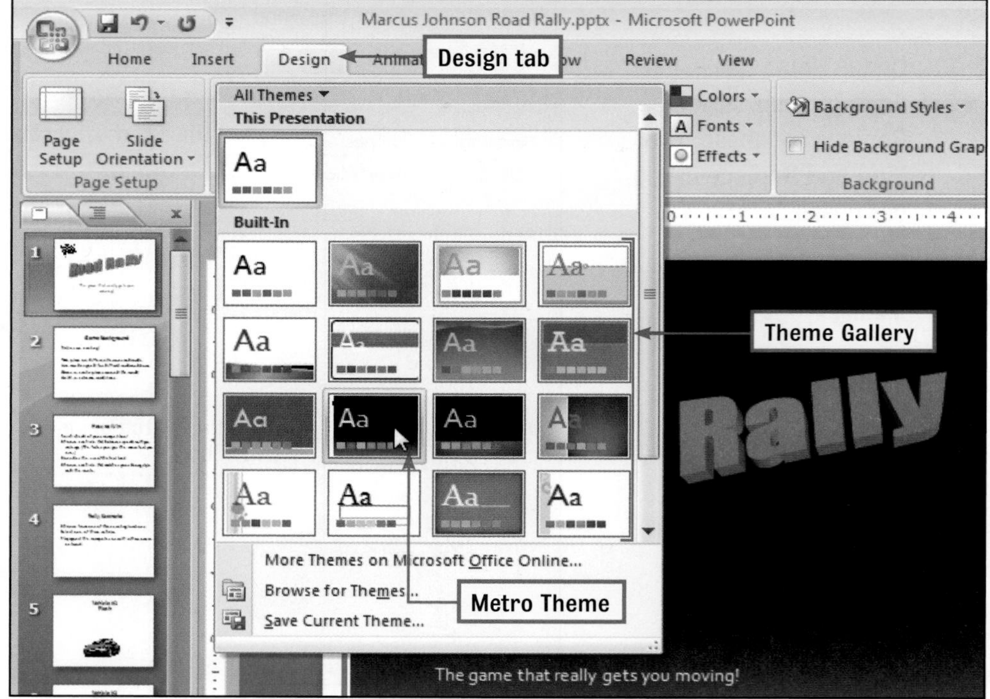

TechSavvy

Create Contrast Effective presentations use contrasting colors. Use light backgrounds with dark text or light text with dark backgrounds.

Exercise 4-5 Edit Your Newsletter

After using the Spelling & Grammar check and proofreading your newsletter, you realize that you have written "Itunes" and "Ipod" instead of "iTunes" and "iPod."

Instead of taking too much time to find and change each "Itunes" and "Ipod," Word has a tool that makes it easy to correct the entire document. Word is capable of scanning the entire document all at once to find words and phrases, and making requested changes for you. This saves time and helps you double-check your own proofreading. Remember to read through the entire document when you are finished to check for other mistakes.

In this exercise, you will use the Find and Replace tool to scan your newsletter and correct your mistakes.

Step-by-Step

1. On the **Home** tab, in the **Editing** group, click the **Replace** command. The **Find and Replace** dialog box opens.
2. In the **Find what** box, key Itunes.
3. In the **Replace with** box, key iTunes.
4. Click the **More** button, then check **Match case** (Figure 4.15).

▼ **Figure 4.15** The Find and Replace command can be used to change one word or every use of the word in a document.

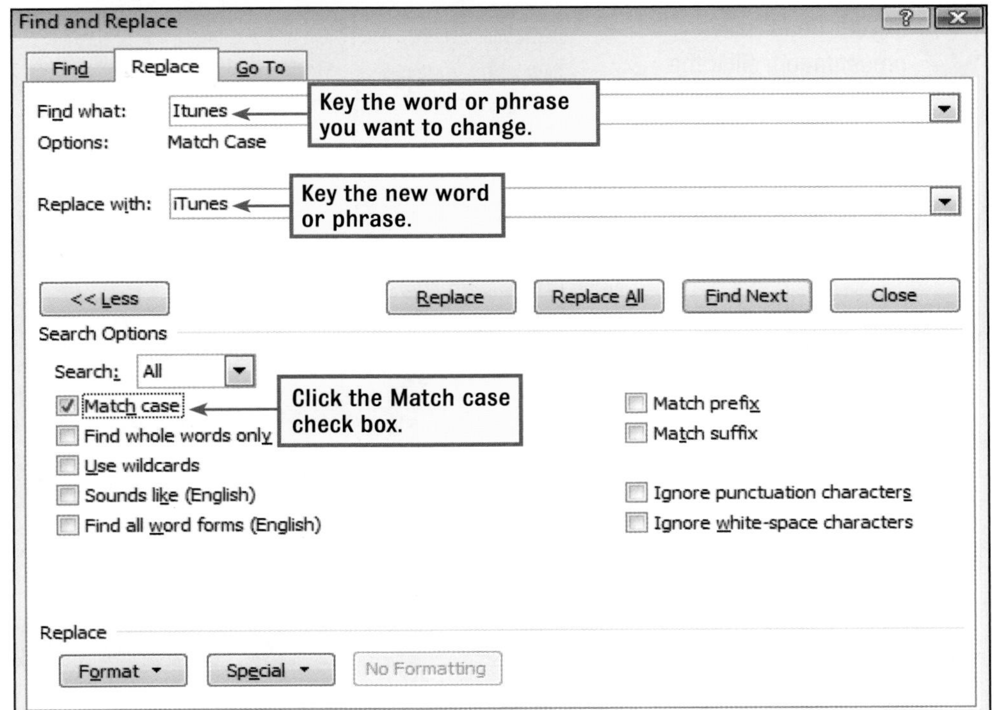

HELP!

Match the Case When finding and replacing text, you may need to specify if letters are uppercase or lowercase. If you do not check the Match case check box, Word will think that *Itunes* and *iTunes* are the same word.

5 On the **Design** tab, in the **Themes** group, click the **More** button.

6 Point to the **Apex** theme, and notice the **Live Preview** (Figure 1.10).

7 Point to and select the **Module** theme.

8 On the **Design** tab, in the **Background** group, click the **Background Styles** button. Select **Style 6**.

▼ **Figure 1.10** The name of each theme displays when you point to the thumbnail.

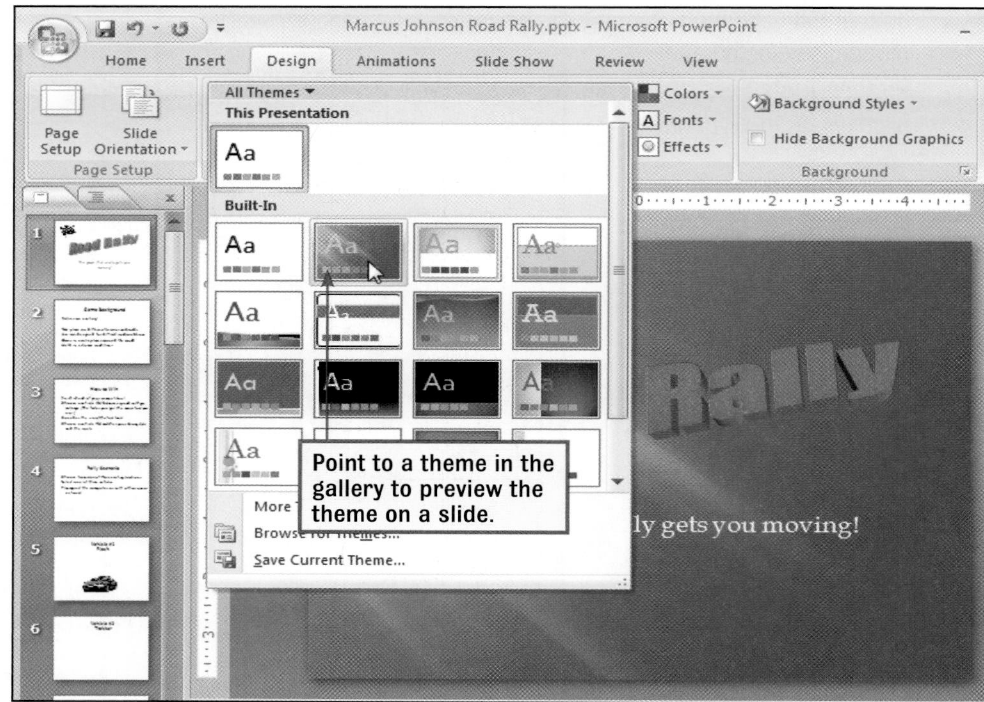

9 The theme is applied to all of your slides (Figure 1.11).

10 **Save** your presentation.

11 Switch to **Slide Show** to view each slide.

▼ **Figure 1.11** After applying a new theme, your screen should look like this.

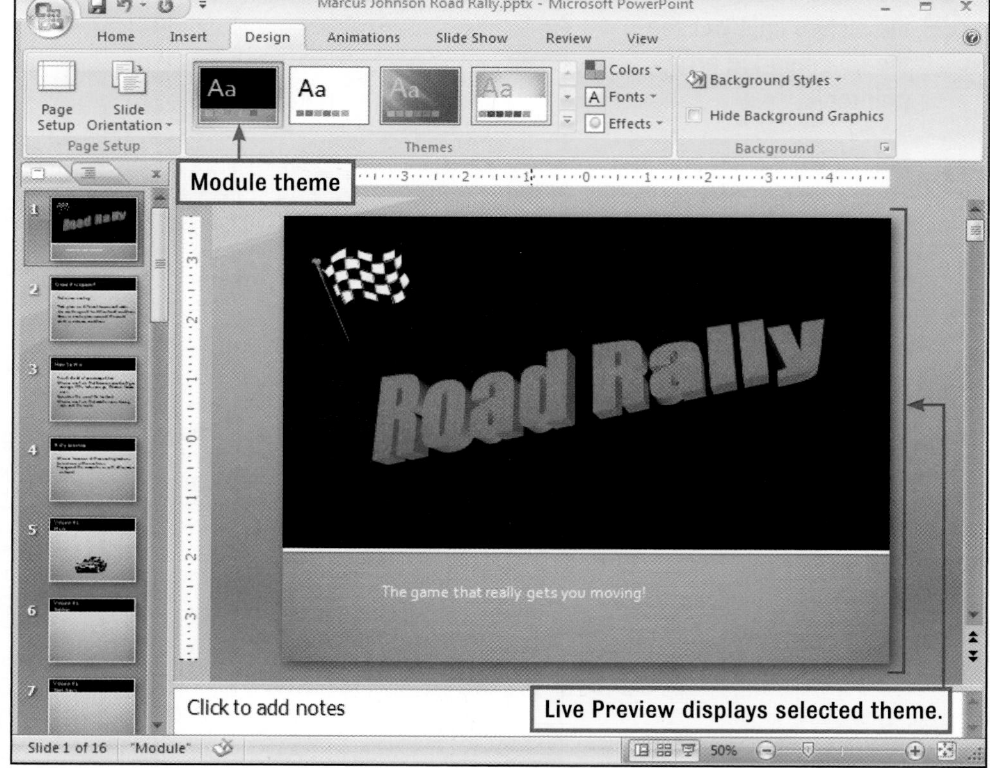

4 Click to select the music note graphic. When a picture is selected, the **Picture Tools Format** tab displays on the Ribbon.

5 On the **Picture Tools Format** tab, in the **Arrange** group, click the **Text Wrapping** button. Then choose **Top and Bottom** (Figure 4.13).

6 Use the **sizing handles** to resize the picture so that all lines of the paragraph above the graphic stay together.

Figure 4.13 Text should wrap around the graphic.

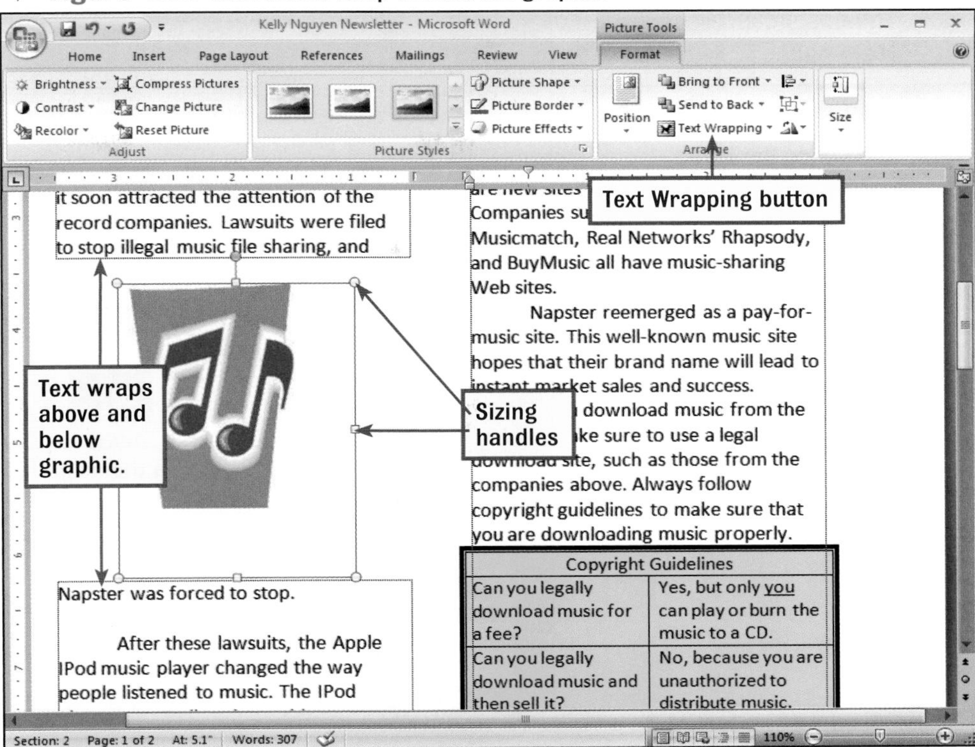

7 Move the mouse over the picture until you see the **four-headed arrow pointer**.

8 Hold down the left button of your mouse, and move the picture to **center** it between the paragraphs. (Figure 4.14).

9 **Save** your newsletter.

Figure 4.14 A graphic can be used to break up the text.

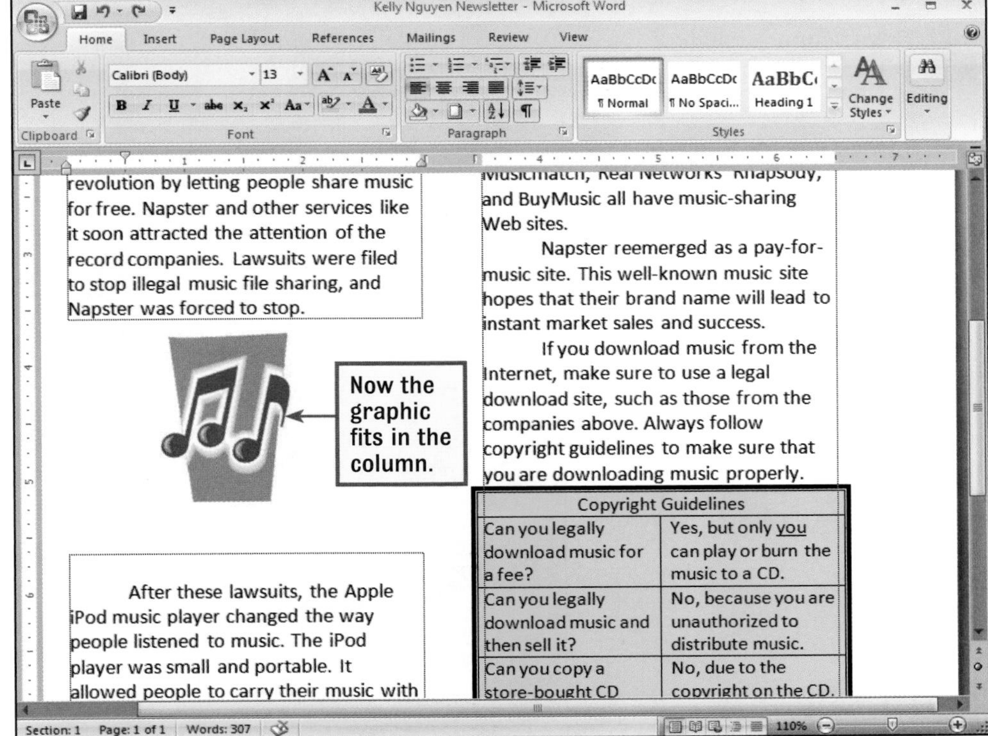

Exercise 1-4 Modify the Slide Master

You can make changes to your entire presentation by using the Slide Master. The Slide Master lets you add a feature to all your slides at once. Using the Slide Master eliminates the need to change each slide individually. You can use it to create your own custom layout.

The Slide Master stores background design, color schemes, and placeholder sizes and positions. It is best to create and edit a Slide Master before you create individual slides.

In this exercise, you will use the Slide Master to add the date and your name to the footer of your presentation. You will also modify the background.

Step-by-Step

1. In your Road Rally presentation, on the **View** tab, in the **Presentation Views** group, click the **Slide Master** button.

2. On the **Insert** tab, in the **Text** group, click the **Date & Time** button.

3. In the **Header and Footer** dialog box, select the **Date and Time** check box, and select the **Fixed** option (Figure 1.12).

4. Click the **Footer** check box.

▼ **Figure 1.12** **By adding the date, you can tell when the presentation was created. If you revise the presentation, you can change the date.**

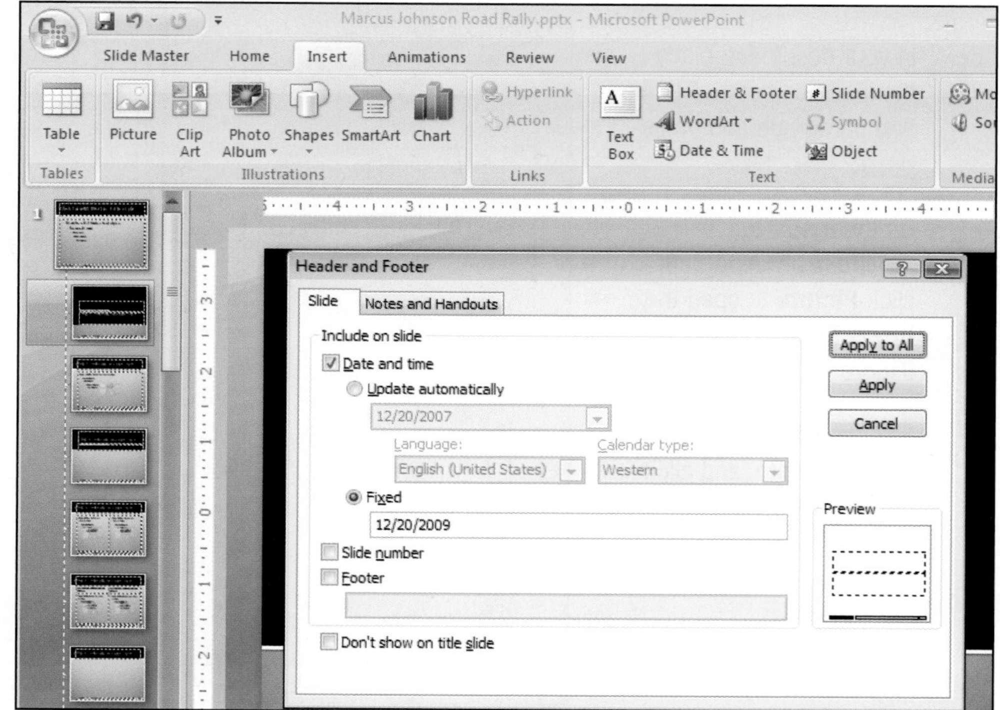

TechSavvy

Customize There are several ways to customize a Slide Master. One way is to add or remove placeholders from a slide layout. To remove a placeholder, click the placeholder border and press **Delete**. To add a placeholder to a slide layout, click the **Insert Placeholder** button. Then select the type of placeholder you want.

Exercise 4-4 Add a Graphic

For a more eye-catching newsletter, add an appropriate graphic. Graphics can help break up the text and make the document more interesting for the reader.

When you insert a picture into the first column, your text will automatically flow into the second column. You may have to reduce or increase the size of the picture so that the page looks balanced and visually appealing. Make sure the text does not flow onto a second page. If it does, edit your text or consider reducing the font size.

In this exercise, you will copy clip art into your newsletter and adjust the size of the clip art. You will then wrap the text above and below the clip art.

Step-by-Step

1. In your document, place the insertion point after the first paragraph and press ENTER.
2. On the **Insert** tab, in the **Illustrations** group, click **Picture** to open the **Insert Picture** dialog box (Figure 4.12).
3. Find the **Data File** named **4I Music Note**, and click **Insert**. The music note graphic appears at your insertion point.

▼ **Figure 4.12** Insert graphics through the Insert tab.

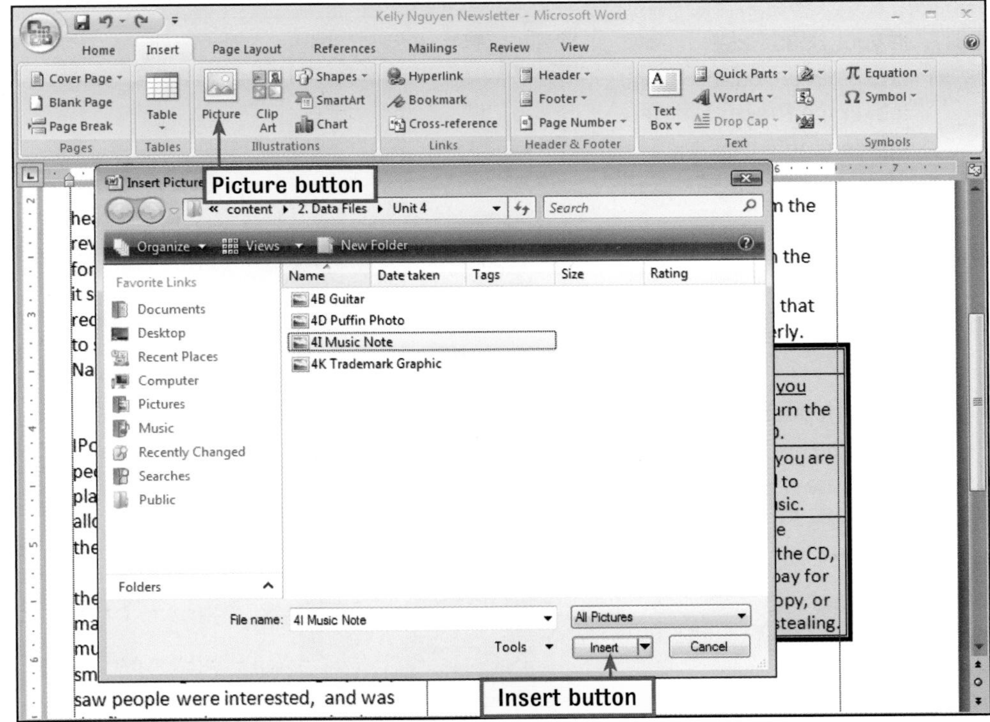

TechSavvy

Borders and Shading You can apply borders and shading to a block of text to make the text stand out. Select the text you want to emphasize. On the **Home** tab, in the **Paragraph** group, click the arrow beside the **Border** button. Click **Borders and Shading**. On the **Borders** tab, choose a **Setting** and a **Style**. Then click the **Shading** tab to select a **Fill** color or **Pattern**.

5. Key your name in the **Footer** text box, and select the **Don't show on the title slide** check box. Then click **Apply to All** (Figure 1.13).

6. Click the **Slide Master** tab. Click the **Module Slide Master** thumbnail. In the **Background** group, click the **Format Background Dialog Box Launcher**. Select the **Solid fill** option. Click the **Color** drop-down arrow, and select **Orange**. Click **Apply to All**. Click **Close**.

7. Click the **Title Slide Layout** thumbnail in the left pane, and select the horizontal line separating the black and orange colors on the slide. On the **Drawing Tools Format** tab, in the **Shape Styles** group, change the **Shape Fill** and the **Shape Outline** to **Red**.

8. Click the **Master Title Style Layout** thumbnail, and change the color of the **horizontal line** to **red**.

9. Click the **Slide Master** tab, and click the **Close Master View** button (Figure 1.14).

10. **Save** the presentation. Notice that the footer displays on every slide in the presentation except the title slide.

▼ **Figure 1.13** You can use the footer to identify the creator of the project.

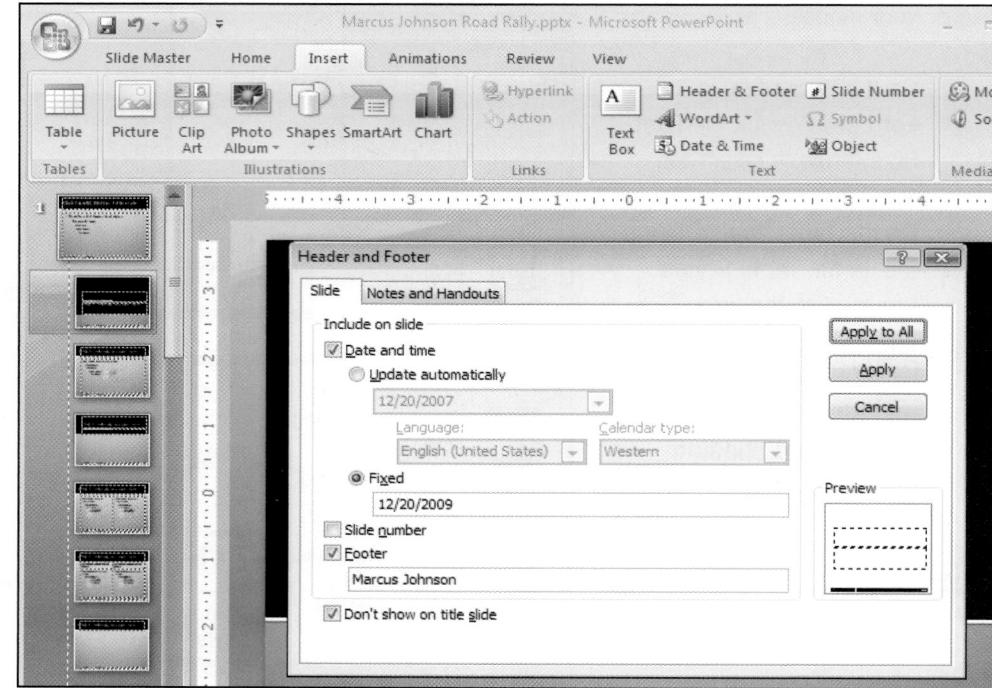

▼ **Figure 1.14** Slide Master View allows you to make changes to all the slides at one time.

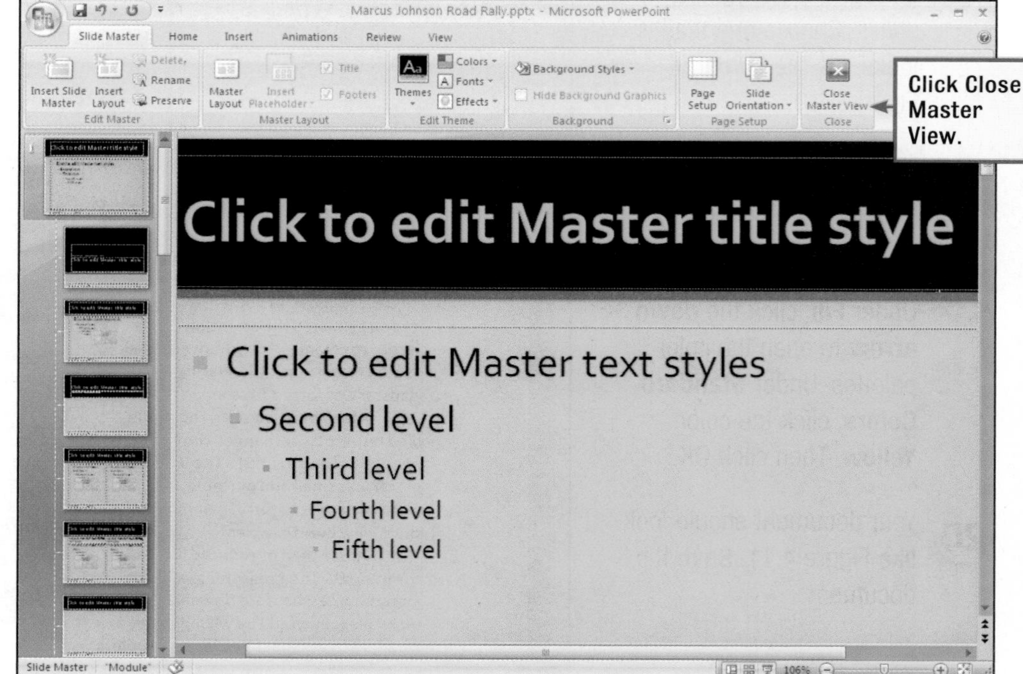

13 Select the whole table with your mouse.

14 On the **Home** tab, in the **Font** group, click the **Font Size** arrow to select **12**.

15 On the **Table Tools Design** tab, in the **Table Styles** group, click the arrow beside the **Borders** button ▦. Then click **Borders and Shading** to open the **Borders and Shading** dialog box (Figure 4.10).

16 Click the **Borders** tab, if necessary.

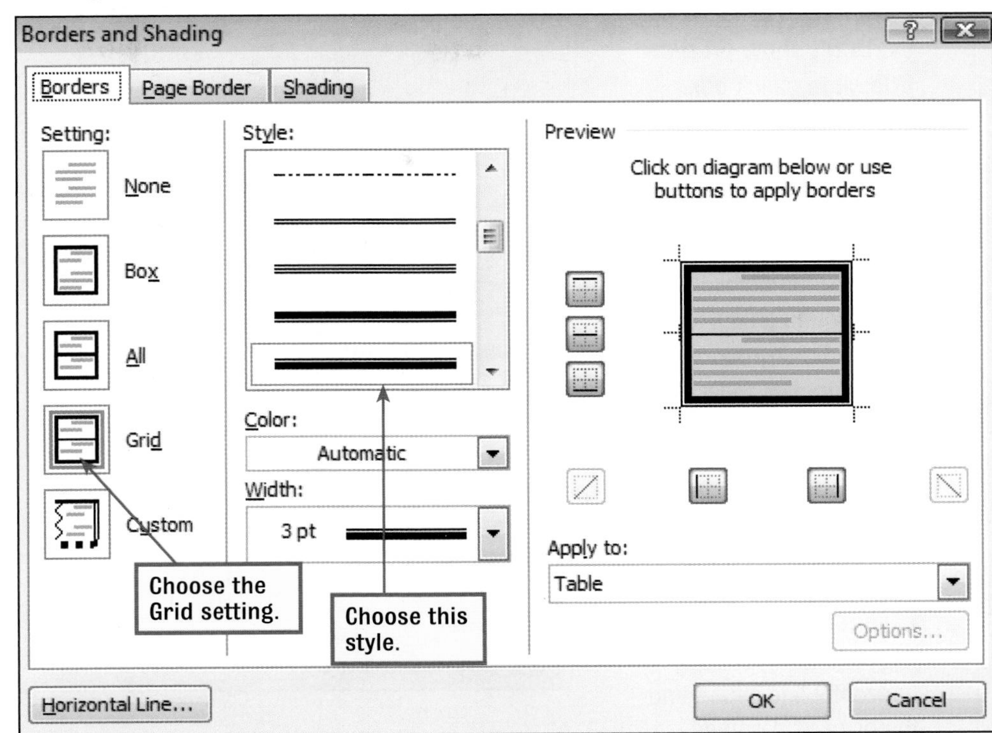

▼ **Figure 4.10** **Use borders and shading to highlight your table.**

17 In the **Style** box, scroll through the border line styles. Choose one that looks like the border in Figure 4.10.

18 Under **Setting**, click **Grid**.

19 Click the **Shading** tab. Under **Fill**, click the **down arrow** to open the color palettes. Under **Standard Colors**, click the color **Yellow**. Then click **OK**.

20 Your document should look like Figure 4.11. **Save** the document.

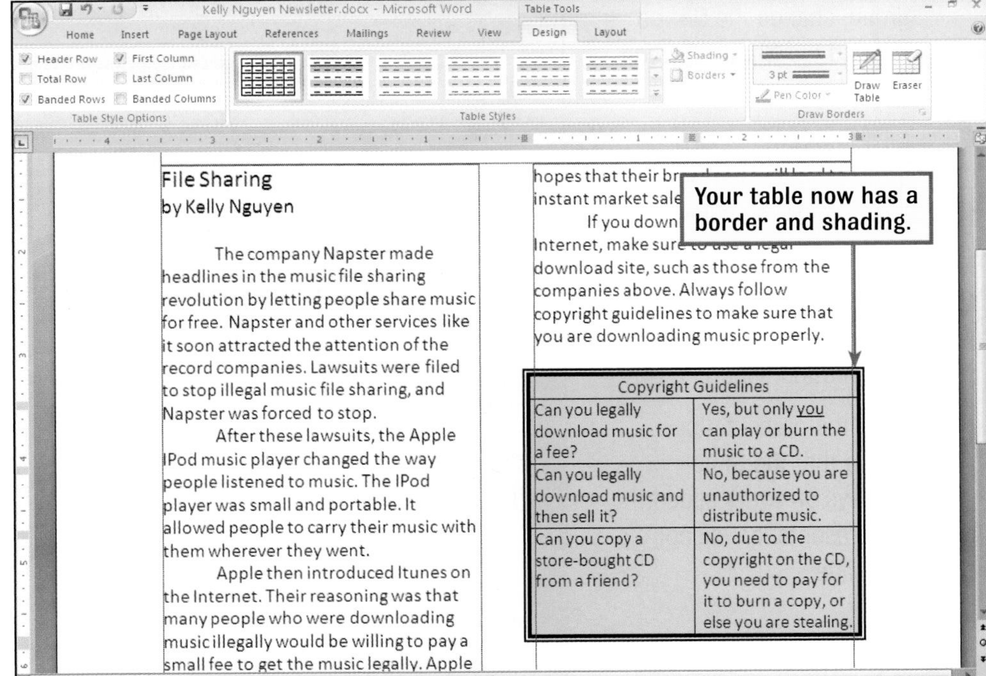

▼ **Figure 4.11** **Your finished table should look like this.**

Exercise 1-5 Navigate Through Your Slides

You can view, edit, and rearrange your slides as you create your presentation. This allows you to make ongoing adjustments to any of the slides, as changes come up.

To make changes to your presentation, you need to be able to view slides and quickly move between them. PowerPoint has a number of ways for you to easily navigate to the slides you need.

In this exercise, you will use different methods to navigate through the slides in a presentation. You will see that you can use either the keyboard or the mouse to move from slide to slide.

Step-by-Step

1. Click **Slide 1** of your Road Rally presentation, and select the text that begins "The game." Change the **Font Color** to **Black** and the **Font Size** to **28**. Apply **bold** formatting.
2. Click the **Slide Show** button on the **status** bar to begin the slide show (Figure 1.15).
3. Click your mouse or press ENTER to advance to the next slide.
4. Press ← to go to the previous slide.

▼ **Figure 1.15** It is recommended that you preview your slide show so that you can make changes, if necessary.

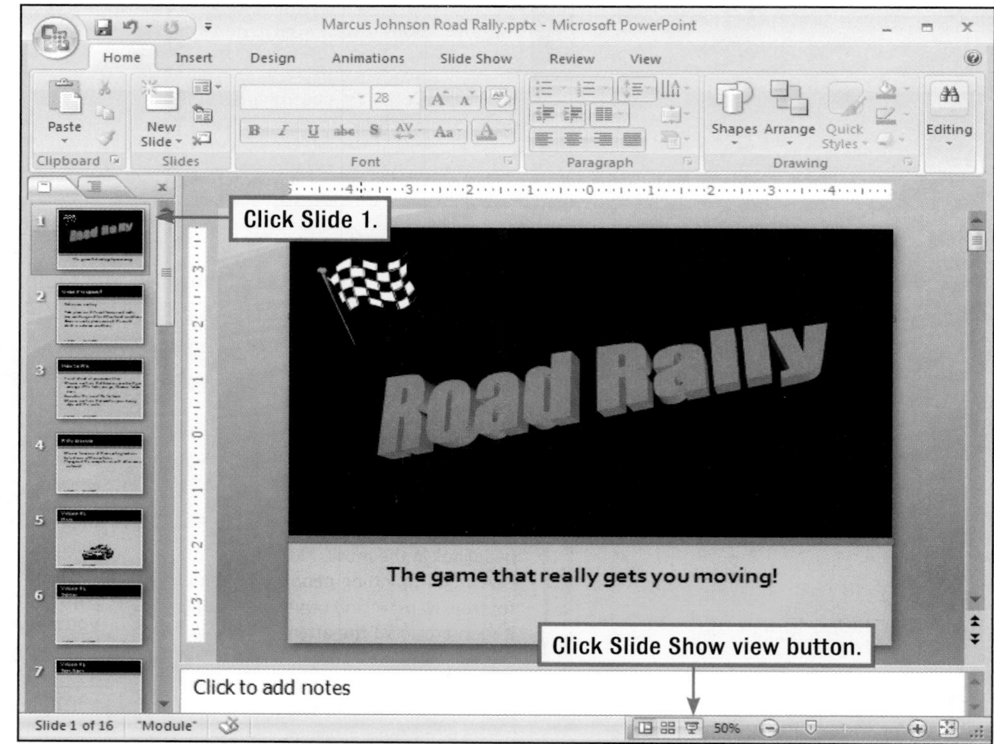

TechSavvy

Comments Some people find it very helpful to keep notes as they create a PowerPoint Presentation or make comments when reviewing a colleague's presentation. Select the slide where you want to add a comment, and click the **Review** tab. Click the **New Comment** button, and key your note. Click outside the comment box when you are finished.

6 The inserted table should look like Figure 4.8. Place the insertion point in the first cell, and select all of the first row (both cells).

7 On the **Layout** tab, in the **Merge** group, click the **Merge Cells** button to combine the two cells into one large cell.

▼ **Figure 4.8** Your table has been inserted into the document.

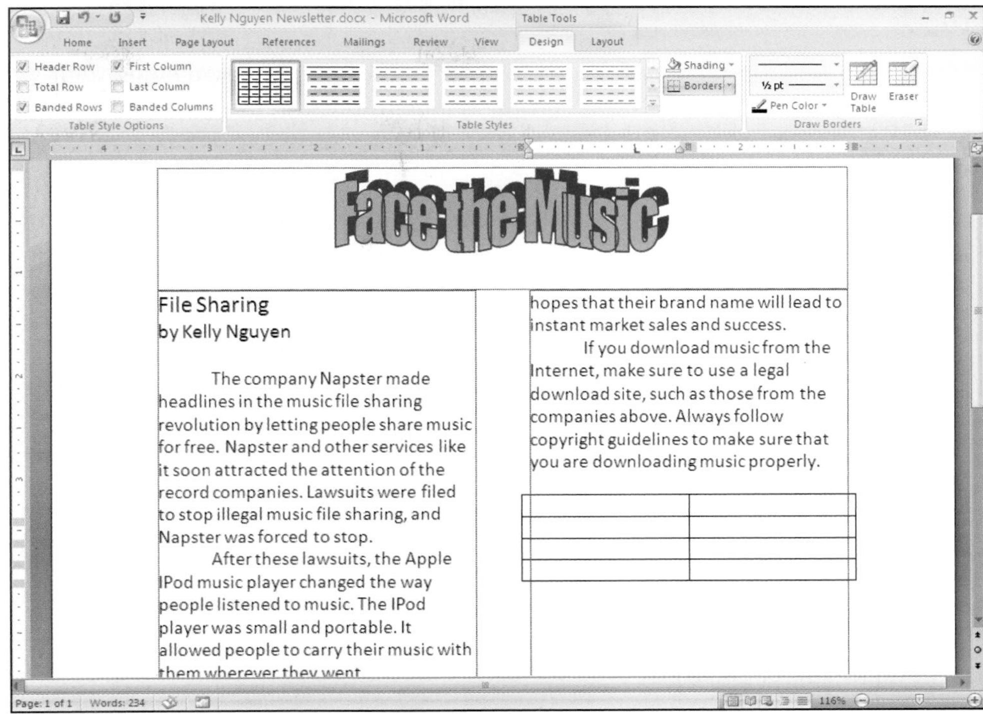

8 In the merged cell, key the table title Copyright Guidelines and **center** it.

9 On the keyboard, use the **arrow** keys to move the insertion point to the top cell in the left column.

10 Key Can you legally download music for a fee?

11 Move your insertion point to the cell to the right and key Yes, but only you can play or burn the music to a CD.

12 Enter the rest of the text from the table shown in Figure 4.9.

▼ **Figure 4.9** Enter the text shown in this table.

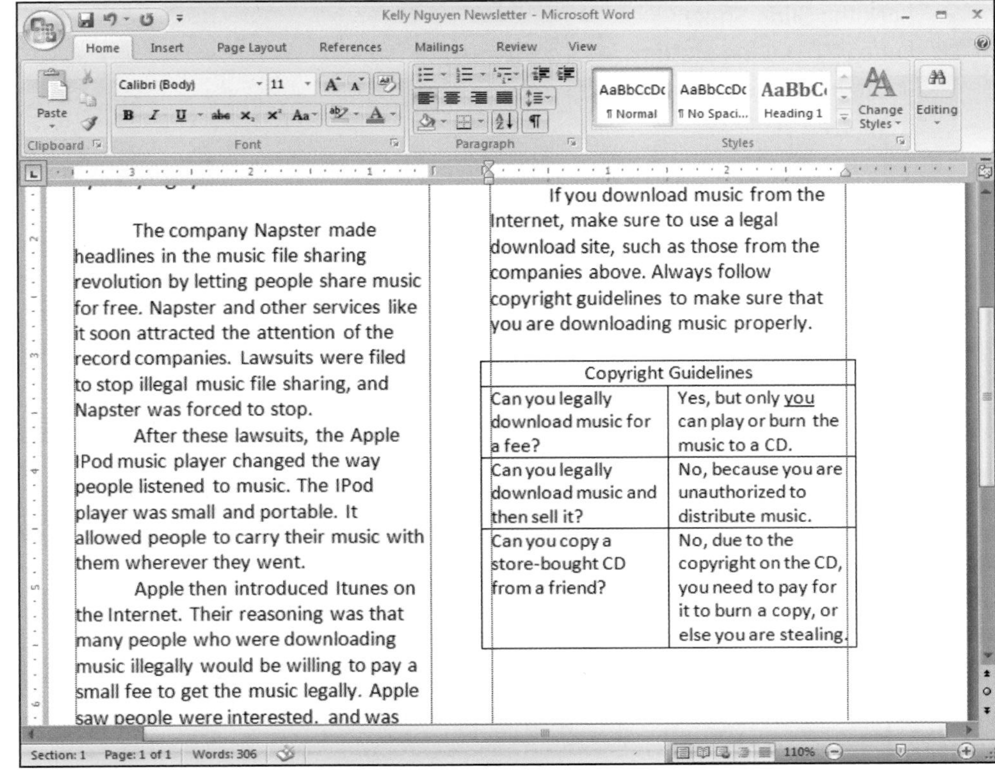

5 While you are viewing the slide show, right-click on a slide to display the **shortcut** menu.

6 Click **Next** (Figure 1.16). This will take you to the next slide.

7 Display the shortcut menu, and click **Previous** to go back to **Slide 1**.

8 Display the shortcut menu, click **Go to Slide**, and click **Slide 3 How to Win**.

▼ **Figure 1.16** You can use the shortcut menu to navigate through the slide show.

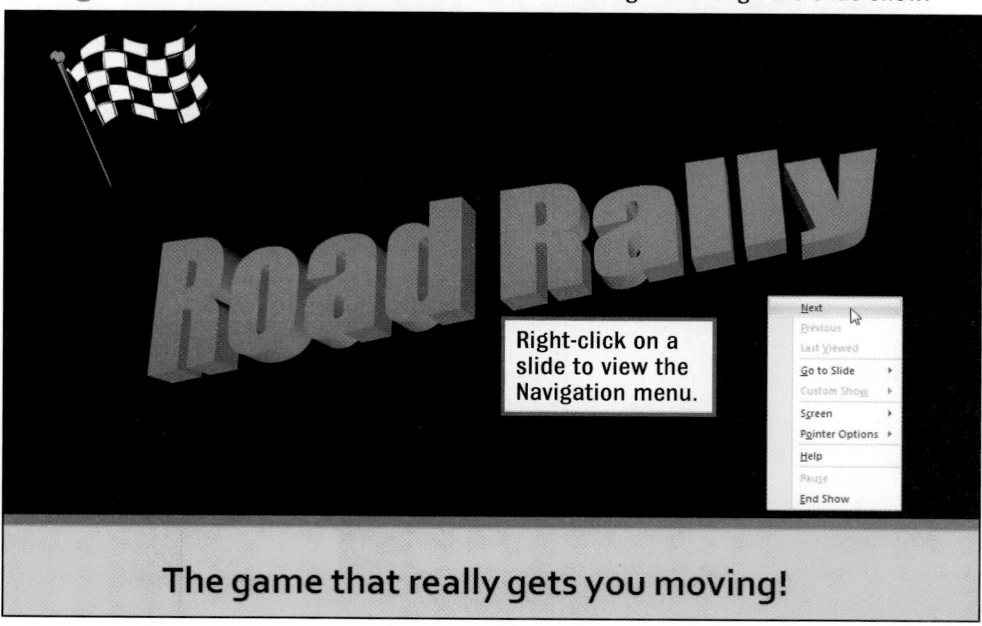

9 Open the shortcut menu, click **End Show** (Figure 1.17). You will be returned to **Normal** view.

10 **Close** the Road Rally presentation.

▼ **Figure 1.17** Use the shortcut menu or press the Escape (Esc) key to return to Normal view.

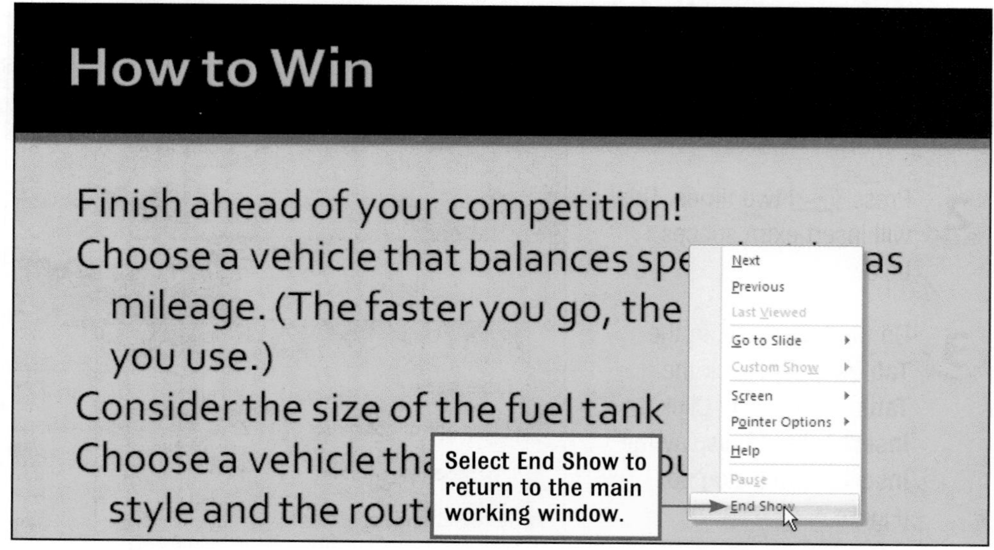

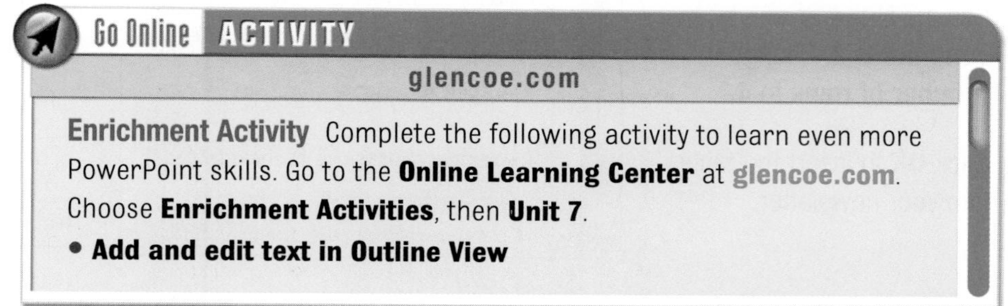

Go Online ACTIVITY

glencoe.com

Enrichment Activity Complete the following activity to learn even more PowerPoint skills. Go to the **Online Learning Center** at **glencoe.com**. Choose **Enrichment Activities**, then **Unit 7**.

- **Add and edit text in Outline View**

Exercise 4-3 Create Tables

A **table** is a grid of rows and columns that organizes complex information so that it is easy to find and understand. A **column** is the information that is arranged vertically (up and down) in the table. A **row** is the information that is arranged horizontally (from left to right). A **cell** is where a column and row cross.

Class Schedule for Monday		
Time	Class	Teacher
8:00-10:00	English	Loh
10:00-12:00	Math	Bonadelli
12:00-12:30	Lunch	
12:30-2:30	Social Studies	Melikian

Row

Cell

Column

In this exercise, you will use Word to create a table for your newsletter. The table you create will need to stand out, so you will also add a distinct border around it and use shading to color the cells.

Step-by-Step

1. In your newsletter, place your insertion point at the end of the article.
2. Press ENTER two times. This will insert extra spaces below your table.
3. On the **Insert** tab, in the **Tables** group, click the **Table** button. Click **Insert Table** to display the **Insert Table** dialog box (Figure 4.7).
4. Change **Number of columns** to **2**. Change **Number of rows** to **4**.
5. Click **OK** to insert the table into your newsletter.

Figure 4.7 Adjust the Insert Table box to look like this.

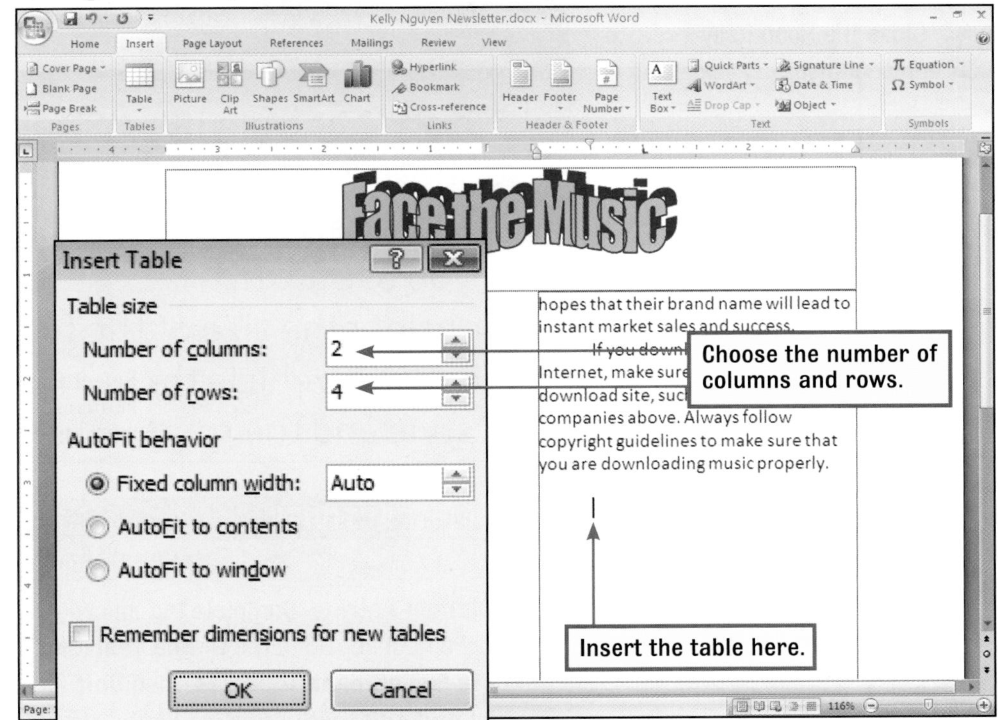

Project 1 Assessment

Key Concepts Check

1. **Identify** What are the different views you can use in PowerPoint?
2. **Describe** What is the purpose of a theme?
3. **Explain** What is the Slide Master?

Critical Thinking

4. **Draw Conclusions** Why is it important for all slides in a presentation to have the same theme?
5. **Cause and Effect** Would you use yellow text on an orange background? Why or why not?

1 Guided Practice

Manage Your Slides Your teacher started to create a PowerPoint presentation about the proper way to give a presentation, but she never finished it. She has given you the job of putting the slides in order and adding a theme to give the presentation a unified look. If you need help, refer back to the exercise in parentheses at the end of the steps.

Step-by-Step

1. **Open** the **Data File** named **7C Present a Presentation**.
2. Click **Slide Sorter** view. (Exercise 1-2)
3. Move **Slide 3** after **Slide 5**, as shown in Figure 1.18. (Exercise 1-2)

▼ **Figure 1.18** Click a slide in Slide Sorter view to move it.

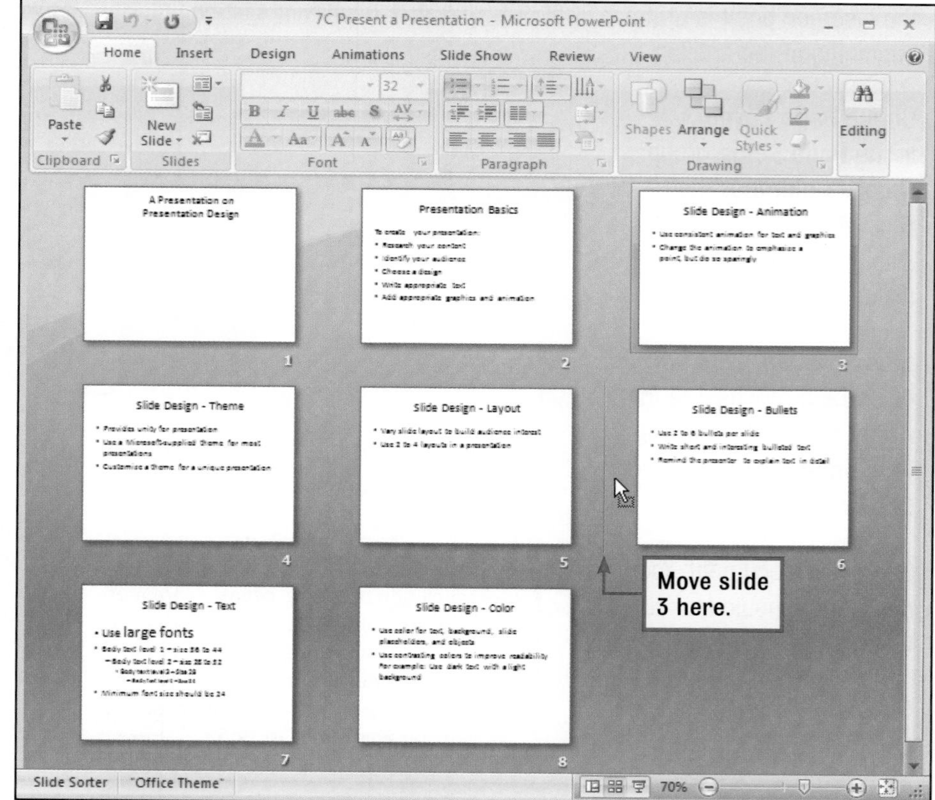

6 Click your newsletter document on the taskbar to switch back to your newsletter file.

7 Verify that the insertion point is two blank lines below the masthead. On the **Home** tab, in the **Paragraph** group, click the **Align Text Left** button, or press CTRL + L to left align the insertion point.

8 On the **Home** tab, in the **Clipboard** group, click the **Paste** button to add the article to your newsletter.

9 Select all the text and set line spacing to **1.0**. Verify the insertion point is at the beginning of the article.

10 On the **Page Layout** tab, in the **Page Setup** group, choose **Columns**. Then click **More Columns** to display the **Columns** dialog box (Figure 4.5).

11 Under **Presets**, click **Two**. Click the arrow next to the **Apply to** box, then choose **This point forward**. Click **OK** (Figure 4.5).

12 **Save** your document. Your newsletter should look like Figure 4.6.

13 **Close** the **4H Article** data file.

Figure 4.5 Add a section break so that your masthead is not forced into the column format.

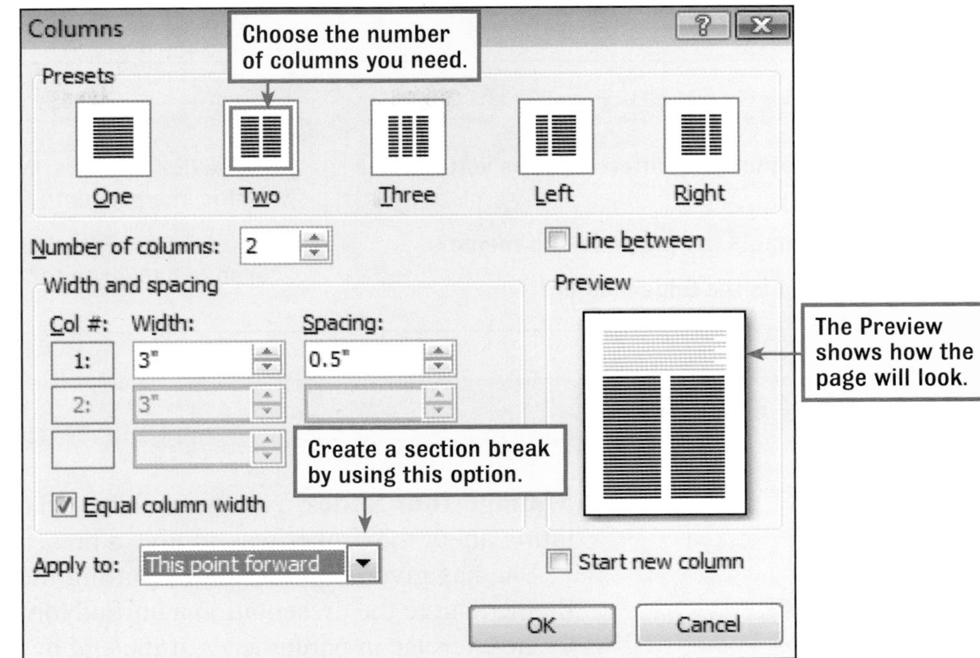

Figure 4.6 Displaying text boundaries lets you see how your columns lay out on the page.

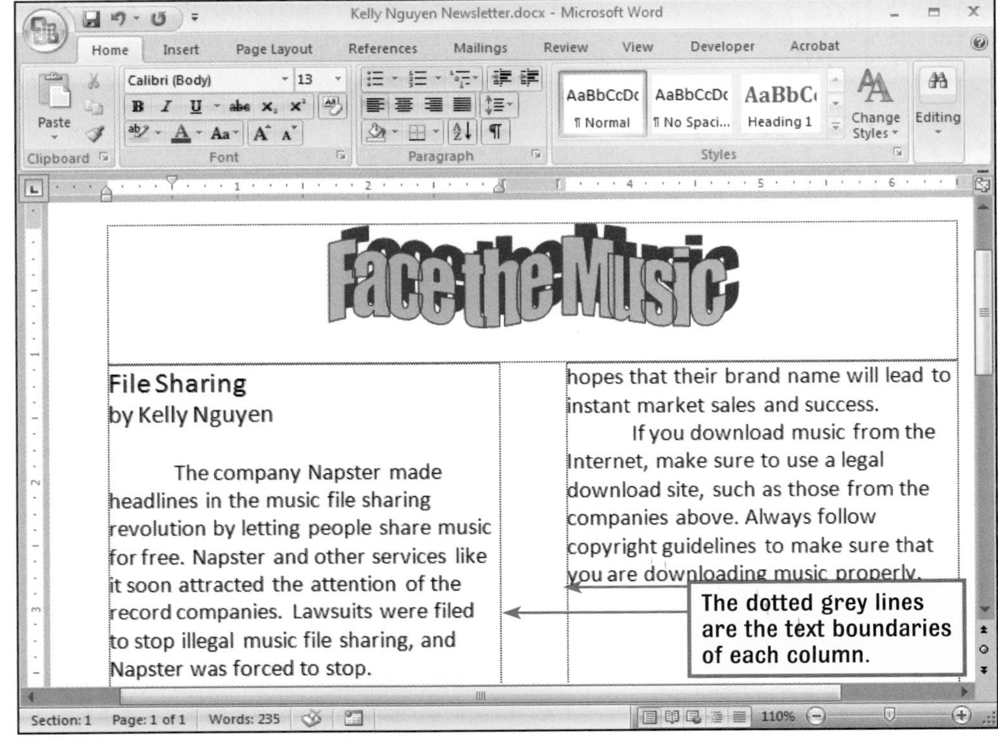

4. Display the **Slide Master**, and click the **Insert** tab. Use the **Header and Footer** button to add a page number to each slide. (Exercise 1-4)

5. Apply a theme of your choosing to the presentation. Figure 1.19 shows one example. (Exercise 1-3)

6. Change the background and apply it to all the slides. (Exercise 1-4)

▼ **Figure 1.19** Choose a theme that is easy to read and is appropriate for the presentation.

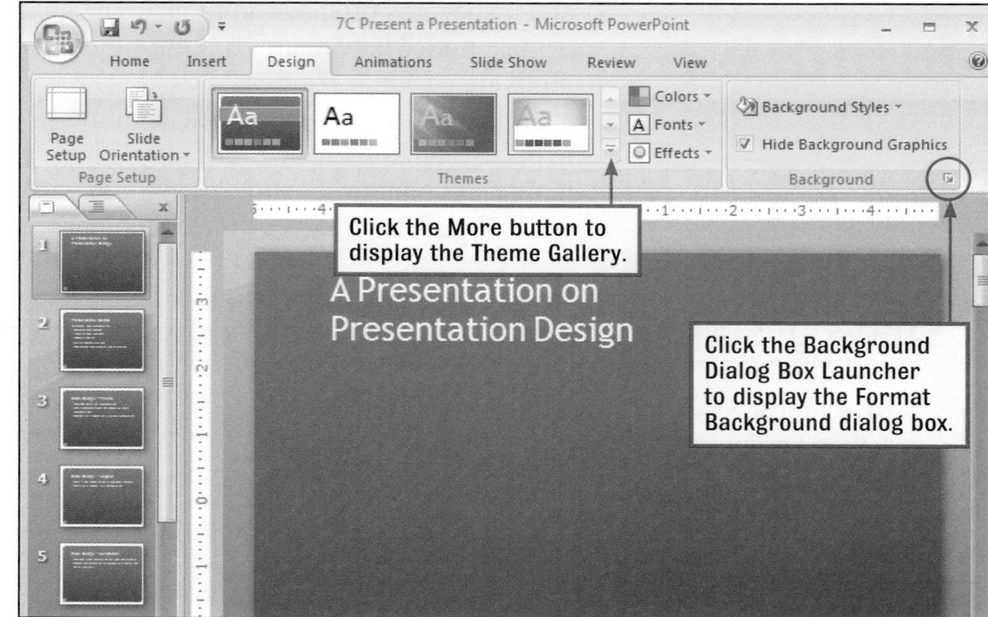

7. Click the **View** tab, and click **Slide Show** to view the presentation (Figure 1.20). (Exercise 1-5)

8. Navigate through the presentation. (Exercise 1-5)

9. **Save** the file as *Your Name* Present a Presentation. (Exercise 1-3)

10. **Exit PowerPoint**.

▼ **Figure 1.20** This is the first screen of the slide presentation.

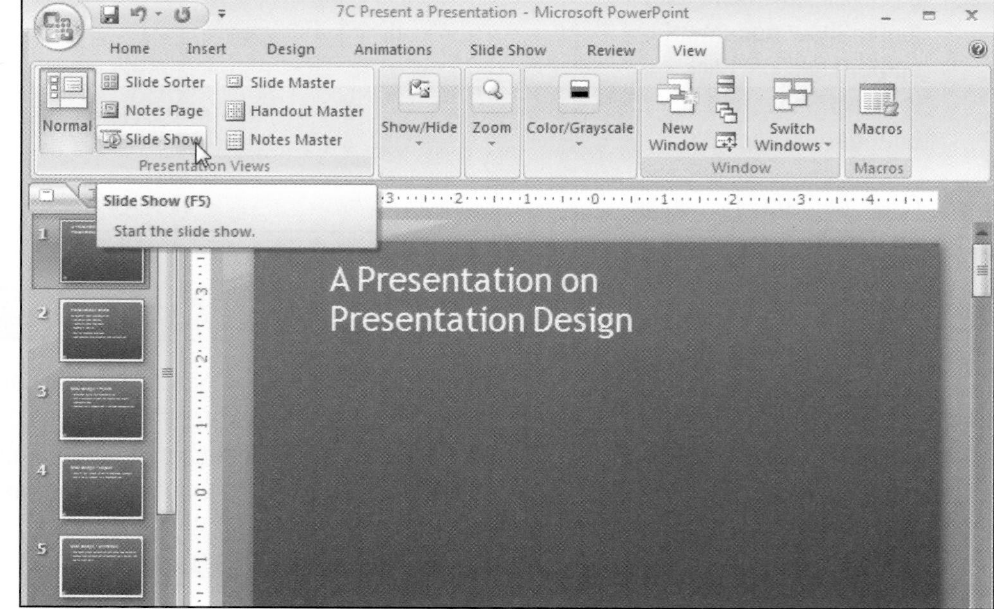

Exercise 4-2 Create Columns

Columns break information into smaller sections so that the reader can easily scan the lines of text. When you have a lot of text, as in a newsletter, it is helpful to lay out the text using two or more columns. Newspapers and magazines often use columns. The next time you read a magazine or a book, notice how many columns of text there are and which formats you think are easier to read.

In this exercise, you will add columns to your newsletter. You will need to place a section break after the masthead so that the masthead is not formatted as columns. Section breaks allow you to apply different formatting styles to different parts of the document.

Step-by-Step

1. Make sure your document is in **Print Layout** view.

2. Click the **Microsoft Office Button**, then click the **Word Options** button to display the **Word Options** dialog box (Figure 4.4).

3. In the **Word Options** dialog box, click **Advanced**. Scroll to the **Show document content** section. Click to select **Show text boundaries**. Click **OK**.

4. Open the **Data File** named **4H Article**.

5. Select the entire article titled **File Sharing** by pressing CTRL + A. On the **Home** tab, in the **Clipboard** group, click the **Copy** button.

Figure 4.4 To view your column boundaries, click the Show text boundaries box.

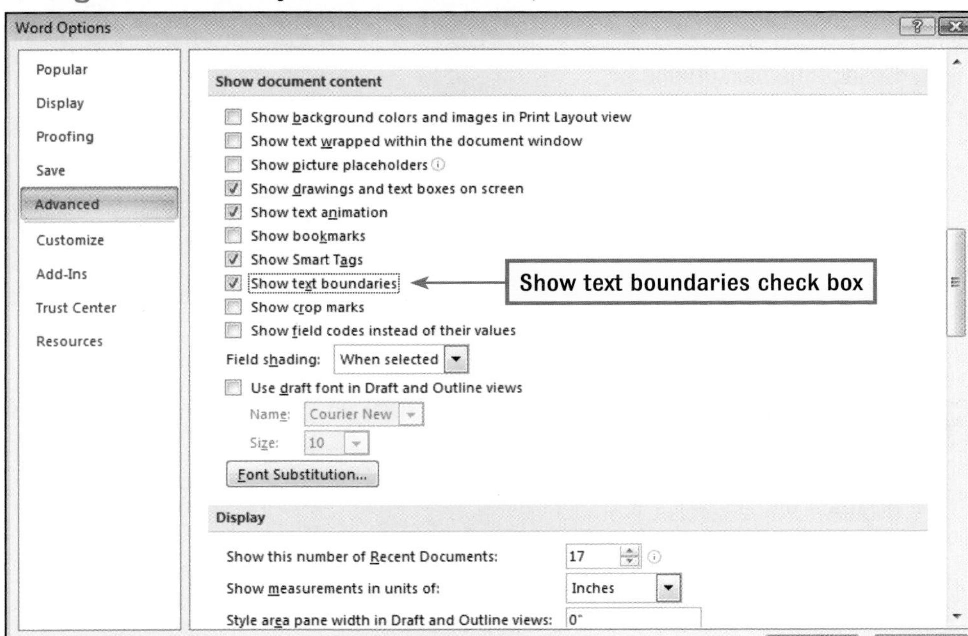
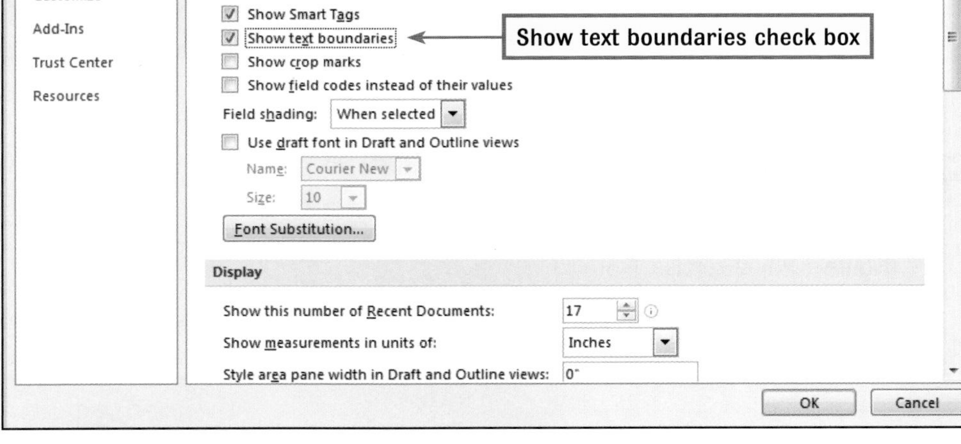

TechSavvy

Columns for Selected Text You can create columns for selected text in a document. First, select the text that you would like formatted in columns. On the **Page Layout** tab, in the **Page Setup** group, click **Columns**, and then choose **More Columns**. In the **Columns** dialog box, in the **Apply to** box, choose **Selected Text**.

Project 1 Assessment

2 Independent Practice ★

English Language Arts Add Text to a Presentation You have been asked to create a presentation about your school.

a. Plan Choose one of the following subjects for your presentation:

- Dress codes at school
- How to succeed on a school team or in a school production
- Ten things you like about school

b. Create Write the text you would use for your slides.

- Create a title slide and six to ten slides with the text you wrote.
- Save your presentation as ***Your Name*** **School Presentation**.

3 Independent Practice ★★

English Language Arts Modify Text in a Presentation Complete Independent Practice 2 above, then modify the slides.

a. Create Apply a theme to all slides.

b. Edit Check your slides for layout and readability.

- Modify the text so that the slides can be easily read.
- Rearrange the slides in a more effective order.
- Change the design elements on all slides.

Independent Practice Use the rubrics for these projects to help create and evaluate your work. Go to the **Online Learning Center** at **glencoe.com**. Choose **Rubrics**, then **Unit 7**.

4 Independent Practice ★★★

English Language Arts Create a Career Presentation Create a presentation about a career in technology.

a. Research Gather information about the career you chose. On note cards, write the following details:

- A description of the career and why it interests you
- The requirements for the career (for example, education, experience)
- The technology you might use in the career

b. Create Use the information to create ten or more slides.

5 On the **Insert** tab, in the **Text** group, click the **WordArt** button. The **WordArt Gallery** appears (Figure 4.2).

6 In the **WordArt Gallery** box, click the **WordArt** style that looks like the one highlighted in Figure 4.2. Click **OK**.

Figure 4.2 WordArt is one of many graphic options on the Ribbon.

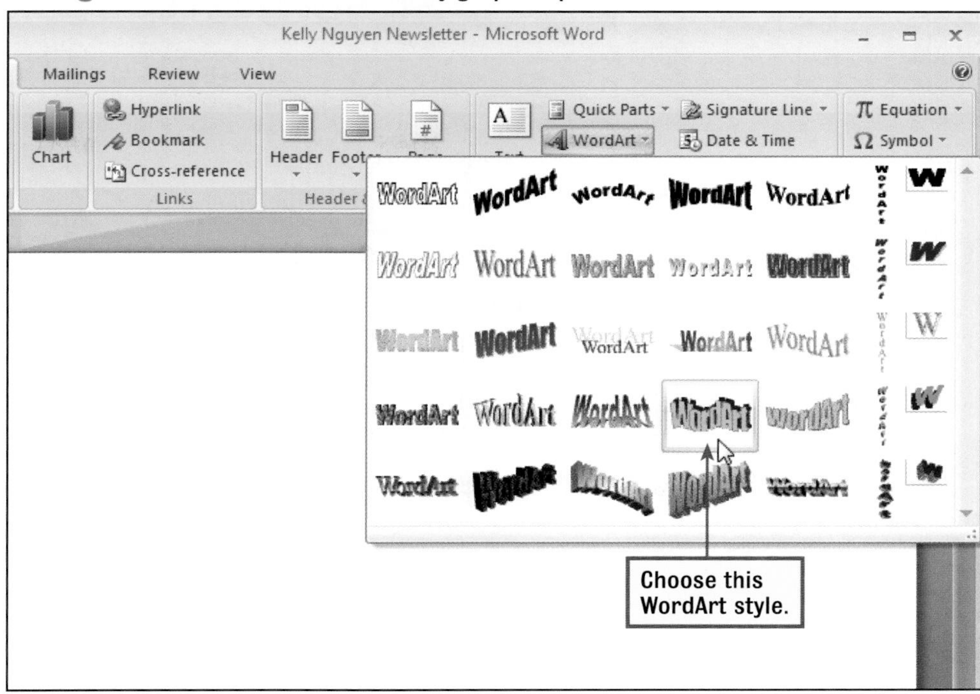

7 In the **Edit WordArt Text** dialog box, key Face the Music. Then click **OK**.

8 On the **Home** tab, in the **Paragraph** group, click the **Center** button, or press CTRL + E to center your masthead.

9 If necessary, click to unselect the WordArt. On the keyboard, press ENTER once.

10 The masthead should look like Figure 4.3. **Save** your document.

Figure 4.3 WordArt gives your document more impact.

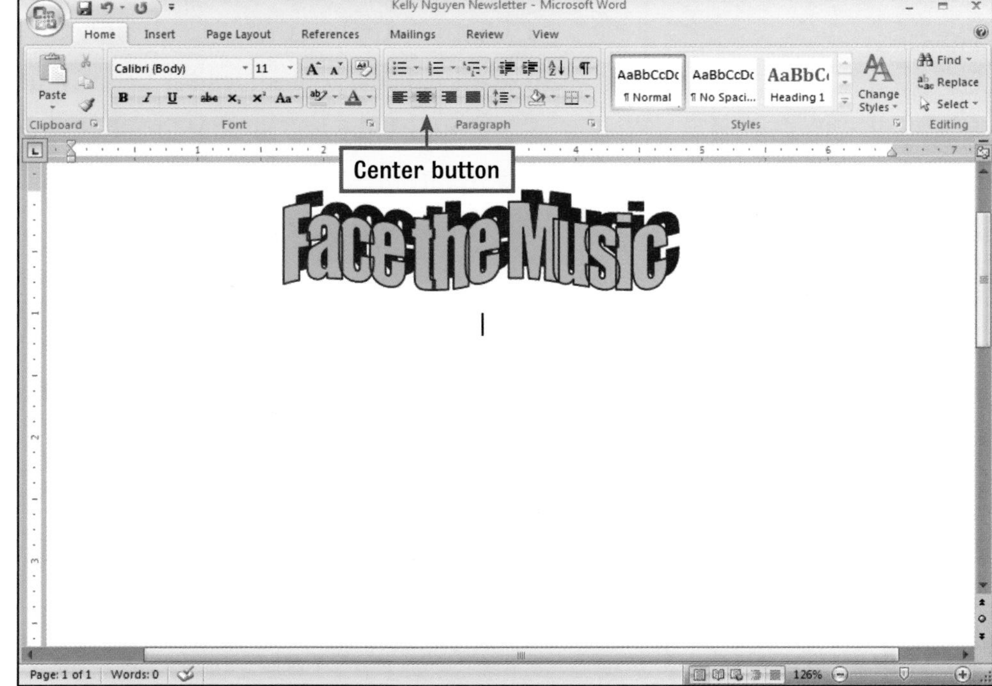

Concepts in Action

Project 2 Enhance a Presentation

Key Concepts

Exercise 2-1

- Apply bullets
- Apply numbering

Exercise 2-2

- Add a table and enter data
- Use borders and shading

Exercise 2-3

- Add a graph

Exercise 2-4

- Apply slide transitions
- Apply custom animation

Exercise 2-5

- Add sounds
- Insert graphics

Vocabulary

Key Terms
legend
transition
animation

Before You Begin

Work with a Buddy
Sometimes it can be difficult to review your own work. A fresh pair of eyes can often spot mistakes quickly. Have a partner review your presentation before you deliver it to your final audience.

In this project, you will continue to format the presentation that you began in Project 1 of this unit. Now you will enhance the presentation and make it more visually appealing by adding tables, graphics, animation, and sound.

Add Tables, Graphs, and Animation

You know that your Road Rally game will be exciting, but how do you get that across to the judges at the video game competition?

To make your presentation both interesting and informative, you will use text, as well as graphics, tables, and animation, to clearly present the game strategies and elements. Each change that you will make to the slide show is designed to help make your presentation easier to follow and understand for your audience. The judges will see the cars that players can choose and maps of the routes they can take. Special effects and sounds will add excitement to the presentation and help the judges see that your idea is the best choice.

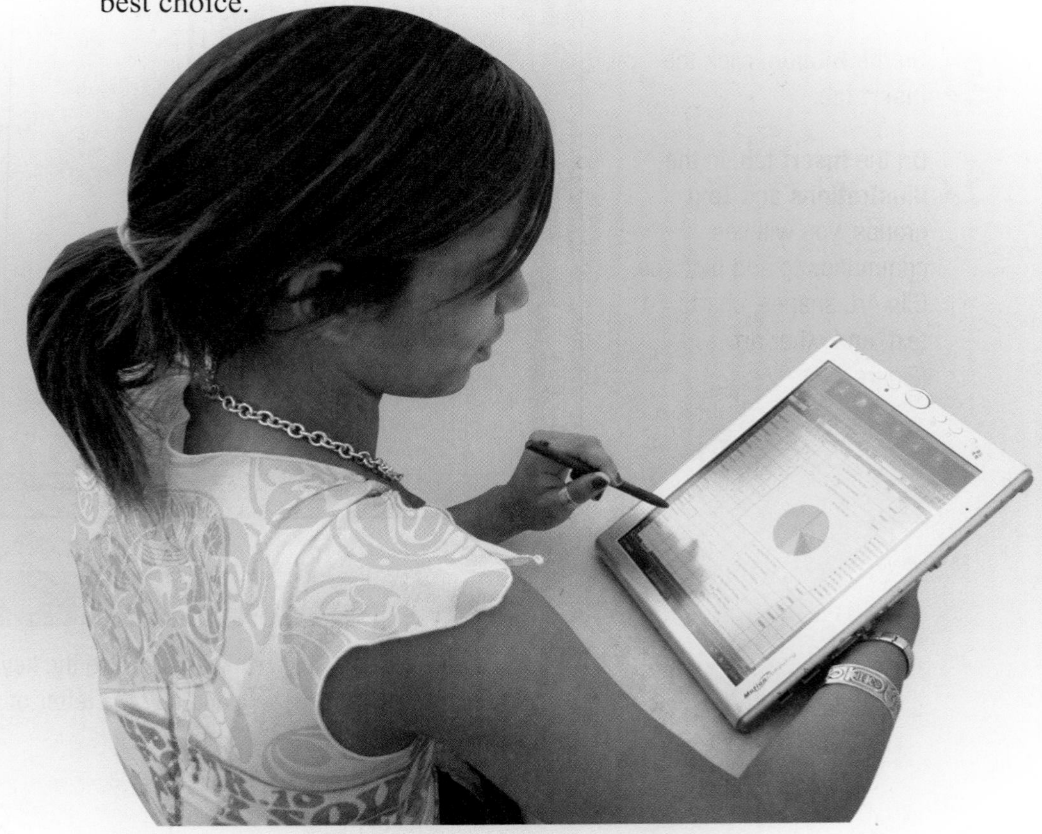

Exercise 4-1 Use WordArt to Create a Masthead

Microsoft Word can be a useful tool for **desktop publishing**. Desktop publishing applications allow you to use text, graphics, photographs, and other features to create newsletters, brochures, Web pages, and similar documents.

A good newsletter should have a masthead. A masthead is another name for the title of the publication that appears at the top of the page. Usually, the masthead will stand out from the rest of the text, using style, color, or size, to grab the reader's attention.

In this exercise, you will use WordArt to create your newsletter's masthead. **WordArt** is a feature in Microsoft Word that allows you to create colorful, eye-catching text by taking your letters or words and changing them into a picture or graphic.

Step-by-Step

1. **Open** a new Microsoft Word document.
2. Save the document as *Your Name* Newsletter.
3. On the **Ribbon**, click the **Insert** tab.
4. On the **Insert** tab, in the **Illustrations** and **Text** groups, you will see commands to add pictures, Clip Art, shapes, charts, text, and other art (Figure 4.1).

▼ **Figure 4.1** The Insert tab includes commands to insert graphic objects.

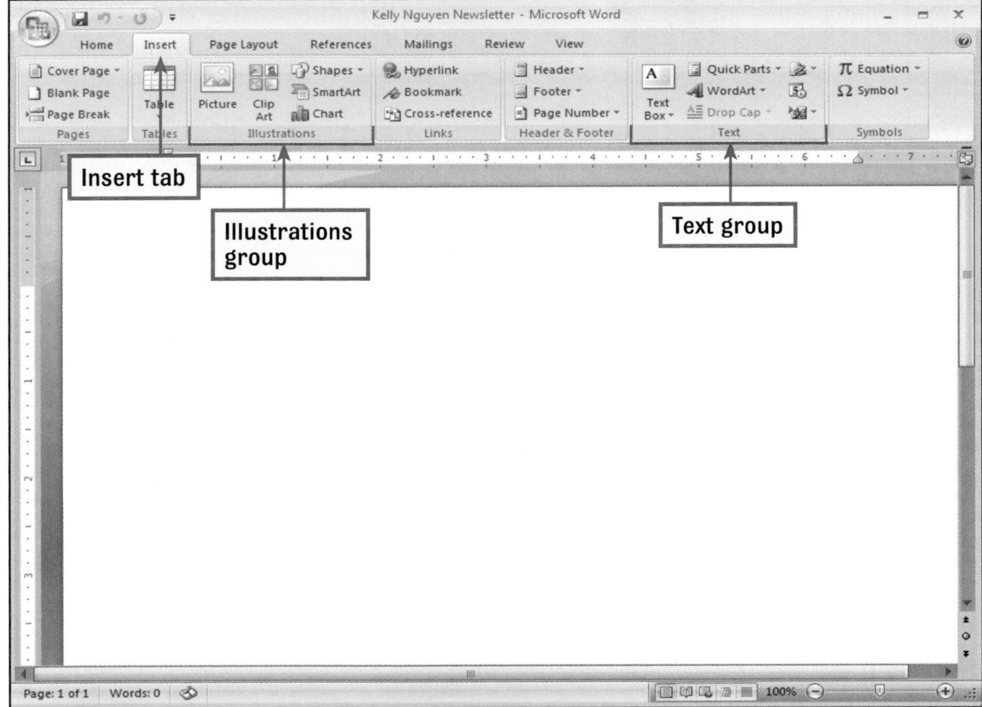

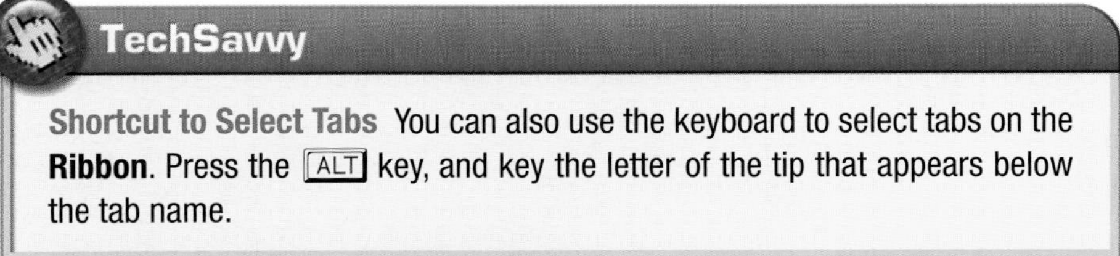

TechSavvy

Shortcut to Select Tabs You can also use the keyboard to select tabs on the **Ribbon**. Press the ALT key, and key the letter of the tip that appears below the tab name.

Exercise 2-1 Create Bulleted and Ordered Lists

Presentations are meant to deliver information in a way that is interesting and easy to understand. If a slide has too much text, the audience will have a hard time reading it while listening to the speaker, or they may find it difficult to focus on the important points. If the slide has too little text, it may not give enough information, or it may look unprofessional.

Presentations often use bulleted and numbered lists so that information can be delivered in short statements. When you use lists in a slide, remember these guidelines:

- Use bullets when the order of the elements in the list is not important.
- Use numbers when the elements need to be in order, as in the steps of a process.
- Use between four and six short bulleted or numbered statements per page. Too many items may be difficult to read.
- Use a font that is easy to read.
- Create short statements that the speaker can explain in more detail during the presentation.

In this exercise, you will apply bullets and numbering to the text on your slides. This will make it easy for the audience to read and understand the important points of your presentation.

Step-by-Step

1. **Open** your **Road Rally** presentation.
2. Click **Slide 2.**
3. Click to position the insertion point in front of the text that begins "Take place." (Figure 2.1).
4. On the **Home** tab, in the **Paragraph** group, click the **Numbering** button. Click to select the first numbering format, and change the **Color** to **Black**. Click **OK**. The text is formatted as a numbered list item.

Figure 2.1 You can number each item on a list one at a time, or you can highlight the whole list, then click the Number button.

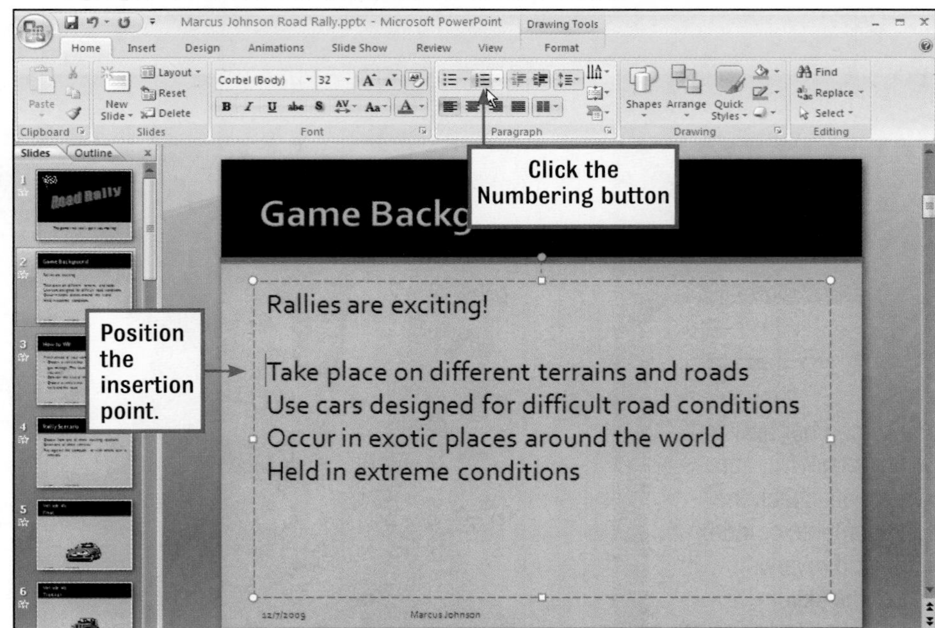

Concepts in Action

Project 4 Create a Newsletter

Key Concepts

Exercise 4-1
- Use WordArt to create a masthead

Exercise 4-2
- Create columns

Exercise 4-3
- Create a table
- Add a border and shading

Exercise 4-4
- Add a graphic

Exercise 4-5
- Use Find and Replace

Exercise 4-6
- Insert a copyright symbol

Exercise 4-7
- Save a Word document as a Web page

Vocabulary

Key Terms
desktop publishing
WordArt
table
column
row
cell

Before You Begin

Reinforce Skills If you cannot remember how to complete a task from an earlier lesson, check the Table of Contents or Index to locate and review how to complete the skill.

In this lesson, you will use a word processing program to create a newsletter about how to avoid piracy by downloading music legally.

Download Music Legally

Your computer is a powerful tool that can be used to research, to create documents, and to share music, pictures, and other files. Some people use their computers to obtain music, movies, and other documents illegally. If you violate copyright laws and terms of use agreements, it is the same as stealing. When you download music for free by file sharing, you could be committing an act of piracy, and you could get into serious trouble.

There are many options available to obtain music legally over the Internet. Your teacher wants you to inform your school about the legal options for sharing music. You decide to create a newsletter about the subject, which you will print and publish as a Web page.

5. Move the insertion point to the beginning of the next line, and repeat step 4.

6. Repeat until all the lines except the first line have numbers. See Figure 2.2.

▼ **Figure 2.2** Notice that numbered lists apply a hanging indent to text.

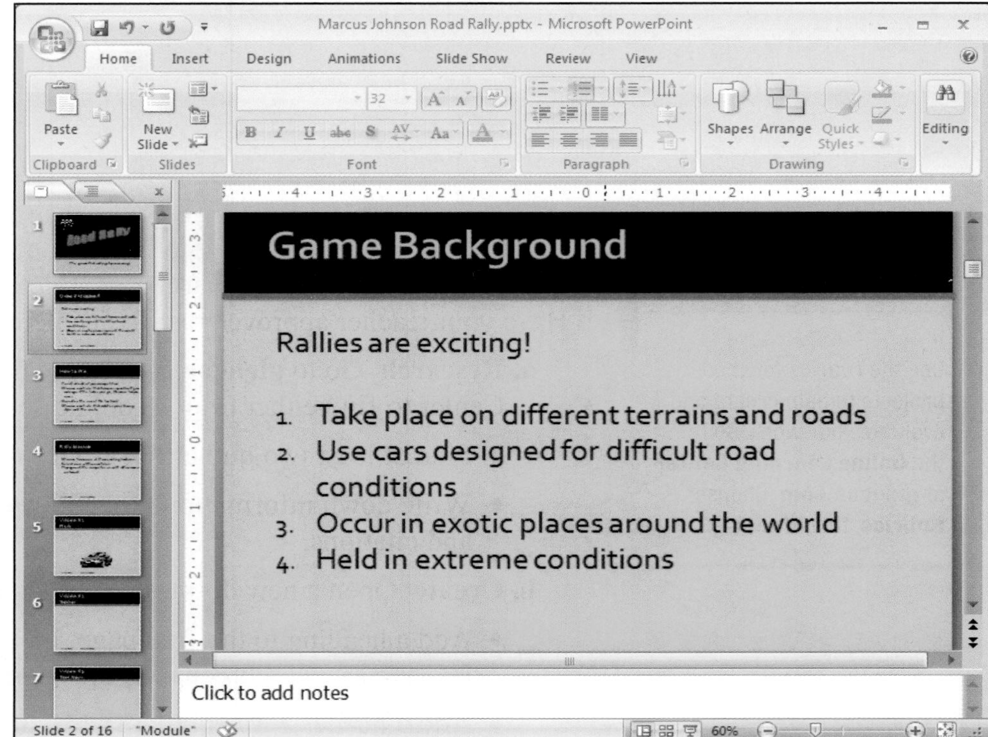

7. Click **Slide 3**.

8. Place the insertion point in front of the first line that begins "Choose a vehicle."

9. On the **Home** tab, in the **Paragraph** group, click the arrow beside the **Bullets** button. Click **Bullets and Numbering**, and click a bullet symbol. Change the bullet **Color** to **Red**. Click **OK**.

10. Repeat steps 8 and 9 for the remaining two lines (Figure 2.3).

11. Add bullets to **Slides 4**, **9**, **11**, **13**, and **16**.

12. **Save** your presentation.

▼ **Figure 2.3** Bulleted text is easier to read.

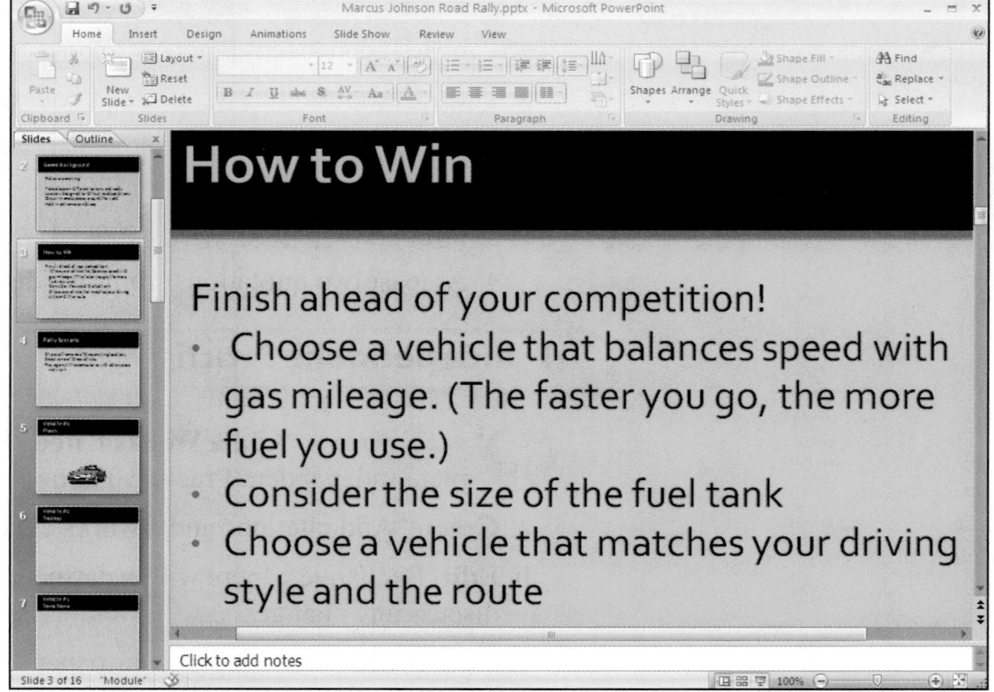

Project 3 Assessment

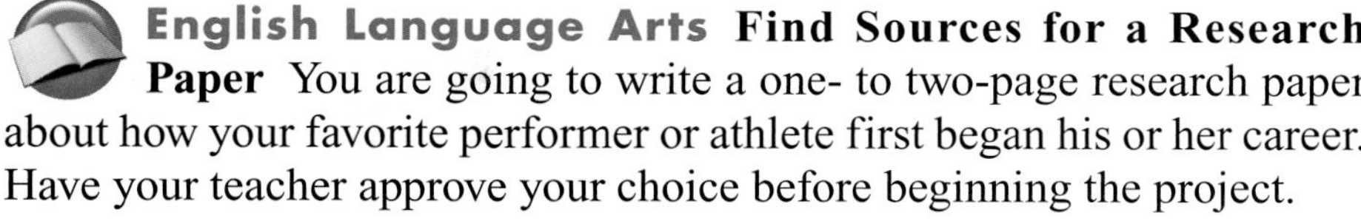

2 Independent Practice

Go Online RUBRICS

glencoe.com

Independent Practice
Use the rubrics for these projects to help create and evaluate your work. Go to the **Online Learning Center** at **glencoe.com**. Choose **Rubrics**, then **Unit 4**.

English Language Arts Find Sources for a Research Paper You are going to write a one- to two-page research paper about how your favorite performer or athlete first began his or her career. Have your teacher approve your choice before beginning the project.

a. Research Go to **glencoe.com** to the book's Online Learning Center to find either print or online sources for information.

- Find at least two quotations from two different sources.
- Write down information you will need for your works cited page and citations.

b. Create Open a new document. Save it as ***Your Name*** **Star Paper**.

- Add a heading to the first page. Include your name, your teacher's name, your class name, the date, and a title.
- Add a header with your last name and page number to all pages.

3 Independent Practice

English Language Arts Write and Format Your Paper Complete Independent Practice 2 above and continue with this project.

a. Plan Compose the first draft of your paper.

b. Create Create an MLA style paper, using the research about your favorite performer or athlete. Include:

- One to two pages, double spaced and properly formatted.
- At least two quotations from two different sources.

4 Independent Practice

Teamwork Add a Works Cited Page and Edit Your Paper Complete Independent Practice 3 above and continue with this project.

a. Create Add citations and a works cited page for the sources used.

b. Edit Exchange papers with a partner, make corrections, and discuss any changes.

c. Revise Make changes to your paper to create a final draft.

Exercise 2-2 Insert a Table

You want your presentation to show the cars that players can choose in the video game. Each car will look different and have different features. Some might work better for a rally in one terrain but not in another. By offering different car choices, your game will be more exciting and your players will not all have to drive the same cars. To clearly show each car's features, you can create a table for your presentation. The table will organize this information so that players can easily decide which car they like best.

In this exercise, you will add a table to a slide. It will show information about what makes each car unique, including gas mileage, fuel tank size, and top speed.

Step-by-Step

1. Click **Slide 5**.
2. Locate and click the **Insert Table** icon in the **Click to Add Text** placeholder (Figure 2.4).
3. In the **Insert Table** box, key 3 for the **columns** and key 2 for the **rows**. Click **OK**.

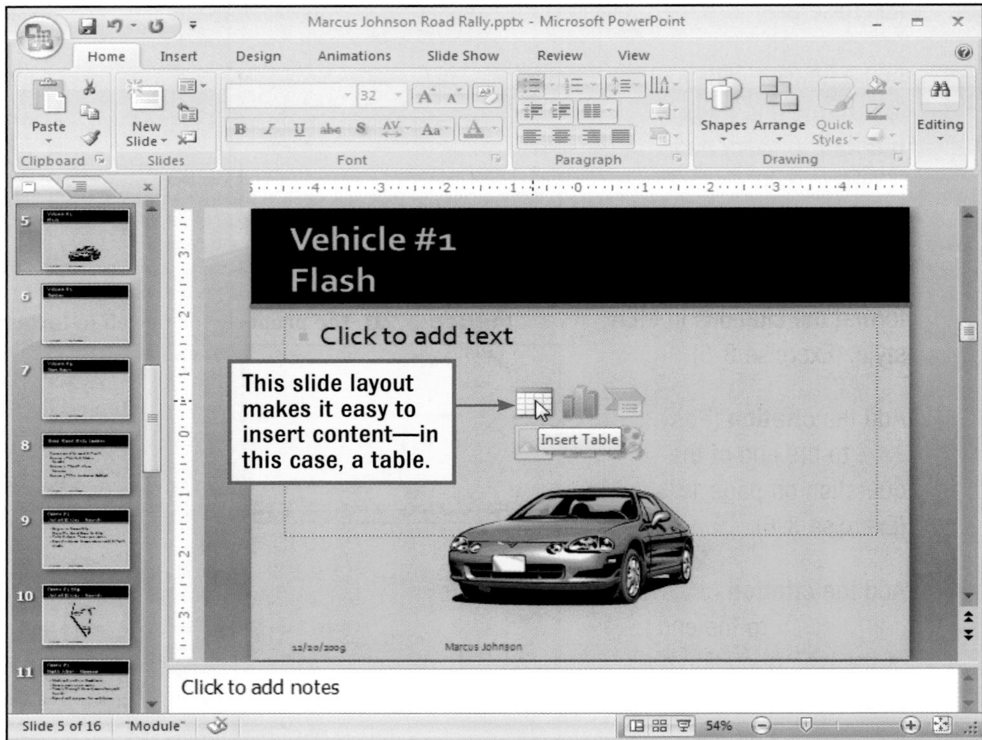

▼ **Figure 2.4** Use the Insert Table icon to add a table.

TechSavvy

Layout Designs Microsoft PowerPoint provides several slide layout designs. When you click the top portion of the **New Slide** button, a **Title and Content** slide layout is inserted automatically. If you click the bottom portion of the **New Slide** button, you can select a slide layout for the new slide. To change the layout of an existing slide, click the arrow beside the **Layout** button.

Project 3 Assessment

5. **Indent** the long quotation **1″** from the margin. (Exercise 3-2)

6. Add a **heading** that includes your name, your teacher's name, your class name, and today's date (Figure 3.19). (Exercise 3-3)

7. Add the **title,** On Top of the World. **Center** the title. (Exercise 3-3)

8. Add a **header** with your **last name** and **page number** to every page. (Exercise 3-4)

9. Add a **page break** before the **works cited list** and format the citations in MLA style. (Exercise 3-5)

10. Add the **citation** (Boehm 152) to the end of the quotation on page 1. (Exercise 3-6)

11. Add the **citation** (Maximilian) to the end of the long quotation on page 2 (Figure 3.20). (Exercise 3-6)

12. **Save** your document.

Figure 3.19 The properly formatted heading and title should look like this.

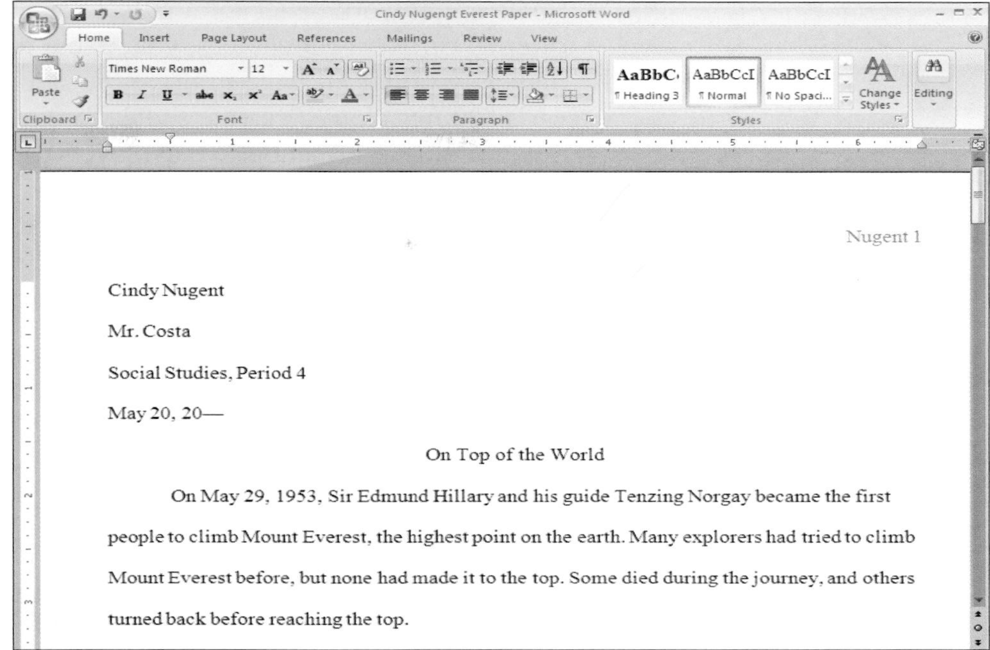

Figure 3.20 The properly formatted in-text citation should look like this.

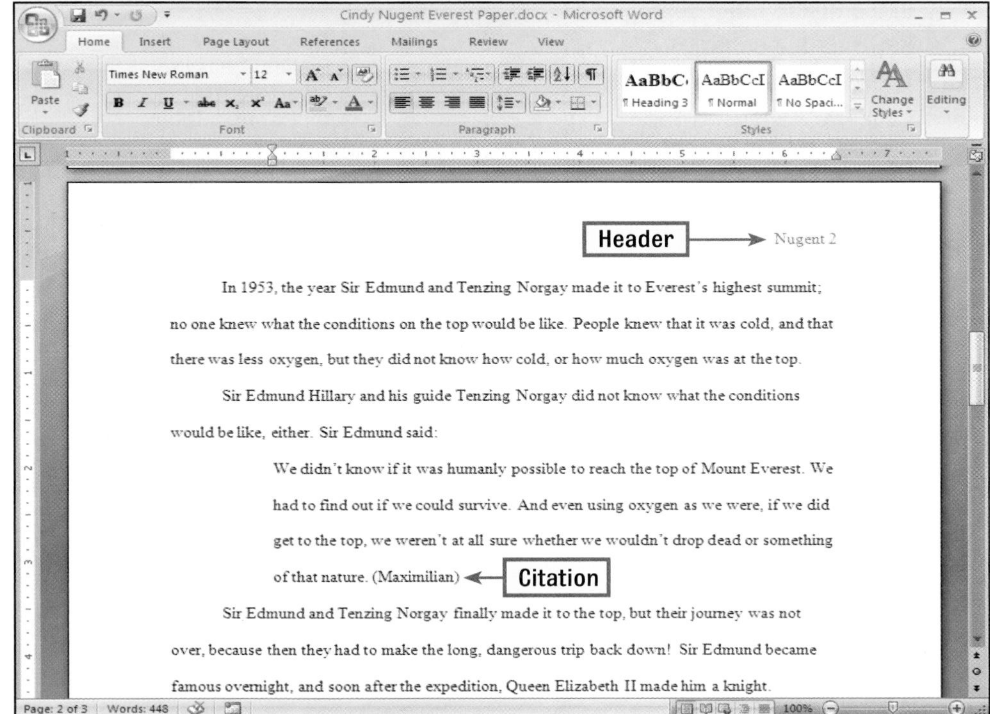

4 Enter the information into the table, as shown in Figure 2.5.

5 Select the text in the table. Change the **Font Size** to **24** pt. and the **Font Color** to **Black**. Click the **Align Center** button.

6 Click the border of the table to select the table.

▼ **Figure 2.5** After formatting the text in the table, your slide should look like this.

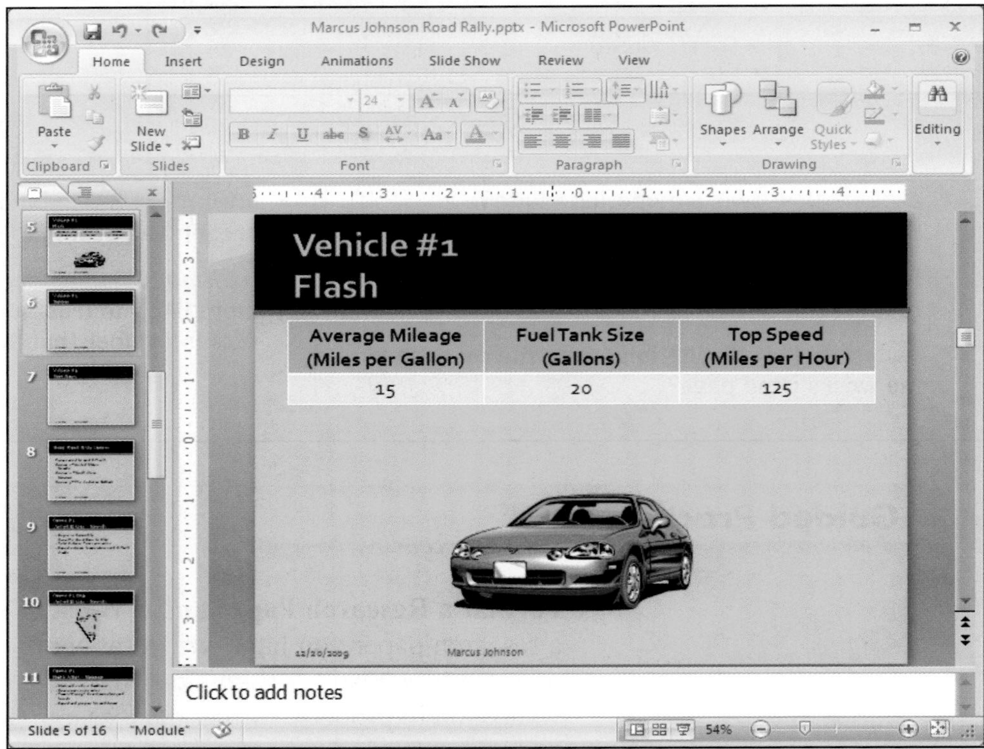

7 On the **Table Tools Layout** tab, in the **Alignment** group, click the **Center Vertically** button (Figure 2.6).

8 On the **Table Tools Design** tab, in the **Table Styles** group, click the **More** button to display the **Table Styles Gallery**.

9 Click the **Red** thumbnail in the first row.

▼ **Figure 2.6** Use the Table Tools Design and Layout tabs to format tables.

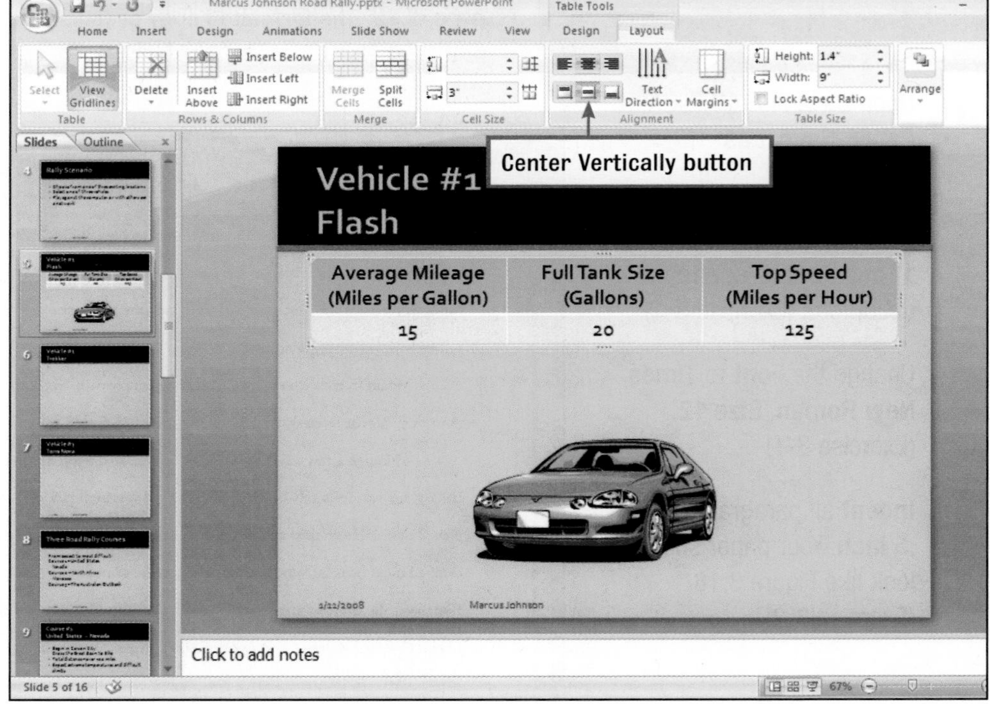

Project 3 Assessment

Key Concepts Check

1. **Explain** How does a quotation relate to a citation?
2. **Identify** How do headers and footers help the readers?
3. **Describe** How do citations refer the reader to the works cited page?

Critical Thinking

4. **Evaluate** Why is standard formatting important in creating a document like a research paper?
5. **Drawing Conclusions** Why would a reader be more likely to trust a paper that cites sources versus a paper that does not?

1 Guided Practice

Format a Research Paper and a Works Cited List You need to format a research paper you have written about the first people to reach the top of Mount Everest, Sir Edmund Hillary and Tenzing Norgay. Your teacher wants you to properly format the research paper and include a heading, a header, and a works cited page. All quotations must be cited. If you need help, refer back to the exercise in parentheses at the end of the step.

Step-by-Step

1. Open **Data File 4G Everest Paper**. **Save** it as *Your Name* Everest Paper.
2. Change the margins to **1″** and **double-space** the document. (Exercise 3-1)
3. Change the **Font** to **Times New Roman**, **Size 12**. (Exercise 3-1)
4. **Indent** all paragraphs **.5 inch**. Your paper should look like Figure 3.18. (Exercise 3-2)

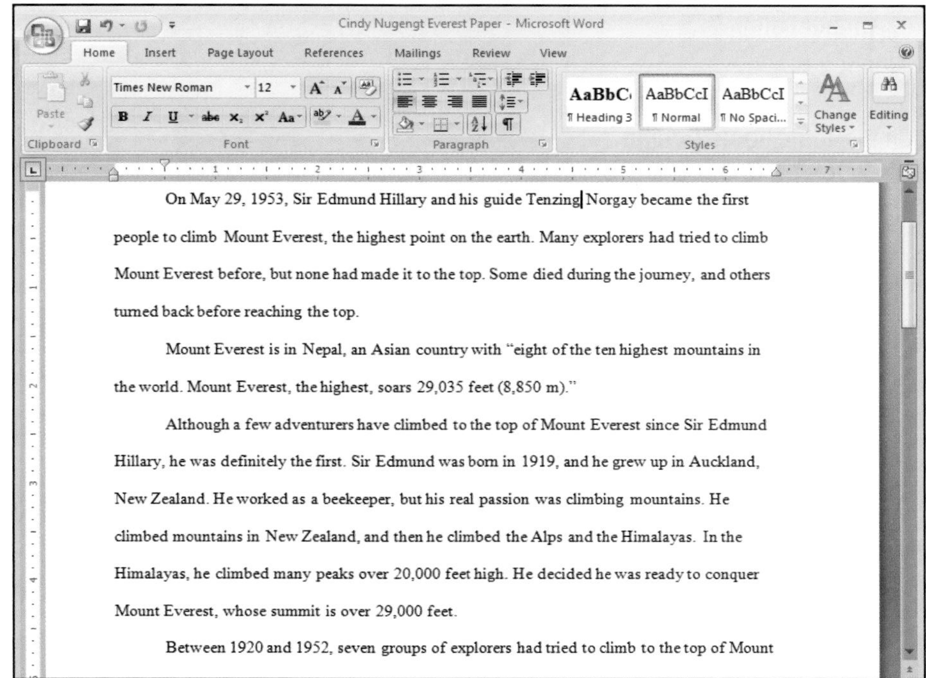

On May 29, 1953, Sir Edmund Hillary and his guide Tenzing Norgay became the first people to climb Mount Everest, the highest point on the earth. Many explorers had tried to climb Mount Everest before, but none had made it to the top. Some died during the journey, and others turned back before reaching the top.

Mount Everest is in Nepal, an Asian country with "eight of the ten highest mountains in the world. Mount Everest, the highest, soars 29,035 feet (8,850 m)."

Although a few adventurers have climbed to the top of Mount Everest since Sir Edmund Hillary, he was definitely the first. Sir Edmund was born in 1919, and he grew up in Auckland, New Zealand. He worked as a beekeeper, but his real passion was climbing mountains. He climbed mountains in New Zealand, and then he climbed the Alps and the Himalayas. In the Himalayas, he climbed many peaks over 20,000 feet high. He decided he was ready to conquer Mount Everest, whose summit is over 29,000 feet.

Between 1920 and 1952, seven groups of explorers had tried to climb to the top of Mount

▼ **Figure 3.18** The formatted body of your paper should look like this document.

10 **Select** the table you created in **Slide 5**.

11 On the **Home** tab, in the **Clipboard** group, click the **Copy** button.

12 Click **Slide 6**, and click the **placeholder border** to select it as shown in Figure 2.7.

13 **Paste** the table into **Slide 6**.

Figure 2.7 Paste the table into Slide 6.

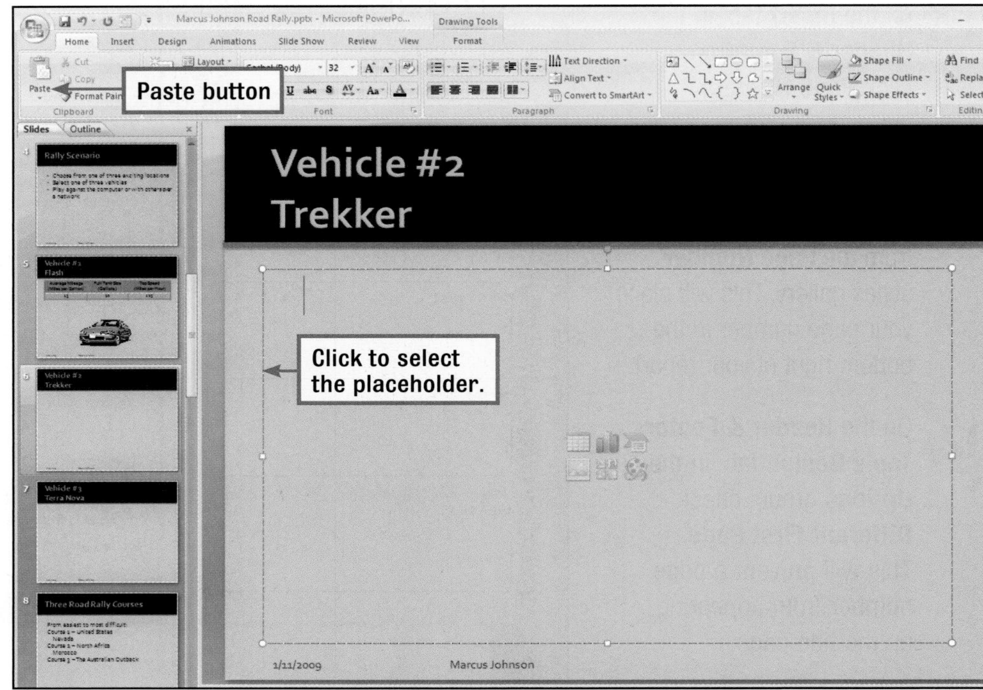

14 **Paste** the same table into **Slide 7**.

15 Enter the information into both tables, as shown in Figure 2.8.

16 **Save** your work.

Figure 2.8 The data in the tables in Slides 6 and 7 should look like this.

10 To insert page numbers, on the **Insert** tab, in the **Header & Footer** group, click **Page Number**.

11 In the drop-down list, click **Bottom of Page**, and then choose **Plain Number 3** from the **Page Number** styles gallery. This will place your page number in the bottom right of your report.

12 On the **Header & Footer Tools Design** tab, in the **Options** group, check **Different First Page**. This will prevent a page number from appearing on the title page.

13 On the Ribbon, locate the **Header & Footer** group. Click the **Page Number** button.

14 Click **Format Page Numbers** to display the **Page Number Format** dialog box.

15 Click **Start at**. Then click the **Down Arrow** to start the numbering at 0 (Figure 3.16). Click **OK**. Click the **Close Header and Footer** button.

16 The numbering in your document should start at 1 on the second page. See Figure 3.17. There should be no number on the title page. **Save** and **close** your document. **Exit Word**.

Figure 3.16 Use the Insert menu to insert page numbers in a footer.

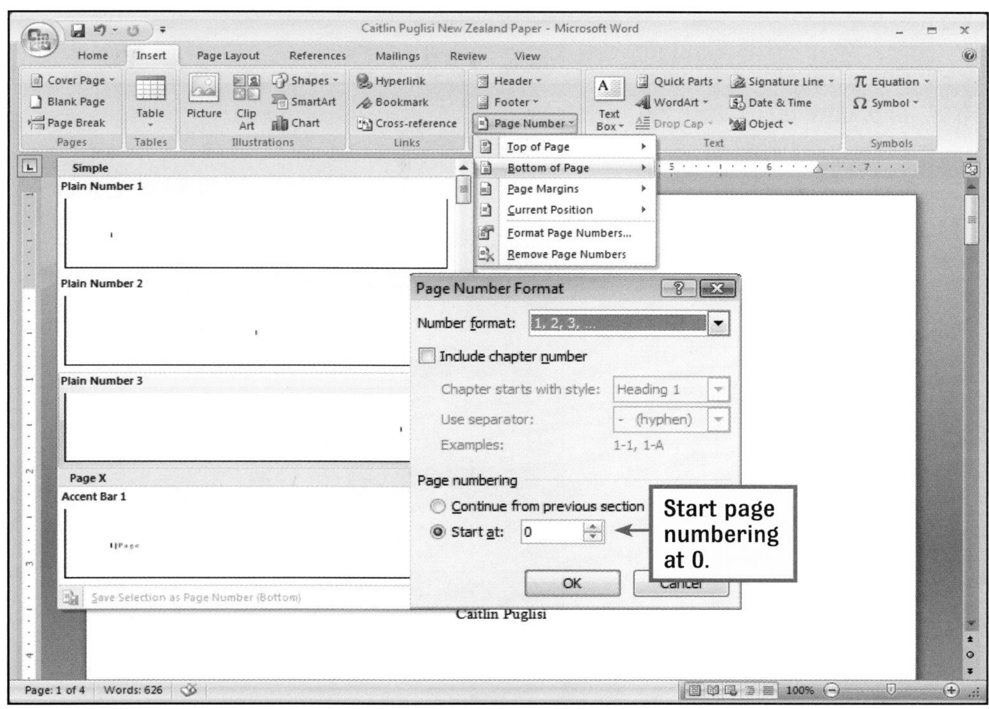

Figure 3.17 The title page does not have a number. The second page is page 1.

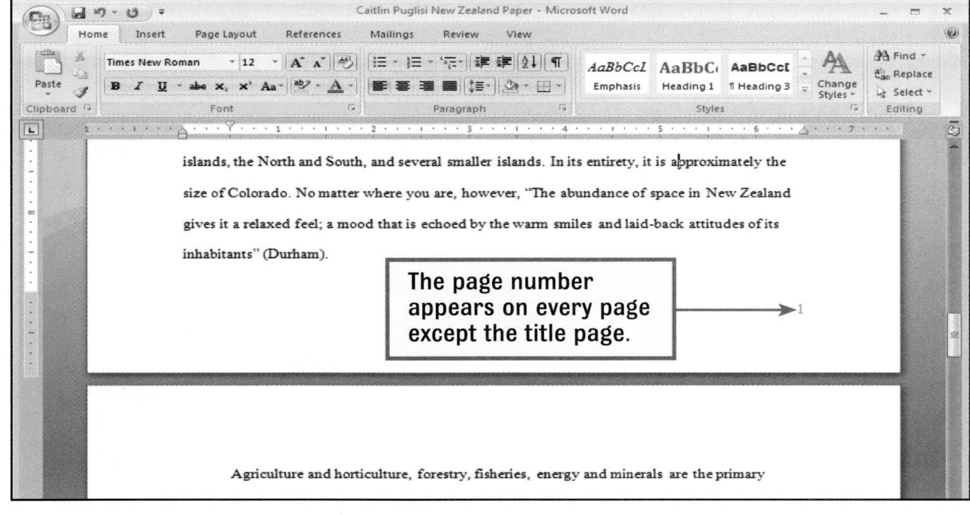

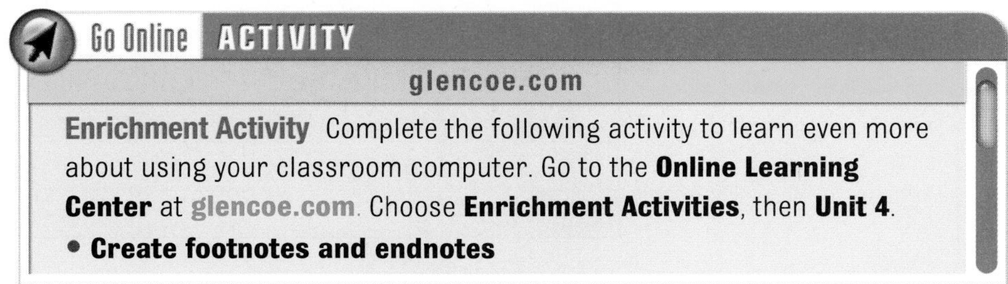

Exercise 2-3 Create a Graph

Graphs, also known as charts, are useful because they communicate complex information in a visual way.

Microsoft PowerPoint uses the following tools to create a graph:

- A **spreadsheet** displays graph data.
- A **chart type** refers to how the information is displayed. Examples include line, bar, and pie charts.
- A **legend** identifies the different data in the chart.

In this exercise, you will add a bar chart to your *Road Rally* presentation. It will compare the fuel mileage (how many miles per gallon the car gets) and fuel tank capacity (how many gallons of fuel the gas tank will hold) for the three cars in the game.

Step-by-Step

1. In your Road Rally presentation, click **Slide 15**.
2. On the **Insert** tab, in the **Illustrations** group, click the **Insert Chart** button. Click the first thumbnail in the **Column** chart type group, and click **OK**.
3. Drag the data range border to include the range A1:C4.
4. Select the text in cells D1 through D5, and right-click the data. Click **Clear Contents** (Figure 2.9). Delete the data in cells in A5 through C5.

▼ **Figure 2.9** Size the data range, and edit the sample data.

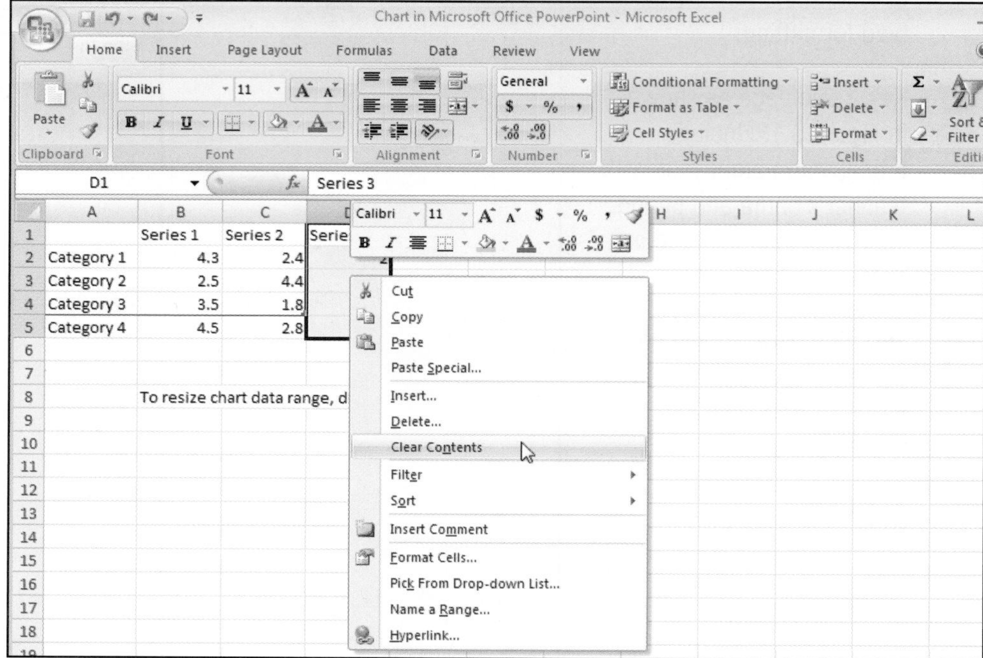

TechSavvy

Add Charts You can add a chart directly to a PowerPoint slide by clicking the **Insert** tab and clicking the **Chart** button. You can also create tables, charts, and graphs in Excel or Word and paste them into PowerPoint.

5 Press the **Up Arrow** [↑] on your keyboard to move to the top of the new page. Your insertion point should be centered.

6 On the **Home** tab, in the **Paragraph** group, click the **Paragraph Dialog Box Launcher**. Change the **Line Spacing** to **Single**, if necessary. Change the **Spacing Before** to **0 pt**, and change the **Spacing After** to **0 pt**. Click **OK**.

7 Key the title. Click the **Bold** button **B** to turn off the bold formatting.

8 Key a title page as shown in Figure 3.15. Include a title, your name, your teacher's name and period, your class name, and the date.

9 Your title page should be centered horizontally and vertically. It should look like Figure 3.15.

▼ **Figure 3.15** **A title page identifies the name of the paper, the writer, and other important information.**

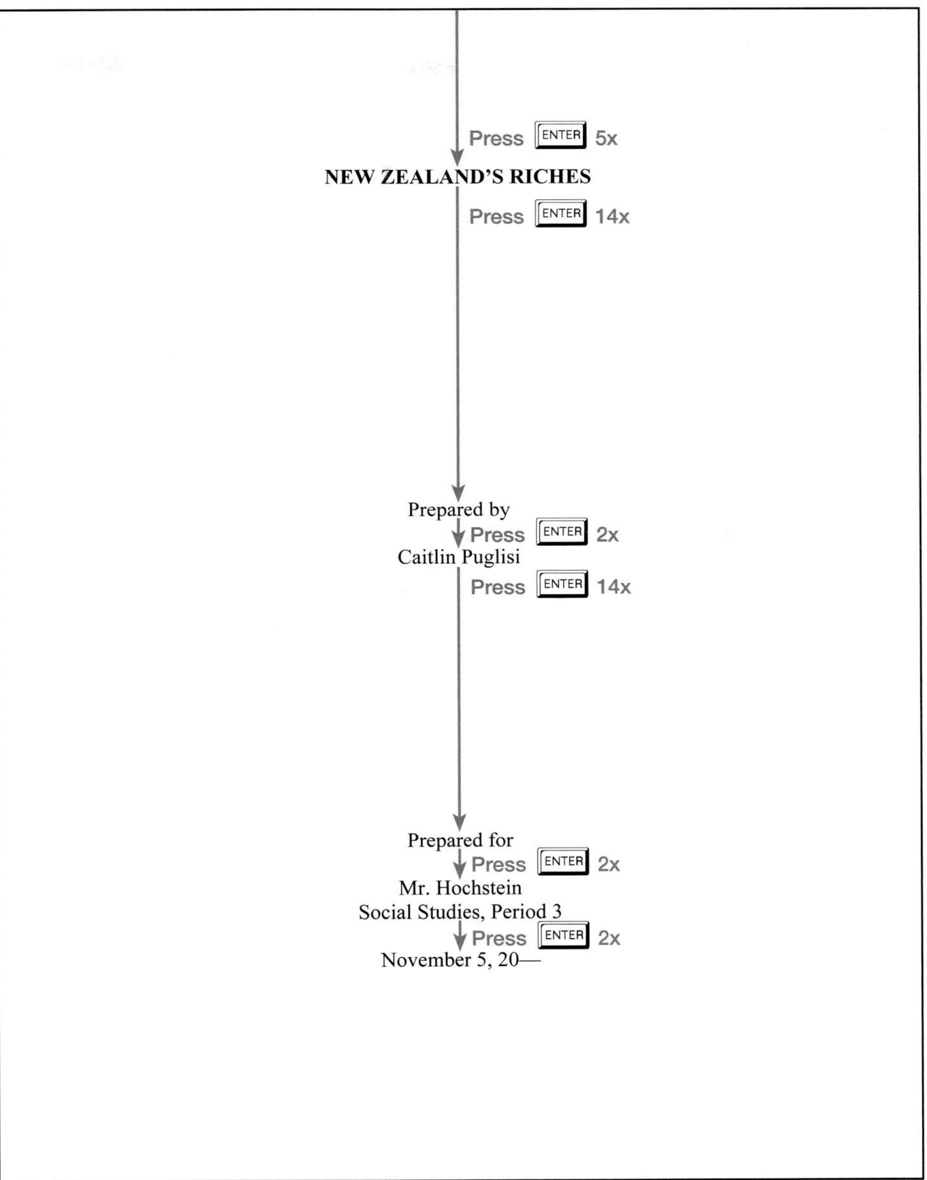

TechSavvy

Page and Section Breaks A *hard page break* is when you start a new page at a specific point by using CTRL + ENTER. A *soft page break* is an automatic page break that is created when the text goes past the end of a page. You can also enter a hard page break from the **Page Layout** tab, **Breaks** command. A *section break* allows you to use different formatting styles in different parts of a document.

5 Key the information into the spreadsheet as shown in Figure 2.10.

6 **AutoFit** the width of the cells. Place your mouse pointer on the divider line between columns **A** and **B** so that the double arrow ⟷ appears. **Double-click** the line to fit to the most efficient width (Figure 2.10).

7 Minimize the spreadsheet window.

8 On the **Chart Tools Design** tab, in the **Data** group, click the **Switch Row/ Column** button. **Close** the spreadsheet window.

9 On the **Chart Tools Design** tab, in the **Chart Styles** group, click the **More** button to display the **Chart Styles** gallery. Click **Style 42**.

10 Your finished slide should look like Figure 2.11.

11 **Save** your work.

Figure 2.10 Use the AutoFit feature to automatically size a column.

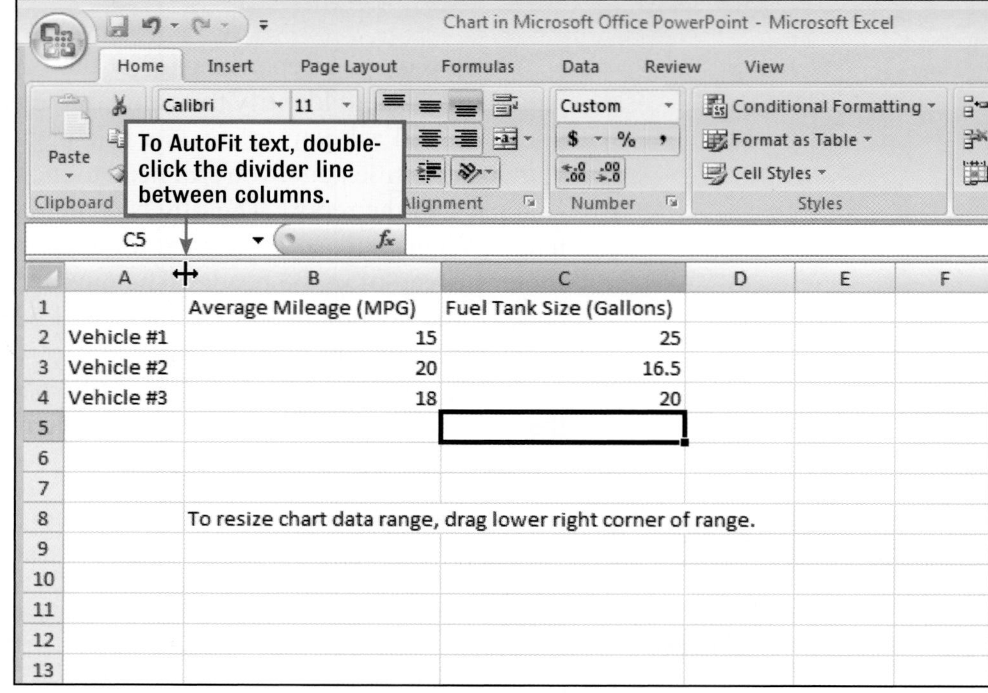

Figure 2.11 The chart is now created in the slide.

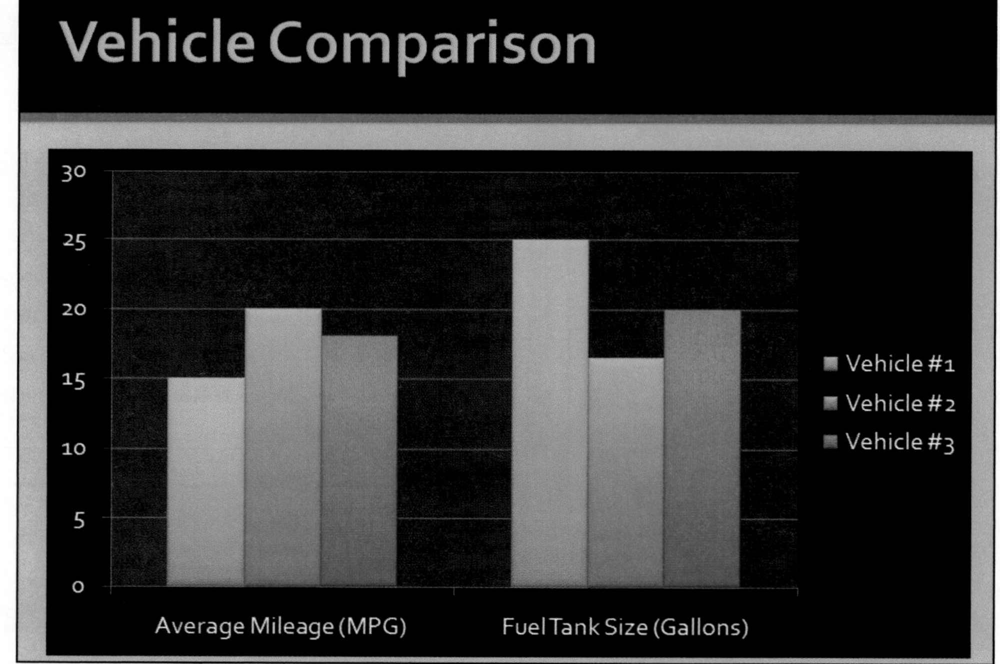

Exercise 3-7 Create a Title Page and Footer

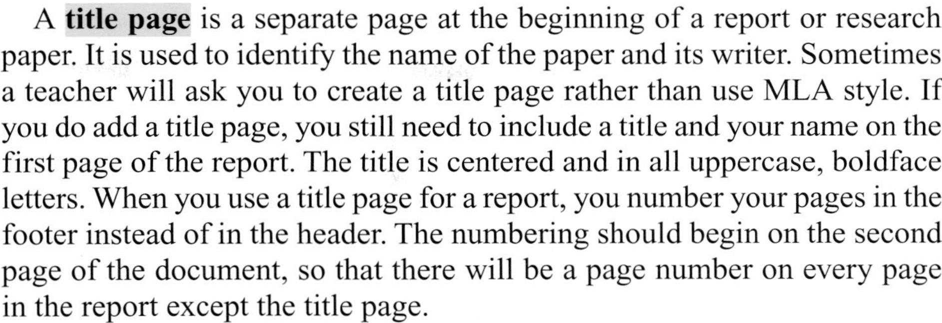

A **title page** is a separate page at the beginning of a report or research paper. It is used to identify the name of the paper and its writer. Sometimes a teacher will ask you to create a title page rather than use MLA style. If you do add a title page, you still need to include a title and your name on the first page of the report. The title is centered and in all uppercase, boldface letters. When you use a title page for a report, you number your pages in the footer instead of in the header. The numbering should begin on the second page of the document, so that there will be a page number on every page in the report except the title page.

In this exercise, you will insert a title page in a report. You will also use the Insert menu to add a footer with page numbers.

Step-by-Step

1. **Open** the **Data File** named **4F New Zealand Paper**.
2. **Save** the file **as** *Your Name New Zealand Paper*.
3. Place your insertion point at the beginning of the document.
4. Press CTRL + ENTER to insert a hard page break. **Note:** You can also click the **Insert** tab, and in the **Pages** group, click the **Blank Page** button to add a page to the document (Figure 3.14).

Figure 3.14 When you insert a page before another page, the new page will have the same formatting as the text where you placed your insertion point.

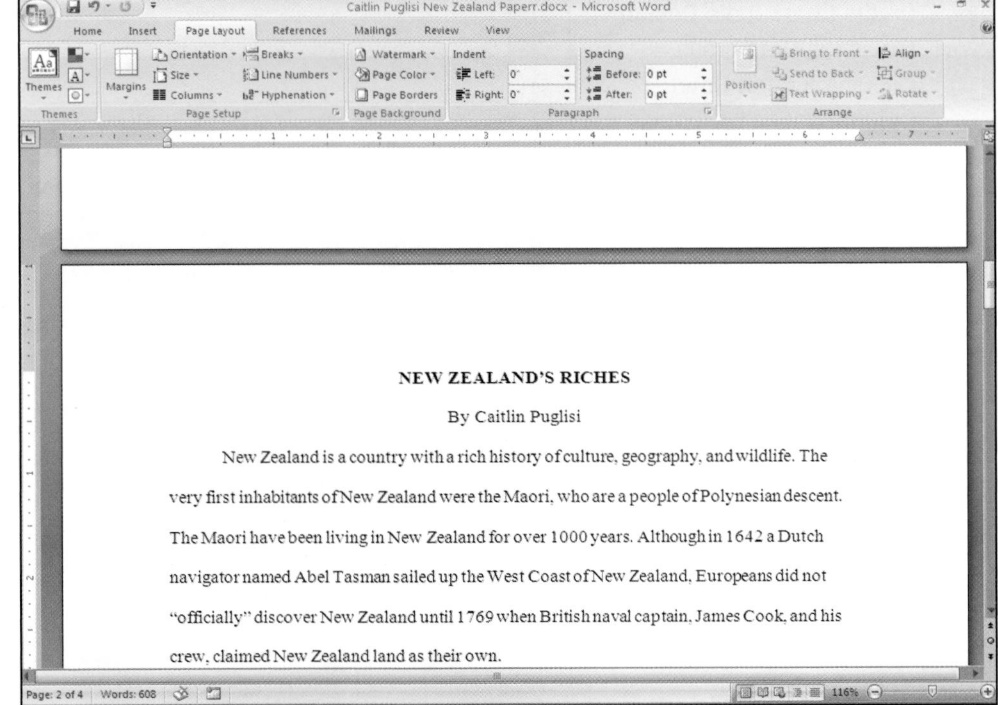

TechSavvy

Title Page or Heading? Ask your teacher if you should format your research report or paper using a title page or the MLA-style heading shown in Exercise 3-3.

Exercise 2-4 Apply Transitions and Animation

You are ready to apply the finishing touches to your presentation. Adding transitions and animation are ways of attracting your audience's attention.

A **transition** is an effect that occurs when you move from one slide to the next. For example, you might want your text to fade in when you move to a new slide. **Animation** refers to effects that are used to display text or other objects on a slide. You can have bullet points appear one by one, or have them glide in from the side.

Transitions and animation can make your presentation more interesting, but if they are used too much, they can be distracting. Here are some design tips to keep in mind:

- Use animation for impact, but only sparingly.
- Apply only one style of slide transition to your presentation.
- Use animation and transitions to help your audience understand the content better, not just to entertain.

In this exercise, you will apply transitions between slides and apply a custom animation to the text on all of your slides.

Step-by-Step

1. Click **Slide 1**.

2. On the **Animations** tab, in the **Transition to This Slide** group, click the **More** button (Figure 2.12).

Figure 2.12 Use the Animations tab to apply slide transitions.

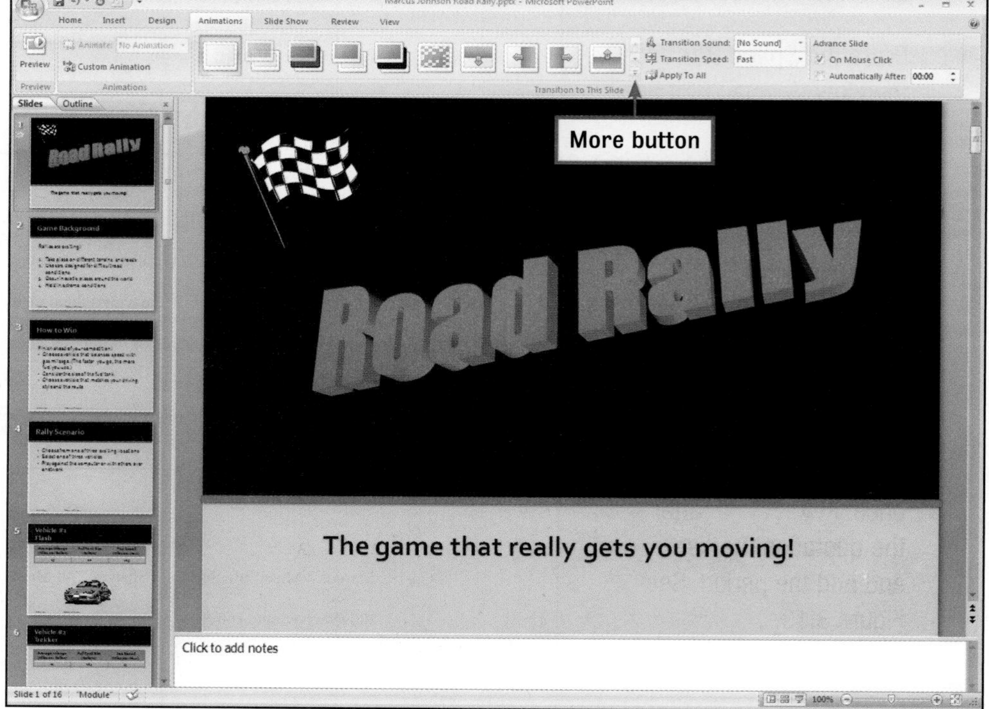

Exercise 3-6 Cite Sources in Your Paper

A works cited page lists all the sources you cited in the body of your research paper. In the body of the paper, you should include an in-text citation that clearly shows which listed source you used for your quotations or information. Cite your source whether you quote someone exactly or rewrite the information in your own words (paraphrase).

Following MLA guidelines, sources are credited at the end of the quotation or cited material. In parentheses, add the author's name and (if it is a print source) the page number where you found the information. For example, if you see the citation (Smith 12) in a paper, you would look for the author Smith in the works cited list and know that the information was from page 12 of Smith's book.

In this exercise, you will create in-text citations in the body of the paper to direct readers to your works cited list.

Step-by-Step

1. In your **Research Paper**, place the insertion point at the end of the indented quotation after the period.
2. Press the **Space Bar** once, then key (Kenna 262). See Figure 3.13.
3. Delete the period at the end of quotation that ends with **copyright holder**. Next, position your insertion point after the ending quotation mark (Figure 3.13).
4. Press the **Space Bar** once. Key (Garcia) after the quotation marks and add the period. See Figure 3.13.
5. **Save** your document.

▼ **Figure 3.13 The in-text citations refer the reader to the works cited list at the end of the document.**

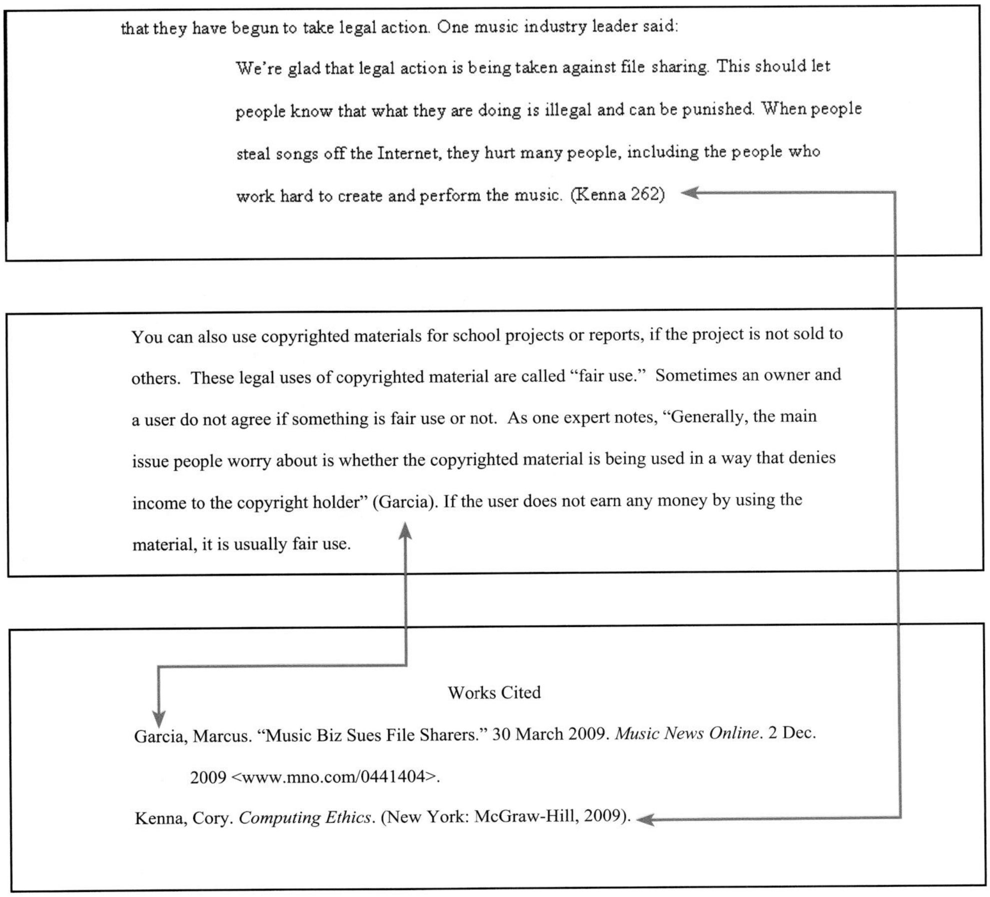

that they have begun to take legal action. One music industry leader said:

> We're glad that legal action is being taken against file sharing. This should let people know that what they are doing is illegal and can be punished. When people steal songs off the Internet, they hurt many people, including the people who work hard to create and perform the music. (Kenna 262)

You can also use copyrighted materials for school projects or reports, if the project is not sold to others. These legal uses of copyrighted material are called "fair use." Sometimes an owner and a user do not agree if something is fair use or not. As one expert notes, "Generally, the main issue people worry about is whether the copyrighted material is being used in a way that denies income to the copyright holder" (Garcia). If the user does not earn any money by using the material, it is usually fair use.

Works Cited

Garcia, Marcus. "Music Biz Sues File Sharers." 30 March 2009. *Music News Online*. 2 Dec. 2009 <www.mno.com/0441404>.

Kenna, Cory. *Computing Ethics*. (New York: McGraw-Hill, 2009).

3 Locate the **Wipes** category, and point to several transition effects to see a preview. Click the **Wipe Down** transition effect in the first row in the **Wipes** category (Figure 2.13).

4 On the Ribbon, click the **Apply To All** button. Click **Slide Show**.

5 Press ENTER to advance to the next slide, and press ESC to end the slide show.

6 Click the **Animations** tab, if necessary. Click **Slide 1**, and click to select the flag graphic.

7 On the **Animations** tab, in the **Animations** group, click the **Custom Animation** button to display the **Custom Animation** pane (Figure 2.14).

8 Click the **Add Effect** button, and click the arrow beside **Entrance**. Click the **Fly-In** effect, and observe the preview.

9 Select the Road Rally placeholder, and apply the Diamond Entrance effect. Apply an animation effect to the subtitle.

10 Close the Custom Animation pane. **Note**: Each object on a slide can be animated. Use animations to emphasize and draw attention. Be careful not to use too many animations.

Figure 2.13 Use transitions to apply a finishing touch to your presentation. Experiment with different speeds.

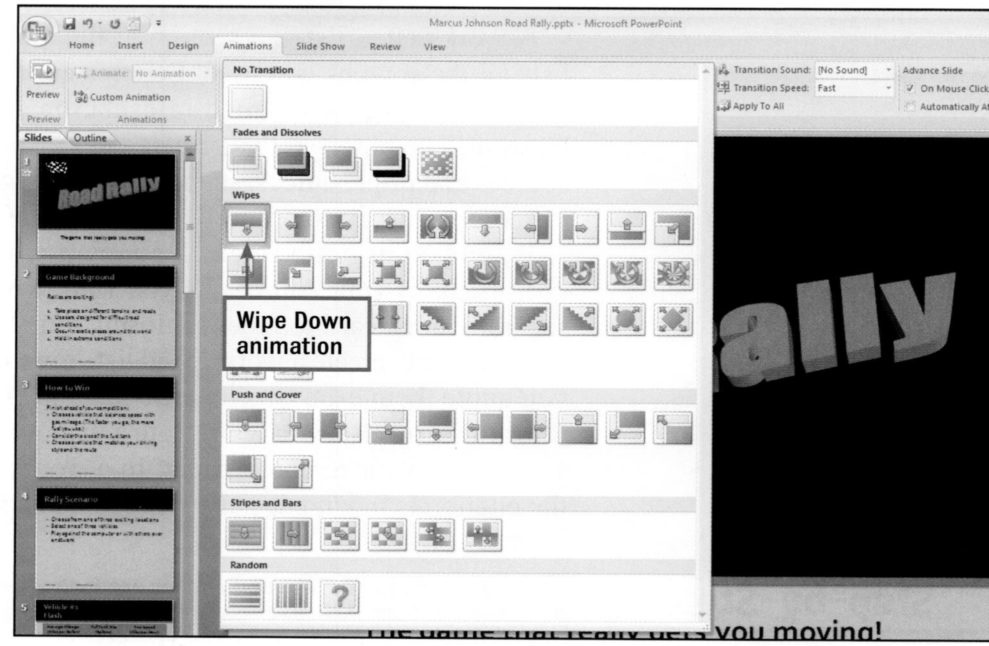

Figure 2.14 Animation can be another way to keep your audience's attention.

Exercise 3-5 Create a Works Cited Page

A works cited list is a section at the end of your research paper that lists all the sources you used. Sources are listed in alphabetical order by author's name. The detailed information about each source is called a **citation**. The report in this project cites different types of sources: online sources and print sources, such as books, magazines, and newspapers. Use the correct format to properly cite each type of source.

When you begin to research a topic for a report or paper, you should keep track of your sources as you find them. It is a good idea to use a separate index card to record information about each source so that later you can easily create a works cited list. You must cite your sources whether you quote them exactly or rewrite them in your own words.

In this exercise, you will create a works cited page to give credit to the sources for your research paper. In a works cited list, the second line of the citation is indented. This is called a hanging indent.

Step-by-Step

1. In your research paper, place your insertion point before the subtitle **Works Cited** near the end of your document.
2. Press CTRL + ENTER to insert a hard page break.
3. Select the two sources in the works cited list.
4. On the ruler, click and drag the bottom indent marker to the half-inch mark, as shown in Figure 3.12.
5. **Save** your document. Your works cited page should look like Figure 3.12.

▼ **Figure 3.12** **Works cited entries are formatted with a hanging indent.**

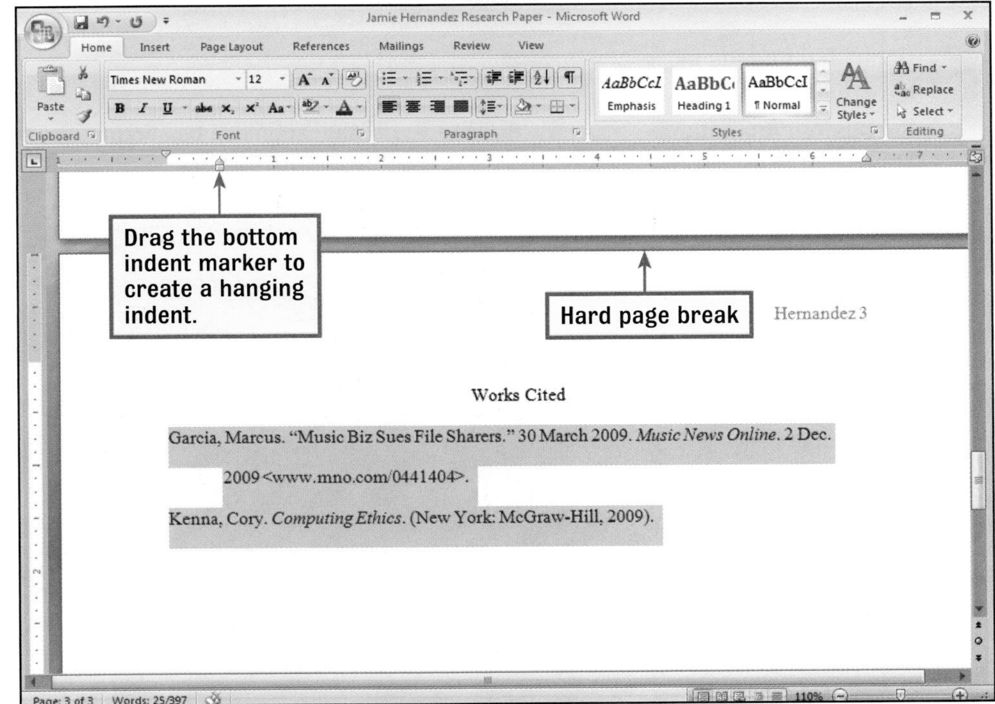

HELP!

Indent Markers To create a hanging indent, move the bottom part of the marker on the ruler. To indent the first line, move the top marker on the ruler.

Exercise 2-5

Add Sound and Graphics

Sound can be an effective tool in delivering a good presentation. It can be used for impact when displaying a specific slide, or it can set the mood for the whole presentation. You can even use background music as the sound for a presentation.

Graphics, or images, are often included in a presentation to add interest and appeal. Graphics can include drawings, charts, diagrams, paintings, and photographs. A type of graphic that is easy to use in a presentation is clip art. Clip Art is available as part of the PowerPoint application and can also be found on the Internet.

In this exercise, you will add a sound file to grab the audience's attention and signal the close of your presentation. You will also add pictures of the cars people can choose in your game.

Step-by-Step

1. Click **Slide 16**.

2. On the **Insert** tab, in the **Media Clips** group, click the arrow on the **Sound** button . Click **Sound from Clip Organizer** (Figure 2.15).

3. In the **Clip Art** task pane, key applause in the **Search for** text box, then click **Go**.

Figure 2.15 The Clip Art pane lets you search for various sounds on your computer or on the Web.

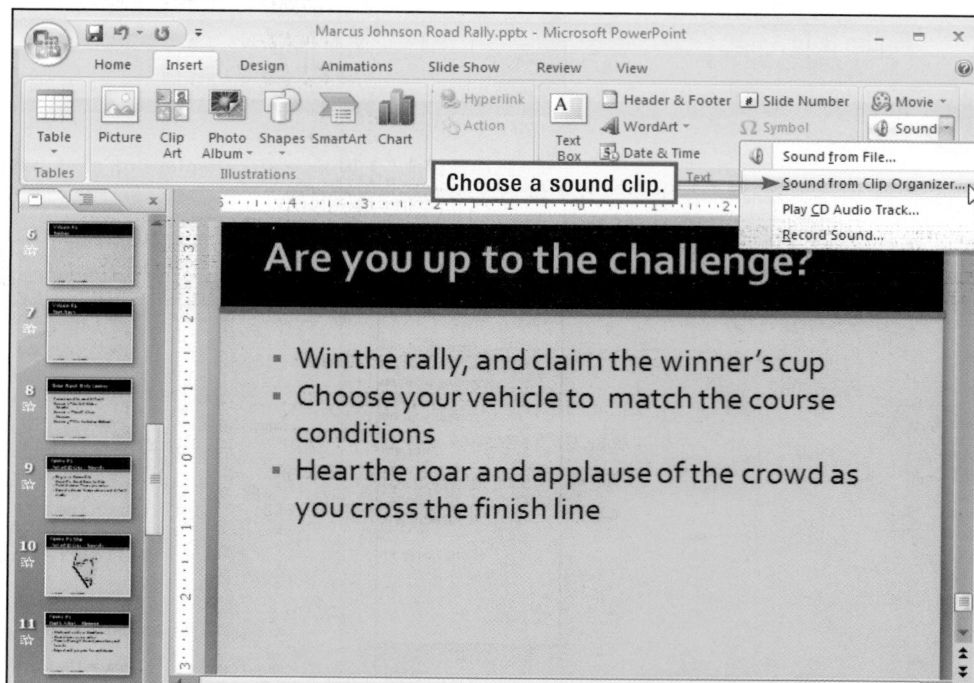

TechSavvy

Add Photos You can use your own images in PowerPoint. For example, take a digital photograph of a nice landscape, upload the image into your Documents folder, then use the Browse function to insert the picture into your presentation.

6. On the **Header & Footer Tools Design** tab, in the **Position** group, verify that the **Header Position from Top** and the **Footer Position from Bottom** are set at **0.5″** (Figure 3.10).

7. Click the **Close Header and Footer** button.

8. Your research paper should have headers on the two pages.

9. Make sure the top of each page looks like Figure 3.11.

10. **Save** your document.

▼ **Figure 3.10** Use the Header and Footer Tools tab to verify header and footer settings.

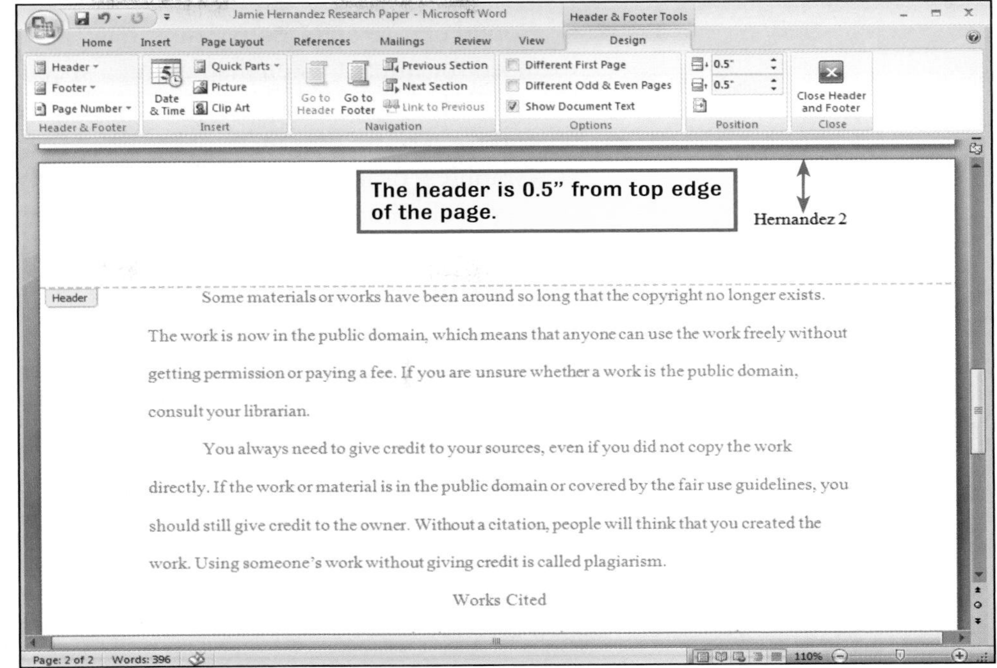

▼ **Figure 3.11** The header displays on each page of the report.

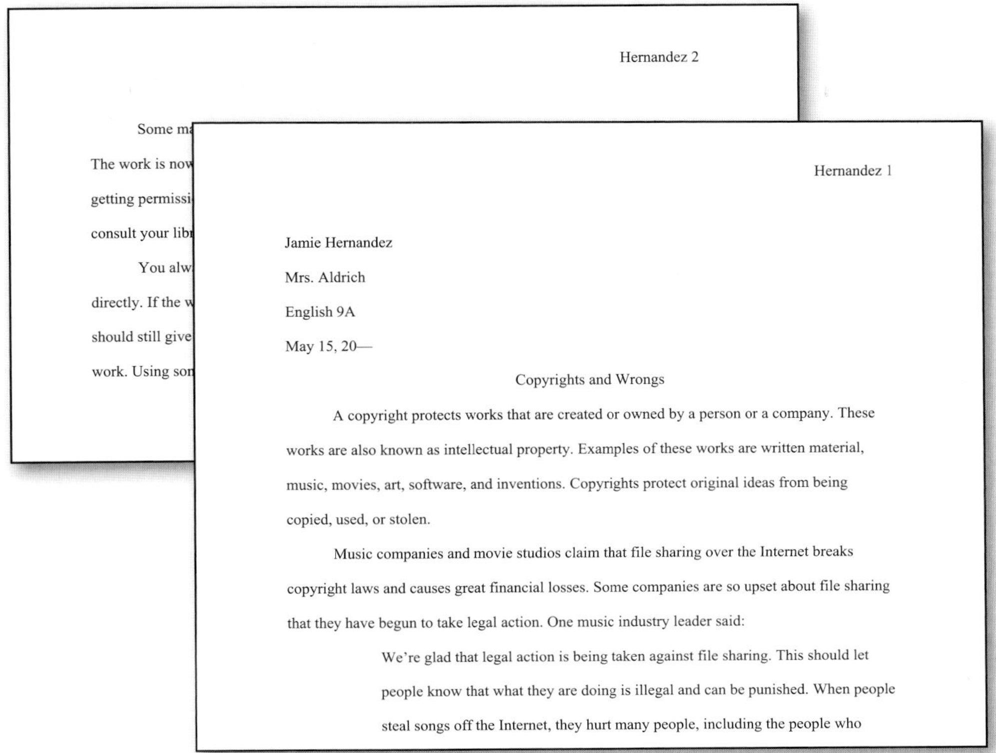

4 Move your mouse over the first clip in the **Clip Art** pane and notice the **ScreenTip, Claps Cheers**. Click the arrow beside the button, and choose **Preview/Properties** (Figure 2.16). Click the **Close** button.

5 Click the **Claps Cheers** button to insert it in the slide.

6 When prompted with the question *How do you want the sound to start in the slide show?* click **Automatically**.

7 A sound icon is displayed on the slide. Drag the **sound icon** to the lower-left corner of the slide.

▼ **Figure 2.16** You can use the drop-down menu to preview the sound.

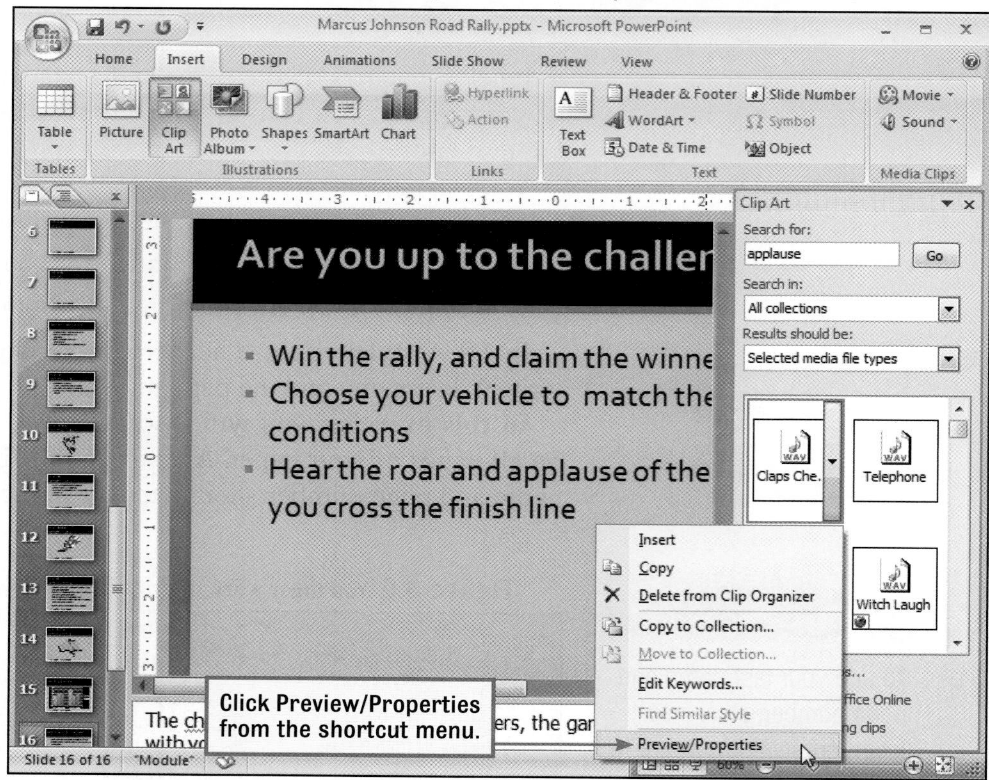

8 Click **Slide 6**.

9 On the **Insert** tab, in the **Illustrations** group, click the **Picture** button. Browse to the **Data File** titled **7D Vehicle Choice2**.

10 Click the file to select it, and click the **Insert** button.

11 Click the image, and drag the lower-right handle downward to make the image larger.

12 Drag the image to center the car under the table (Figure 2.17).

▼ **Figure 2.17** It is easy to resize and move images in PowerPoint.

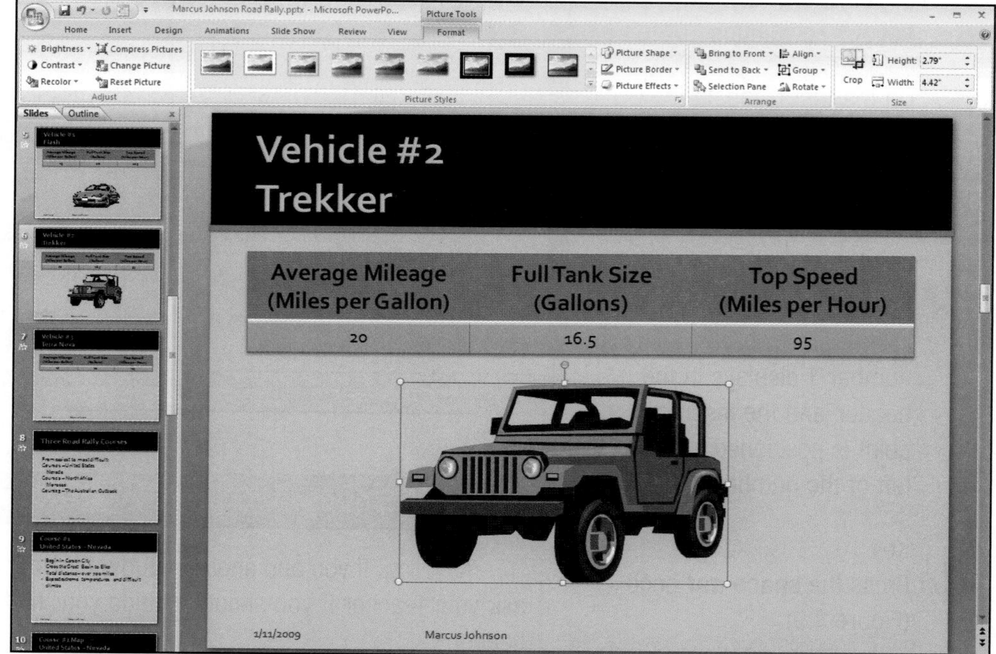

Exercise 3-4 Add a Header

It helps teachers if your name and a page number display on every page of your report. You can do this automatically by using the Header and Footer feature.

You can also use this feature to add the time, date, location of the file, and even the file name in your header or footer.

- A **header** shows information at the top of each page.
- A **footer** shows information at the bottom of each page.

In MLA style, you use headers on all pages. The header includes the writer's last name and the page number.

In this exercise, you will insert text and page numbers into a header on all pages of your paper. According to MLA guidelines, only your last name and page number should appear in the header.

Step-by-Step

1. To add your last name and page number, place your insertion point anywhere in the document.
2. If you are not in **Print Layout** view, click the **Print Layout** view button.
3. On the **Insert** tab, in the **Header & Footer** group, click the **Page Number** command [#].
4. Click **Top of Page**. In the **Page Number** gallery, click **Plain Number 3**. The number **1** displays in the header, and the insertion point is positioned to the left of the number.
5. Key *Your Last Name*. Press the **space bar** once (Figure 3.9).

Figure 3.9 You must work in Print Layout view to see headers and footers.

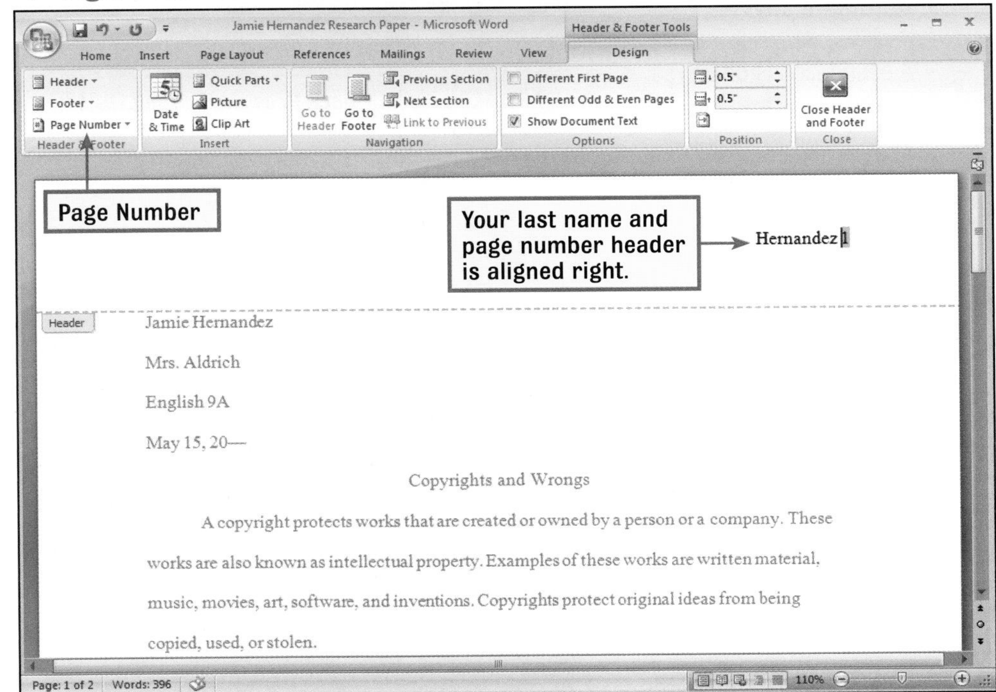

TechSavvy

Header Type If you and another student in your class have the same last name, ask your teacher if you should include your first name or your first initial in the header.

13 Click **Slide 7**.

14 On the **Insert** tab in the **Illustrations** group, click the **Picture** button.

15 Insert the **Data File** titled **7E Vehicle Choice3** (Figure 2.18).

16 Click the image, and drag the lower-right handle downward to make the image larger. **Close** the **Clip Art** task pane.

17 Click the image, and center it under the table (Figure 2.19).

18 Go to the end of the presentation, and insert a new slide. On the **Home** tab, in the **Slides** group, click the **New Slide** drop-down arrow. Choose the **Title Only** layout.

19 Key Thank You! in the title placeholder. Drag the placeholder to center it vertically and horizontally on the slide.

20 Format the placeholder text. Choose your font, font size, and font color. You can also change the fill and outline color of the placeholder as well as apply special effects such as shadow and glow attributes.

21 Add clip art to the slide, and apply animation to each object on the slide.

22 Save your work.

▼ **Figure 2.18** You can insert clips through the Clip Art pane or add images from other sources.

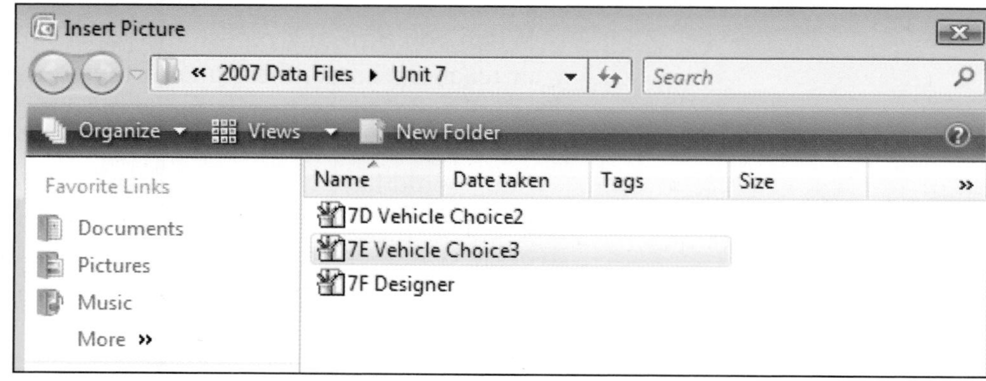

▼ **Figure 2.19** Change the size of an imported image with the sizing handles.

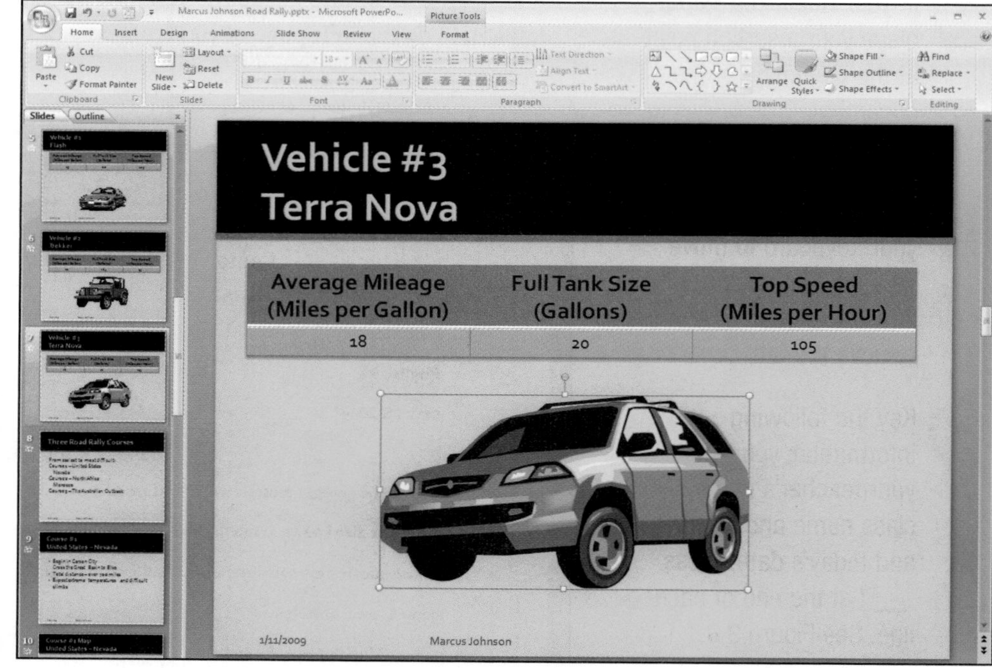

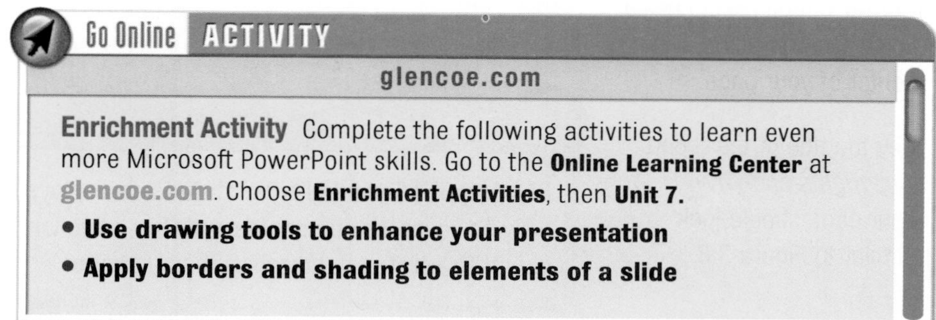

Go Online ACTIVITY

glencoe.com

Enrichment Activity Complete the following activities to learn even more Microsoft PowerPoint skills. Go to the **Online Learning Center** at glencoe.com. Choose **Enrichment Activities**, then **Unit 7.**

- **Use drawing tools to enhance your presentation**
- **Apply borders and shading to elements of a slide**

Exercise 3-3 Create a Heading and a Title

When you turn in a report, the paper must clearly include your name, your teacher's name, the name of the course, and the date you turn it in. This information is often included in a heading at the top of the first page of the report.

You should have a title that describes the content at the top of your report. Some teachers may let you use different fonts and colors in your title to express your creativity, but always follow your teacher's instructions for formatting your reports or papers.

In this exercise, you will add a heading and a title to your report, following MLA guidelines.

Step-by-Step

1. In your **Research Paper**, place your insertion point at the beginning of the document. Press ENTER to create a new line.
2. Press the **Up Arrow** ↑ on your keyboard to move your insertion point to the new line. Press ←BACKSPACE to remove the tab.
3. Key the following information: your name, your teacher's name, your class name and number, and today's date. Press ENTER at the end of each line. See Figure 3.8.
4. Press ENTER. Click the **Center** button to place your insertion point in the center of your page.
5. Key the title of the report *Copyrights and Wrongs*. Your page should look similar to Figure 3.8.

▼ **Figure 3.8** **Always include your name, the teacher's name, the class name, and the date on the first page of your report.**

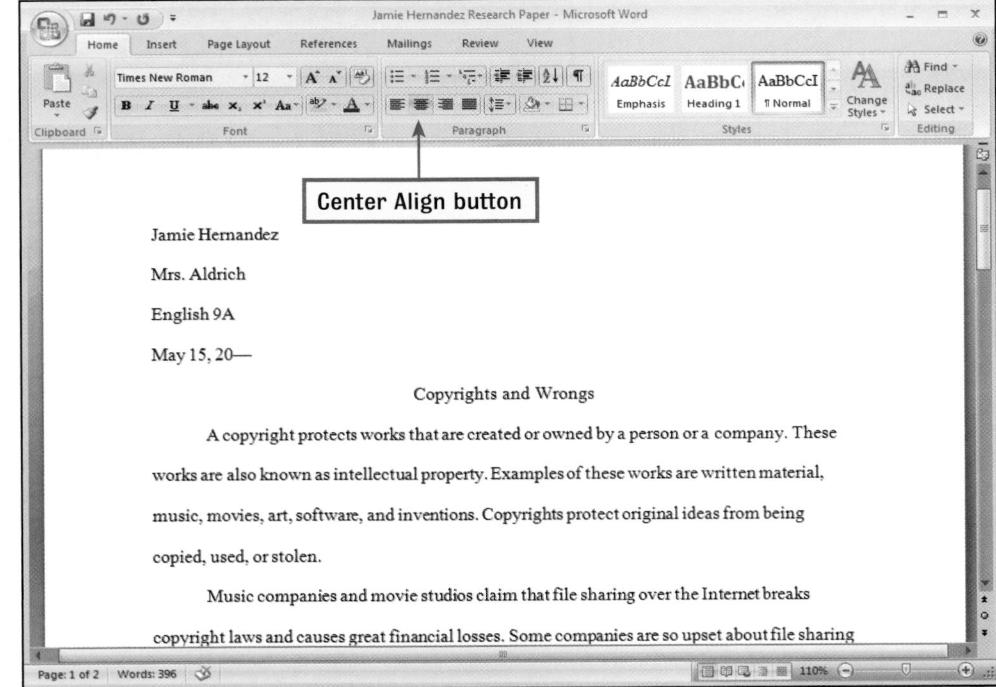

TechSavvy

Word Count By default, the **status** bar displays the total word count automatically. To count the number of words in a selection, select the text that you want to count. The **status** bar displays the number of words in the selection.

Project 2 Assessment

Key Concepts Check

1. **Describe** What are charts and tables used for in a presentation?
2. **Compare** When would you use bulleted lists, and when would you use numbered lists?
3. **Explain** How does a spreadsheet relate to a chart in PowerPoint?

Critical Thinking

4. **Draw Conclusions** Why would you want to use only one type of transition in a presentation?
5. **Cause and Effect** Which should be done first—the presentation design or the presentation content? Explain your answer.

1 Guided Practice

Make Your Presentation More Fun You are helping your teacher finish a PowerPoint presentation about the proper way to give a presentation. You will continue working on the presentation you saved in the Guided Practice for Project 1 (page 323). You will add a slide, change slide transitions, insert a graphic, and add sound. If you need help completing a step, refer back to the exercise in parentheses at the end of the steps.

Step-by-Step

1. **Open** your **Present a Presentation** file in Normal View. (Exercise 1-2)
2. Click **Slide 8**, and insert a new slide. Make sure the new slide has a Title and Context layout. (Exercise 1-1)
3. Key the text shown in Figure 2.20. Make sure the formatting of the new slide matches the rest of the presentation.

Figure 2.20 Click the New Slide button to insert a new slide using Title and Content layout.

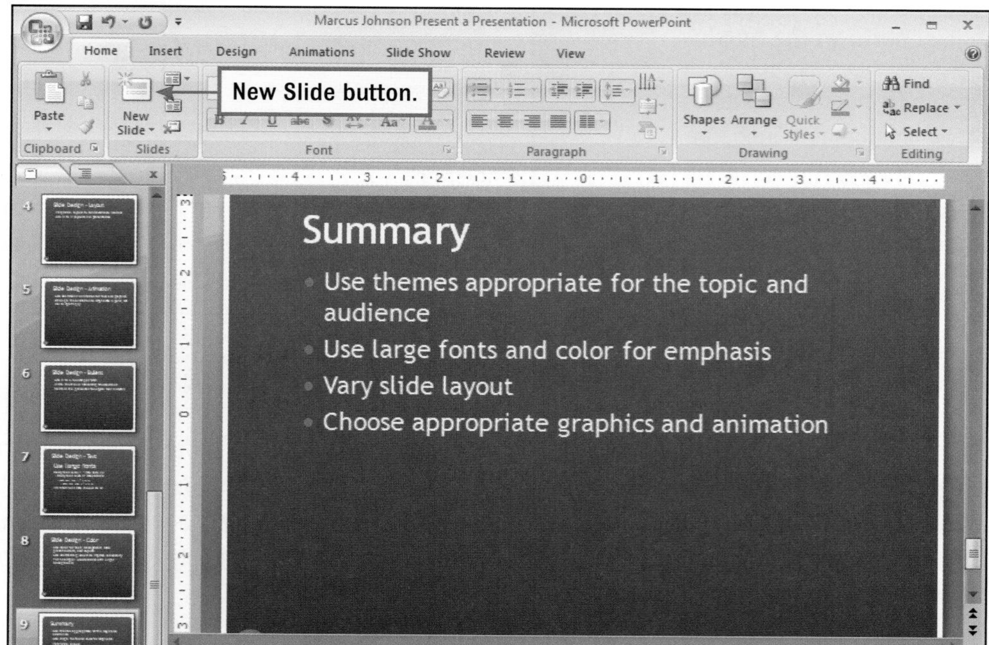

6. On the **Home** tab, in the **Paragraph** group, click the **Show/Hide** button ¶. The ¶ symbol shows where a paragraph ends.

7. Place the insertion point in front of the first paragraph.

8. Press the TAB key on the keyboard to indent the first line of the paragraph (Figure 3.6).

▼ **Figure 3.6** See hidden formatting symbols using the Show/Hide button.

Show/Hide button

Paragraph indent

Dots show space between words.

Paragraph symbol

9. Indent the other paragraphs in the document, except the quote that begins with *We're glad*. See Figure 3.7.

10. Select the entire paragraph that begins with **We're glad** and ends with **perform the music.**

11. To indent the entire quotation 1 inch, on the **Home** tab, in the **Paragraph** group, click **Increase Indent** button twice.

12. Your quote should look like Figure 3.7. **Save** your document.

13. Click **Show/Hide** button ¶ again to hide the formatting symbols.

▼ **Figure 3.7** Long quotations are indented to stand out from the rest of the text.

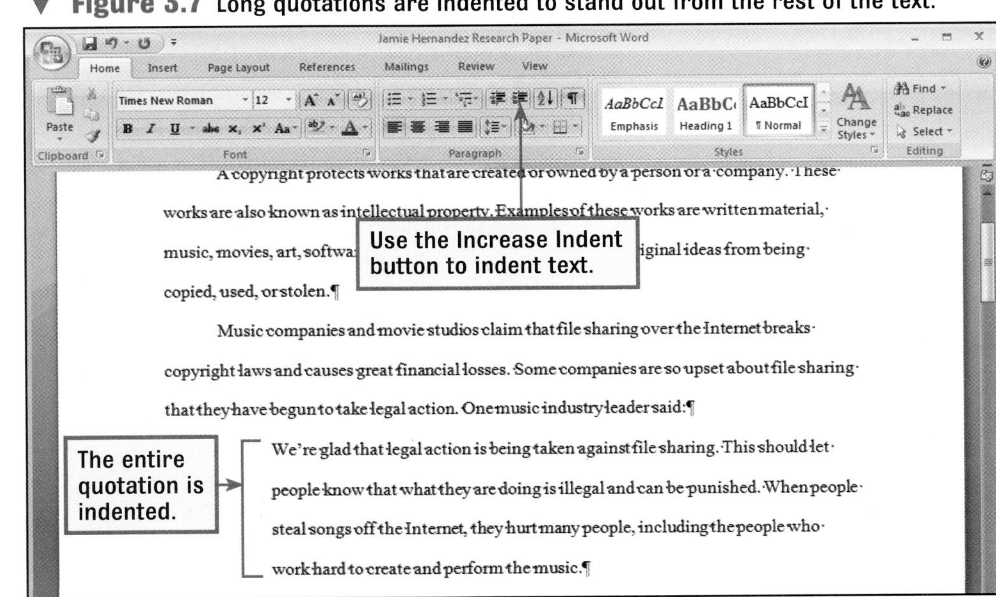

TechSavvy

Long Quotations There are different ways to format a long quotation. In this exercise, you used the Modern Language Association (MLA) style, which is used for research papers. Some teachers prefer a business style, such as Gregg style, where the long quotation is single spaced, with both right and left margins indented half an inch.

4 On the **Animations** tab, in the **Transition to This Slide** group, click the **More** button. (Exercise 2-4)

5 In the **Fade and Dissolves** category, apply the **Fade Smoothly** slide transition to the presentation. See Figure 2.21. Remember to apply the transition to all slides.

6 Select the first slide, and change the slide layout from **Title Only** to **Title Slide**. (Exercise 1-3)

7 Key *Your Name* in the area marked **Click to add subtitle**.

8 Drag the title to the top of the page and the subtitle to the bottom of the page using the four-headed arrow.

9 Click the **Insert** menu, choose **From File**, and click the file titled **7F Designer**. (Exercise 2-5)

10 **Insert** the image onto the title page between the title and subtitle (Figure 2.22).

11 Adjust the placement of the title, subtitle, and image.

12 **Save** your work, and **exit PowerPoint**.

Figure 2.21 Use the Animations tab to change the transitions.

Figure 2.22 Clip art can make your presentation more visually interesting.

Exercise 3-2 Use Tabs to Indent

TechSavvy

What Different Tabs Mean
The tabs on the **Ribbon** help to visually show the organization of the commands in Word. The **Ribbon** tabs look similar and function similar to the way you use folder tabs. Both help you organize the way you work. A tab that is used as an indent visually separates paragraphs for ease in reading.

A **tab** is a set distance for moving the insertion point. An **indent** determines the distance of a paragraph from either the left or right margin.

Research papers often use quotations to support ideas. A **quotation** is the exact words that someone else wrote or said. It must be formatted correctly, and the source must be cited.

- **Short quotations** have quotation marks before and after. For example: "Whether you think you can or whether you think you can't, you're right!" (Henry Ford)
- **Long quotations** are four or more lines. The whole quote is indented, so that it stands out from the rest of the paper.

In this exercise, you will use tabs to indent paragraphs and set indents to format long quotations. You will use the Show/Hide button ¶ to reveal formatting codes (symbols that represent spaces, tabs, returns, breaks, and so on).

Step-by-Step

1. In your **Research Paper** document, on the **Home** tab, in the **Paragraph** group, click the **Paragraph Dialog Box Launcher**. Then click **Tabs**. The **Tabs** dialog box opens (Figure 3.5).
2. The **Default tab stops** box should be set to **0.5″**. (If not, change the setting to **0.5″**.)
3. If there are any numbers in the **Tab stop position** box, highlight them and click **Clear**.
4. Make sure the **Alignment** is set to **left**, and the **Leader** is set to **None**.
5. Click **OK** to return to the document.

▼ **Figure 3.5** Tab stops show how far the insertion point will move.

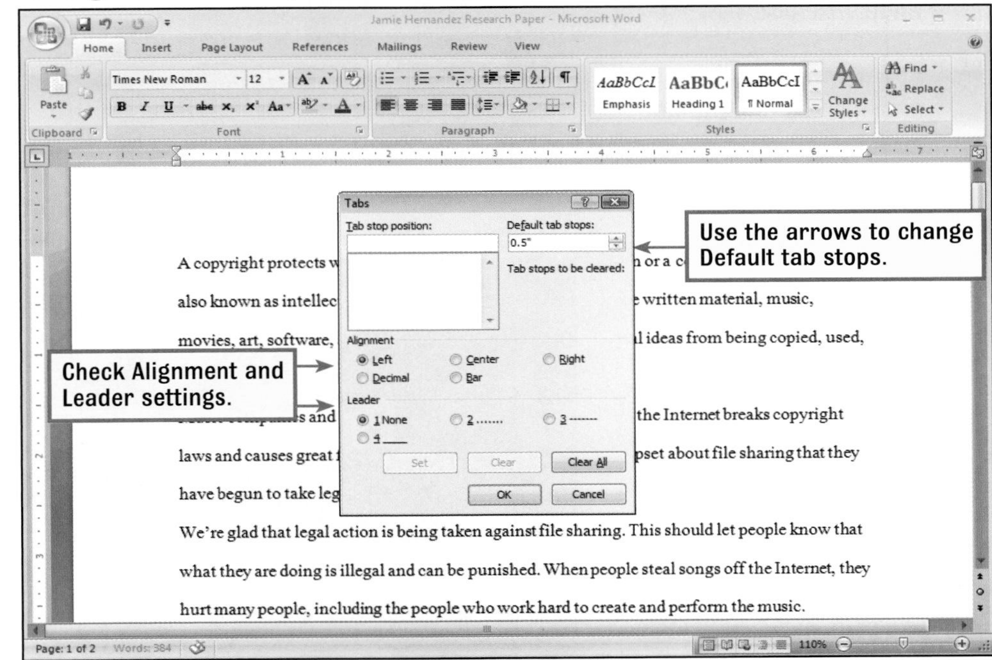

Different Strokes

Ruler Use the ruler to add or delete tabs or to change positions of tab settings. To display the ruler, click the **View Ruler** button above the vertical scroll bar.

Project 2 Assessment

Go Online RUBRICS
glencoe.com

Independent Practice Use the rubrics for these projects to help create and evaluate your work. Go to the **Online Learning Center** at **glencoe.com**. Choose **Rubrics**, then **Unit 7**.

2 Independent Practice ★

English Language Arts **Display Text Effectively** To make your slides more readable, you will add bullets or numbers and apply animation to the school presentation you created in Project 1, Independent Practice 2 (page 325).

a. Create Review the text you wrote.

- Format the text into bulleted or numbered lists.
- Add transitions and animation to the slides.

b. Revise Review the slides to see whether the order still works. Add new slides if you think there is too much text on any of the slides.

3 Independent Practice ★★

Math **Create Tables and Charts** Add visuals to the presentation created in Project 1, Independent Practice 3 (page 325).

a. Plan Think of a table or chart to add to your presentation. For example, you could use a graph to compare the amount of time you spend on an activity or class, or you could create a scheduling chart.

b. Create Where possible, convert text to bulleted or numbered lists.

- Add a new slide to create your table or chart.
- Apply transitions and custom animation to your slides.

4 Independent Practice ★★★

Math **Compare Careers** What kind of jobs can you expect to get in the career of your choice? Add this information to the presentation you created in Project 1, Independent Practice 4 (page 325).

a. Research Use online job postings, your newspaper, or other resources to find information about jobs that relate to your career.

b. Create Organize the jobs into a table that compares the type of work, the companies, and the salaries. Insert the table in a slide.

- Add a bar graph that compares salaries or another job feature.
- Apply transitions and custom animation to your slides.

6. On the keyboard, press CTRL + A to select all of the text in the document.

7. On the **Home** tab, in the **Font** group, change the **Font** to **Times New Roman**.

8. Set the **Font Size** to **12**.

9. To double-space your document, on the **Home** tab, in the **Paragraph** group, click the **Paragraph Dialog Box Launcher**. Then click the **Indents and Spacing** tab.

▼ **Figure 3.3** Make sure all the text is selected before you change the spacing or other paragraph settings.

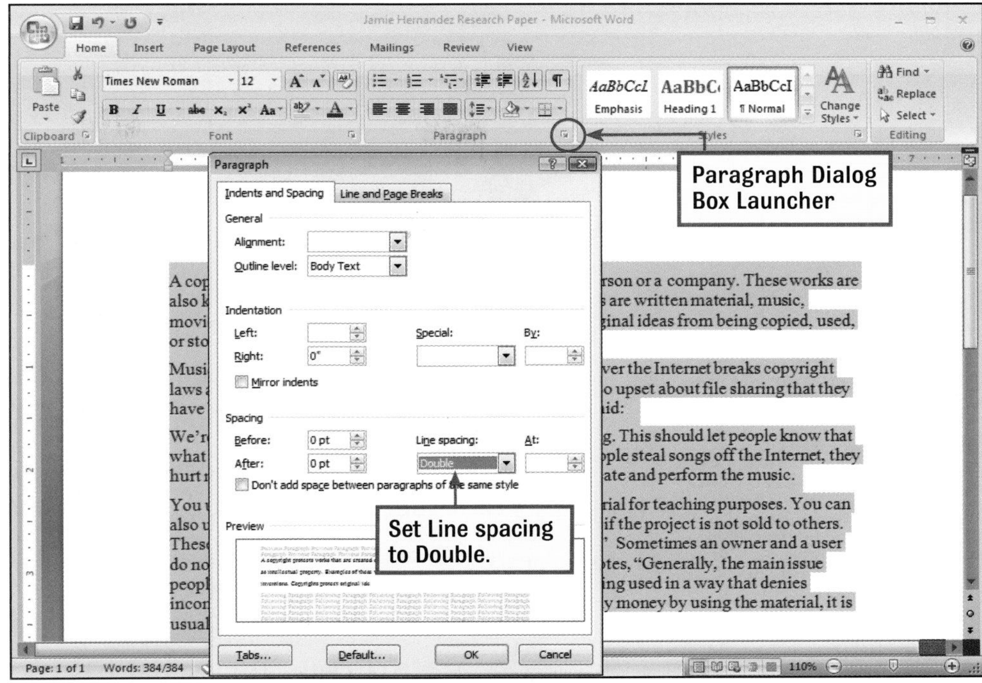

10. Under **Line spacing**, click the arrow, then choose **Double**. Under **Spacing**, change the **Before** and **After** to **0 pt**. Click the **OK** button to close the **Paragraph** dialog box (Figure 3.3).

11. Your document should now look like Figure 3.4.

12. **Save** your document.

▼ **Figure 3.4** Your document is now double spaced.

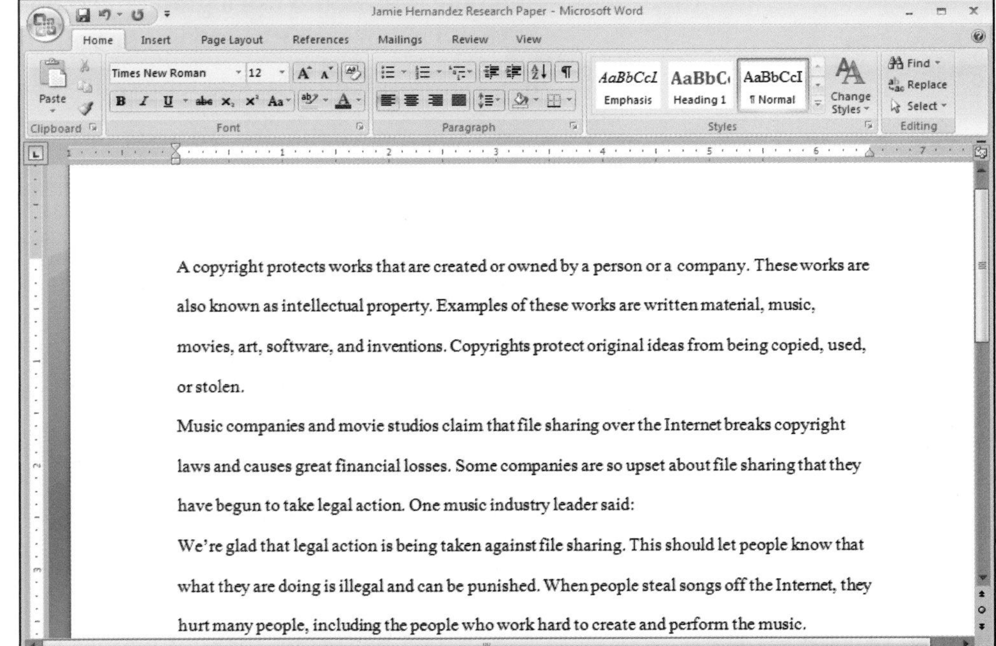

Concepts in Action

Project 3 Deliver a Presentation

Key Concepts

Exercise 3-1

- Create speaker notes
- Delete slides
- Proofread your slides

Exercise 3-2

- Print handouts
- Print speaker notes

Exercise 3-3

- Save your presentation as a Web page
- View your presentation online

Vocabulary

Key Terms
speaker notes
handouts

Before You Begin

Take Good Notes As you complete each exercise, take notes about the skills you are learning. Write down the key skills and how to complete each one. At the end of the project, make sure you can perform each skill. If you have trouble, go back to the exercise and repeat the steps. Then practice on your own.

In this project, you will add the finishing touches to your presentation and make sure that it is error-free. You will prepare to present the slide show to your audience and convert it to a Web page so that others can view it online.

A Lasting Impression

You are satisfied with your presentation about your Road Rally game, but you want to make sure that the judges can clearly see the visuals you have created and remember your important points. Before the presentation, you prepare by printing notes for yourself and handouts for your audience. You also intend to publish the presentation online so that it is available to the competition judges, as well as to other people at the video game company, which is in another city. By preparing ahead of time, you help ensure that the presentation will go smoothly and you will give the audience a good impression of you and your work.

Step-by-Step

1. Open the **Data File** named **4E Research Paper**.

2. Save it as *Your Name* Research Paper.

3. On the **Page Layout** tab, click the **Page Setup Dialog Box Launcher** to display the **Page Setup** dialog box (Figure 3.1).

4. In the **Page Setup** dialog box, click the **Margins** tab.

5. Set the **left** and **right** margins to **1″**, then click **OK**. Your page should look similar to Figure 3.2.

TechSavvy

Dialog Box Launcher The **Dialog Box Launcher** feature expands a **group** command to view the specific features of the **group**. Click the **Dialog Box Launcher** to open a related dialog box. You can make several format decisions quickly and easily.

Figure 3.1 Use 1″ margins on all sides of a research paper or report.

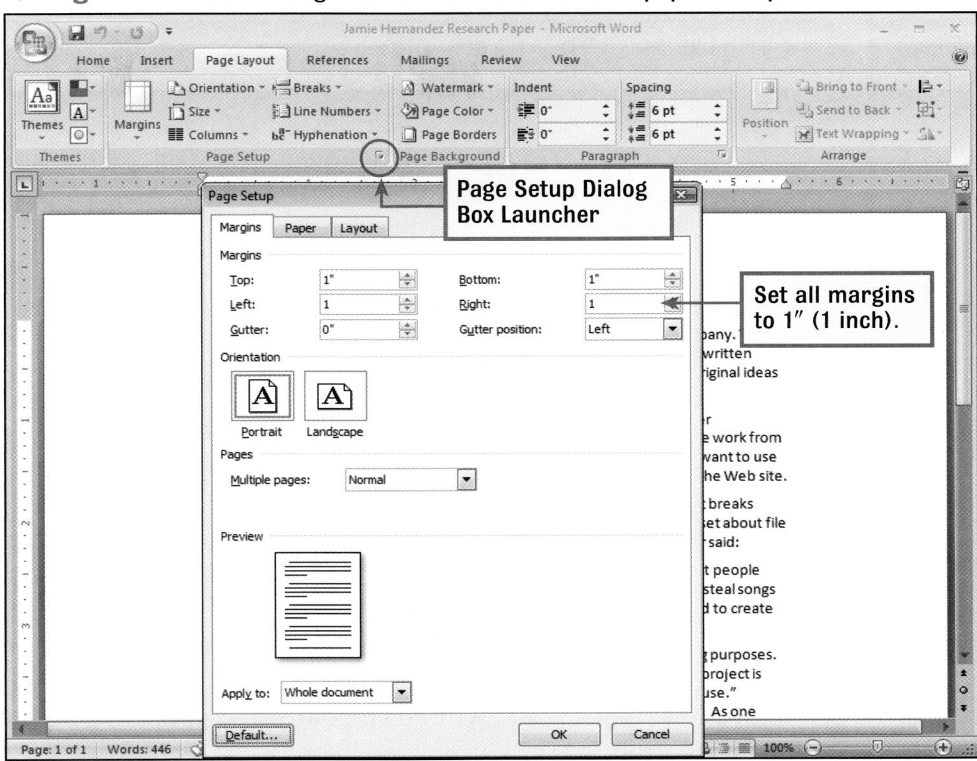

Figure 3.2 Compare the margins here with the figure above. The margins are now 1 inch on both sides.

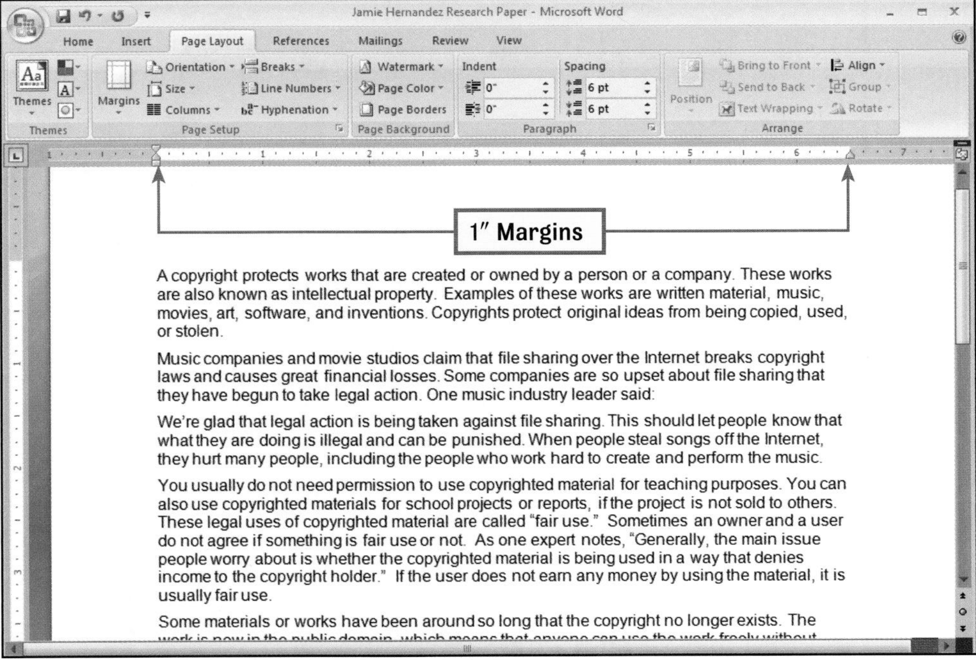

Exercise 3-1 Prepare for the Presentation

No matter how good your PowerPoint slide show is, you need to make sure the spoken part of your presentation is also clear and interesting. A good presenter does not just read the text on a slide. A good presenter elaborates on the bullet points with interesting examples. PowerPoint lets you create **speaker notes**, which are notes that the presenter uses when discussing each slide that is shown.

When printed, the speaker notes appear as text below small pictures of the slides. You can print the notes as handouts for the audience, or you can just use a copy to refer to during your presentation.

In this exercise, you will prepare for your presentation by creating speaker notes, deleting a slide that is no longer necessary, and checking your slides for any errors in spelling and/or grammar.

Step-by-Step

1. In your Road Rally presentation, click **Slide 3**.
2. Click the **Speaker Notes** area below the slide, and key the text shown in Figure 3.1: The game requires more than just good driving skills. The winner has to make good decisions. The player that makes the best decisions and drives the best wins.

▼ **Figure 3.1** Speaker notes are used by the person who gives the presentation.

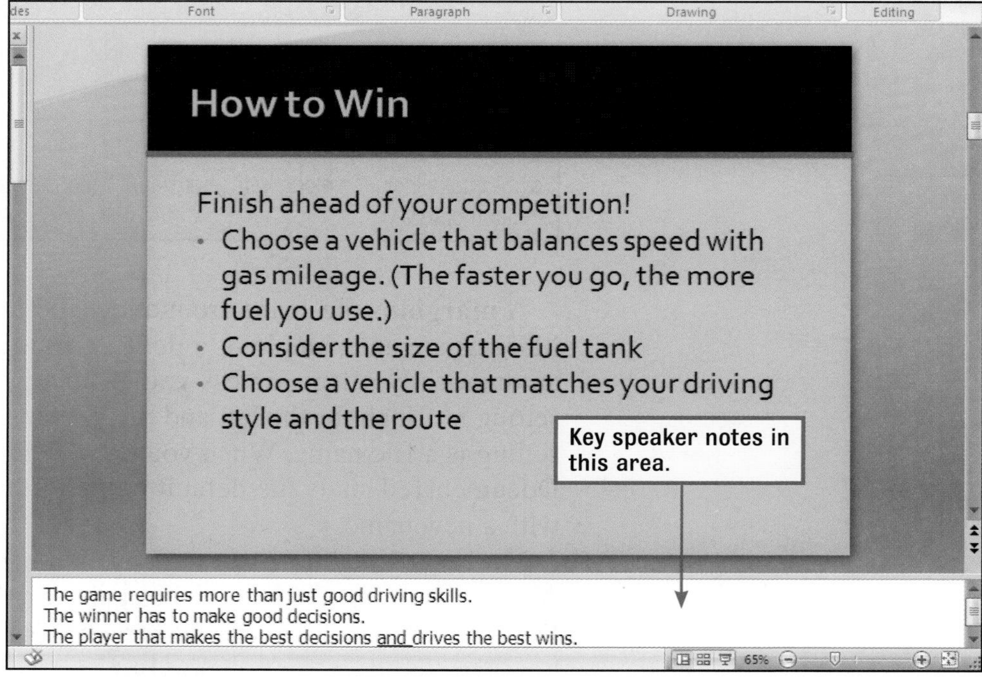

HELP!

Resize the Notes Pane If you have several speaker notes, you might have to enlarge the space where you key the notes. To do so, place your mouse pointer on the line between the slide and the notes. When the pointer becomes a two-headed arrow, drag the line upward.

Exercise 3-1 Format the Body of the Paper

A good report is well researched, clearly written, provides accurate information, and supports conclusions with examples. A good report should also be easy to read. That is why standard proper formatting is so important. When you key your report, follow your teacher's instructions, or follow these formatting guidelines from the Modern Language Association (MLA):

Paper or Report Checklist

- ✔ Margins are 1 inch on all sides.
- ✔ The document is double spaced. (When you double space, there is a blank line between each line of text.)
- ✔ The font is easy to read, such as Times New Roman or Palatino.
- ✔ The font size is 12.
- ✔ Text is aligned left.
- ✔ Text is checked for spelling and grammar.
- ✔ Sources are cited in the body.
- ✔ Sources are listed at the end of the document.
- ✔ A title is included along with your name, your teacher's name, class period, and date.

A **margin** is the space around the sides, top, and bottom of the paper. Margins are an example of a **default** setting, a setting that the computer automatically selects unless you change it. In Word, the default margin setting is 1 inch for the left and right sides. Another example of a default setting is a file name. When you open Word, the first document is called Document1. This is the default name of the document until you save it with a new name.

You can change formats such as alignment and line spacing by using commands on the Ribbon. You can also do the same tasks by clicking the Dialog Box Launcher in the Paragraph group to open the Paragraph dialog box. Use the Paragraph dialog box to accomplish several tasks at once. You can change alignment, indentation, paragraph spacing, and line spacing. Although you will not need to change the spacing between paragraphs in your research paper, the feature is sometimes used in publications. For example, in this book you can see that the spacing between each line of text is slightly smaller than the spacing between each paragraph.

In this exercise, you will practice changing margins, fonts, and line spacing in a report using Microsoft Word.

3 Add the speaker note shown in Figure 3.2 to **Slide 8**.

4 Click **Slide 17**. You are going to delete this slide because you have decided it is no longer needed.

5 Press DELETE. Press CTRL + Z to undo the deletion. You decided to keep the slide.

Figure 3.2 Speaker notes should be easy to read.

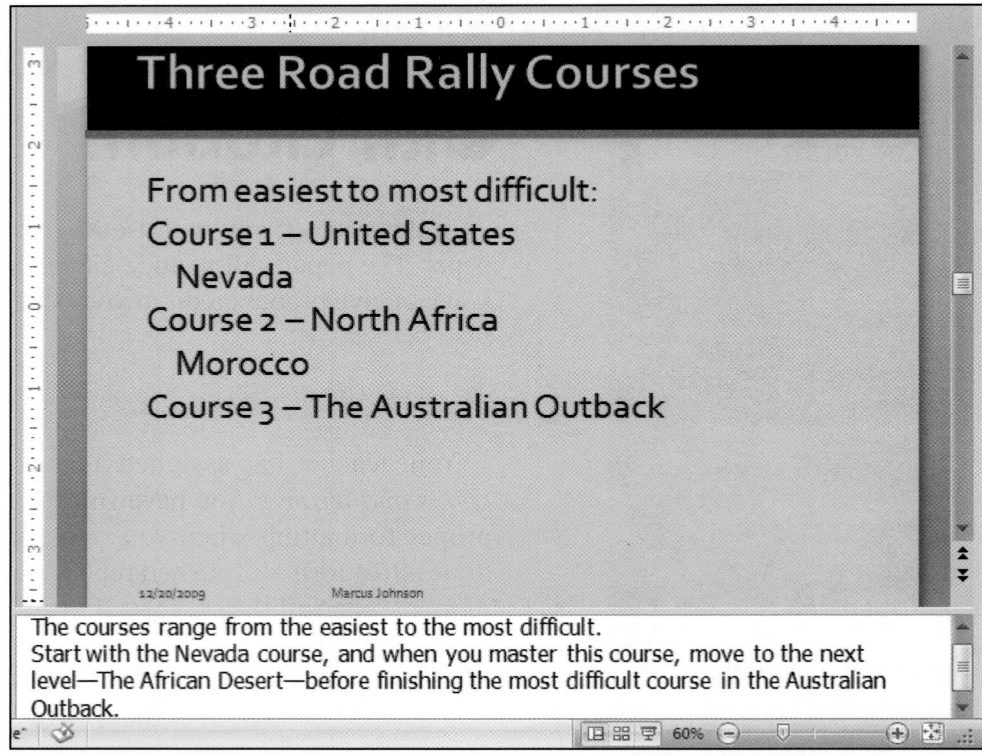

6 Click **Slide 1**.

7 On the **Review** tab, in the **Proofing** group, click the **Spelling** button.

8 As the **Spelling** check goes through your presentation, make any necessary corrections when prompted (Figure 3.3).

9 **Save** your work.

Figure 3.3 Before you make your presentation or print, review your presentation for grammar and spelling errors.

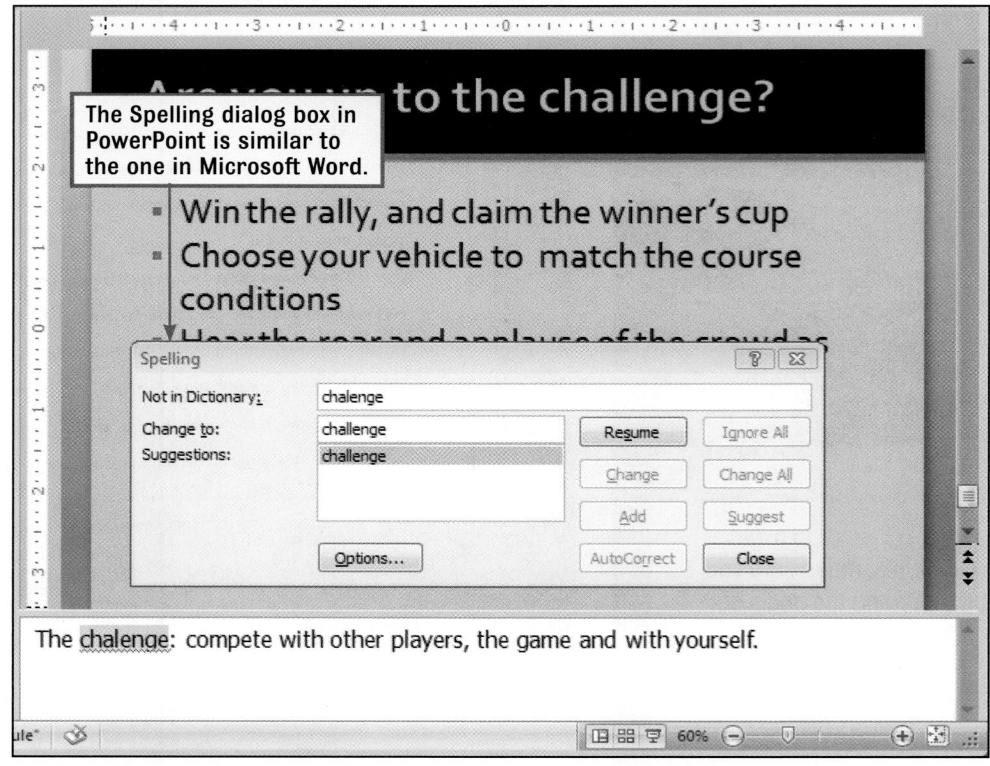

Concepts in Action

Project 3 Format a Research Paper with Citations

Key Concepts

Exercise 3-1
- Format a research paper

Exercise 3-2
- Use tabs

Exercise 3-3
- Create a heading and a title

Exercise 3-4
- Add a header

Exercise 3-5
- Create a works cited page

Exercise 3-6
- Cite a source

Exercise 3-7
- Create a title page and footer

Vocabulary

Key Terms
margin
default
tab
indent
quotation
header
footer
citation
title page

Before You Begin

Think Ahead To avoid problems, make sure you understand the goals of a project before you start working. Ask your teacher if you are not clear about an assignment.

In this project, you will use Microsoft Word to format a research paper. The paper will include citations and a works cited list so that you can give proper credit to your sources of information.

Perfect Your Final Paper

Your teacher has assigned a short research paper called *Copyrights and Wrongs*. You have finished the first draft but did not use proper formatting when you wrote it. Now you have to edit your draft into a formal, finished report that has a heading and a title and properly cites all the sources of information you used.

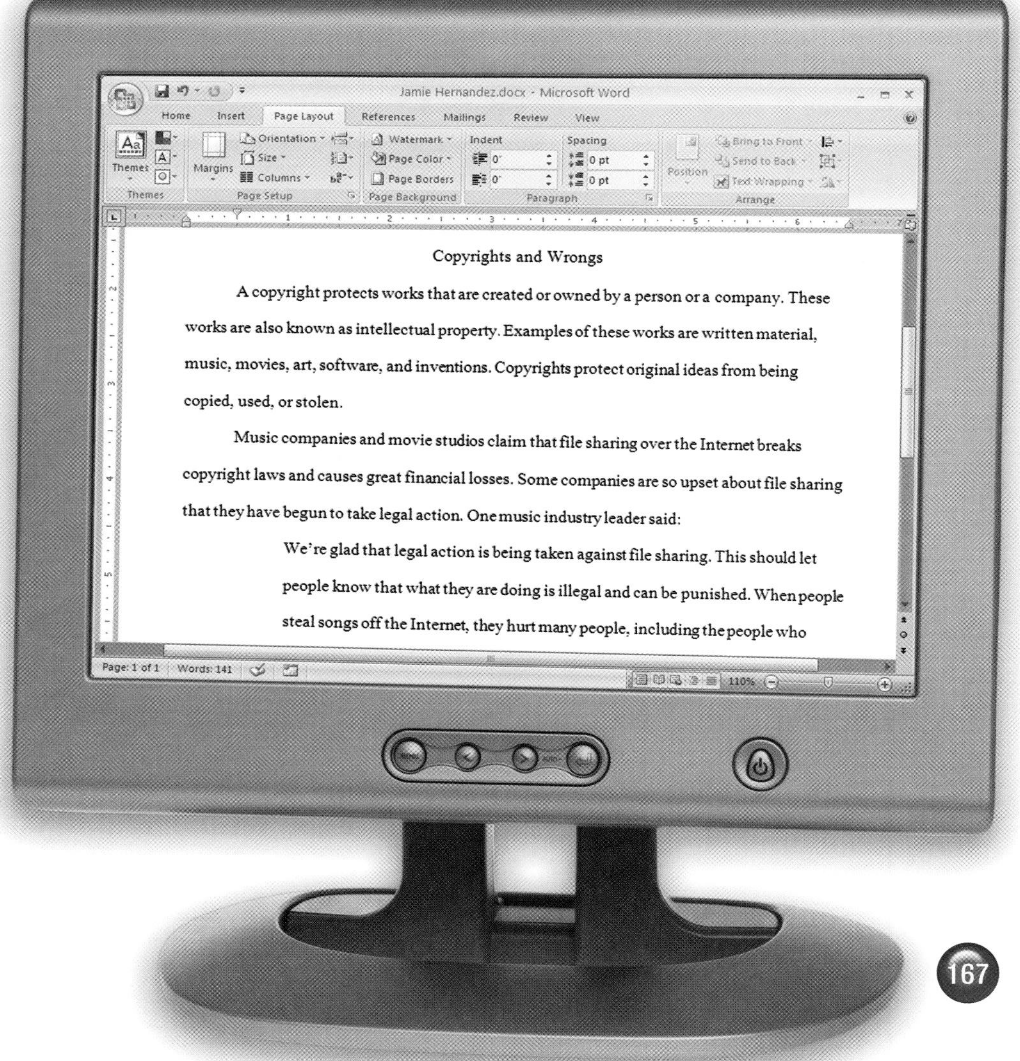

Exercise 3-2 Print Handouts and Speaker Notes

Handouts are printed versions of your slide show. Handouts provide the audience with a convenient place to take notes during a presentation and allow them to take a copy of the presentation with them when it is over.

PowerPoint handouts show between one and nine slides on the page. When you print a lot of slides on each page, they are smaller and harder to read. The most popular handout is a layout with three slides to a page and a place for notes next to each slide.

In this exercise, you will print handouts for the audience and print your own speaker notes. **Note**: Ask for your teacher's permission before you print anything.

Step-by-Step

1. Click the **Microsoft Office Button**, and choose **Print** to display printing options. Click **Print** to open the **Print** dialog box.

2. Under **Print what**, click the drop-down arrow, then choose **Handouts**. See Figure 3.4.

3. In the **Handouts** area, next to **Slides per page**, click the arrow, then choose **3**. See Figure 3.4.

4. Click the **Preview** button. Note how your page will look in the **Preview** layout.

▼ **Figure 3.4** The Print dialog box includes options for printing slides for the presentation, handouts, and speaker's notes.

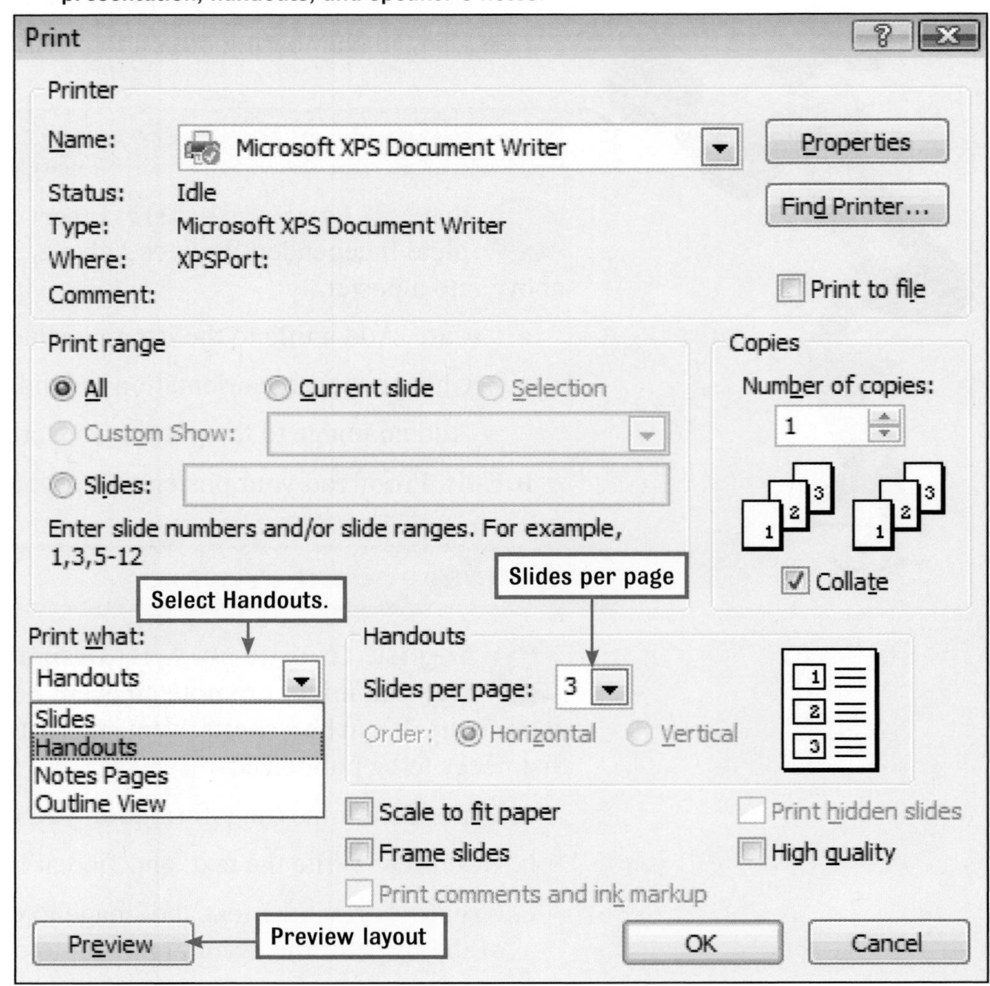

Project 2 Assessment

2 Independent Practice 

Go Online RUBRICS

glencoe.com

Independent Practice Use the rubrics for these projects to help create and evaluate your work. Go to the **Online Learning Center** at **glencoe.com**. Choose **Rubrics**, then **Unit 4**.

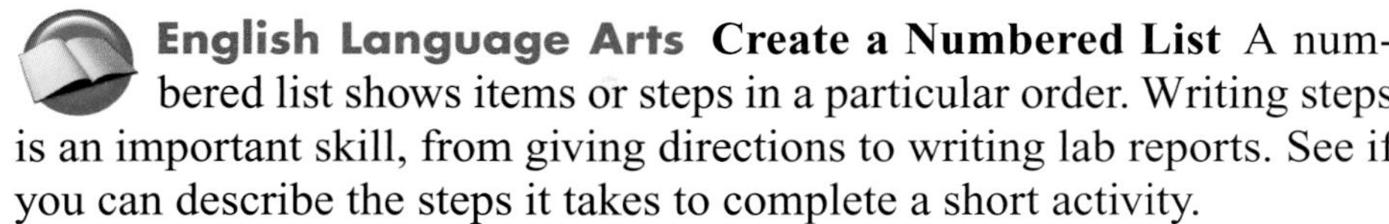

English Language Arts **Create a Numbered List** A numbered list shows items or steps in a particular order. Writing steps is an important skill, from giving directions to writing lab reports. See if you can describe the steps it takes to complete a short activity.

a. Plan Write down ten steps you would use to do one of the following activities, or an activity of your choice:

- Shoot a basketball
- Make a peanut butter and jelly sandwich

b. Create Use Word to create a document.

- Save the document as ***Your Name*** **Poster**.
- Use the Numbering button to create your list.

3 Independent Practice 

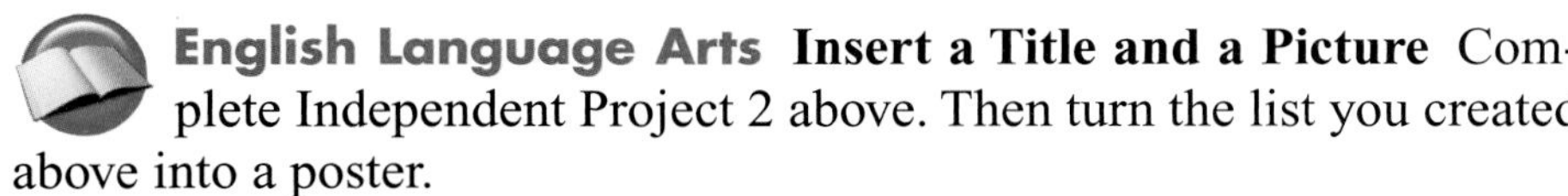

English Language Arts **Insert a Title and a Picture** Complete Independent Project 2 above. Then turn the list you created above into a poster.

a. Create Add a title to the list and center it.

- Change the page orientation to landscape.
- Add an image to the poster. Give credit for the picture source.

b. Edit Proofread your poster and, if your teacher allows, print it.

4 Independent Practice 

English Language Arts **Design a Flyer** Think of a realistic way you might promote an event being put on by your school or community. It can be a sports event, a charity event, a play, or any activity that needs to be publicized.

a. Plan Determine the information you need for the flyer.

b. Research Write the text, and find at least one picture for the flyer.

c. Create Format the text and image to create two different versions of the flyer for the event organizer to choose from.

5 Your handouts should look similar to Figure 3.5. With your teacher's permission, click **Print** and then **OK** to print the handouts.

Figure 3.5 **Your handouts should not show too many slides per page.**

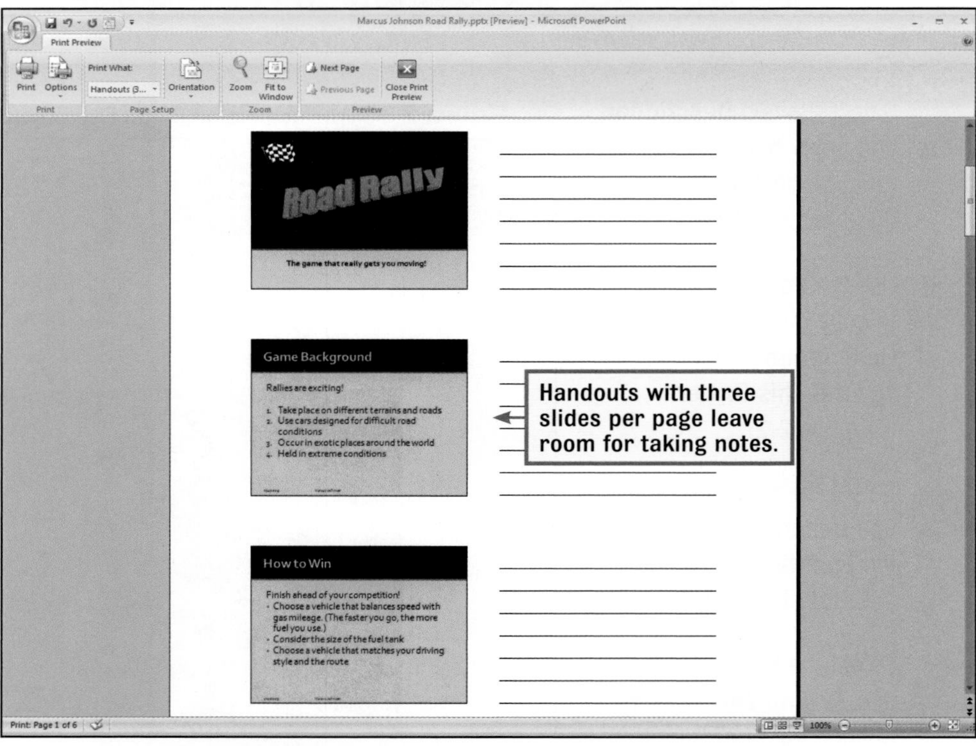

6 To print your speaker notes, click the **Microsoft Office Button**, and choose **Print** from the Print menu.

7 Next to **Print what**, click the arrow, then choose **Notes Pages**.

8 Under **Print Range**, click **Slides**.

9 In the box next to **Slides**, key 3,8 to print the slides on which you added speaker notes.

10 With your teacher's permission, click **OK** to print the speaker notes. They should look similar to Figure 3.6.

Figure 3.6 **Because speaker notes show you the whole slide, you can face your computer (and audience) rather then the screen when presenting.**

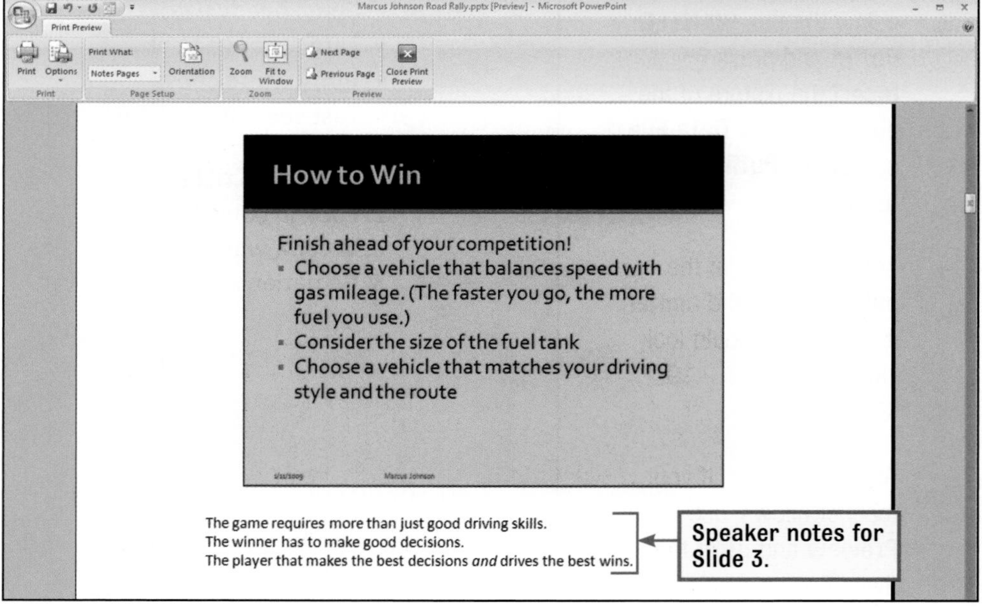

Project 2 Assessment

4. Select the text **Description** and apply **bold** format. Change the **Font Size** to **20**. (Exercise 2-1)

5. Use the **Format Painter** to copy the format of **Description** to the text **To Find This Critter**. (Exercise 2-2)

6. Select the text under the title **Description**. Change the **Font Size** to **18** and add **Bullets**. (Exercise 2-1)

7. Select the text under the title **To Find This Critter**. Change the **Font Size** to **18** and use **Numbering**. (Exercise 2-4)

8. Move your insertion point below the title **WANTED: Puffin** and press ENTER. **Insert** the picture of the puffin from the **Data File** named **4D Puffin Photo**. (Exercise 2-5)

9. Adjust the **size** of the puffin picture and **center** it. Your flyer should look similar to Figure 2.19. (Exercise 2-5)

10. **Save** your work. If your teacher allows, use **Print Preview** and **print** the flyer. (Exercise 2-6)

▼ **Figure 2.19** The completed Puffin Flyer should look similar to this one.

WANTED: Puffin

Description

- Small beady eyes
- Large orange beak
- Puffy white chest
- Last seen in Scotland

To Find This Critter

1. Look in cold climates.
2. Wear a warm coat.
3. Be patient!

Exercise 3-3 Publish as a Web Page

As do other Microsoft Office applications, PowerPoint lets you easily publish your presentation as a Web page. You can take advantage of technology to reach a much larger audience. You do not have to be in the same room with your audience. You do, however, need a computer, access to the Internet or other network, and a place to publish your presentation, such as a Web server.

When you view a presentation with a Web browser, it is much like viewing a Web page. You can view any slide, link to other pages in the presentation or to external Web pages, and view animations and hear sound. **Note**: Always get your teacher's permission before you publish anything as a Web page.

In this exercise, you will save your Road Rally presentation as a Web page, then open it in a browser and view it as a slide show.

Step-by-Step

1. Click the **Microsoft Office Button**, and then choose **Save As**. The **Save As** dialog box displays (Figure 3.7).
2. Next to **File name**, key *Your Name* Road Rally Web Page.
3. In the **Save as type** box, click the arrow, and choose **Single File Web Page**.
4. Click the **Change Title** button, and change the title to *Your Name* Road Rally. Click **OK**.
5. Click the **Publish** button to open the **Publish as Web Page** dialog box.
6. Select the **Complete presentation** option, and deselect the **Display speaker notes** check box.

Figure 3.7 Click the Change Title button if you want a specific title for your presentation.

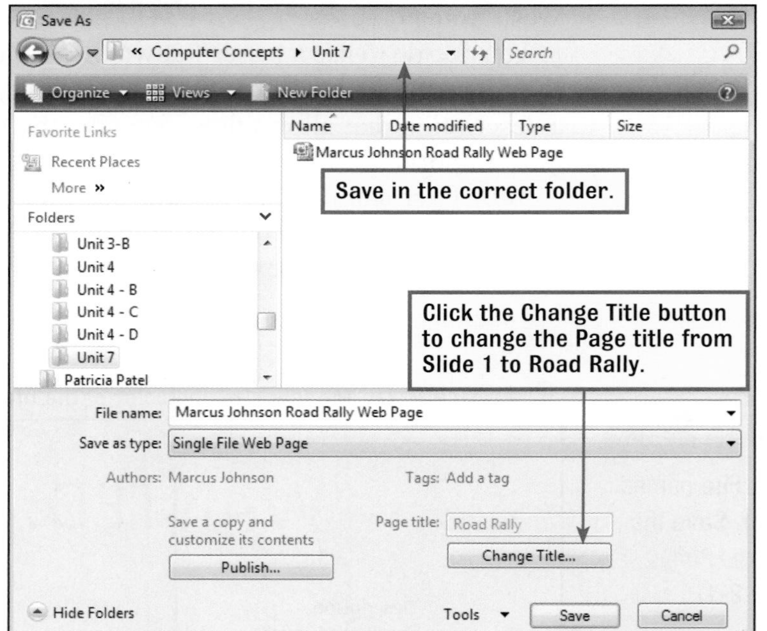

TechSavvy

Updates After you publish a presentation as a Web page, you may want to update it. To do this, first open the original file (the PowerPoint presentation, not the Web page). Then update the presentation and publish it to the Web. If you want only one version of the Web page, give it the same name and save it to the same place so that the new file will overwrite the old one.

Project 2 Assessment

Key Concepts Check

1. **Explain** When should you use a bulleted list, and when should you use a numbered list?
2. **Describe** Why is it important to use Print Preview before you print a document?

Critical Thinking

3. **Draw Conclusions** When would you set the page orientation to landscape rather than portrait?
4. **Evaluate** Describe why it is important to select and use good graphics in a document. List three rules for using graphics effectively.

1 Guided Practice

Create a Wanted Poster You are studying birds in your science class. Your teacher wants you to create a one-page flyer that looks like an Old West "wanted" poster.

You decide to use a lesser-known bird called a puffin as the star of your flyer. The puffin has some unusual features, so you will need to include a description that allows those viewing the flyer to easily understand the most important information.

Your flyer should also visually identify the bird. Therefore, you will need to include a good photo of the puffin. If you need help completing a step, refer back to the exercise in parentheses at the end of the step.

Step-by-Step

1. **Open** the **Data File** named **4C Puffin Flyer**. **Save** the file as *Your Name* Puffin Flyer. (Exercise 2-1)
2. **Center** the text **Wanted: Puffin**, and change the **Font Size** to **48**. (Exercise 2-3)
3. Change the **Font Color** of **WANTED:** to **Red** and **Puffin** to **Brown** (Figure 2.18). (Exercise 2-1)

▼ **Figure 2.18** The font size and color of the title is changed.

WANTED: Puffin

Description
Small beady eyes
Large orange beak
Puffy white chest
Last seen in Scotland

To Find This Critter
Look in cold climates.
Wear a warm coat.
Be patient!

7. Click to select the **Open published Web page in browser** check box.

8. Click the **Web Options** button to open the **Web Options** dialog box. Then click the **General** tab, and select the **Add slide navigation controls** check box.

9. Click the drop-down arrow for the **Colors** text box, and select **Presentation colors (text color)**.

10. Deselect the **Show slide animation while browsing** check box. Then select the **Resize graphics to fit browser window** check box.

11. Click **OK** to close the **Web Options** dialog box, and click the **Publish** button to save the Web page and to close the **Publish as Web Page** dialog box. Your presentation opens as shown in Figure 3.8.

12. In the lower-right corner, click the **Slide Show** button. View your presentation. (Figure 3.9).

13. To end the show, press ESC. **Close Internet Explorer**, and **exit PowerPoint**.

Figure 3.8 Your presentation can be displayed in a Web browser.

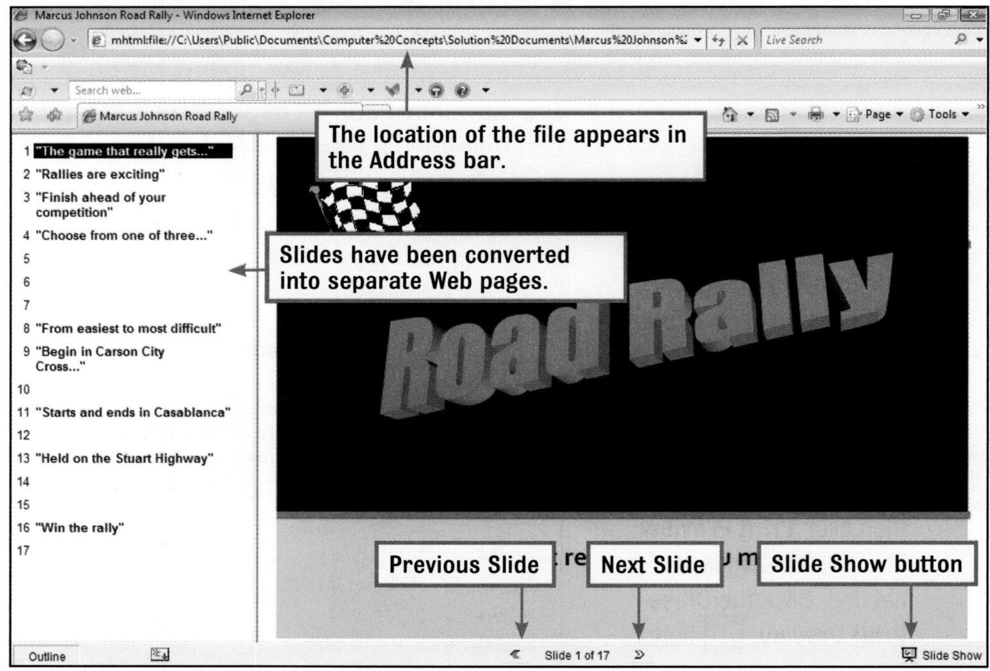

Figure 3.9 The Slide Show view takes up the whole screen.

Exercise 2-6 Print Your Flyer

The Print dialog box includes settings to define a page range, specify the number of copies to print, and change the pages printed per sheet. You can display the Print dialog box by using the Microsoft Office Button or by pressing CTRL + P.

In this exercise, you will use the Print dialog box to change settings before printing your flyer.

Step-by-Step

1. On the **Review** tab, in the **Proofing** group, click the **Spelling & Grammar** button to proof your flyer.
2. Click the **Microsoft Office Button**, select **Print**, and then click **Print Preview**. Make any changes, if needed. Click the **Close Print Preview** button.
3. Click the **Microsoft Office Button**, and click **Print**. The **Print** dialog box opens (Figure 2.17).
4. Identify the parts of the **Print** dialog box in Figure 2.17 on your own screen.
5. Make sure the correct printer is displayed in your **Printer Name** box. (If not, click the arrow and select the correct printer from the menu.)
6. Change the **Number of copies** to **2**.
7. With your teacher's permission, click **OK** to print your flyer.
8. **Close** the document. **Exit Word**.

Figure 2.17 When your document is only one page, you do not have to worry about Page range.

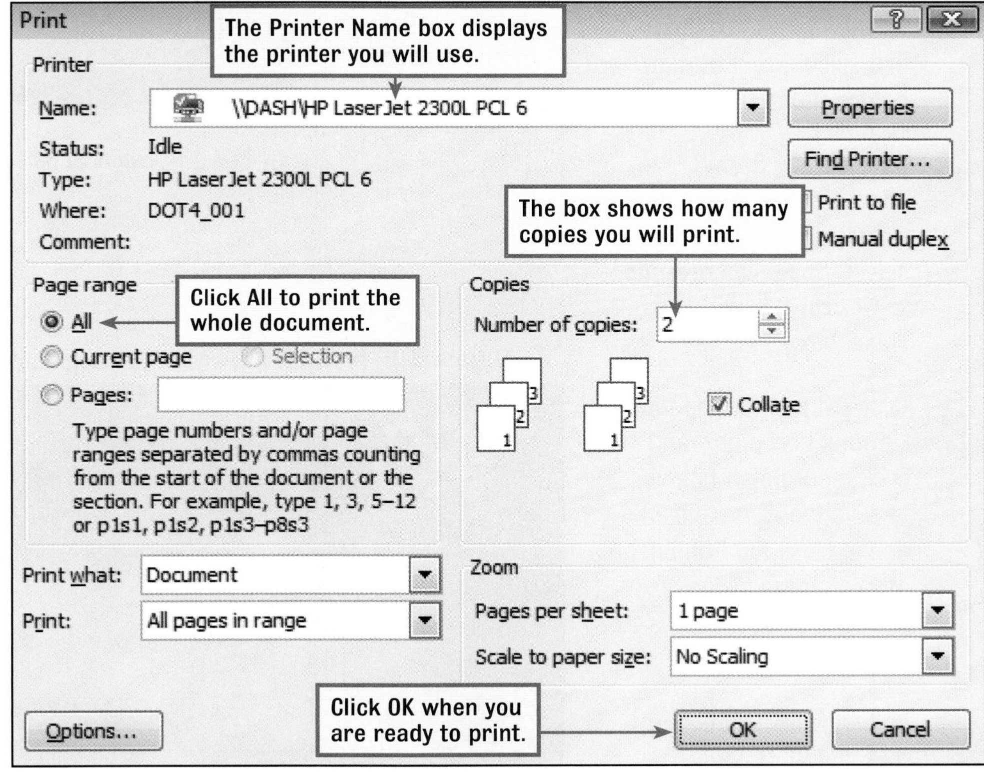

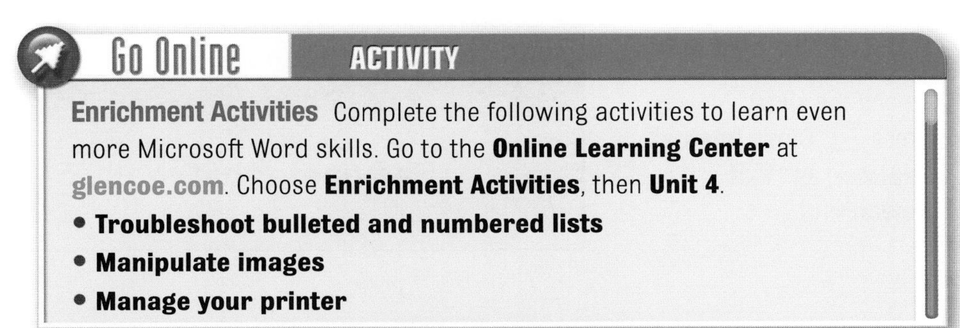

Go Online ACTIVITY

Enrichment Activities Complete the following activities to learn even more Microsoft Word skills. Go to the **Online Learning Center** at glencoe.com. Choose **Enrichment Activities**, then **Unit 4**.

- **Troubleshoot bulleted and numbered lists**
- **Manipulate images**
- **Manage your printer**

Project 3 Assessment

Key Concepts Check

1. **Explain** When do you use speaker notes?
2. **Describe** What are the features of a PowerPoint handout?
3. **Identify** List two ways to navigate through slides that are opened in a Web browser.

Critical Thinking

4. **Draw Conclusions** If you wanted to use your speaker notes as a handout, what kind of notes would you write?
5. **Cause and Effect** What are three advantages to publishing your presentation as a Web page?

1 Guided Practice

Present Your Presentation on Presentations You are ready to give your talk about the proper way to give a presentation. After you add some reminders to yourself in your speaker notes, you plan to print handouts for your classmates. You will also view the presentation using Internet Explorer. If you need help completing a step, refer back to the exercise in parentheses at the end of the steps.

Step-by-Step

1. **Open** your **Present a Presentation** file.
2. Add **speaker notes** to **Slides 3**, **4**, **5**, and **8** (Figure 3.10). The notes should remind you to emphasize certain points and discuss related content that is not on the slide. (Exercise 3-1)
3. **Save** your presentation.

▼ **Figure 3.10** Speaker's notes should help illustrate the content of the slide.

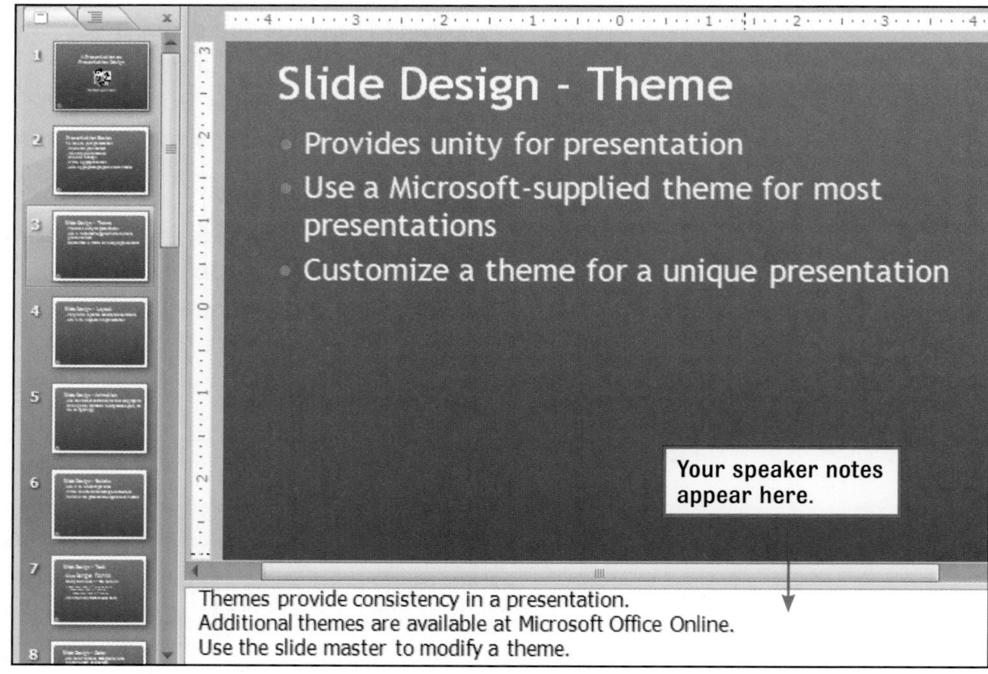

11 At the top left corner of the image, place the pointer over the **sizing handle** until you see a **two-headed arrow** [↘].

12 Hold down the left mouse button and drag the handle downward to make the image small enough to fit in the space. See Figure 2.15.

13 Place the insertion point after **Have a great time!** Press [ENTER] twice.

14 To credit your source, key Photo courtesy of Fender Musical Instruments Corporation. Used with permission.

15 **Select** the text you just keyed. In the **Font** box, click **Calibri.** Click the arrow in the **Font Size** box, then click **12.** Then click the **Bold** button [B] to remove the boldface.

16 Your flyer should look similar to Figure 2.16. **Save** your document.

▼ **Figure 2.15** Use the sizing handles to make the image bigger or smaller.

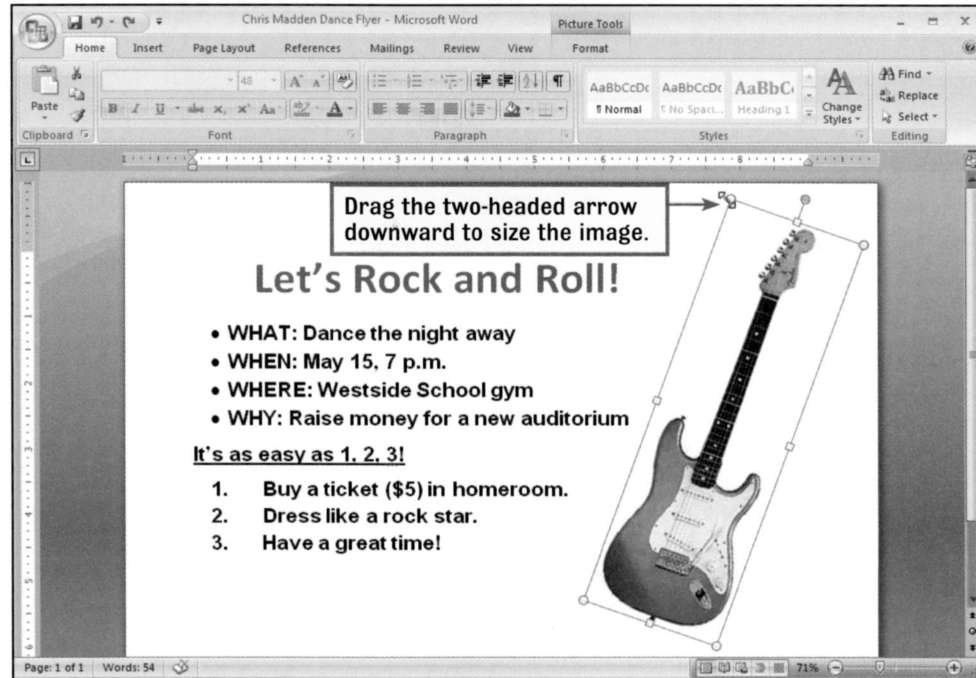

▼ **Figure 2.16** Your finished flyer should be similar to this.

- **WHAT: Dance the night away**
- **WHEN: May 15, 7 p.m.**
- **WHERE: Westside School gym**
- **WHY: Raise money for a new auditorium**

It's as easy as 1, 2, 3!

1. **Buy a ticket ($5) in homeroom.**
2. **Dress like a rock star.**
3. **Have a great time!**

Photo courtesy of Fender Musical Instruments Corporation. Used with permission.

HELP!

Sizing Handles To display sizing handles, or to make them go away again, click your picture. If the top or bottom of your image runs off the page after you resize it, click the picture and drag the image up or down.

Project 3 Assessment

4. Click the **File** menu, and choose **Print**. (Figure 3.11).

5. Print handouts of your presentation for your class. (Select the layout with three slides per page.) Remember to ask your teacher for permission to print. (Exercise 3-2)

▼ **Figure 3.11** **The Print dialog box offers a variety of ways to print your presentation.**

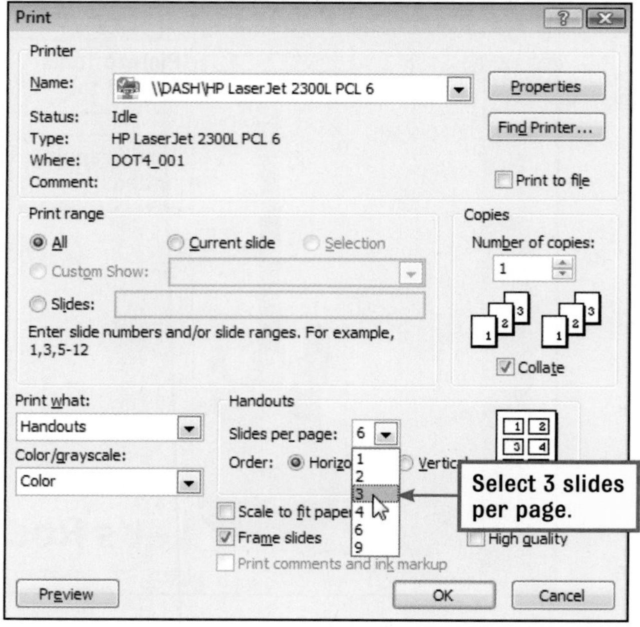

6. **Save** your presentation as a **Web page**. Name the file *Your Name* Presentation Web Page. (Exercise 3-3)

7. **Preview** your PowerPoint file (Figure 3.12). **Close** your presentation.

8. **Exit Internet Explorer**.

▼ **Figure 3.12** **The Internet provides a convenient way to share a presentation.**

4 Click the guitar, if necessary, to display sizing handles and a selection rectangle. See Figure 2.13.

5 Locate the **Picture Tools Format** tab, and click the **Text Wrapping** button. Select **Tight**.

6 Move your pointer over the picture until you see the **four-headed arrow**.

7 Hold down the left mouse button and drag the picture to the right side of the page.

8 When all the text has wrapped to the left of the picture, release the mouse button (Figure 2.14).

9 Click the **green rotation handle** and hold down the left mouse button.

10 Drag the handle so that the guitar tilts to the right, then release the mouse button (Figure 2.14).

Figure 2.13 The Picture Tools Format tab displays on the Ribbon when a picture is selected.

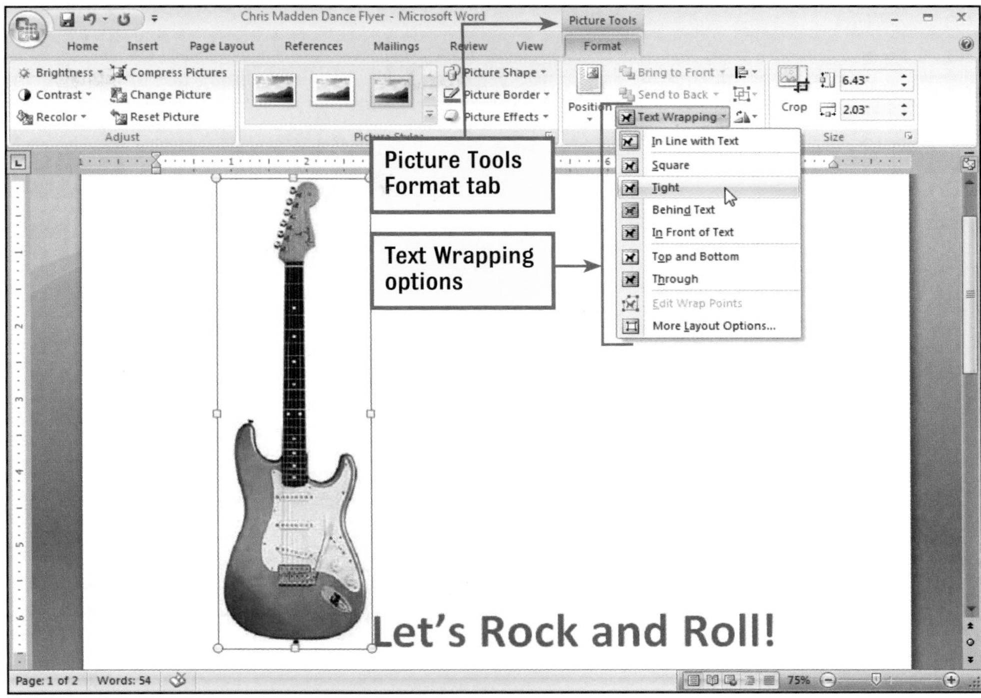

Figure 2.14 You can move or resize an image when you insert it into a document.

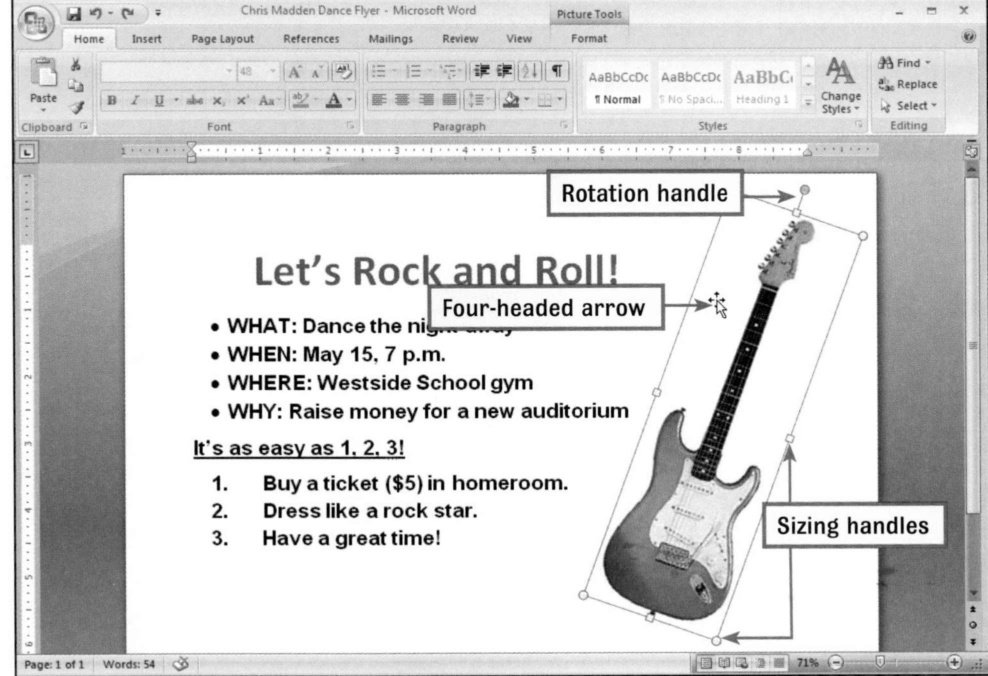

Go Online RUBRICS

glencoe.com

Independent Practice Use the rubrics for these projects to help create and evaluate your work. Go to the **Online Learning Center** at **glencoe.com**. Choose **Rubrics**, then **Unit 7**.

2 Independent Practice

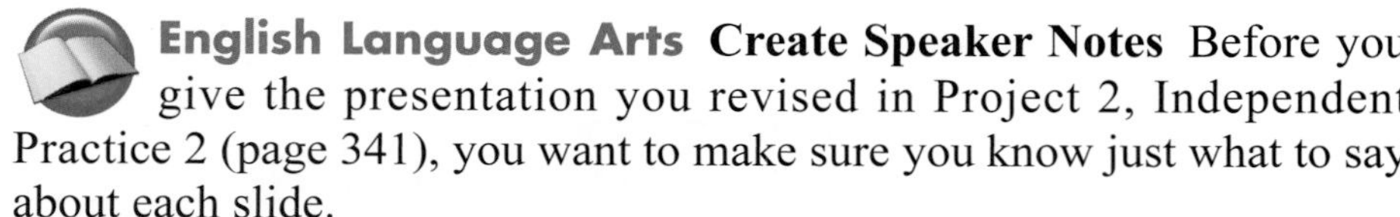

English Language Arts **Create Speaker Notes** Before you give the presentation you revised in Project 2, Independent Practice 2 (page 341), you want to make sure you know just what to say about each slide.

a. Plan Review each slide of your presentation. On a separate piece of paper, write speaker notes about each slide.

b. Create Click each slide, and add your speaker notes. With your teacher's permission, print your speaker notes.

3 Independent Practice

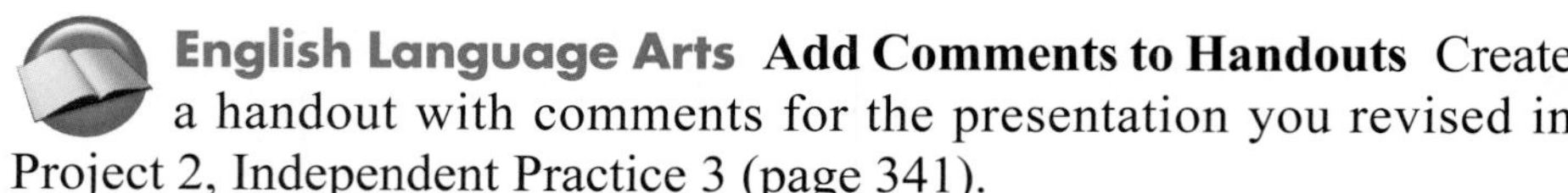

English Language Arts **Add Comments to Handouts** Create a handout with comments for the presentation you revised in Project 2, Independent Practice 3 (page 341).

a. Create For each slide, add comments in the Speaker Notes pane. Provide interesting facts, or add more details about the subject covered on the slide.

b. Revise Proofread your comments and the slides. Make corrections or improvements where necessary.

c. Publish With your teacher's permission, either print your presentation or publish your presentation as a Web page.

4 Independent Practice

English Language Arts **Deliver a Presentation** Add final touches to the presentation you revised in Project 2, Independent Practice 4 (page 341).

a. Create Add more information to your presentation.

- Insert at least three new slides that show why you are interested in and qualified for the career you have chosen.
- Write speaker notes for each slide.

b. Present With your teacher's permission, deliver your presentation to the class. In addition, publish the presentation, with the speaker notes, as a printed handout or as a Web page.

Michelle D. Bridwell/PhotoEdit

Exercise 2-5 Insert a Picture in Your Flyer

Pictures can make your work more interesting and easier to understand. However, when you do use images, use them wisely. Make sure there are not too many images. This can make your document confusing, with too much to focus on. Follow these guidelines when adding pictures to your document.

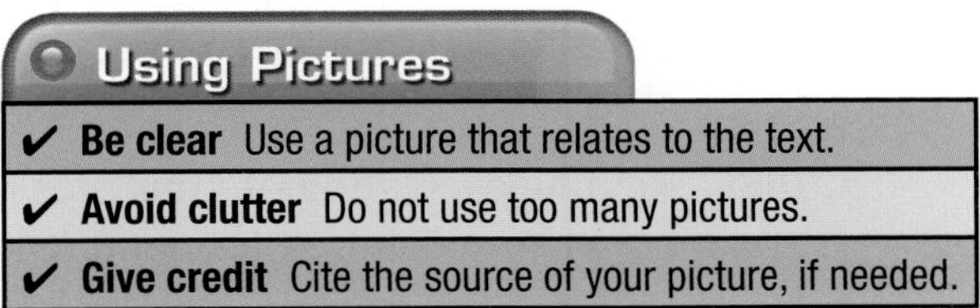

Using Pictures

✔ **Be clear**	Use a picture that relates to the text.
✔ **Avoid clutter**	Do not use too many pictures.
✔ **Give credit**	Cite the source of your picture, if needed.

Word has a number of tools that help you work with pictures. Sizing handles let you make the picture bigger or smaller. Text wrapping makes text flow around the picture. The four-headed arrow [four-headed arrow icon] lets you move the picture around on the page.

In this exercise, you will place a photo of a guitar in your flyer and move it to the position you want.

Step-by-Step

1. Place your insertion point before **Let's Rock and Roll!**

2. On the **Insert** tab, in the **Illustrations** group, choose the **Picture** command (Figure 2.12).

3. **Browse** to the **Data File** named **4B Guitar**. Click **Insert**. The guitar appears on your screen.

▼ **Figure 2.12** **You can insert different kinds of pictures from different locations using the Insert tab.**

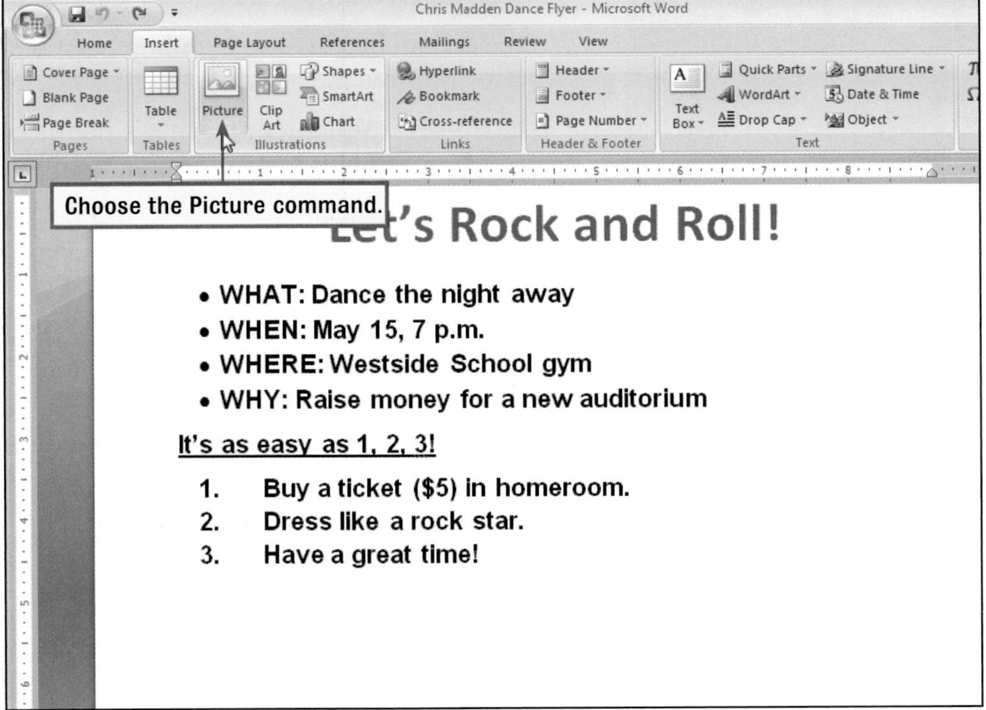

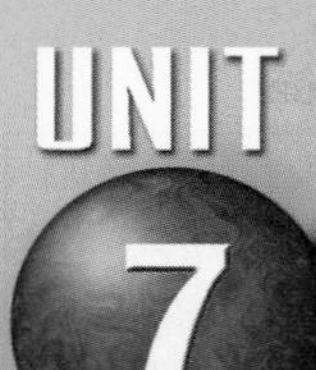

UNIT 7 Projects Across the Curriculum

Use your PowerPoint skills to complete the following projects. Ask your teacher about saving or printing your work.

Project 1 Your Favorite Technology

Science Create a presentation about one type of technology that you would not want to live without. It can be high-tech, such as an MP3 player or a computer, or it can be more basic, such as indoor plumbing.

Research

1. With your teacher's permission, use the Internet or print sources to research your technology. Remember to cite your sources.
2. Write down at least five facts about the history of your chosen technology and five facts about how the technology works.

Create

3. Create a presentation with at least six slides. It should include:
   a. A title slide
   b. Four slides describing how technology works and its history
   c. One slide about why technology is important to you
4. Apply a theme that gives the presentation a consistent look.
5. Add graphics and transitions to your slides.
6. Add speaker's notes that provide extra information that is not included on the slides.

Unit Projects Use the rubrics for these projects to help create and evaluate your work. Go to the **Online Learning Center** at **glencoe.com**. Choose **Rubrics**, then **Unit 7**.

Project 2 Present a News Event

Social Studies Create a presentation that describes and evaluates a newsworthy event, on a school, local, or global level.

Research

1. With your teacher's permission, use the Internet or print sources to research the event. Gather facts, opinions, and images about the event. Remember to cite your sources.

Continued on page 353

5 Place your insertion point at the end of the word **auditorium** (in the fourth bulleted item).

6 Press ENTER two times.

7 Click the **Underline** button U.

8 Key It's as easy as 1, 2, 3!

9 Click the **Underline** button again to stop underlining. Then press ENTER once (Figure 2.10).

Figure 2.10 A Ribbon button changes color when that command is in use.

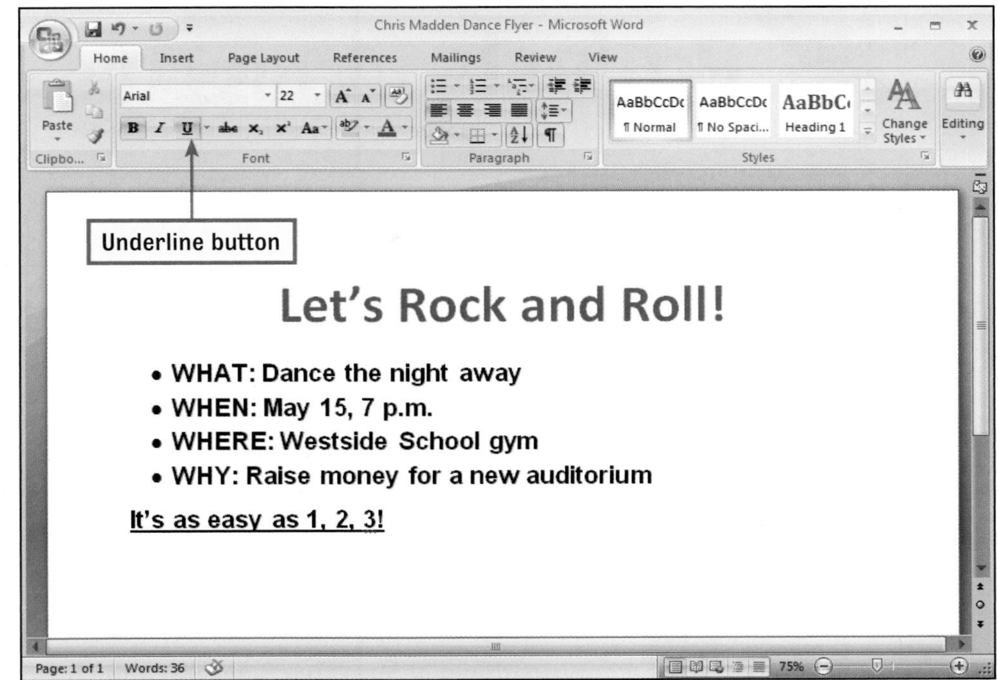

10 Click the **Numbering** button. A number 1 appears.

11 Key Buy a ticket ($5) in homeroom. and press ENTER. A new number should appear on the next line.

12 Key Dress like a rock star. Press ENTER.

13 Key Have a great time!

14 Your document should look like Figure 2.11. **Save** the document.

Figure 2.11 You can add numbers or bullets by first selecting text, then clicking the Numbering or Bullets buttons on the Ribbon.

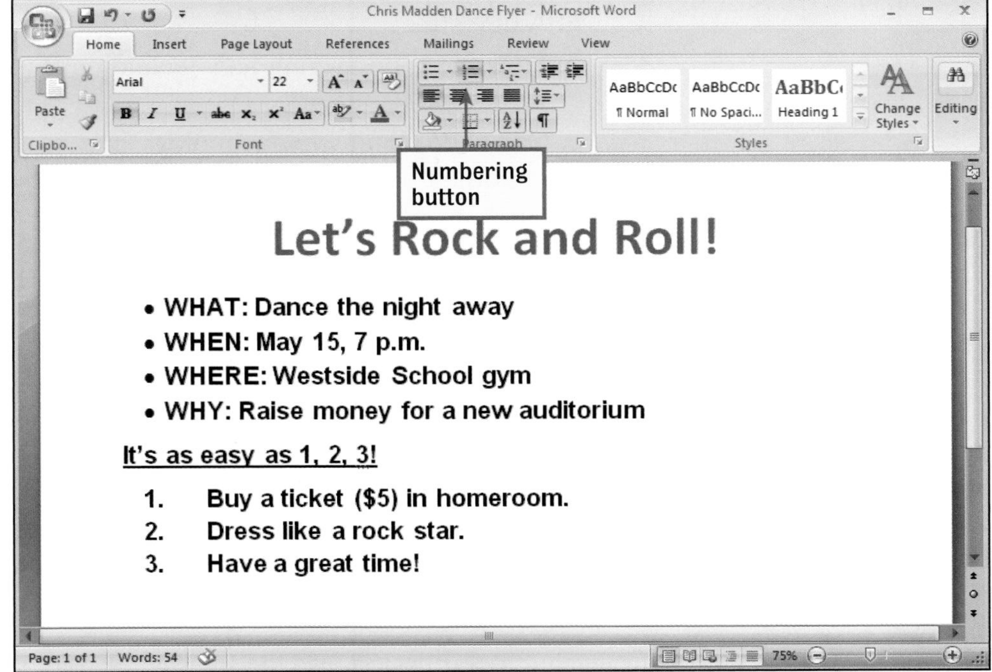

Projects Across the Curriculum

Create

2. Create a presentation with at least ten slides, including a title page. Include a description of the event, the reason the event is important, and images—such as photographs or charts—illustrating different aspects of the event.
3. Apply a theme that gives the presentation a consistent look and feel.
4. Apply animation, transitions, and other special effects to the slides.
5. Add speaker notes that provide information that is not included on the slides.

> **Go Online** **e-REVIEW**
> glencoe.com
> **Assessment** Double-check your knowledge of PowerPoint. Go to the **Online Learning Center** at glencoe.com. Choose **e-Review Quizzes**, and take the **Unit 7 Tech Assess Quiz**.

Project 3 Community Service ★★★

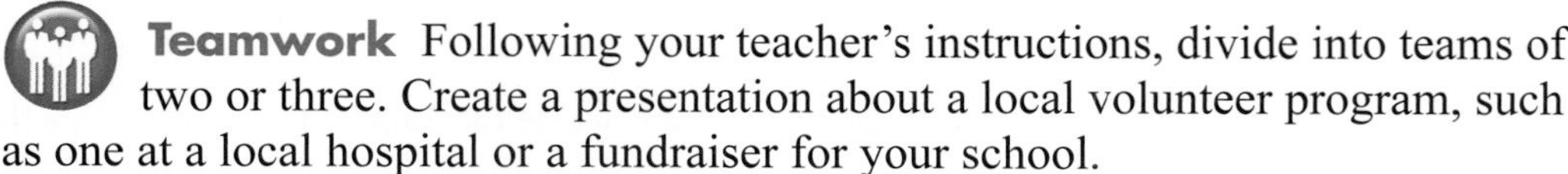

Teamwork Following your teacher's instructions, divide into teams of two or three. Create a presentation about a local volunteer program, such as one at a local hospital or a fundraiser for your school.

Research

1. With your teacher's permission, use the Internet, local publications, or personal contacts to research volunteer opportunities in your community.
2. Take notes describing the organization, the volunteer program, when and where the program is held, and whom to contact.
3. Gather images from the organization's brochures, take your own photos, or use clip art. Cite your sources.

Create

4. Create a presentation with at least 12 slides, including a title page. Include:
   a. All the information and images from your research
   b. Charts or tables to demonstrate the effectiveness of the program
5. Apply a theme and other features that give the presentation a consistent look.
6. Apply animation, transitions, and other effects.
7. Add speaker notes that provide information not included on the slides.

Exercise 2-4 Create Lists

Lists can make information easy to read. They also highlight the most important information. The two kinds of lists you will usually find in documents are **bulleted lists** and **numbered lists**.

Types of Lists

Bulleted List	Numbered List
◆ Inserts dots called bullets before each item	**1.** Inserts a number before each item
◆ Can use other characters, such as diamonds	**2.** Automatically uses consecutive numbers
◆ Presents information in no particular order	**3.** Lists information in specific order, such as steps

In this exercise, you want to make items in your flyer stand out for your reader. You will do this by creating bulleted and numbered lists.

Step-by-Step

1. In the **Dance Flyer** document, select the four lines of text starting with **What**, **When**, **Where**, and **Why** (Figure 2.9).

2. On the **Home** tab, in the **Paragraph** group, click the arrow beside the **Bullets** button.

3. Move your mouse pointer over the styles in the **Bullet Library** for a preview of how the bullets will look in your flyer. Click one of the bullet styles.

4. Review the document. Each line in the list should now begin with a bullet.

▼ **Figure 2.9** **Click the arrow beside the Bullets button to change the style of bullets.**

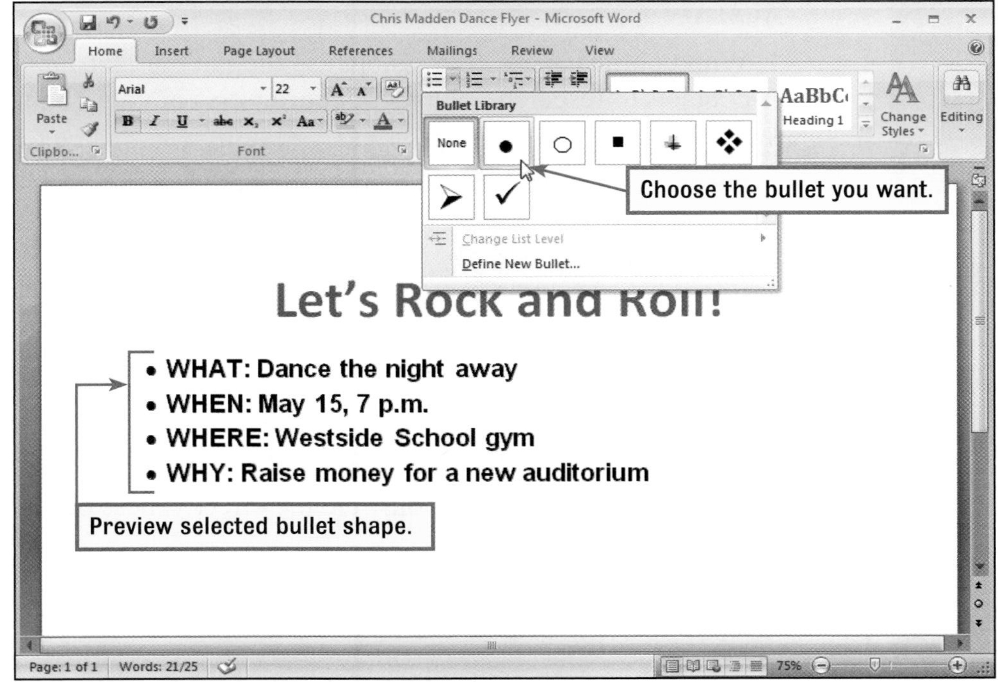

UNIT 7

Build Your Portfolio

Create a Presentation

Preparing for an interview is a critical step when searching for a job. Create a presentation about how to interview for a job. Think about how you dress, how you behave, what you say, and even how you listen.

Research

1. Go to this book's Online Learning Center at **glencoe.com** to find **Web Links** for at least two Web sites that give advice about interviewing for a job.
2. Write the tips you find on index cards, and organize them according to category. For example, you might have tips for dressing correctly, asking good questions, listening well, and so on.

> Go Online RUBRICS
> glencoe.com
>
> **Build Your Portfolio** Use the rubric for this portfolio project to help create and evaluate your work. Go to the **Online Learning Center** at **glencoe.com**. Choose **Rubrics**, then **Unit 7**.

Create

3. Create a PowerPoint presentation with at least ten slides, including a title slide.
   a. Apply a theme and headers or footers that give your slides a consistent look.
   b. Use bulleted and numbered lists to present your information.
   c. Add graphics to illustrate your points. These can be photographs, clip art, tables, or graphs.

4. Add animation and transitions to your presentation.
5. Add speaker notes to each slide.
6. Proofread and edit your presentation and notes. Cite your sources.

Present

7. With your teacher's permission, print the PowerPoint presentation and your speaker notes.
8. With your teacher's permission, save and view your presentation as a Web page.

Step-by-Step

1. In your **Dance Flyer** document, change the **Zoom** dialog box to **75%**.

2. To change the page orientation, click the **Page Layout** tab (Figure 2.7).

3. Click the **Orientation** button.

4. Click **Landscape**. Your document should look similar to Figure 2.8.

Figure 2.7 Click the Page Layout tab to change orientation.

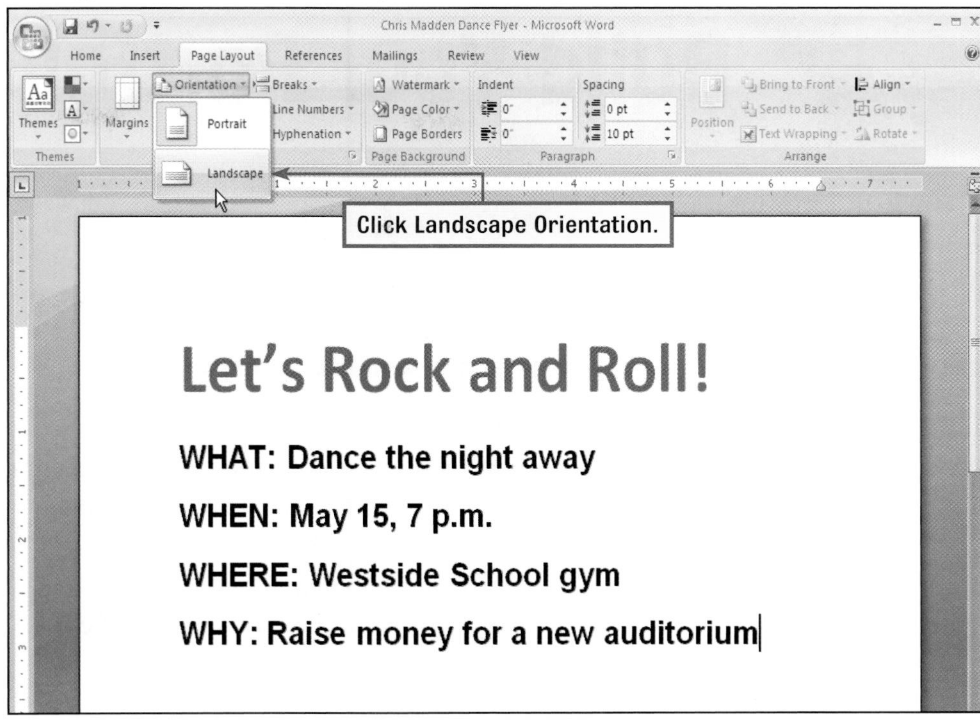

5. Select the text **Let's Rock and Roll!**

6. On the **Home** tab, in the **Paragraph** group, click the **Align Text Right** button. The text should move to the right margin.

7. Click the **Align Text Left** button. The text should move to the left margin.

8. Click the **Center** button. The text should be centered on the page, as in Figure 2.8. **Save** your document.

Figure 2.8 Center alignment is often used for titles.

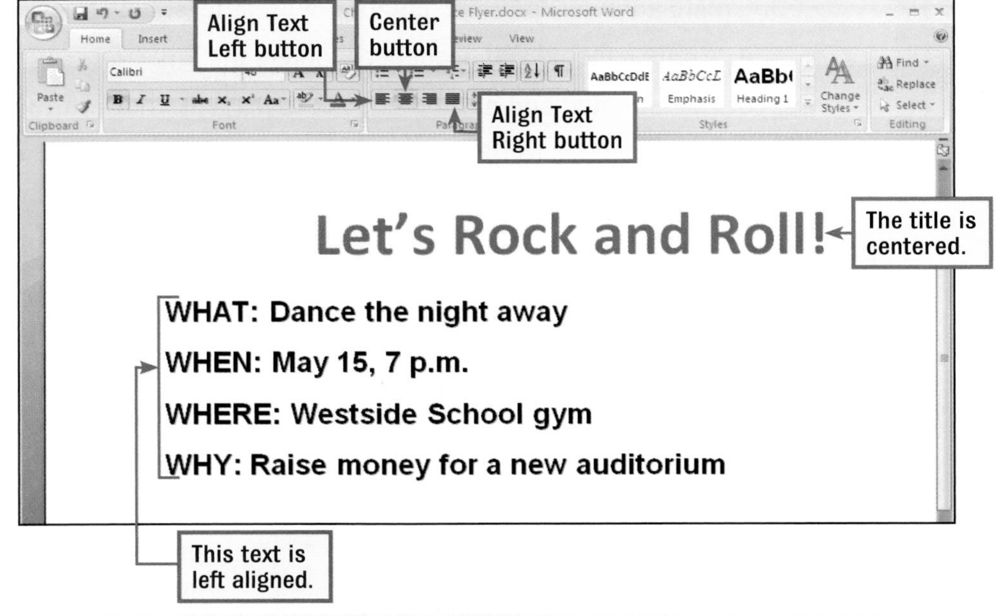

HELP!

Other Ways Use the **Page Layout** tab's **Orientation** button to change orientation, or open the **Page Setup** dialog box, then click the **Margins** tab.

UNIT 8

Integrated Applications

Real World Projects

Go Online **e-QUIZ**

glencoe.com

Starting with You What types of technology do you think you will be using in the future? To find out more, go to the **Online Learning Center** at glencoe.com. Choose **e-Quizzes**, and take the **Unit 8 Pre-Quiz.**

Exercise 2-3 Change Page Orientation and Text Alignment

When you create a document, think about how you want the text to look when you are done. **Orientation** describes the direction of the page or the paper you will print on. You may need to change the orientation of the page to make sure the finished document fits on the page and is easy to read. You can choose to create a document using portrait or landscape orientation, as shown below.

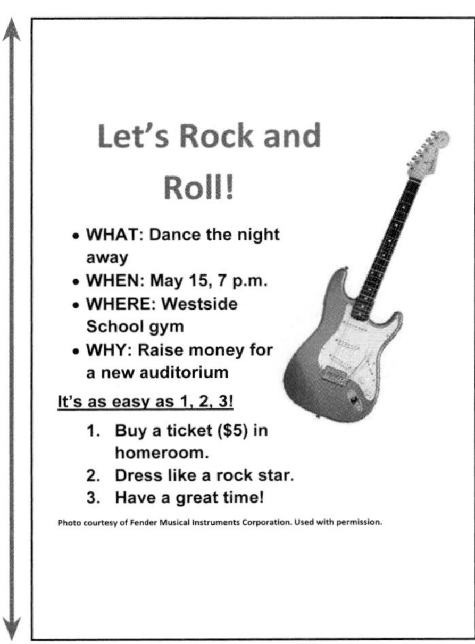

Portrait orientation

Landscape orientation

You can also choose the position of the text on the page. **Alignment** describes whether the text is lined up on the left, right, center, or across the page. In the Paragraph group, you will find four buttons that control alignment, as shown below.

Text Alignment Options

Alignment	Button	Description
Align Text Left		Aligns text on the left margin of the page
Center		Centers text between the left and right margins
Align Text Right		Aligns text on the right margin of the page
Justify		Aligns text across the page from the left margin to the right margin

In this exercise, you will change the orientation and alignment of the text on the page.

Emerging Technologies

Reading Guide

Before You Read

Study with a Buddy Before you read a unit, find a partner and ask each other questions about the topics that will be discussed. (Use the section headings or the "Key Concepts" objectives to identify topics.) Keep these questions in mind when you read and see if you can learn the answers.

Key Concepts

- How to identify current trends in technology
- How to use technology responsibly
- Why access to technology is important

Vocabulary

Key Terms

integrated device
obsolete
electronic waste
accessibility

Academic Vocabulary

trend
benefit
minimize
role

Trends in Technology

The invention of the wheel led to a wheeled cart that could be pulled by an animal. That advancement took a few thousand years. In our era, it seems as though high-tech breakthroughs happen almost daily. The **trend**, or tendency, in technology today is toward devices that are smaller, faster, and more integrated. An **integrated device** performs more than one function.

When compact discs were first introduced, people were amazed that a whole album could fit on a small piece of plastic. Now, thousands of songs fit on a pocket-sized MP3 player, which might play the radio and record your voice.

▲ Many experts think that home robots are the next big advance in technology. What would you like a robot to do for you?

Examples of High-Tech Trends

	SMALLER	FASTER	INTEGRATED
Then	Computers used to take up the space of a whole room.	Early computers could do only basic calculations such as adding, subtracting, multiplying, and dividing.	Not so long ago, you needed a separate cell phone, MP3 player, and PDA to do specific tasks.
Now	Today, some personal computers can clip on to your belt.	Computers today are fast enough to handle movie-making, graphic design, and gaming.	Today you can buy one device that integrates a phone, music player, and PDA.

▲ Technology companies are competing to make the smallest, fastest, and most integrated devices. How will these devices affect your life as a computer user?

Today, many books are written and printed using computer technology. There are even interactive books that can be read on a computer screen rather than on paper. These e-books let users add notes to the text and easily search for information within the book. Eventually you may be able to download all your textbooks and notebooks onto one small computer!

Exercise 2-2 Use the Format Painter

To format text quickly, use the Format Painter button on the Ribbon's Home tab, in the Clipboard group. The Format Painter lets you easily copy formatting from one part of your text to another with the click of a button. After you have formatted text (chosen the font, font size, font color, and so on), you can apply the exact same format to other text.

In this exercise, you will use the Format Painter to copy formatting from one part of your flyer to another.

Step-by-Step

1. In your **Dance Flyer** document, select the text **WHAT: Dance the night away**.
2. On the **Home** tab, in the **Font** group, click the arrow beside the **Font** box, then choose **Arial**.
3. Click the arrow in the **Font Size** box, then choose **22**.
4. Click the **Bold** button **B**. Your text should look like Figure 2.5.
5. Make sure **WHAT: Dance the night away** is still selected. On the **Home** tab, in the **Clipboard** group, click **Format Painter**.
6. Select the next three lines of text, as shown in Figure 2.5.
7. All three lines should now have the same formatting as **WHAT: Dance the night away**.
8. Your screen should look like Figure 2.6. **Save** your document.

▼ **Figure 2.5** Remember to keep your text selected when you apply formatting.

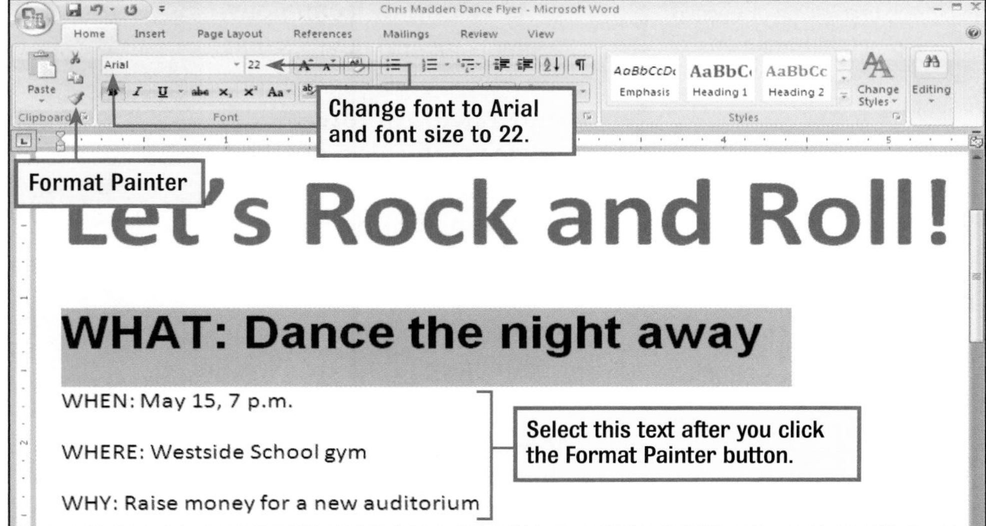

▼ **Figure 2.6** Your final Dance Flyer document should look like this.

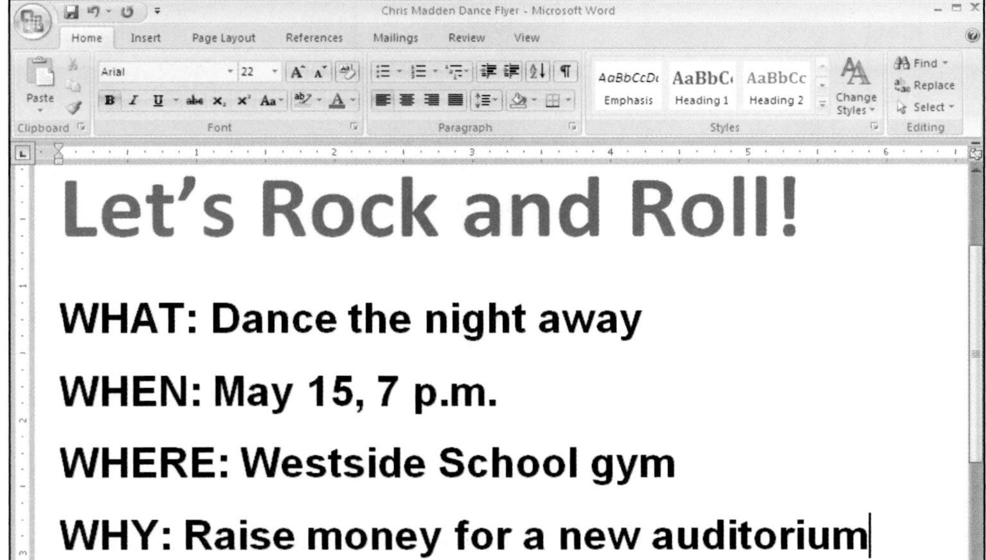

What Does the Future Hold?

Emerging technologies are technologies that are in the process of being developed. Although many of these technologies can be used today, they are being adapted or refined for exciting new uses in the future. The technologies emerging now are already having a big effect on our lives at home, in school, and at work. Below are just a few examples of what we might expect in the years ahead.

Academic Focus

English Language Arts

Read Books Online
Some Web sites allow you to download entire books, such as Jane Austen's *Pride and Prejudice*, that are in the public domain. You can read the entire work on your computer or PDA, and you can even search for keywords to find passages to support your ideas for a book report. When would you choose to read an online book rather than a print book?

NCTE 8 Use information resources to gather information.

Examples of Emerging Technologies

TECHNOLOGY	TODAY	IN THE FUTURE
Robots	• Automate tasks in factories • Do jobs that would be dangerous for people	Home robots may be companions, help clean and care for people, play music, and cook meals.
Wireless networks	• Allow people to connect to the Internet without wires • Let people use wireless computers over limited distances in businesses, homes, and public spaces	Students may use wireless networks to download textbooks and assignments and take part in classes from anywhere in the world—even remote locations.
Virtual reality (an artificial computer environment that mimics a real situation)	• Is used for playing powerful and realistic computer games • Provides a safe way for people to learn how to drive, fly, or perform surgery	Surgeons may operate on patients from remote locations, using virtual reality and cameras to control surgical robots.

▲ The technology we use today will affect our lives even more in the future. **How will wireless networks in the classroom make life easier for students?**

By staying informed about the latest technological changes, you can get the greatest **benefit**, or advantage, from them. Keep up-to-date on new trends by reading magazines, participating in e-mail groups, and visiting Web sites. You never know which breakthroughs will end up making your life easier, safer, and more enjoyable!

Reading Check

1. **Explain** What are integrated devices? Give an example.
2. **Describe** Give two examples of ways that we might use technology in the future.

6. Select the text **Let's Rock and Roll!**

7. On the **Home** tab, in the **Font** group, click the arrow beside the **Font Size** box, and then click **48**. Notice the **Live Preview** when you point to a font size (Figure 2.3).

▼ **Figure 2.3** Font size changes the size of your text.

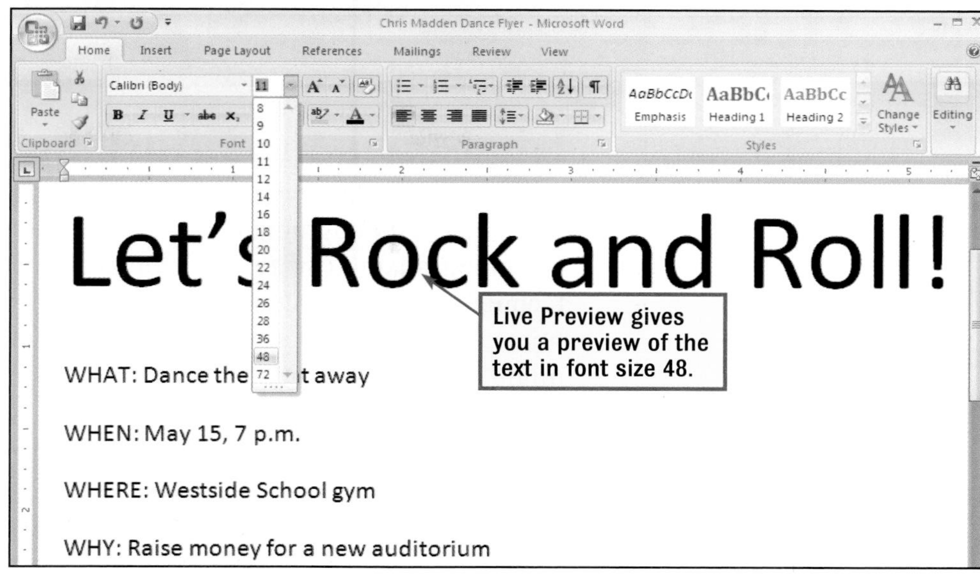

8. On the **Home** tab, in the **Font** group, click the **Font Color** button [A] drop-down arrow, then click a color that will grab people's attention, such as **Blue**.

9. On the **Home** tab, in the **Font** group, click the **Bold** button [B].

10. Click anywhere on the screen to deselect your text.

11. Your text should look like Figure 2.4. **Save** your document.

▼ **Figure 2.4** Use large, bright text so that your flyer can be read from far away.

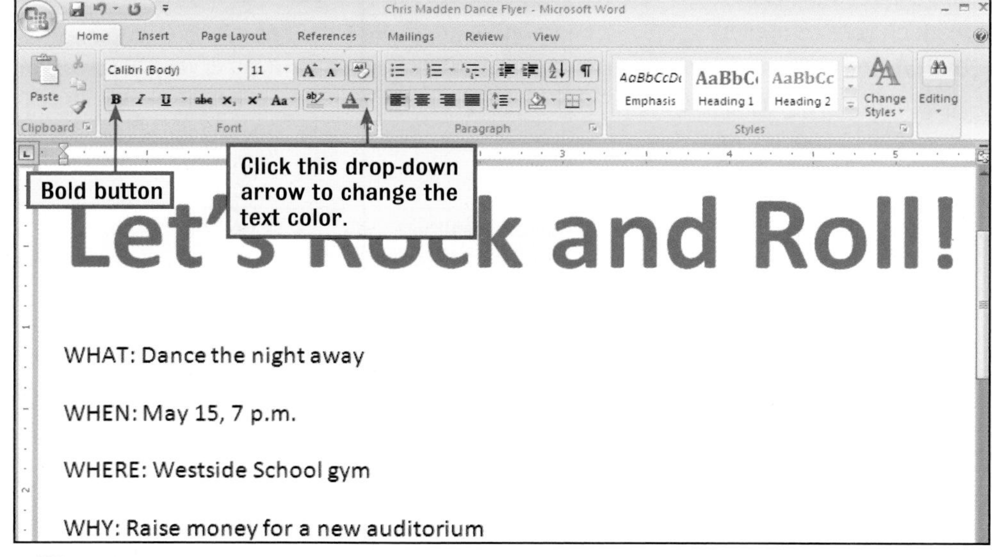

TechSavvy

Live Preview Preview formats, fonts, and styles before you apply them in your document by using **Live Preview**. By pointing to various formatting choices, you can instantly see how those choices would appear on selected text. For example, if you are trying to choose a bullet style, just move the mouse pointer over choices in the **Bullets Library** to see the effect in your document. When you have finished previewing the bullet styles, move the mouse pointer over the style you want and click to apply it.

Use Technology Responsibly

Ethics The information on a computer belongs to the person who put it there. If someone lends you a piece of equipment, make sure you do not view or tamper with any private information. If the equipment is a gift, make sure that all private information has been deleted or moved to another device.

Why It's Important What types of information have you entered into a computer that you would not want others to access?

People have a responsibility to use technology wisely. We have learned this lesson throughout human history. For example, fire can be used for good (cooking, making iron tools, and so on), but it can also be used destructively. Almost any technology, such as cameras, automobiles, or the Internet, can be used for both good and bad purposes.

Computer technology allows us to do many helpful things, but it can sometimes be used to harm people or steal from them. A technology, by itself, is neither good nor bad. It is up to you, the user, to direct the power of technology for helpful, not harmful, purposes. Think about how what you do may affect yourself or others. Consider how you would feel if someone else did something that was hurtful to you.

▲ New technology has made it easier to diagnose medical problems. **Name one type of medical technology and explain its benefits.**

Why Are Ethics Important?

In Units 1 and 4, you learned the importance of ethics—the rules we use to decide how to act. Most people are ethical and treat others fairly. It is important to think and act ethically every time you boot up and use a computer. At home and at school, you probably share your computer with others. The Internet links computers and computer users around the world. An ethical or unethical act, therefore, could reach a very large number of people quickly. This was not possible just a few short years ago.

Even responsible and experienced users of technology need to be careful. Just as you respect other people's privacy online, be sure to protect your own privacy! Using technology is like driving—a good driver is always on the lookout for road hazards. A smart user of technology stays up-to-date about viruses, hackers, and other risks. If you think that your computer may have a virus, contact an adult immediately for help.

Exercise 2-1 Format Text

Good formatting makes your document look better and helps your audience read the information easily. **Format** refers to the way text looks and the way it is arranged on a page. **Font** is the shape of the letters, numbers, and other characters. Word has many fonts to choose from. Some examples are:

Arial	Optima	Papyrus
Brush Script	Gadjet	American Typewriter
CAPITALS	Comic Sans	Times New Roman

In this exercise, you will begin to create a flyer. For the flyer, you will need to format the size, color, and style of selected text.

Student Data File

Step-by-Step

1. **Start Word**. On the **Home** tab, in the **Font** group, identify the buttons shown in Figure 2.1.

2. **Open** the Data File named **4A Dance Flyer**.

3. Click the **Office Button**, then **Save As**. The **Save As** dialog box opens (Figure 2.2).

4. **Save** the **Data File** to the correct location.

5. **Name** the file *Your Name* Dance Flyer. Click **Save**.

Figure 2.1 Use the Font group to change the way text looks.

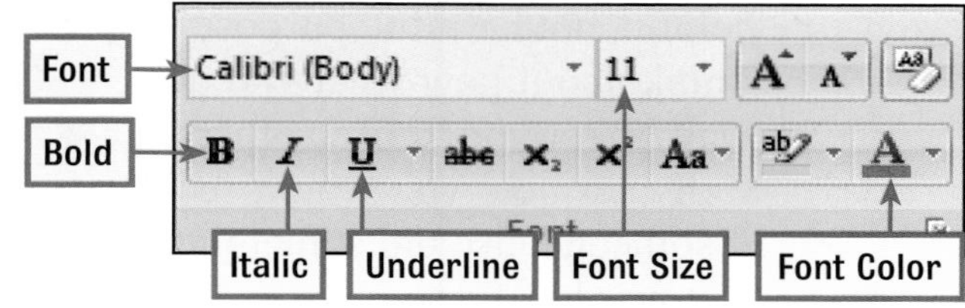

Figure 2.2 Use Save As to save a file in a new location with a new name.

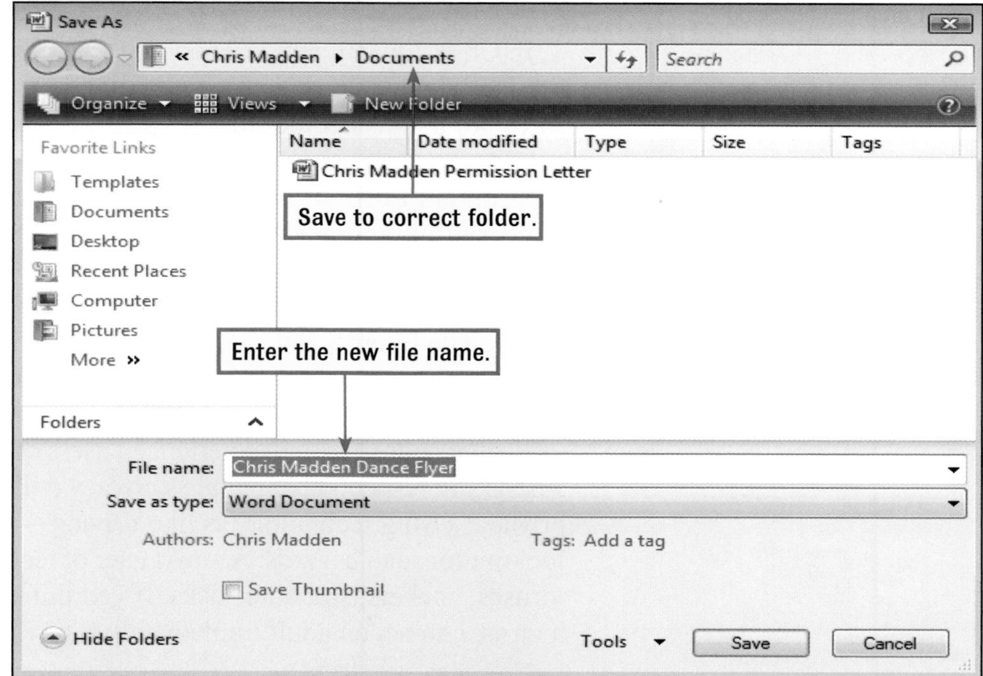

How Does Technology Affect the Environment?

One consequence of rapid technological change is that equipment becomes obsolete very quickly. When technology is **obsolete**, it is no longer useful. Unfortunately, obsolete equipment often becomes **electronic waste**. This refers to all the discarded computers, monitors, and other devices that are thrown away.

Electronic waste is an environmental problem because many devices contain harmful chemicals that can contaminate the air and water near landfills. Taking care of the environment is an important part of being a responsible user of technology. Consider these ways you can **minimize**, or reduce, the environmental impact of your technology:

- Reuse and recycle your printer's paper and ink cartridges.
- Donate used equipment to a charity instead of throwing it away. You can also look for recycling programs offered in your community or by computer manufacturers.
- If you have to throw equipment away, do it safely. For example, computer monitors may contain poisonous lead, so you should learn the best way to dispose of monitors. Many communities have special disposal programs for electronic equipment.

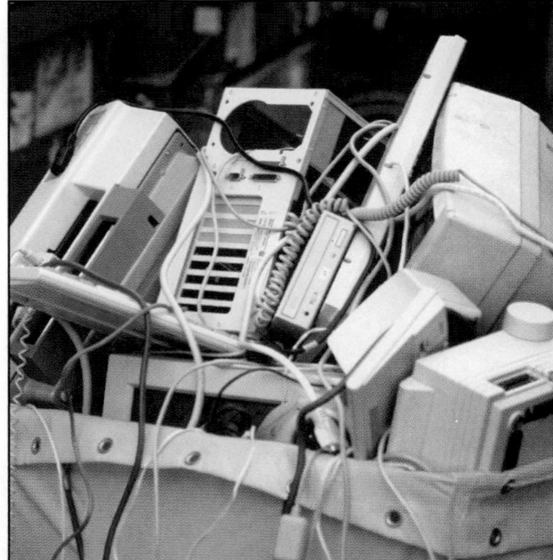

▲ Piles of discarded equipment often end up in landfills. **Why is the amount of electronic waste increasing every year?**

Remember, proper disposal of obsolete technology is a way of acting ethically. Your old computer might be valued by somebody who does not have a computer, or if you choose to recycle, more than 95 percent of a computer can be reused in some way.

Reading Check

1. **Describe** How is using technology similar to driving?
2. **Explain** Why should you be concerned about electronic waste?

Concepts in Action

Project 2 Create a Flyer with a Picture

Key Concepts

Exercise 2-1
- Change font size and color

Exercise 2-2
- Use the Format Painter
- Change fonts

Exercise 2-3
- Change text alignment
- Choose page orientation

Exercise 2-4
- Create bulleted and numbered lists

Exercise 2-5
- Import a picture
- Apply text wrap options
- Rotate and resize a picture

Exercise 2-6
- Print

Vocabulary

Key Terms
format
font
orientation
alignment
bulleted list
numbered list

Before You Begin

Double-Check As you work through each exercise, look at every figure to make sure you complete the steps correctly.

In this project, you will use a word processing program to create a flyer that includes a picture.

Get the Word Out

It is now time to publicize the *Let's Rock and Roll!* dance. Fender gave you permission to use the guitar photo in a flyer. Now you need to create a flyer that will grab people's attention. After all, the more people who go to the dance, the more money there will be for building a new auditorium. You will need to clearly explain when and where the dance will be held, why it is being held, and how to buy tickets. To make these important points stand out, you will use bullets and numbering on your flyer. You will also cite the source of the guitar photo.

Technology and Accessibility

Technology plays a big **role**, or part, in how we work, communicate, learn, and play. Computers and the Internet give you access to job skills, educational opportunities, information, opinions, and more. However, not everyone has the same access to the benefits of technology.

Accessibility refers to how easily available something is. Although it seems as though computers are everywhere, many people living in isolated or poor areas in the United States and throughout the world may not have easy access to computers or the Internet.

▲ In our society, we consider education a basic right for all children. Do you think access to computers and other technology should be a basic right? If so, why?

How Does Accessibility Make a Difference?

Technology helps people all over the world communicate with each other and work together. In particular, the Internet has brought us together as never before. By improving access to technology, we invite more and more people to participate in our global community.

A huge public and private effort is under way to make computer technology accessible to more people. Organizations have donated millions of dollars worth of training, hardware, and software to communities in need in the United States and all around the world. Accessibility to computers has increased due to improvements in areas such as:

- **Affordability** The cost of computers and other devices keeps going down. As this trend continues, more people will be able to afford these tools.
- **Wireless technology** Many homes, businesses, and schools have their own wireless networks. Soon, entire cities will be wirelessly connected, and people living in remote areas will be able to connect without needing wired systems. This means that people will be able to use e-mail and the Internet from anywhere.
- **Public access** Classrooms, libraries, cafes, and other public spaces make it easier for people to use computers for training, creating résumés, and conducting online job searches.
- **Education** The more people learn about technology, the more likely they are to use it themselves. Anyone can be a teacher! Look for ways to share your expertise with others. Teaching someone else also helps you reinforce new ideas and skills.

2 Independent Practice 

English Language Arts **Create and Save a Document** Imagine that you are a graphic designer, and you want to create a flyer to advertise a local dog adoption service.

a. **Research** Go to **glencoe.com** for this book's Online Learning Center to find resources about dogs.
   - Find a suitable picture of a dog on the Web site. With your teacher's permission, print the page where you found the picture.
   - Find the organization's address. (**Hint**: Look for a link called Terms of Use, Permissions, About Our Site, or Contact Us.)

b. **Create** Open a new document. Save it as ***Your Name*** **Dog Letter**.

Go Online RUBRICS

glencoe.com

Independent Practice Use the rubrics for these projects to help create and evaluate your work. Go to the **Online Learning Center** at **glencoe.com**. Choose **Rubrics**, then **Unit 4**.

3 Independent Practice 

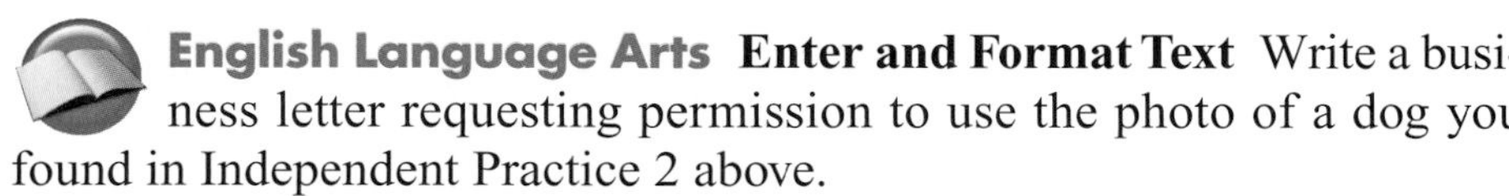

English Language Arts **Enter and Format Text** Write a business letter requesting permission to use the photo of a dog you found in Independent Practice 2 above.

a. **Plan** In the **Dog Letter** document you saved above, include all the parts of a business letter and use the correct format. (**Hint**: See Figure 1.7 on page 140 for help.)

b. **Create** In the body of your letter, include three paragraphs. Each paragraph should have three sentences.
   - Paragraph 1: Identify who you are and your role.
   - Paragraph 2: Describe the photo and how you plan to use it.
   - Paragraph 3: Explain how to contact you.

4 Independent Practice 

English Language Arts **Write a Letter** Think of a realistic way your school can be improved. For example, you might want to paint a student mural on a wall, start a new sports team, or add a salad bar in the cafeteria. Write a business letter to your principal. Describe your idea and explain how it can help the school. Use proper formatting in your business letter. Proofread and edit your letter. If your teacher allows, print the letter and deliver it to your principal.

Go Online ACTIVITY
glencoe.com

Accessibility Learn more about how technology can help people with disabilities and special needs. Go to the **Online Learning Center** at glencoe.com. Choose **Tech Talk Activities**, then **Unit 8**.

How Does Technology Help People with Special Needs?

Special efforts are helping to make technology more accessible to everyone. For example, the Americans with Disabilities Act (ADA) requires government Web sites to have accessibility features (such as voice activation and text magnification). Software companies include accessibility features in their products.

Just about everyone can find a way to use technology, whether facing challenges big or small. The table below describes a few examples.

Technology That Helps People

CHALLENGE	EXAMPLE OF SOLUTION
Hearing impairment	Videophones allow hearing-impaired people to see callers and use sign language.
Sight impairment	Synthetic-speech software can read and enter text.
Mobility challenges	A hands-free mouse allows users to control their computers with head movements.
Learning disabilities	A special "reading pen" can scan text and read the words aloud.

▲ Technology is becoming more accessible to people with disabilities. How can technology make a difference in the education of a person with disabilities?

High-Tech Hero

Stephen Hawking is, perhaps, the most famous scientist of our time. He writes best-selling books and gives speeches all over the world, yet he cannot use a keyboard, and he cannot speak. Hawking has amyotrophic lateral sclerosis (ALS), or Lou Gehrig's disease. He can enter words one by one onto a computer screen using limited hand or head movements. To talk, he enters his words into a voice synthesizer, which then "speaks" through a speaker on his wheelchair. Technology has enabled Hawking to communicate his ideas about the nature and origins of the universe to people around the world.

▲ The scientist Stephen Hawking is an example of how technology can be used to triumph over personal challenges. What would happen if Hawking did not have access to technology?

Reading Check

1. **Identify** What are two ways that technology can meet the needs of people with physical disabilities?
2. **Explain** How can wireless technology improve accessibility?

Project 1 Assessment

5. Key the text as shown in Figure 1.20 for the **salutation** and **body** of the letter. (Exercise 1-3)

6. Key a **closing** using your name. (Exercise 1-3)

7. On the **Page Layout** tab, in the **Paragraph** group, use the command to remove extra spacing between lines in the inside address and closing. (Exercise 1-3)

8. **Copy** the school name in the first paragraph, and **paste** it into the signature. (Exercise 1-4)

9. Use the **Spelling & Grammar** button to proof your letter. (Exercise 1-5)

10. Make any corrections, and **save** your edited letter. (Exercise 1-6)

11. In the **Page Setup** dialog box, check that all **Margins** are **1″**. Change the **Vertical alignment** to **Center**. (Exercise 1-6)

12. Use **Print Preview** to see how the letter will look before printing. If your teacher gives you permission, **print** the letter. (Exercise 1-6)

▼ **Figure 1.20** **Your final letter should look similar to the one below.**

4321 School Street
Wichita, KS 67202
March 15, 20--

Reprints Department Manager
United Media
200 Madison Avenue
New York, NY 10016

Dear Reprints Department Manager:

I am a student at Westside School and I am on the school's Yearbook Committee. We are very excited about our plans for this year's edtion. Humor will play an important part in its success.

Our committee would like to use the attached Peanuts comic strip in our school yearbook. It will be used on a page showing our Writing Club. We plan to print 600 copies of the yearbook. All profits from the yearbook sale will be put into the school's Yearbook Committee fund for next year.

Please let me know if we have permission to use the cartoon, and if so, what the fee to use it would be. I can be contacted at the address above. I will appreciate your help.

Sincerely,

Copy the school name and paste it in the closing.

Lee Davidson
Yearbook Committee
Westside School

Attachment

HELP!

Spelling Remember to space the parts of the letter correctly. Refer to page 140 for an example.

After You Read

Key Concepts Check

1. **Identify** What are three ways that technology is changing?
2. **Define** What is virtual reality, and how might it be used in the future?
3. **Explain** What does it mean to be a responsible user of technology?

Critical Thinking

4. **Evaluate** If you were given the opportunity to use a new wireless device that lets you spy on people, would you use it? Why or why not?
5. **Cause and Effect** What could happen if you threw away an old computer like regular garbage?

21st Century Skills

6. **Evaluate Technology** Go to this book's Online Learning Center **Web Links at glencoe.com** to find resources for portable devices with more than one function (such as a PDA or camera). List the specific features of each device, as well as the price.

Academic Skills

Mathematics

People have experimented with robots for many years.

a. **Calculate** How many years passed between the mechanical musician and the first industrial robot?

b. **Apply** How many of these events have occured since you were born?

Math Concept

Timelines A timeline is useful in displaying important data or information over a time period. This timeline lists events in robotics history.

Starting Hint Find the dates on the line for both the invention of the mechanical musician and the first industrial robot, then subtract to find the difference in years.

NCTM Data Analysis and Probability Select and use appropriate statistical methods to analyze data.

History of Robotics

400 B.C. In ancient Greece, a wooden dove that flaps its wings and flies.

1737 A French-built mechanical "musician" plays 11 different tunes.

1954 The first industrial robot is created for use at a General Motors plant.

1989 Genghis, one of the first walking robots, is created at a U.S. university.

1997 Garry Kasparov, a chess champion, loses to an IBM computer called Deep Blue.

1999 Sony releases an electronic pet dog called Aibo. It sells out in 20 minutes.

2001 The Global Hawk robotic spy plane flies itself from California to Australia.

Go Online e-QUIZ

glencoe.com

Self-Check Assess your understanding of what you have just read. Go to the **Online Learning Center** at glencoe.com. Choose **e-Quizzes**, and take the **Unit 8 Tech Talk Quiz**.

Project 1 Assessment

Key Concepts Check

1. **Identify** What are two Word tools you should use when you proofread and edit a document?
2. **Compare and contrast** What is the difference between the Cut and Delete commands?
3. **Identify** Describe the parts of a business letter.

Critical Thinking

4. **Draw Conclusions** When would it be useful to use a view at 150%, and when would it be better to use a 75% view?
5. **Cause and Effect** Why is it important to proofread your work in addition to using the Spelling & Grammar tool?

1 Guided Practice

Peanuts: ©United Feature Syndicated, Inc.

Create a Business Letter You want to use a Peanuts cartoon in your school yearbook, but you need to ask permission to use it and to find out whether there is a fee. The official Peanuts Web site has a Reprint Information page with an address to use in your letter. If you need help, refer back to the exercise in parentheses at the end of the step.

Step-by-Step

1. **Open** a new Word document. (Exercise 1-1)
2. **Save** the document **as** *Your Name* Cartoon Letter. Save it in the correct folder. (Exercise 1-2)
3. Key your school's **return address** and the **date**. (Exercise 1-3)
4. Key the **inside address**, as shown in Figure 1.19. (Exercise 1-3)

▼ **Figure 1.19** Add your school name and today's date to your letter.

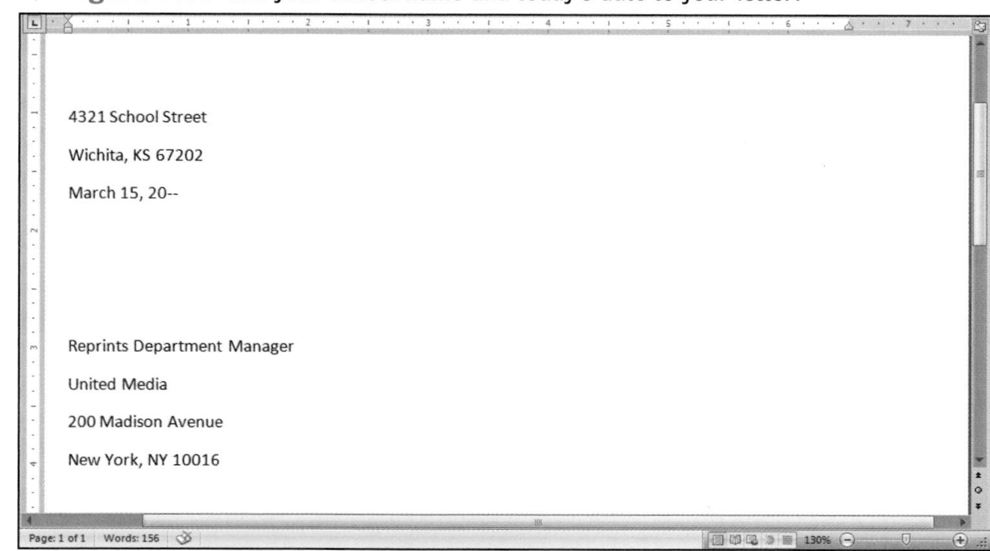

4321 School Street

Wichita, KS 67202

March 15, 20--

Reprints Department Manager

United Media

200 Madison Avenue

New York, NY 10016

Concepts in Action

Project 1

Create a Cell Phone Advertisement

Key Concepts

Exercise 1-1

- Research emerging cell phone technology

Exercise 1-2

- Create and size a text box
- Format a text box

Exercise 1-3

- Use the ruler to modify bullets and margins

Exercise 1-4

- Insert and modify clip art

Exercise 1-5

- Use Drawing Tools to create a logo

Exercise 1-6

- Add layers to a text box

Vocabulary

Key Terms
text box
group
logo

Before You Begin

Office Tools After you learn to use a tool in one Microsoft Office application, the same tool usually works the same way in other Office applications. This makes it easy to use different programs to create a single project.

For this project, you will create an advertisement for a cell phone of the future. You will use your Internet browser and a word processing program.

Calling the Future!

Your company, Future Phones, is creating an advertisement for its new line of cell phones, which uses the very latest in cell phone technology. You will research the latest trends in cell phone technology using your Internet skills and develop a list of features for your new phones. Then, you will create an advertisement for your cell phone using Microsoft Word.

11 Click the **Microsoft Office Button** . Select **Print**, then click **Print Preview** (Figure 1.17).

12 Make sure that your document is only one page.

13 With your teacher's permission, click the **Print** button on the **Print Preview** tab to print your letter (Figure 1.18).

14 On the **Print Preview** tab, in the **Preview** group, click the **Close Print Preview** button .

15 **Save** and **close** the document. **Exit Word**.

TechSavvy

Quick Print The Quick Print option allows you to print right away. The Print dialog box does not open, and the document is sent directly to the default printer. You can use the Quick Print option after you have proofread and know that you do not need to make changes to your document.

Figure 1.17 Use the Print Preview option before you print.

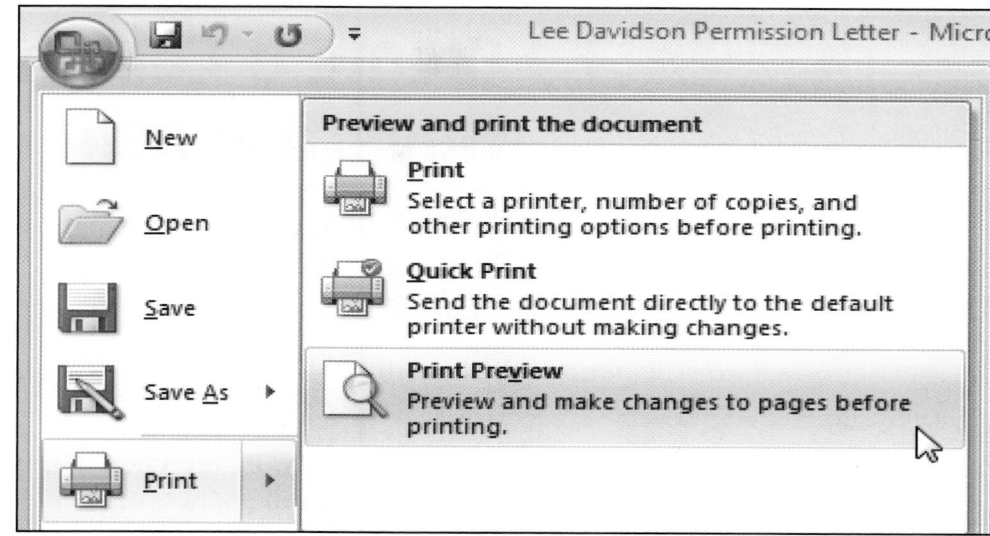

Figure 1.18 Print Preview shows how the document will look when printed.

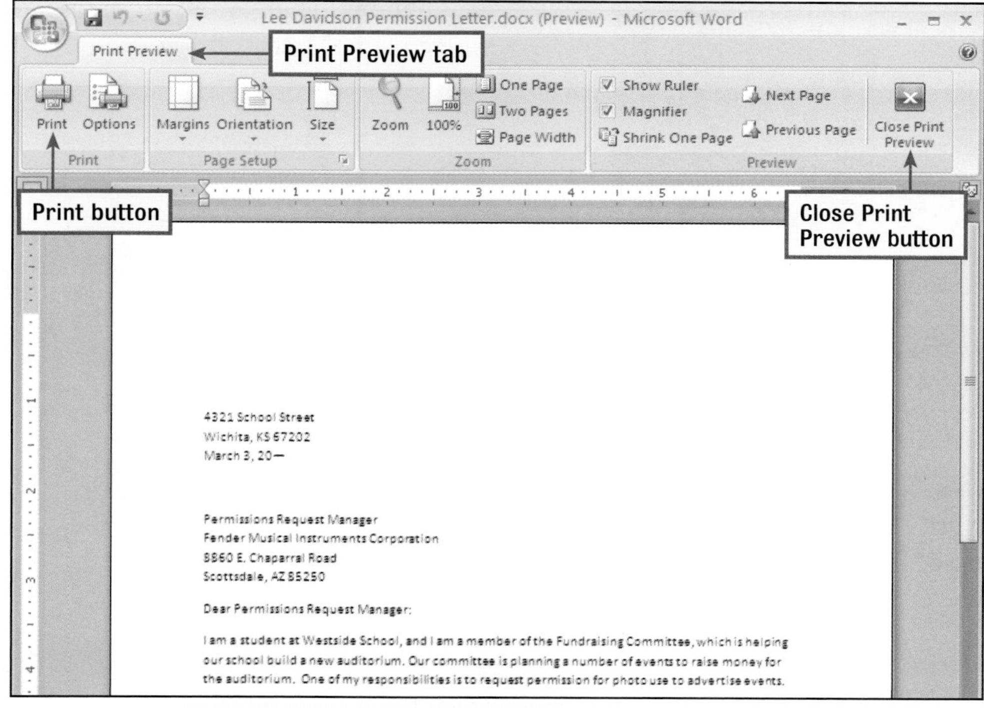

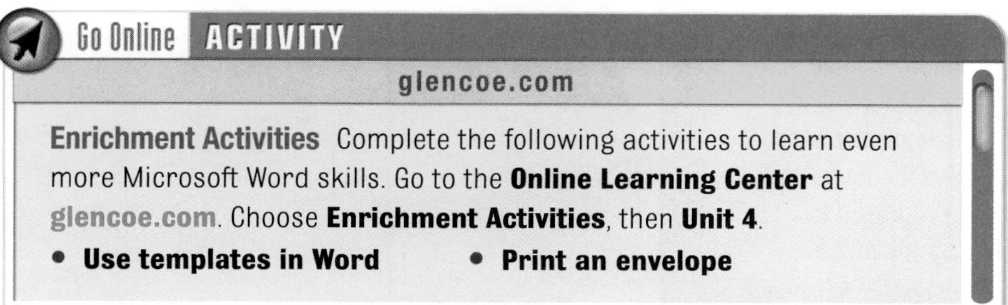

Go Online ACTIVITY

glencoe.com

Enrichment Activities Complete the following activities to learn even more Microsoft Word skills. Go to the **Online Learning Center** at **glencoe.com**. Choose **Enrichment Activities**, then **Unit 4**.

- **Use templates in Word**
- **Print an envelope**

Exercise 1-1 Use Internet Explorer to Research New Technologies

Cell phone makers are constantly developing new phones that combine more and more features in one easy-to-use device. You can easily find information about current and emerging cell phone technology by using the Internet.

In this exercise, you will use your Web browser and a search engine to research emerging cell phone technologies. If you need to review Internet search skills, refer to Unit 3, Project 2 (pages 109–121).

Step-by-Step

1. Follow your teacher's instructions to launch your Web browser. This exercise uses **Internet Explorer**.
2. Ask your teacher which search engine to use. This exercise uses **Google**.
3. In the search window, key future cell phone technology (Figure 1.1).
4. From the results list, choose sites that you think are the most reliable and useful.
5. Select three to five Web sites that you think contain the information you need.
6. Use a pencil and paper, or a word processing program, to create a table like the one in Figure 1.2.
7. In your table, record the information about the sites you visited.

Figure 1.1 Use a search engine such as Google to find information.

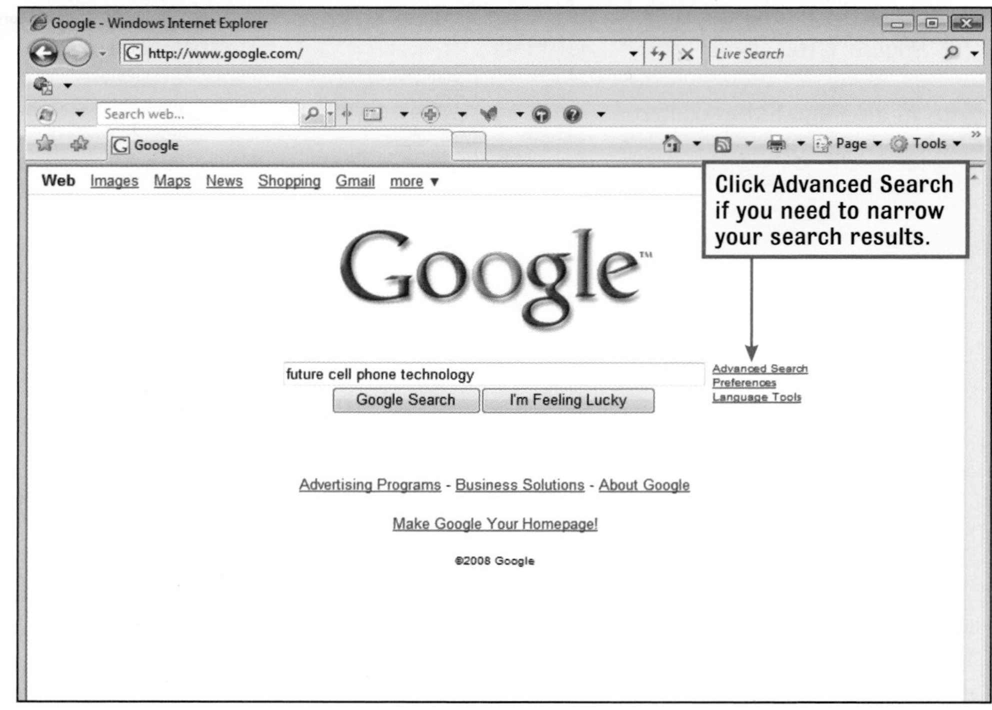

Figure 1.2 Create a table like this on a separate sheet of paper.

Name of Web Site	Site's URL	Why the Site Is Reliable	Name of New Technology	Function of the Technology

7 On the **Page Layout** tab, in the **Page Setup** group, click **Margins**. Then click **Custom Margins**.

8 Click the **Margins** tab, if necessary. Make sure your margins and settings match the settings in Figure 1.16.

9 Click the **Layout** tab. To center your letter on the page, choose **Center** next to **Vertical alignment**. See Figure 1.16.

10 In the **Page Setup** dialog box, click **OK**.

▼ **Figure 1.16** Use the Page Setup dialog box to check margins, change the page size, or adjust layout settings.

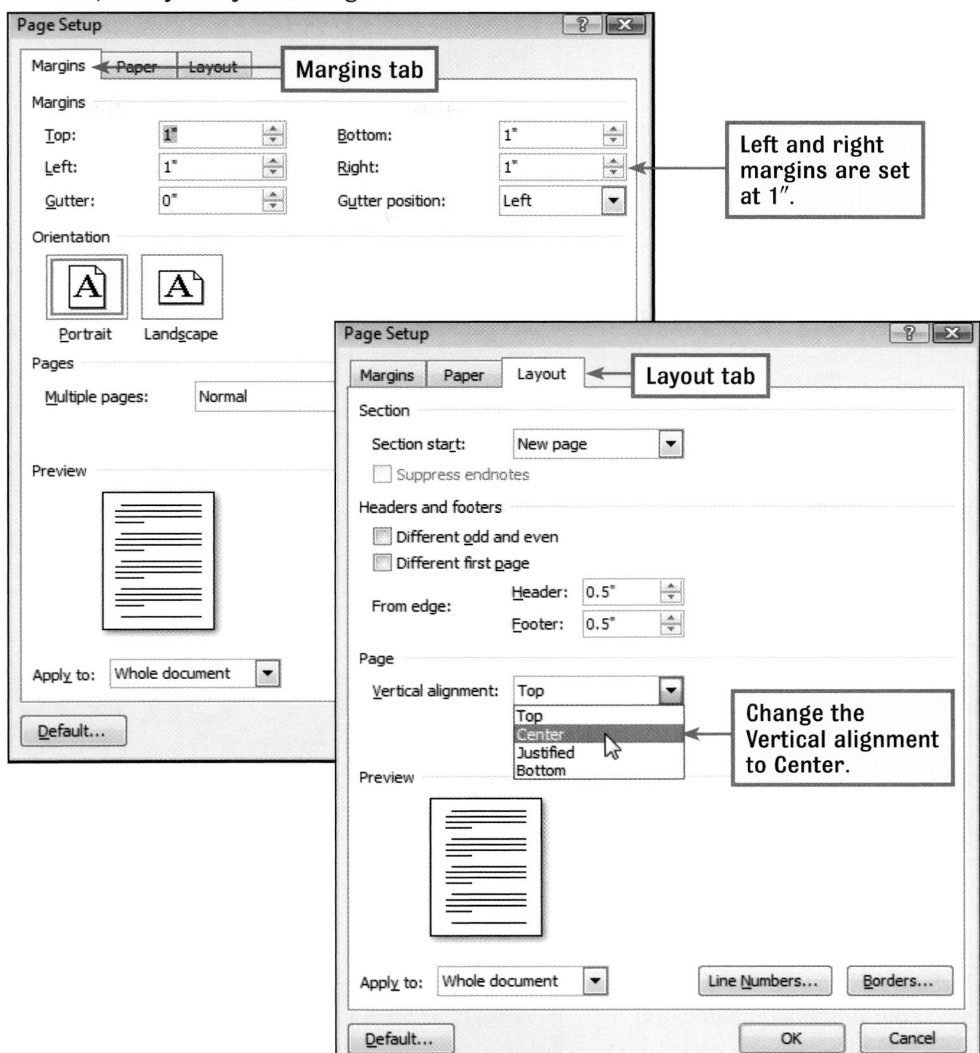

HELP!

Which View Should I Use? Choose the view that you prefer when you write and edit documents.

- **Draft view** is designed for speed of entry and editing. The text and other elements flow in one long, continuous column from one page to the next.
- **Print Layout view** lets you see the margins of your document and check how it will look when printed.
- **Print Preview** shows you at a glance how *all* the pages of your document will look when printed.

Exercise 1-2 Create and Format a Text Box

A printed advertisement usually contains both text and graphics. The text explains a product or service, and graphics add visual interest. Most ads also include a memorable phrase, or slogan, to help people remember the product being sold.

A **text box** is a moveable box that lets you place text anywhere on the page. This lets you customize your document. You can make the text box the exact size you want and also apply effects (like colors and shadows).

In this exercise, you will use your research from the previous exercise to begin creating your cell phone advertisement. You will use Word to create a text box and write about your phone's features. If you need to review Microsoft Word skills, refer to Unit 4, Project 2 (pages 152–166).

Step-by-Step

1. In **Microsoft Word**, create a new blank document.
2. **Save** it **as** *Your Name* Cell Phone Ad.
3. In your Word document, list and describe five new cell phone technologies. **Note**: Use the information from the table you created in Exercise 1-1.
4. Bold the name of each technology. See Figure 1.3 as an example.
5. Select all of the text in the list. Change the **Font** to **Garamond**. Make the **Font Size 14**. **Note:** If you do not have Garamond, use a similar font.

Figure 1.3 Insert a hard return between items in your list.

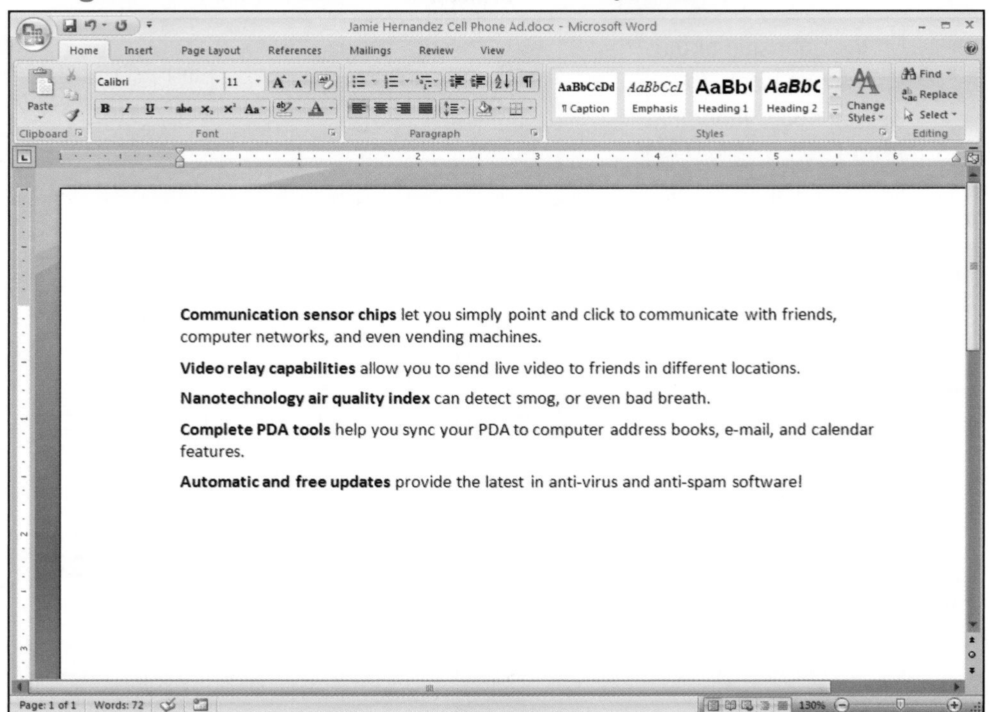

TechSavvy

Microsoft Office 2007 Text Box Gallery You can save your formatted text boxes for use at another time. After you have drawn your text box, select it. On the **Insert** tab, in the **Text** group, click **Text Box**, and choose **Save Selection to the Text Box Gallery**. When you need a text box, click the desired size from the T**ext Box Gallery**.

Exercise 1-6 Preview and Print Your Letter

Word provides many different ways to view your document. Before you print your document, make sure to view the entire document, check the formatting, and make any needed changes.

An average-length business letter should have 1-inch margins on both sides and can be centered vertically, from top to bottom, on the page to make it look professional. Adjust margins accordingly for short or long letters.

In this exercise, you will use the Print Layout view, the Zoom button, and Print Preview to view your letter. You will also use the Page Setup options to center your letter on the page. If your teacher allows, you can print your final letter.

Step-by-Step

1. On the right side of the **status** bar, locate the view buttons. Verify that **Print Layout** view is selected (Figure 1.15).

2. Notice that you can see the page margins and the edges of the page.

3. On the **View** tab, in the **Zoom** group, click the **Zoom** button to display the **Zoom** dialog box.

4. Under **Zoom to**, click **75%**. Click **OK**. You will see more of the screen, but the text will be harder to read (Figure 1.15).

5. On the **status** bar to the right of the view buttons, drag the **Zoom** slider to **200%** to enlarge the text.

6. On the **Zoom** slider, click the **minus** button until the zoom level returns to **100%**.

▼ **Figure 1.15** **Choose Print Layout view to see how your document will look when printed.**

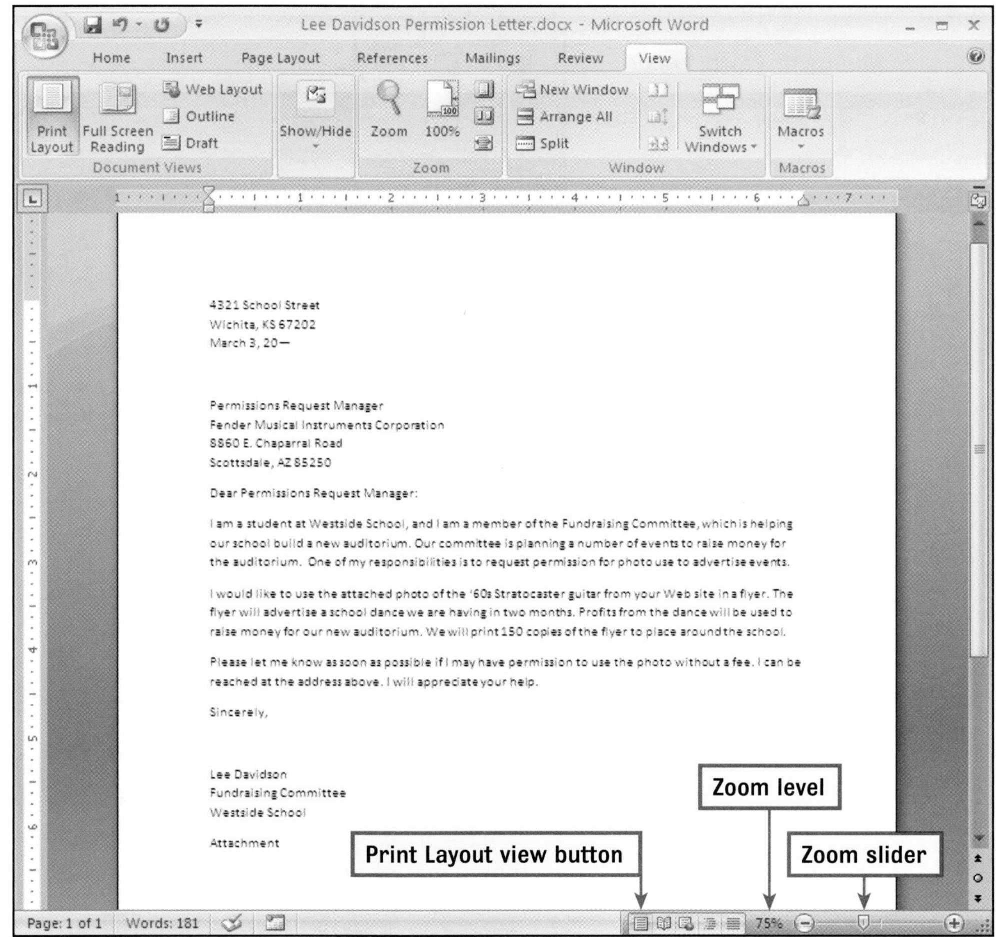

6. Select all the text you keyed, then click the **Insert** tab. In the **Text** group, click **Text Box**. Click **Draw Text Box**. The text box is created around the selected text, and the **Text Box Tools** appear (Figure 1.4).

7. Click the **Format** tab. Then, in the **Size** group, change the **Shape Height** to 5.25. Change the **Shape Width** to 5.75.

Figure 1.4 You can move your text box anywhere on the page.

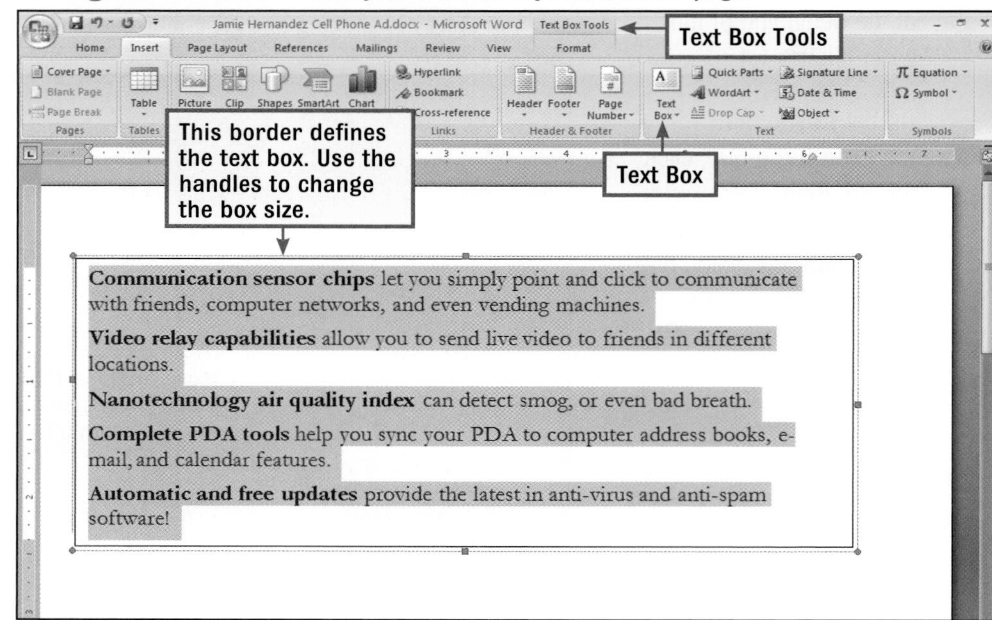

8. With the entire list still selected, click the **Home** tab. Click the **Dialog Box Launcher** for the **Paragraph** group.

9. The **Paragraph** dialog box opens (Figure 1.5). Under **Spacing**, next to **After**, key 8. Click **OK**.

TechSavvy

Resizing Text Boxes If you create a text box from selected text and then add new text to the text box, the box automatically re-sizes to fit the text.

Figure 1.5 Use paragraph formatting to change the spacing before or after a hard return.

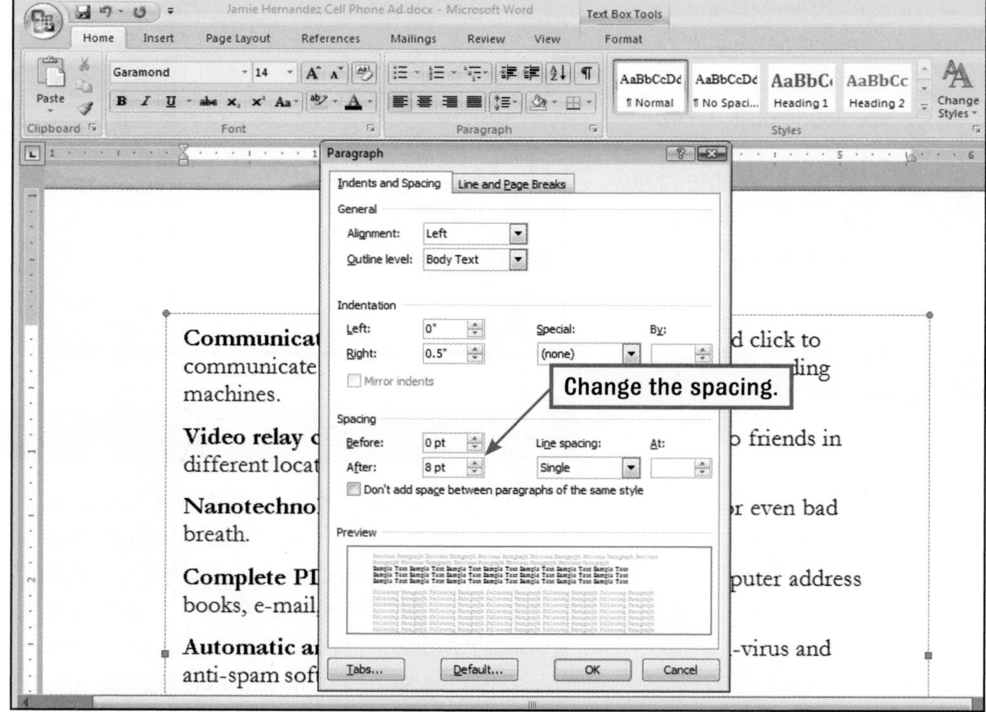

4 Position the insertion point at the beginning of the letter (Figure 1.13).

5 On the **Review** tab, in the **Proofing** group, click the **Spelling & Grammar** button. The **Spelling and Grammar** dialog box displays (Figure 1.14).

▼ **Figure 1.13** **Place your insertion point at the beginning of the document before you start the spelling and grammar check.**

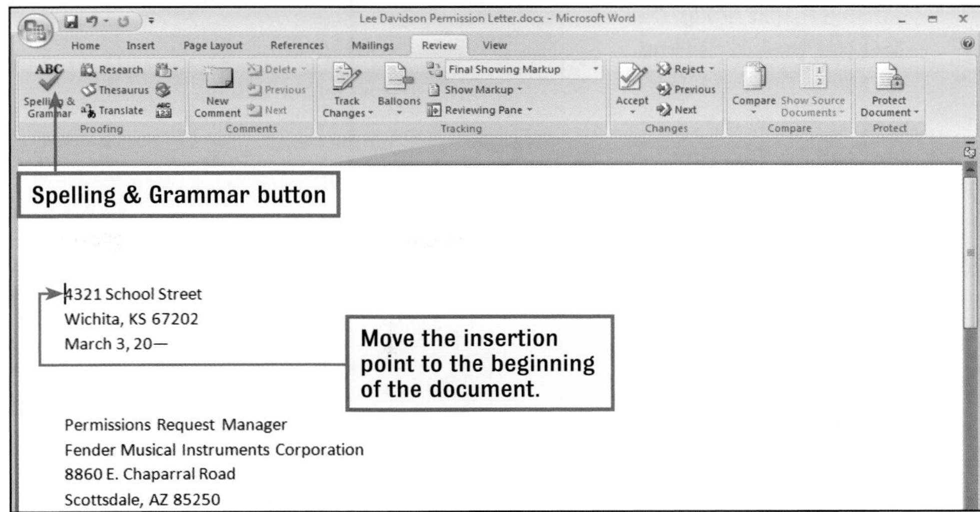

6 To check errors, read any flagged text that appears in the top box. Then check the suggestion in the bottom box.

7 If you agree with the suggested change, click **Change**. The error is corrected (Figure 1.14).

8 If you do not want to make the suggested change, choose **Ignore Once** or **Next Sentence**.

9 **Save** your revised document.

▼ **Figure 1.14** **Word asks you whether you want to fix a possible error.**

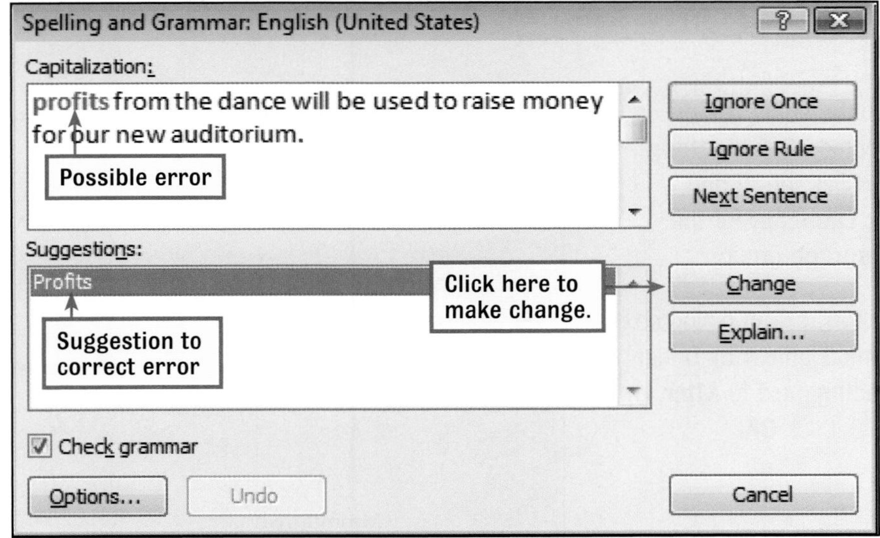

TechSavvy

Spelling & Grammar Tool Never rely on the **Spelling & Grammar** tool to catch every error. Always read the final document yourself. Look at this sentence: *My mother took my too sisters two the pool.* All the words are spelled correctly, but the words *too* and *two* are used incorrectly. It should read: *My mother took my two sisters to the pool.* Look out for homonyms—words that sound the same but have different spellings, such as *two*, *too*, and *to*.

10 After your list, key the slogan: The future is in your hands!

11 **Bold** the slogan.

12 Change the **Font** of the slogan to **Verdana**. **Note**: If you do not have Verdana, use a similar font.

13 Make sure the **Font Size** of the slogan is **14**.

14 Make the slogan's **Font Color Red** (Figure 1.6).

15 On the **Format** tab, in the **Text Box Styles** group, click **Shape Outline** [icon]. Click **No Outline**.

16 Click outside the text box. Save your document. It should look similar to Figure 1.7.

Figure 1.6 Change the format of your slogan to make it stand out.

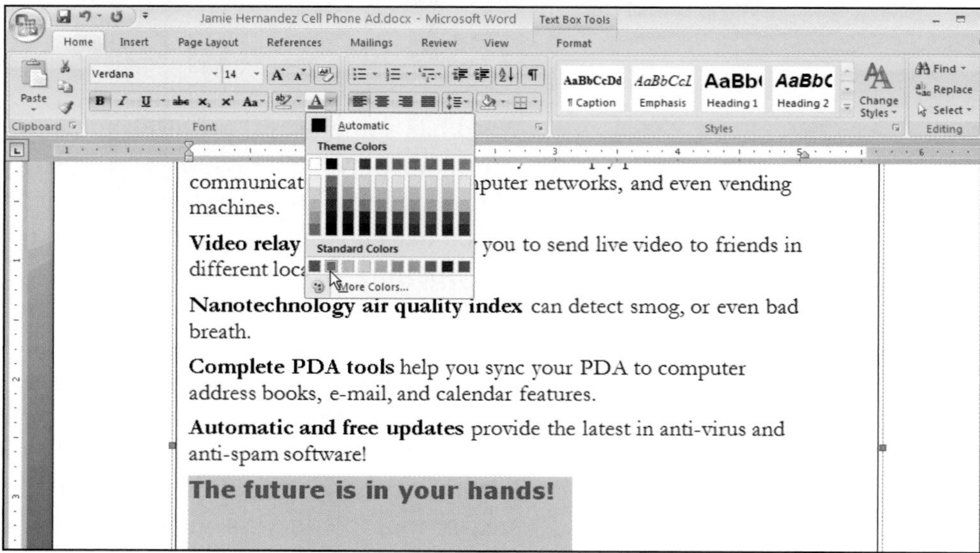

Figure 1.7 The text of the ad is complete.

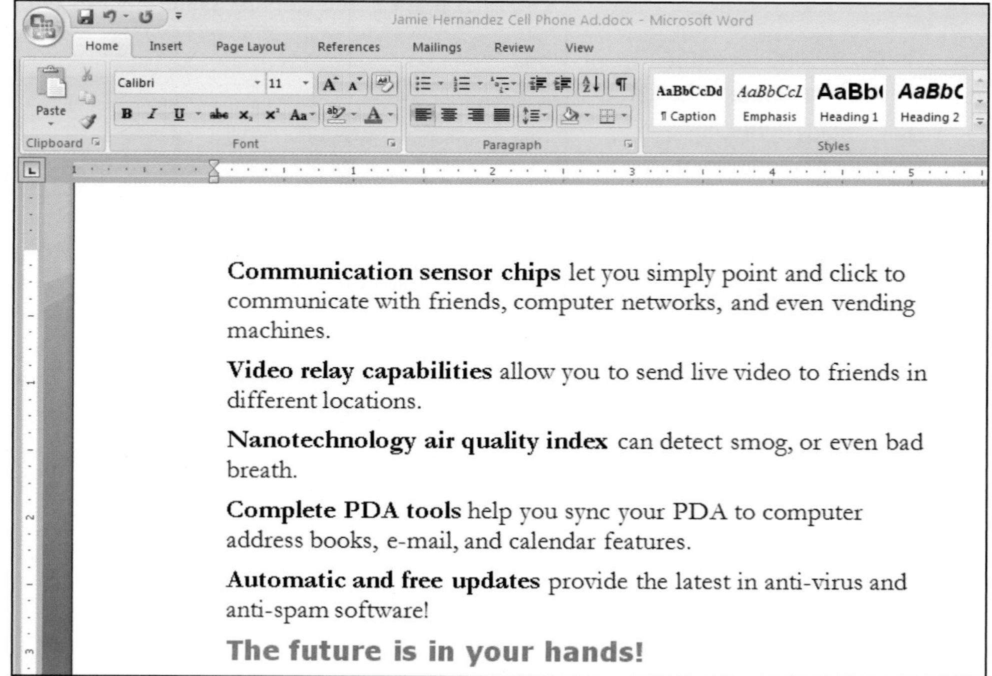

HELP!

Aligning Objects on the Drawing Canvas To align the edges of multiple objects in a drawing canvas, press and hold CTRL to select the objects that you want to align, then click the **Format** tab. In the **Arrange** group, click **Align** [icon] and select an alignment command from the list.

Exercise 1-5 Use the Thesaurus and Check Spelling and Grammar

Word has some useful proofing tools to help you edit documents. The thesaurus displays synonyms for words. **Synonyms** are words that have similar meanings. You might want to use a synonym if you use one word too often or need a word that is easier to understand.

The Spelling & Grammar tool helps you find mistakes in spelling, punctuation, and grammar. Word can also be set to underline words that may be misspelled and phrases that use questionable grammar. When you right-click words or phrases with squiggly underlines, you will see suggestions for changes. Word's proofing tools are helpful, but you should still proofread each document. The tools will not catch every error.

In this exercise, you will use Word's thesaurus and the Spelling & Grammar tool to edit your business letter.

Step-by-Step

1. In the second paragraph of your **Permission Letter** document, right-click anywhere in the word **Proceeds**.
2. Choose **Synonyms** from the drop-down menu. A list of synonyms displays (Figure 1.12).
3. In the list of synonyms, click the word **profits**. It replaces **Proceeds** in the letter.

Figure 1.12 You can find synonyms by right-clicking on a word.

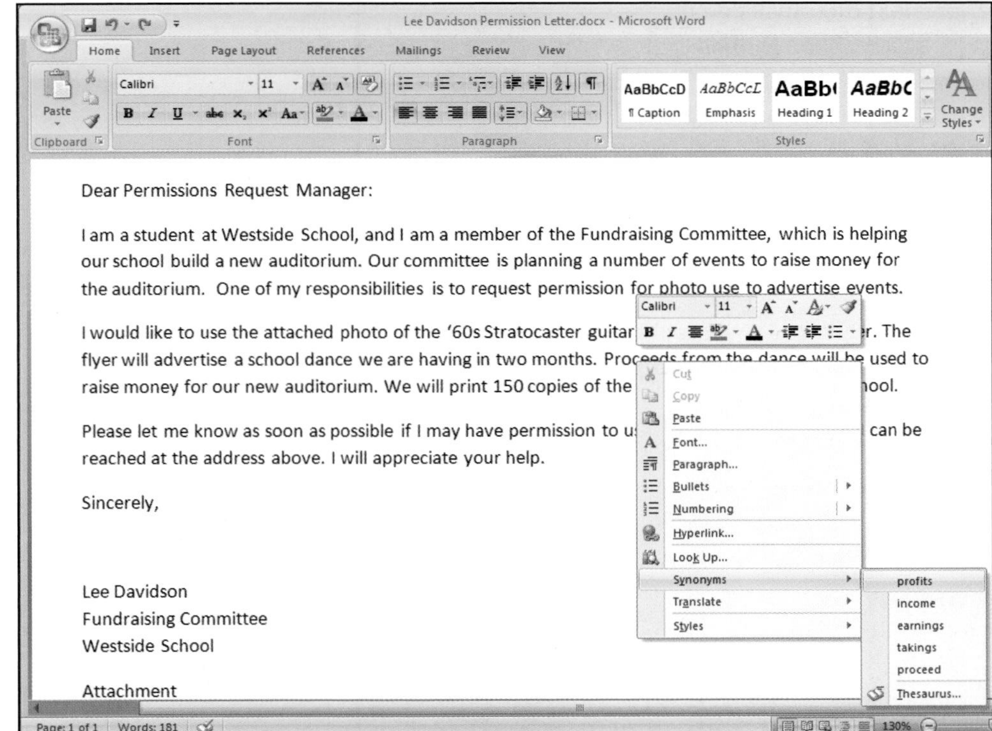

Exercise 1-3 Modify Bullets and Margins

When you add bullets to a document, Microsoft Word automatically changes the Horizontal Ruler (shown below) to make sure the bullets align. When you align items, you make sure they are all in line with each other. You can move the indent markers or the tab stops on the ruler to control how your text aligns, as shown below.

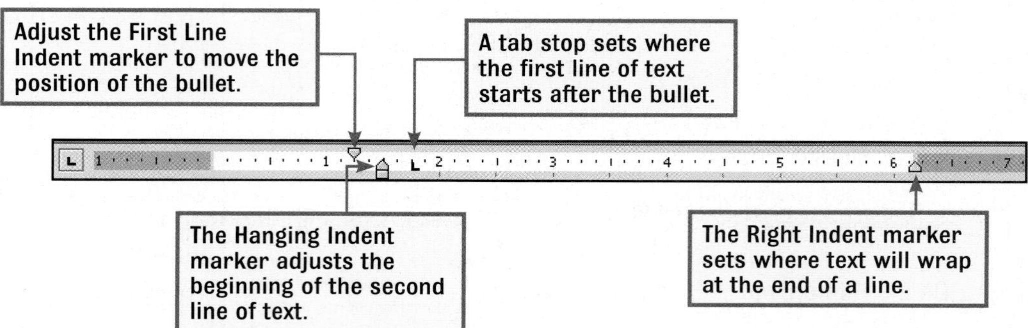

In this exercise, you will use the ruler to modify bullet alignment. If you need to review Microsoft Word skills, see Unit 4, Project 2 (pages 152–166).

Step-by-Step

1. In your Cell Phone Ad, **select** everything in your feature list *except* the red slogan at the end.

2. On the **Home** tab, in the **Paragraph** group, click the **Bullets** button to add bullets to each item in the list (Figure 1.8).

▼ **Figure 1.8** You can change the format of the bullets after you add them.

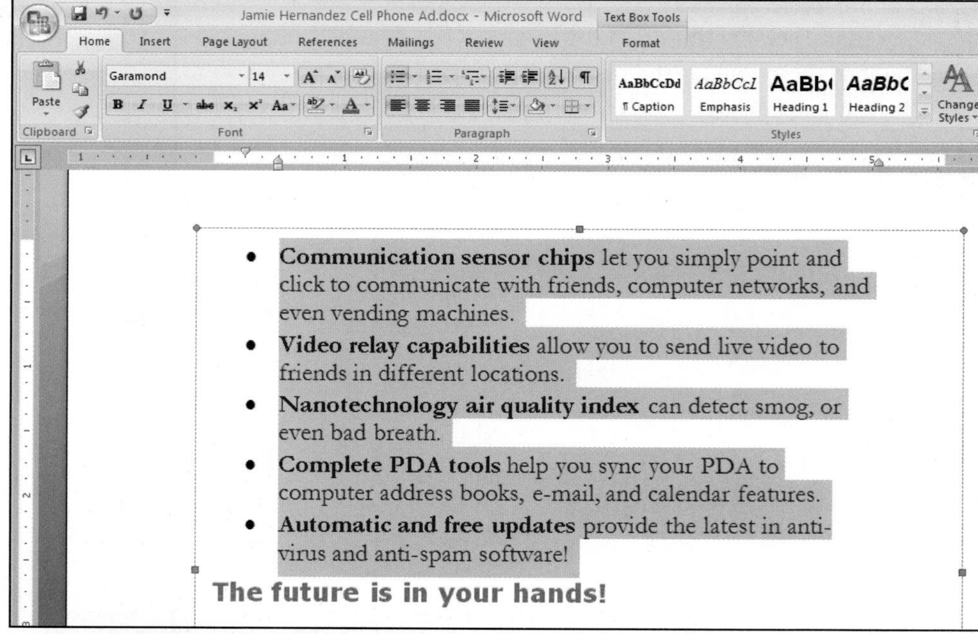

HELP!

Use Format Painter If the last bullet on your list looks different from the others, click any item in the list with the correct bullet style. Click the **Format Painter** button, then the item with the bullet that does not match.

6. Select the text **Fundraising Committee** in the first paragraph.

7. On the **Ribbon**, on the **Home** tab, in the **Clipboard** group, click the **Copy** button to copy the text.

8. Place your insertion point after your name in the letter's closing. Press ENTER to add a blank line below your name.

9. On the **Ribbon**, on the **Home** tab, in the **Clipboard** group, click the **Paste** button (See Figure 1.11).

10. On the **Quick Access Toolbar**, click the **Undo** button to remove the text you just pasted.

11. Click the **Redo** button to restore the text.

12. To repeat your last action, press CTRL + Y.

13. Select the second **Fundraising Committee**, and press the DELETE key. The letter should look like Figure 1.11.

14. **Save** your document.

▼ **Figure 1.11** **The final letter should look like this.**

4321 School Street
Wichita, KS 67202
March 3, 20—

Permissions Request Manager
Fender Musical Instruments Corporation
8860 E. Chaparral Road
Scottsdale, AZ 85250

Dear Permissions Request Manager:

I am a student at Westside School, and I am a member of the Fundraising Committee which is helping our school build a new auditorium. Our committee is planning a number of events to raise money for the auditorium. One of my responsibilities is to request permission for photo use to advertise events.

I would like to use the attached photo of the '60s Stratocaster guitar from your Web site in a flyer. The flyer will advertise a school dance we are having in two months. Proceeds from the dance will be used to raise money for our new auditorium. We will print 150 copies of the flyer to place around the school.

Please let me know as soon as possible if I may have permission to use the photo without a fee. I can be reached at the address above. I will appreciate your help.

Sincerely,

Lee Davidson
Fundraising Committee
Westside School

Attachment

Copy the text in the body and paste it in the signature.

TechSavvy

Inserting Text Verify the position of the insertion point before you begin keying text. If you have selected text, remember that keying text will replace the text selection.

3. With the list still selected, click the first bullet in the list to select all of the bullets.

4. Click the **Home** tab, and launch the dialog box for the **Font** group (Figure 1.9).

5. Change the **Font color** to **Red**, then click **OK** to close the **Font** dialog box. The bullets should now be red.

Figure 1.9 You can format and customize bullets.

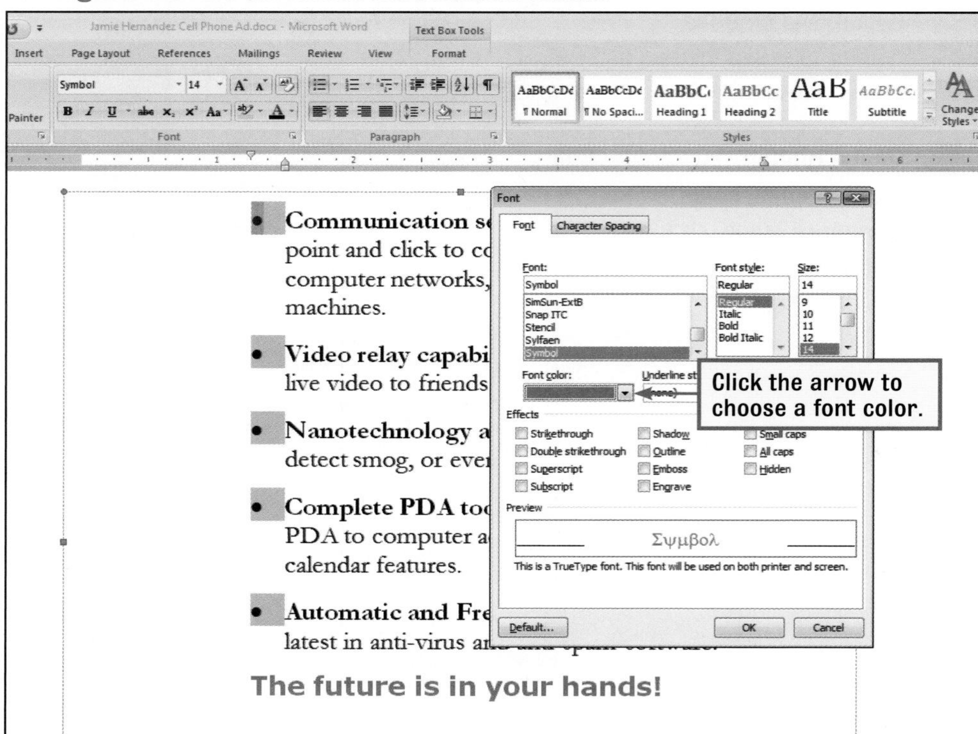

6. Select all of the text on the page, including the last line. On the **Ruler**, drag the **Right Indent** marker to the position shown in Figure 1.10.

7. Adjust the other markers as shown in Figure 1.10.

8. Save your work. It should look similar to Figure 1.10.

Figure 1.10 Use the markers on the ruler to change the bullet settings.

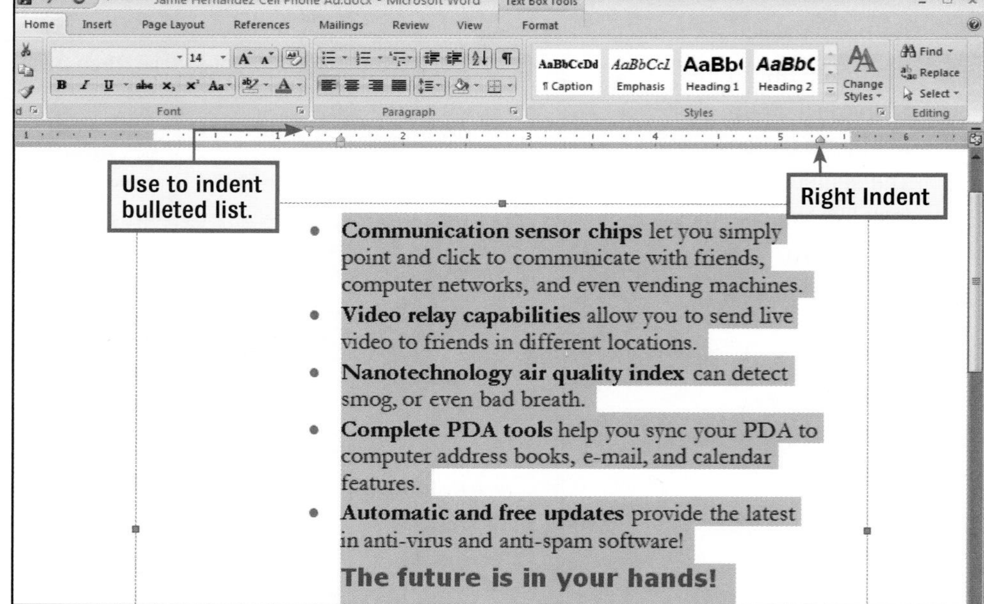

2. Hold down the left mouse button, and drag the pointer to select the text as shown in Figure 1.9.

3. On the **Ribbon**, on the **Home** tab, in the **Clipboard** group, click the **Cut** button. The text disappears.

▼ **Figure 1.9** **You can select text by pressing the Shift key and an arrow key.**

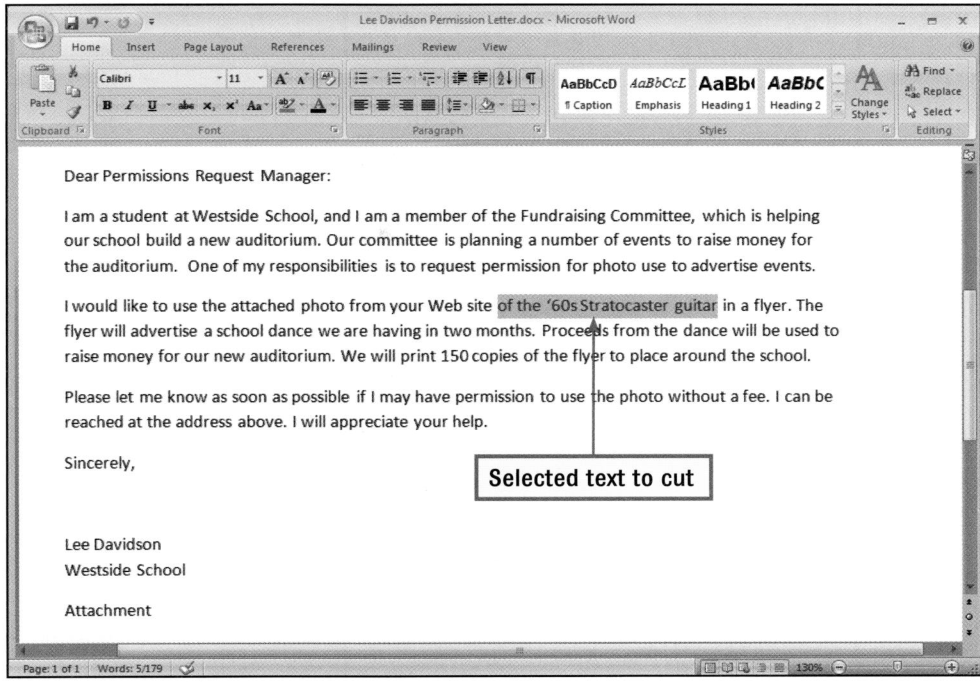

4. Place the insertion point after the text **the attached photo**. (Figure 1.10)

5. On the **Ribbon**, on the **Home** tab, in the **Clipboard** group, click the **Paste** button. The sentence should now look like the one shown in Figure 1.10.

▼ **Figure 1.10** **Make sure to paste text you cut *before* you select and cut more text.**

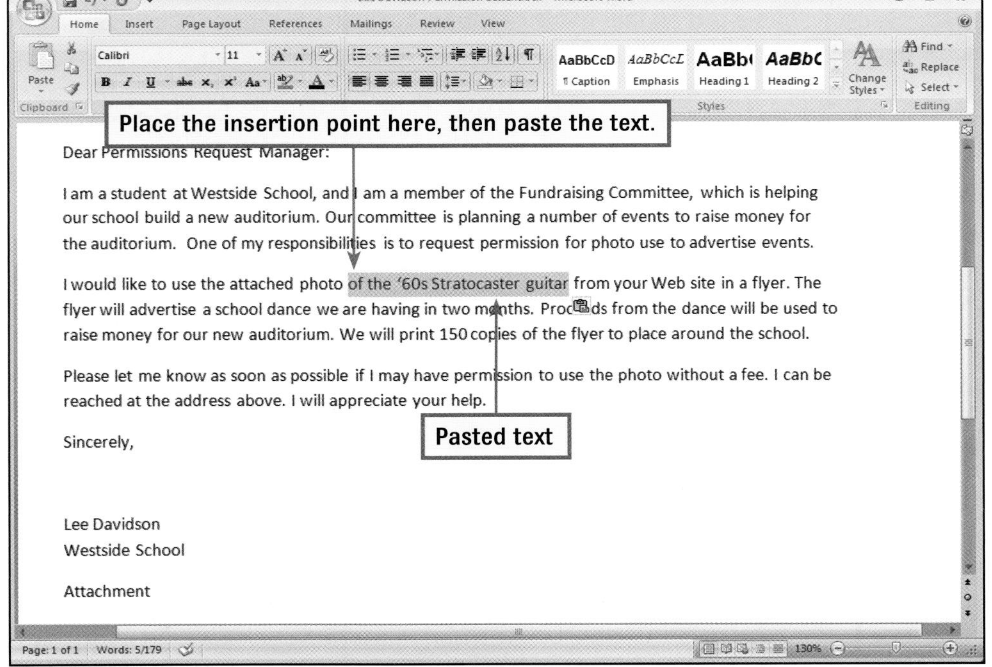

Exercise 1-4 Insert Clip Art

When you use clip art, it is generally *not* a good idea to insert the clip art in text boxes. Make sure that your text box is *not* selected before inserting clip art into your document.

Sometimes you might need to adjust the appearance of clip art to fit your project's needs. With the Drawing Tools in Word, you can **group** objects, which combines separate selected objects into one single object. You can then easily move, resize, or change the appearance of all the parts in a grouped object at once.

In this exercise, you will insert clip art into your advertisement and change its appearance using the group and ungroup tools. If you need to review Microsoft Word skills, refer to Unit 4, Project 4 (pages 184–203).

Step-by-Step

1. To insert clip art outside the text box in your Cell Phone Ad, scroll down and click outside the text box.
2. On the **Insert** tab, in the **Illustrations** group, click the **Clip Art** button.
3. The **Clip Art** task pane is displayed. In the **Search for** box, key cell phone. Click **Go**.
4. Find an image similar to the one in Figure 1.11. Click the image to insert it into your document.
5. Close the **Clip Art** task pane.

Figure 1.11 Insert the clip art outside the text box.

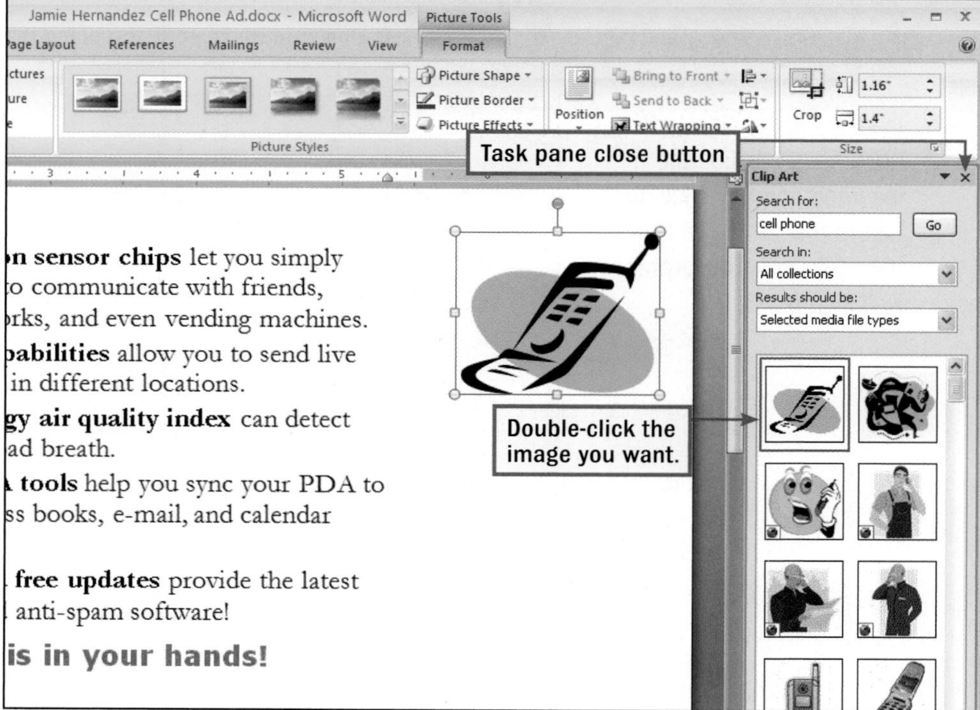

HELP!

Data File If you wish to use the exact piece of clip art shown in the figure above, you can use a data file. Instead of using the Clip Art option in steps 2-5, on the **Insert** tab, in the **Illustrations** group, click **Picture**. Then browse to the **Data File** named **8A Cell Phone,** and click **OK**.

Exercise 1-4 Edit Your Letter

When your business letter is correct and well written, it gives the reader a good impression of you. On the other hand, a poorly organized letter with misspellings and poor grammar presents a negative impression. You should always edit and proofread the letter before you send it.

When you **edit**, you change or rewrite your document to improve it. When you **proofread**, you check to make sure the document makes sense and there are no errors in spelling, grammar, or punctuation. When you edit a document, you may need to cut, copy, or paste text. When you **cut** text, you select and remove it. You can **copy**, or duplicate, text in a document so that it appears exactly the same in another part of your document. After you cut or copy text, you can **paste**, or place, it in a new location.

In this exercise, you will learn to cut, copy, and paste text as you edit the letter you created in the previous exercise.

Step-by-Step

1 In your **Permission Letter** document, position the insertion point by clicking before the phrase **of the '60s Stratocaster guitar**. See Figure 1.8.

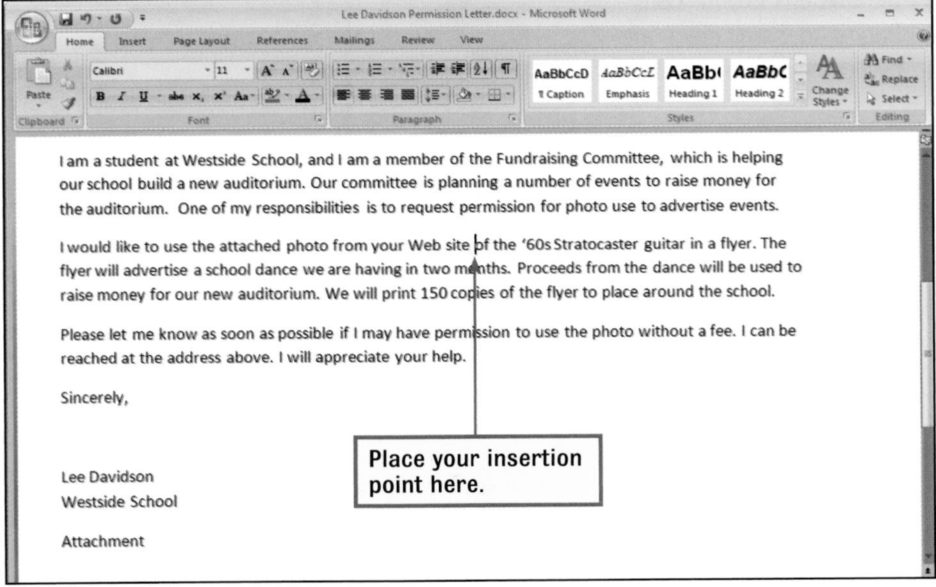

Figure 1.8 Check to make sure you place the insertion point in the correct location.

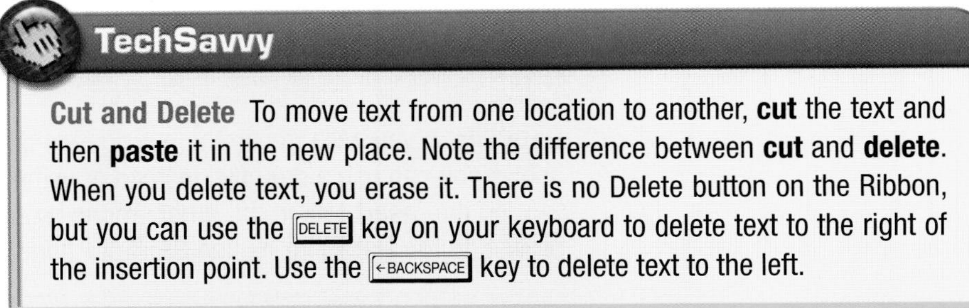

TechSavvy

Cut and Delete To move text from one location to another, **cut** the text and then **paste** it in the new place. Note the difference between **cut** and **delete**. When you delete text, you erase it. There is no Delete button on the Ribbon, but you can use the DELETE key on your keyboard to delete text to the right of the insertion point. Use the ←BACKSPACE key to delete text to the left.

6 Click the **clip art** to display the **Picture Tools**, if necessary.

7 Right-click the **clip art**, and click **Edit Picture**. The **Drawing Tools** appear (Figure 1.12).

Figure 1.12 When clip art is ungrouped, each individual part of the drawing may be moved, recolored, or deleted.

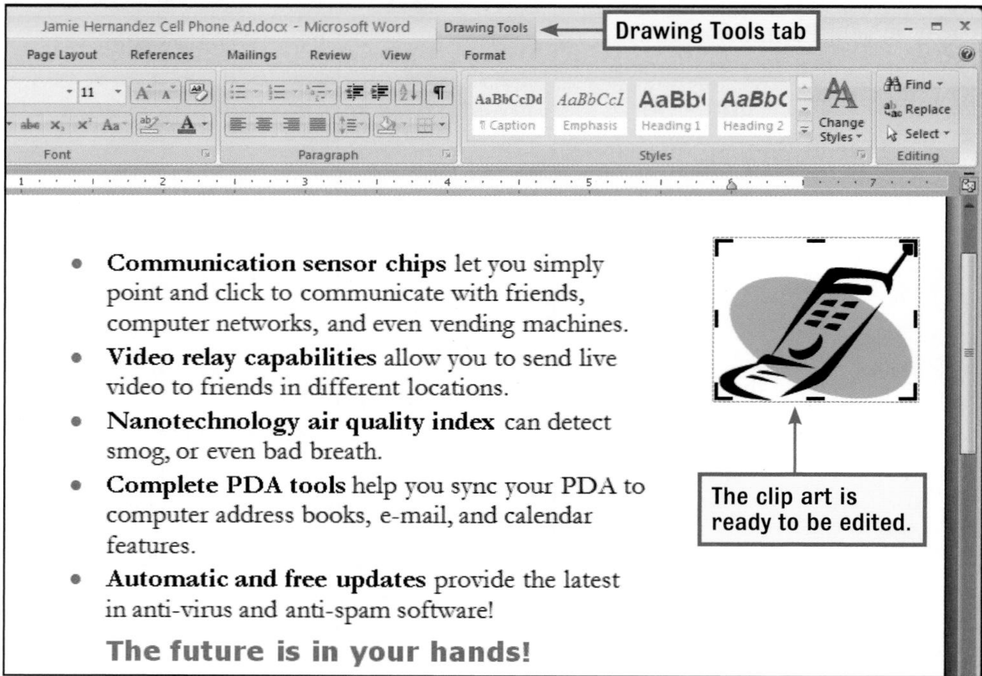

8 Select and click elements that you want to modify within the clip art. Use the **Drawing Tools** to change the **Shape Fill** or the **Shape Outline**. You can delete parts of the clip art, if you want (Figure 1.13).

Figure 1.13 This clip art has been recolored.

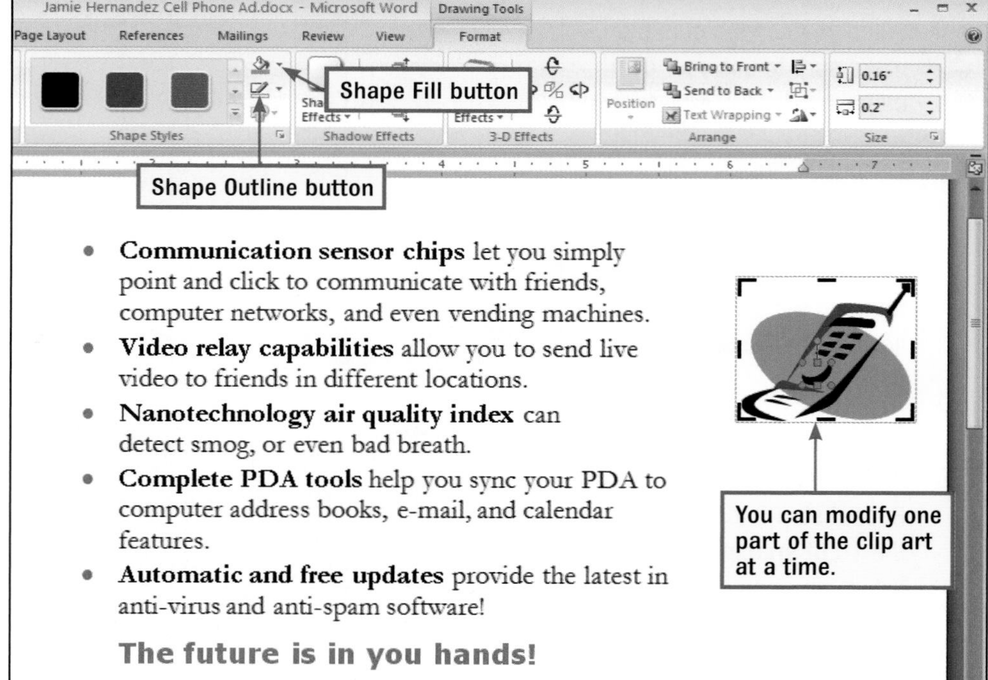

Step-by-Step

1. In your **Permission Letter** document, key and format the text as shown in Figure 1.7.

▼ **Figure 1.7** Your business letter should look similar to this.

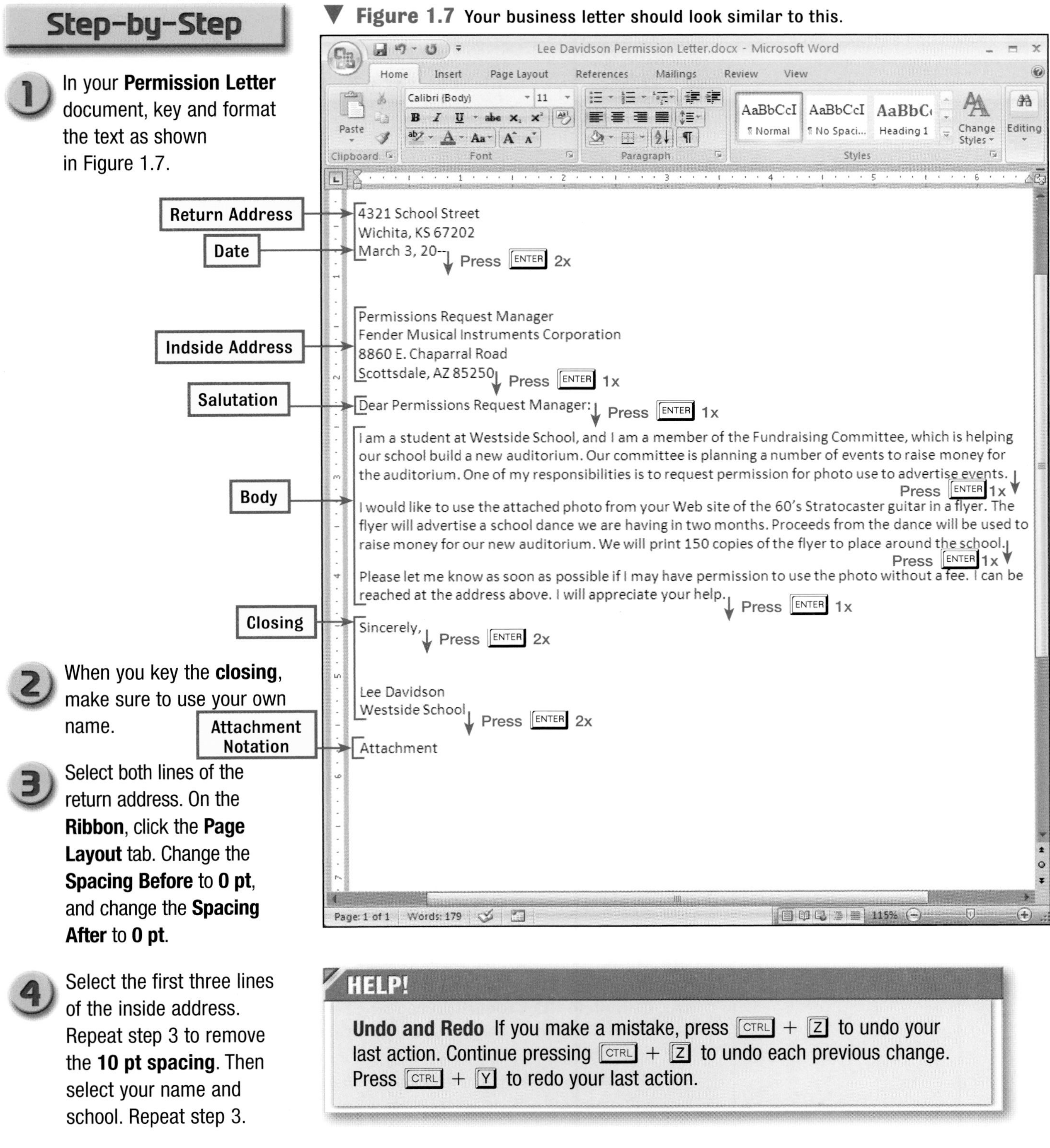

2. When you key the **closing**, make sure to use your own name.

3. Select both lines of the return address. On the **Ribbon**, click the **Page Layout** tab. Change the **Spacing Before** to **0 pt**, and change the **Spacing After** to **0 pt**.

4. Select the first three lines of the inside address. Repeat step 3 to remove the **10 pt spacing**. Then select your name and school. Repeat step 3.

5. Click the **Save** button to save your document.

HELP!

Undo and Redo If you make a mistake, press CTRL + Z to undo your last action. Continue pressing CTRL + Z to undo each previous change. Press CTRL + Y to redo your last action.

9. Click and drag the mouse pointer from the bottom left corner up to the right to draw a box around the cell phone and all its elements (Figure 1.14).

10. Make sure all the elements are selected. On the **Format** tab, in the **Arrange** group, click the **Group** button. **Note**: If you miss any elements when you group the clip art, you can **Ungroup** and repeat step 9. You can also hold down the CTRL key to select the elements that did not fit into the box.

▼ **Figure 1.14** All the elements of the clip art are selected.

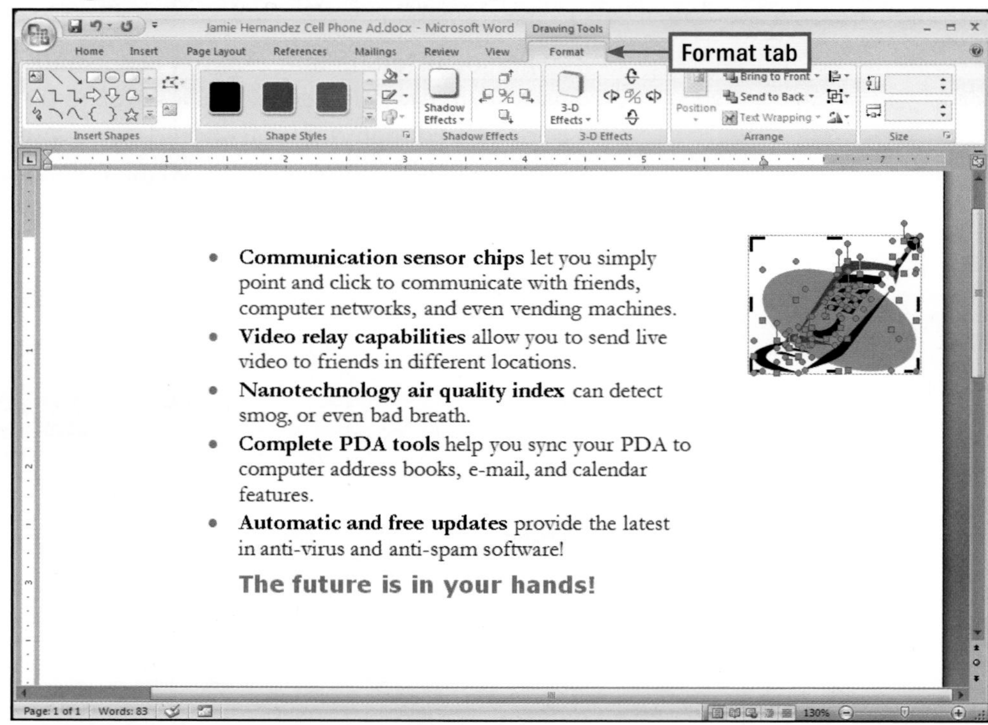

11. Move the clip art and resize it so that your screen looks similar to Figure 1.15.

12. Save your work.

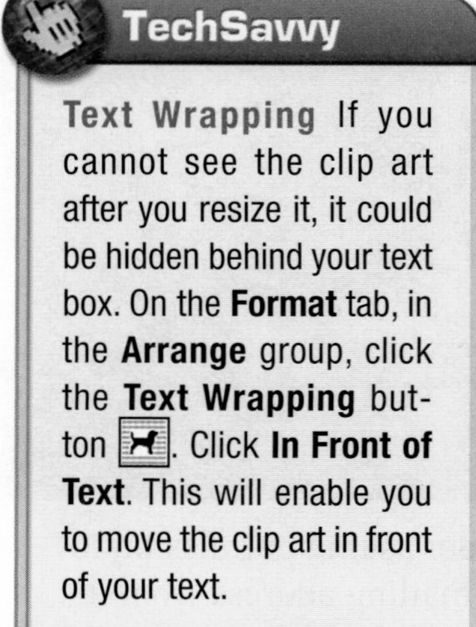

TechSavvy

Text Wrapping If you cannot see the clip art after you resize it, it could be hidden behind your text box. On the **Format** tab, in the **Arrange** group, click the **Text Wrapping** button. Click **In Front of Text**. This will enable you to move the clip art in front of your text.

▼ **Figure 1.15** Resize and position the clip art.

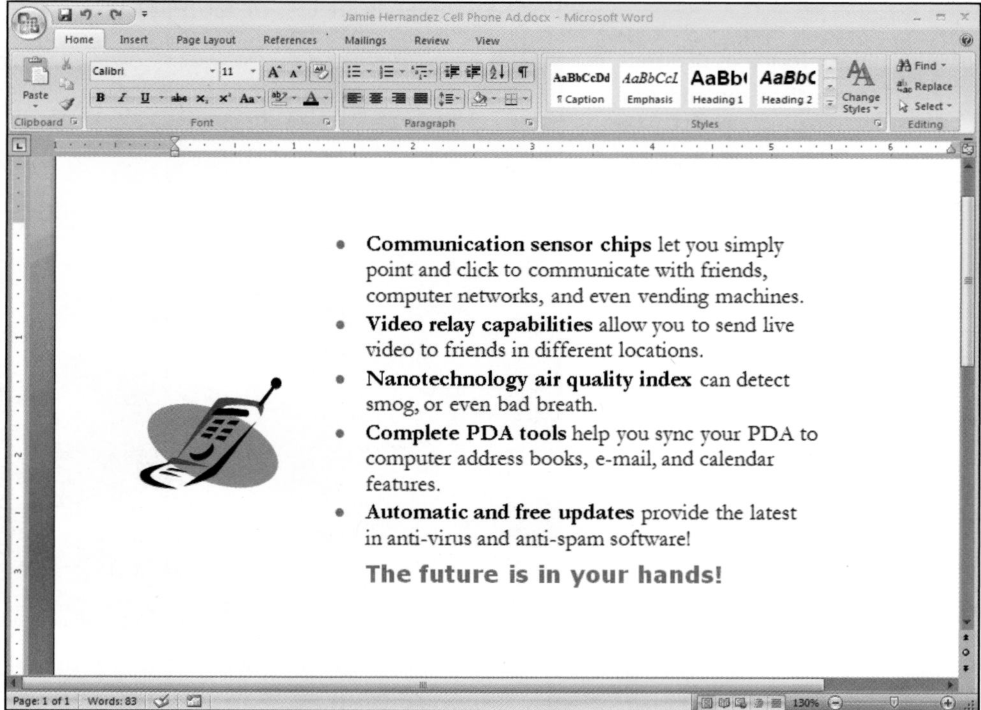

Exercise 1-3 Format a Business Letter

Personal letters and e-mails are usually casual, but a business letter uses formal writing rules and a specific format. To ask permission to use copyrighted material, you should write a formal business letter. Remember these rules whenever you write a business letter:

- **Do** use correct punctuation and spelling.
- **Do not** use slang and abbreviations.
- **Do** use all the parts of a business letter listed below.

Parts of a Business Letter

Part	Description
Return address	Your address, or letterhead if writing for a school, business, or organization
Date	The date the letter was written
Inside address	The address of the person you are writing to
Salutation	The greeting
Body	Message of the letter. A standard business letter includes three paragraphs.
Closing	A goodbye phrase, your name, and your title

When you write a business letter, be sure to use the correct name and address of the person or organization you are writing to. To find a company's address on its Web site, look for a link called Terms of Use, Permission, About Us, or Contact Us.

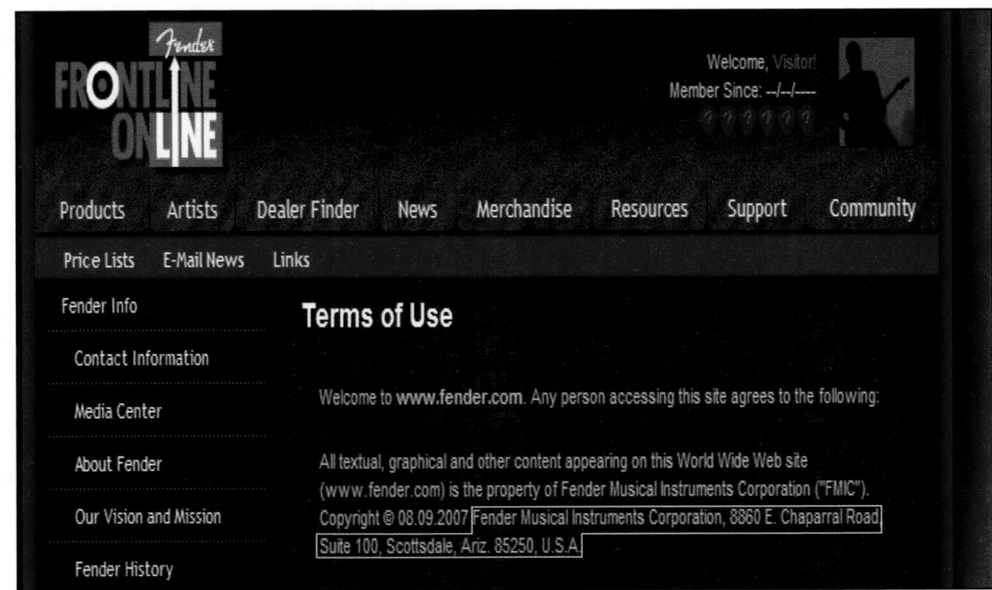

The Fender Terms of Use Web page gives the address you can use to request permission.

In this exercise, you will write a letter to Fender asking permission to use a picture from its Web site. You will use the mailing address from its site, shown above.

Exercise 1-5 Create a Logo with Drawing Tools

A **logo** is a graphic design that is often used to serve as a visual reminder of a company and its services. Logos usually combine graphics and text to create a memorable image. For example, the McDonald's logo uses the company name and the image of the golden arches.

You can create a logo using WordArt instead of keying regular text. This lets you combine the text with drawing elements so that you can easily move or modify the logo.

In this exercise, you will use Word's Drawing Tools to create a logo for your company, Future Phones. **Note:** When you use the Drawing Tools, make sure that your text box is *not selected.* If you need to review Microsoft Word skills, refer to Unit 4, Project 4 (pages 184–203).

Step-by-Step

1. In your Cell Phone Ad, select all of the text in the text box. On the **Home** tab, in the **Paragraph** group, click the **Dialog Box Launcher** to open the **Paragraph** dialog box.

2. In the **Before** box (under Spacing), key 84 pt to create enough room above the text for the logo (Figure 1.16).

3. Click anywhere outside the text box. On the **Insert** tab, in the **Text** group, click the **WordArt** button.

4. In the **WordArt Gallery**, choose the design in the top-left corner.

Figure 1.16 You can insert space before text by formatting the paragraph.

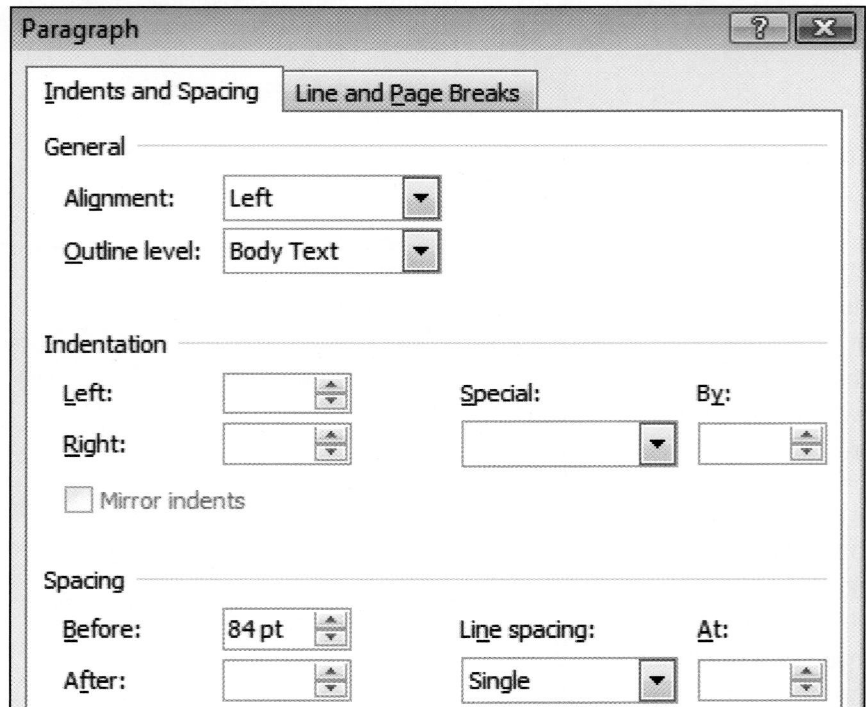

TechSavvy

Point Size Paragraph spacing and font size are sometimes measured in points (pt). **1pt = 1/72 of an inch**.

3. Click the arrow next to the **Documents Folder**. Browse to the folder where your teacher told you to save your files.

4. Remember to name your document! In the **File name** box, key *Your Name Permission Letter*, or follow your teacher's directions (Figure 1.5).

5. Click **Save**. The dialog box closes.

Figure 1.5 Use a file name that is easy to remember.

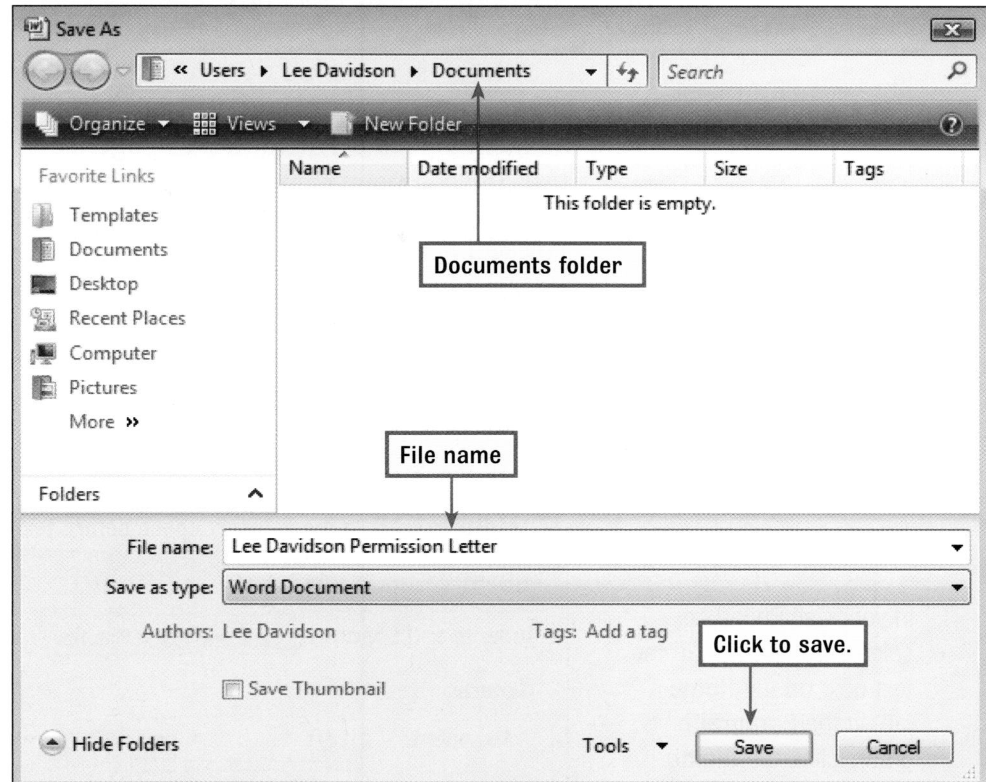

6. Locate the **title** bar at the top of your screen. The **title** bar should now show the name of the document (Figure 1.6).

7. Make sure you saved the file to the right location. Check the folder where the file should be. If it is not there, click the **Office Button**, then choose **Save As**. Then, repeat steps 3 through 5.

Figure 1.6 The document's name is displayed in the title bar.

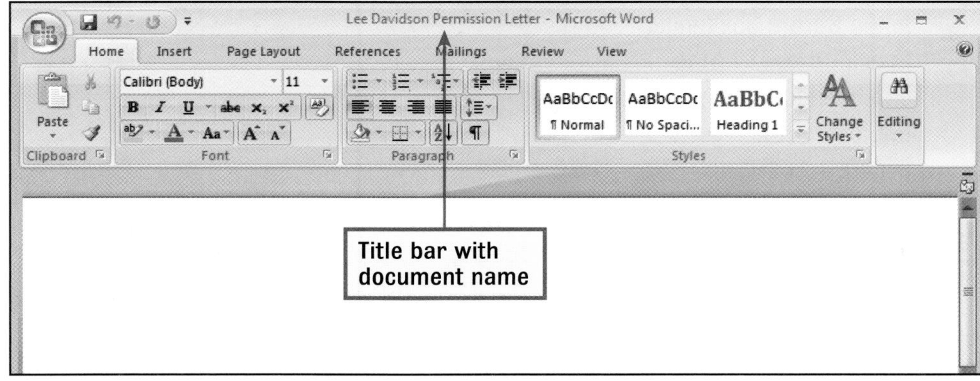

TechSavvy

Create a New Folder You can create a new folder when you save a file. Click the **arrow**, and choose **Save As**. In the **Save As** dialog box, browse to the folder where you want to create a new subfolder. In the **command** bar, click the **New Folder** command. Name the folder, and a subfolder displays. Save your file into the new folder.

5 In the **Edit WordArt Text** box, key Future Phones.

6 Change the **Font** to **Arial** and the **Font Size** to **20**. Make the text **Bold**, and click **OK**.

7 On the **WordArt Tools Format** tab, in the **Arrange** group, choose **Text Wrapping**, and click **In Front of Text**.

8 With the WordArt still selected, on the **WordArt Tools Format** tab, in the **WordArt Styles** group, click the **Change WordArt Shape** button.

9 Click the **Deflate** shape (Figure 1.17).

10 On the **Insert** tab, in the **Illustrations** group, click the **Shapes** button.

11 Under **Basic Shapes**, click the **Moon** shape (Figure 1.18).

Figure 1.17 Customize your logo with the WordArt Tools. Choose a shape that is appropriate for your logo.

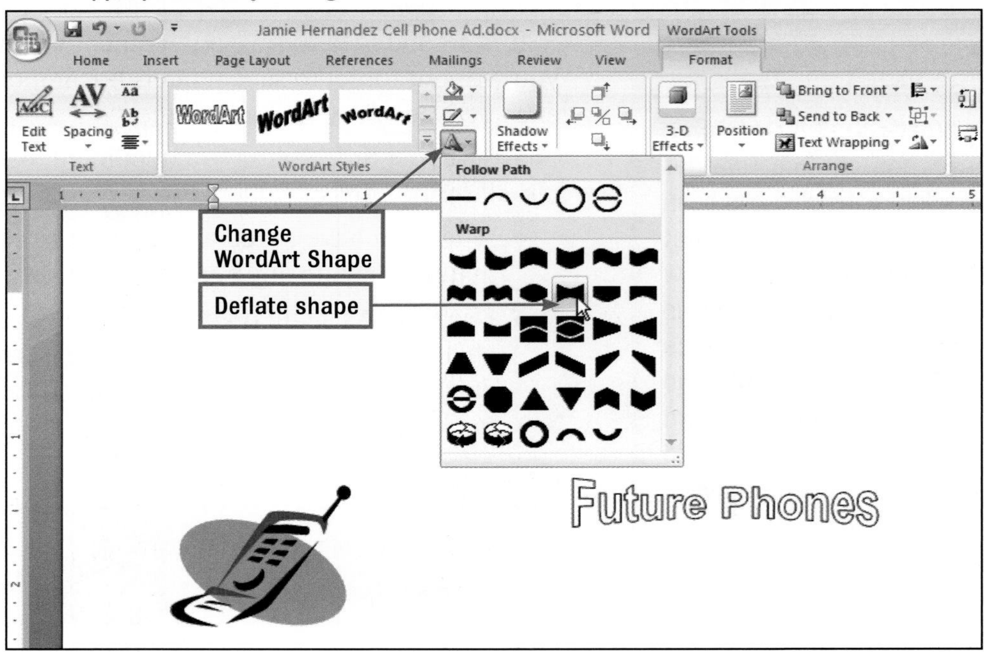

Figure 1.18 It is easy to create many different shapes using Word's Drawing Tools.

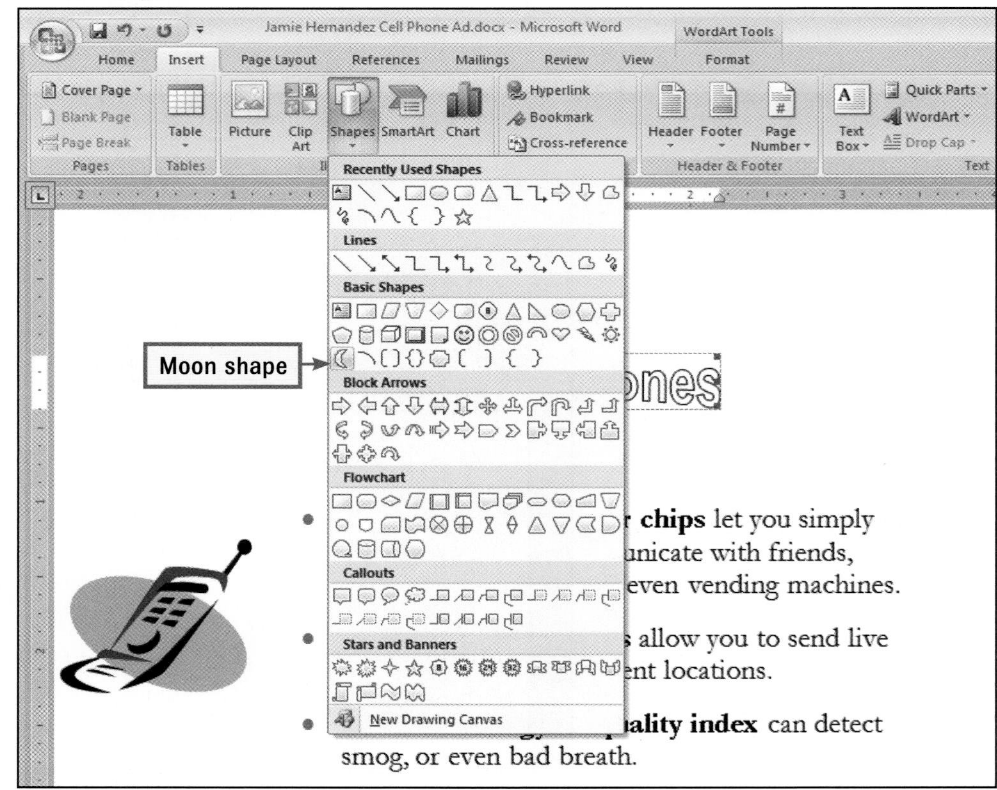

Exercise 1-2 Open and Save a Document

TechSavvy

Word 2007 File Name Extension The familiar ".doc" extension has been used in many different versions of Word. A new XML-based file format is used in Microsoft Office 2007 to improve file and data management and document recovery. Word 2007 documents have a ".docx" extension.

It is a good idea to save a document when you first create it. That way, you will not forget to save it later. It is important to understand the difference between *Save As* and *Save*.

- The first time you save a document, use **Save As** to name it and save it to the correct folder.
- After you have saved a document once, you can use the **Save** command to update any additions and save quickly.
- Use **Save As** again if you want to save a different version of the file or change the location where the file is saved. For example, the second draft of Letter.docx can be renamed Letter2.docx.

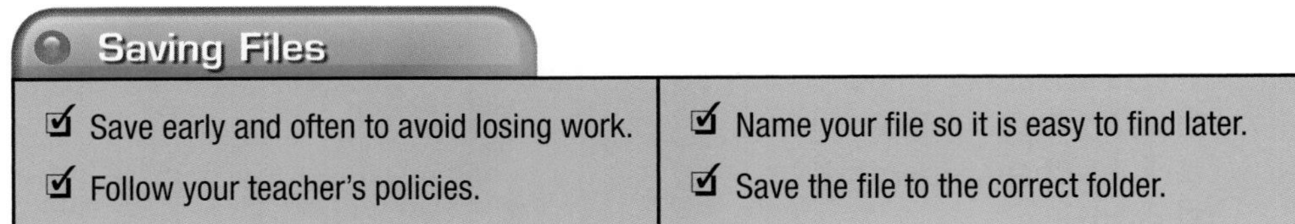

Saving Files

☑ Save early and often to avoid losing work.	☑ Name your file so it is easy to find later.
☑ Follow your teacher's policies.	☑ Save the file to the correct folder.

In this exercise, you will open a new Word document and save it. You will also check to make sure you name the file correctly and save it to the correct location.

Step-by-Step

1. Open a new Word document. **Hint:** Start Word.

2. Locate the **Quick Access Toolbar**, and click the **Save** button (Figure 1.4). Because this is the first time you are saving the document, the **Save As** dialog box opens.

▼ **Figure 1.4** The Quick Access Toolbar provides easy access to your most commonly used command buttons.

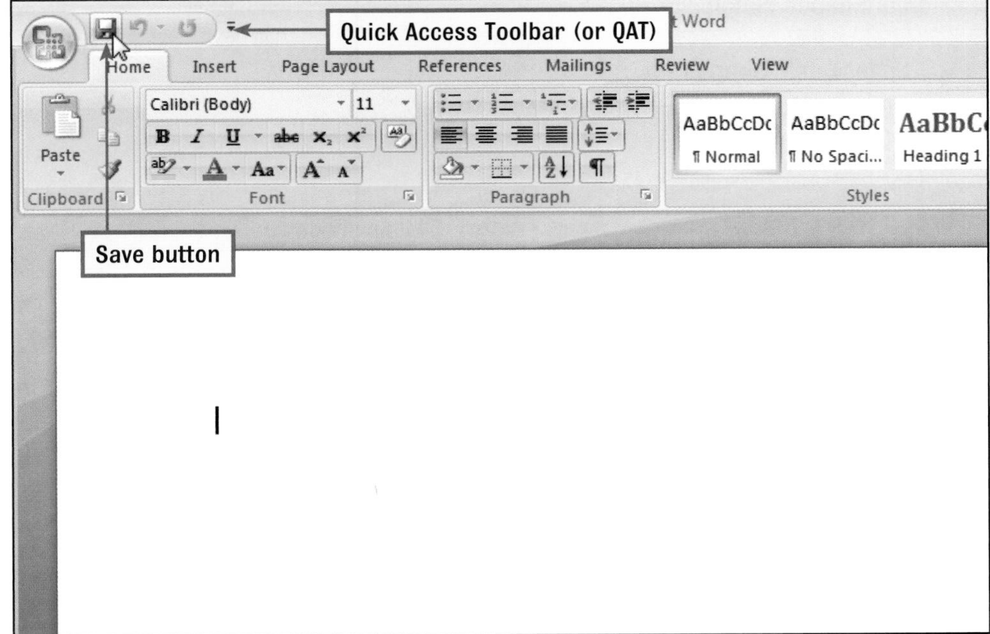

12 Drag the moon to the top-left corner of Future Phones (Figure 1.19). **Note:** If you cannot see the moon's outline, on the **Format** tab, in the **Shape Styles** group, click the **Shape Outline** drop-down arrow. Select **Black, Text 1.**

13 Select the **moon,** and drag the **yellow diamond** to make the shape wider or narrower. Drag the **round handles** to resize it so that the logo looks similar to Figure 1.19.

14 Hold the SHIFT key on your keyboard, and select both the **moon** and the **WordArt**.

15 On the **Format** tab, in the **Arrange** group, click the **Group** button. Then click **Group**.

16 With the grouped moon and shape still selected, on the **Format** tab, in the **Shape Styles** group, click the **Shape Fill** drop-down arrow. Change the color of the logo to **Red.**

17 Position the logo above the bulleted list at the top of your advertisement. Move your cell phone clip art up, if necessary. Your ad should now look similar to Figure 1.20. **Save** your work.

Figure 1.19 You can resize the moon shape using the white handles and the yellow diamond.

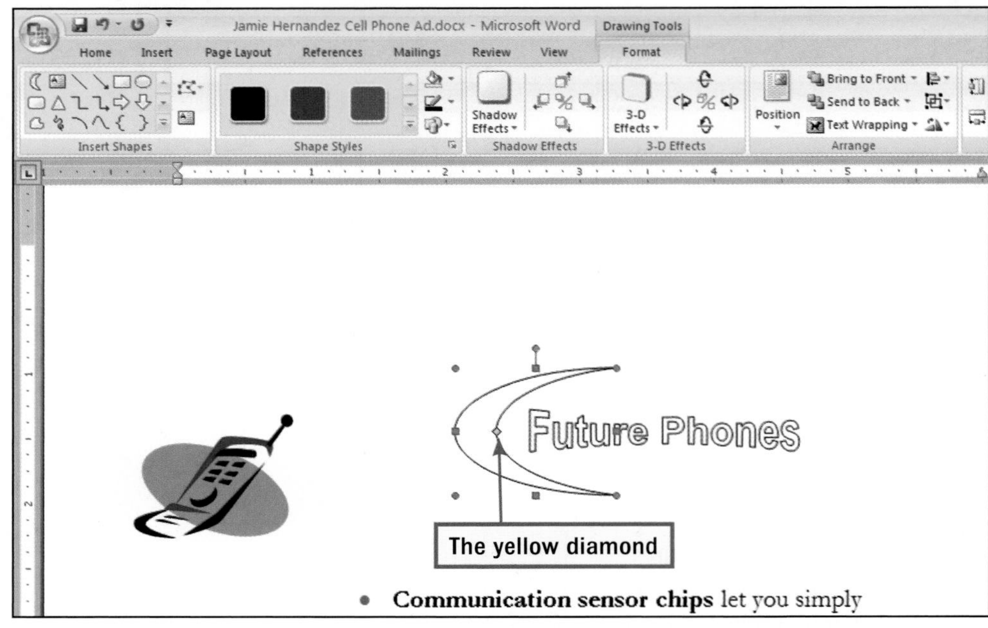

Figure 1.20 The completed logo should now be centered at the top of the ad. If not, click the logo and move it to the correct place.

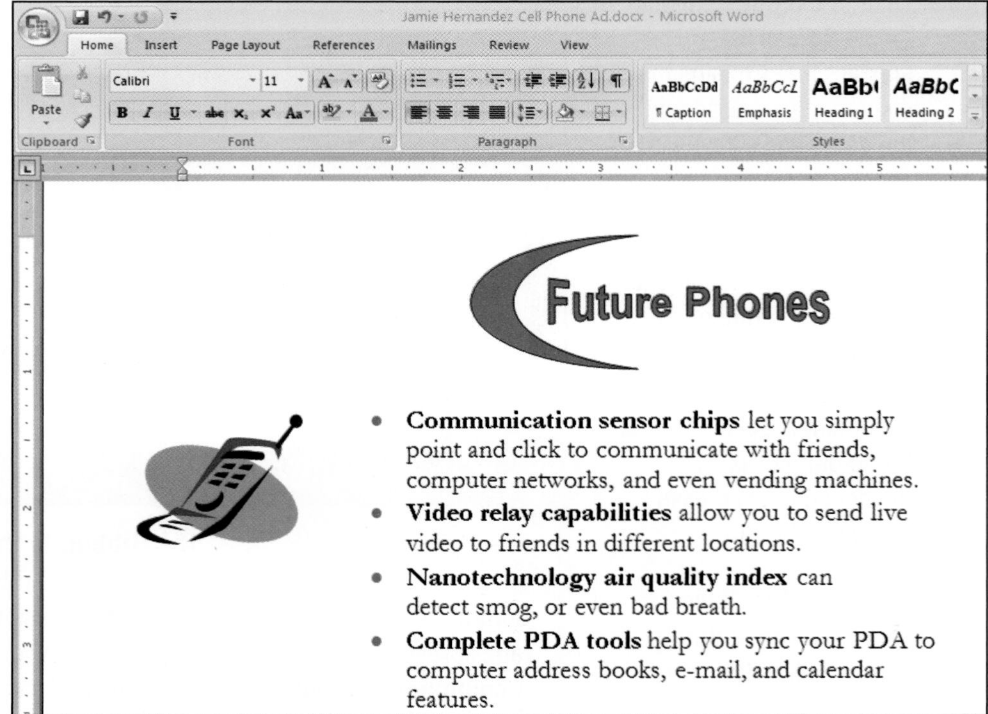

Figure 1.2 Each tab includes related groups of commands.

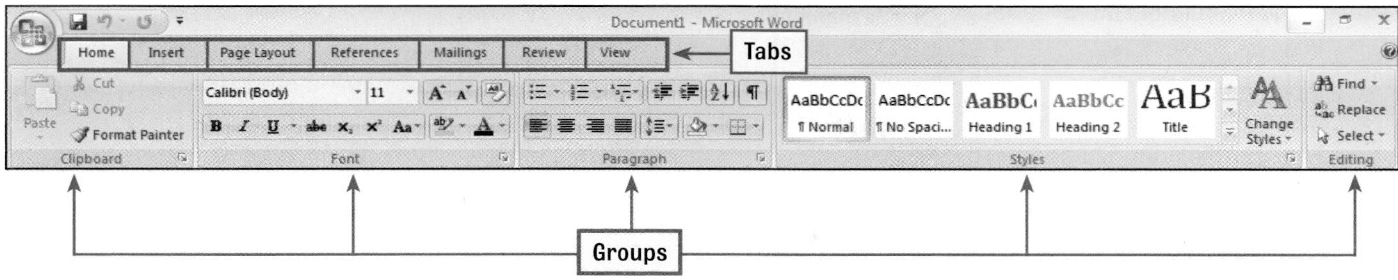

4 On the **Ribbon**, click the **Insert** tab. Then click each of the other tabs. New groups display as you click each tab.

5 On the **Ribbon**, click the **Home** tab. Roll your pointer arrow over the five different groups in the **Home** tab (Figure 1.2).

6 In the **Clipboard** group, point to the **Cut** command. A **ScreenTip** appears that explains the command's purpose and the command's keyboard shortcut.

7 Locate the **Close** button [X]. If multiple documents are open, the **Close** button closes the active document. If only one document is open, the **Close** button closes the document and exits the Word program.

8 To exit Word, click the **Microsoft Office Button**, and click **Exit Word** (Figure 1.3).

Figure 1.3 Click Exit Word to close all your documents and exit Word. Click the Close button to close the active document.

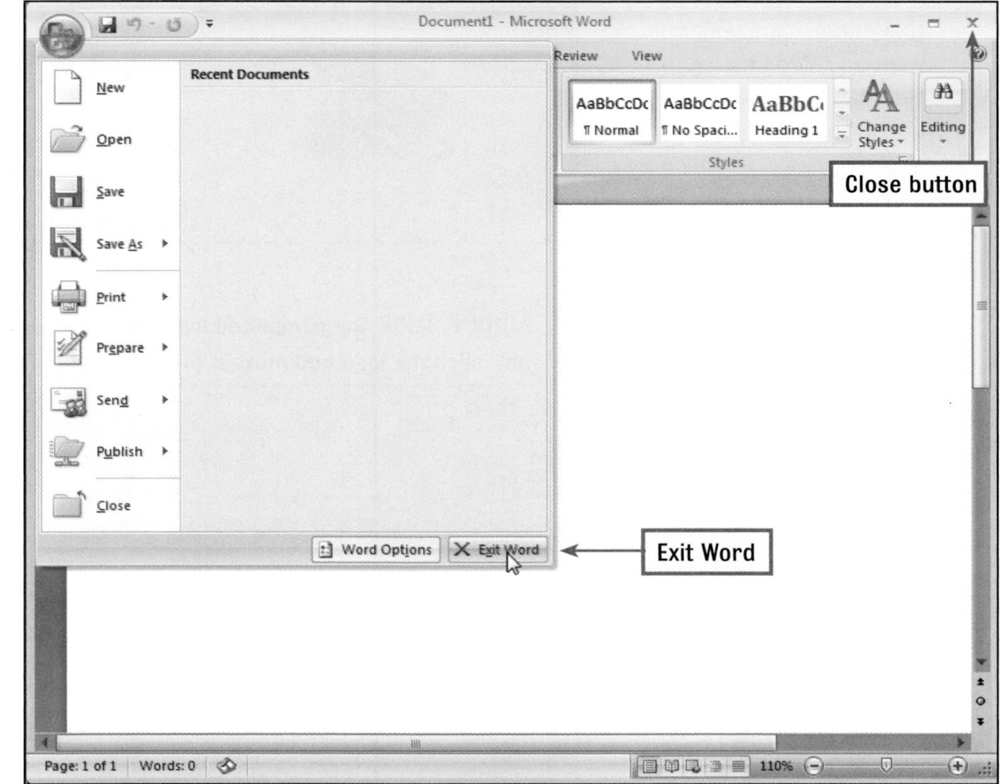

TechSavvy

The Ribbon and the Tabs The **Ribbon** is the focal point for all word processing commands. The three parts of the **Ribbon** are **Tabs**, **Groups**, and **Commands**. There are seven basic tabs across the top of the **Ribbon**. Each tab represents a specific activity area with related groups of commands. A **command** is a button, a dialog box, or a menu that carries out specific functions.

Exercise 1-6 Add Layers to a Text Box

You can use text boxes to place text anywhere you want on the page. You can also layer text boxes over other text boxes. For example, adding a second text box to your advertisement creates a separate section, which looks different from the rest of the advertisement and contains separate text elements. Be careful not to use too many text boxes. Keep the design simple and easy to read.

In this exercise, you will add another text box to your cell phone advertisement and format text within it. If you need to review Microsoft Word skills, refer to Unit 4, Project 2 (pages 152–166).

Step-by-Step

1. In your Cell Phone Ad, on the **Insert** tab, in the **Text** group, click the **Text Box** button [A]. Then select **Draw Text Box** located at the bottom of the **Built-In** gallery.

2. Click the upper-left corner of the ad and drag to create a new text box that extends from the top to the bottom of the ad (Figure 1.21).

3. Select the new text box, if necessary. On the **Format** tab, in the **Text Box Styles** group, click the **Shape Fill** drop-down arrow and select **Orange**.

4. Click the **Shape Outline** drop-down arrow and select **Black, Text 1**.

Figure 1.21 The clip art is hidden behind the new text box. (**Note**: You will correct this in the next exercise.)

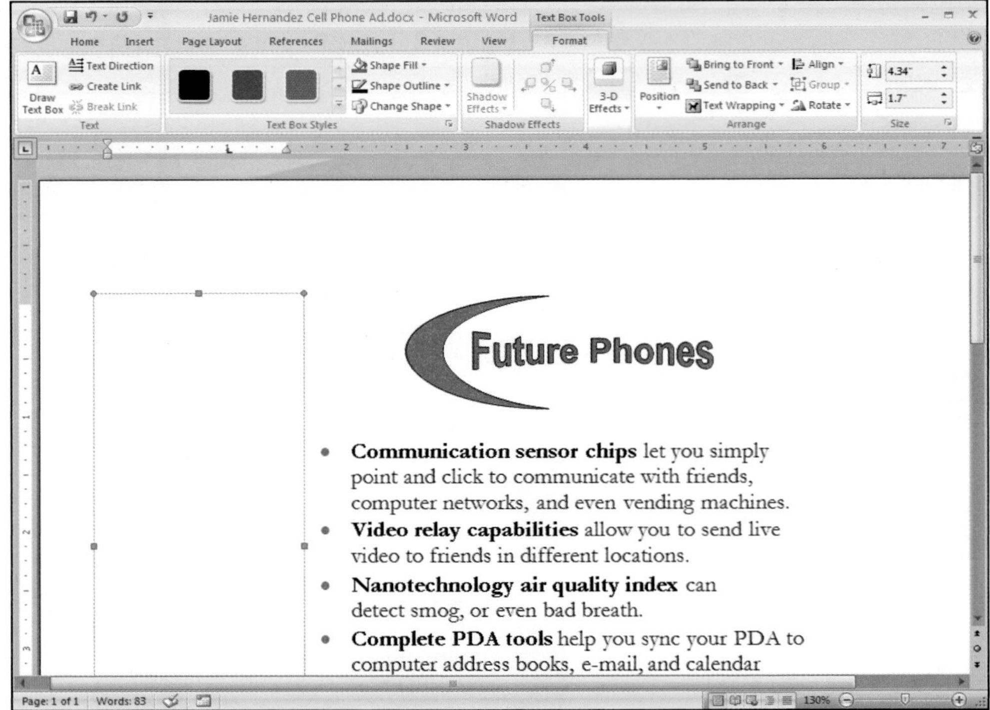

TechSavvy

Add Spaces You can add space above and below text by using hard returns. At the end of a line or a paragraph, press [ENTER] as many times as needed to add space. Note that this method does *not* allow you to control the position of text as precisely as using the **Spacing Before** or **After** option in the **Paragraph** dialog box.

Exercise 1-1 Get to Know Microsoft Word

TechSavvy

Office 2007 Commands The Microsoft Office Button displays a list of commands to create, open, save, and print documents. The Quick Access Toolbar contains frequently used commands and is located to the right of the Microsoft Office Button by default.

Word processing software is used to create and edit text documents. It also has features that make it easy to add graphics to the text. Word processing software can be used to create:

- **Short documents** such as letters, memos, flyers, and essays.
- **Long documents** such as reports and books.
- **Specialized documents** such as newsletters, brochures, and Web pages.

Examples of popular word processing programs include Microsoft Word, Corel WordPerfect, and Microsoft Works.

In this exercise, you will explore the features of Microsoft Word 2007, which is the most widely used word processing software. You will use these features over and over again as you create different documents.

Step-by-Step

1. **Start Microsoft Word.** If you are using Windows XP, please refer to the *Getting Started* pages on pages xlv–xlviii in this book.
2. When Word opens, your screen should show a new document, as in Figure 1.1.
3. On your own screen, find and identify the Word features identified in Figure 1.1.

Figure 1.1 The Ribbon displays commands for tasks you do often.

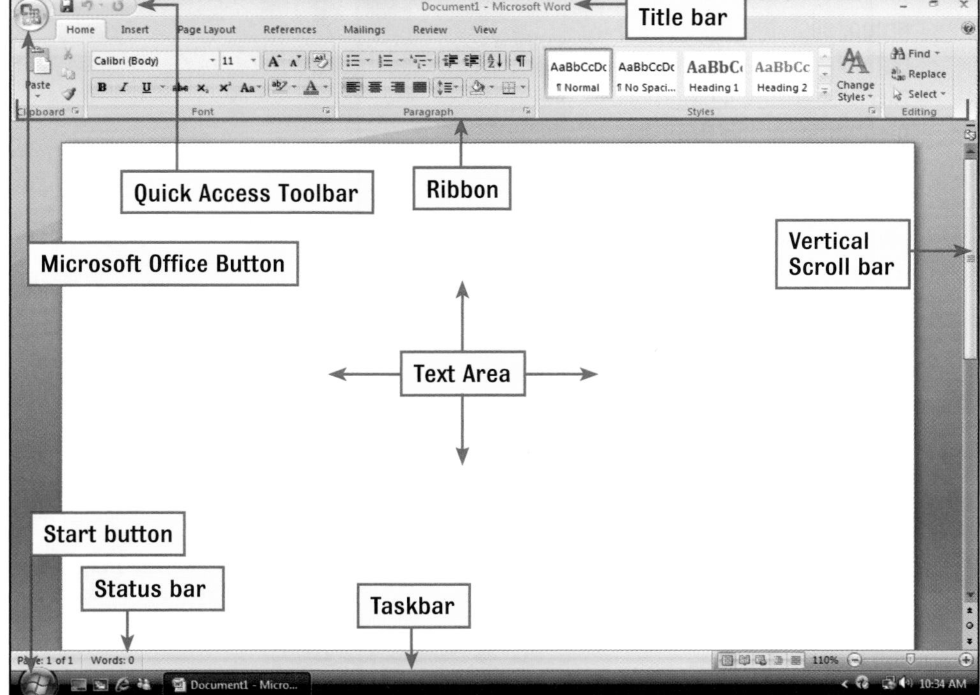

HELP!

What Does This Command Do? To see what each command does, move the mouse pointer slowly over the command. Do not click! The **ScreenTip**, or name, for each command will display.

5 Click inside the new text box.

6 Key a list of three reasons why people should buy your cell phone. See Figure 1.22 as an example.

7 Select all the text you just keyed. Open the **Paragraph** dialog box. In the **Paragraph** dialog box, under **Spacing**, in the **After** box, key 0.

8 Change the **Font** to **Verdana** and the **Font Size** to **12**. Make the text **Bold**. Your ad should look similar to Figure 1.22.

▼ **Figure 1.22** **When you select and change the text in one text box, it does not change the text in the other text boxes.**

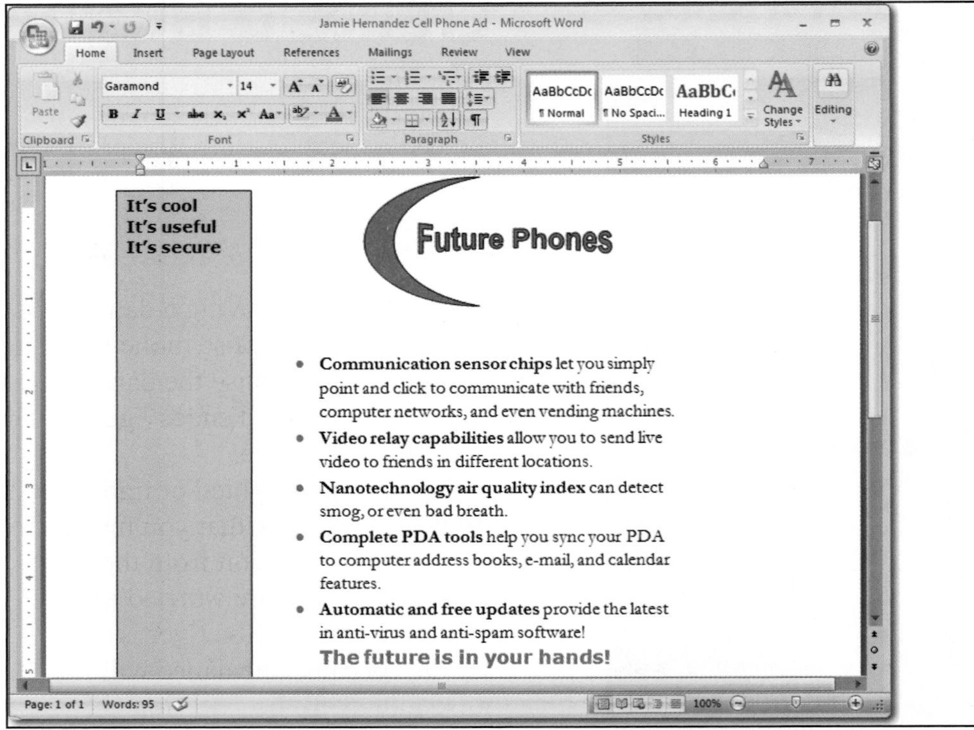

▼ **Figure 1.23** **Add hard returns before and after the new text in the text box.**

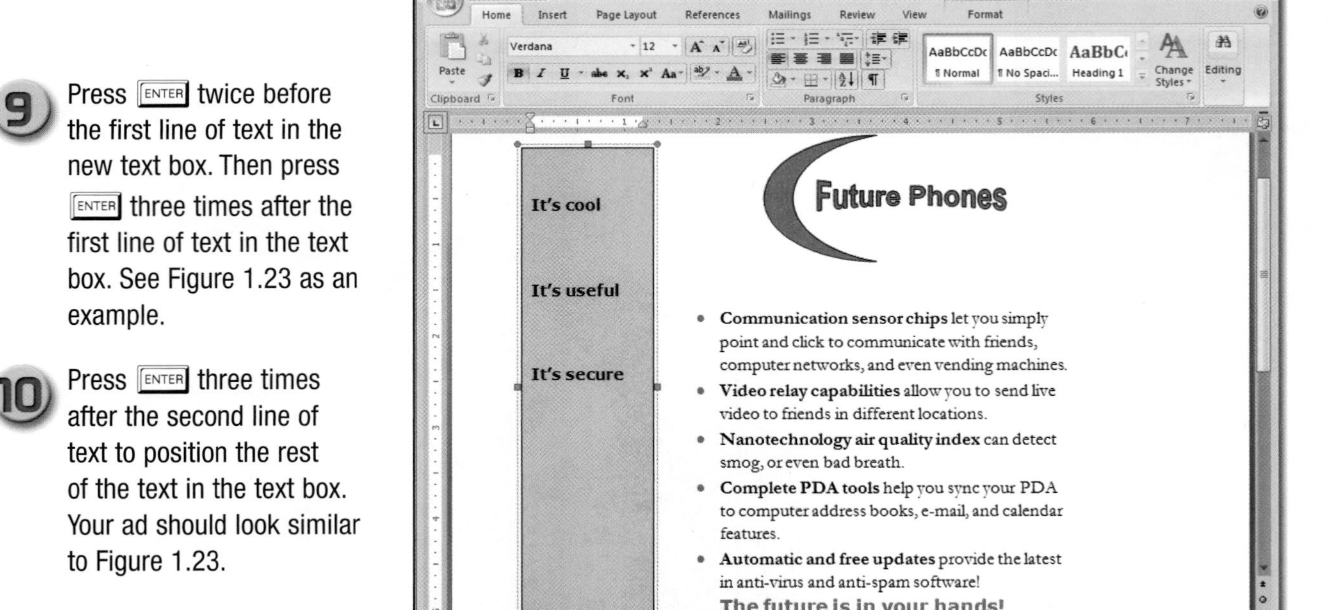

9 Press ENTER twice before the first line of text in the new text box. Then press ENTER three times after the first line of text in the text box. See Figure 1.23 as an example.

10 Press ENTER three times after the second line of text to position the rest of the text in the text box. Your ad should look similar to Figure 1.23.

Concepts in Action

Project 1 Create a Business Letter

Key Concepts

Exercise 1-1

- Explore Microsoft Word Ribbon and commands

Exercise 1-2

- Open and save a document

Exercise 1-3

- Format a business letter
- Enter text

Exercise 1-4

- Select, cut, copy, and paste text

Exercise 1-5

- Use the thesaurus
- Check spelling

Exercise 1-6

- Zoom
- Preview and print

Vocabulary

Key Terms
word processing
edit
proofread
cut
copy
paste
synonym

Before You Begin

Preview Before you begin, review all the figures in the project. This is like having a mental map to help you get to your destination.

For this project, you will use a word processing program to write a business letter asking for permission to use a photo in a flyer.

Let's Rock and Roll!

Your school is having a dance called *Let's Rock and Roll!* to raise money for a new auditorium. To advertise the dance, you want to use a photo of a Fender® guitar from the company's Web site.

To use a copyrighted or trademarked product, you know that you may need to request permission from the copyright holder. You are worried that using the photo in the flyer is not fair use because the dance will raise money. To be safe, you decide to write for permission. In this project, you will create a business letter to ask Fender for permission to use the guitar photo in your flyer.

11 Select the text in the new text box. On the **Home** tab, in the **Font** group, click the **Font Color** drop-down arrow, and then choose **White, Background 1**.

12 With the text still selected, click **Align Text Right** in the **Paragraph** group (Figure 1.24).

13 Select the new text box. The **Text Box Tools** appear. On the **Format** tab, in the **Arrange** group, click the **Send to Back** drop-down arrow. Click **Send Backward**.

Figure 1.24 Change the color and alignment of the text in the text box.

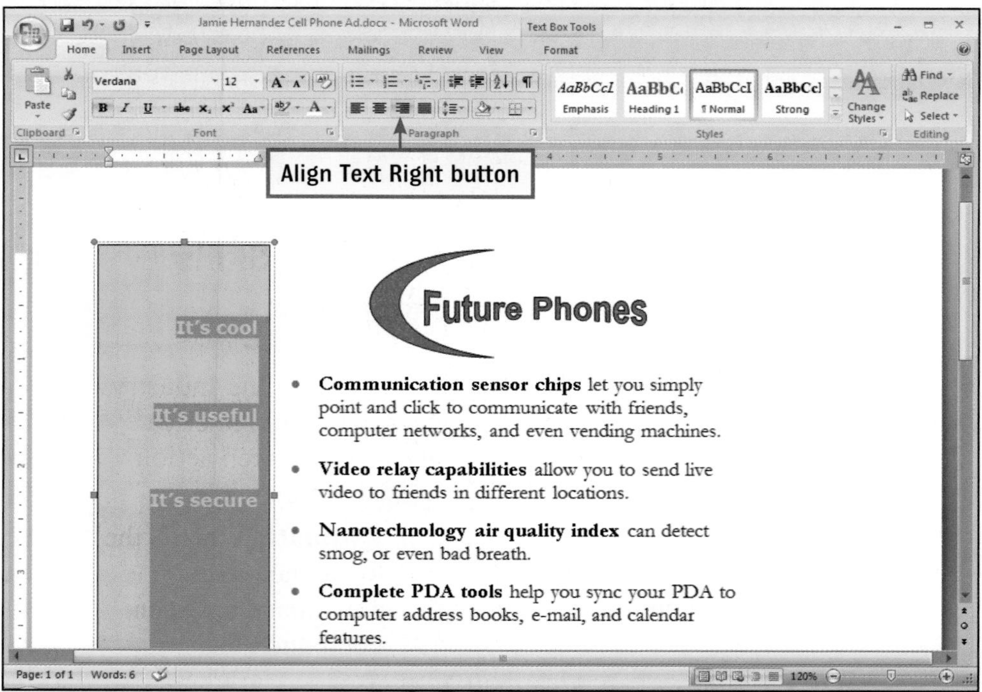

14 Move the clip art down below **It's secure** (Figure 1.25).

15 **Save** your work. **Close** your file.

Figure 1.25 The cell phone clip art is now visible.

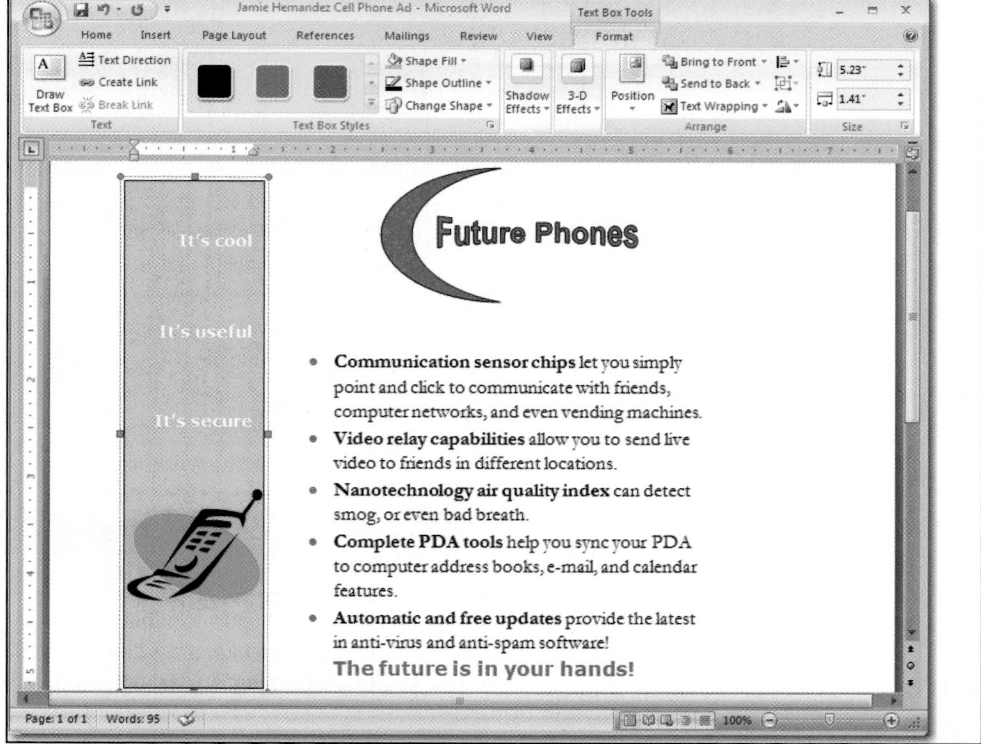

After You Read

Key Concepts Check

1. **Compare and Contrast** What is the difference between piracy and plagiarism?
2. **Describe** How can you tell if an act is unethical?
3. **Explain** What does it mean for a work to be in the public domain?

Critical Thinking

4. **Compare and Contrast** Some people know it is wrong to shoplift but think it is okay to copy a copyrighted CD or DVD.
   a. How is piracy similar to shoplifting?
   b. Why is it wrong to copy a CD or DVD for a friend?

21st Century Skills

5. **Ethics** Your manager has asked you to review the company's terms of use policy. Write a brief summary of your company's policy on software piracy. Include information about the steps the company takes to prevent piracy.

Academic Skills

Mathematics

The Recording Industry Association of America (RIAA) has taken action against piracy.

a. **Estimate** What is the difference in the percentage between 2004 and 2007?

b. **Analyze** Why do you think the percentage of illegal downloading dropped so quickly?

Math Concept

Line Graphs A line graph displays information about quantities that change over time. In this case, the variables are the year and the percentage of youth illegally downloading material.

Starting Hint Find the points on the line for both 2004 and 2007. Then subtract to find the difference in the percentages.

NCTM Data Analysis and Probability Formulate questions that can be addressed with data and collect, organize, and display relevant data to answer them.

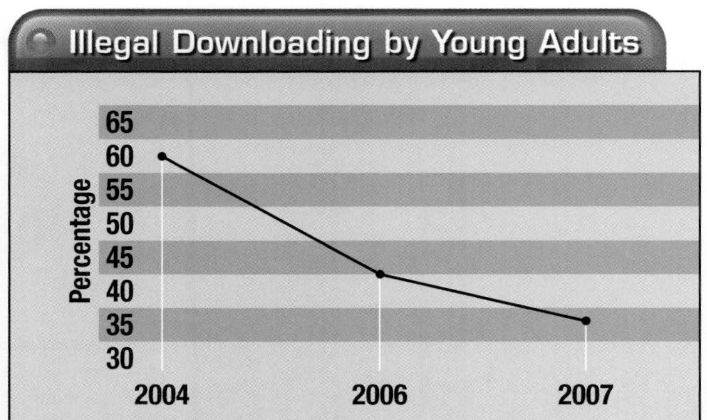

Source: Business Software Alliance

Go Online e-QUIZ

glencoe.com

Self-Check Assess your understanding of what you have just read. Go to the **Online Learning Center** at glencoe.com. Choose **After You Read Quizzes**, and take the **Unit 4 Tech Talk Quiz**.

Project 1 Assessment

Key Concepts Check

1. **Explain** Why would you use a text box in a Word document?
2. **Describe** What happens when you ungroup clip art?
3. **Identify** What elements are combined in a logo?

Critical Thinking

4. **Cause and Effect** Why is it useful to be able to group objects?
5. **Evaluate** You want to add a colorful slogan to a flyer you created. Why might you prefer to use a text box rather than moving your insertion point to add the slogan?

1 Guided Practice

Create an Advertisement You have started your own petsitting business and want to advertise your service to your neighbors. You decide to create an advertisement that will include a description of your service, as well as some of your qualifications. The ad has to be both informative and attractive, so both text and design are important. If you need help, refer back to the exercise in parentheses at the end of the step.

Step-by-Step

1. In Word, create a **New Blank Document**. **Save** it **as** *Your Name* Petsitting Flyer.
2. Change the orientation to **Landscape**. Key the information, and format the text as shown in Figure 1.26.
3. Select the text and create a text box with a height of 5.5 inches and a width of 9 inches. (Exercise 1-2)
4. Select the bulleted text, and set the Indent markers on the ruler as shown in Figure 1.26. (Exercise 1-3)

▼ **Figure 1.26** Use the margins and font styles shown in this figure.

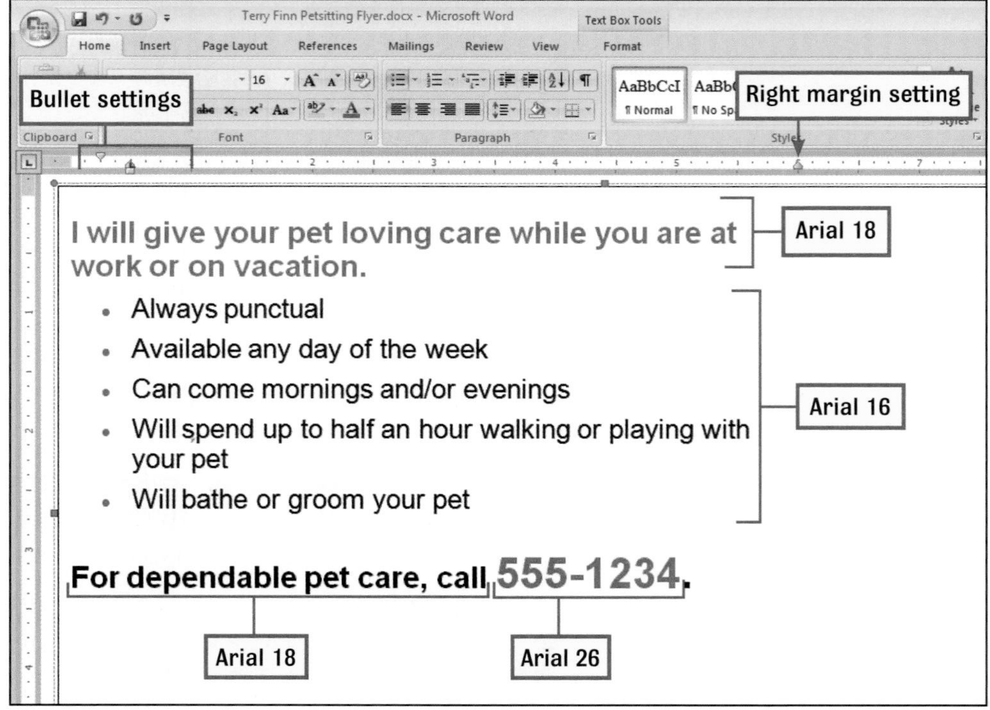

How Do I Cite an Online Source?

The Modern Language Association (MLA) is an organization that has many helpful guidelines for creating reports and citing sources. Although there are other styles for citing sources, teachers often like students to use MLA guidelines to write citations. According to MLA style, when you cite a Web site, include as many of the following details as you can:

- Author's full name, with the last name first
- Title of the article, work, or Web page, in quotation marks
- Complete title of the Web site
- Date of Internet publication or copyright date (look for this at the bottom of the Web page)
- Name of the organization that created or owns the site
- Date you visited the site
- URL (Web address) of the site, in angle brackets

Cite Sources Practice citing print and online sources at the **Online Learning Center** at glencoe.com. Choose **Tech Talk Activities**, then **Unit 4**.

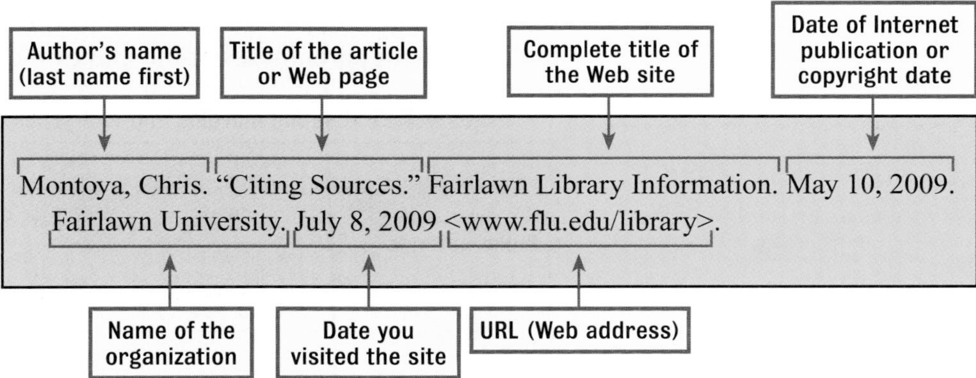

This example shows how to cite an online article. How could you check to make sure the information in this citation is correct?

There are many different kinds of Web sites, and you may not find the same information about each site. The most important thing to remember when citing an online source is to key the URL exactly as it appears in the address bar of your browser. To be safe, you should copy and paste the URL into your citation.

Reading Check

1. **Identify** Where do you list citations in a research paper?
2. **Summarize** Find out your school's policy on plagiarism. Write a paragraph describing the consequences of plagiarizing.

5. Change the **spacing after** each line to **6 pt**. (Exercise 1-2)

6. Change the **spacing before** the first line to **80 pt**. (Exercise 1-5)

7. Create **WordArt** that looks similar to that in Figure 1.27. Remember to create the WordArt outside the text box. (Exercise 1-5)

8. Add a new text box. Change the **Fill Color** to **Blue**. On the **Format** tab, in the **Shadow Effects** group, click the **Shadow Effects** button to add a shadow. See Figure 1.28. (Exercise 1-6)

9. Key the text in the new box, as shown in Figure 1.28. **Center** the text, and change the **spacing after** each item to **3 pt**. (Exercise 1-2)

10. **Insert clip art**. Choose your own, or use **Data File 8B Petsitting**. (Exercise 1-4)

11. **Ungroup** the clip art, and modify the parts as you like. Your flyer should look similar to Figure 1.28. **Save** your flyer. (Exercise 1-4)

▼ **Figure 1.27** Create the WordArt outside the text box, then move it into position.

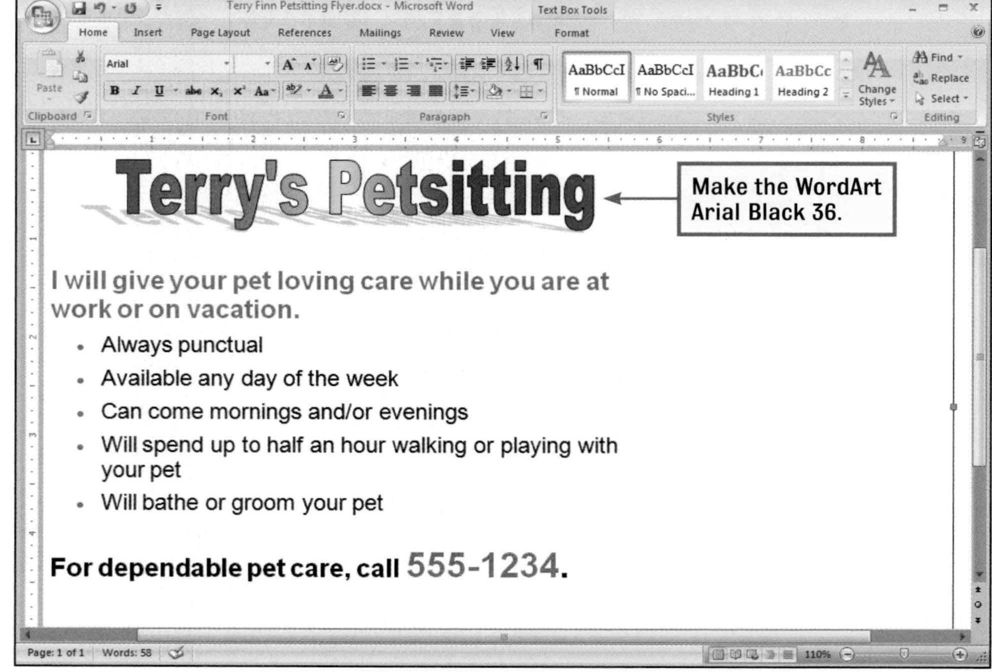

▼ **Figure 1.28** Size your clip art to fit in the new text box.

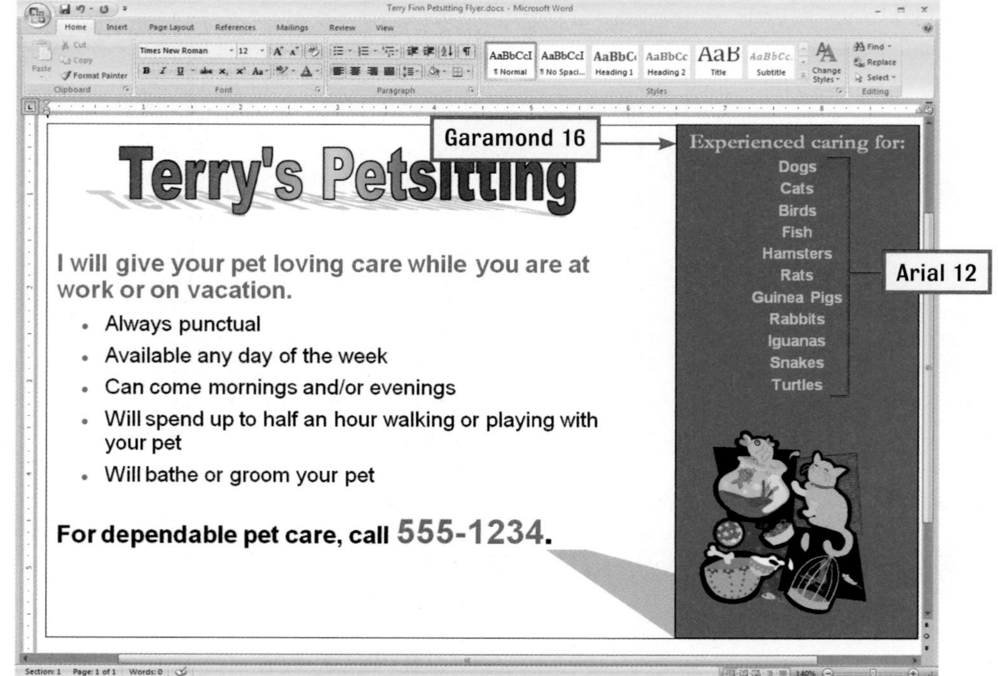

Citing Your Sources

When you use someone else's information, you should cite (give credit to) your sources. This is true even if you change an **image**, a visual representation, or rewrite the information in your own words (paraphrase). Citing your sources is the ethical and legal thing to do.

If you do not cite your sources, you are taking credit for someone else's ideas. This is called plagiarism, and it is illegal.

Why Should I Cite a Source?

When you use material from a book, magazine, newspaper, or Web site in your own reports, presentations, or Web sites, you must cite the sources of the information. Material might include text, graphics, or even someone's original ideas. For example, if you turn to the end of this book, you will find a page that cites the sources for the images in this book.

A citation gives the complete details of the source of your information. Citations help readers know where to look if they want more information about the work where you found the information.

In a research paper, there are a number of ways to cite your sources:

- **Endnotes** credit works that were cited in the body of the paper in the *order in which they were cited*. This numbered list appears on a separate page at the end of your paper.
- A **bibliography** is an alphabetical list of all the sources you use, *whether you cite them or not in the body of your paper*. A bibliography also appears on a separate page at the end of your paper.
- A **works cited page** is the same as a bibliography in format and style, but it lists only the sources *you actually cite in the body of your paper*.

▲ Citing a source is a little like giving an award. How would you feel if someone else got credit for something you had done?

Academic Focus

English Language Arts

Cite Online Sources
Make sure the information you find on a Web site is reliable. Check other sources to see if the information is similar. Find an update or copyright date on the site to see how up-to-date it is. Determine if the site is biased or covers only one side of any issue. Find out who created the site. It may be owned by a company or person trying to sell products or services described on the site. What other decisions would you make before citing an online source?

NCTE 8 Use information sources to gather information and create and communicate knowledge.

Project 1 Assessment

2 Independent Practice 

 Go Online RUBRICS

glencoe.com

Independent Practice
Use the rubrics for these projects to help create and evaluate your work. Go to the **Online Learning Center** at glencoe.com. Choose **Rubrics**, then **Unit 8**.

English Language Arts **Create an Advertisement** You are asked to create a half-page advertisement in your school newspaper for a restaurant.

a. Plan Write the text for your ad. Include a description of the restaurant, a catchy slogan, and its hours and location.

b. Create Use Word to create the advertisement.

- Insert a text box that is 4 inches high and 5 inches wide.
- Key your text into the text box.
- Format the text so that important elements clearly stand out from the rest of the text. Use a second text box if you like.

3 Independent Practice 

English Language Arts **Insert a Logo** Create the restaurant ad in Independent Practice 2 above. Then add elements for visual interest.

a. Research Use Microsoft Word or the Internet to find clip art that illustrates the information in your ad.

b. Create Add a logo and clip art to your advertisement.

- Create your own special logo for the restaurant using WordArt and the Drawing Tools.
- Insert the clip art you researched. Ungroup the clip art, and modify the different elements.

4 Independent Practice 

English Language Arts **Design a PDA Web Page** You want to design a Web page to promote your idea for the personal digital assistant (PDA) of the future.

a. Research With your teacher's permission, use the Internet or print sources to find information about the latest technology used in PDAs.

b. Create Use Word to create an advertisement about the PDA. Write and format text to emphasize the interesting features of your PDA. Use text boxes, clip art, and the Drawing Tools to make the page visually interesting. Save and view the ad as a Web page.

Ethics You usually are allowed to make one backup copy of copyrighted software in case something happens to the original. After that, the number of copies you may make legally depends on the company's policy.

Why It's Important What are some consequences of not making a backup copy of personal software if your computer is damaged?

Copy Software Legally

It might be tempting to buy software and then give it to or share it with whomever you choose. However, software companies have different rules, or policies, about how you can use their products.

STOP Read the software license. Some companies let you install a software program on only one computer.

CAUTION Companies may let you install a program on many machines only if you have a special license.

GO Some companies let you copy and share their software at no cost or for a small fee.

There are also many types of software that software companies *want* to be copied, spread, and used by a lot of different people. Sometimes these products are given out on CDs or DVDs, or they are available online.

Software Options

Type	Description	Examples
Shareware	Can be downloaded or copied if you pay a small fee to the copyright holder.	• WinZip® • Many online games
Freeware	Can be downloaded freely and copied for free.	• Linux® • Instant messaging software • Google™ toolbar

▲ Shareware and freeware can be downloaded and copied with few restrictions. **Why might a company want to offer free software?**

Make sure you obey the law and act ethically. Follow the terms of use when using, copying, or distributing software. Check the copyright agreement or permission information that comes with any copyrighted product.

Reading Check

1. **Evaluate** How are freeware and shareware software different?
2. **Cause and Effect** What would happen if everyone used pirated software rather than bought software?

Concepts in Action

Project 2 Create a Newsletter About Spam

Exercise 2-1

- Find information on a Web site

Exercise 2-2

- Create columns with a break in a Word document
- Insert clip art

Exercise 2-3

- Change text direction
- Use layered text boxes

Exercise 2-4

- Create an Excel spreadsheet and chart

Exercise 2-5

- Link text boxes
- Insert an Excel chart
- Insert page numbers

Vocabulary

Key Terms
fraud
cybercrime
linking

Before You Begin

Spot Similarities If you need help using a Microsoft Office application, use Help and look for tabs, buttons, task panes, and tools that are common to all Office applications.

In this project, you will create a community newsletter that educates readers about Internet spam. You will need to use an Internet browser, Microsoft Excel, and Microsoft Word.

Raising Community Awareness

Spam is commercial e-mail that advertises a product or service. Spam is often compared to junk mail. It can fill up computer e-mail inboxes, and it can take users time to sort through the unwanted e-mails. Although most spam advertises products and services that are legitimate, some spam is illegal. The amount of illegal spam has led to discussion about creating laws and regulations to control it. In this project, you will create a newsletter that describes spam and suggests some solutions to reduce the amount of spam people receive.

Using and Abusing Technology

Some computer users think it is acceptable to copy software, music, or videos from original discs or the Internet, especially if the copies will not be sold. It is NOT acceptable if the works are copyrighted.

Academic Focus

Mathematics

Interpret graphs

Review the bar graph in this article. A bar graph shows the relationship between two sets of data that are graphed as horizontal and vertical bars. Note the graph title, the vertical and horizontal labels, and the bars. Find the top of each vertical bar. Then read the horizontal label to the left of each bar to see the number of pirated units. What conclusions can you draw about disc piracy after reviewing the data?

NCTM Number and Operations Understand numbers, ways of representing numbers, relationships between numbers, and number systems.

What Is Piracy?

Piracy is the act of copying or sharing copyrighted material without permission. Piracy is illegal and unethical, whether you sell the copyrighted material or whether you give it as a gift.

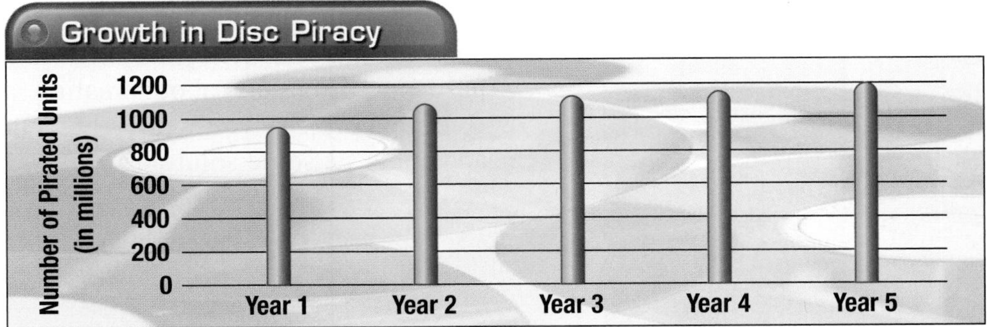

Source: International Federation of the Phonographic Industry

▲ Billions of dollars have been stolen from the creators of copyrighted software, music, films, and books because of piracy. If you were a recording artist, how would you feel about piracy?

It is *not* legal to download copyrighted music and videos and share them for free with other users. This is called **file sharing** (or file swapping). To music companies and movie studios, file sharing often breaks copyright laws and causes great financial losses. Some companies have successfully sued people who swap music and video files.

Music and video producers and artists are trying to find solutions to address the problem. Some possibilities are:

- Make it easy and affordable for music lovers to legally download their favorite tracks from the Web.
- Charge a little more for blank CD-Rs, to make up for money lost due to file sharing.
- Add bonus features to CDs and DVDs so that people will still want to buy them in stores.

Exercise 2-1 Research Spam

The Federal Trade Commission (FTC) is a government agency that investigates crimes such as mail fraud. **Fraud** is a deliberate attempt to trick people into giving money or information.

One type of crime the FTC investigates is Internet fraud, which includes false or misleading spam. Internet fraud is a kind of **cybercrime**, or a crime that is committed with the help of a computer. The FTC's Web site provides information about this topic to interested citizens and consumers.

In this exercise, you will search the FTC Web site to research various issues regarding spam. You will use the Find command to help you in your search. If you need to review Web search skills, refer to Unit 3, Project 2 (Pages 109–121).

Step-by-Step

1. Follow your teacher's instructions to launch your Web browser. This exercise uses **Internet Explorer**.
2. In the **Address bar**, key the URL: http://www.ftc.gov.
3. Under **Consumer Protection**, click the **Consumer Information** tab to see a list of current topics (Figure 2.1).
4. On the **Consumer Information** Web page, find a topic to link to computer- and Internet-related subjects. Click the link, and a list of categories displays.
5. Click the **Spam Email** link. A list of publications about spam displays.

Figure 2.1 On the Federal Trade Commission Web site, find a link to computer- and Internet-related topics.

TechSavvy

Internet Fraud If you or someone you know is the victim of Internet fraud, you should notify the FTC. It maintains a huge online database called Consumer Sentinel, which provides information about incidents of unethical Internet use to law enforcement agencies around the world.

Go Online ACTIVITY
glencoe.com

Ethical Computer Use
Learn about other ethical issues at the **Online Learning Center**. Go to glencoe.com. Choose **Tech Talk Activities**, then **Unit 4**.

Works That Are Legal to Copy

Fair use describes those times when you may use or copy a copyrighted work without asking permission. For example, copyrighted works can be used for the following teaching purposes:

- Teachers may usually copy a few pages of a book to hand out to students to teach a lesson.
- Students may usually include copyrighted material in a school report or presentation to support their research.
- Schools can generally take advantage of copyrighted material for educational purposes as long as they do not make money from it.

Here are two examples of fair use when copyrighted work can be used or copied at home:

- You may listen to a friend's new music CD while visiting his or her house (as long as you do not copy it).
- You may use TiVo®, a digital video recorder (DVR), to record a television program for your own private use.

Public domain describes material that people can use freely without permission. Things that are in the public domain include:

- Material that is so old that the copyright no longer exists.
- Information published by the government.
- Material that the creators have decided to offer free to the public.

If you are not sure whether material is in the public domain or can be used within fair use guidelines, ask your school or local librarian or contact the work's **author** (the one who originates or creates the work).

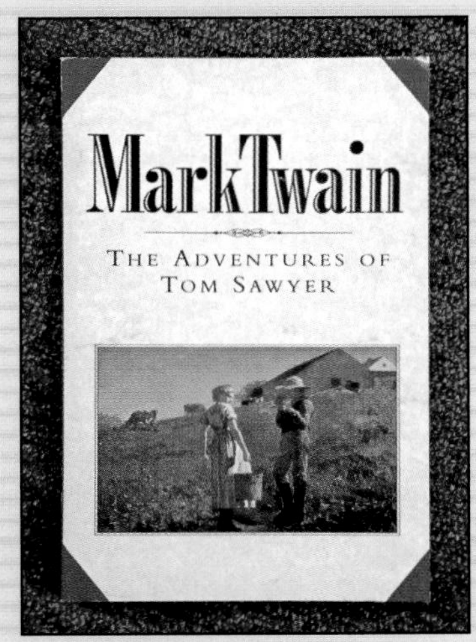

▲ *The Adventures of Tom Sawyer*, first published in 1876, is now in the public domain. Would you need to ask permission before copying part of this book?

Give Credit

Do not forget that even when material falls under fair use or has fallen into the public domain, you should still give credit to the source of the information you copy! (See the article "Citing Your Sources" on pages 131–132 of this Tech Talk for information about how to cite sources.)

Reading Check

1. **Explain** Where would you go on a Web site to find out if you need permission to use material from the site?
2. **Draw Conclusions** Besides loss of money, why might authors care about how others use their work?

6 Press CTRL + F on the keyboard to open the Find tool.

7 In the **Find what** box, key spam. The word **spam** will be highlighted in the results list (Figure 2.2).

Figure 2.2 The Find tool is a convenient way to search a Web page.

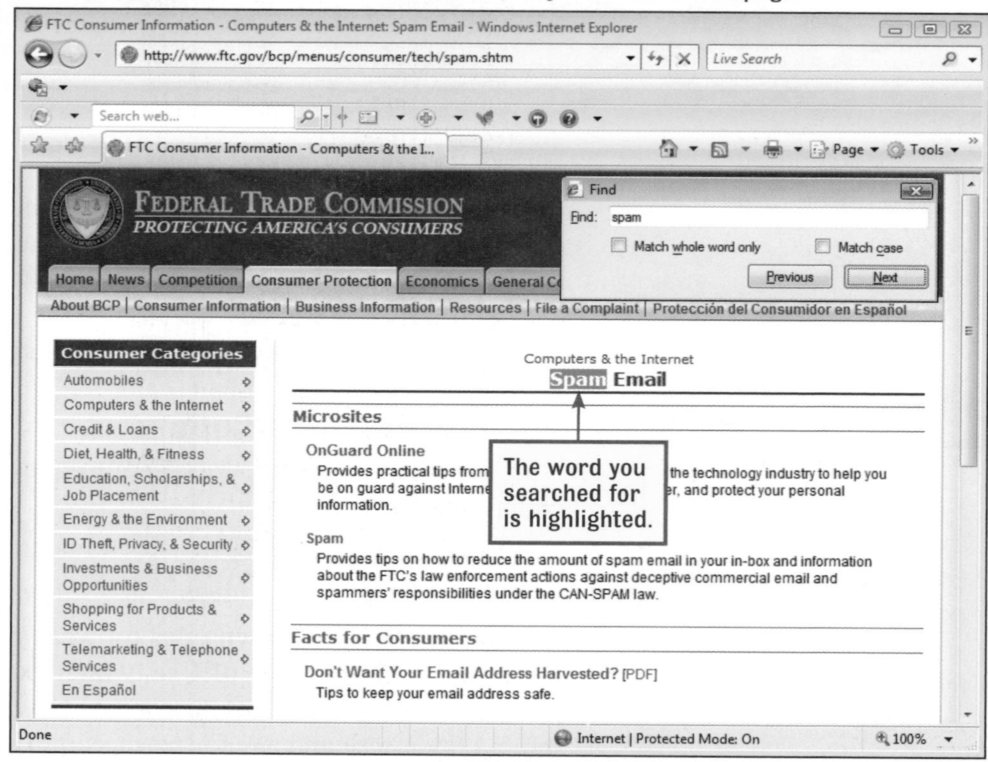

8 In the **Find** dialog box, click **Find Next** to help you look through the results. Choose the publication that you think will answer the questions shown in Figure 2.3.

9 Use pen and paper or Microsoft Word to create a table similar to the one in Figure 2.3.

10 Fill out the table using the information you found on the FTC site or another Web site.

Figure 2.3 Create a table to help organize your research.

TOPIC	NOTES
What is spam, and how is it used?	
In what ways can spam be harmful?	
How can you protect yourself from spam?	
What are some new laws concerning spam?	

TechSavvy

Search with Keywords You can use the Search box on the home page of the FTC site to search for information about spam. If you cannot find suitable results using the keyword *spam*, try using *Internet spam* or *computer spam*. You can also use the same keywords in a search engine such as Yahoo! or Google.

How Can I Copy Legally?

You might find information that you want to copy for public use. However, it might be illegal, and thus unethical, to copy it. If the material is copyrighted, you need permission first. **Permission** is when the owner or creator of a work allows you to use the work in a way that was not its original **purpose**, or the goal or intended outcome of something.

Ethics The first copyright laws were introduced in England in 1709. The term *copyright* comes from a person's *right* to determine who can *copy* his or her work.

Why It's Important Think about work you have done (or would like to do). Do you feel your work should be protected within this definition of the word *copyright*?

Get Permission to Copy

In general, you need permission to copy and use any material that is copyrighted, such as:

- video games
- music
- books
- articles
- photographs
- videos
- software
- TV programs

Web sites have their own rules for what you can and cannot copy. Look for a page called **Terms of Use**, which explains a site's rules regarding permission. If you are not sure whether you are allowed to copy something, play it safe and ask for permission first.

▲ You can usually find a copyright notice or Terms of Use at the bottom of a Web page. Where do you look for copyright and permissions information in a book or magazine?

Exercise 2-2 Work with Columns

In Unit 4, Project 4, you created a newsletter by setting up a newsletter format in Word, then pasting the text into it. You can also do the opposite by creating the articles and then formatting them into a newsletter. You can control how you want the articles to be placed on the page as you create the text.

In this exercise, you will write an article about spam and then begin to format it as a newsletter. If you need to review your Word skills, refer to Unit 4, Project 4 (Pages 184–203).

Step-by-Step

1. **Start Microsoft Word**.
2. Key an original article about spam that is approximately 200 to 250 words. Use your research from Exercise 2-1 to decide on a suitable topic. Be sure to include a title for the article as well as your name.
3. On the **Page Layout** tab, in the **Page Setup** group, click the **Page Setup Dialog Box Launcher** to open the **Page Setup** dialog box. Click the **Margins** tab and, next to **Left**, key 2.5 (Figure 2.4).
4. Click **OK** to close the **Page Setup** dialog box.
5. **Save** your article as *Your Name* Spam Newsletter.

Figure 2.4 Change the left margin of your Word document in the Page Setup dialog box.

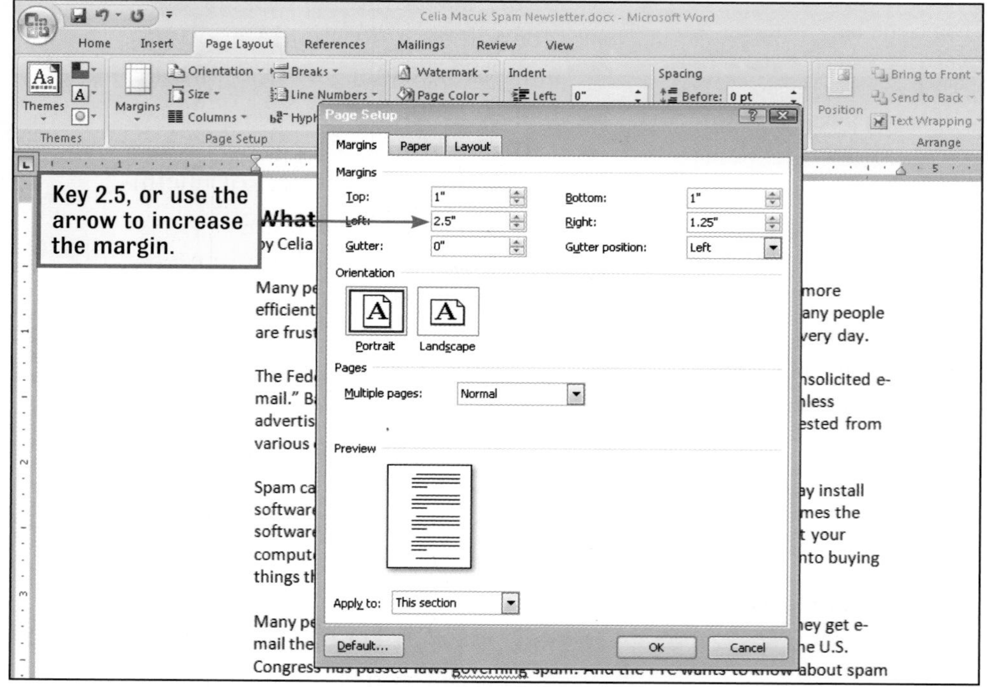

HELP!

Data File If your teacher prefers, you can use a Data File with the article shown in this exercise rather than write your own article. Open the **Data File** named **8C Spam Article,** and save it as ***Your Name* Spam Newsletter**. Then continue with steps 3 to 17.

Exploring Ethics

Reading Guide

Before You Read

Use Bookmarks If you do not understand something you read, mark the page with a bookmark or a sticky note if your teacher allows. Jot down a comment or question about the text. Then come back to it later and reread the section. If you are still unsure, ask your teacher for help or discuss it further in class.

Key Concepts

- Why copyrights are necessary
- How to use technology ethically and legally
- How to cite online sources

Vocabulary

Key Terms

ethics
intellectual property
copyright
trademark
permission
terms of use
fair use
public domain
piracy
file sharing

Academic Vocabulary

symbol
purpose
author
image

Ethics and Technology

Ethics are the rules that we use to define behavior as "right" or "wrong." For example, it is *ethical* to tell the truth. It is *unethical* to cheat on a test or to spread rumors about someone. When you use technology, you should apply the same ethics that you use in other areas of your life.

It is not always easy to know whether an act is ethical or unethical. It helps to ask yourself:

- *What effects will this act have on others?* If the act will harm anyone, there is a good chance that it is unethical.
- *What would be the result if everyone did this?* If everyone did something harmful or dishonest, there could be serious problems. Ethical people lead by example.

▲ Making a poor ethical choice can have serious consequences. What are some of the possible effects of cheating?

What Is Intellectual Property?

The law is designed to help people act ethically. Some laws protect physical property, such as cars, houses, and so on. Other laws are written to protect **intellectual property**, which are ideas and concepts created or owned by a person or company. These could include books, music, movies, software, and inventions. A **copyright** (©) is the legal protection for intellectual property.

Another important type of intellectual property is a **trademark** (™ or ®). A trademark is a name, **symbol**—something that stands for something else, or other feature that identifies a product with a specific owner. Anyone can open a restaurant, but only McDonald's® can legally use the golden arches. That is because the arches are a registered trademark of McDonald's.

6 Select the body of the article, and choose **Calibri, Font Size 10**. Do *not* select the title or byline.

7 With the article still selected, on the **Page Layout** tab, in the **Page Setup** group, click the **Columns** button.

8 Click **Two** (Figure 2.5). Notice that the ruler on your Word screen now has two sections.

▼ **Figure 2.5** Format your newsletter into two columns.

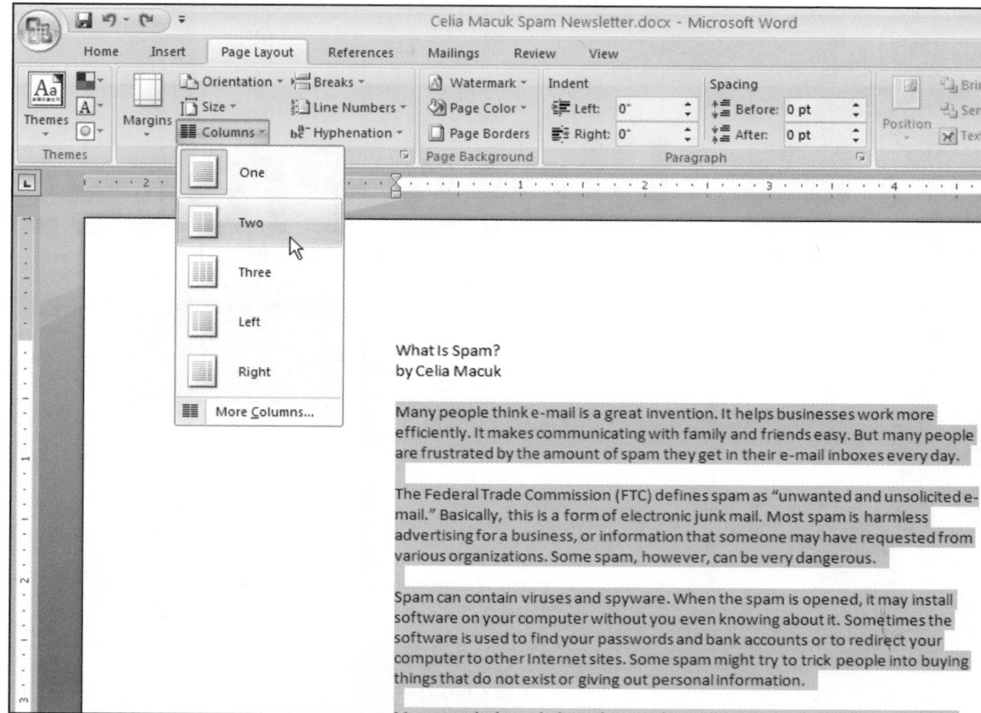

9 **Bold** the title of your article, and choose **Font Size 14**.

10 Place the insertion point in the middle of your article.

11 On the **Page Layout** tab, in the **Page Setup** group, click **Breaks**. Under **Page Breaks**, click **Column**.

12 Check to see if the two columns are roughly the same height. If not, click the **Undo** button and repeat steps 10 and 11 again. Your article should look similar to Figure 2.6.

▼ **Figure 2.6** Insert a column break halfway through your article.

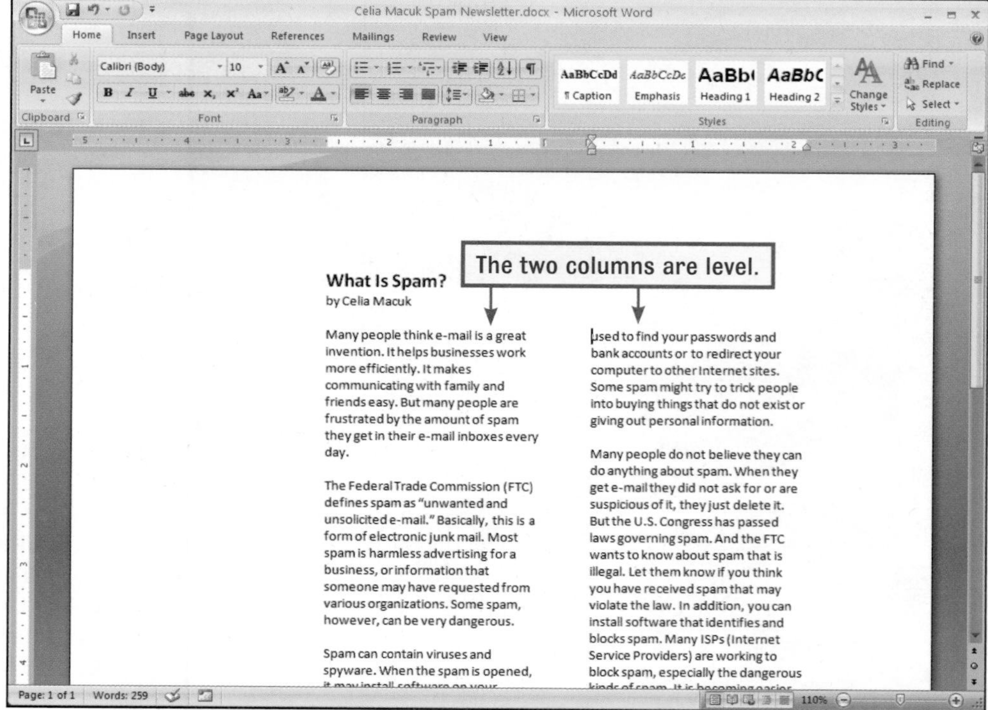

UNIT

4 Word Processing

Real World Projects

Go Online **e-QUIZ**

glencoe.com

Starting with You What do you think it means to use technology ethically? To find out, go to the **Online Learning Center** at glencoe.com. Choose **Before You Read e-Quizzes**, and take the **Unit 4 Pre-Quiz**.

13. Scroll down to the bottom of your article. Click the next available line.

14. On the **Insert** tab, in the **Illustrations** group, click the **Clip Art** button to find your own clip art. (Or click **Insert Picture** to use the **Data File** named **8D Spam Clip Art**.)

15. Click the clip art you inserted, if the **Picture Tools** are not already displayed on your screen.

16. On the **Format tab**, in the **Arrange** group, click **Text Wrapping**. Click **Square**. Handles will be displayed (Figure 2.7)

▼ **Figure 2.7** After you insert the clip art, select the Square wrapping position.

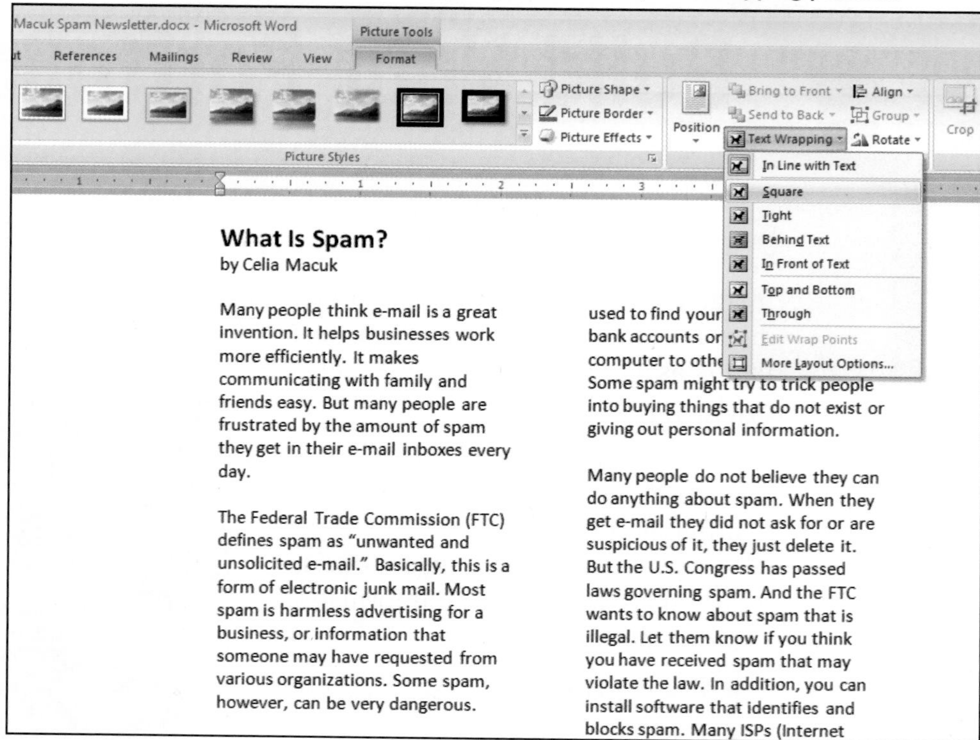

17. Move the clip art between the two columns of text, and resize as needed. Try to keep the columns even. If necessary, add a space at the top of one column.

18. **Save** your newsletter. Your newsletter should look similar to Figure 2.8.

▼ **Figure 2.8** Position the clip art so that it is in the center of your article.

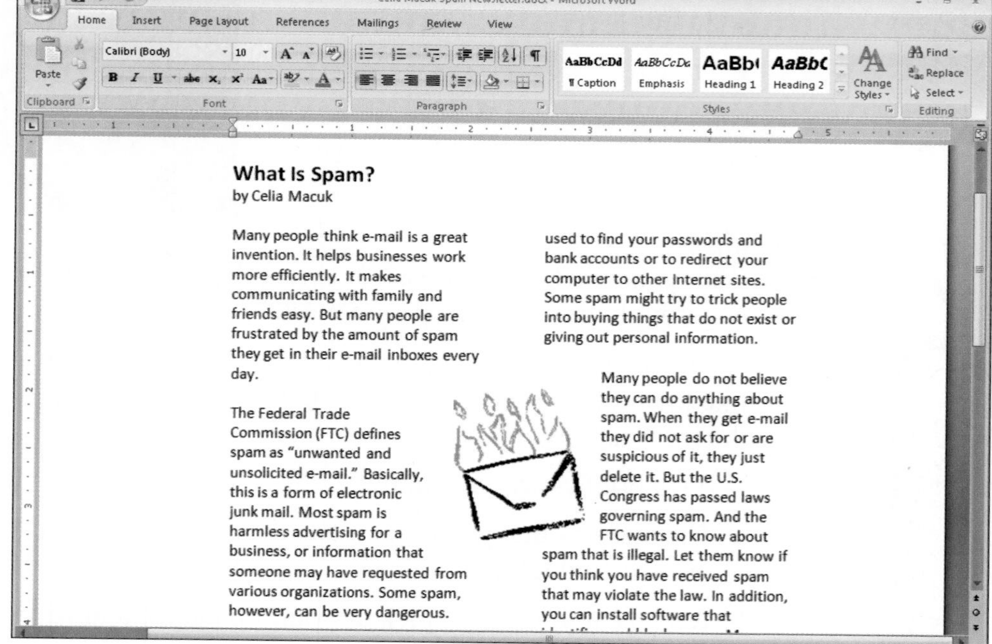

UNIT 3

Build Your Portfolio

Search the Web

Imagine that your family needs a new car, and your parents cannot make up their minds over whether to buy a minivan, an SUV, or a four-door sedan. Using your own family as a model, choose a car that you think best fits your family's lifestyle.

Research

1. After you decide on a style of car, do research to learn about all of the different models.
2. Narrow your search to two models, then do searches to find information about their:
   - Passenger room
   - Gas mileage
   - Storage space
   - Comfort
   - Safety
   - Price
3. Choose at least two Web sites for your information. Save them to your Favorites list.

Create

4. With your teacher's permission, save and print the Web pages with the information you need.
5. Create a chart comparing the features of the two cars you like the best. Make sure you note the sites where you got the information.
6. Write a brief essay explaining:
   a. The features that you think made those sites the most relevant and reliable sources of information
   b. Which car you would pick as your top choice and why

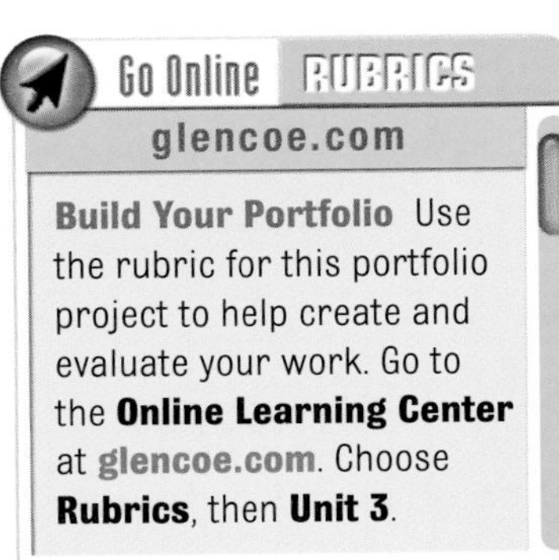

Exercise 2-3 Create a Masthead

A masthead or title will make your newsletter instantly recognizable to your audiences and give it a distinct look. Mastheads are usually at the top of the page, but you can give your newsletter a different look by placing the title along the side.

In this exercise, you will use text boxes and Word's tools to create a professional-looking newsletter title. You will also add color to the title to make it stand out from the rest of the newsletter. A table of contents will let readers know what is in your newsletter. If you need to review your Word skills, refer to Unit 4, Project 4 (pages 184–203).

Step-by-Step

1. On the **Insert** tab, in the **Text** group, click the **Text Box** button, and then select **Draw Text Box**. Click anywhere on the screen and drag the mouse pointer to create a text box of any size.
2. Select the text box, if necessary. On the **Format** tab, in the **Size** group, change the **Shape Height** size to 10.25″.
3. Key 1.35″ in the **Shape Width** box.
4. With the text box selected, on the **Format** tab, in the **Text** group, click the **Text Direction** button. Click **Text Direction** again. Note that the button changes to the left vertical direction (Figure 2.9).

Figure 2.9 Adjust the size and text direction of the text box.

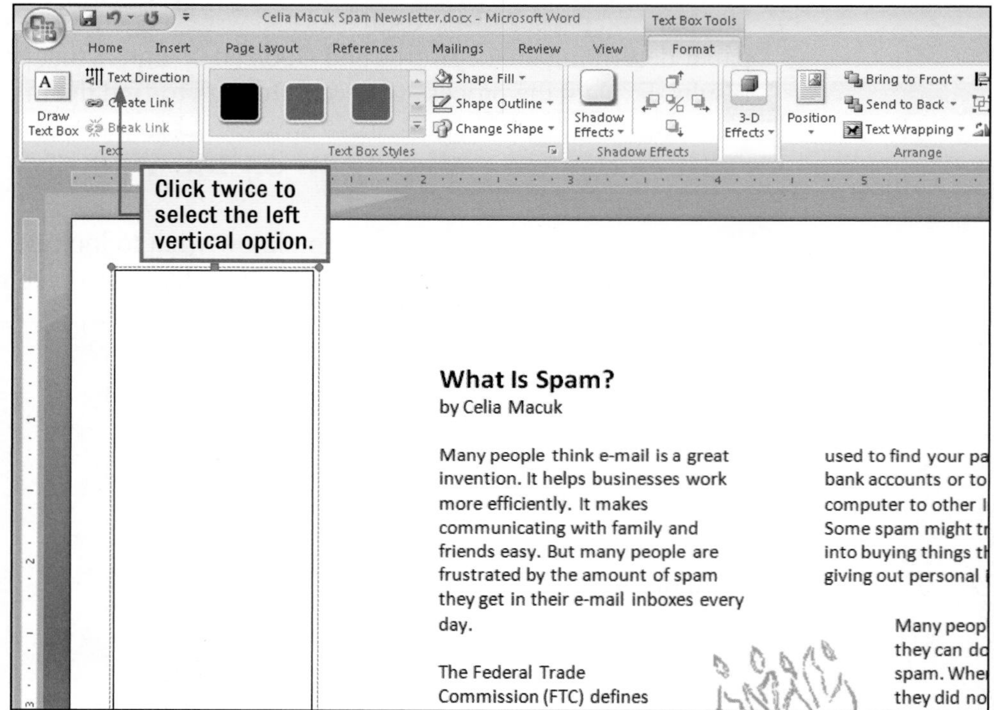

TechSavvy

Resize a Text Box You can easily resize a text box to fit any amount of text. First, right-click the border of the text box. Click **Format Text Box**, then click the **Text Box** tab. Under **Options**, click the **Resize AutoShape to fit text** check box.

Projects Across the Curriculum

Research

1. Do a Boolean search to find the name of the town.
2. Check at least five sites to make sure the town is the same in each. Evaluate the validity of each site.
3. Search through the best sites to find answers to the other questions.

Create

4. Use pen and paper or Microsoft Word to write a one-page paper describing the keywords and Boolean operators that provided the best search results. Explain the process you went through to find the information on the Web.

Go Online e-REVIEW
glencoe.com

Assessment Double-check your Internet skills. Go to the **Online Learning Center** at **glencoe.com**. Choose **e-Review Quizzes**, and take the **Unit 3 Tech Assess Quiz**.

Project 3 Fact and Fiction on the Web ★★★

English Language Arts You know what to look for to find trustworthy sites on the Web. Perform a search in order to evaluate whether Web sites meet the criteria of a good site.

Plan

1. Choose one of the following topics for a search on the Web:
   - Ways to browse the Internet safely
   - A description of a restaurant featuring ethnic food
   - The effects of cell phone use when driving

Research

2. Find four sites that discuss your topic. Evaluate your sites using the four criteria discussed in this unit. The sites should be relevant, reliable, recent, and verifiable.
3. Determine whether the sites meet all the criteria of a good Web site. Review the chart on page 93 for questions to ask and what to look for when you evaluate each site.

Create

4. Make a chart summarizing your evaluation of the four Web sites. Include the name and URL of each Web site and a summary of the information from each of the sites. Be sure to include a column heading for each of the four criteria used to evaluate Web sites: relevant, reliable, recent, and verifiable.

5. In the text box, key the newsletter title: The Spam Report.

6. Select the newsletter title, and format it as **Calibri** at **Font Size 72**.

7. Select the text box. Click the **Shape Fill** drop-down arrow in the **Text Box Styles** group. Click **Orange, Accent 6, Darker 25%**. (Figure 2.10)

8. Create a second text box with a **Height** of **1″** and a **Width** of **1.35″**. **Fill** the text box with a dark yellow.

9. Choose **White Background 1** for **Font Color**, then key *your name*, the *current date*, your *class period*, and Volume 1, Issue 1.

10. Select all the text in the second box, and choose **Calibri** at **Font Size 10**.

11. Center the text. Then launch the **Paragraph** dialog box to change the line spacing to **1.5** (Figure 2.11).

TechSavvy

More Fill Colors If the color you are looking for is not available in the **Shape Fill** gallery, click **More Fill Colors**.

▼ **Figure 2.10** **Format the newsletter title, and change the text box color.**

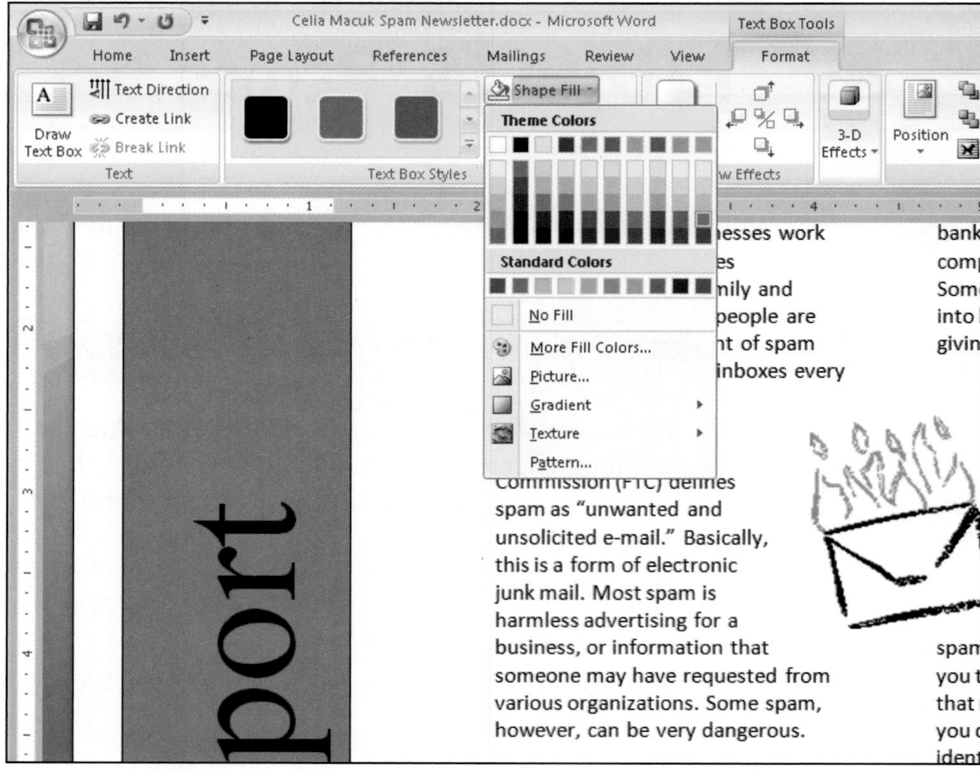

▼ **Figure 2.11** **Create a second text box.**

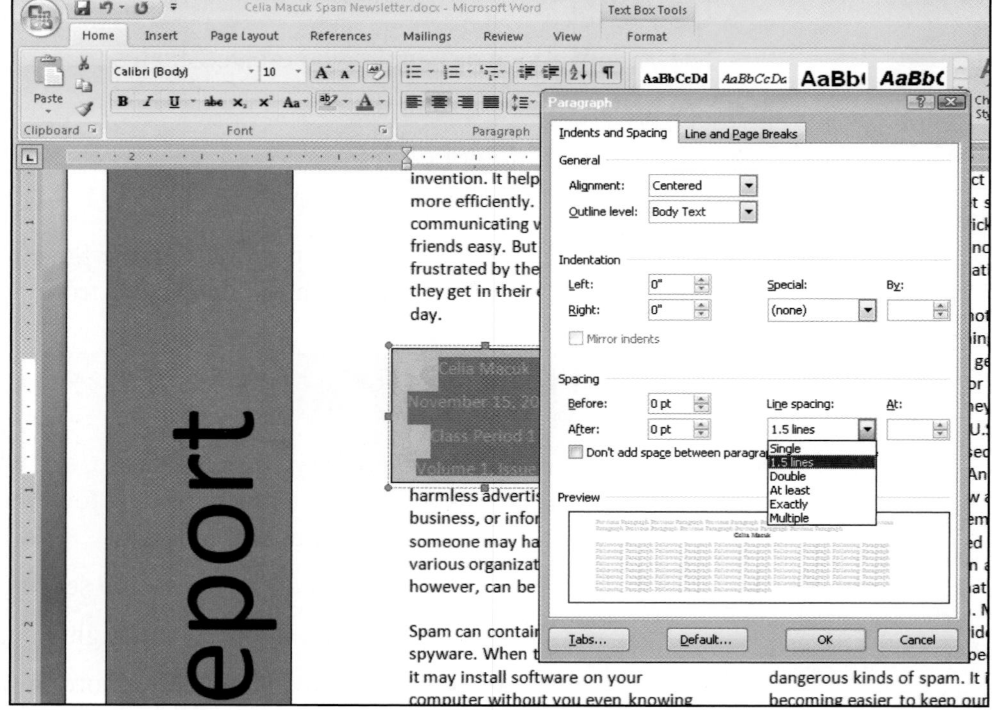

UNIT 3

Projects Across the Curriculum

With your teacher's permission, use your Internet skills to complete the following projects. Ask your teacher about saving or printing a Web site.

Project 1 Search the Web for Lost Wonders

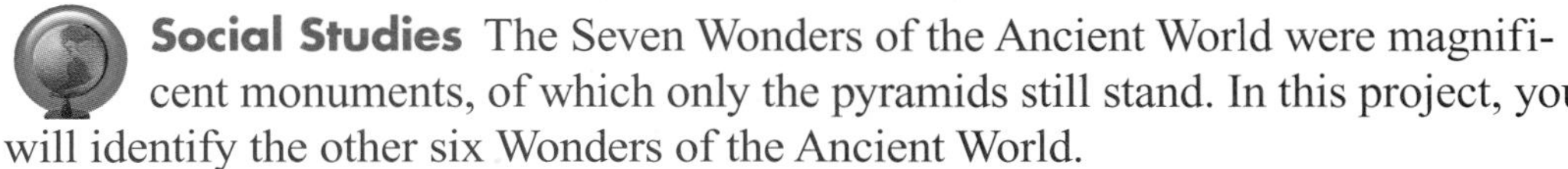

Social Studies The Seven Wonders of the Ancient World were magnificent monuments, of which only the pyramids still stand. In this project, you will identify the other six Wonders of the Ancient World.

Research

1. Do a search to find the Seven Wonders of the Ancient World. Be sure each site is relevant, reliable, recent, and verifiable.
2. Record at least three facts about each of the Seven Wonders.
3. Bookmark at least two Web pages as your sources of information. Then list the following information about the sites:
   - Their names
   - Their URLs
   - The organizations or people who created each site
   - The updates or copyright dates
   - A brief description of each

Create

4. Write a two-page report or make a poster about the Seven Wonders of the Ancient World. Include the information you found from your search.

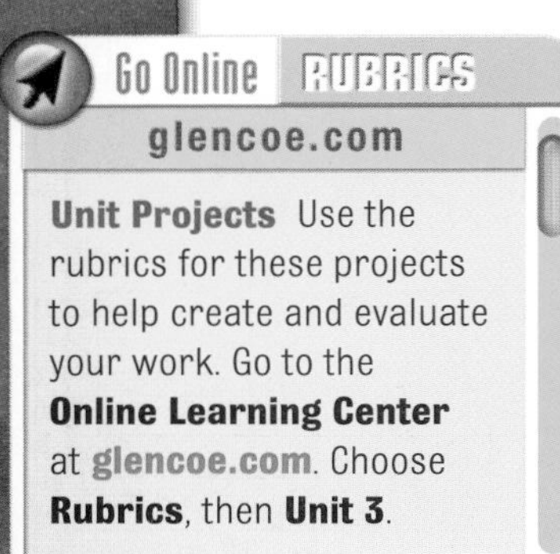

Go Online RUBRICS

glencoe.com

Unit Projects Use the rubrics for these projects to help create and evaluate your work. Go to the **Online Learning Center** at **glencoe.com**. Choose **Rubrics**, then **Unit 3**.

Project 2 Research for Facts on the Web

Teamwork With a classmate, see who can be the first to find the name of the northernmost town in the world and answer the following questions about that town:

- How many months does each season last?
- How long are the days and nights in January and in July?
- What is the average temperature in January and in July?

Continued on page 123

12 Create a third text box with a **Height** of **1.40″** and a **Width** of **1.35″**. Select the new box.

13 Launch the **Paragraph** dialog box, then click **Tabs**. In the **Tab stop position** box, key 1.05. Under **Alignment**, choose **Left**. Under **Leader**, click **2**, then click **Set** and **OK** (Figure 2.12).

14 In the third text box, choose **Calibri** at **Font Size 7**. Then key Other Items in this Issue:.

15 Press [ENTER], then list other features that you might include in your newsletter, with their page numbers. Use the [TAB] key to create a dotted leader between each feature and its page number (Figure 2.13).

16 Change the line spacing to **1.5**. Then move the three text boxes into position so that they look like Figure 2.13.

17 Hold [SHIFT] and select all of the text boxes. On the **Format** tab, in the **Arrange** group, click **Group**. **Note:** Use **Send to Back** if you do not see all of the boxes.

18 **Save** your newsletter. **Close** the file.

▼ **Figure 2.12** Set tab stops in the third text box.

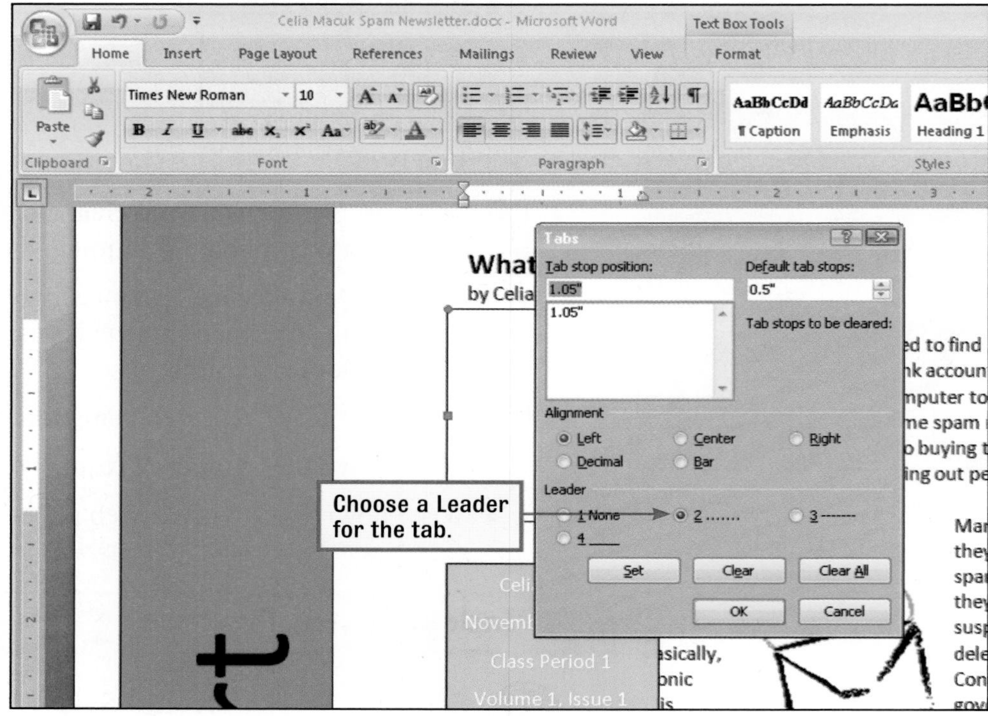

▼ **Figure 2.13** Position the three text boxes and group them.

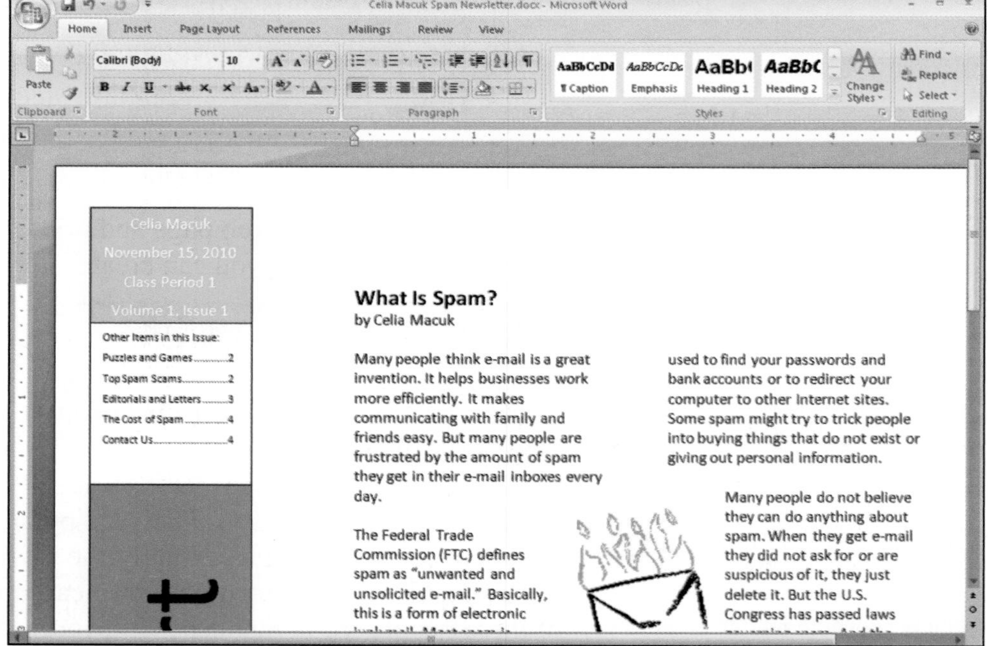

Project 2 Assessment

2 Independent Practice ★

Science **Perform a Web Search** You want to find out how to make your own bubble solution and create large bubbles.

a. Plan With your teacher's permission, figure out three ways to search for this information, first by using one keyword, then two, and then a Boolean search.

b. Research Perform a search using three different search strategies.

- Write down the number of results you get for each search.
- Write down the first five Web pages listed in each of the searches.

3 Independent Practice ★★

Science **Search for and Save a Web Site** Find the Web site that will give you the best information about creating bubbles, as described in Independent Practice 2 above.

a. Research Use the Web results you got in Independent Practice 2:

- Choose three sites that you think are most relevant.
- Evaluate the sites for reliability and relevance.
- After selecting the best site, search the site to find the specific information you need about bubbles.

b. Create Save the Web page and print it, with your teacher's permission. See if you can create a large bubble!

4 Independent Practice ★★★

Social Studies **Search Through Time** You are tracking down the mysterious Dr. Computer, who has disappeared in a time machine. When last heard from, he was staying among a people who lived about a thousand years ago. They had pyramids and a calendar and were excellent astronomers. Eventually the civilization was conquered, and the pyramids were covered with tropical jungles. Today the descendants of these people speak Spanish. With your teacher's permission, do a Web search to find out the people Dr. Computer is living with, his geographic location, and the approximate time period he is living in.

Exercise 2-4 Create a Chart in Excel

Internet fraud can take place through e-mail and Web sites. Sometimes Internet fraud does not begin on the Internet but rather with a phone call or even a letter. Internet fraud rarely begins with a person-to-person meeting. Because the Internet allows anonymity, criminals can use it to hide their identity and reach a large number of victims quickly and easily. Therefore, you should be careful when you are online.

In this exercise, you will create a spreadsheet that shows the sources of Internet fraud. (The data is from the FTC, the Federal Bureau of Investigation (FBI), and other sources.) You will then use the information from the spreadsheet to create a pie chart. If you need to review your Excel skills, refer to Unit 5, Project 3 (pages 239–250).

Step-by-Step

1. **Start Microsoft Excel**.
2. Use the data and headers shown in Figure 2.14 to create a spreadsheet.
3. **Save** your spreadsheet as *Your Name* Fraud Chart.

▼ **Figure 2.14** **Create a spreadsheet showing where Internet fraud most often begins.**

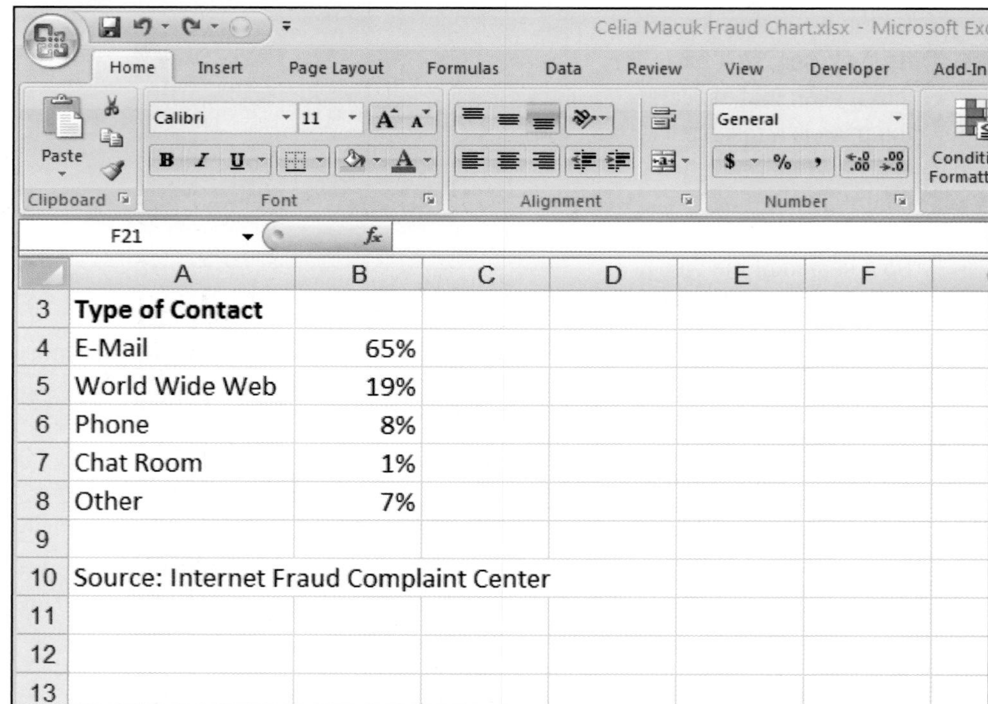

	A	B	C	D	E	F
3	**Type of Contact**					
4	E-Mail	65%				
5	World Wide Web	19%				
6	Phone	8%				
7	Chat Room	1%				
8	Other	7%				
9						
10	Source: Internet Fraud Complaint Center					
11						
12						
13						

HELP!

Data File If your teacher prefers, you can use a Data File with the spreadsheet shown in this exercise rather than create your own spreadsheet. Open the **Data File** named **8E Fraud Data** and save it as ***Your Name* Fraud Chart**. Then create the chart by following steps 4 to 16.

5 Look at three results of your Web search. Do any explain how to care for a hamster? (Exercise 2-2)

6 Narrow your search to find a Web page that explains how to care for golden hamsters (Figures 2.15 and 2.16). Write down the URL, or save it to your Favorites list. (Exercise 2-2)

7 On the Web page you have chosen, look for information that indicates the page is a reliable source. Write down the information. (Exercise 2-2)

8 Do a search of the Web site to find out what you should feed your hamster. (Exercise 2-3)

9 Evaluate the Web page with the information about feeding hamsters. With your teacher's permission, save it as HTML. (Exercise 2-4)

10 **Close your Web browser**.

Figure 2.15 This site provides information about hamsters, but no care tips.

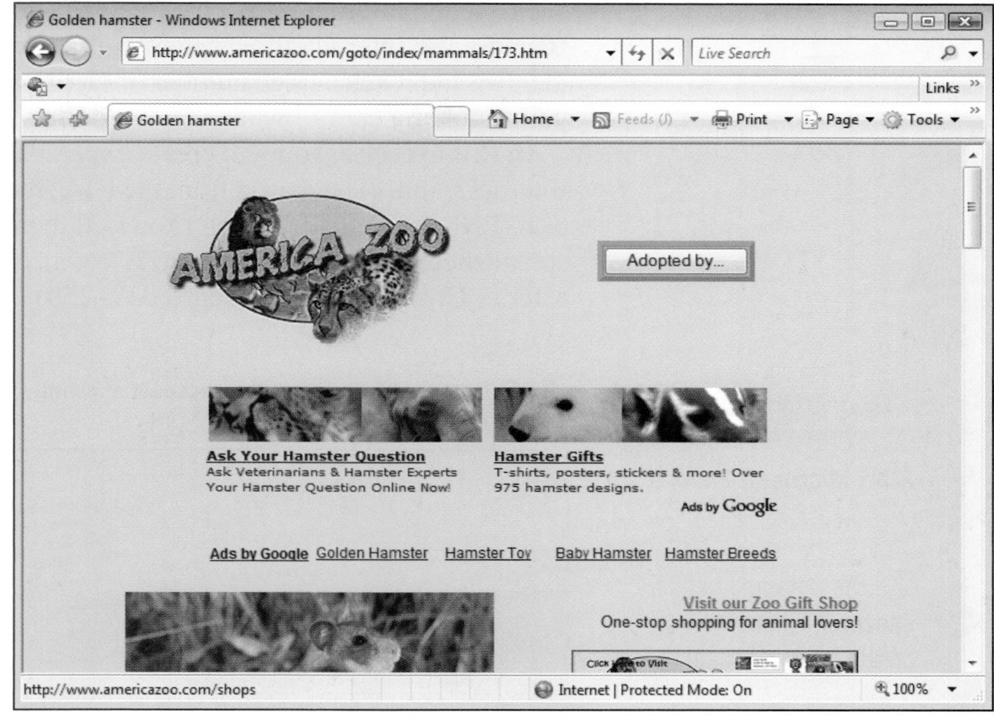

Figure 2.16 This site provides detailed information about caring for hamsters.

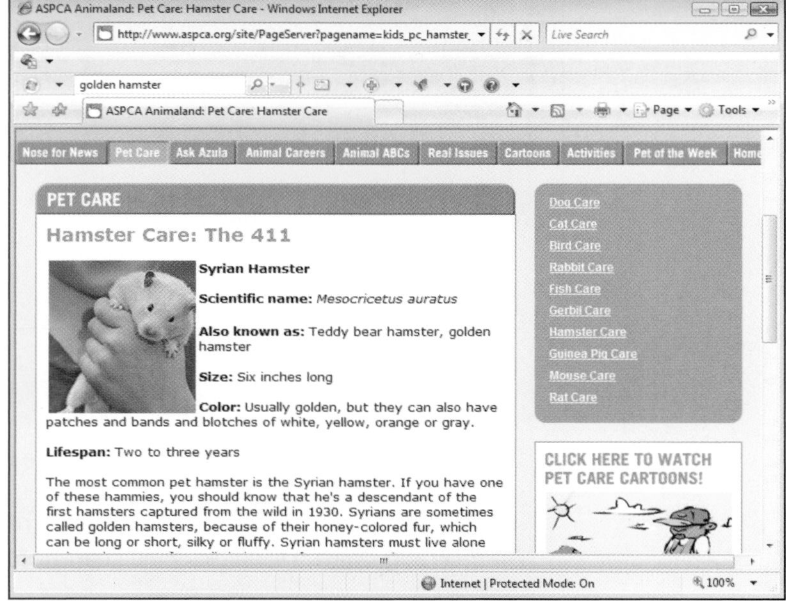

4. Select cells **A4** through **B8** in the spreadsheet.

5. On the **Insert** tab, in the **Charts** group, click the **Pie** button. Under **2-D Pie**, click **Pie** (Figure 2.15).

6. The **Chart Tools** display on the Ribbon, and your chart is embedded in your spreadsheet.

7. On the **Chart Tools Layout** tab, in the **Labels** group, click the **Chart Title** button. Click **Above Chart**, and key How Internet Fraud Begins. Click out of the **Chart Title** box.

Figure 2.15 Create a pie chart using the Charts group.

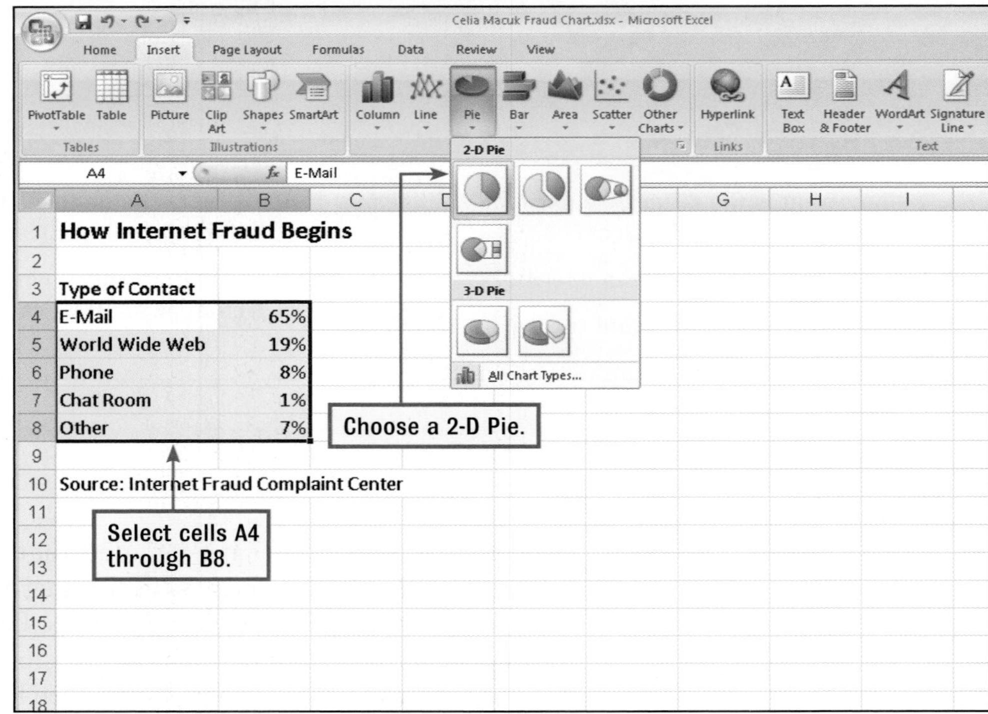

8. On the **Chart Tools Layout** tab, in the **Labels** group, click the **Legend** button. Note that **Show Legend at Right** is selected.

9. On the **Chart Tools Layout** tab, in the **Labels** group, click the **Legend** button. Then click **More Legend Options**. In the **Format Legend** dialog box, click **Border Color**, then select **Solid line**. Click **Close**.

10. On the **Chart Tools Layout** tab, in the **Labels** group, click the **Data Labels** button. Click **Outside End** (Figure 2.16).

Figure 2.16 Your chart displays with a title, legend, and data labels.

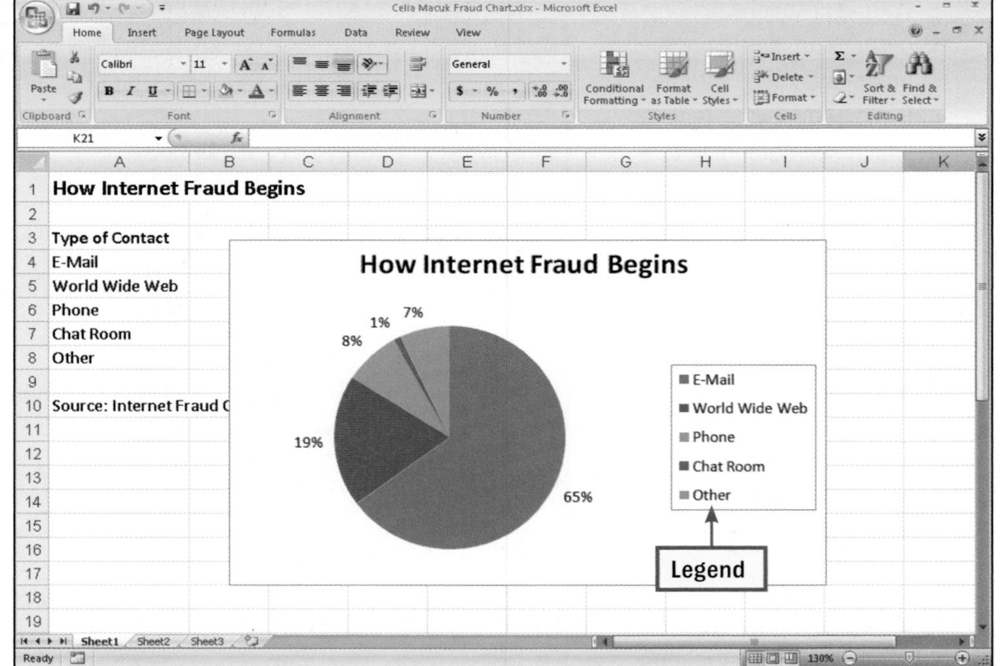

Project 2 Assessment

Key Concepts Check

1. **Define** What is the difference between a Boolean search and a keyword search?
2. **Identify** Name four Boolean operators.
3. **Explain** Why would you want to save a Web page?

Critical Thinking

4. **Evaluate** Name three things you would look for before choosing a Web page in your search results.
5. **Compare** Explain why you might prefer to save a Web page as HTML rather than text.

1 Guided Practice

Search the Web You have decided that a cat is too expensive and difficult to care for. Instead, you decide that a golden hamster would make the ideal pet because it is smaller, easier to keep track of, and requires less maintenance. With your teacher's permission, you will search the Internet to find out how to care for one. If you need help, refer back to the exercise in parentheses at the end of the step.

Step-by-Step

1. With your teacher's permission, start your Web browser such as Internet Explorer. Ask your teacher which search engine to use. This exercise uses Google.
2. In the **Address** bar, key www.google.com or the URL from your teacher. (Exercise 2-1)
3. In the **search** box, key hamster. Note the number of results. (Exercise 2-1)
4. Key golden hamster in the **search** box. Note the number of results and the relevance of each (Figure 2.14). (Exercise 2-2)

▼ **Figure 2.14** The search results for "golden hamster" are displayed.

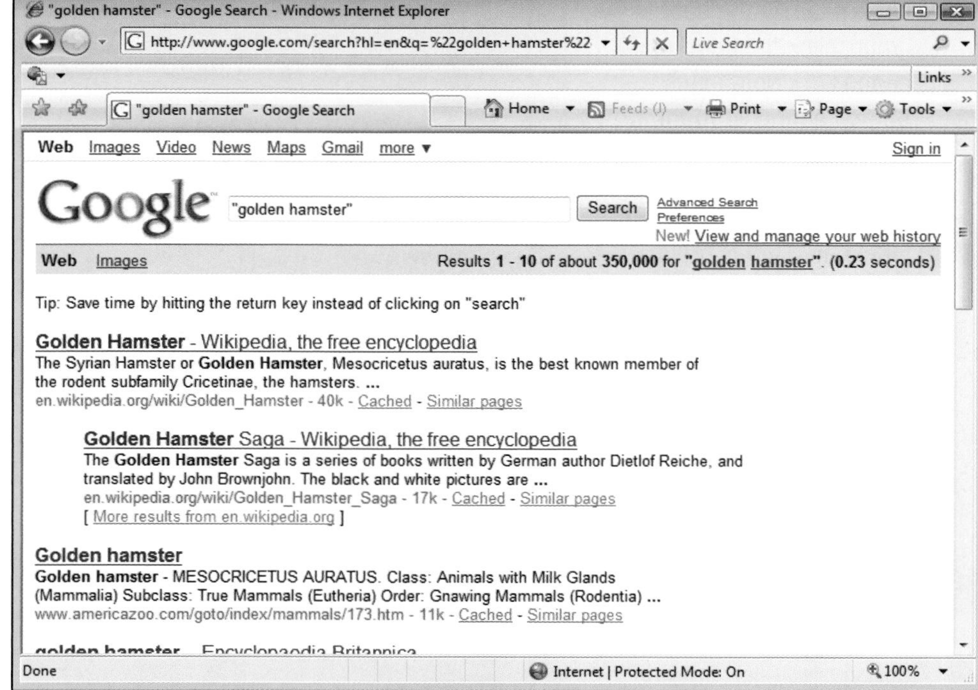

11 You may want to make changes to your chart, including resizing and repositioning objects. Click the chart to display the **Chart Tools** (Figure 2.17).

12 Click right next to the pie to select the **Plot Area**. Resize the plot area by dragging the sizing handles to reduce the size of the plot area.

13 Click a **Data Label**. Note that all labels are selected. Change the **Font Size** to **6**.

▼ **Figure 2.17** Use the sizing handles to resize the chart.

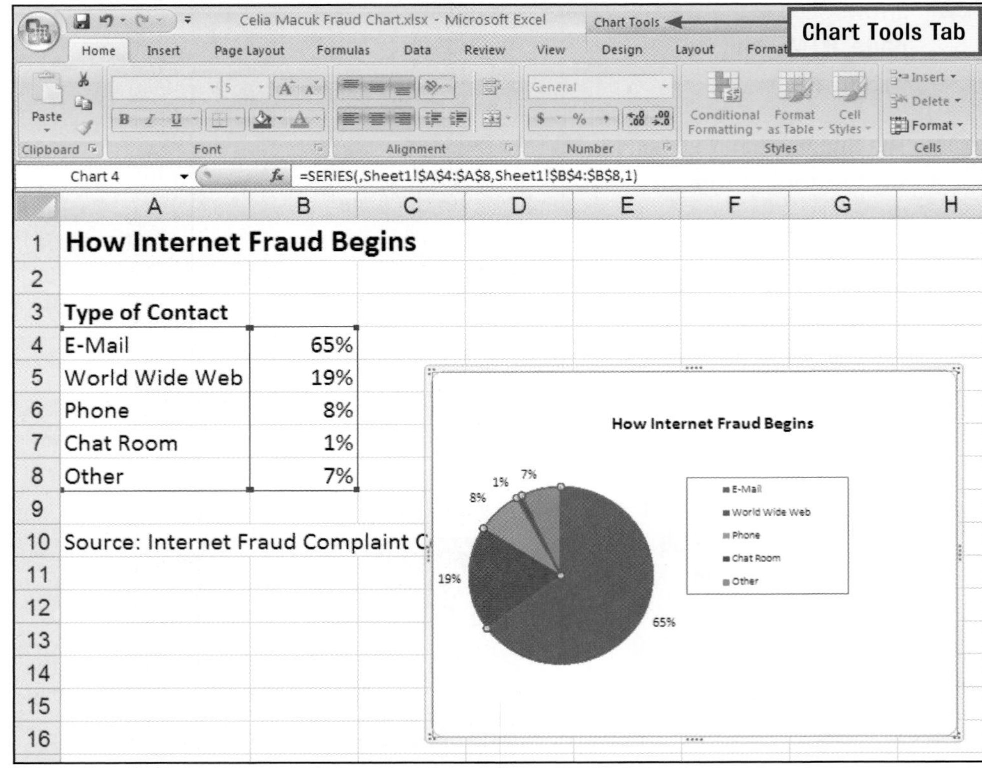

14 Click the **Chart Title**. Change the **Font Size** to **8**. Reposition the title by dragging it with the grab handles (Figure 2.18).

15 Adjust the legend in the same way. Select the legend, and change the legend **Font Size** to **5**.

16 Reduce the size of the chart. See Figure 2.18.

17 **Save** and **close** your spreadsheet.

▼ **Figure 2.18** Change the font size and the size of the chart so that it will fit in your newsletter.

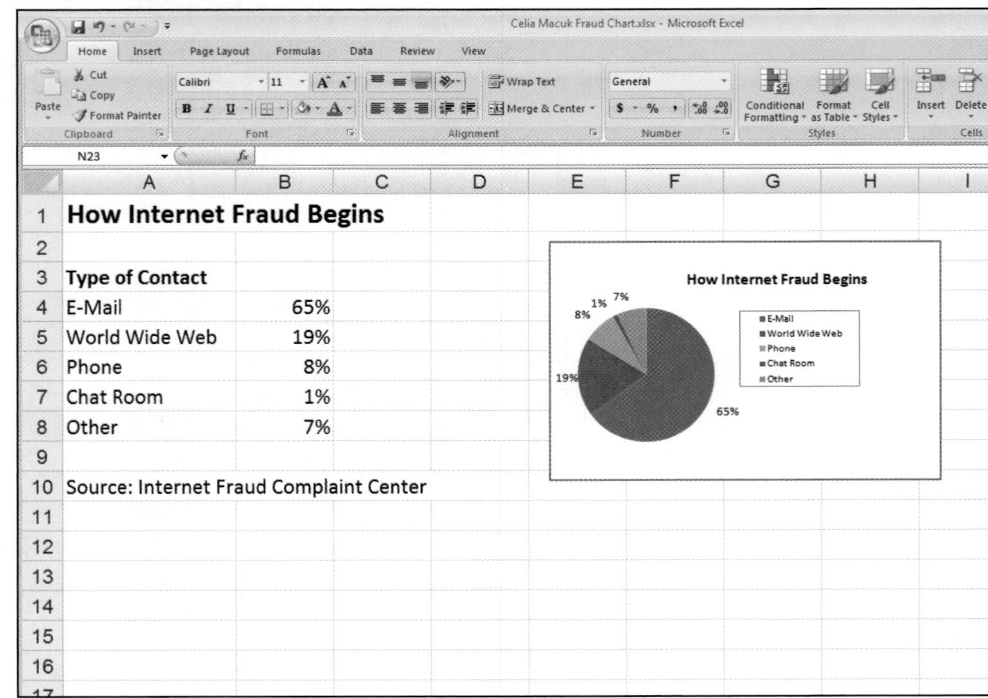

5 Click the **Save as type** arrow. Choose the **Webpage, HTML only** option (Figure 2.12).

6 The **Encoding** box should say **Western European ISO**.

7 Click **Save**, then **close Internet Explorer**.

▼ **Figure 2.12** The Save Webpage box gives you different Save options.

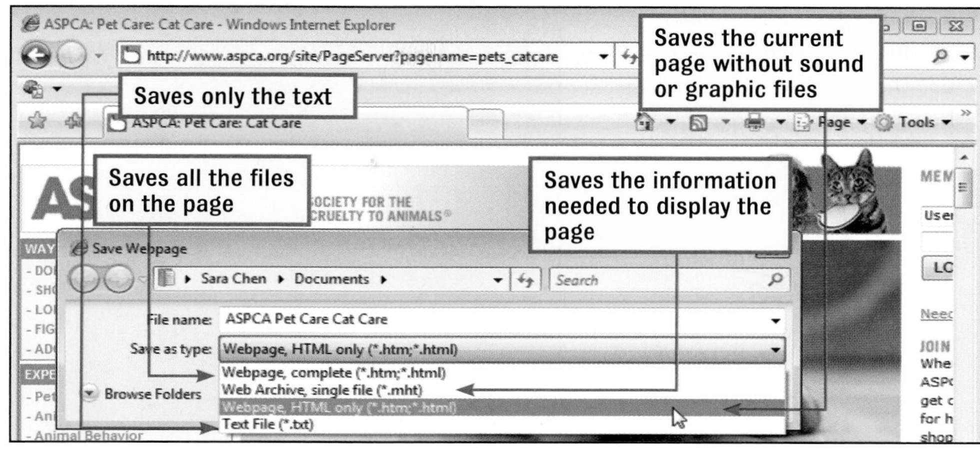

8 Open your student folder and browse to the Web page you just saved.

9 Double-click the Web page file to open it. See whether it opens in a browser (Figure 2.13).

▼ **Figure 2.13** A saved complete Web page looks the same as it did on the Web.

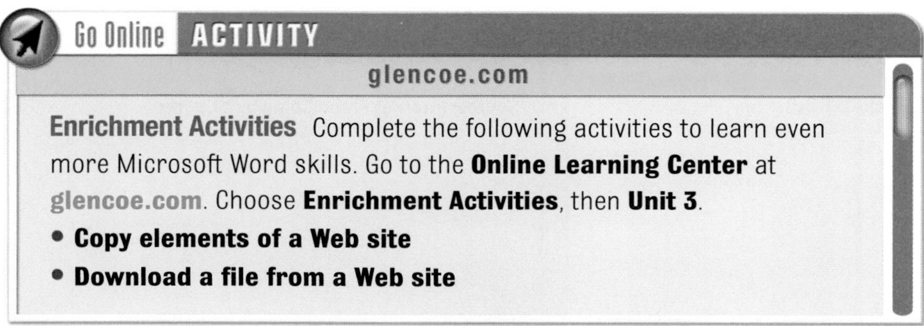

Go Online ACTIVITY

glencoe.com

Enrichment Activities Complete the following activities to learn even more Microsoft Word skills. Go to the **Online Learning Center** at glencoe.com. Choose **Enrichment Activities**, then **Unit 3**.

- **Copy elements of a Web site**
- **Download a file from a Web site**

Exercise 2-5 Create Linked Text Boxes

Text boxes make it easier to place text just where you want it on a page. They can even be linked to create an effect similar to columns. **Linking** is the process of connecting text boxes so that when one box is filled, the text will continue into the linked box. Using linked text boxes, you can continue an article from one column to the next, as in your newsletter. You can also make text flow from a text box on one page to a text box on another page in the same document.

In this exercise, you will continue your newsletter by adding a second article using linked text boxes. The chart you created in the previous exercise will then be inserted into this article. Finally, you will insert page numbers into the newsletter. If you need to review your Word skills, refer to Unit 4, Project 4 (pages 184–203).

Step-by-Step

1. In your **Spam Newsletter** scroll down and add a text box to the bottom-left side of the newsletter.

2. Create a second text box next to the first one. The two boxes should be about the same size (Figure 2.19).

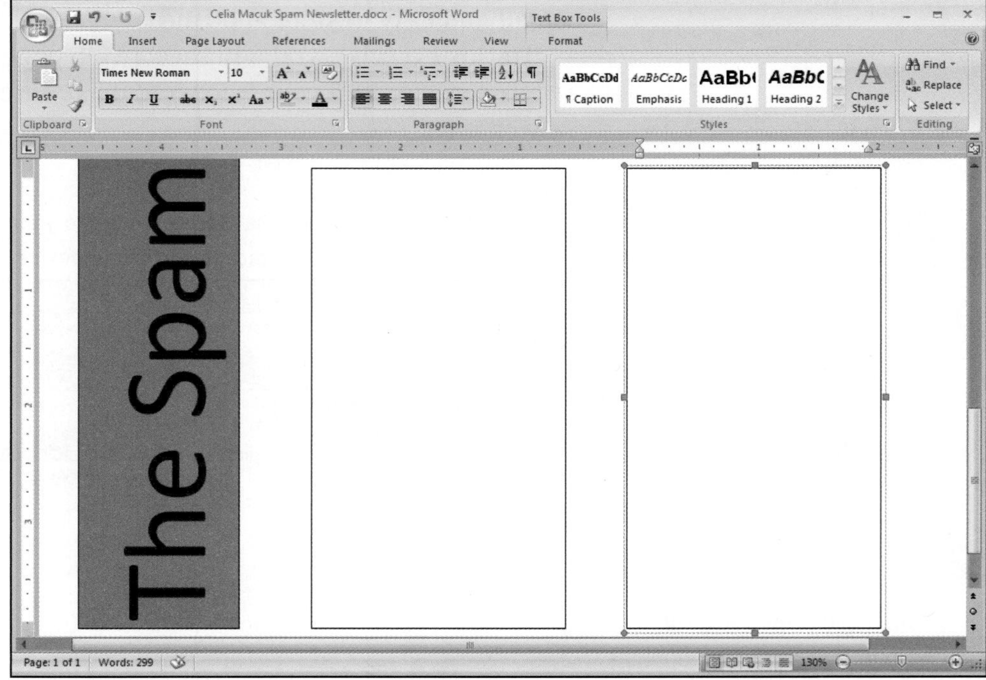

Figure 2.19 Create two text boxes at the bottom of your newsletter.

HELP!

Data File If your teacher prefers, you can use a Data File with the article shown in this exercise rather than write your own article. Open the **Data File** named **8F Spam Article**, and paste it into the text boxes in ***Your Name*** **Spam Newsletter**.

Exercise 2-4 Save a Web Page

You can save a Web page to your computer (or a removable storage device such as a jump drive) just as you would save a document. When you open your saved page, it can be opened in a browser, even if your computer is not connected to the Internet.

There are a number of reasons to save a Web page. For example:

- You may not be able to print the page at your school, or you may be out of printer paper.
- Some Web pages change frequently.

When you save a Web page, you save all of the pieces that make up that page—the text, buttons, pictures, and so on. This can be a large file. To reduce the file size, you can save the page without any sound or video, or you can save it as text, with none of the graphics, pictures, or buttons.

The best way to save most Web pages is as HTML-only files. The saved file looks almost exactly like the original page. Plus, the file is relatively small and easy to store and find.

In this exercise, you will save a Web page about caring for a cat. **Note**: Always check with your teacher to make sure you have permission to save a Web page.

Step-by-Step

1. With your teacher's permission, use your Favorites or History list to go to a page on the Web site you used in Exercise 2-3.
2. Click the **Page** button on the command bar, then click **Save As**. The **Save Webpage** box opens (Figure 2.11).
3. Verify that the **Address** bar displays the correct folder for saving your work.
4. Key a new **File name**, or use the Web page name.

Figure 2.11 You can save a Web page to your computer's hard disk, your school network, or a removable storage device.

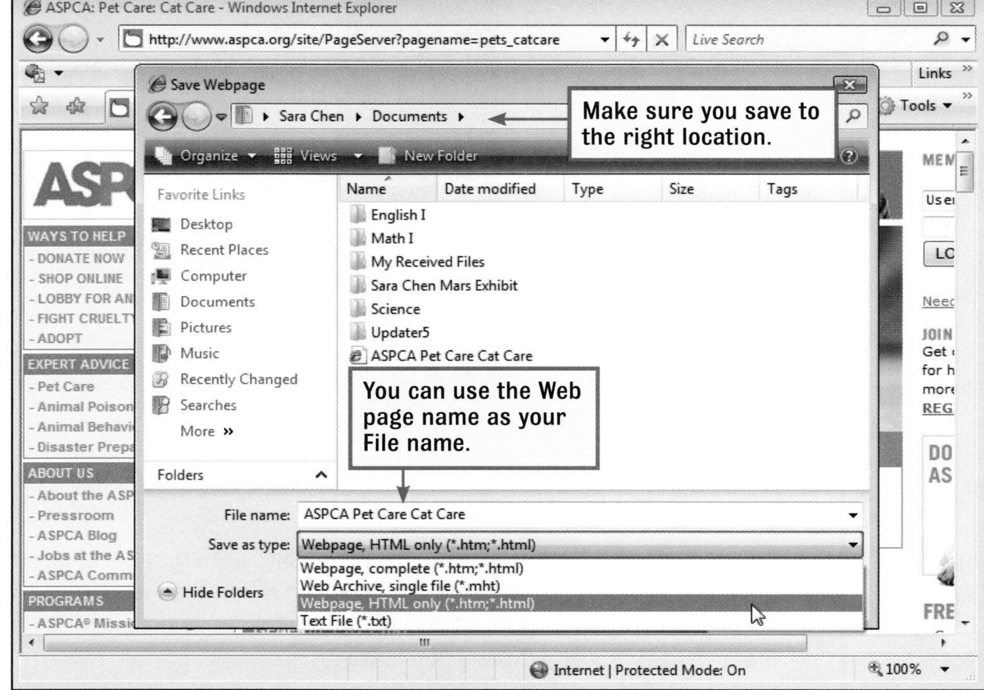

3. Select the first text box. The **Text Box Tools** appear. On the **Format** tab, in the **Text** group, click **Create Link** (Figure 2.20). Your mouse pointer turns into an upright pitcher.

4. Click the second text box to link it to the first. Notice that when you move the upright pitcher to the new text box, the pitcher tips and pours.

5. In the first text box, write a short introduction, followed by a list of four to five specific measures people take to avoid unwanted spam. See Figure 2.21.

6. Format the title of your article as **Calibri**, **Bold**, **Font Size 14**.

7. Format the rest of the article as **Calibri**, **Font Size 10**.

8. Hold SHIFT, and select both text boxes. On the **Format** tab, in the **Text Box Styles** group, click the **Shape Fill** drop-down arrow. Click **No Fill**.

9. Click the **Shape Outline** drop-down arrow, then choose **No Outline**.

Figure 2.20 Click the Create Link button in the Text Group to link the two boxes.

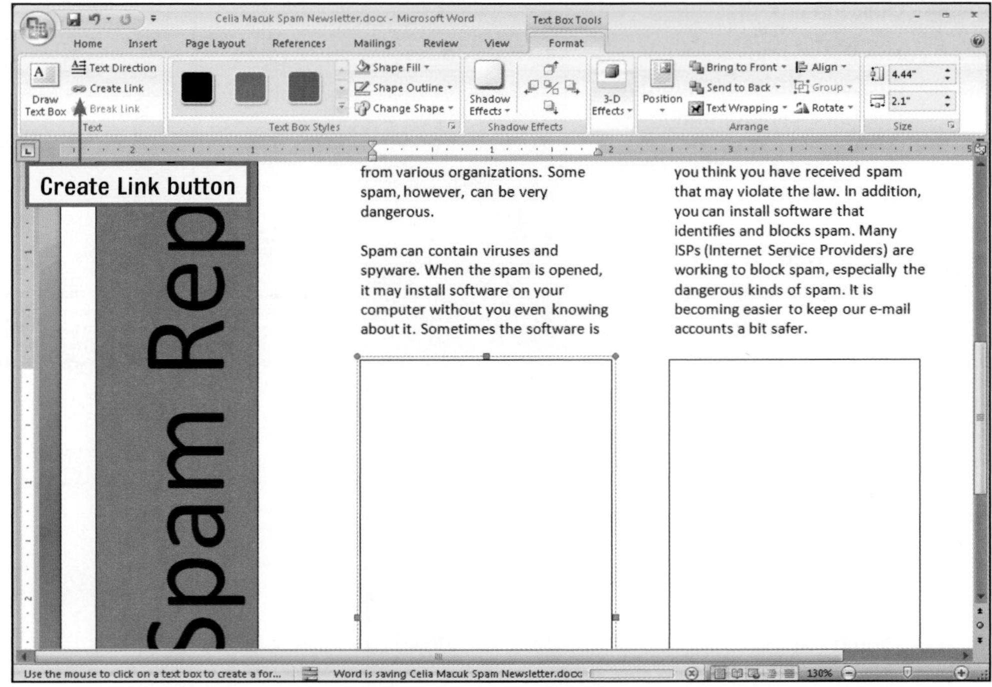

Figure 2.21 Write your text in the first text box, and then format the text boxes.

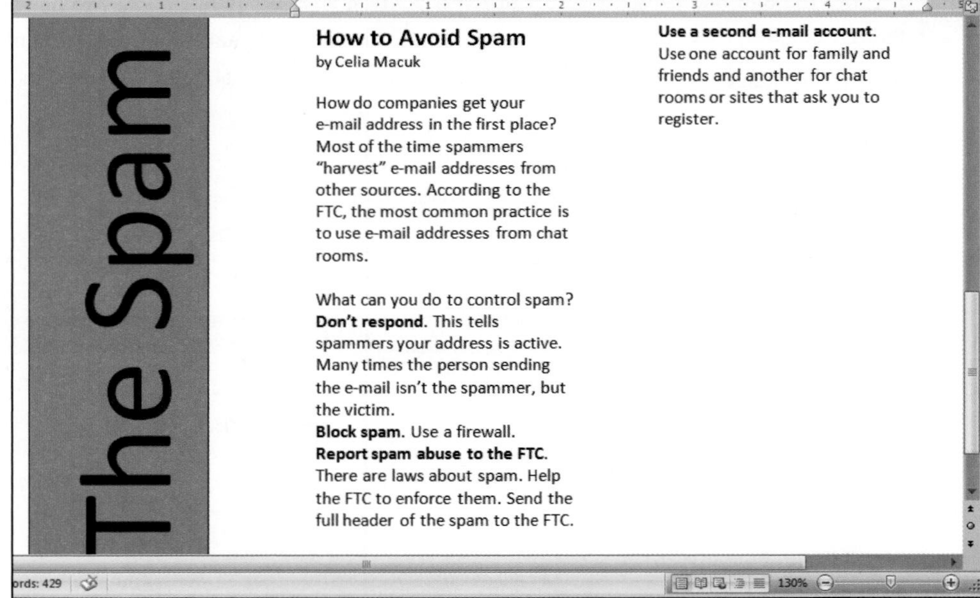

3 In the table of contents, click the link that takes you to the page about cat care. **Note**: Sometimes links display submenus. If so, choose your topic from the submenu.

4 On the Web page, look for links to specific topics related to cat care. Figure 2.9 shows many different aspects of cat care to choose from.

5 Click a link about food or diet. See whether you can find information about what kind of food a cat should eat.

▼ **Figure 2.9** The table of contents is still displayed on the new page.

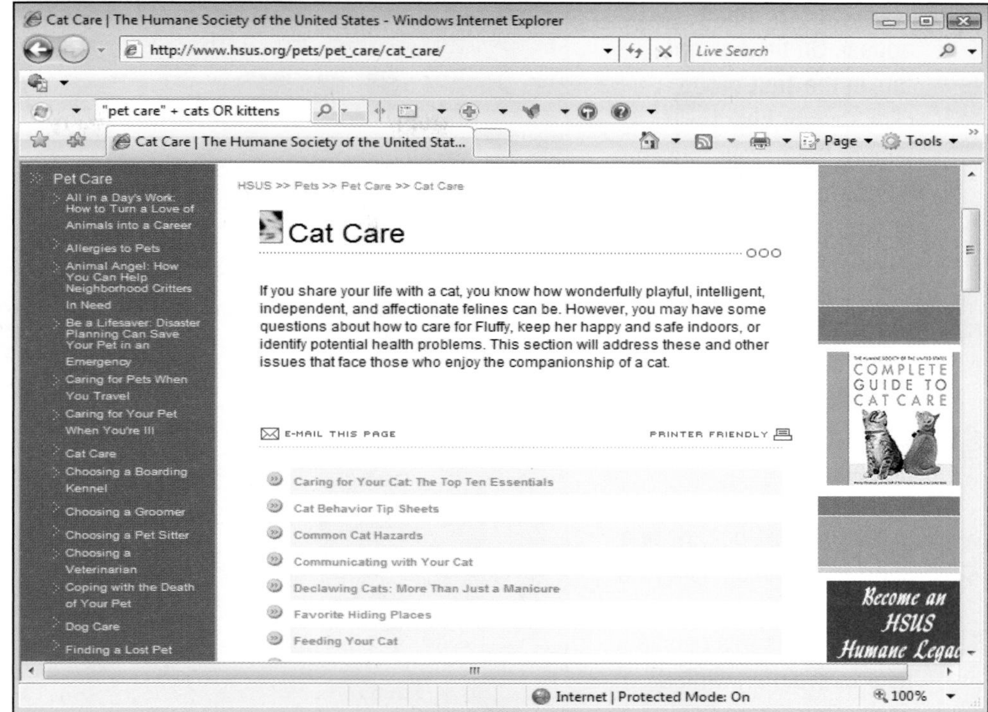

6 If your Web site has a search box, key cat food, then press ENTER.

7 Read the descriptions of the results just as you would when using a search engine.

8 Find the same information about food you found through the table of contents.

9 Click a link that takes you back to the Web site's home page. This link is usually at the top of the page. In Figure 2.10, it is the map icon in the upper-left corner.

▼ **Figure 2.10** A Web site is more likely to be reliable when it is well organized and when it has a number of search options and links that work.

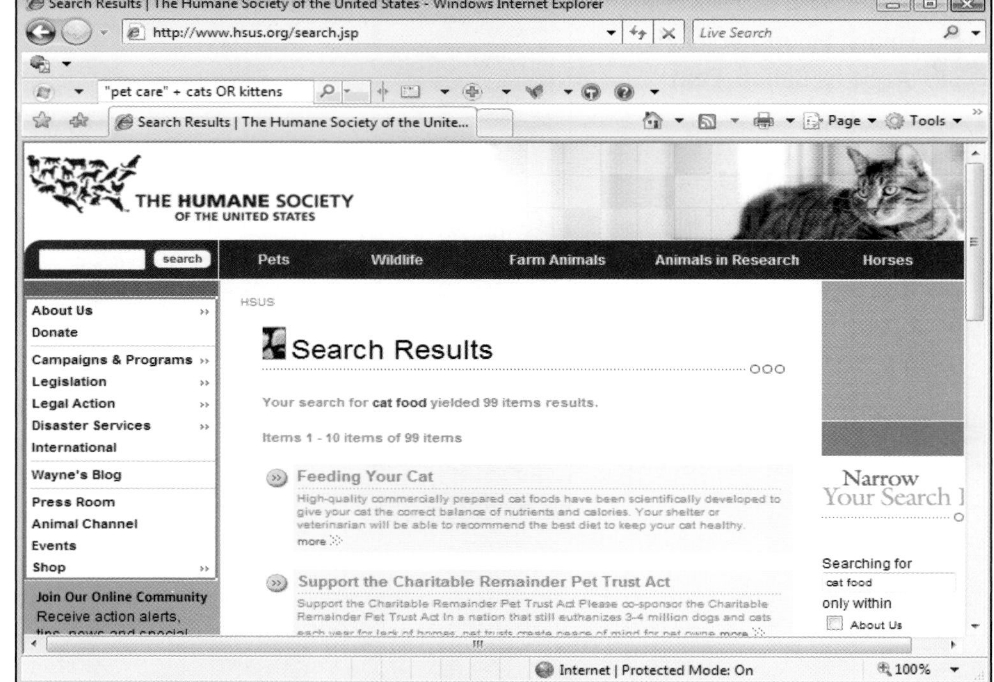

10. **Open** the Excel spreadsheet you created in Exercise 2-4. **Copy** the chart.

11. **Paste** the chart into your newsletter. **Center** it in one of the text boxes at the bottom of the page.

12. The two columns should be roughly equal. If necessary, add spaces to the top of one column. See Figure 2.22 as an example of how your article should look.

13. You may want to adjust your chart, including resizing and repositioning objects so that the chart fits into the text box.

14. On the **Insert tab**, in the **Header & Footer** group, click the **Page Number** button. Click **Bottom of Page**, then select **Plain Number 3**.

15. Save your document. It should look similar to Figure 2.22.

16. With your teacher's permission, print your newsletter.

▼ **Figure 2.22** The Excel chart has been placed in the article.

Celia Macuk
November 15, 2010
Class Period 1
Volume 1, Issue 1

Other Items in this Issue:

The Spam Report

What Is Spam?

by Celia Macuk

Many people think e-mail is a great invention. It helps businesses work more efficiently. It makes communicating with family and friends easy. But many people are frustrated by the amount of spam they get in their e-mail inboxes every day.

The Federal Trade Commission (FTC) defines spam as "unwanted and unsolicited e-mail." Basically, this is a form of electronic junk mail. Most spam is harmless advertising for a business, or information that someone may have requested from various organizations. Some spam, however, can be very dangerous.

Spam can contain viruses and spyware. When the spam is opened, it may install software on your computer without you even knowing about it. Sometimes the software is used to find your passwords and bank accounts or to redirect your computer to other Internet sites. Some spam might try to trick people into buying things that do not exist or giving out personal information.

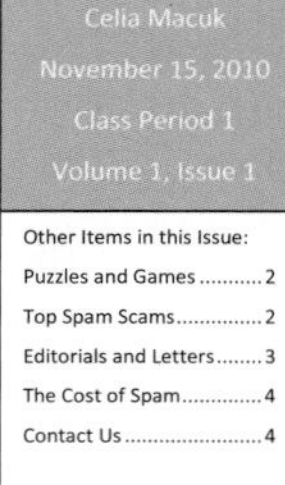

Many people do not believe they can do anything about spam. When they get e-mail they did not ask for or are suspicious of it, they just delete it. But the U.S. Congress has passed laws governing spam. And the FTC wants to know about spam that is illegal. Let them know if you think you have received spam that may violate the law. In addition, you can install software that identifies and blocks spam. Many ISPs (Internet Service Providers) are working to block spam, especially the dangerous kinds of spam. It is becoming easier to keep our e-mail accounts a bit safer.

How to Avoid Spam

by Celia Macuk

How do companies get your e-mail address in the first place? Most of the time spammers "harvest" e-mail addresses from other sources. According to the FTC, the most common practice is to use e-mail addresses from chat rooms.

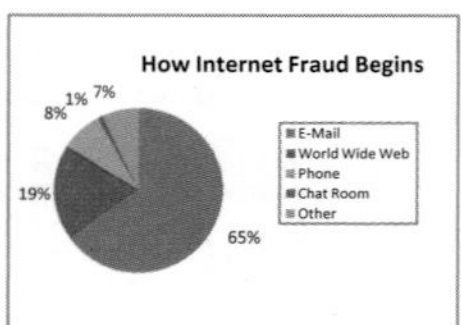

What can you do to control spam? **Don't respond**. This tells spammers your address is active. Many times the person sending the e-mail isn't the spammer, but the victim.
Block spam. Use a firewall.
Report spam abuse to the FTC. There are laws about spam. Help the FTC to enforce them. Send the full header of the spam to the FTC.
Use a second e-mail account. Use one account for family and friends and another for chat rooms or sites that ask you to register.

1

HELP!

Print Preview Remember, before you print, use **Print Preview** to make sure that everything will print properly. If you want to magnify the Print Preview image, check the **Magnifier** box in the **Preview** group to turn the magnifier on or off. You can also zoom the document so that two pages fit in the window. On the **Print Preview** tab, in the **Zoom** group, click the **Two Pages** button.

Exercise 2-3 Search Within a Web Site

When you go to a Web page from your search results, you might not immediately see the information you need. It may not be on the home page itself, or your search result might send you to a subpage within the site. If you are not on the home page, find the link that takes you there. It is usually displayed near the top of the page, and can be text or graphics showing the name of the site.

After you determine that a Web site is reliable, you should explore it to see whether you can find the information you need. Many Web sites have well-organized features that help you find information within that site.

- A **table of contents** shows how the site is organized and lets you link directly to specific topics. The table of contents may appear only on the home page or on every page of the site.
- A **search** box may also appear on some Web sites. Enter keywords into the box to search for information on a site just as you would in a search engine.
- A **site map** is like an index in a book. It lists all the categories of information contained on the entire site. You can usually find a link to the site map on a Web site's home page.

In this exercise, you will use a site's table of contents and search feature to find out about caring for a cat.

Step-by-Step

1. With your teacher's permission, use your Favorites list, History list, or written URL list to go to a cat-care site with search features. It may be different from the site shown in Figure 2.8.

2. Locate the table of contents. In Figure 2.8, the main table of contents is at the top of the page. On some Web sites, it is on the side.

▼ **Figure 2.8** This page offers both a search box and a table of contents.

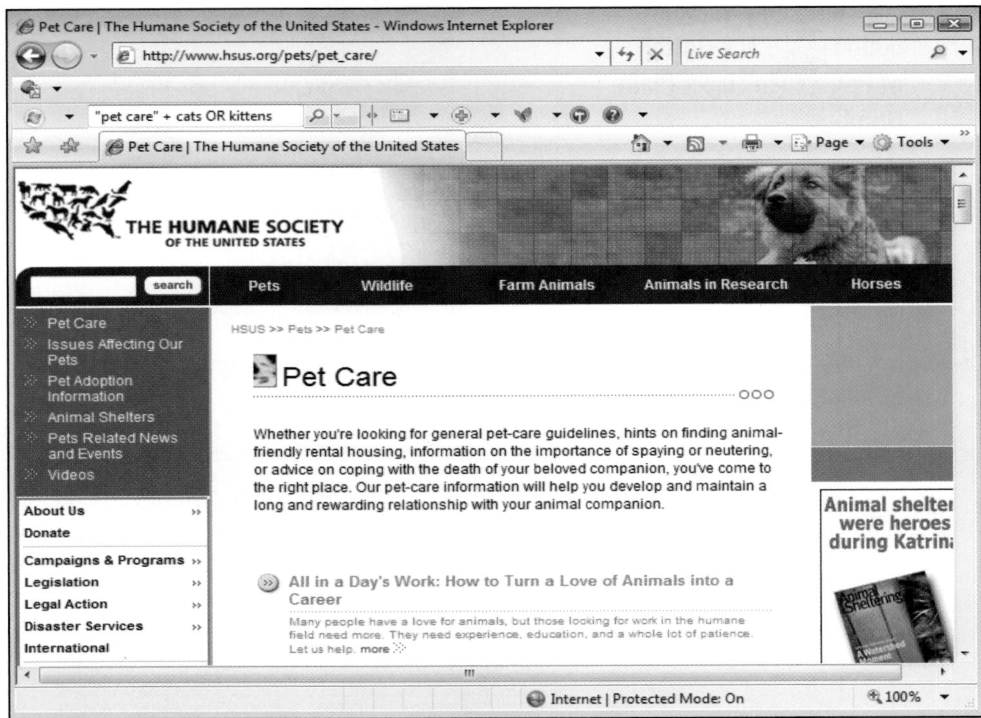

Project 2 Assessment

Key Concepts Check

1. **Define** What is fraud?
2. **Describe** How do you change the text direction?
3. **Explain** What happens to text that is inserted into linked text boxes?

Critical Thinking

4. **Draw Conclusions** What Word tools would you use to format a multi-page, two-column newsletter? Explain your answer.
5. **Identify** Describe two ways to add clip art to a Word document.

1 Guided Practice

Add a Page to Your Newsletter Use your research from Exercise 2-1 to add another page to your newsletter. Your second page should still be in a two-column format, but you will not need to include a masthead. However, you will have to add any new articles or features to the Table of Contents on the first page. If you need help completing a step, refer back to the exercise in parentheses at the end of the step.

Step-by-Step

1. **Open** your **Spam Newsletter**. **Save** it as *Your Name* Newsletter Second Page.
2. Place the insertion point at the end of the first article, and **insert** a **page break** to add a second page. See Figure 2.23.
3. If any of the text boxes from the first page move to the second page, drag them back and place them in the original spot.

Figure 2.23 Place the insertion point at the end of the first article.

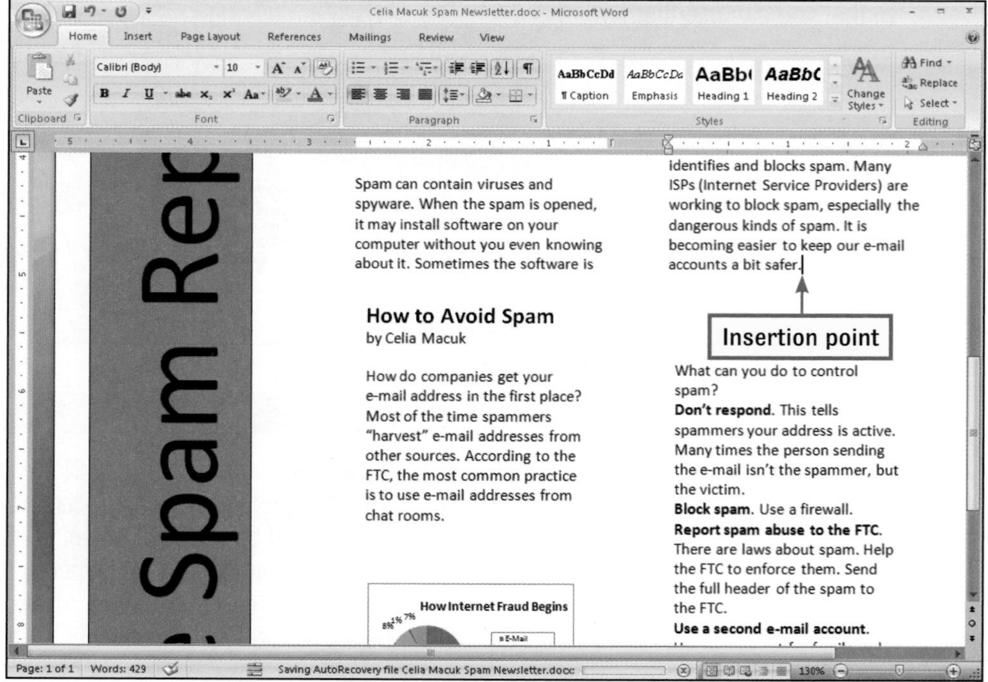

8 Look for update and copyright dates, as well as information about the site's creator and contact information. Scroll to the bottom of the page, if needed (Figure 2.6).

9 **Add** the site to your **Favorites** list, or write down the URL so that you can return to the site.

10 Click the **Back** button to return to the search results page.

11 Evaluate one or two of the other links in your results list. Figure 2.7 shows an example of a Web page that is *not* relevant.

12 **Add** any relevant sites to your **Favorites** list, or record their URLs so that you can use them later.

Figure 2.6 This site gives trustworthy copyright and contact information.

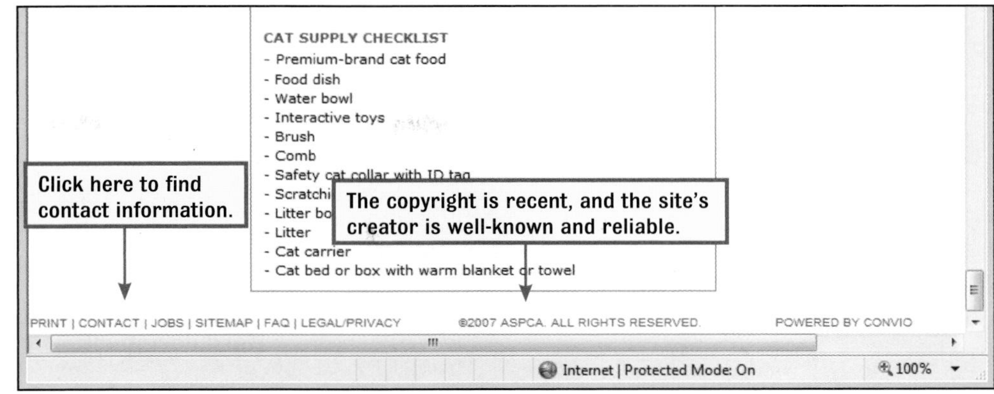

Figure 2.7 Although this site may have useful information, it may be biased in order to sell the company's animal-care products.

HELP!

Web Page Problems If you see a Page Not Found message or another error message, the Web page you are looking for may no longer exist. Check the spelling of the URL and try keying it again. If you still get an error, check to see whether you are connected to the Internet. Sometimes a slowdown or problem on your server can also make it difficult to open a site. Ask your teacher for help.

Project 2 Assessment

4. At the top of the page, write a letter to the editor comparing spam to advertising on the radio or TV (Figure 2.24). Use the same column and text formats as Page 1. (Exercise 2-2)

5. Create a **text box** on Page 2, and **link** it to the text box on Page 1. (Exercise 2-5)

6. Add more information to the second article on Page 1 of your newsletter.

7. The new text should flow to Page 2. At the **end** of the **Page 1 text box**, key (Continued on Page 2). At the **beginning** of the **Page 2 text box**, key How to Avoid Spam (Continued from Page 1).

8. Add a **clip art** image to fill the rest of the page. (Exercise 2-2) Add the **page number** and a **header** with the **name** of the newsletter.

9. Select the grouped text box. **Copy** and **paste** in the left margin on page 2. Ungroup the text boxes. Then delete the dark yellow and white boxes.

10. Add the new features to the **Table of Contents** on the first page, and **save** your newsletter. **Close** the newsletter.

Figure 2.24 Add a header to the second page of your newsletter.

The Spam Report

The Spam Report

Letters to the Editor

Dear Editor,

Recently your newsletter stated that spam should be banned because it costs consumers countless hours in wasted time and is incredibly frustrating. Additionally, you noted that experts estimate that spam accounts for more than 70 percent of all e-mail and costs businesses over $10 billion a year, costs which are passed on to consumers.

While I am as frustrated with spam as you are, I do not believe it should be made illegal. Would you make television or radio advertising illegal? Spam is a kind of advertising and banning it entirely would set a bad example.

I believe the solution is to go after the criminals, not everyone who sends advertising over the Internet. Congress continues to pass laws making it difficult for criminals to use spam to commit crimes. Law enforcement agencies are becoming more effective in enforcing those laws. And companies are developing better software to filter all spam, not just the illegal kind. Most important, the consumer and computer user need to stay informed.

I believe the best solution to the problem of spam is to educate the consumer.

Jennifer Anderson

How to Avoid Spam
(Continued from Page 1)

Report spam abuse to the FTC. There are laws about spam. Help the FTC to enforce them. Send the full header of the spam to the FTC. Go to the FTC site for more information.
Use a second e-mail account. Use one account for family and friends and another for chat rooms or sites that ask you to register. You can often obtain free e-mail accounts through your Internet service provider and Web portals such as MSN Hotmail and SBC Yahoo.
Use common sense. Although the Internet is generally a reliable way to exchange information, criminals keep looking for new ways to use the technology to commit crime. Do what you can to stay one step ahead of them. Update your software, check your system for viruses and spyware, protect your private information, and do not open any e-mail that is suspicious.

2

HELP!

Data Files You can use Data Files to complete the newsletter. For the Letter to the Editor, use **8G Letter to the Editor**. For an expanded second article, use **8H Expanded Article**. For the clip art, use **8I Computer**.

Step-by-Step

1. In your search engine, key "pet care" + cats in the search box, then click **Search** 🔍.

2. Write down the number of search results. Notice that the number is much lower than the search results for *pets* in Exercise 2-1.

3. Key "pet care" + cats OR kittens in the results page search box, then click **Search** 🔍.

4. Check the number of results. Your results page should look similar to Figure 2.4.

5. Read the description of each site on the results page.

6. Click the result that seems most relevant. The Web page you selected appears. **Note**: The page you choose will probably be different from the example shown in Figure 2.5.

7. Read the page to make sure the information is what you need.

Figure 2.4 These are the results of a keyword search for *"pet care" + cats OR kittens*.

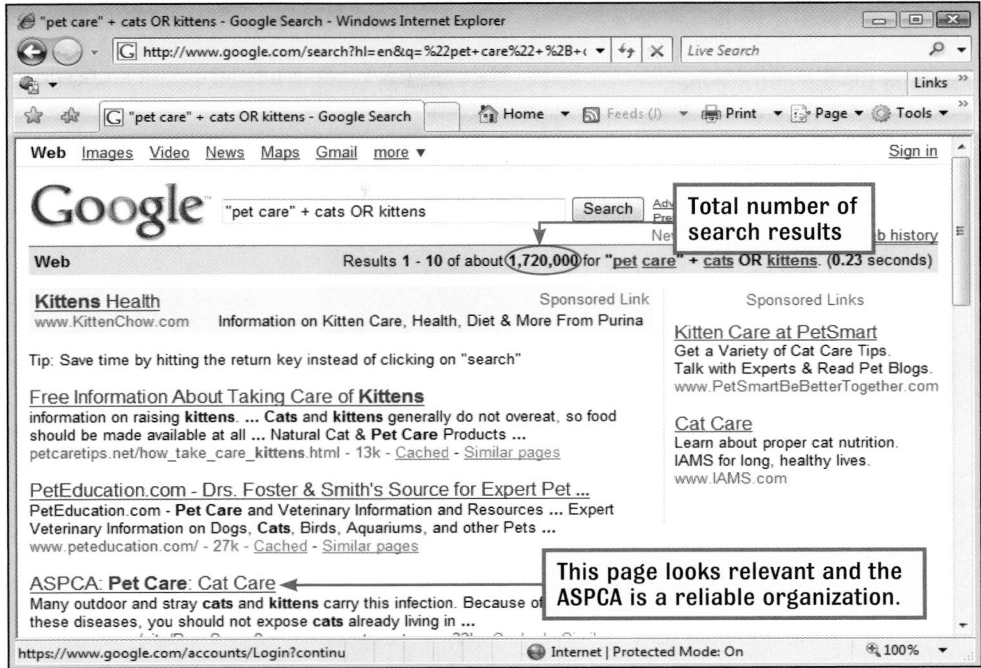

Figure 2.5 Read each search result carefully and choose the page that you think is most relevant.

Project 2 Assessment

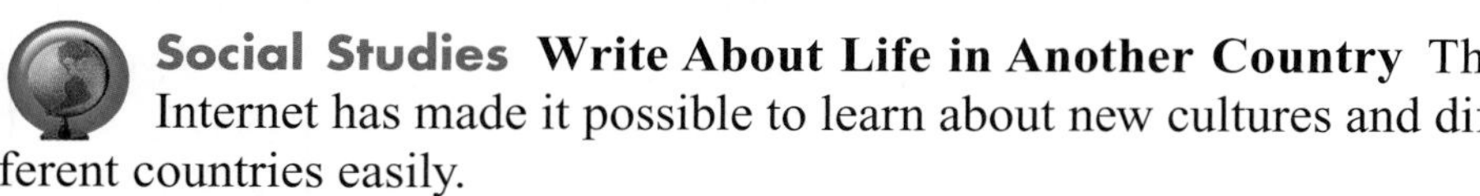

2 Independent Practice ★

Go Online RUBRICS
glencoe.com

Independent Practice
Use the rubrics for these projects to help create and evaluate your work. Go to the **Online Learning Center** at **glencoe.com**. Choose **Rubrics**, then **Unit 8**.

Social Studies **Write About Life in Another Country** The Internet has made it possible to learn about new cultures and different countries easily.

a. Research Use a Web browser aimed at students, such as Yahooligans, to find information about sports, school, food, or any other aspect of life in another country.

b. Create Write two short articles (about 200 words each) about the topic you researched.

3 Independent Practice ★★

Social Studies **Create a Newsletter** Complete Independent Practice 2 above. Then use your completed articles to create a one-page newsletter using Word.

a. Plan Determine how you want to lay out your articles and what graphics you will include.

b. Create Edit your articles to fit onto the page.

- Add a masthead to the newsletter. Include a text box with your name and the date.
- Insert at least one image on the page.

4 Independent Practice ★★★

Math **Plan a Fundraiser** Your class is raising money to buy a digital video camera by holding bake sales every week. Design an announcement in Word to keep your school informed about the sale.

a. Plan Determine how much a camera costs and how many baked goods you must sell every week to afford a camera in two months.

b. Create Explain the reason for the sales and how much each of the treats costs.

- Use text boxes to place your text on the page.
- Add an Excel chart showing how close you are to your goal after three weeks of sales.

Exercise 2-2 Refine a Keyword Search

When you use a search engine, you want to find Web pages that contain useful, or relevant, information. When you use only one keyword to search the Web, you may find that you get a very high number of results, most of which will not be useful. For example, if you want to find information about how to care for a pet, the keyword *pets* might display a Web page about animal care and another that is only advertising lizard cages. Although both are technically about pets, only the one about pet care has the information you will need.

Good keywords will help limit your results. Poor keywords are too general and will give you too many results. To find sites with information about how to take care of a pet, the keyword *pets* is too general. Better keywords would be *pet care*.

To get even better search results, you can do a **Boolean search** (pronounced BOO-lee-an). This is a search that uses keywords plus special symbols to find the exact information you want by eliminating search results that are too general or too broad. Examples of Boolean symbols (also called operators) are shown below.

Boolean Operators

To Find Web Pages with...	Use These Words or Symbols	Example
An exact phrase in quotes	Use quotation marks " "	"Boston terriers" "Siamese cats"
Two or more keywords (the words will not always be near each other on the page)	AND, +, &, or just key a space between words	cats AND dogs cats & dogs cats + dogs cats dogs
One or both keywords	OR, ^	lizards OR snakes lizards ^ snakes
One keyword but not another	NOT, –	cats NOT tigers cats –tigers
A combination of specific information	Use a combination of Boolean operators	"pet care" + lizards OR snakes (will find pages with "pet care" and lizards and pages with "pet care" and snakes)

In this exercise, you will use a Boolean search to narrow your pet care search to a specific pet. After talking with your family, you have chosen to research cats. You will use the guidelines that were described in the Unit 3 Tech Talk (page 93) to evaluate whether the information on a site is relevant, reliable, recent, and verifiable.

Concepts in Action

Project 3 Create a Presentation: Emerging Technologies

Key Concepts

Exercise 3-1
- Use a search engine for research

Exercise 3-2
- Create an outline in Word

Exercise 3-3
- Use a Word outline to create a presentation

Exercise 3-4
- Create a chart in Excel

Exercise 3-5
- Insert a chart and graphics into a presentation

Exercise 3-6
- Add animation and sound to a presentation

Exercise 3-7
- Add speaker notes and edit a presentation

Vocabulary

Key Terms
Outline View

Before You Begin

Use Multiple Programs When you are working with several different programs at one time, you can place your windows side by side. This way, you can easily copy and paste items from one window to another.

In this project, you will use Microsoft Word, Excel, PowerPoint, and the Internet to research and create a presentation about the use of emerging technology in the home.

The Home of the Future

Many of the inventions that scientists envisioned 50 or more years ago are becoming a reality today. Some examples are homes that talk to you, robots that help with difficult tasks, and ovens that can prepare a perfectly cooked dish. Imagine that you work for a company that equips homes with some of these modern advances. In this project, you will research which of these modern products your company might offer. After you have selected some products, you will create a presentation to describe these products to the president of the company.

5 Your results page should look similar to Figure 2.2. Write down the large number of Web pages found.

6 Read the descriptions of the first five results. A description can help you decide whether the Web page could be useful.

7 Click a link in the results list. In Figure 2.3, you can see the page that appears when you click Pets4You.com—Your Online Pet Directory.

Figure 2.2 A keyword that is too general will give you too many results.

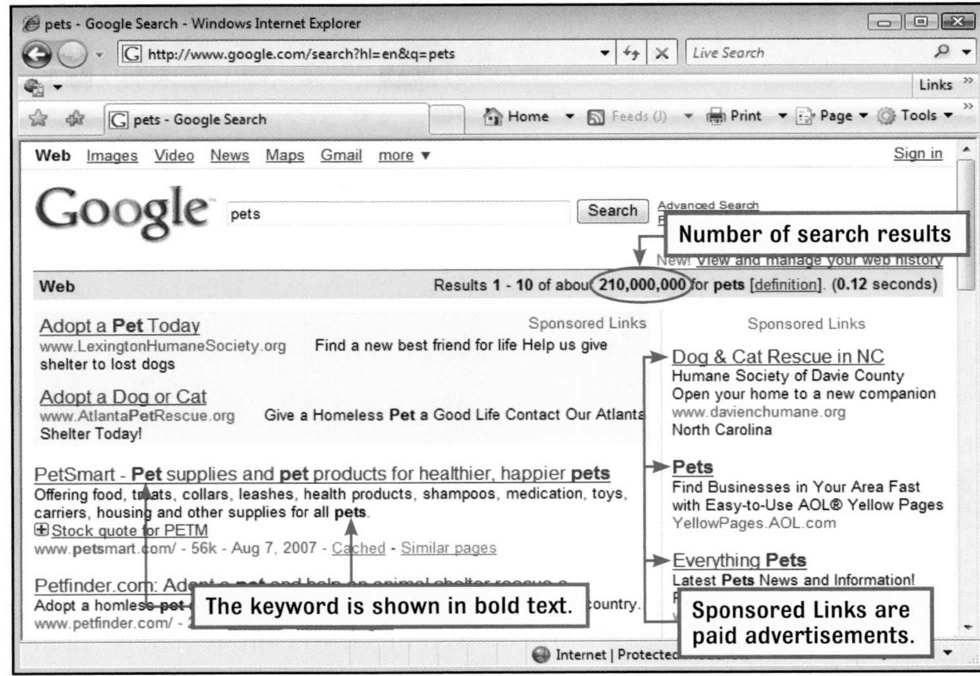

8 Evaluate the relevance of the information on the Web page you chose. **Note**: Drill down or explore outside links. Use your **Back** button to return to the Pets4You home page.

9 If you decide this Web site is not what you need, use the **Back** button to return to your search results and explore other sites.

Figure 2.3 A Web site that does not have the information you were looking for may provide links to more helpful Web sites.

Exercise 3-1 Research New Technologies

An Internet search can produce an overwhelming number of results. Remember, to find relevant sites, you should quickly read the descriptions of the first 10 to 15 results. Do not spend too long looking at each one—simply read the summary detail. If one site does not seem exactly like what you are looking for, move on to the next.

In this exercise, you will use your Web browser to search the Internet for information about the latest advances in home technology. You will later use this information to create a PowerPoint presentation. If you need to review Internet search skills, refer to Unit 3, Project 2 (pages 109–121).

Step-by-Step

1. **Start Internet Explorer**. Ask your teacher which search engine to use. This exercise uses **Google** (Figure 3.1).
2. In the **Search** window, key a phrase such as smart house, home automation, future home robotics, or future assistive technology.
3. From the results list, go to the sites you think will be most reliable.
4. Using pen and paper or Microsoft Word, create a chart similar to the one in Figure 3.2.
5. Use your chart and search results to take notes on at least three interesting facts about emerging home technology.
6. Write down useful URLs, or add the Web site to your Favorites list for later use. Remember to cite your sources.

Figure 3.1 Use a search engine to do your research.

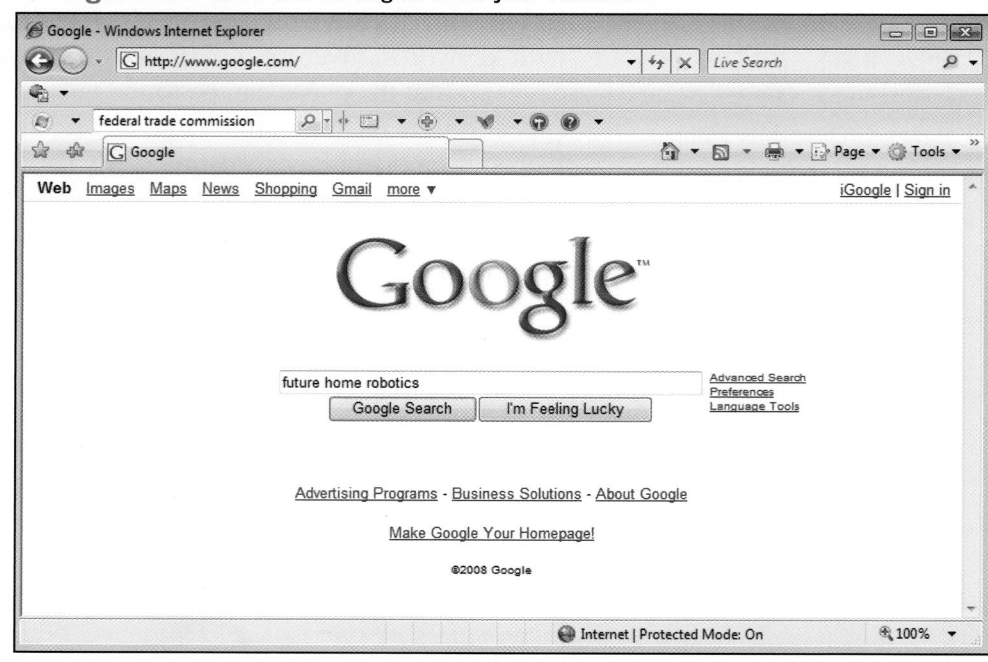

Figure 3.2 Create a table to track your research.

Home Technology	Interesting Facts		
Smart house			
Home automation			
Future home robotics			

Exercise 2-1 Use a Search Engine

TechSavvy

Windows Live Search Microsoft Windows Live Search is a search engine that delivers search results that help you get your answer fast. The program includes tools for helping you quickly find, view, organize, and preview search results. The search preview increases the level of result information on the results page. You can even view search results without moving from page to page.

A **search engine** is a special kind of Web site that lets you search for other Web pages using keywords. A keyword is a word that matches the topic you are looking for. You key the keyword (or keywords) into a search box in the search engine. The search engine then looks through a huge collection of Web pages and gives you a list of pages that contain the keyword or keywords you entered.

There are several different search engines you can use, such as Google™, Yahoo!®, or Windows Live Search®. Using the same keyword in different search engines can give you different results. This is because search engines collect and organize Web pages differently from one another.

A search engine finds results by automatically searching Web pages and looking for keywords on the site itself or by looking for hidden codes with keywords. (Web designers can add keywords when they create Web pages so that the pages can be found even if the keywords do not actually appear on the page.) Search engine companies also hire people to review Web sites and add keywords manually (by hand).

In this exercise, you will use your Web browser and a search engine to find Web sites about pets. You will find that all the results are about *pets*, but not all of the sites will help you learn how to care for them.

Step-by-Step

1. Follow your teacher's instructions to launch the home page of your Web browser. This exercise uses Internet Explorer.
2. Ask your teacher which search engine to use. This exercise uses Google.
3. In the **Address** bar, key www.google.com or the URL from your teacher. Press ENTER to launch the search engine (Figure 2.1).
4. In the search box, key the keyword pets, then click the **Search** button.

Figure 2.1 The home page of Google.com is shown here, but all search engines have common features.

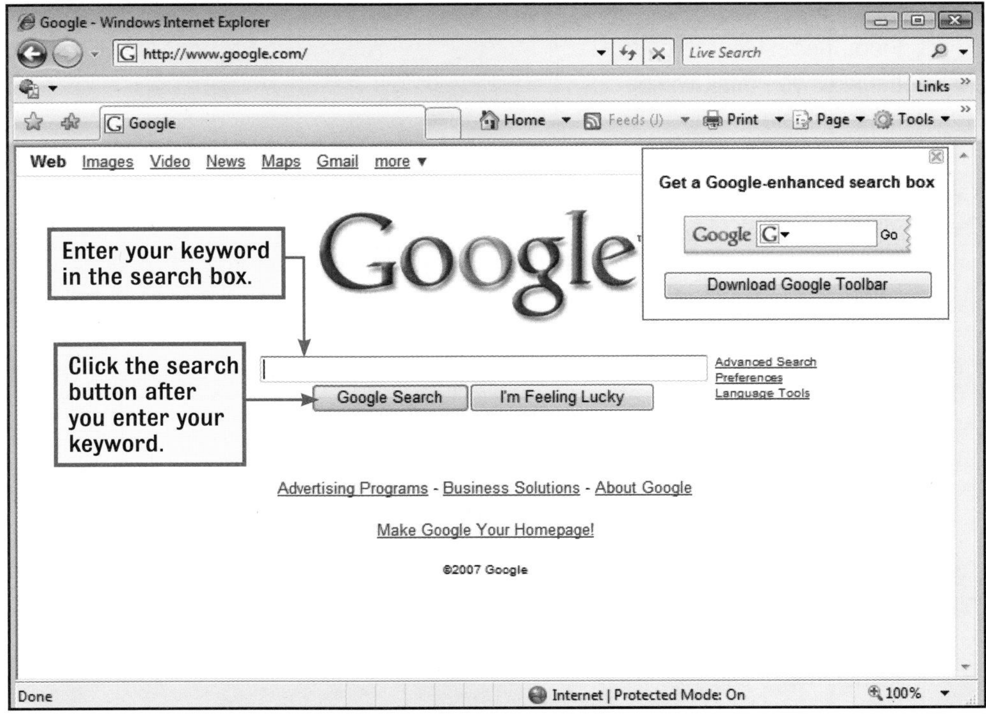

Exercise 3-2 Create an Outline in Word

You can use an outline to organize topics for your reports, papers, presentations, and other assignments. The **Outline View** in Microsoft Word lets you organize a document into headings and body text so that you can easily see how the document is structured. The Outline View will automatically assign a different format to each level of heading. More important items are promoted, or moved up, to a higher level. Supporting items are demoted, or moved down, to a lower level.

For example, you would use a Level 1 heading for the title of a report called *Emerging Technologies*. Then you would demote the following subtitle to a Level 2 heading: *The Home of the Future*. Review Figure 3.4 on page 403 to see how Level 1 and Level 2 headings show the degree of importance of the text. Level 2 headings provide more detail about the main topics.

In this exercise, you will learn to use Word's Outline View to format your document into an outline. In the next exercise, you will see how this Word outline can be imported into PowerPoint to create the content of a presentation quickly.

Step-by-Step

1. **Open** a new blank document in **Microsoft Word**.

2. **Save** your new document as *Your Name* Future Home Outline. Change **Save As Type** to **Rich Text Format**.

3. On the **View** tab, in the **Document View** group, click the **Outline View** button. Notice that the **Outlining** tab appears (Figure 3.3).

4. The **Outline Level** box should read *Level 1*. Key the title for your presentation: Emerging Technologies. Then press ENTER.

Figure 3.3 Format your document in Outline View.

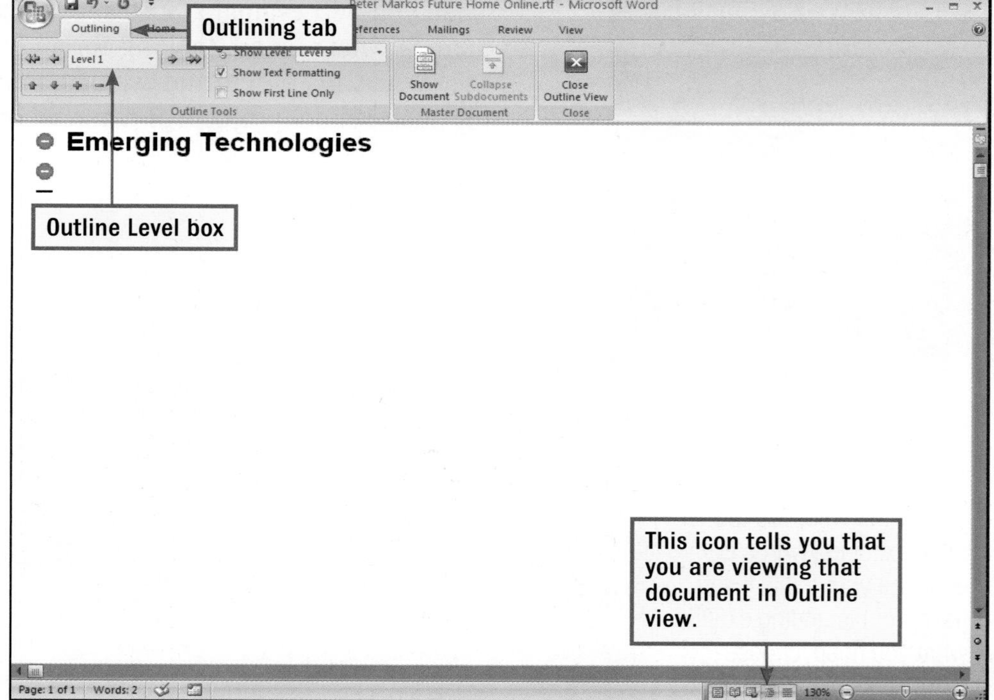

Concepts in Action

Project 2 Search the Internet Effectively

Key Concepts

Exercise 2-1
- Use a search engine to find Web sites
- Perform a keyword search

Exercise 2-2
- Perform a Boolean search
- Evaluate Web sites

Exercise 2-3
- Search a Web site using a table of contents
- Search a Web site using a search box

Exercise 2-4
- Save a Web page
- Open a saved Web page

Vocabulary

Key Terms
search engine
Boolean search

Before You Begin

Choose Your Words Carefully When you search the Web, use the most exact keywords to describe your topic. If you have trouble finding exactly what you need, choose more specific keywords or try a different combination of keywords.

For this project, you will learn how to find information on the Internet using a specific kind of Web site called a search engine. You will learn how to find Web sites quickly and how to evaluate those sites to make sure that the information is relevant and accurate.

Pet Shopping

Imagine that your family decides to get a pet and asks you to find out what kind of pet would be best. You realize there are many factors to consider. You know it will be your responsibility to take care of the pet, so you want to make the right decision.

Fortunately, you have one of the world's greatest sources of information available to you—the Internet. You know the information you need is out there somewhere, but where do you begin? In this project, you will use a search engine to find pet-related Web sites. Then you will evaluate those sites to make sure the information on them is what you are looking for and that it is useful. You can then use these skills to find and evaluate information you find on the Web for other school projects or personal or work-related tasks.

5. On the **Outlining** tab, click the **Demote** button [➔]. Notice that the Outline in the Outline Tools group, Level box displays *Level 2*.

6. Key the subtitle for your presentation: The Home of the Future. Notice that the subtitle's style is different from that of the title. Press [ENTER].

7. In the **Outline Tools group**, click the **Promote** button [⬅].

8. Key the first topic for your presentation. Or use the outline shown here, and key Smart House. Then press [ENTER].

9. In the **Outline Tools** group, click the **Demote** button [➔].

10. Key three subtopics for this category, or use the subtopics shown in Figure 3.4. Remember to press [ENTER] after each subtopic.

11. Repeat steps 7 to 9 until you have entered all of the topics you researched. Or use the outline shown in Figure 3.5.

12. **Save** and **Close** your outline. It should look similar to Figure 3.5.

Figure 3.4 Use the Promote and Demote buttons to create your outline.

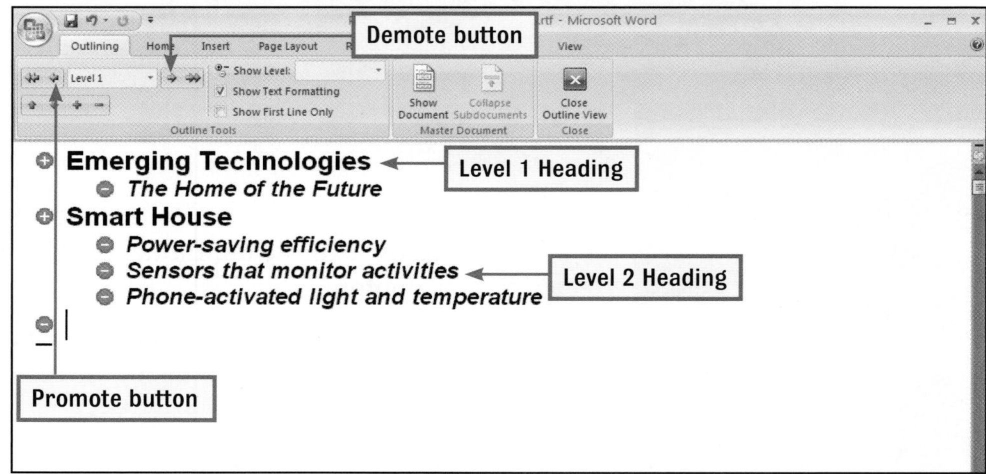

Figure 3.5 The completed outline should look similar to this.

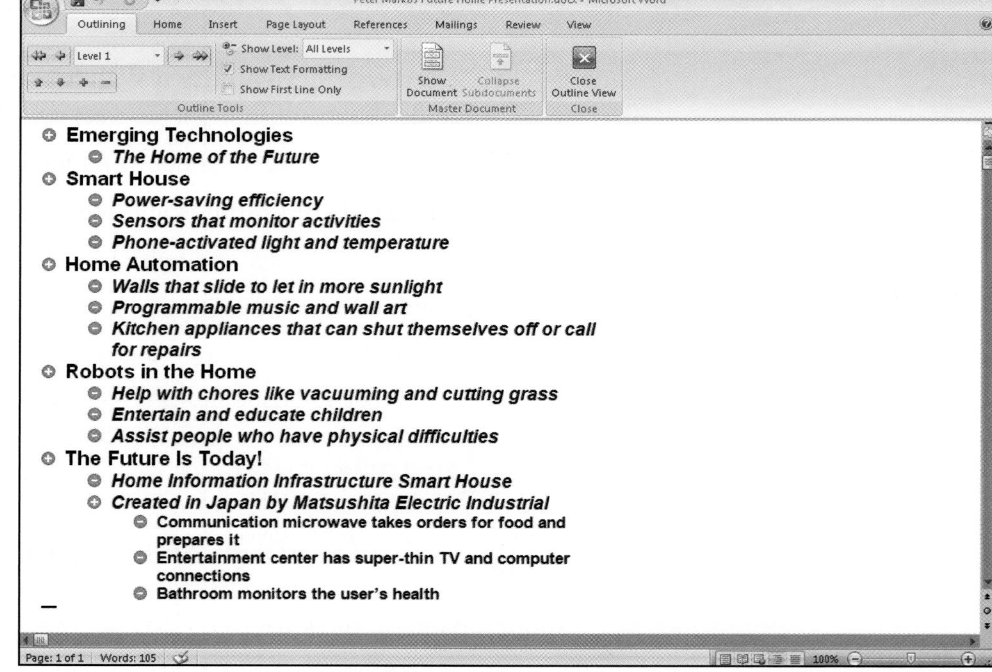

HELP!

Data File If your teacher prefers, you can use the outline shown in this exercise. Open the **Data File** named **8J Future Home Outline** and save it as ***Your Name*** **Future Home Outline**. Then go to step 4 in Exercise 3.3.

Project 1 Assessment

2 Independent Practice 

Social Studies **Explore a Web Site** With your teacher's permission, explore the Library of Congress site to find information about Washington, D.C.

a. **Research** Use links from the home page to find five pages that contain the information about the nation's capitol. Bookmark the five pages.

b. **Create** Create a chart with four columns for the name of the Web page, the URL, a description of the page, and the date of its copyright or last update. Record the information about the five links.

3 Independent Practice 

Teamwork **Evaluate a Web Site** Complete Independent Practice 2, above. With a partner, review the Web sites.

a. **Create** On a separate sheet of paper, create a chart that evaluates:

- What kinds of graphics and media elements are on the page.
- Whether the links and text are easy to read and organized well.
- How the links are arranged to help you find information.

b. **Evaluate** Give each page one to four stars for how well it uses its graphics, text, media, and links, and explain your rating.

Go Online RUBRICS
glencoe.com

Independent Practice
Use the rubrics for these projects to help create and evaluate your work. Go to the **Online Learning Center** at **glencoe.com**. Choose **Rubrics**, then **Unit 3**.

4 Independent Practice 

English Language Arts **Find Contact Information** You want to contact a librarian at the Library of Congress to ask a question about a page on the site.

a. **Research** Explore the links on a page of the Library of Congress site. Think of a question to ask about the page.

b. **Create** Find the contact information on the site, and look for the link that lets you ask a librarian a question.

- When you click the link, use the contact form to write a message to the librarian with your question.
- Print the page. With your teacher's permission, complete the form and e-mail the librarian.

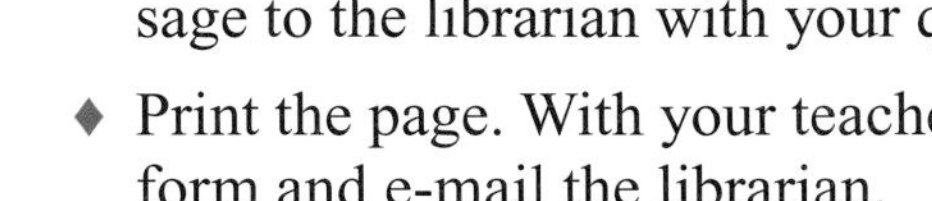

Exercise 3-3 Create a Presentation from an Outline

Microsoft Office makes it possible to create a file in one application and use it for a different purpose in another application. PowerPoint, for example, can convert a Word outline into a presentation. Creating presentations this way can help you effectively organize your ideas and quickly create the skeleton of a presentation.

In this exercise, you will use and modify the outline you created in the previous exercise to create an informative presentation. Each main outline topic will become its own slide in PowerPoint, and each subtopic will become a bulleted list. If you need to review PowerPoint skills, refer to Unit 7, Project 1 (pages 311–325).

Step-by-Step

1. **Open Microsoft PowerPoint**. **Save** your presentation **as** *Your Name Future Home Presentation.*

2. Click the **Microsoft Office Button** and choose **Open**.

3. At the bottom of the **Open** dialog box, change the **Files of type** to **All Outlines** (Figure 3.6).

Figure 3.6 Search for the correct file type.

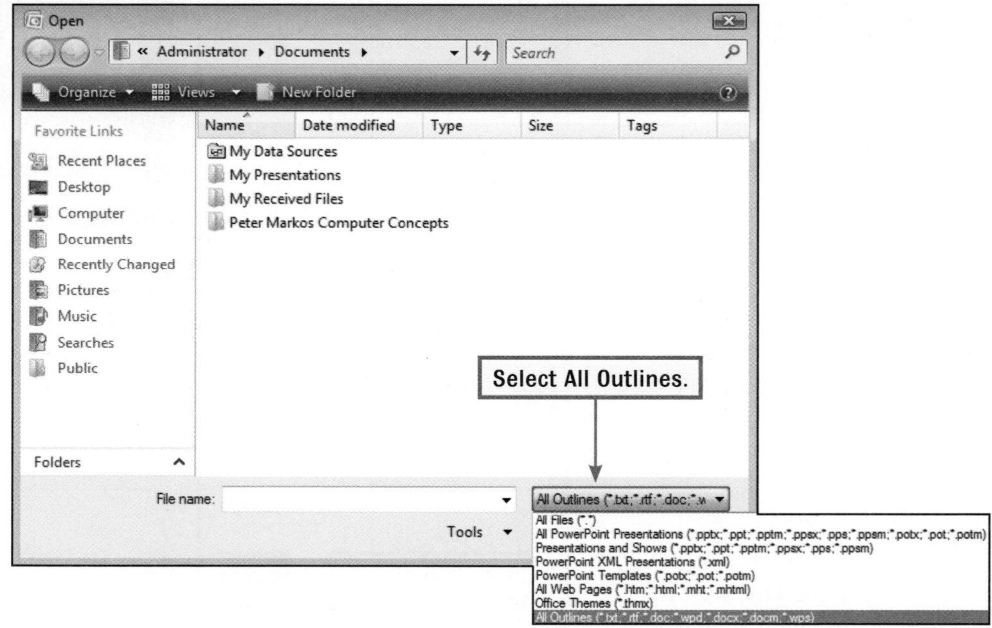

HELP!

Different Versions of PowerPoint If your version of PowerPoint does not have the same features that are shown in this exercise, use Help to find the information you need first. Ask your teacher if you cannot find the answer in Microsoft Office PowerPoint Help.

Project 1 Assessment

4. Use the search results or the arrows to return to the teachers' page. (Exercise 1-2)

5. On the teacher resource page, look for a link to an activities page or a page that shows suggestions for projects. See Figure 1.14 for an example.

6. Click the link. **Add** the page to your **Favorites** list. (Exercise 1-3)

7. Scroll to the bottom of the page. Find information about when the activities were last updated (Figure 1.15).

8. Click a link for one of the activities on the page. Click the **Back** button to return to the list. (Exercise 1-2)

9. Go to at least three activities. When you find an activity you like, view it in **Print Preview.** With your teacher's permission, **print** the page. (Exercise 1-4)

10. Use the **Home** button to return to your browser's home page. (Exercise 1-2)

▼ **Figure 1.14** Your screen might look different from this. If a link does not take you to the information you want, click the Back button.

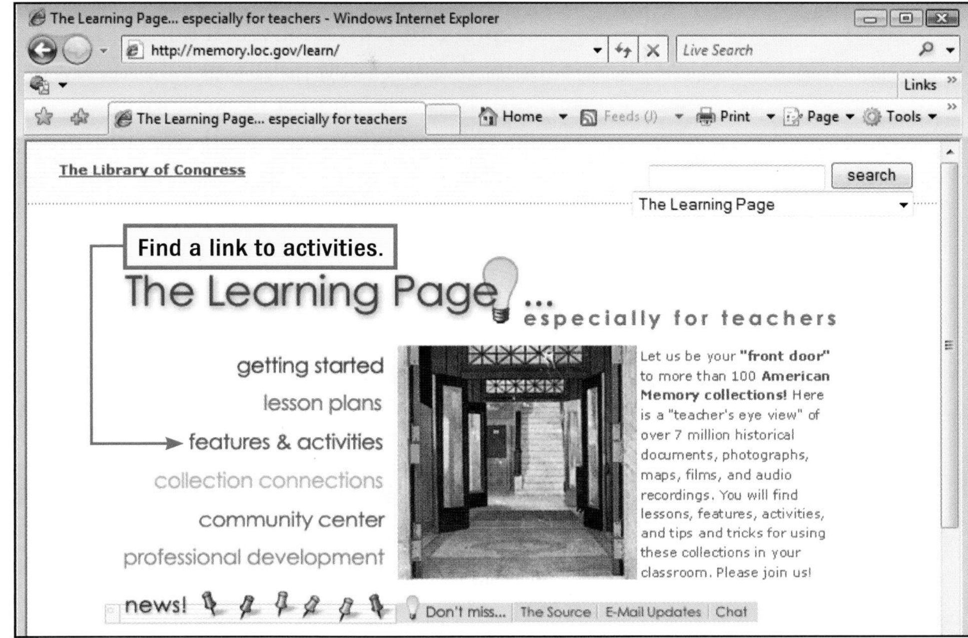

▼ **Figure 1.15** See if your page has a recent update or copyright date.

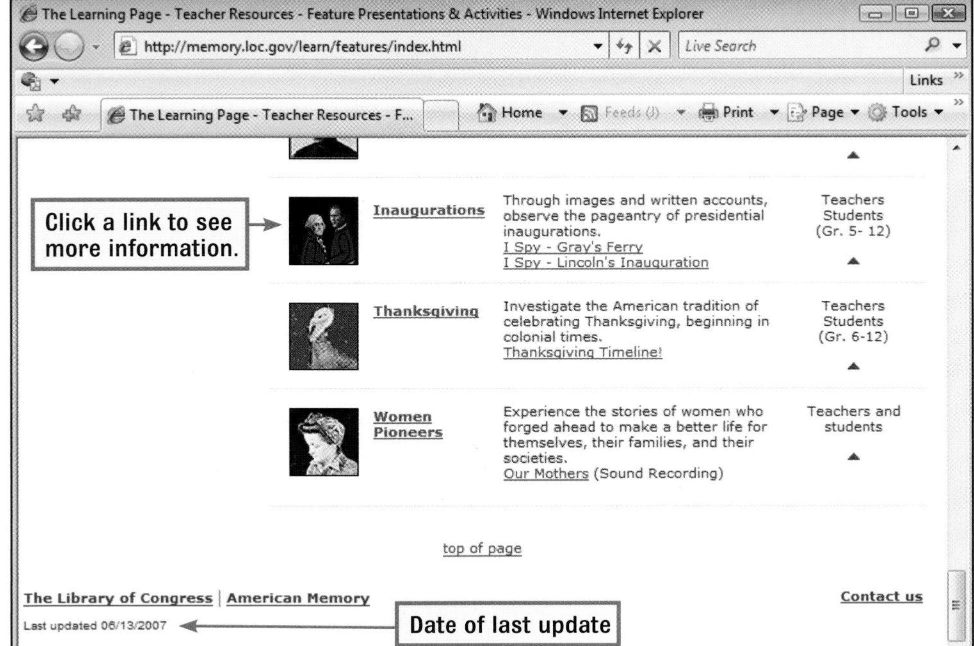

4. Browse to the **Future Home Outline** you created in Exercise 3-2, then click **Open**. **Save** your file **as** *Your Name* Future Home Presentation.

5. The first slide of your PowerPoint presentation should look similar to Figure 3.7. Each of the other slides should also have a Level 1 heading followed by Level 2 bullet points from your outline.

6. On the **Design** tab, in the **Themes** group, choose a **Design Theme**.

7. In the **Background** group, click **Background Styles**.

8. Click the background that you like best. The background should be applied to all of your slides. (Remember to choose a background that works with your text. Text should be readable and clear.)

9. Select **Slide 1**. On the **Home** tab, in the **Slides** group, click **Layout**.

10. Click the **Title Slide** option. Your title slide should look similar to Figure 3.8.

11. **Save** your presentation.

Figure 3.7 Your Future Home outline has been imported into PowerPoint.

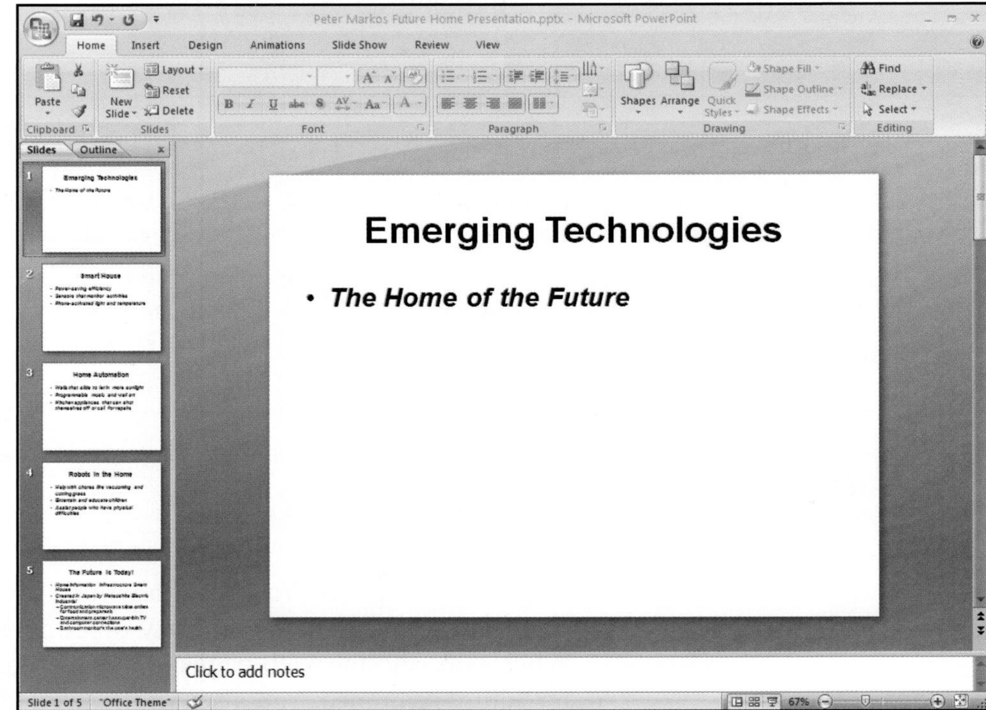

Figure 3.8 Apply a design theme and background style.

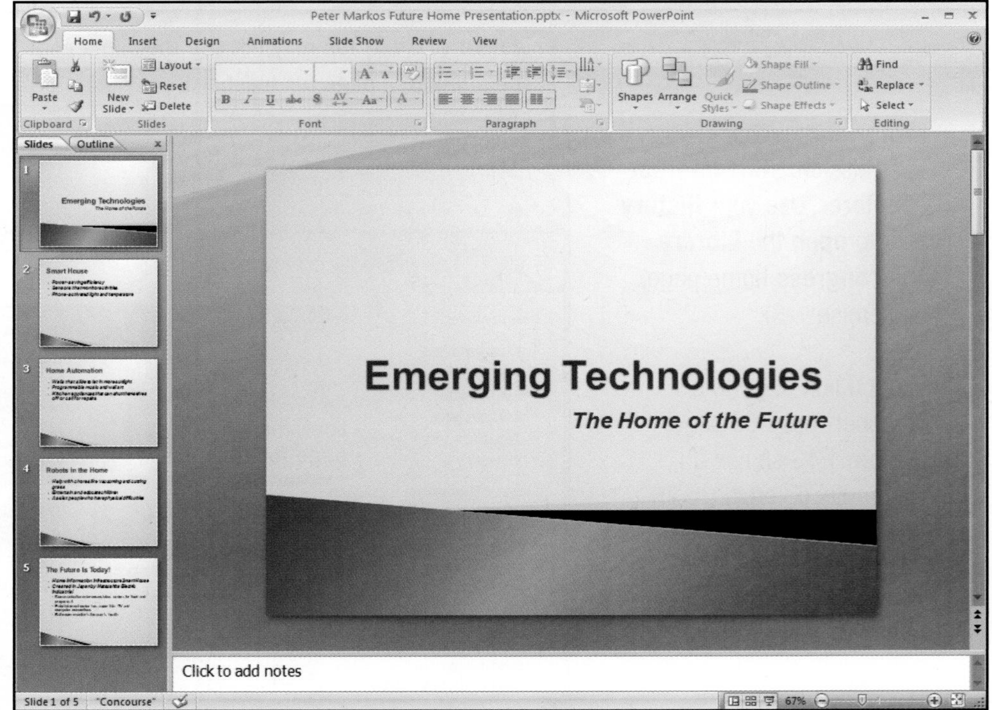

Project 1 Assessment

Key Concepts Check

1. **Identify** Name three kinds of information you might find on a browser's home page.
2. **Compare** What is the difference between the Favorites and History lists in your browser?
3. **Explain** What is a bookmark?

Critical Thinking

4. **Evaluate** Why does a browser's home page usually have links and search boxes?
5. **Make Predictions** What might happen if you did not use Print Preview before you printed a Web page?

1 Guided Practice

Explore a Web Site You need to write a research paper for your history class and want to use the Library of Congress Web site to find a topic. When you find the Web pages you need, you want to create bookmarks for future reference. You also want a printed copy to give to a friend. If you need help completing a step, refer back to the exercise in parentheses at the end of the step.

Step-by-Step

1. With your teacher's permission, **start Internet Explorer**. Use your **History** list to **open** the **Library of Congress** home page. (Exercise 1-3)

2. Find a link to go to a teacher resource page. Figure 1.13 shows an example. (Exercise 1-2)

3. Return to the home page. Key Teachers in the **Search** box. (Exercise 1-2)

▼ **Figure 1.13** You may not see the same page shown here, but there should be a link to a page for teachers.

Exercise 3-4 Create a Chart for Your Presentation

It is often said that a picture is worth a thousand words. This is certainly true of charts and graphs, in which complex information can be easily and efficiently communicated to an audience.

In this exercise, you will create a spreadsheet about household robots. Every year, the United Nations issues a report on the use of robots, both in industry and in the home. You will create a spreadsheet based on information from this report. You will then use the spreadsheet to create a graph to enhance your presentation. If you need to review Excel skills, refer to Unit 5, Project 3 (pages 239–250).

Step-by-Step

1. **Open** a blank worksheet in **Microsoft Excel**. **Save** the worksheet **as** *Your Name* Home Robots.
2. Use the information shown in Figure 3.9 to create a spreadsheet.
3. **Select** cells **A2** to **B7**.

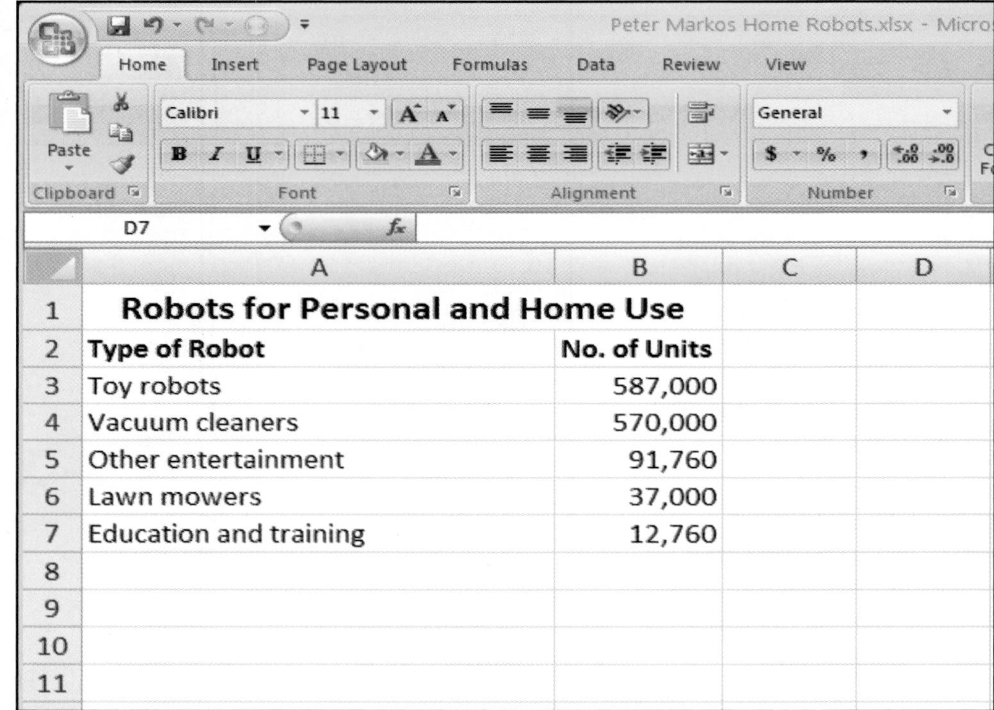

	A	B	C	D
1	Robots for Personal and Home Use			
2	Type of Robot	No. of Units		
3	Toy robots	587,000		
4	Vacuum cleaners	570,000		
5	Other entertainment	91,760		
6	Lawn mowers	37,000		
7	Education and training	12,760		
8				
9				
10				
11				

▼ **Figure 3.9** Create a spreadsheet about robots.

Different Strokes

Selecting Cells Excel provides several ways to select a group of cells. One way is to drag the mouse over the cells you want to select. Another way is to click in one of the corner cells (in Figure 3.9, cell A2). Then, while holding SHIFT, use the directional arrows on the keyboard to select the cells.

8 Click the **Page Setup** button .

9 In the **Page Setup** dialog box, click **Landscape** , then **OK** (Figure 1.11). The whole page can now be viewed.

▼ **Figure 1.11** **Printing in landscape orientation enables you to print the whole page.**

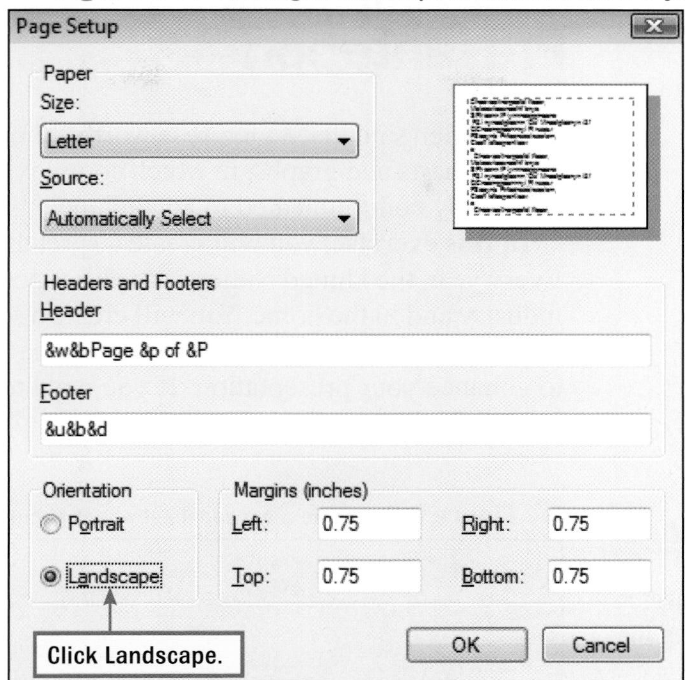

10 In the Print Preview toolbar, click the **Print** button . The Print dialog box appears, as shown in Figure 1.12.

11 Under **Page Range**, click **Pages**. Key 2–3.

12 With your teacher's permission, click **Print** . You will print pages 2 and 3 in landscape orientation.

13 Press , or click the **Close** button , to close Print Preview.

14 **Close Internet Explorer.**

▼ **Figure 1.12** **Use the Print dialog box to choose which pages to print.**

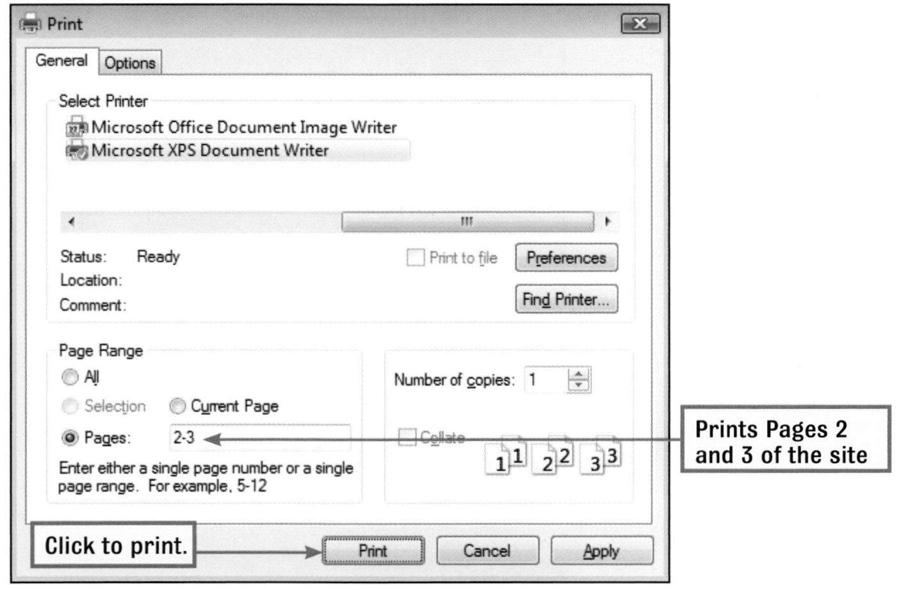

HELP!

URL Headers and Footers You can also open the Page Setup dialog box by clicking the Down arrow next to the Print button. The Page Setup dialog box includes Header and Footer options to print the URL of the page you are viewing.

4. On the **Insert** tab, in the **Charts** group, click the **Column** button [INSERT].

5. Under **3-D Column**, click **3-D Clustered Column**. The **Chart Tools** open.

6. On the **Design** tab, in the **Data** group, click the **Switch Row/Column** button (Figure 3.10).

7. On the **Chart Tools Layout** tab, in the **Labels** group, click the **Chart Title** button. Click **Above Chart**, and key Personal and Home Robots. Press [ENTER].

8. Click the **Legend** button, and then click **More Legend Options**.

9. Click **Border Color**, and select **Solid Line**. Click **Close**.

10. Adjust the size and position of the elements in the chart so that all parts of it are readable.

11. **Save** your work. Your spreadsheet and chart should look similar to Figure 3.11.

▼ **Figure 3.10** Use the Chart Tools to format a 3-D column chart.

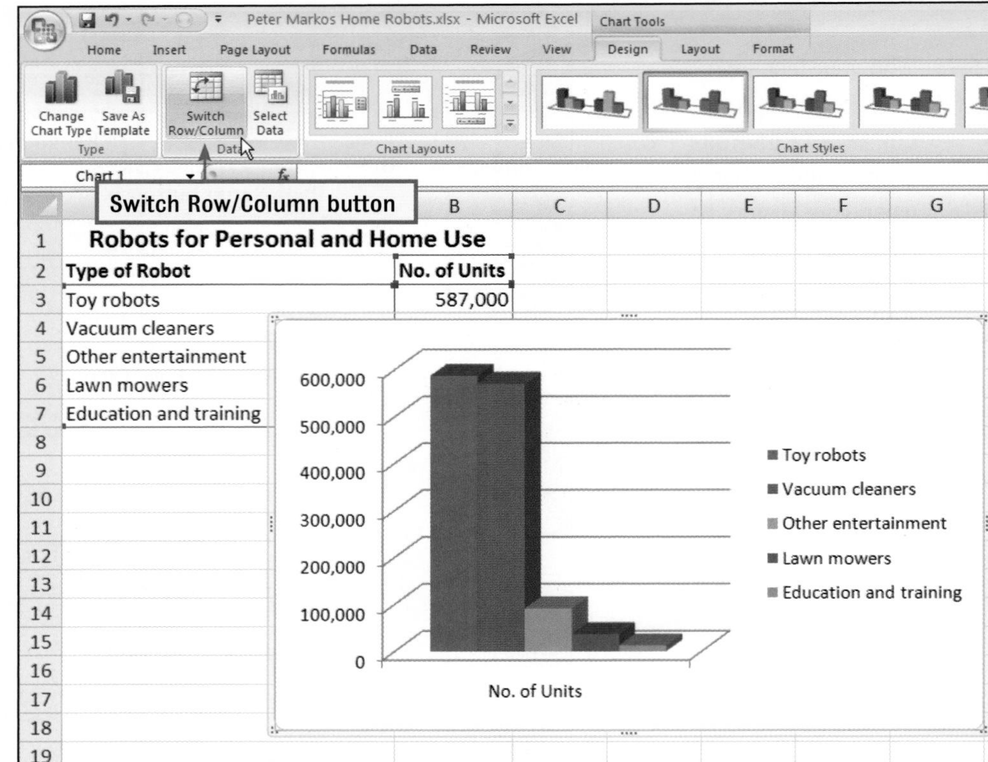

▼ **Figure 3.11** The finished chart should look similar to the one below.

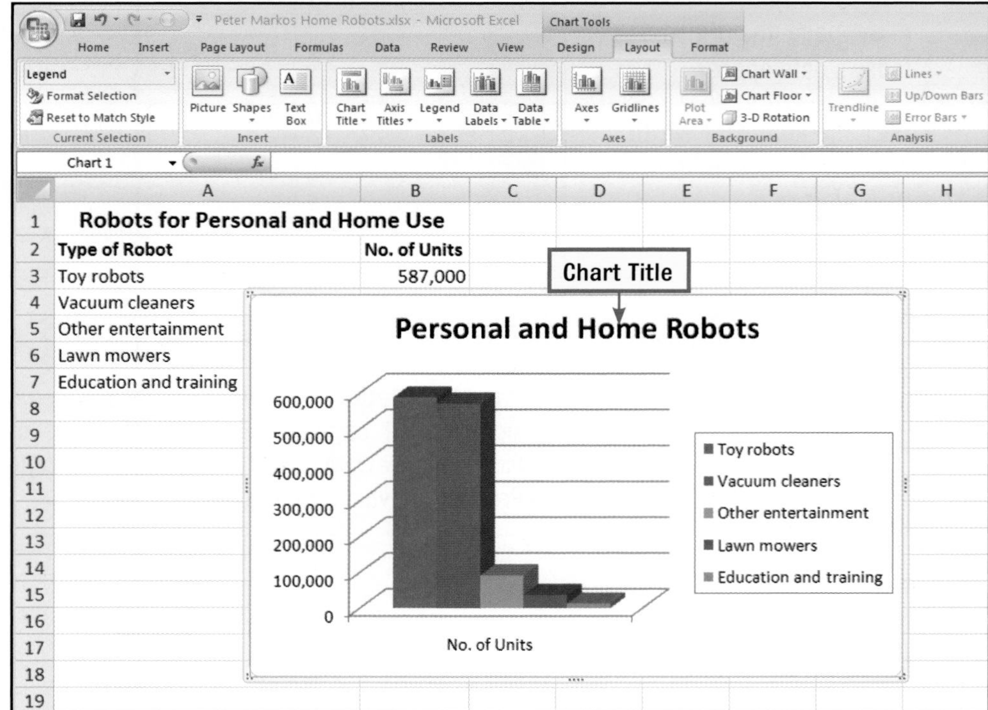

Step-by-Step

1. With your teacher's permission, return to the **Library of Congress home page**, either by using your History or Favorites list, or by keying www.loc.gov in the **Address** bar.

2. On the home page, click the **Site Map** link located at the bottom of the Web page.

3. On the command bar, click the arrow beside the Print button and click **Print Preview.** A new window opens. See Figure 1.10.

4. At the top of the page, notice the name of the Web page. At the bottom of the page, the URL and today's date appear.

5. Click the **View Full Width** button to zoom the Web page to the width of the preview screen.

6. Click the **Next Page** button to view the next page. Click the **First Page** button to go back to page 1, then click the **Last Page** button to jump to the last page.

7. Key 1 in the page number box. Use the page number box to jump to a particular page.

Figure 1.10 Print Preview lets you see how the page will look when it prints.

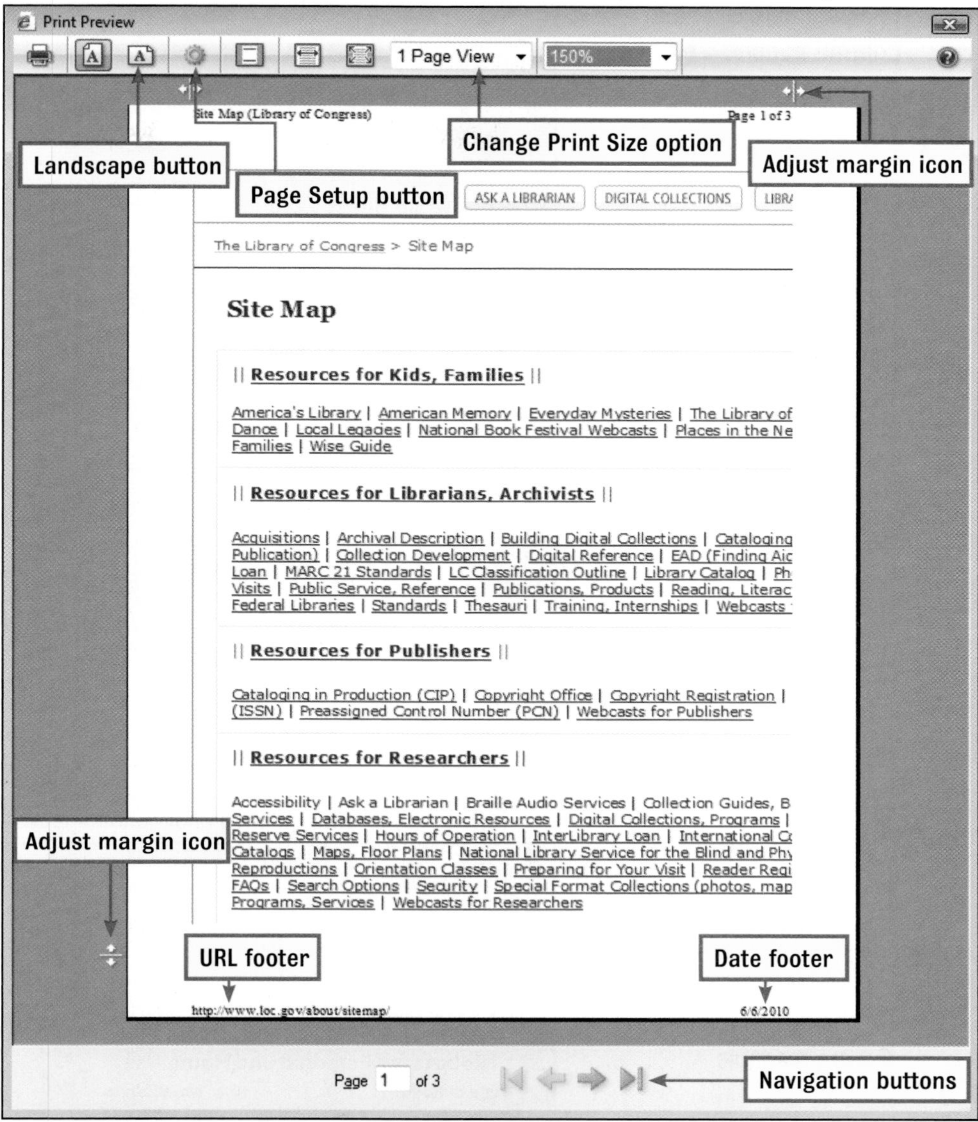

HELP!

Page Orientation The Print Preview screen will often cut off the right side of a Web page when you view the page in portrait view. Switching to landscape view will usually help. Click the Landscape button in Print Preview to avoid losing text.

Exercise 3-5 Insert an Excel Chart and Clip Art

Slide show presentations should capture your audience's interest as well as clearly communicate your ideas. Make sure to use appropriate images, sounds, animation, and possibly even video to further explain your topics.

When using images, make sure they relate to the text on the slide, and that they are easy to see and understand. Use only one or two images. Too many pictures can make the slide too cluttered and be distracting to the audience.

In this exercise, you will add clip art and the Excel chart you created in the previous exercise to enhance your presentation. If you need to review PowerPoint skills, refer to Unit 7, Project 2 (pages 326–341).

Step-by-Step

1. In your Future Homes presentation, select **Slide 4** and add a **new slide** after it.

2. On the **Home** tab, in the **Slides** group, click the **Layout** button. Choose the **Title and Content** format to apply to the new slide (Figure 3.12).

3. Key the title Robots in the Home Today.

▼ **Figure 3.12** **Add a new slide to your presentation and change the format.**

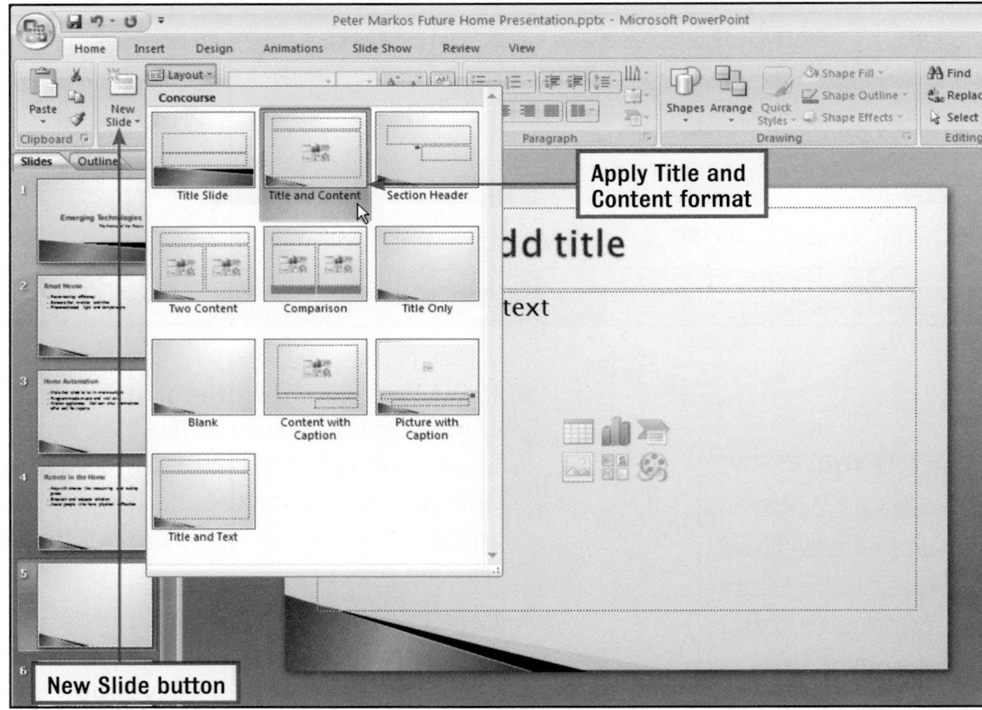

> **HELP!**
>
> **Data File** If your teacher prefers, you can use a Data File with the clip art shown in this exercise instead of finding your own. From your slide, click the **Insert** tab, then click **Insert Picture**. Browse to the **Data Files** named **8K–8M Future Home Clip Art**. Insert each piece of clip art into a separate slide.

Exercise 1-4 Print a Web Page

Sometimes you need to print a Web page so that you have a hard copy of the information you see on the screen. This can be helpful if you need to use the information when you are away from your computer. It can also be helpful because some Web sites are constantly changing, and you may want to print a specific version of a Web page. There are several ways to print a Web page:

- **Browser Print Button** Web browsers have an easy-to-use print option. In Windows Internet Explorer, use the Print button on the command bar. Click the Print button to automatically print the Web page you are viewing. Click the down arrow beside the Print button, or press ALT + R to display print options.

▼ The Windows Internet Explorer Print button is the quickest way to print a page.

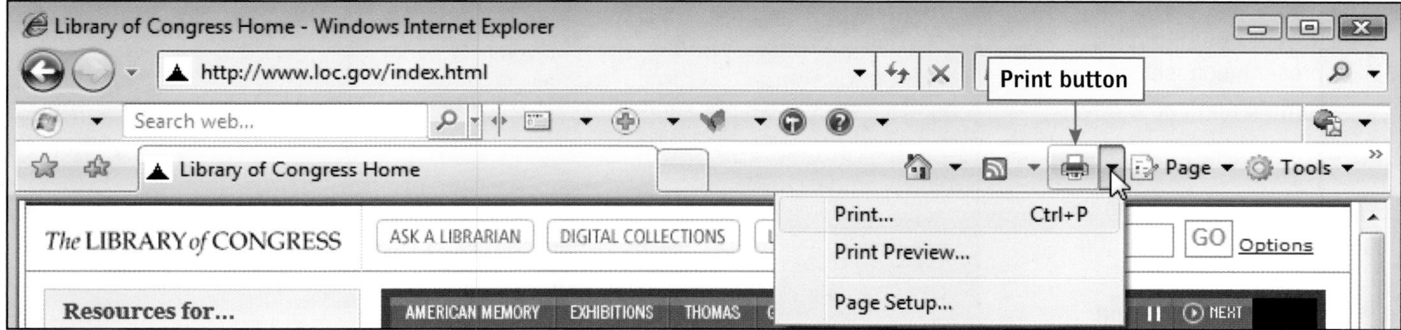

- **Print Preview** Click the arrow to the right of the Print button on the command bar to access the Print Preview command. **Print Preview** allows you to view a page so you can see how it will look when it is printed. You can make sure that you print only the sections you want and that parts of the page are not missing. It is a good way to avoid wasting paper.

▲ Some Web sites provide a printer-friendly version of a Web page that is easy to print.

- **Printer-Friendly Format** Some Web sites have a Printer-Friendly Format link. This option is common on newspaper or magazine Web sites. This link will display a new page that includes the text but usually leaves out graphics and other parts of the page. The link can have a variety of names, including Print Version, Print, and Printer Friendly.

In this exercise, you will use Print Preview to print part of a Web page. Make sure you have your teacher's permission before you print in class.

4 **Open** the **Excel file** you created in Exercise 3-4.

5 On the **Home** tab, in the **Clipboard** group, click the **Copy** button. **Exit** the **Excel file**.

6 Click **Slide 5**. In the **Clipboard** group, click the **Paste** button.

7 Drag the chart to the place you want it on the slide. Resize it if necessary (Figure 3.13).

8 Click **Slide 2**. On the **Insert** tab, in the **Illustrations** group, click the **Clip Art** button.

9 In the **Search for** box, key house (or another key word that relates to the content of your slide).

10 Browse to a clip art selection that you like best, and click it to add it to your presentation (Figure 3.14). You may need to resize or move elements.

11 Repeat steps 8 to 10 to add clip art to at least two other slides in your presentation.

12 **Save** your work.

▼ **Figure 3.13** Insert the chart you created in the previous exercise.

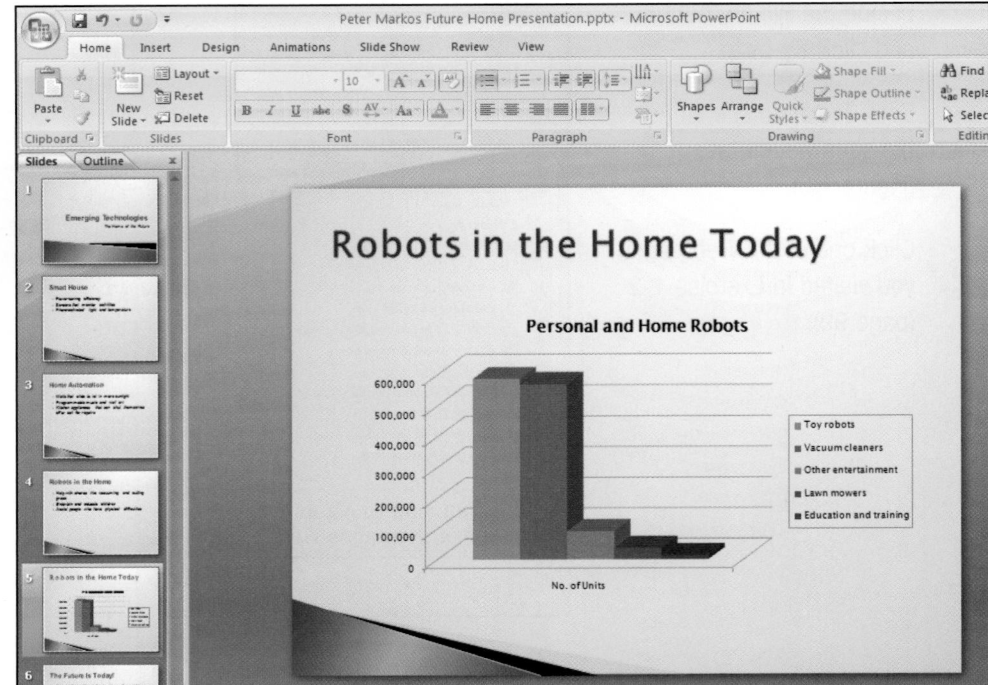

▼ **Figure 3.14** Insert clip art to make your presentation more appealing.

3. Click the down arrow beside the History button, and click **By Date**.

4. Click **Today** to see all the sites visited today (Figure 1.8).

5. Click one of the Web pages you visited in Exercise 1-2 (page 99).

6. On the Explorer command bar, click the **Favorites** button. The History list is replaced by the Favorites list (Figure 1.9).

7. Click the **Add to Favorites** button. Click **Add to Favorites.** The current Web page is now added to the Favorites list.

8. Return to your **History** list. With your teacher's permission, use it to go to two other sites and bookmark them.

9. In your **Favorites** list, click a Web page to go to that site.

10. Click the **Home** button to return to your browser's home page.

Figure 1.8 Click a day to see the History list of visited sites.

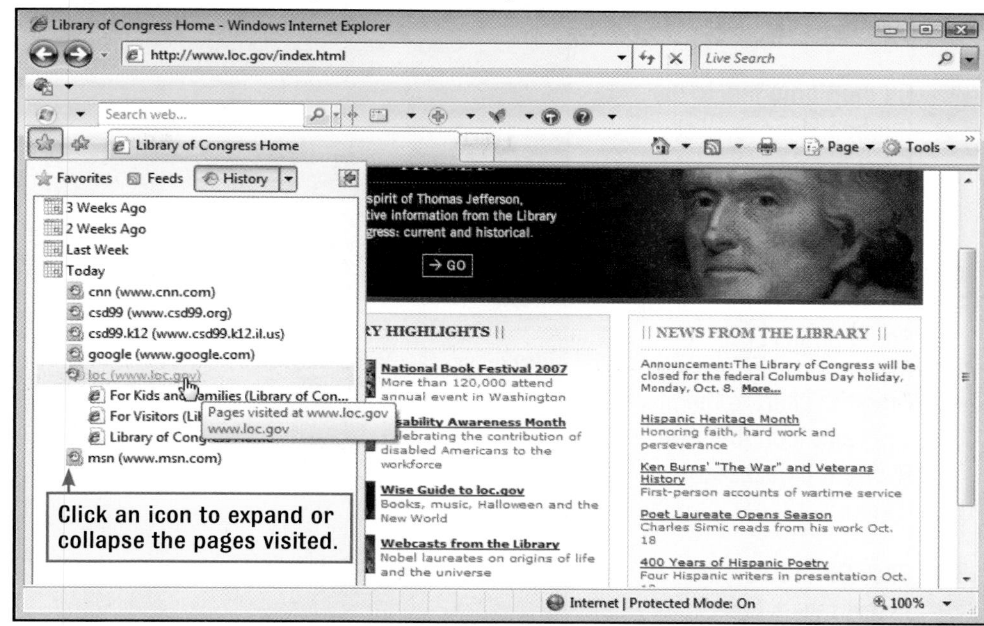

Figure 1.9 Choose what is included in the Favorites list.

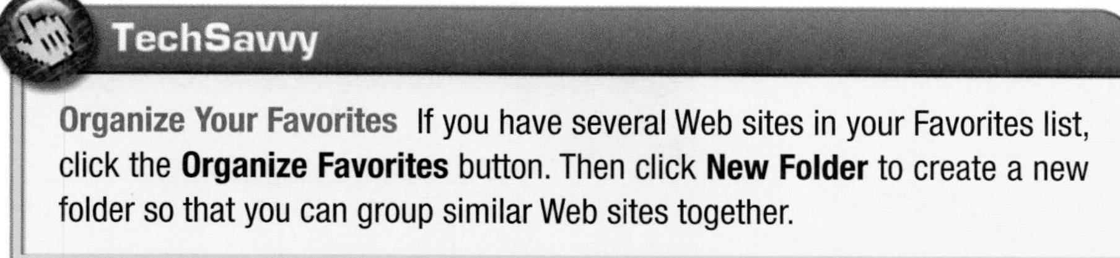

TechSavvy

Organize Your Favorites If you have several Web sites in your Favorites list, click the **Organize Favorites** button. Then click **New Folder** to create a new folder so that you can group similar Web sites together.

Exercise 3-6 Add Animation and Sound

Animation and sound can make a presentation more appealing, but they can also be distracting. Before deciding on what elements to add, think about your audience and the purpose of your presentation. If you are preparing a professional presentation, you might not want sound effects interrupting what you are saying. On the other hand, music or sound could give the slide show a lighter mood.

In this exercise, you will use the Slide Master to add animated elements to all your slides. You will also add sound. Refer to Unit 7, Project 2 (Pages 326–341) if you need to review PowerPoint skills.

Step-by-Step

1. Click any slide in your presentation (except the title slide or Slide 5 with the inserted chart).
2. On the **View** tab, in the **Presentation Views** group, click the **Slide Master** button. See Figure 3.15.
3. To animate the bulleted list, select the text box titled **Click to edit Master text styles**.
4. On the **Animations** tab, in the **Animations** group, click the **Custom Animation** button.
5. In the task pane, click the **Add Effect** button, choose **Entrance**, then click **Fly In.**
6. Under **Modify: Fly In**, choose the **Start**, **Direction**, and **Speed** settings that you like best.
7. On the **Slide Master** tab, in the **Close** group, click the **Close Master View** button.

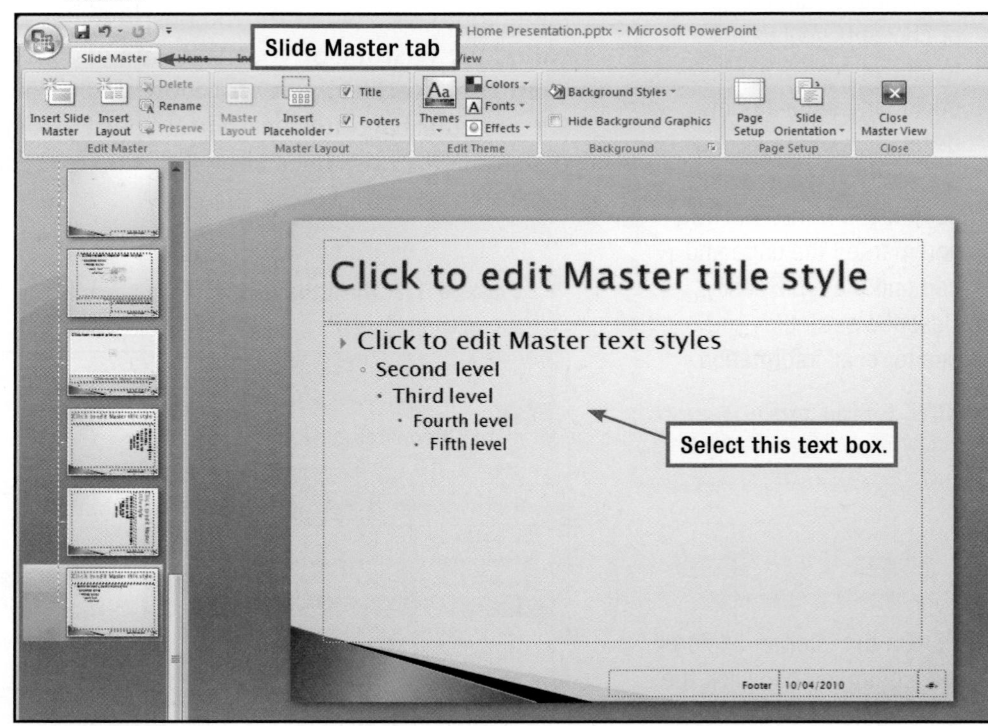

Figure 3.15 Animate the bulleted list in your presentation with the Slide Master.

TechSavvy

Animation Animation is fun to add, but it is easy to get carried away with it. Always use the preview option to make sure your bullets make your presentation look professional and not like a video game. Make sure that any graphics or animation are appropriate and clarify your text. If they are too distracting, you might need to change your animation settings or remove some text from the presentation to simplify it.

Exercise 1-3

Find Web Sites Using History and Favorites

Academic Focus

English Language Arts

Track Your Reading
Bookmarks for your Web browser are similar to the ones you use for textbooks and other reading material. As you read, use pieces of paper or bookmarks to mark pages with terms or concepts you want to study later. On each bookmark, write a brief description of the term or concept you want to study so that you remember why you marked the page and can find the topic easily. Describe strategies you use to recall information.

NCTE 1 Read texts to acquire new information.

When you find a specific Web page that you want to return to later, you can use a bookmark to note the page just as you would in a book. A **bookmark** is a shortcut stored in your browser that takes you directly to a Web page. With a bookmark, you do not have to remember how to navigate to the page or write down the specific URL.

In the Internet Explorer browser, bookmarks are called **Favorites**. You can easily add a Web site to your Favorites list. When you click the Web page name in the Favorites list, the browser goes to that page immediately.

Sometimes you may want to return to a page that you visited but did not add to your Favorites list. Fortunately, your browser keeps track of *every* page you have visited for the past few days or even weeks. This record is called the **History** of your Web site visits.

In this exercise, you will view your browser's History and add useful sites to your Favorites list. **Note**: Your History and Favorites lists may look different from the ones shown in this exercise because each person's list is unique.

Step-by-Step

1. On the Internet Explorer command bar, click the **Favorites Center** button. Click the arrow beside the **History** button (Figure 1.7).

2. Click **By Site**. Notice that site names display in the left pane.

▼ **Figure 1.7** **Click the History drop-down arrow to view options for sorting the History list.**

8 In your presentation, select your last slide.

9 On the **Insert** tab, in the **Media Clips** group, click the **Sound** drop-down arrow. Click **Sound from Clip Organizer**.

10 Choose a sound or music sample you like best, then click it to insert it into the slide.

11 **Close** the **Clip Art** task pane. Select the sound icon on the slide (Figure 3.16).

12 In the **Custom Animation** task pane, click the media clip you chose. Then click the arrow to display the drop-down menu.

13 Choose the play options you want from the menu.

14 Click the **Play** button [Play] to preview the sound.

15 On the **Slide Show** tab, in the **Start Slide Show** group, click **From Beginning** to review your presentation (Figure 3.17).

16 Makes changes as needed. **Close** the **Custom Animation** task pane. **Save** your work.

Figure 3.16 The media clip icon is displayed on the slide.

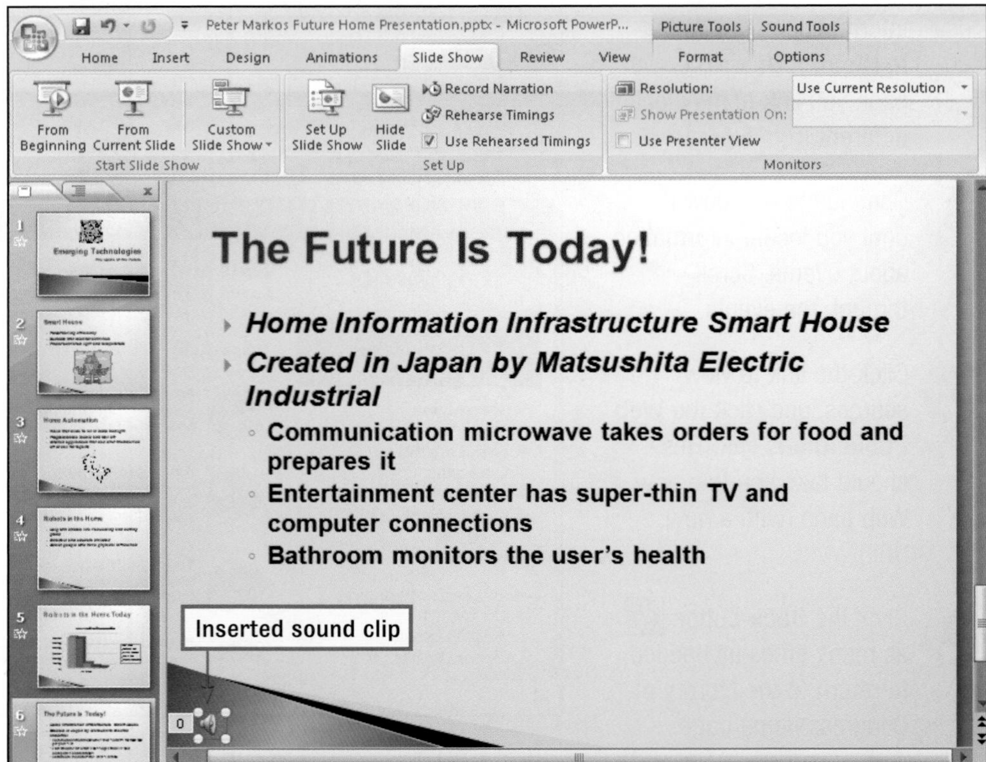

Figure 3.17 Review your finished presentation.

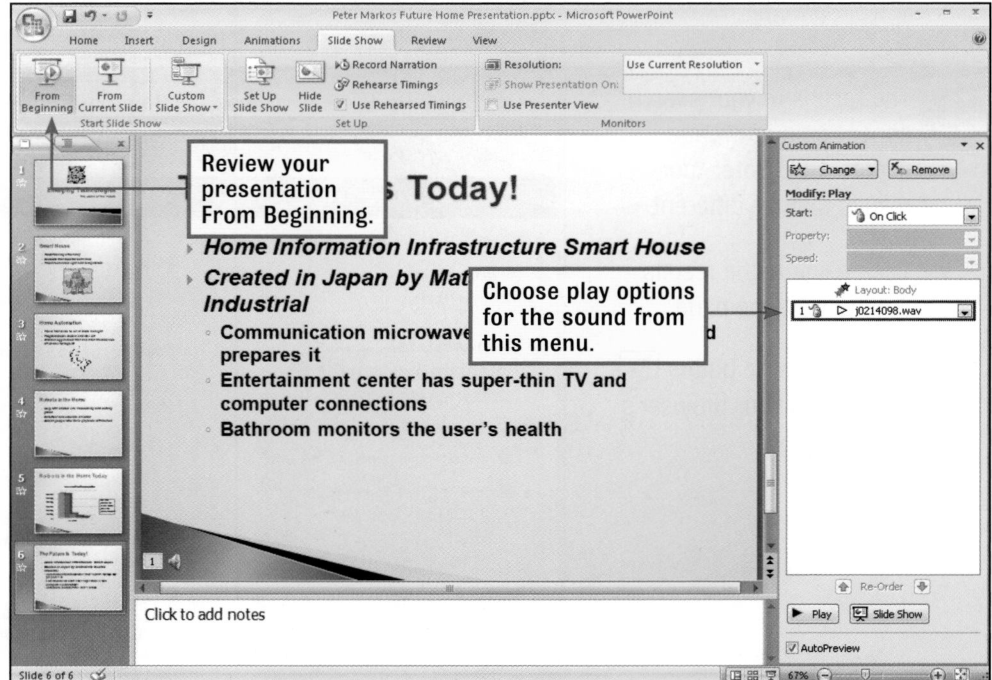

5. Drill down to find information about **Today in History**. **Note:** The Web page you link to may look different from Figure 1.5.

6. Continue to drill down until you locate information about events. Scroll through the events.

7. Click the link to view sources, and click the **Web Publications** link. This should take you to a new Web page (with a new URL).

8. Click the **Back** button as many times as needed to return to the Library of Congress home page.

9. In the **Search** box, in the top-right corner of the screen, key Today in History.

10. The results of your search appear on a new page (Figure 1.6). **Note:** Your results may be different.

11. Click a link in the results area to view the page.

12. Click the **Home** button to return to your browser's home page.

Figure 1.5 As you drill down, links become more and more specific.

Figure 1.6 The Search result can bring up the same Web page that you found by clicking links.

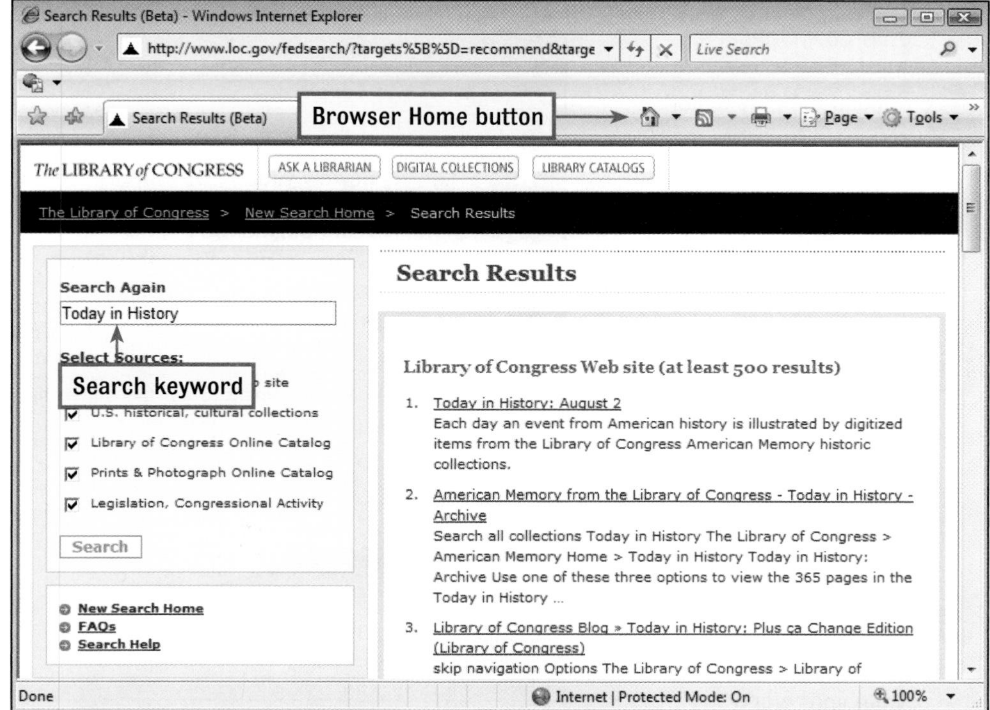

Exercise 3-7 Add Transitions and Speaker Notes

Before you deliver your presentation, it is a good idea to use PowerPoint's Slide Sorter view to make any final changes. You may also want to add speaker notes so that you are prepared to discuss the information on each slide.

In this exercise, you will use the Slide Sorter view to change the order of your slides and to add transitions to your presentation. You will also add speaker notes based on your research notes. If you need to review PowerPoint skills, refer to Unit 7, Project 3 (pages 342–351).

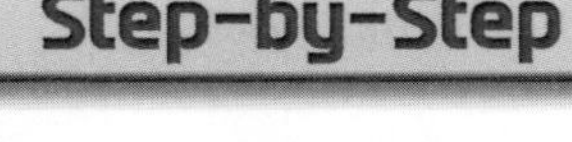

1. In your **Future Home** presentation, on the **View** tab, in the **Presentation Views** group, click the **Slide Sorter** button.
2. Click the **final slide**, and drag it after **Slide 1**.
3. Press CTRL + A to select all the slides.
4. Click the **Animations** tab. The **Transition to This Slide** group displays (Figure 3.18).

Figure 3.18 View your entire presentation with the Slide Sorter view.

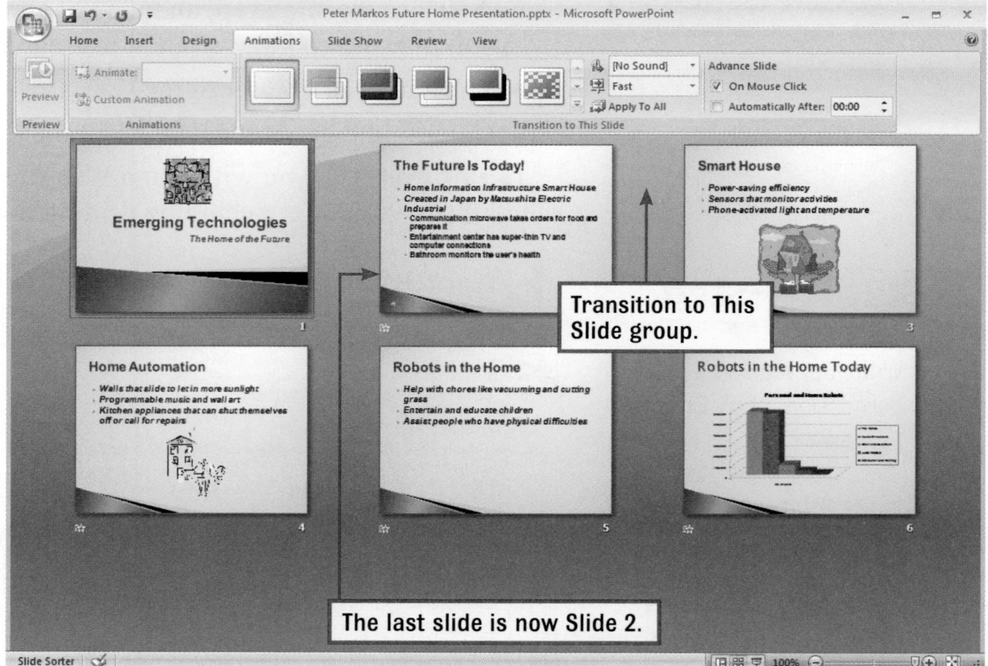

Different Strokes

Start a Slide Show You can use any of these methods to start a slide show:

- **Slide Show tab** On the Slide Show tab, in the **Start Slide Show** group, choose **Start Slide From Beginning**.
- **View tab** On the **View** tab, in the **Presentation Views** group, choose **Slide Show**.
- **Task Panes** Click the **Slide Show** button in the **Custom Animation** task panes.
- **Keyboard** Press F5.

Exercise 1-2 Explore Web Sites

A Web site is made up of individual Web pages, just like a book is made up of many different pages. Each Web site's home page is much like a book cover and a table of contents rolled into one.

When you explore a Web site, you usually start with the home page and **drill down** to find more specific information. To drill down, you click a link that opens a new Web page within the site. From this page, you can choose other links to find even more specific information, and so on.

A Web site's home page often contains the following information:

- Name of the site
- Links to other main areas of the site
- A link to the **site map**, an index of all the main pages in the site that you may use to jump straight to a page without drilling down
- The author or creator of the site
- Copyright date, or the date when the site was last updated

In this exercise, you will visit a Web site and look at different ways to find information on it, including drilling down.

TechSavvy

Home Button The **Home** button on the **command** bar takes you to your browser's home page, not the Web site's home page!

Step-by-Step

1. With your teacher's permission, **start Internet Explorer**.
2. In the **Address** bar, key www.loc.gov.
3. Press ENTER. The Library of Congress home page displays (Figure 1.4).
4. Click the **Visitors** link. A new page appears. **Note**: If you do not see this exact link, click a link about visiting the library.

Figure 1.4 This is the home page for the Library of Congress Web site.

5 Click the drop-down arrow to the right of the slide thumbnails in the **Transition to This Slide** group. Scroll down to the **Random** category and choose **Random Bars Vertical** (Figure 3.19).

6 Click the space after the last slide. On the **Home** tab, in the **Slides** group, click the **New Slide** button.

7 On the **View** tab, in the **Presentation Views** group, click the **Normal** button.

8 Title the new slide Final Thoughts.

9 Key a conclusion that summarizes the main points of your presentation.

10 Click the **Slide Show** button to preview your work and correct errors.

11 Click the **Speaker Notes** area on the bottom of each slide to add notes from your research (Figure 3.20).

12 **Save** your work. With your teacher's permission, print your slides as a handout.

Figure 3.19 Your slide show will use the Random Bars Vertical transition.

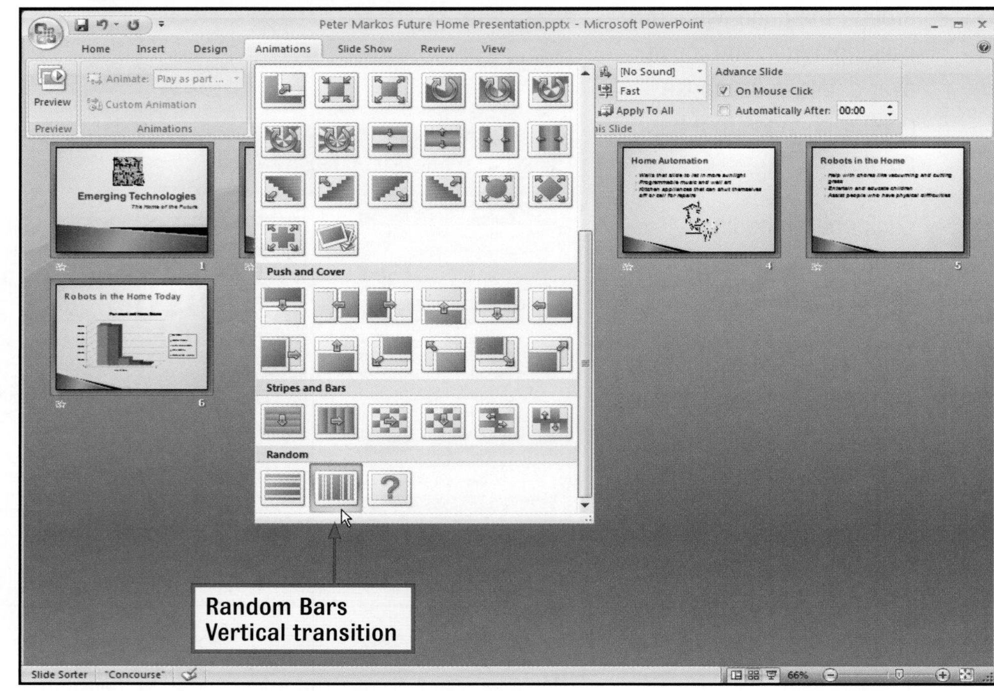

Figure 3.20 You can use speaker notes to add extra information for your presentation.

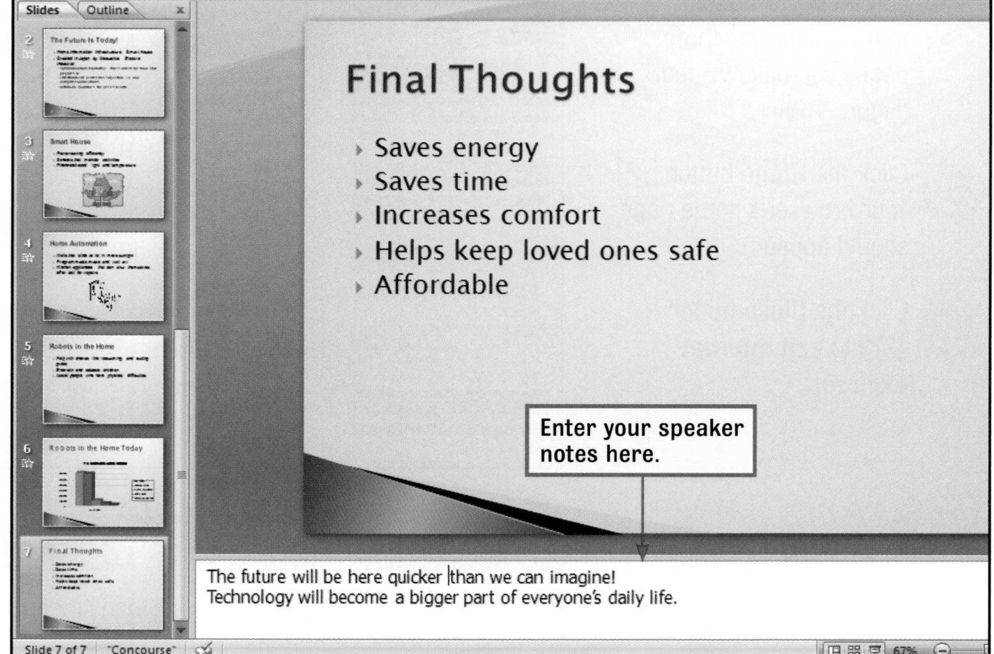

3 Move your mouse pointer around the page, without clicking. When you move over a link, your mouse pointer changes to a hand pointer.

4 Click one of the links. Another Web page now opens (Figure 1.2).

5 Click the **Back** button. This takes you back to the page where you just were (your browser's home page).

6 Click the **Forward** button. This takes you to the second page you visited.

7 Click another link to open a third Web page.

8 Practice using the **Back** and **Forward** buttons to move among the three pages you have visited. (Figure 1.3).

9 Click the **Home** button. Your browser's home page should appear.

10 Click the **Close** button to **exit Internet Explorer**.

Figure 1.2 The mouse pointer changes to a hand when moved over a link.

Figure 1.3 Use the Back, Forward, or Home button to move between pages.

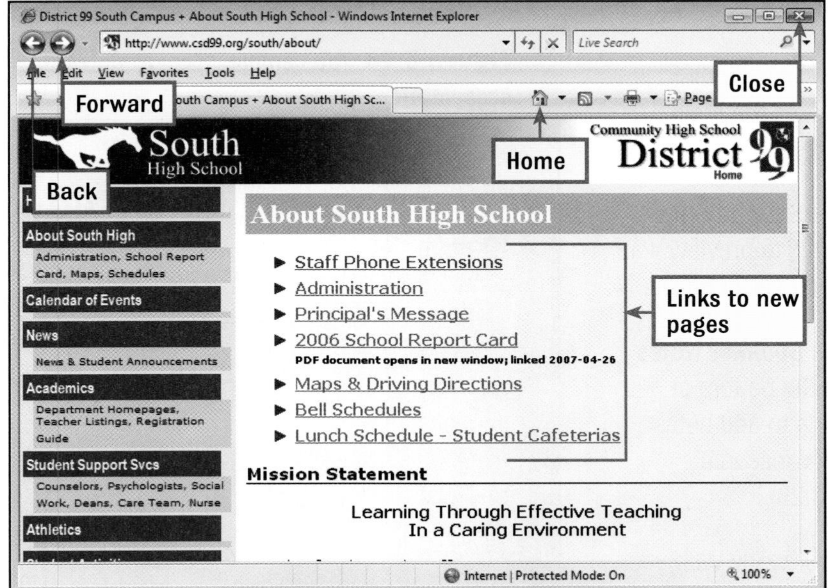

TechSavvy

Refresh Button If your Web page loads incorrectly or seems to stop loading, click the **Refresh** button. In some browsers, the **Refresh** button may be called the **Reload** button, but both buttons do the same thing.

Project 3 Assessment

Key Concepts Check

1. **Define** How does Word's Outline view organize your text?
2. **Identify** What level heading in an outline will start a new slide in PowerPoint?
3. **Discuss** How can Slide Sorter view help you adjust your slide show?

Critical Thinking

4. **Analyze** Why might it be a good idea to create a presentation from a Word outline rather than write it directly onto slides?
5. **Draw Conclusions** How might using the wrong sound effects have a negative impact on your presentation?

1 Guided Practice

Add to Your Presentation You will use the outline you created in Exercise 3-2, add new headings, and then import them into PowerPoint to add slides to your Future Home presentation. If you need help completing a step, refer back to the exercise written in parentheses at the end of the step.

Step-by-Step

1. **Open** your **Future Home outline** in Word. Key the following as a new **Level 1 heading**: Independent Living for Seniors (Figure 3.21). (Exercise 3-2)

2. Key the following as a **Level 2 heading**: Sensors that detect movement. (Exercise 3-2)

3. Key the following as a second **Level 2 heading**: Voice-controlled appliances. **Save** and **Close** your outline. (Exercise 3-2)

▼ **Figure 3.21** Enter new text into your outline.

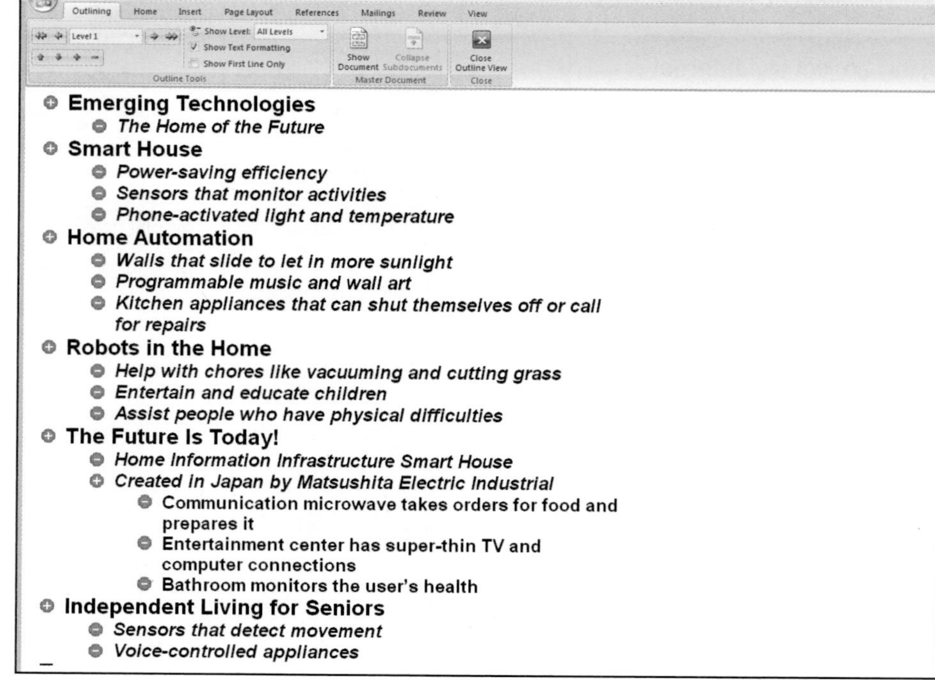

Exercise 1-1 Get to Know Internet Explorer

To find information on the Internet, you will use software called a Web browser. One popular browser is Microsoft Windows Internet Explorer. It can be used with both Microsoft Windows and Macintosh computers.

The first Web page you see when your browser opens is called your **home page**. The home page for your browser usually allows you to do one or more of the following:

- See information you might need every time you use the Internet, such as your school's Web site, research and study tools, news, sports, weather, and so on.
- Use links to other useful sites on the Web
- Search for other helpful Web pages

In this exercise, you will launch your Web browser, view your browser's home page, and navigate between Web pages. **Note**: As you go through the exercises, you may notice differences between your screen and the figures in the steps. This is because information on the Internet is constantly being updated or changed.

Step-by-Step

1. Follow your teacher's instructions to launch the home page of your Web browser. The exercises in this project use **Internet Explorer**.

2. On your screen, identify the parts of a Web browser, as shown in Figure 1.1. **Note**: Your screen may look different from Figure 1.1, but the parts of the Web browser should be the same.

Figure 1.1 You may decide to use the home page of your school's Web site as the home page of your browser.

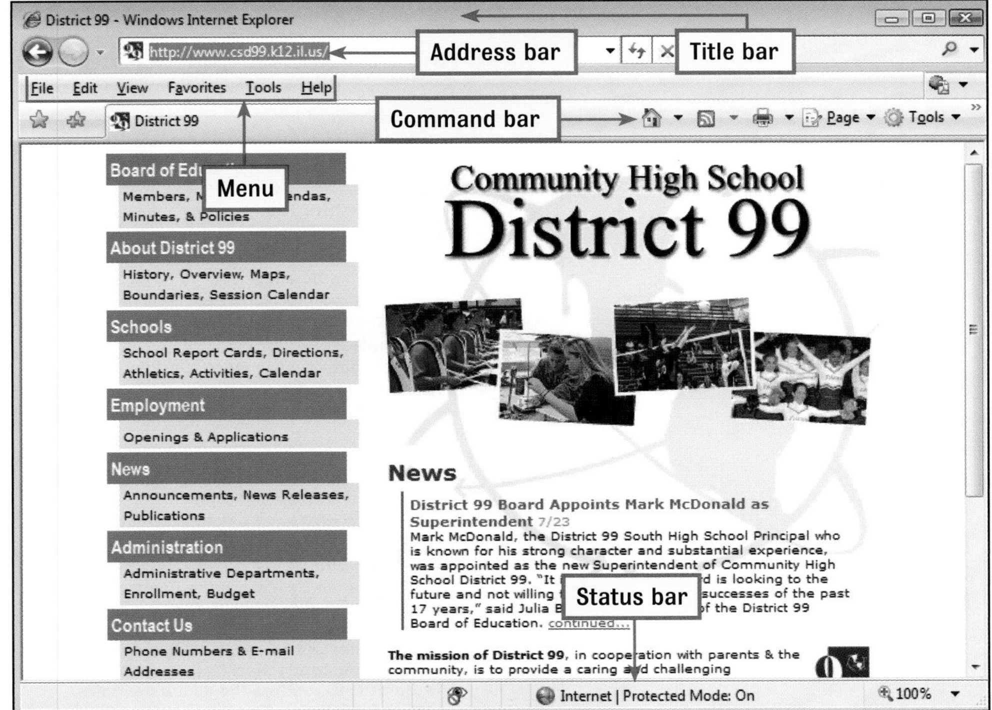

Project 3 Assessment

4. **Open** a new, blank presentation in PowerPoint. Save it as *Your Name* Future Home 2.
5. Create slides from your Word outline. (Exercise 3-3)
6. **Lay out** your first slide as a **title slide**. (Exercise 3-3)
7. Add a new slide after the title slide. Write a brief introduction to your presentation.
8. Add a new **design** to your slides (Figure 3.22). (Exercise 3-3)
9. Add **clip art** to the **title slide** and at least two other slides (Figure 3.23). (Exercise 3-5)
10. Use the **Slide Master** to add animation to your presentation. (Exercise 3-6)
11. Add **sound** to at least two slides. (Exercise 3-6)
12. Add **transitions** to your presentation. (Exercise 3-7)
13. Preview your presentation as a **slide show**. Make any changes, and **save** the document.

▼ **Figure 3.22** Insert a new slide and choose a design.

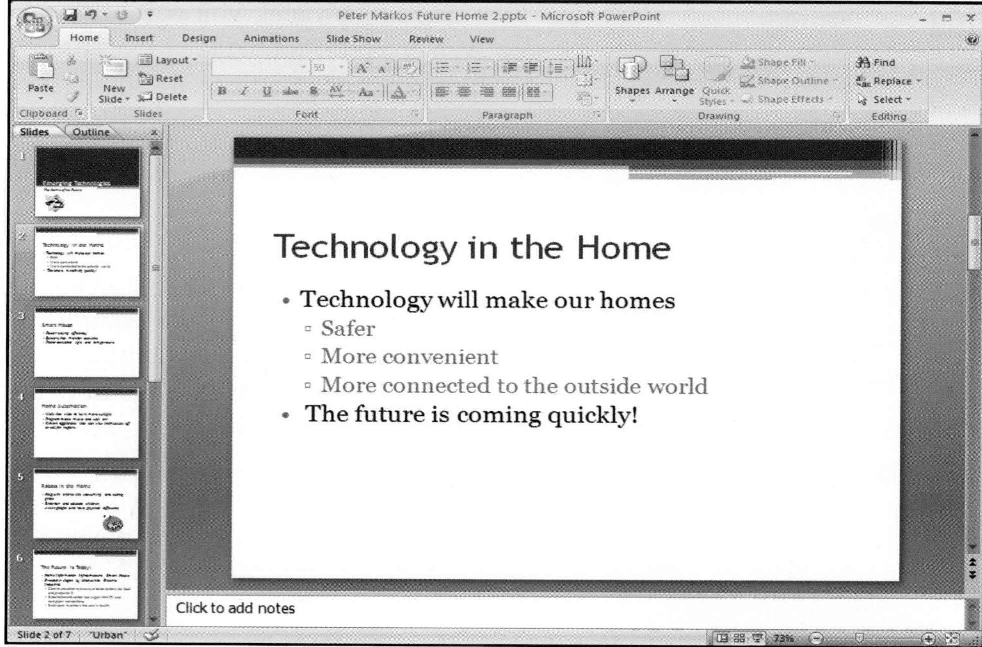

▼ **Figure 3.23** Add clip art, animation, and sound to your presentation.

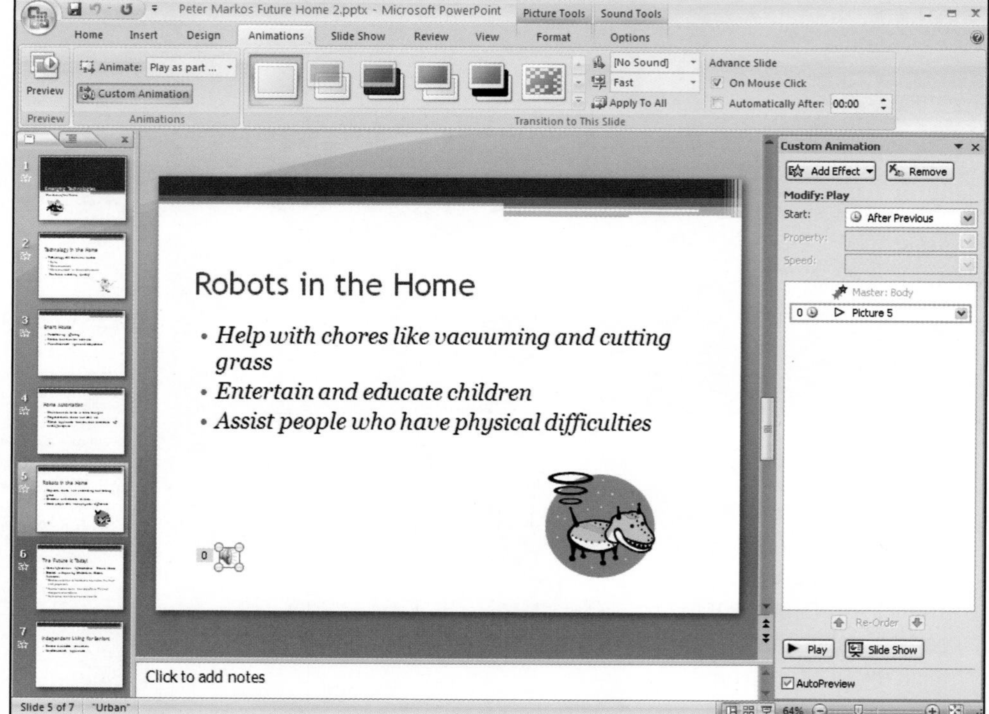

Concepts in Action

Project 1 Use the Internet Safely

Key Concepts

Exercise 1-1

- Open a Web browser
- Navigate a Web site

Exercise 1-2

- Enter a URL to visit a Web site
- Drill down in a Web site
- Perform a search

Exercise 1-3

- View your History list
- Add items to your Favorites list
- Use your Favorites and History lists

Exercise 1-4

- Use Print Preview
- Print a Web page

Vocabulary

Key Terms
home page
drill down
site map
bookmark
Favorites
History
Print Preview

Before You Begin

Expect Change Look at each of the Web pages shown in this project. Predict which pages or parts of pages that you think might change often.

For this project, you will explore, or "surf," the Internet using a Web browser. You will learn how to use Microsoft Windows Internet Explorer and practice safe surfing skills.

Surf's Up!

If you were really going surfing, you would be sure to have the right equipment, use proper techniques, and surf safely. When you surf the Internet, the right equipment (a computer, a Web browser, and Internet access) is essential.

The Web contains billions of pages of information. Some of the pages contain helpful information, some are entertaining, some let you purchase products, and others are inappropriate or even dangerous. This project will help you develop safe surfing skills that will help you find the information you need and determine whether it is accurate and reliable.

Project 3 Assessment

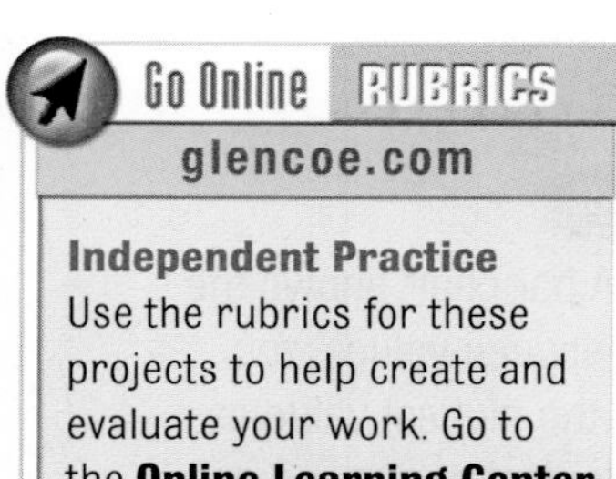

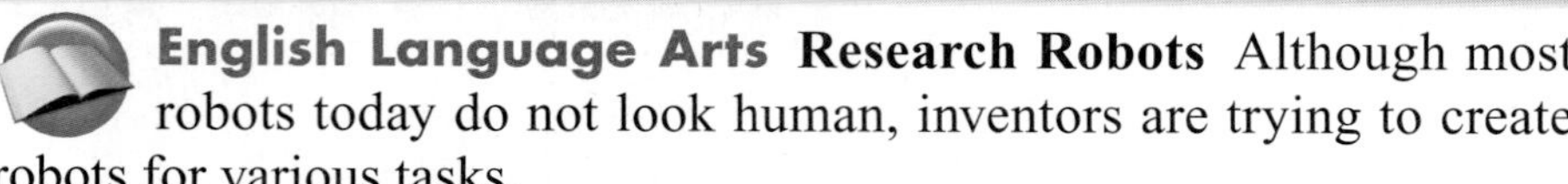

2 Independent Practice ★

English Language Arts Research Robots Although most robots today do not look human, inventors are trying to create robots for various tasks.

a. Research With your teacher's permission, use the Internet to find information about robots that are being used or developed today.

b. Create Use your research to make a slide show about one type of robot.

- Use Word's Outline View to write the content for your slides, then import the outline into a PowerPoint presentation.
- Add a design to your slides.

3 Independent Practice ★★

English Language Arts Enhance Your Robot Presentation Complete Independent Practice 2 above. Add the following features to your presentation.

a. Create Add images, sound effects, animation, and transitions to your slides.

b. Present View your presentation as a slide show.

- Edit your text or rearrange the slides.
- Add speaker notes.

4 Independent Practice ★★★

English Language Arts Present the Classroom of the Future New technology is changing the way we learn. Create a presentation about the classroom of the future.

a. Research With your teacher's permission, use the Internet to find information about how technology has affected our schools, textbooks, and educational options (including online education).

b. Create Use your research to create a PowerPoint presentation that includes images, sounds, animation, and transitions.

- Use Word's Outline View to create the content for your slides.
- Add an Excel chart to one slide, showing how online education is growing.

After You Read

Key Concepts Check

1. **Identify** What are three devices that can be used to connect to the Internet?
2. **Describe** What path might an e-mail take as it travels from one computer to another?
3. **Explain** List two steps you can take to receive less spam.

Critical Thinking

4. **Compare and Contrast** When you want to write to someone, you can use your computer to send an e-mail, or you can send a letter through the mail. What are two similarities and two differences in these methods?

21st Century Skills

5. **Ethics** Go to glencoe.com to this book's Online Learning Center to find **Web Links** for "netiquette." Write down ten rules of netiquette. List the Web addresses (URLs) where you found them.

Academic Skills

Mathematics

Internet usage increases every year, especially among teenagers.

a. **Identify** In which year did users spend the most time on the Internet?

b. **Calculate** What is the usage in hours spent on the Internet between 2007 and 2008?

Math Concept

Bar Chart A bar chart shows the difference between values. You can identify the highest value as well as the lowest one based on the size of the bars.

Starting Hint Find the years on the x-axis. Find the values on the y-axis. Then subtract to find the difference.

NCTM Number and Operations Compute fluently and make reasonable estimates.

Average Internet Usage (Projections)

Hours online: 205, 200, 195, 190, 185, 180

2005, 2006, 2007, 2008, 2009

Source: U.S. Census Bureau, Statistical Abstract of the United States, 2007.

Go Online e-QUIZ

glencoe.com

Self-Check Assess your understanding of what you have just read. Go to the **Online Learning Center** at glencoe.com. Choose **e-Quizzes**, and take the **Unit 3 Tech Talk Quiz**.

UNIT 8

Projects Across the Curriculum

Use your Internet, Word, Excel, and PowerPoint skills to complete the following projects. Ask your teacher about saving or printing your work.

Project 1 Create a Virtual Reality Ad ★

Go Online RUBRICS

glencoe.com

Unit Projects Use the rubrics for these projects to help create and evaluate your work. Go to the **Online Learning Center** at glencoe.com. Choose **Rubrics**, then **Unit 8**.

English Language Arts Virtual reality (VR) is often used in video games and training software. Equipment such as helmets, goggles, or joysticks can let you view and interact with VR. Research and create an advertisement about an example of virtual reality that is in use now or is being developed.

Research

1. With your teacher's permission, use the Internet to choose one example of VR that interests you.
2. Find at least two Web sites that provide relevant and useful information and images. Print or save the Web pages.

Create

3. Design and write an advertisement for the technology that could appear in a magazine. Include:
   - A text box to create an ad that is 5″ by 7″
   - A product name created in WordArt
   - A bulleted list describing the product
   - Clip art or other appropriate images

Project 2 Create a Computer-Use Newsletter ★★

Math How do people in your school use computers? Create a survey and evaluate your data in a spreadsheet. Then share your results in a newsletter.

Plan

1. Use Word to create a computer-use survey. At the top of the survey, key *For which of the following things do you use a computer?* Below this, create a checklist of the following tasks: *entertainment, Internet research, e-mail, instant messaging, word processing, creating spreadsheets, making presentations, creating databases, other.*

Continued on page 418

Caution! Online chat rooms are popular places where people can exchange messages about common interests. Sometimes, adults use these sites and pretend to be teenagers. Make sure you never give out personal information in a chat room. The person you are writing to may not be who he or she seems!

Why It's Important How can you protect your personal information when participating in online chat rooms?

How Safe Is the Internet?

There is a lot of personal information about you, and everyone else, on the Internet. Much of this information is meant to be private and confidential, such as school and hospital records and credit card information.

Companies and other organizations protect this information in a number of ways. Important information is usually kept on **secure**, or safe and protected, computers that people cannot use without permission. A **firewall** is hardware or software that protects a computer or network from intruders.

Protect Your Privacy Online

You may believe that no one knows who you are on the Internet, but that is not always true. You need to be careful about sharing too much personal information. People can sometimes use personal information in illegal, and even dangerous, ways.

Remember that you can protect yourself and your identity while surfing the Internet by using common sense.

- Never give out personal information unless there is a parent or guardian with you at the computer.
- If you decide to give out personal information (your name, phone number, age, and so on), make sure you know to whom you are giving it and that the information will be secure.
- Never give out your Social Security number.
- Use different user names and passwords for different sites.

Restricting Internet Use

There are times when using the Internet is not appropriate. Some companies do not want their employees to visit sites on the Web that are not related to work. Parents also want to be aware of what their children are viewing and to protect them from unsafe sites. Blocking or filtering software prevents a user from viewing certain kinds of sites. Such software can **monitor**, or record, what sites a user has visited.

Reading Check

1. **Identify** How can you tell whether a Web site is trustworthy?
2. **Describe** What are three ways to protect your identity while online?

2. With the help of your teacher, give the survey to 20 people at your school. If possible, include other teachers and administrators in your survey.

Create

3. Use Excel to create a worksheet showing the results of your survey. Label the rows and columns, and add a title. Total the results for each category. Convert your category totals into percentages of your total survey results.
4. Make a pie chart showing the percentage results for each type of computer use.
5. In Word, create a two-column newsletter. Insert the pie chart from above, and summarize your survey results in an article. Add a WordArt title.

> **Go Online e-REVIEW**
> glencoe.com
>
> **Assessment** Double-check your knowledge of Microsoft applications. Go to the **Online Learning Center** at **glencoe.com**. Choose **e-Review Quizzes**, and take the **Unit 8 Tech Assess Quiz**.

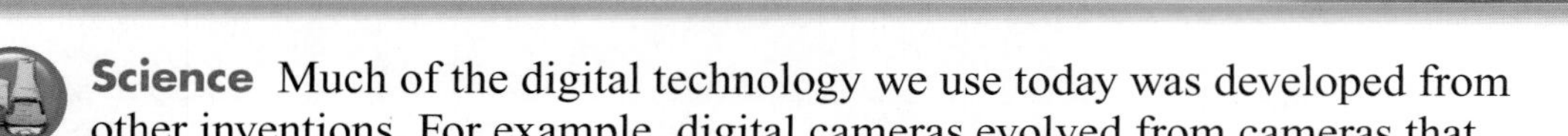

Project 3 Create a Technology Presentation ★★★

Science Much of the digital technology we use today was developed from other inventions. For example, digital cameras evolved from cameras that use film.

Research

1. Use the Internet to learn about the invention of the camera, radio, telephone, or another technology. Trace the development of the technology up to the present.
2. Use Excel to create a worksheet with data that shows the growth of your chosen technology. For example, you might compare the number of standard telephones to cell phones in use over the past 20 years. Convert the data into a chart.

Create

3. Use the Outline View in Word to create an outline for your presentation. Then import the outline into PowerPoint. Explain how the technology was first created, and show how it has developed over the years.
   - Use images, animation, sound effects, and transitions in your slides.
   - Import the Excel chart into your presentation.

Jargon A *blog* (short for Web log) is like an online diary. It is a Web page on which a person can share his or her thoughts with others publicly. Remember that a blog is just one person's opinions and should not be taken as fact.

Why It's Important What topics would you write about for your own blog? Keep in mind that anyone—including friends and family—could read it.

Be Safe on the Internet!

Have you heard the expression "Don't believe everything you read"? This is especially true on the Web. The wonderful thing about the Web is that anyone with basic skills can publish his or her own Web site. This openness, however, also can lead to misuse of the Web. You need to **evaluate**, or assess the value of, Web sites with a critical eye to make sure that the information is accurate and reliable.

Can I Trust the Information on the Web?

The Internet is now the first place where people go when they need to do research. Sometimes, though, so much information is available that it is hard to tell which Web sites you can trust. Here are a few questions to ask in order to evaluate the information you find on a Web site.

What Makes a Good Web Site?

Information Should Be...	Questions to Ask	What to Look For
Relevant	Does the information relate to your topic?	Use precise keywords in a search engine. Check each site to make sure it contains information about your topic.
Reliable	Can the author or publisher of the site be trusted?	Search for the name of the site's creator. Check for negative news stories or reviews that suggest the author should not be trusted.
	Is the owner of the site biased?	Is the site selling products or services? The information may be reliable, but it may not tell both sides of the story.
	Can you contact the author or owner of the site?	There should be a way for you to contact the author or owner of the site. Look for links to Contact Us or About Us.
Recent	Is the information up-to-date?	Look for an update or copyright date at the bottom of the page. If the date is recent, then the information is more likely to be accurate.
Verifiable	Do other sources give you the same information?	Check other sources (both print and Web) to see whether their information is similar.

▲ Always evaluate a site before you use information from it. Why is it important to know who creates or sponsors a site?

UNIT 8

Build Your Portfolio

The Future Is Getting Smaller

The trend in technology to make devices smaller and faster has led to many changes in the way we use technology. Create a presentation about how we use small digital devices today and how you think this technology will develop in the future.

Research

1. With your teacher's permission, use the World Wide Web to find information and images for the latest developments in compact technology. Choose one type of technology, such as cell phones, personal computers, tracking devices, or nanotechnology.
2. Find data for a worksheet about your technology. The data might show the growing use of this technology or compare it to other types of technology.

> **Go Online** RUBRICS
> glencoe.com
>
> **Build Your Portfolio** Use the rubric for this portfolio project to help create and evaluate your work. Go to the **Online Learning Center** at **glencoe.com**. Choose **Rubrics**, then **Unit 8**.

Prepare

3. Create a Word outline that you can use as the basis for your presentation. Your outline should have at least five Level 1 headings. Your final Level 1 heading should introduce your citations.
4. Create a worksheet in Excel from the data you researched. Use the worksheet to create a chart, making sure it supports the information in your presentation.

Create

5. Create a presentation in PowerPoint by importing your Word outline.
   a. Add a design to the slides.
   b. Add your Excel chart to the correct slide and insert appropriate images on at least three other slides.
   c. Add animation, transitions, and sound to your slides.
   d. Edit and add any extra information or slides to your presentation.

Go Online ACTIVITY
glencoe.com

Netiquette To learn rules of netiquette, visit glencoe.com. Choose **Tech Talk Activities**, then **Unit 3**.

How Can I Use E-mail Successfully?

A thoughtful computer user pays attention to netiquette. **Netiquette** refers to the good manners one uses in electronic communications. When you write an e-mail message, remember that the person who will read it cannot hear your voice or see your face. So it is important to write your e-mail messages in a way that will prevent people from misunderstanding you.

It is also important to keep your e-mail messages organized. It does not take long for an in-box to fill up with e-mail. To reduce the clutter, delete old e-mail messages or save the ones you want to your hard drive or a removable storage device. You can also send instant messages using chat software or send text messages and photos from some phones.

Academic Focus
English Language Arts

Say What You Mean
Before you send an e-mail message, read your message once carefully. Make sure that every word is spelled correctly and that your meaning is clear. Unclear messages may confuse or even offend the reader. If you are not sure that your message communicates what you want it to say, ask someone else for feedback on your draft before you send it. How do well developed e-mail communications reflect on you personally?

NCTE 12 Use language to accomplish individual purposes.

Spam

Spam is like junk mail. It is sent in bulk to many people's e-mail accounts. Spam is almost always sent for one reason: to sell you something. Sometimes, spam crosses into illegal or unethical areas. It may try to trick you into buying something that does not even exist. You cannot stop people from sending spam, but you can take steps to avoid receiving it. Never open an e-mail message from someone that you do not know or from an unfamiliar e-mail address.

Avoid Spam

Use Technology	Use Common Sense
• Your ISP can put a "spam filter" on your account, which will stop suspicious e-mails. • Some e-mail software programs have their own spam filters. Learn how to use them. • You can set up your e-mail program to accept e-mail from only certain addresses.	• Do not post your e-mail address on a public site, such as a chatroom. Spammers search the Web for e-mail addresses. • Report instances of spam to your Internet service provider. This will help your ISP crack down on people who send spam.

▲ Spam is a nuisance, but there are ways to avoid it. Why is it important to report spam to your Internet service provider?

Reading Check

1. **Identify** What are three devices that can be used to send e-mail?
2. **Explore** Imagine that a friend receives an e-mail message from a stranger who is selling vitamins through the mail. Your friend is interested in trying them. What would you tell your friend?

Keyboarding Skills

In order to use application software like Microsoft Office successfully, it is helpful to have good keyboarding skills. If you can key text quickly and accurately, you will be more likely to complete assignments quickly.

Proper Techniques

The following Lessons allow you to learn proper keyboarding techniques for the main letters, numbers, and symbols on your keyboard. Before you begin, refer to the figures to make sure your fingers are in the correct position on the keyboard. Look at your book and key the text indicated. Check your screen to make sure you have keyed the text correctly. Try not to look at the keyboard as you key text. For information about ergonomics (how to sit properly while you keyboard), refer to Unit 1, Project 1, pages 12–13.

Go Online ACTIVITY
glencoe.com

Viruses Computer viruses are often spread by e-mail. To learn how to keep your computer from getting "sick" with a virus, visit the **Online Learning Center** at glencoe.com. Choose **Tech Talk Activities**, then **Unit 3**.

Tech Tip E-mail is not the only way to send a fast message to someone. Instant messages also can be sent using chat software on your computer, and you can send text messages and photos from cell phones and PDAs.

Why It's Important Think about a situation in which sending an instant message to a friend would be more effective than sending an e-mail.

How Does E-mail Travel Over the Internet?

Every day, billions of e-mails travel over the Internet. They travel through lots of different networks to arrive at the correct location. It all works because each person has a unique e-mail address and each network has a unique domain name.

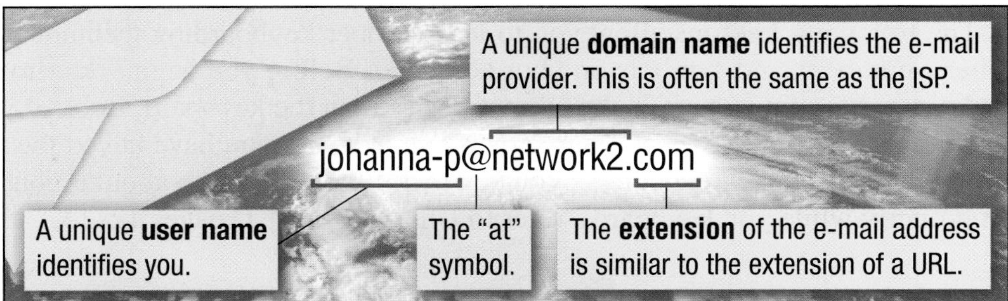

▲ Just as a Web address does, an e-mail address contains an extension (such as .com, .gov, .org) that can help you identify the sender of the e-mail. What would the extension ".edu" tell you about the sender of an e-mail?

When you send an e-mail to a friend, the message might travel through several points before arriving at your friend's computer. The whole process usually takes only a few seconds. Each e-mail message is sent to the correct network that matches the domain name in the e-mail address. Once it arrives at the destination network, it is sorted into the person's mailbox that matches the user name.

Sometimes you do not need the Internet in order to send an e-mail. In an office, for example, one worker can send an e-mail to another without going through the Internet. A company may have its own network that handles the flow of e-mails among its employees.

▲ As an e-mail travels from one computer to another over the Internet, it may pass through several different networks. How do e-mail providers make sure that e-mails get delivered to the proper people?

Lesson 1 New Keys: A S D F J K L ; Space Bar Enter

OBJECTIVE:

- **Learn the home keys, the space bar, and the enter key.**

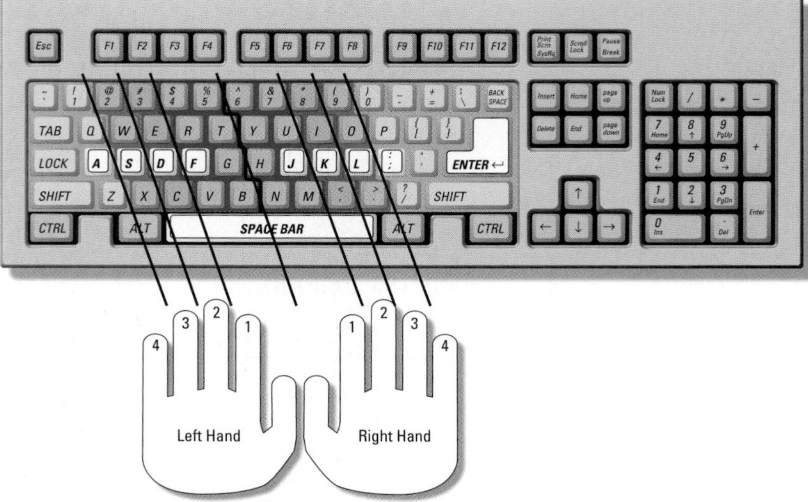

NEW KEYS

A. Home-Key Position

The `A S D F J K L ;` keys are called the home keys. Each finger controls a specific key and is named for its home key: `A` finger, `S` finger, `D` finger, and so on, ending with the Sem finger on the ; (semicolon) key.

1. Place the fingers of your left hand on `A S D` and `F`. Use the illustration as a guide.
2. Place the fingers of your right hand on `J K L ;`. Again, use the illustration as a guide.

You will feel a raised marker on the `F` and `J` keys. These markers will help you keep your fingers on the home keys.

3. Curve your fingers.
4. Using the correct fingers, key each letter as you say it to yourself: `a s d f j k l ;`.
5. Remove your fingers from the keyboard and replace them on the home keys.
6. Key each letter again as you say it: `a s d f j k l ;`.

B. Using Anchors

An anchor is a home key that helps you return each finger to its home-key position after reaching for another key. Try to hold the anchors listed, but be sure to hold the first one, which is most important.

C. Space Bar

The space bar, located at the bottom of the keyboard, is used to insert spaces between letters and words, and after punctuation.

Use E-mail To learn how to use e-mail and Microsoft Outlook, see **Appendix B**. **TechSIM Interactive Tutorials** are available that will let you practice writing and sending e-mail. Ask your teacher whether you should complete the Appendix or the TechSIM Interactive Tutorials.

Why It's Important How has e-mail affected the way in which you communicate with others?

E-mail

Electronic mail (e-mail) is another way that you can share information using the Internet. E-mail is a communication sent from one person to another, or to many people, over the Internet.

Many people now prefer e-mail to regular mail or to phone conversations. E-mail is less expensive than either and often more convenient. E-mail travels across town or around the world in just seconds. Other benefits include:

- **Easy to access** You can send and receive messages or images from any location and with different types of devices.
- **Easy to use** It is simple to send and reply to e-mails. You can also easily share an e-mail with friends.
- **Easy to track** E-mail provides a record of your communications. It is easy to find and save a message you sent or received.

Remember that sometimes it is more helpful to communicate with someone by telephone or face to face. E-mail does not allow someone to hear your tone of voice or see your facial expressions. If you have something especially important to say, consider speaking directly to the person.

How Do I Use E-mail?

There are several ways to write, send, and receive e-mail. The method you choose depends on what kind of computer or device you are using, and whether you are using e-mail at home or somewhere else.

Methods for Using E-mail

E-mail Method	How It Works
Software	Software programs such as Microsoft Outlook or Qualcomm Eudora retrieve your e-mails from the Internet and download them to your computer.
The World Wide Web	Hotmail and Yahoo! let you send and receive e-mails through their Web sites. You do not need any software, and you can connect to your e-mail from any computer with an Internet connection.
Handheld devices	Many cell phones and PDAs can send and receive e-mails.
Integrated applications	Some software applications, such as Lotus Notes, let you perform many tasks, including sending and receiving e-mail.

▲ E-mail can be used at home, at school, at work, and even while taking a walk outside. If you were away from home, how could you check your e-mail?

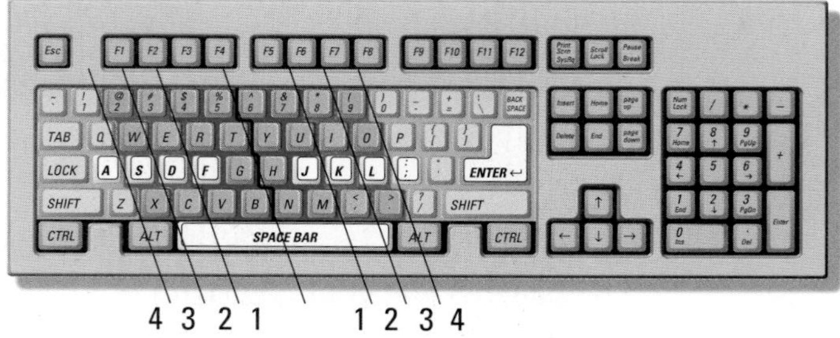

Use the thumb of your writing hand (left or right) to press the space bar.

1. With your fingers on the home keys, key the letters `a s d f`. Then press the space bar once.
2. Key `j k l ;`. Press the space bar once.
3. Key `a s d f`. Press the space bar once; then key `j k l ;`.
4. Repeat Steps 1–3.

D. Enter Key

The ENTER key moves the insertion point to the beginning of a new line. Reach to the ENTER key with the Sem finger. Lightly press the enter key. Return the Sem finger to home position.

Practice using the enter key. Key each line 1 time, pressing the space bar where you see a space and pressing the Enter key at the end of a line.

```
asdf jkl; asdf jkl; asdf jkl;↵
asdf jkl; asdf jkl; asdf jkl;↵
asdf jkl; asdf jkl; asdf jkl;↵
asdf jkl; asdf jkl; asdf jkl;↵
```

E. F J Keys

Key each line 1 time.

Use F and J fingers.

```
1 fff jjj fff jjj fff jjj ff jj ff jj f j↵
2 fff jjj fff jjj fff jjj ff jj ff jj f j↵
```

F. D K Keys

Key each line 1 time.

Use D and K fingers.

```
3 ddd kkk ddd kkk ddd kkk dd kk dd kk d k↵
4 ddd kkk ddd kkk ddd kkk dd kk dd kk d k↵
```

G. S L Keys

Key each line 1 time.

Use S and L fingers.

```
5 sss lll sss lll sss lll ss ll ss ll s l↵
6 sss lll sss lll sss lll ss ll ss ll s l↵
```

H. A ; Keys

Key each line 1 time.

Use A and Sem fingers.

```
7 aaa ;;; aaa ;;; aaa ;;; aa ;; aa ;; a ;↵
8 aaa ;;; aaa ;;; aaa ;;; aa ;; aa ;; a ;↵
```

Go Online ACTIVITY

glencoe.com

The Internet and the Phone Network To learn more about how data travels across the phone network and the Internet, visit **glencoe.com**. Choose **Tech Talk Activities**, then **Unit 3**.

Jargon The speed of data is measured in different units:

- Bits per second (bps)
- Thousands of bits, or kilobits, per second (Kbps)
- Millions of bits, or megabits, per second (Mbps)

The file size and the speed of the network determines how long it takes to send and receive a computer file.

Why It's Important Why is it important that your computer receives large files as quickly as possible?

What Is a Modem?

To connect your computer to the Internet, you need a modem. A modem is a device that lets your computer send data to and receive data from other computers or to a network. Many businesses and schools share a modem over a network. For home users, the three most common types are the telephone modem, DSL modem, and cable modem. Telephone modems provide only low-bandwidth connections. Bandwidth is the rate of data transmission. DSL and cable modems, on the other hand, supply faster high bandwidth (called broadband) connections.

Types of Modems

MODEM	DESCRIPTION
Telephone (or dial-up) modem	A telephone modem connects your computer to the Internet using telephone lines. It is the slowest type of modem, with speeds of up to 56 Kbps.
DSL (Digital Subscriber Line) modem	A DSL modem uses your telephone line to supply a high-speed Internet connection. DSL speeds range from 8 to 24 Mbps, dependent upon the type of connection, service level, and condition of the lines. Unless there are service interruptions, the modem is always connected.
Cable modem	A cable modem uses your cable television lines to supply a high-speed Internet connection. Cable modem service ranges from 384 Kbps to 20 Mbps. As does DSL, the modem always stays connected unless there are service interruptions.

▲ Prices for Internet access can vary a great deal. Why would users pay more for DSL or cable modem service?

What Is a Web Browser?

A **Web browser** is a software program that lets you surf the Web and interact with Web sites. There are several Web browsers to choose from. Some of the more popular are Microsoft Windows Internet Explorer, Netscape, Apple Safari, and Mozilla Firefox. Some Web sites are designed to work with the newest versions of certain browsers. If you are using an older version of a browser to surf the Web, some Web sites might not work as well for you.

Reading Check

1. **Explain** What is the slowest kind of modem?
2. **Describe** What is the purpose of an Internet service provider?

SKILLBUILDING

I. Technique Checkpoint

Technique Checkpoints enable you to practice new keys. They also give you and your teacher a chance to evaluate your keyboarding techniques. Focus on the techniques listed in the margin, such as:

- Use correct fingers.
- Keep eyes on copy.
- Press ENTER without pausing.
- Maintain correct posture.
- Maintain correct arm, hand, and finger position.

Focus on these techniques:
- *Keep eyes on copy.*
- *Keep fingers on home keys.*

Key lines 9 and 10 one time.

```
9  ff jj dd kk ss ll aa ;; f j d k s l a ;↵
10 ff jj dd kk ss ll aa ;; f j d k s l a ;↵
```

J. PRETEST

Key lines 11–12 for 1 minute. Repeat if time permits. Keep your eyes on the copy.

Hold anchor keys.

```
11 sad sad fad fad ask ask lad lad dad dad↵
12 as; as; fall fall alas alas flask flask↵
```

K. PRACTICE

Key lines 13–14 one time. Repeat if time permits.

Leave a blank line after each set of lines (13–14, 15–16, and so on) by pressing ENTER 2 times.

```
13 aaa ddd sad sad aaa sss lll lll all all↵
14 aaa ddd sad sad aaa sss lll lll all all↵↵

15 aaa sss kkk ask ask fff aaa ddd fad fad↵
16 aaa sss kkk ask ask fff aaa ddd fad fad↵↵

17 aaa ddd ddd add add lll aaa ddd lad lad↵
18 aaa ddd ddd add add lll aaa ddd lad lad↵↵

19 aaa sss ;;; as; as; ddd aaa ddd dad dad↵
20 aaa sss ;;; as; as; ddd aaa ddd dad dad↵

21 f fl fla flas flask; l la las lass lass↵
22 f fl fla flas flask; l la las lass lass↵↵

23 f fa fal fall falls; a al ala alas alas↵
24 f fa fal fall falls; a al ala alas alas↵↵
```

L. POSTTEST

Key lines 11–12 for 1 minute. Repeat if time permits. Keep your eyes on the copy. Compare your Posttest results with your Pretest results.

M. End-of-Class Procedure

To keep hardware in good working order, treat it carefully. Your teacher will tell you what should be done at the end of each class period.

Jargon *Protocol* refers to the rules of correct conduct or behavior. *Internet protocol* refers to the technical rules that all computer networks must obey in order to connect successfully to the Internet.

Why It's Important How is protocol, or rules of correct conduct or behavior, important to you?

Getting Connected

You need four things to connect to the Internet from your home or school: a computer, an Internet service provider (ISP), a modem, and communications software. Communications software includes Web browser software, e-mail software, and software that allows your computer to connect to another computer or network.

The number of devices you can use to connect to the Internet keeps growing as the Internet becomes a more important part of people's lives. People can connect to the Internet using:

- Desktop and laptop computers
- Cell phones
- Personal Digital Assistants (PDAs)
- Video game systems

What Is an Internet Service Provider?

An **Internet service provider (ISP)** is a company that sells you access to the Internet, usually for a monthly fee. An ISP gives you your own special user name and password so that you can connect to the Internet securely. ISPs also have a responsibility to provide good service to customers.

Responsibilities of an Internet Service Provider

Responsibility	Why It Matters
Maintain equipment	To offer connections to thousands—even millions—of customers, an ISP has to make sure that its equipment works well.
Provide customer service	If you have a question about your service or you are having trouble connecting to the Internet, your ISP will help you.
Protect the network	An ISP must constantly check its network to make sure there are no security problems.

▲ Customers pay ISPs for Internet access, so the ISPs should provide good service. What might happen if an ISP's equipment breaks down?

Lesson 2 New Keys: H E O

OBJECTIVE:
- Learn the H, E, and O keys.

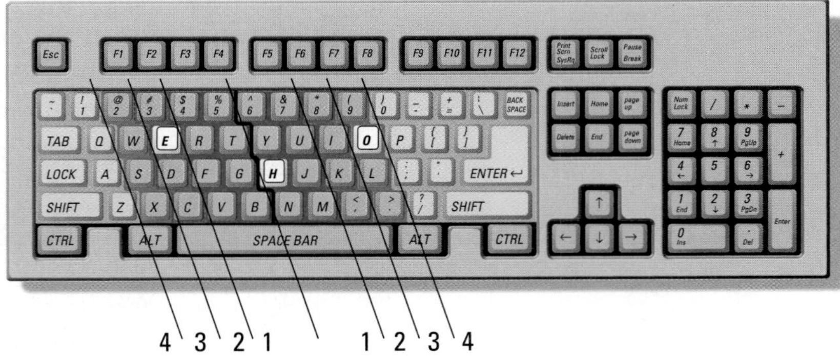

A. Warmup

Key each line 2 times. Leave 1 blank line after each set of lines.

Hold anchor keys
For H anchor ; L K
For E anchor A
For O anchor J or ;

1 ff jj dd kk ss ll aa ;; f j d k s l a ;
2 adds adds fads fads asks asks lads lads

NEW KEYS

B. H Key

Key each line 2 times. Repeat if time permits.

Use J finger.
For H anchor ; L K.

3 jjj jhj jhj hjh jhj jjj jhj jhj hjh jhj
4 jhj ash ash jhj has has jhj had had jhj
5 jhj a lass has; adds a half; a lad had;
6 has a slash; half a sash dad shall dash

C. E Key

Key each line 2 times. Repeat if time permits.

Use D finger.
For D anchor A S.

7 ddd ded ded ede ded ddd ded ded ede ded
8 ded led led ded she she ded he; ded he;
9 ded he led; she fell; he slashes sales;
10 he sees sheds ahead; she sealed a lease

D. O Key

Key each line 2 times. Repeat if time permits.

Use L finger.
For L anchor J K.

11 lll lol lol olo lol lll lol lol olo lol
12 lol odd odd lol hoe hoe lol foe foe lol
13 load sod; hold a foe; old oak hoes; lol
14 she sold odd hooks; he folded old hoses

TECH TALK Going Online

Jargon Web sites from other countries have a two-letter extension identifying the country.

Why It's Important Why is it important for Web sites to be available in different languages?

Extensions

The three-letter extension at the end of a domain name can help you identify the type of Web site you are visiting. For example, schools have a special extension used by educational institutions.

Common URL Extensions

EXTENSION	DESCRIPTION OF SITE	EXAMPLE
.com	Commercial or for-profit business	www.dell.com
.edu	Educational institution	www.harvard.edu
.gov	U.S. government organization	www.usa.gov
.org	Professional or nonprofit organization	www.redcross.org

▲ A URL gives you clues about a Web site's content before you even visit the site. What does the extension ".gov" tell you about a site?

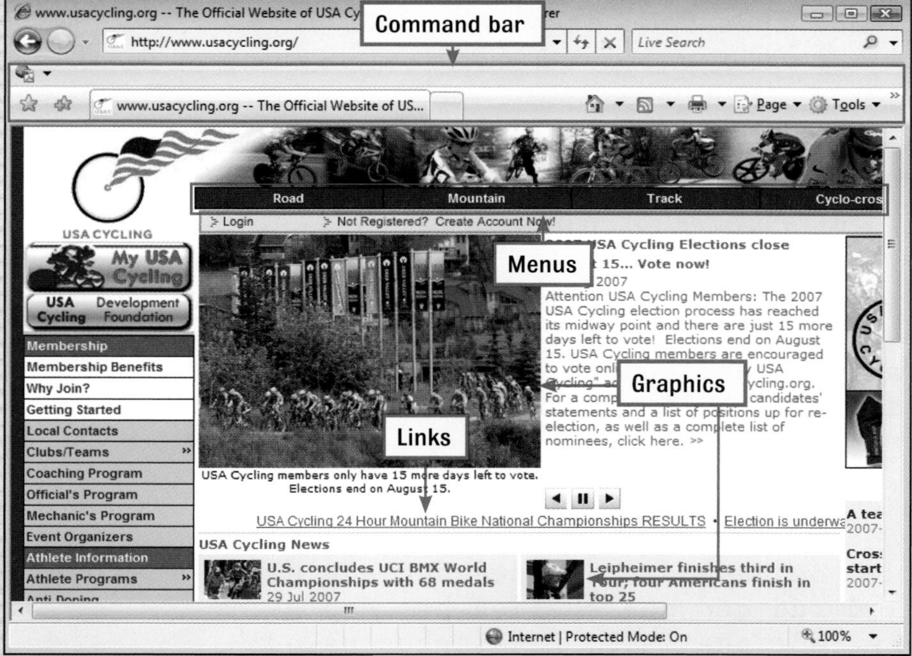

▲ Most Web pages combine words and images. How do graphics make a site more effective?

Parts of a Web Site

A typical Web site contains features that keep users informed and entertained. Many sites have interactive areas where you can enter text, select information, listen to audio, watch video, or play games. Web pages are linked together through hyperlinks, or links, that move you from one online location to another. Links can be graphics or text that is a different color or underlined, as shown to the left. If you move your mouse over a link, the pointer will usually change shape. Click the link to go to a new Web page.

Reading Check

1. **Explain** Why is the Internet frequently compared to a superhighway?
2. **Identify** What are four features that you can find on a Web site?

SKILLBUILDING

E. Technique Checkpoint

Key each line 2 times. Repeat if time permits. Focus on the technique at the left.

Focus on this technique: Press and release each key quickly.

```
15 ddd ded ded ede ded ddd ded ded ede ded
16 lll lol lol olo lol lll lol lol olo lol
17 jjj jhj jhj hjh jhj jjj jhj jhj hjh jhj
18 she has old jokes; he has half a salad;
```

F. PRETEST

Key lines 19–20 for 1 minute. Repeat if time permits. Keep your eyes on the copy.

Hold anchor keys.

```
19 heed jade hoof elf; hash folk head hole
20 seed lake look jell sash hold dead half
```

G. PRACTICE

Key each line 2 times. Repeat if time permits.

When you repeat a line:
- *Speed up as you key the line.*
- *Key it more smoothly.*
- *Leave a blank line after the second line (press ENTER 2 times).*

```
21 heed heed feed feed deed deed seed seed
22 jade jade fade fade fake fake lake lake
23 hoof hoof hood hood hook hook look look
24 elf; elf; self self sell sell jell jell

25 hash hash lash lash dash dash sash sash
26 folk folk fold fold sold sold hold hold
27 head head heal heal deal deal dead dead
28 hole hold hale hale hall hall half half
```

H. POSTTEST

Key lines 19–20 for 1 minute. Repeat if time permits. Keep your eyes on the copy. Compare your Posttest results with your Pretest results.

Going Online

Reading Guide

Before You Read

Same Day Review When you learn something new, look at your notes the same day. If you wait a few days, it will seem much less familiar. A quick review the same day will help you retain the information.

Key Concepts

- How the Internet and the World Wide Web are used
- How computers connect to the Internet
- How e-mail works
- How to stay safe online

Vocabulary

Key Terms

Internet
World Wide Web
Web site
uniform resource locator (URL)
Internet service provider (ISP)
Web browser
electronic mail (e-mail)
netiquette
spam
firewall

Academic Vocabulary

unique
evaluate
secure
monitor

The Internet and the World Wide Web

The **Internet** is a gigantic computer network that connects computers across the world. It has changed the way people communicate, work, and have fun.

The **World Wide Web** (the Web) is only one part of the Internet. It is a way of accessing the huge collection of information, services, and Web sites available through the Internet. Many people think that the Internet and the Web are the same thing, but they are not. If you think of the Internet as a highway, then think of the Web as a car that lets you travel from place to place.

What Is a Web Site?

The World Wide Web is made up of Web sites. A **Web site** is a specific location on the Web that contains a collection of related files and resources by a person, group, or organization. A Web site is made up of individual Web pages, called subpages.

Web Addresses

Just as every home or business has its own address, every Web site has its own address that no other site can use. This address is called a **uniform resource locator (URL)**. If you know the **unique**, or distinctive, address or URL, you can go directly to a Web site. Each Web page also has an address, just as every page in a book has its own page number.

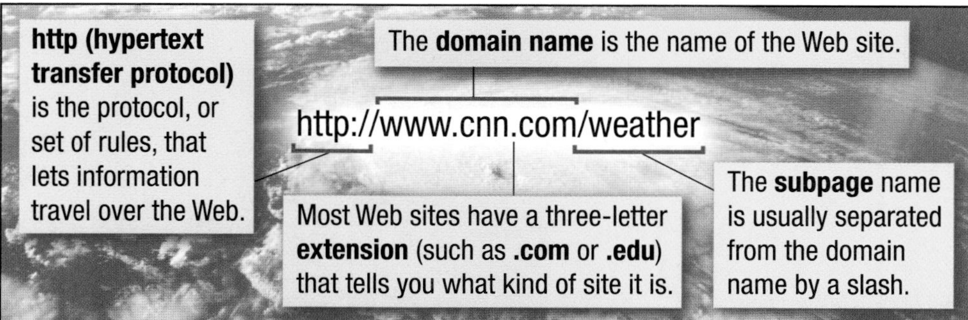

▲ The address of a Web site is also called the URL (uniform resource locator). What is the domain name of this Web site?

Lesson 3 New Keys: M R I

OBJECTIVE:

- Learn the M, R, and I keys.

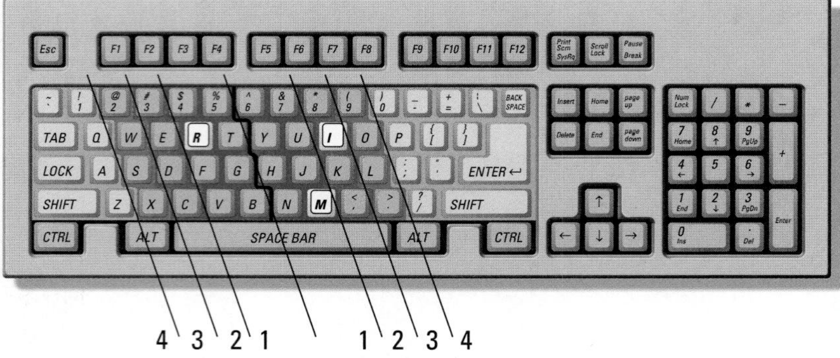

A. Warmup

Key each line 2 times. Leave 1 blank line after each set of lines.

```
1 asdf jkl; heo; asdf jkl; heo; asdf jkl;
2 jade jade fake fake held held lose lose
```

NEW KEYS

B. M Key

Key each line 2 times. Repeat if time permits.

Use J finger.
For M anchor ; L K.

```
3 jjj jmj jmj mjm jmj jjj jmj jmj mjm jmj
4 jmj mom mom jmj mad mad jmj ham ham jmj
5 jmj make a jam; fold a hem; less flame;
6 messes make some moms mad; half a dome;
```

C. R Key

Key each line 2 times. Repeat if time permits.

Use F finger.
For R anchor A S D.

```
7 fff frf frf rfr frf fff frf frf rfr frf
8 frf far far frf for for frf err err frf
9 frf more rooms; for her marks; from me;
10 he reads ahead; more doors are far ajar
```

D. I Key

Key each line 2 times. Repeat if time permits.

Use K finger.
For I anchor ;.

```
11 kkk kik kik iki kik kkk kik kik iki kik
12 kik dim dim kik lid lid kik rim rim kik
13 kik if she did; for his risk; old mill;
14 more mirrors; his middle silo is filled
```

UNIT 3 Using the Internet

Real World Projects

Go Online **e-QUIZ**

glencoe.com

Starting with You Find out why it is important to double-check information you find on the Internet. Go to the **Online Learning Center** at glencoe.com. Choose **e-Quizzes**, and take the **Unit 3 Pre-Quiz**.

SKILLBUILDING

E. Technique Checkpoint

Key each line 2 times. Repeat if time permits. Focus on the techniques at the left.

Focus on these techniques:
- *Fingertips touching home keys.*
- *Wrists up, off keyboard.*

```
15 jjj jmj jmj mjm jmj jjj jmj jmj mjm jmj
16 fff frf frf rfr frf fff frf frf rfr frf
17 kkk kik kik iki kik kkk kik kik iki kik
18 he did; his firm red desk lid is a joke
```

F. PRETEST

Key lines 19–20 for 1 minute. Repeat if time permits. Keep your eyes on the copy.

```
19 joke ride sale same roam aims sire more
20 jars aide dark lame foal elms hire mare
```

G. PRACTICE

Key each line 2 times. Repeat if time permits.

Keep eyes on copy. It will be easier to keep your eyes on the copy if you:
- *Review the charts for key positions and anchors.*
- *Maintain an even pace.*
- *Resist looking up from your copy.*

```
21 joke joke jade jade jams jams jars jars
22 ride ride hide hide side side aide aide
23 sale sale dale dale dare dare dark dark
24 same same fame fame dame dame lame lame

25 roam roam loam loam foam foam foal foal
26 aims aims arms arms alms alms elms elms
27 sire sire dire dire fire fire hire hire
28 more more mire mire mere mere mare mare
```

H. POSTTEST

Key lines 19–20 for 1 minute. Repeat if time permits. Keep your eyes on the copy. Compare your Posttest results with your Pretest results.

UNIT 2

Build Your Portfolio

Create a Photo Album

You want to make it easy for classmates to view all the Mars photos you have collected and organized in this Unit. You decide to create a photo album in Windows.

Research

1. Use Windows Help and Support to learn how to do each of the following tasks. (**Hint**: Use the bold words below as keywords in your search.)
   - Open the **Pictures** folder.
   - Create a **photo album** folder in the Pictures folder.
   - **Print pictures**

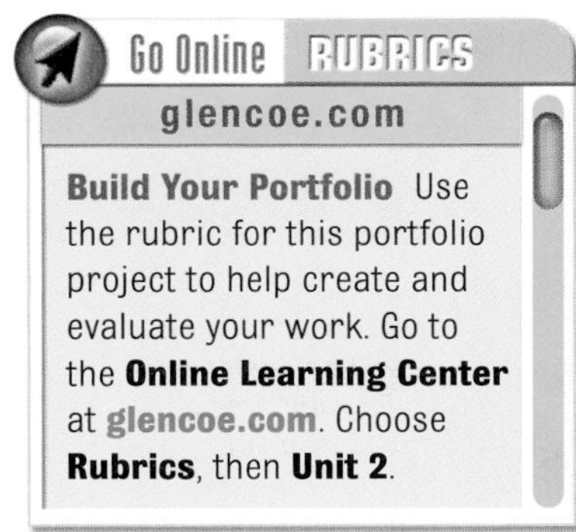

Create

2. Open the Pictures folder.
3. Create a new folder named ***Your Name*** **Mars Album**.
4. Use the Documents folder or search to find the Data File folder named **2A Mars Project**.
   a. In the Data File folder, open the **Mars Pictures** folder.
   b. Copy all the files in the folder.
   c. Close the Documents folder.
5. Paste the Mars picture files into your Mars Album folder.
6. Make the Mars Album folder into a photo album. Follow the Windows Help directions you found in Step 1.
7. View all the photos in the photo album.
8. With your teacher's permission, print all the photos in the photo album.

Lesson 4 New Keys: T N C

OBJECTIVE:

- Learn the T, N, and C keys.

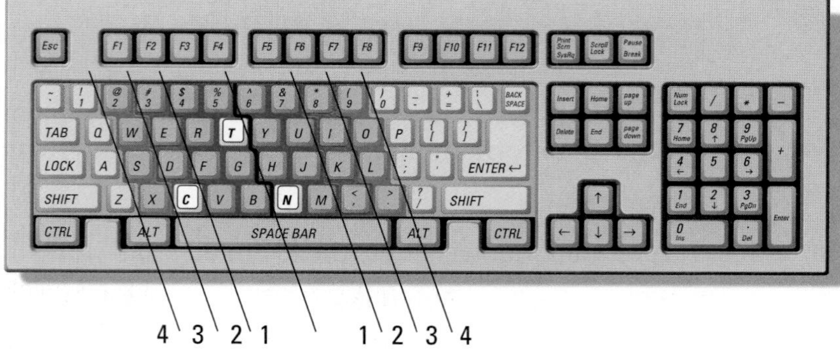

A. Warmup

Key each line 2 times. Leave 1 blank line after each set of lines.

```
1 asdf jkl; heo; mri; asdf jkl; heo; mri;
2 herd herd mild mild safe safe joke joke
```

NEW KEYS

B. T Key

Key each line 2 times. Repeat if time permits.

Use F finger.
Anchor A S D.

```
3 fff ftf ftf tft ftf fff ftf ftf tft ftf
4 ftf kit kit ftf toe toe ftf ate ate ftf
5 ftf it is the; to them; for the; at it;
6 that hat is flat; it ate at least three
```

C. N Key

Key each line 2 times. Repeat if time permits.

Use J finger.
Anchor ; L K.

```
7 jjj jnj jnj njn jnj jjj jnj jnj njn jnj
8 jnj ten ten jnj not not jnj and and jnj
9 jnj nine tones; none inside; on and on;
10 nine kind lines; ten done in an instant
```

UNIT 2

Projects Across the Curriculum

Project 2 Use Help to Explore Windows ★★

English Language Arts You can use Windows Help and Support to search for information about how to use many features of Microsoft Windows.

Research

1. From the following list, choose three tasks you would like to learn how to do:
   - Play music in Windows
   - View photos in Windows
   - Use Windows keyboard shortcuts
   - Add program shortcuts to your desktop
   - Display your computer information
   - Change your screen saver
2. Use Windows Help to search for the information.

Create

3. In your own words, write step-by-step directions describing how to do each task.
4. Exchange your directions with a classmate and see whether you can follow each other's steps. Rewrite your steps if necessary.

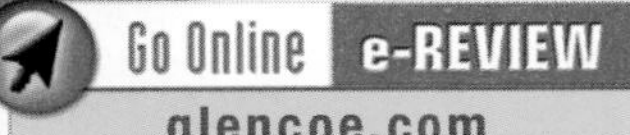

Go Online e-REVIEW

glencoe.com

Assessment Check your knowledge of Windows. Go to the **Online Learning Center** at **glencoe.com**. Choose **e-Review Quizzes,** and take the **Unit 2 Tech Assess Quiz**.

Project 3 Create a Greeting Card ★★★

English Language Arts Use Microsoft Office Word Help to find out how to make a greeting card.

Research

1. Use Windows Office Word Help to find out how to:
   a. Import Clip Art, use WordArt, or use drawing tools to create a design.
   b. Create and print a folded booklet so that when the card is folded in half, the design is on the front and the phrase or poem is on the inside.

Create

2. Write a greeting for the outside of the card and a short phrase for inside.
3. With Word, create the card, using the book fold feature in Page Setup. With your teacher's permission, print your card, using both sides of the same piece of paper if possible.

D. C Key

Key each line 2 times. Repeat if time permits.

Use D finger. Anchor A.

11 ddd dcd dcd cdc dcd ddd dcd dcd cdc dcd
12 dcd ace ace dcd can can dcd arc arc dcd
13 dcd on a deck; in each car; cannot act;
14 act at once; call to cancel the tickets

SKILLBUILDING

E. Technique Checkpoint

Key each line 2 times. Repeat if time permits. Focus on the techniques at the left.

Hold anchor keys. Eyes on copy.

15 fff ftf ftf tft ftf fff ftf ftf tft ftf
16 jjj jnj jnj njn jnj jjj jnj jnj njn jnj
17 ddd dcd dcd cdc dcd ddd dcd dcd cdc dcd
18 the carton of jam is here on this dock;

F. PRETEST

Key lines 19–20 for 1 minute. Repeat if time permits. Keep your eyes on the copy.

19 sail farm jets kick this none care ink;
20 rain hand jots tick then tone came sink

G. PRACTICE

Key each line 2 times. Repeat if time permits.

To increase skill:
- *Keep eyes on copy.*
- *Maintain good posture.*
- *Speed up on the second typing.*

21 sail sail said said raid raid rain rain
22 farm farm harm harm hard hard hand hand
23 jets jets lets lets lots lots jots jots
24 kick kick sick sick lick lick tick tick

25 this this thin thin than than then then
26 none none lone lone done done tone tone
27 care care cake cake cane cane came came
28 ink; ink; link link rink rink sink sink

H. POSTTEST

Key lines 19–20 for 1 minute. Repeat if time permits. Compare your Posttest results with your Pretest results.

UNIT 2

Projects Across the Curriculum

Use pen and paper or computer software to complete the following projects. Ask your teacher about saving or printing your work.

Project 1 Organize Your Computer Components

Science Organize a list of the hardware components and software programs on your computer into a chart that looks similar to the outline of folders and files in a file manager.

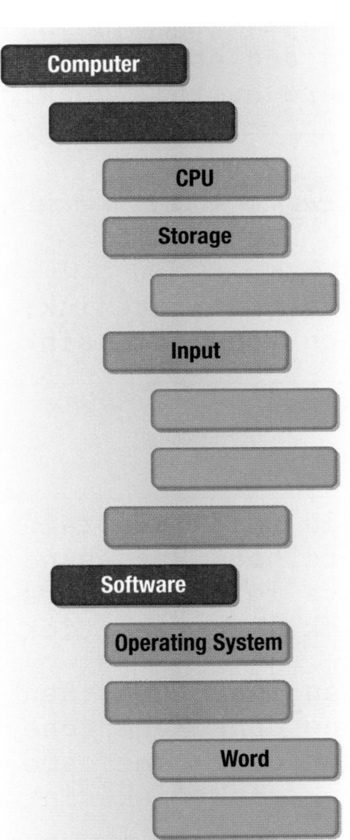

Research

1. On a sheet of paper, write down the hardware components and software programs on your computer. **Hint**: See the Tech Talk on pages 41–50 for help.

Create

2. On a separate sheet of paper, create a chart like the one shown here. Some items are already listed to help you.
    - Add more boxes to your chart where they are necessary.
    - Group similar items together under a single heading.
    - If possible, color code the boxes so that you can tell which items are at the same level.

Revise

3. Check your chart to make sure the components are listed at the correct level. Be sure to check spelling. Make any corrections that are needed.

Continued on page 83

Lesson 5 New Keys: V Right Shift Period (.)

OBJECTIVES:

- Learn the V, right shift, and period keys.
- Learn spacing with the period.
- Figure speed (keying rate in words per minute).

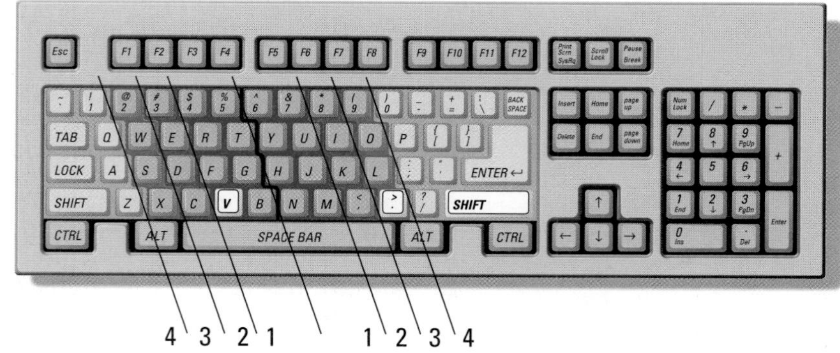

A. Warmup

Key each line 2 times.

```
1 asdf jkl; jh de lo jm fr ki ft jn dc ;;
2 cash free dine jolt milk iron trim star
```

NEW KEYS

B. V Key

Key each line 2 times. Repeat if time permits.

Use F finger.
Anchor A S D.

```
3 fff fvf fvf vfv fvf fff fvf fvf vfv fvf
4 fvf vie vie fvf eve eve fvf via via fvf
5 fvf vie for love; move over; via a van;
6 vote to move; even vitamins have flavor
```

C. Right SHIFT Key

Key each line 2 times. Repeat if time permits.

Use Sem finger.
Anchor J.

```
7 ;;; T;; T;; ;;; C;; C;; ;;; S;; S;; ;;;
8 ;;; Ted Ted ;;; Cal Cal ;;; Sam Sam ;;;
9 ;;; Ed likes Flint; Rick ran; save Tom;
10 Vera loved Florida; Aaron and Sam moved
```

Project 2 Assessment

2 Independent Practice 

Teamwork Compare Search Strategies Use Windows Help to find out how to view your Mars pictures as a slide show.

a. Plan Following your teacher's instruction, form small groups. Each person should choose a different search strategy.

b. Summarize As a group, determine which search method was most effective and why.

- Each team member should write the steps used to conduct his or her search.
- If possible, follow the instructions and create a slide show with the Mars Project Data Files.

3 Independent Practice 

Science Problem Solve You have been asked to create a flowchart in Word to show the steps leading up to the Mars exhibit.

a. Research Use Microsoft Word Help to find out how to create a flowchart.

b. Create Follow the Help instructions to create a flowchart showing at least six steps you would take to create a Mars exhibit.

4 Independent Practice 

glencoe.com

Independent Practice
Use the rubrics for these projects to help create and evaluate your work. Go to the **Online Learning Center** at **glencoe.com**. Choose **Rubrics**, then **Unit 2**.

English Language Arts Peer Challenge Try to stump a classmate by using Help topics to create a quiz.

a. Research Use either Windows Help or Word Help to find interesting information about four topics you would like to learn more about.

b. Create Put together a ten-question quiz about the four topics. (For example, you might ask, "In Word, what Ribbon tab would you use to add borders?")

c. Review Exchange your quiz with a classmate, and take each other's quizzes. Use Windows or Microsoft Help for the answers.

D. . Key

Key each line 2 times. Repeat if time permits.

Use L finger.
Anchor ; or J.

```
11 111 1.1 1.1 .1. 1.1 111 1.1 1.1 .1. 111
12 1.1 Fr. Fr. 1.1 Sr. Sr. 1.1 Dr. Dr. 1.1
13 1.1 std. ctn. div. Ave. Rd. St. Co. vs.
14 Calif. Conn. Tenn. Colo. Fla. Del. Ark.
```

SKILLBUILDING

E. Spacing After Punctuation

Key each line 2 times. Repeat if time permits.

Space once after:
- *A period at the end of a sentence.*
- *A period used with an abbreviation.*
- *A semicolon.*

```
15 The draft is too cold. Close this door.
16 Ask Vera to start a fire. Find a match.
17 Dr. T. Vincent sees me; he made a cast.
18 Ash Rd. is ahead; East Ave. veers left.
```

F. Technique Checkpoint

Key each line 2 times. Focus on the technique at the left.

Hold anchor keys.
Eyes on copy.

```
19 fff fvf fvf vfv fvf fff fvf fvf vfv fvf
20 ;;; T;; T;; ;;; C;; C;; ;;; S;; S;; ;;;
21 111 1.1 1.1 .1. 1.1 111 1.1 1.1 .1. 111
22 Dee voted for vivid vases on her visit.
```

G. Figuring Speed

Keying speed is measured in words per minute (wpm). To determine your keying speed:

- Key for 1 minute.
- Determine the number of words you keyed. Every 5 strokes (characters and spaces) count as 1 word. Therefore, a 40-stroke line equals 8 words. Two 40-stroke lines equal 16 words.
- Use the cumulative word count at the end of lines to determine the number of words in a complete line.

To determine the number of words in an incomplete line:
- Use the word scale below the last line (below line 24 on this page).
- The number over which you stopped keying is the number of words for that line. For example, if you keyed line 23 and completed up to the word vice in line 24, you have keyed 14 words a minute (8 + 6 = 14).

```
23 fold hide fast came hold ride mast fame    8
24 hone rice mask fade none vice task jade   16
   | 1 | 2 | 3 | 4 | 5 | 6 | 7 | 8
```

Project 2 Assessment

5. Click the **Help and Support Home** button to return to the **Windows Help and Support** home page. (Exercise 2-1)

6. **Close** the **Windows Help and Support** window. Start **Microsoft Word**.

7. Press F1 to open the **Word Help** window (Figure 2.16).

8. Click **Working with graphics and charts**, then click **Adding pictures, shapes, WordArt, or clip art** in the Subcategories section.

9. Click **Insert a picture or clip art**. Click the **Home** button to return to the **Word Help** main window. (Exercise 2-3)

10. Click the **Show Table of Contents** button, and click **Working with graphics and charts** (Figure 2.17).

11. Click **Adding pictures, shapes, WordArt, or clip art**. Click **Insert a picture or clip art** (Figure 2.17). (Exercise 2-4)

12. **Close** the **Table of Contents** pane and the **Word Help** window. **Exit Word**.

▼ **Figure 2.16** Use a keyword or phrase in the Search box to find the information you want when searching.

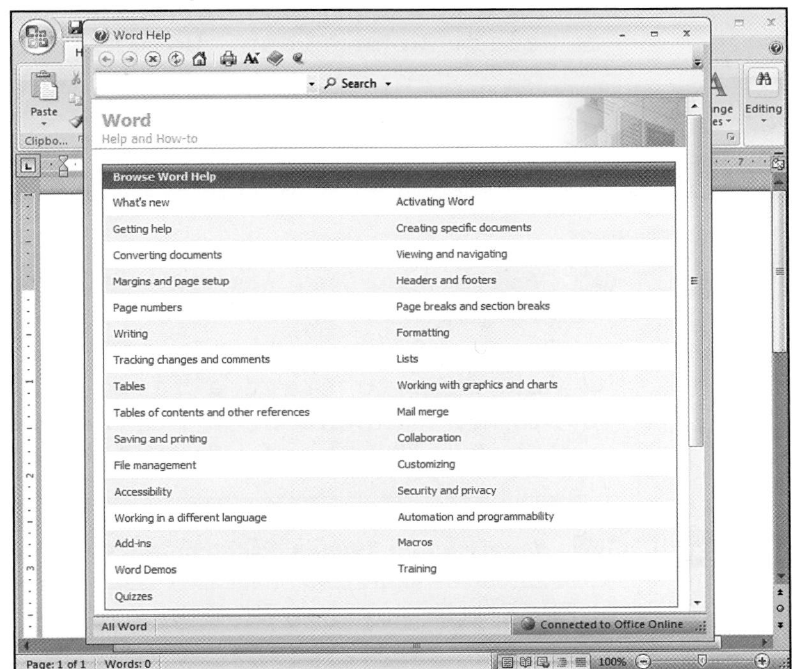

▼ **Figure 2.17** Click a topic to expand the Table of Contents pane.

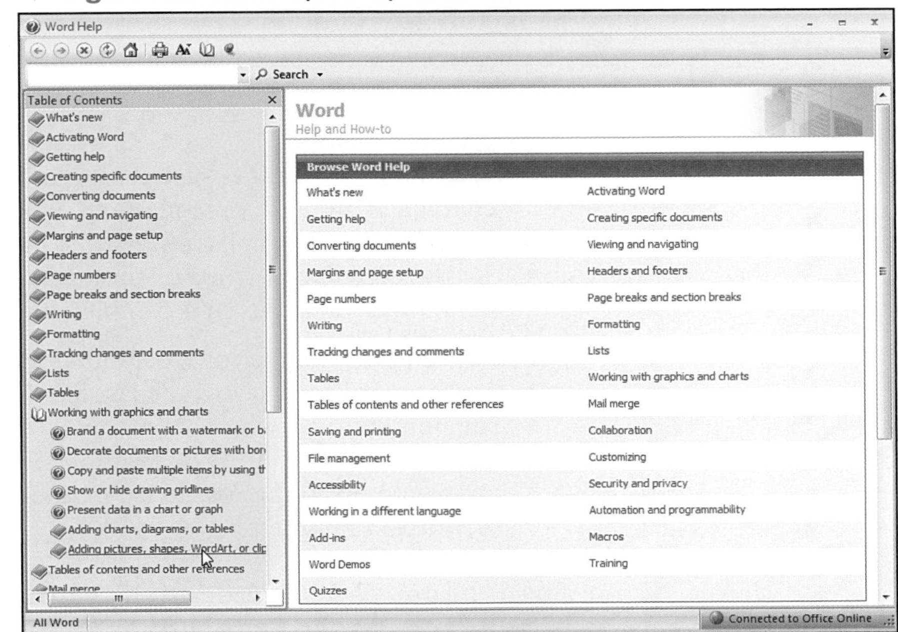

SKILLBUILDING

H. PRETEST

Key lines 23–24 for 1 minute. Repeat if time permits. Note your speed. Keep your eyes on the copy.

```
23 fold hide fast came hold ride mast fame    8
24 hone rice mask fade none vice task jade   16
```

I. PRACTICE

Key each line 2 times. Repeat if time permits.

Build speed on repeated word patterns.

```
25 fold fold hold hold sold sold told told
26 hide hide ride ride rice rice vice vice
27 fast fast mast mast mask mask task task
28 came came fame fame fade fade jade jade

29 last last vast vast cast cast case case
30 mats mats mars mars cars cars jars jars
31 fell fell jell jell sell sell seal seal
32 dive dive five five live live love love
```

J. POSTTEST

Repeat the Pretest. Compare your Posttest results with your Pretest results.

Project 2 Assessment

Key Concepts Check

1. **Describe** What are two ways to find information in the Windows Help and Support window?
2. **Explain** What is the purpose of the F1 shortcut?
3. **List** Name two different ways to find information in Microsoft Office applications.

Critical Thinking

4. **Analyze** Which search method in Office Help do you find to be most efficient? Explain your answer.
5. **Make Predictions** Create a list of three different keyword searches you could use to find information about changing colors on monitors.

1 Guided Practice

Search for Information You need to find out how to save pictures and insert them into a document. If you need help completing a step, refer back to the exercise in parentheses at the end of the step.

Step-by-Step

1. Open the **Windows Help and Support** window.
2. Find information on saving pictures from a Web page. Use the keyword pictures in the **Search** box. (Exercise 2-2)
3. Click the **Save a picture from a webpage** topic to display related topics, as shown in Figure 2.15. (Exercise 2-2)
4. Scroll to the bottom of the window, and click the link to **Print a picture from a webpage**.

▼ **Figure 2.15** Enter a keyword in the Search box to locate related topics.

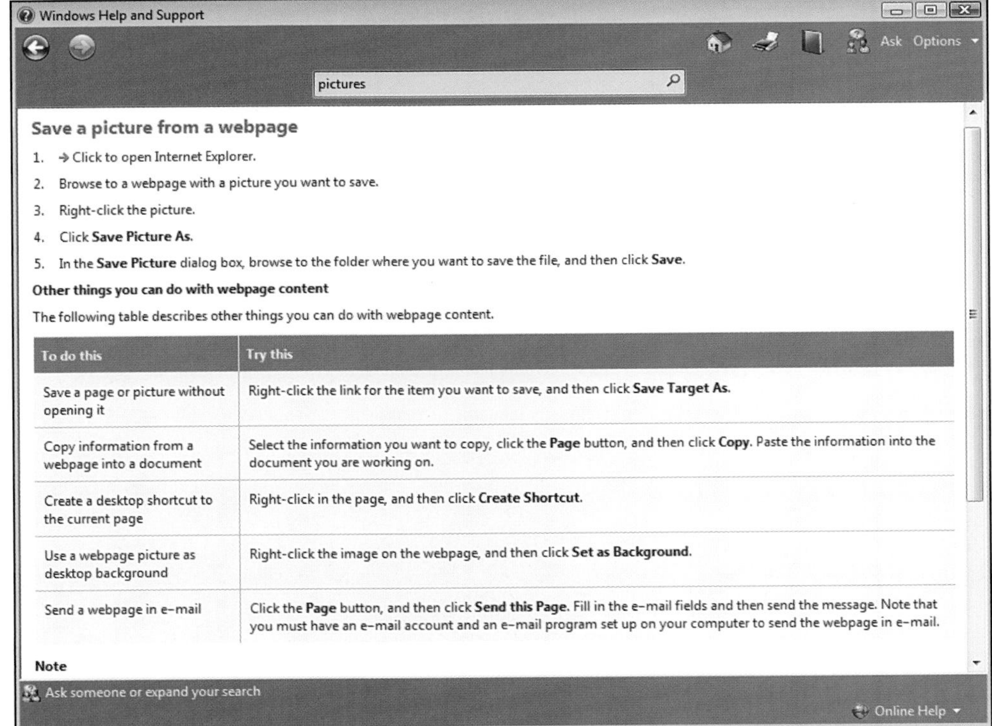

Lesson 6 — New Keys: W Comma (,) G

OBJECTIVES:

- Learn the W, comma, and G keys.
- Learn the spacing with a comma.

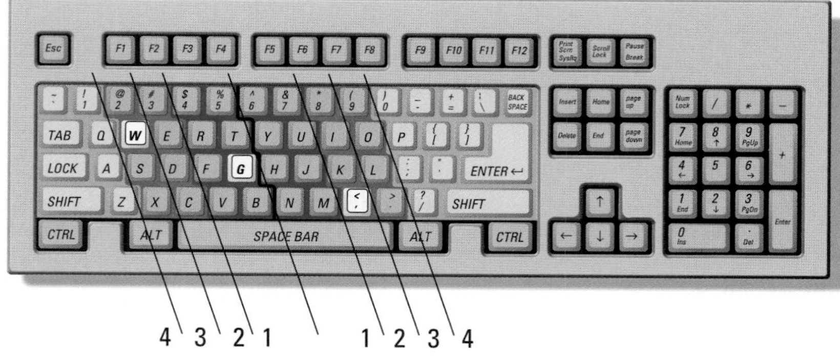

A. Warmup

Key each line 2 times.

1 fail not; jest mist chin Rev. card sake

2 Rick did not join; Val loves that fame.

NEW KEYS

B. W Key

Key each line 2 times. Repeat if time permits.

Use S finger. Anchor F.

3 sss sws sws wsw sws sss sws sws wsw sws

4 sws was was sws own own sws saw saw sws

5 sws white swans swim; sow winter wheat;

6 We watched some whales while we walked.

C. , Key

Key each line 2 times. Repeat if time permits.

Use K finger. Anchor ;. Space once after a comma.

7 kkk k,k k,k ,k, k,k kkk k,k k,k ,k, k,k

8 k,k it, it, k,k or, or, k,k an, an, k,k

9 k,k if it is, two, or three, as soon as

10 Vic, his friend, lives in Rich, Alaska.

D. G Key

Key each line 2 times. Repeat if time permits.

Use F finger. Anchor A S D.

11 fff fgf fgf gfg fgf fff fgf fgf gfg fgf

12 fgf leg leg fgf egg egg fgf get get fgf

13 fgf give a dog, saw a log, sing a song,

14 Gen gets a large sagging gift of games.

3 In the search **Results** list, click **Insert or create a table**. The procedures for inserting or creating a table appear in the window (Figure 2.13).

4 Click the **Home** button [icon] to return to the main **Word Help** window.

5 Review the **Browse Word Help** topics, and click the **Tables** link.

6 Locate the **Subcategories of "Tables"** section, and click the **Creating tables** link.

7 Click the link to **Insert or create a table**.

8 Click the **Home** button to return to the main Word Help window.

9 Click the **Show Table of Contents** button [icon]. The **Table of Contents** pane displays (Figure 2.14).

10 Click the **Tables** topic to display the subtopics. Click the **Creating Tables** topic. Click the **Insert or create a table** topic.

11 Click the **Table of Contents Close** button [X]. **Close** the **Word Help** window.

12 **Exit Microsoft Word**.

Figure 2.13 Click a link to display topics related to the feature you selected.

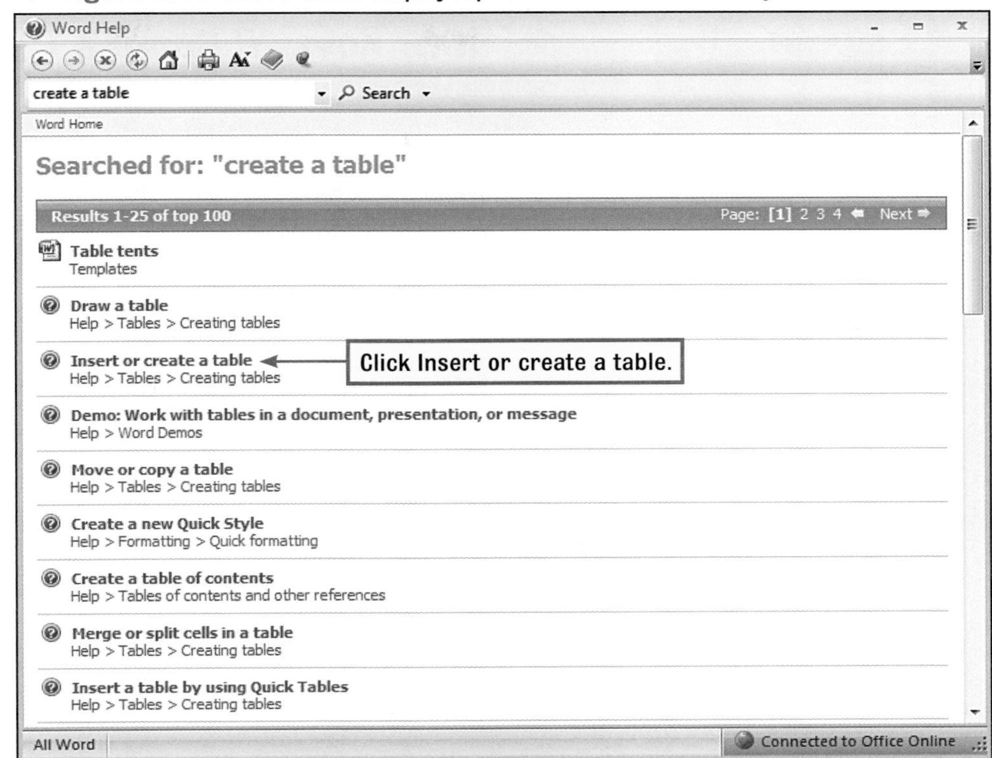

Figure 2.14 Display the Table of Contents pane to view Help topics.

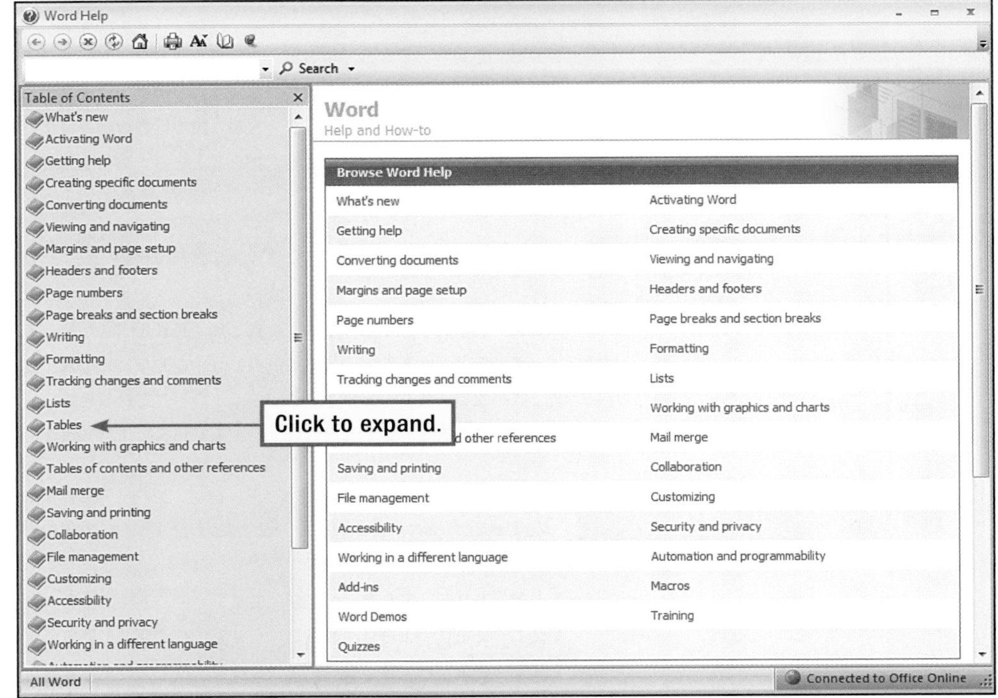

SKILLBUILDING

E. Technique Checkpoint

Technique Checkpoint Key each line 2 times. Repeat if time permits. Focus on the techniques at the left.

Hold anchor keys.
Keep elbows in.

```
15 sss sws sws wsw sws sss sws sws wsw sws
16 kkk k,k k,k ,k, k,k kkk k,k k,k ,k, k,k
17 fff fgf fgf gfg fgf fff fgf fgf gfg fgf
18 Wanda watched the team jog to the glen.
```

F. Counting Errors

Count 1 error for each word, even if it contains several errors. Count as an error:

1. A word with an incorrect character.
2. A word with incorrect spacing after it.
3. A word with incorrect punctuation after it.
4. Each mistake in following directions for spacing or indenting.
5. A word with a space.
6. An omitted word.
7. A repeated word.
8. Transposed (switched in order) words.

Compare these incorrect lines with the correct lines (19–21). Each error is highlighted in color.

```
Frank sold sold Dave old an washing mshcone .
     Carl joked with Al ice, Fran, Edith.
Wamda wore redsocks; Sadie wore green,
```

Key each line 2 times. Proofread carefully and note your errors.

```
19 Frank sold Dave an old washing machine.
20 Carl joked with Alice, Fran, and Edith.
21 Wanda wore red socks; Sadie wore green.
```

G. PRETEST

Take a 1-minute timing on lines 22–23. Note your speed and errors. Keep your eyes on the copy.

```
22 sag, mow, crew elf, down well scow king     8
23 hag, jot, glow ink, tows west snow ring    16
   | 1 | 2 | 3 | 4 | 5 | 6 | 7 | 8
```

Exercise 2-4 Search Microsoft Word Help

Microsoft provides a variety of search options to help you find just what you need quickly. You are able to search for information about an application in a number of ways. You can:

- Scroll through the list of topics in the Word Help window.
- Enter a question, keyword, or phrase in the Word Help Search box.

You can choose where you want to search for Help topics, and you can select an option to search online or offline. Click the Connection Status menu in the lower-right corner of the Word Help dialog box to select an option for displaying Help content.

When you key text in the Search box, try to be specific with your keywords to return a more accurate list of topics. To narrow your search, click the down arrow beside the Search list.

In this exercise, you will use a number of search methods to learn how to create a table. You will see that you can find the exact same information through Help when you search using different methods. When you use Help, choose the Search method that works best for you.

Step-by-Step

1. With your teacher's permission, go to the Online Learning Center at **glencoe.com** to access a **Web Link** for **Microsoft Online Help**.

2. Click in the **Search** box, and key create a table. Press ENTER (Figure 2.12).

Figure 2.12 Use the Connection Status menu to search online.

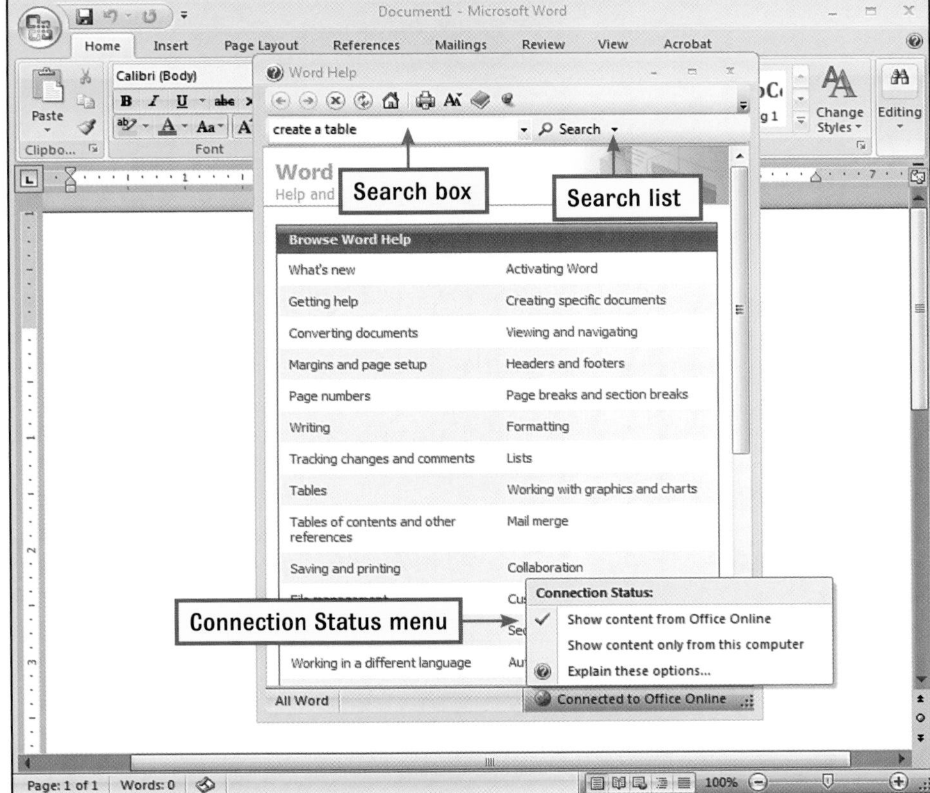

SKILLBUILDING

H. PRETEST

Key each line 2 times. Repeat if time permits.

Focus on:
- *Wrists up; do not rest palms on keyboard.*
- *Fingers curved; move from the home position only when necessary.*

```
24 sag, sag, wag, wag, rag, rag, hag, hag,
25 mow, mow, how, how, hot, hot, jot, jot,
26 crew crew grew grew grow grow glow glow
27 elf, elf, elk, elk, ilk, ilk, ink, ink,

28 down down gown gown town town tows tows
29 well well welt welt went went west west
30 scow scow stow stow show show snow snow
31 king king sing sing wing wing ring ring
```

I. POSTTEST

Repeat the Pretest. Compare your Posttest results with your Pretest results.

5. Press [F1] to open the **Word Offline Help** window. **Close** the **Word Help** window.

6. With your teacher's permission, go to the Online Learning Center at **glencoe.com** to access a **Web Link** for **Microsoft Online Help** (Figure 2.10).

7. In the **Search** box, key table, then press [ENTER].

8. Click the **Back** button to return to the previous screen.

9. Click the **Getting help** link under the **Browse Word Help** heading.

10. Review the topics, then click the **Back** button to return to the **Word Help** main window.

11. Scroll to the bottom of the **Word Help** window, and click the **Training** link to open the **Microsoft Office Online** Web page (Figure 2.11).

12. Click the **Close** button to **exit Microsoft Office Online**.

13. **Close** the **Word Help** window.

Figure 2.10 Search for Help topics by using the Search box or clicking a topic in the Word Help window.

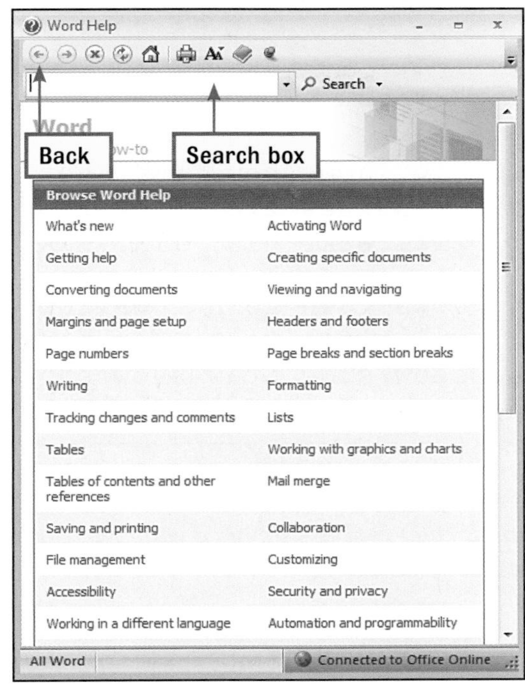

Figure 2.11 Microsoft Office Online provides support and training for every Microsoft Office application.

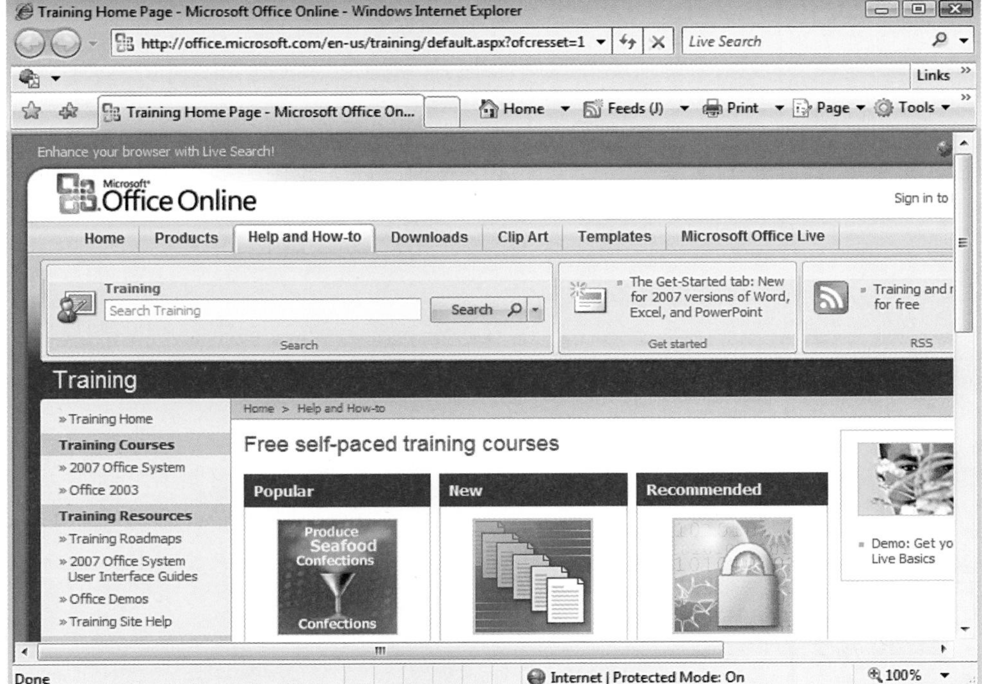

Lesson 7 New Keys: B U Left Shift

OBJECTIVE:
- Learn the B, U, and Left Shift keys.

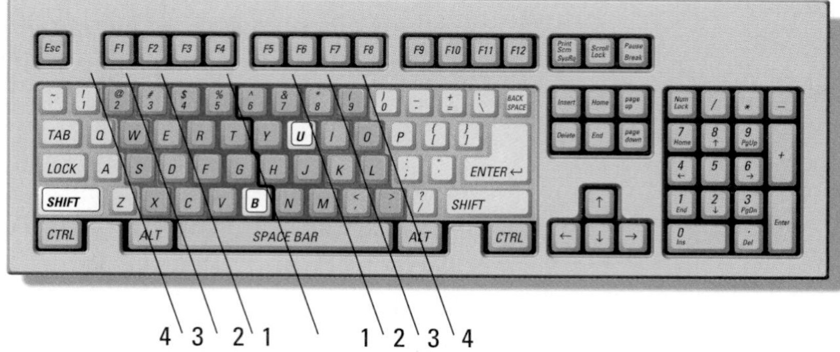

A. Warmup

Key each line 2 times.

```
1 dim logo wags jive foal corn them wags,
2 Wanda mailed the jewels that Carl made.
```

NEW KEYS

B. B Key

Key each line 2 times. Repeat if time permits.

Use F finger.
Anchor A and S.

```
3 fff fbf fbf bfb fbf fff fbf fbf bfb fbf
4 fbf rob rob fbf ebb ebb fbf bag bag fbf
5 fbf a bent bin, a back bend, a big bag,
6 That boat had been in a babbling brook.
```

C. U Key

Key each line 2 times. Repeat if time permits.

Use J finger.
Anchor ; L and K.

```
7 jjj juj juj uju juj jjj juj juj uju juj
8 juj jug jug juj urn urn juj flu flu juj
9 juj jungle bugs, just a job, jumbo jets
10 Students show unusual business success.
```

D. Left SHIFT Key

Key each line 2 times. Repeat if time permits.

Use A finger.
Anchor F.

```
11 aaa Kaa Kaa aaa Jaa Jaa aaa Laa Laa aaa
12 aaa Kim Kim aaa Lee Lee aaa Joe Joe aaa
13 aaa Jan left; Nora ran; Uncle Lee fell;
14 Mari and Ula went to Kansas in October.
```

Exercise 2-3 Get to Know Microsoft Office Help

Microsoft Office Help provides support and information for all Office applications, including Word, Excel, PowerPoint, Access, and Outlook. By using Microsoft Office Help, you can quickly find answers to your questions when you are using one of these applications.

There are three basic ways to use Help in a Microsoft Office application:

- **Microsoft Office Help** lets you search by keyword or browse through a Table of Contents.
- **Keying a question for help** in some versions of Office allows you to use the search box at the top of the screen.
- **Office Online** takes you to Microsoft's Web site to give you the latest information about the applications.

In this exercise, you will learn how to use the different Help options in Microsoft Word. You can then use these skills when you are working in any Microsoft application. **Note**: Your version of Word may not have all of the features in this exercise. Ask your teacher if you have questions.

Step-by-Step

1. Start **Microsoft Word**. **Hint**: Review Exercise 1-4, page 59 if you need help opening Word.
2. Click the **Microsoft Office Word Help** button (Figure 2.9).
3. Locate the notation in the lower-right corner of the Word Help window to determine if you are connected to **Office Online**. If the notation is **Offline**, your help searches are limited to the files stored on your computer.
4. Close the **Word Help** window.

Figure 2.9 Click the Microsoft Office Word Help button to display the Word Help window.

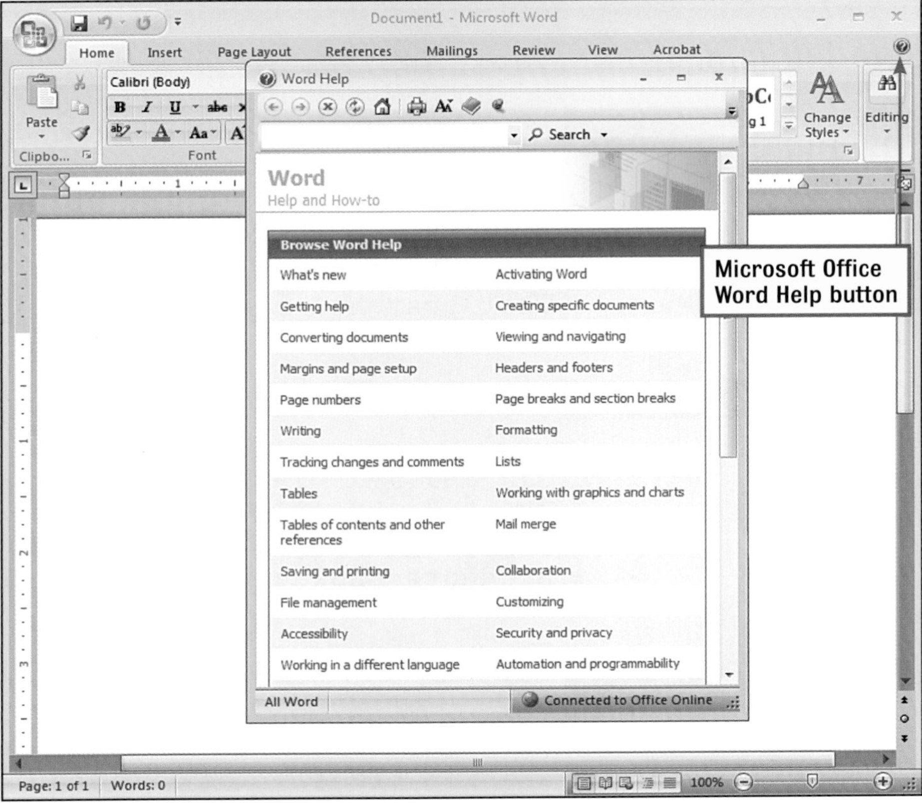

SKILLBUILDING

E. Technique Checkpoint

Key each line 2 times. Repeat if time permits. Focus on the technique at the left.

Keep F or J anchored when shifting.

```
15 fff fbf fbf bfb fbf fff fbf fbf bfb fbf
16 jjj juj juj uju juj jjj juj juj uju juj
17 aaa Kaa Kaa aaa Jaa Jaa aaa Laa Laa aaa
18 Jo told Mike and Nel that she would go.
```

F. PRETEST

Take a 1-minute timing on lines 19–20. Note your speed and errors.

```
19 bran gist vast blot sun, bout just beef    8
20 craw just rest bran sum, dole hunk bear   16
   | 1 | 2 | 3 | 4 | 5 | 6 | 7 | 8
```

G. PRACTICE

Key each line 2 times. Repeat if time permits.

Place your feet:

- *In front of the chair.*
- *Firmly on the floor, square, flat.*
- *Apart, with 6 or 7 inches between the ankles.*
- *One foot a little ahead of the other.*

```
21 bran brad bred brew brow crow crew craw
22 gist list mist must gust dust rust just
23 vast vest jest lest best west nest rest
24 blot blob blow blew bled bred brad bran

25 sun, nun, run, bun, gun, gum, hum, sum,
26 bout boat boot blot bold boll doll dole
27 just dust dusk dunk bunk bulk hulk hunk
28 beef been bean bead beak beam beat bear
```

H. POSTTEST

Repeat the Pretest. Compare your Posttest results with your Pretest results.

10 Click the **Help and Support Home** button.

11 Click the **Table of Contents** icon. Click **Files and folders**. Three subtopics display under Files and folders.

12 Click **Working with files and folders** (Figure 2.7).

13 Locate the paragraph that begins "A file" and notice that file is formatted in green. Click the word ***file***, and a definition displays. Click in the window to hide the definition.

14 Refer to the list of blue links on the right side of the window. The blue links represent major headings in the article. Click **Finding your files**. The heading appears at the top of the window (Figure 2.8).

15 Click the **Close** button to exit **Windows Help and Support**.

▼ **Figure 2.7** Click a link to view topics and subtopics.

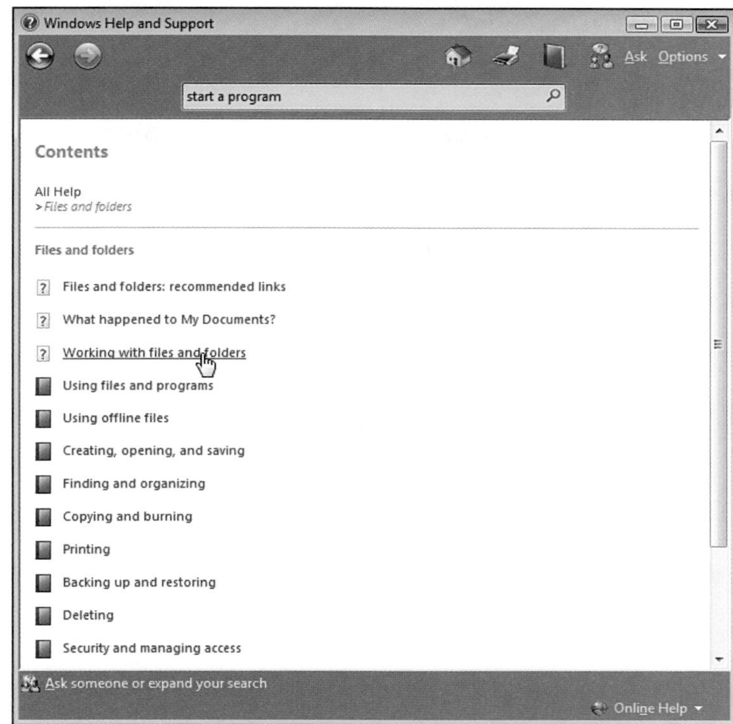

▼ **Figure 2.8** Use heading links to jump to a specific location.

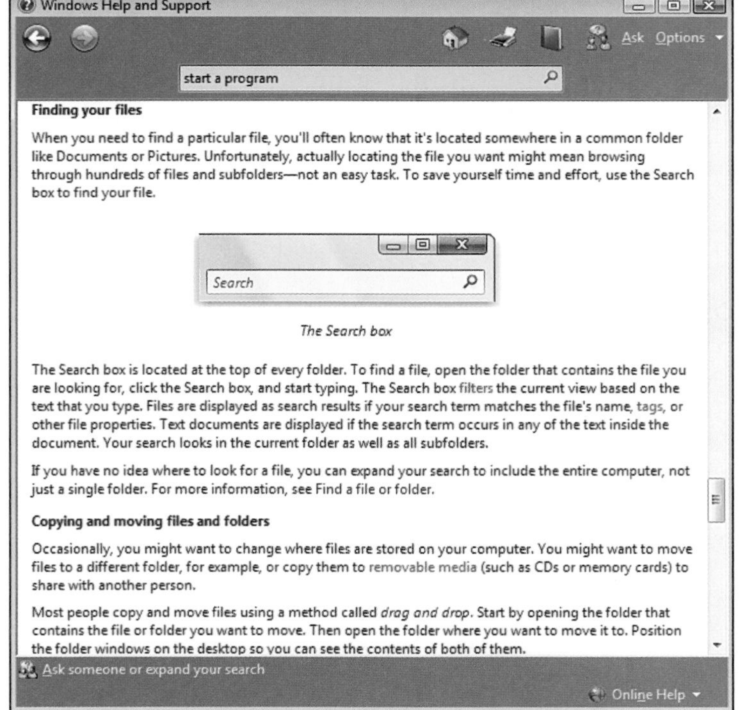

Lesson 8 New Keys: Q /

OBJECTIVE:

- Learn the Q and / (slash or diagonal) keys.

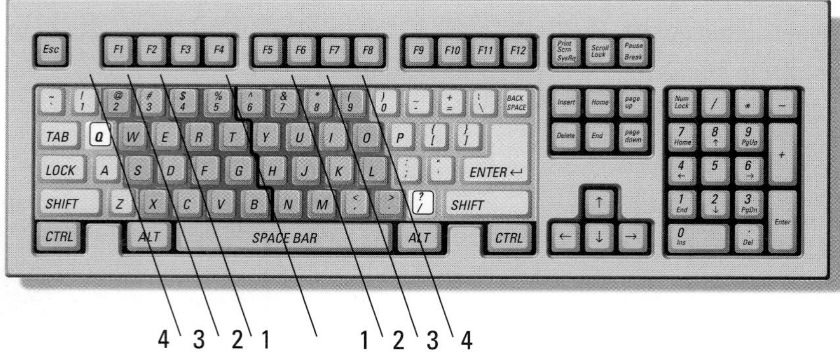

A. Warmup

Key each line 2 times.

```
1 club face when silk mold brag java blue
2 Jana went biking, and Cila waved flags.
```

NEW KEYS

B. Q Key

Key each line 2 times. Repeat if time permits.

Use A finger. Anchor F.

```
3 aaa aqa aqa qaq aqa aaa aqa aqa qaq aqa
4 aqa quo quo aqa qui qui aqa que que aqa
5 aqa quail, quit quick quid, half quest,
6 The quints squabbled on a square quilt.
```

C. / Key

Key each line 2 times. Repeat if time permits.

Use Sem finger. Anchor J. Do not space before or after a slash (diagonal).

```
7 ;;; ;/; ;/; /;/ ;/; ;;; ;/; ;/; /;/ ;/;
8 ;/; her/him ;/; us/them ;/; his/her ;/;
9 ;/; slow/fast, walk/ride, debit/credit,
10 The fall/winter catalog has new colors.
```

4 On the right side of the window, click **Starting a program**. The instructions for starting a program are displayed (Figure 2.5).

5 Following the instructions on how to start a program, **open Microsoft Paint**. (**Hint**: Paint is an Accessory.)

6 To **exit Paint**, click the **Close** button in the upper-right corner.

7 Click the **Help and Support Home** button to return to the **Help and Support** home page.

▼ **Figure 2.5** To learn more about a topic, click the other links.

8 In the **Search** box, key start a program, then press ENTER.

9 Click the link to **Customize the Start menu**. Your screen should resemble Figure 2.6.

▼ **Figure 2.6** Click a link to expand or collapse the steps.

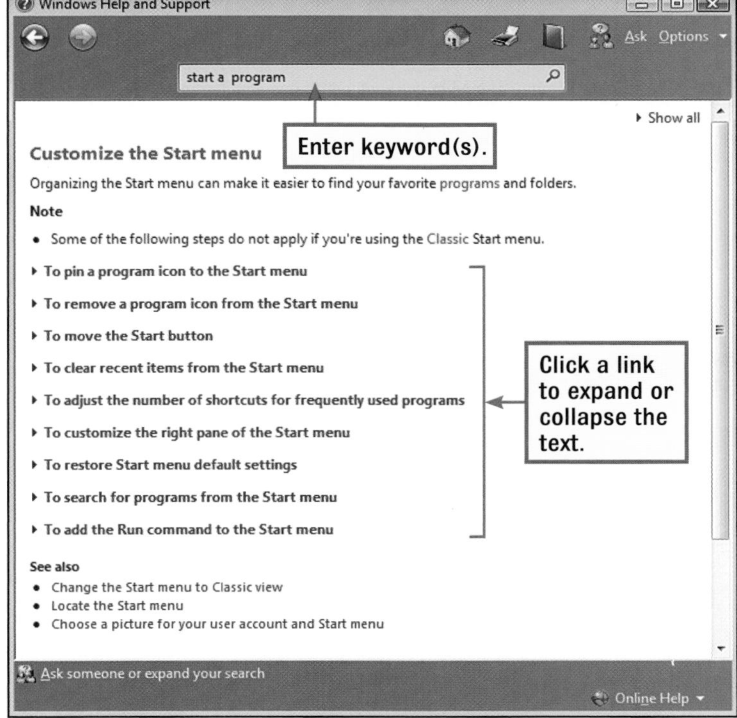

SKILLBUILDING

D. Technique Checkpoint

Key each line 2 times. Repeat if time permits. Focus on the technique at the left.

Keep fingers curved and wrists level.

```
11 aaa aqa aqa qaq aqa aaa aqa aqa qaq aqa
12 ;;; ;/; ;/; /;/ ;/; ;;; ;/; ;/; /;/ ;/;
13 The quick squash squad requested quiet.
14 He/she said that we could do either/or.
```

E. Technique Timings

Take two 30-second timings on each line. Focus on the technique at the left.

Keep your eyes on the copy.

```
15 Louise will lead if she makes the team.
16 Their bands will march at the quadrant.
17 Brad just had time to finish his goals.
18 I was quiet as he glided over the wave.
   | 1 | 2 | 3 | 4 | 5 | 6 | 7 | 8
```

F. PRETEST

Take a 1-minute timing on lines 19–20. Note your speed and errors.

Hold those anchors.

```
19 find/seek boat fate jail cube brad swat     8
20 walk shut quid mile vane aqua slot quit    16
   | 1 | 2 | 3 | 4 | 5 | 6 | 7 | 8
```

G. PRACTICE

Key each line 2 times. Repeat if time permits.

To build skill:
- *Key each line two times.*
- *Speed up the second time you key the line.*

```
21 find/lose cats/dogs hike/bike walk/ride
22 seek/hide soft/hard mice/rats shut/ajar
23 boat goat moat mode rode rude ruin quid
24 fate face race rice nice Nile vile mile

25 jail fail fall gall mall male vale vane
26 cube Cuba tuba tube lube luau quad aqua
27 brad brat brag quag flag flat slat slot
28 swat swam swim slim slid slit suit quit
```

I. POSTTEST

Repeat the Pretest. Compare your Posttest results with your Pretest results.

Exercise 2-2 Perform a Search

A content search is a good place to start if you are new to an operating system. You can browse through a list of categories to find topics that help you learn basic computer tasks.

When you have a general idea of what you are looking for, you can enter a keyword in the Search box. As you key, Windows Vista instantly searches file and application names and the full text of all files. Vista organizes the search results by programs, documents, media, e-mail, and so on.

In this exercise, you will perform a content search and a keyword search to find information about how to open an application. You will then use what you learned to open an application called Microsoft Paint.

Step-by-Step

1. Click the **Start** menu, and choose **Help and Support**.
2. Click the **Windows Basics** icon in the **Windows Help and Support** window. Your screen should look similar to Figure 2.4.
3. Click the **Using programs** link.

▼ **Figure 2.4** Clicking through categories and topics in a content search lets you see how different information is related.

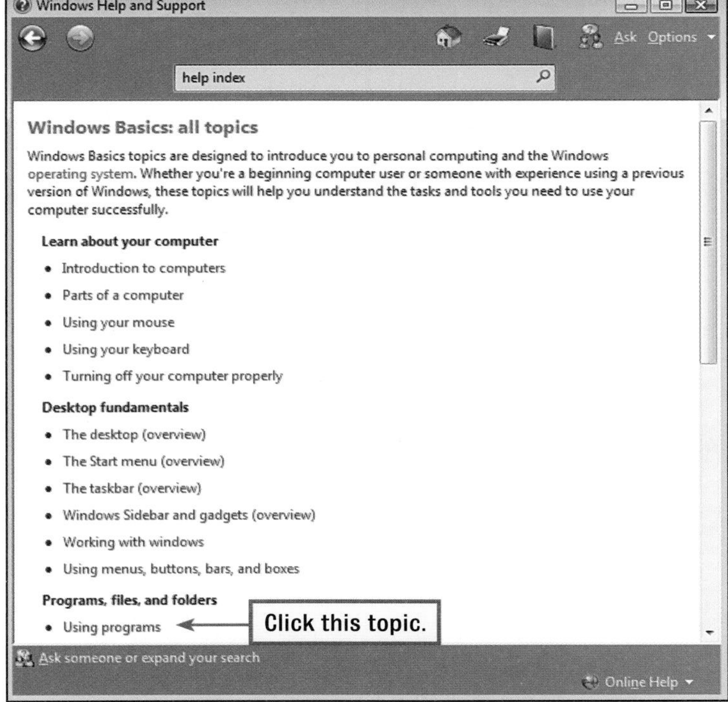

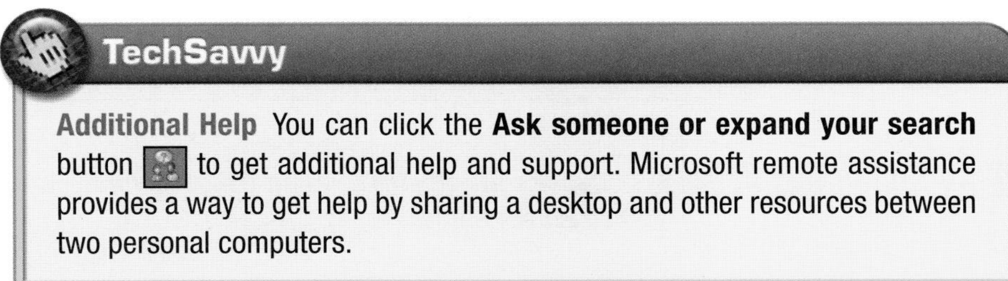

TechSavvy

Additional Help You can click the **Ask someone or expand your search** button to get additional help and support. Microsoft remote assistance provides a way to get help by sharing a desktop and other resources between two personal computers.

Lesson 9 — New Keys: ' "

OBJECTIVES:

- Learn the apostrophe (') and the quotation mark (") keys.
- Improve speed and accuracy.

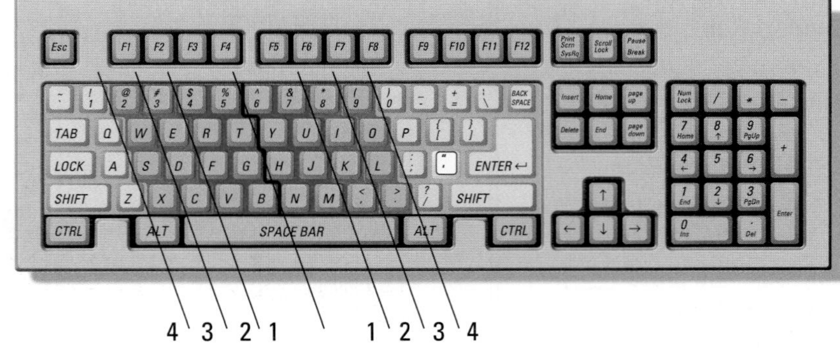

A. Warmup

Key each line 2 times.

1 quill wagon cabin valued helms, and/or;
2 Jake is quite good in math but not Val.

NEW KEYS

B. ' Keys

Key each line 2 times. Repeat if time permits.

Use Sem finger. Anchor J. Do not space before or after an apostrophe within a word.

3 ;;; ;'; ;'; ';' ;'; ;;; ;'; ;'; ';' ;';
4 ;'; he's he's ;'; where's ;'; it's it's
5 ;'; ';' Kit's barn ;'; Ed's car ;'; ';'
6 Bill's car isn't running; it's at Li's.

C. " Keys

Key each line 2 times. Repeat if time permits.

Shift of apostrophe. Use Sem finger. Anchor J.

7 ;;; ;"; ;"; ";" ;"; ;;; ;"; ;"; ";" ;";
8 ;"; "win" "win" ;"; "big" "big" ;"; ";"
9 ;"; "mew" "oink" "woof" "moo" "baa" ";"
10 "Green" means "go"; "red" means "wait."

SKILLBUILDING

D. Technique Checkpoint

Key each line 2 times. Repeat if time permits. Focus on the technique at the left.

Keep your eyes on the copy.

11 ;;; ;'; ;'; ';' ;'; ;;; ;'; ;'; ';' ;';
12 ;;; ;"; ;"; ";" ;"; ;;; ;"; ;"; ";" ;";
13 He said "no thanks," but it was "lame."
14 Rita "forgot," but Milo added "favors."

4 Click the **Printers and printing** link to display the topics for Printers and printing.

5 Click the **Help and Support Home** button to return to the main **Help** window.

6 In the **Windows Help and Support** window, key printing in the **Search Help** box, and press ENTER. The **Windows Help and Support** window displays the search results.

7 Click the **Print a document or file** link as shown in Figure 2.2.

Figure 2.2 You can find more information by clicking Related Topics.

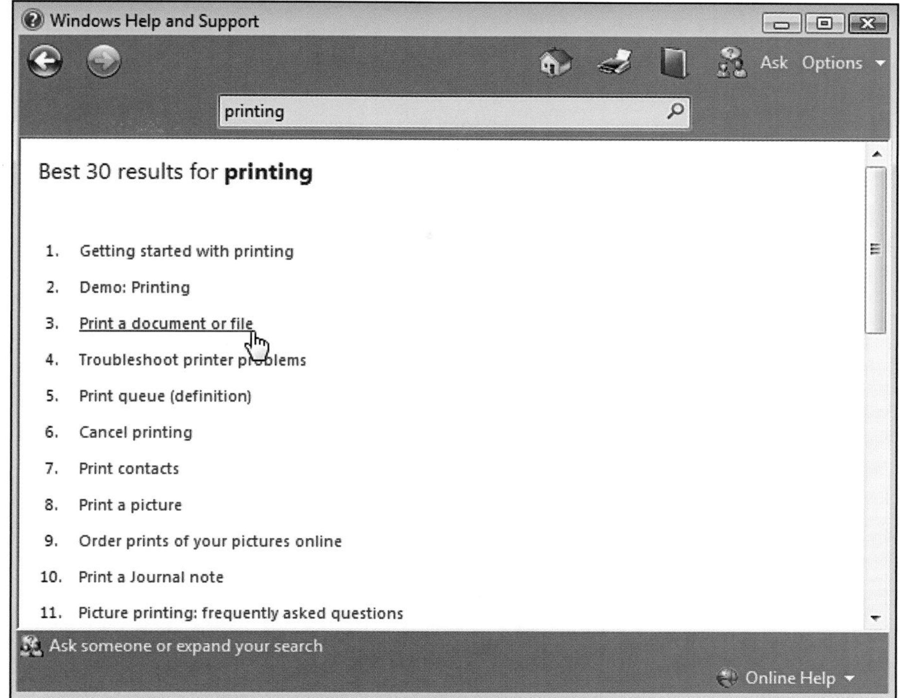

8 Click the **Back** button to return to the printing results window (Figure 2.3).

9 Click the **Forward** button to return to the **Print a document or file** window.

10 To **exit** the **Windows Help and Support** window, click the **Close** button.

Figure 2.3 The Back and Forward buttons can move you to the last page you viewed.

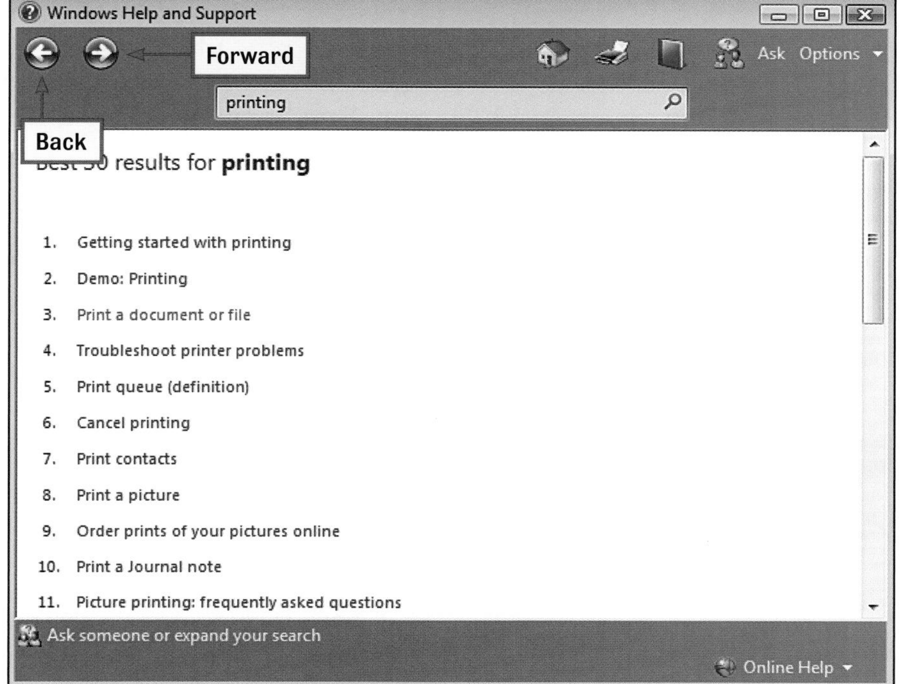

SKILLBUILDING

E. Technique Timings

Take two 30-second timings on each line. Focus on the technique at the left.

Keep your eyes on the copy.

```
15 Robb's clothes and image don't "match."
16 Mr. Quill said, "Wait." Lee did not go.
17 Jane's visit was "quick"; she ran back.
18 I haven't enough time to "quibble" now.
   | 1 | 2 | 3 | 4 | 5 | 6 | 7 | 8
```

F. 12-Second Sprints

Take three 12-second timings on each line. Try to increase your speed on each timing.

```
19 Go to the cabin and get us the dog now.
20 Now is the time to call all men for me.
21 She made a face when she lost the race.
22 Ask them if the vase is safe with them.
   ||||5||||10||||15||||20||||25||||30||||35||||40
```

G. PRETEST

Take a 1-minute timing on lines 23–24. Note your speed and errors.

```
23 We can't "remember" how Bo got bruised.    8
24 Burt's dad "asked" Kurt to assist Ross.   16
   | 1 | 2 | 3 | 4 | 5 | 6 | 7 | 8
```

H. PRACTICE

Key each line 2 times.

```
25 made fade face race lace lice nice mice
26 Burt Nora Will Mame Ross Kurt Olaf Elle
27 he's I've don't can't won't we've she's
28 Bo's dogs Lu's cows Mo's cats Di's rats

29 "mat" "bat" "west" "east" "gone" "tone"
30 He "quit"; she "tried." I hit a "wall."
31 sand/land vane/cane robe/lobe quit/suit
32 asks bask base vase case cast mast last
```

I. POSTTEST

Repeat the Pretest. Compare your Posttest results with your Pretest results.

Exercise 2-1 Get to Know Microsoft Windows Help

Academic Focus

English Language Arts

Get to Know Your Book
A table of contents appears at the front of a book and outlines the content within the book. The first time you open a textbook, skim the table of contents to see how the chapters are organized. Review your textbook's table of contents to see the organization of content. Consider how a table of contents is similar to a content search using Windows Help.

NCTE 8 Use information resources to gather information and create and communicate knowledge.

When you have a problem using the computer, you can ask friends or teachers for help, read the computer manual, or even call a support line. First, though, you should use the Help program in your software.

When you use a Help program, you do a search for a particular topic. Usually a search requires you to key a keyword or scroll to a topic. A **keyword** is a word (or words) keyed into a search box that matches the topic you are looking for. There are two basic types of searches:

- **Content Search** Look for information from a list of categories and topics. This is like using a book's table of contents.
- **Keyword Search** Key one or more keywords. The search results include all of the topics in which the keywords appear.

In this exercise, you will learn about the different ways to search for information using Microsoft Windows Help. **Note**: Your version of Help may look different from the figures in this exercise.

Figure 2.1 Windows Help provides information about using Windows effectively.

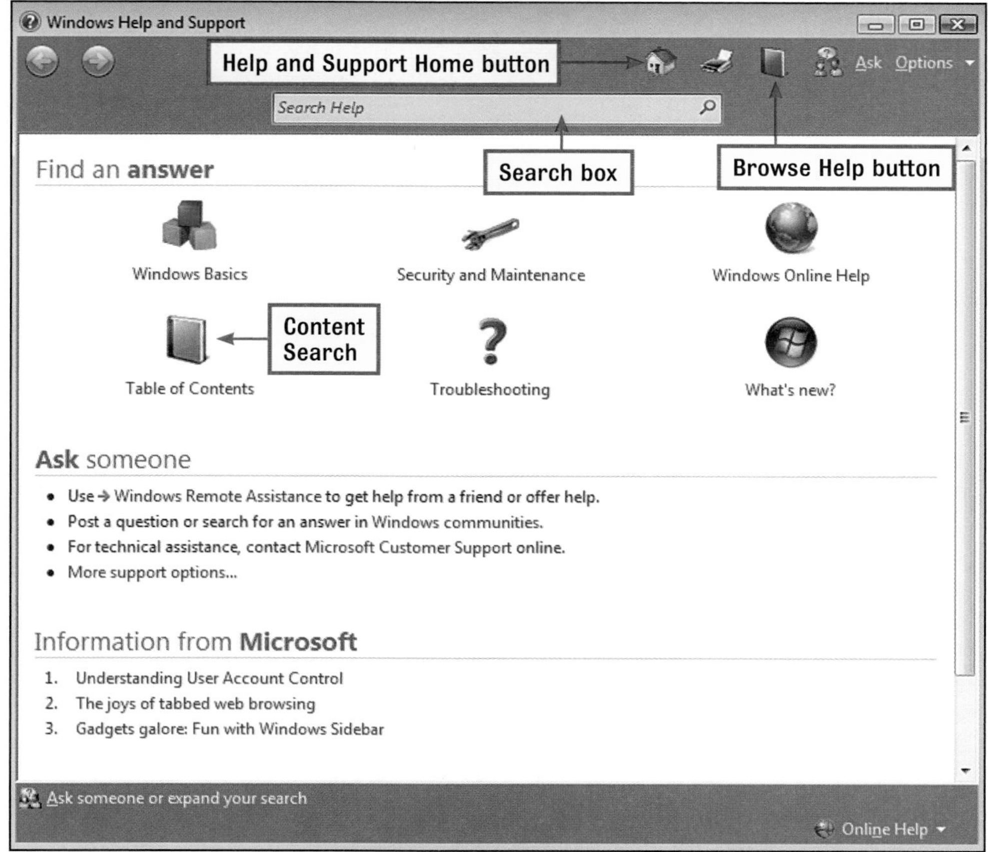

Step-by-Step

1. Click **Start** and choose **Help and Support**. The **Windows Help and Support** window appears (Figure 2.1).
2. Click the **Browse Help** button to view a list of **Help** topics.
3. Scroll through the topics, and locate the **Printers and printing** topic.

Lesson 10 New Keys: P X

OBJECTIVE:

- Learn the P and X keys.

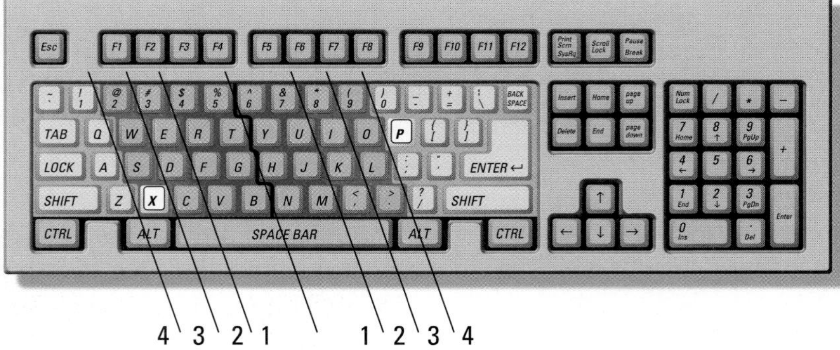

A. Warmup

Key each line 2 times.

1 fade cave what swim quad blot king jars
2 Black liquids vanish from the jug I saw.

NEW KEYS

B. P Key

Key each line 2 times. Repeat if time permits.

Use Sem finger.
Anchor J and K.

3 ;;; ;p; ;p; p;p ;p; ;;; ;p; ;p; p;p ;p;
4 ;p; nap nap ;p; pen pen ;p; ape ape ;p;
5 ;p; perfect plot, a pale page, pen pal,
6 Pam pulled a pouting pup past a puddle.

C. X Key

Key each line 2 times. Repeat if time permits.

Use S finger.
Anchor A or F.

7 sss sxs sxs xsx sxs sss sxs sxs xsx sxs
8 sxs tax tax sxs mix mix sxs axe axe sxs
9 sxs lax taxes, vexed vixen, six Texans,
10 Fix the next six boxes on next weekend.

SKILLBUILDING

D. Technique Checkpoint

Key each line 2 times. Focus on the techniques at the left.

Remember to keep:

- *Wrists up.*
- *Fingers curved.*
- *Feet flat on the floor.*

11 ;;; ;p; ;p; p;p ;p; ;;; ;p; ;p; p;p ;p;
12 sss sxs sxs xsx sxs sss sxs sxs xsx sxs
13 Phil will fix ripped carpets alone now.
14 Go see that duplex before next weekend.

Concepts in Action

Project 2 Use Microsoft Help

Key Concepts

Exercise 2-1
- Open Microsoft Windows Help
- Identify search options

Exercise 2-2
- Perform a content search
- Perform a keyword search

Exercise 2-3
- Open Microsoft Office Help

Exercise 2-4
- Find information in Microsoft Office Help
- Identify keywords and phrases for searches

Vocabulary

Key Terms
keyword
content search
keyword search

Before You Begin

Skills Practice You will use the skills you learn in this unit over and over again. To make sure you understand a skill, try practicing it as soon as you finish each exercise.

In this project, you will use Microsoft Windows Help and Support and Microsoft Office Word Help to find answers to your questions about Microsoft software.

Help Yourself

Sometimes the fastest and easiest way to find answers to your questions is to look for the answers yourself. Learning to use Microsoft Help can help you find answers quickly to most of your questions.

The Mars exhibit you were preparing in the last project is opening in a week, and you need to have some files ready for tomorrow. Suddenly, you come across a computer task that you do not know how to do. No one is around to help you, and you are running late. What should you do? You know you can use the built-in Help features of your software to look for the answers yourself before calling on someone else for more help.

SKILLBUILDING

E. Technique Timings

Take two 30-second timings on each line. Press ENTER at the end of each sentence. Focus on the technique at the left.

Keep your rhythm steady as you reach to the ENTER key and back to home position.

```
15 Pull on the tabs.↵ The box will open.↵
16 Speed is good.↵  Errors are not good.↵
17 Glue the picture.↵  The book is done.↵
18 Get the clothes.↵  Bring me their caps.↵
   | 1 | 2 | 3 | 4 | 5 | 6 | 7 | 8
```

F. PRETEST

Take a 1-minute timing on lines 19–20. Note your speed and errors.

```
19 slag chop gate plop tops bows veal dart      8
20 apex slab gave quit fix, hoax text jell     16
   | 1 | 2 | 3 | 4 | 5 | 6 | 7 | 8
```

G. PRACTICE

Key each line 2 times.

To type faster:
- *Read copy before typing.*
- *Key with smooth strokes.*

```
21 slag flag flap flax flux flex Alex apex
22 chop clop clap clan claw slaw slap slab
23 gate gale pale page pave have cave gave
24 plop flop flip slip ship whip quip quit

25 tops tips sips sits sit, six, mix, fix,
26 bows bowl jowl howl cowl coal coax hoax
27 veal real seal meal meat neat next text
28 dart part park bark balk ball bell jell
```

H. POSTTEST

Repeat the Pretest. Compare your Posttest results with your Pretest results.

Project 1 Assessment

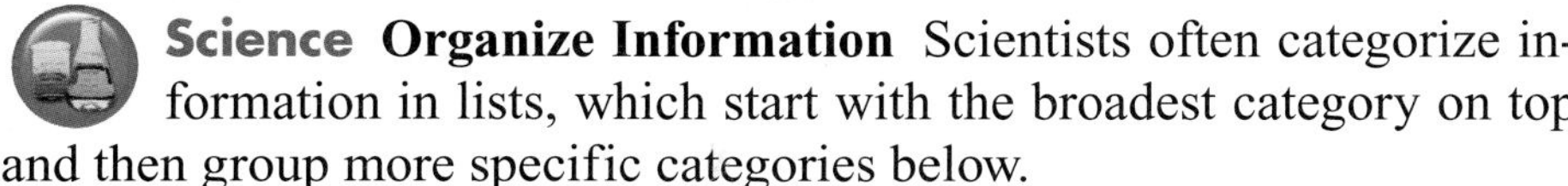

2 Independent Practice

Cookbooks [broadest category]
- **American Food** [cookbook]
  - First Ladies' Favorite Recipes
  - Cajun Cooking
- **International Food** [cookbook]
  - Pasta, Pasta, Pasta,
  - Wok Around the Clock

Sports books [broadest category]
- **Soccer** [sports book]
  - Goalie's Guide to Success
  - What is Offsides?
  - World Cup Greatest Moments

Science **Organize Information** Scientists often categorize information in lists, which start with the broadest category on top and then group more specific categories below.

a. Plan Choose ten of your favorite books, music CDs, or movies. Organize them by type.

b. Create Make a list organizing the books, music, or movies you chose. See the example on this page.

3 Independent Practice

Teamwork **Share Information** Share the list you created in Independent Practice 2 above with a classmate.

a. Evaluate Look at each other's lists.

- Determine which items would be folders and which would be files if these were folders and files on a computer.
- Add to your partner's list two more folders and four more files, putting them at the correct level.

b. Revise Rewrite your list based on your classmate's notes.

4 Independent Practice

Go Online RUBRICS
glencoe.com

Independent Practice
Use the rubrics for these projects to help create and evaluate your work. Go to the **Online Learning Center** at **glencoe.com**. Choose **Rubrics**, then **Unit 2**.

Science **Manage Your Files** Determine how folders and files are organized on your school or home computer.

a. Plan Draw a flowchart showing the structure and categories of the files and folders on either your school or home computer.

b. Evaluate Determine whether this is the best possible organization and how it can be arranged most logically. Create a list of new names for folders, subfolders, and files.

c. Create Create an organizational chart by hand or by using software suggested by your teacher. Compare your new organization with that of your classmates.

Lesson 11 New Keys: Y Tab

OBJECTIVE:
- Learn the Y and the tab keys.

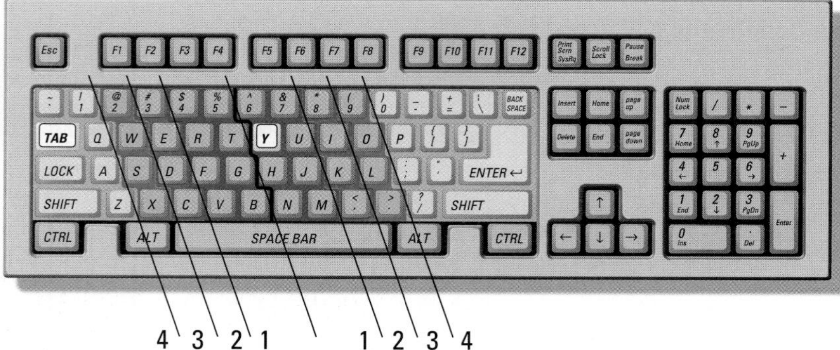

A. Warmup

Key each line 2 times.

1 jibe wing more vase deft lack hex; quid
2 Max just put a pale slab over the gate.

NEW KEYS

B.  Key

Key each line 2 times. Repeat if time permits.

Use J finger. Anchor ; L, and K.

3 jjj jyj jyj yjy jyj jjj jyj jyj yjy jyj
4 jyj yes yes jyj joy joy jyj aye aye jyj
5 jyj yard of yarn, July joy, yellow yam,
6 Shelley yearns to yodel but only yells.

C. Tab Key

The tab key is used to indent paragraphs. The tab key is located to the left of the Q key. Reach to the tab key with the A finger. Keep your other fingers on home keys as you quickly press the tab key.

Pressing the tab key will move the cursor 0.5 inch (the default setting) to the right.

Word wrap automatically moves a word that does not fit on one line down to the next line.

Key each paragraph 2 times. Press Enter only at the end of a paragraph. Repeat if time permits.

7 If you are happy, you will be able
8 to set goals. You will also smile more.
9 The jury was out and no one could
10 leave the room. We all had to stay put.

3. Find and **copy** the **Spirit Mission** folder. **Close** the **Documents** folder. (Exercise 1-3)

4. **Paste** the folder on the desktop, then **rename** it *Your Name* Spirit Mission. (Exercise 1-3)

5. Drag your **Spirit Mission** folder into your **Mars Exhibit** folder. (Exercise 1-3)

6. **Open** the **Mars Exhibit** folder. The Spirit Mission folder should be listed as in Figure 1.23.

Figure 1.23 The Spirit Mission folder is a subfolder of the Mars Exhibit folder.

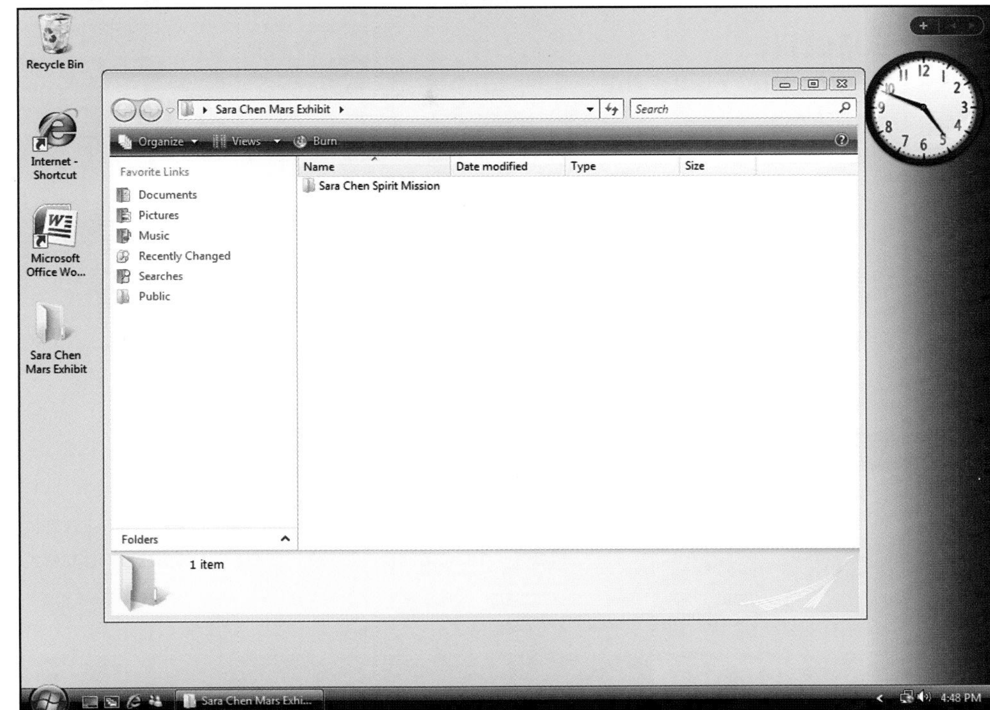

7. Use **Search** to find the file named **Mars Rover**. Your results window should look similar to Figure 1.24. (Exercise 1-6)

8. **Copy** the **Mars Rover** file. Click **Documents** to return to the **Documents** folder.

9. In the **Documents** folder, **paste** the **Mars Rover** file into your **Spirit Mission** folder. (Exercise 1-3)

Figure 1.24 The Search Results window is displayed.

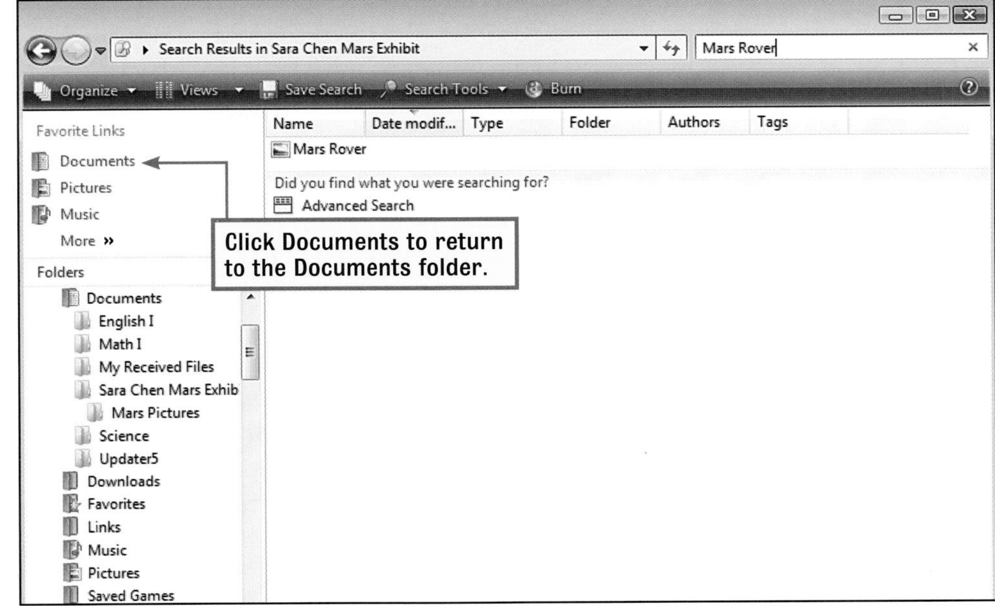

SKILLBUILDING

D. Technique Checkpoint

Key each line 2 times. Focus on the technique at the left. Repeat if time permits.

Keep your eyes on the copy.

11 jjj jyj jyj yjy jyj jjj jyj jyj yjy jyj
12 I saw yards of yellow fabric every day.
13 They happily played in the lonely yard.
14 Yes, the daily reports are ready today.

E. Technique Timings

Take two 30-second timings on each line. Focus on the technique at the left.

Keep your eyes on the copy as you take each timing.

15 Push your fingers to find the keys now.
16 You will see your typing speed improve.
17 Have a goal to type faster than before.
18 Try every day to achieve that new goal.
| 1 | 2 | 3 | 4 | 5 | 6 | 7 | 8

F. PRETEST

Take a 1-minute timing on lines 19–22. Note your speed and errors.

Remember: Press ENTER *only at the end of the paragraph (line 22).*

19 A jury will meet next January to 7
20 get a verdict. People stole costly fuel 15
21 from the boys. We found bags of cards 22
22 next to the mops in the broom closet. 30
| 1 | 2 | 3 | 4 | 5 | 6 | 7 | 8

G. PRACTICE

Key each line 2 times.

23 fuel duel duet suet suit quit quip quid
24 gape nape cape cave wave wage wags bags
25 mops pops maps hops tops toys joys boys
26 rope lope lops laps lips lids kids kiss

27 card cart curt hurt hurl furl fury jury
28 cost most lost lest best test text next
29 slab flab flap flaw flay slay clay play
30 pan, fan, tan, man, can, ran, Dan, Jan,

H. POSTTEST

Repeat the Pretest. Compare your Posttest results with your Pretest results.

Project 1 Assessment

Key Concepts Check

1. **Explain** What is the difference between folders and files?
2. **Identify** What are five search options you can use to do a search?
3. **Describe** What are three steps you can take to avoid losing a file?

Critical Thinking

4. **Cause and Effect** Why is it so important to know the location of a file or folder?
5. **Draw Conclusions** Why would you want to know a document's properties?
6. **Compare and Contrast** What are the advantages and disadvantages of organizing folders on your desktop instead of using the Documents folder?

1 Guided Practice

TechSIM Interactive Tutorials An interactive simulation about file management is available to explore.

Organize Your Files You need to create new folders to organize your files. You will use both the Documents folder and the desktop. If you need help completing a step, refer back to the exercise in parentheses at the end of the step.

Step-by-Step

1. Create a **new folder** on your desktop. Name it *Your Name* Mars Exhibit (Figure 1.22). (Exercise 1-5)

2. Open the **Documents** folder, and open the **Data File** folder named **2A Mars Project**. (Exercise 1-1)

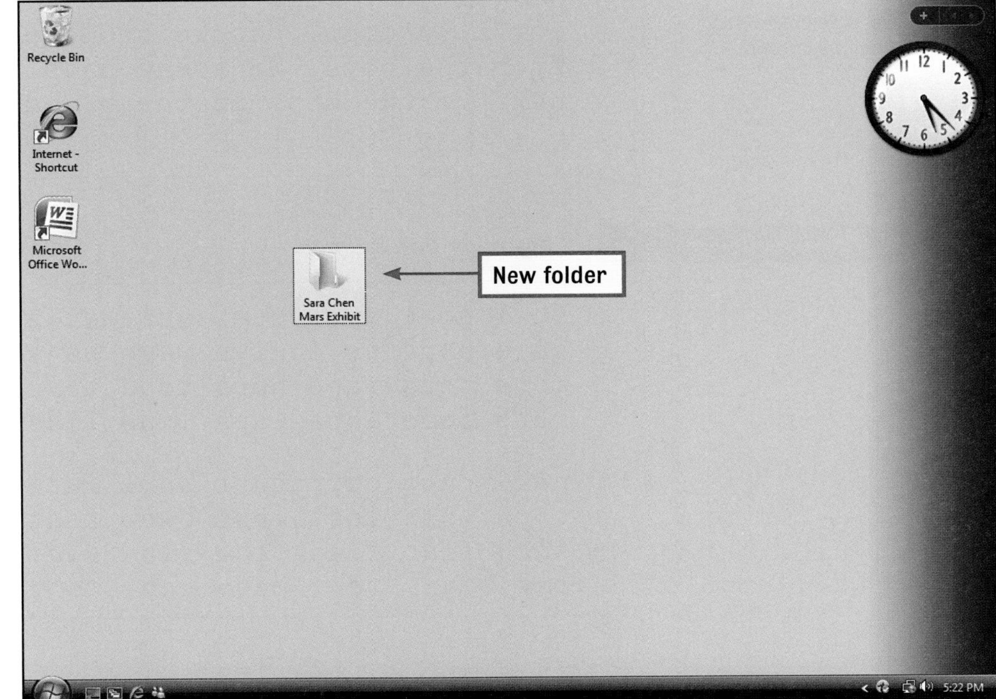

▼ **Figure 1.22** A new folder is created on the desktop.

Lesson 12 New Keys: Z Colon (:)

OBJECTIVE:
- Learn the Z and colon keys.

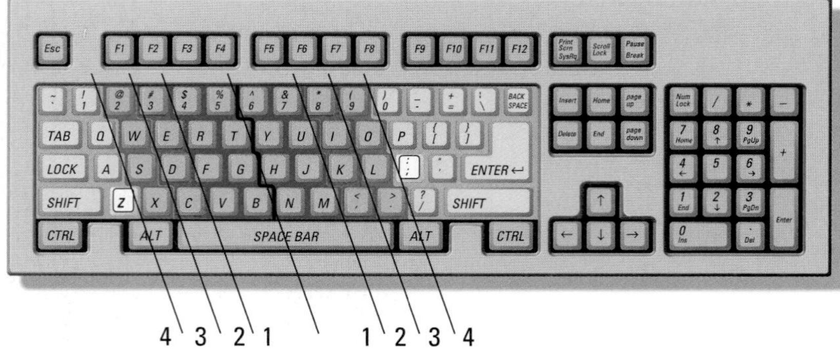

A. Warmup

Key each line 2 times.

```
1 bake chin jogs wave quip dome onyx left
2 His soft big lynx quickly jumped waves.
```

NEW KEYS

B. Z Key

Key each line 2 times. Repeat if time permits.

Use A finger. Anchor F.

```
3 aaa aza aza zaz aza aaa aza aza zaz aza
4 aza zip zip aza zoo zoo aza zap zap aza
5 aza dozing zebu, he zags, dazed zebras,
6 Zachary ate frozen pizza in the gazebo.
```

C. : Key

Key each line 2 times. Repeat if time permits.

Shift of ; Use left shift key. Anchor J. Space once after a colon.

```
7 ;:; ;:; ;:; ;:; ;:; ;:; ;:; ;:; ;:; ;:;
8 Dr. Webb: Mr. Que: Mrs. Downs: Ms. Lia:
9 Mr. Dode: Mrs. Chin: Ms. Finn: Dr. Mai:
10 To: From: Date: Subject: Attention: To:
```

SKILLBUILDING

D. Technique Checkpoint

Key each line 2 times. Repeat if time permits. Focus on the technique at the left.

Keep your elbows close to your body.

```
11 aaa aza aza zaz aza aaa aza aza zaz aza
12 ;:; ;:; ;:; ;:; ;:; ;:; ;:; ;:; ;:; ;:;
13 Zach and zany Hazel visited local zoos.
14 They saw: lazy zebras, apes, and lions.
```

4. Click the **Close** button to close the **Documents** folder.

5. Click the **Start** button. Notice the **Start Search** box above the **Start** button.

6. Key Mars and notice the files and folders that appear in the left pane of the **Start** menu.

7. Click the desktop to close the **Start** menu.

8. Click the **Start** button, and click **Documents**. The **Documents** folder opens.

9. Locate the **Search** box in the **Documents** window (Figure 1.20).

10. Click in the **Search** box, and key Spirit.

11. The Spirit files appear in the **File** list of the window, as shown in Figure 1.21.

12. Click the **Close** button to close the search results window.

Figure 1.20 The Search Results window shows you where the folder is located.

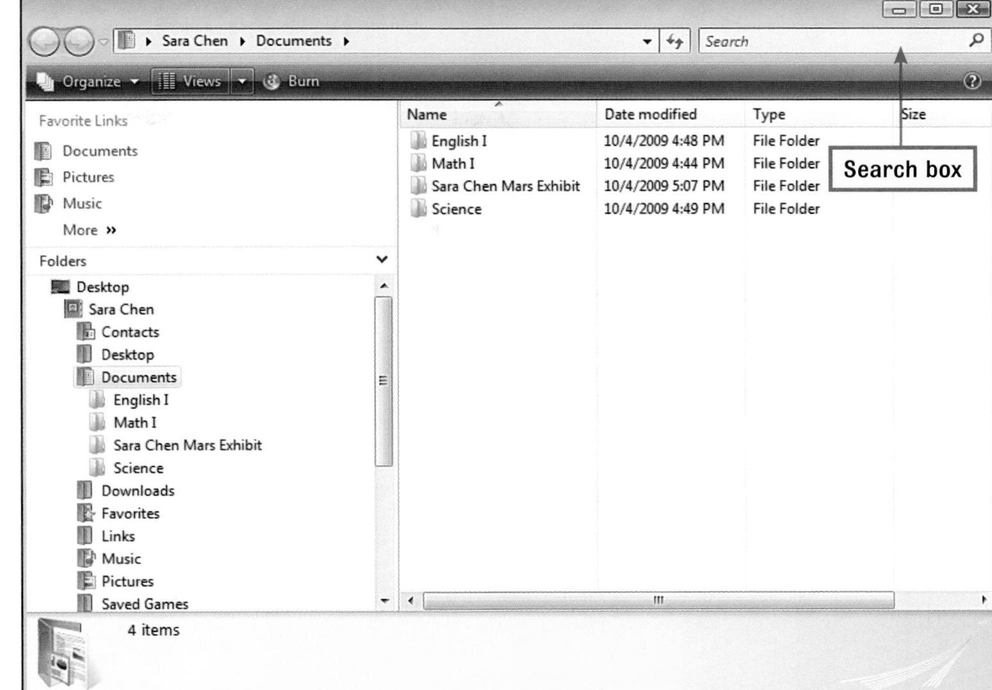

Figure 1.21 You can search for the file itself or the folder it is in.

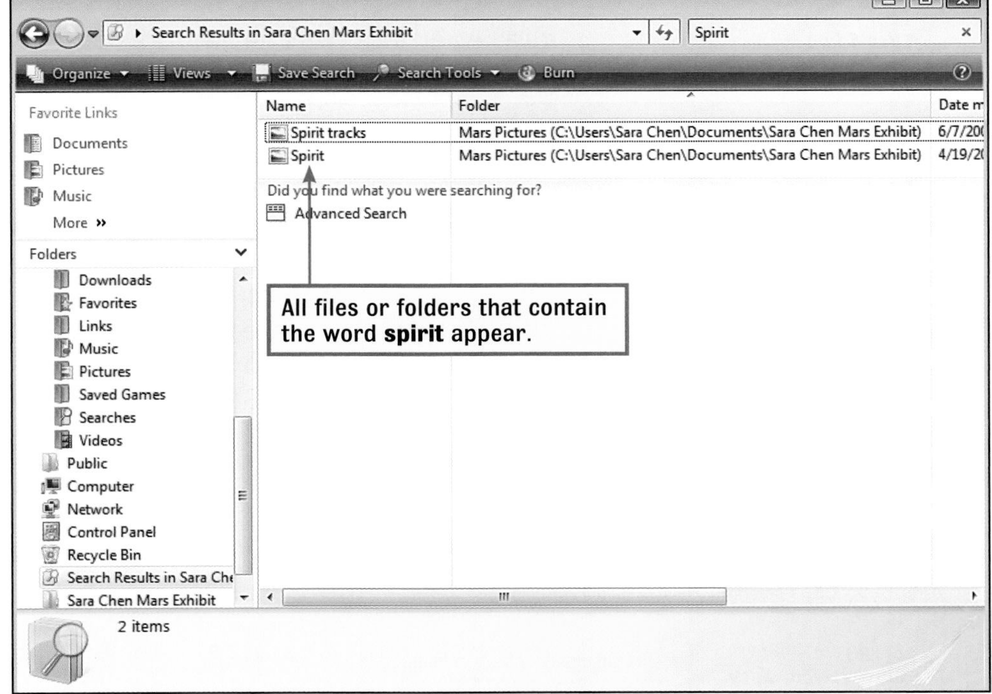

E. Technique Timings

Take two 30-second timings on each line. Focus on the technique at the left.

Keep your elbows in by your sides.

15 Type fast to reach the end of the line.
16 Keep your eyes on the copy as you type.
17 Tests are easy if you know the answers.
18 If they go to the zoo, invite them too.
| 1 | 2 | 3 | 4 | 5 | 6 | 7 | 8

F. PRETEST

Take a 1-minute timing on the paragraph. Note your speed and errors.

Remember to press ENTER *only at the end of the paragraph.*

19 As Inez roamed the ship, she told 7
20 fond tales. She slipped on that waxy 14
21 rung and fell to the deck. She hurt her 22
22 face and was dazed, but felt no pain. 30
| 1 | 2 | 3 | 4 | 5 | 6 | 7 | 8

G. PRACTICE

Key each line 2 times.

Check your posture.

23 waxy wavy wave save rave raze razz jazz
24 ship whip whop shop stop atop atoms At:
25 rung rang sang sing ring ping zing zinc
26 cure pure sure lure lyre byre bytes By:

27 tale kale Kate mate late lace face faze
28 fond pond bond binds bins inns Inez In:
29 gaze game fame same sale dale daze haze
30 roam loam loom zoom boom books took To:

H. POSTTEST

Repeat the Pretest. Compare your Posttest results with your Pretest results.

Exercise 1-6 Search for Files

TechSIM Interactive Tutorials
An interactive simulation about file management is available to explore.

Imagine you have collected hundreds of files for your exhibit. You have created folders and grouped the files, but you have so many folders that you cannot remember where the picture called Spirit is. What would you do?

To find a file, program, or folder, you can search for the lost item using the Search tool.

In this exercise, you will use the Windows Search methods. The table below shows various search methods.

Performing a Search

Search Options	Description	Example	Results
File Name	Key the name you have assigned to a file or folder.	mars rover	The search will display all the files and folders that match **mars rover** exactly.
Kind of File	Key a description of the content. Files are usually documents, pictures, or music.	Document	Search displays all of your text, spreadsheet, presentation, and graphic files.
Type of File	Key the file name extension.	.docx	Displays Word 2007 documents.
*	Use a partial name followed by an asterisk to represent any number of characters.	mars*	Search results include file names, file contents, and file properties containing ***mars*** (e.g., *Mars* photos, *mars*upials, *mars*hall).
Date	Click Advanced and select any date, an exact date, date before, or date after.	Date is after 7/22/2010	The results will return files and folders created after 7/22/2010.

Step-by-Step

1. Click the **Start** button, and click **Search**. The **Search Results** window displays.
2. Click the **Search** text box (Figure 1.19).
3. Key Mars Pictures. As you key text, files and folders appear in the **File** list. Double-click the folder to open it.

Figure 1.19 The Search box is located at the top of every folder.

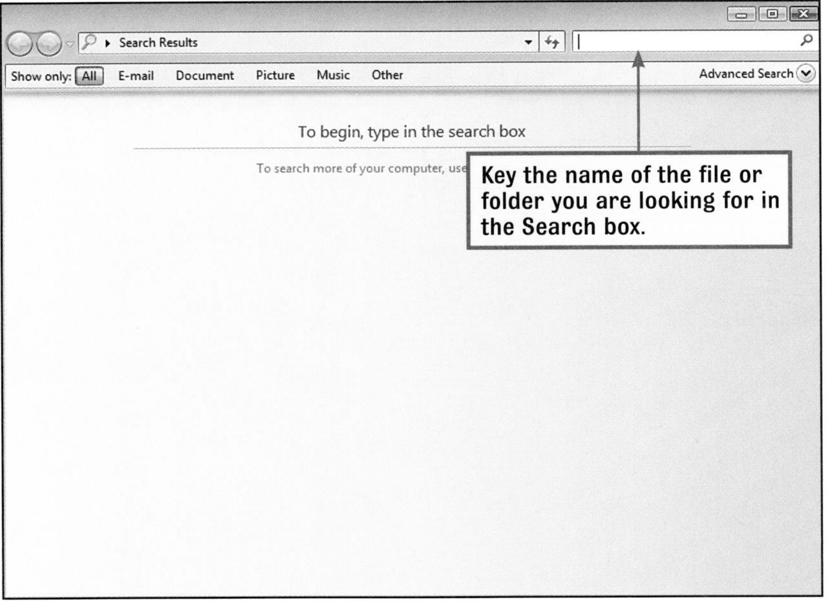

Lesson 13 New Keys: ? Caps Lock

OBJECTIVES:

- Learn the ? key.
- Use the caps lock key to type all-capital letters.
- Compose at the keyboard.

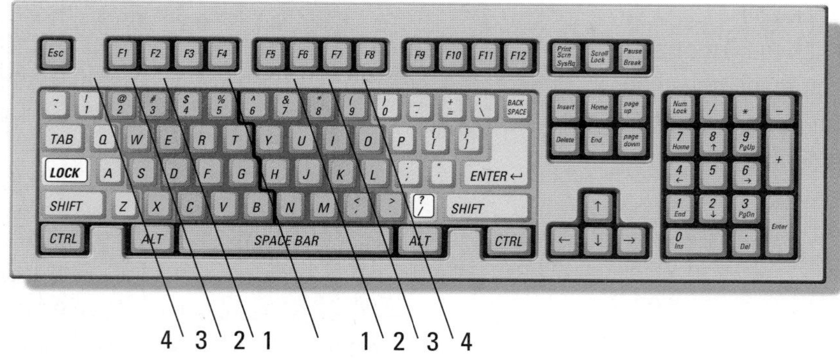

A. Warmup

Key each line 2 times.

Hold those anchors.

```
1 herbs jinx gawk miff vest zinc ploy quad best zoo
2 Dozy oryx have quit jumping over the huge flocks.
3 Lax folks quickly judged the lazy dogs unfit now.
```

NEW KEYS

B. ? Keys

Key each line 2 times. Repeat if time permits.

Shift of /. Use Sem finger and left shift key. Anchor J. Space once after a question mark.

```
4 ;;; ;/; ;/? ;?; ;?; ;;; ;/; ;/? ;?; ;?; ;;; ;/ ;?
5 ;/; ;?; now? now? ;?; how? how? ;?; who? who? ;?;
6 Who? What? Why? Where? When? Next? How many? Now?
7 How can Joe get there? Which way are the outlets?
```

C. Caps Lock Key

Use A finger.

Use the caps lock key to type letters or words in all-capital letters (all caps). You must press the shift key to type symbols appearing on the top half of the number keys.

Key each line 2 times. Repeat if time permits.

```
8 A COMPUTER rapidly scanned most AIRMAIL packages.
9 Another START/STOP safety lever was stuck lately.
10 Was JOSE elected CLASS PRESIDENT today or sooner?
11 You should not answer my door WHEN YOU ARE ALONE.
```

SKILLBUILDING

D. Technique Checkpoint

Key each line 2 times. Repeat if time permits.

Quickly return fingers to home keys after reaching to other keys.

```
12 ;;; ;/; ;/? ;?; ;?; ;;; ;/; ;/? ;?; ;?; ;;; ;/ ;?
13 Did you see HELEN? Did you learn about her crash?
14 Her auto was hit by a TRAIN. She broke BOTH arms.
15 HOW will she manage while both arms are in casts?
```

11 **Double-click** your **Mars Exhibit** folder to **open** it, then click the **Opportunity** folder once.

12 Click the **Organize** command, then choose **Rename**. A box appears around the file name.

13 Key *Your Name* Opportunity in the box, and press ENTER on the keyboard (Figure 1.17).

14 Click the **Close** button [X] to return to the desktop.

15 Right-click the **Mars Exhibit** folder, then choose **Properties** from the menu.

16 Click the **General** tab, and note the folder's type, location, size, and date it was created (Figure 1.18).

17 **Close** the **Properties** box, then right-click the **Mars Exhibit** folder.

18 Click **Delete**, then choose **Yes**. The folder disappears from the desktop.

▼ **Figure 1.17** You follow the same steps to rename either a file or folder.

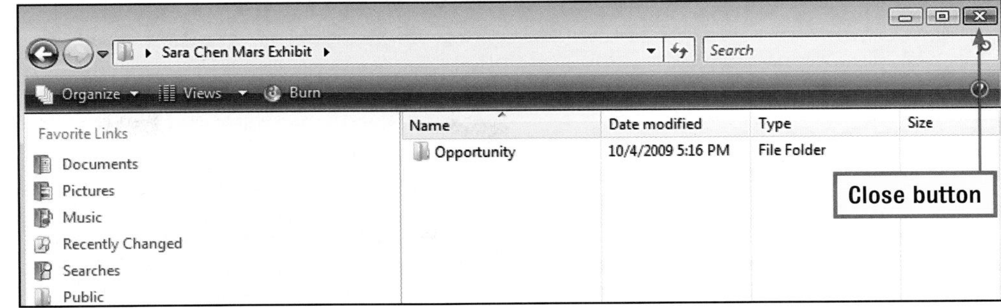

▼ **Figure 1.18** Viewing the properties of a file or folder can help you determine where the item is located and whether it is the latest version.

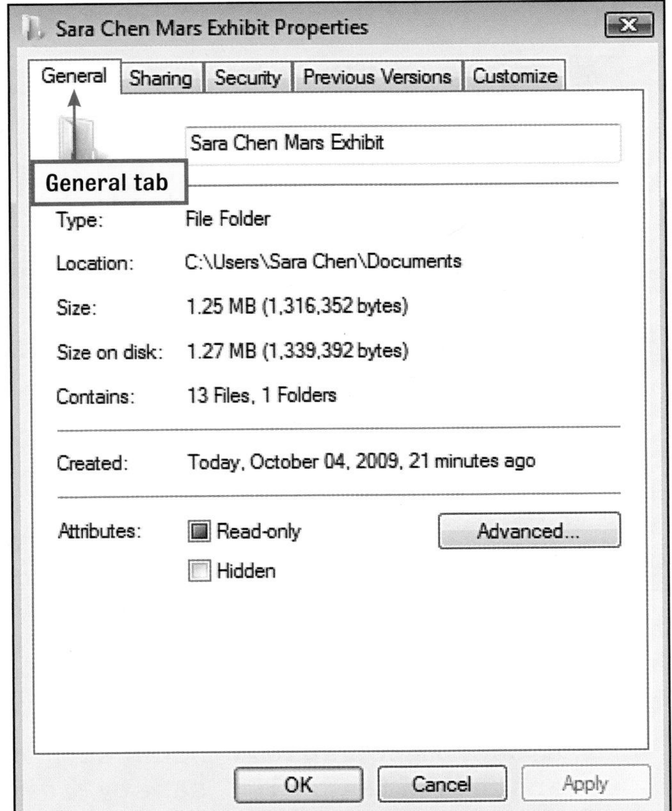

TechSavvy

File Properties Files and folders both have properties. Different types of files might have different properties. For example, a Word document could show a summary, the author, and other properties. A music file might show the title and artist, license information, and even lyrics.

SKILLBUILDING

E. Technique Timings

Take two 30-second timings on each line. Focus on the technique at the left.

Hold those anchors. Quickly return your fingers to home-key position.

```
16 Tony was a better friend than Hope was to Salena.
17 Lu and I were at Camp Piney Forest in early fall.
18 I rode the Rocky Ford train to San Juan in March.
19 Maya, Sue, and Grace were there. It was exciting.
   | 1 | 2 | 3 | 4 | 5 | 6 | 7 | 8 | 9 | 10
```

F. PRETEST

Take a 1-minute timing on the paragraph. Note your speed and errors.

```
20      The blind slats are broken. Can you fix the    9
21 broken ones? My WILY dog jumped out of the window  19
22 which is how this happened. There should be some   29
23 way to stop him. For a young dog, he is AMAZING.   38
   | 1 | 2 | 3 | 4 | 5 | 6 | 7 | 8 | 9 | 10
```

G. PRACTICE

Key each line 2 times.

```
24 slat slit skit suit quit quid quip quiz whiz fizz
25 LASS bass BASE bake CAKE cage PAGE sage SAGA sags
26 maze mare more move wove cove core cure pure pore
27 mix; fix; fin; kin; kind wind wild wily will well

28 cape cane vane sane same sale pale pals pats bats
29 jump pump bump lump limp limb lamb jamb jams hams
30 slow BLOW blot SLOT plot PLOP flop FLIP blip BLOB
31 mite more wire tire hire hide hive jive give five
```

H. POSTTEST

Repeat the Pretest. Compare your Posttest results with your Pretest results.

I. Composing at the Keyboard

Language Link

Answer the following questions with a single word.

Keep your eyes on the screen as you key.

32 What day of the week is today?
33 What is your favorite animal?
34 What is your favorite food?
35 What is your favorite ice cream flavor?
36 What month is your birthday?

4 Open the **Documents** folder by clicking the **Start** button and then clicking **Documents**.

5 Locate the **Data File** folder, and open the **2A Mars Project** file.

6 **Copy** the **Opportunity** folder, and then close the **Documents** folder window. **Hint**: See Exercise 1-2, page 55, to review how to copy folders.

7 **Right-click** the **desktop**, and choose **Paste** (Figure 1.15).

▼ **Figure 1.15** Use Paste to copy a folder onto the desktop.

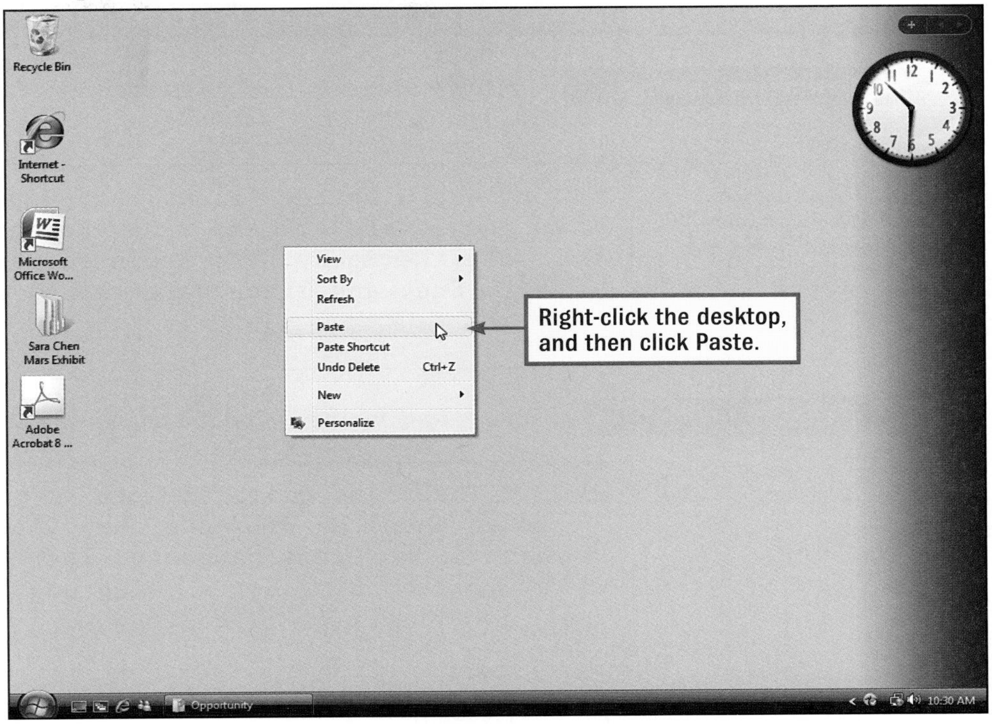

8 The **Opportunity** folder now appears on the desktop (Figure 1.16).

9 Click the **Opportunity** folder and hold down the left mouse button.

10 Drag the **Opportunity** folder on top of your **Mars Exhibit** folder. Release the mouse button when the two folders overlap. The **Opportunity** folder is now inside your **Mars Exhibit** folder.

▼ **Figure 1.16** Use your mouse to drag and drop one folder into another.

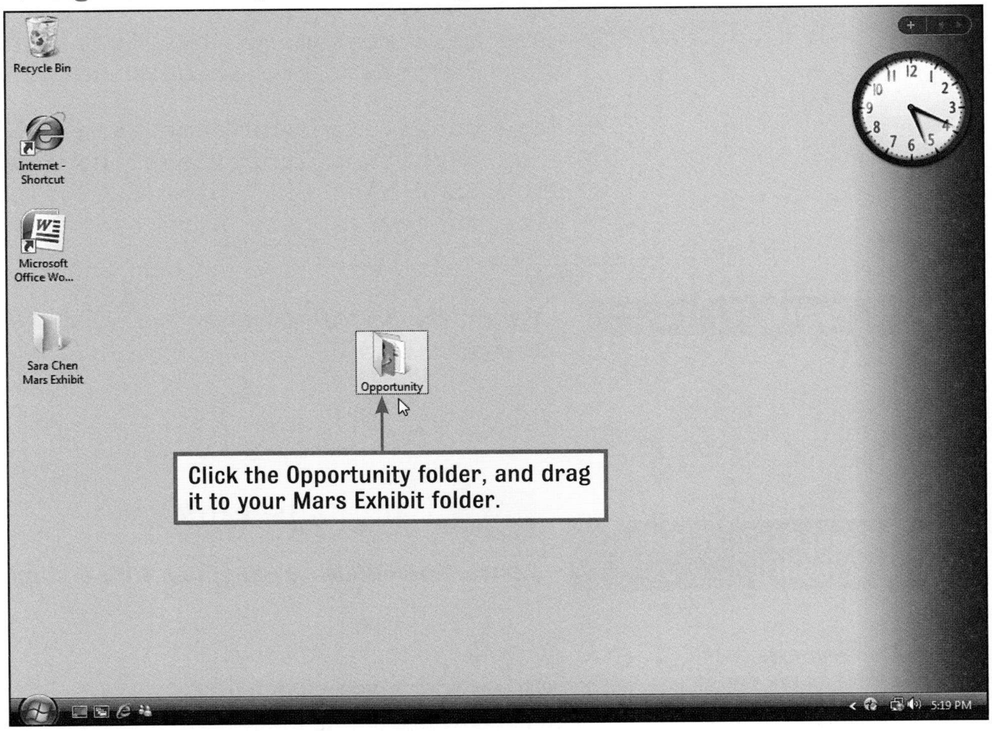

Lesson 14 — New Keys: - _

OBJECTIVES:

- Learn the hyphen (-) and underscore (_) keys.
- Key 25/1'/2e.

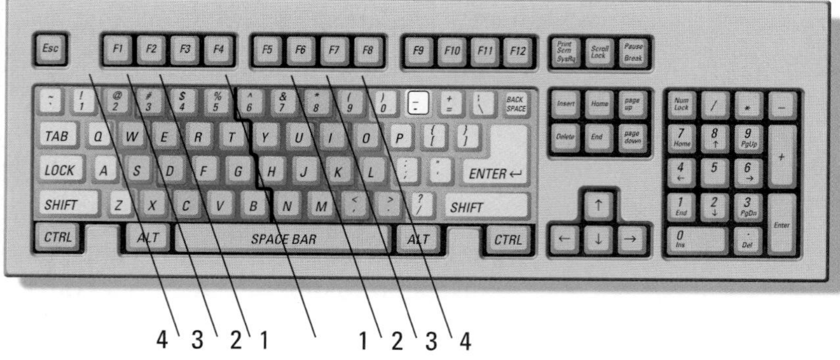

A. Warmup

Key each line 2 times.

```
1 rave jinx tact safe mind glib quit yelp hawk doze
2 We all must be good friends to have good friends.
3 We have quickly gained sixty prizes for best jam.
```

NEW KEYS

B. - Keys

Key each line 2 times. Repeat if time permits.

Use Sem finger. Anchor J. Do not space before or after hyphens.

```
4 ;;; ;p; ;p-; ;-; -;- ;;; ;p; ;p-; ;-; -;- ;;; ;-;
5 ;p- ;-; self-made ;-; one-third ;p- one-sixth ;-;
6 ;p- ;-; part-time ;-; one-tenth ;p- two-party ;-;
7 Self-made Jim stopped at an out-of-the-way place.
```

C. _ Keys (UNDERSCORE)

Key each line 2 times. Repeat if time permits.

Use the Sem finger and the left shift key. Anchor J.

```
8 ;p; ;p- ;-; ;-_; ;-_; ;p-_ _;_ ;p-_ ;-_; ;_; ;p-_
9 ;;; ;p; ;p_; ;_; _;_ ;;; ;p; ;p_; ;_; _;_ ;;; ;_;
10 Quick, create this seven-character line: _______.
11 Be sure to use her e-mail name, jennifer_cochran.
```

SKILLBUILDING

D. Technique Checkpoint

Key each line 2 times. Repeat if time permits. Focus on the techniques at the left.

Keep your feet on the floor, back straight, elbows in.

```
12 ;;; ;p; ;p-; ;-; -;- ;;; ;p; ;p-; ;-; -;- ;;; ;-;
13 ;;; ;p; ;p_; ;_; _;_ ;;; ;p; ;p_; ;_; _;_ ;;; ;_;
14 Are you an easy-going person who gets along well?
15 The new name he now uses for e-mail is jute_rope.
```

Exercise 1-5 Work on the Desktop

TechSIM Interactive Tutorials
An interactive simulation about file management is available to explore.

When you use certain files or folders a lot, you can create shortcuts for them on the desktop. A **shortcut** is an icon that is a direct link to a file or folder. For example, your teachers might put shortcuts to classroom folders or applications on the desktop so that students can access them quickly. This way, you do not have to look through all the files on the school's network.

Try to keep only a few files and folders or shortcuts on your desktop. If the desktop has too many items on it, you may no longer be able to find the items that you need quickly.

In this exercise, you will create, rename, and move files on the desktop instead of using the Documents folder window.

Step-by-Step

1. On the desktop, right-click your mouse. A shortcut menu appears.
2. In the menu, choose **New**, and click **Folder** (Figure 1.14).
3. In the **New Folder** box, key *Your Name* Mars Exhibit, then press ENTER.

▼ **Figure 1.14** **Right-click the desktop to display shortcut menus.**

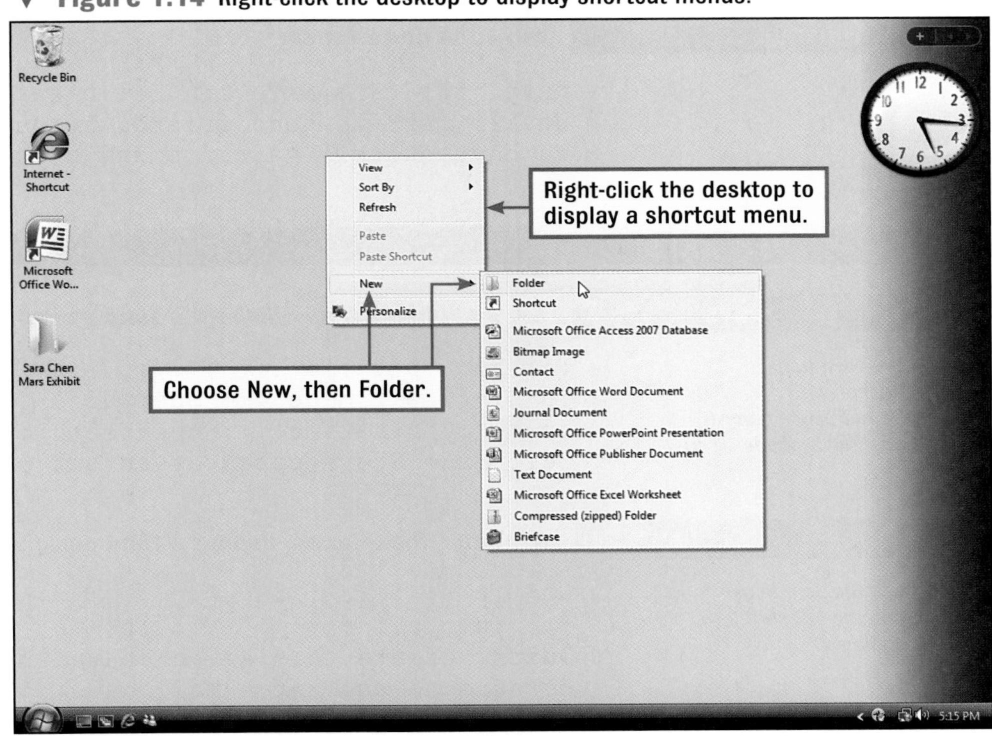

HELP!

How do I navigate on my computer? Use the **Folders** list, which is located in the **Navigation** Pane. The **Navigation** Pane displays on the left side of every folder. Click **Folders** at the bottom of the **Navigation** Pane to open the **Folders** list. Click **Folders** again to close the **Folders** list.

SKILLBUILDING

E. Technique Timings

Take two 30-second timings on each line. Focus on the techniques at the left.

Sit up straight, keep your elbows in, and keep your feet flat on the floor.

16 Steward and Phon drove a car down to the shelter.
17 Ten people helped serve meals to thirty children.
18 They said it was hard work. Jung felt happy then.
19 This might help solve these problems in our city.
| 1 | 2 | 3 | 4 | 5 | 6 | 7 | 8 | 9 | 10

F. PRETEST

Take a 1-minute timing on the paragraph. Note your speed and errors.

20 Look up in the western sky and see how it is 9
21 filled with magnificent pinks and reds as the sun 19
22 begins to set. As the sun sinks below the clouds, 29
23 you will see an amazing display of great colors. 39
| 1 | 2 | 3 | 4 | 5 | 6 | 7 | 8 | 9 | 10

G. PRACTICE

SPEED: If you made 2 or fewer errors on the Pretest, key lines 24–31 two times each.

ACCURACY: If you made more than 2 errors on the Pretest, key lines 24–27 as a group two times. Then, key lines 28–31 as a group two times.

Left and right reaches are a sequence of at least three letters typed by fingers on either the left or the right hand. (lease, think)

24 was raged wheat serve force carts bears cages age
25 tag exact vases rests crank enter greet moves ear
26 was raged wheat serve force carts bears cages age
27 tag exact vases rests crank enter greet moves ear

28 get table stage hired diets gears wages warts rat
29 hop mouth union input polka alone moors tunic joy
30 him looms pumps nouns joked pound allow pours hip
31 lip mopes loose equip moods unite fills alike mop

H. POSTTEST

Repeat the Pretest. Compare your Posttest results with your Pretest results.

I. 1-Minute Timings

Take two 1-minute timings on the paragraph. Note your speed and errors.

Goal: 25/1'/2e

32 We saw where gray lava flowed down a path. 9
33 At the exit, Justin saw trees with no bark and a 19
34 quiet, fuzzy duck looking at me. 25
| 1 | 2 | 3 | 4 | 5 | 6 | 7 | 8 | 9 | 10

5 Click the **Documents** folder in the **Navigation** Pane.

6 Scroll through the folders until you find your own **Mars Exhibit** folder.

7 Double-click the **Mars Exhibit** folder. The folder name appears in the **Address** bar.

8 Click the **File name** box, and key *Your Name* Rover Instruments. (Figure 1.12).

9 Click the **Save** button. You should see the new file name at the top of your Word screen (Figure 1.13).

▼ **Figure 1.12** You can use Save As to save your work to a new drive, such as a floppy disk or a CD-R drive.

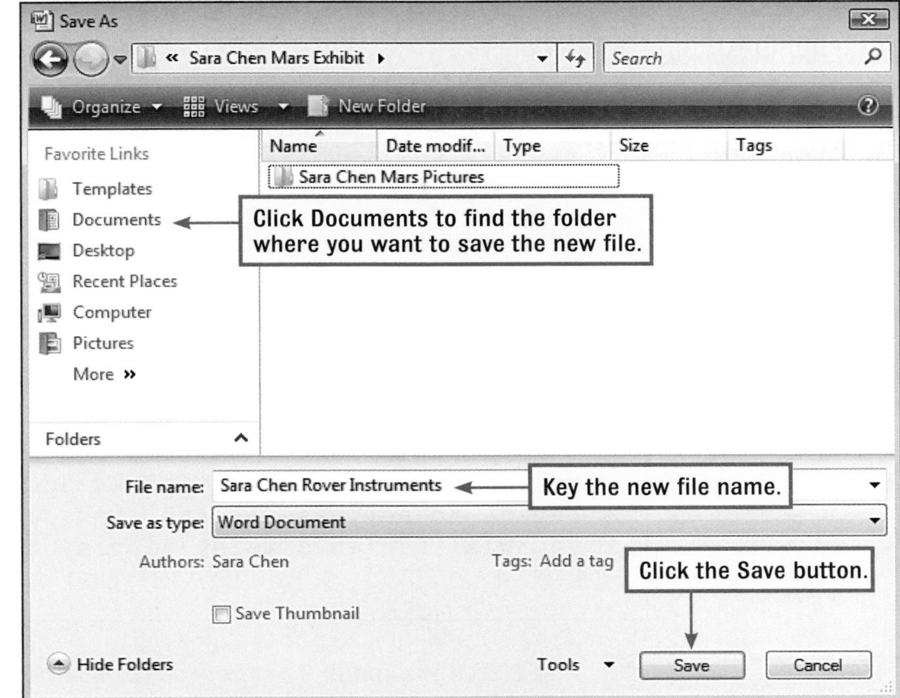

10 Click the blue **Close** button [X] to exit Word.

11 On the taskbar, click the **Opportunity** folder to return to the **Documents** folder window.

12 **Open** your **Mars Exhibit** folder, and click the **Rover Instruments** file you just saved.

13 Click the **Organize** command, and choose **Delete**. In the **Delete File** box, click **Yes**.

14 Click the **Close** button [X] to exit the **Documents** folder window.

▼ **Figure 1.13** The Save As function creates a duplicate of a file.

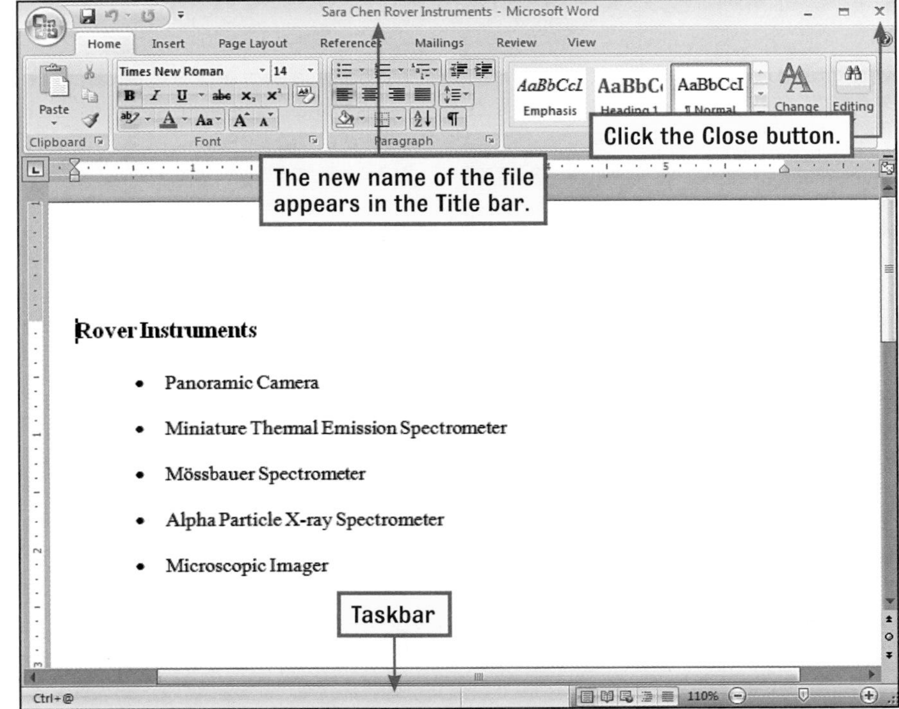

Lesson 15

New Keys: 4 $ 7 &

OBJECTIVES:

- Learn the 4, $, 7, and & keys.
- Refine keyboarding techniques.
- Key 27/2'/4e.

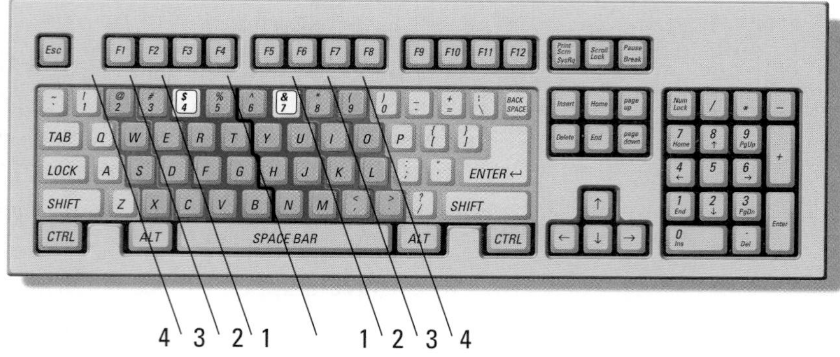

A. Warmup

Key each line 2 times.

Words	1 shot idea jobs corn quip give flex whey maze elks
Speed	2 It is not a good idea to play ball in the street.
Accuracy	3 My joke expert amazed five huge clowns in Quebec.

NEW KEYS

B. 4 and $ Keys

Key each line 2 times. Repeat if time permits.

Use F finger.
Anchor A.

```
4 frf fr4f f4f 444 f4f 4/44 f4f 44.4 f4f 44,444 f4f
5 44 films, 44 foes, 44 flukes, 44 folders, or 4.44
6 I saw 44 ducks, 4 geese, and 4 swans on the lake.
7 Today, our team had 4 runs, 4 hits, and 4 errors.
```

$ is the shift of 4.
Do not space between the $ and the number.

```
8 frf fr4 f4f f4$f f$f f$f $4 $44 $444 f$f f4f $444
9 $444, 44 fish, 4 fans, $44, 444 fellows, $4, $444
10 Jo paid $44 for the oranges and $4 for the pears.
11 They had $444 and spent $44 of it for 4 presents.
```

C. 7 and & Keys

Key each line 2 times. Repeat if time permits.

Use J finger.
Anchor ;.

```
12 juj ju7j j7j 777 j7j 7/77 j7j 77.7 j7j 77,777 j7j
13 77 jokers, 77 joggers, 77 jets, or 7.77, 77 jumps
14 Hank will perform July 4 and 7, not June 4 and 7.
15 On July 4, we celebrated; on August 7, we rested.
```

Use J finger and left shift.
Anchor ;.
Space before and after the ampersand.

```
16 juj ju7 j7j j7&j j&j j&j j& &j& ju7& j&j j7j ju7&
17 7 jugs & 7 jars & 7 jewels & 7 jurors & 7 jungles
18 He thinks he paid $44 & $77 instead of $47 & $74.
19 B & C ordered 744 from Dixon & Sons on January 7.
```

Exercise 1-4 Create a Copy Using Save As

TechSIM Interactive Tutorials
An interactive simulation about file management is available to explore.

In the last two exercises, you copied files and then renamed them. After you copy a file to your folder and rename it, you can work in it and make changes. The original file stays safely in its original location with its original name.

You can also duplicate, or copy, a file by using the **Save As** command. This lets you rename a file and, at the same time, copy the file by saving it to a new location. Use Save As or Copy when you want to make changes to a file and still keep the original. These commands also let you create back up copies of your work on recordable CDs (CD-Rs) or other removable storage devices.

Files have a special three- or four-letter extension after the file name. This tells the computer if the file is a text document, a graphic, a sound clip, and so on. For example, Word 2007 documents have ".docx" at the end. Photograph file names often have ".jpg" on the end. If you rename a file, do not change the file extension or you may not be able to reopen it.

In this exercise, you will use Save As to save a photo from a data file to your own folder and rename it.

Step-by-Step

1. Browse the **Documents** folder window to locate the **Data Files** folder. Open the folder named **2A Mars Project**, then click the **Opportunity** folder.

2. Double-click the **Rover Instruments** file. The file opens in Microsoft Word. **Note**: The Documents folder stays open on your taskbar.

3. Click the **Office Button** (icon). See Figure 1.11.

4. Click **Save As**. **Note**: You can save a copy of the document in various Word formats and other formats.

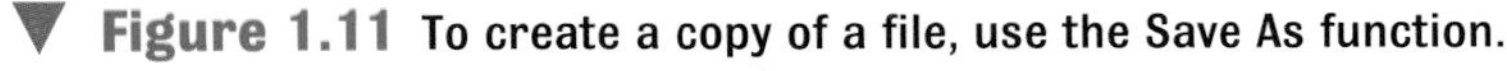
Figure 1.11 To create a copy of a file, use the Save As function.

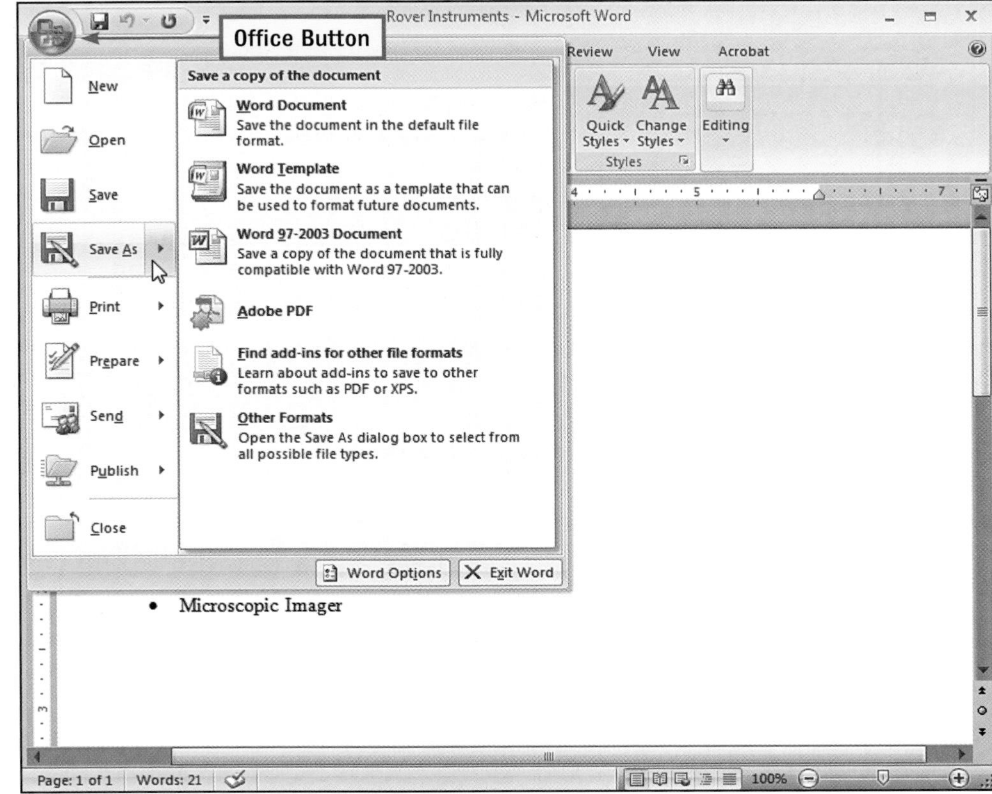

SKILLBUILDING

D. Technique Timings

Take two 30-second timings on each line. Focus on the techniques at the left.

Lines 20 and 21: Keep your eyes on the copy. Lines 22 and 23: Space without pausing.

```
20 Kara saw a ship as she was walking over the hill.
21 Ned says he can mend the urn that fell and broke.
22 The five of us had to get to the bus before noon.
23 Lou said he would be at the game to see us later.
```

E. PRETEST

Take a 1-minute timing on the paragraph. Note your speed and errors.

```
24      Each of us should try to eat healthful food,   9
25 get proper rest, and exercise moderately. All of   19
26 these things will help each of us face life with   29
27 more enthusiasm and more energy.                   35
   | 1 | 2 | 3 | 4 | 5 | 6 | 7 | 8 | 9 | 10
```

F. PRACTICE

SPEED: If you made 2 or fewer errors on the Pretest, key lines 28–35 two times.

ACCURACY: If you made more than 2 errors on the Pretest, type lines 28–31 as a group two times. Then key lines 32–35 as a group two times.

Adjacent Reaches

```
28 tr train tree tried truth troop strum strip stray
29 op open slope opera sloop moped scoop hoped opine
30 er were loner every steer error veers sewer verge
31 po port porter pole pods potter potion pound pout
```

Jump Reaches

```
32 on onion ozone upon honor front spoon phone wrong
33 ex exams exist exact flex exits exalt vexed Texas
34 ve even veers vests verbs leave every verge heave
35 ni nine ninth night nimble nifty nice nickel nighi
```

G. POSTTEST

Repeat the Pretest. Compare your Posttest results with your Pretest results.

4 Return to your own **Mars Exhibit** folder, then click your **Mars Pictures** folder.

5 Click the **Organize** command, then choose **Paste**. The photo is added to your folder.

6 Open your **Mars Pictures** folder, then click the **rover_sundial** file.

7 Click the **Organize** command, then choose **Rename** (Figure 1.9).

▼ **Figure 1.9** Use the File menu to rename files.

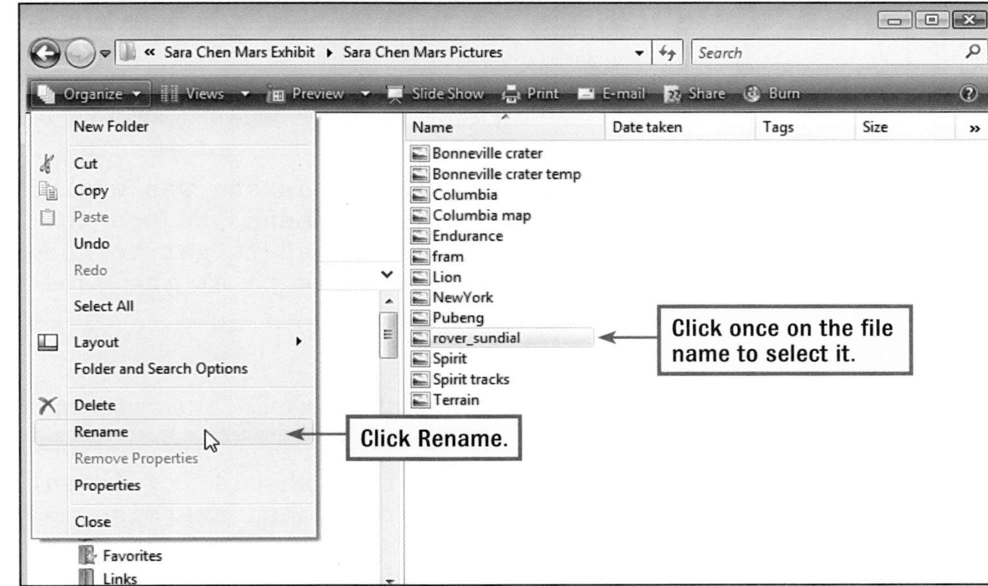

8 Key the new name, Mars Rover, and press ENTER.

9 In the same **Mars Pictures** folder, click the **Terrain** file, then press DELETE on the keyboard.

10 In the **Delete File** box, click **Yes** (Figure 1.10).

▼ **Figure 1.10** Think before you delete a file or folder.

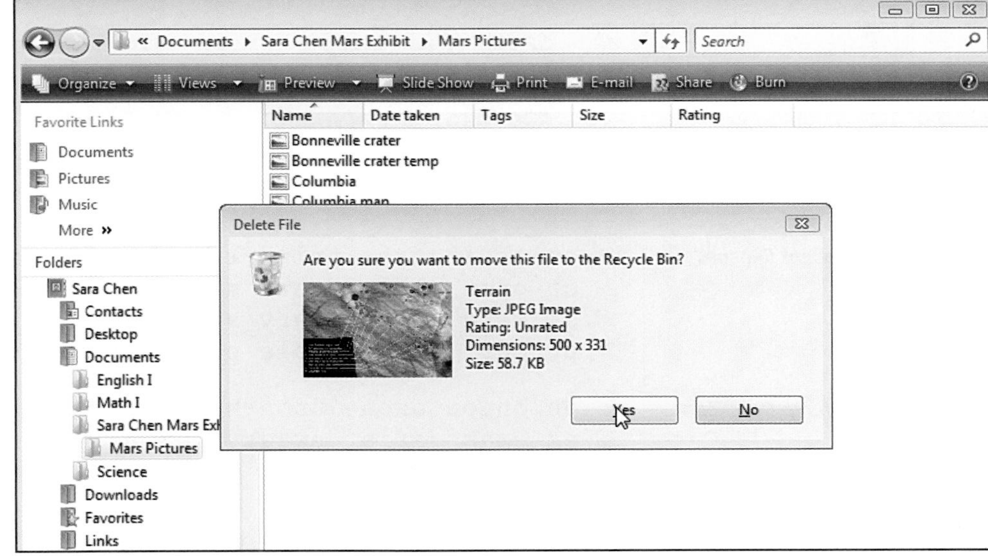

Different Strokes

Selecting Multiple Files To select more than one file in a folder, you can:

- Click the **Organize** command, then click **Select All**.
- Click the first file, press and hold down SHIFT, then click the last file.
- Press and hold down CTRL, then click the files you want.

H. 1-Minute Alpha-numeric Timing

Take a 1-minute timing on the paragraph. Note your speed and errors.

36 Luke sent a $47 check to Computers & Such to 9
37 get a disk with 44 games & 4 special programs for 19
38 7 friends. He saw 47 of his friends at 4 p.m. 28

| 1 | 2 | 3 | 4 | 5 | 6 | 7 | 8 | 9 | 10

I. 2-Minute Timings

Take two 2-minute timings on lines 39–44. Note your speed and errors.

Goal: 27/2'/4e

39 Have you been to our zoo? This is a great 9
40 thing to do in the summer. Bring your lunch to 18
41 eat in the park by the lake. You can watch a bear 28
42 cub perform or just view the zebras. Then explore 38
43 this spot and see the many quail and ducks. Take 48
44 some photos to capture the day. 54

| 1 | 2 | 3 | 4 | 5 | 6 | 7 | 8 | 9 | 10

Exercise 1-3 Work with Files

TechSIM Interactive Tutorials
An interactive simulation about file management is available to explore.

When you move, copy, rename, delete, or organize files, you have to follow the same guidelines as you do when you work with folders. If you are not careful, you can lose files or folders by forgetting where you saved them or what you named them.

When you rewrite or create a new version of a document, you may want to rename it. Often, the easiest way to do this is to add a date "in" the file name. That way, you can easily know that the document with the latest date is the most up-to-date. You can then place all versions of the document into a folder with the same document name.

In this exercise, you will move a file by copying it, then pasting it. You will then practice renaming and deleting the file.

Step-by-Step

1. Browse to your **Data Files** folder, and open the **2A Mars Project** folder.

2. Click the **Opportunity** folder once, then click the file named **rover_sundial**.

3. Click the **Organize** command, then choose **Copy** to copy the **rover_ sundial** file (Figure 1.8).

▼ **Figure 1.8** Use the Organize command to copy and paste files.

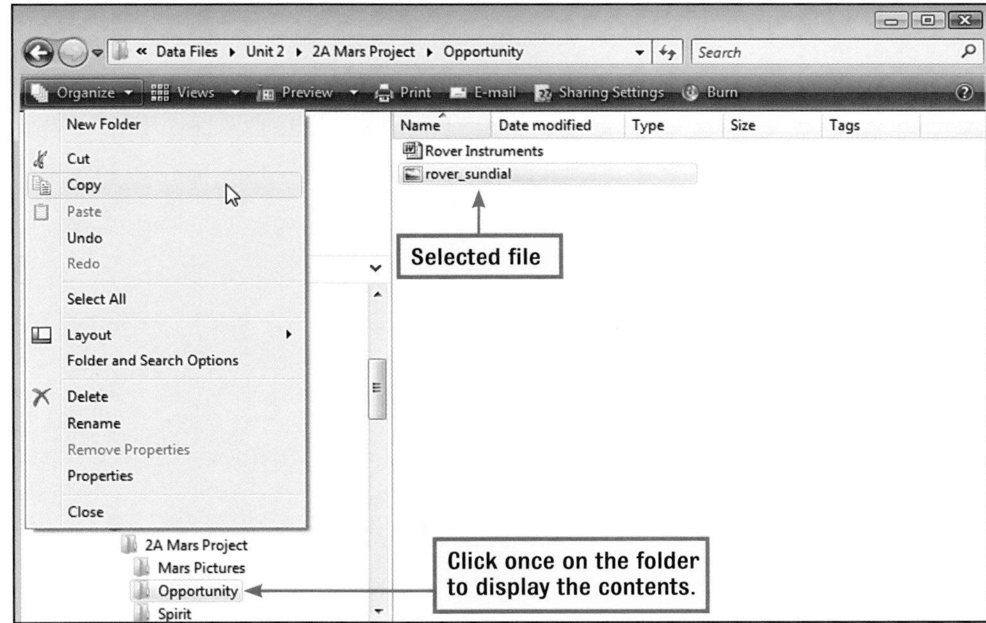

TechSavvy

Recycle Bin To restore a folder or file that you deleted from the hard drive, double-click the **Recycle Bin** icon. Then click the deleted file or folder. Click the **Restore** command. The file or folder will reappear in its original place.

To empty the **Recycle Bin**, double-click the **Recycle Bin** icon. Click the **Empty the Recycle Bin** command. When you delete an item in the **Recycle Bin**, it is permanently deleted and cannot be restored.

Lesson 16 — New Keys: 3 # 8 *

OBJECTIVES:

- Learn the 3, #, 8, and * keys.
- Refine keyboarding skills.
- Key 27/2'/4e.

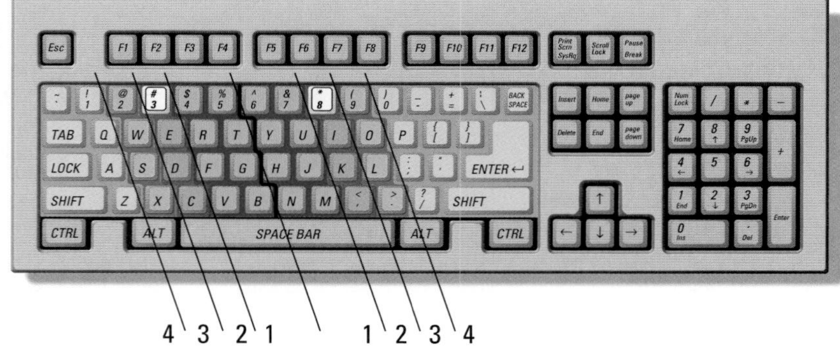

A. Warmup

Key each line 2 times.

Speed	1	The time for Andrew to stop is when the sun sets.
Accuracy	2	Ten foxes quickly jumped high over twelve zebras.
Numbers	3	Lines 47, 77, and 44 were right; line 74 was not.
Symbols	4	Bakes & Deli pays $4, $4.77, and $7.44 for dimes.

NEW KEYS

B. 3 and # Keys

Key each line 2 times. Repeat if time permits.

Use D finger.
Anchor A or F.

```
5 ded de3d d3d 333 d3d 3/33 d3d 33.3 d3d 33,333 d3d
6 33 dimes, 33 dishes, 33 dots, 33 daisies, or 3.33
7 Draw 33 squares, 3,333 rectangles, and 3 circles.
8 They had 333 dogs in 33 kennels for over 3 weeks.
```

The # (number or pound sign) is the shift of 3.
Anchor A or F.
Do not space between the number and #.

```
9 ded de3 d3d d3#d d#d d#d #3 #33 #333 d#d d3d #333
10 #3, 3 dots, #33, 33 dogs, #333, 333 ditches, #333
11 Is Invoice #373 for 344#, 433#, or 343# of fruit?
12 The group used 43# of grade #3 potatoes at lunch.
```

C. 8 and * Keys

Key each line 2 times. Key smoothly as you use the shift keys. Repeat if time permits.

Use K finger.
Anchor ;.

```
13 kik ki8k k8k 888 k8k 8/88 k8k 88.8 k8k 88,888 k8k
14 88 kegs, 88 kilns, 88 knocks, 88 kickers, or 8.88
15 Our zoo has 88 zebras, 38 snakes, and 33 monkeys.
16 The house is at 88 Lake Street, 8 blocks farther.
```

*The * (asterisk) is the shift of 8.*
*Do not space between the word and *.*

```
17 kik ki8 k8k k8*k k*k k*k *8 *88 *888 k*k k8k *888
18 *8, 88 kits, *88, 88 keys, *888, 88 kimonos, *888
19 This manual* and this report* are in the library.
20 Reports* are due in 8 weeks* and should be typed.
```

5 Use the **scroll** bar in the **Navigation** Pane to locate the **Data Files** folder for your class. Follow your teacher's instructions.

6 Click the folder named **2A Mars Project** in the **Navigation** Pane. The contents of the folder appear in the **File** list.

7 Click the **Mars Pictures** folder, and click the **Organize** command. Choose the **Copy** command (Figure 1.6).

8 Scroll the **Navigation** Pane to locate the **Mars Exhibit** folder you created in steps 2-4.

9 Click the folder to select it.

10 Click the **Organize** command, then choose **Paste**. The Mars Pictures folder now appears in your folder as shown in Figure 1.7.

11 Click to select the **Mars Picture** folder.

12 Click the **Organize** command, then choose **Rename**.

13 Key *Your Name* Mars Picture, and press ENTER to rename the folder.

▼ **Figure 1.6** You can use the Organize command to copy, cut, and paste folders.

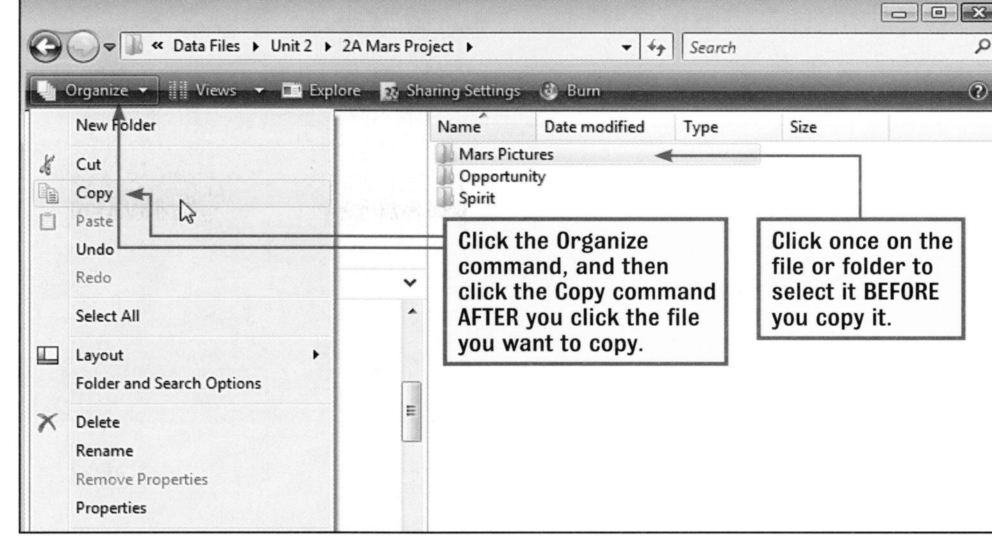

▼ **Figure 1.7.** The right side of the Documents folder shows the contents of the highlighted folder.

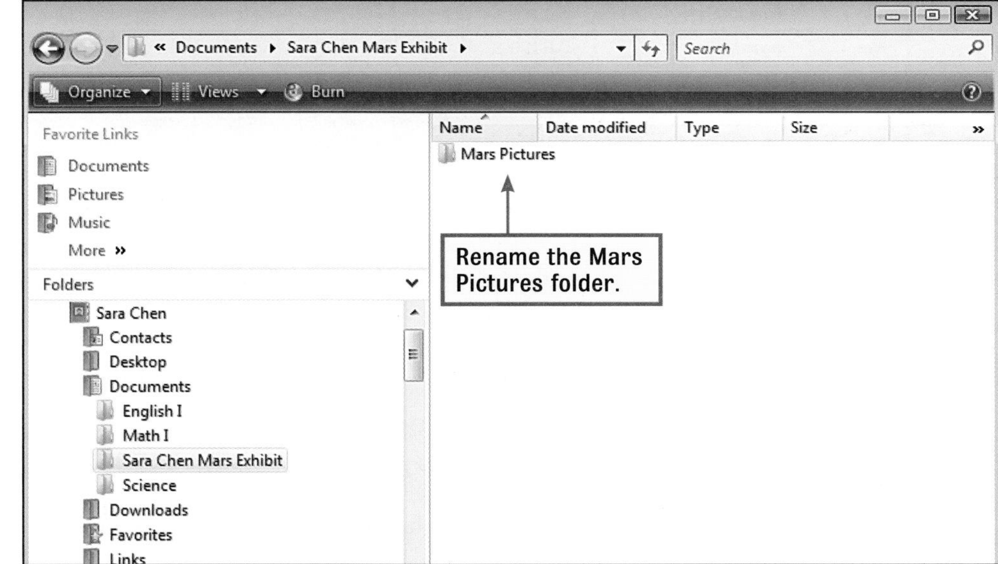

Different Strokes

Moving Files and Folders There are two other ways to move a file or folder.

- Select a file or folder, and right-click to display the **shortcut menu**. Choose **Cut**. Choose the new location, right-click, and choose **Paste**.
- Click the file or folder to select it, and then drag it to the new location.

SKILLBUILDING

D. PRETEST

Take a 1-minute timing on the paragraph. Note your speed and errors.

```
21      Do you brood when you make errors on papers?     9
22 It would be better to figure out what causes the     19
23 errors and to look for corrective drills to help     29
24 you make fewer errors in the future.                 36
   | 1 | 2 | 3 | 4 | 5 | 6 | 7 | 8 | 9 | 10
```

E. PRACTICE

SPEED: If you made 2 or fewer errors on the Pretest, key lines 25–32 two times.

ACCURACY: If you made more than 2 errors on the Pretest, key lines 25–28 as a group two times. Then key lines 29–32 as a group two times.

Double Reaches

```
25 rr errs hurry error furry berry worry terry carry
26 ll bill allay hills chill stall small shell smell
27 tt attar jetty otter utter putty witty butte Otto
28 ff stuff stiff cliff sniff offer scuff fluff buff
```

Alternate Reaches

```
29 is this list fist wish visit whist island raisins
30 so sons some soap sort soles sound bosses costume
31 go gone goat pogo logo bogus agora pagoda doggone
32 fu fun fume fund full fuel fuss furor furry fuzzy
```

F. POSTTEST

Repeat the Pretest. Compare your Posttest results with your Pretest results.

G. Number and Symbol Practice

Key each line 1 time. Repeat if time permits.

```
33 83 doubts, 38 cubs, 37 shrubs, 33 clubs, 34 stubs
34 87 aims, 83 maids, 88 brains, 73 braids, 84 raids

35 78 drinks, 48 brinks, 43 inks, 83 minks, 33 links
36 88 canes, 78 planes, 73 manes, 34 cans, 84 cranes

37 #7 blue, 4# roast, $3 paint, 77 books,* 3 & 4 & 8
38 7# boxes, 38 lists, $4 horse, #8 tree,* 7 & 3 & 4

39 Seek & Find Research sells this book* for $37.84.
40 The geometry test grades were 88, 87, 84, and 83.
```

Exercise 1-2 Work with Folders

TechSIM Interactive Tutorials
An interactive simulation about file management is available to explore.

Use the Documents folder to manage files and folders. Be aware, however, that this folder does not organize them for you. You are responsible for creating a clear structure and easy-to-remember names.

Think of arranging files and folders the way you would arrange drawers of clothing. A folder is like a drawer. You might have one drawer for socks, one drawer for T-shirts, and one drawer for pants. If you keep your clothes in the right drawers, you always know where to find the socks, T-shirts, or pants you want.

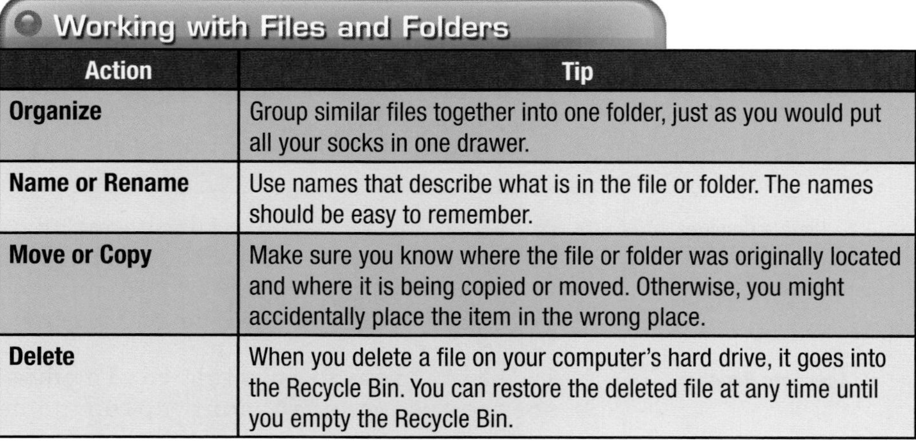

Working with Files and Folders

Action	Tip
Organize	Group similar files together into one folder, just as you would put all your socks in one drawer.
Name or Rename	Use names that describe what is in the file or folder. The names should be easy to remember.
Move or Copy	Make sure you know where the file or folder was originally located and where it is being copied or moved. Otherwise, you might accidentally place the item in the wrong place.
Delete	When you delete a file on your computer's hard drive, it goes into the Recycle Bin. You can restore the deleted file at any time until you empty the Recycle Bin.

Step-by-Step

1. Open the **Documents folder** window, and click the triangle [◢] beside the **Documents** folder to expand the folder contents.
2. Click **Organize** on the toolbar, and click **New Folder**. A new folder appears in the **File** list (right side of the **Documents** folder window).
3. Drag to select **New Folder**, if necessary.
4. Key *Your Name* Mars Exhibit. Press [ENTER] to name the folder. See Figure 1.5.

In this exercise, you will use the Documents folder to create a new folder. You will also copy a folder and paste it into your new folder.

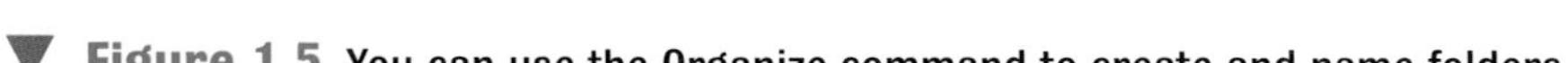

Figure 1.5 You can use the Organize command to create and name folders.

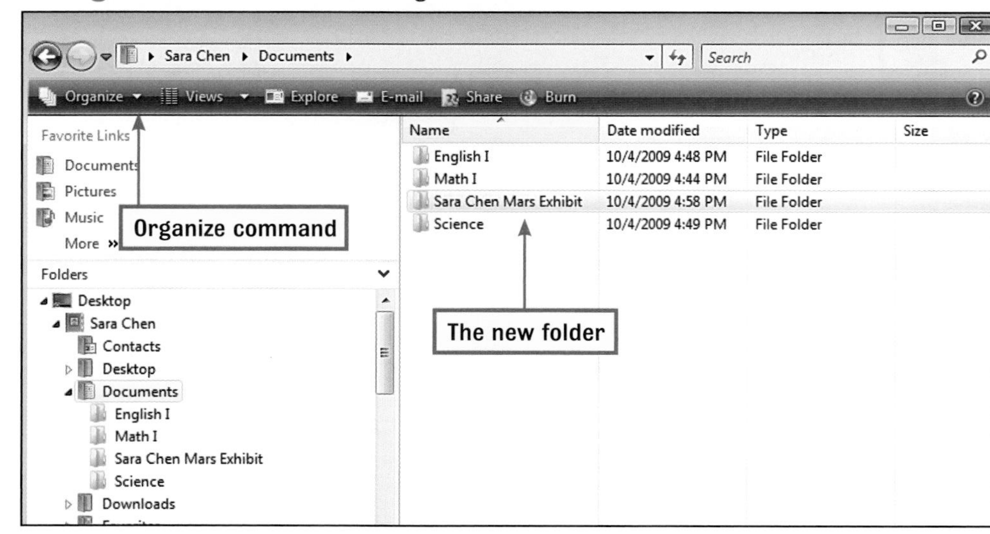

SKILLBUILDING

H. 1-Minute Alphanumeric Timing

Take a 1-minute timing on the paragraph. Note your speed and errors.

```
41      B. Warmsly & J. Barnet paid the $847 charges     9
42  for the closing costs of their home at 3487 Cliff   19
43  Road; claim #47* shows the charge.                  26
    | 1 | 2 | 3 | 4 | 5 | 6 | 7 | 8 | 9 | 10
```

I. 2-Minute Timings

Take two 2-minute timings on lines 44–49. Note your speed and errors.

Goal: 27/2'/4e

```
44      We just want to stay all day in the store to     9
45  see the very new shoe styles. Sue quickly saw the   19
46  mix of zany colors. Jo put on a yellow and green    29
47  pair and looked in a mirror. The shoes had wide     39
48  strips on the soles. We were certain of the good    48
49  brand, so I bought two pair.                        54
    | 1 | 2 | 3 | 4 | 5 | 6 | 7 | 8 | 9 | 10
```

6 To see more information about a folder or file, click the **Views** command. Then choose **Details** (Figure 1.3).

7 To sort the contents of a folder, click a column heading that appears above the folders and files. You can sort by Name, Date modified, Type, or Size.

8 Click the **Name** heading. Figure 1.3 shows the files and folders arranged in alphabetical order by name.

9 To see the contents of a folder, click the folder name in the **Navigation** Pane, or double-click the folder in the **File** list. Figure 1.4 shows the contents of the **English I** folder.

10 Click the **Collapse** arrow [⌄] to the right of the Folders heading to collapse the folder.

TechSavvy

Choose Icon Options Windows Vista provides many options for viewing icons. Click the **Views** command to choose Extra Large Icons, Large Icons, Medium Icons, or Small Icons. Or, choose **Views>Tiles** to see an icon and a description.

▼ **Figure 1.3** Details view shows the size and type of a file or folder and the date it was last modified, or changed.

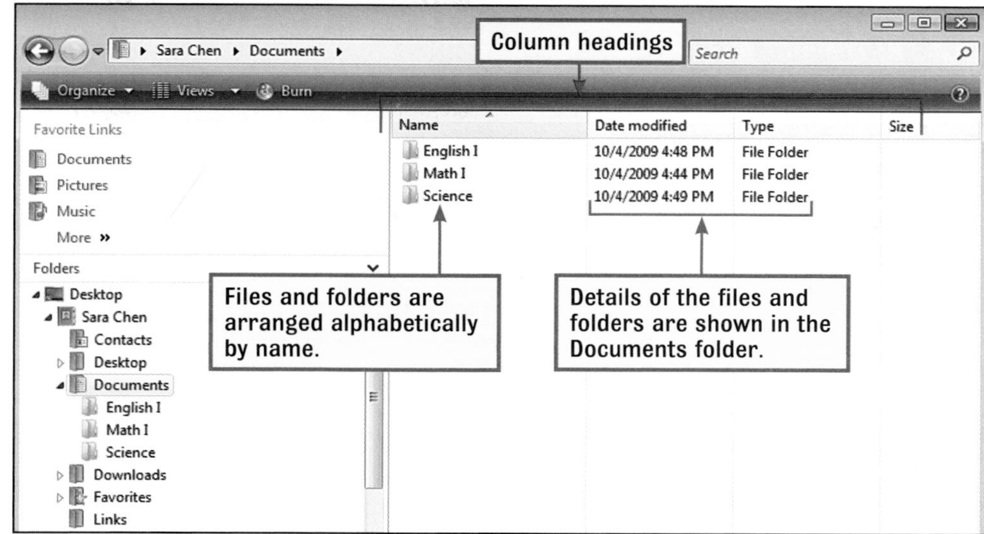

▼ **Figure 1.4** Display the contents of a folder by clicking on it.

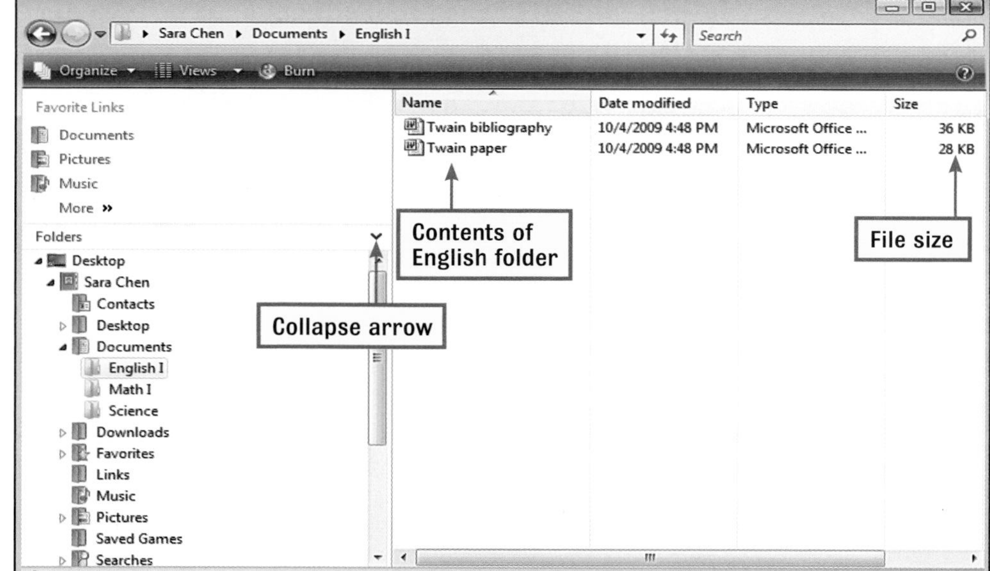

HELP!

Restricted Access Sometimes schools or businesses take safety measures to protect files and restrict the number of people who have access to them. Only those users who know the proper password or who have been given permission may use the file or open the folder.

Lesson 17 New Keys: 2 @ 9 (

OBJECTIVES:

- Learn the 2, @, 9, and (keys.
- Refine keyboarding skills.
- Key 27/2'/4e.

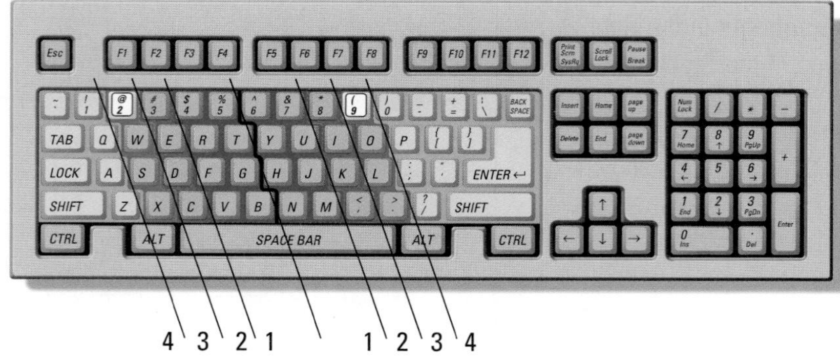

A. Warmup

Key each line 2 times.

Speed 1 The big lake was filled with many ducks and fish.

Accuracy 2 Lazy Jaques picked five boxes of oranges with me.

Numbers 3 The answer is 78 when you add 44 and 34 together.

Symbols 4 Invoices #73 and #48 from C & M Supply were $438.

NEW KEYS

B. 2 and @ Keys

Key each line 2 times. Repeat if time permits.

Use S finger. For 2 and @, anchor F.

5 sws sw2s s2s 222 s2s 22.2 s2s 2/22 s2s 22,222 s2s
6 22 sips, 22 swings, 22 signals, 22 sites, or 2.22
7 Our class used 22 pens, 23 disks, and 24 ribbons.
8 There were 22 people waiting for Bus 22 on May 2.

@ (at) is the shift of 2. Space once before and after @ except when it is used in an e-mail address.

9 sws sw2 s2s s2@s s@s s@s @2 @22 @222 s@s s2s @222
10 @2, 2 sons, @22, 22 sets, @222, 222 sensors, @222
11 Paul said his e-mail address was smith@acc.co.us.
12 She bought 2 @ 22 and sold 22 @ 223 before 2 p.m.

C. 9 and (Keys

Key each line 2 times. Repeat if time permits.

Use L finger. For 9 and (, anchor J.

13 lol lo9l l9l 999 l9l 9/99 l9l 99.9 l9l 99,999 l9l
14 99 laps, 99 loops, 99 lilies, 99 lifters, or 9.99
15 He said 99 times not to ask for the 99 fair fans.
16 They traveled 999 miles on Route 99 over 9 weeks.

The ((opening parenthesis) is the shift of 9. Space once before an opening parenthesis; do not space after it.

17 lol lo9 l9l l9(l l(l l(l (9 (99 (999 l(l l9l (999
18 (9, 9 lots, (99, 99 logs, (999, 999 latches, (999
19 lo9((99((9 lo9(l lo(9(9(9 (9(9(9 l(lo9(l 9(
20 lo9(l9(l 9(9l l((l (9ol 99 lambs, (999, 999 lads

Step-by-Step

1. Click the **Start** button at the bottom left corner of your screen. Click **Documents** in the right pane of the **Start** menu.

2. On your own screen, identify the items shown in Figure 1.1. Your screen may look different depending on how your teacher has files organized.

3. Locate the **Documents** folder in the **Navigation** Pane. Point to and click the **Triangle** ◢ to the left of the folder to expand the **Documents** folder.

4. You can change the way the files are displayed. Click the down arrow beside the **Views** command on the toolbar, and click **Large Icons**. The icons should now look similar to those in Figure 1.2.

5. Click the **Views** command, and choose **List** to see another view.

▼ **Figure 1.1** The right side of the window shows the contents of the expanded folder.

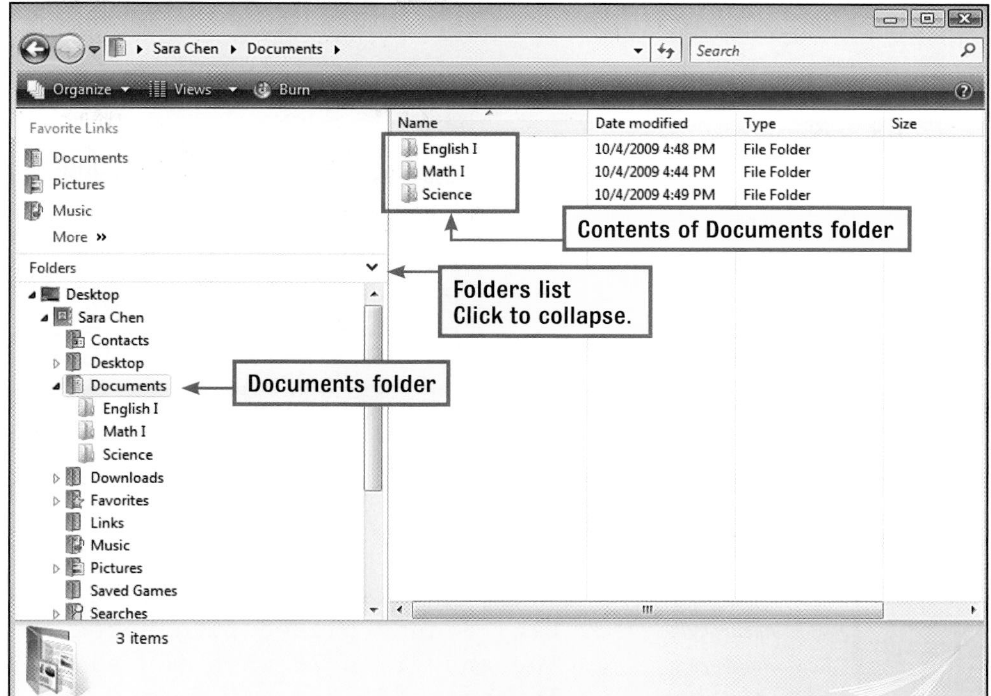

▼ **Figure 1.2** Change the way your folders and files are displayed using the Views command.

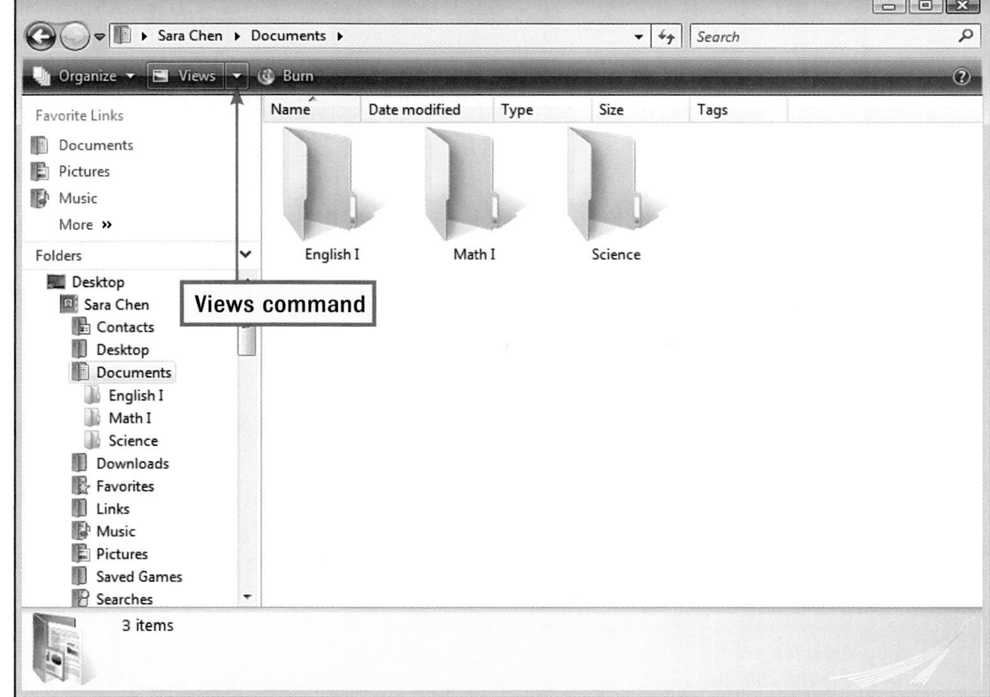

SKILLBUILDING

D. Technique Checkpoint

Key each line 2 times. Focus on the technique at the left.

Keep your eyes on the copy when typing numbers and symbols.

21 sws sw2s s2s 222 s2s 22.2 s2s 2/22 s2s 22,222 s2s
22 sws sw2 s2s s2@s s@s s@s @2 @22 @222 s@s s2s @222
23 lol lo91 191 999 191 9/99 191 99.9 191 99,999 191
24 lol lo9 191 19(1 1(1 1(1 (9 (99 (999 1(1 191 (999

E. PRETEST

Take a 1-minute timing on the paragraph. Note your speed and errors.

25 Were you in the biology group that mixed the 9
26 ragweed seeds with some vegetable seeds? Jon and 19
27 Kim sneezed all month because of that. All of us 29
28 agreed that we must be more careful in the lab. 38

| 1 | 2 | 3 | 4 | 5 | 6 | 7 | 8 | 9 | 10

F. PRACTICE

SPEED: If you made 2 or fewer errors on the Pretest, key lines 29–36 two times each.

ACCURACY: If you made more than 2 errors on the Pretest, key lines 29–32 as a group two times. Then key lines 33–36 as a group two times.

Left Reaches

29 tab wards grace serve wears farce beast crate car
30 far weeds tests seeds tread graze vexed vests saw
31 bar crest feast refer cease dated verge bread gas
32 car career grasses bread creases faded vested tad

Right Reaches

33 you Yukon mummy ninon jolly union minim pylon hum
34 mom nylon milky lumpy puppy holly pulpy plink oil
35 pop oomph jumpy unpin nippy imply hippo pupil nip
36 you union bumpy upon holly hill moon pink ill mop

G. POSTTEST

Repeat the Pretest. Compare your Posttest results with your Pretest results.

Exercise 1-1 Get to Know The Documents Folder

TechSIM Interactive Tutorials
An interactive simulation about file management is available to explore.

TechSavvy

Display the Menu Bar The **Menu Bar** does not display by default. To display the Menu Bar, click **Organize> Layout>Menu Bar**. To turn off the Menu Bar, click **Organize>Layout>Menu Bar**. For quick access, you can also press ALT to display the Menu Bar.

It is very important to save and organize your work so that files are easy to find again for you and others. The Documents folder allows you to organize, move, delete, and copy files on your computer or on your network. You can also display the Menu Bar to assist you with these tasks.

The Documents folder organizes folders and files by always using the same structure. The file structure from the top down starts with the largest storage area (the drive) and ends with the smallest unit of storage (the file).

- A **drive** is the largest storage area. The C: drive is usually the hard drive, but you can have other drives on your school network, or on a separate device, such as your CD drive.
- A **folder** is a place to save and organize files, such as documents or pictures.
- A **file** is a collection of data. Files can be text, graphics, or other types of media such as audio or video clips.

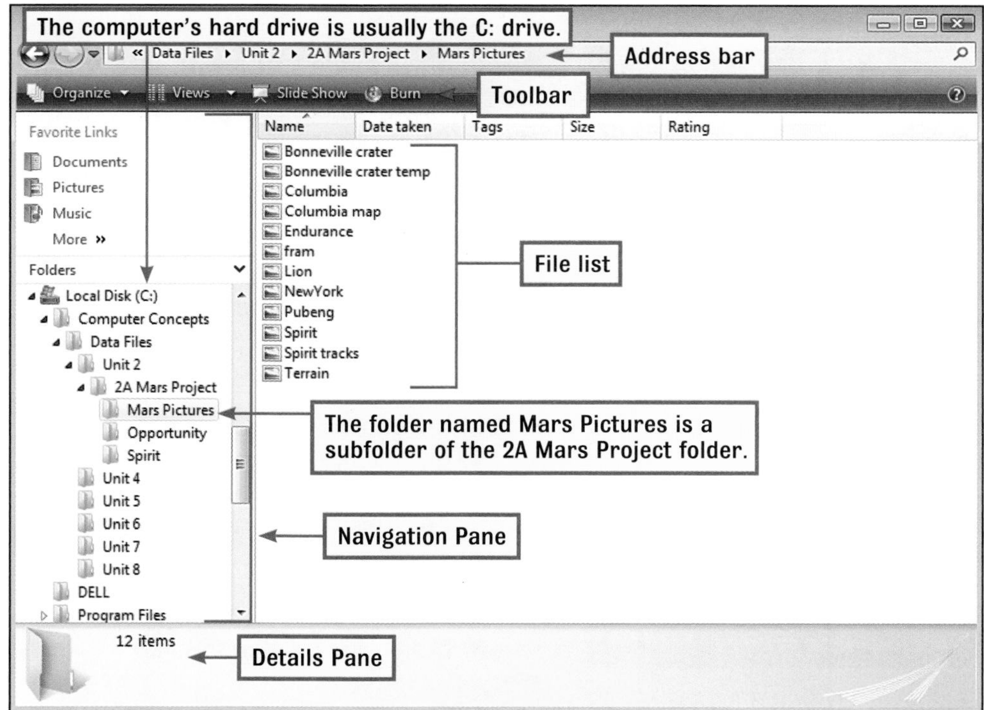

In this exercise, you will use the Documents folder to practice organizing files. You will also display the file's or folder's size, type, and date modified.

SKILLBUILDING

H. 1-Minute Alphanumeric Timing

Take a 1-minute timing on the paragraph. Note your speed and errors.

37	The planned ski tour #4 begins at 2:43 p.m.,	9
38	and tour #3 begins at noon. Every tour costs $43,	19
39	and everyone will end at 7:38 p.m.	26
	| 1 | 2 | 3 | 4 | 5 | 6 | 7 | 8 | 9 | 10	

I. 2-Minute Timings

Take two 2-minute timings on lines 40–45. Note your speed and errors.

Goal: 27/2'/4e

40	It is a joy to end a term with good grades.	9
41	Fall term could be very nice if it were not for	19
42	exams and quizzes. Jan, though, likes to study to	29
43	show how much she has learned. She places great	38
44	value in having high marks. She knows her peers	48
45	admire the grades she achieved.	54
	| 1 | 2 | 3 | 4 | 5 | 6 | 7 | 8 | 9 | 10	

Concepts in Action

Project 1 Use Microsoft Windows

In this project, you will learn how to manage files and folders, find files, and view details about them, called properties.

File Management

Imagine that your class is creating a science exhibit about Mars. NASA has given you permission to use images and information from its Web site. You will need to share the files with your classmates. They need to be able to find these files quickly and easily.

You will learn how to use the Documents folder to group folders and files the same way you would organize material in a file cabinet. Each folder contains files that are related. Keeping your files and folders organized is called file management.

Key Concepts

Exercise 1-1
- Use the Documents folder to view folders and files

Exercise 1-2
- Create, copy, paste, and rename folders

Exercise 1-3
- Copy, paste, rename, and delete files

Exercise 1-4
- Use Save As
- Delete folders

Exercise 1-5
- Manage folders and files on the desktop

Exercise 1-6
- Search for files and folders

Vocabulary

Key Terms
drive
folder
file
Save As
shortcut

Before You Begin

Manage Files You can manage files in the Documents folder or on the desktop. Ask your teacher where you need to organize and save your files for this class.

Lesson 18 NEW KEYS: 1 ! 0)

OBJECTIVES:
- Learn the 1, !, 0, and) keys.
- Refine keyboarding skills.
- Key 27/2'/4e.

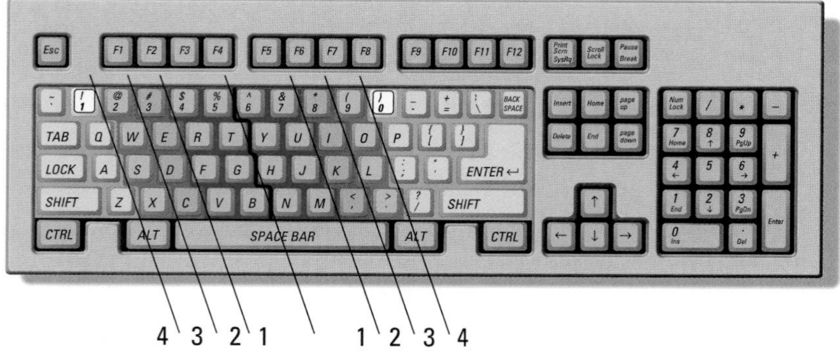

A. Warmup

Key each line 2 times.

Speed	1 The goal of trade schools is to teach job skills.
Accuracy	2 Jess Mendoza quickly plowed six bright vineyards.
Numbers	3 Nate took this new order: 78, 74, 83, 29, and 23.
Symbol	4 Purchase 32# of grass seed today @ $2.98 a pound.

NEW KEYS

B. 1 and ! Keys

Key each line 2 times. Repeat if time permits.

For 1 and !, anchor F. Use A finger. Do not use the lowercase letter l (el) for 1.

5 aqa aq1a a1a 111 a1a 1/11 a1a 11.1 a1a 11,111 a1a
6 11 arms, 11 areas, 11 adages, 11 animals, or 1.11
7 My 11 aides can type 111 pages within 11 minutes.
8 Joann used 11 gallons of gas to travel 111 miles.

! is the shift of 1. Space once after an exclamation point.

9 aqa aq1 a1a a1!a a!a a!a 1! 11! 111! a!a a1a 111!
10 1!, 1 ant, 11! 11 acres, 111! 111 adverbs, 1 area
11 Listen! There was a cry for help! They need help!
12 Look! It's moving! I'm frightened! Run very fast!

C. 0 and) Keys

Key each line 2 times. Repeat if time permits.

Use Sem finger. For 0 and), anchor J. Do not use the capital letter O for 0.

13 ;p; ;p0; ;0; 000 ;0; 1.00 ;0; 20.0 ;0; 30,000 ;0;
14 300 parts, 700 planks, 800 parades, 900 particles
15 Can you add these: 80, 10, 90, 40, 20, 70, & 130?
16 Some emoticons such as :-(or :(use parentheses.

) is the shift of 0 (zero). Space once after a closing parenthesis except when it's followed by punctuation; do not space before it.

17 ;p; ;p0 ;0; ;0); ;); ;););;);;; ;); ;0;);;; ;)
18 ;0; ;0) ;); ;); 10) 20) 30) 40) 70) 80) 90) 1001)
19 The box (the big red one) is just the right size.
20 My friend (you know which one) is arriving early.

After You Read

Key Concepts Check

1. **Identify** What type of memory gets erased when you turn off your computer?
2. **Identify** Name three input devices and three output devices.
3. **Explain** Why is operating system software the most important software on a computer?
4. **Describe** What is a network?

Critical Thinking

5. **Compare and Contrast** How is the human brain like a computer? Give examples.

21st Century Skills

6. **Communication** As an employee, it may be your responsibility to make recommendations for the purchase of new software. Write a paragraph about a software product you would like to try. Describe what the software does and what it will help you do. With your teacher's permission, take an online "tour" of the software.

Academic Skills

Mathematics

Moore's law, named for Intel's co-founder, says that computer processing power doubles about every 18 months.

a. **Compare** How much faster was CPU speed in 2005 than in 2000?

b. **Summarize** Describe how CPU speeds changed from 1995 to 2005.

Math Concept

Plot Points In a line graph, plot points are used to show the relationship between two values.

Starting Hint Place your finger on the plot point labeled "2000." To find out the CPU speed for that year, move your finger in a straight line to the left, then read the value.

NCTM Data Analysis and Probability Formulate questions that can be addressed with data and collect, organize, and display relevant data to answer them.

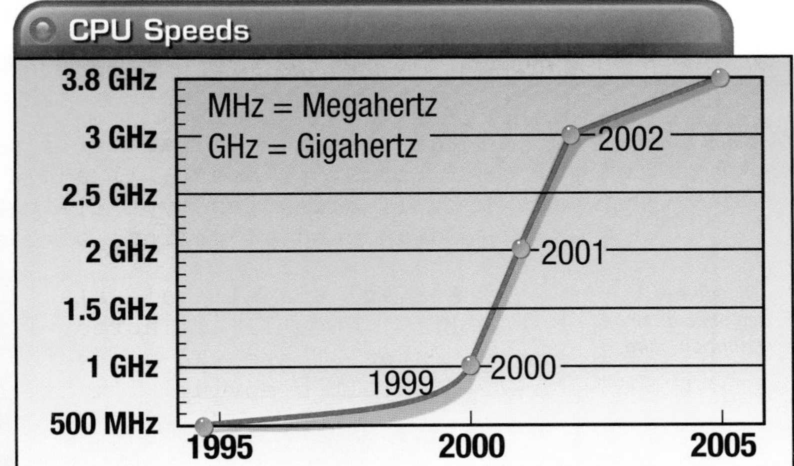

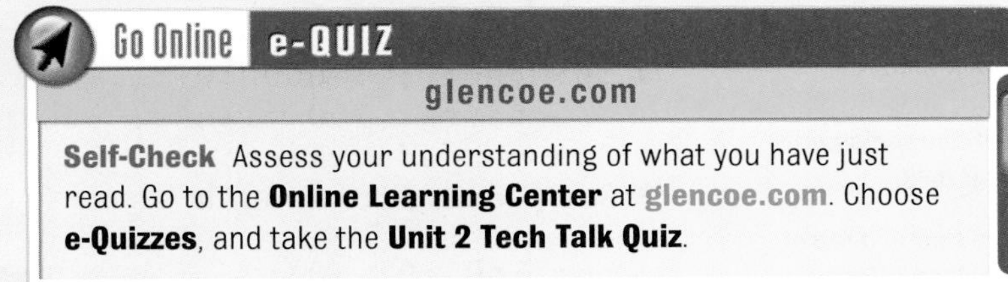

Self-Check Assess your understanding of what you have just read. Go to the **Online Learning Center** at glencoe.com. Choose **e-Quizzes**, and take the **Unit 2 Tech Talk Quiz**.

SKILLBUILDING

D. Technique Checkpoint

Key each line 2 times. Focus on the techniques at the left.

Keep eyes on copy; hold home-key anchors.

```
21 aqa aq1a a1a 111 a1a 1/11 a1a 11.1 a1a 11,111 a1a
22 aqa aq1 a1a a1!a a!a a!a 1! 11! 111! a!a a1a 111!
23 ;p; ;p0; ;0; 000 ;0; 1.00 ;0; 20.0 ;0; 30,000 ;0;
24 p;p p;0 ;0; ;0); ;); ;); );; );;; ;); ;0; );;; ;)
```

E. PRETEST

Take a 1-minute timing on the paragraph. Note your speed and errors.

```
25      Dave and I took our backpacks and started up    9
26 the old mountain trail. Around sunset, we stopped   19
27 to set up camp and have a hot meal. We were very    29
28 tired after such a long day hiking uphill.          37
   | 1 | 2 | 3 | 4 | 5 | 6 | 7 | 8 | 9 | 10
```

F. PRACTICE

SPEED: If you made 2 or fewer errors on the Pretest, key lines 29–36 two times each.

ACCURACY: If you made more than 2 errors on the Pretest, key lines 29–32 as a group two times. Then key lines 33–36 as a group two times.

Up Reaches

```
29 ho shock chose phone shove hover holly homes shot
30 st stair guest stone blast nasty start casts step
31 il lilac filed drill build spill child trail pail
32 de dear redeem warden tide render chide rode dead
```

Down Reaches

```
33 ab squab labor habit cabin cable abate about able
34 ca pecan recap catch carve cable scale scamp camp
35 av ravel gavel avert knave waved paved shave have
36 in ruin invent winner bring shin chin shrink pine
```

G. POSTTEST

Repeat the Pretest. Compare your Posttest results with your Pretest results.

Networks Explore how computer networks work. Go to the **Online Learning Center** at glencoe.com. Choose **Tech Talk Activities**, then **Unit 2**.

Computer Network Basics

A computer **network** is a group of computers connected together. Networks **enable**, or allow, people to share information and resources such as printers, storage devices, and Internet connections. Most large networks, such as the ones in schools and businesses, connect client computers to a central server. This makes a school or company more efficient and also saves money in equipment costs. Networks often are used in classrooms so that students have access to the same information.

A network server is a powerful computer that lets users share storage space and applications. A network server can be a PC or a large mainframe computer. A client computer sends and receives information to and from a server. A client is usually a PC, such as a desktop or laptop computer, or even can be a handheld device such as a PDA.

There are several types of networks. A local-area network (LAN) is a small network that covers a small area, such as an office or school. A wide-area network (WAN) covers a large geographical area, such as an international corporation. The Internet is the biggest network there is, connecting millions of computers around the world. An intranet works like the Internet, but allows only people in the same organization or business to share information. Your school might have its own intranet.

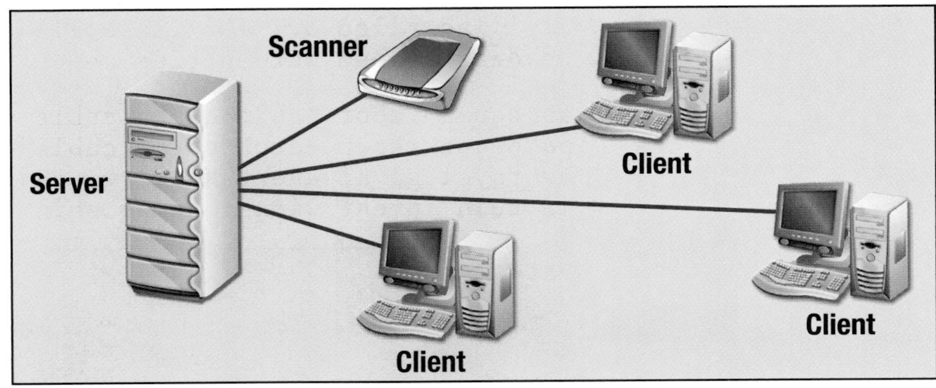

A network allows you to send data back and forth between different computers, servers, storage devices, and shared output devices. What is the difference between a server and a client?

Reading Check

1. **Identify** In a computer network, what do you call the computer that provides shared stored space and applications to other computers?
2. **Explain** Why is it helpful for schools or companies to use a network?

SKILLBUILDING

H. 1-Minute Alphanumeric Timings

Take a 1-minute timing on lines 37–39. Note your speed and errors.

```
37      Joy wanted to get a dozen (12) baseball bats    9
38 @ $4.29 from the sports store at 718 Miner Place.   19
39 When I went, only 10 bats were left.                26
   | 1 | 2 | 3 | 4 | 5 | 6 | 7 | 8 | 9 | 10
```

I. 2-Minute Timings

Take two 2-minute timings on lines 40–45. Note your speed and errors.

Goal: 27/2'/4e

```
40      In the fall of the year, I find pleasure in     9
41 zipping up to the hills to quietly view the trees  19
42 changing colors. Most all aspens turn to shades    29
43 of gold. Oak trees exude tones of red and orange.  39
44 The plants change colors each fall, but all these  49
45 changes are an amazing sight.                      54
   | 1 | 2 | 3 | 4 | 5 | 6 | 7 | 8 | 9 | 10
```

Caution Operating systems are made up of thousands of small computer files. Over time, some of these files can become damaged. This can cause problems such as frequent crashes or error messages. When that happens, you may have to reinstall or upgrade your operating system.

Why It's Important Consider how it would impact you if you were to lose all your information.

What Is an Operating System?

Every computerized device needs an operating system (OS) in order to work. The operating system controls all the other software programs and allows your hardware devices to work properly. There are many kinds of operating systems, though most people use one of these types:

- **Microsoft Windows** is the most popular OS for PCs.
- **Mac OS** is used by Apple computers. It works similarly to Windows, but it has a slightly different appearance, or look.
- **Linux** is a powerful OS often used in large networks and business environments.
- **Handheld operating systems** are used in PDAs, MP3 players, and cell phones. These products use operating systems that were developed specifically for them, called "proprietary software."

When you choose application and utility software for your computer, you need to make sure it will work with your OS. For example, some application software will run only on a Mac, and others will run only on a PC. When computer programs or devices work with each other, they are said to be compatible.

What Is a GUI?

An interface is a point where two things come together. You need an interface to communicate with your computer. To use older operating systems, you had to key all of your commands using a text interface such as MS-DOS (Microsoft-Disk Operating System). Today, your operating system uses a graphical user interface, also called a GUI (pronounced "gooey"). A GUI lets you use a pointing device, such as a mouse, to click images and icons or select commands. The pointer usually displays as a small angled arrow. The Windows operating system and the Mac OS use GUIs. Would you rather key all of your commands or use a mouse to control your computer?

Reading Check

1. **Describe** Name six types of application software, and describe what each one allows you to do.
2. **Identify** What type of software program controls all the other software on your computer?

Lesson 19 New Keys: 5 % 6 ^

OBJECTIVES:

- Learn the 5, %, 6, and ^ keys.
- Refine keyboarding skills.
- Key 27/2'/4e.

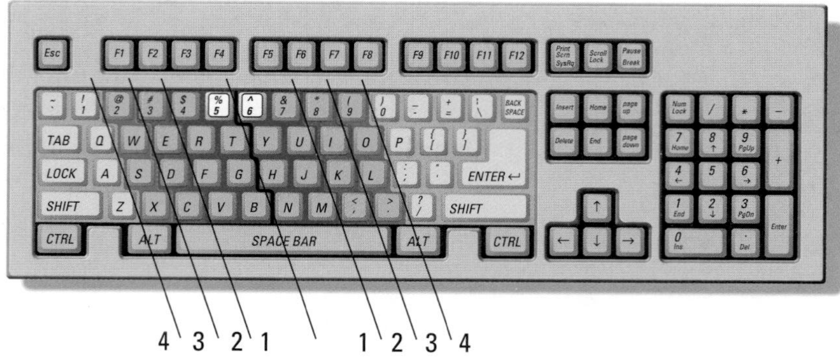

A. Warmup

Key each line 2 times.

Speed 1 Our team at band camp did a new drill for guests.
Accuracy 2 Two jobs require packing five dozen axes monthly.
Numbers 3 Mark read the winning numbers: 190, 874, and 732.
Symbols 4 The shop (J & B) has #10 envelopes* @ $.24 a doz.

NEW KEYS

B. 5 and % Keys

Key each line 2 times. Repeat if time permits.

Use F finger. For 5 and %, anchor A.

5 ftf ft5f f5f 555 f5f 5/55 f5f 55.5 f5f 55,555 f5f
6 55 fins, 55 facts, 55 fields, 55 futures, or 5.55
7 Jo saw 55 bulls, 14 cows, 155 sheep, and 5 goats.
8 I just sold 55 items; his total for today is 555.

% is the shift of 5. The % (percent) is used in statistical data. Do not space between numbers and %

9 ftf ft5 f5f f5%f f%f f%f 5% 55% 555% f%f f5f 555%
10 5%, 5 foes, 55%, 55 fees, 555%, 555 fiddles, 555%
11 The meal is 55% protein, 20% starch, and 25% fat.
12 On June 5, 55% of the students had 5% more skill.

C. 6 and ^ Keys

Key each line 2 times. Repeat if time permits.

Use J finger. For 6 and ^, anchor ;.

13 jyj jy6j j6j 666 j6j 6/66 j6j 66.6 j6j 66,666 j6j
14 66 jaws, 66 jokes, 66 jewels, 66 jackets, or 6.66
15 Her averages were 76.46, 81.66, 86.56, and 96.36.
16 Multiply .66 by .51; the correct answer is .3366.

^ is the shift of 6. The ^ (caret) is used in some programming languages. Do not space between the caret and numbers.

17 jyj jy6 j6j j6^j j^j j^j ^j ^jj ^jjj j^j j6j ^jjj
18 6^, 6 jams, 66^, 66 jets, 666^, 666 jingles, 666^
19 The test problems included these: 75^2, 4^3, 8^6.
20 The ^ (caret) appeared 6 times in a line of code.

Go Online ACTIVITY
glencoe.com

Software Discover more about different types of software. Go to the **Online Learning Center** at glencoe.com. Choose **Tech Talk Activities**, then **Unit 2.**

Software Basics

Software is a set of instructions that makes it possible for your computer to perform tasks. It translates your commands into the language of binary numbers—the 1s and 0s that computers understand. When you key a word, select a menu, or click a button, software sends data to the computer's CPU (Central Processing Unit). Software also can be called a program or an application.

How Do I Use Software?

Most of the software you use will fall into one of these three categories:

- **Operating system (OS) software** is the main program that makes your computer work.
- **Application software** lets you do different tasks on your computer, such as writing reports or sending e-mail.
- **Utility software** helps you **control**, or exercise power over, your computer and keep it in good running condition.

It is important to choose the right software program for the type of task you want to do. The table below can help.

Academic Focus

English Language Arts

Know Your Audience Different software programs help you display data for different audiences. For example, you will likely use a word processing program to write a report for your teacher. To give an oral report on the same topic, you could use a presentation program to display colorful slides. What should you consider when selecting a software program for data preparation?

NCTE 5 Use different writing process elements to communicate effectively.

Types of Application Software

Type of Software	What It Lets You Do	Examples
Web Browsers	Visit Web sites on the Internet	Microsoft Internet Explorer®, Apple Safari®, Netscape®, Mozilla Firefox®
E-mail	Exchange messages and files with other computer users	Microsoft Outlook®, Eudora®
Word Processing	Create letters, term papers, reports, newsletters, and so on.	Microsoft Word®, Corel WordPerfect®
Spreadsheet	Work with numbers and calculations to create tables, charts, and graphs	Microsoft Excel®, Lotus 1-2-3®
Database	Organize and retrieve large amounts of information	Microsoft Access®, FileMaker Pro®
Presentation	Create a slide presentation to show a group of people	Microsoft PowerPoint®, Apple Keynote®

▲ Each task you do on a computer requires a specific kind of software. When would you use spreadsheet software?

D. Technique Timings

Take two 30-second timings on each line. Focus on the technique at the left.

Sit up straight with your feet flat on the floor.

21 Snow leopards are graceful animals with soft fur.

22 They live in the high, rugged mountains of Tibet.

23 These big cats are adept at climbing and leaping.

24 They use their tails to balance on narrow ledges.

E. PRETEST

Take a 1-minute timing on lines 25–28. Note your speed and errors.

25 As a flock, the crows flew to some clumps of 9

26 stalks near the eddy. They seemed to eat the pods 19

27 joyfully as they fed in the field. We like to 28

28 watch them, especially in the morning. 36

| 1 | 2 | 3 | 4 | 5 | 6 | 7 | 8 | 9 | 10

F. PRACTICE

SPEED: If you made 2 or fewer errors on the Pretest, key lines 29–36 two times each.

ACCURACY: If you made more than 2 errors on the Pretest, key lines 29–32 as a group two times. Then key lines 33–36 as a group two times.

Adjacent 29 po pods poem point poise lk hulk silk polka stalk

Jump 30 mp jump pump trump clump cr cram crow crawl creed

Double 31 dd odds eddy daddy caddy tt mitt mutt utter ditto

Consecutive 32 un unit punk funny bunch gr grab agree angry grip

Alternate 33 iv give dive drive wives gl glad glee ogled gland

Left/Right 34 fe fear feat ferns fetal jo joys join joker jolly

Up/Down 35 sw swan sway sweat swift k, ark, ask, tick, wick,

In/Out 36 lu luck blunt fluid lush da dash date sedan panda

G. POSTTEST

Repeat the Pretest. Then compare your Posttest results with your Pretest results.

Tech Tip
1 Kilobyte (KB) = 1,000 bytes
1 Megabyte (MB) = 1,000 KB
1 Gigabyte (GB) = 1,000 MB
1 Terabyte (TB) = 1,000 GB

Why It's Important Think about how many research papers you could store in 1 TB of memory.

Academic Focus

Mathematics

Work with Units Most measurement units can be abbreviated. Memorize common unit abbreviations to prevent confusion.

Prefixes Measurement units often have a prefix—a syllable or two at the beginning of a word—that can give you a clue about the measurement's value. For example, the prefix "kilo" means 1,000, and a "kilobyte" contains 1,000 bytes. Identify other examples of prefixes.

NCTM Measurement Apply appropriate techniques, tools, and formulas to determine measurements.

How Is Information Stored?

If you shut down a computer without saving your work, you will lose your data. Before you save your work, the data is stored in RAM. When you save a file, you move the information from RAM to a **storage device**, such as a hard drive, a server, or a disk. A storage device is like your long-term memory, where you keep memories of important events and your family members' names, for example.

Types of Storage Devices

Storage Device	What It Does	Size
Hard Drive	This is the major storage device inside your computer. It also is known as the hard disk. External hard drives are also available.	40 GB to 320 GB or more
Flash Drives	These portable devices plug directly into a computer's USB port. Some are as small as a pen or a keychain.	256 MB to 4 GB or more
CDs and DVDs	These portable devices store large amounts of information, such as videos.	CD = 700 MB DVD = 4.7 GB to 17 GB
Floppy Disk	This portable device stores smaller files such as text documents.	Floppy disk = 1.44 MB Zip disk = 100 MB to 750 MB

▲ Storage devices come in many sizes. Some are built into a computer, and others are portable. Why would you use portable storage?

You usually store your applications and the files you use all the time on a hard drive. You can use portable storage devices to make backup copies of your files in case your computer crashes, to move files easily from one computer to another, or to store files that are no longer needed on your hard drive.

Reading Check

1. **Explain** How is RAM like your short-term memory?
2. **Explore** If you had a 1 GB file, where could you store it?

SKILLBUILDING

H. 1-Minute Alphanumeric Timings

Take a 1-minute timing on lines 37–39. Note your speed and errors.

Kim ran the 7.96-mile race last week. Yanni 9
ran 14.80 miles. Zeke said the next 5K run will 19
be held on August 14 or August 23. 25

| 1 | 2 | 3 | 4 | 5 | 6 | 7 | 8 | 9 | 10

I. 2-Minute Timings

Take two 2-minute timings on lines 40–45. Note your speed and errors.

As you look for jobs, be quite sure that 9
the way you dress depicts the position that you 18
want. If you hope to obtain an office job, zippy 28
fashions are not for you. Expect to arrive in a 38
clean, pressed business suit. Your clothes should 48
match the job you are trying for. 54

| 1 | 2 | 3 | 4 | 5 | 6 | 7 | 8 | 9 | 10

Storage Learn more about the different kinds of storage devices and how information is stored on your computer. Go to the **Online Learning Center** at glencoe.com. Choose **Tech Talk Activities**, then **Unit 2**.

Computer Memory and Storage Basics

What does a computer do with all the data it processes? A computer stores data in three main places: in its **random-access memory (RAM)**, in its **read-only memory (ROM)**, or on a storage device. A computer mainly uses two different kinds of memory, RAM or ROM, depending on the kind of **task**, or assigned work, the computer is performing.

Types of Computer Memory

Memory Type	What Is It?	How Is It Like Human Memory?
Read-Only Memory (ROM)	This memory is permanent information on your computer. ROM holds your computer's built-in instructions and cannot be erased or changed.	Your brain automatically controls many basic body functions, such as breathing. Similarly, ROM controls the basic functions of your computer.
Random-Access Memory (RAM)	This memory is temporary information that your computer uses only when you work with a particular file. It is erased when you turn off your computer.	RAM is like your short-term memory. Have you ever had to remember something for just a minute, such as a phone number? You used your short-term memory for that task.

▲ Two kinds of computer memory are RAM and ROM. Which type of memory is similar to your short-term memory?

When Do I Use RAM and ROM?

RAM and ROM perform specific tasks that keep your computer running smoothly. For example:

- **ROM works when you turn your computer on or off**. ROM tells the computer how to start up and instructs the operating system (OS) to start. When you turn on or shut down your computer, the computer is using ROM.
- **RAM works when you start and use your software**. After your computer starts, RAM takes over. The computer is using RAM when your operating system starts, and you can see your desktop. If you open a software application such as Microsoft Word and key your name, that information is stored in RAM.

E-mail

Good communication is essential for success in your personal, academic, and professional relationships. The pace of work at a school or a company can be so fast that sometimes e-mail is the best way to communicate. By writing professional e-mails and using Microsoft Outlook, you can keep the lines of communication flowing smoothly.

Microsoft Outlook

The exercises in this Appendix are designed to be completed using Microsoft Outlook. If you use another e-mail application such as Microsoft Outlook Express, or if you subscribe to an e-mail service such as America Online, Hotmail, or Yahoo, you can still follow the steps provided. However, your screen will look different from the ones shown here.

TechSIM™ Technology Simulations

You may not have Outlook or any other e-mail program installed on your computer at school. If this is the case, you may want to use the TechSIM™ Interactive Tutorials—technology simulations that allow you to practice using Outlook to send e-mail. TechSIM Interactive Tutorials are also an excellent option if you are using an older version of Outlook or if your classroom computers all use different e-mail programs. With TechSIM Interactive Tutorials, all students can practice the same skills.

To use the TechSIM Interactive Tutorials, you will need to have Macromedia Flash installed on your computer. Ask your teacher if you should use the TechSIM Interactive Tutorials and how to access them.

Contents

Go Online ACTIVITY
glencoe.com

Input and Output Devices
Learn about other devices that you can use with your computer. Go to the **Online Learning Center** at glencoe.com. Choose **Tech Talk Activities**, then **Unit 2**.

What Are Input and Output Devices?

When you use a computer, information travels from you to the computer and back to you. Input devices and output devices are components that you use to communicate with your computer. **Input** is when a user enters information into a computer. **Output** is when a computer delivers information back to a user.

Types of Input and Output Devices

	Example	Description
Input Devices		A **keyboard** is used to input text and numbers and to send commands to a computer.
Input Devices		A **mouse** is used to click icons and buttons, highlight text, and drag images, text, files, and folders.
Input Devices		A **scanner**, like a photocopier, lets you create an electronic snapshot of an image or a page of text.
Input Devices		Many **digital cameras** connect with computers so that you can download, edit, and e-mail the photos you take.
Input Devices		A **joystick**, used for computer games, controls movement on the screen.
Output Devices		A **monitor** displays the text and graphics that you input or download into your computer.
Output Devices		A **printer** takes electronic information from the computer and produces a paper copy, which also is called a hard copy.
Output Devices		**Speakers** are used to play music on your computer and to give you "alert" sounds as you work.

▲ Some input devices, such as keyboards and mice, are used for everyday tasks. Others, such as joysticks, have more specialized purposes. What is the function of a scanner?

Reading Check

1. **Identify** What are three hardware components that you can see outside the computer and three components that are hidden inside the computer?
2. **Explain** What is the difference between input and output?

Exercise B-1 Get to Know Microsoft Outlook

TechSIM Interactive Tutorials An interactive simulation about e-mail is available to explore.

Microsoft Outlook is a popular e-mail application that lets you share information with others anywhere in the world. It is also a desktop communications program that helps you manage your time and information effectively. In this exercise, you will identify parts of the Outlook screen, including the Navigation Pane, the Inbox, the Reading Pane, the menu bar options, and the toolbar buttons.

Step-by-Step

1. **Start Outlook**. Your screen should look similar to Figure B.1.
2. Locate the **Navigation Pane**.
3. Locate the **Inbox**. The **Inbox** displays e-mail messages you have received.
4. Locate the **Outbox**. This folder stores mail ready to be sent.
5. Locate the **Reading Pane**. This is where you view the message. The pane can be on the side or the bottom of your screen.
6. Move your mouse pointer over each button on the **Standard toolbar** to learn what each button is for.
7. Click on each item on the **menu bar** to see the options available.

Figure B.1 In the Navigation pane, you can select Mail, Calendar, Contacts, or Tasks.

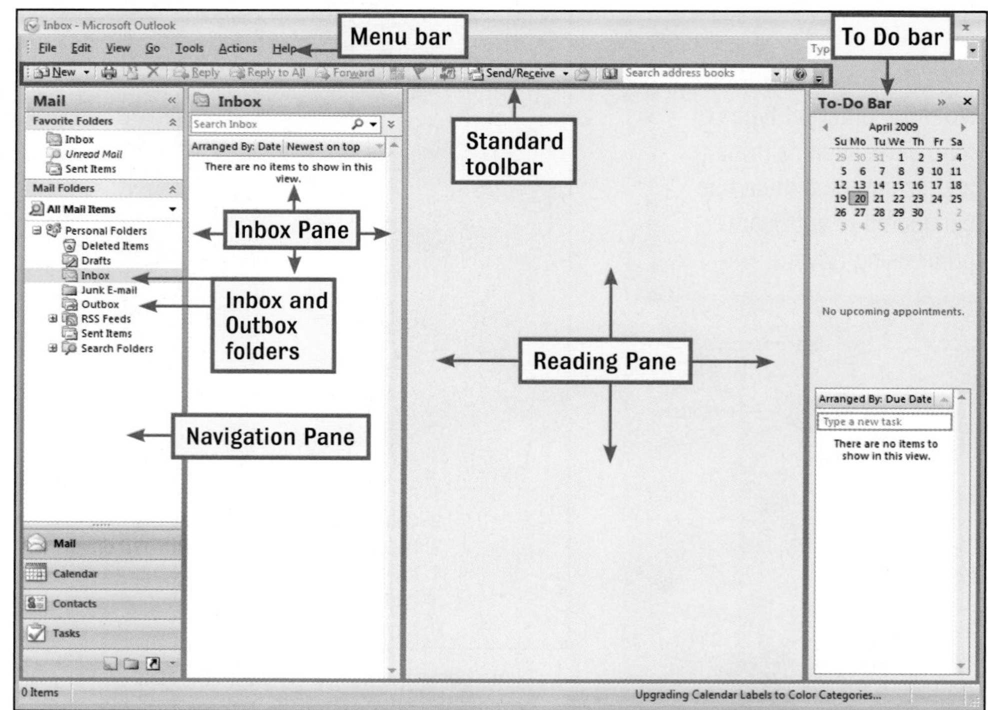

> **HELP!**
>
> **Outlook Help** Use **Outlook Help** to learn more about Outlook features. Locate and click the **Help** button on the **Standard** toolbar. Key text in the **Search** box, and click the **Search** button.

Tech Tip When you add a hardware device to your system for the first time, your computer will either set up the hardware automatically or tell you to install a driver. A *driver* is a special software program that makes the hardware work.

Why It's Important Consider the different types of hardware, such as printers and scanners, that can be connected to your computer using drivers.

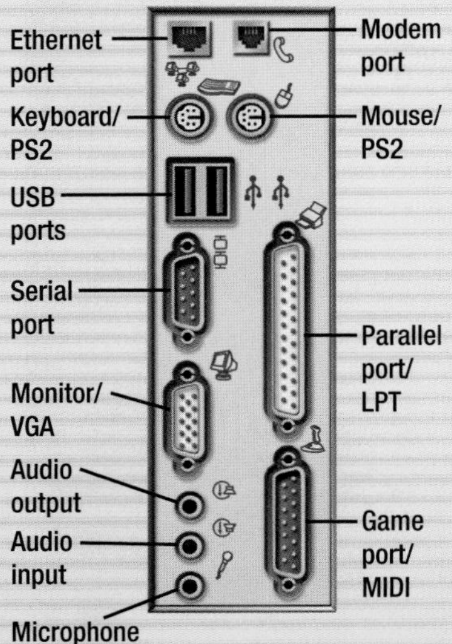

▲ There is usually one area of the computer (often the back of the machine) that contains all of the ports you need to plug in hardware devices. How can you tell which device goes to which port?

Hardware Basics

Hardware is the collection of physical devices that make up your computer system. These devices are also called components.

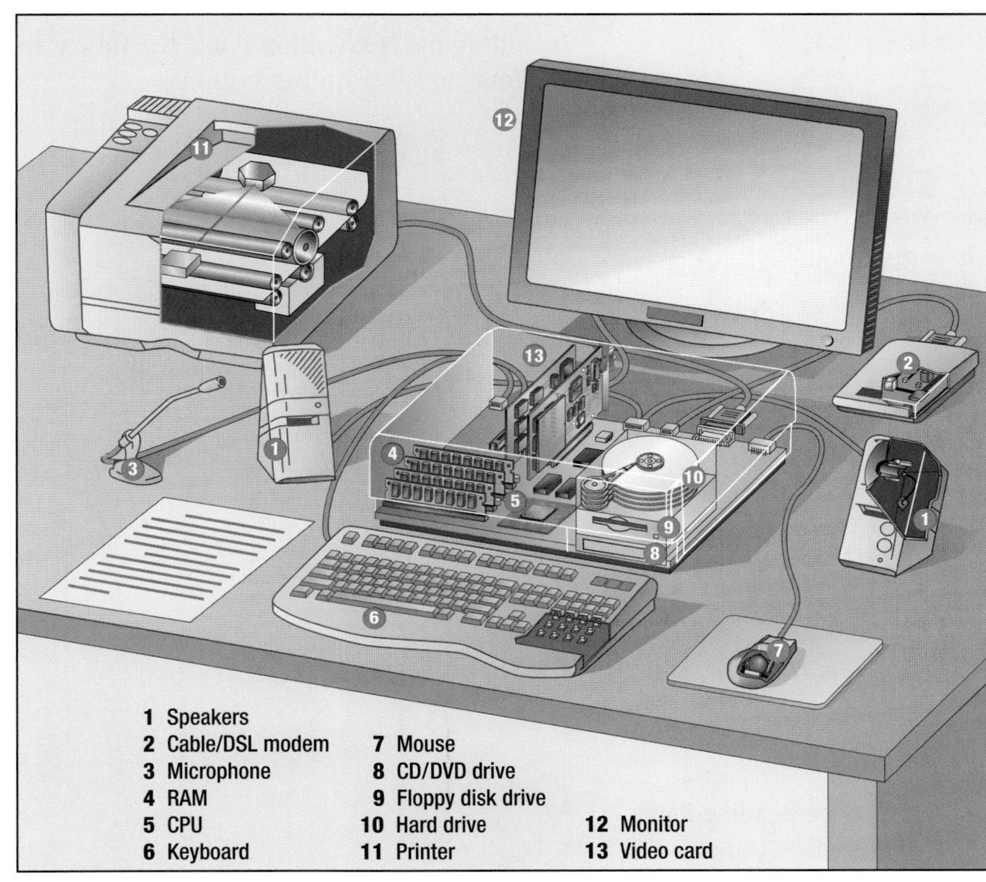

▲ Some components are visible to the user, while other components work behind the scenes. Which of these components do you think are inside your school computer? Which are outside your computer?

How Do I Connect Components?

Many of your hardware devices need to be connected to your computer. Devices such as your monitor and keyboard may have cables with connectors at the end. These connectors are then plugged into a port in the computer. Each port requires its own kind of connector. This makes it easy to know which cable to plug into the correct port.

Exercise B-2 Create an E-mail Message

TechSIM Interactive Tutorials An interactive simulation about e-mail is available to explore.

There are three steps to creating a new e-mail message. First, enter the address for the person to whom you are sending the message. Second, include a brief subject line that tells the recipient what your message is about. Third, write your message in the body of the e-mail.

You may save an e-mail message to send later. Outlook saves a draft of the message that you are writing. You can also save copies of messages that you have completed or sent.

For this exercise, your teacher will assign partners who will e-mail each other.

Step-by-Step

1. On the **Standard** toolbar, click the **New Mail Message** button.
2. On the **To** line, key the e-mail address of your partner.
3. On the **Cc** line, key the e-mail address of your teacher.
4. On the **Subject** line, key Animal Adoption Newsletter.
5. In the body of the e-mail, key the message shown in Figure B.2.

Figure B.2 The subject line should describe the content of the message.

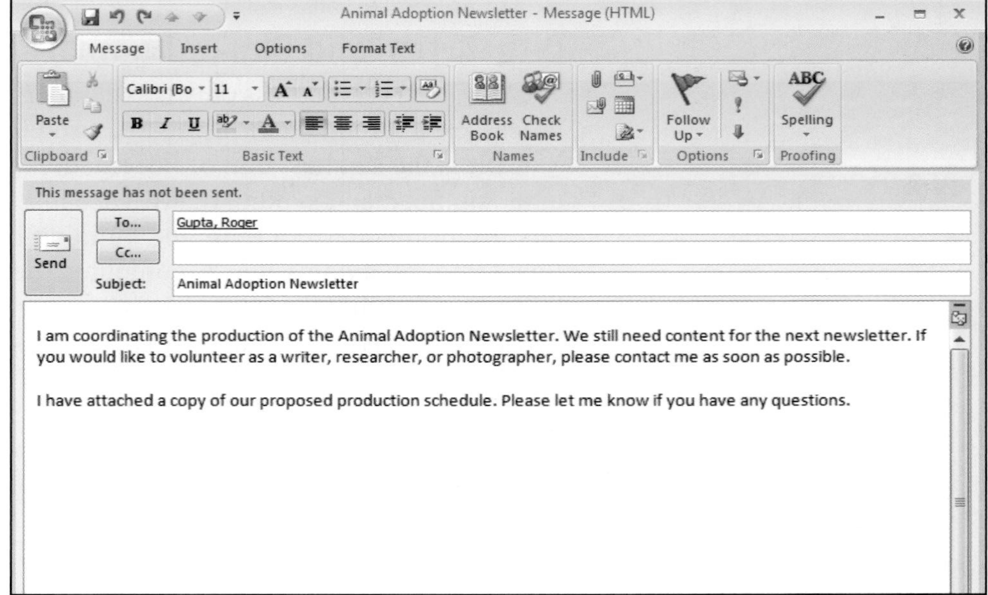

TechSavvy

Copy E-mail Messages When sending a message, you can send a carbon copy (**Cc**) or blind carbon copy (**Bcc**) to other people. Use the Cc address line when you want to send a copy of the message to one or more people. The Cc addresses will appear in every message. When you key an address in the Bcc address line, that person will receive a copy of the message, but the person's address will not be visible to anyone else.

Bits and Bytes Learn how to write your name in bits and bytes. Go to the **Online Learning Center** at **glencoe.com**. Choose **Tech Talk Activities**, then **Unit 2**.

How Does My Computer Work?

When you shoot a basketball, your eyes, brain, and muscles send many signals back and forth. When you use a computer, you send signals to the computer's **central processing unit (CPU)**, which is like the computer's brain. A CPU, or microprocessor, is a small chip that performs calculations and carries out all the instructions you give to your computer. Every time you press a key on the keyboard or move the mouse, you give instructions to the CPU. A faster CPU generally means that a computer can process more data in less time. The process of receiving and carrying out one instruction is called a cycle. The speed of a CPU is measured in:

- Megahertz (MHz)—millions of CPU cycles per second
- Gigahertz (GHz)—billions of CPU cycles per second

Bits, Bytes, and Binary Numbers

Computers can process only two numbers: 1 and 0. All data a computer processes is turned into a string of 1s and 0s called binary numbers.

A **bit** is the smallest unit of information, always either a 1 or a 0. Each letter, number, and symbol that we use in English is represented by eight bits. Eight bits make a **byte**, the building block for all information that flows through a computer. A computer file can contain thousands, millions, or even billions of bytes. A five-page research paper may use 40,000 bytes (or 40 KB). A movie on a DVD holds around five billion bytes (or 5 GB).

The word "cool" in binary numbers

01000011	01001111	01001111	01001100
C	O	O	L

▲ The word "cool" uses four bytes—one for each letter. How many bits does it use?

Reading Check

1. **Compare and Contrast** What are the differences between mainframe computers, minicomputers, and microcomputers?
2. **Identify** What are the only two numbers that a computer can process and what are they called?

6. After you have keyed your message, click the **Close** button [x]. Do not close Outlook!

7. In the dialog box, click **Yes** to save your message as a draft.

8. In the **Navigation** Pane, click **Mail**. Under **All Mail Folders**, click **Drafts** (Figure B.3).

9. Double-click the saved draft of Animal Adoption Newsletter to open it.

10. Click the **Office Button**, and choose **Save As**.

11. Save your file in the location specified by your teacher. Name the file *Your Name* Animal e-mail (Figure B.4). If you are using Windows XP, please refer to the *Getting Started* pages on pages xliv–xlviii in this book.

TechSavvy

Delete a message To delete an e-mail message from your Inbox, click the message to select it, then press the **Delete key** [DELETE] on the keyboard or the **Delete button** on the toolbar.

Figure B.3 The e-mail message is saved as a draft.

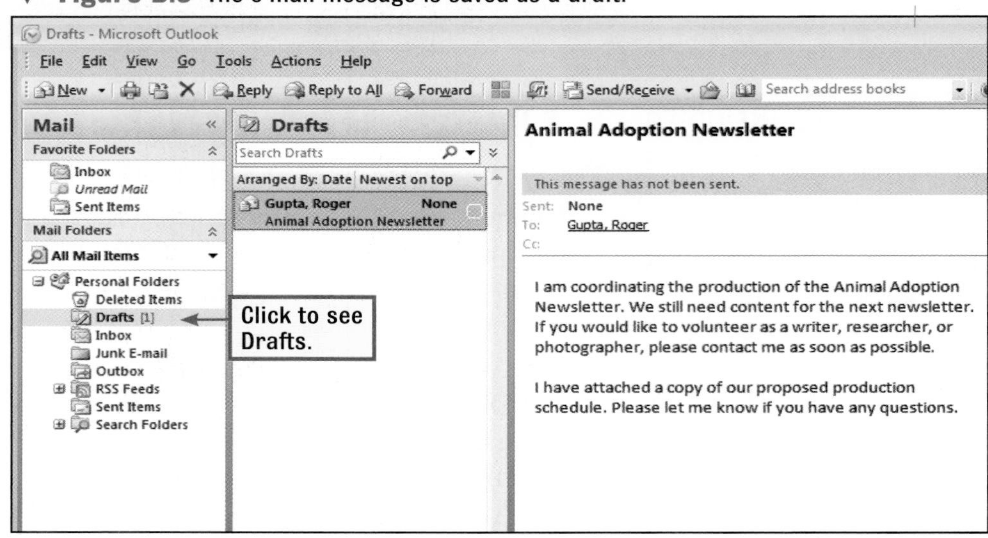

Figure B.4 Use the Save As box to save your e-mail message to your Data folder.

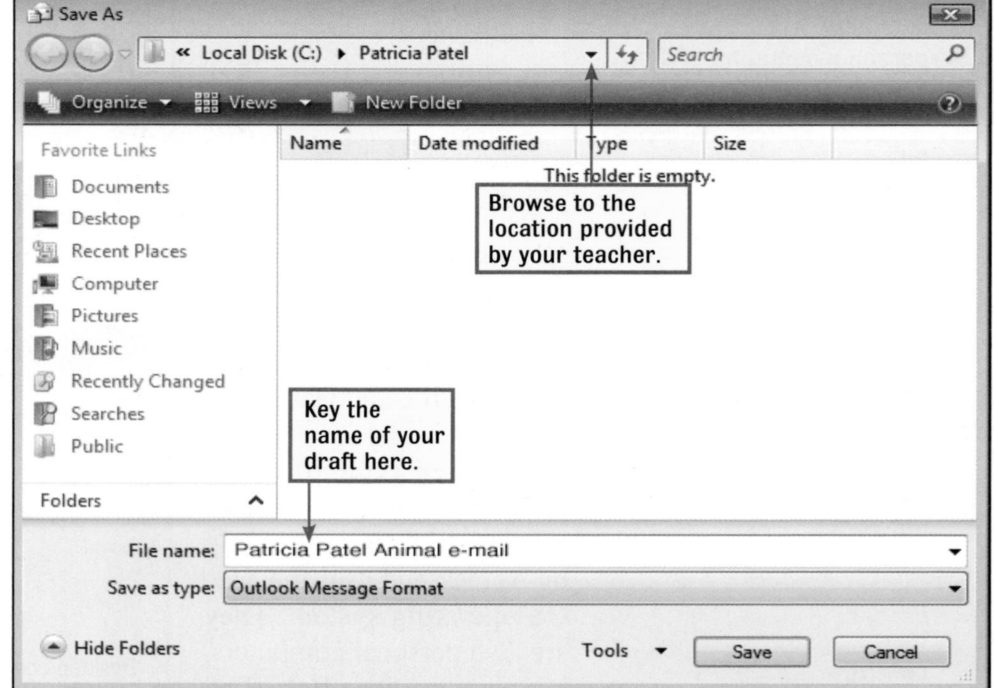

Introducing Your Computer

Reading Guide

Before You Read

Graphic Organizers If you have trouble understanding a concept, organize the information as a chart, table, or diagram.

Key Concepts

- How computers work
- How to identify hardware
- How memory and storage are used
- How to identify software
- How networks work

Vocabulary

Key Terms

computer
personal computer (PC)
central processing unit (CPU)
bit
byte
hardware
input
output
random-access memory (RAM)
read-only memory (ROM)
storage device
software
operating system (OS)
network

Academic Vocabulary

purpose
task
control
enable

Types of Computers

A **computer** is an electronic device that processes data. The earliest computers took up entire rooms. Today, a powerful computer fits in your backpack or even your pocket. Computers can be grouped in several different ways: by size, by **purpose**, or intended use, or by how many people use them.

- A **personal computer (PC)** is used by one person at a time. Desktop and laptop computers, MP3 players, and personal digital assistants (PDAs) are all examples of PCs, which are also called microcomputers.
- A minicomputer can be used by several people to hundreds of people at one time. These computers are often used in small- to medium-sized organizations, such as schools.
- A mainframe, or supercomputer, is so large that it can fill several rooms. These computers are used by thousands of people at the same time in organizations such as corporations and government agencies.

PCs and Macs

Computers also can be grouped by operating system. The term "PC" generally describes a computer that uses Microsoft Windows operating system software. Different companies, such as IBM®, Dell®, and Gateway®, make PCs.

Another type of computer is the Macintosh computer, which is made only by Apple® and uses the Mac OS operating system. They are also personal computers, but they are usually called "Macs" rather than "PCs."

▲ Desktop computers and laptop, or notebook, computers are types of personal computers. Name two other examples of PCs.

Exercise B-3

Attach a File and Send an E-mail Message

TechSIM Interactive Tutorials An interactive simulation about e-mail is available to explore.

An attachment is a file that is added to an e-mail message. An attachment can be a text document, a photo, a music file, or any other type of file. You can use attachments to provide additional information with your message, or to exchange files via e-mail.

If you send a large attachment, make sure the recipient is able to accept it. Some people use e-mail services that do not allow them to receive large attachments. If this is the case, the message and attachment may bounce back to you.

Step-by-Step

1. In your Animal e-mail message, click the **Attach File** button on the Ribbon (Figure B.5).
2. In the **Insert File** dialog box, browse to the **Data File** named **Photos.docx**.

▼ **Figure B.5** **Click the Attach File button to attach a file to your e-mail.**

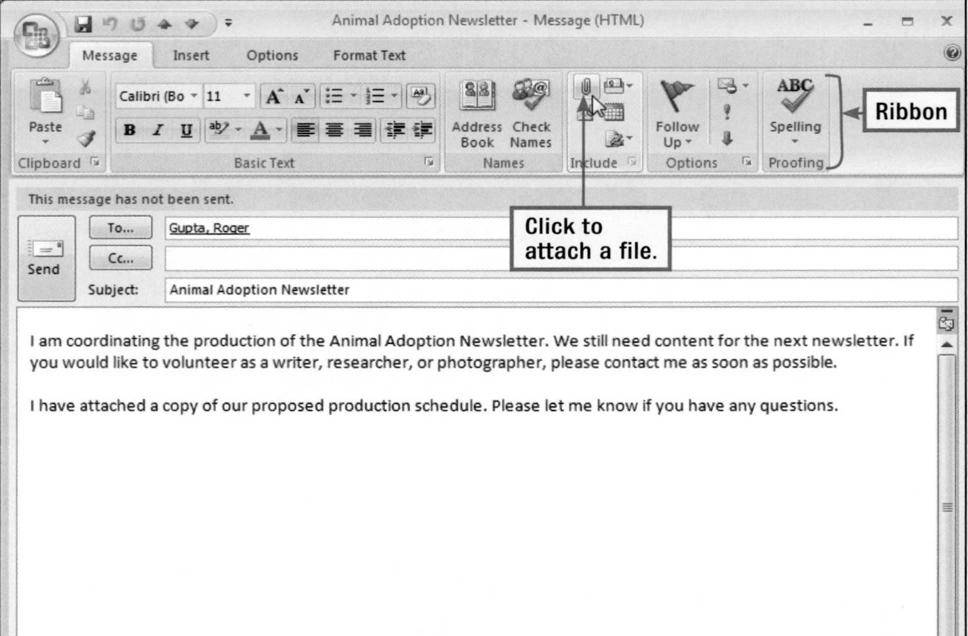

HELP!

Troubleshooting You may sometimes have problems sending, downloading, or viewing e-mail attachments. The fault can be a temporary problem with the e-mail provider or your e-mail application. If you have a problem sending an attachment, reduce the size of the attachment, resend the message, and contact the receiver to make sure the message arrived.

UNIT 2 Computer Hardware and Software

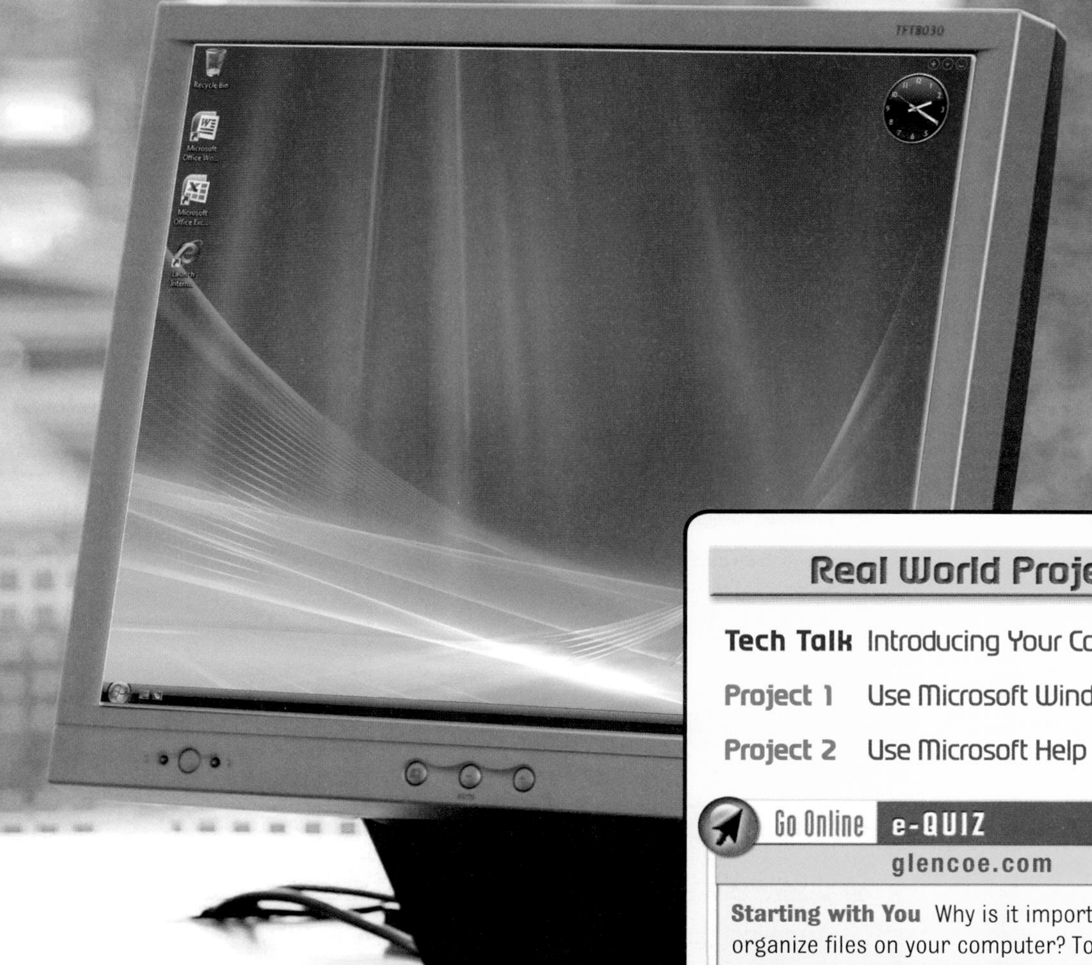

Real World Projects

Go Online e-QUIZ

glencoe.com

Starting with You Why is it important to organize files on your computer? To find out, go to the **Online Learning Center** at glencoe.com. Choose **e-Quizzes**, and take the **Unit 2 Pre-Quiz**.

3. Click **Insert**. The file name will appear in the **Attached** line of your message.

4. Repeat steps 2 and 3 to **insert** the **Data File** titled **Animal.docx**.

5. Right-click the attachment titled **Photos.docx**, then click **Clear**. Your screen should look like Figure B.6.

6. Click **Send** . In your **Sent** items, click to open the message (Figure B.7).

▼ **Figure B.6** A file has been attached to the message.

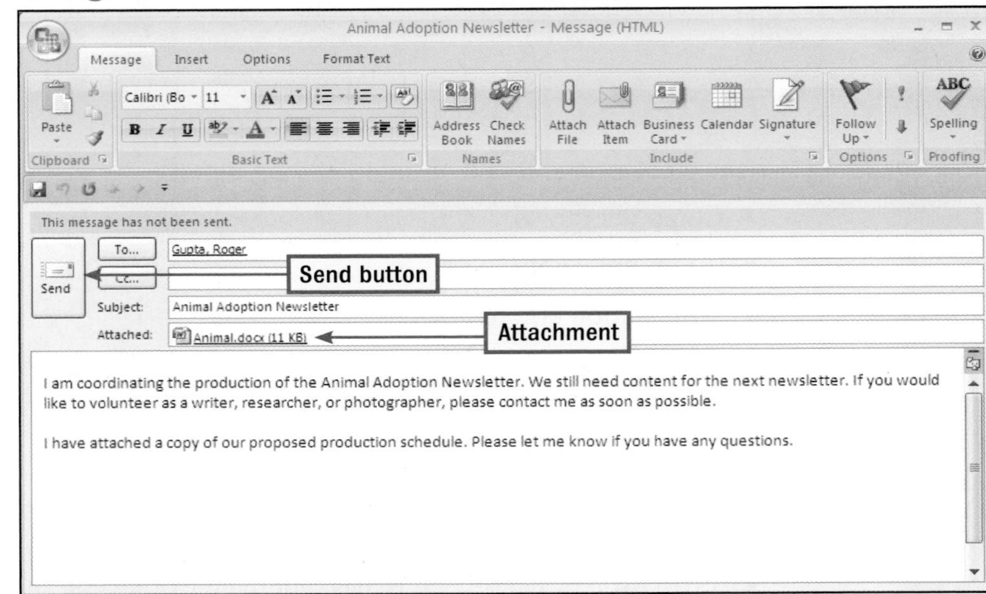

7. In your **Inbox**, find the message sent by your partner. It will have the subject **Animal Adoption Newsletter**.

8. Click the message to open it in the **Reading** Pane.

9. Double-click the attachment titled **Animal.docx** to open it.

10. Click the **File** menu, and **Save** the attachment as *Your Name* Animal Adoption to the location specified by your teacher.

▼ **Figure B.7** The message with attachment has been received.

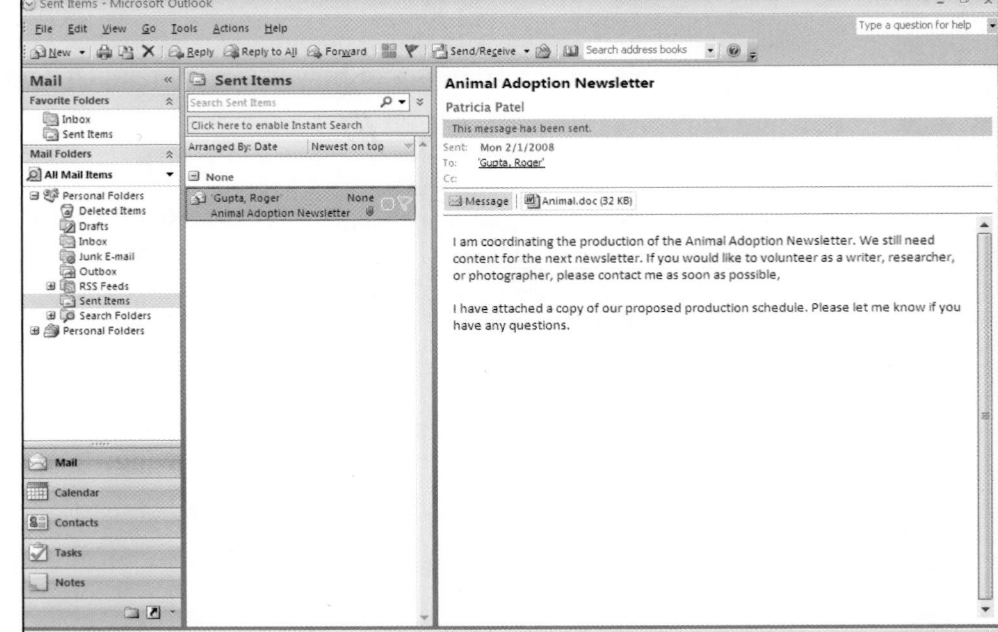

Build Your Portfolio

Create a Poster

Create a poster about one of the following topics:

- Computer ethics
- Computer safety
- Workstation ergonomics

The poster should include both text and art and should communicate a message that you believe is important.

Plan

1. Decide on the topic of your poster.
2. Decide what the message of your poster will be. You can make a poster about one specific issue or list several issues, but the message you send should be clear.

Research

3. Make sure the information on your poster is correct and factual. Use the information in Unit 1 or other print or online sources to back up your message.
4. List any sources that you use. Appendix D, "Reference Guide for Formatting Documents," gives examples of how to list your sources properly.

Be Safe, Not Sorry!

Computer safety is your responsibility.

- **Put computer equipment on sturdy tables.**
- **Sit on sturdy chairs.**
- **Keep the floor clean.**
- **Make sure computer cables are out of the way.**
- **Do not bring food or drinks into the classroom.**

Create

5. Sketch your poster idea on a piece of paper. Include both text and art.
6. If you choose, create your poster using Microsoft Word or another application.
7. Your poster should include the following:
   - At least one image
   - A definition or description of your topic
   - At least six rules that apply to your topic

6. In the new message, Roger Gupta's name appears on the **To** line. (His name is displayed with his e-mail address.)

7. On the **Subject** line, key Photographs.

8. For the message, key I have just seen the first group of photographs. They look wonderful! I can't wait to see the second group. See Figure B.14.

9. Click **Close** [X]. In the warning box, click **No**.

Figure B.14 When you create a new message from a contact card, the contact's e-mail address is automatically added.

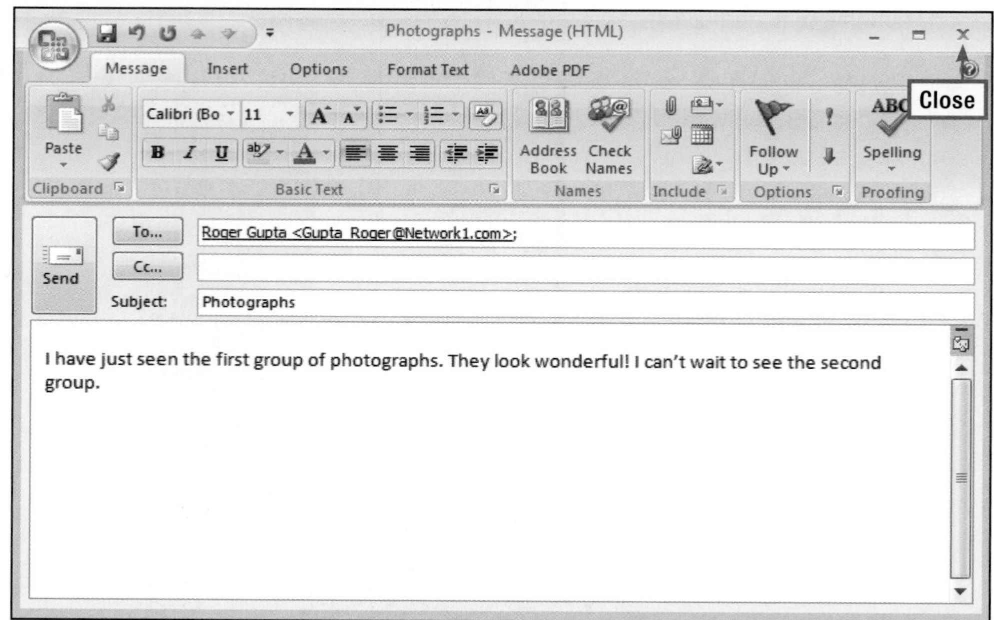

10. The information should be displayed in your **Contacts Pane** (Figure B.15).

11. In the **Contacts** Pane, right-click the **Gupta, Roger** contact card.

12. From the shortcut menu, click **Delete**.

Figure B.15 The Contacts Pane shows a summary of all of your contacts.

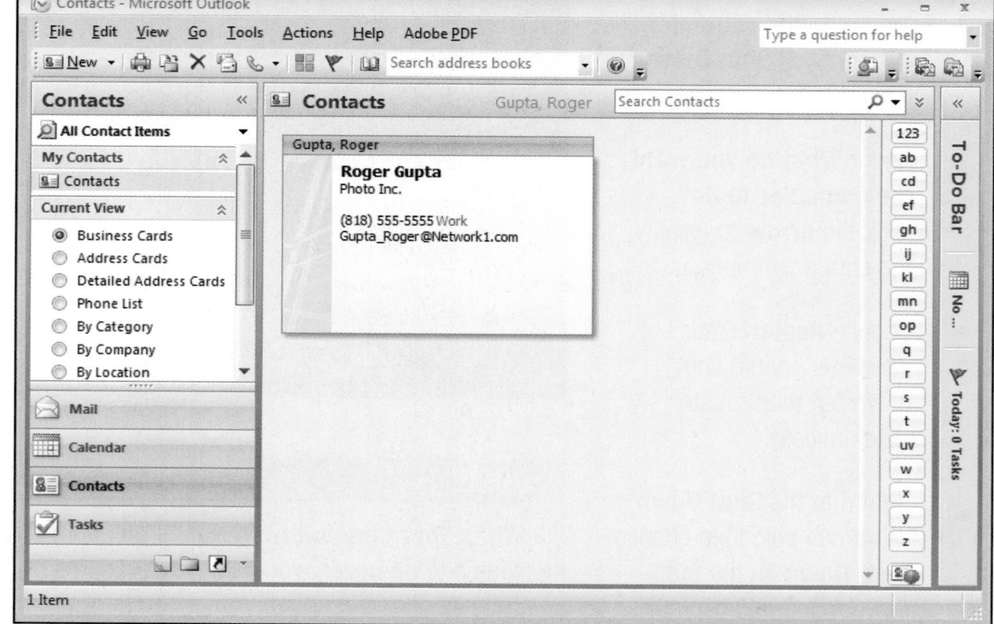

Step-by-Step

1. Click the **Start** button. Point to the arrow beside the **Lock this computer** button (Figure 2.18).

2. If you are logged on to your school's network, choose **Log Off**.

3. In the **Log Off** window, click **Log Off**. Your computer should return to the **Welcome to Windows** or **Log On** screen.

4. **Log** back **on** to Windows.

▼ **Figure 2.18** You can log off from the Start menu or the Shut Down Windows box.

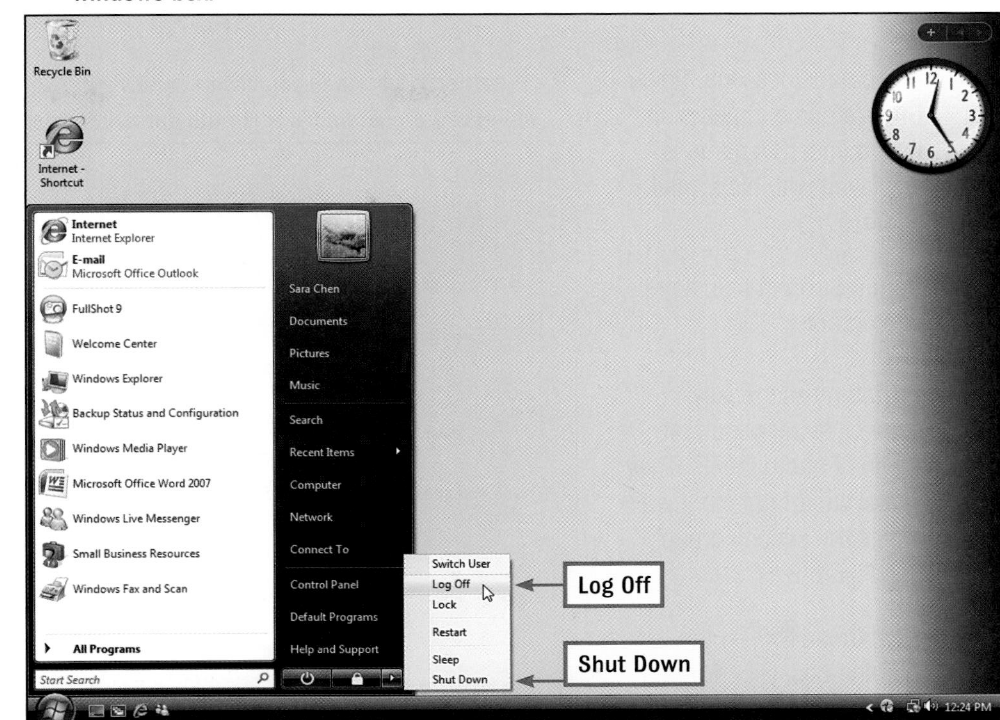

5. Click the **Start** button. Point to the arrow beside the **Lock this computer** button. Click **Shut Down** (Figure 2.19).

6. Under **What do you want the computer to do?**, click the **arrow** to display the shut down options.

7. Choose **Restart**. Your computer should shut down but then restart automatically.

8. Return to the **Shut Down Windows** box, then choose **Shut Down** on the drop-down menu and click **OK**.

▼ **Figure 2.19** Shut Down boxes may not always have a Log off option.

HELP!

When Your Computer Freezes If an application is not working or if it seems to be frozen, you can press CTRL + ALT + DELETE to display a list of options. Click the option to **Start Task Manager**. Click the application in the **Windows Task Manager** window, and then click **End Task**.

Exercise B-8 Adjust E-mail Settings

TechSIM Interactive Tutorials An interactive simulation about e-mail is available to explore.

You can customize Outlook to make it more personal, efficient, and effective. For example, you can attach an automatic signature to all of your messages, containing your name and other information.

Outlook also lets you choose the format of your e-mail messages:

- **Plain Text** format does not allow you to change the font or add graphics in the message body. It is the simplest format and can be read by all users.
- **Rich Text** format allows you to add text formatting.
- **HTML** format lets you use all formatting options, including inserting pictures. HTML format is the default setting for Outlook.

Keep in mind the person you are e-mailing may have problems reading your message if the format is not recognized by their application. For example, if your message is in HTML format, the recipient may not see pictures you inserted or may not be able to read the message at all.

Step-by-Step

1. In the **Inbox**, click the **Tools** menu, then choose **Options**.
2. In the **Options** dialog box, click the **Mail Format** tab. At the bottom of the box, click **Signatures**.
3. In the **Signatures and Stationery** dialog box, click **New**.
4. Key Patricia Patel in the **New Signature** dialog box, and click **OK**.
5. In the **Edit Signature** text box, key the text shown in Figure B.16.

▼ **Figure B.16** Use Signatures to add information to every message you send.

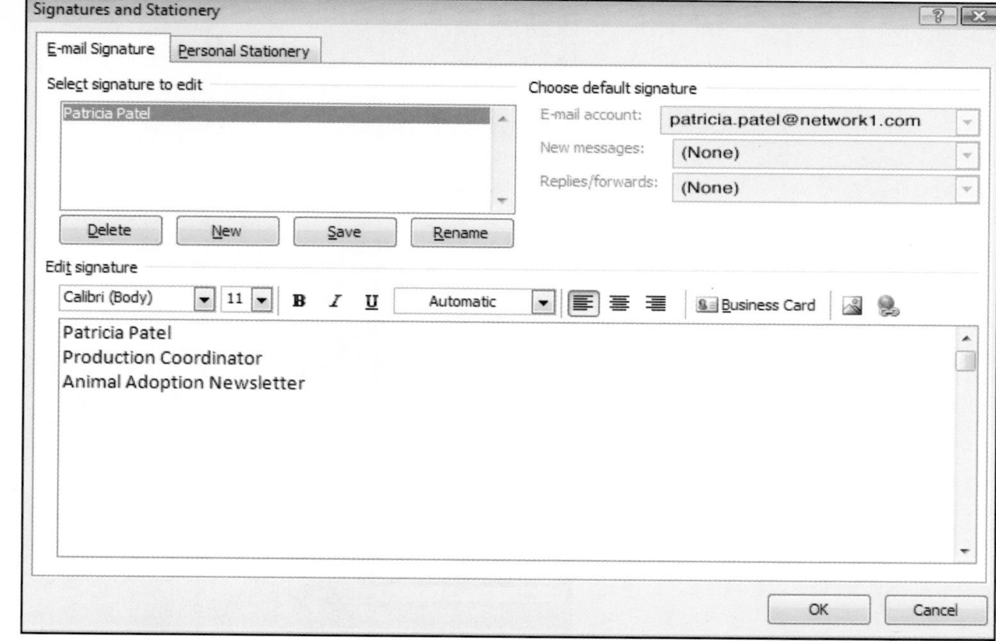

Exercise 2-5 Close Windows

It is important to follow the correct process when you are finished using your computer. If you do not, you might lose your data or damage the computer. You log off or shut down your computer using the Start menu. When you click the arrow beside the Lock button, the following options display:

- **Switch User** changes users. Save files before switching.
- **Log Off** disconnects your account from the network without shutting down the computer.
- **Lock** secures the computer when you need to leave your workstation and to leave all programs and documents open.
- **Restart** shuts down the computer and then automatically starts it again. You might need to do this after you install new software or if your computer is not working properly.
- **Sleep** lets your computer use less power when it is not in use. Your work remains on your computer. Save it before you use this option.
- **Shut Down** automatically logs you off the network. If no one else is going to use the computer after you, it is best to shut down.

TechSavvy

Shortcut Shut Down
An alternative way to shut down or log off your computer is to press ALT + F4. This keyboard shortcut displays the **Shut Down Windows** dialog box. Click the down arrow to display a list of options including **Sleep**, **Switch User**, **Log Off**, **Restart**, and **Shut Down**.

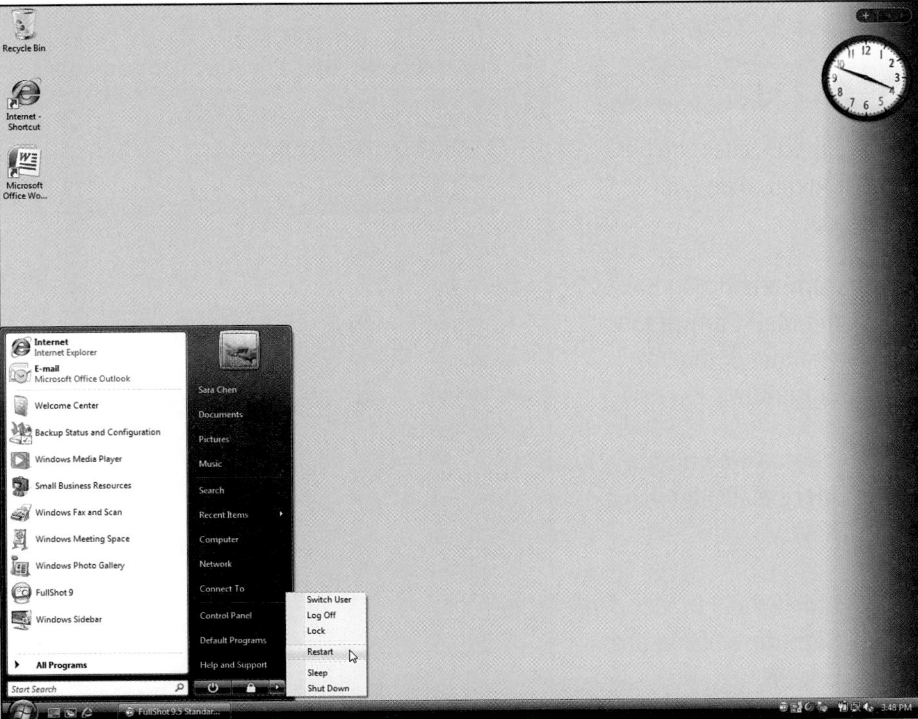

In this exercise, you will use some of Windows' shut down options. You may not be able to do all of them on your classroom computer. Check with your teacher before you begin.

6 Select **Patricia Patel** and click **Font** to open the **Font** dialog box.

7 Under **Font**, click **Lucida Handwriting**, or another font of your choice. Then click **OK**.

8 Click **Finish**, then click **OK** to return to the Inbox.

9 Click the **New Mail Message** button. The signature should be displayed (Figure B.17).

10 On the **Options** tab, in the **Format** group, verify that **HTML** is selected.

11 Click the **Close** button, and do not save the message.

▼ **Figure B.17** The new message has a signature. You can change or delete the signature in each message. Or you can repeat steps 1–8 to change your default signature settings.

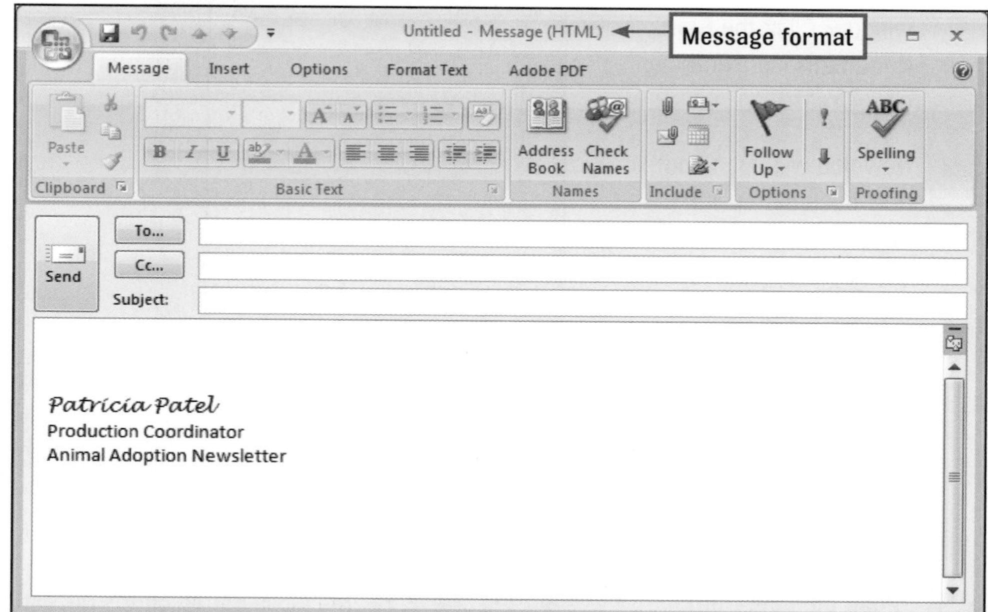

TechSavvy

More Outlook Features Outlook provides other features to make your e-mail application safe and efficient:

Out of Office—If you will not be using your e-mail for a period of time, you might consider turning on the Out of Office feature. When enabled, an e-mail reply is automatically sent for every message you receive, telling the sender that you are not available and explaining when you will return.

Block Spam—Outlook also helps you block unwanted messages from reaching your Inbox. Click the **Tools** menu, and click **Options** to open the **Options** dialog box. Click the **Junk E-mail** button to set Outlook to filter out unwanted e-mail that might contain viruses, advertisements, or messages from specific senders.

15 Click the **Office Button** (icon) at the top left of your screen, as shown in Figure 2.16.

16 Point to and click **New** to open the **New Document** window. Click the **Blank document** icon, and then click **Create**.

17 Now you will open another new document using a keyboard shortcut. Press the CTRL key, and hold it while you press the N key (often written as CTRL + N).

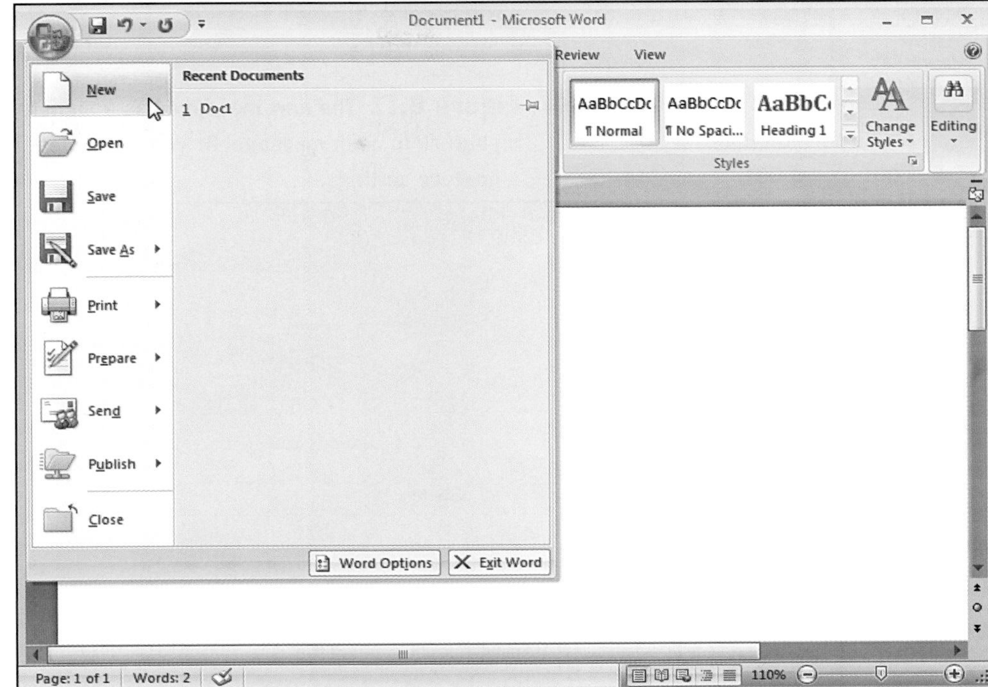

▼ **Figure 2.16** Open a document using your mouse or a keyboard shortcut.

18 **Close** the new Word document by using the keyboard shortcut CTRL + W.

19 Close the next open Word document by clicking the **Close** button (X) in the top-right corner of the window.

20 **Exit Word** and close the document by clicking the **Close** button in the top-right corner of the window (Figure 2.17). When asked "Do you want to save the changes to Document1?", click **No**.

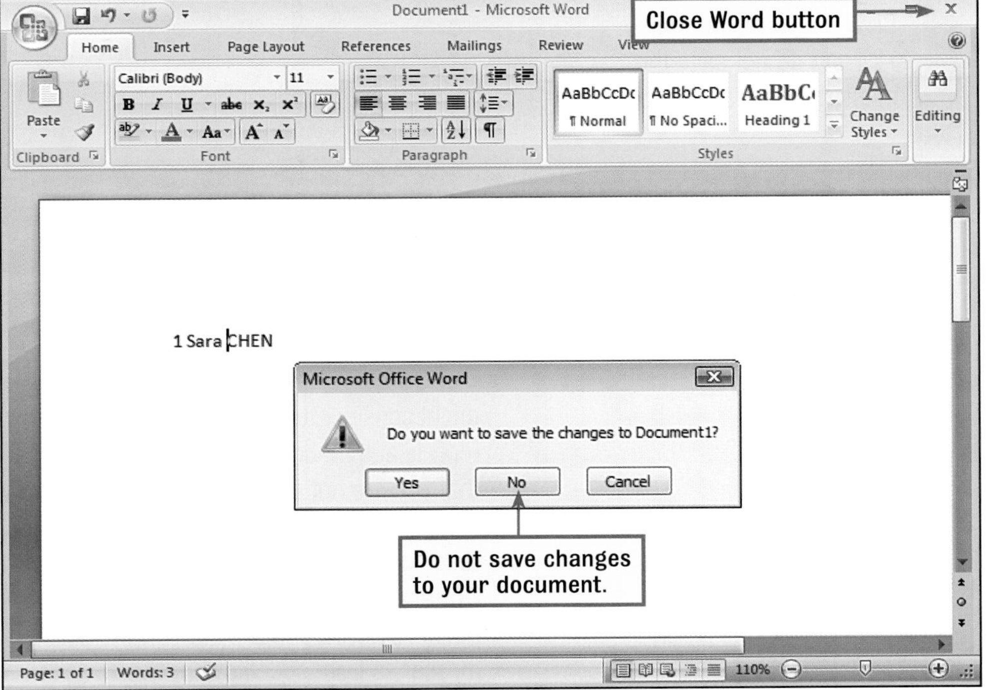

▼ **Figure 2.17** The Close button closes the active window.

Assessment E-mail

Key Concepts Check

1. **Define** What is an attachment?
2. **Identify** What kind of message format can you use to be sure your message will be readable by anybody?
3. **Explain** Why would you save an e-mail?

Critical Thinking

4. **Evaluate** Why is it a good idea to include a signature at the end of your e-mail message?
5. **Compare and Contrast** What is the difference between replying to a message and forwarding a message?

Guided Practice

TechSIM Interactive Tutorials An interactive simulation about e-mail is available to explore.

Step-by-Step

1. **Start Microsoft Outlook.** Create a **New Message**. (Exercise B-2)
2. On the **To** line, key the e-mail address of a classmate assigned by your teacher. (Exercise B-2)
3. On the **Subject** line, key Study Time. (Exercise B-2)
4. In the message body, key the text shown in Figure B.18. (Exercise B-2)

Compose and Send an E-mail Message Follow the steps below to create a new e-mail message and send it to a classmate. If you need help, refer to the exercise in parentheses at the end of the step.

▼ **Figure B.18** Create a new message.

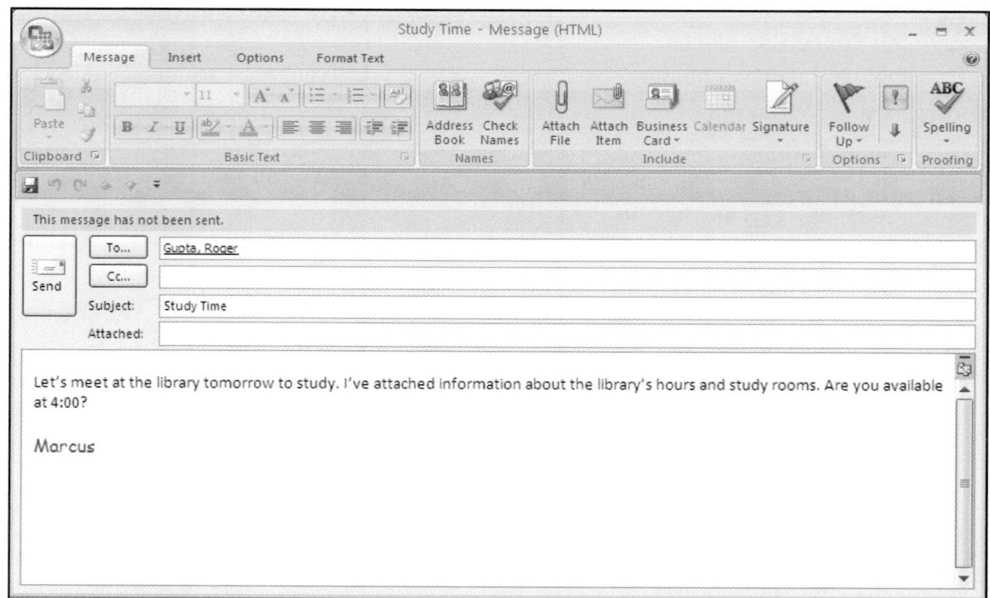

5. Use your **arrow keys** to move the insertion point back to its starting point.

6. Key your name in the document.

7. Press the BACKSPACE key until your name is deleted.

8. Press the CAPS LOCK key. Key your name again. It is uppercase (Figure 2.14).

9. Move the mouse pointer I to the beginning of your name, then click the mouse to insert the insertion point.

10. Key 1, then press the **Space Bar**. Notice how your name moves to the right to insert the 1 and the space.

11. Key 12345, then press the **Space Bar**. Notice that your name continues to move to the right (Figure 2.15).

12. Press the CAPS LOCK key to restore the keyboard to its usual settings.

13. Use the arrow keys or your mouse to move the insertion point to the beginning of the line.

14. Press the DELETE key to **delete** 12345 and the space. Delete your first name. Then rekey the first part of your name.

Figure 2.14 Use the arrow keys or the mouse to move the insertion point without moving or deleting text.

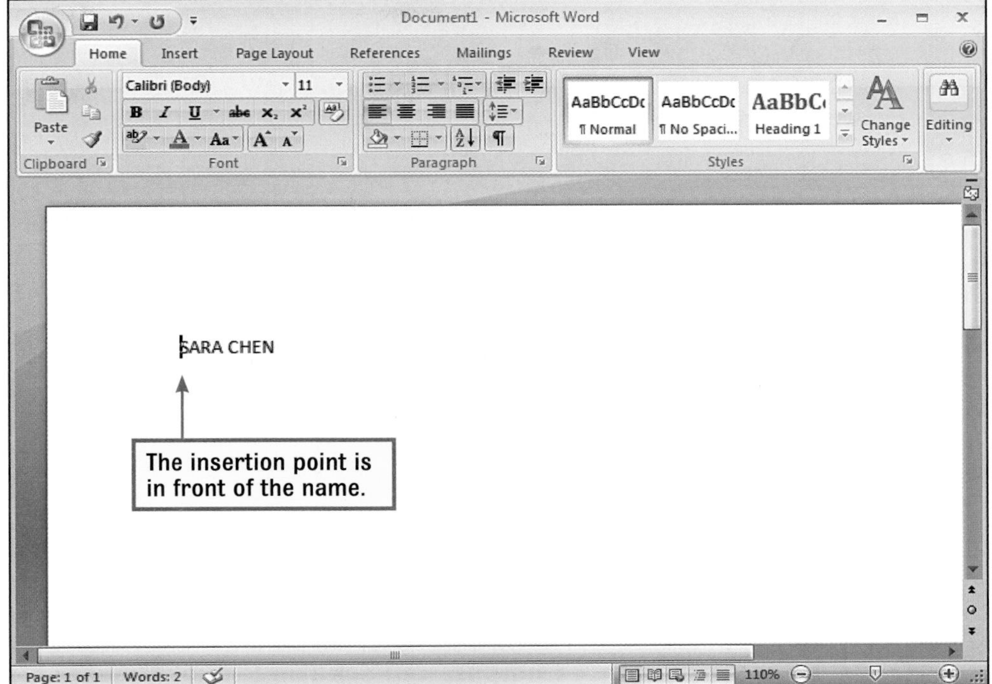

Figure 2.15 To insert text, position the insertion point and key the text.

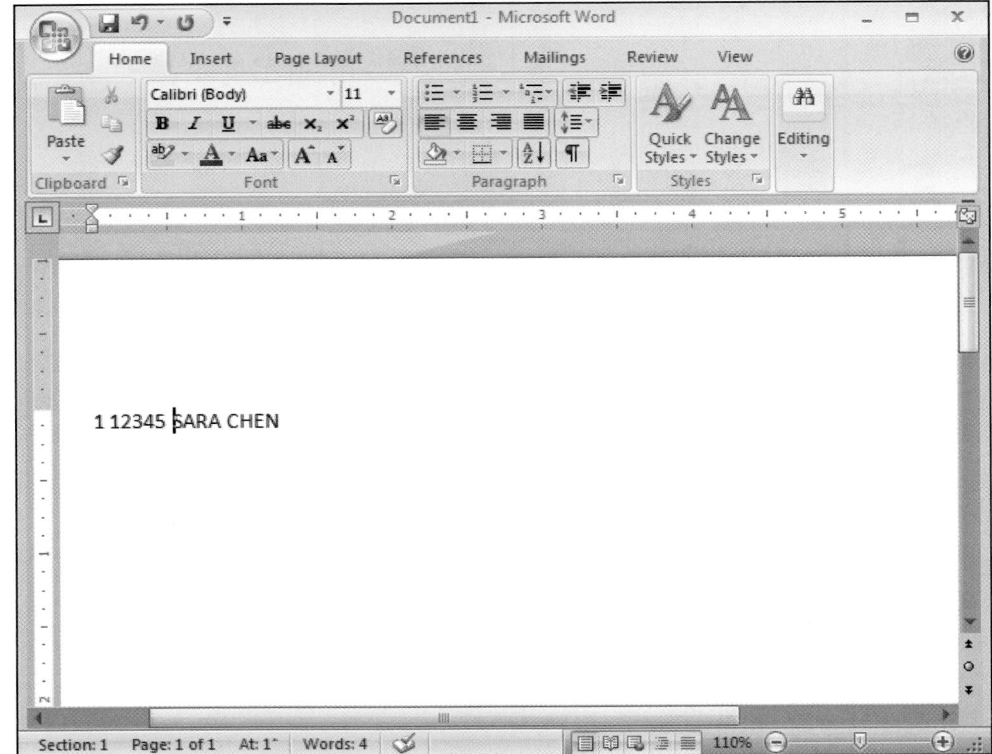

5 **Attach** the **Data File** titled **Study.docx** (Figure B.19). (Exercise B-3)

6 **Send** your e-mail message.

▼ **Figure B.19** Attach a file to your message.

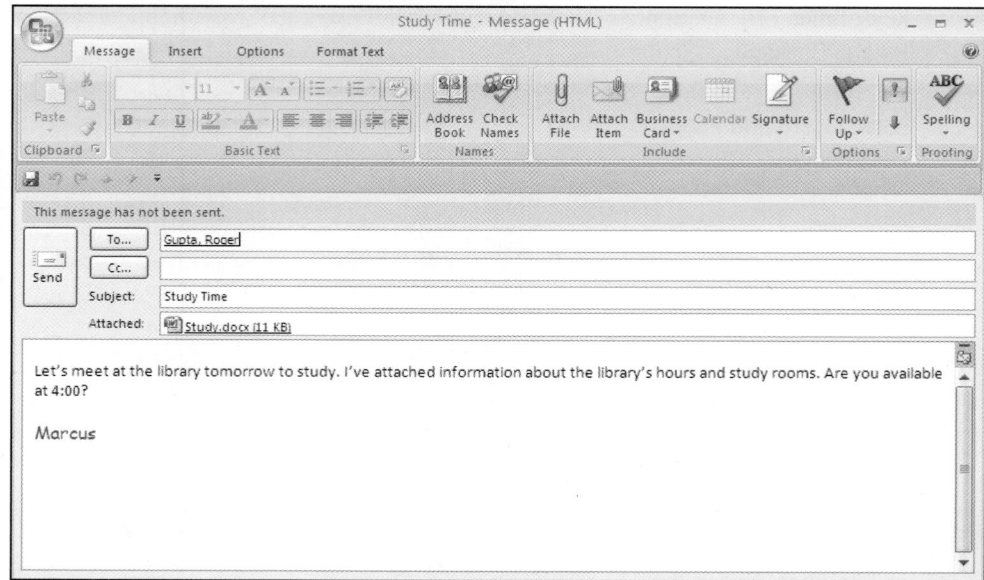

7 In the **Navigation** Pane, click **Contacts**. (Exercise B-7)

8 Create a new contact with the information in Figure B.20. (Exercise B-7)

9 **Close** and **exit** Outlook.

▼ **Figure B.20** Create a new contact.

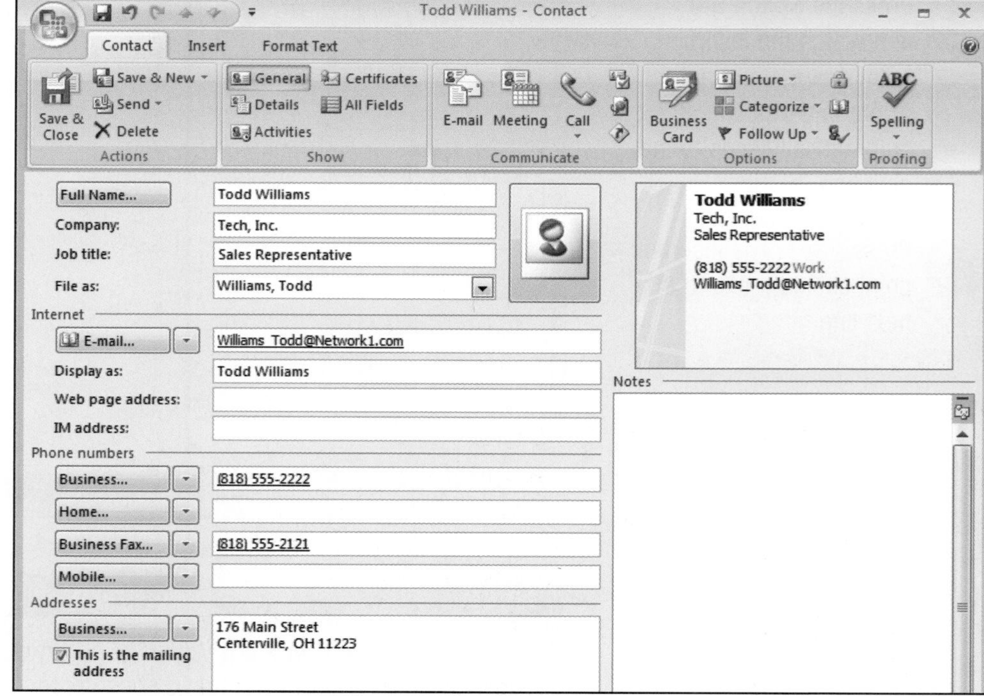

Step-by-Step

1. On your own keyboard, identify the following keys: Enter, Ctrl, Alt, Shift, Delete, Backspace, Space Bar, arrow keys, Tab, Caps Lock, Insert, and Function keys (Figure 2.12).

Figure 2.12 Keyboards may not look the same, but they have the same basic keys.

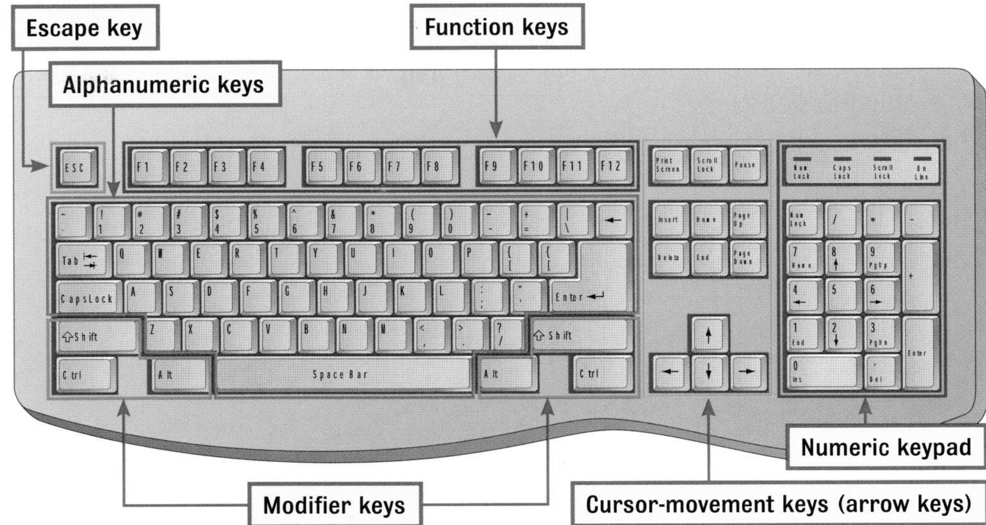

2. On your screen, the blank Word document should still be open. Notice the blinking **insertion point** on your screen (Figure 2.13).

3. Press the **Space Bar**, and watch the insertion point move to the right. At the end of a line, it automatically goes to the next line.

4. Press ENTER. The insertion point should move to the next line.

Figure 2.13 The Word screen displays an insertion point in a blank document.

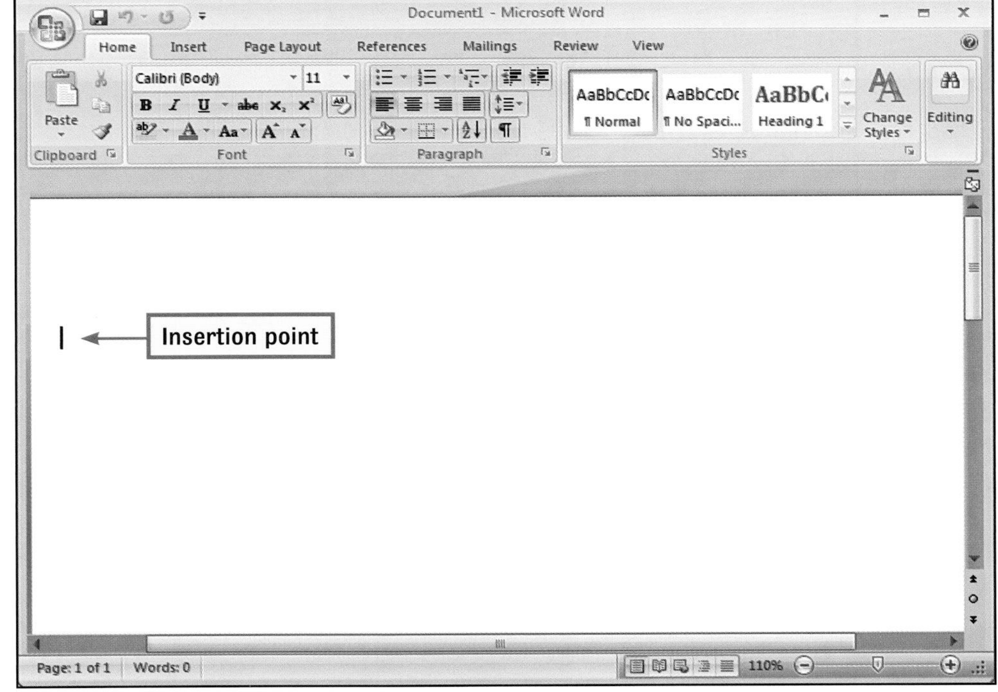

HELP!

Moving the Insertion Point Arrow keys can move the insertion point only where text or spaces have already been entered.

System Settings and the Control Panel

The Control Panel is part of the Microsoft Windows operating system. The Control Panel allows you to change many system settings to customize your computer to suit your needs. For example, you can use it to change the date and time shown on your computer or to change the look of your desktop background.

The following exercises let you practice adjusting system settings on your computer. The figures show examples of Windows Vista. If you use another version of Microsoft Windows, you can still follow the steps, but your screens will look different from the ones shown here.

TechSIM™ Interactive Tutorials

You may not be allowed to change settings on your school computer. If so, you may want to use the optional TechSIM Interactive Tutorials—technology simulations that allow you to practice changing system settings. This is an excellent option if you are using an older version of Windows or if your classroom computers use different operating systems.

To use the TechSIM Interactive Tutorials, you will need to have Macromedia Flash installed on your computer. The TechSIM Interactive Tutorials allow all students to practice the same skills. Ask your teacher if you should use the TechSIM Interactive Tutorials and how to access them.

Contents

Exercise 2-4 Get to Know Your Keyboard

Although you can use your mouse for many computer functions, you still need your keyboard to enter text and numbers. Eventually, you may be able to accurately enter data using your voice or writing on a tablet, but for now, the best way is still by keying this information. **To review keyboarding skills, see Appendix A.**

You can use the keyboard to do many things that can be done by clicking a mouse. For example, you can move the insertion point with either your mouse or a keyboard key. The **insertion point** is the symbol that shows where you will be entering text or data on your screen. It is often a blinking vertical line.

Most of the keys on your keyboard are letters, numbers, or symbols. Besides these, you will need to know the important keys listed in the table below.

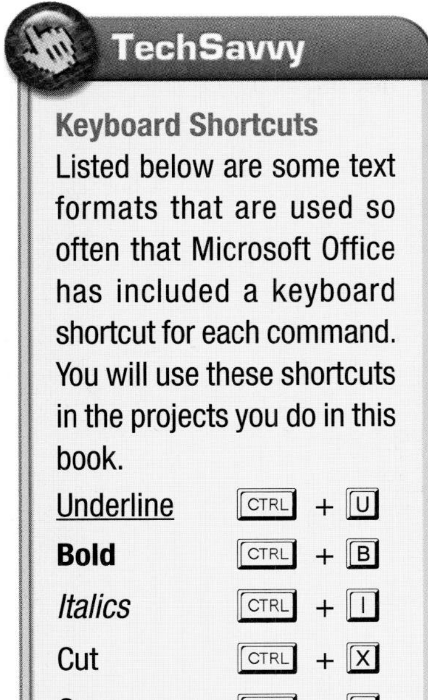

Important Keyboard Keys

Keys	How They Are Used
Enter	This key is used to apply a command or finalize data entry. It is also used to move the insertion point to the next line.
Ctrl (Control), Alt (Alternative), Shift	Modifier keys are used in combination with other keys to issue a command. Shift also makes a letter uppercase.
Delete, Backspace	Erase keys: Delete erases characters to the right of the insertion point, and Backspace erases characters to the left.
Space Bar	This key adds a space at the insertion point.
Arrow keys	These keys move the insertion point up, down, left, or right without creating spaces or deleting text.
Tab	Moves the insertion point or text to a specific point.
Caps Lock	When turned on, this key locks the alphabet keys so that all letters are uppercase.
Insert	When turned off, Insert lets you key over existing text instead of inserting new text that moves any existing text to the right.
Function keys (F1–F12)	These keys can be used for different commands, depending on the program. They are often used with modifier keys.

When you use a keyboard command, it is called a **shortcut**. Shortcuts let you work without the mouse so that you can keep both hands on the keyboard. They often involve use of the Ctrl, Alt, Shift, and Function keys.

In this exercise, you will practice using the keyboard and the mouse to move around in a Word document.

Exercise C-1 Get to Know the Control Panel

TechSIM Interactive Tutorials An interactive simulation about system settings and the Control Panel is available to explore.

The Windows operating system has many useful functions and tools to help you be more productive. Some of these functions can be found in the Control Panel where you can change printers, select Internet options, and much more.

It is likely that many of the system settings on your school's computers can be changed only by teachers or by your school's network administrators. You should only change a setting if you know how it will affect the computer system and the other people who use it.

Do not change any computer settings at school without your teacher's permission!

Step-by-Step

1. Click **Start**, and then click **Control Panel**. See Figure C.1.
2. Locate and click **Classic View**.

Figure C.1 This is the default view of the Control Panel.

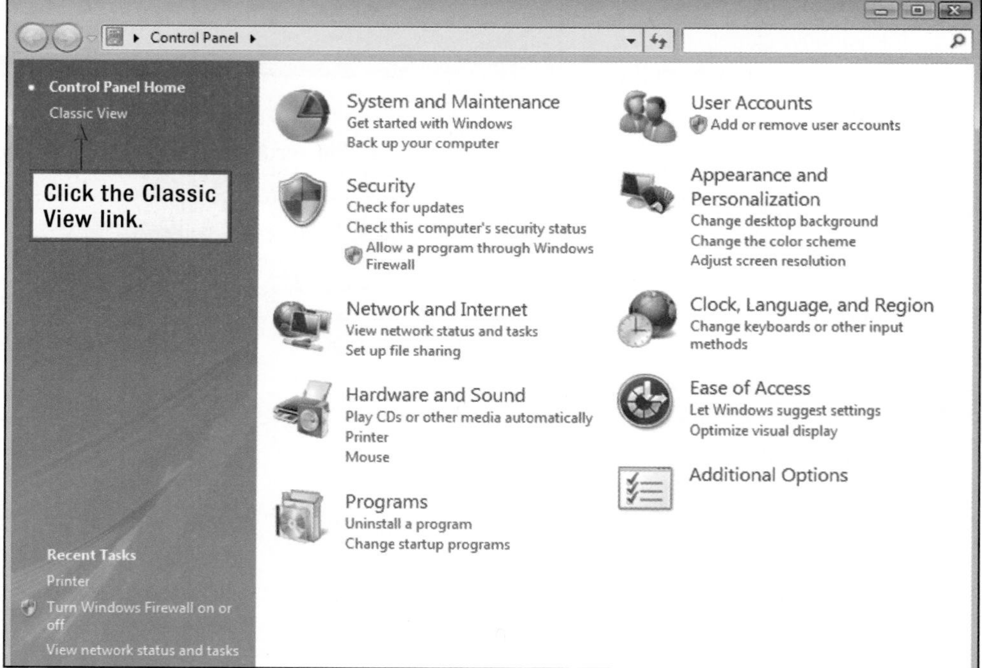

TechSavvy

Views In the Control Panel, you can choose the **Classic View** or the **Control Panel Home** view to access all of the Control Panel's functions and tools. If you are unfamiliar with the Control Panel, it may be easier for you to use the **Control Panel Home** view.

10. Move the mouse pointer over the bottom-right corner of the **Word** screen. Your pointer should change to a two-headed arrow ⤡.

11. Hold down the left mouse button and drag the window frame inward to make the **Word** screen smaller and display **Excel** behind it (Figure 2.10).

12. Click the **Excel** document to bring it to the front of the **Word** window.

13. In the top-right corner of the **Excel** window, click the **Close** button ✕ to exit **Excel**. **Note**: When the window closes, its button disappears from the **taskbar**.

14. Click the **horizontal scroll bar** and drag it to the left and right to see how the screen moves (Figure 2.11).

15. To restore **Word** to its original size, click the **Maximize** button ▭.

16. Click the **vertical scroll bar** on the right side of the document. Drag it up and down (Figure 2.11).

17. Keep Word open for the next exercise.

▼ **Figure 2.10** You can change the size of a window by moving your mouse to the corner and dragging the two-headed arrow pointer.

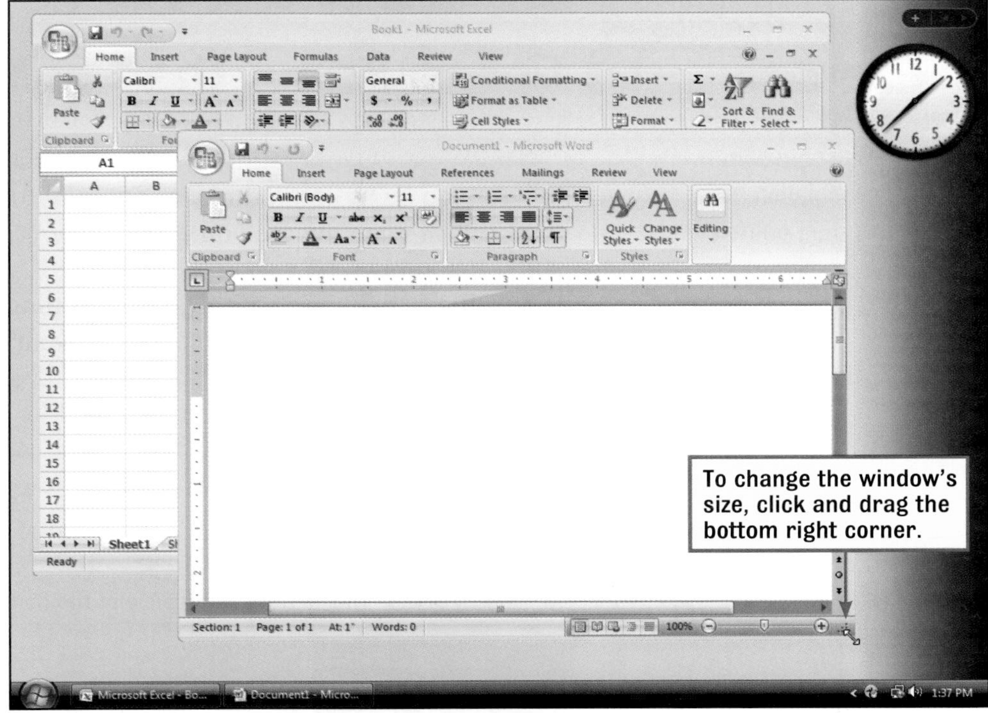

▼ **Figure 2.11** The scroll bars control the position of the document in the window.

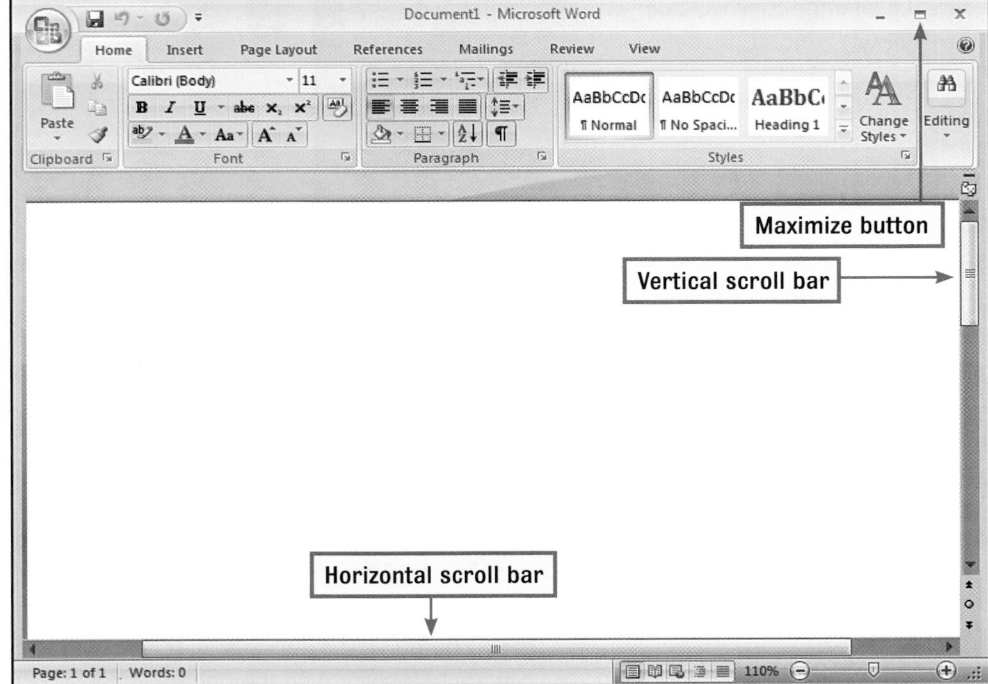

Exercise C-2 Change the Date and Time

TechSIM Interactive Tutorials An interactive simulation about system settings and the Control Panel is available to explore.

Your computer has its own clock for tracking the date and time. The lower-right corner of your screen usually displays the time.

When a document is created or modified, the clock places a time stamp on the document. This time stamp lets you know at what time and date the document was created or last modified. Many people use this time stamp to find the most recent version of a document, so it is important that the computer's clock be accurate. For this exercise, your Control Panel should be in Classic View.

Step-by-Step

1. **Open** the **Control Panel**, and switch to **Classic View**. Double-click **Date and Time**.
2. Click **Change date and time**. Click **Continue**, if prompted. The **Date and Time Settings** dialog box displays (Figure C.2).
3. To change the **month** and **year**, click the right- or left-facing arrows. To change the **day**, click the calendar.
   Note: Click the name of the month to show a list of months or years to select.
4. To change the **time**, click any part of the displayed time to highlight it. Then click the selection arrows to change it.
5. To close the **Date and Time Settings** dialog box without making changes, click **Cancel**. (You would click **OK** to save your changes.)

▼ **Figure C.2** The Date and Time Settings dialog box is a useful tool.

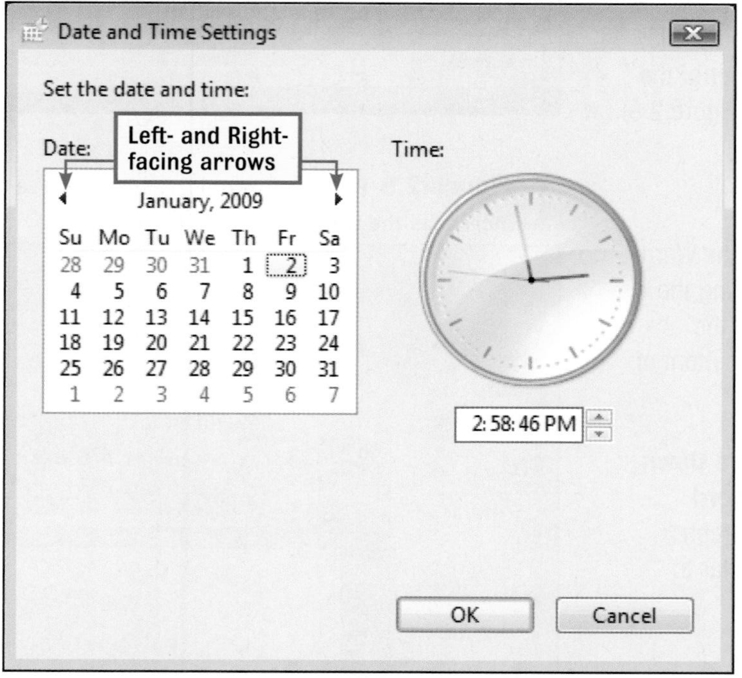

TechSavvy

Caution Unless your teacher instructs you to do so, do *not* change the date or time settings on your computer. Other users of the computer need the date and time to be correct so that the time stamp on their files is accurate.

4 Start **Microsoft Excel** by clicking the **Start** button, choosing **All Programs**, clicking the **Microsoft Office** folder, then clicking **Microsoft Office Excel 2007**.

5 To switch to the Word window, click the **Word** button on the **taskbar** at the bottom of the screen.

6 To bring the Excel window to the front, click the **Excel** button on the **taskbar** (Figure 2.8).

7 Click the **Restore Down** button in the upper-right corner of the **Excel** window (Figure 2.8).

8 Switch back to the Word window by clicking the **Word** button on the **taskbar** at the bottom of the screen.

9 Click the **Restore Down** button on the **Word** window. Your screen should look similar to Figure 2.9.

Figure 2.8 The Excel window opens on top of the Word window.

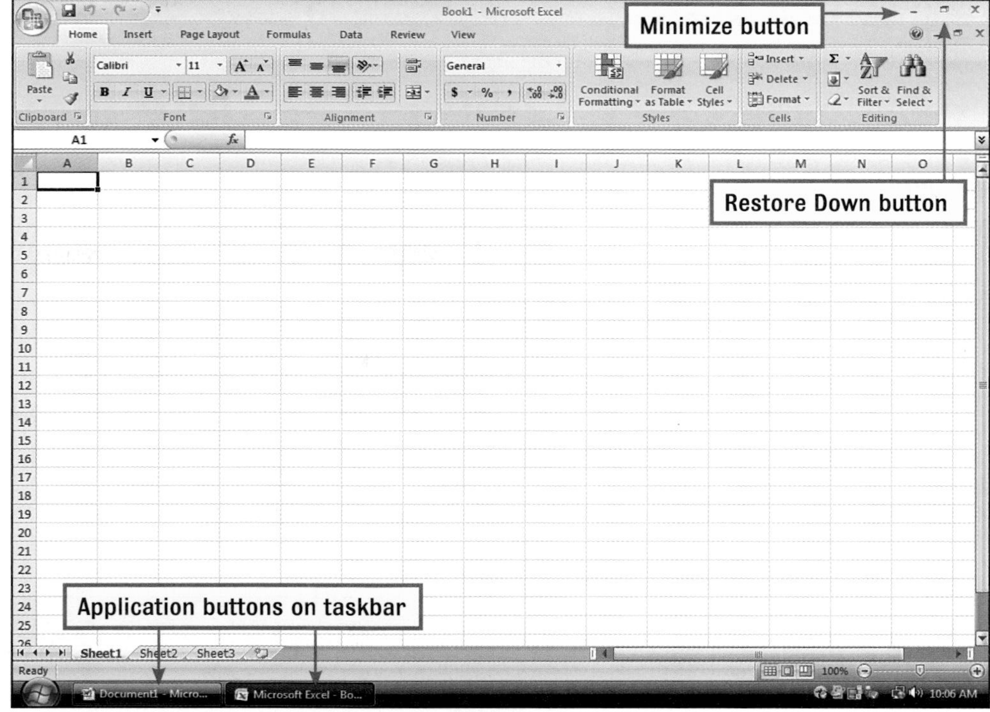

Figure 2.9 Restore Down decreases the size of the window, while Maximize increases the window to its full size.

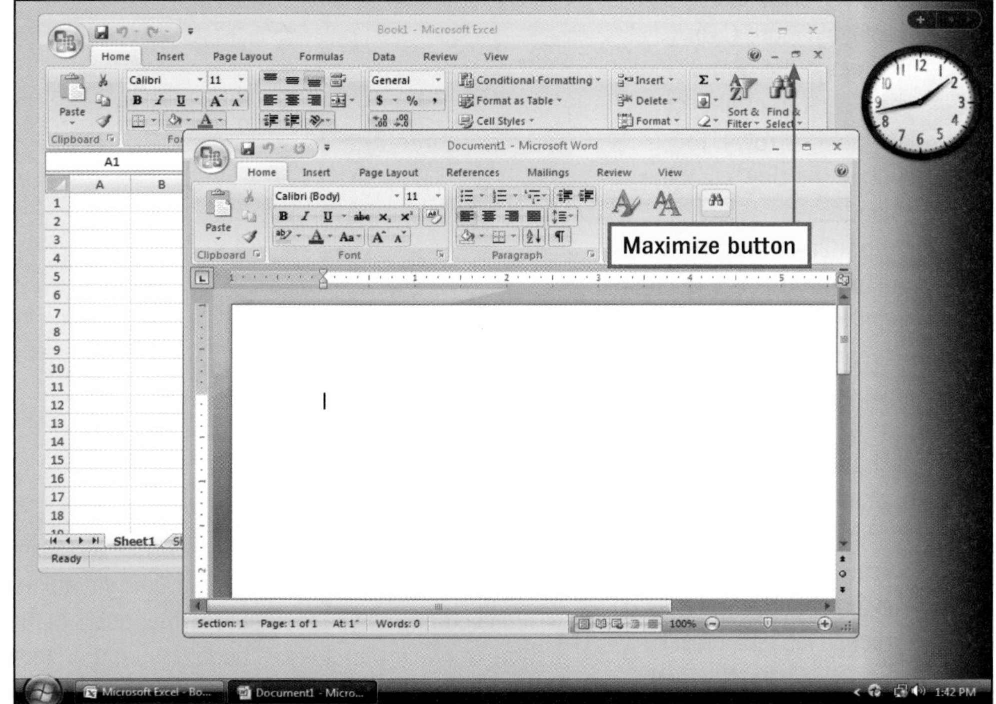

Exercise C-3 Modify the Display

TechSIM Interactive Tutorials An interactive simulation about system settings and the Control Panel is available to explore.

Through the Control Panel, you can view and change your monitor's display, which includes the screen area, screen colors, desktop image, and screen saver. For this exercise, your Control Panel should be in Classic View.

Step-by-Step

1. Open the Control Panel in **Classic View**, and double-click the **Personalization** icon. Click the **Desktop Background** link.
2. Click the drop-down arrow for **Picture Location**, and then click **Sample Pictures** (Figure C.3).
3. Click one of the pictures to apply a new desktop background.
4. Click the **Back** button to return to the **Personalization** settings.
5. Click the **Screen Saver** link to display the **Screen Saver Settings** dialog box. Under **Screen saver**, click the drop-down arrow to display the sample screen savers. Click a screen saver name to see a sample.
6. To close the **Screen Saver Settings** dialog box without saving your changes, click **Cancel**.

Figure C.3 Change your desktop background using the Personalization settings.

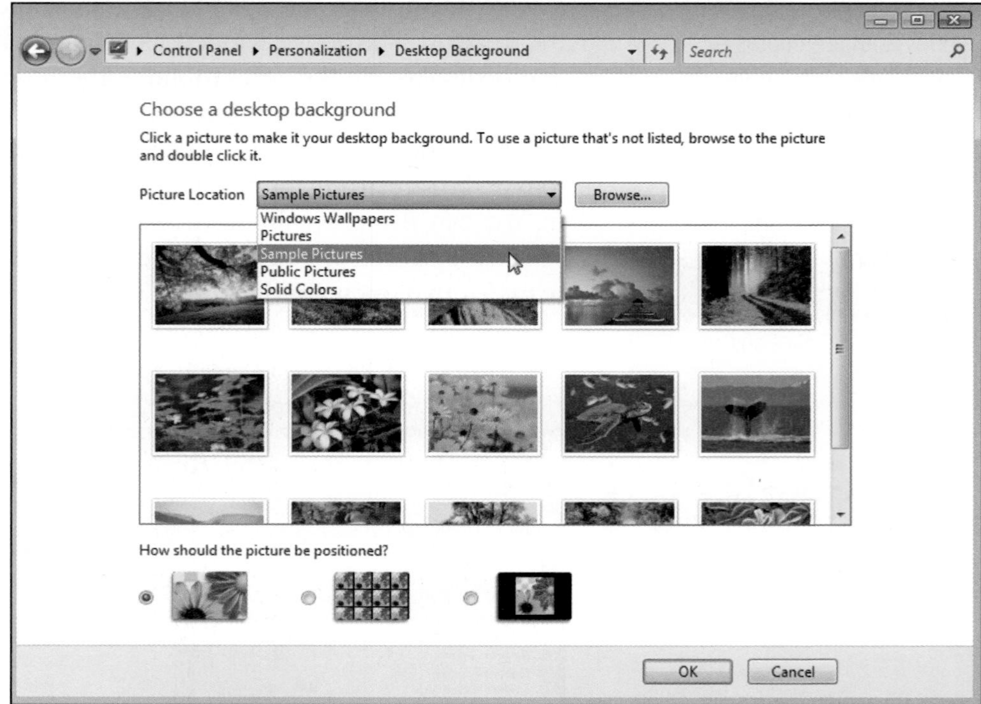

TechSavvy

Desktop Photo Background Turn your favorite photo into your desktop background! Save it to your computer in a graphic format such as *.jpg* or *.gif*. In the **Desktop Background** dialog box, click the **Browse** button. Find your image and select it. You will see a preview of the desktop.

Exercise 2-3 Work with Multiple Applications

Academic Focus

English Language Arts

Metaphors A metaphor uses language to show similarities between two seemingly unrelated things. For example, compare the Microsoft Windows interface and a glass window. Both are contained in a frame and suggest boundaries or limits. Both allow you to think about or imagine something. As a class, share examples of metaphors.

NCTE 6 Apply knowledge of language structure and conventions to discuss texts.

From the Windows desktop, you can open all of the software programs you use on your computer. A **program** is the set of instructions your computer receives in order to carry out its many functions. An **application** is a software program—such as Microsoft Office, Apple Keynote, or Adobe Photoshop—that lets you perform specific tasks such as organizing information, creating reports, or printing a picture.

Whenever you open an application such as Microsoft Word or Excel, it appears as a new window on the screen. A **window** is an area on the computer screen where an application can be viewed and accessed. Use Microsoft Windows to multitask. You can open several windows to complete a project. Applications, system programs, and files display in windows on the desktop. The active window is the application you are currently using, and it displays in the foreground. Other open applications display in the background or as a minimized window with a button on the taskbar.

One of the most important parts of your desktop is the **taskbar** at the bottom of the screen. On the taskbar, you can see what windows you are working in. You can also open any windows that are displayed on the taskbar.

In this exercise, you will make a window smaller and larger and move between two open applications.

Step-by-Step

1. Click the **Start** button to open the **Start** menu.

2. Click **All Programs**. Click the **Microsoft Office** folder, and then click **Microsoft Office Word 2007** (Figure 2.7).

3. Click the **Minimize** button [–] in the upper-right corner of the Word window. The Word window is now visible only as a button on the taskbar.

▼ **Figure 2.7** You may be able to open Microsoft Word directly from the Start menu or from a desktop shortcut.

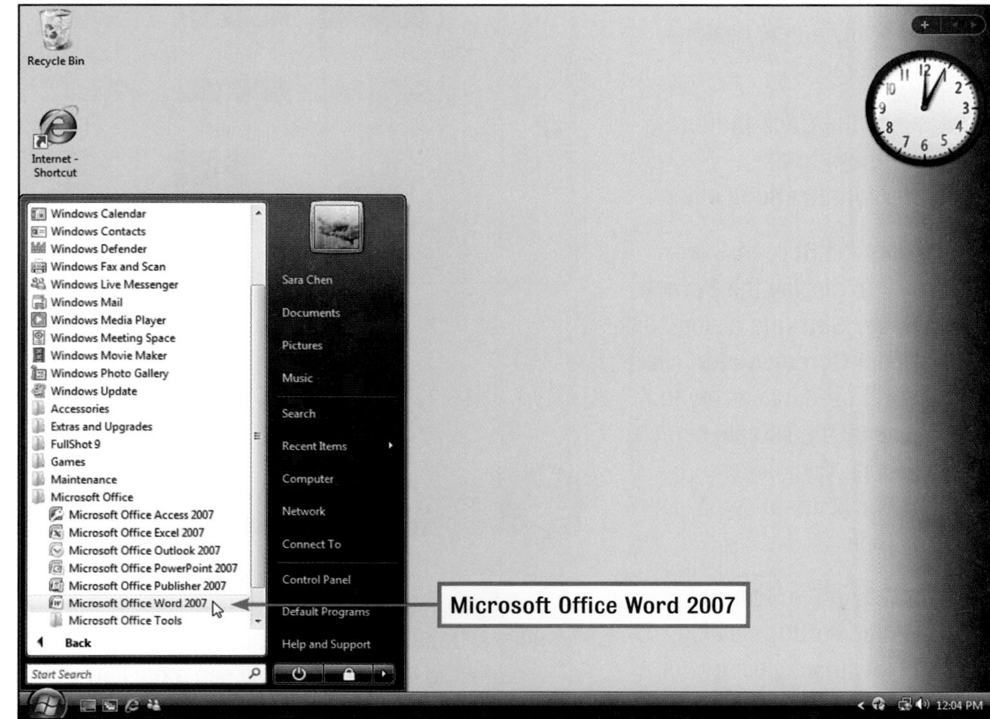

Exercise C-4 Adjust Audio

TechSIM Interactive Tutorials An interactive simulation about system settings and the Control Panel is available to explore.

The Sound dialog box lets you change and view the settings for your speakers, microphone, and other audio devices. For this exercise, your Control Panel should be in Classic View.

Step-by-Step

1. In the Control Panel window, double-click the **Sound** icon. The **Sound** dialog box displays.
2. Click the **Playback** tab, and click the **Speakers** device in the playback device listing. Click the **Properties** button, and click the **Levels** tab (Figure C.4).
3. To adjust the balance and volume of the speakers, click the **Volume Control Balance** button.
4. In the **Balance** dialog box, move both the **Left** and **Right** slide indicators to the middle. Click **OK**.
5. To exit the **Speakers Properties** dialog box without saving your changes, click **Cancel**.
6. To exit the **Sound** dialog box without saving your changes, click **Cancel**.

▼ **Figure C.4** Adjust settings for audio in the Speakers Properties dialog box.

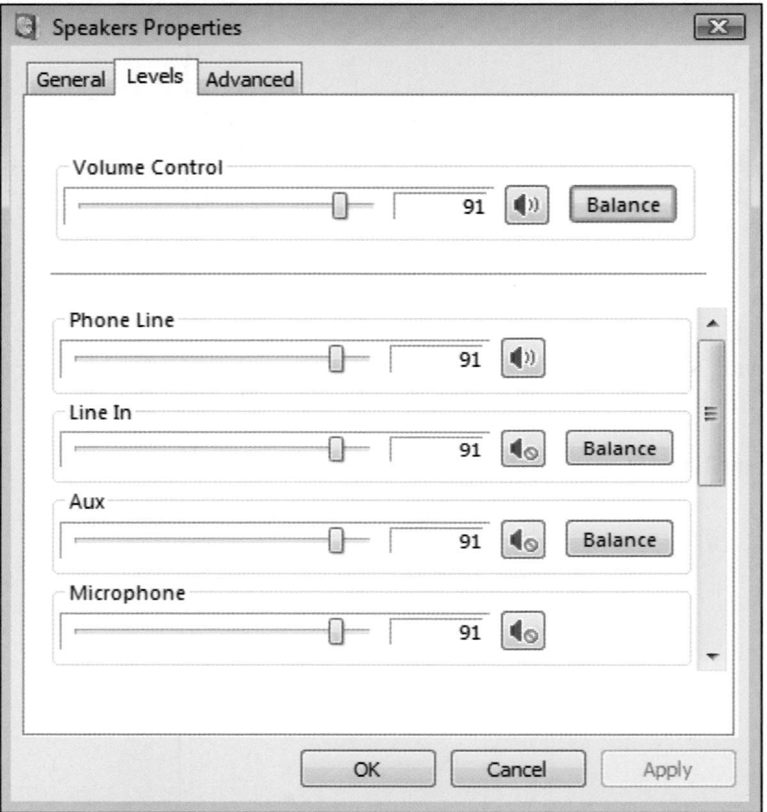

TechSavvy

Control Panel Options You should become familiar with the tools in your Control Panel. For example, you can use the **Fonts** window to add or delete fonts and see all the fonts used in your applications. You can view multimedia devices you might have attached to your computer, such as scanners and cameras or game controllers. The **System** option provides information about your computer system and other settings.

8 On the desktop, right-click the **Recycle Bin** icon. A shortcut menu opens (Figure 2.5).

9 Click **Open**. The **Recycle Bin** opens, and you can see any files or folders that have been deleted (Figure 2.6).

Figure 2.5 When you right-click any feature on the desktop (including the desktop itself), a shortcut menu displays.

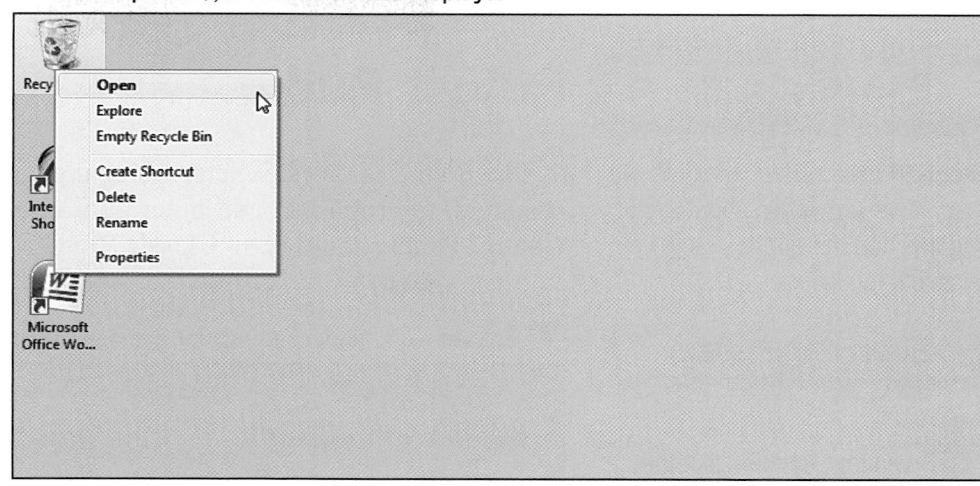

10 To **close** the **Recycle Bin**, click the red **Close** button in the upper-right corner.

11 On the desktop, double-click the **Recycle Bin** icon. The **Recycle Bin** opens.

12 **Close** the **Recycle Bin**.

Figure 2.6 You can open any icon on the desktop by double-clicking it.

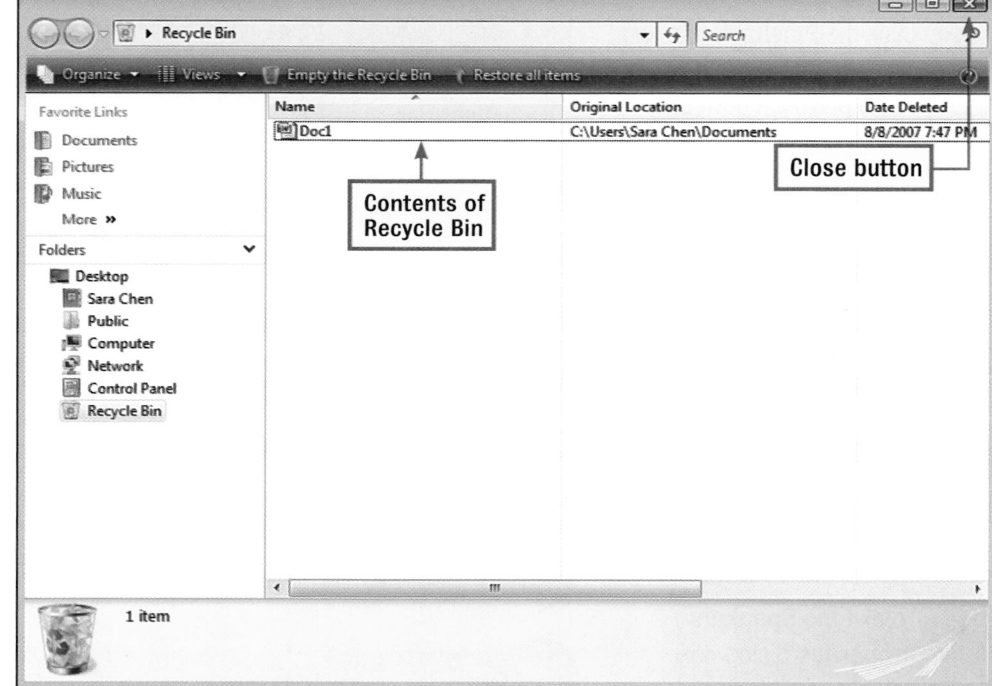

TechSavvy

Add Programs You can add programs to the **Windows Start** menu. Click the **Start** button. Display the program name in the **Start** menu. Right-click the program name, and click **Pin to Start Menu**.

Exercise C-5 Customize the Mouse

TechSIM Interactive Tutorials An interactive simulation about system settings and the Control Panel is available to explore.

Input devices let you enter commands and send information to your computer. The mouse and keyboard are the input devices you probably use the most.

The mouse can be adjusted for both left and right-handed users by changing the buttons you use to click and right-click. You can also change the double-click speed, which is useful for people with limited mobility. For this exercise, your Control Panel should be in Classic View.

Step-by-Step

1. In the Control Panel window, double-click the **Mouse** icon.
2. Click the **Buttons** tab. Under **Double-click speed**, move the slide indicator from **Fast** to the middle of the bar. (Figure C.5).
3. To adjust the speed of movement for the pointer, click the **Pointer Options** tab. Under **Motion**, move the bar from **Fast** to the middle of the bar.
4. To exit the **Mouse Properties** dialog box without saving your changes, click **Cancel**.

Figure C.5 Test the double-click setting by clicking on the folder.

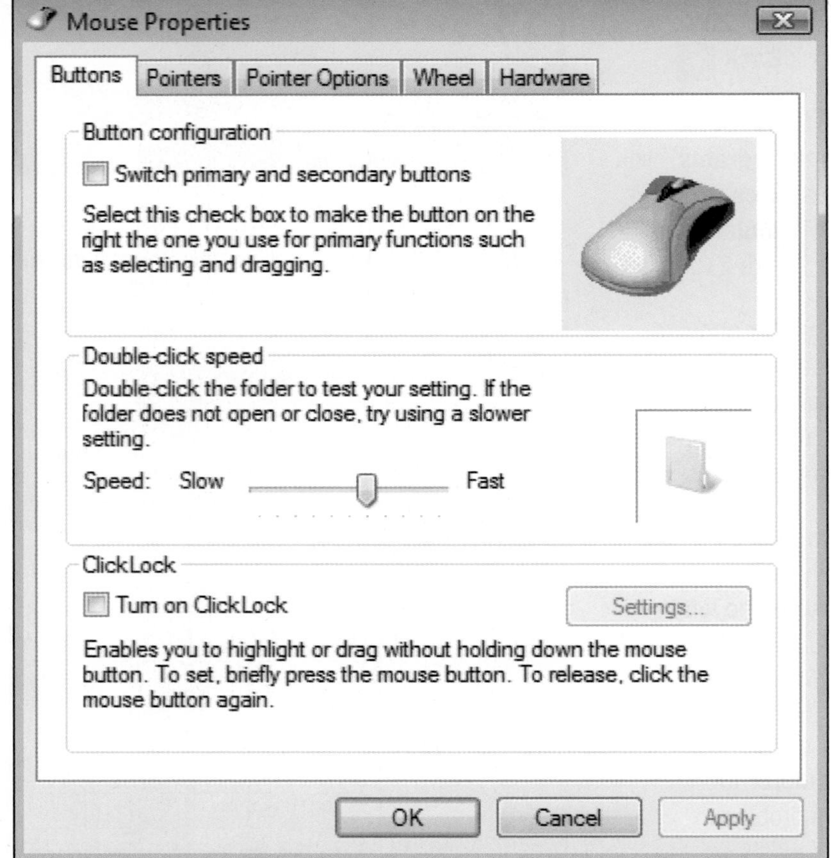

Step-by-Step

1. On the desktop, click the **Start** button to open the **Start** menu. If you are using **Windows XP**, please go to page xliv in the *Getting Started* pages to learn how to complete this step.

2. Click **All Programs** to open the **Programs** menu. **Note:** You can display the menu by resting the mouse pointer over **All Programs**. To return to the Start menu, click **Back** [Back button].

3. Click the **Start** menu, choose **All Programs**, click the **Accessories** folder, and click **Calculator**, as shown in Figure 2.3.

4. The **Calculator** appears on your desktop. Move the mouse pointer to the blue **title** bar at the top of the **Calculator** box.

5. Hold down the left mouse button, and drag the **Calculator** to the left side of your desktop (Figure 2.4).

6. Use your mouse and **Calculator** to solve this problem: 456 + 83 – 201 =

7. To close the **Calculator**, click the red **Close** button [X] in the top-right corner.

Figure 2.3 Click a program to open it.

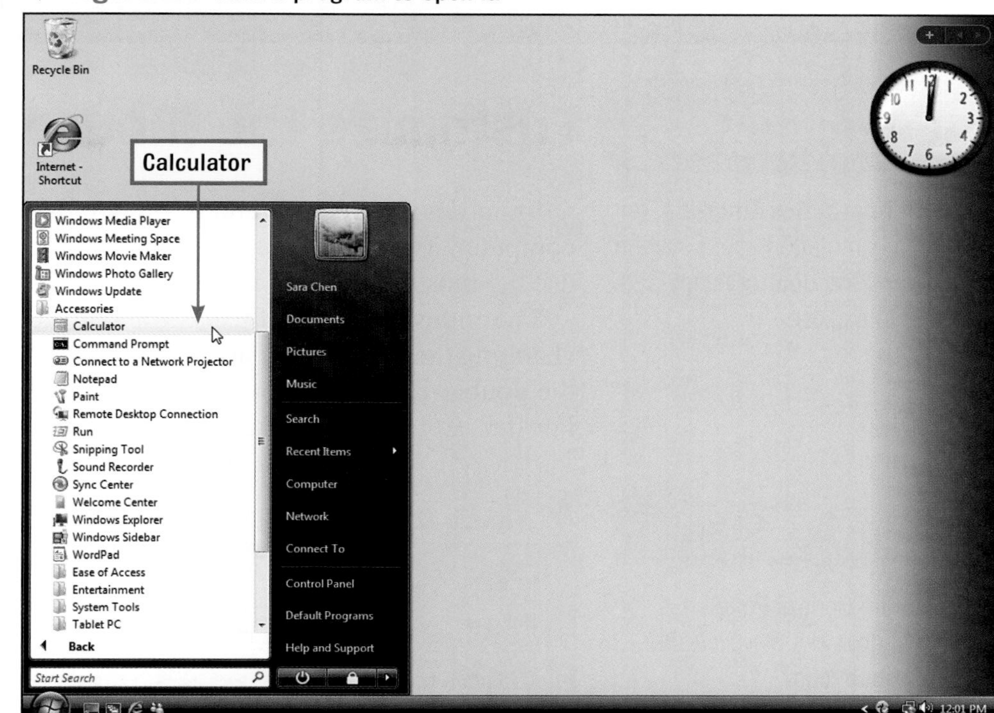

Figure 2.4 You can drag items on the desktop.

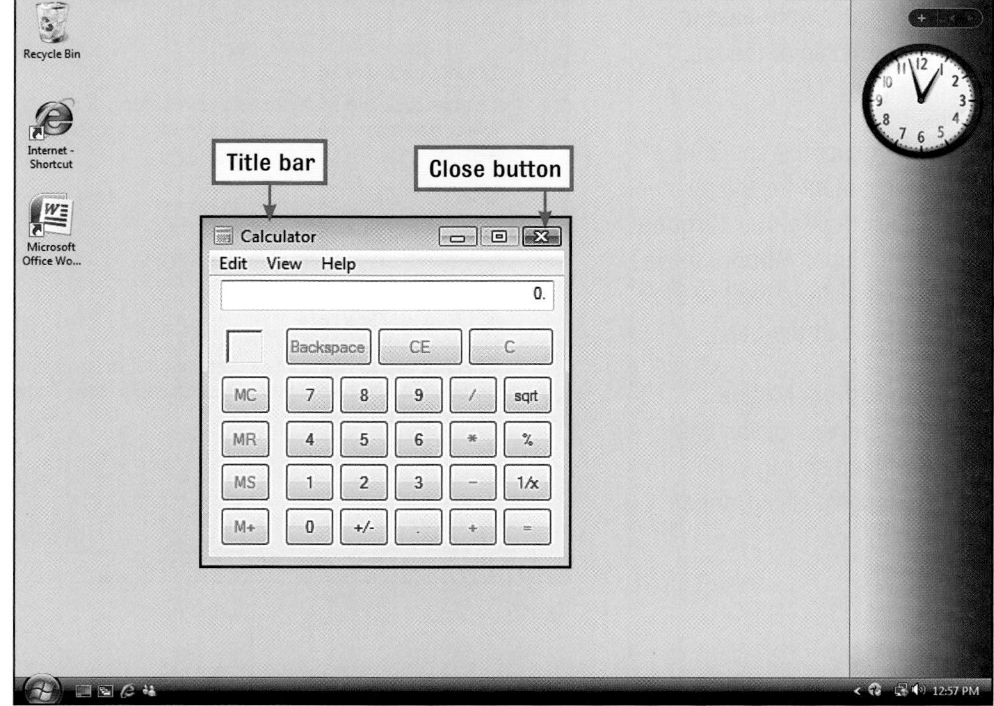

Exercise C-6 Add a Printer

TechSIM Interactive Tutorials An interactive simulation about system settings and the Control Panel is available to explore.

The Control Panel provides a simple way to choose the printer you want to use and to check the progress of printing tasks. From the Printers window, you will see a list of available printers. When you double-click a printer, you can see what is printing, cancel a print job, or correct problems.

You can also add printer connections to your computer, using the Add Printer Wizard. It will help you search for, locate, and test your connection to a new printer. For this exercise, your Control Panel should be in Classic View.

Step-by-Step

1. In the Control Panel window, double-click the **Printers** icon.
2. Click **Add a printer** (Figure C.6). The **Add Printer Wizard** window displays.
3. With your teacher's permission, follow the Wizard's instructions to add a new printer to your computer.
4. Click the **Back** button to return to the **Control Panel** window.

▼ **Figure C.6** This computer is connected to more than one printer.

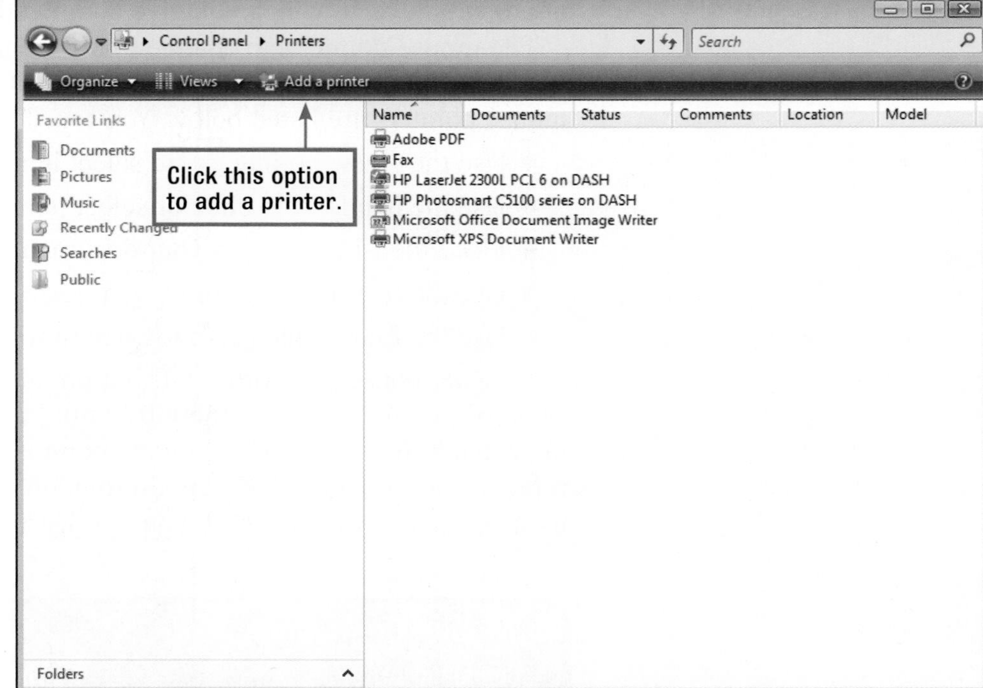

TechSavvy

Caution Unless your teacher instructs you to do so, do *not* change the printer settings on your computer. Doing so might make it difficult for your classmates to print from their computers. Please be considerate of other users.

Exercise 2-2 Get to Know Your Mouse

The mouse and keyboard are the two main devices you use to enter data and commands into your computer. It is very important to understand how to use your mouse if you want to use your computer effectively.

TechSavvy

Mouse Pointer
In Microsoft Vista, the mouse pointer changes to alert you when your mouse is working. When either of the icons below appears, wait for the mouse command to be completed.
Busy
Working in Background

▼ A mouse usually includes a scroll wheel and right and left buttons for clicking.

You use the mouse by pointing to an object on the computer screen and then clicking the object. The object might be a file that you want to open or a menu through which you give commands to the computer.

The mouse pointer can change to different shapes depending on what you are using it for and what it is pointing at. Some of the most common mouse pointers are listed below. You can:

- Use the arrow pointer to select items.
- Use the hand to click or select items.
- Place the I-beam in your document to insert text.
- Use the two-headed arrow to resize objects.
- Use the four-headed arrow to move objects.

A basic mouse has both a left button and a right button for clicking. Most of the time, you use the left button, but the right button has many important functions, too. The mouse commands that are used in this book refer to the way you click the buttons on the mouse. Some mice also include a scroll wheel, which you will learn about in the next exercise.

Mouse Commands

Command	What It Means
Click	Press and release the left button once.
Double-click	Quickly press the left button twice.
Right-click	Press and release the right button once.
Drag	Press the left button and hold it down as you move the mouse.

In this exercise, you will use the desktop and Start menu to practice using your mouse.

Exercise C-7 Internet Options

TechSIM Interactive Tutorials An interactive simulation about system settings and the Control Panel is available to explore.

Internet Explorer comes with default settings that control how it looks and works. You may change these defaults to suit your personal likes and dislikes. For example, you can change the default home page to a Web page of your choice. Do not change any settings without your teacher's permission.

You can also change the settings to protect your privacy while online. When you surf the Web, some Web sites place small files, called cookies, on your computer. Cookies let sites gather personal information about their visitors. When you revisit a site, the cookie tells it who you are. If you go to a site often, you may want the site to have your information so you do not have to reenter the information every time. However, many unwanted sites may also try to place cookies on your computer. You can choose to limit the number of cookies that are placed on your computer by adjusting the privacy setting in the Control Panel.

Step-by-Step

1. With your teacher's permission, in the Control Panel, double-click the **Internet Options** icon.
2. Click the **Privacy** tab. Under **Settings**, move the slider up or down to adjust the level of protection.
3. Click the **General** tab. To remove unwanted cookies, under **Browsing history**, click the **Delete** button. Then click **Delete Cookies**.
4. To change the **Home page**, key the URL of your favorite search engine in the **Address** box. See Figure C.7 as an example.
5. To close the **Internet Properties** dialog box without saving your changes, click **Cancel**.
6. Click the **Close** button to close the Control Panel.

▼ **Figure C.7** Use the Control Panel to change your browser settings.

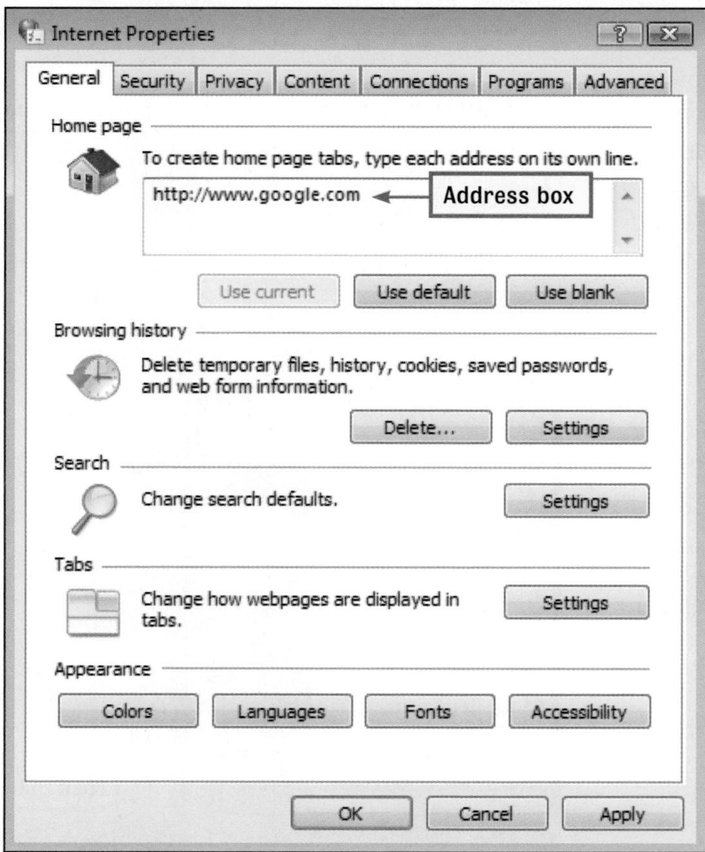

Step-by-Step

1. Following your teacher's instructions, **turn on** your computer.

2. If you need to log on to your computer, key your **user name** and **password** in the **log on** window, then click **OK**.

3. After you are logged on to Windows, your screen should show the **Windows desktop**, which looks similar to Figure 2.1.

4. Identify the following items on your desktop: Start button, icons, Recycle Bin, Time/Date, and Taskbar.

5. Click the **Start** button to display the Start menu. If you are using **Windows XP**, please go to page xliv in the *Getting Started* pages to learn how to complete this step.

6. Find the following menu items: All Programs, Control Panel, Help and Support, and Lock this computer (Figure 2.2).

7. **Close** the **Start** menu by clicking anywhere on the desktop screen.

Figure 2.1 Your computer's desktop screen may look different from this, but it will still include icons, a taskbar, and a Start button.

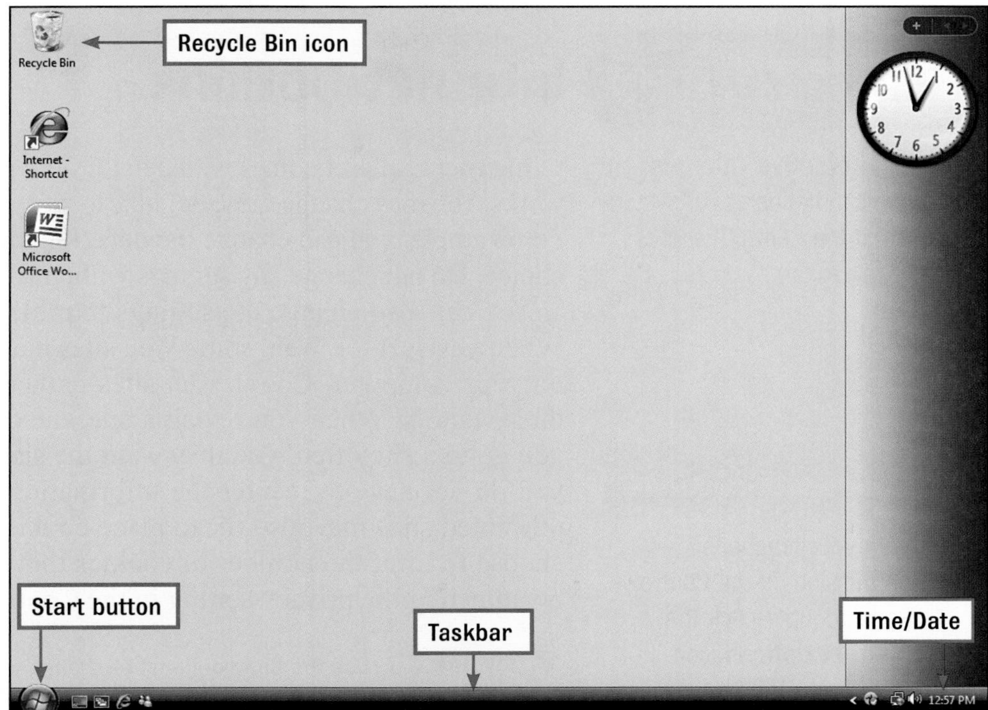

Figure 2.2 From the Start menu, you can open files and programs.

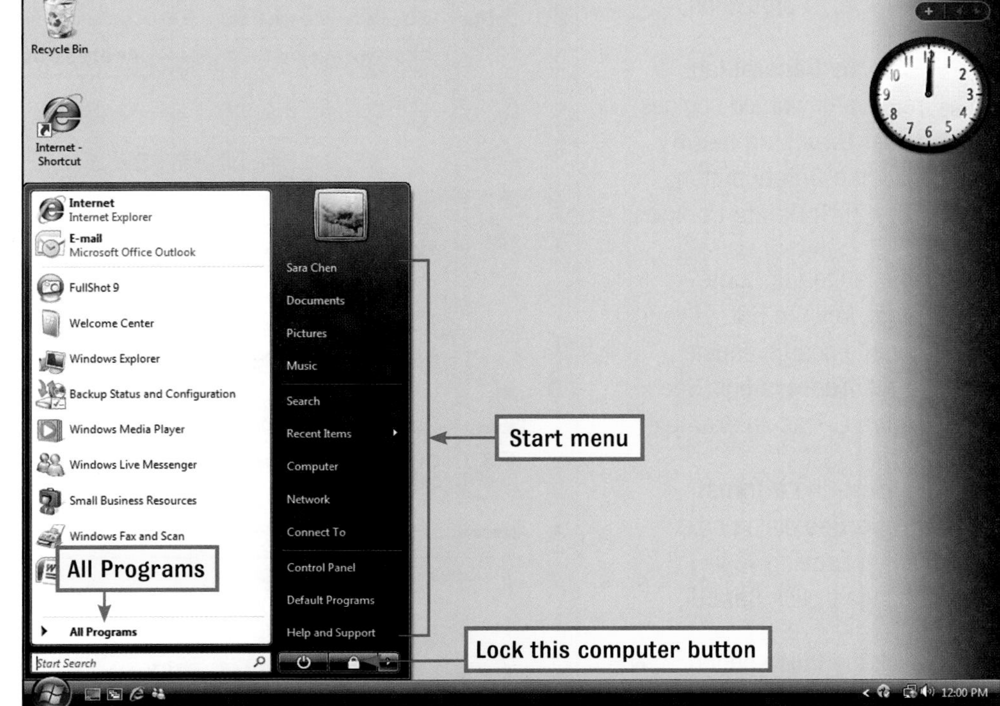

Assessment The Control Panel

Key Concepts Check

1. **Describe** What is the purpose of the Control Panel?
2. **List** What are three mouse settings you can change?
3. **Explain** How would you change the date and time on your computer?

Critical Thinking

4. **Analyze** Why do you think the Control Panel icons are grouped into categories?
5. **Draw Conclusions** What are three reasons a computer user might want to change mouse settings?

Guided Practice

TechSIM Interactive Tutorials An interactive simulation about system settings and the Control Panel is available to explore.

Explore Your Computer Settings Computers should be accessible to everyone. Computer settings can help those who have special needs in hearing, vision, or movement. Follow the steps below to modify your computer settings. Do not change any settings without permission.

Step-by-Step

1. **Open** your **Control Panel**. (Exercise C-1)
2. In the Control Panel window, double-click the **Keyboard** icon. The **Keyboard Properties** dialog box displays.
3. On the **Speed** tab, reduce the **Repeat rate** by moving the slide indicator left. (Figure C.8).
4. To close the **Keyboard Properties** dialog box without saving your changes, click **Cancel**.

▼ **Figure C.8** Slowing the repeat rate helps people with mobility problems.

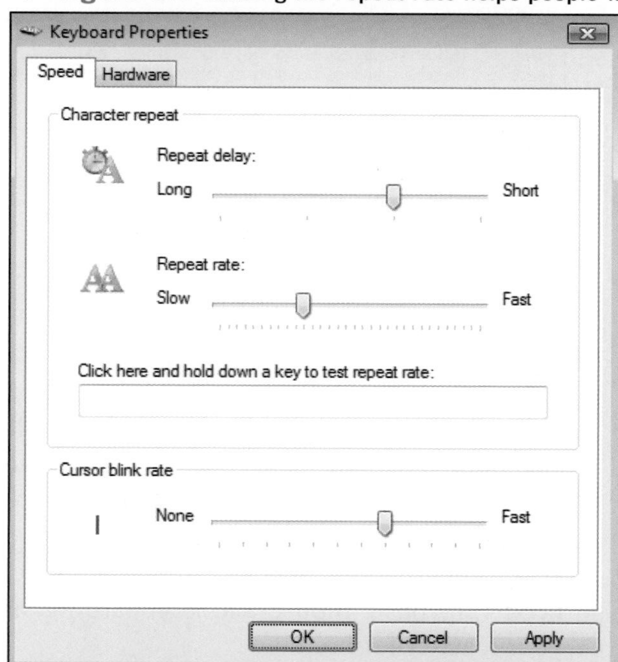

Exercise 2-1 Get to Know the Windows Desktop

When you start Microsoft Windows, the first screen you see is the **desktop**, which is the main work area on a computer. As its name indicates, the desktop is like the top of your desk, with all the files, folders, and programs you need to get started on your work. On your desktop, you will see icons, or shortcuts. An **icon** is a little picture that represents programs, document files, Web links, or other items on the computer. When you double-click an icon, it takes you directly to the program or document.

One of the most important buttons on your desktop is the Start button. This is usually found in the bottom-left corner of your desktop. From the Start button, you can open all the programs you use.

When you turn on your computer, you might not see the Windows desktop right away. Computers at work and at school are often connected to a network so that many users can share files, printers, and Internet access. A user must log on to the network before using the computer.

When you **log on** to your school's network, you key your user name and a password. A user name is a unique name that identifies you to the network. A password is a secret word or set of characters that prevents other people from logging on as you.

◄ When you key your password, dots are displayed so that others cannot see your password. Key your password slowly to avoid mistakes. Make sure the Caps Lock key is off.

By having users log on, a school limits who uses its network. Passwords also protect personal files from being opened, deleted, or changed by other people. You must log on correctly to use your computer.

In this exercise, you will turn on your computer and access Windows according to your teacher's directions. To complete this exercise, you will need very basic mouse and keyboarding skills. If you have trouble, ask your teacher for help.

5. Double-click the **Speech Recognition Options** link in the Control Panel. Then click the **Text to Speech** link in the Navigation Pane.

6. In the **Speech Properties** dialog box, under **Voice selection**, choose a voice and preview it (Figure C.9).

7. **Close** the **Speech Properties** dialog box, and return to the Control Panel Speech Recognition Options window.

8. Click the **Ease of Access Center** link in the Navigation Pane.

9. Click the various links to explore the following control settings: **Use the computer without a display**, **Use the computer without a mouse or keyboard**, **Make the mouse easier to use**, and **Make the keyboard easier to use**.

10. Read the description for each control listed in Step 9, and write each description on a separate piece of paper.

11. **Close** the **Control Panel**.

Figure C.9 The Text to Speech control produces a voice that reads the monitor text aloud.

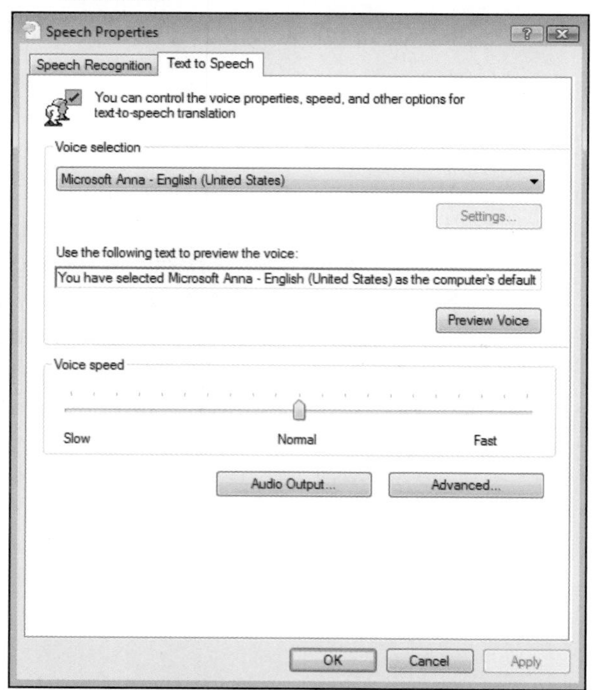

Figure C.10 The Control Panel provides many accessibility options.

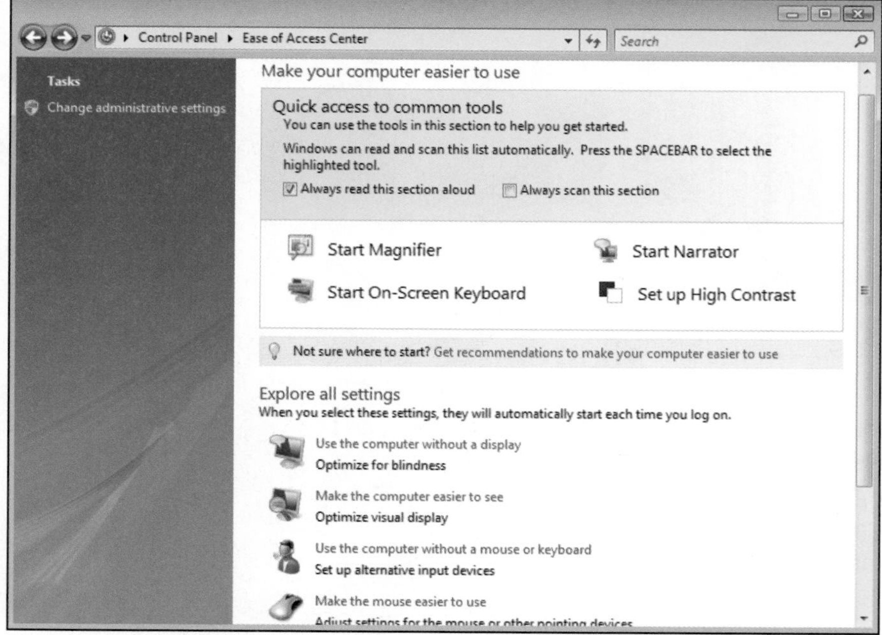

Concepts in Action

Project 2 Operate Your Computer

Key Concepts

Exercise 2-1
- Start the computer
- Log on to Windows
- View the Start menu

Exercise 2-2
- Practice mouse skills

Exercise 2-3
- Open and close an application
- Open multiple applications

Exercise 2-4
- Practice keyboarding skills

Exercise 2-5
- Log off Windows
- Shut down the computer

Vocabulary

Key Terms
desktop
icon
log on
program
application
window
taskbar
insertion point
shortcut

Before You Begin

The Start Menu Use the Start menu to help you open programs and locate folders and files. You can access almost any feature of your computer from the Start menu.

In this project, you will explore the Microsoft Windows desktop. You will open and close programs and move between them.

Getting Started

You start a car by turning a key. This starts the engine, but the car will not go anywhere until the driver puts the car in gear, presses the gas pedal, and steers the car in the right direction.

Similarly, you start a computer by pressing the On switch. You cannot use it, though, without software to make it go and someone to tell it what to do. In this project, you will start your computer and use Microsoft Windows to direct your computer to do what you want it to do.

Reference Guide for Formatting Documents

The information on the following pages will help you format various kinds of documents that you create using Microsoft Word. You can use the proofreaders' marks and the remaining pages to help you edit and proof using any software or handwritten documents.

How to Use the Reference Guide

Use the Contents below to quickly locate the type of document you are creating. Then use the examples shown as a guide to help you format your document properly. The arrows and numbers shown in red on each sample tell you how many times to press Enter or Return on your keyboard to separate items in your document. The letters "ds" indicate double spacing should be used.

Remember that your work should reflect your own original research and content and that the information provided here is for reference purposes only.

Contents

Project 1 Assessment

2 Independent Practice ★

Go Online RUBRICS

glencoe.com

Independent Practice Use the rubrics for these projects to help create and evaluate your work. Go to the **Online Learning Center** at **glencoe.com**. Choose **Rubrics**, then **Unit 1**.

English Language Arts **Identify Safety Issues** Write a brief explanation of the problems that can occur in each of the following scenarios and what you should do to avoid these problems.

- You and a friend start horsing around in the classroom.
- You toss your backpack on the floor behind your chair.
- You decide to fix a problem on the computer without your teacher's help.
- You unplug a computer connection.

3 Independent Practice ★★

English Language Arts **Evaluate a Home Computer** Imagine that your family is thinking of buying a new home computer. Write two paragraphs describing the information your family will need before buying.

- In the first paragraph, describe the devices your family will need for its computer system.
- In the second paragraph, list the steps to safely set up the computer.

4 Independent Practice ★★★

English Language Arts **Evaluate Acceptable Computer Use** Whether in the classroom or at home, you must use common sense to avoid the risks that can occur when using a computer. Write three paragraphs about the issues listed below. Be sure to check your work. Use proper spelling, grammar, and punctuation.

- In the first paragraph, describe the physical safety issues of using a computer.
- In the second paragraph, explain the risks that can occur when using shared computers and computer resources.
- In the third paragraph, describe what you can do to avoid these risks both at school and at home.

Personal Letter

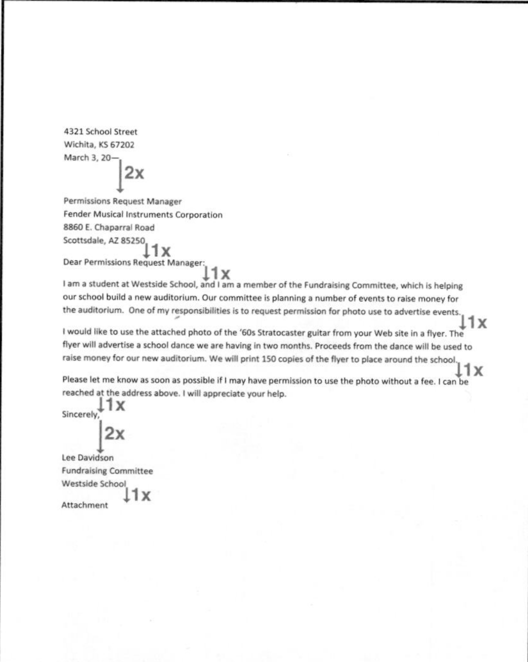

4321 School Street
Wichita, KS 67202
March 3, 20—

Permissions Request Manager
Fender Musical Instruments Corporation
8860 E. Chaparral Road
Scottsdale, AZ 85250

Dear Permissions Request Manager:

I am a student at Westside School, and I am a member of the Fundraising Committee, which is helping our school build a new auditorium. Our committee is planning a number of events to raise money for the auditorium. One of my responsibilities is to request permission for photo use to advertise events.

I would like to use the attached photo of the '60s Stratocaster guitar from your Web site in a flyer. The flyer will advertise a school dance we are having in two months. Proceeds from the dance will be used to raise money for our new auditorium. We will print 150 copies of the flyer to place around the school.

Please let me know as soon as possible if I may have permission to use the photo without a fee. I can be reached at the address above. I will appreciate your help.

Sincerely,

Lee Davidson
Fundraising Committee
Westside School

Attachment

Business Letter

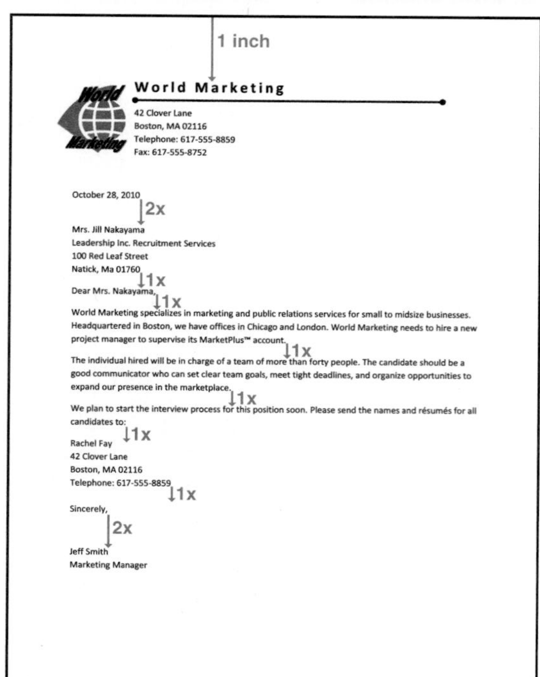

World Marketing
42 Clover Lane
Boston, MA 02116
Telephone: 617-555-8859
Fax: 617-555-8752

October 28, 2010

Mrs. Jill Nakayama
Leadership Inc. Recruitment Services
100 Red Leaf Street
Natick, Ma 01760

Dear Mrs. Nakayama:

World Marketing specializes in marketing and public relations services for small to midsize businesses. Headquartered in Boston, we have offices in Chicago and London. World Marketing needs to hire a new project manager to supervise its MarketPlus™ account.

The individual hired will be in charge of a team of more than forty people. The candidate should be a good communicator who can set clear team goals, meet tight deadlines, and organize opportunities to expand our presence in the marketplace.

We plan to start the interview process for this position soon. Please send the names and résumés for all candidates to:

Rachel Fay
42 Clover Lane
Boston, MA 02116
Telephone: 617-555-8859

Sincerely,

Jeff Smith
Marketing Manager

Personal Business Letter

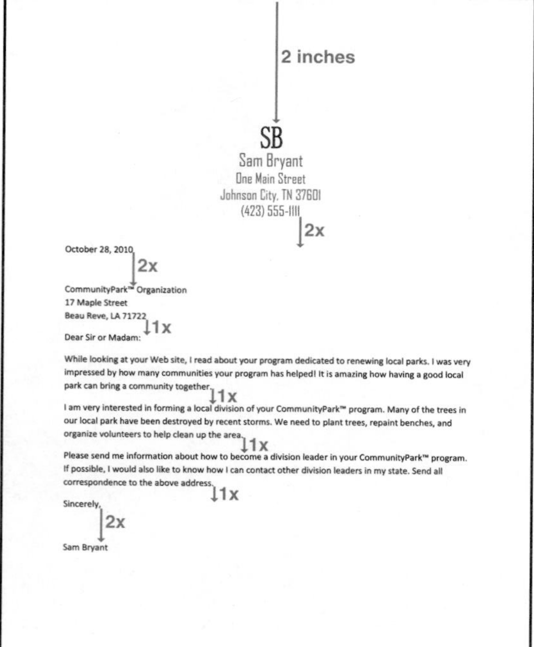

SB
Sam Bryant
One Main Street
Johnson City, TN 37601
(423) 555-1111

October 28, 2010

CommunityPark™ Organization
17 Maple Street
Beau Reve, LA 71722

Dear Sir or Madam:

While looking at your Web site, I read about your program dedicated to renewing local parks. I was very impressed by how many communities your program has helped! It is amazing how having a good local park can bring a community together.

I am very interested in forming a local division of your CommunityPark™ program. Many of the trees in our local park have been destroyed by recent storms. We need to plant trees, repaint benches, and organize volunteers to help clean up the area.

Please send me information about how to become a division leader in your CommunityPark™ program. If possible, I would also like to know how I can contact other division leaders in my state. Send all correspondence to the above address.

Sincerely,

Sam Bryant

Outline

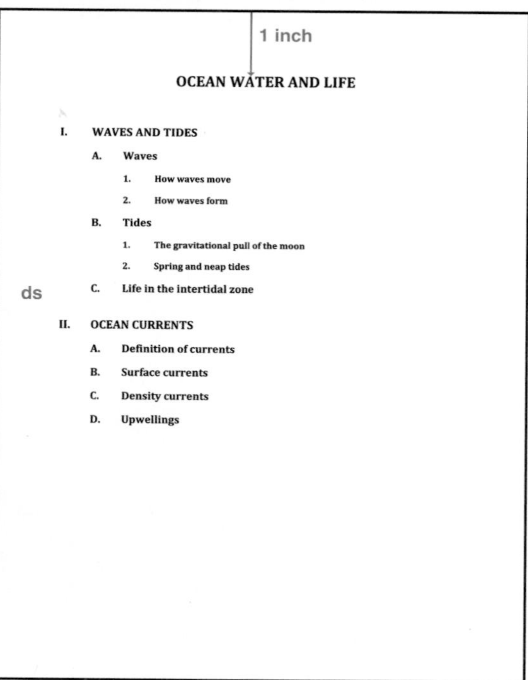

OCEAN WATER AND LIFE

I. WAVES AND TIDES
  A. Waves
    1. How waves move
    2. How waves form
  B. Tides
    1. The gravitational pull of the moon
    2. Spring and neap tides
  C. Life in the intertidal zone

II. OCEAN CURRENTS
  A. Definition of currents
  B. Surface currents
  C. Density currents
  D. Upwellings

Project 1 Assessment

4. Identify six ways that your classroom is set up to be a safe environment. (Exercise 1-2)

5. Make a checklist of ten ergonomic habits you should practice to stay comfortable and safe when using the computer. (Exercise 1-3)

▼ **Figure 1.8** You will work more comfortably and safely if you practice good ergonomic habits.

6. Describe six responsibilities of students in your computer classroom. (Exercise 1-4)

7. Write a five-item acceptable use policy for the other students sharing your workstation. (Exercise 1-4)

▼ **Figure 1.9** Using a computer at school is a privilege.

Newsletter

The Hillside High Gazette

Band Tryouts on Tuesday

Show off your school spirit and your musical talent by joining the band! Band tryouts will be this Tuesday, from 3:30-5:30 in the North field. Please bring your own instrument.

The Hillside High Band is in need of all musicians, especially trumpet and flute players. Band rehearsals will be held every Monday, Wednesday, and Friday after school during football season. Off-season, rehearsals will be held every Monday and Wednesday after school.

The tryouts will be judged by our band leader Mr. Schaefer, as well as by two senior band members in each instrumental group.

Recycling Challenge

Hillside High is proud to announce the first annual Recycling Challenge. Each homeroom class will compete to see who can bring in the most paper, plastic bottles, cans, and boxes. The winning homeroom class will receive a free pizza party.

Items are recycled
Collect items to recycle
Send to recycling plant

Bike Week Continues

The Bicycle Club would like to acknowledge the efforts of Janet McSimmons, Steve Yuan, Maggie Estevez, Jill Pierce, James Mazur, Jason Trevor, and Yolanda Washington, who organized our first annual Bike Week. The event wraps up this Friday with the competition finals.

We had great turnout for all the rides, from spectators and participants alike. Leaders in each category will compete for the grand prize—a free PedalCo bike, helmet, and safety pads. Good luck to all the competitors! Here is a list of events and times to beat.

Event	Type of Bike	Time to Beat
Hills Ride	Mountain Bike	1:05:24
Distance Ride	Road Bike	1:42:07
Obstacle Course	Hybrid	15:32
Beach Ride	Beach Cruiser	37:59
Speed Ride	Racing Bike	25:30

MLA Style Academic Report

1 inch

.5 inch

Last Name 1

Your First and Last Name
1x
Your Teacher's Name
1x
Class
1x
Current Date
1x

King of the Wild Frontier
1x

ds

"Be always sure you are right, then go ahead" (Lofaro 1148d). You're probably wondering what that means. Well, a guy named Davy Crockett used to say that. It is one of his best known quotes. Read on to find out more about this legendary person.

Actually, his name was David Crockett. He was born in a small cabin in Tennessee on August 17, 1786. (*Davy Crockett*). His family lived in a cabin on the banks of the Nolichucky River. Davy had eight brothers and sisters. Four were older and four were younger.

1 inch | 1 inch

Davy lived with his family in Tennessee until he was 13. He went to school, but he didn't like it. He skipped school a lot. He ran away from home because he knew his dad was going to punish him for playing hooky. He joined a cattle drive to make money. He drove the cattle to Virginia almost 300 miles away. He stayed in Virginia and worked a lot of jobs for over two years. He returned to his family in Tennessee when he was 16 (*Davy Crockett Biography*).

When Davy returned home his dad was in debt. Now Davy was 6 feet tall and he could do a man's work. Davy went to work for Daniel Kennedy. Davy's dad owed Daniel 76 dollars and Davy worked for one year to pay the debt (The Texas State Historical Association).

In 1806 Davy married Polly Finley. They had two sons, John Wesley and William. Then Davy went to fight for the Tennessee Volunteer Militia under Andrew Jackson in the Creek Indian War. When he returned home from the war, he found his wife very ill. She died in 1815 (Davy Crockett Birthplace Association).

MLA Style Academic Report cont.

1 inch

.5 inch

Last Name 2

Davy then married Elizabeth Patton in 1817. She was a widow and she had two children of her own, George and Margaret Ann (The Texas State Historical Association).

Davy was well known in Tennessee as a frontiersman. He was a sharpshooter, a famous Indian fighter, and a bear hunter. In 1821, he started his career in politics as a Tennessee legislator. People liked Davy because he had a good humor and they thought he was one of their own. He was re-elected to the Legislature in 1823, but he lost the election in 1825.

ds

1 inch | 1 inch

In 1827 Davy was elected to Congress. He fought for the land bill. The land bill allowed those who settled the land to buy it at a very low cost. He was re-elected to Congress in 1829 and again in 1833, but he lost in 1836 (Lofaro, 1148d).

Many Americans had gone to Texas to settle. In 1835, Davy left his kids, his wife, his brothers, and his sisters to go to Texas. He loved Texas. When the Texans were fighting for their independence from Mexico, Davy joined the fight. He was fighting with a group of Tennessee volunteers defending the Alamo in San Antonio on March 6, 1836 (The Texas State Historical Association). He was 49 years old.

Works Cited

1 inch

.5 inch

Last Name 3

Works Cited

Author Unknown. "Davy Crockett Biography." 6 April 2002. <http://www.infoporium.com/heritage/crockbio.shtml>.

"Davy Crockett." *Microsoft Encarta Online Encyclopedia 2002*. <http://encarta.msn.com>.

Davy Crockett Birthplace Association. "American West-Davy Crockett." 6 April 2002. <http://www.americanwest.com/pages/davycroc.htm>.

Lofaro, Michael A. "Davy Crockett." *The World Book Encyclopedia 2002*. Chicago: World Book, Inc., Vol. 14, pp. 1148d-1149.

The Texas State Historical Association. *The New Handbook of Texas-Online*. "Davy Crockett (1786-1836)-Biography." 6 April 2002. <http://www.alamo-de-parras.welkin.org/history/bios/crockett/crockett.html>.

ds

1 inch | 1 inch

Project 1 Assessment

Key Concepts Check

1. **Identify** What computer devices do you use to send commands to your computer?
2. **Describe** What are ten features of a safe computer classroom?
3. **Define** What is ergonomics?
4. **Explain** Why is an acceptable use policy important in any classroom?

Critical Thinking

5. **Draw Conclusions** Why are computer cables an important safety issue in the classroom?
6. **Evaluate** Why is it practical to have a number of computers sharing a printer?
7. **Cause and Effect** Why should parents have to sign a school's acceptable use policy?

1 Guided Practice

Know Your Computer Classroom Your computer classroom is used by many students, and so is your computer workstation. That means that you have obligations to care for your computer, use it responsibly, and make sure you are considerate of the other students in your class.

Use a separate sheet of paper to complete the following steps. If you need help completing a step, refer back to the exercise in parentheses at the end of the step.

Step-by-Step

1. Make a list of the computer equipment at your workstation. (Exercise 1-1)
2. Add to your list any shared classroom equipment, such as printers, scanners, and so on. (Exercise 1-1)
3. Write a paragraph explaining the classroom policy for using shared equipment. (Exercise 1-4)

▼ **Figure 1.7** A computer lab has equipment that many people share, so be considerate.

Title Page

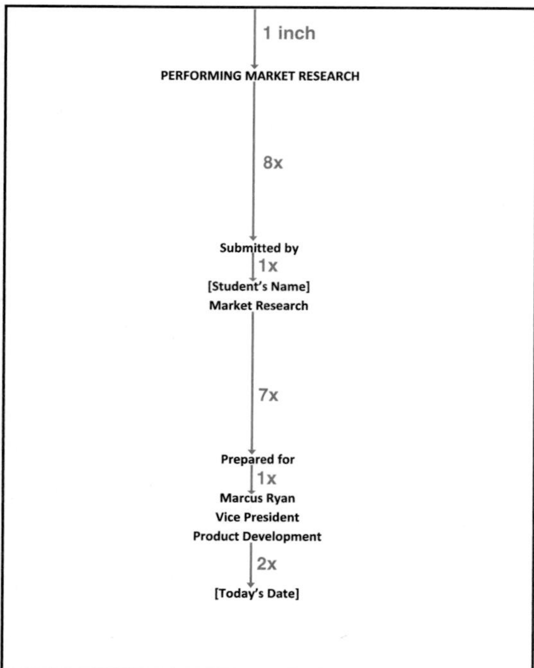

PERFORMING MARKET RESEARCH

Submitted by

[Student's Name]

Market Research

Prepared for

Marcus Ryan

Vice President

Product Development

[Today's Date]

Simple Business Report

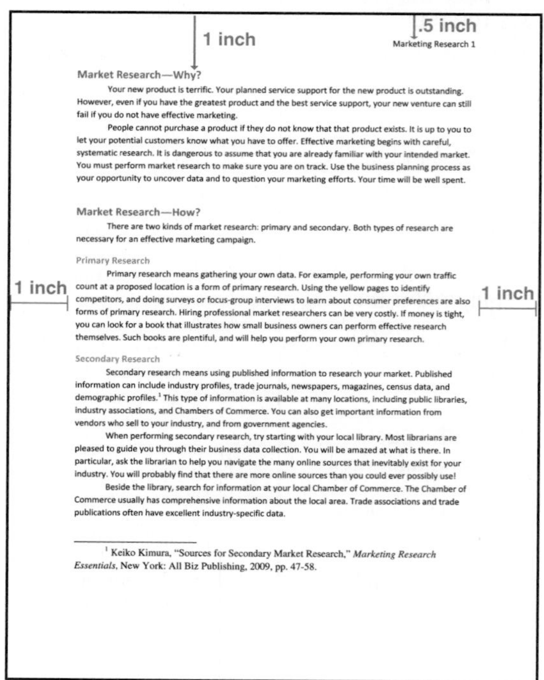

Marketing Research 1

Market Research—Why?

Your new product is terrific. Your planned service support for the new product is outstanding. However, even if you have the greatest product and the best service support, your new venture can still fail if you do not have effective marketing.

People cannot purchase a product if they do not know that that product exists. It is up to you to let your potential customers know what you have to offer. Effective marketing begins with careful, systematic research. It is dangerous to assume that you are already familiar with your intended market. You must perform market research to make sure you are on track. Use the business planning process as your opportunity to uncover data and to question your marketing efforts. Your time will be well spent.

Market Research—How?

There are two kinds of market research: primary and secondary. Both types of research are necessary for an effective marketing campaign.

Primary Research

Primary research means gathering your own data. For example, performing your own traffic count at a proposed location is a form of primary research. Using the yellow pages to identify competitors, and doing surveys or focus-group interviews to learn about consumer preferences are also forms of primary research. Hiring professional market researchers can be very costly. If money is tight, you can look for a book that illustrates how small business owners can perform effective research themselves. Such books are plentiful, and will help you perform your own primary research.

Secondary Research

Secondary research means using published information to research your market. Published information can include industry profiles, trade journals, newspapers, magazines, census data, and demographic profiles.[1] This type of information is available at many locations, including public libraries, industry associations, and Chambers of Commerce. You can also get important information from vendors who sell to your industry, and from government agencies.

When performing secondary research, try starting with your local library. Most librarians are pleased to guide you through their business data collection. You will be amazed at what is there. In particular, ask the librarian to help you navigate the many online sources that inevitably exist for your industry. You will probably find that there are more online sources than you could ever possibly use!

Beside the library, search for information at your local Chamber of Commerce. The Chamber of Commerce usually has comprehensive information about the local area. Trade associations and trade publications often have excellent industry-specific data.

[1] Keiko Kimura, "Sources for Secondary Market Research," *Marketing Research Essentials*, New York: All Biz Publishing, 2009, pp. 47-58.

Simple Business Report (continued)

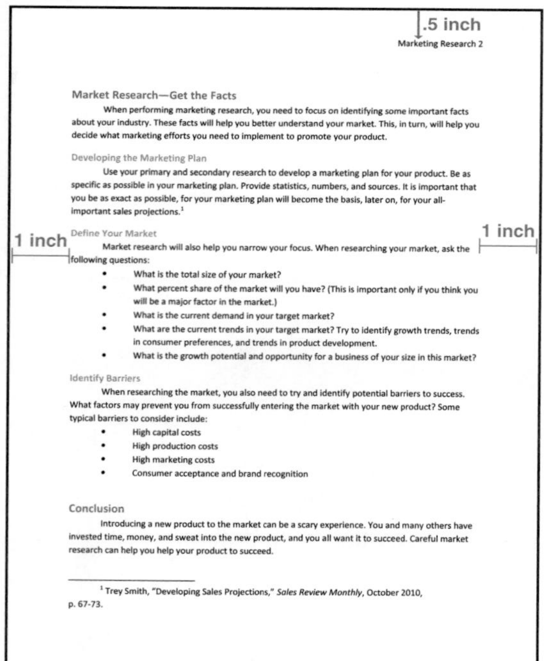

Marketing Research 2

Market Research—Get the Facts

When performing marketing research, you need to focus on identifying some important facts about your industry. These facts will help you better understand your market. This, in turn, will help you decide what marketing efforts you need to implement to promote your product.

Developing the Marketing Plan

Use your primary and secondary research to develop a marketing plan for your product. Be as specific as possible in your marketing plan. Provide statistics, numbers, and sources. It is important that you be as exact as possible, for your marketing plan will become the basis, later on, for your all-important sales projections.[1]

Define Your Market

Market research will also help you narrow your focus. When researching your market, ask the following questions:

- What is the total size of your market?
- What percent share of the market will you have? (This is important only if you think you will be a major factor in the market.)
- What is the current demand in your target market?
- What are the current trends in your target market? Try to identify growth trends, trends in consumer preferences, and trends in product development.
- What is the growth potential and opportunity for a business of your size in this market?

Identify Barriers

When researching the market, you also need to try and identify potential barriers to success. What factors may prevent you from successfully entering the market with your new product? Some typical barriers to consider include:

- High capital costs
- High production costs
- High marketing costs
- Consumer acceptance and brand recognition

Conclusion

Introducing a new product to the market can be a scary experience. You and many others have invested time, money, and sweat into the new product, and you all want it to succeed. Careful market research can help you help your product to succeed.

[1] Trey Smith, "Developing Sales Projections," *Sales Review Monthly*, October 2010, p. 67-73.

Bibliography

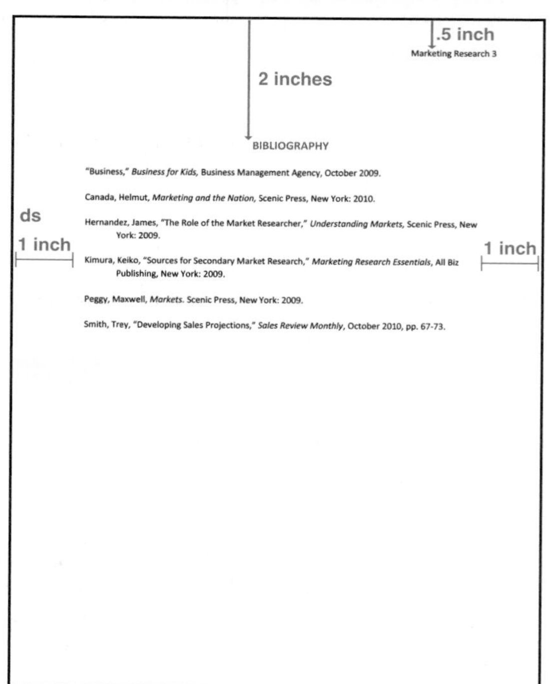

Marketing Research 3

BIBLIOGRAPHY

"Business," *Business for Kids*, Business Management Agency, October 2009.

Canada, Helmut, *Marketing and the Nation*, Scenic Press, New York: 2010.

Hernandez, James, "The Role of the Market Researcher," *Understanding Markets*, Scenic Press, New York: 2009.

Kimura, Keiko, "Sources for Secondary Market Research," *Marketing Research Essentials*, All Biz Publishing, New York: 2009.

Peggy, Maxwell, *Markets*. Scenic Press, New York: 2009.

Smith, Trey, "Developing Sales Projections," *Sales Review Monthly*, October 2010, pp. 67-73.

Step-by-Step

1. On a separate sheet of paper, copy the AUP on this page. Leave room under each item to write notes (Figure 1.6).
2. Read items 1 to 4 in the AUP. Discuss with your teacher the proper care and use of the classroom's computer equipment. On your AUP, write down your responsibilities.
3. Read item 5. With your teacher, discuss which files and folders are for student use on your classroom computer. Write down how to access those files and folders.
4. Read item 6. With your teacher, discuss how to use your computer resources. Write down any restrictions you might need to follow.
5. Read items 7 and 8. With your teacher, discuss the school's policy regarding e-mail and Internet use. Write down those policies.
6. Add any other items that you think should be included on the list.
7. Explain what the final paragraph means and why you have to sign the AUP.

Figure 1.6 An acceptable use policy is an agreement to use computer equipment responsibly.

Acceptable Use Policy (AUP)

1. I will use the computer and school network in a responsible way that will not interfere with others' use.
2. I will ask permission before using computer equipment or accessing the network, a file, or an application.
3. I will not damage the computer or network in any way.
4. I will not change any of the school's computer settings.
5. I will not view or use other people's folders, files, or work without their permission.
6. I will not waste computer resources such as paper, ink, or disk space.
7. I will not intentionally access Internet material that might be objectionable or offensive.
8. I will not use the computer for personal use (checking e-mail, instant messaging, surfing the Web, playing games, and so on) while in class.

I understand that the use of the computer and the Internet is a privilege, not a right, and inappropriate use may result in the canceling of those privileges.

____
Your name (print)

____
Your signature

____
Date

Go Online ACTIVITY

glencoe.com

Enrichment Activity Complete the following activities to learn even more about using your classroom computer. Go to the **Online Learning Center** at **glencoe.com**. Choose **Enrichment Activities**, then **Unit 1**.

- **Protect Your Computer**
- **Computer Care and Maintenance**

Format for Envelopes

A standard large (No. 10) envelope is 9½ by 4⅛ inches. A standard small (No. 6¾) envelope is 6½ by 3⅝ inches. The format shown is recommended by the U.S. Postal Service for mail that will be sorted by an electronic scanning device.

Your Name
4112 Bay View Drive
San Jose, CA 95192

Mrs. Maria Chavez
1021 West Palm Blvd.
San Jose, CA 95192

6021 Brobeck Street • Flint, MI 48532

Mr. Anthony Martinez
Cyber Foundation
4092 Barnes Avenue
Burton, MI 48529

How to Fold Letters

To fold a letter for a small envelope:

1. Place the letter *face up* and fold up the bottom half to 0.5 inch from the top edge of the paper.
2. Fold the right third over to the left.
3. Fold the left third over to 0.5 inch from the right edge of the paper.
4. Insert the last crease into the envelope first, with the flap facing up.

To fold a letter for a large envelope:

1. Place the letter *face up* and fold up the bottom third.
2. Fold the top third down to 0.5 inch from the bottom edge of the paper.
3. Insert the last crease into the envelope first, with the flap facing up.

Exercise 1-4 Use Computers Responsibly

As a responsible computer user, you must be aware of the school and classroom rules for school computer use. Your school, school district, and state have developed rules for safe and proper use of the computers at your school. These rules, called an **acceptable use policy (AUP)**, are created to protect students and staff from dangers that can occur when using computers.

Academic Focus

English Language Arts

Practice Digital Citizenship Responsible, respectful, and acceptable behavior while using technology is as important as learning to use the technology itself. Just as there are laws in our community to help us live safely together, rules must be followed so that everyone can safely use technology. Review the chart in this article with your classmates, and discuss why it is important to practice digital citizenship.

NCTE 12 Use language to accomplish individual purposes.

Be a Responsible Computer User

Inappropriate Action	Result of Inappropriate Action	Appropriate Action
Damaging hardware	Expensive equipment must be replaced.	Respect the computer equipment at your school.
Damaging or deleting software	The computer may not work properly, or it may stop functioning altogether.	Never change software settings or delete software without permission.
Deleting or opening other users' files or folders	Users will not be able to complete assignments.	Use only your own files and folders.
Installing new software	Viruses and other damaging programs may be introduced into the computer or the network.	Always get permission before installing programs.
Visiting inappropriate Web sites and chatrooms	Web content may be offensive to others. Viruses or spyware may be introduced into the computer or the network.	Only visit Web sites that are needed to complete school work. Surf the Web only with permission.
Downloading music or other files without permission or without paying for them	Violates copyright laws. Stealing intellectual property is illegal and may result in criminal action or fines.	Always pay to download music or other files unless they are offered for free.
Copying someone else's work and claiming it as your own	Plagiarism is unethical and illegal.	Always obtain permission, if needed, and cite your sources.
Attempting to use another person's user name or passwords	It is a serious violation of another's privacy or rights. It can also be a cybercrime.	Never use someone else's password or user name.

Your teacher will discuss your school's acceptable use policy. You may be required to sign the policy along with your parents before you may use the school's computers. It is important that you understand and follow the acceptable use policy.

In this exercise, you will evaluate some of the rules found in many acceptable use policies. If your teacher or school has an AUP, you should discuss any additional rules you need to follow.

Contents

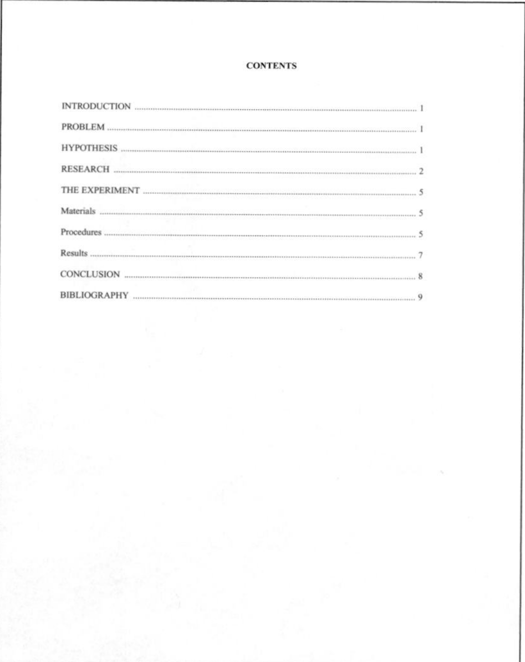

CONTENTS

Boxed Table

Dogs for Adoption

Name	Date Arrived in Shelter	Description
Jack	April 11	5-year-old male; shepherd/lab mix; about 70 pounds; house-trained; good watchdog; great with kids.
Autumn	April 16	3-year-old female; golden retriever; about 75 pounds; house-trained; high energy; needs plenty of exercise.
Tigger	April 16	6-year-old male; terrier mix; about 20 pounds; sweet, friendly, and obedient; good with other dogs; loves to play.
Jasmine	April 18	9-year-old female; sheltie; about 25 pounds; gentle and calm; needs daily exercise and a quiet environment.
Max	April 20	3–4-year-old male; dalmatian mix; about 70 pounds; loves to play with other dogs and needs an area to run and play.
Billy Bob	April 21	5–6-year-old male; beagle; about 30 pounds; a very bright dog; house-trained, active, and good around kids.
Sophie	April 22	1–2-year-old female; collie; about 40 pounds; well-mannered; loves to run and play; short-to-medium hair and is a very pretty dog; gets along with dogs as well as cats.
Molly	April 23	1-year-old female; cocker spaniel mix; about 25 pounds; adorable and happy; playful and energetic; very bright and trainable.

Proofreaders' Marks

Proofreaders' Marks		Draft	Final Copy
⁀	Omit space	data base	database
v or ^	Insert	if he's going (not)	if he's not going,
≡	Capitalize	Maple street	Maple Street
	Delete	a final draft	a draft
#	Insert space	allready to	all ready to
when / if	Change word	and if you (when)	and when you
/	Use lowercase letter	our President	our president
¶	Paragraph	¶ Most of the	Most of the
•••	Don't delete	a true story	a true story
○	Spell out	the only (1)	the only one
∽	Transpose	they all see	they see all

Proofreaders' Marks		Draft	Final Copy
SS	Single-space	ss first line second line	first line second line
ds	Double-space	ds first line second line	first line second line
	Move right	Please send	Please send
	Move left	May I	May I
~~	Bold	Column Heading	**Column Heading**
ital	Italic	ital Time magazine	*Time* magazine
u/l	Underline	u/l Time magazine	Time magazine
	Move as shown	readers will see	readers will see

6. Put your feet flat on the floor. Your knees should be bent at a 90-degree angle, so that your legs form an L shape. (You may have to adjust the seat or place a footrest under your feet.)

7. Rest your back and hips against the back of the chair. Do not slump.

8. Center your body in front of the keyboard. You should be centered on the J key.

9. Position yourself or the monitor so that the monitor is about two feet from your eyes.

10. With your teacher's permission, adjust the monitor so that it is slightly lower than the top of your head, and you look slightly down at the screen.

11. Place your book within easy view of your computer station so that you do not strain your neck trying to see it. If possible, place it on a stand next to your monitor.

12. After you have completed steps 1 to 11, have your partner follow the same steps while sitting at the computer. Help him or her perform each step correctly (Figure 1.5).

Figure 1.5 Practice proper ergonomics at your workstation.

TechSavvy

Monitors Like televisions, most monitors have control knobs or buttons to adjust for brightness, contrast, and other functions. If your monitor does not look right, ask your teacher to help you make the necessary adjustments.

Punctuation and Usage

ALWAYS SPACE ONCE . . .

- After a comma.
  We ordered two printers, one computer, and three monitors.
- After a semicolon.
  They flew to Dallas, Texas; Reno, Nevada; and Rome, New York.
- After a period following someone's initials.
  Mr. A. Henson, Ms. C. Hovey, and Mr. M. Salisbury will attend the meeting.
- After a period following the abbreviation of a single word.
  We will send the package by 7 p.m. next week. [Note: space once after the final period in the "p.m." abbreviation, but do not space after the first period between the two letters.]
- Before a ZIP code.
  Send the package to 892 Maple Street, Grand Forks, ND 58201.
- Before and after an ampersand.
  We were represented by the law firm of Bassett & Johnson; they were represented by the law firm of Crandall & Magnuson.
- After a period at the end of a sentence.
  Don't forget to vote. Vote for the candidate of your choice.
- After a question mark.
  When will you vote? Did you vote last year?
- After an exclamation point.
  Wow! What a performance! It was fantastic!
- After a colon.
  We will attend on the following days: Monday, Wednesday, and Friday.

Punctuation

COMMAS:

1. Use a comma between independent clauses joined by a conjunction. (An independent clause is one that can stand alone as a complete sentence.)
   We requested Brown Industries to change the date, and they did so within five days.
2. Use a comma after an introductory expression (unless it is a short prepositional phrase).
   Before we can make a decision, we must have all the facts.
   In 1992 our nation elected a president.

Exercise 1-3 Practice Proper Ergonomics

Ergonomics is the study of the design of equipment and systems that people use. Some computer equipment, such as keyboards and chairs, is designed for safe computer use. Ergonomics, however, can also include simple practices such as sitting correctly, using proper lighting, and resting your eyes from time to time. Proper ergonomics can improve safety, comfort, and efficiency at work. Good computer ergonomics prevents fatigue and muscle injury, and helps keep you alert and focused.

In this exercise, you will learn how to sit correctly and safely at your computer. Complete these steps with a partner. Take turns to make sure you are each sitting properly.

Step-by-Step

1. Make sure all books, jackets, and other items are stored so that they are not on your lap, or on the floor where you might trip over them.
2. Bend your elbows so that they form a 90-degree angle (an L shape) from your shoulders to your wrist.
3. Rest your hands on the keyboard. Your wrists should be straight, not bent, and not resting on the keyboard or table (Figure 1.3).
4. Place the mouse within easy reach of your hand.
5. Hold the mouse loosely, and use a light touch when you click (Figure 1.4).

▼ **Figure 1.3** The correct placement of your hands on the keyboard can help reduce strain and the possibility of injury.

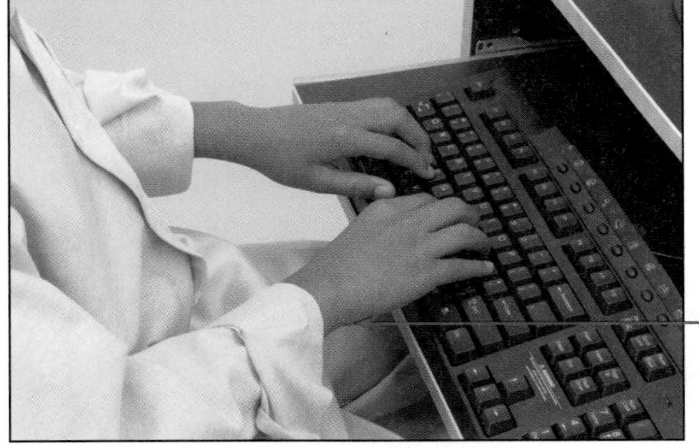

Your wrists should be straight and not rest on the keyboard or table.

▼ **Figure 1.4** For more comfort, use your whole arm and not just your wrist to move the mouse.

Hold the mouse loosely.

Punctuation

3. Use a comma before and after the year in a complete date.
   We will arrive at the plant on June 2, 2010, for the conference.

4. Use a comma before and after a state or country that follows a city (but not before a ZIP Code).
   Joan moved to Vancouver, British Columbia, in September.
   Send the package to Douglasville, GA 30135, by express mail.

5. Use a comma between each item in a series of three or more.
   There are lions, tigers, bears, and zebras at the zoo.

6. Use a comma before and after a transitional expression (such as therefore and however).
   It is critical, therefore, that we finish the project on time.

7. Use a comma before and after a direct quotation.
   When we left, James said, "Let us return to the same location next year."

8. Use a comma before and after a nonessential expression. (A nonessential expression is a word or group of words that may be omitted without changing the basic meaning of the sentence.)
   Let me say, to begin with, that the report has already been finalized.

9. Use a comma between two adjacent adjectives that modify the same noun.
   We need an intelligent, enthusiastic individual for this project.

SEMICOLONS:

1. Use a semicolon to join two closely related independent clauses that are not connected by a conjunction (such as and, but, or nor).
   Students favored the music; teachers did not.

2. Use a semicolon to separate three or more items in a series if any of the items already contain commas.
   Region 1 sent their reports in March, April, and May; and Region 2 sent their reports in September, October, and November.
   The Home room class sent their reports in 1st, 2nd, 3rd, and 4th hour; the history class sent their reports in 4th, 5th, 6th, and 7th hour.

HYPHENS:

1. Hyphenate compound adjectives that come before a noun (unless the first word is an adverb ending in *-ly*).
   We reviewed an up-to-date report on Wednesday.
   We attended a highly rated session on multimedia software.

Exercise 1-2 Operate Computers Safely

As with any type of equipment, you must handle computers correctly. When you learn to drive a car, a teacher or another adult will show you how to operate it safely and with care. In the same way, you need to operate a computer safely or you might be injured or the computer might be damaged. Your classroom or lab should be set up for the safe use of the computers based on the guidelines below.

If you notice any unsafe conditions in the computer lab or in your computer setup at home, notify an adult immediately. Safety issues do not involve only equipment. Your behavior can also affect the safe use of the technology in your classroom.

In this exercise, you will learn how to keep your computer classroom safe and avoid accidents.

Step-by-Step

1. Write down the Guidelines for a Safe Computer Classroom from the checklist on this page, or use guidelines from your teacher (Figure 1.2).
2. Use the guidelines to determine if your classroom is safe for computers.
3. Write down the safety practices used in your classroom.
4. If you find places where you believe safety requirements are not met, write down ways you think safety could be improved.
5. Write down, or discuss with your teacher, what might happen if students do not follow rules in your computer classroom.

▼ **Figure 1.2** **Use these guidelines to keep your computer classroom and equipment safe.**

Guidelines for a Safe Computer Classroom

- ☑ Sturdy tables for the computers, monitors, and other equipment
- ☑ Sturdy chairs for students and other computer users
- ☑ Clean floor, all books and backpacks out of walkways
- ☑ Clean equipment, including monitor screens, keyboards, and mice
- ☑ Computer cables neatly arranged and out of the walkway or seating area
- ☑ Computer cables connected safely to computer equipment and outlets
- ☑ No food or drinks in the classroom
- ☑ Papers and supplies neatly organized
- ☑ Correct lighting to reduce glare and shadow
- ☑ Room temperature that is not too hot or cold (computers need constant temperature)
- ☑ Fire extinguisher or sprinklers in the room

TechSavvy

Caution Never have any liquids or food near your computer. Drinks can spill into the keyboard or computer, ruin the equipment, and create an unpleasant work environment for others. Food anywhere near the computer can invite ants and other bugs to invade your classroom.

2. Hyphenate compound numbers (between twenty-one and ninety-nine) and fractions that are expressed as words.
   We observed twenty-nine fumbles during the football game.
   All teachers reduced their assignments by one-third.

3. Hyphenate words that are divided at the end of a line. Do not divide one-syllable words, contractions, or abbreviations; divide other words only between syllables.
   To appreciate the full significance of rain forests, you must see the entire docu-mentary showing tomorrow in the library.

APOSTROPHES:

1. Use 's to form the possessive of singular nouns.
   The hurricane caused major damage to Georgia's coastline.

2. Use only an apostrophe to form the possessive of plural nouns that end in *s*.
   The investors' goals were outlined in the annual report.

3. Use 's to form the possessive of indefinite pronouns (such as someone's or anybody's); do not use an apostrophe with personal pronouns (such as *hers, his, its, ours, theirs,* and *yours*).
   She was instructed to select anybody's paper for a sample.
   Each computer comes carefully packed in its own container.

COLONS:

Use a colon to introduce explanatory material that follows an independent clause. (An independent clause is one that can stand alone as a complete sentence.)
A computer is useful for three reasons: speed, cost, and power.

DASHES:

Use a dash instead of a comma, semicolon, colon, or parenthesis when you want to convey a more forceful separation of words within a sentence. (If your keyboard has a special dash character, use it. Otherwise, form a dash by typing two hyphens, with no space before, between, or after.)
At this year's student council meeting, the speakers—and topics—were superb.

PERIODS:

Use a period to end a sentence that is a polite request. (Consider a sentence a polite request if you expect the reader to respond by doing as you ask rather than by giving a yes-or-no answer.)
Will you please call me.

Exercise 1-1 Get to Know Your Classroom Computer

Before you use your classroom computer, you should be familiar with its basic equipment. Some computer devices can be used by only one person at a time. Your own computer station may have the devices listed in the first column below. Your computer lab may also have some of the other equipment below that can be shared by more than one person.

- Computer
- Monitor
- Keyboard
- Mouse
- Printer
- Scanner
- Digital camera
- Projector
- Microphones
- Headphones
- Network hubs
- Surge protectors

In this exercise, you will identify and locate the computer equipment in your classroom.

Step-by-Step

1. On a separate sheet of paper, identify the computer devices listed above that you have at your own computer station.
2. Write down the additional computer equipment that is available in your classroom.
3. Draw a map showing the location of each device.
4. Find the cable that connects your computer to the network. On your map, show how each device is hooked up to the other computers and to the computer network. **Hint:** Try to follow the cables on the wall, floor, or ceiling.

▼ **Figure 1.1** **Your workstation may look different from the ones below, but it probably contains the same kinds of equipment.**

Punctuation

QUOTATION MARKS:

1. Use quotation marks around the titles of newspaper articles, magazine articles, chapters in a book, reports, conferences, and similar items.
The best article I found in my research was entitled "Multimedia for Everyone."

2. Use quotation marks around a direct quotation.
Harrison responded by saying, "This decision will not affect our class."

ITALIC (OR UNDERLINE):

Italicize (or underline) the titles of books, magazines, newspapers, and other complete published works.
I read *The Pelican Brief* last month. I read <u>The Pelican Brief</u> last month.

Grammar

AGREEMENT:

1. Use singular verbs and pronouns with singular subjects and plural verbs and pronouns with plural subjects.
I was pleased with the performance of our team.
Reno and Phoenix were selected as the sites for our next two meetings.

2. Some pronouns (*anybody, each, either, everybody, everyone, much, neither, no one, nobody,* and *one*) are always singular and take a singular verb. Other pronouns (*all, any, more, most, none,* and *some*) may be singular or plural, depending on the noun to which they refer.
Each employee is responsible for summarizing the day's activities.
Most of the workers are going to get a substantial pay raise.

3. Disregard any intervening words that come between the subject and verb when establishing agreement.
The box containing the books and pencils has not been found.

4. If two subjects are joined by *or, either / or, nor, neither / nor,* or *not only / but also,* the verb should agree with the subject nearer to the verb.
Neither the players nor the coach is in favor of the decision.

5. The subject *a number* takes a plural verb; *the number* takes a singular verb.
The number of new students has increased to six.
We know that a number of students are in sports.

Concepts in Action

Project 1 Use Your Computer Safely and Responsibly

Key Concepts

Exercise 1-1
- Identify features of your classroom computer

Exercise 1-2
- Operate computers safely

Exercise 1-3
- Practice proper ergonomics

Exercise 1-4
- Use computers responsibly

Vocabulary

Key Terms
ergonomics
acceptable use policy (AUP)

Before You Begin

Survey Before You Read Before you begin reading, quickly preview the content by reading the headings and captions. Look for bolded words and jot down words you do not recognize. Study the figures and graphs. Finally, read the project assessment questions and activities. This will help you pay attention to important concepts and skills as you complete the project.

In this project, you will get an overview of how to use your classroom computer safely and responsibly.

Respect Computers and Other Users

When you use a classroom computer, you are given access to a powerful tool. Computers have fundamentally changed the way people learn, communicate, and have fun. You should use this tool with sound judgment and in an ethical way.

Because the equipment you are using is shared by many people, you are taking on a special responsibility. Computer hardware and software are expensive to buy, maintain, and repair. If they are damaged because of misuse or neglect, it may inconvenience you and other users, or you may not be able to use the computer at all! Be a responsible computer user, just as you expect other people to use computers with care and respect.

Grammar

6. Subjects joined by and take a plural verb unless the compound subject is preceded by *each, every,* or *many a (an).*
   Every man, woman, and child is included in our survey.

7. Verbs that refer to conditions that are impossible or improbable (that is, verbs in the *subjunctive* mood) require the plural form.
   If the total eclipse were to occur tomorrow, it would be the second one this year.

PRONOUNS:

1. Use nominative pronouns (such as *I, he, she, we,* and *they*) as subjects of a sentence or clause.
   They traveled to Minnesota last week but will not return until next month.

2. Use objective pronouns (such as *me, him, her, us,* and *them*) as objects in a sentence or clause.
   The package has been sent to her.

ADJECTIVES AND ADVERBS:

Use comparative adjectives and adverbs (*-er, more,* and *less*) when referring to two nouns; use superlative adjectives and adverbs (*-est, most,* and *least*) when referring to more than two.
Of the two movies you have selected, the shorter one is the more interesting.
The highest of the three mountains is Mt. Everest.

WORD USAGE:

Do not confuse the following pairs of words:

- *Accept* means "to agree to"; *except* means "to leave out."
  *We **accept** your offer for developing the new product.*
  *Everyone **except** Sam and Lisa attended the rally.*

- *Affect* is most often used as a verb meaning "to influence"; *effect* is most often used as a noun meaning "result."
  *Mr. Smith's decision will not **affect** our music class.*
  *It will be weeks before we can assess the **effect** of this decision.*

- *Farther* refers to distance; *further* refers to extent or degree.
  *Did we travel **farther** today than yesterday?*
  *We need to discuss our plans **further**.*

- *Personal* means "private"; *personnel* means "employees."
  *The letters were very **personal** and should not have been read.*
  *We hope that all **personnel** will comply with the new rules.*

After You Read

Key Concepts Check

1. **Define** In your own words, define technology.
2. **Describe** What are two ways that technology works behind the scenes of everyday life?
3. **Identify** What are three ways you can use technology at school?

Critical Thinking

4. **Evaluate** Imagine that a friend tells you about a Web site that sells completed research papers to students. The friend says, "If Web sites like that exist, they must be okay." Based on what you have learned about ethics, how would you respond?

21st Century Skills

5. **Communication** Go to glencoe.com to this book's Online Learning Center to find **Web links** on recent technology. Write one paragraph that identifies the technology, why it is important, and its benefits and drawbacks.

Academic Skills

Mathematics

People have always looked for better ways to communicate.

a. **Compare** How many years passed between the invention of the printing press and that of the Web?

b. **Identify** Name two communication methods that were developed within 100 years after the telegraph.

Math Concept

Time Line A time line displays related events in chronological order. It lists the name of each event as well as the date on which the event took place.

Starting Hint Find the points on the line for both the printing press and the World Wide Web. Then subtract to find the number of years that passed between the two inventions.

NCTM Data Analysis and Probability Formulate questions that can be addressed with data and collect, organize, and display relevant data to answer them.

Communication and Technology

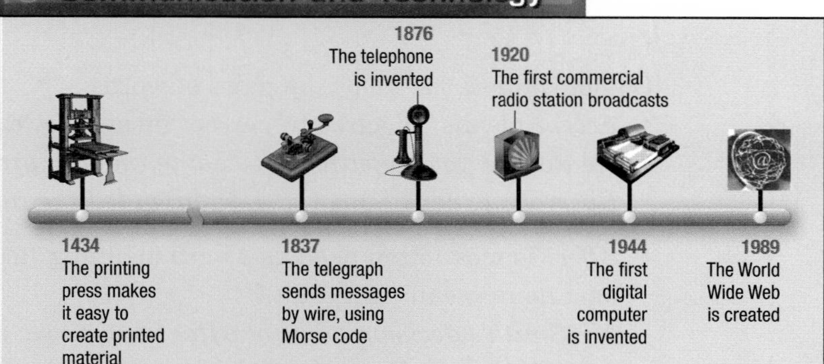

Go Online e-QUIZ

glencoe.com

Self-Check Assess your understanding of what you have just read. Go to the **Online Learning Center** at glencoe.com. Choose **e-Quizzes**, and take the **Unit 1 Tech Talk Quiz**.

Grammar

- *Principal* means "primary"; *principle* means "rule."
  *The **principal** means of research were interviewing and surveying.*
  *They must not violate the **principles** under which our country was founded.*
- *Passed* means "went by"; *past* means "before now."
  *We **passed** another car from our home state.*
  *In the **past**, we always took the same route.*
- *Advice* means "to provide guidance"; *advise* means "help."
  *The **advice** I gave her was simple.*
  *I **advise** you to finish your project.*
- *Council* is a group; *counsel* is a person who provides advice.
  *The student **council** met to discuss graduation.*
  *The court asked that **counsel** be present at the hearing.*
- *Then* means "at that time"; *than* is used for comparisons.
  *He read for a while; **then** he turned out the light.*
  *She reads more books **than** I do.*
- *Its* is the possessive form of it; *it's* is a contraction for it is.
  *We researched the country and **its** people.*
  ***It's** not too late to finish the story.*
- *Two* means "one more than one"; *too* means "also"; *to* means "in a direction."
  *There were **two** people in the boat.*
  *We wished we were on board, **too.***
  *The boat headed out **to** sea.*
- *Stationery* means "paper"; *stationary* means "fixed position."
  *Please buy some **stationery** so that I can write letters.*
  *The **stationary** bike at the health club provides a good workout.*

Mechanics

CAPITALIZATION:

1. Capitalize the first word of a sentence.
   Please prepare a summary.
2. Capitalize proper nouns and adjectives derived from proper nouns. (A proper noun is the official name of a particular person, place, or thing.)
   Judy Hendrix drove to Albuquerque in her new car, a Pontiac.

Go Online ACTIVITY
glencoe.com

Protect Yourself Learn more about using your computer safely at the **Online Learning Center**. Go to **glencoe.com**, and choose **Tech Talk Activities**, then **Unit 1**.

Tech Tip Many stores have a computer station, or kiosk, where you can fill out an electronic job application. Using the kiosk can be the first test to see whether an applicant has the necessary computer skills to work for the store.

Why It's Important Consider the advantages of filling out an electronic job application over a paper application.

What Are the Risks of Using Computers?

Computers give you access to the world, but the reverse is also true: The world can have access to your computer, too. A safe computer user recognizes risks, such as the following:

- **Viruses** A computer **virus** is a program intentionally designed to cause annoyance or damage to computer hardware or software.
- **Hackers** A **hacker** is a person who uses his or her expertise to gain access to other people's computers to get information illegally or do damage.
- **Dishonest people** The Internet is open to anyone, including people who may want to cause harm by giving false or illegal information.

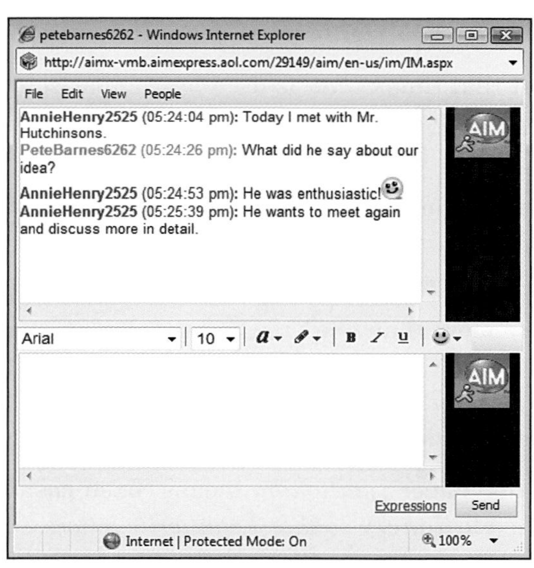

Instant messaging is a favorite activity for many computer users. What common-sense rules should you follow when instant messaging?

When you use a computer, you must be aware of the risks and take the proper precautions. Firewalls and antivirus software can help protect your computer from hackers and viruses. However, you still must use common sense whenever you log on to your computer, when you use the Internet, and when you share files with other people.

Reading Check

1. **Explain** What are the consequences of acting unethically?
2. **Draw Conclusions** Why should you be careful about the information you send or receive over the Internet?

Mechanics

3. Capitalize the names of the days of the week, months, holidays, and religious days (but do not capitalize the names of the seasons).
   On Thursday, November 25, we will celebrate Thanksgiving, the most popular fall holiday.

4. Capitalize nouns followed by a number or letter (except for the nouns *line, note, page, paragraph,* and *size*).
   Please read Chapter 5, but not page 94.

5. Capitalize compass points (such as *north, south,* or *northeast*) only when they designate definite regions.
   The Crenshaws will vacation in the Northeast this summer.
   We will have to drive north to reach the closest Canadian border.

6. Capitalize common organizational terms (such as *advertising department* and *finance committee*) when they are the actual names of the units in the writer's own organization and when they are preceded by the word *the*.
   The quarterly report from the Advertising Department will be presented today.

7. Capitalize the names of specific course titles but not the names of subjects or areas of study.
   I have enrolled in Accounting 201 and will also take a marketing course.

NUMBER EXPRESSION:

1. In general, spell out numbers 1 through 10, and use figures for numbers above 10.
   We have rented two movies for tonight.
   The decision was reached after 27 precincts had sent in their results.

2. Use figures for:
   - Dates (use *st, d,* or *th* only if the day precedes the month).
     We will drive to the camp on the 23d of May.
     The tax report is due on April 15.
   - All numbers if two or more related numbers both above and below ten are used in the same sentence.
     Mr. Carter sent in 7 receipts; Ms. Cantrell sent in 22 receipts.
   - Measurements (time, money, distance, weight, and percentage).
     At 10 a.m. we delivered the $500 coin bank in a 17-pound container.
   - Mixed numbers.
     Our sales are up 9½ percent over last year.

Responsible Use of Technology

Ethics are the principles and standards we use to decide how to act. People generally assume that other people will act toward them in an ethical manner. The consequences of acting unethically **vary**, or differ. They can range from losing a friend to losing a job to even being arrested. Ethics also help you predict how a person will behave toward you. Telling the truth is ethical, and lying is unethical. We usually assume that people are not lying.

▲ "With great power comes great responsibility." How do these words of advice from the movie *Spiderman* apply to technology and ethics?

Academic Focus

English Language Arts

Cite Sources Responsibly When researching a topic for a report, search on the Internet to find reliable information to support your ideas. Then, use your own words to describe what you discover. Be sure to cite your sources, and never copy text directly from a Web site without proper attribution. Why is it unethical to not cite your sources?

NCTE 8 Use information resources to gather information and create and communicate knowledge.

How Can I Use Computers Ethically?

Your behavior while using a computer is also guided by ethics. Make sure you follow these ethical guidelines:

Computer Use Guidelines

Respect the privacy of others	Do not open any files or e-mails that are not your own, unless you have permission to do so.
Be honest	Use a computer and Internet access to do your own work. Some students may use computers and the Internet to cheat on schoolwork. Students who do this are likely to get caught.
Treat people fairly	Conflicts should be worked out face to face. Do not use Web sites, e-mail, or chatrooms to harm someone's reputation. Never damage someone's computer or files on purpose.
Pay your fair share	You might hear about ways to get commercial software or music for free, but this is usually illegal.

▲ Many of the ethical issues you face when using technology are similar to ethical issues in other aspects of your life. How else might you apply the guidelines in this table to your life?

When you sit down at a computer to work or to go online, remind yourself of the importance of acting ethically. Also, be aware that you could be the victim of someone else's unethical conduct. If you believe that someone is acting unethically, notify an adult, such as your teacher or a parent or guardian.

3. Spell out:

- Numbers used as the first word in a sentence.
  Seventy people attended the conference in San Diego last week.
- The smaller of two adjacent numbers.
  We have ordered two 5-pound packages for the meeting.
- The words millions and billions in even amounts (do not use decimals with even amounts).
  The lottery is worth 28 million this month.
- Fractions.
  About one-half of the audience responded to the questionnaire.

ABBREVIATIONS:

1. In nontechnical writing, do not abbreviate common nouns (such as *dept.* or *pkg.*), compass points, units of measure, or the names of months, days of the week, cities, or states (except in addresses).
The Sales Department will meet on Tuesday, March 7, in Tempe, Arizona.

2. In lowercase abbreviations made up of single initials, use a period after each initial but no internal spaces.
We will be including several states (e.g., Maine, New Hampshire, Vermont, Massachusetts, and Connecticut).

3. In all-capital abbreviations made up of single initials, do not use periods or internal spaces. (Exception: Keep the periods in most academic degrees and in abbreviations of geographic names other than two-letter state abbreviations.)
You need to call the EEO office for clarification on that issue.

Jargon The Digital Divide is the social and financial gap between people who do have computer access and those who do not. Although plenty of people live without computers, computer skills and access can make it easier to find a job or exchange information with others.

Why It's Important Consider how having access to a computer impacts your daily life.

How Is Technology Used at Home?

Stereos, refrigerators, telephones, televisions, microwave ovens, MP3 players, security systems, and computers are all part of our daily lives. Most of these technologies use microchips to control how they work. Computers are especially useful because they can be used for many different purposes. You can use them to:

- Communicate instantly with friends and family
- Find information
- Listen to music and watch movies
- Play video games
- Take pictures and create home movies

How Is Technology Used at Work?

Technology is everywhere in the workplace. Office workers use computers to create documents and stay on schedule. Sales people use computers to track sales and place orders. Businesses use databases to track products, workers, and customers. Industrial workers use high-tech machinery to make a variety of products.

Many careers require a solid knowledge of technology. What kinds of technology are shown in this photo?

Some people do not even have to go into the office to work anymore. They can **telecommute**, which means to work from home or another location with the help of cell phones, fax machines, and the Internet.

Having a solid knowledge of technology is one key to a great career. Most jobs today require at least basic computer knowledge. So, the more you learn now, the better off you will be later. Also, your computer skills can help you find the right job. You can search for a job on the Internet and apply for jobs online.

Reading Check

1. **Describe** What are three good reasons to learn about technology?
2. **Cause and Effect** If you leave high school with very few computer skills, what problems might you face in the future?

IC³ Standards and Correlations

Internet and Computing Core Certification (IC³) standards provide a solid foundation for the productive use of computer hardware, software, and the Internet. The objectives are divided into three modules: Computing Fundamentals, Key Applications, and Living Online. The following pages describe the IC³ 2005 standards and objectives and where they are met in this course.

Correlation to IC³ (Internet and Computing Core Certification) 2005 Standard

The following abbreviations are used in the correlation to help you locate information quickly:

SE Student Edition
TRM Teacher Resource Manual
OLC Online Learning Center (Go to glencoe.com)
GO TT Go Online Tech Talk Activity
GO EA Go Online Enrichment Activity
SIM TechSIM™ **Interactive Tutorials** (Available on the TechSIM Interactive Tutorials CD or at glencoe.com)

All learners can master the IC³ objectives that are thoroughly covered in this course. Students who wish to become officially IC³ certified must take and pass IC³ exams covering the three modules. For more information about Certiport, and IC³ objectives, and IC³ exams, please visit www.certiport.com.

Contents

Technology and You

Technology is always changing. That is why you need to keep learning new skills—to keep up with the changing world around you. The more confident you are when you work with technology, the more productive you will be at home, at school, and at work.

We are living in the information age. What can computers help you do with all that information?

- **Collect it!** The Internet is a powerful tool for gathering information.
- **Organize it!** Instead of using file cabinets, you can save your documents on the computer so that you or others can find them easily.
- **Communicate it!** E-mail, instant messaging, and Web sites are just a few ways that computers can help you share information.

How Is Technology Used at School?

Students learn to use technology—and then they use technology to learn. Educators have recognized that computers can make education more effective and exciting for students.

Students can use computers and the Internet to take classes without ever going to a classroom. This is called e-learning or distance learning. It is a popular choice for students who have full-time jobs.

Academic Focus

English Language Arts

Research with Technology The computer is one of many resources you can use to obtain information. Reports, class presentations, and group projects all require research. When your research is completed, use software applications to communicate what you have learned. Review the chart in this article. Discuss with your classmates other types of school assignments that you can do on a computer and how the computer can help you do the assignments.

NCTE 8 Use information resources to gather information and create and communicate knowledge.

Computer Use in School

School Assignment	How Computers Can Help You
Research a specific subject for a school report.	Use the Internet to find the information you need.
Write a report for school.	Use word processing software to create text documents.
Create a presentation to deliver in class.	Use presentation software that lets you display text and graphics. You can even include music and videos.
Work with partners on a project.	Use e-mail or instant messaging to work with teammates outside the classroom.
Keep track of similar information, or compare and contrast information.	Use spreadsheet software to record information. Create charts and graphs that compare data.

▲ Computers can help you with your work in all your subjects. How would you use e-mail to help you with classwork?

IC^3 - Module 1: Computing Fundamentals

Total Domains: 3 Total Objectives: 9

Standardized Coding Number	Objectives & Abbreviated Skill Sets	Performance Based	Location (Page #)
Domain 1.0: Computer Hardware	This domain includes the knowledge and skills required to identify different types of computers and computing devices, the components of a personal computer (including internal components such as microprocessors) and how these components function and interact. The domain also includes the knowledge and skills relating to computer storage, performance and maintenance procedures.		
Objective 1.1	Identify types of computers, how they process information and how individual computers interact with other computing systems and devices		
IC^3-1 1.1.1	Categorize types of computers based on their size, power and purpose	No	SE 41
IC^3-1 1.1.2	Identify types of microcomputers	No	SE 41
IC^3-1 1.1.3	Identify other types of computing devic-es	No	SE 3
IC^3-1 1.1.4	Identify the role of the central process-ing unit	No	SE 42, 43
IC^3-1 1.1.5	Identify how the speed of the micropro-cessor is measured	No	SE 42
IC^3-1 1.1.6	Identify the role of types of memory and storage and the purpose of each, includ-ing RAM, ROM, and CD ROMs	No	SE 45, 45 (GO) OLC GO TT 2.2
IC^3-1 1.1.7	Identify concepts related to how memory is measured, including bits, bytes and megabytes	No	SE 42, 46 (Real World)
IC^3-1 1.1.8	Identify the flow of information between storage devices (such as floppy or hard disks) to the microprocessor and RAM in relation to everyday computer opera-tions	No	SE 45
IC^3-1 1.1.9	Identify the differences between large systems and desktop computers and appropriate uses for large vs. small sys-tems	No	SE 49
IC^3-1 1.1.10	Identify that computers integrate into larger systems in a variety of ways	No	SE 49

Go Online ACTIVITY
glencoe.com

History of Computers
Learn about the history of computers at the **Online Learning Center**. Go to **glencoe.com**. Choose **Tech Talk Activities**, then **Unit 1**.

Jargon *Google* is the name of the Web site for one of the most popular search engines on the Web. When people talk about "googling" something, they simply mean using the Google Web site to search for information.

Why It's Important Think about how "googling" key words could help you find information about a topic for a school report.

How Do I Use Technology?

Often we are not aware of how technology works behind the scenes. Computers keep track of the books in your library. They make it possible for weather forecasters to **predict**, or declare, whether you will need an umbrella. In law enforcement, computers help police officers track their cases. In medicine, doctors use them to monitor patients.

The "brain" of every computerized **device**, or tool, is a **microprocessor**, also called a microchip. A microprocessor is a tiny computer chip that receives instructions and carries them out. Calculators, for example, use microprocessors to add and subtract.

Technology Behind the Scenes

Technology	How Technology Is Used
Automated Teller Machines (ATMs)	• An ATM card has a magnetic strip that contains information about an account. • The ATM reads the strip and asks the bank's main computer for permission to take money out of the account. • The ATM then lets customers withdraw money.
Cars	• To improve safety, microchips are placed in sensors that control antilock brakes and air bags. • To make cars more efficient, microchip sensors in the engine control how the car uses gas. • To make driving easier, microchips control global positioning systems and cruise control.
Cash Registers	• A cashier scans the bar code on an item using a special bar code-reading device. • A microchip in the cash register sends the bar code number to the store's main computer. • The store's computer looks up the price and sends it back to the cash register in a split second. • The computer tells the store to order more of the product so that the store does not run out of inventory.

▲ Computers are part of our daily lives, even if you cannot see them working. What types of computer technology are found in a grocery store?

Reading Check

1. **Define** What is a microprocessor?
2. **Summarize** How would your life be different without technology?

Standardized Coding Number	Objectives & Abbreviated Skill Sets	Performance Based	Location (Page #)
IC^3-1 1.1.11	Identify how computers share data, files, hardware, and software	No	SE 212
Objective 1.2	Identify the function of computer hardware components		
IC^3-1 1.2.1	Identify the types and purposes of external computer components, including standard input and output devices	No	SE 43
IC^3-1 1.2.2	Identify the types and purposes of internal computer components	No	SE 43, 485
IC^3-1 1.2.3	Identify the types and purposes of specialized input devices (e.g. digital cameras and touch screens)	No	SE 44 (GO) OLC GO TT 2.5
IC^3-1 1.2.4	Identify the types and purposes of specialized output devices (e.g. projectors)	No	SE 44 (GO) OLC GO TT 2.5 TRM 158
IC^3-1 1.2.5	Identify the types and purposes of storage media (e.g. DVDs and network drives)	No	SE 45 (GO), 46 OLC GO TT 2.2
IC^3-1 1.2.6	Identify ports used to connect input and output devices to a computer (e.g. USB ports and Ethernet ports)	No	SE 43
IC^3-1 1.2.7	Identify how hardware devices are installed on a computer system	No	SE 43, 43 (Real World)
Objective 1.3	Identify the factors that go into an individual or organizational decision on how to purchase computer equipment		
IC^3-1 1.3.1	Identify criteria for selecting a personal computer	No	SE 209
IC^3-1 1.3.2	Identify factors that affect computer performance	No	SE 211
IC^3-1 1.3.3	Identify hardware and software considerations when purchasing a computer	No	SE 209-211
IC^3-1 1.3.4	Identify other factors that go into decisions to purchase a computer including warranties and support agreements	No	SE 49 (GO), 210 (GO) OLC GO TT 2.4, GO TT 5.1
Objective 1.4	Identify how to maintain computer equipment and solve common problems relating to computer hardware		
IC^3-1 1.4.1	Identify how to protect computer hardware from theft or damage	No	SE 15 (GO) OLC GO EA 1.1

Computers and You

Reading Guide

Before You Read

Vocabulary Journal As you read, you will come across a number of important key terms. To help you understand these words and recall their meanings, draw four columns on a piece of paper and label them: *Key Terms*, *What is it?*, *What else is it like?*. *What are some examples?* Then, write down each key term you see and answer the questions.

Key Concepts

- How technology affects your everyday life
- How technology is used at home, school, and work
- How you can use technology ethically and safely

Vocabulary

Key Terms

technology
microprocessor
telecommute
ethics
virus
hacker

Academic Vocabulary

communicate
predict
device
vary

Technology in Our Lives

Technology is the use of science to solve practical problems. Technology affects us in so many ways because it is everywhere. The cars, computers, and electronic gadgets that surround you every day are products of technology.

The use of technology goes back much farther than you might think. Ancient peoples who used sundials and created calendars to keep track of time were the technological experts of their eras. When farmers first used plows to grow crops, they applied technology to solve the problem of providing food for their families. It is only in the past 50 or so years, however, that technology really has changed the way people work, play, and **communicate**, or stay in touch.

Technology Solves Problems

Problem	Technology	Solution
How can we create a standard measurement of time?		A sundial marks the position of the sun at specific times of the day.
How can one person prepare and plant a field?		A plow, pulled by an animal, turns the soil so that seeds can be planted.
How can people make calls when they are away from their home or office?		Cell phones allow people to communicate over long distances without the need for wires.

▲ Technology has always been an important part of human progress. What new technology would you like to see developed?

Technology has become such an essential part of our daily lives that when computers are not working, it can become more difficult to do everyday tasks, whether you are trying to finish your homework or pump gas at the gas station.

Standardized Coding Number	Objectives & Abbreviated Skill Sets	Performance Based	Location (Page #)
IC^3-1 1.4.2	Identify factors that can cause damage to computer hardware or media (e.g. heat and humidity)	No	SE 15 (GO) OLC GO EA 1.2
IC^3-1 1.4.3	Identify how to protect computer hardware from fluctuations in the power supply, power outages, and other electrical issues	No	SE 15 (GO) OLC GO EA 1.2
IC^3-1 1.4.4	Identify common problems associated with computer hardware such as inoperable hardware devices	No	SE 15 (GO) OLC GO EA 1.2
IC^3-1 1.4.5	Identify common problems that can occur if hardware is not maintained properly	No	SE 15 (GO) OLC GO EA 1.2
IC^3-1 1.4.6	Identify maintenance that can be performed routinely by users such as cleaning and defragmenting hard drives	No	SE 15 (GO) OLC GO EA 1.2
IC^3-1 1.4.7	Identify maintenance that should ONLY be performed by experienced professionals	No	SE 15 (GO) OLC GO EA 1.2
IC^3-1 1.4.8	Identify the steps required to solve computer-related problems	No	SE 15 (GO) OLC GO EA 1.2
Domain 2.0: Computer Software	This domain includes the knowledge and skills required to identify how software works, software categories such as operating systems, applications and utilities, fundamental concepts and best uses of each type of software, and which application is best used for a specific purpose.		
Objective 2.1	Identify how software and hardware work together to perform computing tasks and how software is developed and upgraded		
IC^3-1 2.1.1	Identify how hardware and software interact	No	SE 41, 44, 47 (GO) OLC GO TT 2.3 TRM 158
IC^3-1 2.1.2	Identify simple terms and concepts related to the software development process	No	SE 47 (GO) OLC GO TT 2.3
IC^3-1 2.1.3	Identify issues relating to software upgrades such as pros and cons and methods to upgrade	No	SE 47 (GO) OLC GO TT 2.3

UNIT 1

Technology in Your Life

Real World Projects

Go Online **e-QUIZ**

glencoe.com

Starting with You To find out how many times a day you use technology, go to the **Online Learning Center** at glencoe.com. Choose **e-Quizzes**, and take the **Unit 1 Pre-Quiz**.

Standardized Coding Number	Objectives & Abbreviated Skill Sets	Performance Based	Location (Page #)
Objective 2.2	Identify different types of software, general concepts relating to software categories, and the tasks to which each type of software is most suited or not suited		
IC^3-1 2.2.1	Identify fundamental concepts relating to word processing and common uses for word-processing applications	No	SE 135, 139, 141, 146
IC^3-1 2.2.2	Identify fundamental concepts relating to spreadsheets and common uses for spreadsheet applications	No	SE 215, 218, 240–244
IC^3-1 2.2.3	Identify fundamental concepts relating to presentation software and common uses for presentation applications	No	SE 312–348
IC^3-1 2.2.4	Identify fundamental concepts relating to databases and common uses for database applications	No	SE 267–275
IC^3-1 2.2.5	Identify fundamental concepts relating to graphic and multimedia programs and common uses for graphic or multimedia software	No	SE 45 (GO), 47 (GO),59, 135,160–162, 373–375 OLC GO TT 2.2, GO TT 2.3 TRM 161
IC^3-1 2.2.6	Identify the types and purposes of different utility programs	No	SE 15 (GO), 47 (GO) OLC GO EA 1.2, GO TT 2.3
IC^3-1 2.2.7	Identify other types of software	No	SE 47 (GO) OLC GO TT 2.3
IC^3-1 2.2.8	Identify how to select the appropriate application(s) for a particular purpose, and problems that can arise if the wrong software product is used for a particular purpose	No	SE 47

Operating Your Computer

Computer Concepts in Action was written to reach a wide range of computer users with various levels of computer experience. Access to a computer, the Internet, and Microsoft Windows and Microsoft Office software are an important part of the course.

Recommended Hardware and Software

Specific directions and illustrations are given for Microsoft Windows Vista and Microsoft Office 2007, but teachers can easily tailor activities to previous versions of the Windows and Office software. (Note to Macintosh users: Most material in this text book can be modified for use in Mac platform. However, Windows and Access coverage will not be applicable for the MacOS.)

Equipment Needs

	Hardware	Software
Required	• Computer • Color monitor • (Make sure your equipment meets or exceeds the system requirements of your software.) • Mouse • Keyboard	• Microsoft Windows Vista, XP, 2000, or 98 • Internet browser (such as Microsoft Internet Explorer, Netscape Navigator, and so on.) • Microsoft Office 2007, 2003, XP, or 2000 (Note: Microsoft Office includes Word, Excel, Access, and PowerPoint.) • Word 2007, 2003, XP (or 2002), or 2000 • Microsoft Excel 2007, 2003, XP (or 2002), or 2000 • Microsoft Access 2007, 2003, XP (or 2002), or 2000 • Microsoft PowerPoint 2007, 2003, XP (or 2002), or 2000
Recommended	• Floppy drive, CD drive, or DVD drive • CD burner, or Zip drive, or other storage drive and media • Printer • Scanner • Microphone	• Microsoft Outlook 2007, 2003, 2002, or 2000 (Note: Outlook may be included in your version of Microsoft Office.)

Using Student Data Files

To complete some exercises in this book, Data Files are required.

- When you see the Data File icon, locate the needed files before beginning the exercise.
- Data Files are available on the Online Learning Center at glencoe.com and on the Teacher Resource DVD. Your teacher will tell you where to find these files.
- Some exercises require you to continue working on a file you created in an earlier exercise. If you are absent and cannot complete the previous exercise, your teacher may choose to provide you with the Solution File for the missed exercise. Solution Files are also available on the Online Learning Center and the Teacher Resource DVD.

Standardized Coding Number	Objectives & Abbreviated Skill Sets	Performance Based	Location (Page #)
Domain 3.0: Using an Operating System	This domain includes the knowledge and skills required to perform the most frequently used functions of an operating system. Elements include the ability to install and run software, control the workspace (desktop), perform file management and change system settings (display, date and time settings, etc.). For purposes of this domain, the operating system used as an example for performance based questions is Windows, the most popular PC operating system.		
Objective 3.1	Identify what an operating system is and how it works, and solve common problems related to operating systems		
IC^3-1 3.1.1	Identify the purpose of an operating system and the difference between operating system and application software	No	SE 48
IC^3-1 3.1.2	Identify different operating systems including DOS, Windows and Macintosh	No	SE 48
IC^3-1 3.1.3	Identify the difference between interacting with character-based and graphical operating systems	No	SE 48
IC^3-1 3.1.4	Identify the capabilities and limitations imposed by the operating system	No	SE 48
IC^3-1 3.1.5	Identify and solve common problems related to operating systems	No	SE 20, 47, 48 (Real World)
Objective 3.2	Manipulate and control the Windows desktop, files and disks		
IC^3-1 3.2.1	Identify elements of the Windows desktop	No	SE 21, 52, 61–63
IC^3-1 3.2.2	Manipulate windows such as minimizing windows	Yes	SE 25–27
IC^3-1 3.2.3	Shut down, Logoff, and restart the computer	Yes	SE 20, 32, 33 (Help)
IC^3-1 3.2.4	Use the Windows Start menu and Taskbar	Yes	SE 21-23, 24 (Real World), 25, 70–71
IC^3-1 3.2.5	Manipulate desktop folders and icons	Yes	SE 61–63 SIM A-1, A-5
IC^3-1 3.2.6	Manage files using the Windows Explorer/File Manager	Yes	SE 20, 52–61, 63–65 TRM 164 SIM A-1, A-2, A-3, A-5, A-6
IC^3-1 3.2.7	Identify precautions one should take when manipulating files including using standardized naming conventions	No	SE 45 (GO), 57, 59, 475 OLC GO TT 2.2 TRM 164 SIM A-3

Operate Microsoft Office 2007 Using Windows XP (Continued)

Use Windows XP and Insert SmartArt

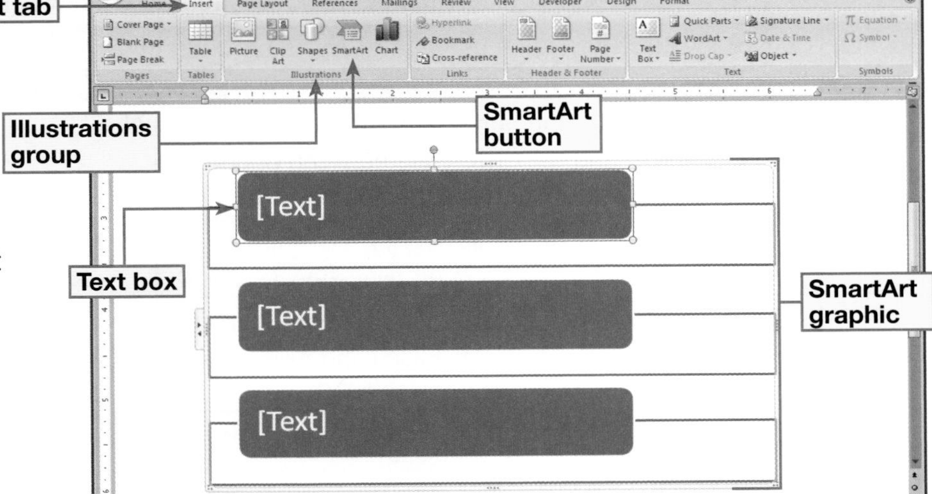

1. Click where you want to insert the SmartArt graphic.
2. On the Ribbon, on the Insert tab, in the Illustrations group, select the SmartArt button.
3. In the Choose a SmartArt Graphic dialog box, select the type and layout of the SmartArt graphic.
4. The graphic will appear in the area that you designated. On the left side of the SmartArt graphic is the Text Pane Launcher. Click the Launcher to enter text into the graphic.
5. The Text pane will open either on the left or right side of the graphic, depending on the space available. Key your text into the appropriate spots in the Text pane. The Live Preview function shows the text in the graphic as you key it in the Text pane.
6. To close the Text pane, select the Text pane close button in the top-right corner of the pane.

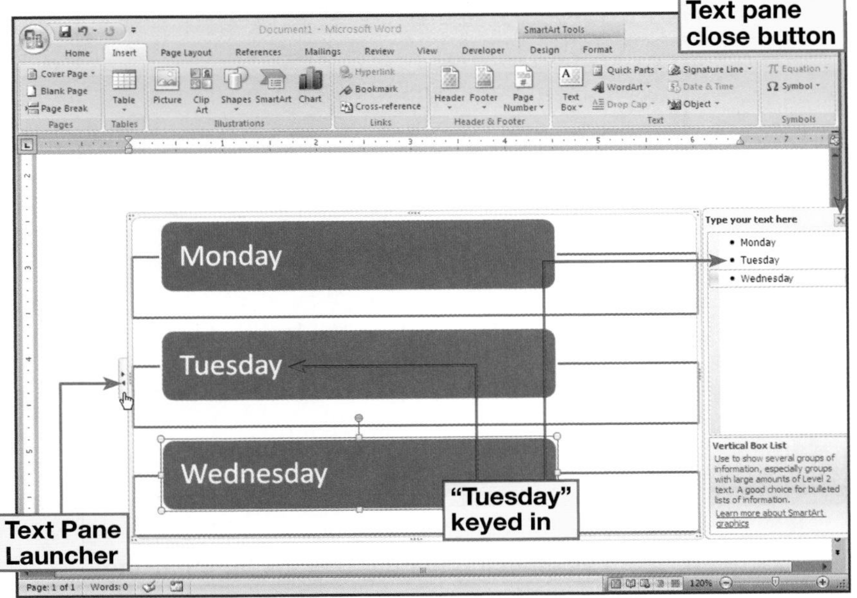

Standardized Coding Number	Objectives & Abbreviated Skill Sets	Performance Based	Location (Page #)
IC^3-1 3.2.8	Solve common problems associated with working with files	No	SE 45 (GO), 54, 57, 59, 135 OLC GO TT 2.2 SIM A-1, A-3
Objective 3.3	Identify how to change system settings, install and remove software		
IC^3-1 3.3.1	Display control panels	Yes	SE 484 SIM C-1
IC^3-1 3.3.2	Identify different control panel settings	No	SE 484 SIM C-1
IC^3-1 3.3.3	Change simple control panel settings such as date and time settings	Yes	SE 484 (TechSavvy), 485–488 SIM C-2, C-3, C-4, C-5
IC^3-1 3.3.4	Display and update a list of installed printers	Yes	SE 489 SIM C-5
IC^3-1 3.3.5	Identify precautions regarding changing system settings	No	SE 484 SIM C-1
IC^3-1 3.3.6	Install software including installing updates from online sources	Yes	TRM 154, 157
IC^3-1 3.3.7	Identify common problems associated with installing and running applications	No	SE 47 (GO) OLC GO TT 2.3

For more information about IC^3 and the Exam Objectives, visit certiport.com.

Operate Microsoft Office 2007 Using Windows XP (Continued)

Use Windows XP to Save a Document (Continued)

Sometimes you might want to use the Save As function instead of the Save function. The Save As and Save functions perform differently. The Save function will replace the original file with the new file. The Save As function will leave the original document as it was and will save the revised document as a separate file with a new name.

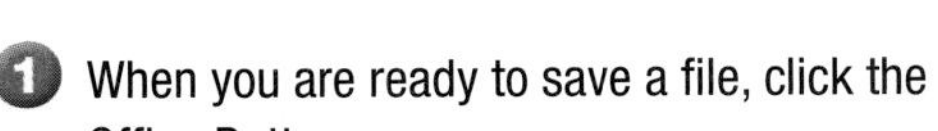

1. When you are ready to save a file, click the Office Button.
2. On the Office menu, select Save As. The Save As dialog box will open.
3. In the Save As dialog box, select the Save in box drop-down arrow. Ask your teacher where the file should be saved, and navigate to that location.
4. Double-click the name of the save location. The name should now be the only item located in the Save in box.
5. In the File name box, key the name under which you would like to save the file. Give the file a new name that distinguishes it from the original document. Click the Save button in the lower-right corner to save your file.

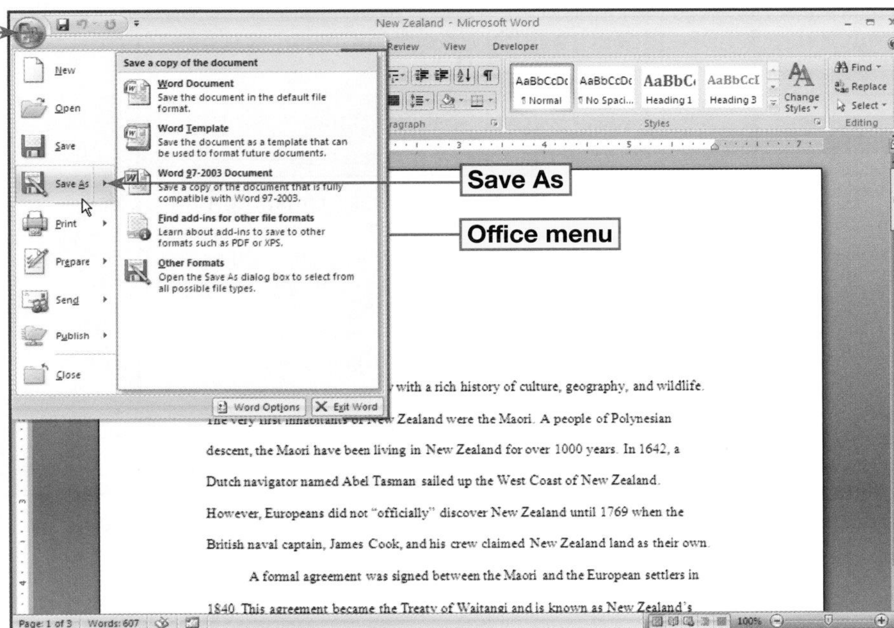

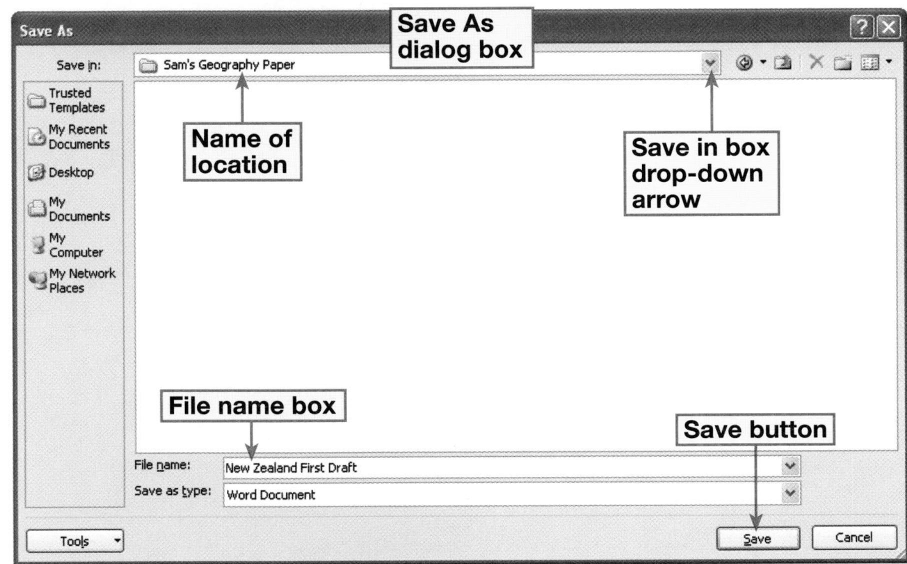

IC^3 - Module 2: Key Applications

Total Domains: 4 Total Objectives: 9

Standardized Coding Number	Objectives & Abbreviated Skill Sets	Performance Based	Location (Page #)
Domain 1.0: Common Program Functions	This domain includes the knowledge and skills required to perform functions common to all Windows applications with an emphasis on the common functionality of the Microsoft Office applications Word, Excel and PowerPoint. Skills and knowledge covered in this domain will concentrate on those features considered basic and - to the largest extent possible - applicable to all Windows-based word processors, spreadsheets and presentation programs. Elements include the ability to start and exit either the Word or Excel application, modify the display of toolbars and other on-screen elements, use online help, and perform file management, editing, formatting and printing functions common to Word, Excel, PowerPoint and most Windows applications.		
Objective 1.1	Be able to start and exit a Windows application and utilize sources of online help		
IC^3-2 1.1.1	Start a Windows application	Yes	SE 135, 216, 312
IC^3-2 1.1.2	Exit a Windows application	Yes	SE 136, 224, 324
IC^3-2 1.1.3	Identify and prioritize help resources, including online help within software and contacting a help desk	No	SE 70–72, 72 (TechSavvy), 73–78
IC^3-2 1.1.4	Use various forms of automated help	Yes	SE 70–72, 72 (TechSavvy), 73–78
Objective 1.2	Identify common on-screen elements of Windows applications, change application settings and manage files within an application		
IC^3-2 1.2.1	Identify on-screen elements common to Windows applications (e.g. menus, toolbars and document windows)	No	SE 21, 23, 52, 135, 136, 138, 215–216
IC^3-2 1.2.2	Display or hide toolbars	Yes	SE 135, 136
IC^3-2 1.2.3	Switch between open documents	Yes	SE 25–26
IC^3-2 1.2.4	Change views	Yes	SE 146–147
IC^3-2 1.2.5	Change magnification level	Yes	SE 146
IC^3-2 1.2.6	Create files	Yes	SE 135–138, 148 (GO), 317–319 OLC GO EA 4.1
IC^3-2 1.2.7	Open files within an application and from the Windows desktop, identify file extensions including .xls or .doc	Yes	SE 20, 25, 52–63, 137, 153, 215 TRM 161
IC^3-2 1.2.8	Save files in specified locations/formats	Yes	SE 55–56, 61–63, 137–138, 143, 148 (GO), 199–200 OLC GO EA 4.1
IC^3-2 1.2.9	Close files	Yes	SE 137–138, 148

Operate Microsoft Office 2007 Using Windows XP (Continued)

Use Windows XP to Open a Document (Continued)

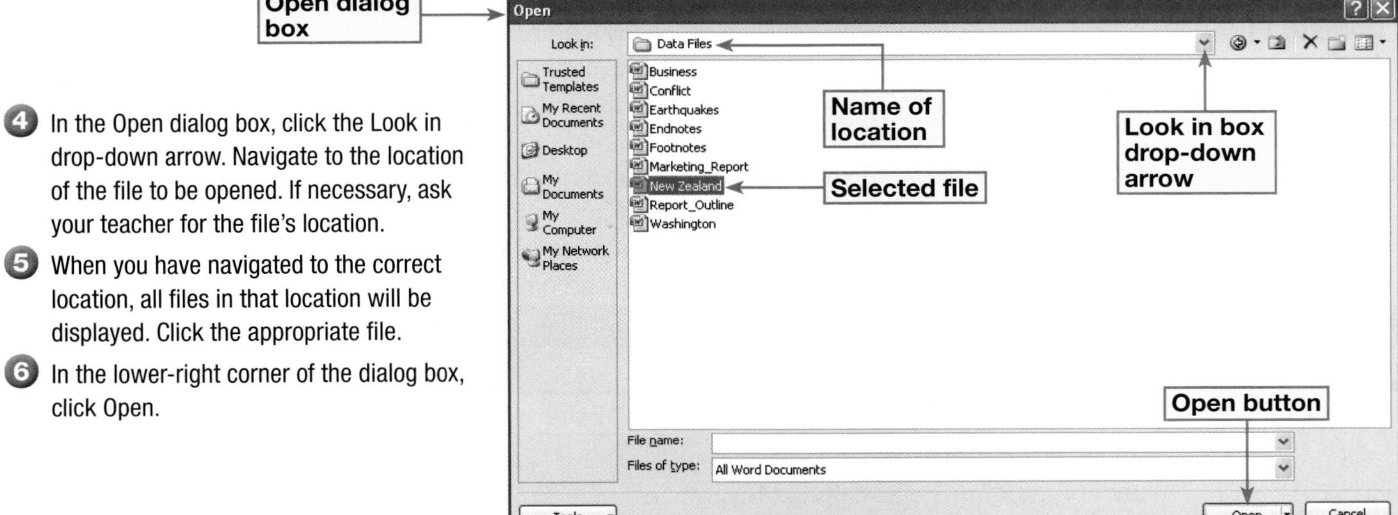

4. In the Open dialog box, click the Look in drop-down arrow. Navigate to the location of the file to be opened. If necessary, ask your teacher for the file's location.
5. When you have navigated to the correct location, all files in that location will be displayed. Click the appropriate file.
6. In the lower-right corner of the dialog box, click Open.

Use Windows XP to Save a Document

1. When you are ready to save a file, click the Office Button to display the Office menu.
2. In the Office menu, click Save. If the file has been saved before, it will be saved, with your changes, to the same location with the same file name. If the file has not been saved before, the Save As dialog box will open.
3. In the Save As dialog box, select the Save in box drop-down arrow. Ask your teacher where the file should be saved, and navigate to that location.
4. Double-click the name of the save location. The name should now be the only item located in the Save in box.
5. In the File name box, key the name under which you would like to save the file. Click the Save button in the lower-right corner.

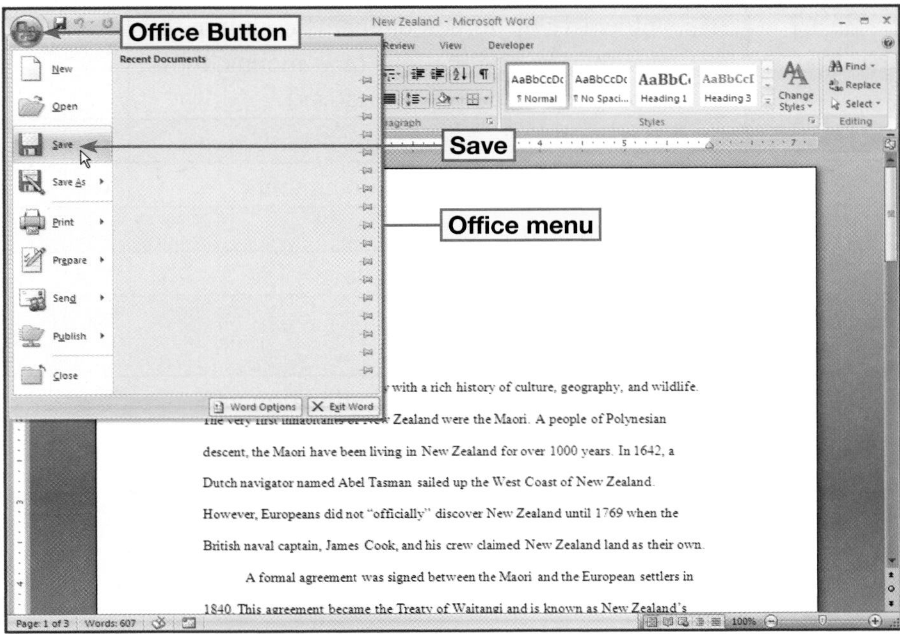

Standardized Coding Number	Objectives & Abbreviated Skill Sets	Performance Based	Location (Page #)
IC^3-2 1.2.10	Identify and solve common problems relating to working with files (e.g. product or version incompatibility)	No	SE 48, 57 (TechSavvy), 59, 479 SIM A-4
Objective 1.3	Perform common editing and formatting functions		
IC^3-2 1.3.1	Navigate around open files using scroll bars, keyboard shortcuts, etc.	Yes	SE 27, 215, 217–218, 322 TRM 335
IC^3-2 1.3.2	Insert text and numbers in a file	Yes	SE 140, 218, 313
IC^3-2 1.3.3	Perform simple editing (e.g. cut, copy and move information)	Yes	SE 141 (TechSavvy), 141–143
IC^3-2 1.3.4	Use the Undo, Redo, and Repeat commands	Yes	SE 140 (Help)
IC^3-2 1.3.5	Find information	Yes	SE 194–195
IC^3-2 1.3.6	Replace information	Yes	SE 194–195
IC^3-2 1.3.7	Check spelling	Yes	SE 144–145
IC^3-2 1.3.8	Perform simple text formatting	Yes	SE 153–157, 196–197
IC^3-2 1.3.9	Insert pictures into a file	Yes	SE 160–162, 192–193
IC^3-2 1.3.10	Modify pictures in a file	Yes	SE 161–162, 163 (GO), 192 OLC GO EA 4.4
IC^3-2 1.3.11	Add drawn objects into a file, including creating and modifying objects	Yes	SE 329, 330, 374–375
Objective 1.4	Perform common printing functions		
IC^3-2 1.4.1	Format a document for printing	Yes	SE 157, 163 (GO), 169 OLC GO EA 4.5
IC^3-2 1.4.2	Preview a file before printing	Yes	SE 103
IC^3-2 1.4.3	Print files, specifying common print options	Yes	SE 163
IC^3-2 1.4.4	Manage printing and print jobs	Yes	SE 163 (GO) OLC GO EA 4.5
IC^3-2 1.4.5	Identify and solve common problems associated with printing	Yes	SE 163 (GO) OLC GO EA 4.5

Operate Microsoft Office 2007 Using Windows XP (Continued)

Use Windows XP to Start a Program (Continued)

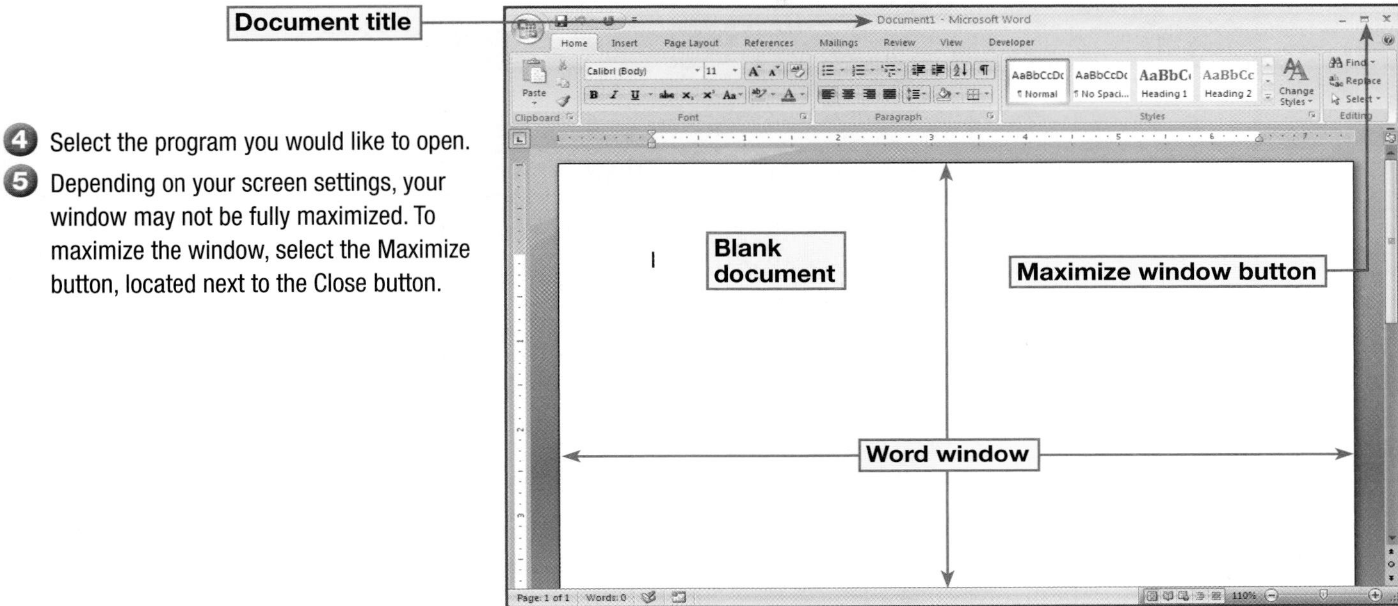

4. Select the program you would like to open.
5. Depending on your screen settings, your window may not be fully maximized. To maximize the window, select the Maximize button, located next to the Close button.

Use Windows XP to Open a Document

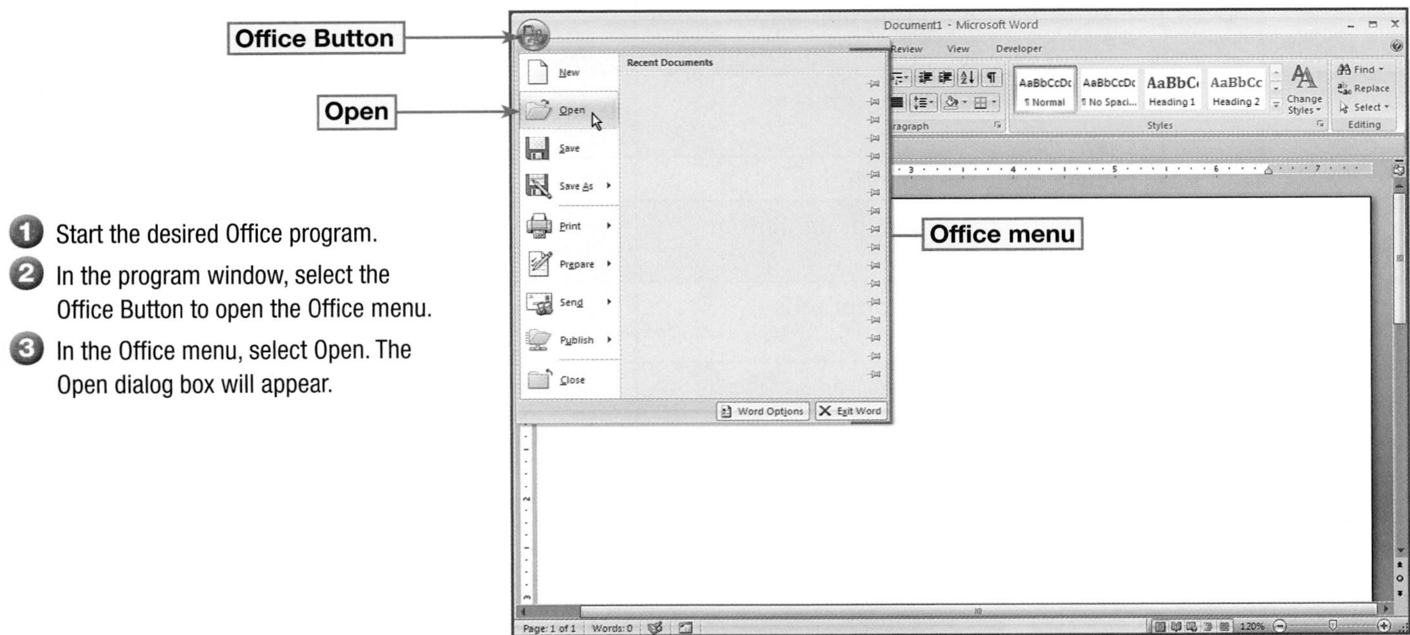

1. Start the desired Office program.
2. In the program window, select the Office Button to open the Office menu.
3. In the Office menu, select Open. The Open dialog box will appear.

Standardized Coding Number	Objectives & Abbreviated Skill Sets	Performance Based	Location (Page #)
Domain 2.0: Word Processing Functions	This domain includes the knowledge and skills required to perform functions specific to creating documents with a word processor (as opposed to common functions such as those identified in Domain 1: Common Program Functions). Elements include paragraph formatting (including line spacing, indenting and creating bulleted or numbered lists), document formatting (including headers and footers), applying styles and other automatic formatting options, creating tables, applying borders and shading to text and tables.		
Objective 2.1	Be able to format text and documents including the ability to use automatic formatting tools		
IC^3-2 2.1.1	Identify on-screen formatting information, including breaks, paragraph markers, etc.	Yes	SE 171–172
IC^3-2 2.1.2	Select word, line, paragraph, document	Yes	SE 143, 176
IC^3-2 2.1.3	Change line and paragraph spacing	Yes	SE 168–170
IC^3-2 2.1.4	Indent text	Yes	SE 171–172
IC^3-2 2.1.5	Create and modify bulleted and numbered lists	Yes	SE 158–159, 163 (GO) OLC GO EA 4.5
IC^3-2 2.1.6	Use outline structure to format a document	Yes	SE 402–403
IC^3-2 2.1.7	Insert symbols/special characters	Yes	SE 196–198
IC^3-2 2.1.8	Insert date and time	Yes	SE 200 (GO), 316 OLC GO EA 4.9
IC^3-2 2.1.9	Insert, view and print document comments	Yes	SE 200 (GO) OLC GO EA 4.9
IC^3-2 2.1.10	Display the ruler	Yes	SE 171, 368
IC^3-2 2.1.11	Use tabs	Yes	SE 171–172
IC^3-2 2.1.12	Insert and delete a page break or section break	Yes	SE 178, 187-188
IC^3-2 2.1.13	Insert, modify, and format page numbers	Yes	SE 178–180
IC^3-2 2.1.14	Create, modify, and format headers and footers	Yes	SE 174–175
IC^3-2 2.1.15	Create, modify, and format footnotes and endnotes	Yes	SE 131, 180 (GO) OLC GO EA 4.6
IC^3-2 2.1.16	Apply borders and shading to text paragraphs	Yes	SE 192
IC^3-2 2.1.17	Create, modify and apply styles	Yes	SE 200 (GO) OLC GO EA 4.7
IC^3-2 2.1.18	Copy formatting (Format Painter)	Yes	SE 155

Operate Microsoft Office 2007 Using Windows XP

Glencoe's *Computer Concepts in Action* has been created and written to show Microsoft Office 2007 on the new Windows Vista operating system. Microsoft Office 2007 can also be used with the Windows XP operating system.

Most tasks can be completed on either operating system with the instructions in this book. However, there are a few tasks that have slightly different instructions or may not look exactly the same as in the textbook. This section shows the steps needed to complete these tasks with Windows XP.

The following steps are shown using Microsoft Word 2007, but the steps apply to all Office 2007 applications. Depending on how hardware and software was installed on your computer, you may need to ask your teacher for further instruction.

Use Windows XP to Start a Program

1. In the Windows taskbar, click the Start button.
2. In the Start menu, select Programs.
3. In the Programs menu, select Microsoft Office.

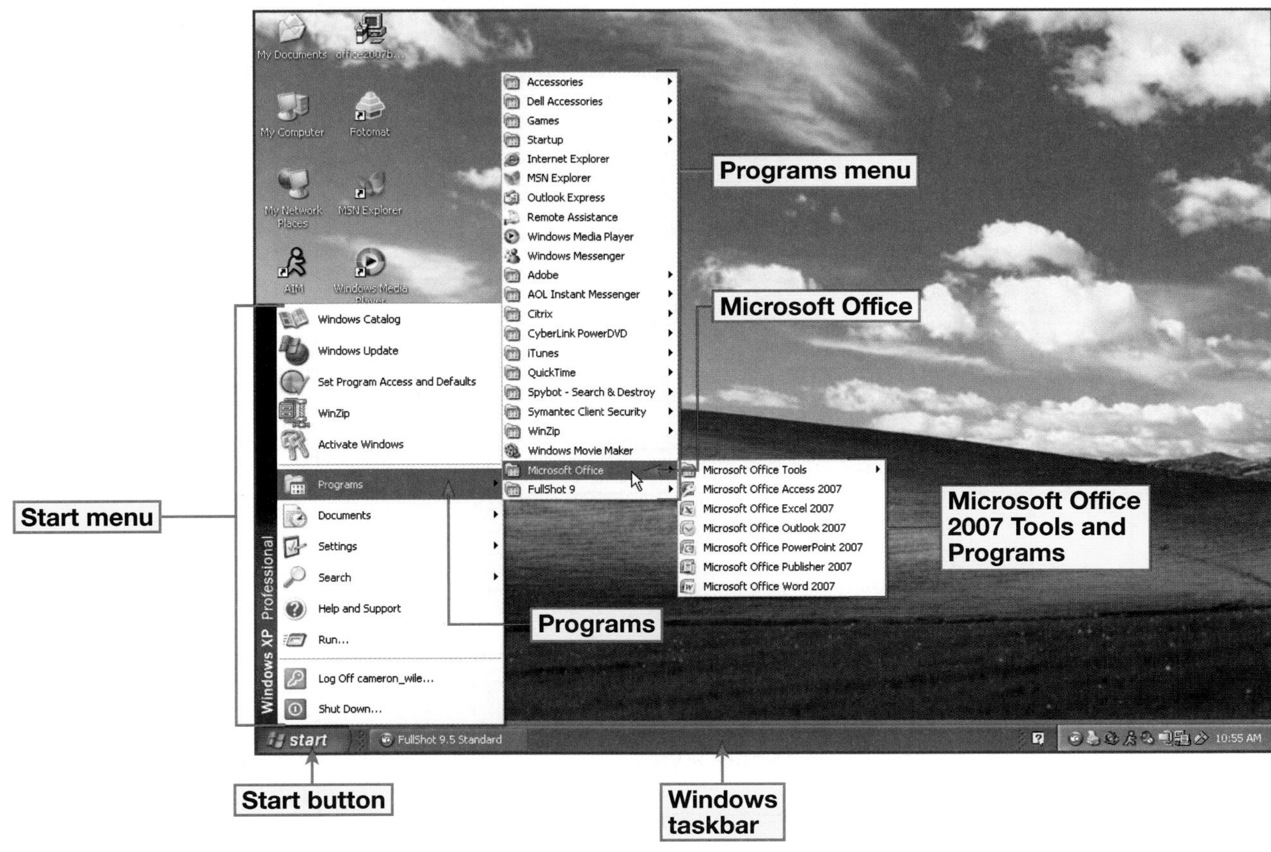

Standardized Coding Number	Objectives & Abbreviated Skill Sets	Performance Based	Location (Page #)
IC^3-2 2.1.19	Use language tools	Yes	SE 144–145
IC^3-2 2.1.20	Use track changes in a document	Yes	SE 200 (GO) OLC GO EA 4.9
IC^3-2 2.1.21	Display document statistics	Yes	SE 173
Objective 2.2	Be able to insert, edit and format tables in a document		
IC^3-2 2.2.1	Create a table	Yes	SE 189, 200 (GO) OLC GO EA 4.8
IC^3-2 2.2.2	Insert and edit data in a table	Yes	SE 190–191
IC^3-2 2.2.3	Modify table structure	Yes	SE 190, 200 (GO), 219, 222, OLC GO EA 4.8
IC^3-2 2.2.4	Format tables	Yes	SE 189–191, 200 (GO) OLC GO EA 4.8
IC^3-2 2.2.5	Sort data in a table	Yes	SE 240–241
Domain 3.0: Spreadsheet Functions	This domain includes the knowledge and skills required to analyze information in an electronic spreadsheet and to format information using functions specific to spreadsheet formatting (as opposed to common formatting functions included in Domain 1). Elements include the ability to use formulas and functions, sort data, modify the structure of an electronic worksheet, and edit and format data in worksheet cells. Elements also include the ability to display information graphically using charts, and to analyze worksheet data as it appears in tables or graphs.		
Objective 3.1	Be able to modify worksheet data and structure and format data in a worksheet		
IC^3-2 3.1.1	Identify how a table of data is organized in a spreadsheet	No	SE 215, 218
IC^3-2 3.1.2	Select information with the keyboard and mouse including selecting rows, columns, and worksheets	Yes	SE 218–219, 224
IC^3-2 3.1.3	Insert and modify data	Yes	SE 218–219
IC^3-2 3.1.4	Modify table structure	Yes	SE 219, 222, 222 (TechSavvy), 223 TRM 228
IC^3-2 3.1.5	Identify and change number formats, including currency, date and time, and percentage formats	Yes	SE 229–230
IC^3-2 3.1.6	Apply borders and shading to cells	Yes	SE 218
IC^3-2 3.1.7	Specify cell alignment (e.g. wrapping text within a cell)	Yes	SE 223–224 TRM 228
IC^3-2 3.1.8	Apply table AutoFormats	Yes	SE 200 (GO) OLC GO EA 4.8

Security Tools

Microsoft Office 2007 includes new security features that protect your documents and computer from hacking and identity theft.

Mark as Final

After you have finished a document, you can use the Mark as Final command to make the document read-only, which prevents any changes from being made. This allows you to share the document with others without the fear of anything being lost or changed.

The Mark as Final command is located in the Microsoft Office Button menu, in the Prepare section.

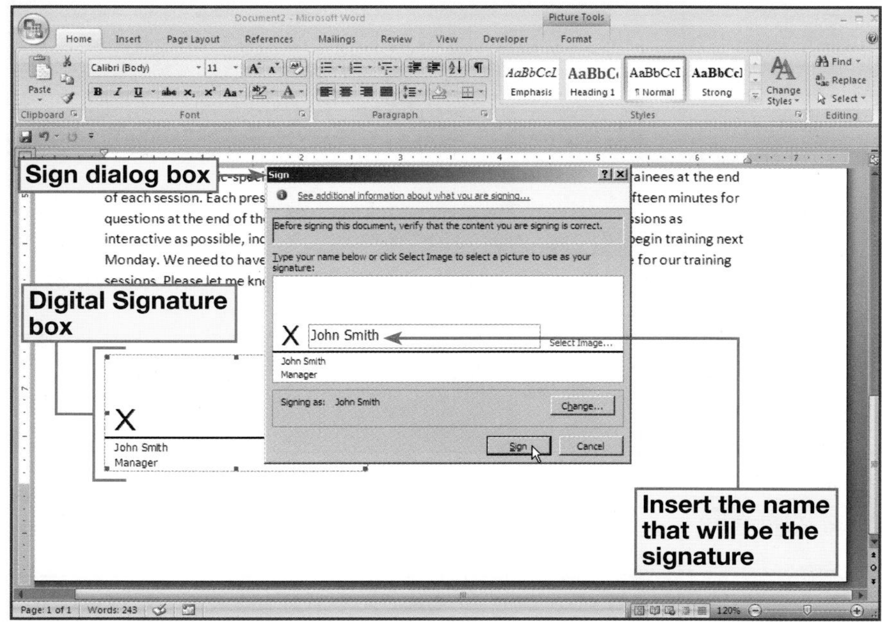

Digital Signatures

You can also digitally sign a document to authenticate any digital information that you create, such as documents, e-mails, macros, and databases. Cryptography assures that the content has not been changed since the document was signed.

Standardized Coding Number	Objectives & Abbreviated Skill Sets	Performance Based	Location (Page #)
Objective 3.2	Be able to sort data, manipulate data using formulas and functions and add and modify charts in a worksheet.		
IC^3-2 3.2.1	Sort worksheet data	Yes	SE 240–241, 243 (TechSavvy)
IC^3-2 3.2.2	Demonstrate an understanding of absolute vs. relative cell addresses	No	SE 234, 234 (TechSavvy), 235
IC^3-2 3.2.3	Insert arithmetic formulas into worksheet cells	Yes	SE 229–230, 235 (GO) OLC GO EA 5.1 TRM 233
IC^3-2 3.2.4	Demonstrate how to use common worksheet functions (e.g. SUM, AVERAGE, and COUNT)	Yes	SE 231–233
IC^3-2 3.2.5	Insert formulas that include worksheet functions into cells	Yes	SE 235 (GO) OLC GO EA 5.1
IC^3-2 3.2.6	Modify formulas and functions	Yes	SE 235 (GO) OLC GO EA 5.1
IC^3-2 3.2.7	Use AutoSum	Yes	SE 231–233
IC^3-2 3.2.8	Identify common errors made when using formulas and functions	No	SE 235 (GO) OLC GO EA 5.1
IC^3-2 3.2.9	Draw simple conclusions based on tabular data in a worksheet	No	SE 239–247
IC^3-2 3.2.10	Insert and modify charts in a worksheet	Yes	SE 240, 242, 244–247
IC^3-2 3.2.11	Be able to identify if a presented chart accurately represents worksheet data shown in a table	No	SE 244
IC^3-2 3.2.12	Identify appropriate chart types for presenting different types of information	No	SE 244

Quick Styles

While themes change the overall colors, fonts, and effects of a document, Quick Styles determine how those elements are combined and which color, font, and effect will be the dominant style. Roll your pointer over each Quick Style to get a Live Preview.

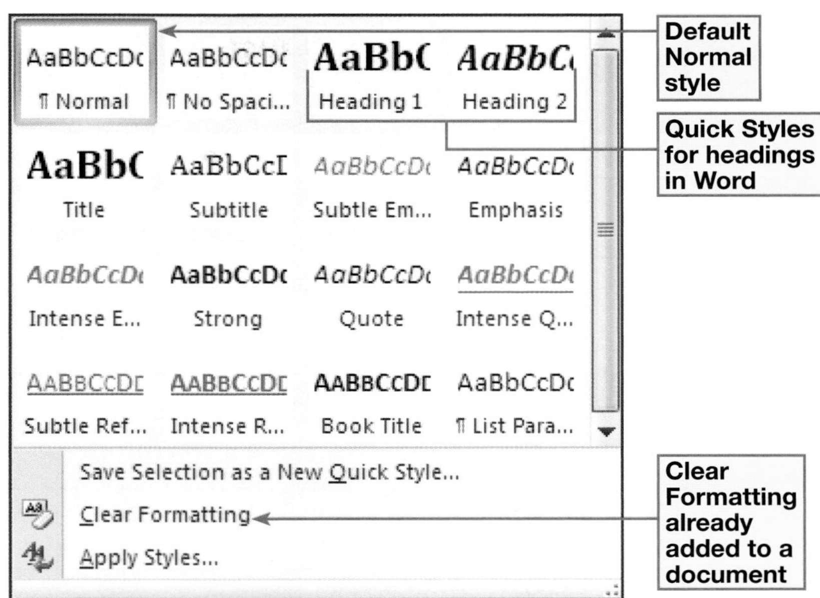

Word 2007 allows you to choose from specific styles for headings, quotations, and titles, or you can choose from a Style Set list to format your entire document. You can even choose a Style Set first and then apply Quick Styles to some elements.

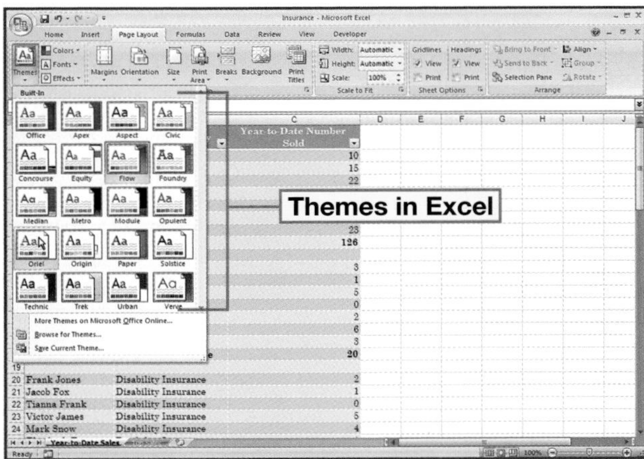

Excel 2007 offers cell styles that work like Quick Styles. In the Themes group, click the Themes drop-down arrow to choose a theme.

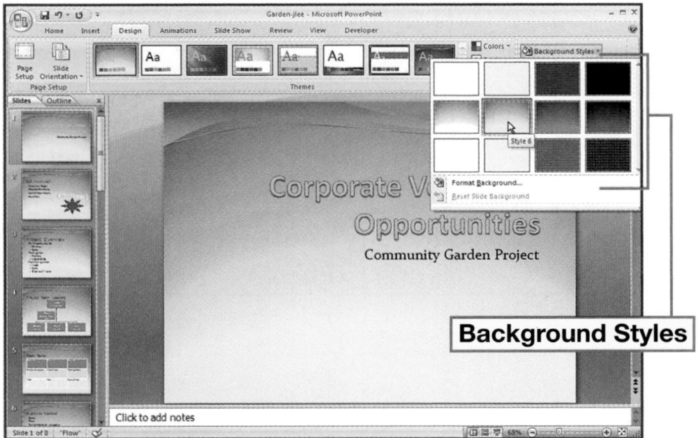

PowerPoint 2007 uses Quick Styles with the Background Styles function, located on the Design tab. The background styles can be used with any of the themes in PowerPoint.

Standardized Coding Number	Objectives & Abbreviated Skill Sets	Performance Based	Location (Page #)
Domain 4.0: Communicating with Presentation Software	This domain includes the knowledge and skills required to communicate effectively with presentation software such as Microsoft PowerPoint, and to use simple functions specific to creating and editing presentations (as opposed to common functions included in Domain 1: Common Program Functions). Elements include the ability to create and modify slides in a presentation, create different types of presentation output and identify the most effective ways to use a presentation program to communicate with others.		
Objective 4.1	Be able to create and format simple presentations		
IC^3-2 4.1.1	Identify effective design principles for simple presentations	No	SE 317, 317 (TechSavvy), 327
IC^3-2 4.1.2	Manage slides (e.g. delete a slide)	Yes	SE 313, 322 (GO), 344 OLC GO EA 7.3
IC^3-2 4.1.3	Add information to a slide	Yes	SE 314, 322 (GO), 327, 329, 336–338, 338 (GO) OLC GO EA 7.1, GO EA 7.3
IC^3-2 4.1.4	Change slide view	Yes	SE 314–316
IC^3-2 4.1.5	Change slide layout	Yes	SE 315
IC^3-2 4.1.6	Modify a slide background	Yes	SE 317–318
IC^3-2 4.1.7	Assign transitions to slides	Yes	SE 334–335
IC^3-2 4.1.8	Change the order of slides in a presentation	Yes	SE 314–315, 323
IC^3-2 4.1.9	Create different output elements (speaker's notes, handouts, etc.)	Yes	SE 342–346
IC^3-2 4.1.10	Preview the slide show presentation	Yes	SE 321
IC^3-2 4.1.11	Navigate an on-screen slide show	Yes	SE 321–322

For more information about IC^3 and the Exam Objectives, visit certiport.com.

Design and Layout Tools

The enhanced design and layout functions in Microsoft Office 2007 allow you to produce professional-looking documents quickly and easily.

Themes

Themes can be applied with one click to provide consistent fonts, charts, shapes, tables, and so on throughout an entire document.

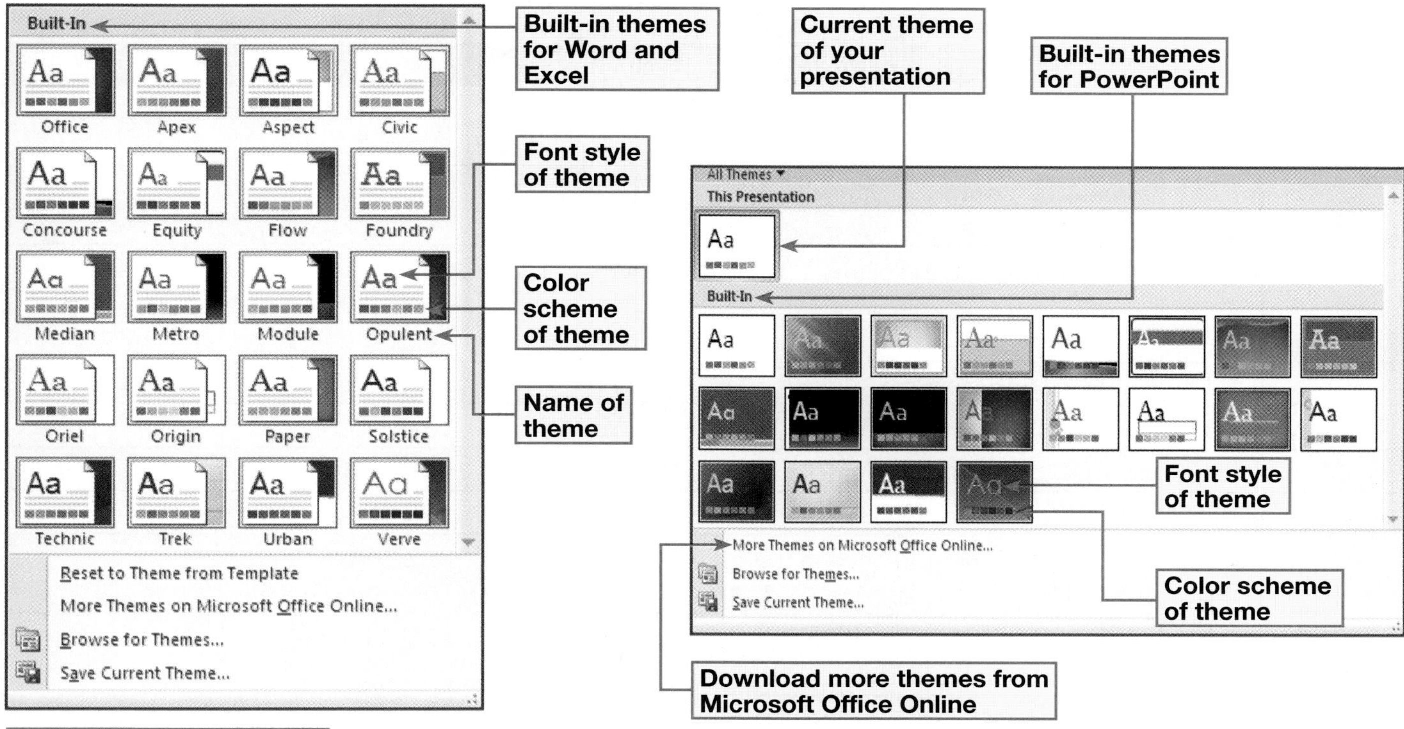

Preview of theme applied to document

The entire document is linked to a theme. If the theme is changed, new colors, fonts, and effects are applied to the entire document.

Microsoft Office 2007 also allows you to see how a theme would look in a document without applying the theme. As the pointer is rolled over each theme, the document changes to show a Live Preview of what it would look like with each theme. Additional themes are available through Microsoft Office Online.

IC^3 - Module 3: Living Online

Total Domains: 4 Total Objectives: 11

Standardized Coding Number	Objectives & Abbreviated Skill Sets	Performance Based	Location (Page #)
Domain 1.0: Networks and the Internet	This domain includes the knowledge of common terminology associated with computer networks and the Internet, components and benefits of networked computers, the difference between different types of networks (for example, LAN and WAN), and how computer networks fit into other communications networks (like the telephone network and the Internet).		
Objective 1.1	Identify network fundamentals and the benefits and risks of network computing		
IC^3-3 1.1.1	Identify terminology relating to telecommunications, networks, and the Internet	No	SE 49 (GO) 86–91 OLC GO TT 2.4
IC^3-3 1.1.2	Identify types of networks	No	SE 49
IC^3-3 1.1.3	Identify how networks work	No	SE 49 (GO) OLC GO TT 2.4
IC^3-3 1.1.4	Identify benefits of networked computing	No	SE 49
IC^3-3 1.1.5	Identify the risks of networked computing	No	SE 264 (GO) OLC GO TT 6.1
IC^3-3 1.1.6	Identify fundamental principles of security on a network	No	SE 264 (GO) OLC GO TT 6.1
Objective 1.2	Identify the relationship between computer networks, other communications networks (like the telephone network) and the Internet		
IC^3-3 1.2.1	Identify the different ways the telephone system is used to transmit information	No	SE 89 (GO) OLC GO TT 3.1
IC^3-3 1.2.2	Identify that telecommunication devices such as modems convert information from analog to digital and digital to analog formats	No	SE 89 (GO) OLC GO TT 3.1
IC^3-3 1.2.3	Identify the units used to measure data transmission rates	No	SE 89 (Real World)
IC^3-3 1.2.4	Identify the Internet as a "super network" of smaller computer networks and that computers connect to the Internet via the "onramp" of a smaller computer network	No	SE 89 (GO) OLC GO TT 3.1
IC^3-3 1.2.5	Identify the hardware and software required to connect to the Internet	No	SE 89

Contextual Tabs

Contextual tabs appear only when you work with certain objects. Contextual tabs are available with objects such as charts, tables, and pictures.

In Microsoft Word 2007 and Microsoft PowerPoint 2007, the Picture Tools contextual tab appears when you insert a picture into a document or slide. Included in the Picture Tools tab is the Format tab, which contains groups to help you adjust, place, and style the picture.

When you have finished working with the picture, select an area outside of the picture's boundaries. The Picture Tools tab disappears.

In Microsoft Excel 2007, the Chart Tools contextual tab appears when you want to insert a chart into a worksheet. Included in the Chart Tools tab are the Design, Layout, and Format tabs, which all contain groups to help you insert a chart.

When you have finished working on the chart and select an area outside of the chart's boundaries, the Chart Tools tab disappears.

Word Ribbon

PowerPoint Ribbon

Excel Ribbon

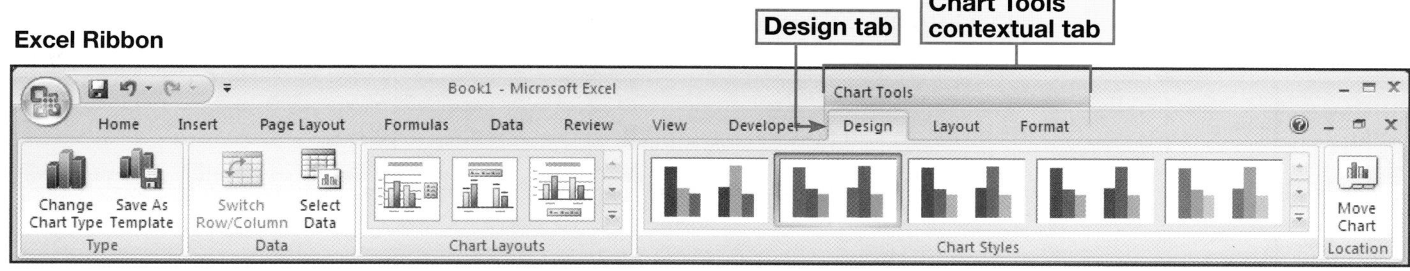

Standardized Coding Number	Objectives & Abbreviated Skill Sets	Performance Based	Location (Page #)
IC^3-3 1.2.6	Identify different types of Internet connections and the advantages and disadvantages of each connection type	No	SE 89
IC^3-3 1.2.7	Identify the roles and responsibilities of an Internet Service Provider (ISP)	No	SE 88
Domain 2.0: Electronic Mail	This domain includes the knowledge and skills required to identify how electronic mail works, the makeup of an e-mail address and other communications methods such as instant messaging. The domain also includes the ability to use an electronic mail software package and to identify the "rules of the road" (i.e., "netiquette") regarding the use of electronic mail.		
Objective 2.1	Identify how electronic mail works		
IC^3-3 2.1.1	Identify how electronic mail works on a network and on the Internet	No	SE 91
IC^3-3 2.1.2	Identify the components of an electronic mail message	No	SE 469, 469 (TechSavvy), 470–472 SIM B-2, B-3
IC^3-3 2.1.3	Identify the components of an electronic mail address	No	SE 87, 91
IC^3-3 2.1.4	Identify when to use different electronic mail options	No	SE 469 (TechSavvy), 473, 473 (TechSavvy), 474 SIM B-2, B-3, B-4, B-5
IC^3-3 2.1.5	Identify different ways electronic mail is accessed	No	SE 90
IC^3-3 2.1.6	Identify the difference between standard electronic mail and other forms of messaging, such as paging or Instant Messaging	No	SE 92
Objective 2.2	Identify how to use an electronic mail application		
IC^3-3 2.2.1	Read and send electronic mail messages	Yes	SE 469–470, 472–473, 473 (TechSavvy), 474–475 SIM B-2, B-3, B-4, B-5, B-6
IC^3-3 2.2.2	Identify ways to supplement a mail message with additional information	No	SE 471, 472 SIM B-3
IC^3-3 2.2.3	Manage attachments	Yes	SE 471–472 SIM B-3
IC^3-3 2.2.4	Manage mail	Yes	SE 468, 470, 470 (TechSavvy), 472, 475 SIM B-1, B-2, B-4, B-5, B-6

The Mini Toolbar

The Mini Toolbar appears when you select text and enables you to format the text at the point of use in the document instead of with the Ribbon. The Mini Toolbar includes fonts, font styles, font size, alignment, indentation, bullets, and text color.

When text is selected, the Mini Toolbar is semitransparent until you roll your pointer over it. When the pointer rests on the toolbar, it becomes opaque.

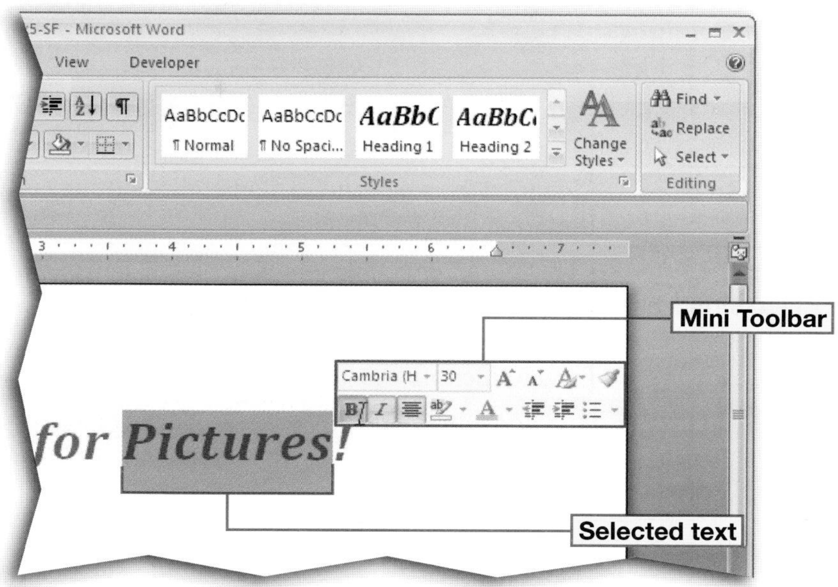

Options Dialog box

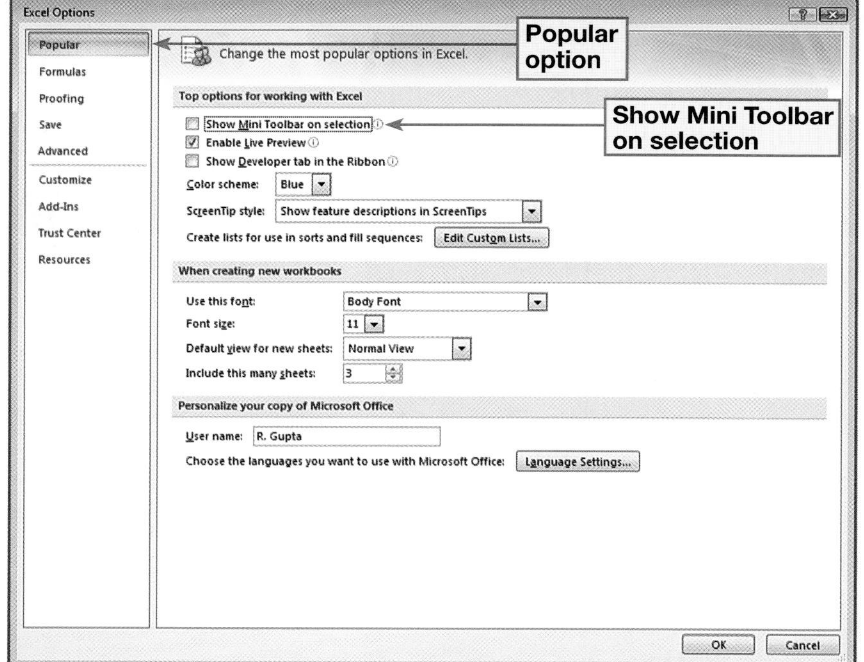

To turn off the Mini Toolbar:

- Click the Microsoft Office Button
- Select the application's Options button in the lower-right corner
- Select Popular from the listing of options
- Clear the Show Mini Toolbar on selection check box.

To turn the Mini Toolbar back on:

- Click the Microsoft Office Button
- Select the application's Options button in the lower-right corner
- Select Popular from the listing of options
- Select the Show Mini Toolbar on selection check box

Standardized Coding Number	Objectives & Abbreviated Skill Sets	Performance Based	Location (Page #)
IC^3-3 2.2.5	Manage addresses	Yes	SE 477, 478 SIM B-7, B-8
IC^3-3 2.2.6	Identify the purpose of frequently used mail-configuration options	No	SE 479, 480 SIM B-8
Objective 2.3	Identify the appropriate use of e-mail and e-mail related "netiquette"		
IC^3-3 2.3.1	Identify the advantages of electronic mail	No	SE 90 TRM 155
IC^3-3 2.3.2	Identify common problems associated with electronic mail	No	SE 90, 91 (GO), 92, 92 (GO), 473, 480 OLC GO TT 3.2, GO TT 3.3 SIM B-2, B-3, B-4
IC^3-3 2.3.3	Identify the elements of professional and effective e-mail messages	No	SE 92 (GO), 469, 479 OLC GO TT 3.3 SIM B-1, B-2, B-8
IC^3-3 2.3.4	Identify when other forms of correspondence are more appropriate than e-mail	No	SE 92 (GO) OLC GO TT 3.3 TRM 155
IC^3-3 2.3.5	Identify when to include information from an original e-mail message in a response as a method of tracking the "history" of e-mail communication	No	SE 473–474 SIM B-4
IC^3-3 2.3.6	Identify appropriate use of e-mail attachments and other supplementary information	No	SE 471, 473–474 SIM B-3
IC^3-3 2.3.7	Identify issues regarding unsolicited e-mail ("spam") and how to minimize or control unsolicited mail	No	SE 92
IC^3-3 2.3.8	Identify effective procedures for ensuring the safe and effective use of electronic mail	No	SE 91 (GO), 92 (GO), 264 (GO), 475 OLC GO TT 3.2, GO TT 3.3, GO TT 6.1
Domain 3.0: Using the Internet	This domain includes the knowledge the skills required to identify information and resources that are available on the Internet and use a Web browsing application. Elements include the ability to identify elements of Web pages and Web sites and how to determine the quality of information found online. Elements also include the ability to use a Web browsing application such as Microsoft Internet Explorer® to browse the Internet.		

Zoom Settings

The zoom level of the screen increases or reduces the size of objects within the window. When proofreading a Word document, you might want a higher zoom level in order to see the text more clearly. When working in a large Excel worksheet, you might want a lower zoom level to see all of the data at once.

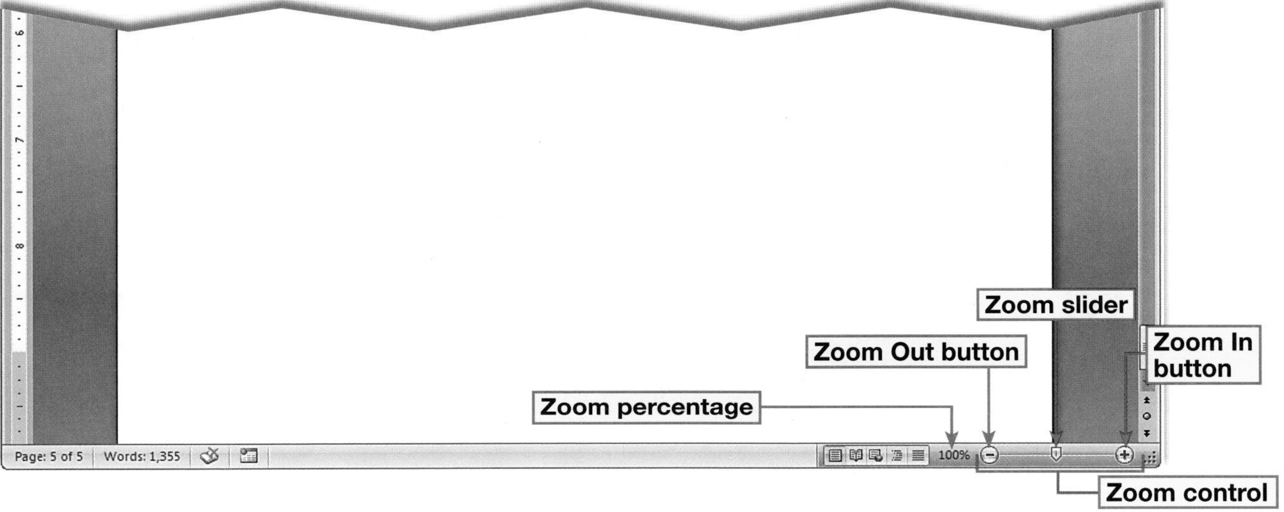

To adjust the zoom level of a program window, use the **Zoom control** at the lower-right corner of the window.

- Click the Zoom In or Zoom Out button to increase or decrease the size of the items on screen by 10 percent increments.
- You can also use the slider to select a specific zoom amount.

You can also adjust the zoom level in the **Zoom dialog box.** To access the Zoom dialog box:

- Click the View tab.
- In the Zoom group, select the Zoom button.

The Zoom dialog box allows you to select a preset zoom level or to enter a specific custom zoom level.

Zoom dialog box

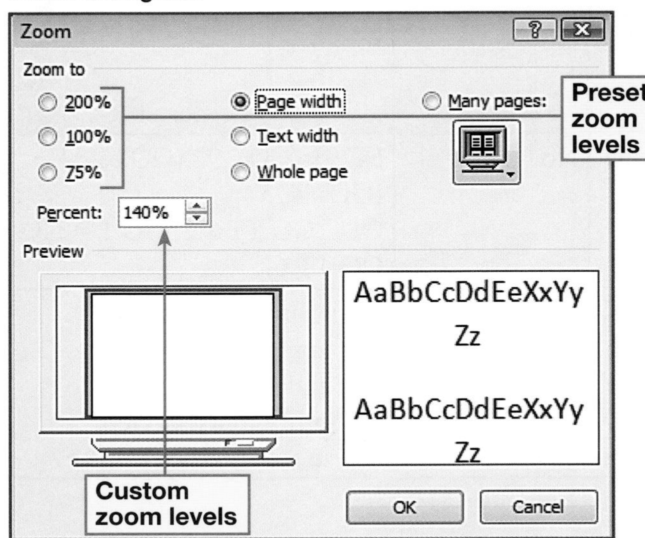

Standardized Coding Number	Objectives & Abbreviated Skill Sets	Performance Based	Location (Page #)
Objective 3.1	Identify different types of information sources on the Internet		
IC^3-3 3.1.1	Identify terminology related to the Internet	No	SE 86–94 TRM 163
IC^3-3 3.1.2	Identify the purpose of a browser in accessing information on the World Wide Web	No	SE 89
IC^3-3 3.1.3	Identify different elements of a Web site	No	SE 87, 97–98
IC^3-3 3.1.4	Identify different types of Web sites by their extensions, and the purposes of different types of sites	No	SE 87, 87 (Real World)
IC^3-3 3.1.5	Identify the difference between secure and unsecure Web sites (such as password-protected sites or sites secure for online transactions) and how to tell if a Web site is secure	No	SE 263–264 (GO) OLC GO TT 6.1
IC^3-3 3.1.6	Identify different ways of communicating and corresponding via the Internet	No	SE 94 TRM 155
Objective 3.2	Be able to use a Web browsing application		
IC^3-3 3.2.1	Identify the make-up of a Web address/ Uniform Resource Locator (URL)	No	SE 86–87
IC^3-3 3.2.2	Navigate the Web using a browser	Yes	SE 97–99, 99 (TechSavvy)
IC^3-3 3.2.3	Reload/Refresh the view of a Web page	Yes	SE 98 (TechSavvy)
IC^3-3 3.2.4	Show a history of recently visited Web sites and delete the list of recently visited Web sites	Yes	SE 101–102 TRM 161
IC^3-3 3.2.5	Find specific information on a Web site	Yes	SE 99
IC^3-3 3.2.6	Manage Bookmarked sites/Favorite sites	Yes	SE 101–102, 102 (TechSavvy)
IC^3-3 3.2.7	Save the content of a Web site for offline browsing	Yes	SE 117–118
IC^3-3 3.2.8	Copy elements of a Web site including copying text or media to another application	Yes	SE 118 (GO) OLC EA 3.1
IC^3-3 3.2.9	Print all or specified parts of a Web site	Yes	SE 103–105
IC^3-3 3.2.10	Download a file from a Web site to a specified location	Yes	SE 118 (GO) OLC GO EA 3.1
IC^3-3 3.2.11	Identify settings that can be modified in a Web browser application	Yes	SE 490 SIM C-7

The Quick Access Toolbar

The Quick Access Toolbar (or QAT) contains frequently used commands. The default location of the QAT is in the upper-left corner of the screen, next to the Microsoft Office Button. To maximize the work area on your screen, keep the Quick Access Toolbar in its default location.

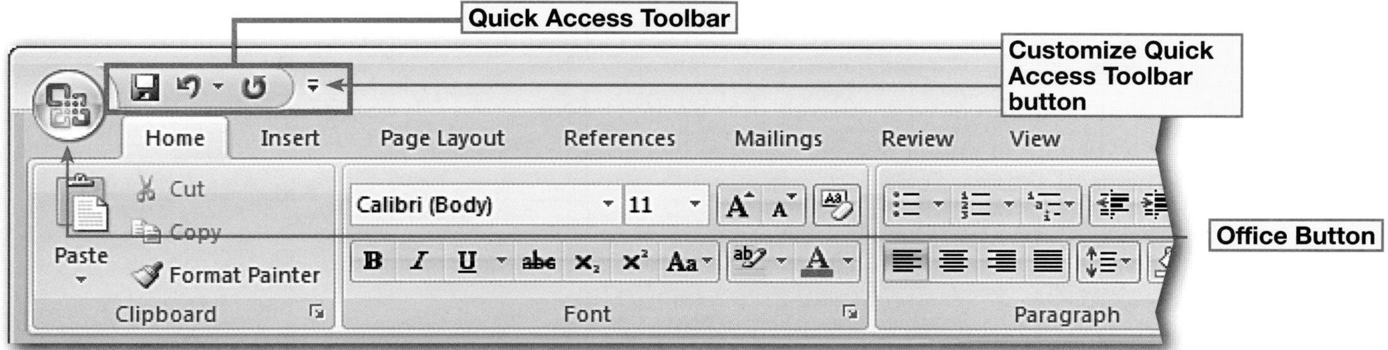

The **Quick Access Toolbar is customizable**, which means that you can add any command to it. To add a command to the Quick Access Toolbar:

- Click the appropriate tab
- Locate the command you want to add
- Right-click the command
- Select Add to Quick Access Toolbar from the shortcut menu

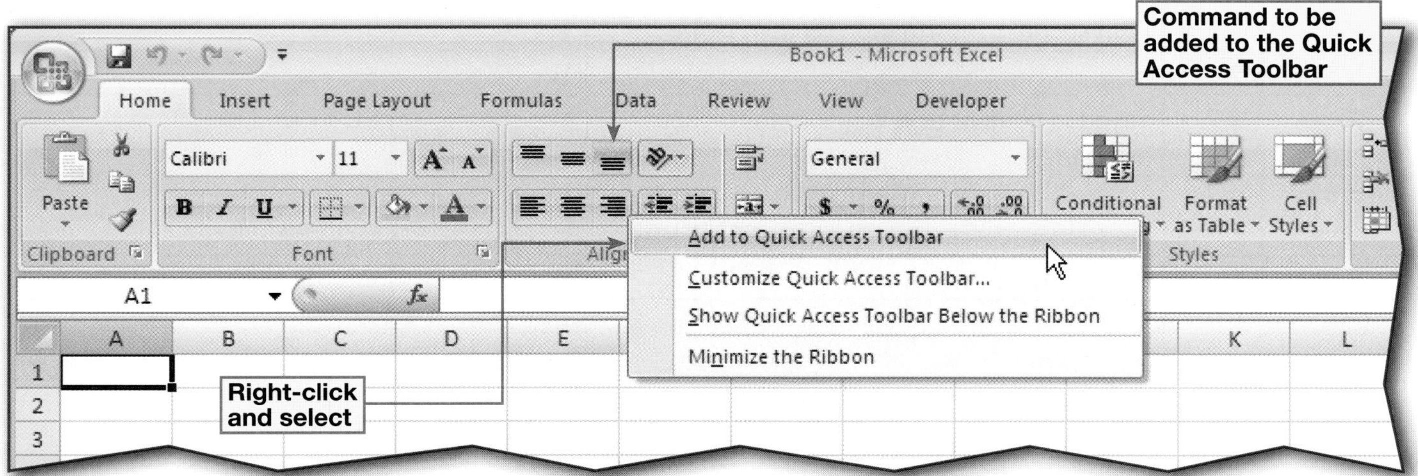

Standardized Coding Number	Objectives & Abbreviated Skill Sets	Performance Based	Location (Page #)
IC3-3 3.2.12	Identify problems associated with using a Web browser	No	SE 89, 114, 261
Objective 3.3	Be able to search the Internet for information		
IC3-3 3.3.1	Identify the ways a search engine classifies and looks for Web sites	No	SE 110
IC3-3 3.3.2	Identify other ways of searching for information on the Web	No	SE 115–116
IC3-3 3.3.3	Use a search engine to search for information based on specified keywords	Yes	SE 110–111
IC3-3 3.3.4	Search effectively	Yes	SE 110, 112–114
IC3-3 3.3.5	Identify issues regarding the quality of information found on the Internet	No	SE 93
IC3-3 3.3.6	Identify how to evaluate the quality of information found on the Web	No	SE 93
Domain 4.0: The Impact of Computing and the Internet on Society	This domain includes the knowledge and skills required to identify the benefits and risks of computing and the role of the Internet in many areas of society, from home and work to school and recreation. Elements include the ability to identify how computers and the Internet are used in different aspects of work, school, and home and how these areas of society are impacted by the availability of computer technology and online resources.		
Objective 4.1	Identify how computers are used in different areas of work, school and home		
IC3-3 4.1.1	Identify how computers and the Internet are used to collect, organize, and evaluate information and promote learning	No	SE 3–5
IC3-3 4.1.2	Identify the technology and processes involved with computers operating "behind the scenes" in everyday activities	No	SE 3
IC3-3 4.1.3	Identify the impact of electronic commerce (e-commerce) on business, individuals, and governments	No	SE 255–256
IC3-3 4.1.4	Identify technologies that support or provide opportunities to the disabled and disadvantaged such as voice recognition	No	SE 361
Objective 4.2	Identify the risks of using computer hardware and software		
IC3-3 4.2.1	Identify how to maintain a safe working environment that complies with legal health and safety rules	No	SE 11, 11 (TechSavvy), 12

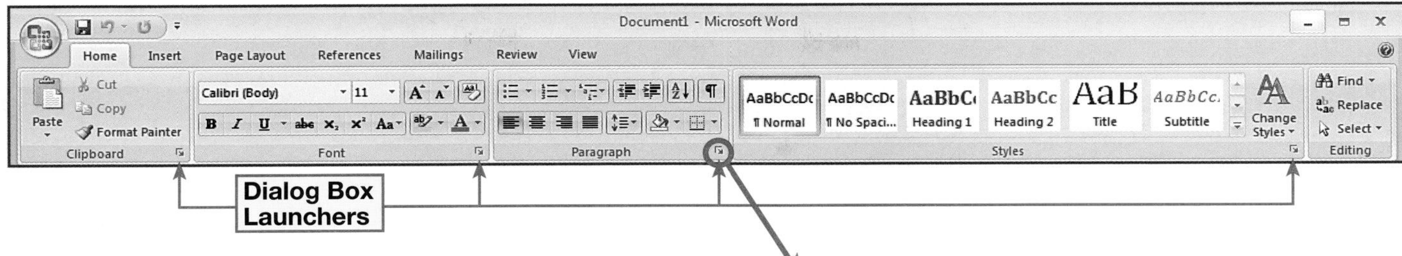

The Dialog Box Launcher

In Office 2007, the dialog boxes have been moved to the appropriate groups in the Ribbon. If a dialog box is available, the **Dialog Box Launcher** will be in the bottom right corner of the group and will open a dialog box with the same name as the group. For example, the Paragraph group's Dialog Box Launcher opens the Paragraph dialog box.

Paragraph Dialog Box

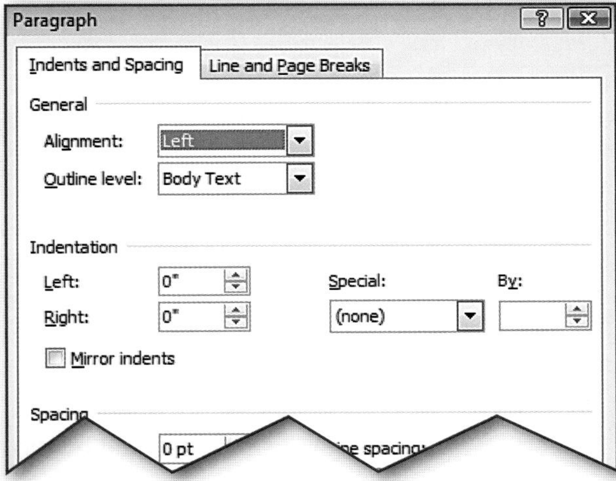

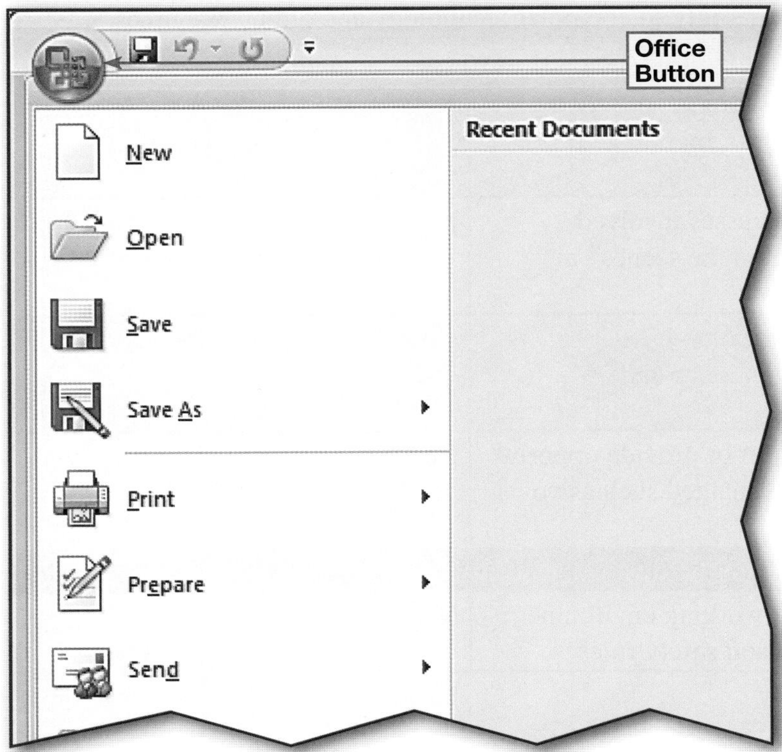

The Microsoft Office Button

The Microsoft Office Button, located in the upper-left corner of Microsoft Word, Excel, Access, and PowerPoint, replaces the File menu. You can use the Office Button to open, save, and print your files. The Publish command, new in Office 2007, also allows you to save your file to a server or to sign your document digitally.

Standardized Coding Number	Objectives & Abbreviated Skill Sets	Performance Based	Location (Page #)
IC³-3 4.2.2	Identify injuries that can result from the use of computers for long periods of time	No	SE 12–13
IC³-3 4.2.3	Identify risks to personal and organizational data	No	SE 264 (GO) OLC GO TT 6.1
IC³-3 4.2.4	Identify software threats, including viruses and WORMS	No	SE 91 (GO) OLC GO TT 3.2
Objective 4.3	Identify how to use computers and the Internet safely, legally, ethically and responsibly		
IC³-3 4.3.1	Identify reasons for restricting access to files, storage devices, computers, networks, and certain Internet sites	No	SE 94
IC³-3 4.3.2	Identify concepts related to intellectual property laws including copyrights, trademarks, and plagiarism	No	SE 126, 128 (GO), 131; OLC GO TT 4.1
IC³-3 4.3.3	Identify the principles regarding when information can or cannot be considered personal, including the difference between computer systems owned by schools or businesses that may have rules and guidelines as to who owns data stored on the system, and computers owned by individuals	No	SE 128 (GO) OLC GO TT 4.1
IC³-3 4.3.4	Identify how to avoid hazards regarding electronic commerce, including giving credit card information only on secure sites	No	SE 263
IC³-3 4.3.5	Identify how to protect privacy and personal security online, including understanding how Web sites track your activity online using "cookies" and other "behind-the-scenes" systems	No	SE 262–263
IC³-3 4.3.6	Identify how to find information about rules regarding the use of computers and the Internet, including laws, use policies at school, and company guidelines at places of employment	No	SE 14–15
IC³-3 4.3.7	Identify how to stay informed about changes and advancements in technology	No	SE 357
IC³-3 4.3.8	Identify how to be a responsible user of computers and the Internet	No	SE 358–360

For more information about IC³ and the Exam Objectives, visit certiport.com.

The **Access Ribbon** makes it easy to create and use a database:

- You can insert records into a datasheet with the Records group on the Home tab.
- You can then use the Database Tools tab to examine the records more closely.
- The Show/Hide group, located in the Database Tools tab, allows you to see relationships between multiple records as well as multiple databases.

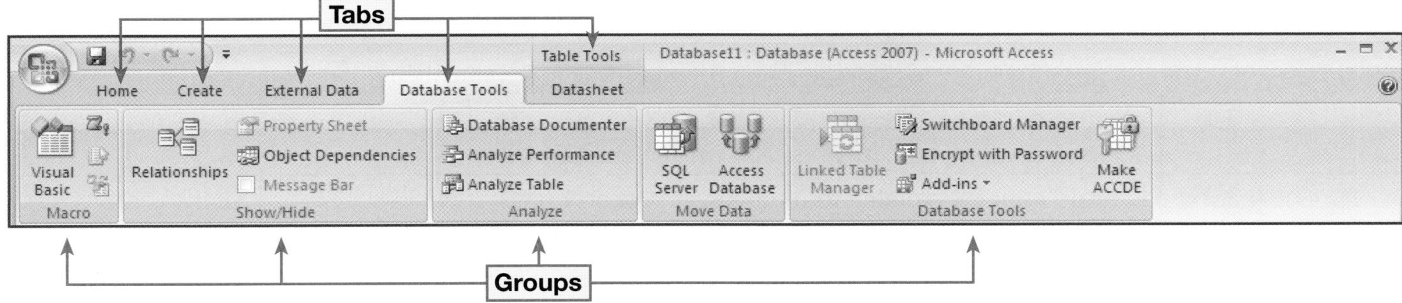

The **PowerPoint Ribbon** helps you to design and create presentations with ease:

- You can manage a presentation with the Slide Show tab, which includes the Set Up group and the Start Slide Show group.
- The other tabs separate the basic areas of presentations, such as design and animation, and enable you to create a visual and informative slide show.

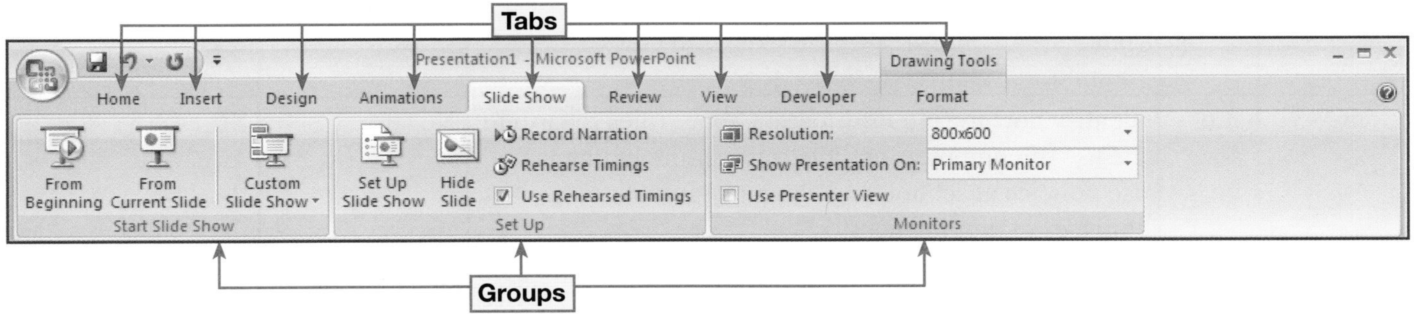

English

How to use the glossary:

1. Look for the term that you want to find in the left column. Its definition appears immediately after the term.
2. The Spanish equivalent of each term and its definition appear in the right column. Other acceptable translations of English terms appear in parentheses.

Español

Cómo usar el glosario en español:

1. Busca el término en inglés que desees encontrar.
2. El término en español, junto con la definición, se encuentra en la columna de la derecha. Otras traducciones aceptables de los términos en inglés se encuentran en parentesis.

A

Acceptable Use Policy (AUP) The rules for safe and proper use of the computers at your school. (p. 14)

accessibility A way of making technology available to all people, despite physical, geographical, or other limitations. (p. 360)

active window The visible application or icon currently in use. (p. 25)

affect To produce an effect upon. (p. 212)

align To line items up or arrange items along a line. (p. 156)

alignment The arrangement of text lined up along the left, center, right, or across the page. (p. 156)

animation The simulated effects used to move text or other objects on a slide. (p. 334)

application A software program that lets you perform specific tasks, like organizing information, creating reports, or printing a picture. (p. 25)

arithmetic operator A symbol that represents a specific action such as adding, subtracting, multiplying, or dividing. (p. 229)

arrow key Key on the keyboard used to move the cursor or insertion point on the screen. (p. 29)

ascending sort To arrange data in order from A to Z, or from smallest number to greatest number. (p. 240)

author One who originates or creates a work. (p. 127)

AutoFit In Excel, a function that can automatically change the width of a column to fit the longest entry or change the height or a row to fit the font. (p. 221)

Política de Uso Aceptable Reglas para el uso seguro y adecuado de las computadoras de tu escuela. (p. 14)

accesibilidad Una manera de asegurar que la tecnología esté disponible a todos, a pesar de las limitaciones físicas, geográficas u otras limitaciones. (p. 360)

ventana activa La aplicación visible o icono de uso en ese momento. (p. 25)

afectar Producir un efecto sobre algo. (p. 212)

alinear Poner en línea los objetos o arreglarlos en una línea. (p. 156)

alineación El arreglo de un texto hacia la izquierda, al centro, a la derecha o a lo ancho de la página. (p. 156)

animación Efectos simulados que se usan para mover un texto u otros objetos en una diapositiva. (p. 334)

aplicación Programa que te permite realizar tareas específicas como organizar la información, crear reportes o imprimir una imagen. (p. 25)

operador aritmético Símbolo que representa una acción específica como sumar, restar, multiplicar o dividir. (p. 229)

teclas de flechas Teclas que se usan para mover el cursor o punto de inserción en la pantalla. (p. 29)

orden ascendente Arreglar los datos en orden de la A a la Z o bien del número más pequeño al más grande. (p. 240)

autor El que es causa primera de alguna cosa. (p. 127)

Autoajustar En Excel es una función que modifica automáticamente el ancho de una columna para que quepa la entrada más extensa o cambia la altura de una fila para que quepa el tipo de fuente. (p. 221)

New Features in Microsoft Office 2007

Microsoft Office 2007 is a collection of software applications, including Word, Excel, Access, and PowerPoint. Like previous versions of Office, Microsoft Office 2007 allows you to create, communicate, and work in a productive manner. Office 2007 contains new features that allow users to create and format documents with greater ease and with a more professional look.

Interface Tools

The Office Ribbon

The Microsoft Office 2007 interface is based around a new tool called the **Ribbon.** The Ribbon groups tools by their functions. The Ribbon is broken into three different portions:

- The **tabs** are divided among the different tasks you can do in an application.
- The **groups** within each tab break the tasks into subtasks. The groups replace the menus used in previous versions of Office.
- The **buttons** within each group carry out commands or display menus of subcommands.

The **Word Ribbon** provides you with related tasks for formatting text. For example, on the Home tab, every task related to fonts is in the Font group. Next to the Font group is the Paragraph group, where you can format text. Other tabs, such as Page Layout and Review, contain tools for those areas.

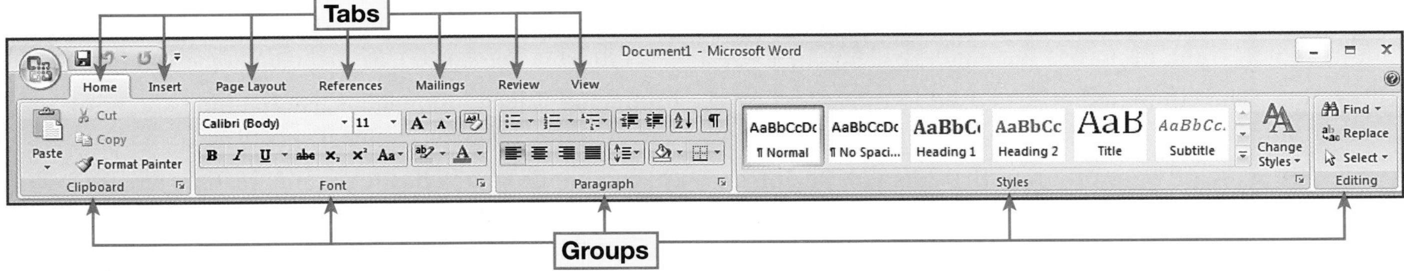

The **Excel Ribbon** allows you to find related tasks involving cell formatting. For example, on the Formulas tab, you can find all major commands involving functions in the Function Library group.

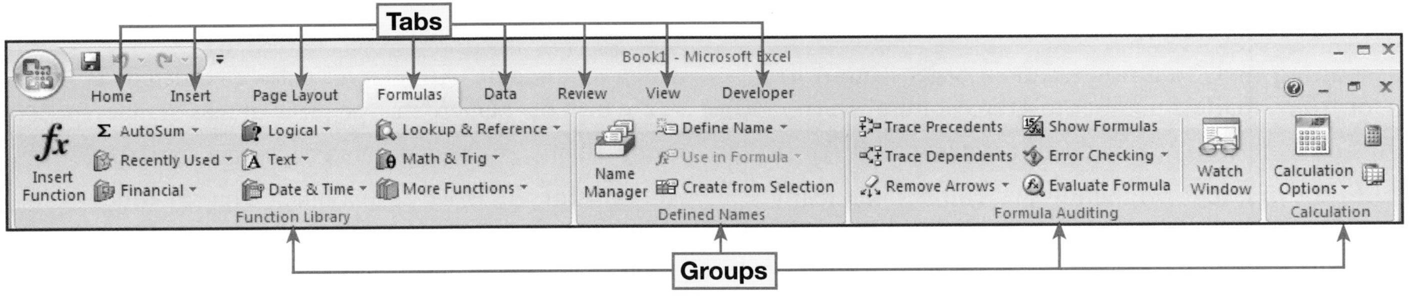

English	Español
AutoSum In Excel, a function that adds a column of numbers above or a row of numbers to the left. (p. 231)	**Autosuma** En Excel es una función que suma una columna de números arriba o una fila de números a la izquierda. (p. 231)
aware Having or showing realization. (p. 263)	**conciente** Tener o demostrar comprensión. (p. 263)

B

English	Español
background An image, like a pattern or a picture, displayed on or used as the desktop (also known as wallpaper). (p. 486)	**fondo (o segundo plano)** Una imagen tal como un patrón o una pintura que se exhibe o se usa en la computadora. También se conoce como papel tapiz. (p. 486)
banner ad A graphical advertisement that takes you to another Web site when you click on it. (p. 260)	**banner publicitario** Anuncio comercial gráfico que lleva hacia otro sitio web cuando haces clic en él. (p. 260)
benefit An advantage. (p. 357)	**beneficio** Ventaja. (p. 357)
binary number The string of 1's and 0's that a computer uses to read and write data. (p. 42)	**binario (o binaria)** Las cadenas de 1 y 0 que usa una computadora para leer y escribir datos. (p. 42)
bit The smallest unit of information, always either a 1 or 0. (p. 42)	**bit** La unidad más pequeña de información que siempre es 1 ó 0. (p. 42)
bookmark A shortcut that takes you directly to a Web page. (p. 101)	**marcador** Método abreviado que te lleva directamente a una página web. (p. 101)
Boolean search A search that uses keywords plus special symbols to find more exact results. (p. 112)	**búsqueda booleana** Búsqueda que utiliza palabras clave más símbolos especiales para encontrar resultados más exactos. (p. 112)
border A format tool that displays a line on any side of an element, often used to separate or distinguish. (p. 191)	**borde** Herramienta de formato que muestra una línea en algún lugar de un elemento y se usa para separar o distinguir. (p. 191)
browser *See* Web browser. (p. 89)	**explorador (o navegador)** *Ver* explorador o navegador de web. (p. 89)
bulleted list A series of text that uses characters, such as dots or diamonds, to present information in no particular order. (p. 158)	**lista con viñetas** Serie de textos en que se usan caracteres como puntos o diamantes para presentar la información sin seguir un orden particular. (p. 158)
business-to-business A business that uses the Web to sell goods and services to other businesses. (p. 259)	**negocio a negocio** Negocio que usa la web para vender bienes y servicios a otros negocios. (p. 259)
business-to-consumer A business that uses the Web to sell things to individual customers. (p. 259)	**negocio a consumidor** Negocio que usa la web para vender objetos a clientes individuales. (p. 259)
byte A byte is 8 bits and is the building block for all other units of information. (p. 42)	**byte** Un byte se compone de 8 bits y es el bloque básico para todas las otras unidades de información. (p. 42)

Locate Appropriate Print and Nonprint Information

In your research, try to use a variety of sources. Because different sources present information in different ways, your research project will be more interesting and balanced when you read a variety of sources.

Literature and Textbooks These texts include any book used as a basis for instruction or a source of information.

Book Indexes A book index, or a bibliography, is an alphabetical listing of books. Some book indexes list books on specific subjects. Others are more general. Some list a variety of topics or resources.

Periodicals Magazines and journals are issued at regular intervals, such as weekly or monthly. One way to locate information in magazines is to use the *Readers' Guide to Periodical Literature.* This guide is available in print form in most libraries.

Technical Manuals A manual is a guide, or handbook, intended to give instruction on how to perform a task or operation. A vehicle owner's manual might give information on how to operate and service a car.

Reference Books Reference books include encyclopedias and almanacs, and are used to locate specific pieces of information.

Electronic Encyclopedias, Databases, and the Internet There are many ways to locate extensive information using your computer. Infotrac, for instance, acts as an online readers guide. CD-ROM encyclopedias can provide easy access to all subjects.

Organize and Convert Information

As you gather information from different sources, taking careful notes, you will need to think about how to **synthesize** the information, or convert it into a unified whole, as well as how to change it into a form your audience will easily understand and that will meet your assignment guidelines.

1. First, ask yourself what you want your audience to know.
2. Then, think about a pattern of organization, a structure that will best show your main ideas. You might ask yourself the following questions:
   - When comparing items or ideas, what graphic aids can I use?
   - When showing the reasons something happened and the effects of certain actions, what text structure would be best?
   - How can I briefly and clearly show important information to my audience?
   - Would an illustration or even a cartoon help to make a certain point?

English	Español
C	
cell The box formed at the intersection of a row and a column, either in a table or a spreadsheet. (p. 189)	**celda** El área que se forma en la intersección de una fila y una columna, ya sea en una tabla o en una hoja de cálculo. (p. 189)
cell address The column letter and row number for each cell. (p. 225)	**dirección de celda** La letra de la columna y el número de la fila de cada celda. (p. 225)
cell pointer In Excel, a square border that indicates an active cell. (p. 215)	**puntero de celda** En Excel es el rectángulo que indica una celda activa. (p. 215)
central processing unit (CPU) A small chip that performs calculations and carries out all instructions given to a computer (also known as microprocessor). (p. 42)	**unidad central de procesamiento (CPU)** Es un chip que realiza cálculos y lleva a cabo las instrucciones que se le dan a la computadora. También se llama microprocesador. (p. 42)
chart A graphic tool used to compare data in a worksheet (also known as a graph). (p. 244)	**gráfica (o gráfico)** Herramienta gráfica que se usa para comparar datos en una hoja de trabajo. (p. 244)
citation A method to provide information about a source used or quoted for a research paper. (p. 176)	**cita** Método para proporcionar información acerca de una fuente usada o mencionada en un documento de investigación. (p. 176)
click-through The number of people moving from one Web site to another, usually because of on-line advertising. (p. 261)	**click-through** El número de personas que se trasladan de un sitio web a otro generalmente debido a publicidad en Internet. (p. 261)
client A customer or patron. (p. 49)	**cliente** El que utiliza los servicios de una entidad. (p. 49)
Clip art Prepared pictures and other artwork that can be inserted into a document. (p. 336)	**imágenes prediseñadas** Son imágenes artísticas prediseñadas que pueden insertarse en un documento. (p. 336)
column Information arranged vertically. (p. 189)	**columna** Información arreglada verticalmente. (p. 189)
communicate To transmit information. (p. 2)	**comunicar** Transmitir información. (p. 2)
Compact Disc (CD) A small optical storage device on which data, such as music, text, or graphic images, is digitally encoded. (p. 46)	**disco compacto (CD)** Disco para almacenamiento óptico de datos, música, textos o imágenes gráficas que se codifican digitalmente. (p. 46)
component A piece of hardware that is part of a computer system. (p. 208)	**componente** Pieza de hardware que es parte del sistema de cómputo. (p. 208)
computer An electronic device that receives, processes, and stores data, and produces a result. (p. 41)	**computadora (o computador)** Dispositivo electrónico que recibe, procesa y almacena datos y produce un resultado. (p. 41)

Draw Conclusions

A conclusion is a general statement you can make and explain with reasoning, or with supporting details from a text. If you read a story describing a sport in which five players bounce a ball and throw it through a high hoop, you may conclude that the sport is basketball.

Analyze

To understand persuasive nonfiction (a text that discusses facts and opinions to arrive at a conclusion), you need to analyze statements and examples to see if they support the main idea. To understand an informational text (such as a textbook, which gives you information, not opinions), you need to keep track of how the ideas are organized to find the main points.

Hint: Use your graphic organizers and notes charts.

Distinguish Facts and Opinions

Learning to determine the difference between facts and opinions is one of the most important reading skills you can learn. A fact is a statement that can be proven. An opinion is what the writer believes. A writer may support opinions with facts, but an opinion cannot be proven. For example:

Fact: California produces fruit and other agricultural products.

Opinion: California produces the best fruit and other agricultural products.

Evaluate

Would you seriously consider an article on nuclear fission if you knew it was written by a comedic actor? If you need to rely on accurate information, you need to find out who wrote what you are reading and why. Where did the writer get information? Is the information one-sided? Can you verify the information?

Reading for Research

You will need to **read actively** in order to research a topic. You might also need to generate an interesting, relevant, and researchable **question** on your own and locate appropriate print and nonprint information from a wide variety of sources. Then you will need to **categorize** that information, evaluate it, and **organize** it in a new way in order to produce a research project for a specific audience. Finally, **draw conclusions** about your original research question. These conclusions may lead you to other areas for further inquiry.

English

computer system The combination of hardware, software, and data working together. (p. 41)

consumer A person who buys products. (p. 255)

consumer-to-consumer A business transaction where one individual uses the Web to sell goods and services to another individual. (p. 259)

content search To seek out information from a list of categories and topics. (p. 70)

control To exercise power or influence over something. (p. 47)

cookie A file of information about you that a Web site stores on your computer. (p. 262)

copy To duplicate data from one location to another. (p. 141)

copyright A type of legal protection for works that are created or owned by a person or a company. (p. 126)

crash To stop functioning properly. (p. 48)

criteria The characteristics that define your data, such as a name, a color, or a date. (p. 240)

cut To remove data from one area and store it so that it can be placed to a different location. (p. 141)

cybercrime An crime that is committed with the help of a computer. (p. 383)

Español

sistema de computación (o sistema de cómputo) La combinación del hardware, programas y datos en conjunto. (p. 41)

consumidor Persona que compra productos. (p. 255)

consumidor a consumidor Transacción de negocios en la que un individuo usa la web para vender bienes y servicios a otro individuo. (p. 259)

búsqueda de contenido Buscar información a partir de una lista de categorías y temas. (p. 70)

controlar Ejercitar poder o influir en algo. (p. 47)

cookie Pequeño archivo de información sobre ti que el sitio web almacena en tu computadora. (p. 262)

copiar Duplicar datos de un lugar a otro. (p. 141)

derechos de autor (o derechos reservados) Forma de protección legal para trabajos que crea una persona o que son propiedad de una compañía. (p. 126)

caerse el sistema Dejar de funcionar adecuadamente. (p. 48)

criterios Características que definen tus datos como un nombre, un color o una fecha. (p. 240)

cortar Borrar datos de un área y almacenarlos para pegarlos en otro lugar. (p. 141)

ciberdelito Delito que se comete con ayuda de una computadora. (p. 383)

D

data Factual or numerical information, often organized to be analyzed or used to make a decision. (p. 264)

database A software program that organizes data or information so that it can be quickly found and displayed. (p. 264)

data series A range of cells you decide to include into a chart. (p. 245)

datos Información de hechos o datos organizada casi siempre para analizarse o para tomar una decisión. (p. 264)

base de datos Programa de software que organiza datos o información para encontrarla rápidamente y mostrarla. (p. 264)

serie de datos Conjunto de celdas que decides incluir en una gráfica. (p. 245)

Cause and Effect

Writers use the cause and effect structure to explore the reasons for something happening and to examine the results, or consequences, of events.

Signal words: so, because, as a result, therefore, for the following reasons

Problem and Solution

When they organize text around the question "how?", writers state a problem and suggest solutions.

Signal words: how, help, problem, obstruction, overcome, difficulty, need, attempt, have to, must

Sequence

Sequencing tells you the order in which to consider thoughts or facts. Examples of sequencing are:

Chronological order refers to the order in which events take place.

Signal words: first, next, then, finally

Spatial order describes the organization of things in space (to describe a room, for example).

Signal words: above, below, behind, next to

Order of importance lists things or thoughts from the most important to the least important (or the other way around).

Signal words: principal, central, main, important, fundamental

▶ Reading for Meaning

It is important to think about what you are reading to get the most information out of a text, to understand the consequences of what the text says, to remember the content, and to form your own opinion about what the content means.

Interpret

Interpreting is asking yourself, "What is the writer really saying?" and then using what you already know to answer that question.

Infer

Writers do not always directly state everything they want you to understand. By providing clues and details, they sometimes imply certain information. An **inference** involves using your reason and experience to develop the idea on your own, based on what an author implies or suggests. When drawing inferences, be sure that you have accurately based your guesses on supporting details from the text. If you cannot point to a place in the selection to help back up your inference, you may need to rethink your guess.

English

data type The kind of information displayed in a field. (p. 269)

default A setting the computer automatically selects unless you change it. (p. 168)

delete To permanently erase data. (p. 28)

demonstrate To illustrate and explain. (p. 309)

descending sort To arrange data in order from Z to A, or greatest number to smallest number. (p. 240)

desktop The main work area on a computer that holds the most used and needed files, folders, and programs. (p. 20)

desktop publishing A special feature or software that lets you create documents, newsletters, flyers, and similar documents. (p. 185)

determine To settle on or decide by choice of alternatives or possibilities. (p. 208)

device A piece of equipment. (p. 3)

disk The magnetic medium on which data is stored. (p. 46)

digital video disk (DVD) A high-density compact disk for storing large amounts of data, especially high-resolution audio-visual material. (p. 46)

disk drive The hardware that finds, reads, and writes information to and from a disk. (p. 46)

document A file produced by an application, such as a text document, spreadsheet, or graphic file. (p. 52)

Español

tipo de datos Tipo de información mostrada en un campo. (p. 269)

predeterminado Configuración que la computadora selecciona automáticamente a menos que tú la cambies. (p. 168)

borrar (o suprimir) Borrar datos permanentemente. (p. 28)

demostrar Ilustrar y explicar. (p. 309)

orden descendente Arreglar los datos de la Z a la A o del número mayor al menor. (p. 240)

escritorio (o fondo de la pantalla) Área principal de trabajo en una computadora que tiene los archivos, carpetas y programas que más se usan. (p. 20)

edición por computadora Es una característica especial o un programa que te permite crear documentos, boletines, volantes y otros documentos semejantes. (p. 185)

determinar Resolver o decidir por convicción. (p. 208)

dispositivo Pieza del equipo. (p. 3)

disco Medio magnético donde se almacenan los datos. (p. 46)

disco video digital (DVD) Disco compacto de alta densidad para almacenar grandes cantidades de datos, especialmente material audio visual de alta resolución. (p. 46)

unidad de disco Hardware que encuentra, lee y escribe información de un disco o la almacena en un disco. (p. 46)

documento Archivo producido por una aplicación tal como un documento de texto, una hoja de cálculo o un archivo gráfico. (p. 52)

Clarify

If you feel you do not understand meaning (through questioning), try these techniques:

What to Do When You Do Not Understand

- Reread confusing parts of the text.
- Diagram (chart) relationships between chunks of text, ideas, and sentences.
- Look up unfamiliar words.
- Talk out the text to yourself.
- Read the passage once more.

Review

Take time to stop and review what you have read. Use your note-taking tools (graphic organizers or Cornell notes charts). Also, review and consider your KWL chart.

Monitor Your Comprehension

Continue to check your understanding by using the following two strategies:

Summarize Pause and tell yourself the main ideas of the text and the key supporting details. Try to answer the following questions: Who? What? When? Where? Why? How?

Paraphrase Pause, close the book, and try to retell what you have just read in your own words. It might help to pretend you are explaining the text to someone who has not read it and does not know the material.

Understanding Text Structure

Good writers do not just put together sentences and paragraphs. They organize their writing with a specific purpose in mind. That organization is called text structure. When you understand and follow the structure of a text, it is easier to remember the information you are reading. There are many ways text may be structured. Watch for **signal words**. They will help you follow the text's organization. Also, remember to use these techniques when you write.

Compare and Contrast

The compare and contrast structure shows similarities and differences between people, things, and ideas. This is often used to demonstrate that things that seem alike are really different, or vice versa.

Signal words: similarly, more, less, on the one hand/on the other hand, in contrast, but, however

English / Español

domain The portion of a Web site address that identifies the type of site. For example, the *.com* in *www.google.com* is the domain name, which indicates that this is a type of commercial site. (p. 86)

dominio Porción de la dirección del sitio web que identifica el tipo de sitio. Por ejemplo, en *www.google.com*, el *.com* es el nombre del dominio e indica que es un sitio comercial. (p. 86)

domain name The identification of a Web site within a particular domain. For example, the *google* in *www.google.com* is the Web site's name in the .com domain. (p. 86)

nombre de dominio Es la identificación de un sitio web en un dominio particular. Por ejemplo, en *www.google.com*, *google* es el nombre del sitio en el dominio .com. (p. 86)

double-click To press the mouse button twice quickly. (p. 22)

hacer doble clic (o pulsar dos veces) Presionar el botón del ratón dos veces rápidamente. (p. 22)

download To retrieve a file from a remote computer. (p. 90)

bajar (o descargar, transferir) Recuperar u obtener un archivo de una computadora remota. (p. 90)

drag To move or copy a selected element using the mouse. (p. 22)

arrastrar Mover o copiar un elemento seleccionado usando el ratón. (p. 22)

drill down To move from general information to more detailed information by exploring a series of folders, drop-down menus, or Web pages. (p. 99)

perforar (o hacer navegación descendente) Ir de información general a información más detallada explorando una serie de carpetas, menús desplegables o páginas web. (p. 99)

drive The largest storage area. (p. 52)

unidad El área de almacenamiento más grande. (p. 52)

driver A special software program that makes hardware work. (p. 43)

controlador Programa especial que hace que funcione el hardware. (p. 43)

E

e-commerce Business, buying, and selling performed over the Internet. (p. 255)

comercio electrónico Negocios de compra y venta que se hacen por medio de Internet. (p. 255)

edit To change, improve, or rewrite a document. (p. 141)

editar Cambiar, mejorar o volver a escribir un documento. (p. 141)

electronic job market The collection of Web sites that help people find various jobs and companies find employees. (p. 307)

mercado electrónico de trabajo El conjunto de sitios web que ayudan a las personas a encontrar trabajo y a las compañías a encontrar empleados. (p. 307)

electronic mail (e-mail) A communication sent from one person to another over the Internet. (p. 90)

correo electrónico (e-mail) Comunicación enviada de una persona a otra por medio de Internet. (p. 90)

electronic waste Obsolete equipment, including all the discarded computers, monitors, and other devices that are thrown away. (p. 359)

basura electrónica Equipo obsoleto que incluye las computadoras, los monitores y otro equipo que se desecha. (p. 359)

enable To make possible, practical, or easy. (p. 49)

permitir Hacer posible, práctico o sencillo. (p. 49)

Taking Notes

Cornell Note-Taking System There are many methods for note taking. The **Cornell Note-Taking System** is a well-known method that can help you organize what you read. To the right is a diagram that shows how the Cornell Note-Taking System organizes information.

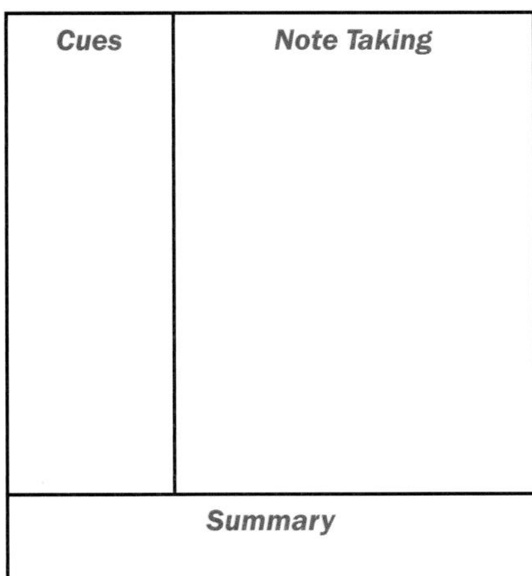

Graphic Organizers Using a graphic organizer to retell content in a visual representation will help you remember and retain content. You might make a **chart** or **diagram**, organizing what you have read. Here are some examples of graphic organizers:

Venn diagrams When mapping out a compare-and-contrast text structure, you can use a Venn diagram. The outer portions of the circles will show how two characters, ideas, or items contrast, or are different, and the overlapping part will compare two things, or show how they are similar.

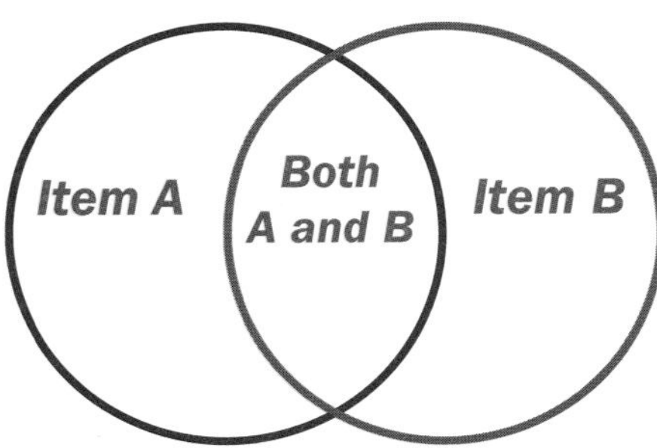

Flow charts To help you track the sequence of events, or cause and effect, use a flow chart. Arrange ideas or events in their logical, sequential order. Then draw arrows between your ideas to indicate how one idea or event flows into another.

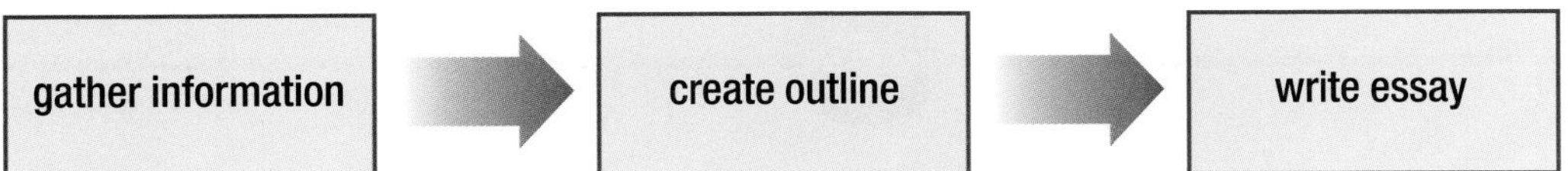

Visualize

Try to form a mental picture of scenes, characters, and events as you read. Use the details and descriptions the author gives you. If you can **visualize** what you read, it will be more interesting and you will remember it better.

Question

Ask yourself questions about the text as you read. Ask yourself about the importance of the sentences, how they relate to one another, if you understand what you just read, and what you think is going to come next.

English / Español

encryption A way to keep information secure by scrambling it as it is being transmitted over a network or over the Internet. (p. 263)

encriptación (o texto cifrado) Es una forma segura de guardar la información codificándola conforme se transmite por una red de comunicaciones o por Internet. (p. 263)

endnote A note at the end of an article, chapter, or book that comments on or cites a reference for a part of the text. (p. 131)

notas finales Son notas al final de un artículo, capítulo o libro en que se comenta o cita una referencia para una parte del texto. (p. 131)

ergonomics The study and design of equipment and systems that people use to improve safety, comfort, and efficiency. (p. 12)

ergonomía Estudio y diseño de equipo y sistemas que se usa para incrementar la seguridad, la comodidad y la eficiencia. (p. 12)

ethics The rules that we use to define behavior as "right" or "wrong." (p. 126)

ética Reglas que usamos para definir una conducta como "buena" o "mala." (p. 126)

evaluate To determine the significance. (p. 93)

evaluar Determinar la importancia. (p. 93)

expert Someone with special knowledge or ability. (p. 264)

experto Persona con un conocimiento o habilidad especial. (p. 264)

F

fair use The times when you can use copyrighted material without permission or payment. (p. 128)

uso justo (o uso razonable) Situaciones en las que puedes usar material con derechos reservados sin necesidad de permiso o pago alguno. (p. 128)

Favorites Internet Explorer's term for Web site bookmarks. (p. 101)

Favoritos Término de Internet Explorer para indicar un marcador en el sitio web. (p. 101)

fee A sum paid or charged for a service. (p. 210)

cuota Suma pagada o cobrada por un servicio. (p. 210)

field In Access, the information contained within each record. (p. 267)

campo En Access es la información contenida en cada registro. (p. 267)

file A collection of data. (p. 52)

archivo (o fichero) Colección de datos. (p. 52)

file sharing To give, receive, or exchange music, videos, or other files with other computer or Web users. (p. 129)

compartir archivos Entregar, recibir o intercambiar música, videos u otros archivos con otros usuarios de computadoras o de Internet. (p. 129)

fill handle The small square at the bottom of the cell pointer used to copy contents by clicking and dragging into another desired cell. (p. 220)

manija de llenado El pequeño cuadro localizado en la parte inferior del puntero de la celda, que se usa para copiar el contenido haciendo clic y arrastrando hacia otra celda. (p. 220)

Reading for detail involves careful reading while paying attention to text structure and monitoring your understanding. Read for detail when you are learning concepts, following complicated directions, or preparing to analyze a text.

Techniques to Understand and Remember What You Read

Preview

Before beginning a selection, it is helpful to **preview** what you are about to read.

Previewing Strategies

- Read the title, headings, and subheadings of the selection.
- Look at the illustrations and notice how the text is organized.
- Skim the selection: Take a glance at the whole thing.
- Decide what the main idea might be.
- Predict what the selection will be about.

Predict

Have you ever read a mystery, decided who committed the crime, and then changed your mind as more clues were revealed? You were adjusting your predictions. Did you smile when you found out you guessed the murderer? You were verifying your predictions.

As you read, take educated guesses about story events and outcomes; that is, **make predictions** before and during reading. This will help you focus your attention on the text and it will improve your understanding.

Determine the Main Idea

When you look for the **main idea**, you are looking for the most important statement in a text. Depending on what kind of text you are reading, the main idea can be located at the very beginning (as in news stories in a newspaper or a magazine) or at the end (as in a scientific research document). Ask yourself:

- What is each sentence about?
- Is there one sentence that is more important than all the others?
- What idea do details support or point out?

English

file name A name assigned to a file for identification. (p. 52)

filter To limit information to the specific data or criteria you want. (p. 242)

Filter By Form In Access, a tool that displays all records that match two or more values or criteria at once. (p. 285)

Filter By Selection In Access, a tool that displays all records that match a specific value or criteria you set. (p. 283)

firewall Hardware or software that protects a computer or network from intruders, especially from over the Internet. (p. 94)

folder A place to organize files. (p. 52)

font The shape of letters, numbers, and other characters as they appear on the page. (p. 153)

footer Document information that appears at the bottom of each page. (p. 174)

form An arrangement of fields from a table that makes it easy for anyone to enter data. (p. 291)

format The appearance and arrangement of text on a page. (p. 153)

Format Painter In Word, a tool to apply previously paragraph formatting onto other text. (p. 165)

formula In Excel, the relationship between cells, such as adding or dividing the contents of cells in an arithmetic equation. (p. 229)

fraud A deliberate attempt to trick people into giving money or information. (p. 383)

freeware Software made freely available to the public by the publisher. (p. 130)

function An automatic formula in an arithmetic operation. (p. 231)

function key Key on the keyboard used to give shortcut command to the computer. (p. 29)

Español

nombre de archivo Nombre asignado a un archivo para su identificación. (p. 52)

filtrar Limitar la información a los datos específicos o a los criterios que tú quieras. (p. 242)

filtro por formulario En Access es una herramienta que muestra todos los registros que coinciden con dos o más valores o criterios al mismo tiempo. (p. 285)

filtro por selección En Access es una herramienta que muestra todos los registros que coinciden con un valor o criterio específico establecido por ti. (p. 283)

firewall Hardware o programa que protege una computadora o una red contra los intrusos, especialmente los de Internet. (p. 94)

carpeta Lugar para organizar archivos. (p. 52)

fuente Forma de las letras, números y otros caracteres tal como aparecen en la página. (p. 153)

pie de página Documento de información que aparece en la parte de abajo de cada página. (p. 174)

formulario Arreglo de campos en una tabla que facilita la entrada de datos. (p. 291)

formato El aspecto y arreglo del texto en una página. (p. 153)

Copiar Formato En Word es una herramienta que se usa para aplicar el mismo formato de párrafos anteriores en otro texto. (p. 165)

fórmula En Excel es la relación entre las celdas, por ejemplo, la suma o la división del contenido de las celdas en una ecuación aritmética. (p. 229)

fraude Intento deliberado de engañar a una persona para que proporcione dinero o información. (p. 383)

freeware Programas de software que las casas editoriales ofrecen gratuitamente al público. (p. 130)

función Fórmula automática en una operación aritmética. (p. 231)

teclas de función Teclas del teclado usadas para proporcionar accesos rápidos a comandos de la computadora. (p. 29)

Understanding What You Read

Reading comprehension means understanding—deriving meaning from—what you have read. Using a variety of strategies can help you improve your comprehension and make reading more interesting and more fun.

Read for a Reason

To get the greatest benefit from what you read, you should **establish a purpose for reading**. In school, you have many reasons for reading. Some of them are:

- To learn and understand new information
- To find specific information
- To review before a test
- To complete an assignment
- To prepare (research) before you write

As your reading skills improve, you will notice that you apply different strategies to fit the different purposes for reading. For example, if you are reading for entertainment, you might read quickly, but if you read to gather information or follow directions, you might read more slowly, take notes, construct a graphic organizer, or reread sections of text.

Draw on Personal Background

Drawing on personal background may also be called activating prior knowledge. Before you start reading a text, ask yourself questions like these:

- What have I heard or read about this topic?
- Do I have any personal experience relating to this topic?

Using a KWL Chart A KWL chart is a good device for organizing information you gather before, during, and after reading. In the first column, list what you already **know**, then list what you **want** to know in the middle column. Use the third column when you review and you assess what you **learned**. You can also add more columns to record places where you found information and places where you can look for more information.

K (What I already know)	W (What I want to know)	L (What I have learned)

Adjust Your Reading Speed Your reading speed is a key factor in how well you understand what you are reading. You will need to adjust your speed depending on your reading purpose.

Scanning means running your eyes quickly over the material to look for words or phrases. Scan when you need a specific piece of information.

Skimming means reading a passage quickly to find its main idea or to get an overview. Skim a text when you preview to determine what the material is about.

English	Español
G	
grammar check A word processing tool that points out possible mistaken uses of grammar in a document. (p. 144)	**revisión de gramática** Herramienta del procesador de palabras que señala posibles usos incorrectos de la gramática en un documento. (p. 144)
graphic Items other than text, including photos, clip art, and drawing objects. (p. 185)	**gráfico** Objetos distintos del texto, tales como fotografías, imágenes prediseñadas y objetos de dibujo. (p. 185)
group To combine separate selected objects into one single object. (p. 370)	**agrupar** Combinar distintos objetos seleccionados en un solo objeto. (p. 370)
H	
hacker One who uses programming skills to gain illegal access to a computer network or file. (p. 7)	**pirata informático** Persona que usa sus habilidades de programación para obtener acceso ilegal a una red de computadoras o a un archivo. (p. 7)
handout In PowerPoint, printed version of a slide show. (p. 345)	**páginas de notas** En PowerPoint, versiones impresas de una presentación con diapositivas. (p. 345)
hard disk (also hard disk drive) A rigid storage device fixed permanently within a computer. (p. 46)	**disco duro (también unidad de disco duro)** Dispositivo rígido de almacenamiento instalado permanentemente dentro de una computadora. (p. 46)
hardware The physical devices that make up a computer system. (p. 43)	**hardware** Dispositivos físicos que forman parte de una computadora. (p. 43)
header Document information that appears at the top of each page. (p. 174)	**encabezado** Información de un documento que aparece en la parte superior de cada página. (p. 174)
hiding In Excel, to eliminate rows or columns that do not contain specific data or criteria. (p. 242)	**ocultar** En Excel, eliminar filas o columnas que no contienen datos o criterios específicos. (p. 242)
history A record kept by a browser of every Web page visited in the past few days or weeks. (p. 101)	**historia** Registro que lleva un navegador de cada página web visitada en los días o semanas pasados. (p. 101)
home page The first Web page an Internet browser is set to access when opened. (p. 97)	**página de inicio** La primera página web que se establece en un navegador para que la acceda al abrirse. (p. 97)
hyperlink Text or object on a Web page that forwards to another location on the Internet. (p. 98)	**hipervínculo (o hiperenlace)** Texto u objetos que en una página web llevan a otra dirección en Internet. (p. 98)

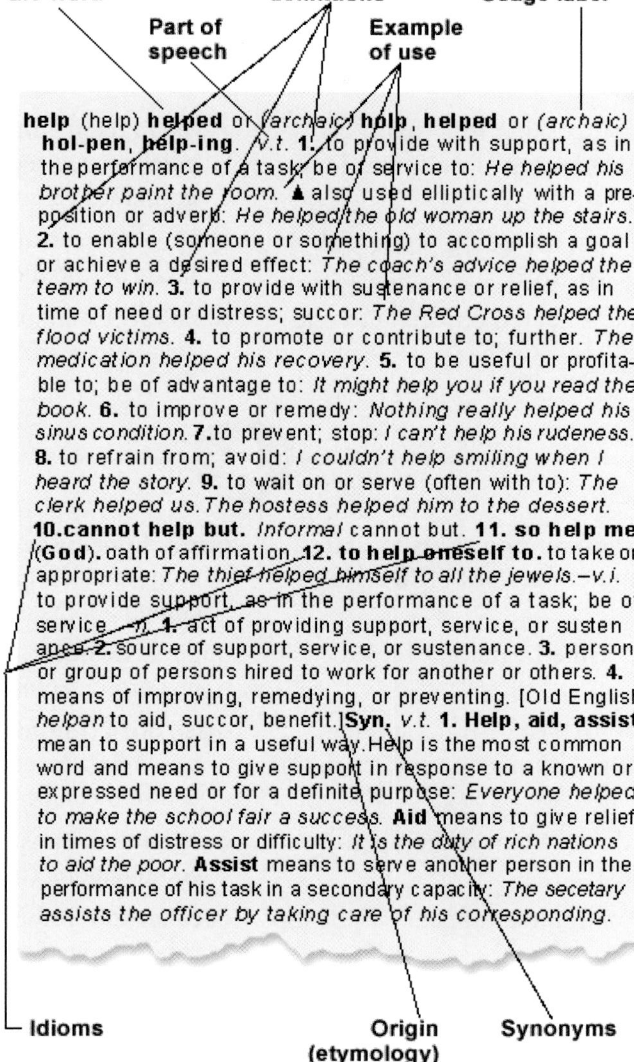

help (help) **helped** or *(archaic)* **holp**, **helped** or *(archaic)* **hol-pen**, **help-ing**. *v.t.* **1.** to provide with support, as in the performance of a task; be of service to: *He helped his brother paint the room.* ▲ also used elliptically with a preposition or adverb: *He helped the old woman up the stairs.* **2.** to enable (someone or something) to accomplish a goal or achieve a desired effect: *The coach's advice helped the team to win.* **3.** to provide with sustenance or relief, as in time of need or distress; succor: *The Red Cross helped the flood victims.* **4.** to promote or contribute to; further. *The medication helped his recovery.* **5.** to be useful or profitable to; be of advantage to: *It might help you if you read the book.* **6.** to improve or remedy: *Nothing really helped his sinus condition.* **7.** to prevent; stop: *I can't help his rudeness.* **8.** to refrain from; avoid: *I couldn't help smiling when I heard the story.* **9.** to wait on or serve (often with to): *The clerk helped us. The hostess helped him to the dessert.* **10. cannot help but.** *Informal* cannot but. **11. so help me (God).** oath of affirmation. **12. to help oneself to.** to take or appropriate: *The thief helped himself to all the jewels.*—*v.i.* to provide support, as in the performance of a task; be of service.—*n.* **1.** act of providing support, service, or sustenance. **2.** source of support, service, or sustenance. **3.** person or group of persons hired to work for another or others. **4.** means of improving, remedying, or preventing. [Old English *helpan* to aid, succor, benefit.] **Syn.** *v.t.* **1. Help, aid, assist** mean to support in a useful way. Help is the most common word and means to give support in response to a known or expressed need or for a definite purpose: *Everyone helped to make the school fair a success.* **Aid** means to give relief in times of distress or difficulty: *It is the duty of rich nations to aid the poor.* **Assist** means to serve another person in the performance of his task in a secondary capacity: *The secetary assists the officer by taking care of his corresponding.*

Using Dictionaries A dictionary provides the meaning or meanings of a word. Look at the sample dictionary entry above to see what other information it provides.

Thesauruses and Specialized Reference Books A thesaurus provides synonyms and often antonyms. Specialized dictionaries, such as *Barron's Dictionary of Business Terms* or *Black's Law Dictionary,* list terms and expressions that are not commonly included in a general dictionary. You can also use online dictionaries.

Glossaries Many textbooks and technical works contain condensed dictionaries that provide an alphabetical listing of words used in the text and their specific definitions.

English	Español
I	
icon A small picture or graphic that visually represents programs, document files, Web links, or other items on the computer. (p. 20)	**icono** Pequeña imagen o gráfico que representa visualmente programas, archivos de documentos, enlaces web u otros objetos en la computadora. (p. 20)
image A visual representation. (p. 131)	**imagen** Una representacíon visual. (p. 131)
indent The distance of a paragraph from either the left or right margin. (p. 171)	**sangría** Distancia de un párrafo desde el margen izquierdo o el derecho. (p. 171)
index search To seek out information from an alphabetical list of keywords. (p. 70)	**búsqueda índice** Localizar información en una lista alfabética de palabras clave. (p. 70)
Information technology (IT) The creation and installation of computer systems and software. (p. 305)	**tecnología de la información (TI)** Creación e instalación de sistemas de cómputo y software. (p. 305)
input Information entered into a computer. (p. 44)	**datos de entrada** Información ingresada en la computadora. (p. 44)
insertion point The symbol (often a blinking vertical line) on the screen where text or data is to be entered. (p. 28)	**punto de inserción** Símbolo (comúnmente una línea vertical parpadeante) en la pantalla donde debe ingresarse el texto o la información. (p. 28)
integrated device A piece of equipment, hardware, or machinery that performs more than one function. (p. 356)	**dispositivo integrado** Equipo, hardware o maquinaria que efectúa más de una función. (p. 356)
intellectual property Ideas and concepts created or owned by a person or company (including books, music, movies, software, inventions, and trademarks). (p. 126)	**propiedad intelectual** Ideas y conceptos creados o que posee una persona o compañía (incluyendo libros, música, películas, software, inventos y marcas registradas). (p. 126)
Internet The computer network that connects computers across the world. (p. 86)	**Internet** La red de computadoras que conecta equipos de cómputo alrededor del mundo. (p. 86)
Internet service provider (ISP) A company that provides access to the Internet, usually for a monthly fee. (p. 88)	**proveedor de servicios de Internet (ISP)** Una compañía que proporciona acceso a Internet, normalmente mediante el cobro de una tarifa mensual. (p. 88)
intranet Internal network that uses protocols similar to that of the Internet. (p. 49)	**intranet** Red interna que usa protocolos similares a los de Internet. (p. 49)
J	
joystick Input device that controls the movement of objects on the screen. (p. 44)	**palanca de mando** Dispositivo de entrada que controla el movimiento de objetos en la pantalla. (p. 44)

Use Context to Determine Meaning

The best way to expand and extend your vocabulary is to read widely, listen carefully, and participate in a rich variety of discussions. When reading on your own, though, you can often figure out the meanings of new words by looking at their **context**, the other words and sentences that surround them.

Tips for Using Context

Look for clues such as:

A synonym or an explanation of the unknown word in the sentence:
*Elise's shop specialized in **millinery**, or **hats for women**.*

A reference to what the word is or is not like:
*An **archaeologist**, like a **historian**, deals with the past.*

A general topic associated with the word:
*The **cooking** teacher discussed the best way to **braise** meat.*

A description or action associated with the word:
*He used the **shovel** to **dig up** the garden.*

Predict a Possible Meaning

Another way to determine the meaning of a word is to take the word apart. If you understand the meaning of the **base**, or **root**, part of a word, and also know the meanings of key syllables added either to the beginning or end of the base word, you can usually figure out what the word means.

Word Origins Since Latin, Greek, and Anglo-Saxon roots are the basis for much of our English vocabulary, having some background in languages can be a useful vocabulary tool. For example, *astronomy* comes from the Greek root *astro*, which means "relating to the stars." *Stellar* also has a meaning referring to stars, but its origin is Latin. Knowing root words in other languages can help you determine meanings, derivations, and spellings in English.

Prefixes and Suffixes A prefix is a word part that can be added to the beginning of a word. For example, the prefix *semi* means "half" or "partial," so *semicircle* means "half a circle." A suffix is a word part that can be added to the end of a word. Adding a suffix often changes a word from one part of speech to another.

Recognize Word Meanings Across Subjects
Have you learned a new word in one class and then noticed it in your reading for other subjects? The word might not mean exactly the same thing in each class, but you can use the meaning you already know to help you understand the word's meaning in another subject area.

English	Español
K	
keyboard Common input device for entering data into and delivering commands to a computer. (p. 44)	**teclado** Dispositivo común de entrada para ingresar datos y enviar órdenes a la computadora. (p. 44)
keyword A word (or words) used in a search to match a desired topic. (p. 70)	**palabra clave** Palabra (o palabras) que se usan en una búsqueda para localizar un tema específico. (p. 70)
keyword search To seek information through a database, like Help and Support topics, by keying in words or phrases that match your topic. (p. 70)	**búsqueda por palabra clave** Localizar información por medio de una base de datos, como temas de Ayuda y Soporte, ingresando palabras o frases que correspondan al tema. (p. 70)
L	
landscape orientation Document orientation formatted with the long edge of the page along the top. (p. 156)	**orientación horizontal** Orientación del documento con la parte más amplia de la página en la parte superior. (p. 156)
legend A guide that identifies the different data in a chart. (p. 332)	**leyenda** Guía que identifica los distintos datos en una tabla. (p. 332)
link Pointer in a hypertext document or Help window that connects with other hypertext documents or that jumps you to other Help entries. (p. 98)	**vínculo (o enlace)** Apuntadores en un documento de hipertexto o ventana de Ayuda que conectan con otros documentos o que dirigen hacia otros temas de la Ayuda. (p. 98)
linking The process of connecting text boxes so that when one box is filled, the text will continue into the connected box. (p. 394)	**vinculación** Proceso de conectar cuadros de texto de modo que cuando uno se llene el texto continúe en el cuadro conectado. (p. 394)
local area network (LAN) A series of connected personal computers, workstations, and other devices such as printers or scanners within an office or building. (p. 49)	**red de área local (LAN)** Una serie de computadoras personales, estaciones de trabajo y otros dispositivos tales como impresoras o escáneres conectados en una misma oficina o edificio. (p. 49)
log off To exit a network without turning off the computer so a different user can log on. (p. 32)	**cerrar sesión** Salir de una red sin apagar la computadora para que otro usuario pueda iniciar una sesión. (p. 32)
log on To access a network, usually by keying in a username and password. (p. 20)	**iniciar sesión** Ingresar a una red, normalmente proporcionando un nombre de usuario y una contraseña. (p. 20)
logo A graphic design often used as a visual reminder of a company and its services. (p. 373)	**logotipo** Diseño gráfico que se usa como recordatorio visual de una compañía y de sus servicios. (p. 373)

Reading: What's in It for You?

What role does reading play in your life? The possibilities are countless. Are you on a sports team? Perhaps you like to read about the latest news and statistics in your sport or find out about new training techniques. Are you looking for a part-time job? You might be looking for advice about résumé writing, interview techniques, or information about a company. Are you enrolled in an English class, an algebra class, or a business class? Then your assignments require a lot of reading.

Improving or Fine-tuning Your Reading Skills Will:

- Improve your grades
- Allow you to read faster and more efficiently
- Improve your study skills
- Help you remember more information accurately
- Improve your writing

The Reading Process

Good reading skills build on one another, overlap, and spiral around in much the same way that a winding staircase goes around and around while leading you to a higher place. This handbook is designed to help you find and use the tools you will need **before**, **during**, and **after** reading.

Strategies You Can Use

- Identify, understand, and learn new words
- Understand why you read
- Take a quick look at the whole text
- Try to predict what you are about to read
- Take breaks while you read and ask yourself questions about the text
- Take notes
- Keep thinking about what will come next
- Summarize

Vocabulary Development

Word identification and vocabulary skills are the building blocks of the reading and the writing process. By learning to use a variety of strategies to build your word skills and vocabulary, you will become a stronger reader.

English	Español
M	
margin The blank space at the top, bottom, and sides of a document. (p. 168)	**margen** El espacio vacío de las partes superior, inferior y laterales del documento. (p. 168)
memory A unit of a computer's motherboard that stores data. (p. 45)	**memoria** Unidad dentro de la tarjeta madre de una computadora que sirve para almacenar datos. (p. 45)
menu A list of commands or options grouped under specific headings or titles. (p. 21)	**menú** Lista de comandos u opciones agrupadas bajo encabezados o títulos específicos. (p. 21)
merge cells In Excel, to combine two or more cells into a single cell. (p. 190)	**combinar celdas** En Excel, agrupar dos o más celdas en una misma celda. (p. 190)
microcomputer A type of computer designed for use by a single user (also known as *personal computer* or *desktop computer*). (p. 41)	**microcomputadora** Un tipo de computadora diseñada para un solo usuario (también conocida como *computadora personal* o *computadora de escritorio*). (p. 41)
microprocessor A tiny microchip that acts as the "brain" of a computer by receiving instructions and then carrying them out. (p. 3)	**microprocesador** Diminuto microcircuito o chip que actúa como el "cerebro" de una computadora al recibir órdenes y luego ejecutarlas. (p. 3)
minicomputer A type of computer designed to serve multiple users and process significant amounts of data. (p. 41)	**minicomputadora** Tipo de computadora diseñada para servir a múltiples usuarios y procesar cantidades grandes de información. (p. 41)
minimize To reduce or keep to a minimum. (p. 359)	**minimizar** Reducir o mantener al mínimo. (p. 359)
modem The hardware that connects a computer to the Internet. (p. 89)	**módem** Hardware que conecta una computadora con Internet. (p. 89)
monitor (1) A video display screen. (p. 44)	**observar (1)** Pantalla de video. (p. 44)
monitor (2) To watch, keep track of, or check. (p. 94)	**observar (2)** Vigilar, dar seguimiento, reviser. (p. 94)
mouse A single-hand-held pointing device that serves as an alternative to the keyboard in communicating instructions. (p. 22)	**ratón** Dispositivo apuntador que se usa con una sola mano y sirve como alternativa en lugar del teclado para comunicar instrucciones. (p. 22)
N	
netiquette The rules or manners used in electronic communications. (p. 92)	**etiqueta en la red** Reglas y buenos modales usados en las comunicaciones electrónicas. (p. 92)
network A group of computers connected together. (p. 49)	**red** Grupo de computadoras conectadas unas con otras. (p. 49)
numbered list A series of text that uses numbers to present information in a particular order. (p. 158)	**lista numerada** Serie de texto que usa números para presentar información en un orden específico. (p. 158)

Prepare *for* Academic Success!

National Language Arts Standards

To help incorporate literacy skills (reading, writing, listening, and speaking) into *Glencoe Computer Concepts in Action*, each project includes opportunities to reinforce language arts skills. These skills have been developed into standards by the *National Council of Teachers of English and International Reading Association*.

- Read texts to acquire new information.
- Read literature to build an understanding of the human experience.
- Apply strategies to interpret texts.
- Use written language to communicate effectively.
- Use different writing process elements to communicate effectively.
- Apply knowledge of language structure and conventions to discuss texts.
- Conduct research and gather, evaluate, and synthesize data to communicate discoveries.
- Use information resources to gather information and create and communicate knowledge.
- Develop an understanding of diversity in language used across cultures.
- Use first language to develop competency in English language arts and develop an understanding of content across the curriculum.
- Participate as members of literacy communities.
- Use language to accomplish individual purposes.

National Math Standards

Glencoe's Computer Concepts in Action textbook provides students with opportunities to practice the math skills indicated in the national math standards developed by the *National Council of Teachers of Mathematics*. The basic skills are:

- Number and Operations
- Algebra
- Geometry
- Measurement
- Data Analysis and Probability
- Problem Solving
- Communication
- Connections
- Representation

English

O

obsolete No longer useful. (p. 359)

operating system The overall program that controls all the other software programs and allows hardware devices to work properly. (p. 47)

orientation The direction of the page or paper a document will print on. (p. 156)

Outline View In Word, a visual setting that lets you organize a document into headings and body text so that you can easily see how the document is organized. (p. 402)

output The information a computer delivers back to the user. (p. 44)

P

password A secret word that protects access to a network or computer. (p. 20)

paste To place copied or cut text or graphics to a different location. (p. 141)

percentage The result obtained by multiplying. (p. 255)

performance The measurement of how fast a computer works. (p. 211)

permission Consent or authorization by the owner or creator to use his or her work in a way that was not its original purpose. (p. 127)

personal computer (PC) A computer that is used by one person at a time. (p. 41)

personal digital assistant (PDA) A small, portable type of computer (also known as a palmtop computer). (p. 48)

piracy The act of copying or sharing copyrighted material without permission. (p. 129)

Español

O

obsoleto Que ya no es útil. (p. 359)

sistema operativo El programa general que controla todos los demás programas de software y permite que los dispositivos de hardware funcionen adecuadamente. (p. 47)

orientación Dirección de la página o papel en que se va a imprimir un documento. (p. 156)

Vista esquema En Word es un parámetro visual que te permite organizar un documento en encabezados y cuerpo del texto para que puedas ver fácilmente cómo está organizado el documento. (p. 402)

datos de salida Información que la computadora entrega al usuario como resultado. (p. 44)

P

contraseña Palabra secreta que protege el acceso a una red o computadora. (p. 20)

pegar Colocar en un lugar distinto el texto o gráficos previamente copiados o cortados. (p. 141)

porcentaje Resultado obtenido de una multiplicación. (p. 255)

rendimiento La medida de rapidez del funcionamiento de una computadora. (p. 211)

permiso Consentimiento o autorización que otorga el dueño o creador para usar su trabajo de una manera diferente de su propósito original. (p. 127)

computadora personal (PC) Computadora que se usa por una sola persona a la vez. (p. 41)

asistente personal digital (PDA) Tipo pequeño y portátil de computadora conocido también como computadora palmtop. (p. 48)

piratería El acto de duplicar o compartir material con derechos reservados sin permiso. (p. 129)

IC^3 Module 2 – Key Applications

The exam objectives cover the following areas:

Common Program Functions

- Be able to start and exit a Windows application and utilize sources of online help
- Identify common on-screen elements of Windows applications, change application settings, and manage files within an application
- Perform common editing and formatting functions
- Perform common printing functions

Word Processing Functions

- Be able to format text and documents including the ability to use automatic formatting tools
- Be able to insert, edit, and format tables in a document

Spreadsheet Functions

- Be able to modify worksheet data and structure and format data in a worksheet
- Be able to sort data, manipulate data using formulas and functions, and add and modify charts in a worksheet

Presentation Software

- Be able to create and format simple presentations

IC^3 Module 3 – Living Online

The exam objectives cover the following areas:

Networks and the Internet

- Identify network fundamentals and the benefits and risks of network computing
- Identify the relationship between computer networks, other communications networks (like the telephone network), and the Internet

Electronic Mail

- Identify how electronic mail works
- Identify how to use an electronic mail application
- Identify the appropriate use of e-mail and e-mail related "netiquette"

Using the Internet

- Identify different types of information sources on the Internet
- Be able to use a Web browsing application
- Be able to search the Internet for information

The Impact of Computing and the Internet on Society

- Identify how computers are used in different areas of work, school, and home
- Identify the risks of using computer hardware and software
- Identify how to use the Internet safely, legally, and responsibly

English	Español
plagiarism To take credit for someone else's ideas. (p. 131)	**plagio** Acreditarse las ideas de otra persona. (p. 131)
pointer An on-screen symbol that lets the user select a command when positioned on the appropriate button or icon. (p. 22)	**puntero (o apuntador)** Símbolo en la pantalla que permite al usuario seleccionar un comando al colocarlo en el botón o icono apropiado. (p. 22)
policy A definite course or method of action selected from among alternatives and in light of given conditions to guide and determine present and future decisions. (p. 212)	**política** Curso definido o método de acción seleccionado de entre varias alternativas a la luz de condiciones específicas para guiar y determinar decisiones presentes y futures. (p. 212)
pop-up ad A small Web page containing an advertisement that suddenly appears on your screen when you are using a Web site. (p. 261)	**publicidad pop-up (o anuncio contextual)** Pequeña página web que contiene un anuncio publicitario y que aparece repentinamente en tu pantalla cuando estás visitando un sitio web. (p. 261)
port The hardware and associated circuitry that links one piece of hardware, computer, or device with another. (p. 43)	**puerto** El hardware y circuitos relacionados que unen una pieza de hardware, computadora o dispositivo con otro. (p. 43)
portrait orientation Document orientation formatted with the short edge of the page along the top. (p. 156)	**orientación vertical** Orientación del documento con la parte más angosta de la página en la parte superior. (p. 156)
predict To declare or indicate in advance. (p. 3)	**predecir** Declarar o indicar por adelantado. (p. 3)
presentation software A program that uses words, pictures, sound, and video to support a speech, lecture, or public presentation. (p. 312)	**programa de presentación** Programa que usa palabras, imágenes, sonido y video para hacer una presentación, un discurso o una conferencia en público. (p. 312)
primary key A unique number created when a new record is added to a database. (p. 269)	**llave principal (o clave principal)** Número único creado cuando se añade un nuevo registro a una base de datos. (p. 269)
print To transfer data to a paper-based format. (p. 163)	**imprimir** Transferir datos al papel. (p. 163)
Print Preview A browser function used to see how a document or Web page is going to appear on paper. (p. 103)	**Vista preliminar** Es una función del navegador que se usa para ver cómo se imprimirá en papel un documento o página web. (p. 103)
printer An output device that transfers data to a paper-based format. (p. 44)	**impresora** Dispositivo de salida que se usa para transferir datos al papel. (p. 44)
program The set of instructions a computer receives in order to carry out its many functions. (p. 25)	**programa** Conjunto de instrucciones que recibe una computadora para ejecutar sus muchas funciones. (p. 25)
proofread To check a document for spelling, grammar, and punctuation to see if everything makes sense. (p. 141)	**corrección de pruebas** Verificar la ortografía, la gramática y la puntuación de un documento para asegurarse de que está correcto. (p. 141)

Certiport and IC^3 (Internet and Computing Core Certification)

Another national technology standard known as IC^3 has been developed by Certiport, a globally-recognized company that provides services and certification. They also provide the Microsoft Office Specialist (MOS) certification and many other technology certifications.

IC^3 standards provide a solid foundation for the productive use of computer hardware, software, and the Internet. The objectives are divided into three modules: Computing Fundamentals, Key Applications, and Living Online. The skills addressed in these modules are summarized in the following pages, and provide the framework for activities found in this textbook. For a complete list of the IC^3 objectives and where they are met in this course, see Appendix E on page 507.

All learners can master the IC^3 objectives that are thoroughly covered in this course. Students who wish to become officially IC^3 certified must take and pass IC^3 exams covering the three modules. For more information about Certiport and IC^3 objectives and IC^3 exams, please visit www.certiport.com.

IC^3 Module 1 – Computing Fundamentals Foundation Standards for Students

The exam objectives cover the following areas:

Computer Hardware

- Identify types of computers, how they process information, and how individual computers interact with other computing systems and devices
- Identify the function of computer hardware components
- Identify the factors that go into an individual or organizational decision on how to purchase computer equipment
- Identify how to maintain computer equipment and solve common problems relating to computer hardware

Computer Software

- Identify how software and hardware work together to perform computing tasks and how software is developed and upgraded
- Identify different types of software, general concepts relating to software categories, and the tasks to which each type of software is most suited or not suited
- Identify fundamental concepts relating to database applications

Using an Operating System

- Identify what an operating system is and how it works, and solve common problems related to operating systems
- Manipulate and control the Windows desktop, files, and disks
- Identify how to change system settings, and install and remove software

English

public domain That material which people can freely use without asking permission. (p. 128)

purpose The goal or intended outcome of something. (p. 41, 127)

pursue Employing measures to obtain or accomplish. (p. 308)

Q

query A database feature that locates records based on certain criteria. (p. 283)

quotation The use of the exact words that someone else spoke, wrote, or communicated. (p. 171)

R

random access memory (RAM) The temporary information that a computer uses only when it works with a particular file. (p. 45)

range A selected group of cells. (p. 221)

read only memory (ROM) The permanent information on your hard drive. (p. 45)

record In Access, all of the information about a person or an event. Each row in a table is a record. (p. 267)

recycle bin A computer's "trash can", represented by an icon on the desktop, where deleted files are stored temporarily. (p. 24)

relational databases Programs that make it possible to organize and quickly find information entered on a number of tables. (p. 273)

relative addressing The change a formula makes when it is moved or copied to other cells with different data. (p. 234)

Español

dominio público Material que se puede usar libremente sin solicitar permiso. (p. 128)

propósito Objetivo o resultado deseado de algo. (p. 41, 127)

perseguir Emplear medidas para obtener o lograr. (p. 308)

Q

consulta Característica de la base de datos que localiza registros según ciertos criterios. (p. 283)

cita textual Uso de las palabras exactas que una persona pronunció, escribió o comunicó. (p. 171)

R

memoria de acceso aleatorio (RAM) Información temporal que usa una computadora sólo cuando trabaja con un archivo particular. (p. 45)

rango Grupo seleccionado de celdas. (p. 221)

memoria de sólo lectura (ROM) Información permanente en la unidad de disco duro. (p. 45)

registro En Access es toda la información sobre una persona o evento. Cada fila de una tabla es un registro. (p. 267)

papelera de reciclaje Es el "bote de basura" de la computadora, está representado por un icono en el escritorio y es donde se guardan temporalmente los archivos ya borrados. (p. 24)

bases de datos relacionales Programas que permiten organizar y encontrar rápidamente la información ingresada en cierto número de tablas. (p. 273)

direccionamiento relativo Cambio en una fórmula cuando se mueve o se copia a otras celdas con diferentes datos. (p. 234)

④ Critical Thinking, Problem-Solving, and Decision-Making

Students use critical thinking skills to plan and conduct research, manage projects, solve problems and make informed decisions using appropriate digital tools and resources. Students:

- **a.** identify and define authentic problems and significant questions for investigation.
- **b.** plan and manage activities to develop a solution or complete a project.
- **c.** collect and analyze data to identify solutions and/or make informed decisions.
- **d.** use multiple processes and diverse perspectives to explore alternative solutions.

⑤ Digital Citizenship

Students understand human, cultural, and societal issues related to technology and practice legal and ethical behavior. Students:

- **a.** advocate and practice safe, legal, and responsible use of information and technology.
- **b.** exhibit a positive attitude toward using technology that supports collaboration, learning, and productivity.
- **c.** demonstrate personal responsibility for lifelong learning.
- **d.** exhibit leadership for digital citizenship.

⑥ Technology Operations and Concepts

Students demonstrate a sound understanding of technology concepts, systems and operations. Students:

- **a.** understand and use technology systems.
- **b.** select and use applications effectively and productively.
- **c.** troubleshoot systems and applications.
- **d.** transfer current knowledge to learning of new technologies.

English	Español
report A printable summary of information. (p. 295)	**informe (o reporte)** Resumen de información que puede imprimirse. (p. 295)
require Demand as necessary or essential. (p. 305)	**requerir** Exigir como necesario o esencial. (p. 305)
restart To shut down a computer and automatically start it again. (p. 32)	**reiniciar** Apagar una computadora y encenderla de nuevo automáticamente. (p. 32)
right click To press and release the right mouse button. (p. 22)	**hacer clic derecho** Presionar y soltar el botón derecho del ratón. (p. 22)
role A function or part performed, especially in a particular operation or process. (p. 360)	**papel** Función o parte representada, especialmente en una operación o proceso particular. (p. 360)
row Information organized horizontally. (p. 189)	**fila** Información organizada horizontalmente. (p. 189)

S

English	Español
Save As A command to rename a file at the same time as moving it to a new location. (p. 59)	**Guardar como** Comando para renombrar un archivo y al mismo tiempo moverlo a otro lugar. (p. 59)
scanner Hardware that digitally encodes text, graphics, and photographs. (p. 41)	**escáner (o digitalizador)** Hardware que codifica digitalmente texto, gráficas y fotografías. (p. 41)
scroll To move through a list, block of text, or any other material larger than the current window or screen. (p. 27)	**desplazar** Mover una lista, bloque de texto o cualquier otro material más grande que la ventana o pantalla en uso. (p. 27)
scroll bar The bar on the right side or bottom of a window that can bring different parts of a document into view. (p. 27)	**barra de desplazamiento** Barra a la derecha o en la parte inferior de una ventana que logra que se vean diferentes partes de un documento. (p. 27)
search engine A Web site used to seek out other Web pages using keywords. (p. 110)	**buscador (o máquina de búsqueda)** Sitio web que se usa para buscar otros sitios en la web mediante el uso de palabras clave. (p. 110)
secure Free from risk or loss. (p. 94)	**seguro** Libre de riesgo o pérdida. (p. 94)
server A computer that handles requests for data, e-mail, file transfers, and other network services from other computers (clients). (p. 49)	**servidor** Computadora que recibe solicitudes de datos, correo electrónico, transferencias de archivos y otros servicios, de otras computadoras (clientes). (p. 49)
shareware Copyrighted software that is available free of charge, usually on a trial basis and with the condition that users pay a fee for continued use and support. (p. 130)	**shareware** Programa con derechos reservados que se ofrece gratuitamente para ser probado con la condición de que el usuario pague una tarifa para usarlo posteriormente y obtener soporte. (p. 130)
shortcut (1) A direct link to a file or folder. (p. 61)	**acceso directo** Vínculo que lleva directamente a un archivo o carpeta. (p. 61)

National Educational Technology Standards and Performance Indicators for Students

The NETS are divided into the six broad categories that are listed below. Activities in the book meet the standards within each category.

1 Creativity and Innovation

Students demonstrate creative thinking, construct knowledge, and develop innovative products and processes using technology. Students:

- **a.** apply existing knowledge to generate new ideas, products, or processes.
- **b.** create original works as a means of personal or group expression.
- **c.** use models and simulations to explore complex systems and issues.
- **d.** identify trends and forecast possibilities.

2 Communication and Collaboration

Students use digital media and environments to communicate and work collaboratively, including at a distance, to support individual learning and contribute to the learning of others. Students:

- **a.** interact, collaborate, and publish with peers, experts or others employing a variety of digital environments and media.
- **b.** communicate information and ideas effectively to multiple audiences using a variety of media and formats.
- **c.** develop cultural understanding and global awareness by engaging with learners of other cultures.
- **d.** contribute to project teams to produce original works or solve problems.

3 Research and Information Fluency

Students apply digital tools to gather, evaluate, and use information. Students:

- **a.** plan strategies to guide inquiry.
- **b.** locate, organize, analyze, evaluate, synthesize, and ethically use information from a variety of sources and media.
- **c.** evaluate and select information sources and digital tools based on the appropriateness to specific tasks.
- **d.** process data and report results.

English

shortcut (2) A keyboard command that takes the place of using the mouse. (p. 28)

shutdown To turn off the computer safely. (p. 32)

site map An index of the main pages in a Web site, used to jump straight to a page without drilling down. (p. 99)

slide In PowerPoint, one frame of text or images in a series presentation. (p. 312)

Slide Master In PowerPoint, a view setting that allows changes to text, graphics, or background on all slides at once. (p. 314)

software A computer program that contains a set of instructions that make it possible for your computer to perform tasks. (p. 47)

sort To arrange, classify, or separate from others according to class, kind, or size. (p. 240)

sorting To rearrange data in a particular order, such as alphabetical or numerical. (p. 240)

spam Unwanted e-mail sent by an unknown person or business. (p. 92)

speaker notes In PowerPoint, the presenter's comment or explanation for each slide in a presentation. (p. 343)

spell check A tool that checks for spelling errors in documents. (p. 144)

spreadsheet A grid of rows and columns containing numbers, text, and formulas. (p. 215)

Start button A Windows screen element found on the taskbar that displays the start menu when selected. (p. 21)

Start menu A Windows menu that provides tools to locate documents, find Help, change system settings, and run programs. (p. 21)

Español

método abreviado Comando del teclado que substituye el uso del ratón. (p. 28)

apagar Apagar la computadora con seguridad. (p. 32)

mapa del sitio Índice de las páginas principales de un sitio web que se usa para ir directamente a una página sin necesidad de navegar en sentido descendente. (p. 99)

diapositiva En PowerPoint es un cuadro de texto o imágenes que forma parte de una serie en una presentación. (p. 312)

Clasificador de diapositivas En PowerPoint es una opción de vista de la presentación que permite hacer cambios al texto, a los gráficos o al fondo en todas las diapositivas al mismo tiempo. (p. 314)

software (o programa) Programa de cómputo que contiene un conjunto de instrucciones que permiten a tu computadora efectuar tareas. (p. 47)

ordenar Arreglar, clasificar o separar del resto de acuerdo a la clase, tipo o tamaño. (p. 240)

ordenamiento Volver a arreglar la información en un orden específico, como alfabético o numérico. (p. 240)

correo no solicitado (o correo basura) Correo electrónico no deseado que envía una persona o compañía desconocida. (p. 92)

notas del expositor En PowerPoint son los comentarios o explicaciones hechas por el presentador en cada una de las diapositivas de la presentación. (p. 343)

revisión de ortografía Herramienta que revisa errores ortográficos en los documentos. (p. 144)

hoja de cálculo Cuadriculado de filas y columnas que contiene números, texto y fórmulas. (p. 215)

botón de inicio En Windows es un elemento de pantalla que se encuentra en la barra de tareas y muestra el menú de inicio al seleccionarse. (p. 21)

menú de inicio En Windows es un menú que proporciona herramientas para localizar documentos, encontrar ayuda, modificar parámetros del sistema y correr programas. (p. 21)

Prepare for 21st Century Success!

ISTE and NETS

The International Society for Technology in Education (ISTE) has developed National Educational Technology Standards to define educational technology standards for students (NETS•S). The activities in this book are designed to meet ISTE standards.

NETS•S Standards

To live, learn, and work successfully in an increasingly complex and information-rich society, students must be able to use technology effectively. Althought the ISTE standards identify skills that students can practice and master in school, the skills are also used outside of school, at home, and at work. For more information about ISTE and the NETS, please visit **www.iste.org**.

English

storage device Hardware that saves data onto a hard drive, a server, or a disk. (p. 46)

suggest To mention or imply as a possibility. (p. 262)

summary An abstract, abridgement, or compendium. (p. 307)

supercomputer The largest and fastest type of computer, capable of storing and processing tremendous volumes of data. (p. 41)

symbol Specialized character or picture, such as © and ®, that represents something else by association. (p. 126, 196)

Español

dispositivo de almacenamiento Hardware que guarda información en una unidad de disco duro, un servidor o un disco. (p. 46)

sugerir Mencionar o insinuar algo como una posibilidad. (p. 262)

resumen Sinopsis, sumario o compendio. (p. 307)

supercomputadora El tipo de computadora más grande y rápido, capaz de almacenar y procesar cantidades enormes de información. (p. 41)

símbolo Caractere especiales o dibujos, como © y ®, que representan algo más por asociación. (p. 126, 196)

T

tab A set distance for moving the insertion point (also known as indent). (p. 171)

table A grid of rows and columns that organizes complex information so that it is easy to find and understand. (p. 189, 267)

task A usually assigned piece of work often to be finished within a certain time. (p. 45)

taskbar A visual element on the desktop that displays the Start button, available applications, and active programs. (p. 25)

technology The use of science to solve practical problems. (p. 2)

telecommute To work from home or another location with the help of communication tools, such as a cell phone, fax machine, and the Internet. (p. 5)

Terms of Use The rules regarding permission to use copyrighted material. (p. 127)

text box In a document, a moveable square graphic that lets you place text anywhere on the page without having to create tables, columns, or setting tab stops. (p. 365)

tabulación Distancia establecida para mover el punto de inserción (también conocida como sangría). (p. 171)

tabla Un cuadriculado de filas y columnas que organiza información compleja para que sea más fácil de encontrar y entender. (p. 189, 267)

tarea Trabajo asignado que por lo común debe terminarse en un tiempo específico. (p. 45)

barra de tareas Elemento visual en el escritorio que muestra el botón de inicio, las aplicaciones disponibles y los programas activos. (p. 25)

tecnología Uso de la ciencia para resolver problemas prácticos. (p. 2)

teletrabajo Trabajar desde la casa u otro lugar con la ayuda de herramientas de comunicación, tales como teléfono celular, fax e Internet. (p. 5)

Términos de Uso Reglas que rigen el permiso para usar material con derechos reservados. (p. 127)

cuadro de texto En un documento es un gráfico cuadrado y movible que permite colocar texto en cualquier parte de la página sin tener que crear tablas, columnas o establecer paradas del tabulador. (p. 365)

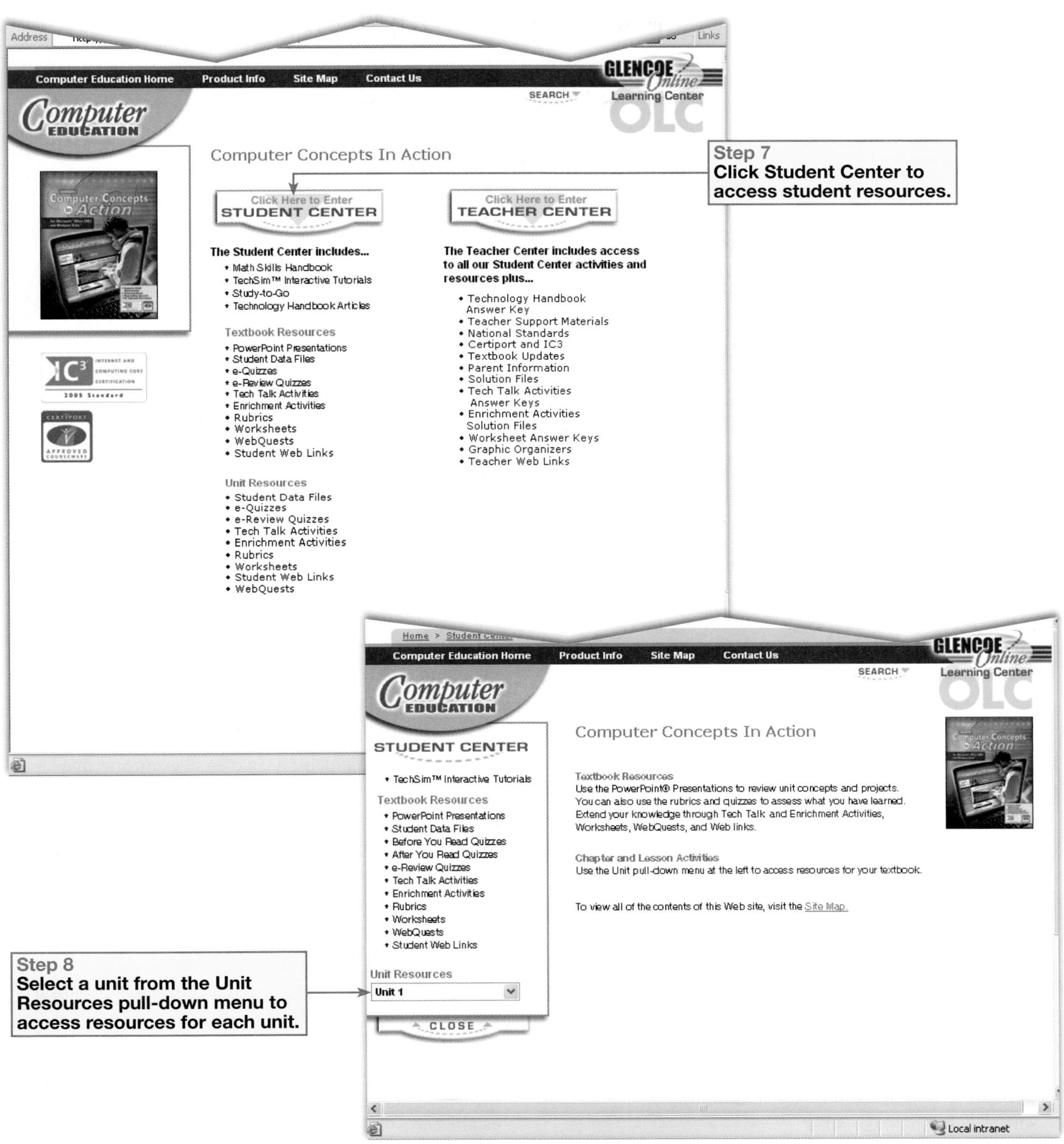

Address
Links
Computer Education Home
Product Info
Site Map
Contact Us
GLENCOE Online Learning Center
SEARCH
Computer EDUCATION
Computer Concepts In Action
Step 7
Click Student Center to access student resources.
Click Here to Enter STUDENT CENTER
Click Here to Enter TEACHER CENTER
The Student Center includes...
• Math Skills Handbook
• TechSim™ Interactive Tutorials
• Study-to-Go
• Technology Handbook Articles
Textbook Resources
• PowerPoint Presentations
• Student Data Files
• e-Quizzes
• e-Review Quizzes
• Tech Talk Activities
• Enrichment Activities
• Rubrics
• Worksheets
• WebQuests
• Student Web Links
Unit Resources
• Student Data Files
• e-Quizzes
• e-Review Quizzes
• Tech Talk Activities
• Enrichment Activities
• Rubrics
• Worksheets
• Student Web Links
• WebQuests
The Teacher Center includes access to all our Student Center activities and resources plus...
• Technology Handbook Answer Key
• Teacher Support Materials
• National Standards
• Certiport and IC3
• Textbook Updates
• Parent Information
• Solution Files
• Tech Talk Activities Answer Keys
• Enrichment Activities Solution Files
• Worksheet Answer Keys
• Graphic Organizers
• Teacher Web Links
Home > Student Center
STUDENT CENTER
• TechSim™ Interactive Tutorials
Textbook Resources
• PowerPoint Presentations
• Student Data Files
• Before You Read Quizzes
• After You Read Quizzes
• e-Review Quizzes
• Tech Talk Activities
• Enrichment Activities
• Rubrics
• Worksheets
• WebQuests
• Student Web Links
Unit Resources
Unit 1
CLOSE
Textbook Resources
Use the PowerPoint® Presentations to review unit concepts and projects. You can also use the rubrics and quizzes to assess what you have learned. Extend your knowledge through Tech Talk and Enrichment Activities, Worksheets, WebQuests, and Web links.
Chapter and Lesson Activities
Use the Unit pull-down menu at the left to access resources for your textbook.
To view all of the contents of this Web site, visit the Site Map.
Step 8
Select a unit from the Unit Resources pull-down menu to access resources for each unit.
Local intranet

English

title bar The horizontal band that displays the name of an application window, a document window, or a dialog box. (p. 23)

title page The first page of a report used to identify the name of the paper and its writer. (p. 178)

trademark A name, symbol, or other feature that identifies a product with a specific owner. (p. 126)

transition In PowerPoint, the effects or animation that move from one slide to the next slide. (p. 334)

trend A prevailing tendency or inclination. (p. 356)

U

uniform resource locator (URL) A Web site's own unique Internet address that no other Web site can use. (p. 86)

unique Distinctively characteristic. (p. 86)

user name A unique name that identifies a user to a network. (p. 20)

V

vary To make differences between items. (p. 6)

view A setting that displays how the user sees and interacts with the application or operating system. (p. 136)

virus A program intentionally designed to cause annoyance or damage to a computer or software. (p. 7)

W

warranty A manufacturer's promises to pay for specific repairs, offer replacements, or refund money for a certain length of time. (p. 210)

Español

barra de título Banda horizontal que muestra el nombre de una ventana de aplicación, una ventana de documento o una ventana de diálogo. (p. 23)

página de título Primera página de un informa usada para identificar el nombre del trabajo y su autor. (p. 178)

marca registrada Nombre, símbolo u otra característica que identifica a un producto con su dueño. (p. 126)

transición En PowerPoint son los efectos o animación que aparecen de una diapositiva a la siguiente. (p. 334)

tendencia Propensión o inclinación predominante. (p. 356).

U

localizador de recurso uniforme (URL) La dirección única de Internet de un sitio web que ningún otro sitio puede usar. (p. 86)

único Con características distintivas. (p. 86)

nombre de usuario Nombre único que identifica a un usuario en una red de computadoras. (p. 20)

V

variar Crear diferencias entre artículos. (p. 6)

vista Es un parámetro que indica cómo un usuario ve e interactúa con la aplicación o sistema operativo. (p. 136)

virus Programa diseñado intencionalmente para causar molestias o daños a una computadora o programa. (p. 7)

W

garantía Promesa del fabricante de pagar reparaciones específicas, ofrecer reemplazos o devolver el dinero dentro de cierto límite de tiempo. (p. 210)

Online Learning Center

Follow these steps to access the textbook resources on the Student Online Learning Center.

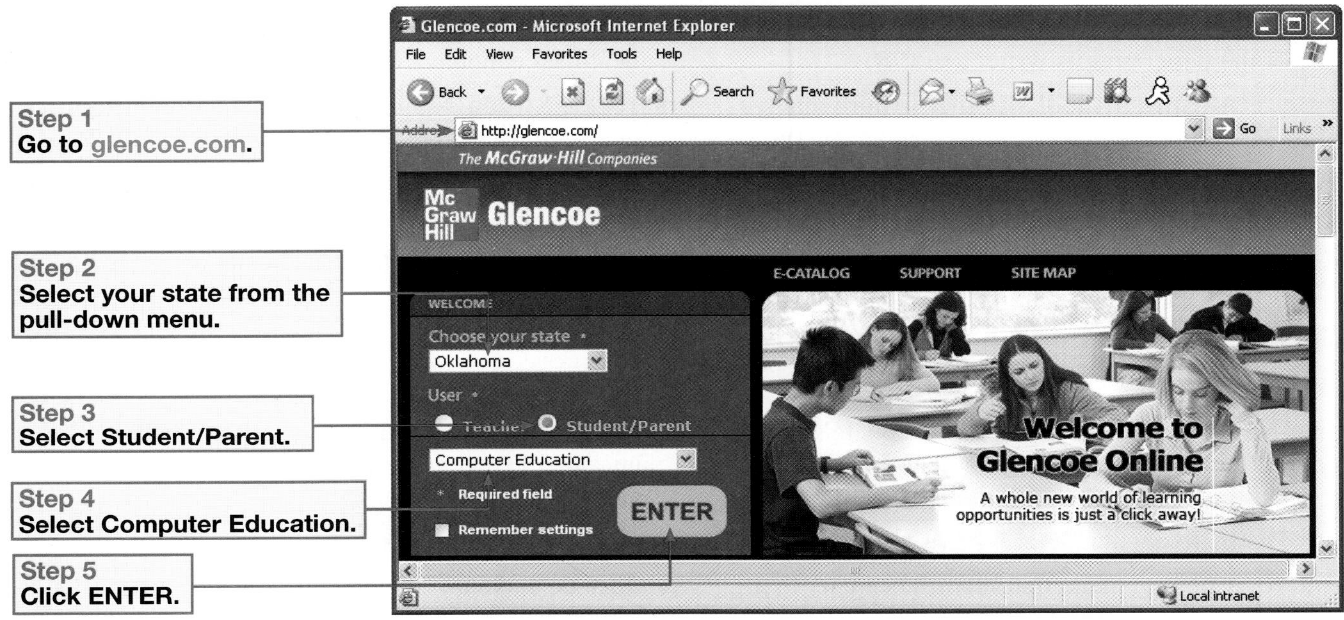

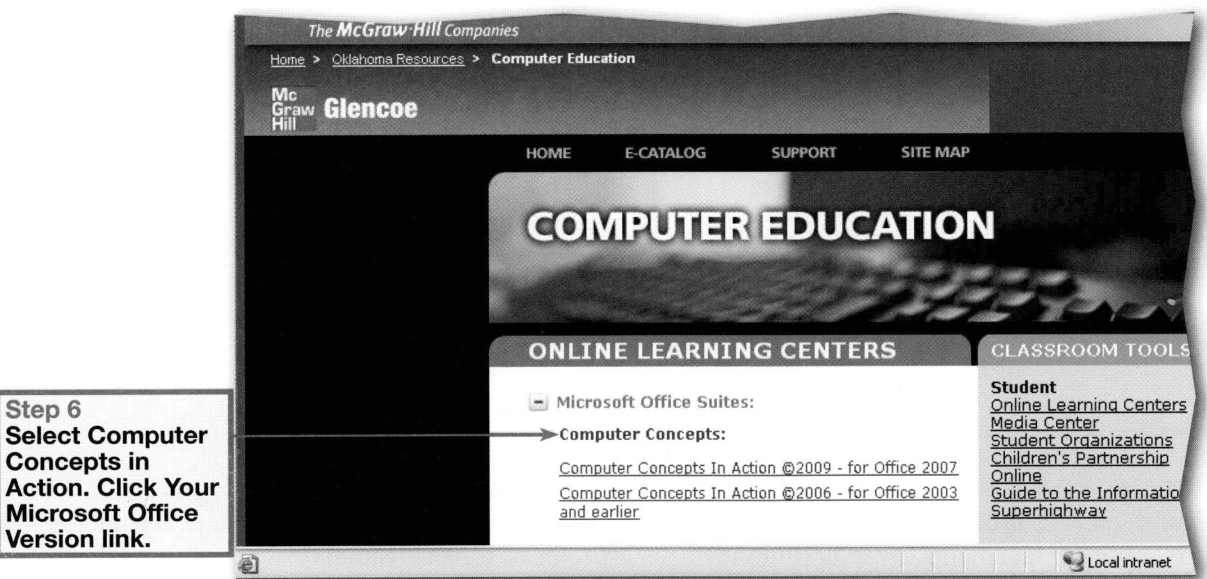

English

Web browser A software program that can surf the Web and interact with Web sites. (p. 89)

Web site A specific location on the Web that contains a group of related files and resources. (p. 86)

window An area on the computer screen where an application can be viewed and accessed. (p. 25)

wizard A tool that gives directions or a number of steps needed to create a product, such as a form. (p. 291)

word processing program A program used to create, edit, and print documents. (p. 135)

WordArt In Word, a tool that creates colorful, eye-catching text. (p. 185)

workbook In Excel, a file that contains worksheets. (p. 215)

worksheet In Excel, a table of data that is organized into columns and rows. (p. 215)

works cited list A method of providing public information about the sources used in a document that follows the guidelines and recommendations set out by the Modern Language Association (MLA). (p. 131)

World Wide Web The huge collection of information, services, and Web sites accessible through the Internet. (p. 86)

wrap In a document, when text hits the right margin and automatically moves to the next line. (p. 161)

Español

navegador de Internet Programa de software que se usa para navegar en Internet e interactuar con sitios web. (p. 89)

sitio web Lugar específico en Internet que contiene un grupo de archivos y recursos relacionados entre sí. (p. 86)

ventana Área en la pantalla de la computadora donde puede verse y usarse una aplicación. (p. 25)

asistente Herramienta que proporciona las guías o los pasos necesarios para crear un producto, tal como un formulario. (p. 291)

programa procesador de palabras Programa usado para crear, editar e imprimir documentos. (p. 135)

WordArt En Word es una herramienta con la que se crea texto colorido y llamativo. (p. 185)

libro de trabajo En Excel es un archivo que contiene hojas de trabajo. (p. 215)

hoja de trabajo En Excel es una tabla de datos organizada en columnas y filas. (p. 215)

lista de obras citadas Método para proporcionar información pública acerca de las fuentes usadas en un documento, que sigue los lineamientos y recomendaciones establecidos por la Asociación de Lenguas Modernas (MLA). (p. 131)

Red Mundial La enorme cantidad de información, servicios y sitios web disponibles en Internet. (p. 86)

ajuste de línea En un documento es cuando el texto alcanza el margen derecho y automáticamente se mueve a la siguiente línea. (p. 161)

What Is Your Computer Concepts Skill Rating?

POINTS	SKILL RATING
90 to 100	You really know how to let your textbook work for you!
70 to 89	Researching and organizing are skills you possess!
Less than 70	Consider working with your teacher or classmates to learn how to use your book more effectively—you will gain skills you can use your whole life.

1. Going online, using the Internet safely, searching the Internet effectively
2. Three
3. By reading it first, you know what skills will be covered in the project. It is easier to understand what you are doing if you know its purpose first.
4. You can create a chart or diagram to help understand and reinforce difficult concepts.
5. The Go Online feature
6. Skills reading timelines, graphs, and charts.
7. Key Concepts Check, Critical Thinking, Guided Practice, Independent Practice
8. A rubric
9. Independent Practice in the Project Assessment and Projects Across the Curriculum in the Unit Assessment
10. Appendix D

A

B

C

Take the Computer Concepts Challenge!

Many features in this text—such as color headings, illustrations with captions, tables and charts—have been carefully created to help you read, understand, and remember key ideas and concepts. Taking advantage of these features can help you improve your reading and study skills.

Get Started

The scavenger hunt on these pages highlights features that will help you get the most out of your textbook. Collect points as you complete each step.

1. What are the major topics you expect to learn about in Unit 3? [10 points. *Hint: Contents in Brief at the beginning of the Unit gives you at-a-glance information about the topics covered in the Unit.*]
2. How many **Reading Checks** are in the **Tech Talk** in Unit 1? [10 points]
3. What is the purpose of **Key Concepts** on page 9? Why is it important? [10 points]
4. What is the study tip you learned from the **Before You Read** on page 41? [10 points]
5. What feature in the **Tech Talk** articles and the **Projects** sends you to the Web to learn more about special topics? [10 points]
6. What types of skills are needed to successfully complete the **Math Concept** activity, such as the one on page 8? [10 points]
7. What are the four main parts of the **Project Assessment**? [10 points.]
8. What **online tool** will help you check the project you create in **Build Your Portfolio**? [10 points]
9. Where in each unit can you find projects that you can use for your other school subjects like English, social studies, math, and science? [10 points]
10. In which **Appendix** can you find the correct way to format a research paper? [10 points]

D

To The Student

Why Study Computer Concepts?

For many students, computers have become a basic part of daily life. By understanding how to use computers and the software that runs them, you will learn skills that will help you in school and in your career.

Computer Concepts in Action is intended to help you develop skills needed to succeed in school and throughout your life. This textbook was written and designed to help you achieve each of the following goals:

Become a 21st Century Citizen

- ◆ Understand how to use technology wisely and safely.
- ◆ Understand how computers and the Internet work.
- ◆ Evaluate the accuracy and usefulness of information on the Web.
- ◆ Find and share information quickly, safely, and ethically.

Become an Effective Computer User

- ◆ Demonstrate your understanding of Microsoft Office software, including Word, Excel, PowerPoint, and Access.
- ◆ Become a skilled and creative user of Microsoft Word, Excel, PowerPoint, and Access.
- ◆ Create interesting projects using both individual applications and integrated applications.
- ◆ Become an effective researcher using the resources of the World Wide Web.
- ◆ Become an expert at navigating the Web and evaluating Web sites.
- ◆ Offer constructive feedback to improve your own and others' projects.

Develop Learning and Study Skills for All Subjects

- ◆ Improve reading comprehension with both guided and independent reading strategies.
- ◆ Develop critical thinking skills.
- ◆ Build teamwork skills.
- ◆ Integrate technology skills across the curriculum.

E

F

G

H

UNIT 7 Presentations 304

M

Table of Contents

N

O

P

Table of Contents

UNIT 4 Word Processing 125

T

Table of Contents

UNIT 3 Using the Internet 85

Table of Contents

PHOTO CREDITS

Frontmatter and Text: Age Fotostock Royalty Free, **1**; Scott Barrow/Imagestate **126**; Ed Bock/Corbis **ix**, **239**, **358**; Michelle D. Bridwell/PhotoEdit **351**; Paul Burns/Getty Images, **355**; Don Carstens/Imagestate **289**; William Castner/Imagestate **252**; Patrick Clear/PhotoEdit **326**; © Columbia/Sony Pictures J.C.C./MPTV **6**; Corbis **204**; Royalty-Free/Corbis **121**, **207**, **301(r)**, **308**, **363**; Thomas Michael Corcoran/PhotoEdit **208**; Digital Art/Corbis **400**; Duomo/Corbis **183**; Najlah Feanny/Corbis **228**; Ron Fehling/Masterfile **342**; Jon Feingersh/Masterfile **18**, **305**; Freelance Consulting Services Pty Ltd/Corbis **122**; Tim Fuller Photography **x**, **19**, **124**, **416**; Comstock Images (Royalty Free)/Getty Images **341**; Getty Images **205**, **278**; Getty Images Royalty Free **85**, **125**; Glencoe Stock **165**; Spencer Grant/PhotoEdit **128**; David Hall/Masterfile **151**; Handout/Reuters/Corbis **51**; Noel Hendrickson/Getty Images, **304**; Courtesy of Hewlett Packard **v**, **22**, **167**, **41(2)**, **418**; Walter Hodges/Corbis **69**; Dana Hursey/Masterfile **5**; The Image Bank/Getty Images **382**; Bob Kramer/Index Stock **134**; Lisette LeBon/Superstock **325**; Lester Lefkowitz/Corbis **9**; Jo Lillini/Corbis **311**; Lawerence Manning/Corbis **96**; Lou Manna/Imagestate **238**; Masterfile (Royalty-Free) **17(b)**; MedioImages/Superstock **108**; Mug ShotsCorbis **108**; David Muir/Masterfile **109**; Michael Newman/PhotoEdit **10**; Richard T. Nowitz/Corbis **399**; Owaki-Kulla/Corbis **300**; Michael Wade Perry **165**; Jose Luis Pelaez/Corbis **16**; Photodisc Green (Royalty-Free)/Getty Images **417**; Photo edit, **254**; H. Prinz/Corbis **184**; Roger Ressmeyer/Corbis **81**; Photo disc/ Royalty-Free/Getty Images **xiv**; SW Productions/Brand X Pictures/PictureQuest **iv**, **x**, **360**; The Scotsman/Corbis Sygma **361**; Chuck Savage/Corbis **152**; Stockbyte/Superstock **vi**, **88**; Eriko Sugita/Corbis **356**; Think Stock LLC/Index Stock **38**; Thinkstock (Royalty-Free) **251**; Courtesy of Toshiba **40**; A & J Verkaik/Corbis **301(l)**; Dana White/PhotoEdit **203**; Lee White Photography **214**, **266**, **290**, **354**; David Young Wolf/PhotoEdit **xi**, **xii**, **131**, **166**, **206**, **267**, **353**, **381**, **419**.

ILLUSTRATION CREDITS

© 2004 United Media **149**; All other Illustrations by Gary Hespenheide Design.

Table of Contents

SCREEN CAPTURE CREDITS

Abbreviation Key: MS = Screen shots used by permission from Microsoft Corporation.

Cover: www.trailpeak.com

© 2007 MS Explorer, **20**, **87**, **97–107**, **110**, **111**, **113–120**, **123**, **127**; © 2007 MS Windows Vista, **21**, **23–26**, **32–34**, **52–58**, **61–67**, **70–74**, **76**, **79**, **84**, **404**; © 2007 MS Excel, **26**, **27**, **215–237**, **240–242**, **245–250**, **253**, **332**, **333**, **391–393**, **406**, **407**; © 2007 MS Word, **26**, **27**, **29–31**, **35**, **59**, **60**, **75–78**, **80**, **135–138**, **141**, **142**, **144–149**, **153–155**, **157–163**, **167**, **169–176**, **178**, **180–182**, **185–197**, **199–201**, **365–380**, **385–390**, **394–397**, **402–405**, **414**; © 2007 MS Access, **268–272**, **274–277**, **281–288**, **291–299**; © 2007 MS PowerPoint, **312–324**, **327–331**, **333–340**, **343–350**, **408–413**, **415**; © 2007 MS Outlook, **280**; © 2007 MS Windows Vista Media Player, **36**; © 2008 Microsoft Corporation Inc. (Web site), **76 (b)**; © 2008 USA Cycling, Incorporated, **87**; © Community High School District, **99**, **97**, **98**; © Library of Congress, **99–107**; © 2008 Google, **110**, **111**, **113**, **119**, **261**, **364**, **401**; © Pets4You.com, **111**; © 2008 ASPCA. All Rights Reserved, **113**, **114**, **117**, **118**, **120**; © 1998–2008 PetCareRX.com, **114**; © 2008 The Humane Society of the United States. All rights reserved, **115**, **116**; © 2005–2006 Americazoo.com, **120**; © 2008 olivegarden.com, **123**; © Glencoe/McGraw-Hill. All Rights Reserved, **127**; © 2008 Fender Musical Instruments Corporation. All rights reserved, **134**, **139**, **156**, **161**; © 1996–2008, Amazon.com, Inc., **255**; © 2007 Cub Foods, **257**; © 2008 Adidas, **258**; © 1997–2008 Buy.com Inc. All rights reserved, **258**; © 2008 Billboard.com, Nielsen Business Media, Inc. All rights reserved, **260**; © 2007 Marvel Characters, Inc. All rights reserved, **261**; © 1997–2008 Barnesandnoble.com llc, **263**; © CareerBuilder.com, **307**; Federal Trade Commission, **383**, **384**.

About the Author

Stephen Haag is a professor and Chair of the Department of Information Technology and Electronic Commerce in the Daniels College of Business at the University of Denver. He is also the Director of the Masters of Science in Information Technology program and the Director of the MBA program. Stephen holds a B.B.A. and M.B.A. from West Texas State University and a Ph.D. from the University of Texas at Arlington. He also holds the IC^3 certification. Stephen has been teaching in the classroom since 1982 and publishing textbooks since 1984. He is the author of numerous articles and over 40 books, including *The I-Series Computing Concepts* (and 18 other books within *The I-Series*), *Management Information Systems for the Information Age, and Information Technology: Tomorrow's Advantage Today* (with Peter Keen). Stephen lives in Highlands Ranch, Colorado, with his wife and four sons. When not teaching and writing, Stephen is a trainer for the federal government, helping managers effectively develop and assess technology metrics.

Academic Consultants

Erik Amerikaner
Mesa Verde Middle School
Moorpark, California

Linda Mallinson
Mid Florida Tech Center
Orlando, Florida

Teresa M. Peterman
Grand Valley State University
Allendale, Michigan

Marilyn L. Satterwhite
Professor Business and Technology Division
Danville Area Community College
Danville, Illinois

Diane Williamson
Raleigh Egypt Middle School
Memphis, Tennessee

Contributors

Jonathon Fine
Writer/Editor
Portland, Oregon

Bob Goldhamer
Technology Curriculum Developer
Los Angeles, California

Kevin Niemeyer
KLEB Intermediate School, Klein ISD
Houston, Texas

Michael Wade Perry
Chapel Hill High School
Douglasville, Georgia

Jack E. Johnson, Ph.D.
Department of Management and Business Systems
State University of West Georgia
Carrollton, Georgia

Judith Chiri-Mulkey
Department of Computer Information Systems
Pikes Peak Community College
Colorado Springs, Colorado

Delores Sykes Cotton
Detroit Public Schools
Detroit, Michigan

Carole G. Stanley, M.Ed.
Rains Junior High School
Emory, Texas

Academic Reviewers

Jeffrey S. Aronsky
La Mesa Junior High School
Santa Clarita, California

Marsha Bass
Art Institute of Pittsburg
Elkhart, Indiana

James T. Davis
A. Crawford Mosley High School
Lynn Haven, Florida

Michelle Endsley
Brinkley Middle School
Jackson, Mississippi

Cathy R. L. Gaspard
Foothill Technology High School
Ventura, California

Leah Goldman
White Knoll Middle School
W. Columbia, South Carolina

Anita Bliss Greenhut
Halsey Junior High 157
Rego Park, New York

Linda Robinson
Winter Haven High School
WInter Haven, Florida

Lisa Rogers
Forney Middle School
Forney, Texas

Laura Scanlon
Pioneer Ridge Freshmen Center
Chaska, Minnesota

Jearline H. Spence
Leesville Road Middle School
Raleigh, North Carolina

Jennifer Wegner
Mishicot High School
Mishicot, Wisconsin

Mina B. Williams
Alexander Graham Middle School
Charlotte, North Carolina

Lillian Willis
Scarlet Oaks Cdc Vocational School
Cincinnati, Ohio